CAPACITY UTILIZATION RATE, MANUFACTURING   **PERCENT**

1966 67 68 69 70 71 72 73 74 75 76 77 78 79 80 81 82 83 84 85 86 87 88 89 90 91 92 93 1994

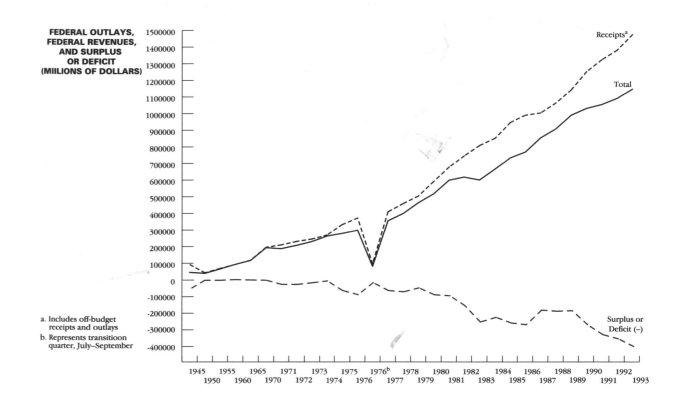

FEDERAL OUTLAYS, FEDERAL REVENUES, AND SURPLUS OR DEFICIT (MIILIONS OF DOLLARS)

Receipts[a]

Total

Surplus or Deficit (–)

a. Includes off-budget receipts and outlays
b. Represents transitioon quarter, July–September

1945 1955 1965 1971 1973 1975 1976[b] 1978 1980 1982 1984 1986 1988 1990 1992
1950 1960 1970 1972 1974 1976 1977 1979 1981 1983 1985 1987 1989 1991 1993

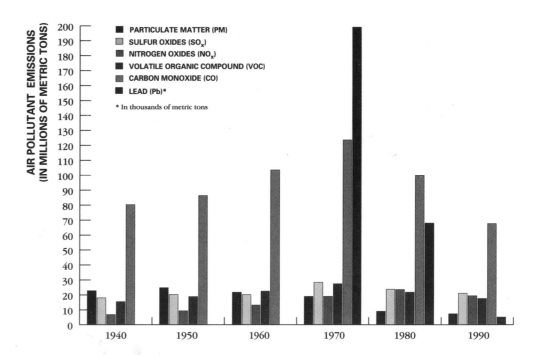

AIR POLLUTANT EMISSIONS (IN MILLIONS OF METRIC TONS)

- ■ PARTICULATE MATTER (PM)
- ■ SULFUR OXIDES (SOₓ)
- ■ NITROGEN OXIDES (NOₓ)
- ■ VOLATILE ORGANIC COMPOUND (VOC)
- ■ CARBON MONOXIDE (CO)
- ■ LEAD (Pb)*

* In thousands of metric tons

1940 1950 1960 1970 1980 1990

Modern Economics

Modern Economics

JAN S. HOGENDORN
The Grossman Professor of Economics
Colby College

Prentice-Hall, Englewood Cliffs, New Jersey 07632

Production Manager: Andrea G. Mulligan, Benchmark Productions
Production Editor: Alisa M. Andreola, Benchmark Productions
In-house Project Liasion: Alana Zdinak
Acquistions Editor: Leah Jewell
Assistant Editor: Teresa Cohan
Editorial Assistant: Elizabeth Becker
Interior Designer: Ed Smith and Benchamrk Productions
Cover Designer: Maria Lang
Cover Photos: Woodland Stream: © Tony Stone Worldwide, Silhoutte of oil refinery lit up at dusk, orange sky, Texas USA: Terry Vina/ © Tony Stone Worldwide, Sri Lanka, vendor standing by fruit stall: Hugh Sitton/ © Tony Stone Worldwide, Grenda, St. Georges, fruit and vegetable stalls at open air market: Doug Armand/ © Tony Stone Worldwide, USA, New York City, Wall Street, Stock Exchange building, flag in front: Greg Pease/ © Tony Stone Worldwide,

Set in 12-point Garamond ITC by Benchmark Productions

Printed in the United States of America

10 9 8 7 6 5 4 3 2 1

ISBN 0-13-103995-4

Prentice-Hall International (UK) Limited, London
Prentice-Hall of Austrailia Pty. Limited, Sydney
Prentice-Hall Canada Inc., Toronto
Prentice-Hall Hispanoamericana, S. A. Mexico
Prentice-Hall of India Private Limited, New Delhi
Prentice-Hall of Japan, Inc., Tokyo
Simon & Schuster Asia Ptc. Ltd., Singapore
Editora Prentice-Hall do Brasil., Rio de Janerio

To Christiaan Hogendorn
who, at the end, contributed

TABLE OF CONTENTS

Part 2 ■ Microeconomics

Part 3 ■ Macroeconomics

Chapter 19

MONEY AND THE BANKING SYSTEM **477**

Chapter 20

THE TOOLS OF MONETARY POLICY **503**

Part 4 ■ International Economic Experience

PREFACE

I set out to write this book because I believe that something is seriously amiss with today's standard principles of economics books. The text when I took the introductory course at Wesleyan University was the third edition of Paul Samuelson's *Economics*. It was about 750 pages in length.. Nowadays, the standard texts are typically over 1000 pages long with some running to over 1200, with their diagrams, captions, and tables often printed in the margin to keep them from running much longer yet. Their weight alone, over 4 lbs., is more than double Samuelson's 2 lbs. The length and the weight have a direct impact on cost; these books are quite expensive. Moreover, economics has never been an easy subject. When I took that introductory course at Wesleyan, its difficulty was recognized by not allowing first-year students to enroll. This practice was followed at most colleges and universities. Now almost everywhere the course has been opened up to first-year students, who are often the majority in the classroom.

So, compared to when I took the course, the major texts now attempt to present almost twice as much material to an audience that is younger than it used to be. Some of this material, especially the macroeconomics, is more difficult than was formerly the case.

How did this happen? I have no question that the students of today are bright and motivated and curious. But I do not believe that they have sufficient time on their hands to handle nearly twice as much harder material than formerly. Judging by college entrance scores, students are no smarter than they were two and three decades ago. I certainly have seen no evidence that they spend more time on their studies, either. Yet the authors of the hefty economics textbooks seem to assume, contrary to my experience, that students are both smarter and blessed with more time.

I believe that competitive economic forces have caused this evolution toward large-size texts. in order to capture and hold their share of the market, authors and publishers seem to assume that their books must be comprehensive. They include almost everything that is relevant, apparently believing that to omit anything might mean the loss of an adoption by this or that group of instructors. I suggest that this trend toward encyclopedic inclusion of material, even when it is very difficult, has not been helpful either to students or to the profession of economics. Students are swamped with the doubling of detail, often I fear at the cost of a firm grasp of the basic principles. They complain about the length of their texts, and in all probability many actually do not find the time to read all of their assignments. Indeed, many instructors, I among them, often do not even try to include long sections of the large volumes, a reasonable response except that this wastes students' money and may leave gaps in essential knowledge.

With these thoughts in mind, I set out to write a book that preserved the essential rigor of first-year economics while cutting back by about a quarter to a third on the size, the weight, and the cost. My hope is that the book's combination of conciseness and readability will mean that students will actually enjoy reading it. I believe that many of my colleagues who teach—and like to teach—the principles of economics will welcome a text that presents the basic principles in a more concise format. The more limited compass will allow instructors the time to expand, illustrate, and discuss the material in ways not so feasible with the bulky texts. For the normal two-semester micro-macro sequence, the brevity will allow instructors freedom to shape the material according to their individual desires. The book's shorter length also makes it appropriate for use at the colleges and universities that prefer to offer principles as a one-term course.

To achieve conciseness and intellectual precision at the same time, I have tried to be rigorous in two senses. I have included material at a level so that students who major in economics have the necessary tools to make them competitive in upper-level economics courses. But I have also carefully excluded unnecessary detail and technical material that will be forgotten (with enthusiasm) after the final examination. This book is not economics made simple, a watered-down version of the subject. Instructors who may need a simplified text should look elsewhere. Instead, I have tried to present the rigor and elegance of economics while at the same time economizing on unnecessary or confusing complexity.

I believe strongly that the first-year economics text ought to be interesting and readable. Sometimes, we economists in our enthusiasm for our subject and its logical way of thinking tend to forget that a great many people, undoubtedly including college students, view economics as the "dismal science." From the beginning of this project, I have wanted it to be a literary effort as well as a pedagogical one. In particular, the footnotes and boxed material have been my venue for adding human interest to the text, my attempt to show that economics is anything but dismal.

In addition to conciseness and readability, I have pursued two other goals. I have tried to place a greater emphasis on the lessons of economic history than has been apparent in the principles course in recent years. History is an excellent test of ideas, it contributes to understanding, it ties economics to liberal learning, and it is intrinsically interesting in its own right. I have, therefore, frequently woven historical example into the presentation.

I have also integrated international aspects of economics at many points throughout the text, in addition to presenting international material in the last few chapters where it has traditionally been placed. To understand the increased globalization of the world economy, American institutions and practices have to be put into a much broader perspective that used to be the case. I have, therefore, tried to work the global components into the narrative.

Writing a principles text is challenging, but I have felt it all worth while because economists these days are seldom able or even willing to talk very successfully to non-economists. I contend that this must not only be done, but done well. Consider that all professional economists had to be introduced to the discipline in a way that captured their interest. The principles of economics textbooks that attracted them to the major had to be among the most important books they ever read. Moreover, a principles text may well be the only time an economist is able to address in any depth the people who do not major in economics but who make their careers in business, teaching, and government, and who vote. The major opportunity for economists to convey knowledge about their discipline, and encourage thinking about economic issues, is the first-year course. That course is the ultimate line of defense against seduction of the public by false prophets and economic hucksters, and the best hope that reasonable economic policies will be adopted and damaging ones rejected.

Jan Hogendorn
East Vassalboro, Maine

ACKNOWLEDGEMENTS

This book first took shape in the form of several sample chapters sent to Gary Burke, the economics editor at Mayfield Publishing Co. in Palo Alto, California. Gary, who is quite knowledgeable about economics, liked the concept of a shorter text, liked what he saw, and liked the first reviews, and so I signed on the dotted line and publication went forward. Over a year of reviewing and editing went by, and the book was nearing publication when I received a surprising series of phone calls. Prentice-Hall was purchasing the rights to the book!

It was of course satisfying, akin to getting off a Vespa and climbing into a V-8. Suddenly I had a new and much larger team of Prentice-Hall editors (led initially by Stephen Dietrich), support staff, and not least, a large marketing and sales force. Stephen Dietrich's faith in a shorter book, as strong as Gary Burke's earlier, made me believe I was on the right track.

In writing the book, I have received a tremendous amount of support and encouragement both from economists I knew and those that I didn't. Among the Mayfield reviewers, Paul Barkley at Washington State contributed substantially, and nearly every chapter reflects his painstaking suggestions. I was also first in contact with David Moewes of Concordia College, the author of the student guide, during the Mayfield days, which also included reviewers from the Universities of Arizona, Florida, and Michigan, and Penn State University, whose names I have not been able to retrieve from Mayfield.

The Prentice-Hall reviewers, listed alphabetically, included F. Trenary Dolbear, Jr., of Brandeis, Lisa M. Grobac of California State at Long Beach, Jim Lee of Fort Hayes State, Arthur E. Kartman of San Diego State, Leonard Lardara of the University of Rhode Island, Harold McClure of Villanova, Norma Morgan of Curry College, Joseph L. Moore of Arkansas Tech, Rachel A. Nugent of Pacific Lutheran, William C. O'Connor of Western Montana, Anthony Pizelo of Spokane Community College, Christina D. Romer of the University of California at Berkeley, David Rose of the University of Missouri, Ruth Shen of San Francisco State, Robert Whaples of Wake Forest, Leonard White of the University of Arkansas, David Zimmerman of Williams, and Jeffrey A. Zimmerman of Clarkson (who ended up doing the instructor's manual). I was struck by the care and conscientiousness of the reviews, and almost all of these reviewers will recognize that many times I adopted their suggestions.

Prentice-Hall (as well as Mayfield earlier) made it possible for me to utilize as consultants several Colby College economists, whom I would otherwise have found it embarrassing to hector so often. In the micro section, Clifford Reid commented on all the chapters and Jim Meehan assisted with those on industrial organization. In macro, David Findlay and Michael Donihue allowed me all the time I wanted for fruitful discussions of the current state of macro modelling, and their advice often finds reflection in the macro section. In more specific areas, other economists at Colby were helpful. The chapter on environmental economics draws heavily on the work of my colleague in the next office, Tom Tietenberg; the historical material has benefited from a quarter-century of association with Hank Gemery, Colby's economic historian; and Randy Nelson provided some of the information on productivity decline.

My developmental editors were Ev Sims for the micro half of the book and Becky Kohn for both sections. At Prentice-Hall, the following were the most involved with the project on a day-to-day basis: Liz Becker, Teresa Cohan, Leah Jewell, Alana Zdinak and Ray Mullaney. At Benchmark in Boston, where the book was produced, Andrea Mulligan and I were in contact nearly every day for weeks. My thanks to her for keeping her sense of humor when schedules were tight.

My students were on the front line for this book, either on the receiving end for the test runs in my micro and macro classes, or as research assistants. My assistants have looked up information, helped with computer work, and done considerable proofreading. Over recent years, these assistants included Clover Burns, Azeen Chamarbagwala Siddhartha Choudhury, Steve Dimitriou, Meg Ewing, Lesley Eydenberg, Karen Floyd, Susan Hale, Tracy Mungeam, Kristen Pettersen, Katherine Rogers, Kristen Russo, and Kristen Sullivan.

Joyce Matthews, the secretary of the Colby economics department for many years, had the task of packaging up and sending everything from first-draft chapters to second-pass proofs. (I hope Joyce owns some Fed Ex stock.)

My wife Dianne had to put up with my endless calls for synonyms and advice on how to hyphenate. My son Chris, a recent economics graduate from Swarthmore College, gave me an economics student's perspective on every chapter, made valuable comments, and is the author of the end-of-chapter questions.

▶ ADAPTING THE BOOK TO DIFFERENT COURSES

The chapter layout is designed for a one-year or one-semester principles course that follows a micro-macro sequence. Instructors who are teaching one semester of macroeconomics, or who wish to follow a macro-micro sequence, can utilize the following order (which has been class-tested with success several times). Chapters 1 and 2 should be assigned first. Taken together, these are an introduction to the subject that gives students a grounding in micro. That will then enable them to read the macro section, Chapters 14-26. The international sections, Chapters 27-30, can be read either with the micro or the macro part of the course.

What Is Economics?

OVERALL OBJECTIVE: To see that economics is the study of making choices when the alternatives are limited by scarce resources.

MORE SPECIFICALLY:

- To show that choice involves five main questions that any economic system must answer: what to produce, how to produce, for whom to produce, are resources being used efficiently, and is the economy growing or stagnant?
- To explain the difference between microeconomics (the study of individual economic decisions at the level of a person, firm, or industry) and macroeconomics (the study of aggregate economic topics such as growth, inflation, and unemployment).
- To discuss what economic models are and how economists use them.
- To use a single economic model, the production possibilities curve, to give an introduction to opportunity costs, economic efficiency, and economic growth caused by changes in the factors of production.

In an ideal world, every want, including food, health care, education, recreation, housing, police protection, defense, and all other goods and services, would always be satisfied. This ideal world would have an economy of boundless resources to produce everything in any desired quantity. Even time would not limit human activity. There would be no need to study economics and no economic problems. Obviously, we do not live in this ideal world. Each day we must face decisions about what to choose and how to allocate scarce resources to the production of what we want most. *Economics is the study of making choices when the alternatives are limited by scarce resources*. Choice and scarcity go together hand-in-glove, both in government and in private life. Choosing is necessary because objects of desire are scarce.

Every issue involving economics, including the central policy questions of our times, arises because resources are finite and choices have to be made. With sufficient resources we could eliminate poverty, pollution, unemployment, government budget deficits, and all other economic problems. Unfortunately, it is not possible to conceive of all scarcities disappearing. Making choices in the face of scarce resources will always be part of the human condition because humans are able to produce only a small portion of what they desire. This is the basic economic problem, and analysis of this problem in all its many aspects is what professional economists do.

▶ THE FIVE MAIN QUESTIONS OF ECONOMICS

The choices we must make because productive resources are scarce can be divided into five different categories:

1) *What to produce?* Which goods among the endless possibilities will a society decide upon, and in what quantity; what decision-making process will be used to arrive at the answer?
2) *How to produce?* This question concerns the methods that a society can use to undertake its production. Usually an item can be produced with various different techniques; a lot of labor and only a few machines, as in a Chinese irrigation project, or a lot of machinery and very few workers, as in the United States.
3) *For whom to produce?* This question concerns the distribution of the output. Who in a particular society will get the goods and services that are produced?
4) *Is a society using its productive resources fully and efficiently?* Anything less will mean unemployment of people, machines, and other productive agents.
5) *Is an economy growing or stagnant?* Growth means greater output and potentially higher levels of living for a society; stagnation removes that possibility for improvement. These main questions of economics are central to the study of the entire subject. We return to them again and again throughout this book.

▶ MICROECONOMICS AND MACROECONOMICS

The economic choices we face can be divided into two areas of study, **microeconomics** and **macroeconomics**. Microeconomics (from Greek *mikros,* meaning "small") is the study of individual economic decisions. It considers how resources are allocated by the actions of individual decision-making units. Microeconomics takes a nation's income and output—its "economic pie," so to speak—as given, and asks how that pie is divided by product, how to minimize the resources used in producing the pie, and how individuals get their share of it. The first three questions on our list are topics in microeconomics, while the fourth bridges the gap between micro and macro.

Macroeconomics (from Greek *makros*, meaning "large") is the study of the whole economic pie. What determines the size of a nation's income and output and what causes them to fluctuate—how large is the pie and what is happening to its dimensions—are macro topics. So are the great national problems such as rapid inflation or high unemployment or stagnating growth. The last two questions on our list involve macro issues.

Note some strangeness and ambiguity: the study of decision-making by AT&T or General Motors is a micro study; an examination of inflation and unemployment in the Bahamas belongs to macro. Each of the companies is far larger in money terms than the entire Bahamian economy! Size is not the issue here, however. Whether an issue is micro or macro depends on whether the discussion concerns units within an economy (micro) or an entire economy (macro).

▶ THE PRODUCTION POSSIBILITIES CURVE

Having looked at what economics is, let us now begin our study of what economists do. That frequently involves the construction of economic theories, or **models**, that lead to logical thinking about economic issues and allow analyses of these issues. One simple model, known as the **production possibilities curve (PPC)**, is very helpful for illustrating the central subject of economics; that is, how choices must be made among scarce economic alternatives. We will begin with a very simple case that enlists the help of Robinson Crusoe, marooned by shipwreck on his lonely island.[1] A "Crusoe economy" is a good starting point for a production possibilities curve. His land area is fixed, his supply of tools is not easily altered, and the number of working hours available to him is limited to the time he can stay awake. There is no money supply to consider. After seeing how the curve works for Crusoe, we will apply its lessons to national economies.

Now to Crusoe's choices. With resources scarce (limited tools, time, labor, and managerial ability), Crusoe cannot have everything he wants. Take his food supply as an example. The island is lush with mango trees, and his lagoon teems with fish. At the very most, Crusoe might *want* to eat 300 mangoes and 200 fish every month. Unfortunately for him, Crusoe cannot obtain these quantities. He has discovered that even by using all his working time picking mangoes, he cannot get 300 per month. Nor, even if he transferred all his working time to catching fish, could he get 200 fish per month.

A production possibilities model starts with data on what actually can be obtained—the alternatives that are feasible. If Crusoe were to sit down on the sand for a few moments, he might be able to sketch out the beginnings of a table, or schedule, that displays these alternatives. He knows his maximum possible output of mangoes in a month is 200 when all his time is spent on mango production, and so he will write 200 mangoes in the first column of figures (see Table 1.1). Since no time is left to catch fish, he writes 0 fish in that column.

Crusoe then considers what would happen if he spent all his time catching fish. Here he predicts the result will be 100 fish per month, and, of course, 0 mangoes.

TABLE 1.1
Crusoe's production alternatives.

	All time spent picking mangoes	All time spent catching fish
Mangoes picked	200	0
Fish caught	0	100

---

1.   Daniel Defoe's famous novel, *The Life and Strange Surprizing Adventures of Robinson Crusoe*, was published in 1719-1720. It has long been a tradition in economics to illustrate the simplest form of an economy that could be constructed, an individual in isolation, with Crusoe. The first use of the castaway for this purpose was in the 1830s. He still rates a full page in the *The New Palgrave: A Dictionary of Economics*, London, 1987. Economists typically ignore details such as Crusoe's considerable waste of time getting organized, the advantage to him of being able to salvage a wide range of items from his wrecked ship, and the eventual addition of as many as six people (including Man Friday) to his little community.

The data in the table can be illustrated on a diagram, as in Figure 1.1. Mangoes are plotted on the vertical (Y) axis running from 0 up to 200, and fish are plotted on the horizontal (X) axis running from 0 to 100. Crusoe's production possibility of 200 mangoes and 0 fish is the point labeled **A** on the diagram, while 0 mangoes and 100 fish is the point marked **F**. (Readers who would benefit from a review of how to read graphs can consult the appendix to this chapter.)

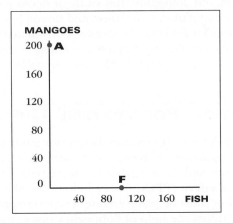

Figure 1.1. Mango and fish production when Crusoe specializes completely. If Crusoe spends all his time producing mangoes, his total output would be 200 mangoes and 0 fish. Point **A** shows 200 mangoes and 0 fish. If he spends all his time producing fish, his total output would be 100 fish and 0 mangoes. Point **F** shows 100 fish and 0 mangoes.

Of course, Crusoe knows that he is not limited to just these two possibilities. He can divide his labor time between fish and mangoes, getting some of each. Even his tools can be shifted between occupations to some extent. For example, the poles that support his fish nets can be employed to knock mangoes off the trees, and the knife that cleans the fish can also cut the fruit. There will be many alternative combinations of fish and mangoes that Crusoe can obtain if he ceases to specialize in one or the other. As long as he is using all his labor time at peak efficiency, however, he can never get more mangoes without giving up some fish. Nor can he ever get more fish without giving up some mangoes. Crusoe thus faces the universal constraint that economics deals with. The scarcity of resources (labor time, tools, and so forth) will not permit him to produce more of both items; he can increase his output of one product only at the cost of losing some output of the other product.[2]

As he gains experience and studies his choices, Crusoe will have more data available on his production possibilities. Assume he finds that he can produce the various combinations shown in Table 1.2.

TABLE 1.2
Various combinations of mangoes and fish that Crusoe could produce.

	A	B	C	D	E	F
Mangoes	200	190	160	120	80	0
Fish	0	20	50	75	90	100

These data in Table 1.2 can be plotted on the same sort of diagram used earlier in Figure 1.1. Various points from **A** to **F** on Figure 1.2's panel **a** show the production possibilities that are open to Crusoe. In between these examples are other feasible possibilities. If we investigated every single alternative, there would soon be so many points that they would appear as a continuous curve, as in panel **a**. Economists call this curve the **production possibilities curve** or sometimes the "production frontier." Any point on the curve could be reached by Crusoe if he employed efficiently the resources available to him.

2.　　　We assume that the resources available to Crusoe cannot be increased—no "Fridays" will appear, as Man Friday did in Defoe's novel, to share the work—and that his technique of production will not be improved.

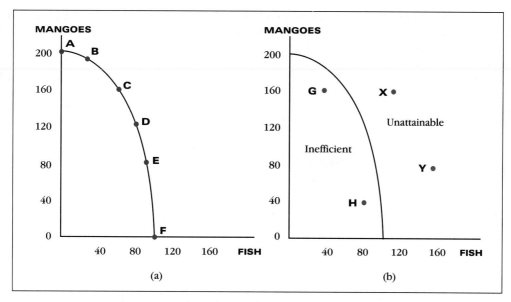

Figure 1.2 Crusoe's production possibilities curve. In panel **a**, we see the various combinations of mangoes and fish that Crusoe can produce. They are shown here as points **A** to **F**, all of which lie along a curve called the production possibilities curve. In panel **b**, we see that points within Crusoe's production possibilities curve are inefficient in that more of both mangoes and fish could be obtained. Points outside the curve show production levels higher than can actually be attained.

Now move to Figure 1.2's panel **b**, which duplicates the production possibilities curve shown in panel **a**. Not only can Crusoe obtain any combination of mangoes or fish along the curve, he can also acquire any combination *inside* the curve, as at point **G** (160 mangoes, 40 fish) or point **H** (40 mangoes, 80 fish). But production anywhere within this curve is less than what could be produced with the resources available, so such choices would involve letting some resources stand idle. (Perhaps he has been too lazy to repair the holes that have developed in his fish nets.) Combinations *outside* the curve, as at point **X** (160 mangoes, 120 fish) or point **Y** (80 mangoes, 160 fish) cannot be attained because not enough resources are available to yield these quantities.

This simple model reveals an important proposition of modern economics: Cost is properly defined as **opportunity cost**, meaning whatever has to be given up to obtain something. Crusoe's little economy does not use money, so he can have no money costs of production. All the same, there is a definite cost whenever he raises his output of mangoes. That cost is a reduction in the quantity of fish that can be caught. Similarly, the cost of raising fish production is some quantity of mangoes that must go unpicked. A general rule of economics, for nations as for Crusoe, is that every production choice involves an opportunity cost, the possible alternative production that has to be given up.[3] In Figure 1.2, opportunity cost is shown whenever Crusoe changes his output decision by moving along his production possibilities curve.

In his optimistic first days on the island, Crusoe may have thought that the trade-off between mangoes and fish—the sacrifice of the one as he increases the production of the other—would be simple. He believed it would make no difference whether lots of fish or lots of mangoes were produced. He assumed that a fixed amount of one could always be sacrificed to gain a fixed amount of the other. But our castaway's life, and in this regard the life of a modern economy, is *not* so simple. As he studies the data, he sees that something unexpected is happening along his production possibilities curve. The trade-off changes along the curve; it is not constant. Crusoe has learned another central lesson of economics: Opportunity costs usually increase disproportionately as one engages increasingly in some given activity.

---

3.   Opportunity cost is treated in more detail in Chapter 6, where we will emphasize that it is not necessarily the same as money cost.

As Table 1.2 and Figure 1.2 show, to acquire more fish, an ever greater sacrifice of mangoes must be made. For example, moving from **A** to **B** in Table 1.2 means that 20 more fish are acquired at an opportunity cost of 10 mangoes. But moving from **E** to **F** means that only 10 more fish are acquired at a cost of 80 mangoes. Similarly, the decision to increase the number of mangoes picked will have an opportunity cost that will always be increasing. Why does this happen? In Crusoe's case, the reasoning is straightforward. Say he picks only a few mangoes and spends almost all of his time fishing, putting him far down on the production possibilities curve, at **W** in Figure 1.3.

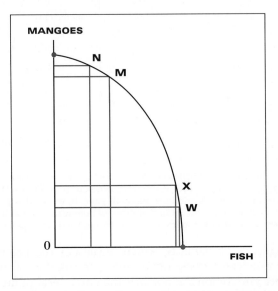

Figure 1.3. Crusoe's opportunity costs. Crusoe discovers that when he produces many fish but just a few mangoes (point **W**), he can then move to point **X** with many more mangoes acquired at little cost in forgone fish. But when Crusoe already produces numerous mangoes (point **M**), then raising mango production further is costly, requiring the sacrifice of many fish (point **N**). On this production possibilities curve, opportunity costs increase.

Here at point **W**, he need give up only very little of the time he spends fishing in order to gather some mangoes on the ground or to pick them when they are in reach. Raising his mango output to **X** on the curve can be accomplished with only a small sacrifice of fish. Now consider point **M**. Here extra mangoes are much harder to come by, as a great many are already being harvested. Crusoe has to shake the trees or even climb into them to obtain his large output. Any addition to mango production, as at point **N**, will involve a long, hot climb high into the trees, which takes away from time spent fishing.[4] The result is that between **M** and **N** on the curve, a great many fish must be sacrificed to obtain a very small increase in mangoes. A curve bowed outward (concave to the origin) always exhibits this principle of increasing costs.

---

4.   Time is not the only problem. Tools also pose a difficulty. Crusoe is now at the point where he must take resources away from their most productive use and transfer them to an activity where they are used with less efficiency. For example, the fish net is considerably more effective in catching fish than it is in catching falling mangoes.

CONSTANT COSTS AND DECREASING COSTS

If instead of increasing costs, the trade-off for Crusoe is always the same no matter how much he produces of either item, then opportunity costs are constant. Production possibilities would then be shown by a straight line, as in Figure 1.4. Beyond Crusoe's horizons, mass production techniques and "learning by doing" may sometimes lead to *decreasing* costs. Here, specialization brings increased efficiency and reduces costs. The curve showing this is convex to the origin, as in Figure 1.5, rather than concave to the origin as in the model of increasing costs.

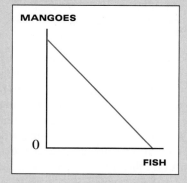

Figure 1.4. **A constant-cost PPC.**
More fish are always obtained with the same sacrifice of mangoes. Opportunity costs are constant.

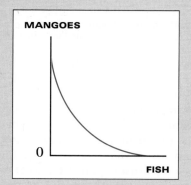

Figure 1.5. **A decreasing-cost PPC.**
More fish are obtained with a decreasing sacrifice of mangoes. Opportunity costs decrease.

PRODUCTION POSSIBILITIES CURVES FOR NATIONS

We can now dispense with the services of Mr. Crusoe, leaving him to his fish and his mangoes. The production possibilities framework developed with his help can now be applied to the analysis of modern economies. One form of this analysis, the "guns-and-butter" trade-off between military goods and civilian production, is especially revealing. Every country with a defense establishment faces a trade-off between devoting resources to its military and devoting them to peaceful purposes. This is shown in Figure 1.6, with guns on the vertical axis and butter on the horizontal. A guns-and-butter diagram of production possibilities repeats and reinforces the insights into the economic problem faced by Robinson Crusoe: *the necessity for making choices because resources are scarce*. All nations face that critical economic problem. The issue can, as discussed earlier, be addressed in the form of five main questions: what to produce, how to produce, who gets the goods, whether resources are used efficiently, and whether (and how) to grow? The implications of each can be seen with guns-butter production possibilities curves for nations.

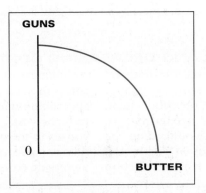

Figure 1.6. The guns-and-butter trade-off. A production possibilities curve can be used to show the trade-off between military production (guns) and production for civilian purposes (butter).

Take first the question "what to produce?" Just as in a Crusoe economy, a nation must face the economic constraint that many possible combinations of guns and butter output would call for more resources than society has available. Points **X** and **Y** on Figure 1.7 represent such cases. These points might be desired, just as Crusoe wanted more mangoes and fish than he had the ability to produce, but they cannot be reached given the scarcity of resources. Points such as these lie outside the production possibilities curve. Instead, the problem of choosing what to produce must focus on *attainable* objectives—points **A**, **B**, **C**, and **D** are all attainable combinations. But, as we saw for Crusoe, points **C** and **D** would not be efficient choices.

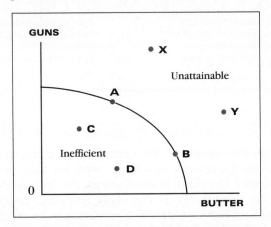

Figure 1.7. Economic problems illustrated with the guns-butter trade-off. As in a Crusoe economy, points within a production possibilities curve must involve inefficiency in production, while points outside the curve represent levels of production that are unattainable given the quantity of resources that are available.

Another lesson that carries over from Crusoe to nations is that for individuals, the real cost (opportunity cost) of acquiring more of an item is the forgone alternatives—the sacrifice—of other items. This is not necessarily the same as the money spent on the item. Consider the cost of going to college. The money cost of tuition, fees, and books make up only a part of the total opportunity cost. Had you not decided to go to college, you could have taken paid employment. So the expense of going to college far exceeds the bills that you pay.[5] By the same token, when the U.S. government utilized a draft in World War II, the Korean War, and Vietnam, the cost to the

---

5.   Don't let this be discouraging—the average lifetime earnings of college graduates surpass that of high school graduates by a wide margin. According to the World Bank's *World Development Report 1987,* p. 64, even when all opportunity costs are taken into account, the rate of return on money spent for higher education in developed countries is about 11% per year. This is much higher than the return that would be earned if the money were put in a bank account and allowed to earn interest.

draftees was not just the discomfort and the danger, but the loss of wages. The wages the government paid the draftees were much lower than what many would have made in civilian life.

As we also saw with Crusoe, *increasing opportunity cost* is standard in most economic activity. Obtaining larger and larger amounts of any product, with the quantity of resources and technology unchanging, will usually require greater and greater sacrifices.[6]

The questions "how to produce?" and "is production efficient?" also can be shown using the model of the production possibilities curve. Points **C** and **D** on Figure 1.7, inside the curve, illustrate the principle. Some production techniques will yield less output than others, and some types of economic organization may result in unemployment of labor, land, and machines. In either case, society could obtain more output than it is currently producing. If organization or technology, or both, are inefficient, then the combination of guns and butter will, like points **C** and **D**, fall below the production possibilities curve. Any unemployment of a country's stock of resources, or inefficient use of them if employed, will result in a combination of outputs represented by a point *below* the curve. The answer to the question "how to produce?" involves a search for efficient methods of production. An economy producing on its production possibilities curve has obviously adopted an economic system and economic policies that facilitate the full employment of labor and other resources. Henceforth, we will define **inefficiency in production** as a condition in which a greater amount of output could be produced using a given amount of labor, land, and machines all working at a reasonable pace. Productive inefficiency is illustrated by a position within (under) a production possibilities curve.[7]

How the Same Events May Have Quite Different Economic Results

The concepts of opportunity costs and efficiency as illustrated by production possibilities curves allow for some piercing insights into many great historical and current experiences. For example, we can use PPCs to understand how the U.S. economy was affected in a very different way by two episodes of rapid rearmament. Consider the significantly different U.S. experience during World War II in the 1940s and the Vietnam War in the 1960s. In 1940, the United States was just coming out of the Great Depression of the 1930s and unemployment was still very high, at about 15% of the labor force. The huge rearmament program that began in 1940 was achieved *along with* a general rise in living standards (though the rise was slight). Both were possible at the same time because of the unemployment of resources. As Figure 1.8 shows, when starting from a position of unemployment at point **A** it is possible to obtain more guns (**AB**), more butter (**AD**), or more of both at the same time (**AC**), anywhere along the curve between **B** and **D**.

In 1966 the situation was very different. U.S. unemployment was only a quarter of what it had been in 1940 (and well below what it is now), at 3.8% of the labor force. When U.S. military expenditures leaped in support of the Vietnam War, the United States was very much closer to its production possibilities curve than it had been before World War II. It faced the problem that any increase in military production had to be at the sacrifice of some civilian output, as in the movement from **D** toward **C** in Figure 1.8.

6.   The training of an economist focuses especially on the recognition of costs. Harry S. Truman, the president who established the U.S. Council of Economic Advisors just after World War II, heard so often from these advisors that "on the one hand" such and such a problem would follow from a policy proposal, while "on the other hand" there would be these other consequences from an alternative policy, that he plaintively asked for a one-armed economist. (The story has been told of other famous public figures as well, but it seems particularly apt for the earthy Truman.) Truman's discomfort is, or should be, shared by all politicians whose decisions have an economic impact. Most of these decisions will involve costs as well as benefits.

7.   Later we shall see that there is another kind of inefficiency, in allocation. Allocative inefficiency can exist even if production is efficient. This is seen most easily if one of the axes is "food" and none is produced. In that case, production would be at one end of the curve. The production itself would be efficient, temporarily at any rate, but the allocation of the production between goods would not be. By comparison to this situation, points such as **C** or **D** in Figure 1.7 would be much more desirable; people would have something to eat even though production is inefficient.

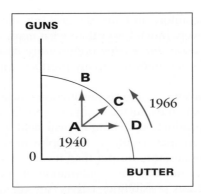

Figure 1.8. The different experience of the United States in World War II and the Vietnam War.
The United States, with significant unemployment of resources in 1940, could obtain more guns, and more butter as well, by putting the idle resources back to work. In 1966, with the economy much closer to full employment, the country could achieve more guns only by sacrificing butter.

Neither President Johnson nor Congress was willing to make that sacrifice. In effect, both wanted to reach an unattainable point beyond the production possibilities curve. The result was economic difficulty, the effect of which lasted for over a decade. Thus, the armament program of 1940 was readily absorbed by the economy, while the armament program of 1966 and subsequent years resulted in severe economic problems, the memory of which still haunts U.S. economic policymakers.

From this we see that countries with slack in their economies caused by unemployment or technological inefficiencies suffer from reduced output but have some room to maneuver if they have to increase output quickly. Countries operating with an efficient economy, and thus operating on or near their production possibilities curves, maximize their present output but must face difficult sacrifices if production has to be reallocated quickly. (Economists do not, however, recommend maintaining substantial permanent slack as insurance against emergencies, because the present costs of such a policy would be far too great.)

By the 1990s the guns-butter model was being used to analyze a *dividend*, not a sacrifice. A "peace dividend" flowing from East-West detente was resulting in massive cuts in defense spending in both NATO and the former Communist countries. Resources were being freed from military production and applied to peaceful uses. This peace dividend involves a movement from **B** toward **A** in Figure 1.9.

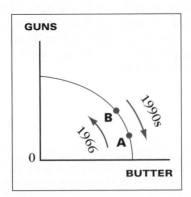

Figure 1.9. Guns for butter, 1990s. Instead of butter for guns, as during the Vietnam War of the 1960s, in the 1990s guns were being traded for butter.

ECONOMIC GROWTH AND PRODUCTION POSSIBILITIES CURVES

Production possibilities curves can also help us understand issues concerning economic growth.[8] Is growth desirable? Is growth taking place? Why is it occurring? These questions were not important in a Crusoe model because we assumed that the quantity and quality of resources at his disposal did not change. For a national economy, however, we will want to know what will happen when more resources become available.

The Factors of Production

First, we need to be clear about how we define the word **resources**. Most people think of resources as natural resources—coal, iron, oil, and the like—but much more is included in the term as it is used by economists. To avoid any misunderstanding, we shall use the substitute phrase **factors of production**. These factors are broad categories that give a convenient way to classify the resource inputs of an economy. Commonly, there are said to be five factors of production: *labor, land, capital, technology, and entrepreneurship.*

Labor represents human physical effort which is in turn influenced by skills, education, and natural talent. **Land** includes aspects such as arable acreage, minerals, water, and other natural resources. Traditionally, land was considered as more fixed in supply than the other factors and was looked at as the gift of nature, the factor unaltered by any other factor. Nowadays we realize that applications of capital and technology can affect both the quantity and quality of land. **Capital** is anything man-made that is produced and used for further production, thus increasing future output. Machines, roads, and buildings, as well as tools, are all examples of capital. (Inventories of unsold goods are also considered to be capital and, indeed, without inventories many types of production would come to a halt.) Education and skills give a capital aspect to labor and are sometimes called "human capital."[9] (Economists use the word **investment** to describe the creation of new capital.) **Technology** is the word used to indicate the application of practical or scientific knowledge to production. Fundamentally, it refers to the way the factors of production are combined. (Thus, we speak of "labor-intensive" or "capital-intensive" or "knowledge-intensive" technologies.) Most commonly, technological change is associated with increases in the effectiveness of physical capital, but the term is broader than that. Along with transformations in machinery, equipment, communications, and transport, technology is also embodied in the seeds and methods used in agriculture, in the provision of marketing facilities and the organization of marketing, and indeed, in virtually any economic activity. **Entrepreneurship** refers to activities of entrepreneurs, who play three roles, all vital to the production process: first, as initiators or innovators who begin a project; second, as organizers whose aim is efficiency in production; and third, as risk takers, risking funds, reputation, or both on a project. These aspects of entrepreneurship need not always be embodied inthesame person; for example, in large corporations the various tasks are shared by a group of managers and stockholders.

The existence of the factors of production—labor, land, capital, technology, and entrepreneurship—do not depend in any way on the type of economy being considered. The (former) communist countries had the same kinds of factors as the United States and the other western market economies—so did Crusoe on his island.

The Factors of Production and Economic Growth

With this background, let us return to the question of growth. What would be expected to happen over time to the factors? In a Crusoe economy, nothing except perhaps the manufacture

---

8.   The third main question of economics "who gets the goods?" is not easily answered within the framework of production possibilities curves, and consideration of it is postponed here.

9.   As suggested, land and capital may also be intertwined. For example, an acre of original and irreproducible farmland might have once been covered with boulders that had to be removed and large trees that had to be cut and their stumps uprooted. Or it might have been tidal flats or swampland (or even, in the Netherlands, the bed of the sea) that had to be filled or drained. Minerals might require deep and expensive mining to reach them. The land and capital aspects are not always easy to separate.

of a few more tools until he dies or is rescued. The *world*, however, has experienced considerable change in its stock of factors, especially during the nineteenth and twentieth centuries.

1) There has been an increase in the size of the labor force as population has grown, along with enhanced quality of labor as educational standards have improved.
2) New land was brought into production through the clearing of forests, the plowing of prairies, irrigation, and the draining of wetlands. New natural resources were discovered in the last century at rates far surpassing those of all other centuries put together.
3) There has been tremendous investment in new capital, resulting in an increased use of machines and other capital. As a result, large portions of the world have become industrialized.
4) Great improvements in technology have revolutionized production methods, marketing, communications, and transportation. In recent years this has been the most important of all the changes.
5) Entrepreneurial services have increased in amount as a larger population brought more opportunities for entrepreneurs to establish new firms. More debatably, improved education has made entrepreneurs more effective.

All this means that a production possibilities curve that is accurate at this moment will not be accurate in a few months or years when more and better factors of production are available. The normal expectation is that, with the passage of time, the curve will shift outward all along its length as shown in Figure 1.10. It is important to realize that the outward shift is a shift in possibilities only. There is no universal rule ensuring that production will actually take place at some point on the new curve. Some of the new factors of production might remain unemployed, or if employed, they might be used inefficiently. Either way, an outward movement of the curve never guarantees that the actual point of production will change in the same degree.

One complication can occur when the curve shifts outward. What if the new factors of production are better adapted to producing one of the goods (say butter) than the other (guns)? In this case, the curve will move outward a greater distance along the butter axis than along the guns axis as in Figure 1.11.

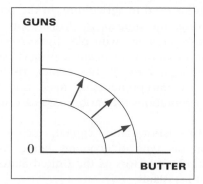

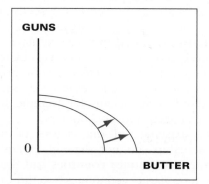

Figure 1.10. An increase in factors moves the PPC outward. An increase in land, labor, capital, technology, or entrepreneurship will move the PPC outward, meaning that greater production of butter, guns, or any combination of the two is now possible.

Figure 1.11. An increase in factors better suited for butter production. If new machines, new skills, etc., increase production of butter more than that of guns, then the PPC will move out further along the butter axis.

Under certain circumstances, the production possibilities curve might shift inward, as in Figure 1.12.

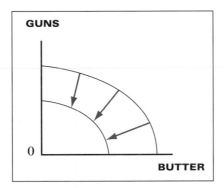

Figure 1.12. A decrease in factors moves the PPC inward. A decrease in the quantity or quality of any factor of production will mean reduced production possibilities and an inward movement of the PPC.

For this to occur, there would have to be widespread reductions in the quantity or quality of labor, land, capital, or entrepreneurial ability. Three obvious cases of this come to mind. A destructive war, such as World Wars I and II, or even smaller ones such as in Vietnam and Bosnia, would kill or wound large numbers, waste natural resources, and ruin much capital. A depopulating disease, such as the Black Death of the fourteenth century, would reduce the supply of labor and managerial talent. Finally, exhaustion of important natural resources like crude oil, copper, tin, and uranium would have a similar effect on the production possibilities curve. Of course, simultaneous changes may partly or wholly offset these effects. War may be accompanied by rapid technological progress. The disappearance of an essential natural resource may spur the search for substitutes. Unless such changes occur, however, the production possibilities curve will move inward.

THE CHOICE OF CAPITAL GOODS OR CONSUMPTION GOODS

Economic growth occurs when the factors of production are augmented and put to use. There are choices connected with growth, however, because any society has some control over how fast it grows. One critical choice is between the output of capital goods that will increase future consumption, and the output of consumption goods that are consumed now. We can analyze the problem with production possibilities curves. Figure 1.13 shows two mythical countries, each starting with exactly the same production possibilities curve but each making different choices of capital goods production and consumption.

Instead of guns and butter on the axes, we now show output of capital goods vertically and consumption goods horizontally. The point marked P_o in panel **a** shows the initial choice made by Poveria. This choice involves substantial capital formation but great sacrifices in terms of restricted current consumption. Meanwhile, the point P_e in panel **b** shows the original choice made by Penuristan, whose people prefer a high level of current consumption and invest only enough to keep their capital stock from wearing out.

Given this situation, a first impression might be that Poveria has made a silly decision. Capital goods are desirable, but why consume less than Penuristan does? The reason is made clear on further examining the same figures. It can be seen in panel **b** that Penuristan, which has only been producing enough capital to replace that which has worn out, has not raised its production possibilities curve at all over the last twenty years. It is still at P_e on its original curve. In contrast, Poveria has managed through capital formation to raise its curve significantly from its former position, which was originally identical to Penuristan's, but now runs through a point P_o' in panel **a**. Its initial sacrifices now allow it not only to forge ahead in current consumption, but even to retain its lead in capital formation. To equal Poveria's performance, Penuristan would have had to reach point P_e', but it was unable to do so. This is a good example of the trade-off in the growth process. Restricting consumption at one time period in Poveria has meant greater consumption than could have been attained in a subsequent time period.

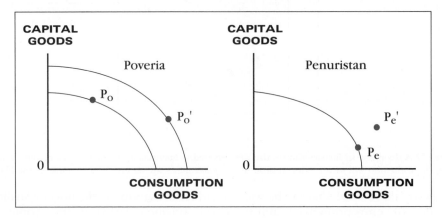

Figure 1.13. **The reason for Poveria's choice of more capital goods.** At point P_o, Poveria chooses to produce fewer consumption goods than Penuristan (P_e) because that allows it to produce more capital goods than Penuristan. Poveria's leaders hope that in time its new capital will allow greater economic growth and a larger output of both capital and consumption goods (at P_o') than Penuristan can enjoy (still at P_e).

ECONOMIC MODELS

Throughout this discussion of production possibilities curves we have been using an economic model that attempts to advance understanding by simplifying reality. The PPC was the first of many models to be found in the following pages. This section is a brief discussion of what economic models are and how economists use them to facilitate their thinking.[10]

Economic models provide a way to render some aspect of an economy less complex than it really is. They help economists to identify causes and effects, explain various economic phenomena, and make useful economic predictions. Models are not in themselves the truth, but they are engines for discovering the truth. Economic modeling can involve verbal descriptions, or mathematical equations, or geometric diagrams of the sort used for the production possibilities curves. Geometric models can deal with only a small number of variables because they are generally limited to two dimensions. Calculus allows an unlimited number of variables to be considered and is thus central to advanced economics. Whatever form models take, they have the same goal in view.

A good analogy to an economic model is a map. A map is a model that uses assumptions (such as 1 inch = 100 miles) to simplify and predict, but some maps are more useful than others for the purpose at hand. The scale for a map that shows you to how to drive from your apartment in Manhattan to JFK Airport would be utterly useless for a map used to sail a ship from Yokohama to New York. That same scale would be equally useless for showing how much ground is taken up by the buildings between 15th and 16th Streets on Flatbush Avenue in Brooklyn. Drawing maps to different scales is akin to simplifying reality to the required degree—sorting out the relevant facts from the irrelevant. Because a map selects the key facts from an unwieldy mass of information, we arrive most efficiently at our destination. In short, a map *is* a model, like an economic model, except that it is designed for different purposes.

---

10.   Most economists use the words economic theory and economic law as almost complete synonyms with economic model. The term "law" is now largely outdated and is used mainly—but not always—to refer to some of the most respected models developed by economists during the nineteenth century. That the term "law" has gone out of fashion in economics is a healthy development recognizing that the discipline cannot be reduced to a series of immutable laws like gravity or the diffusion of gases. A less familiar word, paradigm, is often used for the collection of related models or theories that make up a tradition or "school of thought." Thus, Marxist economic models, taken together, make up the "Marxist paradigm."

Our discussion of maps helps us to view an objection sometimes made against economic models of all types, namely, that they are not realistic. This charge represents a misunderstanding of what models are intended to do. If a model were truly realistic, then like a map that showed reality itself, it would be enormous and utterly useless for practical purposes. Models, therefore, aim at finding the right abstractions and making accurate predictions and interpretations. They do not attempt to describe every aspect of reality.

How then do we ever judge a model? When do we conclude that it is important?[11] Four tests may be proposed. First, is the model coherent? If conclusions do not flow logically from the assumptions and argument, then the model is internally inconsistent and not coherent. A wall map of the United States purporting to show the actual shape of the country, but with one or more states drawn to a different scale from that used to draw the others, would be internally inconsistent.

Second, the model must be testable with evidence from the real world (the test of correspondence). Are any of the assumptions contrary to fact? If so, then successful prediction from this model must be in spite of the incorrect assumptions. Conclusions should be testable empirically. A useful model makes accurate and significant predictions based on a few key facts abstracted from the complexities of reality. In economics, a model can never achieve the status of 100% certainty. Even after ten thousand tests for accuracy, more testing might uncover a rare exception—especially since we are dealing with human beings and not laws of physics. Still, should a model make accurate predictions time after time over long periods, it has passed its most important test. Maps must face the same challenge. When explorers showed there was no unfrozen Northwest Passage from the Atlantic to the Pacific, and that the Nile did not rise in West Africa, many nineteenth-century maps had to be discarded. So it is with economic models.

Third, the model is of greater significance and importance if it can pass a test of comprehensiveness. The more facts that the model can account for, the more confidence that the model is comprehensive rather than a special case only. A map showing just toll highways would be seriously inadequate for getting from New York to Philadelphia.

Finally, a model should be frugal (the test of parsimony). Can any element or assumption of the model be dropped with no loss of ability to explain? If so, it *should* be dropped as it does not add to the model's explanatory power. (To get you from New York to Philadelphia, road maps do not need to show railway tracks; it reduces clutter and increases utility if they are not included.)

In short, the test of coherence checks the internal consistency of the logic employed; no empirical verification is involved at this stage. The test of correspondence checks the output of the model with empirical reality. The test of comprehensiveness checks to see what is unexplained by the model to determine whether it is identifying special cases only. The test of parsimony aims to pare away the parts of a theory not needed to explain observable reality.

CETERIS PARIBUS: AN IMPORTANT ASSUMPTION IN ECONOMICS

An important special case of model building in economics is the frequent use of the assumption that "all other things are equal," **ceteris paribus** in Latin. We have already encountered a *ceteris paribus* assumption, implicitly, in discussing the Crusoe economy. When looking at Crusoe's PPC, we assumed no change in labor availability (no other castaways arrive), no additions to capital, no devastating hurricane to uproot the mango trees, and so on. It would be difficult to proceed without this valuable simplification which, by abstracting from the incidentals of real life, allows us to keep a model within manageable bounds. "Other things being equal" is a phrase frequently found in the work of economists, in effect allowing us to conduct experiments in economic reasoning.

---

11.   Milton Friedman, a Nobel prize-winning economist who spent his career at the University of Chicago, is the most influential modern writer on the subject. The discussion in his *Essays in Positive Economics* is perhaps the best-known treatment of the field. The paragraphs that follow are distilled from Friedman's work and Alfred S. Eichner's concluding essay in the book edited by him, *Why Economics Is Not Yet a Science*, Armonk, N.Y., 1983.

POSITIVE AND NORMATIVE STATEMENTS

One last consideration in the theorizing of economists is the distinction between positive and normative statements. A **positive statement** is a statement of what is, and is thus testable by factual evidence. "The earth revolves around the sun" is an example. "Families with incomes over $100,000 a year pay an average tax rate of 26%" is another. (Here a major task of the economist is to distinguish between assertions that are valid and those that are not, and more narrowly to determine *when* an assertion is valid and when it is not.) In contrast, a **normative statement** is an expression of belief in what ought to be. Normative opinions cannot be tested by an appeal to the facts. "The rich ought to pay higher taxes" is a normative statement. "Ought to" or "should" are the identifying marks of a normative expression.

Economists have their own normative values, of course, and they often differ in their value judgments—just as does the general public. Yet the training of an economist is particularly well suited to distinguishing between positive and normative; in detecting when private interest lies behind public proposals; in seeing that many a statement of fact conceals a value judgment. For a politician, it is high art to pass off a normative position as a positive one. For the economist, correct identification and exposure of value judgments are part of the job.

 ## LOOKING AHEAD

This book's strategy is to move immediately to microeconomics—the study of individual economic decisions—and then to consider macroeconomics—the whole rather than individual units. The reason for so doing is that a solid grounding in micro principles, especially the model of supply and demand studied in the chapters just ahead, is of great assistance in providing a foundation for macro studies. Following a sequence of micro and then macro yields gains, by conserving on the labor of both students and instructors, but with only inconsequential costs in forgone opportunities. How better to begin an economics textbook than by practicing what we preach.

SUMMARY

1) Economics is the study of making choices when the alternatives are limited by scarce resources.
2) The choices that must be made because resources are finite can be divided into five main questions that any economic system must answer: what to produce, how to produce, for whom to produce, are resources being used efficiently, and is the economy growing or stagnant?
3) Economics consists of two major areas: microeconomics (the study of individual economic decisions at the level of a person, firm, or industry) and macroeconomics (the study of aggregate economic topics such as growth, inflation, and unemployment).
4) A single economic model, the production possibilities curve, can be used to introduce a number of key concepts in economics. Economists define costs as opportunity cost. This is illustrated by the movement along a PPC; the rise in the production of one good is at the cost of the reduced output of another. Production is efficient when a country is producing on its PPC. If it is producing at a point below the curve, production is inefficient. Production levels outside the PPC are unattainable.

5) Economic growth is caused by changes in the quantity or quality of the factors of production. These factor inputs to production are labor, land, capital, technology, and entrepreneurship.

6) Economic models are abstractions that simplify reality and allow meaningful predictions to be made. This word model means the same thing as theory. This chapter shows how economic models can be compared to road maps, which have the same purpose of simplification and useful prediction.

APPENDIX
READING GRAPHS

All the graphs in this book utilize a horizontal (or X) axis running rightward from the graph's origin, and a vertical (or Y) axis running upward from a common point that is called the origin.[12] These axes permit us to measure the quantities of two different variables on the same graph. For example, say we want to measure how many mangoes and how many fish are available to Robinson Crusoe. We can measure mangoes along the vertical (Y) axis of Figure 1A.1 and fish along the horizontal (X) axis of the figure.

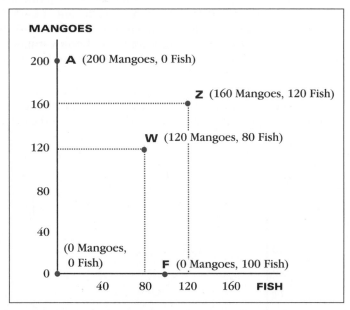

Figure 1A.1. **Locating coordinate points.** Graphs utilize a horizontal (or X) axis running rightward from an origin, and a vertical (or Y) axis running upward from that same origin. Any given combination of the item measured along the horizontal axis and the item measured along the vertical can be shown as a coordinate point positioned in the graph's space.

---

12.   A useful way to keep straight which axis is X and which is Y is to recall that the letter Y has a long vertical portion; the Y axis is the vertical one.

Any actual combination of mangoes and fish can be plotted as a coordinate point on the graph. Let us first picture a situation where 0 mangoes and 0 fish are available. That would be at a point of 0 on the mango axis and 0 on the fish axis, at the graph's origin. Now say we want to picture a situation of 200 mangoes but still no fish. The coordinate point in this case would be at 200 on the mango axis, but at 0 on the fish axis. This point is labeled **A** in Figure 1A.1. What if we want to show 0 mangoes but 100 fish? Now the coordinate point would be at 0 on the mango axis, but at 100 on the fish axis. This point is labeled **F** in the figure.

Any combination that involves positive amounts of both mangoes and fish would yield coordinate points lying upward and to the right of the graph's origin. Say we want to picture 120 mangoes and 80 fish. Consider how point **W** does exactly this. Read the number on the vertical axis that indicates the height of **W** above the origin. That number is 120. Now read the number on the horizontal axis that indicates how far to the right of the origin **W** is. That number is 80. So, point **W** is the coordinate point that indicates 120 mangoes and 80 fish. Check your understanding of this by identifying the quantity of mangoes and fish indicated by point **Z**. Looking at the vertical axis, we see that **Z** indicates 160 mangoes. Looking at the horizontal axis, we see that **Z** indicates 120 fish. *Any* quantity of mangoes and fish can be indicated by these means. The technique described here is central to most of the figures in this book.

FITTING LINES THROUGH KNOWN POINTS

Sometimes data points may indicate a pattern, as in Figure 1A.2, that shows a hypothetical relationship between vehicle weight and the miles obtained per gallon of fuel. Say that experiments have produced good data for vehicle weights of 2,500, 3,000, and 3,500 lbs., as shown by points **A**, **B**, and **C** in the figure. There seems to be an obvious correlation: The heavier the car, the lower the miles per gallon. But what about intermediate points, such as car weights between 3,000 lbs. and 3,500 lbs.? If there is sufficient reason to believe that the relationship is a consistent one, then a line can be drawn through the known points **A**, **B**, and **C**. This implies that the consistent relationship would hold for unknown values, such as 3,250 lbs., as well as for the known ones. Fitting a line or curve to known points is standard technique for economists.

Notice that the figure also employs another standard convention of drawing graphs. No cars are built so light as just 500 lbs., so including this part of the range of weights would foolishly waste space on the page. The two little hash marks // indicate a break along the horizontal axis.

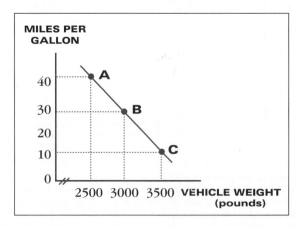

Figure 1A.2. Fitting a line through known points. In the figure, a line fitted through points **A**, **B**, and **C** suggests that known values can be extrapolated to unknown ones. Also note the break along the horizontal axis marked //, indicating that weights up to 2,500 lbs. have been omitted to save space.

ILLUSTRATING CAUSE-AND-EFFECT RELATIONSHIPS

Economists often use graphs to illustrate cause-and-effect relationships. Usually, though not always, the independent variable (that is, the variable that is believed to be the cause of some result) is placed on the horizontal (X) axis. The dependent variable (the variable that is affected by some cause) is usually placed on the vertical (Y) axis. In panel **a** of Figure 1A.3, the length of a bridge is the independent variable and cost of the bridge is the dependent variable. On average, the (hypothetical) cost of a bridge increases as its length increases, so the relationship is positive; the line relating bridge length and cost is positively sloped.[13] (Here it is obvious that length is the cause and higher cost is the effect, and not the other way around. An increase in cost did not cause the bridge to get longer. In many other cases, however, it is not so clear which is cause and which is effect—a major reason why professional economists must have a thorough grounding in statistical technique.)

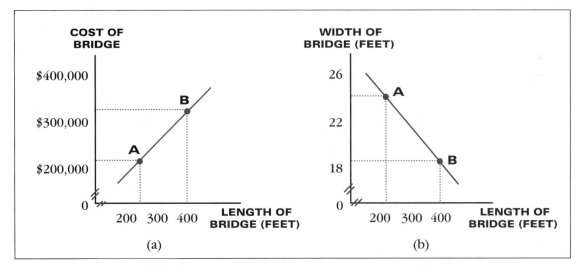

Figure 1A.3. **Cause-and-effect relationships.** Graphs can be used to show cause-and-effect relationships. In panel **a**, the relationship is positive, and the curve slopes upward. Bridge length, the independent variable, is on the horizontal (or X) axis. Bridge cost is on the vertical (or Y) axis. Longer bridges are more costly. In panel **b**, the relationship between the length of bridges and their width is negative. Longer bridges are frequently built to narrower widths. The curve showing the relationship slopes downward.

In panel **b** of Figure 1A.3, the relationship (again hypothetical) between the length of bridges and the width of bridges is negative. Longer bridges are frequently built to a narrower width. The length is clearly the cause of the narrow width (because of costs, of course). No one would argue that a narrower width causes bridges to get longer. So an increase in length, the independent variable, causes a decrease in width, the dependent variable. The line relating the two has a negative slope.

WHEN SLOPES ARE INCREASING OR DECREASING

Often the relationship involves a curve rather than a straight line. What difference would it make if the rate of increase or decrease changes? Panel **a** of Figure 1A.4 indicates that as bridge length increases, bridge costs rise at an ever faster rate. (Perhaps construction techniques become more complex as bridges have to span ever wider gaps, raising costs greatly.) In that case, the curve showing the relationship has an increasing slope, sloping more steeply upward at higher bridge

---

13.   *Warning:* Do not use the data on bridge lengths, costs, and widths in this section in your engineering courses. They are completely hypothetical.

lengths. Check the figure to see what the upward slope implies. See how the movement from point **A** (200 feet) to point **B** (250 feet) involves a horizontal movement rightward from **A** of 50 feet as measured along the horizontal axis. Using letters to show this, as is frequently done, the increase in length of 50 feet can be indicated by the distance **AW**. That causes a rise in costs of $10,000, from $190,000 to $200,000, as measured along the vertical axis, or a distance of **WB**. Now consider a rise in bridge length from 400 to 450 feet, read on the graph as a distance of **CX**. That causes a much greater rise in costs, from $300,000 to $380,000 as seen on the vertical axis. This is the same as the distance **XD**. The curve is rising at an increasing rate; bridge costs balloon as they span greater gaps.

In panel **b**, we discuss a slope that is decreasing, but more gradually. That is, its slope is falling at an ever slower rate. Perhaps the reason is that no one wants to build a bridge narrower than one lane, for then you couldn't take a car across it. So although the width of bridges tends to decrease as bridge length increases, the narrowing slows as length increases. The curve showing the relationship has a decreasing slope, but with the slope becoming shallower at longer lengths. Using letters to show this, an increase in length from 200 feet to 250 feet can be indicated by the distance **AW** in panel **b**. That is associated with a fall in width of 5 feet, from 25 to 20, as measured along the vertical axis, or a distance of **WB**. Now consider a rise in bridge length from 400 to 450 feet, read on the graph as a distance of **CX**. That is associated with a much smaller narrowing of width, just 1 foot, from 12 feet to 11 feet as seen on the vertical axis. This is the same as the distance **XD**. The curve is falling at a decreasing rate; on average, bridges are narrower as they are longer, but the narrowing slows down as their width approaches the one lane that would accommodate a car.

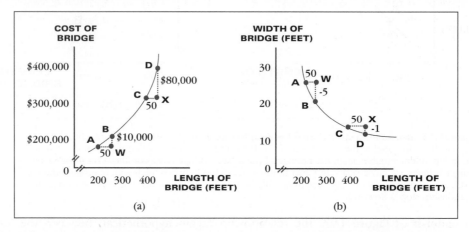

Figure 1A.4. Increasing and decreasing slopes. In panel **a**, the curve is rising at an increasing rate. Any given increase in the length of bridges causes a greater increase in costs when the bridges are already long. In panel **b**, the curve is falling at a decreasing rate. Any given increase in bridge length is associated with a narrowing of width, but at a decreasing rate because there is some minimum width below which the bridge will be useless.

Later in the book, it will sometimes be useful to measure the slope of the lines in the figures we use. With a straight line, the calculation is easy. Imagine we are driving a car up a mountain pass, and that the ascent of the road is indicated by the line in Figure 1A.5. What is the slope of this line (that is, the slope of the upgrade)? Measuring the numerical value of slopes involves dividing the *rise* by the *run*, that is, the distance by which the line rises vertically for some given horizontal movement. In panel **a**, we can see that if we travel a horizontal distance of 10 miles (the run), we have ascended a distance of 2 miles (the rise). Dividing the rise by the run yields $2/10$, $= 1/5$, or a 20% upgrade. Around the world, steep hills are often marked "1:5 slope" or "20% grade." Economists have many uses for these values, as we shall see.

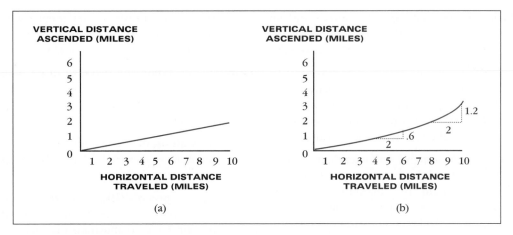

Figure 1A.5. Measuring slopes. Measuring the slope of a line involves dividing the rise by the run. In panel **a**, a highway rises 2 miles for every 10 miles of horizontal travel, so the slope is $\frac{2}{10} = \frac{1}{5} = 20\%$. In panel **b**, the upgrade is increasing. Lower down on the pass, the slope indicated by the little triangle is only $\frac{.6}{2} = \frac{3}{10} = 30\%$, while higher up the slope is $\frac{1.2}{2} = \frac{6}{10} = 60\%$. Better keep your car off the top part of that road; try a burro instead.

The little triangles we used to illustrate changing slopes in the last section are valuable for calculating the numerical value of slopes along a curve rather than a straight line. Look at panel **b** of Figure 1A.5. In the area between 4 and 6 miles, the road is rising by .6 of a mile for every 2 miles of horizontal distance, or a slope of $\frac{.6}{2} = \frac{3}{10} = 30\%$. Higher up, in the area between 8 and 10 miles, the road is rising by 1.2 miles for every 2 miles of horizontal distance, or a slope of $\frac{1.2}{2} = \frac{6}{10} = 60\%$. The slope has changed. This is now a very steep road, so watch out.

These slopes also allow us to clarify a point concerning how percentage changes are expressed by economists. We understand that an increase in slope from 50% to 60% represents a rise in the road from 1 mile per 2 miles traveled to 1.2 miles for every 2 miles traveled. But what is the increase in percentage terms? Some would say the rise from 50% to 60% is an increase of 10%, but 10% of 50 is only 5, not 10, so inaccuracy is involved in this way of describing it. For strict accuracy, it is better to say that the rise from 50% to 60% is an increase of 10 percentage points. That is the method employed in the rest of the book.

CONCLUSION

Economics employs a considerable amount of graphical analysis, so it is necessary to be familiar with the techniques used. This appendix has explored several key features involved in reading graphs, features that are encountered throughout the book. For our purposes, the ones covered in this appendix are the most important ones. Later, we will encounter several further techniques having to do with reading graphs. These are explained as they arise.

Chapter Key Words

Capital: The factor of production that is man-made and helps to increase future output.

Ceteris paribus: Latin, meaning all other things are equal. Useful simplification allowing economists to conduct experiments in economic reasoning.

Economics: The social science that studies the making of choices when the alternatives involve scarce resources.

Entrepreneurship: The factor of production involving initiation of projects, organization, and risk-taking.

Factors of production: Resources of an economy used in the production process, including labor, land, capital, technology, and entrepreneurship.

Guns and butter: A phrase that illustrates the "trade-off" problems of economics. Achieving more production of one item will be at the expense of some other item.

Inefficiency: Productive inefficiency involves a failure to use the factors of production so as to obtain the maximum possible output. It is shown by a point inside a country's production-possibilities curve.

Investment: The creation of new capital.

Land: The factor of production that includes arable acreage, minerals, water, and other natural resources.

Macroeconomics: The study of aggregate economic problems that tend to affect a whole economy.

Microeconomics: The study of economic problems at the individual level of a person, firm, or industry.

Models: Abstractions that simplify reality and allow meaningful predictions to be made; model has the same meaning as theory.

Normative statement: A statement of what ought to be, a value judgment. Not testable by factual evidence. See *positive statement.*

Opportunity cost: The real cost of production measured in terms of the alternative production that has to be given up to obtain something.

Positive statement: A statement of what is, testable by factual evidence. See *normative statement.*

Production possibilities curve: A curve illustrating an economy's potential output. Used to illustrate the answers to several of the basic questions of economics, the existence of unemployment and/or inefficiency, and the doctrine of opportunity cost.

Technology: The application of practical or scientific knowledge to production; the manner in which the factors of production are combined.

Chapter Questions

1) The citizens of Utopia are lucky to live in a country where every resource (including labor) is boundless and even time is not a limitation. One Utopian proposes that the country hire her to become Utopia's first economist. Using the five main questions of economics, explain why her job would not be very interesting. Would she be hired anyway?

2) Explain why each of the following is a microeconomic or macroeconomic topic: U.S. inflation is running above 10%; apple prices rise by more than 10%; the president vows to cut the U.S. unemployment rate; Microsoft plans to hire more workers.

3) A small pizzeria sells pizza and stromboli. Use the data in the following table to plot points on a graph. Then smoothly connect the points to show the production possibilities curve for the pizzeria. Put pizza on the horizontal axis and strombolis on the vertical axis.

Possible combinations of pizza and stromboli that can be produced in one day.				
Pizza	100	95	60	40	0
Stromboli	0	40	95	110	120

Suppose that one day the pizzeria makes 50 pizzas and 60 strombolis. Plot this point on your diagram. Is it efficient? Now suppose that a person orders 80 pizzas and 70 strombolis for a large party. Could the pizzeria fill the order?

4) Use the data from Question 3 to answer the following questions. If the pizzeria is currently making 0 pizzas and 120 strombolis, what is the opportunity cost of making 40 more pizzas? Now suppose the pizzeria is making 60 pizzas and 95 strombolis. What is the opportunity cost of making 40 more pizzas? Try to explain why the opportunity cost might change.

5) Concordia and Harmonia are two rich nations that are economic rivals. Concordia's economy is running at peak efficiency, while Harmonia's is deep in recession with 18% unemployment. Harmonia's president proposes a massive space program to restore national pride, and Concordia's prime minister responds by creating one as well. A few years later, the citizens of Concordia elect a new majority in parliament, complaining that spending on the space program has lowered their standard of living. Meanwhile, Harmonia's citizens applaud their space program as a great success at getting the nation back on its feet.

Draw PPCs for Concordia and Harmonia, with space equipment on the horizontal axis and consumer goods on the vertical axis. Using the experience of the United States in World War II and the Vietnam War as a guide, show the points where Concordia and Harmonia started from when they began their space programs. Explain why Harmonians were much more supportive of their space program.

6) Draw a PPC for two goods: parks and roads. The only factor of production that parks require is land. Roads require land as well, and they also need capital in the form of asphalt, signposts, and street lights. Assume that neither parks nor roads need labor, technology, or entrepreneurship. Show what would happen to the PPC if the amount of capital increased. Then show what would happen if a natural disaster decreased the amount of land available?

7) Recall from the reading that Poveria made the choice to produce more capital goods and fewer consumption goods. One night a Poverian family sits down to dinner and the grandfather attacks the government policy, stating that more consumption goods should be produced. His grand-daughter in high school supports the policy, claiming that it is a wise investment. Explain why they are both right from the point of view of self-interest.

8) An economist proposes the following simple model. A small Florida orange crop occurs only when there are floods in the Midwest and/or freezing temperatures in Florida. The economist tests the model with data on flooding, temperatures, and the orange crop, and finds that it predicts quite accurately. But critics of the model claim that it fails the tests of coherence, comprehensiveness, and parsimony. Explain why it fails these three tests. Why might it pass an empirical test?

9) Explain why each of the following statements is positive or normative. You will probably disagree with some of the statements.

   a. General Motors must build electric cars because of a new California law.
   b. General Motors should build electric cars.
   c. Job-training programs should be created in order to raise the self-esteem of the unemployed.
   d. A survey of participants in job-training programs showed that the programs raised their self-esteem.
   e. Research suggests that job-training pros should reduce unemployment.
   f. The government should not waste its money funding medical research.
   g. Medical research has never led to developments that have saved lives.

CHAPTER 2

The Market System

OVERALL OBJECTIVE: To present a model of how a market system operates, with prices determined by demand and supply signalling the answers to the basic economic questions, and to explore the reasons why the development of a market system was impeded for many centuries.

MORE SPECIFICALLY:

- To show that the traditional economic systems that preceded the widespread emergence of markets, though perhaps reasonably suited to the times, prevented much economic growth. They lacked openness to trade, benefitted little from capital formation and technical improvement, and were subject to diminishing returns and diseconomies of small scale.
- To describe the process by which markets emerged to become the paramount economic system.
- To show how a maximizing principle underlies the behavior of both consumers and producers, so allowing a market system to work.
- To build a model of a market system operating through prices set by demand and supply. Revenues, costs, and profits in the markets for factor inputs and the markets for goods and services are the guiding signals that determine what will be produced, how it will be produced, and who gets the production.

Any economy must decide *what* to produce, *how* to produce it, and *who* will receive the output once it is produced. In most parts of the world, the answers are determined within a **market system** of prices established by the forces of demand and supply. In a market system, prices signal what buyers want and what the costs of production are, profits motivate production decisions, and income is the incentive for work. The emergence of markets and prices to provide answers to economic questions, and the appearance of social and governmental institutions to support such a system, may well comprise the single most important development in the history of economics. But the predominance of the market system was never a foregone conclusion, and it took many centuries to evolve. Indeed, it is *still* evolving in quite a number of countries.

The general subject of this chapter is why the development of a market system was so important to human progress. First we examine the barriers to the emergence of markets. Then we discuss how these barriers were overcome and why markets developed when they did. Finally, by means of a model, we explore how the market system works.

► BARRIERS TO THE EMERGENCE OF MARKETS AND PRICES

Markets, though not faultless, are a powerful mechanism for directing the production of what consumers want at the lowest possible cost and with the least necessity for governments to become involved in economic management. Markets also promote dynamic change, including capital formation, technical change, and acquisition of training and new skills. The emergence of markets was slow and uncertain, however, with powerful forces causing the delay. A number of these forces still exist, and understanding what they are and how they historically retarded economic development gives a better understanding of the economic problems of today.

TRADITIONAL ECONOMIES

In the beginning of economic relations among peoples, and for many thousands of years thereafter, economic decisions were not driven primarily by markets and prices, and the **traditional economy** predominated. The early evolution of economic relations was not conducive to a market form of organization. Buying and selling, prices, and profits played only a small role. The barriers to the emergence of markets proved so overwhelming that no society had an economy based primarily on markets until at least the sixteenth or seventeenth centuries.[1]

Even in the absence of written histories of early societies, the explanation for the slow development of markets is reasonably clear. Excavations of sites occupied by early humans reveal that the family groups that peopled the sites were largely self-sufficient. Subsistence production of a family's own food, clothing, and shelter prevailed.[2] The emergence of market transactions on any scale was an extremely slow process. Some village specialization of labor did exist from earliest times, clear because many stone spear points can be identified as the product of the same individual. Some production of nonsubsistence output by specialists existed as well, as demonstrated by cave paintings showing the hand of the same artist, or by decorative ornaments for the body recognizably the work of the same talented person. Thus, even before the last Ice Age, 10 to 20 thousand years ago, exchange via barter methods, with one good exchanged directly for

---

1.　　A warning is in order when examining the emergence of markets from traditional economies. It is easy to slip into the false assumption that tradition and markets have, or have had, an independent existence and can be examined in pure form. In human history, the shifts in economic systems are of degree, not of kind. One can speak of a system *predominating,* but not of a system *excluding* the others. Even changes in degree of importance often took hundreds of years to accomplish, as seen in this section. Pure economic systems exist only in the form of models.

2.　　The term "primitive economies" was once much used to describe these societies. But the term has been largely rejected by scholars, not only because it was demeaning, but because so-called primitive economies actually developed a wide variety of rather sophisticated methods for dealing with economic problems.

another, must have supported the specialized labor of at least a few skilled artisans, and some commerce in goods and services was taking place with neighbors in the immediate vicinity.

Growing specialization and more frequent exchanges of goods and services notwithstanding, the appearance of a full-fledged market system was delayed for many centuries. Traditional economies remained based on extended families or (at most) villages, largely closed, self-sufficient peasant communities.[3] Tradition shaped the answers to the basic economic questions concerning "what," how," and "for whom." Long-standing community standards dictated the type of work to be followed, the amount of work to be done, and how this work was to be divided between the sexes. Kinship ties and ancestor worship required obedience to social norms, and religious ceremonies and ritual influenced both production and consumption.

A visitor thrust back in time to a society based on tradition would find it easy to identify the outstanding features. That society would produce what it had produced before, with prices and markets having little impact on day-to-day life. Sons and daughters would follow fathers and mothers into the same pursuits, working with little capital and techniques of production that would be largely unchanged from those of the distant past. (As long as circumstances did not change too greatly, however, these techniques would often be reasonably well suited to the available resources.) Society's distribution of production, and hence income, was based primarily on membership in the community. Ownership of land was a hazy concept, with the land held communally by a village or tribe or clan or descent group, and with farm animals, trees, and other property often "owned" in the same way.

A wide range of factors delayed or prevented the emergence of markets.

1) The world was overwhelmingly rural and, until relatively modern times, most production was subsistence production carried on for use by farmers and workers in the countryside.[4] At least a few cities existed as early as 6000–7000 BC and all the ancient civilizations had at least some urban development. Where they existed, cities always furthered the growth of trade, the division of labor among occupations, and the provision of more specialized tools. But the proportion of the population that could be considered as urban was low, usually well under 10%.

2) The growth of markets was inhibited by customary rules of class, caste, and status. Lineages carefully traced through descent groups figured prominently in most traditional economies and meant that labor would not be attracted into new occupations or pushed out of old ones by differences in wages. In Rome, the long-standing principle of sons following fathers into occupations was a social norm so powerful that at some periods it was enforced by law for certain key occupations. The guilds of medieval Europe, with membership in many trades and crafts determined by family lines, were a continuation

---

3.   The origin of the word economics reflects this idea of a simpler structure of families and villages. The word is derived from the ancient Greek *oikonomia*, meaning the management of a household or family.

4.   The importance of settled agriculture shows that the ideas of opportunity costs and substituting cheaper for dearer appeared very early in mankind's history. A major shift from a food supply based on hunting to one based on settled agriculture occurred some eight to ten thousand years ago when, independently in a number of far-separated locations including China, Mesopotamia, and Middle America, hunting grew more costly relative to farming. The reasons included perhaps some pressure from human population growth and the beginnings of town life, some spread of agricultural technique, and some major reductions in numbers among the animals hunted (including extinction of the ancient bison, the mammoth, and the mastodon) which may have involved over-hunting. Several millennia later, after the Spanish Conquistadores introduced the horse to North America, the use of that animal by Native Americans lowered the opportunity cost of hunting sufficiently so that some (the Cheyenne, the Arapahoe) virtually abandoned the practice of agriculture.

of this principle. In such a setting, market-induced wage changes had little ability to attract individuals from one occupation to another. Life would simply continue to follow the old track.[5]

Feudalism and slavery had the same effect. Slavery was widespread throughout the ancient world, and semifeudal or feudal systems flourished in the Roman Empire, lasted late into the eighteenth century in France and Germany, and until 1861 in Russia. Slaves were bound to their masters, just as serfs were to their "landlords." Slaves and serfs often practiced agricultural techniques that would not have been out of place on pre-Roman farms.

3) Traditional economies usually had autocratic rulers of one sort or another: chiefs, clan patriarchs, castes or classes of nobles, warriors, and priests. The rulers were seldom responsive to any sort of democratic process whereby economic exploitation could be alleviated or reversed, and their rigidity further solidified the influence of custom and tradition in economic decision making.

For example, in the great empires of the Middle East, including Sumeria (4500 BC and before), Assyria, and Babylonia, the ruling class of allied priests and warriors was so important in economic life that these empires have been called "temple and palace economies." In Egypt, first under the Pharaohs and later under the Ptolemeys, a vast traditional and peasant subsistence economy coexisted under substantial state direction and control. Especially in Ptolemaic Egypt, royal ownership of agricultural land was combined with bureaucratic ordering of what crops to grow. Significant state control was exercised over commerce, mines were owned by the government, there were state olive oil and banking monopolies, high tariffs and export duties were placed on foreign trade, and taxation was generally steep. Later, the Roman Empire also developed a surprisingly high level of state direction of the economy, superimposed on a mostly rural, mostly subsistence substructure.

It is important to note that a ruling class will have an easier time exercising economic power when subsistence agriculture makes up so much of total production. Before the development of market economies, manufacturing and mining were small-scale and much simpler to direct. They were still key sectors, however, and the substantial state supervision and control reduced the likelihood that economic decisions would ever be made largely by markets and prices.

4) Early economies were largely closed systems. The difficulties and dangers of transport ensured that international and interregional trade would be of small importance for many centuries. Only a few goods could stand the universal high cost of transport. Some metals (especially copper), salt, stone axes, seashells (which were thought to have magical properties), and amber were among the limited range of goods involved in the earliest long-distance commerce. Later, many more goods were involved, but high transport costs continued to limit the marketing of items produced at a distance.

5) The mechanics of exchange were difficult and inhibited marketing. Modern money in the form of coins did not evolve until about 600 BC. (Paper money and bank accounts did not become important until over 2000 years later.) Trade thus had to involve either barter or inconvenient quasi-moneys such as seashells or beads that might be acceptable only in

---

5.   The power of tradition in determining one's occupation is particularly clear in view of the choices made when surnames came to be taken four or five centuries ago. At that time, population growth was making the numbers of "Johns of Lincoln" or "Margarets of Salisbury" overly large. Among the many familiar Anglo-Saxon surnames that show the impact of economic tradition are Archer, Baker, Bishop, Brewer, Bulger (a task in pipe-making), Butler, Carpenter, Carrier, Carter, Cartwright, Chamberlain, Chandler (provider of candles), Clark or Clarke (meaning clerk), Cook or Cooke, Cooper (a part of barrel-making that involves fitting the rings), Currier, Eisenhower (English: iron-worker), Farmer (German: Bauer), Fisher, Fletcher (arrow-maker), Forrester (and Foster, which has the same meaning), Gardiner or Gardner, Hooper, Hunter, Kitchener, Mason, Miller, Parker, Plummer, Porter, Potter, Sawyer, Sargent, Shepherd (German: Schaeffer), Schumacher (Shoemaker), Shriver (writer), Smith, Stewart or Stuart (meaning steward), Taylor (German: Schneider, Snider), Thatcher, Walker (meaning a peddler who travels on foot), Weaver, and Wright. When other languages and cultures are included, the list becomes much longer yet.

limited areas, or were themselves difficult to transport in quantity.[6] Prices were not considered fixed even for a single transaction, but had to be established for every sale by a process of bargaining or haggling. Credit, though it existed long before modern money, was rudimentary.

6) Almost all early philosophers, religious leaders, rulers, and even the proto-economists themselves, had views that ran *contrary* to the development of a market system. The great thinkers, for the most part, took the traditional form of organization for granted. The eminent Greek philosophers Plato and Aristotle both accepted slavery as rational and defensible, for example. In the thirteenth century, St. Thomas Aquinas (1225–1274) and numerous other "preclassical" scholars who wrote on economics, worked to inhibit the emergence of a market system in a number of ways. Aquinas in particular wrote disdainfully of trade and commerce, and he condemned the selfishness that propels markets, and indeed is necessary to make them work. Aquinas and his intellectual followers believed in a duty to transact at a "just price," meaning a price sufficient to keep the seller at his customary or traditional station in life. Profit was denounced as evidence of acquisitiveness and as socially disruptive. Such notions became part of the teachings propagated by the established religion. Earning interest was forbidden by the Church. This limited borrowing and lending for investment, while the religious opposition to the profit motive and support for the traditional economy created both an intellectual and social barrier to the flowering of a market system.[7]

DISADVANTAGES OF TRADITIONAL SYSTEMS

Tradition as a system of economics is still widely encountered in many less-developed countries (LDCs we shall call them for short), especially in South Asia and in Africa.[8] For the most part, however, its surviving vestiges are in rapid retreat everywhere.

Economic decision making by traditional means placed severe constraints on economic progress. The traditional institutions, customs, and religious attitudes were not of the sort that rewarded efficiency and penalized inefficiency. On the whole, there was no mechanism to promote the economically proficient and wipe out economic ineptitude. When markets and prices emerge to guide economic decision making, these particular constraints are mostly broken and economic growth becomes more rapid. The four most significant constraints imposed by traditional systems are the lack of openness; the lack of capital formation, technical change, and learning; diminishing returns; and the diseconomies of small-scale production.

Lack of Openness

The closed nature of family and village economies, feudal barriers to movement, and high transport costs prevented specialization. People were not able to produce what they could do best in exchange for products from other regions or countries whose products they could not produce so well. Lack of trade meant knowledge of new products and new methods of production would not flow smoothly and easily to other areas even when such improvements did occur. New products from the outside were not readily available, and so there was not much reason for people to increase their efforts in order to acquire the new goods. The **gains from trade** were lost.

---

6. Barter could be carried out, however, by means of "assortment bargaining" that exhibited some aspects of today's money. A pile of stone axes brought by one trader could be valued as so much salt; a lump of copper brought by another trader as so much salt; and a trade could go forward if the difference in the salt value was made up by goods thrown into the balance. No salt needed to change hands; the salt was used merely as a "unit of account." Assortment bargaining appears to have long preceded actual money. At other times and places, a good might achieve such prominence in trade that some of it would be carried to facilitate transactions. Thus, the salt value of the difference noted above might be paid over in real salt. Historically, iron bars, copper rods, lengths of cloth, special seashells (the cowrie), and the salt of our example served this purpose, among others. By such methods the inconvenience of barter was reduced.

7. In Asia, there was a similar Confucian dislike of marketing activity.

8. It should also be said that tradition has not disappeared to the extent we like to believe even in today's developed countries, where in particular occupations prejudices involving gender and race can be seen as a throwback to a caste or class view of occupational specialization.

It is true that self-sufficiency has always had a certain appeal, as with the idealism of Rousseau's "noble savage," Thoreau's *Walden,* and the back-to-the-land movement of the 1960s and 1970s. Yet self-sufficiency is costly. Later in the book we will explore the important principle called *comparative advantage,* which illustrates how gains will accrue from trade because the trade allows specialization to occur. Understanding comparative advantage requires some development of micro theory, so for now suffice it to say that an individual or region or country unable to trade with its neighbors would have to produce everything it consumed, involving the sacrifice of the greater output that could be obtained from specializing on the output in which producers are most efficient. Figure 2.1 suggests how damaging this might be. See how Fabrica in panel **a** has a clear advantage in producing cloth rather than wheat. If all its resources were devoted to cloth production, it could produce 100 bales of cloth, but if all of its resources were turned to wheat production it could produce only 20 bushels of wheat. A production possibilities curve running from 100 cloth to 20 wheat shows Fabrica's alternatives.

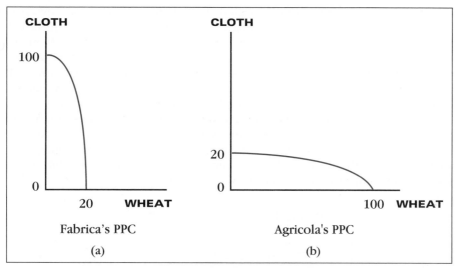

Figure 2.1. **The gains from trade.** In panel **a**, we see that Fabrica is more efficient at producing cloth than wheat, while in panel **b** we see that Agricola is more efficient at producing wheat than cloth. If each country specializes in what it can do best, the two together can produce more than they otherwise could. They can then trade with one another—Fabrica exporting cloth and importing wheat, and Agricola exporting wheat and importing cloth. Each country will enjoy gains from trade.

Fabrica's neighbor, Agricola, faces different production conditions as shown in panel **b**. All of Agricola's resources if employed on cloth production, which is difficult in Agricola, would yield only 20 bales of cloth. Conditions for wheat farming, however, are relatively more favorable. If all Agricola's resources were devoted to wheat production, 100 bushels of wheat would be the result.

If each country specialized in what it did best, Fabrica in cloth and Agricola in wheat, the two together could produce far more than they could if they produced each good separately. Their "world" could have 100 bales of cloth *and* 100 bushels of wheat if they specialized, whereas if they did not, Fabrica would have to feed itself and Agricola clothe its people from their own inefficient production of these items. If they could export some of what can be produced with advantage, and import what cannot be, both countries would end up ahead.

If you are not yet convinced, ask yourself how your level of living would change if your state or county had to produce for itself everything that was consumed. Resources would have to be transferred to producing items that would be difficult to make in your locality, items which you presently buy from other areas that have specialized in making these goods. If there is not much arable land in your state, you would have problems providing for your food supply. But with trade, Kansas and Iowa are happy to sell you grain; Florida and California will sell you fruit; Wisconsin will sell you cheese; and so forth.

Lack of Capital Formation, Technological Improvement, and Learning

The inflexibility of the traditional system, the Church's determined stand against charging interest, and the absence of sufficient motives for personal gain meant capital formation was slow. It also left little latitude for learning or the development of new skills and new technologies. A visitor to a European (or Chinese or Native American) community in the year 1300 probably would not have noticed a larger capital stock than had been present on a similar visit a thousand years before. In some cases, the capital stock was much reduced, as with the famous roads of the Roman empire, by 1300 turned into muddy tracks, their paving stones sunk out of sight. The people would not have been noticeably better educated either, and the technology would have been remarkably similar. The production possibilities curves of traditional economies moved out with agonizing slowness.

Diminishing Returns

In the traditional economies, the problem called **diminishing returns** was always close to the surface. This concept is one of the most familiar in economics, and one that affects all economies. The "law of diminishing returns to a factor" suggests that production will be subject to a constraint. If any *one* factor of production (the variable one) is increased in increments of the same quantity, while all the other factors are held constant, eventually returns will diminish. That is, total output will increase for every same-size increase of a variable factor, but each increment to total output will be smaller than the last. For example, if Robinson Crusoe were joined by another marooned sailor, and then another, and another, but the quantity of tools, the number of trees, and the supply of fish nets stayed the same, then there would be diminishing returns to labor and the island economy's PPC would have an appearance similar to that of Figure 2.2. Each new worker would add something to production, but less than the last one did. The production possibilities curve shifts out by ever smaller increments, from curve 1 to 2 to 3 to 4.[9]

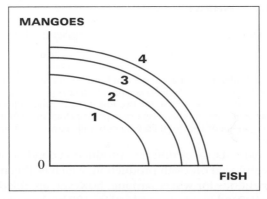

Figure 2.2. Diminishing returns to a factor (labor) seen on a production possibilities curve. If a variable factor of production is increased in increments of the same quantity while all the other factors are held constant, then each resulting increase in total output will be smaller than the last. The PPC moves out as shown.

9.　　*Technical note:* This principle of diminishing returns to a factor now allows us to explain with greater technical accuracy why increasing costs, shown by the bowed-outward concave-to-origin shape of the production possibilities curve, would occur. Remember from the last chapter how Crusoe had to give up ever more mangoes to get a given increment of fish, and vice versa? One major reason why is that the two products will very likely use the available factors in different proportions: more capital, say, in fishing where the nets are so important, more labor for picking and climbing in mango production. At the outside limit, assume that no capital at all is used in mango output, with all the capital used in fishing. In that case, transferring production by increments from mangoes to fish must mean that more and more labor is being shifted to work with a fixed capital stock. The result will ordinarily be diminishing returns to labor, making it ever more costly to raise fish output, and thus showing the relationship between increasing costs and diminishing returns.

If all factors increase at the same time, then diminishing returns to a factor will not occur. If on Crusoe's island the capital stock grows and education improves as more marooned sailors come ashore, then the diminishing returns to labor can be avoided. But this is precisely the result that traditional economies everywhere had trouble delivering. Their stock of resources was relatively fixed, their learning limited, their technology stagnant, and their level of enterprise low. If population growth occurred within some traditional economy, that economy would all too likely encounter diminishing returns. Simultaneous growth in all the factors of production, especially enterprise and technology, would keep the constraint from binding, but alterations in the economic system would be necessary before that could be provided.

Diseconomies of Small Scale

Production in traditional economies was usually very small in scale. Farms were limited in size, artisans labored mostly in workshops instead of factories, and lack of power and technical shortcomings in metallurgy limited the size of the few factories that did exist. The small size of the market limited the growth of factories in any case. Traditional economies thus could not realize **economies of scale.** This is the term used by economists to describe the lower costs and greater efficiency that may be available only to larger-scale enterprises. If Crusoe and a multitude of fellow castaways could have utilized mass-production techniques and economies in buying and handling large stocks of inputs, they could have realized economies of scale and become much more productive.

In Figure 2.3 we show how economies of scale can be illustrated with a production possibilities curve. Assume that a given increment to all factors of production (say a 10% increase in labor, 10% more capital, and 10% more natural resources) occurs at the same time. That would move the production possibilities curve outward from 1 to 2. Now consider that *another* 10% addition is made to all the factors of production. If scale economies from larger operations exist, that would cause the PPC to shift outward by an increasing increment (for example, from 2 to 3). Yet another 10% increase in the factors might result in a movement to 3 to 4, and so on. (Alternatively, there might be *dis*economies to larger-scale operations if larger and ever larger operations become relatively less economical because of management problems. That case would be illustrated by a diagram exactly the same as Figure 2.2.)

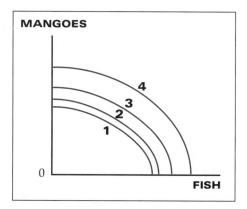

Figure 2.3. Economies of scale from larger-size operation. If all factors increase in increments of 10%, but the resulting output produced by those factors grows by ever greater increments, then economies of scale have been realized. The PPC moves out as shown.

All these considerations, especially the low investment in new capital, the extreme waste of human talent, and the stagnant methods, brought high likelihood that traditional economies would be permanently retarded by inefficiencies. Because of these inefficiencies, economic growth was very slow and living standards remained low.

▶ THE EMERGENCE OF THE MARKET ECONOMY

When "the market" first appeared, or even when it began to exercise significant influence in the making of economic decisions, is not known, but it was certainly a very early development. We have already seen that exchange by barter methods occurred long before written records referred to it. Even in the early temple and palace economies of the ancient Middle Eastern empires, some exchange by means of markets was being carried on at a lower level than could be easily reached by officials and bureaucrats.[10] Though the details are sparse, the limited foreign trade of the ancient empires—even early Sumeria was importing copper from as far away as Oman, Anatolia, and the Caucasus Mountains—must have involved market transactions. Similar findings concerning the existence of markets have been made for the early dynasties of China as well. Merchants and traders bought and sold in these markets, the profits from their dealings serving as their income and allowing them to buy the production of others.

The invention of a convenient form of money around 600 BC, probably in the Kingdom of Lydia that forms part of what is now Turkey, aided considerably in the early growth of markets. Coinage expedited exchange by means of price rather than by barter, and thus made market transactions considerably more convenient.

Marketing was in evidence in the Roman Republic at least as early as the first trustworthy records (fourth century BC). In spite of its state control and large subsistence sector, Rome of the first and second centuries AD had a significant free-enterprise sector engaged in vigorous market activity, and with a high proportion of transactions in that sector carried on by means of money. Cities such as Alexandria became commercial emporia the likes of which had not been seen before. Still, the economy of rural manorial estates predominated, and in any case a long retreat from marketing ensued with Europe's Dark Age from about 600 to 1200.

THE MARKET EXPANDS

A constellation of events in the late Middle Ages caused the market system to expand. The expansion extended through the Renaissance and into the modern period of European history. By the eighteenth century, the market system predominated. To this day, the enlargement continues, both in the less-developed countries and in the former Communist countries, and direction of economic activity by markets and prices is not likely to be seriously challenged in the foreseeable future. Although the exact reasons for the development and expansion of the market system remain subject to debate, six events stand out.

1) *Improvements occurred in transport and motive power.* Horses, which are faster than oxen and do not need to be used in teams, could not be used effectively to pull anything until the invention of the horse collar sometime during the Middle Ages. That led to more efficient plowing and more widespread use of the four-wheel wagon. A series of maritime innovations (the compass, improved sailing rig, deeper hulls for merchant ships) revolutionized the carriage of cargoes by sea.

2) *Advances in agriculture.* A movement to the three-field system in farming allowed farm output to grow by as much as a third or more. The older two-field system kept one field fallow while the other was planted, but from the eleventh century it was found that the land bore just as well when it was divided into three fields, one kept fallow every year, the second planted in grasses, and the third in grain. Heavy plows, unknown to the Romans, facilitated the cultivation of these fields.

---

10.   Recent archaeological work indicates, for example, that the reputation of ancient Sumeria as an economy completely controlled by priests and warriors has to be modified. To some limited degree, both markets and flexible prices existed there during the period between 4000 and 3000 BC.

3) *Population growth.* Between the years 1000 and 1300, population growth led to greater urbanization and growing markets. Without the first "agricultural revolution" mentioned previously, supporting that increased population would have been difficult.

4) *Expanded wants and improved markets.* Beginning in 1096, the Crusades introduced both Christians and Muslims to new goods (and also new ways of doing things). Explorers like Marco Polo and others brought news of what the Far East had to offer. With transport easier, merchants began to gather at trade fairs and then in cities that began to serve as commercial emporia. To buy these goods, money had to be earned. Sellers more frequently became "price-makers," announcing and adhering to temporarily fixed prices without the necessity for bargaining or haggling over each transaction.[11] The appearance of seemingly modern and sophisticated devices of the market such as checks, credit instruments, and accounting procedures accompanied these developments.

5) *The growth of capitalist production.* Growing numbers of merchant capitalists found they could increase output by means of a new method. Instead of leaving production in the hands of independent craftsmen and guild artisans, it proved advantageous to the capitalist (and the artisan, too) to provide artisans with raw materials and pay a fee to them for making the products. This "putting-out system" helped cut costs of production and made goods more available while simultaneously boosting merchants' profits. It was well on the way to superseding independent handicraft production by the end of the sixteenth century. That, in turn, meant the creation of a larger paid labor force than before. Combined with the increase in trade and commerce, it also meant that profit was becoming established as the primary motive in decisions involving production. The onset of the Black Death (bubonic plague) in Europe caused a temporary disruption in the spread of marketing during the fourteenth century, but it also caused labor shortages and hence rising wages that eventually widened the market still further.

6) *The breakup of the manor.* By the sixteenth century, the feudal manor was being undermined and its customs and traditions were breaking up. This was essential in the emergence of market economies because the growing cities had to have food and raw materials. New wants meant that the lords of the manor needed to earn incomes to supply their needs and, fortunately for them, they could sell food to the cities. More and more, tenants paid rent and many hired labor themselves.

THE TURNING POINT IN THE DEVELOPMENT OF THE MARKET SYSTEM

In Europe, the sixteenth and seventeenth centuries marked the turning point for the market system. It was a time of accelerating social and economic change, certainly not everywhere, but widely enough to make an enormous mark.

The Changing Role of Institutions

The Church had already long been wavering in its condemnation of acquisitiveness, profits, and the payment of interest. The birth of Protestantism, and the so-called "Protestant ethic," brought considerably more acceptance of these activities. The institutions of government changed roles as well, steadily coming to encourage the utilization of entrepreneurial talent and initiative. More and more, competition was allowed and encouraged, economic decision making at the individual level was permitted, while new patent laws encouraged innovation. Significantly, the property rights of merchant capitalists became better recognized, important because private property ownership, especially of land, natural resources, and buildings, was found to be an

---

11.   It is said that by the seventeenth century fortunes were made as firms followed the practice of announcing prices and sticking to them for some time. Consumers apparently considered individually bargained, highly flexible prices to be an annoyance, and rewarded with their custom the firms that established fixed prices.

effective way to increase earnings. Contract enforcement came to be provided by court systems, another contribution of government. Without property rights and the sanctity of contracts, the growth of long-term investment would have been slow and halting. Developments in banking meant that entrepreneurs were better able to borrow on commercial terms. The growing use of **debt financing** of businesses meant that owners did not have to depend solely on their own or their families' resources. Finally, new developments in bankruptcy law began to lift the risk that a single bad experience would lead to lifelong indebtedness.

Changing Forms of Business Organization

Before the seventeenth century, the only common forms of business organization were single proprietorships (that is, firms owned by single individuals) and partnerships owned by groups of people, often members of the same family. These forms of organization survive and thrive today, of course. But they also had in common a major disadvantage. The owner of a single proprietorship, or each partner in a partnership, was liable for all the debts of the firm. Say a firm had taken out loans to finance a business venture or had bills outstanding when some commercial disaster struck. In that case, the creditors of the firm could lay claim to all the property of the owner or of each of the partners, up to the amount of the outstanding debt. This meant a high degree of risk. Even if the firm had no debts at all, if it failed, the owner or the partners would suffer large losses because the ownership was so concentrated.

In the seventeenth century, the corporate form of organization was emerging. Corporations were owned by their shareholders, who held shares of stock in them. The shareholders had a vote in their management proportional to the number of shares that they owned. Under the corporate form of organization, firms could obtain financing from the sale of their stock (called **equity financing**). The new system brought several advantages. First, if large numbers of people had purchased shares in the same corporation, then the risk of failure would be spread widely and the chance of loss for any single individual was reduced. Second, the losses to investors from projects that went wrong were restricted to just the amount already invested. Creditors could not lay any further claim to shareholder's assets beyond that amount, which limited their risks.[12] Third, the shareholder could diversify risks still further by buying just a little stock in several different companies. So equity financing was far safer for the shareholder than being a proprietor or partner. In addition, the shareholders as owners of the corporation would share in the corporation's profits through the payment of dividends on the stock. These attributes made stockholding financially attractive and allowed corporations to raise much more money for capital investment. They were a major contributor to the emergence of the market system.

THE RISE OF MODERN INDUSTRY

The "end of the beginning" for the market system was the dawning of modern industry that began in the eighteenth century in Great Britain. Use of the familiar term **industrial revolution** to describe this process is debatable; many economic historians emphasize the long continuity of industrial development, and they are quite right. Yet something of importance was certainly taking place in Britain during the half-century before the year 1800. During this period, inventors began to apply mechanical knowledge as never before. Their technical skills led to the development of large-scale machinery powered by water and steam and the wide use of new materials like iron and steel. Without the new materials, the new machines could not have been built. Without the new forms of power in the form of improved water wheels and coal-fired steam engines, they could not have been run. Without the favorable conditions discussed in the last section, the innovations would not have been adopted or even contemplated.

---

12.   That is why corporations used to be called "limited liability companies," and why in Britain they still have "Ltd." after their names.

Government, for the most part, did not stand in the way of these industrial changes. The banking system had developed sufficiently to provide large flows of debt financing, and the profits from the sale of consumer goods—especially the textiles that were produced by Britain's largest industry—could be plowed back into investment as well.[13] The investment went not just to factories and machinery, but also to canals, roads, ships, and, within a few years, railroads. The improved transportation lowered costs and widened markets. Within a few decades, Britain produced two-thirds of the world's coal, half or more of its cotton cloth, coal, iron, and steel, and 40% of its hardware. True, the general impression of a revolution can be overdone. The technical advances built on many antecedents extending back for centuries, and they were not necessarily British in origin. The process was slow—as late as 1850 there were more shoemakers in Britain than there were factory workers. The growth of output was relatively slow as well, averaging only a little more than 1% a year during the century after 1780. Many social problems arose, and the "dark satanic mills" with their often ruthless child labor probably did not much improve the majority's living standards for a considerable time. By hindsight, however, this was the price paid for the replacement of stagnant tradition by a system that promoted dynamic economic growth.

In short, an unprecedented period of industrialization had begun. Slowly modern industries spread, first to the rest of Europe and the United States, and later to Japan. To this day, that spread continues as poor countries continue their own industrialization.

The Importance of Knowledge and Technology

Though there were many components to the rise of modern industry, the key ingredient was the new industrial technology. The cooperation of inventors and entrepreneurs lay at the core of the process, as scientifically educated researchers fed new ideas to entrepreneurs. In Britain, most of the scientific education was on-the-job, not in schools. (In fact, only from 1870 was there was any government financing at all for British education, and at that time half the population had not received any formal education at all. As late as the 1920s, only 12% of the eligible age group was enrolled in secondary school. It was Germany, later in the nineteenth centuries, that pioneered scientifically based education in the technical high schools.) Yet in Britain during the dawn of the industrial age, sufficient training and experience had become available to fuel an outpouring of new technical ideas. Knowledge and technology were the driving forces behind the appearance of modern industry.

ADAM SMITH AND THE MARKET ECONOMY

Together, all the facilitating developments in religion, government, business organization and financing, and the application of knowledge and technology to industry accelerated the expansion of the market system. The growing markets began to deliver economies of scale and gains from trade, while the increasing technological change, improving education (at least for the elite), and better infrastructure of transport and communication stimulated growth and helped to offset diminishing returns. Intellectual opinion began to recognize that the changes were revolutionary. Foremost among these intellectuals was Adam Smith (1723–1790), the professor of moral philosophy (in which subject economics was then included) at the University of Glasgow in Scotland.

---

13.   Equity financing was, however, not central to this rise of modern industry. Because of financial scandals earlier in the eighteenth century, new corporations had to be approved by Parliament until 1825. The ability of equity financing to cut the risk of investment and increase the flow of funds was not realized until after the repeal of that provision, so the firms that carried out the industrial awakening were mostly sole proprietorships and partnerships.

In 1776, Smith's *The Wealth of Nations* introduced a well-thought-out framework of ideas concerning how a market system operates. He was the first to give a satisfactory explanation of the newly emerging market system. A lucid writer and brilliant communicator, Smith became the first of the "classical" economists, as he and his successors came to be called.[14] With his view of economics as the search for "the greatest happiness for the greatest number,"[15] and his distaste for those who manipulate political power for economic ends, he was able to draw together many strands of disorganized earlier thought into understandable description and analysis of the market system. The influence of this analysis is still felt after more than two centuries, and Smith is deservedly accorded the title of founder of the subject as we now know it.[16]

In *The Wealth of Nations,* Smith concentrated his analysis on the questions that today we (aptly) call classical. The greatest of the classical questions was, "Can a society in which each person seeks his own selfish ends serve to enhance the general welfare?" Smith answered yes. He believed that "the uniform, constant and uninterrupted effort of every man to better his condition" is "the principle from which public and national, as well as private opulence is originally derived."[17] Every individual, Smith reasoned, seeks to find the most advantageous employment of himself and his capital.

It was this line of inquiry that eventually led the classical economists to the basic theories of market prices determined by demand and supply, the advantages of a division of labor, and many other models that remain central to the study of microeconomics. In his most memorable turn of phrase, Smith advanced the notion that the market was an "invisible hand" solving problems of pricing, allocation, and distribution. The phrase encompassed most economic research until the middle of the twentieth century. Smith was also alert to flaws in the market. He insisted that a government role in economic life was a necessity. Were government to fail in providing law and order, then the resulting injustice could keep the market system from working properly and halt its benefits. He believed that government institutions were required to do what the market cannot or will not do. (If he had been writing in the twentieth century, he would surely have illustrated this point with the social costs of pollution that dog the market system.) Smith was also concerned with the potential for monopolizing combinations on the part of the managers and owners of business firms. He was suspicious of them and warned that constant vigilance was needed to guard against such combinations. Today, both social costs and monopoly behavior have a major role in the study of microeconomics.

The maturation of a market system opened up avenues for economic advancement that had been blocked for many centuries. Rightly, markets and marketing form the core of today's microeconomics.

---

14.   *The Wealth of Nations* would be entitled to survive permanently because of its prose style alone. Every interested person should give it a try, though admittedly there will not be a miniseries.

15.   The phrase "greatest happiness for the greatest number" is thought to have been coined by Adam Smith's own instructor at Glasgow, Professor Hutcheson.

16.   See Chapter 3 of Robert Heilbroner, *The Worldly Philosophers,* for many anecdotes on the life and times of Adam Smith. As the son of a customs official and himself holding the post of collector of customs for Scotland, he had plenty of on-the-job training for his profession.

17.   Adam Smith, *The Wealth of Nations,* London, 1776, Cannan edn., vol. 1, bk. 2, ch. 3, p. 325.

THE CHALLENGE OF THE COMMUNIST COMMAND ECONOMY AND ITS REPULSE

Since the time of Adam Smith, only one great challenge has ever been mounted against the predominance of the market system. It is now fair to say that this Communist challenge has failed, but only after a struggle that occupied three-quarters of the twentieth century. The German economist and philosopher Karl Marx (1818–1883) believed that the disadvantages of the market system—particularly the concentration of wealth and power in the hands of capitalists, monopolizing behavior, and impoverishment of workers—were so great that fundamental reform was called for. He and his followers (mostly the latter, including Friedrich Engels and especially Vladimir Lenin) advocated tearing up the market system and replacing it with a **command economy** based on state supervision and control. Marx was little concerned with the structure such an economy would have, and died over 30 years before Lenin suddenly in 1917 received the opportunity to put the theory into practice.

The new USSR became both the first and the most famous example of the Communist command system. Most prices were fixed by the government and were not altered for many years at a time, thus playing no role in answering the questions "what, how, and for whom?" Decisions as to what goods to produce and what factor inputs to use were made by the political authorities, and since the state owned the means of production, the orders were followed. The decisions were made in various government ministries which had charge of production, all coordinated by a central planning agency. The techniques of production were likewise dictated by the planning authorities to the factories and farms. Wages and salaries were also established by central direction. Investment, especially in heavy industry, was emphasized at the expense of consumption.[18]

The command system was transplanted to many parts of the globe. China, Cuba, all of Eastern Europe, North Korea, and Vietnam had generally similar command economies. For a time these systems had undeniable successes. Soviet military might (a product of its command economy) brought Hitler's war machine (the product of Germany's market system) to a halt. Soviet scientists were first in space; China after 1949 got along with little foreign contact and fought the United States to a standstill in Korea; further south and two decades later, Vietnam did likewise. It was possible to say that the command economy was an entirely viable alternative to the market.

By the 1990s, however, the command system had collapsed almost everywhere, and even in countries like China that still call themselves Communist, many principles of the market had been adopted. As we shall investigate later in the book, the command economy's recent record of slow growth and lower standards of living for most people had proved intolerable to the people who had to live under the system.

---

18. We have already noted that economic systems are never found in pure form. Even in the full flower of the Soviet planned economy, market transactions in the USSR, including many legal ones, were common. (Note that an Israeli kibbutz, or monastery or nunnery, or nuclear family, or typical large U.S. corporation or college or university, or even the U.S. government itself including the military, the highways, and the courts, does many things only indirectly linked to market principles. All contain elements of an internal command system.)

▶ A MODEL OF A MARKET SYSTEM

Almost all of the world's countries are now market economies. The market system's answers to the three basic questions involving choice, the "what," "how," and "for whom" of microeconomics, are central to the next 11 chapters. At this point, we begin our study of how a market economy works.[19]

WHAT UNDERLIES THE MARKET MECHANISM'S EFFECTIVENESS?

Behind the concept of a market are two important observations about human character and behavior. The first is that incentives matter and that individuals seek to maximize their own welfare. The second is that prices for goods and services and for factors of production are flexible in a reasonably predictable way associated with the demand and supply of the buyers and sellers in the market. These two observations are central, for together they make a market system workable. If neither observation were accurate, the effectiveness of the market system would be undermined.

The Maximizing Principle

A market system is effective because of the maximizing behavior of both consumers and producers. This is the elemental concept that people will take the opportunity to gain an economic advantage if it is offered to them. In practical terms, the observation means that people will prefer higher incomes for a given amount of effort in whatever activity they undertake. This **maximizing principle** is also called the economizing principle.

For consumers, the principle means that within the constraints that they face, they will strive to maximize their utility or satisfaction. In their choice of what to do with their time, they will have to balance labor against leisure, making the choice they consider brings the most satisfaction. (All work and no play is not much fun; all play and no work soon leaves one very hungry.) Following the same principle, consumers will prefer to pay lower prices for a given amount of utility from anything they purchase. Paying anything more absorbs income that has other uses, and so means a level of living lower than what could be attained. For producers, the maximizing principle means that within the constraints of what they can produce, they will attempt to achieve the highest possible income from their activity. In the words of the old phrase, they will strive to "buy low and sell high," for that will maximize sellers' incomes.

A fundamental economic principle is that maximizing behavior is the source of the benefits of a market system. What these benefits are is explored in the sections that follow.

WHAT IS A MARKET?

In modeling a market system, the first task is to define what a market is. A market exists in the context of a geographical setting where prices are determined by buyers and sellers coming together. This geographical area can be international, as for passenger aircraft, wheat, great soccer players, or foreign currencies, with the buyers and sellers linked electronically over long distances. It can be strictly local as with small-town newspapers or highly perishable fresh-baked bread. Or, it can be any size in between.

Markets exist both for *goods* and *services,* and for the *factors of production.* Markets for tangible *goods* include those for automobiles, food, ballpoint pens, computers, and VCRs. Markets for intangible *services* include the ticket for a bus ride, a trip to the doctor or beauty parlor, the taking out of an insurance policy. The goods and services produced by an economy

---

19.   "Capitalism" and "free enterprise" are two other terms often used loosely to mean the same thing as "the market system." Neither term serves the purpose as well, however. Significant accumulation of capital has certainly been part of the market system's attractiveness, but it is not strictly necessary for such a system to operate. Free enterprise can be an inaccurate and misleading term if a market works imperfectly, say because of monopoly power—there can still be a market system even when the market is not entirely free. Calling the mechanism the market system avoids these difficulties.

are the output of that economy's production process. Markets also deal in the factors of production employed by firms to produce goods and services. These factors of production, which are the inputs to an economy's production, are labor, land including natural resources, capital such as new highways, new machines, or new factories, technology, and entrepreneurial ability, as defined in Chapter 1. The expenses incurred by firms to buy or hire these factors of production— wages and salaries for labor, rent for land, the expenses for capital and technology defined conventionally as interest, and profit which is the return to entrepreneurial ability—are the *costs* to firms of producing output.

HOW MARKETS WORK

We have seen that the main observation underlying a market system is that people strive to maximize their satisfaction. Higher incomes are preferred to lower; buyers prefer lower prices to higher ones; sellers prefer greater profits to lesser. A model of how economic decisions are made in a market system can be constructed on this foundation. The model sees decision making as dependent on two central concepts, *costs* and *revenues,* and the difference between the two, which is *profits.* This relationship, which underlies the basic processes of microeconomics, can be seen in both the market for factor inputs and in the market for goods and services.

The Market for Factor Inputs

Anytime a firm produces output of goods and services it incurs costs for hiring factors of production. Indeed, for any type of output, it should be able to arrive at the *total cost* (TC) of the factor inputs used for production. This total cost will be made up of so much labor employed at the prevailing wage level, of land and natural resources at their going price or rental value, and of the additional expense for capital, technology, and entrepreneurship at their current rate of return. In each of these cases there is a factor market. Total cost can be written as an equation: the quantity of labor employed (Q_L) times the price of labor (P_L); the quantity of land utilized (Q_N) times the cost of land (P_N); the quantity of capital used (Q_K) times the cost of capital (P_K); the quantity of technology purchased (Q_T) times the cost of technology (P_T); and the quantity of entrepreneurship (Q_E) times the price of entrepreneurs' services (P_E). Therefore,

$$TC = (Q_L \times P_L) + (Q_N \times P_N) + (Q_K \times P_K) + (Q_T \times P_T) + (Q_E \times P_E).$$

This can be reduced and written as a single equation, $TC = Q_f \times P_f$, with the subscript "f" referring to all the factors of production. The total cost of output is equal to the quantity of the factors of production utilized multiplied by the average price of those factors.

The Market for Goods and Services

These costs have been incurred because firms in turn will sell the output they produce on a market for goods and services. By doing so, they will obtain revenue. The amount of this revenue can be established by multiplying the quantity of goods and services sold (Q_p) by the average price at which each was sold (P_p). The result is the figure for the *total revenue* (TR) of that business. Thus, we can write

$$TR = Q_p \times P_p.$$

Assuming that entrepreneurs seek higher incomes in preference to lower, then firms will have a keen interest in the *difference* between total revenue and total cost. Subtracting TC from TR will leave a remainder that belongs to the entrepreneurs: This is the **total profit** (TP_r) of the firm. We write

$$TR - TC = TP_r.$$

Thus, the profits of firms are determined in a market for goods and services that establishes revenues, and in a market for factors that simultaneously establishes costs.

This method for finding the total profit of firms also allows the determination of the amount of income earned by the factors of production. Notice once again the TC, or total cost, element in the formula. Costs to a firm represent income to the factors: wages to the workers who supplied the labor, rent to the landlord supplying the land, and so forth. The people who possess factors of production will thus find that their incomes, too, are determined in the market process.

How a Market System Answers the Basic Economic Questions

This model of revenues, costs, and profits allows us to explain how the market system answers the basic questions of economics: what goods will be produced, how will they be produced, and who gets the goods?

1) *What will firms produce?* Entrepreneurs as a group face an enormous range of goods and services, the output of which they could conceivably undertake. Supply-and-demand conditions for each possible product and for the factors of production used to produce them will most likely be different, however. Some possible outputs will yield higher revenues in relation to their costs than will other items, and so will be more profitable to produce. Profit as determined by TR – TC is the incentive for production in a market economy. Within their abilities, firms choose to produce those items they believe will yield them the greatest profit. A major implication is that to be successful, firms in a market system must produce what buyers want.

2) *What production techniques will be utilized once the decision to produce a certain good or provide a certain service has been made?* Here, too, profit is pivotal. The technique that can produce a certain quantity and quality of a good and at the same time minimize the total cost element in $TR - TC = TP_r$ will tend to maximize a firm's profits. The incentive to adopt a technique is its profitability.

3) *How will the goods and services, once produced, be allocated among the members of society?* Again, by the action of markets. Those individuals who command scarce factors of production much demanded by business, and those willing to work hard, will find that their incomes (wages, salaries, rents, and so forth) are higher than the incomes of those who command factors in plentiful supply and not much in demand, or who are unwilling to work hard. In a market system, those with the higher incomes are able to purchase the greater share of output. Just as with production, incentives propel decisions. It follows that some of those earning low incomes will be led by self-interest to attempt to shift the factors of production under their command into pursuits where they will earn higher incomes.

The end result is that the basic questions what, how, and for whom are answered by the pursuit of personal gain. The gain for entrepreneurs decides what is to be produced and how (and not any abstract concept of "social need"), while the gain to the other factors of production attracts them to their employment.

High income differentials are a characteristic of a market system. Only limited numbers of people have the enterprise and resources to become capitalists, or the rare talents that command high salaries, or the ownership of lucrative deposits of natural resources, and so on.

THE ELEMENTS
OF PRICE DETERMINATION

The total revenues and total costs discussed in the last section can be determined only with knowledge of the prices of goods, services, and the factors of production. In a market system, flexible prices reflecting changes in markets are the key to the decision-making process. They give the signals to which market participants respond. Now we must discuss how these prices are determined. The mechanism of price determination involves the demand and supply of buyers and sellers. **Demand** is the intensity of wanting something. **Supply** is the abundance or scarcity of something.

In general, the model suggests that changes in demand or supply, or both, will alter the market price. Take first a change in demand. If consumers want to buy a greater amount of a good or service, all other things being equal, we would expect its price to rise. Similarly, when the managers and owners of firms want to hire more labor, or rent more land, we can expect wages or rents to rise. The opposite is also true: Reduced wants lead predictably to lower prices. Now consider how prices respond to changes in supply. If a good or service or factor of production becomes scarce, all other things being equal, there will be an expectation that its price will rise. If instead of scarcity there is glut in a market, then the price of the good, service, or factor will be expected to fall.

We now turn to the study of these concepts. In the remainder of this chapter, we give a brief overview of how demand and supply determine market prices of both output and the factors of production. Then in the next two chapters we undertake a much more detailed examination of these famous concepts.

THE DEMAND CURVE

We begin with demand. What determines the quantity that people will demand of a certain item during some given time period? The tastes of buyers plays a part. So does the price of the item, the amount of income available to buyers, the prices of other goods that might be purchased instead, and the number of buyers in the market. If we use a *ceteris paribus* assumption, holding all these variables constant *except for price,* a predictable result emerges: A higher price causes a lower quantity to be demanded, and a lower price causes a higher quantity to be demanded. In Figure 2.4, price is shown on the vertical (Y) axis and quantity demanded is shown on the horizontal (X) axis. Notice that a high price, such as $2.00 per unit, is coordinated with a low quantity demanded, such as 10 units per day, at point **A**. A low price, such as $1.00 per unit, is coordinated with a high quantity demanded, 20 units per day, at point **B**. Points **A** and **B** are points on a **demand curve,** and all the other various combinations of prices and quantities in this diagram lie along the same curve, which has the standard downward slope of most demand curves. That slope indicates a negative relationship between price and quantity demanded: Higher quantities are demanded at lower prices, and lower quantities at higher prices.

If we relax the *ceteris paribus* assumption and permit one or more of the nonprice determinants of demand to change, the demand curve will move to a new position. Consider what would happen if buyers' desire for this item grew stronger, or if buyers' income rose. At any given price, high or low, there would be a greater demand for it. We see in Figure 2.5 a rightward shift in the demand curve, from D_1 to D_2. If the desire of buyers for the item became weaker, or if buyers' income fell, the demand curve would shift to the left.

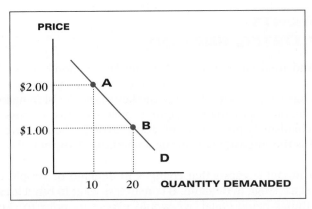

Figure 2.4. A demand curve. Higher quantities are demanded at lower prices, and lower quantities at higher prices.

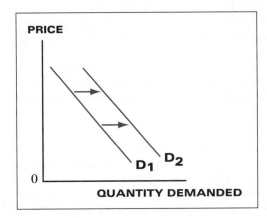

Figure 2.5. A change in demand. The demand curve will shift to a new position when one or more of the underlying nonprice determinants of demand changes.

THE SUPPLY CURVE

The supply of an item during some given time period also depends on a number of circumstances. What are the goals of the firm supplying the item? Maximum profit? Prestige? A quiet life for the owners? The price that the seller receives for the item also is important, as are the costs of the factors of production employed in producing it. The technology used, the prices of other items that could be produced instead, and the number of firms in the industry are other determinants of supply. If we use a *ceteris paribus* assumption, holding all these variables constant *except for price,* a predictable result emerges: A higher price leads to a larger quantity supplied and a lower price leads to a smaller quantity supplied. In Figure 2.6, we see a higher price of $2.00 per unit might be associated with a larger quantity supplied, 20 per day, as at point **A**. A lower price, $1.00 per unit, is associated with a lower quantity supplied, 10 per day, as at point **B**. An upward slope of the **supply curve,** reflecting a positive relationship between price and quantity supplied, is considered to be standard.

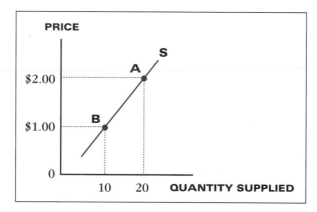

Figure 2.6. A supply curve. Higher quantities are supplied at higher prices, and lower quantities at lower prices.

Any change in a nonprice determinant of supply would cause the supply curve to move to a new position. If labor costs were to decline, for example, or if a technological advance were adopted, supply would increase, and the supply curve S_1 would shift rightward to S_2 (see Figure 2.7).

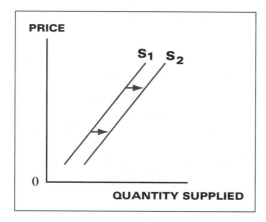

Figure 2.7. A change in supply. The supply curve will move to a new position when one or more of the underlying nonprice determinants of supply changes.

SURPLUSES AND SHORTAGES
CAUSE A MOVEMENT TOWARD EQUILIBRIUM

Figure 2.8 brings the demand curve and the supply curve together in the same diagram. Now we can analyze how price responds to market forces. At the low price of $0.50 per unit, the quantity demanded will be larger than the quantity supplied. As a result, there will be excess demand, called a **shortage.** Many people who cannot buy as much as they would like will now be willing to pay more than $0.50. Suppliers are quick to realize that they can charge more than $0.50. The price rises until eventually the quantity supplied and the quantity demanded become equal at the so-called **equilibrium price,** $1.50 per unit in Figure 2.8. This point where the supply and demand curves cross is the equilibrium, marked with an "E" in the figure.

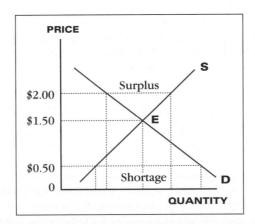

Figure 2.8. The movement to equilibrium. Above the equilibrium price, there will be a surplus, while below the equilibrium there will be a shortage. Surpluses cause sellers to cut the price, while shortages cause them to raise the price.

At the higher price of $2.00 per unit, the quantity supplied is greater than the quantity demanded. As a result, there is excess supply, and firms will accumulate an unsold **surplus.** Those unwanted inventories cost money to store and tie up funds that have other uses. In this case, the pressure on price will be downward. The price will fall until the quantity supplied and the quantity demanded meet at the equilibrium price of $1.50 per unit.

CHANGES IN SUPPLY OR
DEMAND CAUSE A CHANGE IN PRICE

Whenever one of the nonprice determinants of demand (perhaps income) or supply (perhaps labor costs) changes, one or both of the curves will move to a new position. That shift in the position of the curve will create additional pressures to move price toward a new equilibrium. In Figure 2.9's panel **a**, an increase in demand from D_1 to D_2 would result in a shortage at the old price $1.50 and would move the price up to a new equilibrium (E') of $1.75. In panel **b**, an increase in supply from S_1 to S_2 would cause a surplus at the old price $1.50 and would move the price down to a new equilibrium (E") of $1.25.

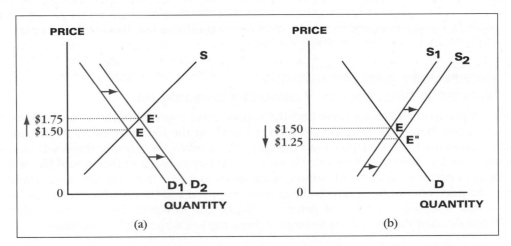

Figure 2.9. Shifts in demand and supply cause a change in price. An increase in demand (rightward shift of the demand curve) causes the equilibrium price to rise. An increase in supply (rightward shift of the supply curve) causes the equilibrium price to fall.

This model of demand and supply as determinants of market price is central to economics. In the next two chapters, we examine the demand and supply mechanism in greater detail, filling in the gaps and answering the questions that must arise from the brief discussion in the section just completed.

► THE RESULTS OF THE MARKET SYSTEM

The establishment of the market system had an overwhelming result. Because the market system bestows greater rewards on productive than unproductive activity, it allowed an escape from the stagnation and diminishing returns of the traditional economy. Markets have certainly not conquered all parts of all economies. Everywhere some elements of tradition still survive, whether in the form of kinship or political influence or personal relations—predominantly in Africa, Latin America, and South Asia, but in all the developed countries as well. In some places government bureaucracies are more important than the market in the making of economic decisions—again to a degree in every nation, but far more so in the remaining Communist countries, some countries that once were Communist, and some LDCs. When these conditions become intrusive, then the efficiency with which an economy operates, and its ability to deliver a higher standard of living to *most* of its members, appears almost universally to decline. Economic sclerosis may be brought about by government regulations that serve the self-interest of the few, or barriers to foreign trade, or trade union militancy. These, together with the monopolizing behavior that worried Adam Smith, and costs to society such as those of pollution, congestion, and the like, can bring reversals of the dynamism promised by the market.

But it remains true that the evolution of the market system and the new attitudes and values that accompanied it proffered an environment that rewards productive activity, stimulates the formation of capital through investment, encourages the acquisition of knowledge, skills, and education, and leads to learning-by-doing. Its atomized decision making by many different firms in many different industries produces new ideas, new experiments, and trials that promote the technical change so central to economic growth. These are major virtues that alternative systems have not been able to deliver.

Yet governments must play an important role. The essential tasks are (1) to define that role in such a way that governments help to preserve the advantages of the market, acting where possible as a force for stability; (2) for governments to provide some services that the market cannot; (3) to ensure that costs to society of a social nature (such as pollution and congestion) do not foul the nest; (4) to keep the monopolizing behavior that Adam Smith worried about under control; and finally (5) to take care that if vast differences in income develop, they do not cause the losers to disappear into a permanent and embittered underclass. These central tasks of appreciating and preserving the benefits of the market while limiting its costs form the core of microeconomics.

SUMMARY

1) Although markets appeared very early in human existence, it took many centuries for a market system to predominate. For the most part, tradition determined what would be produced, how to produce it, and who would get the goods.

2) Traditional economies were handicapped by their loose definition of property rights and their limited use of money. They were largely unable to deliver gains from trade, nor did they facilitate much capital formation or technical improvement. They were especially subject to diminishing returns, the situation where the addition of units of a factor of production causes the additions to output to rise more and more slowly. Because the industries within traditional economies were usually small, economies of scale could seldom be realized.

3) After expansion in the Middle Ages, the market system reached a sixteenth-century turning point during which governments became more receptive to its emergence. The subsequent development of private property rights, new forms of financing for firms, and the application of knowledge and technology to production all facilitated the spread of the market system.

4) Adam Smith, founder of economics as we know it, was the first writer to present a coherent model of how a market system works. For their effectiveness, markets depend on the principle that people strive to maximize their satisfaction. There is a market for factor inputs and a market for goods and services. Factor incomes and the profits of firms determine what is produced, how to produce it, and who gets the production. With knowledge about market prices, total revenues, total costs, and total profits can be calculated. These are the key ingredients in the decision making of market participants. Firms produce the goods that bring in the greatest profit and adopt the techniques that minimize costs. People with the higher incomes can command the greater quantity of goods and services.

5) Prices, which give the signals in a market system, are determined by the interaction of demand and supply. Prices are pushed toward equilibrium by the excess demand (shortages) or excess supply (surpluses) that develop at price levels different from equilibrium.

6) Markets have facilitated growth by rewarding productive activity. But in some cases they fail to provide certain goods, or are subject to monopolizing behavior, or result in environmental costs, or are unable to keep an underclass from developing. In such cases of market failure, governments must play a role.

Chapter Key Words

Command economy: A system where government direction is utilized to determine what is produced, how production is managed, who receives the output that is produced, and how growth is obtained.

Debt financing: With the development of banks, financing for new firms and the expansion of old ones could be obtained through loans on commercial terms. Such debt financing added significantly to the availability of funds, which previously came mostly from owners' own resources or family funds.

Demand: The intensity of wanting something; the quantity of a good or service that people want to buy in a given time period.

Demand curve: A curve showing how the quantity demanded of an item varies as price changes, all other determinants of demand being held constant.

Diminishing returns (to a factor): The idea that if additional inputs of one factor of production (the variable one) are added incrementally while all the other factors are held constant, then eventually each resulting addition to total output will be smaller than the last.

Economies of scale: The idea that lower costs and greater efficiency may be available to larger-size enterprises.

Equilibrium price: In the model of demand and supply, the price where the quantity demanded and the quantity supplied of an item are equal. Any other price will result in either a shortage or a surplus, so that there is a tendency for prices to move toward equilibrium in a market system.

Equity financing: Financing available to corporations, involving the sale of the corporation's stock. Revolutionary when first introduced because it substantially cut risks for investors, so leading to considerably greater flows of financing to firms that were organized as corporations.

Gains from trade: The idea that self-sufficiency is costly, and that gains will accrue from trade. Countries can export what they can produce cheaply at home to countries where the items are expensive, and import items that are expensive at home but cheap abroad. Because countries can specialize in what they do best, trade can increase total world output.

Industrial revolution: A somewhat controversial term applied to the rise of modern industry in Britain during and after the second half of the eighteenth century. Based on the application of knowledge and skills to innovating activity, such as the extensive use of machinery powered by water and steam and the wide use of new materials like iron and steel.

Market system: A system where the prices of what is produced, together with the profits, wages, and other income to the factors of production, play the main role in determining what will be produced, how production is managed, who receives the output that is produced, and how growth is obtained.

Shortage (excess demand): A situation that develops when the price of an item is below the *equilibrium price* (which see). Tends to cause prices to rise toward the equilibrium.

Surplus (excess supply): A situation that develops when the price of an item is above the equilibrium price (which see). Tends to cause prices to fall toward the equilibrium.

Supply: The quantity of a good or service that firms want to sell in a given time period.

Supply curve: A curve showing how the quantity supplied of an item varies as price changes, all other determinants of supply being held constant.

Total profit: The entrepreneurs' reward for producing output; a major factor motivating what is to be produced in a market system. Measured by the difference between total revenue from sales (TR) and the total costs of production (TC); hence $TR-TC = TPr$.

Traditional economy: A system whereby custom and tradition are the main determinants of what will be produced, how production is managed, who receives the output that is produced, and how growth is obtained.

Chapter Questions

1) Suppose you live in a traditional society more than one thousand years ago. You have a great stroke of vision that a market economy would benefit your people. Describe the factors that will tend to prevent you from making your vision a reality.

2) Gluttonia and Guzzlia are two nations that do not trade with one another. Draw smooth, bowed-out PPCs for both countries using the following data: Gluttonia can produce 120 units of food and no units of drink, 40 food and 40 drink, or no food and 45 drink; Guzzlia can produce 45 food and no drink, 40 food and 40 drink, or no food and 120 drink. Suppose that the people in both countries require 40 units of food and 40 units of drink to survive. What is the combined production of food and drink for the two countries? Now suppose that the countries begin trading. What is the new maximum combined production of food and drink?

3a) An Iowa farm can produce corn or soybeans along a typical bowed-out PPC. In the 1930s when labor was very cheap, the farmer employed many more hired hands to work on his farm, but he found that each hired hand increased output by a smaller amount. What is the name for this effect? Show how the PPC shifts as each hand is hired.

3b) By the 1970s the farmer's daughter had taken over the farm. Crop prices were high, so she bought new fields and acquired more tractors and equipment, as well as hired more help. She found that each time she expanded all elements of the farm, her output increased by a greater increment. What is the name for this effect? Show how the PPC shifts as the farm is expanded more and more.

4) You are the distant descendent of the visionary mentioned in Question 1. Your family told you of his ideas about market economies, but they always dismissed them as foolishness. However, you are living in sixteenth-century Europe, and studying the last 500 years of history you begin to see some wisdom in your ancestor's ideas. What are the changes that have led you to this new way of thinking?

5) If you were an investor in the seventeenth or eighteenth centuries, why would you prefer the new corporations over a partnership? If you wanted to start a business of your own, why would you also prefer the corporation to a single proprietorship or partnership?

6) Major Motors (MM) is a small automobile and truck company. Its owners can choose to produce either cars or trucks, but not both. The MM plant can make 100 trucks using 120 workers, 500 tons of steel, 10 acres of land, and medium-level technology. The other choice is to make 420 cars using 170 workers, 105 tons of steel, 20 acres of land, and high technology. Trucks sell for $50,000 each, cars sell for $15,000. One worker gets paid $30,000, a ton of steel costs $1,000, an acre of land costs $10,000, medium technology costs $250,000, and high technology costs $600,000. Using this data, determine whether MM should choose to produce cars or trucks.

7) Draw a demand curve for apples, assuming that *ceteris paribus* people buy more apples when the price is lower. Also draw the supply curve for apples, making the *ceteris paribus* assumption that apple producers will grow more apples when the price is higher. Now suppose that a volcanic eruption in Washington State destroys a large portion of the apple crop. Show what happens to the supply curve. Is there now a surplus or a shortage of apples? Explain what will happen to bring the apple market back to equilibrium.

Demand and Supply I:

The Concept of Demand

OVERALL OBJECTIVE: To develop the technical skills needed to understand demand curves and the various elasticities that attach to them.

MORE SPECIFICALLY:

- To establish that the determinants of demand are the taste for an item, its price, the level of buyers' income, the price of other goods, expectations, and the number of buyers.
- To construct demand curves, showing that movements along them (changes in quantity demanded) are caused by a change in the price of the item, while shifts in their position (change in demand) are caused by a change in one of the nonprice determinants.
- To demonstrate that demand curves normally slope downward and to the right because of diminishing marginal utility, and that demand curves for individuals can be added horizontally to obtain market demand curves.
- To show how the various elasticities of demand are defined and measured, and what difference it makes.

As we found in the last chapter, the prices of goods and services, along with the incomes earned by factors of production, provide the mechanism by which the market system operates. Prices reflect both the intensity of wanting an object (demand) and the scarcity of that object (supply). This chapter examines in detail the concept of demand, while the next considers the concept of supply and then goes on to analyze the market mechanism for price determination.

▶ THE CONCEPT OF DEMAND

To economists, demand is a measure of the intensity with which a particular good or service is wanted. Demand is a flow concept that requires a time horizon. It is not a static number like 500 apples; unless we specify a time period, it is meaningless to say that the demand for apples is 500. Rather, we would have to indicate that there is a demand for 500 apples *per day* or *per week.* In diagramming demand, the quantity measured along the horizontal axis is understood to be in some given period of time.

What establishes the level of demand? There are six main **determinants of demand,** some of which were mentioned in the previous chapter.

1) *The taste or preference for an item.* The greater the liking for a product, the greater the demand. For some goods, taste has been stable for decades or even centuries (cabbages, hammers, tables and chairs), while for other goods, taste has been notoriously changeable over time and from country to country. Frisbees were invented in the 1930s, but there was no appreciable demand for them until they became popular in the late 1950s; snowmobiles are popular in the United States but are detested in Norway; hot tubs are common in Japan, while in the United States they are a luxury item. The French enjoy eating raw snails and frogs' legs, while most Americans approach such foods with caution.[1]

2) *The price of a good or a service.* A rising price for a product almost always causes a decline in the quantity demanded, and a falling price almost always causes an increase in the quantity demanded. This is likely to be true even when common sense says it is not. For example, you probably wouldn't buy a second copy of your daily newspaper if its price dropped 5¢. But what about the *total* demand for newspapers? New readers would be attracted by the lower price and more copies would be sold.

3) *The level of buyers' income.* The higher a buyer's income, the greater the quantity of goods and services that buyer is likely to purchase. The lower the income, the lower the quantity purchased. This relationship wherein the demand for goods rises as income increases is so common that economists use the term *normal good* to describe it. *Inferior goods* do not follow this pattern. Consumer demand for an inferior good declines as buyers' income rises. Horse meat and firewood are examples of inferior goods. (Circumstances may change, however, and a good that is an inferior good one year may be a normal good the next year. A world oil shortage could conceivably make firewood into a normal good.)[2] Whether a good is normal or inferior, the basic point is that income is a determinant of demand.

---

1.   Until recently, economists have had little to say on the subject of how tastes are formed; they have assumed that consumers know what they want and take tastes as given. Recent work by scholars including Tibor Scitovsky of Stanford University, Shlomo Maital of the Israel Institute of Technology, and Paul Romer of the University of California links concepts from economics to others from psychology and biology in an attempt to explain what establishes tastes. But much remains to be explored on this frontier of the discipline.

2.   The epitome of the inferior good was the reclaimed wool named shoddy, obtained by salvaging old woolen garments and used in uniforms by unscrupulous contractors during the Civil War. We now employ the word shoddy for any sort of inferior merchandise.

4) The price of other goods. The effect of price changes for other goods on the demand for a product depends on whether other products are substitutes or complements.

Substitutes are products that perform the same function; butter and margarine are examples. Other things being equal, a rise in the price of margarine will almost certainly lead to an increase in the demand for butter. Some substitutes are so similar that they are almost indistinguishable, such as cane sugar and beet sugar, or T-bone steak and sirloin steak. Others are less alike but serve much the same purpose, like bricks and lumber, copper and aluminum, or Cadillacs and Subarus. In any case, goods are substitutes when a rise in the price of one product leads to an increase in the demand for another, or conversely when a decline in the price of one product leads to a decline in the demand for another.

Complements are dissimilar products that are used together. Examples of complements are lamps and light bulbs, electric toasters and electricity, cars and gasoline, razors and razor blades. In each case, a decline in the price of one of the complements leads to an increase in the demand for the other.

A change in the price of one good can also influence the demand for another good indirectly, through the so-called **income effect.** A decline in the price of a good, though it does not actually raise a household's cash income, acts as if it does, because the purchase of that good at its now-lower price will leave the part of income once spent on it available for the purchase of other goods. So the decline in price is likely to influence the demand for other goods, however slightly, even when the goods involved are neither substitutes nor complements. For example, suppose the price of an automobile a family had decided to buy were to drop by 10%, so that a $12,000 car would cost only $10,800. The income of the family would effectively rise by $1,200, which could be spent to buy other goods.

5) *Expectations of future prices, income, and quality.* All other things being equal, if the price of a good is expected to rise, many consumers will choose to buy now rather than later. Conversely, if a price decline is likely, buyers will tend to postpone purchases until the decline has actually taken place. Expectations of higher or lower future income are also likely to affect the demand for a particular good. If you are reasonably sure of getting a substantial pay raise next month, you may be prompted to go out and buy a greater amount of a product than you would otherwise have done. Similarly, if you expect a new technical advance to be available next month in a computer that you want to buy, you might delay your purchase until then.

6) *Number of buyers.* Other things being equal, the demand for a product increases as the number of buyers rises.

THE DEMAND CURVE

Economists use demand curves to model how the market mechanism works. To construct a demand curve, we select *one* of the determinants of demand and temporarily hold all the others constant. Particular interest attaches to the relationship between the price of a good and the demand for that good. Assuming that the other determinants of demand do not change, we can focus on the relationship between the price of a good and the quantity that will be demanded over a specified time period.

To show graphically the inverse relation between price and quantity demanded, we can construct a demand curve based on the hypothetical data shown in Table 3.1, which is a *demand schedule* for cauliflower.

TABLE 3.1
The price and quantity demanded of cauliflower.

	If the price per pound is	Then the pounds demanded by a buyer in one month will be
A	$2.00	0
B	1.50	2
C	1.00	6
D	0.50	10
E	0	18*

*The high quantity at $0 price would result not only from eating lots of cauliflower, but from all sorts of unusual purposes: to make relish, to feed the dog, to put out for the birds, etc. To persuade people to take more than what they voluntarily would at $0 price, it might be necessary to pay them something. The price would thus become negative.

In Figure 3.1, the vertical (Y) axis shows price ranging from $0 to $2.00, and the horizontal (X) axis shows quantity demanded ranging from 0 to 18 pounds. Points **A**, **B**, **C**, **D**, and **E** correspond to the data in Table 3.1. For example, point **A** shows that at a high price of $2.00 per pound, the quantity demanded is 0. Point **D** shows that at a low price of $.50 per pound, quantity demanded is 10 pounds.

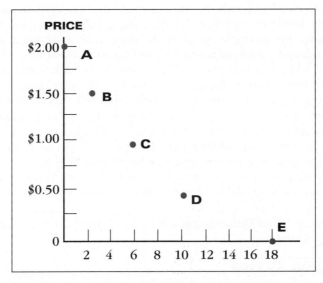

Figure 3.1. Prices and quantity demanded. The figure shows coordinate points for the quantity demanded at various prices.

If data were available for all possible prices, we would have so many points that they would form a continuous curve, as shown in Figure 3.2. This is called a *demand curve*. Depending on the data, a demand curve might be a straight line, a curve concave to the origin, or some other shape.[3]

---

3.   *Historical note:* The British economist Alfred Marshall, the inventor of supply and demand curves, had the unusual notion that quantity demanded was the independent variable: A change in quantity demanded causes a change in price. According to convention, in drawing diagrams the independent variable was and is shown on the horizontal (X) axis, so that is where Marshall put quantity demanded. To this day, in a practice that seems strange to mathematicians, economists still put quantity demanded on the horizontal axis even though it is now considered to be the dependent variable: A change in price causes a change in quantity demanded.

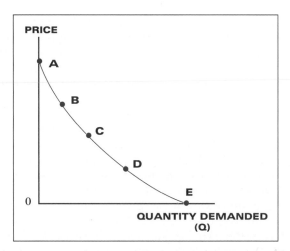

Figure 3.2. A demand curve. A line connecting the coordinate points in the previous diagram is a demand curve that relates price and quantity demanded.

WHY DEMAND CURVES SLOPE DOWN AND TO THE RIGHT

That people will buy more of an item as its price falls and will buy less as it rises seems to be common sense. Economists use the concept called *diminishing marginal utility* to explain more rigorously why this is so. Related ideas that trace the reasons why we buy more of something as its price declines are the *substitution effect* of a price change and the *income effect* of a price change.

Diminishing Marginal Utility

Diminishing marginal utility is a central principle of the theory of demand. It explains why demand curves slope downward. Marginal utility is an idea involving the additional satisfaction we receive by consuming another unit of some good. Marginal utility tends to decline as we consume more and more units. A Pepsi tastes great after a workout, and the second one brings almost as much satisfaction as the first. But the third surely brings less additional satisfaction than did the second, and a sixth will probably bring acute distress. Virtually everything follows the same pattern; psychologically, our capacity to appreciate a good thing declines as we get more of it.[4]

How does diminishing marginal utility explain why the demand curve has its downward slope? Say there is a Pepsi machine at the tennis court that fills a cup with a good quarter-pint gulp of 4 fluid ounces for 25¢. How many cups will we choose to buy after a match? Begin by realizing that the satisfaction we get from buying a cup will have to be at least as great as the price we pay for it; otherwise we will not buy it. To buy the first cup for 25¢, we must believe we are going to get at least 25¢ worth of satisfaction (utility) from the drink. If we are really not very thirsty and estimate that we would get only 15¢ worth of satisfaction from that first drink, we will not spend our money on the Pepsi. We will spend it on something else that will give us our money's worth—perhaps a lemonade from the same machine, or perhaps something we buy later. The key point is that we will buy the Pepsi only if the satisfaction we receive is worth at least as much to us as the price we have to pay. But if we are very thirsty, the 25¢ price for a cup will seem a great bargain. We might estimate that we would get as much as $3.00 worth of pleasure from that first gulp. If we had to pay that much, we would. Clearly, 25¢ for our first taste is not too high a price to pay, and we insert the first quarter.

4.　　Even what appear to be exceptions—for example, getting the last postage stamp in a series for your stamp collection and realizing what great pleasure that last stamp has brought you—is not really an exception because another *complete* series will surely bring less satisfaction than the first did.

What about spending another 25¢ for a second cup? Just as we noted above, a second one will be nice, but not as nice as the first—we are already cooled off a little and are feeling a little more full. Similarly, each additional cup leaves us a little cooler and a little fuller. A table will help in exploring the issue of how many 25¢ cups of Pepsi we would logically choose to drink after the tennis match. See in Table 3.2 that, obviously, if we do not buy a first cup of Pepsi, we will get no satisfaction (utility) at all from it. Now what if we *do* buy a first cup? In terms of satisfaction received, let us say that first cup would be worth $3.00 to us, as above. The total utility from 1 cup is thus $3.00, as shown in the second column. That means that the extra, or marginal, utility in going from 0 cups to 1 is $3.00. What about buying cup number 2? Let's say we would have been willing to pay $4.25 for the two cups together. That means the marginal utility of buying the second cup is $1.25. The second cup brought far less marginal utility than the first. A third cup brings only 75¢ worth of additional pleasure. A fourth brings 25¢ more; in fact, because its price was 25¢, from our point of view it was just worth buying. A fifth cup leaves us with little additional pleasure; we would have paid only $5.35 for five cups, just 10¢ more than the $5.25 for four, so the marginal utility of the fifth cup was just 10¢. That is less than the 25¢ we have to pay for it, so, not getting our money's worth for this cup, we will not buy it. A sixth cup would definitely make us feel too full, reducing our well-being. We would be willing to pay less for six cups than for five; the marginal utility of the sixth cup is a negative 25¢.

TABLE 3.2
Determining total and marginal utility.

Pepsi Purchased from Machine (4-ounce cups)	Total Utility (in dollars)	Marginal Utility (in dollars)
0	0	
		3.00
1	3.00	
		1.25
2	4.25	
		0.75
3	5.00	
		0.25
4	5.25	
		0.10
5	5.35	
		−0.25
6	5.10	

The main lesson from this is that we will buy the first, second, and third and fourth cup, for in these cases, the extra utility from buying it is either the same or greater than the purchase price. But we will not buy more than four, because the extra utility brought by another cupful is less than the purchase price (and becomes negative when we reach six or more). The general rule is that a consumer who wants to maximize the satisfaction received from money spent will purchase additional items up to the point where the marginal utility from the purchase is equal to the price, or **MU = P.** Check your understanding by asking why we did not maximize our *total* utility (at $5.35) by drinking a fifth cupful. The answer: buying a fifth cup does add some total satisfaction, but less than the 25¢ we have to pay to buy it. We would not be getting our money's worth.

What if the price changed? What would happen then? Say that instead of 25¢ per cup, the price of the Pepsi was $1.25 per cup. Looking at the table, we see that the marginal utility of the second cup would have been equal to the price—we would have bought two cups. What if the price had been much lower, only 10¢ per cup? In that case, we would have bought five, because the marginal utility of the fifth cup is also 10¢.

The rule that we purchase goods up to the point where the price is equal to the good's (diminishing) marginal utility is central to determining the slope and position of the demand curve. In the example above, when the price of the Pepsi was 25¢, we bought four cups. When it was $1.25, we bought three. When it was 10¢, we bought five. This is exactly the information that we need to construct a demand curve. Indeed, every point along a demand curve mirrors the underlying marginal utilities. The concept of marginal utility is basic to the construction of demand curves for all items.

Marginal utility has other uses as well. As the accompanying discussion explains, it allows us to determine the optimal combination of all the various goods that are purchased.

USING MARGINAL UTILITY TO FIND THE OPTIMAL COMBINATION OF PURCHASES

The idea of marginal utility allows us to explore what combination of purchases of various goods would leave us as individuals with the greatest total amount of satisfaction (utility). With a given amount of spending, a consumer could buy a little clothing and a lot of food, perhaps, or a lot of clothing and somewhat less food. How can someone achieve the *combination* of purchases that involves the greatest satisfaction from a given amount of money? Using marginal utility, we can make a revealing calculation.

Take an example. Assume that you can buy a unit of clothing and a unit of food for $1 each. Assume further that in consuming a given quantity of a good, the last unit of clothing purchased brings you marginal utility of $2, and the last unit of food you buy conveys marginal utility of $1. In that case, the last dollar you spend on clothing is yielding you more satisfaction than the last dollar you spend on food. If you want to maximize your utility, you would choose to buy less food and more clothing.

It makes good sense to substitute a product that yields more utility per dollar spent for a product that yields less utility per dollar spent. Remember, however, that buying a greater amount of clothing will cause its marginal utility to fall (see Table 3.2), while purchasing less food will raise its MU. (The less food you have, the more satisfaction the last unit of food will bring to you.) So the marginal utilities of the two products move toward one another. *Only when the last dollar spent on clothing and the last dollar spent on food yield exactly the same amount of additional satisfaction (MU) has the consumer attained the optimal combination of purchases.*

In the real world, the prices of a unit of clothing and a unit of food are not likely to be the same. The price of some given article of clothing may be far more than the price of a lunch. We take account of this by using the following formula, in which **C** stands for clothing and **F** for food. The formula identifies the satisfaction-maximizing combination of the two products by indicating the additional utility obtained per dollar spent on each product.

$$\frac{MU_C}{P_C} = \frac{MU_F}{P_F}$$

For example, say clothing is expensive compared to food. The formula tells us that to maximize our satisfaction, it would be economically sensible to buy a large quantity of cheap food, thus bringing the MU of food quite low, and a smaller quantity of expensive clothing, meaning that the MU of clothing will be high. The consumer's task will be to substitute clothing for food, or food for clothing, until the MUs per dollar spent on these products are equal. Here to maximize satisfaction per dollar spent, consumers must buy more food than clothing.

If by contrast food is relatively expensive and clothing is relatively cheap, it would be economically sensible to consume a different bundle of goods. With P_F high and P_C low, MU_F will have to be high and MU_C low to bring about equality in the formula. So to maximize their welfare, consumers would have to buy a relatively larger quantity of clothing, resulting in a lower MU_C, and a relatively smaller quantity of food, resulting in a higher MU_F.

What if there are more than two goods to consider, say entertainment and transportation in addition to clothing and food? The analysis remains the same: Obtain the greatest amount of satisfaction per dollar spent.

We simply expand the formula to accommodate the additional objects. The general formula for any number of goods is:

$$\frac{MU_A}{P_A} = \frac{MU_B}{P_B} = \frac{MU_C}{P_C} = \cdots = \frac{MU_N}{P_N}$$

Notice that consumers do not need to have heard the theory or have seen the algebra in order to behave in the predicted way. They merely need to be attempting to maximize their satisfaction per dollar that they spend. This maximizing rule is implicit in our analysis of the market mechanism.

Substitution and Income Effects

Marginal utility analysis underlies the position and slope of demand curves. Two further concepts that emerge from utility analysis, the *substitution effect* and the *income effect,* help to explain why demand curves have a downward slope. The **substitution effect** suggests that when the price of a good falls, the good becomes a more attractive purchase than are substitutes whose prices do not fall. In other words, we demand more of the good and less of its substitutes. As we have already seen, the **income effect** means that a lower price for a good raises the purchasing power of buyers. Because they pay less of their income for the good, they now have more available for additional spending. Though much of this additional spending will be on other goods, some of it may be spent on the good whose price fell, leading to an increase in the amount of that good that is demanded. The substitution effect and the income effect explain that lower prices lead to a greater quantity demanded of a good and, therefore, why an individual's demand curve slopes downward. For the market as a whole, very often the increase in quantity demanded as the price falls is because new customers are attracted by a price decline. Recall the example of a daily newspaper that cuts its price; its higher sales are the result of more new subscribers, not additional purchases of papers by old subscribers who already take the paper. A rigorous treatment of substitution and income effects requires the use of a more advanced technique than is appropriate for some principles courses. This technique, which utilizes so-called *indifference curves,* is presented in an appendix to this chapter.

ADDING DEMAND CURVES HORIZONTALLY TO FIND MARKET DEMAND

Thus far we have sometimes referred to the demand curve for a single buyer, and at other times to the demand curve for an entire market composed of many buyers. What is the relationship between the two? By adding together individual demand curves we can obtain the demand curve for an entire market. Consider Figure 3.3.

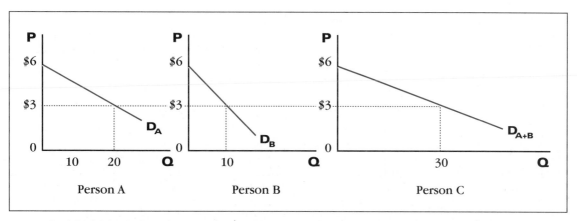

Figure 3.3. Adding demand curves horizontally. The demand curve for an entire market is the horizontal addition of the demand curves for each individual buyer in that market.

Two buyers, A and B, have the demand curves for a particular good shown in the first and second panels. We can calculate their total demand at a given price by adding their respective demands horizontally. At a price of $6, neither A nor B has any demand for the good. So their combined demand at that price is zero. At $3, A wants 20 units and B wants 10. So their total demand—that is, the market demand of A and B together—is 20 + 10 = 30. At any other price, we can calculate market demand in the same way. This technique allows us in concept to determine the market demand by adding together the individual demand curves of all the participants in the market.

DO DEMAND CURVES ALWAYS SLOPE DOWNWARD?

The notion that buyers demand less of a good when its price rises and more of a good when its price falls suggests that demand curves *always* slope downward from upper left to lower right. Economists have devoted considerable attention to an exception, the case of one producer among many where the demand curve is a horizontal line. That case is explored in the next section. Sometimes the suggestion is made that demand curves might even slope upward, with a higher price leading to a *higher* quantity demanded. Several possibilities are discussed in the accompanying box.

The Horizontal Demand Curve

Imagine a producer whose output is only a tiny fraction of the total output flowing to the market. Farmer Robinson in Iowa, for example, produces a corn crop that is only a small part of the total corn produced annually in the United States. What if you asked him to describe the demand for his corn? He would reply, "Well, my corn is the same as anyone else's. You can't tell it apart from the rest once it's in the bins in Des Moines or Chicago. Furthermore, I could sell my entire crop today, at whatever the market price happens to be. Even if I could produce 50 times more I could still take it to market and sell it all at the same market price. My production is way too small to affect the national market. But if I raised my asking price over the market price, even by a penny or two, I couldn't sell a single bushel. Buyers could get whatever they wanted at the market price from the hundreds of thousands of other farmers who grow identical corn."

Farmer Robinson would be correct in his description of the demand for *his small share of the U.S. corn market*. The demand curve for his corn is quite different from the demand for corn in the market as a whole, as shown in Figure 3.4. Any slight rise in price above the level $2.00 per bushel will mean a zero quantity demanded, but at the price of $2.00, Robinson can sell whatever he produces.

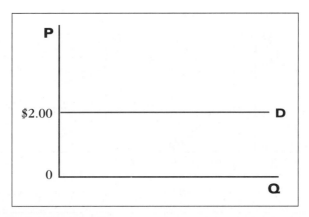

Figure 3.4. A horizontal demand curve. The demand curve for the product of a single small seller in a very large market is a horizontal line. If this seller tried to raise the price, quantity demanded would disappear. Asking a lower price would not make sense because this seller can already sell all that is produced at $2.00 per bushel.

Note, however, that for the entire corn market, a falling price will lead to a greater quantity demanded of the corn produced by all farmers, and a rising price will lead to a smaller quantity demanded.

DO DEMAND CURVES EVER SLOPE UPWARD?

Economists have suggested several cases where demand curves might slope upward, with a higher price leading to a *higher* quantity demanded. The three most important are discussed here, along with the reasons why many economists are skeptical.

 ### VEBLEN GOODS

Thorstein Veblen (1857–1929) developed the idea of *conspicuous consumption* in his book *The Theory of the Leisure Class*, first published in 1899. Veblen suggested that certain prestige goods that are not in demand at a low price may become much desired at a high price. Fashions and cosmetics are excellent examples. A recent article in *Newsweek* reported on the race to market the highest-priced beauty cream. The beauty cream Re-Nutriv, which sold for $115 per 1-pound jar, was outsold by a newcomer, Novessence, which sold for $150 in the 11 1/2-ounce jar. The Astro Villager, located across from the Astrodome in Houston, Texas, advertises that its penthouse is "the world's most expensive hotel suite."[5] Presumably this indicates a willingness to boost the price in order to increase the quantity demanded.

Although the demand curves for **Veblen goods** may slope upward for many individual consumers, the effect is largely overcome by more orthodox behavior. Take diamonds for example: some people may desire diamonds less when their price falls, but industrial users of diamonds would be pleased with the lower prices and would use more of them in a wide range of industrial applications. Even an individual who wants a Ferrari because of its great

---

5.   For your $4000 per night, admittedly you do get a Lane of Lanterns, six bedrooms including the Lady Chatterly Room, a Calliope Bath, a Bouquet Bath, a Roman Bath, a shower for six in the Crusader Room, a gold toilet, and a marble library. As its advertising states, "almost anything is possible in the unique and varied atmosphere of this penthouse suite," though one does wonder how many people read in the marble library.

expense might choose to buy from a dealer willing to take $20,000 off rather than pay list price at another dealership. In any case, some economists have also implied a logical fallacy in the idea of a Veblen good. If the price change is somehow associated with a change in consumer taste for the good, that would be a violation of the *ceteris paribus* assumption and would result in a shift of the demand curve, as discussed in Chapter 2.

 ## "LEMONS"

The demand curve for goods with "lemons" (disappointments) included among them might also be unusual. Say you are buying a used car today and you find one on a lot with a suspiciously low price tag. Because you fear that you have encountered a potential lemon, the low price will make you less likely to buy, so that the demand curve slopes upward. This is known as the Lemon Theory, first proposed by George Akerlof of the University of California. In such cases, risk and uncertainty are the issue. "Normal" demand curves do not imply that risk increases as price declines, possibly outweighing the low price. If the risks *were* known, high-risk used cars and low-risk used cars would each have different downward-sloping demand curves.

GIFFEN GOODS

The only unambiguous and market-wide example of upward sloping demand, with a price rise causing an increase in the quantity of a commodity demanded, is the so-called **Giffen good** named for a nineteenth-century British economist, Sir Robert Giffen (1837–1910). During the Irish famine of 1845–1849, airborne spores turned potatoes overnight into a black, rotting mass. At the time, the Irish were overwhelmingly dependent on potatoes for food. There was a very unusual reaction to the higher price caused by the scarcity, so it is said. As the price of potatoes rose, the demand for potatoes rose as well. Why? Because potatoes were still the cheapest food item available in spite of the price increase. Since they continued to be less expensive than alternative foods, they continued to serve as the dietary staple. Their higher cost required a larger outlay on them, leaving a smaller proportion of income available to spend on "luxury" foods such as vegetables, meat, and fruit. Now that people were relatively poorer (an example of the income effect), they bought fewer luxury foods and more potatoes.[6]

Economists have usually been willing to admit that Giffen goods are logically possible and *might* exist. But the evidence that they actually *do* exist is very thin. Goods that take up a sufficiently large proportion of consumers' income are rare, and a diligent search for actual cases has not turned up convincing examples.

---

6.   Curiously, there is no evidence that Sir Robert Giffen actually conceived the idea that is now associated with his name. Giffen did study the demand for bread among British workers during an economic slump, but he did not apparently hypothesize an upward-sloping demand curve. The myth is entrenched, however. Fortunately, it is as good as the truth for a teaching tool.

INFORMATION CONVEYED BY A DEMAND CURVE

A demand curve can be used to show at a glance what happens when price changes. In Figure 3.5, we see that a decline in price (with no change in any of the other determinants of demand), from $1.50 per unit to $1.00 per unit, leads to an increase in the quantity demanded from 10 units to 25 units. Such a movement along a given stationary demand curve is referred to as a **change in quantity demanded**; it is shown here as a movement from point **a** to point **b**.

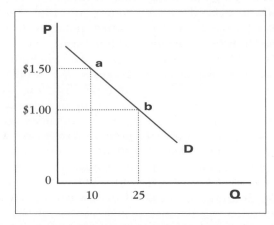

Figure 3.5. A change in price leads to a change in quantity demanded. The expression *change in quantity demanded* is used when a change in price leads to a new quantity along a demand curve.

A demand curve can also be used to show what happens when we suspend the assumption that tastes, income, and the other nonprice determinants of demand remain constant. With the *ceteris paribus* assumption relaxed, the demand curve itself is free to move. In Figure 3.6, suppose D_1 is the demand curve for cauliflower with the nonprice determinants of demand held constant. What would happen if consumers developed a greater liking for cauliflower? Or if their income increased and cauliflower is a normal good? Or if the price of a substitute for cauliflower rose sharply? Or if a rumor spread that the price of cauliflower would rise next week? Or if the country's population grew? In each case, the demand curve for cauliflower would shift to the right. In Figure 3.6, the demand curve would shift from D_1 to D_2. Larger incomes, a greater desire to buy, and so forth, will result in an expanded demand even at a high price such as $1.50 per head. Where formerly consumers wanted only a quantity of 10 heads of cauliflower at a price of $1.50, now they want to buy 20 heads. At a low price, such as $0.50, consumers who previously wanted 30 cauliflowers will now purchase 40. Such a rightward shift of the demand curve is caused by some change in one or more of the underlying determinants of demand.[7]

In Figure 3.7, the demand curve has shifted leftward in response to a *decreased* desire to buy, lower income, or other changes in the nonprice determinants that work to reduce demand. A leftward or rightward shift of the demand curve is referred to as a **change in demand.**

---

7.   It is tidy to show the shift as parallel but it need not be so. For example, demand might shift further to the right at lower prices than at higher prices. In that case, the slope of D_2 would be shallower than that of D_1. The rightward shift in the demand curve from D_1 to D_2 could also be described as an upward shift, or rise. That is, for any given quantity on the horizontal axis, greater demand would mean that consumers would be willing to pay a higher price as measured on the vertical axis. What this text calls a "rightward shift in the demand curve" might also be described as an "upward shift" or a "shift upward and to the right." In each case, the meaning is the same.

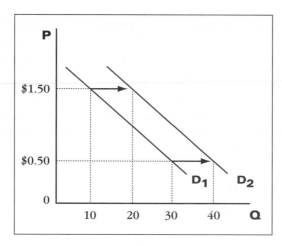

Figure 3.6. An increase in demand. The expression *change in demand* refers to a shift of the demand curve. This figure shows an increase in demand.

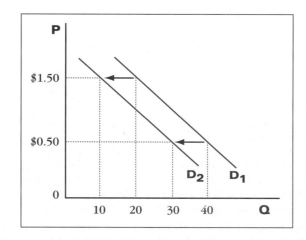

Figure 3.7. A decrease in demand. This figure also shows a change in demand, in this case a decrease.

► ELASTICITY OF DEMAND

The word *elasticity* refers to the reaction of something in response to a force exerted on it. A rubber band is said to be very elastic when a given pull stretches it a long way, whereas another rubber band is not very elastic if the same pull stretches it only a little. Economists use the term *elasticity* in a similar way to describe a response to a force. The concept helps us to see how demand curves figure in economic decision making.

PRICE ELASTICITY OF DEMAND

The concept of **price elasticity of demand** involves the degree to which a price change causes a change in quantity demanded and, therefore, in the total revenue that sellers receive.

At any point along a demand curve, we can calculate how much revenue sellers receive from buyers who purchase a given quantity at a given price. In Figure 3.8, the total revenue earned is equal to price times quantity, or TR = P x Q. If 10 units of the same good are sold to buyers at $5 for each unit, then the total revenue of sellers is $50. Using a basic principle of geometry, we know that multiplying a horizontal side of a right-angled figure times a vertical side yields the area of the resulting rectangle. So P x Q must be equal to the shaded area in the diagram. This rectangular area is equal to the total revenue earned. Similarly, 8 units sold at $7 each results in a total revenue of $56, and 18 units sold at $2 each yields total revenue of $36. In each case, the resulting total revenue can be seen as a rectangle formed by multiplying P x Q.

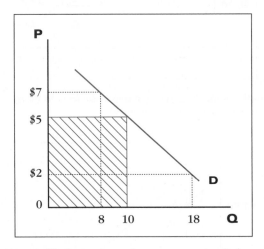

Figure 3.8. **Finding total revenue.** Total revenue can be seen as a rectangle formed when the price is multiplied by the quantity demanded.

As we have noted, the degree to which quantity demanded responds to a change in price, and thus the degree to which the total revenue received changes, involves the price elasticity of demand. To see price elasticity in action, consider what would happen if price is reduced along a given demand curve. There are only three possibilities: (1) many more items will be sold, so that the increase in total revenue will far outweigh any loss caused by the price reduction; (2) just enough more items will be sold so that the increase in total revenue exactly matches the loss caused by the price reduction; and (3) only a few more items may be sold, or even no more, so that total revenue will decline as a result of the price reduction. In each case, the responsiveness of quantity demanded and consequently of total revenue to the price change is different, meaning that the price elasticity of demand is different.

The three cases are illustrated in Figure 3.9. In each situation we start out with a price (P) of $4 per unit and a quantity demanded (Q) of 60, so that total revenue amounts to $4 x 60 = $240, and we then lower price to $3 per unit. Panel **a** shows that the decline in price leads to a new quantity demanded of 100. Since $3 x 100 = $300, total revenue has risen. The gain outweighs the loss, as shown by the increased size of the P x Q rectangle. This is an example of *elastic demand.* Panel **b** shows that the decline in price leads to a quantity demanded of 80. Because the increase in quantity demanded is just balanced by the loss from the price reduction, total revenue remains the same at $3 x 80 = $240. The rectangles are of the same size. This is an example of *unitary elasticity.* (The choice of that term will be explained shortly.) Panel **c** shows that the decline in price leads to a quantity demanded of 70. Since $3 x 70 = $210, total revenue has fallen. The loss outweighs the gain, as shown by the decreased size of the P x Q rectangle. This is an example of *inelastic demand.*

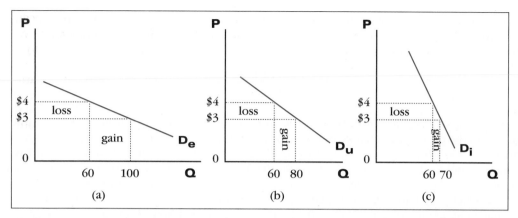

Figure 3.9. Elastic demand, unitary elasticity, and inelastic demand. Panel **a** shows *elastic demand;* a price decrease has caused an increase in total revenue. Panel **b** shows *unitary elasticity,* with a price decrease leaving total revenue the same as before. Panel **c** shows *inelastic demand;* a price decrease has caused a fall in total revenue.

Calculating Price Elasticity

How revenue responds to price changes is so important that precise estimates are often made. To show how, let the symbol ε_d stand for the price elasticity of demand.[8] The formal method for calculating ε_d is then:

$$\varepsilon_d = \frac{\text{percentage change in quantity demanded.}}{\text{percentage change in price}}$$

If the result is greater than 1, then the percentage change in quantity demanded (Q) must be larger than the percentage change in price (P). So the price reduction will *increase* total revenue, and demand is elastic in this price range. If the result is 1, the percentage change in Q must equal the percentage change in P. The price reduction will not alter total revenue. Here demand exhibits *unitary elasticity*. (The use of the term unitary reflects the fact that the numerical elasticity is 1.) If the result is less than 1, the percentage change in Q must be less than the percentage change in P. The price reduction will *reduce* revenue, and demand is *inelastic* in this price range. Note that in each case, because the percentage change in quantity moves in the opposite direction to the percentage change in price, the resulting elasticities are really negative. By convention, however, price elasticities are usually written without the minus sign.[9]

Unless we use differential calculus to calculate the price elasticity of demand or have an equation for the curve, we face a problem involving the accuracy of the percentage changes. For example, if a price falls from 10¢ to 8¢, and then rises again from 8¢ to 10¢, is that a fall of $^2/_{10} = 20\%$ followed by a rise of $^2/_8 = 25\%$? Our conventional quick method of calculation would seem to make it so, yet ought not the percentages be the same? To avoid this inexactness, we split the difference by taking as a base the average of the higher price and the lower price:

$$\frac{10¢ + 8¢}{2} = \frac{18¢}{2} = 9¢.$$

---

8.   The use of ε which is the Greek letter epsilon, and of other Greek letters elsewhere in the text, reflects the role of calculus in the origins of many concepts in economics.

9.   To allow for this, the formula can be shown as an absolute value, $\varepsilon_d = \left| \frac{\%\Delta Q}{\%\Delta P} \right|$.

The percentage change would then be 2¢ on a base of 9¢, or $\frac{2}{9}$ = 22%. We can use the same procedure to calculate the (nearly) exact percentage change in quantity demanded. So we can write the elasticity formula as follows, with the symbol Δ meaning "change in":

$$\varepsilon_d = \frac{\Delta Q / [(Q_1 + Q_2) / 2]}{\Delta P / [(P_1 + P_2) / 2]} .$$

Now let us use this formula with the three different examples of elasticity. In panel **a** of Figure 3.10, the percentage change in quantity demanded is $\frac{6}{6}$ = 100% and the percentage change in price is $\frac{2}{3}$ = 66%. Since the result of dividing 100 by 66 is greater than 1, demand is price-elastic. In panel **b**, the percentage change in quantity is $\frac{2}{9}$ = 22%, and the percentage change in price is also $\frac{2}{9}$ = 22%. The result of dividing 22 by 22 is 1, and the case is one of unitary elasticity. In panel **c**, the percentage change in quantity is $\frac{20}{200}$ = $\frac{1}{10}$ = 10%, and the percentage change in price is $\frac{2}{19}$ = 10.5%. The result of dividing 10 by 10.5 is less than 1, and demand is price-inelastic.

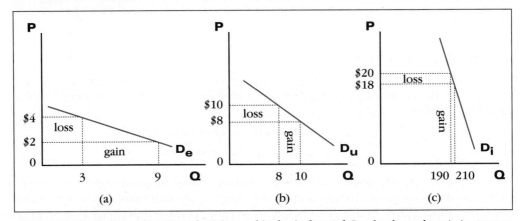

Figure 3.10. Elastic demand, unitary elasticity, and inelastic demand. Panel **a** shows the gain in revenue from the increased quantity outweighing the loss because the price was cut; demand is elastic. Panel **b** shows the gain and loss are the same; the elasticity of demand is unitary. Panel **c** shows the gain in revenue from the increased quantity is less than the loss because the price was cut; demand is inelastic.

Here is a complete sample calculation based on the last case, panel **c**. Say the price of an item rises from $18 to $20, and as a result the quantity demanded falls from 210 units to 190. The price elasticity of demand for this change is:

$$\frac{20 / [(210+190) / 2]}{2 / [(18+20) / 2]} = \frac{20/200}{2/19} = \frac{.100}{.105} = 0.95.$$

So demand is slightly price-inelastic; a price cut will lower total revenue a little, and a price increase will mean a small rise in total revenue.

Some actual price elasticities of demand when prices are changed slightly from prevailing levels are shown in Table 3.3:

TABLE 3.3
Sample price elasticities of demand.

Inelastic		Unitary Elasticity		Elastic	
Potatoes	0.3	Beef	1.0	Electricity	1.3
Clothing	0.6	Beer	1.0	Cars	2.1
Gasoline	0.6			Sporting goods	2.4
Medical care	0.8				

Sources: Mostly from E. Lazear and R. Michael, "Family Size and the Distribution of Real Per Capita Income," *American Economic Review,* March 1980, Table 2; and H. Houthakker and L. Taylor, *Consumer Demand in the United States,* Cambridge, Mass., 1970, Table 3.2.

Elasticities Vary Along a Demand Curve

A warning: You cannot judge the price elasticity of demand simply by noting the flatness or steepness of a demand curve. Take the example illustrated by Figure 3.11.

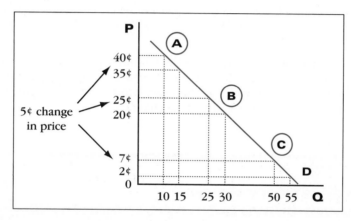

Figure 3.11.Elasticity at different points along the same demand curve. Around **A**, the percentage change in quantity is high and the percentage change in price is low; demand is elastic. Around **B**, the percentage change in quantity and price are about the same; the elasticity of demand is approximately unitary. Around **C**, the percentage change in quantity is low and the percentage change in price is high; demand is inelastic.

In the area around **A** on the diagram, a 5¢ decline in price causes a relatively small percentage change in price and a very large percentage change in quantity demanded. What is the price elasticity of demand? High, with a considerable increase in total revenue. Now take the area around **B** on the *same* demand curve. Here the percentage changes in price and quantity demanded are about equal. This is the sign of unitary elasticity. In the area around **C**, the percentage change in price is large and the percentage change in quantity demanded is small. Here demand is inelastic, with the reduction in price causing a decline in total revenue.

In fact, price elasticity along a straight-line demand curve varies from infinity at the price axis to 0 at the quantity axis, with all other elasticities in between. To show this, we start where the demand curve intersects the price axis in Figure 3.12, and lower the price a little.[10] Quantity then rises from 0, which is an infinite percentage change. Infinity (the percentage change in quantity) divided by a finite number (the percentage change in price) yields an elasticity of infinity.

---

10.   The symbol ∞ stands for infinity; > means greater than; and < means less than.

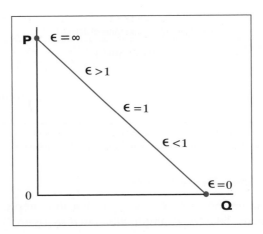

Figure 3.12. Different Elasticities Along the Same Demand Curve. Along a straight-line demand curve that runs from axis to axis, the price elasticity of demand ranges from ∞ at the top to 1 at the midpoint to 0 at the bottom.

Conversely, where the demand curve intersects the quantity axis, let us raise the price a little. That rise is an infinite percentage change; the percentage change in quantity is finite. A finite number divided by infinity equals 0. Meanwhile, at the exact center of the straight line any (very small) change in price will result in an equal percentage change in quantity; elasticity is unitary.[11]

FINDING ELASTICITY WHEN THE DEMAND CURVE IS NOT A STRAIGHT LINE

This division of a straight-line demand curve into an elastic, unitary, and inelastic range will serve to identify the elasticity of a given point along a demand *curve* as well. By drawing a tangent line to a curve (see Figure 3.13), we can discover whether the point is above or below the midpoint of the line.

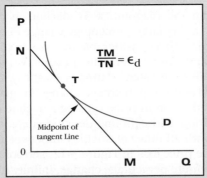

Figure 3.13. Measuring elasticity along a demand curve. The price elasticity of demand at any point along a demand curve can be expressed as the value of the ratio TM/TN.

The ratio $\frac{TM}{TN}$ is the numerical elasticity: if TM = TN, elasticity is unitary; if TM > TN as in the figure, point T is in the elastic range; if TM < TN, point T is in the inelastic range.

---

11.   A geometric property of a straight line drawn from Y axis to X axis is that very slight movements from the center point of the line involve the same percentage change along the two axes.

In general, elasticity *changes* along a demand curve, and the shape, slope, or position of a curve does *not* immediately reveal what the elasticity is at a *given* point. The most we can say is that in some given price range, demand is elastic or inelastic, as in Figure 3.14.

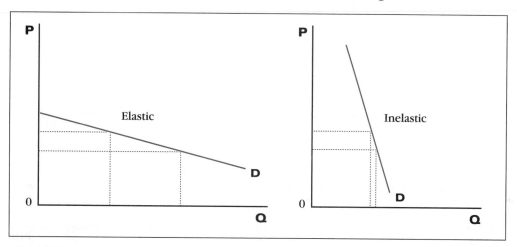

Figure 3.14. **Different curves, same price range.** Along two straight line demand curves, a given price change results in a more elastic response along the shallower curve.

Where we are dealing with the same demand curve as in Figure 3.15, we can tell that a price change in the top part of the curve is in the elastic range, while a price change in the bottom part of the curve is in the inelastic range.

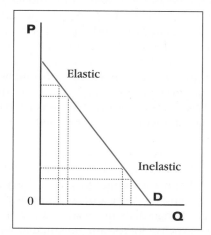

Figure 3.15. **Same curve, different prices.** Along the same demand curve, the price elasticity of demand is greater for a price change further up the curve and less for a price change lower down the curve.

These simple rules allow us to make some further deductions. When two straight-line demand curves intersect, as in panel **a** of Figure 3.16, at the point of intersection, elasticity must always be higher along the flatter of the two curves. On that flatter curve, the point of intersection must be further along toward, or in, the upper half of the curve. Similarly, where there are two parallel straight-line demand curves, as in panel **b**, the inner one must be the more elastic for a given price change because we are dealing with a higher position on that inner curve.

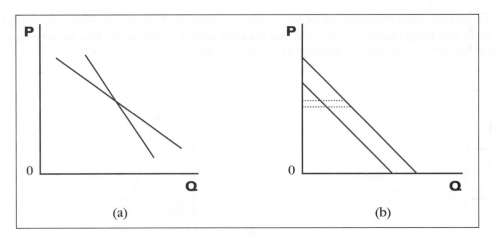

Figure 3.16. Further deductions about elasticity. At the intersection of two straight-line demand curves, the flatter curve is more elastic. The inner of two parallel demand curves is more elastic than the outer one.

In three exceptional cases the demand curve has the same elasticity throughout its range.

1) The first of these, shown in panel **a** of Figure 3.17, is a horizontal line. Recall that this shows the demand facing one producer of many in a market. The market will take any quantity a single producer will sell, but the price change is 0. Because a finite number divided by 0 equals infinity, the elasticity of such a curve is infinite.[12] A horizontal demand curve is said to be *perfectly elastic*.

2) The second exception is the *perfectly inelastic* demand curve, where the same quantity is demanded no matter what happens to the price. The demand curve is thus a vertical line, as in panel **b**. The finite change in price and the 0 change in quantity means, following the elasticity formula, that $\varepsilon_d = 0$. Insulin for a diabetic is a common example of perfect or near-perfect inelasticity because high prices will not curtail demand nor will low prices increase it. Heroin for an addict is also an example (though for the heroin market as a whole, a lower price would attract more users). Salt is another often suggested case because a limited amount is necessary for life. Yet it is probably not a very good example of perfect inelasticity; more of it would surely be used to melt ice on roads and driveways if its price fell substantially.

3) The third exception is the unusual case of a curve called a *rectangular hyperbola*. Any such curve, which approaches each axis asymptotically (that is, always coming closer but never touching) as in panel **c**, has a strange property. Every rectangle drawn to it has the same area. Because such rectangles represent revenue, as they are always a price multiplied by a quantity, a price change does not lead to a revenue change. That, of course, is our definition of unitary elasticity. So, for any rectangular hyperbola, $\varepsilon_d = 1$ throughout its length.

---

12.   Strictly speaking, we cannot divide by 0. But the limit as the divisor *approaches* 0 is infinity.

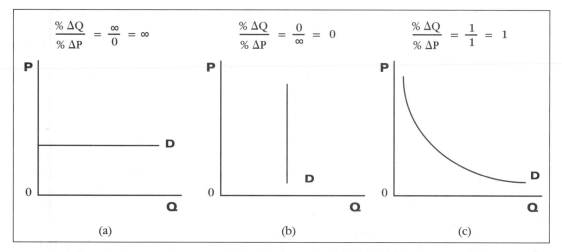

Figure 3.17. Demand curves that are perfectly elastic, perfectly inelastic, and of unitary elasticity throughout their length. A horizontal demand curve (panel **a**) is perfectly elastic throughout its length. A vertical demand curve (panel **b**) is perfectly inelastic throughout its length. A demand curve that is a rectangular hyperbola (panel **c**) exhibits unitary elasticity throughout its length.

What Determines the Elasticity of a Good?

Within a given price range, why does raising or lowering the price have a much greater effect on the quantity demanded of some goods than of others? In short, what is it that makes the demand for a good elastic or inelastic? The demand for a good is likely to be more *inelastic* for a given price change if one or more of the following conditions prevails:

1) You have a great need for a good and there are no substitutes. The demand for food in general, or insulin, or salt, or for subway tickets in New York and London, is likely to be inelastic. Conversely, butter, Toyotas, and Coca-Cola all have good substitutes (margarine, Subaru, Pepsi-Cola), and thus the need for these goods is not so great. We would expect the demand for all of these to be relatively elastic. Time also plays a role where substitution is concerned. In the frost belt of Maine or Minnesota, it may not be possible to substitute wood heat for fuel oil in a short time period, but the shift *may* be possible if there is enough time for the adjustment to be made. The longer the time period, the more elastic demand is likely to be.
2) You spend a small percentage of your income on some necessary item. Nails are a small proportion of the expenditure on the house you are building; because you have to have them, their price can rise quite a bit without much curtailing your demand.
3) The good is a nondurable good. Consider that if it were a durable good, such as a refrigerator, and refrigerator prices rose, then you could probably keep the old one in service somewhat longer. The quantity demanded would decline more sharply with a price rise than would be true if you couldn't keep your old one in service any longer. So durables generally have a more elastic demand, and nondurables such as bread, milk, and diapers for the baby, have a lower elasticity.

In a sense, elasticity depends on how precisely we define a good. "Food" certainly has an inelastic demand because there are no substitutes and great need. But "meat" has a higher elasticity (less need, closer substitutes). "Steak" has a very much higher elasticity, and "T-bone steak" even higher. (Most people would probably agree that sirloin steak and T-bone steak are almost perfect substitutes; and that however much you believe you "need" meat, it is unlikely that you will feel your need for T-bone steak is as great as that.)

The concept of price elasticity of demand is one of the most important in all of economics. Where elasticity is high, changes in price signal large movements in how much consumers buy, and firms face quite significant market responses if they alter price. Conversely, low elasticity means that even large price changes may have little effect on quantity demanded. The signals given by price are then less powerful. Price elasticity of demand figures importantly in many of the subject areas discussed in the remainder of the book.

INCOME ELASTICITY OF DEMAND

So far we have focused on changes in price with the nonprice determinants of demand held constant under a *ceteris paribus* assumption. Now we will see what happens when we hold all determinants (including price) constant *except for income.* Figure 3.18 shows the effect of a change in income on quantity demanded. This time quantity demanded is on the vertical axis.[13]

The curve labeled **A** shows the usual expectation: A rise in income leads to a rise in quantity demanded. As we mentioned earlier, such behavior defines a *normal good.* The same is true of curve **B** up to a point, but the downward bend indicates that when income rises beyond the level of the arrow, quantity demanded begins to *fall.* Such behavior defines an *inferior good.* These curves are called **Engel curves** after Ernst Engel, a nineteenth-century Prussian statistician who discovered in the course of his research that the percentage of income spent on food declines as income increases. Fortunately, later writers decided to use his name for the curves; otherwise, textbook authors might call them "income-consumption curves," a cumbersome term that a few actually use.

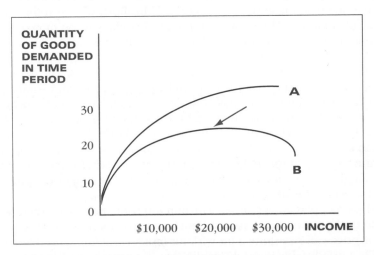

Figure 3.18. Engel curves. Curves that show how the quantity demand changes as income changes are called Engel Curves. Curve **A** indicates a normal good throughout the length of the curve. Curve **B** shows a normal good until the downward bend, beyond which the good is inferior.

Where there is an Engel curve, there is also an elasticity, but it is an income elasticity rather than a price elasticity. If we let ε_y stand for the **income elasticity of demand,** then:

$$\varepsilon_y = \frac{\text{percentage change in quantity demanded}}{\text{percentage change in income}}$$

---

13. Marshall did not invent this curve, so the independent variable, the level of income, is in its proper place on the horizontal axis.

If a rise in income causes the quantity demanded of a good to *rise,* the income elasticity of demand must be a positive number and the good is a normal good. If a rise in income causes quantity demanded to *decline,* the income elasticity is negative and the good is an inferior good. A further convenient definition is that when income rises, but in percentage terms the quantity demanded rises by more, so income elasticity >1, then the good is income-elastic. Income-elastic goods are luxuries, wanted more as people become better off. If quantity demanded rises, but by less than the income increase, then income elasticity <1 but >0, and the good is income-inelastic. Income-inelastic goods are necessities. With cuts in income, the consumption of them does not fall very much. The position of all these elasticities is shown on Figure 3.19.

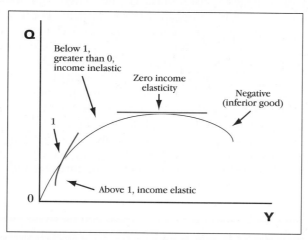

Figure 3.19. Income elasticity of demand. Income elasticities can be read along an Engel Curve as shown in the figure.

Some actual income elasticities of demand, all for the United States except as noted, are shown in Table 3.4.

TABLE 3.4
Income elasticities of demand for sample goods.

Inferior		Normal, inelastic		Normal, elastic	
Potatoes	–0.2	Wine (France)	0.1	Wine (U.S.)	1.4
		Food (U.S.)	0.2	Consumer durables	1.8
		Cheese	0.4	Medical care	1.9
		Cigarettes	0.8	Taxi rides	2.8
		Food (India)	0.8	Sporting goods	3.7
		Shelter	0.9		

Source: Mostly from E. Lazear and R. Michael, "Family Size and the Distribution of Real Per Capita Income," *American Economic Review,* March 1980, Table 2; and H. Houthakker and L. Taylor, *Consumer Demand in the United States,* Cambridge, Mass., 1970, Table 3.2.

CROSS ELASTICITY OF DEMAND

What do you think would happen to the quantity demanded of video cassettes if the price of video cassette recorders fell? What would happen to the quantity demanded of meat if fish prices fell? We can analyze such questions by means of the ***cross elasticity of demand,*** often called the cross-price elasticity of demand. If we let ε_{xy} stand for the cross elasticity of demand, with Y the item whose price changes and X the item the quantity demanded of which changes as a result, then:

$$\varepsilon_{xy} = \frac{\text{percentage change in quantity demanded of X}}{\text{percentage change in price of Y}}$$

There are three possibilities. (1) A rise in the price of Y will cause a rise in the quantity demanded of X. Consumers will shift away from Y (meat perhaps) in favor of X (fish perhaps). The positive percentage changes in both the numerator and the denominator yield a positive cross elasticity, because $\frac{+}{+} = +$. Positive cross elasticity shows that the goods are substitutes. (2) A rise in the price of Y will cause a decline in the quantity demanded of X. Discouraging consumption of one (VCRs perhaps) discourages consumption of the other (videotapes). A negative number divided by a positive number yields a negative cross elasticity, because $\frac{-}{+} = -$. Negative cross elasticity shows that the two goods are complements. (3) A change in the price of Y causes no change in the quantity demanded of X. Zero divided by a positive number yields a result of zero. A cross elasticity of zero means that the two goods (perhaps VCRs and dog food) are in no way related to each other. They are neither substitutes nor complements.

One example of an actual cross elasticity is +0.01 when considering the demand for meat as the price of fish changes. (So meat and fish are indeed substitutes, though just barely.) Another is the cross elasticity of –0.04 when considering the demand for meat as the price of tobacco changes. (The two are complements; perhaps smokers are dying for a cigarette after their roast beef for dinner.)[14] Typically, cross elasticities are much smaller than price elasticities because a change in a good's own price usually has a greater influence on the quantity demanded of the good than would a change in the price of some other good.

A SUMMARY TABLE OF DEMAND ELASTICITIES

It is helpful to have a summary table of the various elasticities of demand. This box provides it. Below, Q = quantity, P = price, Y = income, and x and y are two different goods.

Type	Formula	Range	Curve
Price elasticity of demand	%ΔQ/%ΔP	∞, perfectly elastic	where demand curve hits y axis; also a horizontal demand curve
		over 1, elastic	upper half of straight-line demand curve
		1, unitary	mid-point of straight-line demand curve; also a rectangular hyperbola
		0-1, inelastic	lower half of straight-line demand curve
		0, perfectly inelastic	where demand curve hits x axis; also a vertical demand curve
Income elasticity of demand	%ΔQ/%ΔY	over 1, normal, income elastic (luxury)	rising Engel curve, quantity demanded increasing faster than income
		0-1, normal, income inelastic (necessity)	rising Engel curve, quantity demanded increasing more slowly than income
		0	Engel curve is flat
		negative, inferior good	Engel curve slopes down
Cross elasticity of demand	%ΔQx/%ΔPy	positive, substitutes	no curve is drawn
		negative, complements	no curve is drawn

14.   From A.P. Barten, "Consumer Demand Functions under Conditions of Almost Additive Preferences," *Econometrica*, January–April 1964, Table XV (except for the humor).

CONCLUSION

This chapter has examined the essential concept of demand which, with supply, determines market prices. We have shown how demand curves are constructed, how movements along these curves differ from shifts in the curves themselves, how the elasticities of demand are measured, and why elasticities make a difference. In the next chapter, we move to the discussion of supply, and then use demand and supply together to analyze the mechanism of market pricing.

SUMMARY

1) The determinants of demand are the taste for an item, the price of the item, the level of buyers' income, the price of other goods, expectations, and the number of buyers.

2) A demand curve can be constructed by holding all the determinants of demand constant except for price, and then allowing price to vary. A movement along a demand curve (a change in quantity demanded) is caused by a change in the price of the item, while a shift in the position of the demand curve (a change in demand) is caused by a change in one of the nonprice determinants.

3) Demand curves normally slope downward and to the right because of diminishing marginal utility, and the associated substitution effect and income effect. Individuals' demand curves can be added horizontally to obtain market demand curves.

4) The price elasticity of demand, measured as $\%\Delta Q/\%\Delta P$ (with Q = quantity and P = price), shows how responsive the quantity demanded is to a price change. A large response indicates high elasticity; a small response indicates inelasticity. All conceivable elasticities from infinity to 0 are present along a straight-line demand curve that runs from axis to axis.

5) The income elasticity of demand, $\%\Delta Q/\%\Delta Y$ (with Y = income), shows how quantity demanded changes as a result of a change in income. With normal goods, the quantity demanded rises as income rises, while with inferior goods, the quantity demanded falls as income rises.

6) Cross elasticity of demand, measured as $\%\Delta Q_x/\%\Delta P_y$ (with x = good x and y = good y), measures the degree to which a change in the price of one good alters the quantity demanded of another. If a fall in the price of x leads to a fall in the quantity demanded of y, the goods are substitutes. If a fall in the price of x leads to a rise in the quantity demanded of y, the goods are complements.

APPENDIX
INDIFFERENCE CURVES

Indifference curves are a technical tool for explaining the position and slope of demand curves. With such curves, the substitution and income effects discussed in the chapter can be explained more fully.

An indifference curve traces out all the combinations of two goods that are equally satisfactory to an individual. Ask yourself, what various quantities of food and clothing would leave you feeling equally well-off. You would say, clearly there is a trade-off here. I need to eat, and I have to have something to wear, but up to a point I would be willing to take some more clothing and give up some food. But I would have to be compensated with more and more clothing because eventually giving up food will make my diet less exciting. If I gave up *too* much food, I could even get hungry. Eventually, another sweater won't compensate me for a lost lunch. In the same way, I'm willing to take more food in exchange for clothing up to a point, but eventually I'll be a little threadbare, and it will take a lot of food to persuade me to give up any more of my clothes.

Let us draw a curve that plots the various amounts of food and clothing that would leave you completely indifferent. Figure 3A.1 shows an indifference curve, IC_1. This curve shows that you would be equally satisfied with 15 units of food and 8 units of clothing, or 10 units of food and 12 units of clothing, or any other combination indicated by the curve.

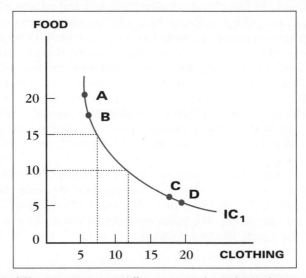

Figure 3A.1. An indifference curve. An indifference curve shows the combinations of two goods that leave a consumer equally satisfied. The convex-to-the-origin shape reflects diminishing marginal utility.

The convex-to-the-origin shape of the curve is important. If we assume the fundamental principle discussed in the body of the chapter, that the marginal utility of an item diminishes as more of it is consumed, then indifference curves will be convex. See how at **A** you would be willing to give up quite a lot of food in order to get a little more clothing, in a trade-off that would move you to **B**. But if you already had a lot of clothing but not much food, as at **C**, then you are far less interested in losing any more food. So you would have to be compensated with much more clothing in order to move to a point like **D**. The implication is that the marginal utility of clothing falls as you get more of it, while the marginal utility of food rises as you have less of it.

Indifference curve IC_1 is just one of many possible curves. There would be other combinations that would leave you indifferent, but with both more food and more clothing, so that you would clearly be better off. In Figure 3A.2, IC_2 is a higher indifference curve than IC_1. Here is another set of combinations of food and clothing that would leave you indifferent, but at a higher level of satisfaction overall. You would prefer any combination along it to any combination along IC_1. Similarly, IC_0 is a lower indifference curve; each combination of food and clothing along it represents a lower level of satisfaction compared to curve IC_1.

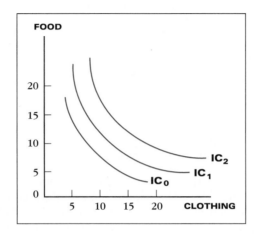

Figure 3A.2. A map of indifference curves. The further outward and to the right an indifference curve is located, the higher level of satisfaction it shows.

To utilize indifference curves, the next step is to ask how much income you have to spend on food and clothing. In Figure 3A.3, we draw a *budget constraint* that in effect measures how much income is available to you for your spending on these items. In the figure, assume that if you spent your entire income on food, the price of food is such that you have enough to buy 20 units of food. That would leave you consuming at point **A.** If, however, you spent your entire income on clothing, assume that, given the price of clothing, you could buy 15 units. That would leave you consuming at point **D.** Because 20 units of food are worth as much as 15 units of clothing, the price of one more unit of food is 3/4 of a unit of clothing. So we can draw a budget line connecting **A** and **D** that traces out all the combinations of consumption that are open to you. For example, you have enough income to buy the combination of food and clothing indicated by point **B,** and also enough to buy the combination indicated by point **C.** You do not have enough income to buy combinations of food and clothing upward and to the right from this budget constraint.

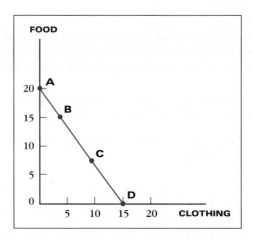

Figure 3A.3. A budget constraint. Assume that if you spent all of your income on food, you could buy 20 units of food. That would put you at point **A**. Or if you spent all of your income on clothing, you could buy 15 units of clothing. That would put you at point **D**. A budget line running from **A** to **D** would show all the combinations of food and clothing, such as **B** and **C**, that you could purchase with your income.

In Figure 3A.4 we combine the budget constraint from Figure 3A.3 with our "map" of indifference curves from Figure 3A.2. The logic of the budget constraint is that it shows the highest level of consumption that is possible given your income. The logic of the indifference curves is that the further out you go (say to IC_2 rather than IC_1), the higher the level of satisfaction you will attain. It follows that the highest level of satisfaction that you can actually reach, given your limited income, is identified by the point where the budget constraint just touches the highest indifference curve that is reachable. That point, a tangency, is point **E** on IC_1 in Figure 3A.4. To maximize your satisfaction, you would choose to consume 12 units of food and 6 of clothing.

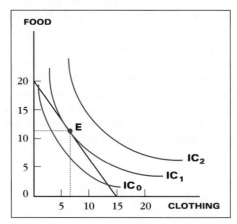

Figure 3A.4. Combining indifference curves with a budget constraint. The highest level of satisfaction you can reach is the point where the budget constraint just touches the outermost reachable indifference curve. The combination of food and clothing at point **E** (12 food and 6 clothing) is thus the consumption choice that will maximize your satisfaction.

What would cause you to change your decision? Let us first ask what would happen if the prices of food and clothing change, with food getting cheaper and clothing more expensive. Whereas you used to be able to buy 20 food if you spent all of your income on that item, now you can buy 24 of the now cheaper food with the same amount of income. But you can buy only 12 of the now more expensive clothing, rather than 15 as before, if you spend of all your income on clothing. That means the price of 1 food is 1/2 a unit of clothing, and the new budget constraint runs from 24 food to 12 clothing. Would this price change alter your choice of how much food and clothing to buy? Figure 3A.5 shows that the answer is yes. Your new budget constraint just touches the same indifference curve, IC_1, at point **E'**. You would choose to consume 16 units of food and 4 units of clothing, more food because it has become cheaper, and less clothing because it has become more expensive. You have substituted some food for clothing. This is the *substitution effect* introduced in the body of the chapter.

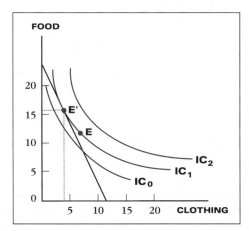

Figure 3A.5. The substitution effect. Consider what would happen if food becomes cheaper, so that you could buy 24 units instead of 20 with your income, while clothing becomes more expensive so you could purchase only 12 instead of 15. Your new budget constraint runs from 24 to 12. Your highest reachable level of satisfaction would now be at point **E'**. You would maximize your welfare by consuming 16 food and 4 clothing, more food and less clothing than at point **E**.

Try another case where changing circumstances would cause you to alter the decision pictured in Figure 3A.4. Say your income is cut so that if you spend all of your income on food, you could now buy only 12 units, or if on clothing, only 9 units. The relative prices of the two items are the same as initially; 1 food still gets you 3/4 of a unit of clothing. But your reduced income has moved your budget constraint downward and to the left, to a position running from 12 food to 9 clothing in Figure 3A.6. What would happen now? You would no longer be able to reach a level of satisfaction as high as that along indifference curve IC_1. Now the highest curve you can reach is IC_0. Here, at **E''**, you would choose to consume 8 units of food and 3 of clothing. Your reduced income has caused you to consume less of both goods compared to point **E**. This is the *income effect,* introduced earlier in the chapter.

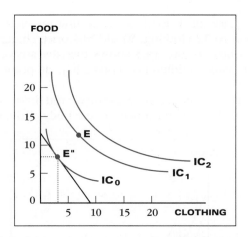

Figure 3A.6. The income effect. Consider what would happen if your income fell so that you could buy only 12 units of food with all your income, or only 9 units of clothing. Your new budget constraint runs from 12 food to 9 clothing. Your highest reachable level of satisfaction would now be at point **E″** on indifference curve IC_0. You would maximize your welfare by consuming 8 food and 3 clothing, less food and less clothing than at point **E**.

Now we are able to connect the discussion of substitution and income effects in this appendix to the construction and explication of demand curves. Together, the substitution and income effects allow us to explain exactly what happens when the price of *just one good* changes. Look at Figure 3A.7, where we start at the same position as in Figure 3A.4. If you spent all of your income on food, you could buy 20 units; all on clothing would get you 15 units. You would consume the quantities of food and clothing indicated by the coordinate point **E**. Now we raise the price of clothing. You can only buy 9 clothing with all of your income, rather than 15. The price of food has, however, not changed. You could still buy 20 food if you spent all of your income on that item. The new budget constraint runs from 20 food to 9 clothing.

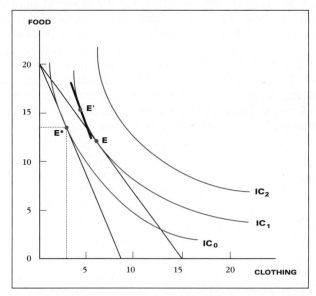

Figure 3A.7. A change in the price of a good changes the quantity purchased because of the substitution effect and the income effect. Starting at **E**, what would happen if the price of clothing were to rise? That would shift the budget constraint from 20 food to 15 clothing to 20 to 9. The highest level of satisfaction you can now reach is point **E***. The movement from **E** to **E′** is due to the substitution effect, while the movement from **E′** to **E*** is due to the income effect. The two effects together explain why the consumption of clothing falls as its price rises.

What is the result of the rise in the price of clothing? Examine Figure 3A.7. The budget line now hits indifference curve IC_0 instead of IC_1. You will consume at point **E***. Look carefully. See how point **E*** involves a fall in your consumption of clothing, from 6 units to 3 units. Now we can provide a rigorous explanation of why this is so. Part of the fall in your clothing consumption is because of the substitution effect. The rise in the price of clothing caused you to substitute food for clothing. We can locate exactly what role substitution played by holding your income constant. If your income were held constant, you would remain on IC_1, the original indifference curve. However, you would move to a different point on that curve because of the price change. We show this by drawing a line at the new price ratio of 20:9 but keeping it tangent to indifference curve IC_1. That is the heavy black line in Figure 3A.7. With income constant, you would have moved from **E** to **E'**, purchasing less clothing and more food. This movement is the substitution effect. Of course, we know that income is not constant. The higher price means that effectively you have less income than before and, therefore, you move to a lower indifference curve. The income effect is represented by the fall from **E'** on IC_1 to **E*** on IC_0.

The upshot is that as the price of clothing rises, you tend to buy less clothing because of the substitution effect and the income effect. The substitution effect caused you to buy less clothing and more food. The income effect caused you to buy still less clothing, and less food, too. The combined effect explains why as the price of clothing rises you buy less of it, and vice versa.

Chapter Key Words

Change in demand: A shift in the demand curve caused by a change in any of the underlying determinants of demand except price.

Change in quantity demanded: A movement along a demand curve caused by a change in price.

Complement: A good which is related to another good, so that an increase in the price of one will lead to a decrease in demand for the other. A complementary good has a negative cross elasticity of demand.

Cross elasticity of demand: A concept that relates numerically the reaction in quantity demanded to a change in the price of another good. The formula for the cross elasticity of demand is $\%\Delta Qx/\%\Delta Py$ (with Qx = quantity demanded of good x and Py = the price of good y).

Determinants of demand: Taste for the good, price of the good, buyers' income, prices of substitutes or complements, expectations of the future, and the number of buyers.

Diminishing marginal utility: The idea that the additional satisfaction received from consuming another unit of some product declines. Explains the shape of the demand curve.

Giffen good: An exception to the rule that demand curves slope downward; occurs when income effect overpowers substitution effect. Because consumers cannot now afford to buy expensive foods, they must purchase more of the cheaper food because its price has risen.

Engel curves: Curves indicating how changes in income alter the quantity demanded. Upward-sloping Engel curves indicate normal goods; downward-sloping ones indicate inferior goods.

Income effect: The idea that a lower price for a good has the effect of raising purchasing power so that more of the good is purchased; helps to explain the downward slope of demand curves.

Income elasticity of demand: The concept that relates numerically the reaction in quantity demanded to a change in income. The formula for the income elasticity of demand is %ΔQ/%ΔY (with Q = quantity demanded and Y = income).

Price elasticity of demand: The concept that relates numerically the reaction in quantity demanded to a change in the price of a good. The formula for the price elasticity of demand is %ΔQ/%ΔP (with Q = quantity and P = price).

Substitute: A good which is related to another good, so that an increase in the price of one will lead to an increase in demand for the other. A good that is a substitute for another has a positive cross elasticity of demand.

Substitution effect: The idea that when the price of a good falls, consumers will purchase more of it and less of the substitutes for that good whose prices have not changed; helps to explain the downward slope of demand curves.

Veblen goods: A possible exception to the rule that demand curves slope downward; idea is that the quantity demanded of prestige goods may rise if their price increases.

Chapter Questions

1) A motorist has a downward-sloping demand curve for gasoline. Explain how each of the following changes would shift the demand curve:
   a) An ad campaign by an environmental group convinces the motorist to drive less.
   b) The motorist receives a significant pay raise (and gasoline is a normal good).
   c) Bus fares are reduced in the motorist's city.
   d) A discount car repair shop opens near the motorist's home.
   e) The newspaper reports that OPEC leaders plan to limit oil production.
   f) Exceptionally good weather causes bumper harvests, and the prices of many foods drop.

2) After graduating from college, you rent a small, unfurnished apartment where you will live alone. Immediately you find that you have no place to sit, so you decide to buy some chairs. The following table gives the total utility in dollars that you derive from various numbers of chairs:

Number of Chairs	Total Utility (in dollars)
0	0
1	200
2	275
3	325
4	355
5	370
6	365

Calculate the marginal utility of each chair and try to give an intuitive explanation for the values. Then use the marginal utilities to draw your demand curve for chairs.

3) A lobster fisherman in Maine buys a bigger boat with better equipment. The improvements almost double his catch of lobsters, yet he sells the lobsters for the same price as he did before. In fact he could sell any number of lobsters at that price. Draw the demand curve for the lobsterman's catch. Why does it look the way it does? A family living in Baltimore loves to eat lobster. Would their demand curve for lobster look like the one the lobsterman faces? Would the demand curve for the whole lobster market look like the one the lobsterman faces?

4) Suppose that pens and pencils are substitutes. The price of pens falls by 40¢ and the quantity of pens sold rises by 100,000. At the same time, the quantity of pencils sold falls by 20,000. Has the pen market experienced a change in the quantity demanded or a change in demand? How about the pencil market? Explain your answers.

5) You are the owner of a TV dealership where business is booming. You contemplate raising your prices so that you will make more money. However, your economic consultant warns you that demand for your TVs is price elastic. Why should this concern you? Should you go through with your price increase?

6) In the winter, the price of lettuce falls from 95¢ to 85¢ per head, and quantity demanded rises from 100 heads per day to 150 heads per day at a local grocery. Calculate the price elasticity of demand for lettuce. The next summer, prices are lower because the lettuce can be grown locally. The price falls from 45¢ to 35¢ per head. The quantity demanded rises from 350 heads per day to 400 heads. Again calculate the price elasticity of demand for lettuce. In which case was the demand for lettuce elastic? Suppose that the demand curve for lettuce was exactly the same in both winter and summer. How can it be that the elasticities were different?

7) You are planning to open a store in a small Colorado town in the mountains. A ski resort has just opened nearby, and the average income in the area is increasing rapidly. All other things being equal, should you open a bulk potato outlet or an imported wine shop? Illustrate your answer with Engel curves.

8) Suppose a British family that was earning £20,000 suffers a bad setback and its income falls to £10,000. Its tea consumption falls from 10 bags per day to 8 bags per day. Calculate the income elasticity of tea. Is tea an inferior good, a necessity, or a luxury for the British family?

9) The price of movies in a certain city rises from $5.00 to $8.00. As a result, the number of video rentals per evening rises from 10,000 to 12,000. Calculate the cross elasticity of demand for video rentals with respect to movie prices. Are movies and videos substitutes or complements?

Demand and Supply II:

The Concept of Supply, the Market Mechanism

OVERALL OBJECTIVE: To develop the technical skills needed to understand supply curves, to show how demand and supply curves determine market prices, and to undertake some analysis with these curves.

MORE SPECIFICALLY:

- To establish that the determinants of supply are the objectives of the firm, the price received for its output, the price of goods that can be substituted in production, expectations, the prices of the factors of production, the level of technology, and the number of sellers.
- To construct supply curves, showing that movements along them (changes in quantity supplied) are caused by a change in the price of the item, while shifts in their position (change in supply) are caused by a change in one of the nonprice determinants.
- To demonstrate that supply curves normally slope upward and to the right because of rising costs and that supply curves for firms can be added horizontally to obtain market supply curves.
- To show how the elasticity of supply is defined and measured, and what difference it makes.
- To show how the demand and supply curves together indicate an equilibrium price, and how prices are pushed toward this equilibrium by excess supply (surpluses) when price is above equilibrium and by excess demand (shortages) when price is below equilibrium.
- To investigate the concept of allocative inefficiency and show how such inefficiency develops when prices are not allowed to find their market equilibrium.
- To use the tools acquired in this chapter to analyze deliberate shifts in the demand or supply curves: OPEC's restriction of the oil supply, consumer boycotts, and government sales taxes and subsidies.

This chapter shows how supply curves are constructed and why they appear as they do. It then goes on to discuss how demand and supply together determine market prices, which are the central signaling device of a market system. Finally, it traces some of the analysis that flows from that use of these valuable ideas.

THE CONCEPT OF SUPPLY

Demand and supply together determine market price. The concept of supply is in many ways similar to the concept of demand. Just as we did in the last chapter with demand, we can define supply in a sentence, note its relation to a time period, identify the determinants of its magnitude, show it diagrammatically, and distinguish between movement along a stationary supply curve and a shift in the position of the curve itself.

Supply is defined as the quantity of a good or service sellers wish to sell on the market. As with demand, supply is a flow concept that must be considered within a time horizon—so much *per hour* or *per year*. What are the **determinants of supply**? Consider the case of the Welkin Ring Company, a maker of engagement, wedding, and college class rings.

1) *The objectives of the firm.* Before any other determinant of supply can be assessed, we need to know about the Welkin Company's objective. If it is to maximize profit, then the difference between the revenues earned from sales and the costs of production, which determines the profit earned, will be central. Does the Welkin family seek recognition? In this case, they may want to have every young person wearing a Welkin ring even if this means the company will fail to maximize profit. Perhaps the family prefers a quiet life. They may choose to avoid risk, earning enough to be comfortable, but not maximizing their profit. Economists have traditionally assumed that, like consumers, firms are maximizers, attempting to maximize their profits. As we shall see, if profit maximization is assumed to be the goal, the conclusions when modeling firms' behavior are explicit and mathematically tractable. We shall also see that there are strong pressures that drive a firm toward profit maximization.

2) *The price at which a firm can sell its product.* If firms are profit-maximizers, or even if they just want to avoid losses, the *price* of the items sold will be important. The price will affect the firm's revenues. With all other things being equal, a higher price will allow the Welkin Company to earn higher revenue and so higher profit on each ring sold. The company can take advantage of this by increasing its output of the item with a high price and producing less of other commodities. Higher prices may also attract new firms into the industry, thereby increasing supply.

3) *The price of goods that can be substituted in production.* The supply of college rings will be affected by a fall or rise in the price of the firm's wedding bands. If greater competition, or fewer weddings, force the Welkin Company to reduce the wedding band price, that will lower revenue and hence profit earned on them, and will lead the firm to produce more college rings. A rise in the wedding band price will lead to fewer college rings and more wedding bands. In many areas, the supply of a good is affected by the price of goods that can be substituted in production: for the farmer, corn or soybeans; for the rancher, cattle or sheep (and within these categories, milk or beef, or wool or lamb); for the shipbuilder, container ships or tankers; for Detroit, small four-cylinder cars or large six-cylinder cars.[1]

---

1.   More rarely, there are also complements in production. In the refining of gasoline, the refinery gets an irreducible minimum quantity of kerosene as part of the process. A rise in the price of gasoline that leads to a greater quantity of gasoline supplied would therefore also mean an increase in the supply of kerosene.

4) *Expectations.* Not only prices now, but expectations concerning future prices make a difference for revenues and profits, and hence for supply. If the Welkin Company's managers expect that next month college rings will be rising in price while wedding bands fall, they will surely alter production now. The company might raise its current output of college rings and hold them in inventory in order to sell them later at the higher price.

5) *Prices of the factors of production.* Supply also depends on the prices of the factors of production (labor, land, capital, etc.) that the firm uses. If the skilled labor needed to engrave class rings goes up in price, *ceteris paribus*, Welkin's costs of production will rise, profits on the sale of college rings will decline, and the company will cut back on its output.

6) *The level of technology.* A technical advance in ring production may affect costs and the level of profit, thus leading to an increase in supply. For example, inventions (discovery of new methods) and innovations (adapting of inventions to make them useful in the production process) both have an influence on supply. In Welkin's case, a newly developed stamping machine may make it much cheaper to produce rings and prompt the company to increase its supply.

7) *The number of producers.* Finally, a change in the number of producers can affect supply: More firms like the Welkin Company will produce more rings.

 ## THE SUPPLY CURVE

We can construct a diagram to show what happens when any of these determinants undergoes a change. As in the case of demand, our study of the market mechanism leads us to a special interest in one of these, namely, the relation between price and the quantity supplied. Invoking the *ceteris paribus* assumption and holding the other six determinants constant, the quantity supplied of a good will depend only on the price of that good. We can then ask for some given period of time what quantity of a good a seller will supply to the market at different prices.

Under usual circumstances, the Welkin Company will supply a greater quantity of college rings to the market at higher prices than at lower prices, as shown in Table 4.1. Why? One way of looking at it is that if all production costs are held constant, an increase in the price will mean more profit per ring produced. To obtain a higher total profit, the firm will choose to increase the quantity supplied.

TABLE 4.1
The price and quantity supplied of college class rings.

	If the price per ring is:	The annual quantity supplied will be:
A	$200	1000
B	$150	700
C	$100	400

The idea that a greater quantity supplied and a higher price are logically related can also be looked at as the outcome of the diminishing returns to a factor of production noted in Chapter 2. Producing a greater quantity will probably cause *diminishing returns* to set in. If the amount of some factor of production is fixed, at least for the immediate future (the stock of machinery and factory space, for example), then adding more and more labor is likely to mean overtime and night shifts will be necessary. Tired workers trying to do their job in close quarters will be less efficient workers; thus, each additional worker brings a smaller increase in output than the previous one. So if Welkin decides to increase production by a certain amount, price will have to rise to allow the firm to take on more of the labor whose contribution is now less productive than it would otherwise have been.

Figure 4.1 plots the data listed in Table 4.1 with price on the vertical axis and quantity supplied on the horizontal. Points **A**, **B**, and **C** correspond to the figures in the table. If we could plot all such points they would form a *supply curve*, labeled S.[2] (A warning: We will see in Chapter 7 that if there is little or no competition among suppliers in markets, then the firm or firms in that market may not have a conventional supply curve.)

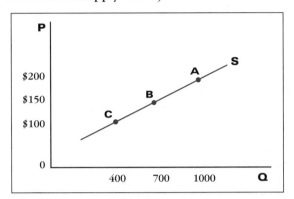

Figure 4.1. A supply curve. A line connecting coordinate points of price and quantity supplied is a supply curve.

Adding Supply Curves Horizontally to Find Market Supply

To determine the total market supply contributed by all the sellers of the same good, we proceed as we did in determining total market demand. We simply add together, horizontally, all the supply curves of the individual sellers. In Figure 4.2, panel **a** shows the supply curve of the Welkin Ring Company, and panel **b** shows the supply curve of another supplier, the Nibelungen Ring Company. Panel **c** shows the two added together.

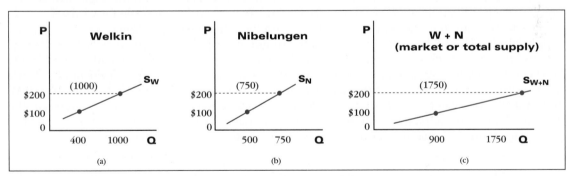

Figure 4.2. Adding supply curves horizontally. The supply curve for an entire market is the horizontal addition of the supply curves for each individual seller in that market.

At a given price on the vertical axis, the quantity supplied by the two-firm market is equal to the quantity supplied by the first firm plus the quantity supplied by the second firm. At a price of $200, Welkin's quantity of 1000 plus Nibelungen's 750 give a total of 1750. The quantities are summed horizontally on the diagram as shown by the dotted lines. If the price had been $100, then $S_W = 400$, $S_N = 500$, and $S_{W+N} = 900$.

Elasticity of Supply

How quantity supplied responds to price changes is an important question with consequences in many areas of economics. To measure the **elasticity of supply** we use the same technique employed to measure the elasticity of demand. If we let ε_s stand for the elasticity of supply, then:

---

2.   As with demand, depending on the data, a supply curve could be linear or exhibit curvature.

$$\mathcal{E}_s = \frac{\text{percentage change in quantity supplied}}{\text{percentage change in price}}.$$

To calculate the percentage changes as accurately as possible, the formula may be written:

$$\mathcal{E}s = \frac{\Delta Q / [(Q_1 + Q_2) / 2]}{\Delta P / [(P_1 + P_2) / 2]}.$$

Identifying the elasticity of supply on a diagram is easier than identifying the elasticity of demand. By mathematical rule, straight lines exhibit infallible properties depending on where they intersect the axes of the diagram. Try it with the easiest case: the line labeled S_2 in each panel of Figure 4.3. S_2 is drawn with a slope of 45° in all three panels; in panel **a** it bisects the 90° angle at the origin. Therefore, along S_2 in panel **a**, a distance of 10 on the vertical (Y or price) axis must correspond to a distance of 10 on the horizontal (X or quantity) axis, as shown by point **A**.

Now raise the price from $10 to $12. The quantity supplied responds by moving from 10 to 12. Using the elasticity formula just above, the percentage changes in price and quantity are the same ($\frac{2}{11} = \frac{2}{11}$). This is a case of unitary elasticity of supply.

Next move to panel **b**. Here the price change of $10 to $12 is the same as before, but it occurs along a line S_2 located closer to the vertical price axis. The resulting rise in quantity supplied is from 6 to 8. The percentage change when the quantity supplied moves from 6 to 8 is greater than the percentage change in price from $10 to $12 ($\frac{2}{7} > \frac{2}{11}$). This is a case of elastic supply, with elasticity greater than one.

Finally, move to panel **c**. Here the price change from $10 to $12 is again the same as before, but it occurs along a line S_2 located further away from the vertical price axis. The resulting rise in quantity supplied is from 12 to 14. The percentage change when the quantity supplied moves from 12 to 14 is smaller than the percentage change in price from $10 to $12 ($\frac{2}{13} < \frac{2}{11}$). This is a case of inelastic supply, with elasticity less than 1. The same geometric logic works with upward-rising straight lines of *any* slope. Try it with curves S_1 and S_3 and see for yourself.

The rule for the elasticity of supply is therefore rather simple. When any straight-line supply curve such as S_1, S_2, or S_3 intersects the origin, as in panel **a**, then any given percentage increase in price causes an identical percentage increase in quantity supplied, and elasticity must be unitary. When any straight-line supply curve intersects the vertical axis, as in panel **b**, then a given percentage increase in price causes a greater percentage change in quantity supplied, and elasticity is greater than 1, or elastic. When any curve such as S_1, S_2, or S_3 intersects the horizontal axis, as in panel **c**, then a given percentage increase in price causes a smaller percentage change in quantity supplied; elasticity is less than 1 and supply is inelastic.

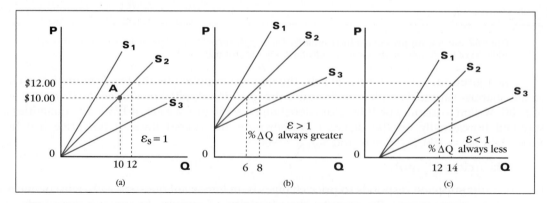

Figure 4.3. Unitary elasticity of supply, elastic supply, and inelastic supply. Any straight-line supply curve that intersects the origin exhibits unitary elasticity of supply (panel **a**). A supply curve that intersects the vertical axis exhibits elastic supply (panel **b**). A supply curve that intersects the horizontal axis exhibits inelastic supply (panel **c**).

FINDING ELASTICITY WHEN THE SUPPLY CURVE IS NOT A STRAIGHT LINE

These rules are also useful for finding the elasticity when a price change occurs along a supply *curve*. By drawing a tangent line to a supply curve (see Figure 4.4), we can discover the elasticity for a price change around that point. For example, in the figure when the price changes from $1.00 to $1.05, a tangent extended from the supply curve hits the origin and, therefore, the elasticity for this price change is 1. When the price changes from $0.60 to $0.65, a tangent extended from the supply curve hits the vertical (y) axis and, therefore, the elasticity for this price change is greater than 1. When the price changes from $2.00 to $2.05, a tangent extended from the supply curve hits the horizontal (x) axis and, therefore, the elasticity for this price change is less than 1.

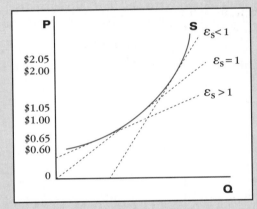

Figure 4.4. Measuring elasticity along a supply curve. The elasticity of supply at any point along a supply curve is indicated by whether a line tangent to the curve hits the vertical axis, the horizontal axis, or the origin.

DO SUPPLY CURVES ALWAYS SLOPE UPWARD?

Ordinarily, market supply curves slope upward from lower left to upper right. But, as with market demand curves, there are certain exceptions. Three of those special cases are the horizontal supply curve, the vertical supply curve, and the "backward-bending" supply curve.

1) *The horizontal supply curve.* If production costs do not rise appreciably as output is increased, suppliers will be able to step up production even without the promise of higher price. Say output is profitable at a price of P in Figure 4.5 for some easily reproducible item such as nails, pins, or pencils. In such so-called "constant cost" cases, firms can increase their output considerably with little extra effort. A few more people running the existing machinery faster and longer might raise yearly output by many millions. Within wide limits, firms might be capable of supplying any quantity at price P. In the range of output where this is so, the supply curve will be a horizontal line and supply will be *perfectly elastic*. A change in quantity can occur, but a change in price does not; numerically, %ΔQ is a positive number while %ΔP = 0. When a positive number is divided by 0, the result is infinity.[3] Therefore, along a horizontal supply curve ε_s = infinity.

---

3.   Strictly, the result approaches infinity.

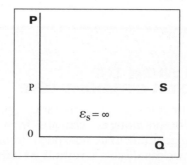

Figure 4.5. Perfectly elastic supply. A horizontal supply curve is perfectly elastic throughout its length.

2) *The vertical supply curve.* The exact opposite is the case where the quantity supplied is fixed no matter what the price. There are many possible examples, ranging from paintings and sculptures by old masters to guitars once owned by Elvis Presley, to plots of land at a particular intersection (Hollywood and Vine). In each case, whether the price is high or low, the quantity that can be supplied is fixed, and price changes cause no response on the part of the supplier. In Figure 4.6 the supply curve reflecting this is a vertical line. Such a supply curve is called *perfectly inelastic*. Since %ΔQ is 0 (no change occurs in the quantity supplied) while %ΔP is positive, and since 0/+ = 0, therefore ε_s = 0.

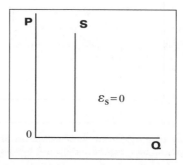

Figure 4.6. Perfectly inelastic (fixed) supply. A vertical supply curve is perfectly inelastic throughout its length.

3) *The backward-bending supply curve.* A **backward-bending supply curve**, like the one shown in Figure 4.7, is sometimes found in labor markets. In an unpleasant occupation—mining, for example—workers may dislike their work so much that a rise in wages will cause them to work fewer hours and use more time for leisure. At the higher wage the individual miners may prefer to work fewer hours for the same total income, as shown by the backward-bend above the arrow in Figure 4.7. Such behavior has also been reported in several less developed countries where workers come to the cities from villages with the aim of earning a certain income; once they have earned it, they return to their homes. At the other end of the income scale, the supply curve for adult labor in a rich country like the United States may also bend backward (though only slightly) because, at higher and higher wage levels, leisure time becomes more and more affordable.[4] The backward bend may also apply to recipients of Social Security benefits who are limited to a certain amount of outside income that they can earn without forfeiting their benefits. Because of this, higher pay in a job may lead a Social Security recipient to work fewer hours. Finally, national governments of oil-producing states might

---

4.   Though true of adult male labor in the United States, this description is not true of females or teenagers. Twenty-eight studies of males in the U.S. labor force show that on average a 10% wage increase results in a reduction of 0.6% in the quantity of labor supplied. Twenty-two studies of women show a reversed result: on average a 10% wage increase results in an increase of 9.4% in the quantity of labor supplied. See the survey by Ingemar Hanson and Charles Stuart, "Tax Revenue and the Marginal Cost of Public Funds," *Journal of Public Economics,* August 1985.

produce less if they had a target level for revenue and the price of oil rose. With oil prices higher, they will be able to reach their target by pumping less oil.

Whatever the example, if price rises past the point where the supply curve begins to bend backward, shown in the figure by the arrow and vertical tangent line at price P*, then the elasticity of supply will be negative (−/+ = −). In cases where the supply curve is backward-bending, price changes will have surprising results if they occur along the portion of the curve that slopes upward and to the left: a higher price reduces the quantity supplied, while a lower price raises it.

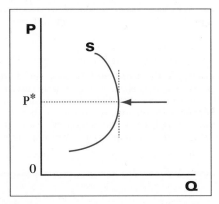

Figure 4.7. A backward-bending supply curve. Elasticity above the arrow is negative; a higher price reduces the quantity supplied, while a lower price raises it.

TIME AND SUPPLY CURVES: THE SHORT RUN AND THE LONG RUN

Alfred Marshall pointed out that elasticity of supply often changes over time, as suppliers have an opportunity to adjust to circumstances. Consider the supply of fish in a fishing port late in the day when the boats are already back in the harbor. What is the shape of the supply curve? Because no greater quantity will be available until tomorrow, even if price were to rise considerably, we can predict a perfectly inelastic vertical curve (as in panel **a** of Figure 4.8). This is called the *momentary period*, a period of time too short to allow suppliers to adjust their quantity supplied. In the **short run**, some adjustments are possible. Larger crews can be hired, more nets can be rented or purchased, and higher prices will elicit larger quantities, as in panel **b**. In the **long run**, there is enough time to adjust all factors of production, including the building of new boats, the opening of new wharfs, and the construction of new processing plants. (We can, in fact, *define* the long run as the period of time needed for adjusting the quantity of all factors of production, including capital.) The long-run supply curve will be perfectly elastic (horizontal) if costs do not rise with increased output, as in panel **c**. If, however, the purchase or hire of additional factors raises the prices of those factors, then the supply curve will be upward sloping, as with the dashed line in that figure.

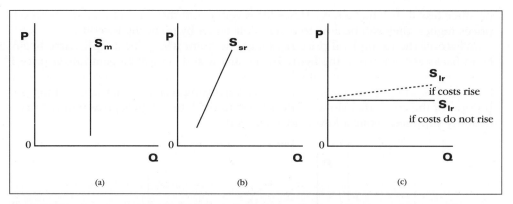

Figure 4.8. **The momentary period, the short run, and the long run.** In the momentary period, suppliers have no time to respond to price changes and the supply curve is perfectly inelastic, a vertical line as in panel **a**. In the short run, with time available, a rise in price will cause suppliers to respond with a greater quantity, seen in panel **c**. In the long run (panel **c**), there is enough time to adjust all factors of production. The long-run supply curve will be perfectly elastic (horizontal) if costs do not rise with increased output. If costs do rise, the supply curve will slope upward.

A SUMMARY TABLE OF SUPPLY ELASTICITIES

This table summarizes the various price elasticities of supply.
Supply elasticities are clearly less complex than demand elasticities.

Type	Formula	Range	Curve
Price elasticity of supply	%ΔQs/%ΔP	∞, perfectly elastic	supply curve is horizontal; constant costs
		over 1, elastic	tangent to supply curve hits y axis
		1, unitary	tangent to supply curve hits origin
		0-1, inelastic	tangent to supply curve hits x axis
		0, perfectly inelastic	supply curve is vertical; fixed supply
		negative	backward-bending supply curve

INFORMATION CONVEYED BY A SUPPLY CURVE

As with demand curves, a supply curve can be used to convey a variety of information. For example, it shows the result of a price change in a given time period when the other determinants of supply are held constant. In Figure 4.9, a decline in price from $2.00 per unit to $1.00 results in a decrease in quantity supplied from 40 units to 20. Such a movement along a stationary supply curve is referred to as a **change in quantity supplied**.

Like the demand curve, the supply curve is a pliant tool that is capable of reflecting changes in underlying assumptions. Suppose we relax the assumption that all the determinants of supply except price are held constant and say that labor costs fall. In that case, the supply curve itself is free to move to a new position. The result will be an increase in supply, as shown in Figure 4.10. The curve has shifted to the right, indicating that a larger quantity will be available at each of the various prices.[5]

---

5.   This rightward shift in the supply curve can also be described as a downward shift, or fall. At any given quantity along the horizontal axis, a greater supply would mean that producers would charge a lower price as measured on the vertical axis. What this text calls a "rightward shift in the supply curve" might also be described as a "downward shift" or a "shift downward and to the right." The meaning of all of these is the same.

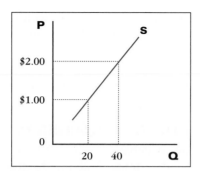

Figure 4.9. A change in quantity supplied. The expression change in quantity supplied is used when a change in price leads to a new quantity along a supply curve.

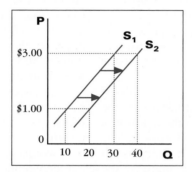

Figure 4.10. A change in supply. The expression *change in supply* is used for a shift of the supply curve. This figure shows an increase in supply.

Sellers who previously were willing to market a quantity of only 30 units at a price of $3.00 are now willing to sell 40. Sellers who formerly marketed 10 units at a price of $1.00 are now inclined to supply a higher quantity 20.

The same rightward shift in the supply curve would flow from changes in other determinants of supply such as (1) a decline in the market price of a substitute in production,[6] (2) an advance in technology, (3) rising expectations among producers that changes in price or technology will soon occur, and (4) an increase in the number of suppliers.

A shift in the position of the supply curve in response to a change in one or more of the nonprice determinants of supply is referred to as a **change in supply**. (What would cause a *leftward* shift of the supply curve?)

CONCLUSION

We have now acquired the technical background that we need to analyze the market mechanism for price determination. That involves putting the demand curve and the supply curve together on the same diagram, as we see in the next section.

▶ DEMAND AND SUPPLY TOGETHER

The demand curve and the supply curve for an item work together to establish that item's market price. This model of price determination was formulated by Alfred Marshall (1842–1924), a professor at Cambridge University in England. His theory of price determined by demand and

---

6.   Or a rise in the price of a complement in production.

supply solved the intellectual puzzle as to why an item with immense utility could command a low or zero price while an item of less utility could command a very high price. That puzzle is discussed in the accompanying box.

THE DEBATE OVER WHAT DETERMINES PRICE

Few questions in economics were debated longer than the question of what determines the price of an object. It took many years for economists to explain why something with very high utility, such as the air we breathe, (we die in a few minutes without it), could have a low or even zero price, whereas the price of a single "useless" painting by Rembrandt was not only high, but rising over time.

Adam Smith's theory of price, formulated in the eighteenth century, declared that the price of an object represented the amount of labor that had gone into producing it. The price differential between a Rembrandt painting and air could be explained by the fact that Rembrandt took a great deal of time to create a painting, but no labor goes into the manufacture of air. This "labor theory of value" had an extraordinary life span. Karl Marx used it in *Das Kapital*, and Marxian economists still treat it as a central proposition.

There were always doubters, however. To say that the value of an item depended entirely on the labor that went into it seemed to run counter to experience. What about the natural resources used to make the object, or the machine that fashioned it? Did these really contribute to the value of an item only the labor value involved in extracting the resource or making the machine? And how are we to explain why many goods produced with a great expenditure of labor do *not* command a high price? A hand-made coat too long or too short for current tastes, for example, or a scale model of Notre Dame cathedral made of toothpicks, may represent large amounts of labor, but the market price at which each could be sold would probably be quite low. Although Marxian economists have continued to look for ways to explain such problems within the framework of a labor theory of value, their efforts have failed to be accepted except among the Marxians themselves.

For non-Marxian economists, Alfred Marshall's model of demand and supply, which first appeared in his *Principles of Economics* published in 1890, laid the labor theory to rest.

To see how market price is determined, we bring the demand curve and the supply curve together in the same diagram. Both curves must relate to a particular market, a geographical area where buyers and sellers can transact business. If the product cannot be shipped—a haircut or a house painting, for example—the market may be no larger than a neighborhood. For products difficult to transport, a city and its suburbs may be the limit. For others (aircraft, maritime insurance, oil, wheat, currencies), the market is worldwide, linked by computer and telex networks.

SURPLUSES AND SHORTAGES

If the curves have their normal slopes, as in Figure 4.11, they tell us that of all the possible prices along the vertical axis, only *one* price (P_E, or $0.75) will result in a quantity supplied equal to the quantity demanded. At any other price there will be either a surplus (excess supply) with the quantity supplied greater than the quantity demanded, or a shortage (excess demand) with the quantity supplied less than the quantity demanded.

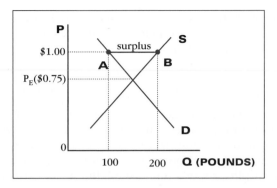

Figure 4.11. A surplus arises when the price selected is too high. At a price above the equilibrium, the quantity supplied is greater than the quantity demanded—in other words, a surplus.

Consider the seller. In a market system, sellers can ask whatever price they want for their wares, but consumers are under no obligation to pay what they ask. Suppose that in the market for cauliflower, suppliers choose to sell at a price of $1.00 per pound. They soon discover that though they are ready to provide 200 pounds of cauliflower per day at that price (point **B** on the supply curve), buyers are willing to buy only 100 pounds per day (point **A**).

The horizontal distance **AB** represents the 100 pounds of cauliflower that go unsold at a price of $1.00. The quantity supplied is greater than the quantity demanded. So a *surplus* emerges. Sellers do not like to be saddled with unsold goods. No profit is being earned from their sale, and storage and spoilage both cost money. So to be rid of the excess supply, the sellers decide to cut the price.

What will happen if they slash the price to $0.25 per pound the next day? At that price, as Figure 4.12 shows, the sellers are willing to put only 90 pounds of cauliflower on the market per day. Some of them decide to give up the cauliflower market altogether and turn to other activities. Consumers, however, are pleased with this price and increase their purchases. In the diagram the quantity they demand is 175 pounds, which is 85 pounds more per day than the quantity supplied at $0.25 per pound. The horizontal distance **WX** represents the *shortage* that emerges at that price.

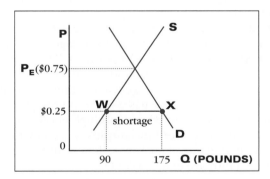

Figure 4.12. A shortage arises when the price selected is too low. At a price below the equilibrium, the quantity demanded is greater than the quantity supplied—in other words, a shortage.

Too little cauliflower is now on sale to satisfy all the people in the market who want to buy it at this low price. The situation of excess demand is not a stable one. Sellers see that they can raise their price, thus increasing their profit, while dissatisfied buyers unable to purchase as much as they want will offer more money for an extra pound or two.

In short, any price above the intersection of the demand and supply curves will result in excess supply (a surplus), while any price below that intersection will result in excess demand (a shortage). Shortages and surpluses when prices are not at the equilibrium are the conditions that cause the price to change.

THE PATH TO EQUILIBRIUM

In Figure 4.13, prices above the intersection of the curves (labeled **E**) will result in an excess of quantity supplied over quantity demanded—that is, a surplus. At a price of $1.00 per pound the size of the surplus as measured by the horizontal distance between the curves is large, **HJ** = 100 units. A downward pressure is exerted on price, which firms may mark down to, say, $0.80 per pound. At that price, the surplus is much diminished, but it still exists (**FG** = 20 units).

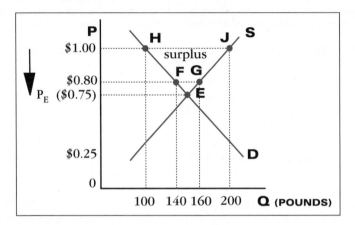

Figure 4.13. **Any price above the intersection yields a surplus.** The surpluses that occur at prices above the equilibrium bring pressures on sellers to cut their prices, which move toward the equilibrium.

Market forces still exert pressure on the sellers to lower their price.[7] The process is self-reinforcing because sellers who are slow to cut their price while others are cutting theirs will find that the demand for their output has evaporated. The downward pressure on price continues until the remaining surplus vanishes.

Looking now at Figure 4.14, we see that any price *below* P_E will cause an excess of quantity demanded over quantity supplied—that is, a shortage. Say at a price of $0.10 per pound the magnitude of the shortage is large (**KL** = 170 pounds). That would cause firms to mark up their prices. If the rise is to $0.40 per pound, then the shortage is reduced, here to **MN** = 100 pounds. Even so, this smaller shortage will continue to create an upward pressure on price that will disappear only when the price has risen to point P_E.

In Figure 4.15, a price at the level marked P_E is high enough to avoid the shortage caused by excess demand, and low enough to avoid the surplus caused by excess supply. The "**E**" stands for **equilibrium**—the point at which the quantity sellers want to supply (150) and the quantity that buyers want to consume (150) are equal, as at Q_E.

---

7.   In certain industries it may be common to find that the price reductions in response to an unsold surplus come in the somewhat disguised form of manufacturers' rebates or better finance terms. Both tactics are familiar in the market for automobiles, for example. Students sometimes point out that during inflation prices rarely go down. Since prices are *relative* to one another, however, a price that rises by less than the average during inflation has actually fallen in relative terms. Note that the elementary model of supply and demand says nothing about the speed of the adjustment, which may be rapid or slow. The length of time taken to complete the adjustment may well differ considerably among industries.

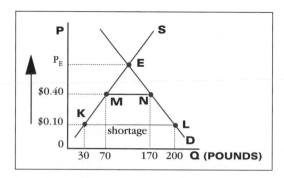

Figure 4.14. Any price below the intersection results in a shortage. The shortages that occur at prices below the equilibrium bring pressures on sellers to raise their prices and buyers to offer more, which moves the price toward the equilibrium.

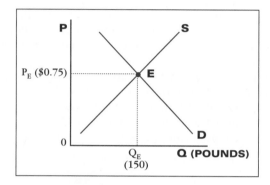

Figure 4.15. Equilibrium. At the equilibrium price, the quantity supplied (150) is the same as the quantity demanded. There is neither shortage nor surplus.

The idea of equilibrium price is central to the market system. At that price the forces of demand and supply interact to "clear the market." Without human command or conscious direction, the pressures that lead to an equilibrium price will provide signals to the participants in the market. Consumers and producers respond to these signals by changing the quantity they demand and supply. Their responses work automatically to eliminate shortages and surpluses.

WHEN UNDERLYING CONDITIONS CHANGE, THE EQUILIBRIUM IS ALTERED

The mechanism is flexible and steers markets toward equilibrium whenever a change occurs in the underlying conditions of demand and supply. In Figure 4.15, the price of cauliflower is $0.75 per pound at equilibrium. What will happen if the demand for cauliflower changes significantly? A booming economy might raise consumer income, for example. Or consumers might decide cauliflower is healthy for them, and that they should eat more of it. Or the price of broccoli rises, and the two are substitutes. In each case, the demand for cauliflower will increase. Figure 4.16 shows the rightward movement of the demand curve to D_2 and the resulting higher equilibrium price P_2.

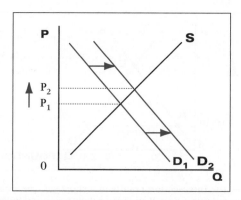

Figure 4.16. A shift in demand alters the equilibrium. An increase in demand moves the equilibrium price to a higher level.

With standard-shaped curves, a rise in demand with unchanged supply will raise the equilibrium price, and a decline in demand will lower the equilibrium price. There is no guarantee that any one seller will charge the equilibrium price exactly, but economic pressure is moving sellers toward that position.

The mechanism is equally responsive to changes in supply. Assume that a spell of perfect weather increases the cauliflower harvest, or the cost of farm labor declines, or new mechanized methods bring economies to the operation. Such events lead to an increase in supply, shown as a rightward movement of the supply curve to S_2 in Figure 4.17. A supply increase with unchanged demand causes a decline in the equilibrium price from P_1 to P_2.

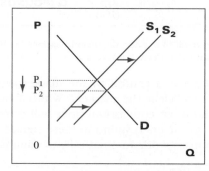

Figure 4.17. A shift in supply alters the equilibrium. An increase in supply moves the equilibrium price to a lower level.

With standard-shaped curves, a rise in supply will shift the supply curve to the right and will lower the equilibrium price, and a decline in supply will shift the supply curve to the left and will raise the equilibrium price. Thus, any change in *either* supply or demand will result in a new equilibrium.

With nonstandard curves, however, a change in the position of a curve may have a different effect on the equilibrium price. If the supply curve is perfectly elastic (horizontal), for example, an increase in demand will increase quantity but leave price unaltered. If supply is fixed, with the supply curve vertical (perfectly inelastic), then a change in demand will affect only the price, since no more of the product can be supplied. If the supply curve is backward-bending, an increase in demand will reduce the quantity supplied as price rises. You may want to draw these diagrams for yourself, and also consider what happens when supply changes along a perfectly elastic (horizontal) demand curve or along a perfectly inelastic (vertical) demand curve.

THE WIDE APPLICABILITY OF THE MECHANISM

The adaptability of the mechanism of demand and supply is truly extraordinary. It works as well for intangibles and services as it does for tangible goods: there is a supply, demand, and equilibrium price for insurance policies, airline tickets, and trips to the dentist. The stock market is a vivid case of minute-to-minute variations in price. So is the foreign exchange market, where the equilibrium price of currencies is in constant flux. One day, the British pound is priced at £1 = $1.55, while the next day it is priced at £1 = $1.54. The supply of British pounds is furnished by people who want to buy dollars so that they can purchase U.S. goods, or travel in the United States, or invest in American enterprises, or deposit their money in U.S. banks to earn a high rate of interest. The demand for British pounds is furnished by Americans who want to buy British goods, or travel in Britain, invest in British enterprises, or deposit money in British banks to earn a high interest rate. Figure 4.18 shows how supply and demand lead to an equilibrium price of pounds in terms of dollars.

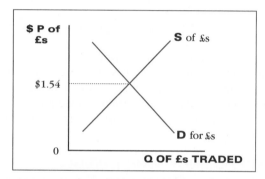

Figure 4.18. Demand and supply in the foreign exchange market. The market for British pounds behaves just like that for wheat or any other commodity. There is a demand, a supply, and an equilibrium price (in this case £1 = $1.54).

The mechanism affects the markets for the factors of production just as it does the markets for goods and services. The same diagrams used to examine the price of cauliflower or British pounds can be used to examine the salaries of nurses or computer programmers, the price of land in a subdivision, the cost of a copper mine, or the price of a machine. The market system pushes these prices toward an equilibrium in the same manner that it does for the prices of goods and services. Surpluses and shortages emerge when prices are above or below equilibrium. In fact, you will probably find that market forces will have a significant impact on your choice of what occupation to enter, and whether to stay.

We can extend supply and demand analysis to more exotic cases as well. Why, for example, do used postage stamps such as the British Guiana one-penny magenta or Mauritius Island two-penny "Post Paid"—each at the end of the stamp collector's rainbow—cost millions of dollars today? The answer: very low supply coupled with intense demand from rich collectors. Why does a used 5¢ President Eisenhower stamp vintage 1965 cost less than 5¢? The answer: enormous supply overwhelms demand. Why did the price of Model T and Model A Fords built in the 1920s and 1930s fall in the late 1980s (by as much as 30%) while the price of certain Chevelles, Plymouth Barracudas, and Pontiac GTOs from the 1960s and 1970s rose sharply? The answer: collectors were buying the cars they remembered with nostalgia rather than cars that had gone out of use long before they were born. Their demand for the newer cars was increasing while the demand for the older ones was falling.[8]

---

8.   For verification see "Classic 'Muscle Cars' Replace Model T's as Hot Collectibles: Autos From '20s and '30s Lose Value as Baby Boomers Redefine What's Vintage," *Wall Street Journal*, March 20, 1990.

The mechanism works for illegal transactions as well as legal ones. It explains why Colombians can realize only about $1,100 from the coca paste that will make a pound of cocaine, whereas that same pound when processed (very cheaply) into pure cocaine and landed in New York City will sell for about $5,000, while the retail street price for the pound of cocaine is about $41,000.[9] At every stage, the mechanism of demand and supply sets an equilibrium price. The prices are clearly affected not only by the costs of processing, distribution, and transport, just as is true of everything else, but by different degrees of risk, drug dealers' market power at the various locations of the transactions, dangerous and unorthodox transport conditions, and the need to pay more "protection money" in some places than in others.

The market mechanism is most in evidence, however, in the mundane activities of millions of buyers and sellers trading in millions of goods and services every day. Whenever the market mechanism operates unimpaired, and whatever its faults, it serves as an automatic regulator of surpluses and shortages.

▶ THE CONCEPT OF ALLOCATIVE INEFFICIENCY

There is an old saying, "you can't interfere with supply and demand," but this is quite wrong. You certainly can. We can now develop the tools that allow us to see what happens when something intervenes or interferes with the mechanism of market prices. Because prices will cease to reflect true wants and scarcities, economic consequences will ensue that are often predictable. These consequences include not only the shortages or surpluses already discussed, but also *allocative inefficiency*.

ALLOCATIVE INEFFICIENCY WHEN MARKETS ARE PREVENTED FROM REACHING EQUILIBRIUM

Intervention or interference with equilibrium prices and quantities determined in a free market can come in a number of ways. It might involve private actions by monopolists who rig a market by setting prices and quantities in order to raise their profits, as we discuss in Chapters 7 and 8. Or it might come from coordinated decisions to restrict supply (OPEC and oil) or demand (consumer boycotts) as discussed at the end of this chapter. Or it may involve a government decision to set prices and quantities independently of market forces, as examined in the next chapter. Whatever the cause, the act of preventing markets from reaching equilibrium is likely to give rise to the condition called **allocative inefficiency**.

The term allocative inefficiency means that resources are being allocated to production in such a way that, all other things being equal, the benefits to society are less than they would be if the price were market-determined. Allocative inefficiency is not the same as the inefficiency in production discussed in Chapter 1. Where *production* is inefficient, some of the factors of production are either unemployed or are not working at full capacity. Unemployed labor, idle factories, long unauthorized coffee breaks for workers, and afternoons at the golf course for managers are all examples of productive inefficiency. In terms of production possibilities curves, the point of (inefficient) production falls somewhere below the curve.

Allocative inefficiency is different. In this case, all factors of production may be fully employed, and production may be efficient. The allocative inefficiency stems not from the conditions of production, but from the production of a different quantity and at a different price from what would prevail in a free market. With curves for demand and supply, it is possible to identify the harm from allocative inefficiency.

---

9.   The prices are calculated from figures in *The Economist,* July 21, 1990.

Consumer Surplus and Producer Surplus

We have already seen how the concept of marginal utility underlies demand curves. In fact, *both* demand and supply curves say something useful about the welfare or satisfaction associated with buying and selling goods and services at their equilibrium price. Figure 4.19 shows a demand curve for light bulbs with an equilibrium price of $1.00 each. Consumers who purchase a bulb at that price must obtain at least $1.00 worth of satisfaction or utility from the good; otherwise they would not have made the purchase. Consumers who believe their satisfaction would be less than $1.00 would not buy at all. Those consumers are represented by the part of the demand curve below and to the right of point E.

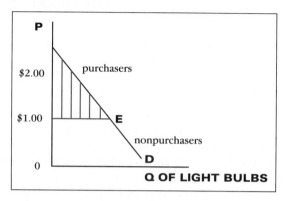

Figure 4.19. Consumer surplus. Many buyers would be willing to pay more than the market price for some given item. These buyers glean a consumer surplus. In the figure, total consumer surplus is the shaded triangular area above the market price and under the demand curve.

Some of the consumers who pay $1.00 for a bulb would have been willing to pay a higher price. Notice that there is still some demand at $2.00 per bulb. But all they have to pay is the *market* price of $1.00. In a real sense, they have obtained a **consumer surplus** equal to $1, the difference between what they would have been *willing* to pay and what they actually *did* pay. Similarly, consumers willing to pay $1.50 or $1.25 per bulb would enjoy a surplus, though it would be lower. Only where the price line at $1.00 approaches and then meets the demand curve are there consumers who receive little or, finally, no surplus. For them, the price is a close measure of the satisfaction or utility they obtain from the purchase. The shaded triangle in Figure 4.19 represents the *total* consumer surplus. It is fair to add that rather than use gas lamps or some other inferior substitute, many consumers might be willing to pay—if they had to—much more than $2 per bulb. If the diagram were drawn to show significant demand remaining at $10, and some even at $100, then the triangle of consumer surplus would be considerably larger than that shown in Figure 4.19.

We can use a supply curve to demonstrate that a **producer surplus** also may emerge at the equilibrium price, as shown in Figure 4.20. Here, the equilibrium price received by producers of light bulbs is again $1.00. A few of the suppliers, however, perhaps those who work harder or have more productive machinery, would have been willing to supply bulbs at a price of 75¢ or even 40¢. Because they receive the full market price of $1.00, they are obtaining a *producer surplus* equal to the difference. The shaded triangle in Figure 4.20 represents the *total* producer surplus.[10]

---

10.   Later in the book, we shall see that economists commonly use the term *economic rent* to describe the producer surplus.

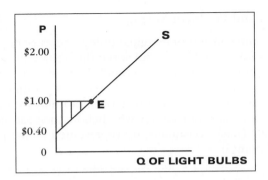

Figure 4.20. Producer surplus. Many sellers would be willing to produce at a lower price than the market price for some given item. These sellers garner a producer surplus. In the figure, total producer surplus is the triangular area under the market price and above the supply curve.

Using Consumer and Producer Surplus to Show Allocative Inefficiency

Consumer and producer surplus help explain why interference in a free-market equilibrium causes society to lose some of its welfare or satisfaction. Imposing a price and a quantity of production that is not at the equilibrium will involve an allocative inefficiency. To see how large this inefficiency is, consider Figure 4.21. At the free-market equilibrium price P_e and quantity Q_e, the total of the consumer and producer surplus would equal area **A** plus area **B**.[11] Be careful with the term consumer surplus, which is a concept having to do with the welfare or satisfaction of consumers. Its meaning is entirely different from the surplus, or excess supply that arises when the price is above the equilibrium, and which was described earlier in the chapter.

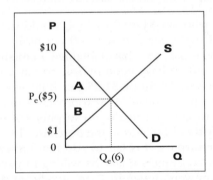

Figure 4.21. Total surplus at the equilibrium price. At price P_e consumer surplus is area **A** and producer surplus is area **B**.

Now consider some interference with a free market. What would happen, for example, if the government imposed a price ceiling (that is, a level that by law cannot be exceeded) and set the price below the equilibrium P_e, say at P_1 in panel **a** of Figure 4.22. At that price, the quantity supplied would be only Q_1. At price P_1 and quantity Q_1, the consumer surplus (the area over the price but under the demand curve) would be area **A+B**, and the producer surplus would be area **C**. The total surplus would be area **A+B+C**, which is less, by the amount of the triangular area **F**, than the total surplus shown in Figure 4.21. The result is similar if government limits

11.   Sometimes students ask how these surpluses can actually be measured, other than using graph paper and counting the little squares. Actually, the problem is an easy one solvable by means of the geometry of triangles. In Figure 4.21, the dollar value of the consumer surplus (area **A**) can be calculated as follows: P_e = $5, and the demand curve hits the vertical axis at $10. The demand curve is a straight line, so the triangle **A** is a right triangle with a base of 6 (read on the horizontal quantity axis) and a height of $5 on the vertical price axis. The area of a right triangle is $\frac{1}{2}$ x base x height, or in the case at hand $\frac{1}{2}$ x 6 x $5 = $15. The total amount of the consumer surplus is $15. When the supply curve is a straight line, the producer surplus of area **B** can be calculated in the same way. Try the calculation for yourself. (It comes out to $\frac{1}{2}$ x 6 x $4 = $12.)

production to Q_1 and allows price to rise to P_2, as in panel **b**. Here producer surplus would be equal to areas **B+C** and consumer surplus would be equal to area **A**. Again the total surplus **A+B+C** would be less by the amount of the triangular area **F** than the total surplus at equilibrium, as shown in Figure 4.21.

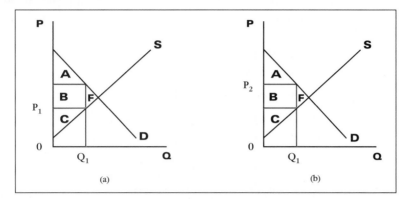

Figure 4.22. **Total surplus is reduced when either price or quantity is moved from the equilibrium.** In panel **a**, if government fixes the price at P_1, then the total surplus **A+B+C** is lower by area F than what it would have been at equilibrium. In panel **b**, if government fixes the quantity at Q_1, then it is also the case that the total surplus **A+B+C** is lower by area F than what it would have been at equilibrium.

In both panels of Figure 4.22 there is an allocative inefficiency equal to the area of the triangle **F**. The example, and the significance of area **F**, is enlarged upon in Figure 4.23. Here, assume that the government for some reason has limited the output of a certain good to just 90 units. That limit of 90 units leaves some unsatisfied consumers who would have been willing to pay a price higher than would have been necessary to persuade suppliers to market a larger quantity. See how the demand curve indicates that some buyer would be willing to pay 60¢ for the 90th unit, while some supplier would be willing to produce it for only 40¢. The total satisfaction of buyers and sellers cannot be maximized when production is limited to only 90 units. The same logic applies to the *whole triangular area* where the demand curve lies above the supply curve. A 95th unit would also bring more satisfaction to some consumer, as reflected by the price that consumer would be willing to pay for it, than it would cost some firm to produce it. The triangle represents the total allocative inefficiency caused by the government interference. (Allocative inefficiency is often called a **deadweight loss**, and sometimes a *welfare loss* or *efficiency loss*.) Note that the triangle grows smaller as larger amounts are produced, and it disappears when output reaches the equilibrium level (here 100 units). At market equilibrium, no consumer would pay more for the last unit produced (the 100th) than what is necessary to persuade suppliers to produce it.

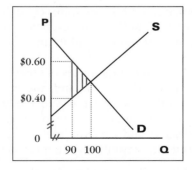

Figure 4.23. **Allocative inefficiency is a triangular area.** All the units from 90 to 99 would bring more satisfaction to consumers, as reflected by the price they would be willing to pay for these units, than it would cost firms to produce them. The triangular area thus represents an allocative inefficiency or deadweight loss.

The logic is the same if firms are persuaded (say by a government subsidy) to produce a quantity larger than equilibrium quantity. That also creates an allocative inefficiency, as shown in Figure 4.24. In this case consumers are not willing to pay as much for the last unit being produced (the 110th) as it took to persuade suppliers to produce it. Again the triangle represents the allocative inefficiency, which becomes smaller and eventually disappears as the quantity is adjusted leftward toward equilibrium.

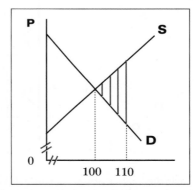

Figure 4.24. Allocative inefficiency when output exceeds the equilibrium level. All the units from 101 to 110 would bring less satisfaction to consumers, as reflected by the price they would be willing to pay, than it would cost firms to produce them. The triangular area thus represents an allocative inefficiency or deadweight loss.

► APPLYING THE TOOLS TO POLICY ISSUES

The tools of demand, supply, and allocative inefficiency allow for striking insights into numerous policy issues. Here we will apply them to three areas, each of which involves deliberate shifting of one of the curves. The first case is when producers shift the supply curve, as with OPEC and the damaging rise in oil prices in the 1970s and 1980s. The second case is a shift in the demand curve when consumers engage in boycotts and governments in embargoes. The third case is a shift in the supply curve when governments impose sales taxes or grant subsidies. Generally, the public has found it difficult to understand these issues in the abstract, but they become much clearer when the tools of demand and supply are applied.

OPEC AND THE OIL CRISES

How the supply curve might be manipulated to raise price is dramatically illustrated by the behavior of the Organization of Petroleum Exporting Countries (OPEC). In 1973 and 1979, OPEC moved to restrict the supply of oil and so raise its price. OPEC strategy was the work of a small group in a small number of countries, but for a time this cartel brought the industrial world to its knees. The episode demonstrated as perhaps never before how external forces can have a profound effect on the allocation of resources within an economy. Our analysis works well in explaining OPEC's tactics.

Figure 4.25 shows that if the member countries of OPEC could agree to reduce the quantity of petroleum pumped at any price, they could shift the world's supply curve from S_1 to S_c ("c" for cartel). As a result, the equilibrium price would rise from P_1 to P_c, as the equilibrium quantity falls from Q_1 to Q_c. The magnitude of the price rise would depend both on how drastically supply could be restricted and on how inelastic demand turned out to be. (With inelastic demand, consumers would not rapidly reduce their use of petroleum as the supply falls, and price would rise further.)

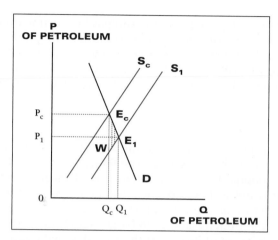

Figure 4.25. **The OPEC cartel in action.** OPEC's restrictions on supply raised the price of oil, especially during the 1970s. The allocative inefficiency is shown by the shaded triangle.

OPEC was extremely successful at first; in 1973–1975, a 10% restriction of output caused a threefold increase in prices to about $12–$13 per barrel. OPEC disrupted the oil markets once again in 1979–1980 when the Iran/Iraq war caused a sharp cutback in the output of these two OPEC member nations, and the other members deliberately did not make up the difference. The result of this second OPEC crisis was that the price of crude oil eventually reached $34 per barrel. It was history's most successful combination in restraint of trade.

The resulting allocative inefficiency is represented by the triangle WE_cE_1 in the figure. This triangle shows that consumers would have been willing to pay more for the quantity from Q_c to Q_1 than it would have cost the oil-producing countries to pump it, as shown by the supply curve before the restriction (S_1). But these consumers were squeezed out of the market by the price rise.

By 1985, however, OPEC's success had begun to erode. As the price of oil rose from $3 to $34 per barrel, consumers learned to economize by buying smaller, fuel-efficient cars, more insulation for their attics, and more energy-efficient appliances. The U.S. Congress passed a mandatory mileage standard of 26.5 miles per gallon on average for new cars from 1990. World petroleum use in market economies fell 11% between 1979 and 1985. Meanwhile, the high price of petroleum prompted nonmember nations to step up production. The great North Sea fields, Alaska, and above all Mexico came on line to share in the profits. Just as demand was falling from D_1 to D_2, supply was rising from S_c to S_2, as shown in Figure 4.26, with a resulting downward pressure on the oil price.

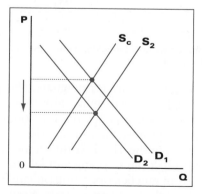

Figure 4.26. **The supply and demand response to OPEC.** Consumers responded to OPEC by reducing their demand. On the supply side, OPEC had trouble maintaining discipline, and new sources of petroleum were developed outside of OPEC.

OPEC could have kept the price high by cutting its production even more, but it was unable to do so. The price plummeted from $28 per barrel in late 1985 to $9 per barrel in mid-1986. OPEC hastily cobbled together some new supply limitations in 1986–1987, and the price moved up again to $18. But overproduction set in once again, and by late 1988 the price was down to $12. Except for some reduced supply and panic buying that temporarily accompanied Iraq's invasion of Kuwait in 1990, oil prices have been relatively moderate ever since.

Embargoes

Embargoes, where one or more countries halt the sale of goods to another country or group of them, are analytically similar to the OPEC case. The limitation on supply drives up the price of the item in the embargoed country. Usually the intent is to damage or punish that country; unlike OPEC, the main motive is not to boost profits. The embargo by many countries of exports to South Africa because of *apartheid*, the U.S. embargoes on exports to Castro's Cuba and Haiti after Aristide's expulsion, and the United Nations embargoes on trade with Iraq following its invasion of Kuwait, and on Serbia because of its role in the Yugoslav civil war are all cases in point. (Many imports from these countries were embargoed as well, which is akin to the boycotts discussed in the next section.)

CONSUMER BOYCOTTS

In 1880, Captain Charles Boycott, a land agent in County Mayo, Ireland, had a dispute with his tenants over their rent. Offended, the local population decided to have nothing more to do with him. Thus the Captain's name entered the English language and many other languages as well.

When consumers engage in a **boycott**, they will not buy from the person or firm or country they are attempting to influence. If a consumer boycott succeeds, price will decline, as shown in Figure 4.27. Here, as consumer demand shifts leftward from D_1 to D_2, price falls from P_1 to P_2.

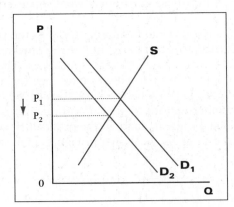

Figure 4.27. A consumer boycott. A boycott is intended to move the demand curve to the left and so reduce the price that the producer will receive.

In famous incidents at Montgomery and Birmingham, Alabama, blacks boycotted city buses and businesses during their struggle for civil rights. More recently, boycotts were mounted by consumers against California lettuce, Hormel Spam, and Coors Beer (all involving trade-union disputes), meat in supermarkets to protest high meat prices in 1973, and the products of the Nestlé Corporation over its activities in the Third World. In the early 1990s, boycotts were waged against canned tuna in an effort to halt the trapping and killing of dolphins; against Burger King because of its purchase of meat from ranches operating on land cleared from tropical rain forest; and against companies that use animals in laboratory tests. Nestlé, Star-Kist Tuna, and Burger King all capitulated. (So did Captain Boycott, who left Ireland for good.) But consumer boycotts have to be sustained if their effect is to last. Otherwise, the demand curve will inch to the right and the price will creep up again. Only so long as demand is kept depressed will the effect of a boycott continue to be felt.

SELLERS' RESPONSE TO A BOYCOTT MAY ALTER THE OUTCOME

Sellers might not look on passively as a boycott builds against them. In 1973 when consumers organized the meat boycott referred to earlier, sellers launched a sellers' boycott of their own in response. Cattle producers, emulating OPEC's supply restrictions, simply held their steers off the market while waiting for the consumer action to collapse. The economic effect was interesting: meat prices actually changed very little

because the effect of the consumer boycott was just about balanced by the effect of the supplier boycott. As Figure 4.28 shows, the decrease in demand from D_1 to D_2 was approximately countered by a simultaneous decrease in supply from S_1 to S_2. There was, however, one major difference. At the new equilibrium E_2 the quantity of meat bought and sold was down substantially, from Q_1 to Q_2.

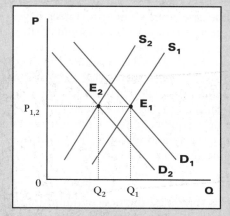

Figure 4.28. **A supplier boycott in response to a consumer boycott.** Sellers may not take a consumer boycott sitting down. In the figure, they have responded with a boycott of their own that reduces supply and works to restore the price.

WHO PAYS A SALES TAX? WHO GETS A SUBSIDY?

Our analysis works well in exploring what the effect of sales taxes and subsidies is on market prices. Without our tools, it would be extremely difficult to explain these effects, which are not especially intuitive.

It might appear at first glance that buyers pay the entire sales tax. Actually, at least in the short run, a sales tax is usually *shared* by buyer and seller. Figure 4.29 shows the demand and supply curves for a given good. The equilibrium price is P_1 and the equilibrium quantity exchanged is Q_1.

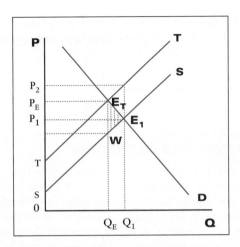

Figure 4.29. Who pays a sales tax? A sales tax is usually shared between buyer and seller, at least in the short run. The allocative inefficiency is shown by the shaded triangle.

Now a sales tax is imposed that requires a fixed amount **ST** to be paid on every unit sold. As a result, the supply curve **S** will shift upward to position **T**. The distance between curve **T** and curve **S** is exactly **ST**.[12] The reason why **S** shifts to **T** is that if sellers are to continue to supply quantity Q_1, they will have to be paid the price they would previously have been willing to receive plus the amount of the new tax. Before the tax, price P_1 brought forth a quantity supplied of Q_1 from suppliers. Now, because of the tax, consumers will have to pay P_2 to get a quantity Q_1. This new price of P_2 is equal to the old price P_1 plus the amount of the tax P_1P_2.

Suppliers would be satisfied to raise their price to P_2 and continue to sell the old quantity Q_1. But note that the new higher price will cut back the quantity demanded. Price P_2 is not an equilibrium. The attempt to charge that price will result in a surplus. To avoid that, sellers will have to lower the price. The new equilibrium is at the intersection of the new supply curve (**T**) and the old demand curve, at price P_e and quantity Q_e. In short, sellers could not raise the price high enough to cover the whole sales tax.

How the Tax Is Shared

The figure shows how the tax is shared. At the new equilibrium quantity Q_e, the tax is P_nP_e = **ST**. Consumers pay part of this amount but not all. They used to pay P_1 but now they must pay P_e, a rise of P_1P_e. Sellers also pay part. They used to receive P_1 but now they receive only P_n, a decrease of P_nP_1. Of the whole tax P_nP_e, P_nP_1 is paid by sellers and P_1P_e by consumers. (In the long run, however, marginal firms may go out of business because some of the burden of the sales tax has fallen on them. The reduction in the number of firms may thus limit supply, so that eventually the price may rise by the full amount of the tax. In such a long-run case, the tax would be borne entirely by the consumer.)

Like any other interference with market equilibrium, sales taxes create an element of allocative inefficiency. The shaded triangle WE_TE_1 in Figure 4.29 shows that consumers on the demand curve between Q_1 and Q_e would have been willing to pay a higher price for the good than it would have cost suppliers to produce it. The imposition of the sales tax means the market does not allocate resources to production with the same efficiency as a free market.

The extent to which the tax is shared between the consumer and producer depends on the elasticities involved. Panel **a** of Figure 4.30 shows what happens when a sales tax is imposed on a commodity for which demand is perfectly inelastic, insulin perhaps. Here the price rises by the full amount of the tax; which means that the consumer pays the entire tax. In panel **b**, demand

---

12   Technically, this is an "excise tax" of fixed amount. The normal state sales tax is a percentage of the sales price. To illustrate a sales tax we would have to draw TT diverging from SS at higher quantities.

for the commodity—perhaps a certain kind of fish—is perfectly elastic. If suppliers of that fish raise the price, their customers will stop buying it and purchase other types of fish. Here the supplier must pay the entire tax. In panel **c**, a tax is imposed on a product that is highly elastic in supply, perhaps ballpoint pens. If the producers of that product had to pay any part of that tax, they would shift production to something else—felt-tip pens instead of ballpoints, for example. Here the price rises by the full amount of the tax, which means that the consumer again pays the entire tax. Finally, if supply is perfectly inelastic, as in panel **d**, the supply curve is already vertical and thus cannot be pushed upward. Here there is no change in price and the supplier must absorb the entire tax.

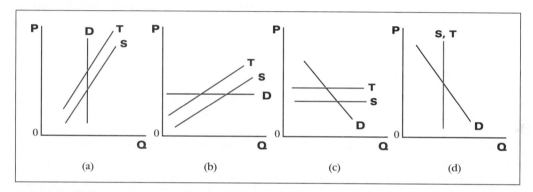

(a)   (b)   (c)   (d)

Figure 4.30. Sales taxes on products with different elasticities of supply and demand. In panels **a** and **c**, the price rises by the full amount of the sales tax, which means that the tax is paid by the buyer; in panels **b** and **d**, the price stays the same, so the seller pays the tax.

Who Receives a Subsidy?

A subsidy paid by the government, say 1¢ per kilowatt-hour of wind-generated electricity, is the opposite of a sales tax. Who receives the subsidy? In Figure 4.31, the original equilibrium price is P_1. If the government provides a subsidy equal to the distance SS_{sub}, the supply curve will shift from S to S_{sub}.

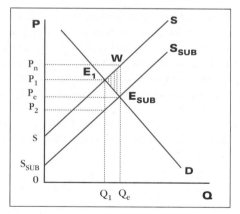

Figure 4.31. Who receives a subsidy? A subsidy is usually shared between buyer and seller. It typically involves an allocative inefficiency as shown by the shaded triangle.

Suppliers who receive that subsidy, which is equivalent to P_1P_2 per unit, will be willing to supply the old quantity Q_1 at the lower price P_2, since the government is providing the difference between the old price P_1 and the new price P_2. But P_2 is not an equilibrium price because the quantity demanded at that price exceeds the quantity supplied. Consequently, price will gravitate to P_e, and quantity will move to Q_e, with the subsidy equal to $E_{sub}W = P_eP_n$. The supplier does not receive the entire subsidy, however; the increase in receipts per unit is only P_1P_n. The consumer receives part of it because the price paid has fallen from P_1 to P_e. (In the long run, new firms may be attracted to the business because of the subsidy. The greater number of firms may increase supply, so that eventually the price may fall by the full amount of the subsidy. In that long-run situation, the subsidy accrues entirely to the consumer.)

Like a sales tax, subsidies create an element of allocative inefficiency. Consider the shaded triangle E_1WE_{sub} in Figure 4.31. In a free market, consumers on the demand curve between Q_1 and Q_e would not be willing to pay a price as high as the cost of producing the good. The market with a subsidy is not allocating resources to production with the same efficiency as a free market. Also, as with sales taxes, subsidies can be analyzed when the supply and demand curves have unusual slopes.[13]

 ## CONCLUSION

The demand and supply mechanism introduced in this chapter and the previous one is central to the microeconomic analysis of a market economy. Its concepts of equilibrium, surplus, shortage, and allocative inefficiency provide us with powerful tools that can be used to explain what goes on around us in the world of public affairs and business. We have put these tools immediately to work by looking at several cases where the curves are deliberately shifted by producers, consumers, or governments. In the next chapter we discuss a different class of cases, where governments intervene to fix prices at levels different from what demand and supply would dictate. The immediately following chapters use the tools developed in this chapter to analyze the behavior of firms, including those that have some degree of market power and those that cause environmental problems.

SUMMARY

1) The determinants of supply are the objectives of the firm, the price received for its output, the price of goods that can be substituted in production, expectations, the prices of the factors of production, the level of technology, and the number of sellers.
2) A supply curve can be constructed by holding all the determinants of supply constant except for price, and then allowing price to vary. A movement along a supply curve (a change in quantity supplied) is caused by a change in the price of the item, while a shift in the position of the supply curve (a change in supply) is caused by a change in one of the nonprice determinants.
3) Supply curves normally slope upward and to the right because of rising costs. The supply curves of individual firms can be added horizontally to obtain market supply curves.

---

13.   Simply look back at Figure 4.30, call T the original supply curve, and call S the supply curve when shifted downward by a subsidy. In Figure 4.30's panel **a**, if demand is perfectly inelastic (insulin), then the price falls by the full amount of the subsidy, which thus accrues entirely to consumers. In panel **b**, if demand is perfectly elastic (one particular type of fish), then price will not fall so producers keep the entire subsidy. In panel **c**, supply is perfectly elastic (ballpoint pens) and the price falls by the full amount of the subsidy, consumers taking it all. Finally, in panel **d** the perfectly inelastic supply curve is already vertical, so it cannot be moved upward. Price does not change; the supplier pockets the whole of the subsidy.

4) The price elasticity of supply, measured as %ΔQs/%ΔP, shows how responsive the quantity supplied is to a price change. A large response indicates elastic supply; a small response indicates inelastic supply. Straight-line supply curves that hit the origin exhibit unitary elasticity; curves that hit the vertical axis are elastic, while curves that hit the horizontal axis are inelastic. Elasticity usually increases over time; in the momentary period, suppliers cannot make adjustments, in the short run, some but not all factors of production can be adjusted, while in the long run all factors can be adjusted.

5) Together, demand and supply are the mechanism through which the market equilibrium is determined. Prices are pushed toward this equilibrium. At any price above equilibrium, excess supply (surpluses) cause the price to fall. At any price below equilibrium, excess demand (shortages) cause prices to rise. Shifts in either curve cause the equilibrium price to change.

6) Allocative inefficiency (deadweight loss) develops when prices are not allowed to find their market equilibrium. The point is made by comparing the size of the consumer surplus (area below the demand curve but above the price) and producer surplus (area above the supply curve but below the price) in a free market to a situation when the market price is not charged. The total of consumer and producer surplus is smaller in the latter case.

7) The tools of this chapter allow us to analyze deliberate shifts in the demand or supply curves. OPEC's restriction of the oil supply raised oil prices. Consumer boycotts shift the demand curve leftward and so lower the prices received by boycotted firms. Government sales taxes and subsidies shift the supply curve and typically result in a sharing of the tax burden or benefit of the subsidy by producers and consumers.

Chapter Key Words

Allocative inefficiency: The notion that society loses some of its "welfare" or "satisfaction" when interference in a free-market equilibrium is made. Imposing a price and a quantity of production that is not at the equilibrium will involve an allocative inefficiency because the sum of consumer and producer surplus will be smaller than it would be at the equilibrium price and quantity. Allocative inefficiency means the same thing as deadweight loss.

Backward-bending supply curve: Above the bend in the supply curve, a higher price leads to a lower quantity supplied. Examples might include dirty or dangerous labor, the work of Social Security recipients, and the production of petroleum by a country that wants to achieve a target income.

Boycott: An attempt to influence economic behavior by refusing to buy (or sometimes sell) a commodity.

Change in quantity supplied: A movement along a supply curve caused by a change in price.

Change in supply: A shift in the supply curve caused by a change in any of the underlying determinants of supply except price.

Consumer surplus: The idea that some consumers would pay more than the equilibrium price for an item, and so will reap a surplus. Geometrically, a triangular area below the demand curve but above the price.

Deadweight loss: The loss to society caused by interference with a free-market equilibrium. Has the same meaning as allocative inefficiency, which see.

Determinants of supply: The objectives of the producer, the selling price, the costs of production, changes in the price of goods that can be substituted in production, expectations for the future, and the techniques of production.

Elasticity of supply: The concept that a given percentage change in price will induce the same percentage change in quantity (unitary elasticity), or a larger percentage change in quantity (elastic), or a smaller percentage change in quantity (inelastic).

Equilibrium: In the model of demand and supply, that price where the quantity demanded and the quantity supplied of an item are equal. Any other price will result in either a shortage or a surplus, so that in a market system there is a tendency for prices to move toward equilibrium.

Long run: A period of time long enough to alter the availability of all the factors of production, including capital.

Price elasticity of supply: The concept that relates numerically the reaction in quantity supplied to a change in the price of a good. The formula for the price elasticity of supply is $\%\Delta Qs/\%\Delta P$.

Producer surplus: The idea that some producers would still produce at a price less than the equilibrium for an item, and so reap a surplus. Geometrically, a triangular area above the supply curve but below the price.

Short run: A period of time too short for the availability of all the factors of production to be altered.

Chapter Questions

1) Kiwi Computer is an upstart computer and video monitor manufacturer in New Zealand. It has typical upward sloping supply curves for computers and monitors. How would the supply curve for computers shift if:
    a) the price of monitors suddenly rises?
    b) Kiwi's managers expect computer prices to rise in one month?
    c) there is a shortage of technical labor in New Zealand that drives up wages?
    d) Kiwi finds a way to put far more chips on the same circuit board, reducing costs considerably?
2) You run a paper mill with two very expensive paper machines. The more intensely you run the machines, the more maintenance they need, raising your costs considerably. What is the name for this situation? Why will it cause your supply curve to slope up?
3) A mail-order catalog increases the price of a sweater from $35 to $45. As a result, the sweater manufacturer increases output from 30,000 to 40,000 sweaters. What is the elasticity of supply? Does this manufacturer's supply curve intercept the horizontal or vertical axis?
4) Rather than continue to study economics, you decide to become an artist. You are discovered at an art show, and suddenly all the collectors there want to buy your paintings. What is your elasticity of supply when you are still at the art show (assuming you do not paint exceptionally fast)? What is your elasticity in the weeks or months following the show? What is your elasticity over your entire lifetime?

5) The market for VCRs is initially in equilibrium. Then there is a technological advance that lowers the cost of producing VCRs. Assuming demand remains unchanged, use diagrams to show the path to a new equilibrium. Will price and quantity be higher or lower than before?

6) It is the day before Thanksgiving, and 50 people want to buy $100 standby tickets on a flight to Milwaukee. However, the supply of standby seats is fixed at just 15. If the airline can change the price of the seats, explain and show graphically how the situation could be resolved.

7) The market for digital watches has standard demand and supply curves. Over time, technology has improved and the supply curve has been shifting to the right. On a diagram, show the initial consumer and producer surpluses. Has consumer surplus grown or shrunk as technology has improved? Can you say for certain what has happened to producer surplus?

8) Governments often put a ceiling on the price of food. Draw demand and supply curves for food, and add a price ceiling that is below the equilibrium price. Show the consumer and producer surpluses with and without the price ceiling. What is the allocative inefficiency of the price ceiling? Look at your diagram carefully. Can you see why consumers would lobby for the price ceiling?

9) In 1993 the federal government raised the gas tax by 4.9¢ per gallon. At a certain Pennsylvania gas station, the price rose from $0.99 to $1.04 the day the tax took effect. Over the next week it remained at $1.04, but then it fell back to $1.02. Explain why this happened using a diagram. Show the allocative inefficiency of the tax.

When Government Intervenes

OVERALL OBJECTIVE: To use the tools of economic analysis to understand the consequences that ensue when government establishes price ceilings and price floors.

MORE SPECIFICALLY:

- To demonstrate that price controls may have to be adopted in grave emergencies, but that side effects are likely to ensue. These include shortages, queues, allocative inefficiency, black markets, and possibly a system of rationing to distribute scarce goods. It is difficult to judge exactly how serious an emergency must be before price controls bring more benefits to society than costs.
- To show that rent controls mandating maximum rentals and taxicab regulations that license a fixed number of cabs and enforce maximum rates will typically cause shortages of housing and available taxis.
- To explore the consequences of the three main ways to aid farmers: price supports, deficiency payments, and supply restrictions.
- To investigate the effects of minimum wage laws. Though widely supported by the public, such laws may have the unwanted result of creating unemployment.
- To discuss why health care has become so expensive in the United States, and why government is at once part of the problem and part of the solution.

Government has an important role to play if the free market is to work. Even the economists with the strongest faith in free markets usually believe that it must guarantee law and order, see that contracts are honored, regulate the banking system and financial markets, maintain a supply of money, and provide public education. It must also be ready to intervene when the market fails to give acceptable results, as in policing monopolies and protecting the environment. Without these interventions, the market mechanism would not work nearly as well.

Other forms of government intervention are less obviously for the common good. For political reasons, sometimes based on ethical and humane concerns but sometimes based on the lobbying success of powerful private interest groups, direct intervention in the operation of free markets is sometimes undertaken to change the equilibrium price or quantity. Often the results include surpluses or shortages and allocative inefficiency.

These adverse results can occur even when the intervention may be justified by the benefits it brings to the public welfare. Shortage or surplus and allocative inefficiency receive a good deal of emphasis in this chapter, thus serving to illustrate once more that economics is a study of trade-offs. In emphasizing the disadvantages, there is some danger of giving the impression that economists as a group are anti-government. To counter this impression, remember that many forms of government intervention, such as those noted in the first paragraph, do not give rise to shortage, surplus, and allocative inefficiency. Further, even damaging consequences almost always have offsetting benefits of one sort or another that caused the intervention to be undertaken in the first place.

Examples of government interference with free-market equilibrium are common in microeconomics. Grouped together in this chapter are a number of cases of interference with the market that involve either price ceilings or price floors set by the government. The cases involving legal price ceilings that cannot be exceeded are (1) general price controls and rationing, (2) rent controls, and (3) taxicab regulation. The cases involving price floors are (4) programs to boost farmers' incomes, and (5) minimum wage laws. The chapter concludes with a sixth case, the most important one currently in the United States. This is the broader question of government involvement in providing medical care. In all of these cases, the tools of demand, supply, elasticity, and allocative efficiency allow for illuminating analysis and prediction. Once a person has studied the principles of economics, none of these questions ever looks quite the same.

▶ PRICE CONTROLS AND RATIONING

In emergencies, particularly in time of war, food, clothing, fuel, and other essential items may be in short supply as a result of labor shortages, diversion of the items to military uses, and embargoes of critical imports. Hoarding by consumers anticipating shortages may elevate demand considerably. As demand and supply shifts cause prices to soar, only consumers with high incomes will be able to afford certain necessities. In effect, the market price will ration the small supply to consumers who are willing and able to pay. To avoid a catastrophic breakdown of morale, governments may respond with **price controls** that fix the prices of necessities. Our task in this section is twofold: first, to analyze what the results of price controls are likely to be, and second, to ask whether they should be employed to counter emergencies more minor than, say, a full-scale war.

We begin with an analysis of price controls. In wartime, government might decide, for example, to fix the price of gasoline substantially below the free-market equilibrium price. Figure 5.1 shows that during a period of acute shortage, the price of gasoline, as determined by demand and supply, might rise to $4.00 per gallon. What would happen if the government established a price ceiling at a much lower level—perhaps at $1.00 per gallon? At that price, the amount producers are willing to supply is only 1 million gallons per day, while consumers would like to purchase 3 million gallons. The excess demand of 2 million gallons makes itself felt as a shortage.

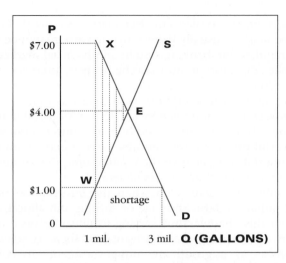

Figure 5.1. **Price controls.** A price ceiling at $1.00, below the equilibrium price of $4.00, results in a shortage and causes allocative inefficiency equal to the shaded triangle in the figure.

This interference with equilibrium price gives rise to an allocative inefficiency (deadweight loss) represented by the triangle **WXE**. Some consumers are willing to pay a much higher price to obtain what they want, but, because of the price control, they cannot. Unable to satisfy their needs, they suffer a loss of satisfaction. Meanwhile, other consumers regard gasoline as not worth much more to them than the controlled price of $1.00, but when they find it on sale, they will buy it. If the government had allowed a market price to be charged, the allocative inefficiency would have been avoided.

FURTHER EFFECTS OF PRICE CONTROLS

When price controls are put in place, sellers have a strong incentive to evade or ignore them. If the good controlled is closely defined, sellers may try to alter its appearance and shift it to a noncontrolled category. For example, when France imposed price controls on bread loaves and croissants during the late 1970s, French bakeries gave a new shape to the croissant, called it "le Barre" after the premier who had introduced the controls, and so avoided the price ceiling— at least until the controls were extended to cover the new offering, which promptly disappeared from the shops.

Black Markets

Some consumers and suppliers evade price controls by resorting to the illegal **black market**, where goods are bought and sold above the official price. The simplest case would be if production is easily policed but resale is difficult to monitor. In Figure 5.1, say the government can easily supervise sales from petroleum refineries at a fixed price of $1.00. The resulting quantity of gasoline is 1 million gallons. If consumers do not fear being caught in illegal transactions, they would be willing to pay a black-market price of $7.00 per gallon for this quantity. As before, the allocative inefficiency is equal to the triangle **WXE**.

Actually, the black-market price will often not be easy to predict. Many consumers and producers will find concealment of their actions difficult, will fear police action, and will suffer pangs of conscience. Neither the demand nor the supply on the black market will be as large as it would be without price controls. The black-market demand and supply curves are thus likely to be different than the curves in a free market, both probably lying somewhere to the left of the demand and supply curves in a free market. The black market has its own equilibrium price, at P_{bm} in Figure 5.2. That price might be lower, in the same range, or higher than the free-market equilibrium price would have been (P_h), depending on the shape and position of the black market curves.

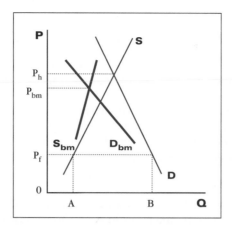

Figure 5.2. Black-market equilibrium. The black-market equilibrium price will not necessarily be the same as the free-market equilibrium price. It depends on the position of the black-market supply and demand curves, which are greatly affected by the risks of illegal trading.

Black markets are most likely to arise when an inefficient, corrupt bureaucracy attempts to police a public that has no incentive to comply.[1] Price controls are least likely to lead to a black market when a patriotic public supports the controls and when government enforcement of them is tough.

Shortages

Even where there is general reluctance to participate in a black market, price controls are still likely to have some adverse and visible side effects. Remember that they are associated with shortages. One does not have to look back to World War II for examples of how such shortages are manifested. As recently as 1979, the U.S. government had price controls in place on gasoline at a time when OPEC cut back on supplies exported to the United States. Because the public regarded OPEC's action as a threat, there was general support for the controls and little in the way of a black market. But a strange thing happened—strange at least to the large part of the population that had not taken an economics course. Suddenly, some filling stations had no gas available. At many gas stations, customers found they had to wait in line for an hour or more.[2] The gasoline shortage ended when the price controls were lifted.

Predictably, behavior changes to accommodate the fact that less of the product is available than people want to buy at the going price. Many stations with the "no gas" signs had simply pumped all the gas people asked for on a first-come, first-served basis until they ran out. Others set a daily quota for themselves and closed after selling that amount. Yet others engaged in so-called "seller rationing." A station manager might sell only to friends and familiar customers, telling all others that supplies were exhausted. Needless to say, this generates great hostility. To find the car ahead of you and the car beside you getting gas when you are told there isn't any is an upsetting experience.

First-come, first-served by sellers until the supply runs out is the usual procedure. Such behavior inevitably produces **queues**. This word, taken from the long braided hair worn by Chinese men during the Manchu Dynasty, was given a new and popular application by the British, particularly during the First World War of 1914–1918. The long lines of customers standing for

---

1.   Or where the police believe the crime is not very serious. Illegal ticket scalping almost always occurs at Madonna concerts, the Olympics, the World Series, Superbowl games, and so forth. The organizers do not charge what the market will bear, probably to avoid adverse publicity. Scalpers know they can resell tickets for much more—5 to 15 times more is not unusual—than their original price. The police often just look the other way.

2.   Perhaps fittingly, even OPEC countries with price controls on gasoline faced shortages. "The petrol crisis in the northern emirate [of the United Arab Emirates] has become more acute," said *Newsweek* in March 1980; "most filling stations have closed down." The stations' managers were at the time seeking "permission of the authorities concerned to increase petrol prices."

hours outside shops waiting for supplies to arrive resembled a queue, so it was said. But queueing up is not only time consuming but haphazard in its selection of who must do without. Those with the greater responsibilities and less leisure find it costly in terms of lost time. In Poland during the food shortages of the early 1980s, a new occupation sprang up: retirees who for a fee would stand in a queue for you. They were called *stacz*, Polish for "one who waits." The rate at which the queues for different goods moved became common knowledge in Poland just before the end of Communist rule. Average time-in-queue per day in Poland was 63 minutes in 1966, 98 minutes in 1976, and from all accounts much longer yet in the mid-1980s according to a Polish survey reported in *The Economist*.[3] With the return to market pricing by the new Polish government in 1990, the queues disappeared.

Rationing

To avoid the inconvenience of widespread queueing and the unfairness of seller rationing, the government may institute a system of official **rationing**. This can be done by issuing ration books containing coupons for each good, say a gallon of gasoline or a pound of meat. In the situation shown in Figure 5.2, the quantity of coupons issued would be exactly equal to **A**. To make a purchase, the buyer would need enough money to pay the money price P_f per unit and a ration coupon to pay the "coupon price." Demand is thus artificially restricted to a quantity no greater than the amount **A**, and the price will (in the legal market) be under no pressure to rise beyond P_f. Such a system was first implemented on a large scale in World War I, when it was used for scarce products in all the belligerent countries and in many neutral countries as well.

When the United States resorted to rationing at the start of World War II, it soon became apparent that when certain goods were rationed, shortages arose among other goods that were not originally in short supply. Workers in the booming defense industries could not spend their rising incomes on scarce rationed goods. For example, if rationing prevented them from spending their money on meat, they might spend it on an unrationed substitute such as fish. When the increased demand boosted fish prices, the authorities were forced to extend the rationing to fish. The process was called "spreading the shortages"; it led to *point rationing,* as explored in the box.

POINT RATIONING

Eventually during World War II, most countries adopted point rationing, a more-sophisticated scheme that made it unnecessary to issue separate coupons for separate items such as shirts, socks, coats, and shoes. Point rationing was invented by Nazi Germany but spread rapidly to Britain and then to the United States. Under point rationing, coupons of a certain point value would be issued, say, for clothing. Consumers could choose from among all the various sorts of clothes where to "spend" their points. If pants were in shorter supply than shirts, pants would be assigned a higher point value. If the government needed to cut clothes consumption drastically, say by half, it would double the value of the points needed to make a purchase or halve the number of points distributed. In Britain during the worst days of World War II, average allowances were cut to one quart of milk per family per week, and one egg per month!

---

3.   June 25, 1988. All the former Communist countries used price controls. The longest continuous period for widespread price controls in a single country was in the old Soviet Union, from 1917 until 1991, during which time most prices were set by government. At the time of writing, some of the USSR's successor republics still maintained many price controls in spite of repeated announcements that prices would be freed.

Meat and bacon rationing continued in Britain until July 1954, nine years after the end of the war.

In the United States, the rationing system was administered by the Office of Price Administration (OPA), which employed thousands of economists stationed in offices in every major city and town. The ration coupons, red for meat and butter, blue for fruits and vegetables, and so forth, are collector's items today. If you ever see one, look at it closely. The bombers, tanks, and so on pictured on them were antique by the standards of the 1940s and would have fared poorly on the battlefields of Europe. The stamps were apparently designed much earlier and held for an emergency.

An idea that emerged after World War II was to make the ration coupons transferable, allowing them to be bought and sold on a so-called "white market." The U.S. government considered setting up a rationing system of this type during the oil crises of the 1970s. Under the plan, those who felt they did not need as much gasoline as their allotted ration could sell their coupons to those who thought they needed more. That system would have prevented a black market from emerging and would have made unnecessary much of the bureaucracy that would have been needed to police it. It did not, however, receive a trial.[4]

SHOULD PRICE CONTROLS BE ADOPTED TO COUNTER MORE MODEST EMERGENCIES?

A difficult question concerns how serious an emergency has to be to justify the use of price controls. Few economists would oppose price controls on food and clothing in a full-scale war or famine, for who would stand by and watch people starve and go unclothed while the wealthy continued to eat and dress well? The problem comes when the emergency is not so serious as that.

Good examples of a debatable use of price controls can be found in the aftermath of Hurricane Hugo, which hit Charleston, South Carolina, in September 1989, and Hurricane Andrew, which hit southern Florida in August 1992. In the aftermath of these great storms, state and local authorities decided to place controls on the prices of certain items. Consider the price controls on chain saws and ice (for keeping freezers cold as long as the power outage continued). There were substantial arguments against them. People with a tree blocking their driveway had a greater need for a chainsaw than did people with a limb lying on their lawn, and they would have been willing to pay for it. People with $1000 of food in their freezer would have been willing to pay much more for ice than people with $50 worth of food. Yet the price controls made it impossible for these disparate demands to be satisfied. The result was considerable allocative inefficiency. Furthermore, higher prices would have attracted a much greater quantity supplied in a much shorter period of time. But there were also strong arguments that favored the imposition of controls. Without them, sellers would practice price gouging. People did not have complete information; the saws and the ice were needed in a hurry; ice that was actually available three blocks away for $10 was being priced at $50 by profiteers going door-to-door with pickup trucks. There is reason on both sides of the argument. The decision to adopt or not to adopt price

---

4.   Ration coupons were actually printed in 1974—5 billion of them. There was some comic relief when it was found that the coupons, which bore a portrait of George Washington, activated change-making machines as if they were dollar bills. They were never distributed and sat in storage for years. In 1984 it was decided to shred and bury them. In Europe, too, gas-rationing plans were held in readiness during the OPEC crisis. Only in the Netherlands was rationing actually adopted. It was soon abandoned, however, because motorists swarmed over the borders to buy unrationed fuel in Belgium and Germany. A few countries, including Australia and France, instituted price controls on gasoline (but not rationing) in the aftermath of Iraq's invasion of Kuwait in 1990.

controls in situations like these is essentially political, involving a weighing of the costs against the benefits. The responsibility of economists is to provide the fullest possible knowledge of the likely economic consequences of those decisions.

In the case of the gasoline shortage of 1979–1980, many would now argue that a fairly modest price increase would have cleared the market and saved millions of motorists millions of hours of aggravating waits in the gas lines. In this reading, the delays caused considerably more harm than any moderate price increase would have caused.

▶ RENT CONTROLS

City governments often impose controls on the rents that can be charged for apartments and houses. Their declared reason for doing so is to make the housing market "fair." Political reality suggests it is because there are far more tenants who vote than there are landlords. Rent controls have an unintended effect, as Figure 5.3 shows. If the controlled rent is higher than the equilibrium rent R_e that would exist in the absence of government action, the rent control will have no effect. A rent ceiling *below* equilibrium, however, as at R_{max}, will cause a shortage of rental housing equal to Q_1Q_2, because the quantity demanded is greater than it would be at equilibrium while the quantity supplied is reduced by the artificially low return to landlords.

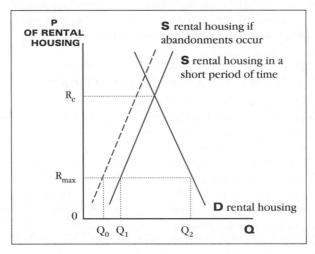

Figure 5.3. Rent control. Rent control that puts a ceiling on the rent that can be charged typically causes a shortage of rental housing and leads to a slowdown in the construction (or even the abandonment) of such housing.

New York City has had rent control since 1943. (It was adopted during wartime. External forces are often the proximate cause of rent control's first adoption.) At present it applies to about a third of the city's housing units; much of the rest is under a "rent stabilization program." Washington, D.C., Los Angeles, San Francisco, London, Paris, and Rome also have rent controls, along with about 150 other cities and counties in the United States. About 10% of all U.S. housing is affected.

Cities with rent controls have experienced chronic housing shortages. In New York City, the vacancy rate for apartments (currently 2%) is usually from a third to a half of the vacancy rates in cities without controls. This is hardly surprising, when the median controlled apartment rent in midtown Manhattan in 1985 was $476 per month even though uncontrolled small studio apartments were commonly renting for about $1000 per month. Among the lucky beneficiaries was said to be a mayor of New York City, who was found by the press to be paying a controlled $351-a-month rental for an apartment in Greenwich Village that observers believed would have brought $1500 in a free market. (The controls do not take location into account; the same maximum is imposed on an apartment in Harlem as on an apartment on Central Park West.)

Many landlords have responded to the controls by letting their rental properties deteriorate. Entire buildings are being abandoned every year because it does not pay landlords to keep them up; the total of such abandonments are believed to have reached the 300,000 mark. A 1991 U.S. government study charges that the controls are thereby connected with homelessness. In Figure 5.3 note that in the long run the abandonment of buildings will shift the supply curve to the left, making the shortage greater, Q_0Q_2, than it is in the short run. New York City permits rents to be raised 15% when there is a change in tenants—an obvious incentive for landlords to get rid of tenants on a revolving basis, perhaps by cutting back on the heat. A black market in rent-controlled housing has also developed, taking the form of "key money" (a quasi-bribe of cash) and the compulsory purchase of battered furniture at high prices. Tenants acquiesce in these landlord demands because they are eager to find a place to live. Conversion of rental housing to offices, or to condominiums owned rather than rented by their residents, has become rampant.

Among the strongest rent controls in the United States are those in effect in Berkeley, California, and Cambridge, Massachusetts. By 1984 a Berkeley ordinance passed in 1980 had led to the loss of 31% of the city's rental housing. Berkeley is the only U.S. city to control office and shop rents as well as apartment and house rents. Currently, there is a movement to control the sale price of houses as well. (Berkeley's voters elected a more moderate rent board in 1990, and that city is now allowing rents to rise.) Cambridge, where 77% of residents are renters, also has strong rent controls. Landlords dissatisfied with low rents cannot decide to leave an apartment vacant. Heavy fines are levied if they do.

Why does the public put up with such results? Remember the many voters who live in rent-controlled housing and want to keep it that way. Meanwhile, many people who are willing to pay higher rents do not vote in city contests because they are unable to live there; they cannot find a city apartment to rent. Those people are the victims of allocative inefficiency. (The total amount of that inefficiency would be a triangular area, the left side of which would run up to the demand curve from Q_1 in Figure 5.3.)

Few U.S. cities have scrapped their rent controls altogether. But some are now persuaded that the costs of the controls to society are greater than the benefits. Boston, for instance, enacted "vacancy decontrol" in 1976. A change of tenants automatically frees a rental unit from control. Other cities use "rent regulation," which allows adjustments for inflation, tax changes, improvements, and differences in location. The Reagan administration, which opposed rent controls, suggested that cuts be made in federal funding to cities that retained them, but no action was taken.

► TAXICAB REGULATION

In many large U.S. cities—almost 90% of those with 50,000 or more people—municipal governments regulate taxicab fares. This is a curious situation because the regulations typically create a shortage by controlling prices and at the same time exacerbate the shortage by controlling the supply of taxis. In Chicago, for example, fares are kept to some fixed maximum, such as P_{max} in Figure 5.4. That would itself cause a shortage. But the city government has issued only 4,600 taxi licenses in recent years. (The licenses are transferrable and can be bought and sold.) Thus, the supply curve turns vertical (completely inelastic) at the point where no more licenses can be issued, making the shortage worse. Normally the shortage would be Q_1Q_2 at P_{max}. On a rainy day, when demand rises but supply remains fixed, the shortage might be as much as Q_1Q_3.

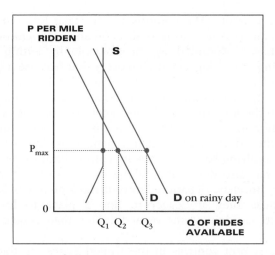

Figure 5.4. **Taxicab regulation.** The figure shows why it is hard to find a cab in Chicago on a rainy day. Not only does the city government control taxi fares, but it places a legal limit on the permitted number of cabs.

New York City also restricts the number of "medallions," as its taxi licenses are called. Under the Haas Law of 1937, the number of medallions in existence has been frozen for many years at 11,787. Almost double that number of cabs were on the streets in the early 1930s. As in Chicago, the medallions can be bought and sold; one originally cost $10, but in 1992 the price was $140,000—and that cost is, of course, built into the structure of taxi fares. Cab companies that have paid over $100,000 for many of their medallions would furiously resist deregulation.[5] If just anybody could get into the business, the price of medallions would sink to zero. Cities that want to deregulate may find that the only way to do so is to buy back all the medallions at vast expense, perhaps with a temporary tax on fares. Once a government begins to tamper with the price mechanism there may be no comfortable way to back out.

▶ BOOSTING FARMERS' INCOMES

Up to this point we have been discussing price ceilings that establish legal maxima for prices. Now we take up price floors that establish a minimum level for prices. A classic case involves government intervention in agriculture.

Farming was once the textbook example of a free market populated by millions of competing participants. Pervasive government intervention in both developed and underdeveloped countries has made that market far less free than it once was. The United States first adopted agricultural income and price supports in the 1930s.

Several arguments have been advanced in support of programs to boost farmers' incomes. These include producing enough food at home to keep from becoming overly dependent on foreign supplies, keeping the countryside nicely cultivated and not letting it grow up in weeds and brush, and the preservation of family farms. It is true that during the Great Depression, farm support programs brought relief to many farmers who were being driven off their land by the collapse of prices. Today, however, the main reason for the existence of programs to boost farm income is that farmers have political clout. However expensive these programs are, legislators are loathe to tamper with them for fear of the political revenge that would be exacted on them. (This is even more true in Europe and Japan than in the United States at the present time.)

---

5.   In Boston, a city government decision to raise the number of medallions by 300 from its 1990 figure of 1,525 was immediately challenged in court by the taxi companies. In New York City, the opposition to deregulation would have an ethical side to it: increasing numbers of immigrant families have pooled their slender resources to make a down payment on an expensive New York City taxi medallion with the balance financed by a bank loan. The families often keep their one cab running 18 or 20 hours a day, 7 days a week.

PRICE SUPPORTS

There are three main ways of raising farmers' incomes, as can be seen from U.S. policy at various times. One method, with origins in the 1930s, is through **price supports**. Assume that the Department of Agriculture decides to raise the price of corn from the equilibrium price P_e to price P_h, as shown in Figure 5.5. It can do so by buying up a portion of the crop **AB** (the same as Q_1Q_2 on the horizontal axis) and holding it in storage. The government thus reduces the quantity supplied to the market from the original Q_e to Q_1, and as a result of the reduction in quantity the price rises to P_h, as seen along the demand curve.

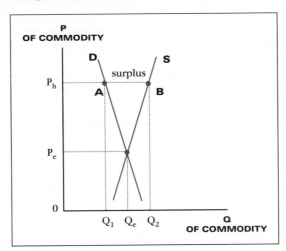

Figure 5.5. A price support. Price supports paid to farmers mean that government must acquire and store a stockpile of surplus commodities.

Such intervention entails serious costs. Because consumers have to pay the higher-than-market price P_h, they consume less, cutting back their consumption of corn to Q_1. The government must pay for the purchase of the crop, at a cost of Q_1ABQ_2. It must also pay the cost of storing the crop. The U.S. corn and wheat surpluses held in stock in June 1988 (a high point) were well over five billion bushels, about two-thirds of the annual harvest of each crop; the quantity of butter, cheese, and milk products being held in surplus was $2\frac{1}{2}$ billion pounds. Much of the surplus was stored in giant bins that loomed over the Midwestern landscape. Such surpluses are sometimes useful, of course, as during World War II, or when drought struck in the summer of 1988. The depletion of U.S. grain stocks associated with that drought brought these stocks down to levels lower than had been reached in several years. But the stocks were never intended to be an emergency stockpile, nor have they ever been managed as such. That they are sometimes useful is mere accident.

THE STRANGE " EAU CLAIRE RULE"

Government intervention into milk marketing goes well beyond "normal" price support. Under rules dating back to the 1930s, the U.S. Secretary of Agriculture sets the minimum price that can be charged for milk. (Milk is the only product subject to such a rule.) According to obscure logic concerning the need for the south to have a nearby source of milk for its cities, national prices are based on the Eau Claire, Wisconsin, price of milk with a bonus allowed the further a dairy farm is from that city. The Eau Claire rule supports milk production where it would otherwise be uneconomic: it thrives in Florida, for example, where milk prices are high because the distance from Eau Claire is great. The federal rule also makes it impossible to ship milk from regions where it is abundant to regions where it is not. Even though milk is now easy to ship long distances, milk prices vary widely from state to state.

DEFICIENCY PAYMENTS

Another means of raising the income of farmers is through so-called **deficiency payments**, which have been used in the United States since 1973 for several main crops (wheat, corn, barley, oats, sorghum). To implement this scheme, the Department of Agriculture sets a *target price*, say $4.30 per bushel of wheat, as shown in Figure 5.6.

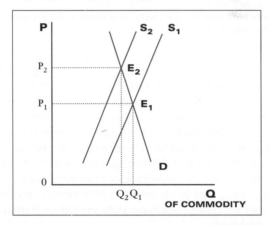

Figure 5.6. A **deficiency payment.** Deficiency payments that top up the price a farmer receives do not involve purchase of surplus commodities, but they cause the market price to decline and production to increase as well. They are therefore expensive.

If the market price would otherwise have been $4.20, the wheat farmer gets a check for 10¢ per bushel as a deficiency payment. As a result, there is likely to be an increase in quantity supplied, from Q_1 to Q_2, as farmers move up their supply curve. That larger quantity will bring the market price down to $4.10, as seen on the demand curve. Now the deficiency payment rises to 20¢ per bushel.

Deficiency payments have certain advantages over price-support programs. For one thing, the government does not have to buy and store any surpluses. Moreover, the cost of the program is easier to identify because the deficiency payment comes solely from the government and consumers do not pay a higher price as is true with price supports. In the diagram, the entire cost is the 20¢ deficiency payment WX on a quantity of Q_2, for a total of ABWX. Consumers actually pay *less* than they would under a price-support program because the crop is sold for what the market will bear. Typically, government pays more under this plan than it does under price supports because the rise in output and the resulting fall in the price paid by consumers raise the tab.[6]

COSTS OF THE U.S. PROGRAM

Agricultural assistance programs represent an astonishingly expensive use of consumer and taxpayer money, with U.S. costs reaching $75 billion in 1990. Remember that these costs are an amalgam of higher prices paid by consumers ($28 billion in 1990) and higher tax bills to finance the purchase of surpluses, to cover storage costs, and to fund deficiency payments ($47 billion). A farm bill passed in 1985 favored deficiency payments over price supports, causing a large increase in the cost of the programs. Consumers benefited from falling prices, but direct cash outlays to farmers shot up. *All* farm bills, it seems, turn out to be more expensive than anticipated. The farm bill that had been in force until 1985 cost almost six times its original $11 billion budget over a period of four years. (Another new farm bill passed in 1990 has succeeded in reducing cash outlays to farmers somewhat, though only from $17 billion in 1989 to $15 billion in 1992.)

Not all the money spent by the government on agricultural support finds its way to farmers. Some of it goes to the cost of administering the programs, storage, collecting taxes, and keeping resources in farming that would find more efficient use elsewhere. For 1985, it has been calculated that U.S. farmers received as transfers of revenue only about three-quarters of the total cost of agricultural support.

Another type of cost comes from the increase in land prices and rental values associated with programs to boost the income of farmers. As farming becomes more rewarding, the price of farmland and its rental value also rise. Economic modeling in the mid-1980s suggested that a $1-billion permanent rise in payments to farmers through various U.S. farm programs raises the average price of an acre of farmland by $15.21.

OUTPUT RESTRICTIONS AND INPUT RESTRICTIONS

In a third type of program to raise farm income, the government restricts either the output of a commodity or the inputs used to produce a commodity. Either way, the intent is to reduce supply. In Figure 5.7, a fall in a commodity's supply will increase price and, therefore, raise farmers' income if the supply change occurs on the inelastic portion of the demand curve. At the original price P_1, farmers earn $0P_1E_1Q_1$. But if supply is restricted to supply curve S_2, then the price rises to P_2 and farmers' income rises to $0P_2E_2Q_2$. (Remember that a higher price will *raise* income if demand is inelastic, but *lower* it if demand is elastic. Demand for farm commodities as a whole is thought to be relatively inelastic because food is a necessity.)

Notice that if supply restriction does succeed in raising the price of a commodity, imports from abroad must also be restricted. Otherwise, additional supplies will flow in as prices rise.

The first modern experiments with output restrictions in the United States took place in the 1930s, when 10 million acres of cotton were plowed under to boost cotton prices and 6 million piglets were killed to raise the price of pork. This happened during the Great Depression, when many thousands of Americans were going to bed hungry every night. Under present output restriction programs, the government assigns production quotas to farmers for crops such as peanuts, tobacco, and sugar. Such quotas are widely used in Canada as well as in the United States.

---

6.   This conclusion is correct if, as is usually the case and as illustrated in the diagrams, short-run supply and demand in agriculture are relatively inelastic. If they are elastic, price supports will be the more costly alternative for the government.

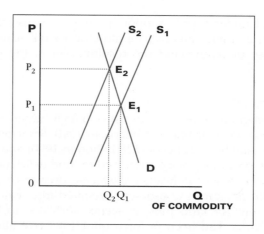

Figure 5.7. A restriction on output. Restrictions on output move the supply curve to the left, raising the equilibrium price.

A variety of costs are incurred in output restriction. First, *cash payments* are made to farmers to persuade them to plow crops under or to slaughter livestock. Second, the decreased supply means that consumers must pay a *higher price* for the commodity, P_2 in Figure 5.7. Third, the country is deprived of the *forgone production*. Fourth, the quotas assigned to the owner of a farm are usually sold when the farm is sold. The value of these quotas is incorporated into *land values and rents*, which are higher as a result. In some cases the quota tickets are the most valuable asset on a farm. In British Columbia, for example, the right to sell the milk from a cow recently cost eight times more than the cow itself, while in Ontario the quota for a 25,000-chicken egg farm cost $580,000 and the quota for 40 acres of tobacco cost $310,000. Finally, the *cost of policing the quotas* is an expense to taxpayers. (The federal officials who supervise the 44,000 U.S. farmers who are licensed to grow peanuts and the interlopers who try to do so illegally have been called the "peanut police.")

Instead of limiting output itself, input quotas can be used to reduce production.[7] For example, the "soil bank" of President Eisenhower's administration limited the supply of grain by paying farmers to take land out of use, and the 1985 farm bill limited the supply of milk by buying out and slaughtering the herds of participating farmers. Both were voluntary programs.

"Acreage set-asides," which call for the removal of land from cultivation, experienced a lively resurgence in the 1980s. The Reagan administration expanded the existing program in an attempt to cut the cost of price supports and deficiency payments. Farmers were paid (in kind, with surplus commodities taken from government storage) to idle their land. The land set aside eventually amounted to 43% of the nation's corn acreage and 35% of its wheat acreage, a total area equal to half of Indiana plus all of Illinois plus all of Iowa. Although land retirement has been scaled back since then, it is still in effect; recently, about one-sixth of all U.S. farmland (61 million acres) was lying idle in response to one government program or another.

Under acreage restriction, the percentage cuts in output are typically less than the percentage cuts in acreage because of a phenomenon called "slippage." Farmers take their poorest land out of production and cultivate their good land more intensively. The strongest proponents of acreage restriction seem to be farmers who choose not to participate in the voluntary programs, but who hope to sell all they can grow at the anticipated higher prices.

GOVERNMENT INTERVENTION IN OTHER COUNTRIES

Other countries have been even more active than the United States in finding expensive ways to intervene in agriculture. Government subsidies, which in 1991 made up 30% of total farmer

---

7. The first restriction on input in North America dates as far back as 1613, when Virginia's colonial government limited tobacco acreage.

income in the United States, comprise 66% of that income in Japan and 49% in the European Community (EC, or Common Market). By contrast, Australia's subsidies are much smaller (15%) while New Zealand's are very low (4%).

Japan

Japan's price-support program creates even greater disequilibrium than the U.S. program. Japanese farms are inefficiently small, with 80% of all farms averaging just three acres in size. For the expensive food produced on these small plots, Japan spends about 20% of its income, well above the 13% of income spent on food in the United States. Because the Japanese government relies more on price supports than on deficiency payments, the cost to consumers accounts for 82% of the cost of the whole program, against a little over a third in the United States. A pound of steak costs over $40 in Japanese supermarkets, and farmers receive some eight or nine times the U.S. price for rice. To protect their price-support programs, the Japanese impose strict limitations on imports. In 1991, for example, officials of a U.S. company were threatened with arrest for illegally importing 10 pounds of rice to exhibit at a trade show. Beef and citrus fruits are also expensive, and both are the subjects of major trade disputes with the United States. Recently, the Japanese government has been paying farmers to limit their output of citrus fruits by uprooting citrus trees from former rice paddies which the government had previously paid farmers to remove from rice production.

The European Community's Common Agricultural Policy

The most expensive intervention of all is that of the European Community, under its so-called **Common Agricultural Policy (CAP)**. Its main tool has been price supports. Until reforms in 1992–1993, neither deficiency payments nor output restrictions were much used. The main protected commodities are wheat, dairy products, beef, wine, and sugar, all of which are much higher in price within the EC than in world trade. Wheat, for example, was recently priced at $225 per metric ton within the EC at a time when the world price was as low as $75. Surpluses are the inevitable result. Over 70% of all the EC's official spending goes to buy and store these surpluses, which are referred to as "mountains." (The wine surplus is called a "lake.") The mountains are enormous and the lake is deep. Their size is shown in Table 5.1.

TABLE 5.1
Size of EC surplus commodity "mountains" and "lakes."

Cereal grains	18 million metric tons (record high)
Beef	0.7 million metric tons (record high)
Butter	0.3 million metric tons
Milk powder	0.3 million metric tons
Wine	80 million liters

Source: EC Commission. The data are for January 1991. The figure for butter has been as high as 1.2 million metric tons in 1987, while wine was 740 million liters in 1988. There is also a "manure mountain" produced by the surplus livestock.

The EC has struggled to rid itself of these huge, unwanted surpluses, and schemes abound for possible uses. About a third of all table wine production is currently being turned into industrial alcohol. Butter has been used for axle grease, in soap, in paint, and as a processed cooking oil. On occasion it has been fed to cows, which then produce more butter. Portions have simply been thrown away, and some has been donated to African famine relief. Mostly, however, the surpluses are exported at subsidized prices that compensate the EC for only a small fraction of its acquisition costs.

The costs to other countries from these subsidized exports are very large. The United States, Canada, Australia, New Zealand, and Argentina have all lost many of their European markets because of slumping exports to the EC and have lost markets elsewhere because of the

EC's own exports of cheap surplus commodities. The EC share of total U.S. agricultural exports was 35% in 1960, but only 22% in 1980. The EC was a net importer of dairy products, sugar, and beef as late as 1974; now it is the world's largest exporter of dairy products, poultry, eggs, and veal. It is number two in beef exports and number three in wheat exports. It now produces about 25% more sugar (from sugar beets, not cane) than it consumes. This makes it the free world's largest exporter of sugar, all subsidized, of course, and deprives poor countries of one of their largest export markets. The CAP, cause of constant bickering with the rest of the world, stands as a monument to the unwillingness of farmers to give up aid and to the willingness of politicians to provide it.

WHAT NEEDS TO BE DONE?

A possible solution to the farm-support dilemma would be for government to provide direct income support to farm families without regard to the level of production. Though seldom employed anywhere in the world, direct income subsidies would be simple and effective. The payment of income supplements could require the phasing out of uneconomical farms and provide recipients with retraining and relocation allowances, thus reversing policies that keep inefficient amounts of labor and capital in farming. Targeting subsidies to those in need would ensure that aid does not go to those who could thrive without it, thereby cutting costs by at least half. Moreover, such subsidies could be used to keep land open around cities and to advance sound conservation practices. There would be no surpluses, no crop restrictions, no price-boosting effects, and the costs to society would be not only lower but clearly visible.

Large Farmers Have the Most to Lose

The prospects for such reform are not bright, however. Large, well-to-do farmers would lobby hard against it. Supports set at levels to keep marginal farmers in business, as they now are, are highly lucrative for the more efficient farmers with the lowest costs. At present, the more farmers produce, the more they receive in benefits. In fact, less than 20% of U.S. farmers get any federal farm subsidies at all because of rules that exclude small, part-time operations and hobby farms.

Though there is a cap of $50,000 on what each farmer can receive in deficiency payments, no limits have been placed on what a farmer can receive in price-support payments, in the dairy program, for acreage set-asides, or in federal subsidies for growing cotton and rice. Even the $50,000 cap can easily be evaded by dividing a farm up among business associates or family members. Administration attempts to lower the cap on deficiency payments to $20,000 and to put a ceiling of $500,000 on price-support payments have been bitterly resisted by the farm lobby and up to now have been defeated. Department of Agriculture statistics reveal that the biggest 1% of U.S. farm producers receive about 30% of all the farm subsidies, with half of that (15%) going to farmers with net worth of over $1 million dollars.

Adding to the irony of this "welfare" going to many who are already rich, the poor spend a greater percentage of their income on food than does anyone else. The schemes that raise price are thus inequitable as well as inefficient. In the mid-1980s the world spent about $185 billion annually to support its farmers. Surely it should get more for its money than an outcome where too many resources are kept in farming. Those resources could be released, if governments were ever to find the courage to do it, for use in other areas where the market reveals that the output is wanted. Once again, the moral is clear: When government has once intervened, backing out may be extremely difficult.

LOW-PRICE POLICIES IN LDC AGRICULTURE

Paradoxically, many of the less-developed countries (LDCs) maintain policies that keep the prices of farm products well *below* the free market price. Higher prices, of course, would increase the food supply in these countries, where food is desperately needed. Why do these countries' governments keep prices below market levels? The policies are usually the result of the political influence of urban workers, who benefit from cheap food. The low prices foisted on farmers by government action, together with the high barriers to imports of farm commodities imposed by rich countries that want to protect their price-support schemes, have served unforgivably to discourage food output in many a hungry land.

REFLECTIONS ON THE THEORY OF PUBLIC CHOICE

The analysis of the various forms of government intervention has come to be known as the "theory of public choice." Why do governments intervene in markets when the consequences so often seem to go counter to the public interest? One answer might be simple ignorance of the consequences. Another might be that intervention improves legislators' chances for reelection.

The political case for government intervention is often very strong. In the case of price supports for farm products, for example, the costs to the public are obscure, but the benefits to farmers are highly visible. Price supports mean that the public must spend a few dollars more per person on bread or milk or peanuts, but they also mean that many farmers receive thousands of dollars in additional income. Thus, the farm lobby reports for duty every time a farm bill comes up for consideration. Meanwhile, the members of the public at large, if they are aware of the bill at all, assume that the cost to each person will be relatively small and, therefore, put up little or no opposition.

Moreover, representation in Congress is not fully proportional to population. A vote in rural North Dakota counts for more than a vote in urban Maryland. Both states elect two members to the Senate, even though North Dakota's population is much smaller than Maryland's. Given the large number of rural states in the South, Midwest, and West, the Senate understandably takes a generous view toward agricultural support. The political strength of farmers makes it possible for committee agendas to be molded in ways that promote agricultural programs, and senators from farm states are sometimes willing to back a bill that will benefit Maryland in return for Maryland's promise not to block a generous farm bill. In other countries, the situation is even more unbalanced. Japan's farm bloc consists of just 5% of the voters, but because of the way voting districts are drawn they have 25% of the voting power in the legislature. Japanese farmers are unprecedentedly powerful in politics.

When government interventions in free markets on balance cause a loss to society, it is usually certain that the interventions continue because they deliver benefits to small and committed groups. Education, public arousal, and voting reform are all possible remedies. Yet dubious government interventions with accompanying inefficiency and high cost remain common, highlighting the difficulties involved in making rational public choices in the political arena.

MINIMUM-WAGE LAWS

Minimum-wage laws are among the most familiar examples of government interference with market equilibrium. Most countries, but not all, have minimum-wage-laws. Among those that do not are Britain, Denmark, Switzerland, and Germany. The first minimum wage in the United States was set at 25¢ per hour in 1938. It rose gradually over the years and from 1981 to 1990 it stood at $3.35 per hour. On April 1, 1991 it was raised to $4.25 per hour. (In the United States, the states are permitted to set a minimum wage higher than the federal minimum if they so desire. Currently, 12 states have done so.)

Hardly any issue in microeconomics has been more hotly debated. Democrats usually favor minimum-wage increases as a way of aiding poor workers. Republicans argue that increases cause unemployment and inflation. (Polls usually report that three-quarters or more of the public favors an increase.) Economists typically view the alleged benefits of the minimum wage as questionable and its alleged costs as exaggerated. These positions can be explored to advantage with the use of demand and supply curves for labor.

A CRITIQUE OF MINIMUM-WAGE LAWS

Let us first criticize the position that raising the minimum wage will help those in poverty to a better life. The first objection is that, of the 5 million or so minimum-wage recipients in the United States, only about 15% are poor as defined by the federal government. Eighty-five percent belong to families that earn more than the federally defined poverty-level income, and 70% belong to families that earn half again more than that level. Many of the recipients are middle-class young people; about two-thirds of the recipients are under 24 years of age, and more than half of these are teenagers. Spouses supplementing the earnings of a major breadwinner make up another important group. Most recipients of the minimum wage work only part-time, with only one-third working full-time—the part-timers are not usually trying to subsist on the minimum wage alone.

Even the working poor would not be assisted if an increase in the minimum wage cost them their jobs. Consider the demand and supply analysis in Figure 5.8. When the minimum wage is set *below* the market wage actually being paid in an occupation (W_e), then the legislation will have no effect on wages. If the mandated minimum is *above* the market wage, however, the case is different.

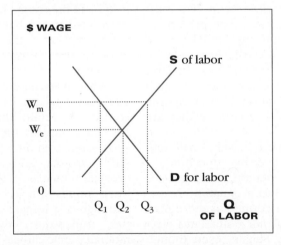

Figure 5.8. **A minimum wage.** Because a minimum wage establishes a floor above the equilibrium, some employers will choose to lay off some of their now more expensive workers. The more elastic the curves, the greater the problem.

The total number of workers who manage to find jobs at the minimum wage W_m is Q_1. But if the minimum wage were not in effect, the total number who would find employment would be Q_2. In response to the minimum wage, employers tend to substitute machines and other productive factors for the higher-priced labor, which causes the fall in the quantity of workers demanded. The more elastic the demand for labor, the greater this substitution will be. Indeed, we would expect the demand curve to become more elastic over time as employers make adjustments that were not open to them in the short run. Moreover, the higher wage attracts additional workers who want jobs in this occupation, so quantity supplied rises from Q_2 to Q_3. At wage W_m, therefore, a quantity of labor Q_1Q_3 will seek jobs but will not find them.

This effect will be especially apparent among teenagers, minority groups, and retirees who want to supplement their incomes. These groups, which are heavily represented among workers earning the minimum wage, are often regarded as marginal by employers and are the first to be laid off when labor costs are cut. (Minorities and the elderly are, of course, protected by anti-discrimination laws, but to avoid any impact on their employment these laws would have to work with complete success.) The minimum-wage law is obviously of little help to the teenagers who cannot find jobs because wages have been boosted. In fact, the unemployment rate for teenagers is usually about double the national average, while the unemployment rate for black teenagers is about four or five times the national average.

Evidence on the Effect of Minimum-Wage Laws

According to recent studies, teenage employment falls by 1 to 3% following a 10% increase in the minimum wage. Moreover, discouraged teens unable to find jobs frequently abandon their search for work.

A study by the National Bureau of Economic Research covering the years 1973–1978 suggests unemployment would have been 4% lower in the age group 16–24 and 7% lower in the age group 16–19, if no minimum wage had been in force.[8] The NBER study points out that the most important loss might not be the unearned wages, but instead the loss of job skills that would have been acquired through on-the-job training. These skills are believed by many economists to be the key to higher income in the future. The study did, however, cast doubt on one often-argued business objection to the minimum wage: it found no identifiable tendency for wages already higher than the minimum to be pushed up by a modest increase in that minimum. (This point is controversial, however.) Another NBER study states that after the 1980–1981 minimum-wage increases, affected workers whose wages were above the old minimum but below the new one were 3% to 4% more likely to be unemployed after one year than were other workers. In Canada, where each province sets its own minimum wage, the pattern is similar, according to a recent report from the Economic Council of Canada. In particular, young and uneducated workers find fewer job opportunities as the minimum wage rises.

THE MINIMUM WAGE AND BLACK FARM HANDS IN THE RURAL SOUTH

When the federal minimum wage was extended to agricultural labor in 1967, thousands of blacks in the South lost their jobs as hired farm hands. Employers faced with the new $1.15 per *hour* minimum wage had been accustomed to hiring blacks for $3.00 per *day*. The poverty of these farm hands and their families was clearly a national disgrace, but attacking it by means of a minimum-wage law caused damage to them, which was clearly not the intent of the law. Employers chose to use chemical herbicides rather than to continue their large-scale hiring of labor for hand-weeding. This dislocation of labor fueled the last great migration of blacks from the South to the inner cities of the North.[9]

---

8.   See Charles Brown, Curtis Gilroy, and Andrew Kohen, "The Effect of the Minimum Wage on Employment and Unemployment," *Journal of Economic Literature*, Vol. 22, June 1982, pp. 487–528. Employment would be more affected by changes in the minimum wage if wages were the only way in which labor is compensated. Fringe benefits such as rest periods, flexibility in hours, training on the job, and company discounts for employees are also part of compensation. If minimum wages rise, such fringe benefits might be cut back in response, so that total compensation is less affected or perhaps not affected at all.

9.   See Nicholas Lemann, *The Promised Land: The Great Black Migration and How It Changed America*, New York, 1991, p. 287.

Ideas for Reform

Several attempts have been made to eliminate the side effects of minimum-wage legislation on young people. The Dutch government was one of the first to act, forced to because the minimum wage in the Netherlands is pegged at about 70% of the average wage earned in that country, one of the world's highest. The effects on youths have been particularly severe. Acting on the belief that the high minimum was harmful to young people, the Dutch government has lowered it for workers under the age of 23. For every year below that age, the minimum is reduced by 15%. Following the introduction of the "youth minimum," unemployment among young people declined. Several other European countries have also adopted a youth differential.

In the United States, youth sub-minimum wages have been difficult to adopt. Possibly the inaction has been due to the argument that a lower youth minimum might lead to problems among very low-skill adult workers, who might be replaced with lower-cost teenagers if a youth minimum were in effect. Finally, in April, 1991 a youth training wage of $3.61 per hour for young people between the ages of 16 and 19 was adopted for their first six months of work.

Economists have attempted to model how much more employment would be created for young workers by a more comprehensive U.S. youth minimum. One study from the Federal Reserve Bank of Chicago suggests that a 25% cut in the minimum wage would raise teenage employment by 14%.

DAMAGE MIGHT BE LIMITED

All the above has been critical of minimum wages. However, there is another side to the coin. A moderate increase of a dollar or so in the U.S. minimum under present conditions, with only 4% of all employees receiving it, is likely to have far more limited effects than would have been true in 1980 when the figure was 11%. With equilibrium wages in most occupations and most areas well above $4.25 per hour, damaging consequences of a rise would be constrained. This is especially true of high-wage areas such as cities or the Northeast. There a further limited rise in the minimum wage, say to the $4.75 per hour recommended by Secretary of Labor Robert Reich, would probably have only marginal effects. The consequences in lower-wage regions (the South, rural areas generally) would likely be more severe. For example, it is believed that the effect of minimum-wage increases on employment is particularly strong in low-wage Puerto Rico.

More general damage would probably flow from a much larger increase, say to $6 or above. The combination of unemployment and the rise in prices in the economy as business costs increase would then be more severe, while the results of a $10 or $20 minimum could be economically catastrophic. The continuing debate concerning a limited 50¢ or $1.00 per hour rise is, to the contrary, more political than economic. Neither the costs nor the benefits are likely to be nearly as great as the politicians in either camp would have it.

Public support for increased minimum wages still seems high, with the lack of opposition probably explained by the failure of those who lose their jobs because of an increase to identify minimum wages as the cause of their unemployment. (Even if they *did* identify the cause, those who earn only the minimum wage have little political clout.) Others charge that economists who criticize the minimum wage are insensitive to the plight of the poor. As in any group, perhaps some are, but many others would reply that if poverty is to be attacked by government, it ought to be done in a manner that will not result in the loss of jobs. Specifically, altering the Social Security payroll tax so that it does not take so much from the pockets of the poor would serve well in this regard. (Other measures such as income transfers and tax credits to low-income workers would avoid the boost in labor costs caused by minimum wages and would not cause the job losses associated with minimum wage increases. They would, however, introduce other market interferences with distortions of their own that would have to be examined with care.) Yet the debate over the minimum wage continues, a clear victory of political symbolism over economic rationality.

In each case discussed thus far in this chapter, government intervention in the market may be more or less justified by social welfare considerations. The point is not that such intervention should be avoided. It is instead that whenever such intervention is undertaken, we can be reasonably certain that shortages will develop when prices are fixed below equilibrium, surpluses will occur when the fixed price is above equilibrium, and in either case, allocative inefficiency will appear. Some interventions are necessary, but it is the responsibility of economists to make clear all of the consequences, costs as well as benefits, that can be identified.

► HEALTH CARE

We have left for last the hybrid case of health care. This subject, too, is a study of government intervention, made directly in some countries, but mostly indirectly through the tax laws in the United States. Currently, the economics of health care is surrounded by anticipation, as the United States debates what to do with its system. The reform of the U.S. health care system is likely to be in the spotlight for some time to come.

Government intervention in the delivery of health care represents a huge retreat from free-market pricing in what is literally a vital sector of the economy. As late as 1960, people in the United States were still paying about 60% of all their health care expenditures directly for services rendered, but by 1989 the figure had fallen to under 25%. The government, either by granting tax breaks to private insurance companies or by direct financing from taxation, has assumed wide responsibility for health care. We can use the tools of demand and supply to analyze the effects of that policy and suggest why the problems have grown so vast.

Few doubt that the cost of medical care in a developed country would be high no matter what policies the government adopted. The demand for health services is both price-inelastic and income-elastic. On the supply side, health care is costly because it calls for a large input of highly skilled labor from doctors and nurses and because many sophisticated techniques performed with expensive equipment have come into widespread use, such as dialysis machines, CAT-scanners, and organ transplants. The high costs are reflected in the prices charged to patients.

Because the expenses associated with the treatment of a major illness are now simply too great to be borne individually except by the rich, government involvement in health care is the norm in the developed countries. Worldwide, three systems are currently in use:

1) Health insurance is provided, mostly by employers, perhaps supplemented by insurance from private companies. The government encourages individuals to buy private insurance by exempting part of the cost (the employers' share of health insurance is not counted as part of the employees' taxable income). Government insures the elderly and the poor directly. Doctors and hospitals are left in the private sector. This is the mostly private system that up to now has prevailed in the United States.

2) Health care for all is provided by the government and is financed through taxation. Doctors are government employees and hospitals are public. (People are free to make their own arrangements with doctors in the small private sector if they can afford to do so.) This is the system followed by Great Britain, with its National Health Service; Sweden and Italy have somewhat similar systems. The U.S. Veteran's Administration operates along the same lines.

3) The government provides health care financed by taxes and/or requires people to buy insurance from regulated semipublic insurance funds. Doctors and hospitals are private. A variation on this scheme was instituted over a hundred years ago by Bismarck in Germany, and other variations are now employed by Canada, France, the Netherlands, and Japan.

THE U.S. SYSTEM OF HEALTH CARE

The U.S. system of health care is currently undergoing critical scrutiny, and persistent pressure for reform has arisen. Its shortcomings are severe. For one, not everybody is insured. Perhaps 37 million people, about 14% of the population, are not insured at all. Many of them are low-income but not poor people who cannot afford private insurance and work for small employers who do not provide insurance. Also included are people with chronic conditions such as high blood pressure, whom insurance companies often refuse to insure. The companies are trying to avoid what is known as **adverse selection**, the idea that those who are already ill or run the greatest risk of becoming so will have the greatest desire to buy insurance. Yet people who, for whatever reason, are without health insurance may face financial catastrophe if they become ill. No other developed country tolerates such a deficiency in its health care system.

A second shortcoming is the extraordinary cost of health care in the United States. From 1960 to 1990, spending on health care rose by a factor of 23.6, while spending for all purposes rose by a factor of only 9.6. As Table 5.2 shows, spending on health care as a percentage of the nation's total spending is considerably higher than it is in other developed countries.

TABLE 5.2

Spending on health care as a percent of total spending, 1989, and in dollars spent annually per capita, 1990.

Country	% of Spending	$ per capita	Country	% of Spending	$ per capita
United States	11.8	2,566	Germany	8.2	1,287
Canada	8.7	1,795	Japan	6.7	1,113
France	8.7	1,379	Britain	5.8	909

Source: The Economist, July 6, 1991, and the *Wall Street Journal,* January 20, 1993. Total spending is defined as gross domestic product (see Chapter 15 for details).

In 1990 the U.S. percentage reached 12.4%; by 1992 it was over 13%; without reform, the figure could reach 20% within a few years, over twice as much as in any other country. The ever-higher costs of private insurance drive it out of reach for some. Employers, who usually pay part of the insurance costs, find their outlays mounting rapidly. Often they prefer to hire part-time employees who do not qualify for full benefits, or they ask current employees to work overtime rather than hiring new ones. Job shifting is discouraged because it is too risky to give up your present insurance while you look for other employment.

Reasons for the High Cost of Health Care in the United States

Ironically, one of the major reasons for the high cost of health care in the United States is that the availability of private insurance and of the government's Medicare and Medicaid plans has fostered the idea among both patients and providers of care that the cost of treatment is low. Because the bills are mostly paid by insurance of one kind or another, there has been little concern about costs. Neither doctors, hospitals, nor patients have had to worry about the cost of each unit of care or the total quantity of care delivered. The costs could be largely passed on to a third party such as an insurance company or the government. This is an example of what is called the **moral hazard** of insurance—someone else is paying the bills, so people with insurance may as well demand whatever treatment that will possibly do any good.

The situation is explored in Figure 5.9. If patients had to pay the equilibrium price P_e for care, they would demand the quantity of treatment Q_e. But if third parties such as private insurance companies and the government pay most of the bills, so that patients pay only P_1 out of their own pockets for treatment, then the quantity of care they demand will increase to Q_1. That quantity is much higher than if patients were bearing some of the costs themselves. (For an example of the results, there are 3.3 very expensive open-heart surgical units per million people in the United States, compared to 1.2 in Canada and 0.7 in Germany where different systems are in operation.)

Because so much care is demanded, the cost of supplying it is driven up, in the figure to C_1. This is the amount that suppliers of treatment have to receive in order to provide a quantity Q_1. The benefits of the additional care may be very low compared to the additional cost, but doctors and hospitals will urge and dutifully deliver the treatment, knowing they will be reimbursed, and patients will choose it because it appears to be low in cost.

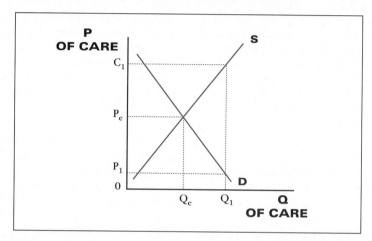

Figure 5.9. Why the cost of health care is high. If those with insurance find that their own out-of-pocket health care costs are small, then these people will demand a high quantity Q_1 rather than the lower quantity Q_e if they had to make all the payments themselves. Because so much care is demanded, the cost of the care is boosted to C_1 on the diagram.

For a long time the public tended to ignore the increasing national burden of cost. The increase in private insurance premiums and the rise in taxes to finance Medicare and Medicaid were so attenuated by the large numbers making the payments that they were hardly noticed. In any case, those costs usually do not become visible until sometime in the future and are not connected with any individual decision on what care should be provided.

Despite the steadily rising cost of health care in the United States, the nation's health ranking is not impressive. The U.S. population has lower life expectancy than four of the countries shown in Table 5.2 and is no healthier on other measures. This is due in part to the large number of people who lack health insurance and in part to the low benefits accruing from the additional care delivered.

In recent years, the trend has been to make patients responsible for more of their costs. Nowadays, private insurance companies usually build a per-year or per-sickness deductible clause into their policies which requires patients to pay a certain sum or a certain percentage of the bill up to some fixed limit. The spread of Health Maintenance Organizations (HMOs), staffed by physicians who are compensated by an annual membership fee, has also helped to curtail the rise in physicians' costs. But these reforms have merely slowed the acceleration in health care costs and have done nothing for the millions of people who lack health insurance of any kind.

HEALTH CARE ABROAD

Several other countries have instituted health care systems that provide universal coverage, keep costs under control, and yet seem to leave voters reasonably satisfied. Under Great Britain's National Health Service, everyone is eligible for coverage, and charges to patients are either nonexistent or very low. During its early years, spending was open-ended, but since 1949 the NHS has kept costs down by adopting fixed annual budgets that imply a kind of rationing. For example, patients seeking nonemergency treatment face long waiting periods, and certain treatments—including dialysis for elderly patients, expensive treatment for infertility, and plastic surgery— are unavailable from the NHS. Moreover, hospital expenditures for maintenance and new equipment are strictly policed. These constraints are the trade-off for universal coverage and low cost.[10] The NHS is nonetheless very popular among the British, and even conservative Margaret Thatcher mounted no major attack on it.

Canada's tax-financed national health plan, which dates back to 1971, allows people free choice of doctors and hospitals, which remain in the private sector. The government pays the bills from tax revenues. The Canadian plan has attracted much U.S. attention because it provides health care to the entire population at a per-person cost much lower than in the United States. One limit on outlays is that, as in Britain, hospitals are required to operate on fixed annual budgets, which has brought some delays in treatment and some shortages of equipment. Another reason for the lower costs is that administrative overhead is carefully controlled. Fewer people are needed to cope with the paperwork and form-filling that plague the U.S. system. According to one study, only 11¢ of every Canadian health care dollar goes for administrative expenses, compared to 24¢ in the United States. Polls indicate a high level of public satisfaction with the Canadian plan.

In Germany's health care system, everyone under a certain income level (recently $41,000) must buy, and most others do buy, insurance from one of many private "sickness funds." The premium, half of which is paid by employers, is the same percentage of income (13%) for everyone, so the better off, in effect, subsidize the poor. Premiums for the jobless are paid as part of unemployment compensation. The government requires that a national budget for health care be set annually through negotiations among the sickness funds, doctors, and hospitals. Costs are kept under control and coverage is practically universal.

THE CLINTON HEALTH CARE PLAN

It seems inevitable that the U.S. health care system will soon undergo major changes. In his first week in office, President Clinton named his wife Hillary to chair a committee tasked with proposing a solution, and the committee reported in mid-1993. The primary elements in the Clinton plan are as follows: (1) The entire population would be covered; you would still be insured if you lose your job or change jobs. There would be no risk rating or exclusions, insurers and providers would have to charge the same fee for everyone, and by the start of 1995 health insurance would involve a single standardized form. (2) Large networks of buyers of health insurance, including firms, HMOs, insurance companies, and individuals, would band together in

---

10.   Sweden, a richer country than Britain, also rations hospital services. There the waiting period for elective surgery is long. In the United States, the state of Oregon's new Medicaid plan is also tantamount to rationing. That plan will rank treatments according to their effectiveness and will exclude from coverage those below a certain cutoff figure for effectiveness. The Bush administration blocked the implementation of this plan, but the Clinton administration has allowed it to go forward.

regional health alliances to buy care from hospital and doctor groups. Because of their size, these alliances would have bargaining strength in terms of price and quality that only big companies currently have. (Firms with more than 5,000 workers would be free to do their own bargaining, much as they are now.) This idea is called "managed competition." (3) Employers would be required to pay for 80% of the health insurance for their workers and dependents. (4) The government would cover the health care costs of the jobless and would subsidize the insurance of the employees of small businesses that could not afford to pay for the coverage.

How to finance the increased costs under the plan was still very much up in the air at the time of writing. A "sin tax" on cigarettes and alcohol was a possibility. To hold down costs, the Clinton plan involves caps on insurance premiums, in effect requiring an overall national budget for health care somewhat resembling the cost controls in Canada and Germany. If spending runs up against the caps, they would have to be raised (requiring the small-business subsidy to rise), or the government would have to pay the bill (so budget deficit would rise or taxes would have to be raised), or controls on services delivered would have to be imposed, or doctor and hospital income would have to be reduced. These cost difficulties have led to several competing proposals that do not cover the population completely but which would be less costly. Whatever compromise emerges is likely to be a pioneering idea with no close parallel in other countries.

HIGH COSTS WILL SURELY PERSIST

It is obvious that passage of this or any plan will be contentious. Whatever the course of reform, however, the cost problem is likely to persist. For one reason, the population of the United States is aging, and medical spending on people over the age of 65 is 4.2 times greater than it is for those under 65. Another reason is that continuing advances in medical technology will inevitably bring higher costs. Some procedures are likely to result in economies, but many others will represent new forms of treatment that simply were not possible before. The much higher spending on them will be a net addition to health care costs.

▶ CONCLUSION

In this chapter we have used the concepts of demand, supply, elasticity, surplus, shortage, and allocative inefficiency to analyze a wide variety of government interferences with free-market equilibrium. Such interference usually creates either a surplus or a shortage, together with some degree of allocative inefficiency.

But to those who proposed the intervention in the first place, the benefits of the action must have seemed greater than the costs. Whether the effects of the intervention outweigh the resulting inefficiency is a question that must be resolved by the political system. Such decisions should be taken with full awareness of the consequences, and with the understanding that intervention, once undertaken, creates vested interests and is hard to reverse. The mechanism of demand and supply is extremely useful for analyzing such questions.

SUMMARY

1) Price controls are justified in grave emergencies, for few would agree to see people starve and go unclothed while the wealthy continue to eat and dress well. But side effects from price controls are likely, including shortages, queues, allocative inefficiency, and black markets. Possibly a system of rationing will be needed to distribute scarce goods. It is difficult to judge exactly how serious an emergency must be before price controls bring more benefits to society than costs.

2) Rent controls that put a maximum on the rental price of apartments will typically increase the quantity of housing that people demand while decreasing the quantity supplied, and so create a housing shortage.

3) Taxi fares are often regulated, and some cities limit the number of cabs permitted to take to the road. Together, these two restrictions often make it difficult to find a cab.

4) The three main ways to aid farmers are price supports, deficiency payments, and supply restrictions. Price supports cause a surplus of commodities to develop, deficiency payments are expensive, while supply restriction typically has to be enforced by means of quotas that require policing. Price supports are especially disruptive to world markets because the surplus is often exported for what the market will bear.

5) Minimum-wage laws are widely supported by the public, but they carry the risk that a wage higher than equilibrium will cause unemployment. Increases in the minimum may cause employers to hire less labor and utilize more capital.

6) Health care is a major economic problem for the United States today. The U.S. system is insurance-based, but large numbers of people do not have insurance. Built-in circumstances have caused the bill for health care to rise in an extraordinary way. A great debate is currently underway on President Clinton's proposals for a change in the system.

Chapter Key Words

Adverse selection: Characteristic of the market for insurance. Sick people will be more eager to buy health insurance than will those who are well, while insurance companies will be less eager to insure them.

Black market: An illegal market in which goods are sold above the official price ceiling during a period of government price control.

Common Agricultural Policy (CAP): The program within the European Community to boost farmers' incomes mainly by means of price supports. Because the surpluses acquired as a part of the CAP have been dumped on world markets, they have disrupted world trade.

Deficiency payments: A government program to raise farmers' incomes by making payments to them on the basis of how much they produce.

Moral hazard: Characteristic of the market for insurance. One example is that because the insurance company is paying the bills, those with health insurance will want all the treatment that will possibly do them any good.

Price controls: For various reasons, including fairness for lower-income groups, governments may impose a legal price ceiling below the equilibrium price. Will usually result in shortages.

Price supports: A government program to raise farmers' incomes by purchase of some of their crop. Results in surplus stocks.

Queues: The lines that form outside shops and stores when price controls create shortages.

Rationing: Government action to restrict demand during a period of price control.

Chapter Questions

1) You live in a coastal city and a hurricane has just passed through. Trees are down everywhere, and demand for chain saws is suddenly very high. The market equilibrium price would be $600 per saw. However, the authorities impose a price ceiling of $300, and at that price sellers supply only a few saws. A fallen tree has blocked your driveway, and you calculate that the cost to you of not being able to get out is $1200. Why would you object to the price control?

2) You are still the homeowner from Question 1. After fuming at the authorities to no avail, you hear from a friend that chain saws are being sold out of the back of a pickup truck for $500 apiece. How is it that there are not only chain saws available, but at less than the $600 market clearing price? Chain saws are being sold out of pickups in other cities nearby. Can you be sure that the price elsewhere will be less than $600 as well?

3) You move to a city with rent controls. It takes you a month to find an apartment, and when you do you have to buy some old living room furniture from your landlord. Your view across the street is an ugly abandoned apartment building. Yet in the next election, you vote to continue rent controls. Explain all these experiences.

4) Carefully draw the supply curve for taxi rides in Boston under the medallion system. Draw the demand curve and show the equilibrium price. If Boston successfully increased the number of medallions, how would the supply curve change? What would be the new equilibrium price? Show what would happen if Boston completely deregulated the taxicab market.

5) The market clearing price of corn is $3.50 per bushel. The government decides the price should be $4.00 per bushel. It can choose to raise the price through price supports, deficiency payments, or output quotas. If you were a corn farmer, would you prefer some methods of raising prices to others? What if you were a consumer and you were worried only about the price you pay for corn? Show your reasoning with diagrams.

6) You are a black teenager working at a fast-food franchise in South Philadelphia. Why aren't you thrilled with the possibility of an increase in the state of Pennsylvania minimum wage?

7) A friend of yours was self-employed, and she was so healthy that she never bothered to purchase health insurance. A month ago she started working at a large corporation that provides employee health insurance. All of a sudden she has to go to the doctor very often. Explain your friend's behavior and give the name of this phenomenon. How does it relate to the U.S. health care crisis?

Revenues and Costs of the Firm

And the
Case of
Perfect
Competition

OVERALL OBJECTIVE: Overall objective: To analyze the revenues and costs of the firm, and then show how a perfectly competitive firm would use this information to determine its quantity of output.

MORE SPECIFICALLY:

■ To show that a firm's total revenue is found by multiplying the quantity it produces times the price at which the production is sold, while its marginal revenue is the extra revenue obtained from the sale of another unit of output.

■ To discuss how economists define costs as opportunity costs, and demonstrate how super-normal profit is the difference between total revenue and total (opportunity) cost.

■ To explore costs in the short run and long run, explain the meaning of fixed and variable costs, investigate total, average, and marginal costs, and draw curves for these.

■ To show how concepts such as the division of labor, economies of scale, and diseconomies of scale affect cost curves.

■ To investigate the form of industrial organization called perfect competition, establishing the necessary assumptions that underlie it, discussing why such firms will produce where price and, therefore, marginal revenue equal marginal cost, and establishing that a firm's marginal cost curve is its supply curve.

■ To trace how perfectly competitive firms that want to maximize profits will react to changing prices, raising the quantity they produce as price rises and lowering it as price declines; how some firms will enter or exit the industry in the presence of profits or losses; and why economists frequently utilize the system of perfect competition as a benchmark against which to measure other forms of market organization.

We have seen that the price mechanism works as a signaling device. Producers use prices to determine the costs of the factors of production, the revenue they will receive from selling their product, and the profit they will earn on the transaction. How producers react to price signals is a central topic of microeconomics. Their reactions depend on how an industry is organized, in particular on the degree of competition that is present. We could, for example, construct a model of a market in which just one producing firm is responsible for the total supply produced by an entire industry. Alternatively, we could construct a model in which only a small number of firms are responsible for the industry's total output. Finally, we could model a situation where an industry's output is produced by a very large number of firms in constant competition with each other.

In each of these forms of industrial organization, a primary question is what price a firm would charge and the quantity of output that it would produce if it wants to maximize its profits. As we shall see, the analysis of profit maximization differs depending on the degree of competition within an industry. But whether this is intense or completely absent, two elements in the analysis are the same. A firm will need to know its *total revenue* at various quantities of production and the *total costs* associated with those quantities in order to determine its resulting *total profit,* according to the formula that links these, $TR - TC = TP_r$. In this chapter we turn first to the calculation of revenue, and then to the costs of production. Our findings will help us to determine the behavior of firms in any type of industry, whether the degree of competition is intense, weak, or nonexistent. In the second half of this chapter, we apply our knowledge of revenues and costs to industries with a very high degree of competition. (We shall call such industries "perfectly competitive.") In the two subsequent chapters, we do the same for the industries, called "imperfectly competitive," where the degree of competition among firms is not so great.

▶ REVENUE FROM PRODUCTION

Knowledge of the revenue a firm earns from its production is, along with its costs, essential for calculating the firm's total profit. Revenue is therefore a key element in determining what quantity a firm will decide to produce.

TOTAL REVENUE

A firm's total revenue from its production is essentially simple to calculate, as we saw in Chapter 2. We need to know the price of a product (P_p) and the quantity sold of that product (Q_p). The result of multiplying the two is the total revenue (TR) of that firm; $TR = Q_p \times P_p$. If 50 units of an item are sold at a price of $2.00 each, the total revenue earned is $100.

In Chapter 3, we learned how to picture this by using the firm's demand curve and some simple geometry. Panel **a** of Figure 6.1 shows a quantity of 50 units and a price of $2 each. Multiplying 50 × $2 involves multiplying the horizontal side of a rectangle by the vertical side. The total revenue of 50 × $2 = $100 is therefore equal to the area of the shaded rectangle in the figure.

Perhaps the demand curve is not downward-sloping, as in panel **b**. Here we see the horizontal (perfectly elastic) demand curve of a single small producer among many—a perfect competitor. Remember Farmer Robinson from Chapter 3? His portion of the U.S. corn crop was so insignificant that his sales of corn have no effect on the market price. The demand curve facing him indicates he could sell any quantity at $2 per bushel, but nothing at all if he raised his price even by just a little. This makes no difference for the calculation and viewing of total revenue. Robinson sells 50 bushels at $2 each, so total revenue is 50 × $2 = $100, and the resulting rectangle has an area equal to $100.

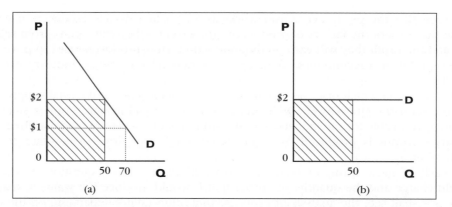

Figure 6.1. Calculating total revenue. The calculation of total revenue involves multiplying the price times the quantity sold. Total revenue is thus seen as a shaded rectangle in the figure. For the calculation, it does not matter if the firm is a perfect competitor, as in panel **b**, or whether it is not, as in panel **a**. The calculation is the same.

MARGINAL REVENUE

For tracing the behavior of a firm, it is important to know how its total revenue changes as it chooses to sell different quantities. This information involves another measure of revenue, the marginal revenue of a firm. **Marginal revenue (MR)** *is the addition to total revenue resulting from the sale of an extra unit of output.*

The slope of the demand curve makes quite a difference for calculating a firm's marginal revenue. Look at the two panels of Figure 6.1 to see how this is so. When a firm is a perfect competitor, as in panel **b**, marginal revenue is easy to determine. Each additional unit sold always brings extra revenue that is exactly the same as the price of the good. Another item sold for $2 brings additional revenue of $2 to the competitive firm. The marginal revenue is constant, identical to the constant price.

A firm that is an imperfect competitor differs from a perfectly competitive firm in a critical way. The demand curve facing it is downward-sloping as in panel **a**, indicating that its decisions to change the quantity it sells do affect the price of its product. If an imperfect competitor raises its output, the price will fall. The firm is big enough so that it has to cut its price to persuade consumers to buy a greater quantity of its output. See in panel **a** how an increase in sales from 50 to 70 required a cut in prices from $2 to $1 per unit. That means the firm's marginal revenue cannot be the same as price, as was true of a perfect competitor. Extra units sold cause the price to fall; the additional revenue earned from selling another unit will be *less* than the original price.

When we examine perfect and imperfect competition in detail, later in this chapter and in the next, we will make considerable use of the concept of marginal revenue. For a perfect competitor we have seen that marginal revenue is the same as the selling price. When a firm is not a perfect competitor, its marginal revenue will be less than its selling price. In the next chapter, we will show in detail how to calculate the marginal revenue of an imperfect competitor.

▶ COSTS OF PRODUCTION

We now turn to the costs of production, for without knowledge of costs as well as revenues, it will be impossible to determine whether it is profitable to produce something. We saw as early as Chapter 1 that there is a great difference between the concept of cost as usually understood by the public and as understood by economists. In measuring cost, economists include more than the actual cash outlays incurred during production. This broader definition of costs is essential to obtain a correct measurement of total profits.

Cash outlays, which people commonly think of as costs, are an important component of total cost and must be carefully recorded. Accountants will usually find it easy to keep a record of wages and salaries for workers, outlays for raw materials and power, and spending on buildings, machines, insurance, business taxes, and the like. Once these cash outlays are subtracted from the firm's revenue, what is left over is the firm's *accounting profit*.

But what if the owners of the firm spend many evenings and weekends working but without drawing a salary for their efforts? Because they could have spent their time working for some other firm that would have paid them, they are sacrificing income by doing the work without pay. The *implicit wage* they could have earned by working elsewhere for pay is not an actual cash outlay, but it is an opportunity cost of production that must be subtracted from total revenues in order to find the true level of profit.

Other opportunity costs must also be considered. Everyone would agree that if a firm rents its buildings and land from others, the rental payments are part of the firm's costs. What if the firm *owns* the buildings and land where it conducts its business? It might rent them to some other firm. The rent forgone by the decision to use the buildings and land is also a sacrifice, an opportunity cost that must be subtracted from total revenues.

The firm's own financial capital invested in the operation also involves an opportunity cost. The funds tied up in the business could be put to some alternative use, placed perhaps in a money-market savings account or government bond where they would earn interest. The *implicit interest* on those funds also must be recognized as an opportunity cost. Finally, the entrepreneurial services contributed by the owners of the company—initiating projects, organizing them, and bearing the risk of failure—also involve an opportunity cost. The return to entrepreneurship is profit. The owners could have obtained earnings for their entrepreneurial efforts in some other occupation. There must be some minimal amount of return they would have to receive, or else they would liquidate the company and take their services elsewhere. Also, the investors would have to be paid some minimum return to keep their money invested in the company.

The minimal return just sufficient to keep the entrepreneurs with the business is an opportunity cost to the firm. Economists call this opportunity cost of entrepreneurship **normal profit.** Only after all costs including this necessary minimum return to entrepreneurship are subtracted from revenues do we find the **super-normal profit** that economists mean when they use the word "profit."[1] Frequently, the term "economic rent" is used as a synonym, for reasons to be explored in Chapter 12. Henceforth, whenever costs are referred to in this book the word will mean opportunity costs, including both actual cash outlays and the noncash implicit costs of not employing factors in their best alternative use. The accompanying box summarizes the discussion.

"COSTS" AS DEFINED BY ECONOMISTS ARE OPPORTUNITY COSTS

Total revenue
- All explicit (cash) costs of production
= "Accounting profit"
- All additional implicit (noncash) opportunity costs (including normal profit)
= Super-normal profit (also called economic rent)

1.　　　Other names sometimes encountered are abnormal, economic, pure, excess, or real profit. It is fair to point out that many aspects of opportunity cost have become widely accepted among accountants, whose notions of accounting profit are in a number of applications now much closer to super-normal profit than they used to be.

Now we must ask what happens to the costs of production when the firm expands or contracts its output. To answer that question, we must introduce time into the discussion. The behavior of costs will be different depending on whether the firm has sufficient time to increase or decrease the size of its factory and other production facilities.

SHORT-RUN COSTS

Economists define the *short run* as a period during which at least one factor of production is fixed in amount. (Often this factor is capital, especially the size of the factory or other production facility and the amount of the machinery and other equipment. It might, however, be any other factor that cannot be easily adjusted, such as farmland.) The firm can alter its output even with one factor fixed—say the size of the factory—by making more or less intensive use of its machinery, by changing the number of workers it employs, or by altering the input of fuel and raw materials. The short run is by no means the same period of time for all industries. A producer of cement, for example, may find it relatively easy to build a bigger plant and to add equipment, so that the short run might be only a few months. A shipping firm operating supertankers might find that its short-run period is several years if it has to build a new one—tankers take a long time to construct.

Fixed, Variable, and Total Costs

In the short run with plant size held fixed, the firm encounters two types of costs. Some costs are incurred even when a plant is standing idle and will remain the same when the plant is producing large quantities of output. These **fixed costs** do not depend on the amount produced. They include rent or, if the firm owns its plant, funds to cover depreciation and eventual replacement. Other fixed costs are insurance on the buildings, costs of maintenance and security, interest on outstanding loans, property taxes, and the salaries of managerial personnel under long-term contract. They also include the various opportunity costs we mentioned previously, such as the return that could have been earned by using the firm's funds elsewhere, renting to others the land and buildings owned by the firm, and the normal profit needed to retain entrepreneurial talent.

Table 6.1 lists total fixed costs, assumed here to be $100, in column 2. These fixed costs do not vary with the quantity produced.

TABLE 6.1
Short-run costs of the firm.

(1) Quantity Produced	(2) Total Fixed Costs TFC	(3) Total Variable Costs TVC	(4) Total Costs TC = TFC + TVC
0	$100	$0	$100
1	100	25	125
2	100	50	150
3	100	75	175
4	100	100	200
5	100	125	225
6	100	150	250
7	100	175	275
8	100	200	300
9	100	225	325
10	100	250	350
11	100	275	375
12	100	300	400

Figure 6.2 diagrams total fixed cost (TFC) as a horizontal line at $100. It is unaffected by the level of output.

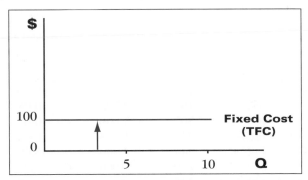

Figure 6.2. Total fixed cost. The total fixed cost of a firm does not depend on the amount produced. It is thus shown as a horizontal line in the figure.

The second type of costs incurred by the firm in the short run are **variable costs** incurred only because production takes place. Examples already discussed include the cost of raw materials and energy, wages, and any other cost that rises as production increases. Total variable costs (TVC) are $0 at 0 output and rise as output rises, as shown in the third column of Table 6.1. Figure 6.3 shows TVC as a positively sloped line starting from the origin. Notice that when there is no output there are no variable costs.

Fixed costs and variable costs added together give **total costs (TC)** at any level of output; TC = TFC + TVC, as shown in Table 6.1. See in the table, and also in Figure 6.3, that at 8 units of output, total fixed costs of $100 plus total variable costs of $200 equal total costs of $300. Line TC parallels line TVC because fixed costs are a constant to which variable costs are added at any level of output.

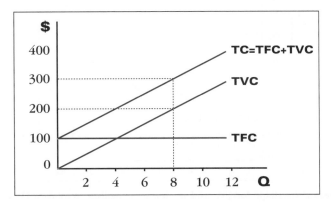

Figure 6.3. TFC + TVC = total costs. Total variable cost is $0 at 0 output and rises as output rises. Adding TVC to TFC yields total cost (TC), an upward-sloping line with the same slope as TVC.

Although we have shown TC and TVC as straight lines, the situation is more complicated in the real world. A firm that starts up production will probably find its variable costs do not increase at the same rate as the quantity produced rises. Table 6.2 shows the pattern that is more likely to emerge under actual production conditions. Notice that the variable costs in column 3 always rise but that the rate of increase slows and then speeds up again.

TABLE 6.2
Costs of the firm, reflecting more realism.

(1) Quantity	(2) Total Fixed Costs TFC	(3) Total Variable Costs TVC	(4) Total Costs TC = TFC+TVC	(5) Average Fixed Costs AFC = TFC/Q = (2) ÷ (1)	(6) Average Variable Costs AVC = TVC/Q = (3) ÷ (1)	(7) Average Total Cost ATC =TC/Q= AFC+AVC = (4)÷(1) = (5)+(6)
0	$100	$0	$100	$∞	$0.00	$∞
1	100	60	160	100.00	60.00	160.00
2	100	100	200	50.00	50.00	100.00
3	100	120	220	33.33	40.00	73.33
4	100	144	244	25.00	36.00	61.00
5	100	170	270	20.00	34.00	54.00
6	100	220	320	16.66	36.66	53.33
7	100	280	380	14.28	40.00	54.28
8	100	360	460	12.50	45.00	57.50
9	100	460	560	11.11	51.11	62.22
10	100	580	680	10.00	58.00	68.00
11	100	740	840	9.09	76.36	85.45
12	100	1060	1160	8.33	96.66	104.99

In Figure 6.4, we see that as output increases, the TVC curve rises rapidly at first, then turns more level, and then rises rapidly once again. Because TVC is added on top of a straight-line TFC to obtain the curve for TC, TC itself will show the same curvature as TVC.

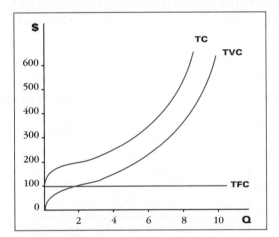

Figure 6.4. A characteristic shape for TVC and TC. It is more realistic to think of TVC as rising rapidly at first, then turning more level, and then rising rapidly once again. Because TVC has this shape, TC does as well since a constant amount (TFC) has been added to TVC to obtain it.

There are two main reasons for the slowing of the increase in both total variable cost and total cost as output increases over some range of output: the division of labor and economies in the use of plant and equipment. The **division of labor** implies that each worker is more efficient when performing a single operation than when performing several operations. In pin manufacturing, to use Adam Smith's famous example, workers could make complete pins by themselves. But if they specialize in different tasks—some cutting the metal, some fashioning the heads, some shaping the body and point—they can produce more pins in the same amount of time. They would not need to shift from task to task and tool to tool and would become more proficient in performing a single operation. Division of labor tends to be attractive to managers. It allows them to purchase exactly the "right" kind of labor that is needed. For example, one worker assigned to do an entire job might need to possess both great strength and great skill, but this combination of talents might be uncommon and thus costly. With a division of labor, a firm can hire some workers that have great strength and others that have great skill. Separating the traits enables the hiring to be accomplished at lower cost.

Economies in the use of plant and equipment also influence the rate at which the TVC and TC curves rise. Often, plant and equipment cannot be reduced below some minimum practical size, and trained people must be paid to run them. But at low output levels, the machines and the people tending them may be operating far below their full capacity. Both might be capable of stepping up their pace with little increase in cost as output rises.[2] Thus, the TVC and TC curves enter a relatively flat area. As output rises, however, there comes a point where costs (both TVC and TC) begin to climb more rapidly once again. In Figure 6.5, that point occurs when output has reached 3 units. The major reason for this increase in costs is that rising production begins to impose an overload on the available plant and equipment. Machines are being run too fast, work space becomes crowded, confusion sets in, and accidents occur. Recall that we are still speaking of the short run, a period in which the plant and equipment cannot be altered in size. We have here an example of the diminishing returns to a factor, which we discussed in Chapter 2. As more and more labor and raw materials are added to a fixed stock of plant and equipment, output continues to grow, but at a slower rate. Each additional worker added, each additional ton of coal used for fuel, costs as much as the last, but the increase in output is slowing down. Increments to output become more costly, so the TVC and the TC curves both rise more steeply, as shown in Figure 6.5.

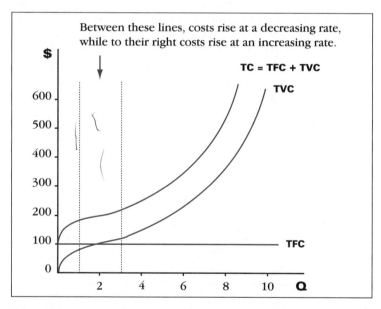

Figure 6.5. Total cost rises more rapidly beyond a certain output. Within a given plant, that is, in the short run, TVC and hence TC rise more slowly, due to the division of labor and better opportunities to overcome indivisibility of plant and equipment. Then they rise rapidly as output approaches the capacity of the plant.

2   Part-time renting of machines and hiring of labor may be a way for the company to avoid this constraint, but it is often difficult to acquire specialized machines and skilled people for short periods of time.

Average Costs

Once we know total costs, we can calculate a number of refinements. The **fixed cost** per unit, or *average fixed cost (AFC)*, is total fixed cost divided by quantity produced: AFC = TFC/Q. Since fixed costs are the same at any level of output, average fixed costs must decline steadily as output rises. When only a few units are being produced, AFC is high, but as a greater quantity is produced, AFC falls. Business managers call this "spreading the overhead." Column 5 of Table 6.2 shows the results, which are plotted in Figure 6.6. If total fixed costs are $100, the AFC of producing 2 units is $50, and the AFC of producing 10 units is only $10.

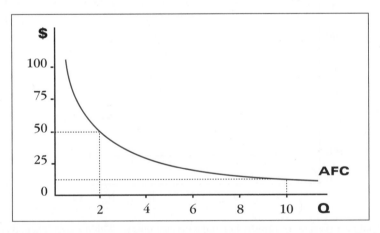

Figure 6.6. Average fixed cost. Total fixed cost being a given amount, dividing that figure by the quantity results in a lower average figure as more is produced. The curve for AFC thus slopes downward.

Average variable cost (AVC) is total variable cost divided by quantity produced: AVC = TVC/Q. Remember that after some level of output has been achieved, division of labor and more efficient use of plant and equipment cause total variable costs to rise more slowly than they did at first. Thus, AVC will fall for a time, as shown at the top of column 6 of Table 6.2 and by

Figure 6.7. When 2 units are produced, AVC is $50; when output rises to 4 units, AVC is $36. As output comes to be large within the bounds of a given-sized plant, AVC begins to rise, as shown in the lower part of column 6; when output is 11 units, AVC is $76. A curve for AVC plotted from these data is U-shaped, as in Figure 6.7.

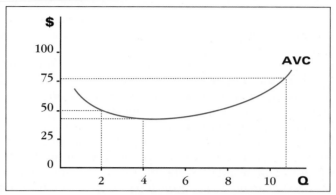

Figure 6.7. Average variable cost. AVC has a U shape. As output increases from low levels, AVC falls because of more division of labor and more efficient use of plant and equipment. As the maximum productive capacity of the firm is approached, ATC rises.

Average total cost (ATC) is total cost divided by quantity produced: ATC = TC/Q. Since total cost = fixed cost plus variable cost, then average total cost must equal average fixed cost plus average variable cost, or ATC = AFC + AVC. Our data produce an ATC curve that is U-shaped. At low levels of output ATC is high, because the small number of units produced must absorb all the fixed costs. As output rises, however, the spreading of the overhead, together with the decline in AVC, causes ATC to fall. Finally, as plant capacity is reached, ATC rises, as shown in Figure 6.8. Remember that ATC = AFC + AVC. Then notice that at every level of output in the figure, ATC is drawn as the vertical addition of AFC and AVC: for example, at 5 units of output, AFC is $20, AVC is $34, and ATC is $54.

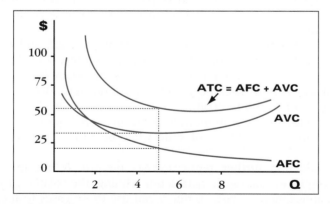

Figure 6.8. Average total cost. ATC is total cost divided by quantity produced. The curve is U-shaped; at low levels of output ATC is high because the small number of units produced must absorb all the fixed costs. As output rises, the spreading of the overhead, together with the decline in AVC, causes ATC to fall. Finally, as plant capacity is approached, ATC rises.

The average total cost curve is important in the analysis to come. Henceforth when we say **average cost,** average total cost is what we mean.

LONG-RUN COSTS

So far, we have been talking only about costs in the *short run,* a period too short for the firm to adjust its plant and equipment to accommodate changes in output. In the *long run,* however, both plant and equipment are variable. If expansion is limited by the constraints of size and the capacity of the machinery, the firm has time to acquire a larger plant and more equipment. Conversely, if its machines and structures are too large for profitable operation, the firm has time to replace them with smaller ones. In the long run, there are no fixed costs—all costs are variable.

Large-scale operations may reduce unit costs, so that the output of a new larger plant is cheaper on average than the output from the smaller plant it replaced. Why would such *increasing returns to scale* or **economies of scale** occur? There are two ways to approach the answer. First, we could assume that all inputs are supplied on a competitive basis. The firm pays the same price for its inputs no matter what its size. This is the standard assumption. Alternatively, we could assume that the size of a plant has some bearing on the prices it pays for inputs.

If we adopt the first assumption of competitive markets for inputs, then when economies of scale occur they will not be the result of being able to acquire inputs at a lower price. The scale economies must be due to the ability to reorganize production within large plants. The primary reason is that in plants of large size, mass production with assembly lines can be utilized. In mass production, the division of labor can be carried ever further, with new tasks created to improve efficiency. Larger, more specialized machinery can be installed and used at its most efficient speed.

Mass production with assembly lines is actually a combination of two different developments, "continuous flow" and interchangeability of parts. Continuous flow production is credited to Oliver Evans, whose 1785 grain mill in rural Delaware moved the raw material, milled grain, and finished products on a system of conveyors. After the Civil War the concept flowered in the famous stockyards of Chicago. The first known use of interchangeable parts occurred when Eli Whitney contracted to produce muskets at Whitneyville, Connecticut (outside New Haven), in 1798.[3] Before that time, tolerances were so inexact that craftsmen would custom-fit each part; the barrel from one musket might not fit the stock of another, even if the two muskets were ostensibly the same model. Interchangeability of parts flowered before the Civil War at the Colt arms works in Hartford, the Waltham watch factory in Massachusetts, and Cyrus McCormick's reaper works in Chicago.

The maturity of mass production came at the Highland Park and River Rouge plants in Detroit, where Henry Ford built the Model T. Ford's momentous contribution was to combine continuous flow production and interchangeable parts in assembly lines where the division of labor and use of specialized machinery could be optimized. Most modern manufacturing involving mass production exhibits economies of scale as plant size expands. (Redesigning the assembly line to allow for less monotonous "team work," pioneered by Volvo and Saab in Sweden, can still capture economies of scale while being more appealing to workers. The idea has spread.)

Large-scale production further reduces costs because it becomes possible to utilize by-products. For example, in small-scale petroleum refining, the volatile gases produced may be burned off into the atmosphere. A large refinery can use those gases to fuel its own processes, thereby reducing energy costs significantly.

Finally, many structures such as a building, a ship, or a storage tank, can be doubled in size without doubling the cost of construction because surface area does not increase at the same rate as internal volume. Here again, economies of scale may be found.

---

3.   The claim is disputed by some economic historians, who give the honor to the French arsenal at Vergennes on the outskirts of Paris. In either case, muskets were involved.

If we adopt the alternative assumption that input prices might change as a plant's size is enlarged, then another reason for scale economies emerges. Large-scale purchases of raw materials and equipment may induce suppliers to grant price discounts on big orders. In that case, larger plants will have lower average costs.

Whatever their source, economies of scale mean that average total costs, henceforth labeled simply AC, are lower for larger plants. In Figure 6.9, AC_1 is the cost curve for a small plant and AC_2 is the cost curve for a larger plant. A yet larger plant would have an even lower cost curve, further out to the right in the figure, and so on.

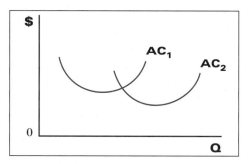

Figure 6.9. **Economies of scale.** If larger plants can produce output at lower average costs, economies of scale exist and a larger-size plant has an AC curve below that of a smaller-size plant.

Are There Diseconomies of Scale in the Long Run?

Are economies of scale a permanent feature of the expansion in plant size? Or, as plant size is expanded do the average costs of production eventually stop falling and rise again? Remember that in the long run crowding in the factory or overutilization of machines can be corrected by adding more space or acquiring more machinery. Yet in the real world we note that actual industries do *not* exhibit a taste for plant giantism. Even the largest firms, which could concentrate their production in one plant instead of spreading it among several, most frequently do not do so. Their managers must believe that plants can indeed grow so large that the average cost of producing in them may rise.

Why is it logical for these managers to believe that, whatever the product produced, the cost per unit eventually will begin to rise as scale increases? The reasons underlying *decreasing returns to scale* or **diseconomies of scale** depend on the assumptions used. If factor markets are always competitive, so that inputs can be added as needed with no change in their price, then scale diseconomies would have two causes. First, extremely large plants will require squadrons of managerial and supervisory staff organized on complex hierarchical lines. The delegation of authority may be diffuse, with decision making by committees so complicated and slow that efficiency suffers and costs rise. Even if managerial talent is always available for hiring at an unchanging price, and is added as plant size expands, the flow of information begins to be obstructed. To overcome the obstacle, "supermanagers" and internal information systems can be added, but these will raise costs. Second, the surface area-to-volume rule that a building, ship, storage tank, or other structure when doubled in size costs less than twice as much to construct, loses force and reverses itself as size becomes extremely large. Architects find that the ever increasing size of buildings requires more and more stabilization of the underlying subsoil; shipping firms find that the average costs of operating ever larger ships start to rise because the ships require internal reinforcement and cannot enter most harbors; storage tanks built larger than a certain size run the risk of collapse, and so on.

If we alter the basic assumption and allow that input markets may not be perfect, then the case for an upturn in average costs becomes more convincing. Especially in regard to management, the ability needed to run a gigantic business concern efficiently is not readily available. Ever larger plants would require hiring more managers capable of doing so, and at the outside limit—perhaps the factory equivalent of the Normandy Invasion—only a handful of people might have the requisite ability. Though the managerial problem would probably be the first to surface if input markets are imperfect, *any* input used by a giant plant could ultimately be the source of difficulty. For example, the ever greater output produced by a firm would continually increase the demand for *all* the factors of production, including land, labor, buildings, raw materials, and other inputs, as well as managerial skills. There would presumably come a time when these needs begin to raise prices in factor markets, meaning higher costs for very large plants. (But see the following for the lack of empirical evidence on the subject.)

Diagramming Long-Run Average Costs

Figure 6.10 shows a plausible outcome: economies of scale accompanying increases in plant size, but eventually giving way to diseconomies of scale as plants grow extremely large. Here, the average cost curves for ever larger plants reach a minimum at curve AC_5 (note the arrow) and then rise to curve AC_8. An "envelope curve" that just touches each short-run curve forms a **long-run average cost** curve (LRAC) that reveals how average costs behave over a range of plant sizes.[4]

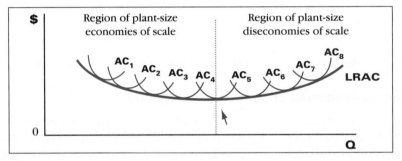

Figure 6.10. The long-run average cost curve. The LRAC curve is an envelope of many short-run AC curves, each showing a different-size plant. When LRAC is falling, plant-size economies of scale exist. When the LRAC is rising, diseconomies of scale have set in.

Diseconomies of scale such as those shown to the right of the vertical line in the figure *are very seldom observed in practice*. Empirical research with existing plants of different sizes suggests that the LRAC curves usually exhibit a long, flat extension to the right, with no upturn for large-size plants. The owners and managers of firms have presumably been intelligent enough to avoid the problems that are likely to occur with plants that are "too large." But an upturn surely *would* take place if plant sizes were expanded to sufficiently giant proportions.

In some industries, economies of scale set in at relatively low levels of output. The cost curve then flattens out for a long distance thereafter (before presumably turning upward when diseconomies of scale are encountered at extremely large quantities). In such cases, the "minimum efficient scale" where the cost curve turns flat would involve relatively low output. Beyond that point, firms could vary significantly in size while still remaining efficient; over this range small and large firms may exist within the same industry. If new entrants are quicker to establish themselves than existing firms are to expand as the industry grows, then many small firms are likely to characterize an industry. If existing firms are quicker off the mark, then a lower number of larger firms is more likely.

In some industries—motor vehicles, petrochemicals, and metal milling, for example— a firm must achieve a very large size before it realizes the minimum efficient scale of lowest average costs. In such industries, where economies of scale are great, plants will grow to a size so large that only a few can supply the entire market. This is a major reason why perfect competition cannot exist in some industries.

---

4   Notice that the LRAC curve does not run through the lowest point of the short-run AC curves. Instead, it just touches the AC curves, to the left of their lowest points in the region of plant-size economies of scale, at its lowest point when short-run average cost is at a minimum, and to the right of their lowest points in the region of plant-size diseconomies of scale.

In yet other industries, diseconomies of scale set in at fairly low levels of output. Retail stores, for example, generally find it inefficient to stock too many classes of goods (say fresh food, hardware, books, computers, and clothing) in any considerable quantity under one roof. The supermarket may carry books, but only a few of them, and the bookstore may have a rack or two of sweatshirts, but no more. The specific knowledge and bulk-ordering that are needed for efficiency are easier to cultivate in a more specialized setting.

MARGINAL COST

One last aspect of costs is extremely useful in predicting how profit-maximizing firms will behave. That is the concept of marginal cost. **Marginal cost (MC)** *is the extra cost of producing an additional unit of output.* Column 3 of Table 6.3 shows how marginal cost is determined. Notice that the figures for marginal cost are placed midway between the units of output. Moving from no output (total cost = $100) to the production of 1 unit (total cost = $160) brings an additional cost of $60, so the figure $60 is positioned between 0 and 1 units of output. The second unit produced brings an additional cost of $40, and so on.

TABLE 6.3
Determining marginal costs.

(1) Quantity	(2) Total Cost	(3) Marginal Cost (cost of producing one additional unit)
0	$100	
		$60
1	160	
		40
2	200	
		20
3	220	
		24
4	244	
		26
5	270	
		50
6	320	
		60
7	380	
		80
8	460	
		100
9	560	
		120
10	680	
		160
11	840	
		320
12	1160	

Figure 6.11 plots the figures listed in column 3. The marginal cost curve falls at first, reaches a turning point, and then rises. In the range where marginal cost is falling, to the left of the lowest point on the MC curve, each additional unit of output costs *less* to produce than the previous one. Where the MC curve levels off, at the curve's lowest point, each additional unit costs *the same* to produce as the previous one. In the range where the MC curve is rising, to the right of its lowest point, each additional unit of output costs *more* to produce than the previous one.

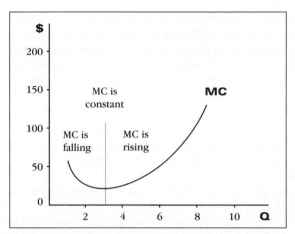

Figure 6.11. The shape of the marginal cost curve. Marginal cost is the extra cost of producing one more unit of output. Where MC is falling each additional unit of output costs less to produce than the previous one. Where it levels off, each additional unit costs the same to produce as the previous one. Where it is rising, each additional unit of output costs more to produce than the previous one.

CONCLUSION

With the knowledge of revenues and costs developed in this chapter, we now have the tools that will allow us to analyze the decisions made by profit-maximizing firms. In particular, what quantity will a firm decide to produce? Why will it decide to do so? The remainder of this chapter considers the answers in the case of perfect competition, while the next two consider the answers when competition is less than perfect.

▶ PERFECT COMPETITION

There are good reasons for starting our study of market types with the model called **perfect** (or pure) **competition,** where so many firms compete with each other that no single one can influence the market price. We begin with perfect competition not because it is found very frequently, but because the model is relatively simple to construct and gives well-defined predictions about how firms will behave. Furthermore, because the forces operating in a perfectly competitive market tend to drive an economy toward efficiency in its operation, it serves as a convenient benchmark against which to compare other forms of industrial organization. Keep in mind that a benchmark for comparison is not the same as a goal to be attained. As we shall see in Chapters 7 and 8 when we discuss imperfect markets, in many cases perfect competition would be counterproductive even if it were possible.

Recall the meaning of the term perfect competition. By definition, the number of sellers in the market must be so large that no one of them can influence the market price. A single farm is too small to affect the market price for corn. Each farmer takes the market price as given. No seller can increase sales by lowering price because a perfectly competitive firm can sell any amount it chooses to at the *current* market price. Moreover, if any one seller raised its price when others did not, that seller would cease to sell anything. Buyers would simply make their purchases from the other sellers who have kept their price unchanged. The demand curve facing the firm is horizontal, reflecting that the firm is a "price-taker" rather than a "price-maker."

For perfect competition to exist, three conditions must be present. First, the sellers must be selling an identical or "homogeneous" product. If one farmer's wheat differed from another's, buyers might be willing to pay more for the variety they prefer. It follows that among perfectly competitive firms there is no need for brand-name advertising: Why bother to advertise when the goods sold are identical and when sales depend entirely on market price?

Another requirement for perfect competition is that new firms must find it easy to enter the industry. If entry is not easy, then when the market for a product grows, some of the already established firms may enlarge their share of the market, and the degree of competition may decline. ("Easy entry" does not mean "no cost." New firms will need capital before they can start operating. Rather, it means simply that new firms have access to bank loans or other financing on reasonable terms, and government rules and regulations are not a serious barrier to entry.) If entry is easy, exit will be easy, too, a point that becomes important later in the chapter.

The third requirement for competition to be perfect is that knowledge of market conditions must be sufficiently widespread so that sellers cannot rely on lack of information among buyers about competing alternatives to boost their own prices. If the customers of a firm are unaware that another firm a block away is charging a lower price for the same good, and do not find out, then price differences for the same good may perpetuate themselves and the market for that good is not perfectly competitive.

All these circumstances taken together are quite restrictive. They obviously do not apply to any kind of "big business." Perhaps the best example of perfect competition is farming when government does not intervene to fix prices. Most fruits and vegetables produced by truck and market gardeners generally follow this model. Even when government does intervene to fix farm prices, the product will still be largely homogeneous, there will still be considerable freedom of entry and exit, and information about the market will still be widespread. This means that even when agriculture is controlled, the markets for agricultural commodities in many cases approach perfect competition, with individual producers facing a horizontal demand curve. Other markets that are more or less perfectly competitive are those for some common raw materials like lumber, some simple standardized electronic parts such as 16K computer memory chips, many sorts of secondhand goods, and, importantly, stocks, bonds, and foreign currencies (at the wholesale level). It is fair to say that perfect competition is uncommon in the economies of modern developed countries. Firms that are not perfect competitors may still face a good deal of competition, however. Indeed, it is estimated that some three-quarters of total U.S. private sector output is produced by firms under conditions of considerable competition.[5] But most of these firms are not perfect competitors, as we shall see.

THE SUPPLY DECISIONS OF A PERFECTLY COMPETITIVE FIRM

With the information on a firm's revenues and costs developed earlier in the chapter, we are now able to determine the quantity of output that a perfectly competitive firm will produce if it is a profit maximizer.

Under perfect competition, as we have seen, the price charged by a firm will not vary whether sales are small or large. So the firm can easily calculate total revenue by multiplying price times quantity sold, as shown in Table 6.4.

TABLE 6.4
Total revenue from sales, perfectly competitive firm.

Quantity sold	Price	Total revenue
0	$10	$0
10	10	100
20	10	200
30	10	300
40	10	400
50	10	500
60	10	600

5.   Estimate of 76.7% for 1980 by William G. Shepherd of the University of Massachusetts, "Causes of Increased Competition in the U.S. Economy, 1939-1980," *Review of Economics and Statistics*, Vol. 64, No. 4, November 1982, p. 618. The figure has been rising; Shepherd's estimate was only a little over half (56.3%) in 1958 and 52.4% in 1939.

The perfectly elastic (horizontal) demand curve in Figure 6.12 reflects the prices and quantities in the table. The different quantities sold are shown along the horizontal axis and the unchanging price of $10 is shown on the vertical axis.

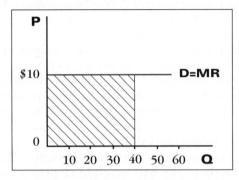

Figure 6.12. **The perfectly elastic (horizontal) demand curve.** The horizontal (perfectly elastic demand) signifies that a firm is in an environment of perfect competition. Because each additional unit sold at the unchanging price of $10 brings the firm $10 in extra revenue, the demand curve is also the curve showing the firm's marginal revenue. Total revenue, which is price times quantity, is the area of the shaded rectangle.

Let us assume that 40 units are sold at a price of $10 per unit. In that case, total revenue is the quantity 40 multiplied by the price of $10, or $400 as seen by the area of the shaded rectangle. We know that each additional sale of one more unit raises total revenue by $10 because that is the price at which the unit can be sold. This is the firm's marginal revenue, which is equal to the price. In fact, the demand curve will also serve as the curve showing marginal revenue, so in Figure 6.12 we label it D = MR. All essential information on the firm's revenues can be ascertained from the position of the firm's horizontal (perfectly elastic) demand curve, which is also the marginal revenue curve.

The firm's costs are illustrated by the cost curves constructed earlier in the chapter. The key cost curves for this analysis are the marginal cost (MC) curve and the average cost (AC) curve. To solve the problem of what quantity of output will maximize profit, we need to make simultaneous use of the demand curve (which shows revenue), the marginal cost curve, and, a little later, the average cost curve.

HOW THE MC CURVE AND
THE DEMAND CURVE DETERMINE THE QUANTITY PRODUCED

How does a perfectly competitive firm that wants to maximize its profits determine the quantity to produce? In Figure 6.13, the price of the output sold is $10 per unit. What if the firm decides to produce and sell 30 units? The price it receives for the last unit produced, the 30th, is also the marginal revenue from that last sale. This revenue ($10) is higher than the cost of producing it ($7). So the firm obtains more revenue from the last unit produced than it cost the firm to produce it. The firm is not earning all the profit it could earn, because if it chose to produce a 31st unit, a 32nd unit, and so on, up to the 40th unit, the price of each of those units (and the marginal revenue earned from producing each) would still exceed the cost of producing it. Total profit will be increased by each unit of greater output until the 40th unit is reached. Unless output is as high as point **E** in the figure, total profit cannot be at a maximum.

If the firm decided to produce *more* than 40 units, however, that would also prevent profits from being maximized. For example, if a 45th unit is produced, the cost of that unit ($12) would be more than the price at which it could be sold ($10), and thus more than the $10 marginal revenue earned from producing it. So the firm would suffer a loss on that unit and could increase profit by not producing it. That is true for any unit for which the marginal cost exceeds the sale price. Thus the profit-maximizing equilibrium for a firm under perfect competition is the point at which marginal cost and marginal revenue are equal, **MC = MR,** which is at point **E** in Figure 6.13. (Because the price is the same as the marginal revenue, we could also say the profit-maximizing equilibrium is where MC = P. For perfect competition, these two ways of identifying the equilibrium are one and the same.)

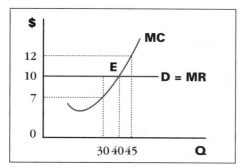

Figure 6.13. What quantity will be produced by a perfectly competitive firm? The profit-maximizing equilibrium for a firm under perfect competition is MC = MR (with MR equal to the price P, and shown by the position of the demand curve D). If MC ≠ MR, profit cannot be maximized. If the cost of producing the last unit is higher than the marginal revenue, it adds to profit if the last unit is not produced. If the cost of producing the last unit is lower than the marginal revenue, producing another unit will add to profit.

Check Table 6.5 to confirm that the firm pictured in Figure 6.13 will maximize its profits by producing 40 units of output. The table shows the data for the units of output clustered around 40 to demonstrate this. See how a decision to produce 36 units and no more would result in a loss of 50¢ that could have been earned from producing the 37th unit. If that 37th unit had been produced, it would have brought in revenue of $10 but would have cost only $9.50 to make, meaning that 50¢ in potential profit has been sacrificed. Similarly, 35¢ was lost by not producing the 38th unit, and 20¢ on the 39th, for a total of $1.05 in sacrifice of profits. A decision to produce 43 units would also involve a sacrifice of $1.05 in profits. That 43rd unit brought in revenue of $10, but that was not enough to cover the $10.50 cost of producing it, so the firm's profitability was reduced by 50¢. Similarly, 35¢ was lost from producing the 42nd unit and 20¢ on the 41st. Only when the marginal revenue earned from producing the last unit is exactly equal to the marginal cost of its production is profit at a maximum. At that level of output—40 units, marked by the arrow—no profit has been sacrificed.

TABLE 6.5
Confirming that the output level where MC = MR maximizes profits.

Quantity sold (Q)	Price (P)	Marginal Revenue (MR)	Marginal Cost (MC)	Lost profit on each unit
37	$10	$10	$9.50	−$0.50
38	10	10	9.65	−$0.35
39	10	10	9.80	−$0.20
→ 40	10	10	10.00	0
41	10	10	10.20	−$0.20
42	10	10	10.35	−$0.35
43	10	10	10.50	−$0.50

What If the Market Price Changes?

If the market price were to rise, say to $12 as in Figure 6.14, the firm would face a new demand curve, D_2, horizontal at $12 per unit. Now if the firm produced *fewer than* 45 units, the marginal cost of the last unit produced would be less than the price and hence marginal revenue received from selling it. So the firm would not be maximizing profits. If it produced *more than* 45 units, the marginal cost of the last item would be greater than its price and hence marginal revenue. So again, the firm would not be maximizing profit. Only at point E_2, where MC = MR, would the firm attain its profit-maximizing equilibrium.

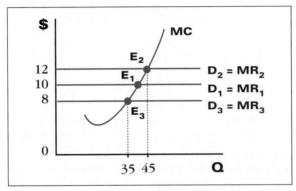

Figure 6.14. What if the price changes? If the price rises to $12, the profit-maximizing level of output where MC = MR would rise to 45. If the price falls to $8, the profit-maximizing level of output where MC = MR would decline to 35. The marginal cost curve is acting as if it were this firm's supply curve, which indeed it is.

What happens if the market price falls to, say, $8? The firm now faces yet another demand curve, D_3, horizontal at $8 per unit. In order to maximize profit at this price the firm must choose output 35, at E_3, where MC = MR.

All this builds to a clear conclusion: Whenever the market price changes, and with it the position of the horizontal demand curve, a new equilibrium output will be established at the point where MC = MR. That conclusion has a major implication: price changes drive quantity changes along the upward-sloping marginal cost curve just as if it were the firm's supply curve. In fact, that is exactly the case. *The marginal cost curve of a perfectly competitive firm is the same as that firm's supply curve* as long as the firm is producing any output at all. (As we will see, price may fall so low that it becomes economically rational for a firm to shut down. So at some point the firm's marginal cost curve ceases to be identical to its supply curve.) The fact that a firm's supply curve reflects exactly the cost of the resources required for the production of each additional unit of output is significant in many areas of microeconomics.

Because a competitive firm's marginal cost curve is also its supply curve, the marginal cost curves for all the firms in the industry when added together horizontally must give the supply curve for the whole industry. (Recall that in Chapter 4 we added firms' supply curves horizontally to find the supply curve for the whole industry.)

Putting MC and AC Together

By bringing the marginal cost curve and the average cost curve together on the same diagram, we can obtain important information about a firm's decisions. Panels **a** and **b** in Figure 6.15 show how the two curves relate to each other.

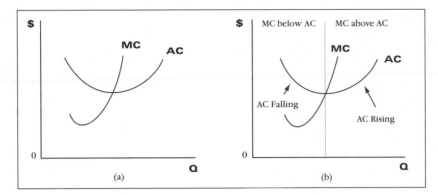

Figure 6.15. The relationship between the average and marginal cost curves. The MC cuts through the AC curve at the latter's lowest point. It does so because when MC is less than AC, the last unit produced must be pulling the average down, whereas when MC is greater than AC, the last unit produced must be pulling the average up.

Notice that the MC curve cuts through the AC curve at the latter's lowest point. It must always do so because when marginal cost is less than average cost, the last unit produced must be pulling the average down. Conversely, when marginal cost exceeds average cost, the last unit produced must be pulling the average up. In panel **b** of Figure 6.15, to the left of the vertical line, MC is less than AC, so AC is falling. To the right of that line, MC is more than AC, so AC is rising.

To demonstrate the relationship between marginal and average, we can take an example from baseball. Say Frank Thomas is batting .333 for the season, which means that he will get 33.3 hits for every 100 times at bat. But what if in today's game—the *marginal* game—he goes 2 for 5 and so bats .400 today. Clearly his performance today will pull his season's average up. But if he goes only 1 for 5 today, that is only .200 and his season's average will be pulled down. The average will remain the same only when the marginal equals the average. It follows that marginal cost equals average cost where average cost is not changing. That point is at the bottom of the AC curve, as in panel **b** of Figure 6.15. The same logic applies to average total cost and to average variable cost: MC intersects both the ATC curve and the AVC curve at their lowest points.

The Shut-Down Rule

If the market price falls, a profit-maximizing firm will produce less. If the fall is far enough, the firm will eventually decide to halt production and shut down. The **shut-down rule** indicating when this will happen is interesting and not intuitively obvious. Assume that in the short run the market price and thus the demand curve facing the firm begin to drop and continue to do so. The firm will supply less and less output to the market, as shown by the successive intersections of the MC curve and the demand curve in Figure 6.17, first at Q_1, then at Q_2, and then at Q_3. When price drops below P_c, notice that the firm is suffering a loss, because average total costs are no longer being covered. In the face of these losses, the firm has two choices. It can keep producing, thus continuing to incur both fixed and variable costs. Or it can shut down, producing nothing and incurring only fixed costs but no variable costs. According to the shut-down rule, the firm should continue to produce so long as it is making enough to cover its variable costs plus a little more. By doing so the firm will be gleaning some revenue over and above its variable costs that will help reduce the burden of its fixed costs. Only when the price sinks below P^*, where variable costs can no longer be covered, should the firm shut down. Below P^*, the loss from producing plus the fixed costs make the balance sheet worse than it would have been if the firm had halted production.[6] When that shut-down happens, output is immediately zero, and the firm's marginal cost curve is no longer identical to its supply curve.

---

6.   This shut-down rule is the reason why in a declining industry, outmoded and obsolescent plant and equipment are often kept in use. Management may be attempting to reduce the burden of the unavoidable fixed costs by continuing operation, even when production is unprofitable. The same reason explains why in some countries, including the United States, obsolete plants such as those that use open-hearth furnaces for steelmaking have been kept in production even after their technology has been far surpassed (by oxygen steelmaking).

THE RELATIONSHIP BETWEEN MC AND AVC

The relationship between MC and AVC can be seen in another way. In Figure 6.16, notice that the two curves begin at the same point, X.

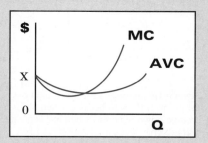

Figure 6.16. **How the marginal and average cost curves relate to one another.** The MC and AVC curves start at the same point. The average variable cost of the first unit of output is the same as the extra cost incurred from going from 0 units to 1 unit of output.

The very first unit produced means that total variable costs of $X are incurred, and $X ÷ 1 = AVC. That first unit produced also raises total cost by $X; $X = ΔTC = MC. So at that first unit, AVC = MC. The curves start together. After that, a second unit costs less to produce than the average (MC < AVC), so AVC must fall. When a unit costs more to produce than the average (MC > AVC), AVC must rise.

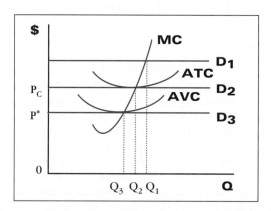

Figure 6.17. **The shut-down rule.** A firm will not shut down if it can earn enough to more than cover its AVC. It will shut down when it can no longer cover AVC.

In the long run, there are no fixed costs. All costs are variable. If prices sink below average cost, plant and equipment can be sold off and managers and owners can leave the business. So in the long run, firms will exit the industry unless they can at least break even, covering all their costs.

THE MODEL OF ENTRY AND EXIT UNDER PERFECT COMPETITION

The model of perfect competition allows us to predict the position toward which an industry will be propelled. Let us take one firm out of many in some given industry and analyze its behavior. Panel **b** of Figure 6.18 shows the marginal and average cost curves for that firm. The demand curve facing the firm is perfectly elastic. It is positioned at the equilibrium market price, P_1, that has been established by industry supply and demand, as shown in panel **a**. (Notice that the scales differ along the horizontal axes of panels **a** and **b**. On the left, panel **a** shows quantity for the industry in millions, while panel **b** shows the quantity for the individual firm in hundreds.) For a perfect competitor, price is the same as marginal revenue, so the demand curve and the marginal revenue curve are the same.

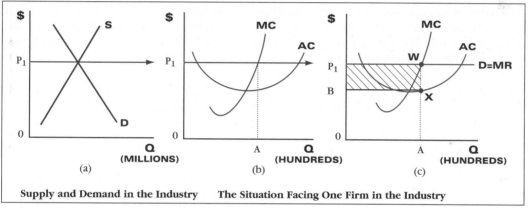

Supply and Demand in the Industry   The Situation Facing One Firm in the Industry

Figure 6.18. Perfect competition in the short run. Because the price it receives is above AC, the single firm in panels **b** and **c** earns a super-normal profit.

Faced with this situation, the firm in panels **b** and **c** will produce quantity A at price P_1, for it is there that MC = MR. At that quantity, panel **c** shows that average cost per unit is only B while the price received (which is the same as marginal revenue) is P_1. On each of the units produced (from 0 to A), the firm is earning an extra or super-normal profit equal to BP_1. Total profit of BP_1 per unit on each of 0A units (with 0A = BX) can be represented as a shaded rectangle formed by BP_1 × BX. The area of this rectangle is BP_1WX. As we have seen, the super-normal profit shown here is in addition to the "normal" profit needed to keep the entrepreneurs active in their current employment. Normal profit is an opportunity cost, and along with all other opportunity costs it is included in the average cost curve.

We can identify the super-normal profit by another method. Total revenue is equal to price times quantity, or the distances $0P_1$ × 0A, which equals a rectangle $0P_1$WA. Total cost is B per unit (as indicated on the AC curve) times A units, which equals rectangle 0BXA. Since TR – TC = total profit, then $0P_1$WA – 0BXA = BP_1WX.

The super-normal profit available to the firms in this industry will prove attractive to entrepreneurs outside the industry. As long as entry is free (a requirement of perfect competition), then new firms will enter in search of this profit. The result will be an increase in industry supply from S_1 to S_2 as shown in panel **a** of Figure 6.19, and a resulting decrease in price (and hence marginal revenue) from P_1 to P_2.

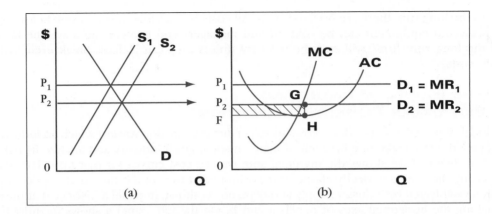

Figure 6.19. Adjustment under perfect competition. Super-normal profit, as seen in panel **b**, causes an increase in supply and a cut in price in panel **a**.

Each firm in the industry will now face demand curve D_2, as shown in Figure 6.19's panel **b**. Even so, each firm is still earning a profit equal to FP_2GH (calculated as above by first finding the point of profit maximization where $MR = MC$). This super-normal profit, though smaller, will still provide an incentive for new firms to enter. So supply will continue to expand (as shown in panel **a** of Figure 6.20) and price (and MR) will be forced down further, to P_3.

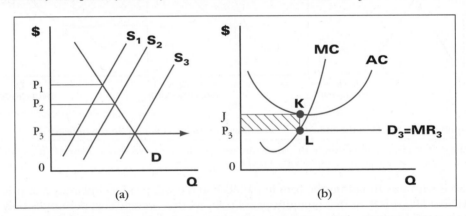

Figure 6.20. Further adjustment under perfect competition. If because of new entrants supply increases so far in panel **a** that the price (and hence MR) falls below average cost, then a single firm will earn a loss as in panel **b**.

At this price and marginal revenue, with perfectly elastic demand curve D_3, a firm in the industry will not be making even a normal return. In fact, it will be suffering a *loss* of P_3JKL. Consequently, some firms, perhaps the weakest ones or those whose entrepreneurs are quick to spot other opportunities, will exit the industry. As shown in panel **a** of Figure 6.21, supply will fall to S_4 and price will rise to P_4. Demand (and marginal revenue) will rise to D_4, as in panel **b**.

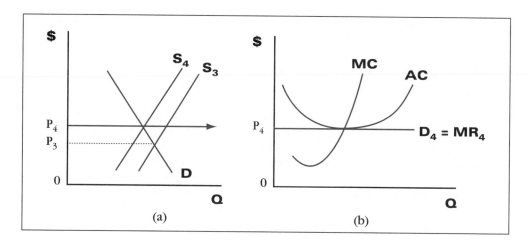

Figure 6.21. Equilibrium under perfect competition. Equilibrium is reached when supply and demand in panel **a** are such that a single firm's price and marginal revenue equals its average cost in panel **b**. There is no further incentive for firms to enter or to exit the industry.

At price P_4, with the demand curve facing a firm just touching the lowest point on its average cost curve and no super-normal profit or loss, there is no further incentive for firms to enter or to exit the industry. The firm in a perfectly competitive market has reached equilibrium. At that equilibrium, $P = MR = MC = AC$.

Competition Pushes Firms Toward Optimal Size

In considering equilibrium under perfect competition, we must recall the distinction made earlier between the short run, when plant size is fixed, and the long run, when time is available to alter the scale of operations. The plant size with the AC curve shown in all the figures from Figure 6.14 on may not be the plant built to optimum scale. A larger plant might result in economies of scale, with a correspondingly lower cost per unit. Figure 6.22 suggests the economic motivation to build such a plant. Given the same market price, and hence the same demand (and marginal revenue) curve, the profit APWX earned by the small-size plant with cost curve AC_1 would be far overshadowed by the profit BPYZ that could be earned if a larger-scale plant with lower cost curve AC_2 was built.

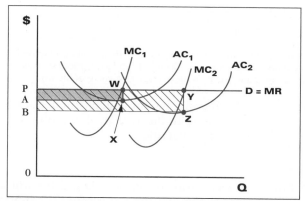

Figure 6.22. Changing plant size to maximize profits under perfect competition. Adjustment under perfect competition includes movements in the average cost curve. Firms that find they can realize economies of scale by building larger plants will have a motive to do so.

A firm intent on maximizing profit could decide to expand its scale of operations to capture the even greater profit made possible by economies of scale. (However, if economies of scale are very large, some firms may grow to a size where they can influence the market as a whole. In that case, perfect competition would cease to exist in the industry, as we shall see in the next chapter.)

What Happens If Overall Consumer Demand Changes?

How will a competitive industry originally in equilibrium react to variations in overall consumer demand? If the demand curve in panel **a** of Figure 6.21 were to shift, individual firms would feel the effect at once. That is because the new level of demand will alter the market price and hence the position of the perfectly elastic demand curve facing each firm. Profit will increase as price rises (or will decline as price falls); and new firms will be attracted into the industry (or else expelled from it). Market supply will change because of the entry or exit of firms, and super-normal profit and loss will both be eliminated. The firms in the industry will once more be at equilibrium, at the bottom of their U-shaped average cost curves.

The Effect of Entry on Costs

Entry by new firms into a perfectly competitive industry may or may not have an effect on the prices (costs) of the factors of production. If there is *no* such effect, the firms will face average cost curves no higher than before. Long-run supply will then be highly elastic—perfectly elastic if there is no rise in costs at all. But if the entry of new firms results in a bidding up of factor prices—the wages of skilled labor, for example, or the prices of raw materials—entry will mean not only a fall in the demand curve facing the individual firm, but a simultaneous rise in the average cost curves of the individual firms (see Figure 6.23).

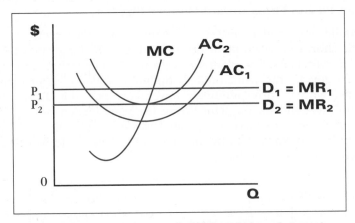

Figure 6.23. Competitive equilibrium when entry of new firms bids up factor prices.
If under perfect competition the entry of new firms bids up factor prices such as the wages of labor or the prices of raw materials, then the average cost curve of the firm will rise.

Equilibrium will be as before, with super-normal profit eliminated, but the equilibrium will occur at a higher price because costs have risen. In this case the long-run supply curve of the industry will be upward-sloping instead of perfectly elastic.

CONCLUSION

To conclude: A competitive firm faced with rising or falling price will adjust its output so as to maximize its profits. If the firms in the industry are earning super-normal profits, new firms will enter the industry until those profits are eliminated. That will occur when the price (shown by the perfectly elastic demand curve) touches the minimum point of the AC curve, where the MC curve cuts through it. Thus equilibrium under perfect competition occurs where $P = MR = MC = AC$.

We would not expect the perfectly competitive equilibrium to be long lasting. Any shift in either the industry supply curve or the industry demand curve—any change in weather that affects crops, or any change in wages, or costs of a raw material, or consumer taste, or income, or any other determinant of either supply or demand—will change the price and thus the position of the demand curve facing individual firms. A new process will begin in which profits or losses occur, firms move in or out, and a new equilibrium is approached. The setting is never static, always moving. Equilibrium is a mobile target rather than a fixed position.

ADVANTAGES FLOWING FROM PERFECT COMPETITION

Generations of economists have seen advantages in an industrial structure that is perfectly competitive. It is important to appreciate why.

Reaction to Changing Wants and Changing Costs

Under perfect competition, the economic system reacts to changing demand and to changing cost levels. If the demand for a product increases, both its price and the profit accruing to its suppliers rise. Higher profit attracts additional firms, and the supply of the product increases. It is hard to imagine other economic systems—for example, traditional economies or centrally planned command economies as discussed in Chapter 2—reacting so quickly to changes in consumer tastes and costs.

Minimization of Costs of Production, Elimination of Super-Normal Profits

A perfectly competitive system works to minimize production costs, and because of competition, super-normal profits are eliminated. If the firms within an industry have similar cost curves, the ones that fail to reduce cost per unit to its lowest feasible level incur a loss.[7] This is true both in the short run and in the long run. In the long run, firms that fail to take advantage of economies of scale will lose sales to firms that do. The firms that build plants able to capture economies of scale can cut prices and enlarge their share of the market. Under perfect competition, all firms that want to survive must adopt the most efficient cost-cutting techniques.

The minimization of production costs and the elimination of super-normal profits both mean that consumers will be charged the lowest product prices consistent with the survival of the firms in the industry. In the process, scarce resources that are high in price are conserved, and abundant resources that are low in price are more utilized.

Promotion of Economic Efficiency

Perfect competition promotes *efficiency in production* by encouraging firms to use the most productive, lowest-cost techniques and to adopt a scale of operations at which costs are minimized. Moreover it promotes *allocative efficiency,* the production of "just the right amount" of a good.

---

7   If some firms have lower costs than others for one reason or another—more efficient management or a better location, for example—then such firms may not move to the lowest point on their average cost curves. We will return to the subject in the next chapter.

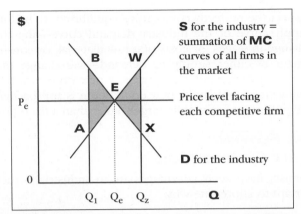

Figure 6.24. Allocative inefficiency when output is not at competitive equilibrium. At the perfectly competitive equilibrium, supply equals demand, production is allocatively efficient, and "just the right amount" of a good is being produced. But when output is not at competitive equilibrium, allocative inefficiency is seen as a triangle between the demand and supply curves.

In Figure 6.24, at the perfectly competitive equilibrium the industry supply and demand curves intersect at point E and each firm in the industry faces price P_e. All the firms in the industry taken together produce quantity Q_e. For each firm, price equals marginal cost. At quantity Q_e, with P = MC, consumers are willing to pay exactly what it cost suppliers to produce the product (including normal profit).

For any quantity less than Q_e, such as Q_1 where P > MC, consumers are willing to pay more for the product, as indicated along the industry's downward-sloping demand curve, than it would cost suppliers to produce it, as indicated along the industry's upward-sloping supply curve. At any quantity greater than Q_e, such as Q_2 where MC > P, production of these units costs more (shown along the industry supply curve) than people are willing to pay for them (shown along the industry demand curve).

Thus, any quantity other than Q_e involves inefficient allocation. Following our analysis in Chapter 4, the total amount of allocative inefficiency is measured by the size of a triangle between the demand and supply curves. At output Q_1, that amount is ABE. At output Q_2, it is EWX. The more markets in an economy that approach perfect competition, the more closely that economy will approach allocative efficiency.

Absence of Government Control

Finally, the free entry and exit that characterize perfect competition are consistent with a large amount of freedom to pursue economic alternatives. A system of perfect competition eliminates the need for a controlling or managing apparatus of government to issue licenses and permits for production, and makes it pointless for people to try to obtain these by bribing government officials. The result is less opportunity for corruption in public service.

Perfect Competition as a Benchmark

This concurrence of advantages explains why economists frequently use perfect competition as a benchmark against which to compare other models of market organization. In addition, this model is relatively simple to master and produces a clear-cut outcome.[8] Its role as benchmark and its basic simplicity make it the appropriate model with which to begin the study of market organization. As we shall see, however, "benchmark" does not mean "goal to be attained" and "simplicity" does not mean "frequently found." There are numerous reasons why perfect competition is not common, and why damage would ensue if many sectors of the economy suddenly became perfectly competitive. These considerations play a major part in the next chapter.

---

8   The model of perfect competition also finds use in advanced economics, where *general* equilibrium in *all product and factor markets* can be analyzed mathematically. Kenneth Arrow of Stanford University and Gerard Debreu of the University of California at Berkeley won Nobel Prizes in economics (in 1972 and 1983, respectively) in part for their "Arrow-Debreu" model of general equilibrium under perfect competition.

SUMMARY

1) We can find a firm's total revenue by multiplying the quantity it produces times the price at which the production is sold. The firm's marginal revenue is the extra revenue obtained from the sale of another unit of output.

2) Cost as defined by economists is opportunity cost, including both the explicit cash costs of production and the implicit noncash costs of opportunities forgone. Super-normal profit is the difference between total revenue and total (opportunity) cost.

3) Costs in the short run are within a fixed plant size, while in the long run the plant size can expand or contract.

4) Fixed costs are those incurred even if the firm produces nothing, while variable costs are incurred because things are produced. In the short run, firms will shut down if they cannot cover their variable costs; in the long run all costs are variable, so the same rule applies. Average cost is the cost per unit of production, or TC/Q; marginal cost is the extra cost for an additional unit of output. The marginal cost curve cuts through the lowest point of the U-shaped average cost curve.

5) Under perfect competition, no single firm is large enough to influence the market price. The demand curve facing such a firm is horizontal (perfectly elastic). A perfectly competitive firm maximizes its profits by producing the quantity of output where the price and, therefore, the marginal revenue, equals marginal cost, or P = MR = MC; the MC curve is therefore the supply curve for such a firm.

6) Perfectly competitive firms that want to maximize profits will raise the quantity they produce if the price rises, and lower it if the price declines. Some firms will enter the industry if there are profits to be made, while some will exit if losses occur. The entry and exit shifts the industry's supply curve and so alters the price, leading the industry to an equilibrium. That equilibrium of price and output is at the point where the demand curve, the marginal cost curve, and the average cost curve all touch at the bottom of the U-shaped average cost curve. P = MR = MC = AC.

7) Economists often hold up perfect competition as a benchmark against which to measure other forms of market organization because of its ability to react to changing wants and changing costs, the way it works to minimize production costs and eliminate super-normal profits, and its promotion of economic efficiency.

Chapter Key Words

Average cost: See *average total cost.*

Average total cost: The average cost per unit of production; often called simply "average cost." Thus, if 10 units are produced at a total cost of $20, average total cost is $20/10 = $2. A perfectly competitive firm will tend to produce at the minimum level of average total cost.

Diseconomies of scale: As the size of a plant grows in the long run, there comes a time when economies of scale cease to be realized due to the pressure of a large plant on resource prices and also management difficulties. Larger plants may then exhibit higher average costs.

Division of labor: The process described by Adam Smith whereby labor specializes in various tasks, gaining in efficiency and contributing to economies of scale.

Economies of scale: Larger plants may allow for more division of labor, use of more specialized machines, mass-production techniques, the utilization of by-products, and economies in large-scale purchases of raw materials. So as the size of a plant grows in the long run, costs per unit of output may fall.

Fixed cost: The costs incurred by the firm in the short run even if nothing is produced. Includes rent, insurance, salaries, and various opportunity costs. By definition, for any given scale of operation, fixed costs are constant. There are no fixed costs in the long run.

Long-run average cost: The average cost over a period of time sufficiently long so that all the factors of production used by a firm can be varied in amount. In the long run, plant size can be reduced or expanded.

Marginal cost (MC): The additional cost of producing one more unit of output. Important for determining a firm's profit-maximizing output (which under perfect competition is where marginal cost equals price).

Marginal revenue (MR): The extra revenue from selling one more unit of output. Under perfect competition, the same as the price of the product. Under imperfect competition, less than the price of the product.

Perfect competition: A situation under which the number of sellers in a market is so large that no single firm can influence the market price. The demand curve facing a perfectly competitive firm is a horizontal line.

Short-run average cost: The average cost over a period of time too short for a firm to alter its plant size, although other inputs can be varied in quantity.

Shut-down rule: The rule that a firm will shut down its operation if the price it receives for its product is not enough to cover its average variable cost.

Super-normal profit (sometimes called abnormal, economic, pure, excess, or real profit): The excess of total revenue over total cost when total cost is defined to include all opportunity costs including normal profit. The pursuit of super-normal profits cause firms' managers to decide what quantity of output to produce and what techniques of production to use.

Total cost (TC): In the short run, the fixed costs plus the variable costs of a firm's operation. In the long run equal to the firm's variable cost.

Total revenue (TR): The total amount of a firm's sales revenues, calculated as the quantity of an item produced by the firm times the price at which the units were sold. $TR = Q_p \times P_p$. A firm's profit is determined by subtracting its total costs from its total revenue.

Variable cost: In the short run, costs incurred because production takes place. At zero output there are no variable costs. In the long run, all costs are variable.

Chapter Questions

1) In northern Minnesota the equilibrium price of a 2' x 4' board is $2, and the market for such boards is perfectly competitive. Bunyan's saw mill currently sells 600 2' x 4's every day. What is Bunyan's total revenue? If Bunyan's produced one more board, what would be the marginal revenue of that board?

2) Your college offers you a campus job at $5 per hour for 300 hours, but instead you choose to start a small business. You buy a very used car and drive other students downtown for a fee. In your first year you spend 300 hours on your business and you bring in $2,500. You pay $500 in gas for the year and the car only cost $800, so you figure that you have made a handsome profit. But your friend who took economics claims that you have lost money. Explain the discrepancy.

3) You are a British spy in World War I. You suspect that Germany has reached a level of technical expertise that will allow it to produce battleships at a very fast rate. In economic terms, you worry that the marginal cost of a battleship is fairly low. You know that last year Germany had fixed costs equivalent to £3 million for its battleship program. It produced two battleships, with a total variable cost of £3 million. This year your intelligence estimate is that fixed costs have not changed. You believe that three battleships were produced, and you think that the average variable cost of each ship was £1.5 million. Can you sort out this data to find the marginal cost of a battleship?

4) We know that the average *fixed* cost curve must be downward-sloping because each additional unit of production "spreads the overhead" a little more. We assume that total variable costs rise quickly, then slowly, then quickly again, so we can also say that the average *variable* cost curve is U-shaped. How do we know that the average *total* cost curve is U-shaped, too?

5) Behemoth Enterprises was a very large company. Its main plant building covered two counties in Texas, and it employed 2 million people. But Behemoth fell on hard times and had to cut back over the course of several years. It reduced its plant size to half a county and cut back its workforce to 500,000 people. The new plant actually had lower production costs than the old one. Draw Behemoth's long-run average cost curve. Show the short-run average cost curves for the big old plant and the smaller new one. Why did Behemoth cut costs by scaling down its plant?

6) Bud, the owner of Bud's Machinery Co., tells you, "The average cost of one of my electric motors is $23, and I can sell them for $25, so I make a profit." You say to Bud, "But how much extra did it cost to produce the last motor, and what was the marginal revenue from that motor?" Bud says, "Well, it cost $30 extra, and since the basic electric motor market is very competitive I get $25 no matter how many motors I produce." Show Bud his average and marginal cost curves, his marginal revenue curve, and explain why he should cut back production.

7) Draw the marginal cost, average variable cost, and average total cost curves for a typical company. Why do you know exactly how to draw the intersections of the MC curve and the AC curves? Show a price where the firm makes a profit. Show a price where the firm makes a loss and will shut down immediately. Show a price where the firm loses money but does not shut down in the short run. Explain why the firm would behave this way.

8) Demand for vegetables rises because of health concerns. Price goes up, and New Jersey truck farmers suddenly are making large profits. One farmer says, "I've got it made, I'll be making big bucks like this for the rest of my career." Is she right, or will something happen to reduce her profits? Use a diagram of market supply and demand for vegetables and a diagram of this farmer's marginal and average costs to show what will happen.

9)   As a way to cut the budget, Congress is considering abolishing the National Bureau of Rubber Stamp Plant Sizing. This bureau has the task of telling the otherwise perfectly competitive producers of rubber stamps what size factories to build. The chairman of the bureau tries to defend himself by saying, "There are economies of scale in this industry. Without our guidance, there would be too many small, inefficient producers." You are called to testify against the bureau. Show why perfect competition would prevent the small, inefficient plants from surviving.

Imperfect Markets I:

Why They

Exist and

the Case of

Monopoly

OVERALL OBJECTIVE: Overall objective: To begin the study of imperfect markets by examining the reasons why they exist and considering the case of monopoly (a single seller).

MORE SPECIFICALLY:

- To explain that imperfectly competitive firms face a downward-sloping demand curve; for them, a greater quantity sold causes the price received to fall, while a smaller quantity causes prices to rise.

- To examine the causes of imperfections in markets, which include imperfect information, high transactions costs in interfirm trade, economies of scale, government regulation, patents and copyrights, tariffs and quotas, superior management, control of an essential resource, and high entry costs.

- To show that a profit-maximizing monopoly will choose to produce the quantity of output where marginal revenue equals marginal cost, so charging a higher price than it would if the firm were perfectly competitive.

- To trace the probable economic consequences of monopoly on output (lower), costs (higher), price (higher), profits (increased), the distribution of income (less equal), rent-seeking activity (increased), efficiency of production (decreased), and allocative efficiency (decreased).

- To investigate why price discrimination may be profitable and when it is possible.

Perfectly competitive firms are "price-takers" with no control over the price they receive. But perfect competition is rare in modern economies, for reasons that we trace in this chapter. Rather frequently, firms can gain some measure of control over the price they charge, becoming "price-makers" rather than "price-takers." When this is so, the resulting market is called an imperfect market.[1]

One main feature distinguishes imperfect markets from those that are perfectly competitive. Changes in output by a firm that is an imperfect competitor affect the price of its product, but a perfectly competitive firm has no influence on the market. A perfect competitor dares not raise its price above what other sellers are charging, for then all sales will be lost to those competitors. It will not lower its price, because it can already sell all it can produce at the prevailing market price. If an *imperfect* competitor raises its price, however, some people will indeed cease to buy its product, but others will be willing to pay the higher amount. And if it lowers its price, it will increase its sales.

An imperfect competitor's demand curve for its product is therefore downward-sloping. As Figure 7.1 shows, an imperfect competitor can produce various quantities of output, but every change it makes will alter the price it can charge. If it produces and sells Q_1, it can charge price P_1.[2] However, if it raises its output to Q_2 and tries to sell that amount, it "spoils" the price. To sell this larger quantity the firm will have to reduce its price to P_2. Conversely, if it restores output to Q_1, it can again charge P_1.

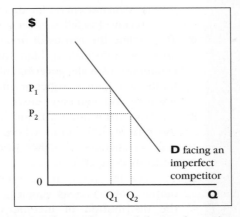

Figure 7.1. An imperfect competitor faces a downward-sloping demand curve. An imperfect competitor's downward-sloping demand curve indicates that it is large enough so that its decisions to raise or lower quantity will force it to change its price.

The degree of control a firm may have over price can vary greatly, from slight to substantial. If it is slight, the demand curve will have a very shallow slope. A price increase by a single firm will cause most of its customers to take their business to other firms, while lower prices will attract many buyers from other firms. If a firm's degree of control over price is substantial—perhaps it is the only seller, a monopoly—its demand curve will be steeper. If it raises its price, it will not lose customers to the competition because there isn't any; if it lowers its prices, there are no other firms from which to attract customers. In short, the elasticity of the demand curve facing a firm is a good indicator of the degree of competition in an industry.

1.   As suggested in the preceding chapter, "perfect" does not necessarily mean "desirable" nor does "imperfect" necessarily mean "to be avoided."

2.   In this section, "production" has the same meaning as "sales." Additions to and subtractions from inventory will be discussed later in the book.

► THE CAUSES OF MARKET IMPERFECTION

The reasons why a market may be imperfect are varied. Some of them are frequently encountered, while others are relatively rare. The conditions can and often do occur simultaneously; that is, a market may be imperfect for several of the reasons discussed here. In this section, we discuss the causes of market imperfection.

IMPERFECT INFORMATION

The first condition under which the firm may exercise some control over price prevails when consumers have **imperfect information** about the product the firm is marketing. Because consumers are generalists, it takes time for them to acquire knowledge about products and to shop around for the best price. "Time is money"; it would be irrational for consumers to devote more of their valuable time on such pursuits than what they are likely to gain from doing so. (The principle that the search for information will continue as long as the additional benefit is greater than the extra cost of continuing the search is known as the *optimal search rule*.) The prevalence of imperfect information among buyers gives firms an opportunity to introduce and maintain different prices for what are essentially the same products.

WHEN IMPERFECT INFORMATION WILL BE IMPORTANT

We would expect imperfect information to be more important the smaller the percentage of consumers' budgets spent on a given item. The less spent on that item, the lower the payoff in expending the effort to find the lowest price. Less search effort by buyers would have the effect of decreasing the pressure on suppliers to charge the same price for the item.

There is abundant anecdotal information that producers frequently follow practices that would not exist if information were more widely available. In the case of flour, for example, a famous company is known to package exactly the same product in different containers, label them with different names, and price them differently. A student at the author's college visiting the factory of a well-known spaghetti-maker discovered that the spaghetti coming off the line and being boxed as a "store brand" destined for sale at a lower price was exactly the same as the maker's own "name brand" for sale at a higher price. Companies follow this practice as an inexpensive way to capture the demand of two groups of consumers: those who want a high-quality product and believe that high price correlates with high quality, and those looking for the more ordinary (hence lower-price) item. Because either way, the item represents a relatively small expenditure to buyers and the makers can assume that these buyers will not spend much time checking out their assumptions. (Note that if a company puts the name brand into stores more quickly and makes sure the boxes do not stay on the shelf for long, while not taking such care with the store brand, then a price premium may be justified after all.)

Because incomplete information is widespread, consumers are certain to make mistakes. To avoid disappointment, they will often rely on the firm's reputation when they make purchases. A firm that is regarded as honest and reliable is in a position to charge a premium for its products. In a way, consumers who take the firm's reputation into account are "insuring" against the consequences of imperfect information. Again, conditions favor the likelihood of price differentials for the same product, and the market will be imperfect rather than perfectly competitive.

TRANSACTIONS COSTS

A firm's **transactions costs** are another reason why it might obtain some control over the price it charges.[3] Each firm must decide whether to buy the inputs it needs, such as raw materials and semifinished items, from other firms or to produce them itself. In other words, it must decide whether to "make or buy." Firms that choose to make most of their inputs will probably be larger and consequently may be in a position to exercise some degree of market power.

Assuming a firm could either make or buy, what would cause it to make? It might do so if buying involves greater transactions costs. Four separate costs of transacting can be identified. (1) *Brokerage,* the cost of matching buyer and seller. Acquiring information, for firms as well as for consumers, takes time and costs money. Sometimes the firm pays the cost directly, as when it hires a broker or an agent. Often the cost is shared by buyer and seller as they seek to locate and obtain information about each other. (2) *Contracting,* the cost of drawing up contracts to cover the contingencies of buying and selling, and then monitoring and enforcing them. A good deal of haggling may be necessary; a careful watch on performance has to be kept; and lawyers' fees tend to be high. (3) *Risk,* the cost arising from nondelivery, cheating on the part of the supplier, and overcharging. (4) The *loss of commercial secrets* to competitors who observe what inputs the firm is buying.

Large firms that make their inputs rather than buying them can *internalize* these transactions costs. When its inputs are made by the firm itself, there is a good chance that knowledge will be improved, with less need for brokerage, for haggling, for contracts and lawyers. Risks of nondelivery may be reduced. The firm knows that the goals of the provider of the input and the producer of the output are the same or at least similar; suppliers are not constantly trying to "steal a march." Its commercial secrets will be safer. A firm will weigh these possible benefits against the costs of internalizing the transactions, mainly that administration becomes more complex and more diffuse as an operation grows larger and involves more diverse production.

Even if firms decide to buy rather than make, they may develop strong links with a few trusted suppliers rather than shopping around for the lowest price. When firms do decide to reduce their transactions costs by internalizing them or by linking themselves to a favored small group of suppliers, they deal with a smaller number of firms, which in consequence will tend to move the industry away from perfect competition.

ECONOMIES OF SCALE

Another way in which a firm can exercise some control over price involves **economies of scale.** If a firm commands significant economies of scale, its average costs will decline as output increases, at least up to some level. Scale economies were noticed by Adam Smith, but in his time virtually all production was small in scale so he did not anticipate how important they would become. Scale economies are closely associated with the modern era of large mass-production industries. In Figure 7.2, for example, the average cost curve AC falls steadily from the low output level of 1,000 units to the high output level of 15,000 units. At that point, all economies of scale have been achieved, and AC turns up again.

---

3. Analysis of transactions costs was pioneered by Ronald Coase of the University of Chicago, winner of the 1991 Nobel Prize in Economics.

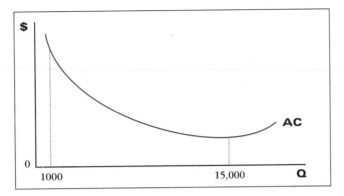

Figure 7.2. Economies of scale may bring a considerable reduction in average costs. In the figure, large economies of scale exist, with average cost continuing to drop until production hits a quite high level. Minimum cost may be reached at a level of output so high that perfect competition is impossible in this industry.

When economies of scale are significant, a firm may gain some control over the price it charges. In Figure 7.3, the demand curve D_1 represents the entire market demand for a product that is being produced under conditions of decreasing cost.

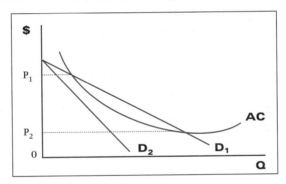

Figure 7.3. No room for two firms. In the figure there is enough demand so that one firm could charge a price that equals or exceeds AC, but not enough demand for two firms to do so. Perfect competition would not be possible in this industry.

If just one firm were the only producer in the industry, it could make a super-normal profit by charging any price between P_1 and P_2. Throughout that range the price is above the cost per unit. Now assume that another firm enters the industry and captures half the sales. Each company now faces a demand that is just half of what it was when only one firm commanded the entire market. Demand curve D_2 fits this description. At any given price, the quantity demanded along curve D_2 is exactly half what it was along D_1. Now neither firm can make a profit because there is no price that will cover the cost of production. The demand curve faced by both firms—curve D_2—lies below AC all along its length. In short, one firm can exist profitably in this industry and will have some freedom to choose the price it charges. Two firms cannot survive. The situation here is what is called a **natural monopoly**.[4]

---

4.   The weaker or less aggressive firm will presumably be forced to merge with the stronger or be driven out of existence. Natural monopolies occur because of technological circumstances coupled with free-market conditions. Other explanations of monopoly depend on an *absence* of free-market conditions.

The scale of operation does not have to be large in absolute terms for a natural monopoly to arise. For example, the general store in Caratunk, Maine (population 100), has some market power. The reason is that Caratunk generates insufficient demand to support two general stores, and there are no competing establishments for many miles around. The store can set its prices higher than would be true in a competitive market.[5]

Scale economies had been noticed for centuries, but they first became an important element in firms' achievement of market power in the nineteenth century, as discussed in the box.

SCALE ECONOMIES APPEARED IN THE NINETEENTH CENTURY

The wide appearance of scale economies was mainly a nineteenth-century development. In the United States, custom shoemakers found that they could not compete with the mass-produced machine-made shoes of Lynn, Massachusetts; village flour mills were beaten out by Pillsbury, Washburn, and others; farm implements could be made more cheaply by the large McCormick, Oliver, and Ames concerns than by the local blacksmith; small distillers were overwhelmed by the large-scale distilleries of Peoria and Baltimore; similar scale economies in the hands of Armour, Morris, and Swift crushed small-town meat packing all across the country. The predominance of the Duke family in tobacco, of Rockefeller's Standard Oil in kerosene, of the Studebakers in wagon building, of Pittsburgh and Bethlehem, Pennsylvania, in steel making, of Baldwin and Lima in the building of railroad locomotives, and a wide variety of other industries as well, all illustrate how economies of scale emerged as a major force for lower production costs—hence affording a new path to market power.

GOVERNMENT AS A SOURCE OF MARKET POWER

Governments have historically granted private firms protection against competition in many different fields. When they were founded in the seventeenth century, the British and Dutch East India Companies and the Hudson's Bay Company were based on government grants of monopoly power. Adam Smith's advocacy of free markets played a major role in ending these statutory monopolies, but governments still grant monopoly power for certain reasons.

Regulated Industries

When the government recognizes that large economies of scale exist in a certain industry, as in the case of natural monopoly mentioned previously, it may eliminate competition by regulating the industry.[6] In many regulated industries, a public utility franchise is granted to a single company. Typically, the regulated industry accepts some supervision and control over its

---

5.   A major reason why Caratunk cannot support another store is high opportunity costs. If these had been very low—that is, if the potential owners of competing stores had no better alternatives to starting up a store—then a much smaller demand might be sufficient to keep more than one store in existence. Thus, in the poorer parts of China or Africa, one finds sellers of goods in village markets dealing in very small quantities under highly competitive conditions, whereas in North America or Europe the greater opportunity costs may cause a market of the same size to be a natural monopoly.

6.   Breaking up a natural monopoly into a number of smaller firms, say by means of government antitrust laws meant to encourage competition, would be damaging because it would lead to higher production costs.

rates in return for a guarantee that no competitor will enter its market. The government usually resorts to this practice when the duplication of expensive capital facilities would be wasteful. Imagine the inconvenience of having to write separate checks to two or more telephone companies for service, and the wasted expenditure on wires and poles strung by competing phone and electricity companies.[7] The tangle of overhead wires and cables seen in old pictures of New York City and other cities shows what happens when two or three competing phone and power companies each strings its own set of wires. Not visible in the pictures are the duplicated central exchanges, generating facilities, and the like.

Other examples of public utilities include water, natural gas systems, and public transport systems. The phrase "public utility" is a little misleading because ownership frequently remains in private hands. However, the government itself sometimes owns and operates utilities, though less commonly in the United States than elsewhere. Even in the United States, the government owns and operates the postal system, most waterworks and sewage systems, many hydroelectric dams in the southeastern and western states, Amtrak, and most highways.

Whether owned privately or by government, utilities that are regarded as natural monopolies are often granted protection against the entry of competing rivals. Competition would result in reduced economies of scale and would greatly increase expenditures on a wasteful duplication of facilities. Here is a case where an increased number of competing firms might cause serious damage to the economy.

Patents and Copyrights

Other government grants—**patents** and **copyrights**—have the ability to bestow market power on private firms. Patents originated in seventeenth-century Britain. They give the patent holder exclusive rights to the use of an invention for 17 years in the United States, for 20 years in Great Britain and most of western Europe, and for shorter periods in most other countries.[8] Patents are typically nonrenewable.

Intended to reward and encourage invention, patent legislation has led to market control by a single firm in several industries. In the United States, the Eastman patents in photography, the Edison patents in light bulbs, the Bell patents in telephones, Alcoa in aluminum, National Cash Register, and the control of the shoe industry by the United Shoe Machinery Company with its 6,000 patents, are all cases from an earlier era that led to domination of an industry by the holder of the patents.

The 17-year duration of patents is rather misleading, because a company that continues research on a basic invention may develop many patentable improvements and thus prolong its market domination years after the original patents have expired. More recent patents in such fields as computers (IBM) and photocopying (Xerox) have led to the emergence of new industrial empires. In the pharmaceuticals industry, profitable patents have been granted for the treatment of ailments ranging from acne (Roche's Acutane) to AIDS (Burroughs and Wellcome's AZT).

Copyrights serve much the same purpose as patents. Formerly of concern only to authors, playwrights, composers, photographers, artists, and sculptors, copyrights are now important for originators of computer software as well. Copyrights in the United States extend for 28 years, renewable for another 28. (In many other countries, a copyright lasts for 50 years after the death of its holder.)

---

7.   Mexico City was until quite recently a case of a locale with two telephone companies, duplicate phones in most major offices, and duplicate billing.

8.   The original British law of 1624 granted coverage for 14 years. The British colonies in North America were subject to the law of 1624, and the United States continued to use the 14-year figure following its independence. The U.S. law was changed to 17 years in 1861. Numerous nations grant a shorter period of patent protection. The average for 45 countries not including the United States and western Europe is only 11 years. A new international agreement will, if ratified, standardize the period of protection at 20 years.

Tariffs and Quotas

Finally, governments impose tariffs and quotas to discourage competition. These policy tools prevent foreign firms from competing on the same terms as domestic firms and, by restricting supply, may make it possible for domestic firms to raise their prices. Firms that are unable to achieve market power in the presence of unrestricted foreign competition may be able to do so in a domestic economy protected by trade barriers. We analyze barriers to foreign trade in Chapter 27.

SUPERIOR MANAGEMENT

Yet another source of market imperfection is the superior quality of management that may reside in some of an industry's firms. Even under conditions that would otherwise be competitive, better management might keep some firms' cost curves lower than others, so that the firms with the lower costs earn super-normal profits for long periods. Occasionally, a truly talented entrepreneur with insight and vision, motivation, ability to develop wanted products, and capacity for utilizing new techniques and new methods of organization can win significant market control and lead a firm to preeminence in its field.

The genius of Henry Ford provides an obvious example. In 1910–1911 there were nearly 300 car manufacturers in the United States. By 1929 there were only 23. A major reason for this great shakeout was that in the early 1920s, Ford was selling more cars than all his competitors put together. Ford's success might appear to be only another example of the economies of scale argument discussed earlier. But it was also due to his management skill. He pioneered production-line assembly. First at his Highland Park plant, and later at the much larger Willow Run factory, which still produces cars in Detroit, Ford used a moving assembly line to carry the semifinished product from workstation to workstation. He also organized a complex network of suppliers and established assembly plants at a number of dispersed locations. These advances allowed the price of a Model T Ford to drop from $950 in 1909, the year after the assembly-line technique was introduced, to $360 in 1916 and $240 in 1925.

More recent examples of entrepreneurs whose talents have led to market dominance include Edwin Land at Polaroid, Steve Jobs at Apple Computer, and JVC's Shizuo Takano and Yuma Shiraishi, the developers of the VCR. In addition to their technical expertise, these entrepreneurs had a broad vision of the market and how to reach it.

Of course the market power derived from superior management will vanish if successive managers lack the entrepreneurial gift. Even Henry Ford himself lost his touch. "A customer can have any color as long as it's black," he once remarked. He resisted the idea of trade-ins and refused to allow a self-starter to be installed in the Model T. He held out for the "planetary" transmission rather than the conventional gearshift (the car usually crept forward even when it was in neutral), and for a mechanical brake that gripped the drive shaft rather than hydraulic brakes on the wheels.

Finally it became obvious even to Henry Ford that the Model T had to be replaced, but introducing a new model (the Model A in 1927) proved to be difficult. The machine tools with which the "T" was built were permanent fixtures. They had to be torn out and new ones installed when the new car was put into production, leaving Willow Run a temporary ruin. The "A" never matched the great success of the "T", and by the late 1930s, the Ford Motor Company is said to have been perhaps the poorest managed and least efficient large corporation in the market economies. Richard S. Tedlow graphically described it as "a brontosaurus of big business, living off its fat, governed by a tiny brain, blubbering its way through the tar pits of life." After Henry Ford died (in 1947), the problems extended to another generation of managers. The Ford product named after his son, the Edsel, became one of the legendary failures in U.S. economic history. The Ford experience demonstrates that managerial superiority can be a fragile and impermanent route to market dominance.

CONTROL OF AN ESSENTIAL RESOURCE

The control of some essential resources, either natural or man-made in the form of knowledge, may enable a firm (or government) to command market power. Among natural resources, the control of oil reserves has brought significant influence over price to a lucky or far-sighted few. Other natural resources where competition has been precluded by control over supply include nickel, almost all the reserves of which were at one time owned by Canada's International Nickel Company; molybdenum, most of which is produced by the American Metal Climax Corporation; magnesium; radium; and sulphur. Most of the planet's helium is produced by the U.S. Bureau of Mines, largely in the area around Amarillo, Texas. The De Beers diamond concern in South Africa controls the marketing of most of the world's high-quality diamond supply, as discussed in the accompanying box.

DE BEERS CONSOLIDATED MINES: A FAMOUS MONOPOLY

De Beers Consolidated Mines, Ltd., is the most well-known current example of a firm with monopoly power based on natural resource control. The firm was founded by Cecil Rhodes, who later devoted some of his immense fortune to funding the famous Rhodes scholarships at Oxford University. (It was named for two brothers on whose South African land diamonds had been found in the 1870s.) The company markets some 80% of the world's diamonds, produced in its own South African mines and purchased under contract from the mines of most other diamond-producing countries. Its selling organization, based in Amsterdam, carefully manages the supply of diamonds to the world's buyers, so boosting their price. De Beers currently faces the danger that the diamond production of the former USSR might eventually be marketed outside its framework, posing a danger to its monopoly power.

In many industries, the control of technical knowledge serves to limit competition. Knowledge of processes and procedures may be carefully guarded and difficult for outsiders to acquire, and patents and copyrights may make it illegal to copy such "proprietary knowledge." Entry into a wide variety of "high tech" industries—including aerospace, computers, and pharmaceuticals—is inhibited by the difficulty of acquiring information about the relevant technologies.

THE HIGH COST OF ENTRY

High cost of entry can discourage entrepreneurs from attempting to enter an industry. Where large buildings, expensive machines, or extensive landholdings are needed, the number of competitors is likely to be small even when profits are high. Unknown entrepreneurs may be turned away by banks because of insufficient security, and their inexperience may make their stock unsaleable.[9]

---

9. Charles Duryea, the pioneer U.S. automaker, was refused small loans by bankers. His company was never much of a success. Will Durant, who dreamed of production on a large scale and later was able to put together General Motors, was told by a banker to "keep those notions to himself if he ever wanted to borrow money." James Couzens, the treasurer of the fledgling Ford Motor Company, was thrown out of so many banks in Detroit trying to raise money for Ford that he was once found weeping on a curb.

As an example of the deterrent effect of high capital costs, when Alexander Graham Bell's telephone patents expired in 1894, independent telephone companies sprang up all over the United States to compete with Bell's AT&T. But AT&T would not allow them to utilize its long-distance trunk lines. Because it would have been far too expensive for the independents to string their own trunk lines, the only way they could offer long-distance service was by connecting their local lines at the perimeters of their territories and routing calls through the operators of several different companies. By 1904 people could make a call from Cleveland to St. Louis by this method, but the service was slow and the lines were plagued by static. Eventually, the independents gave up long-distance service altogether. AT&T retained its monopoly based on the high cost of entry until the availability of microwave transmission in the 1980s made it profitable for competitors like MCI and Sprint to provide long-distance service. (A major court case in 1982 resulted in a voluntary decision by AT&T to allow competing companies to connect with its local service lines. Otherwise, firms like MCI and Sprint could not have entered the long-distance market without providing their own local service as well.)

Sometimes established firms may make entry more costly for newcomers. One predatory tactic, for the most part now illegal under the antitrust laws, is selective price cutting. At the turn of the century, John D. Rockefeller's Standard Oil Company made tactical reductions in local prices to levels that discouraged new entrants and forced smaller refineries either to merge with Standard or to leave the field altogether. In the rate wars of the late nineteenth and early twentieth centuries, railroads reduced their charges in order to erode the profit margins of potential or actual competitors.[10] Price wars in local markets for gasoline used to be quite common before the appearance of OPEC and still occur from time to time. (We will have more to say about "predatory pricing," some of it skeptical, in the next chapter.)

A more ordinary practice is the use of **exclusive dealerships.** The cost of introducing a new make of car is huge, in part because of the need to establish and maintain a nationwide organization of exclusive dealers. That cost element helps explain why no new U.S. automaker has successfully entered the market since the 1930s.[11] (The last to try was Kaiser-Frazer, which gave up in 1953.) Foreign automakers face the same problem, though to a lesser degree because car dealers are often eager to market a line of popular imported autos along with a domestic make. "Dodge-Toyota," "Pontiac-Isuzu," "Chevrolet-Nissan," and "Ford-Honda" dealers all appear in the author's local small city phone book. The costs of arranging dealerships are still significant, however, when new foreign firms attempt to enter the market.

Finally, the cost of entry into any industry in which advertising is important is invariably higher than otherwise. The established brand names of cigarettes, for example, are so familiar to the smoking public that a newcomer must be advertised on a grand scale if it is to attract attention. It is estimated that the advertising costs for launching a new brand of cigarettes in the United States run to about $50 million. Here, too, the high cost of entry bolsters the market power of already-established firms.

---

10.   A famous rate war in 1885 between Commodore Vanderbilt and the Pennsylvania Railroad resulted in Vanderbilt starting a new line (the South Pennsylvania Railroad) with many tunnels between Pittsburgh and Harrisburg. The rate war ended with a truce, the unfinished new line was abandoned, but you can see it today because its derelict tunnels were purchased, cleaned out, and used for the Pennsylvania Turnpike. The most dramatic of all rate wars took place in India, in 1946, when the India State Railways actually paid shippers to use their line.

11.   Henry Ford was active here, too. The Ford Motor Company had a major role in establishing exclusive franchised dealers as the standard in the auto market. Before that, you would buy your new car from a hardware store or livery stable, wagon dealer or bicycle shop, each marketing several different makes. You could even buy by mail order from a firm like Sears. Criticism of the franchise system as leading to diseconomies of small scale, and annoyance from not being offered a fixed price have been made in recent years, but that system is deeply entrenched. U.S. automakers only rarely grant franchises to dealers who already sell the cars of a competing U.S. company, and many states have laws backing up the practice. In the United States, Porsche's attempt in 1984 to market its cars by means of direct contact between the main office and potential buyers was abandoned as lawsuits from Porsche dealers mounted up. In Japan, however, door-to-door marketing of new cars is standard practice, with negotiations taking place in the buyer's home. Recently, the U.S. system has been undergoing some change. Some "mega-dealers," mostly in large cities, have persuaded manufacturers to grant them several franchises, the cars often displayed in side-by-side showrooms or in auto malls.

All these reasons why the cost of entry to an industry may be high are important in explaining imperfect competition. Where entry is costly, an enterprise must obtain considerable financing just to get a start. Once "sunk" into capital such as machines and buildings, the money cannot easily be transferred to other uses. The risks of attempting to compete are boosted, perhaps considerably, because any loss if an enterprise does not prove to be profitable will be magnified by the possible loss of some or most of the sunk capital. Entry by competing firms may thus be deterred.

Conclusion

Each of the considerations discussed to this point in the chapter—incomplete information, high transactions costs, economies of scale, government grants of market power, superior management, control of an essential resource, and high costs of entry—is an imperfection in the market that can prevent an industry from being perfectly competitive. The remainder of this chapter together with the next three analyze the variations in economic organization where competition is imperfect.

▶ The Special Case of Monopoly

At the furthest limit of imperfect competition, a firm may be the *only* seller in its industry and is known as a **monopoly.** (The word monopoly comes from the Greek *monos polein,* which means single seller.) In today's economy, unregulated monopoly is rare, with monopoly firms estimated to produce no more than 2% or so of the nation's output. Not very long ago, however, complete or virtually complete monopolies existed in several industries.[12]

Even though present-day examples of monopoly are hard to find, studying the case of monopoly is useful. It is a relatively simple model of a polar case, just as was the other polar case, perfect competition. The tools developed in the study of these two extremes enable us to investigate the vast middle ground—the world of department stores and supermarkets, medium-size and large businesses.

Because a monopoly firm is the only firm in its industry, the demand curve for the product of a monopoly must be the same as the demand curve for the industry. Like almost all demand curves for whole industries, it will be downward-sloping. A monopoly can produce various quantities of output, but every change it makes will alter the price it can charge. If it raises its output and tries to sell that amount, it will have to reduce its price. If it reduces its output, it can charge a higher price.

This necessary alteration in prices when a monopoly changes its output means that a monopoly firm cannot calculate its sales revenues in the same way as a perfect competitor. For the competitor, additional output is sold at the same market price as before, and reducing output does not change the price either. If a monopoly raises output and thus causes a fall in price, then possibly this lower price, even when multiplied by the higher quantity produced, may result in total revenue lower than before. The monopoly's marginal revenue (the extra revenue from selling another unit of output) would in this case be negative. Recall from Chapter 3 that lowering price along the inelastic portion of a demand curve (lower half) will reduce total revenue despite the higher quantity produced. But if the price is lowered and the quantity increases along the *elastic* portion (upper half) of the demand curve, total revenue will *rise.* This relationship has a direct bearing on the monopoly's attempt to maximize its profits.

---

12.   William G. Shepherd estimates that monopoly production was 2.5% of total U.S. output in 1980, compared to 3.1% in 1958 and 6.2% in 1939. See his "Causes of Increased Competition in the U.S. Economy, 1939–1980," *Review of Economics and Statistics,* Vol. 64, No. 4, November 1982, p. 618. Shepherd states that in practice, the firms involved are certain utilities and producers of some patented goods.

A MONOPOLY'S COSTS AND REVENUES

In order to analyze how a monopoly maximizes profit, we must examine both its costs and its revenues. Figure 7.4 shows a U-shaped average cost curve and a marginal cost curve cutting across it in the usual way. Remember that cost curves are constructed from numbers that are essentially engineering data. Moving from perfect competition to monopoly does not mean a change in the logic underlying these curves, nor does it involve any fundamental alteration in their shapes, though the scale of operations may be much bigger.

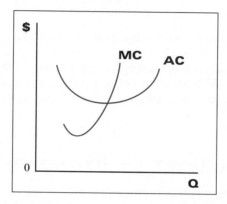

Figure 7.4. The monopoly's cost curves are familiar. The AC and MC curves for a monopoly do not differ in their appearance from those of a firm under perfect competition, though the quantity of output is likely to be much larger.

The demand curve facing the monopoly is, however, different from that under perfect competition because, as we have seen, the firm's demand curve is also the demand curve for the entire industry. It has a downward slope, as in Figure 7.5. As with any demand curve, we can calculate total revenue at a given price by multiplying price times quantity: P x Q = TR. Thus, if 3 units are sold for $10 each, the total revenue earned is 3 x $10 = $30; if 4 units are sold for $9 each, the total revenue earned is 4 x $9 = $36.

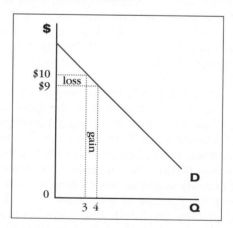

Figure 7.5. Finding a monopoly's total revenue. A monopoly's total revenue can be found by multiplying price times quantity. Unlike under perfect competition, however, a greater quantity will involve a lower price.

A MONOPOLY'S MARGINAL REVENUE

From the information on total revenue we can determine a monopoly's *marginal revenue,* which is essential for determining the quantity of output a profit-maximizing monopoly will choose to produce. Recall from Chapter 6 that **marginal revenue (MR)** is *the addition to total revenue resulting from the sale of one more unit of output.* When we discussed perfect competition, we found that marginal revenue was easy to calculate because in that situation MR is the same as the price of the good. The competitive firm can always sell one more unit for the same price as all the previous units it sold. So the curve showing marginal revenue is the same as the firm's horizontal demand curve.

For a monopoly, however, marginal revenue is *not* the same as price. In Figure 7.5, note that the third unit can be sold for $10, but in order to sell the fourth unit the monopoly must cut its price to $9. The firm had been selling the first 3 units for $10 each. With the price cut to $9, it gains $9 from selling the fourth item but loses $1 each on the sale of units 1, 2, and 3, or $3 in all. In net terms, the gain of $9 and the loss of $3 result in extra receipts from the sale of the last item (marginal revenue) of $6. Another way of reaching that same conclusion is to say that originally the total revenue was 3 units x $10 = $30 and that the new total revenue is 4 units x $9 = $36, or a marginal revenue of $6 from selling an additional unit.

So for a monopoly, marginal revenue is the addition to total revenue from selling an additional unit. Marginal revenue can also be calculated by taking the price of the last (nth) unit sold and subtracting from it the loss in revenue on previous units resulting from the reduction in price. These two methods yield the same result.

Positioning the Marginal Revenue Curve

Fortunately, it is easy to position a curve for marginal revenue on a diagram. Figure 7.6 shows a straight-line demand curve.

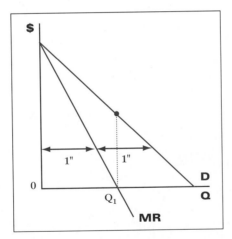

Figure 7.6. The marginal revenue curve of a monopoly. A monopoly's MR lies below its demand curve, indicating that a price cut means more sales but also means a lower price on what was being sold before. So marginal revenue is not as great as price. When the demand curve is a straight line, the MR curve is also a straight line located halfway between the demand curve and the vertical axis.

In Chapter 3 we saw that the price elasticity of a straight-line demand curve is unitary at the line's exact center. Therefore, a very small price change at this point will leave total revenue unchanged. The marginal revenue associated with that price change must be 0, as at quantity Q_1 in the figure. Where the demand curve is elastic (upper part), a price cut will increase the firm's total revenue and marginal revenue is positive. Where the demand curve is inelastic (lower part), the reverse is true; a price cut will decrease total revenue and marginal revenue is negative. Conveniently, when the demand curve is a straight line, the marginal revenue curve associated with it is also a straight line that runs halfway between the vertical axis and the demand curve itself, as shown in the figure.[13]

PROFIT MAXIMIZATION FOR A MONOPOLY

We now have all the information we need to find the price and quantity of output at which a monopoly will maximize its profit. That position occurs where marginal revenue equals marginal cost, MR = MC. The logic is the same as when we analyzed perfect competition: if the revenue generated by the last item sold is greater than the cost of producing it, then the firm's total profit will be increased by expanding output. But if the last item costs more to produce than the revenue generated by its sale, then total profit will be diminished by producing it.

Check this conclusion by considering Figure 7.7, which combines the demand curve and the marginal revenue curve of a monopoly with its average cost and marginal cost curves. Could an output of 290 units rather than 300 possibly maximize profits? It could not. See how the revenue from selling the last, or 290th, unit as identified on the MR curve at K is slightly higher than the cost of producing that 290th unit, shown on the MC curve at L. The marginal revenue from a 291st unit also would be greater than the MC of producing it. If only 290 units are produced, some profit is being sacrificed. The same is true of a 292nd unit, a 293rd, and so forth up to 300 units where there is no remaining profit left to take.

Now consider a decision to produce 310 units. This cannot maximize profits either. The 310th unit cost more to produce, at M on the MC curve, than the revenue obtained from its sale, N on the MR curve. Production of the 310th unit must have involved a loss, and total profits cannot be maximized if that unit is produced. The same is true of the 309th, the 308th, and so forth. It will increase overall profits if these and all other units above 300 are not produced. Only where MC = MR, at 300 units in Figure 7.7, are profits maximized. This is a monopoly's equilibrium level of output.

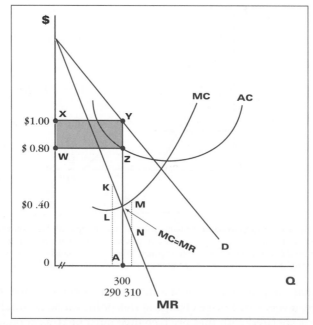

Figure 7.7. Calculating a monopoly's profit. A monopoly's super-normal profit is maximized at the quantity of output where MC = MR. The price is determined by running a line vertically upward from that quantity to the demand curve, and then over to the vertical axis. The profit is equal to the area of the shaded rectangle.

---

13.   The geometric proof of this takes more space than is appropriate. Geometry texts can be consulted by those interested in pursuing the proof.

As always, cost is defined as opportunity cost, including normal profit just sufficient to keep the entrepreneurs with the firm. Maximum profit occurs where MC = MR. In the figure, this is at an output level of 300 units. What can this monopoly charge if it produces 300 units? A quick guess might be $0.40, where MC and MR cross. At that price, however, the quantity demanded would be far more than 300, so $0.40 could not be an equilibrium price. Actually, the demand curve tells us that the monopoly could charge a price of $1.00 per unit without creating an unwanted surplus or shortage. Even though the market will bear a price of $1.00 for the 300 units, note that producing those units *costs* the firm only $0.80 per unit, as the average *cost* curve shows. This leaves the monopoly with a super-normal profit of $1.00–$0.80 per unit, or $0.20 per unit. In total this is: $0.20 profit per unit times 300 units = $60.

We can put this arithmetic into more general terms by making use of the geometry of rectangles. In Figure 7.7, the profit per unit is the distance from W to X. The number of units is the distance from 0 to A, which is the same as X to Y. Multiplying one side of a rectangle WX by another side XY gives the area of that rectangle, WXYZ. WXYZ is thus the total profit of the monopoly at the profit-maximizing equilibrium.

The logic can be checked by another means. We know that total revenue minus total cost equals total (super-normal) profit. In Figure 7.7 the monopoly firm's total revenue is found by multiplying the price per unit ($1.00, the distance from 0 to X) by the number of units (300, the distance from 0 to A). Total revenue is thus $300, the area of the rectangle 0XYA. Total cost is found by multiplying the cost per unit ($0.80, the distance from 0 to W) by the number of units (300, the distance from 0 to A). Total cost is thus $240, the area of the rectangle 0WZA. Total revenue $300 minus total cost of $240 equals total profit $60; in terms of the rectangles total revenue 0XYA minus total cost 0WZA equals the remainder, the shaded rectangle WXYZ, which is the total profit.

Notice that equilibrium for a monopoly must always occur in the elastic range (upper half) of the demand curve. Any output greater than that, beyond the halfway point on the demand curve, would mean that marginal revenue was negative. In that range, every additional unit produced would reduce revenues, and every reduction of a unit produced would raise revenues.

THE ECONOMIC CONSEQUENCES OF MONOPOLY

The logic underlying the price and quantity decisions that maximize profit for a monopoly reveal that in several major respects, monopolies may be inherently unfavorable to the consuming public, though they surely benefit their owners, the managers who run them, and the factors of production they employ. Much depends, however, on how important economies of scale are in a given industry. We illustrate monopoly's consequences in Figure 7.8. By assumption, the demand curve is drawn through the lowest point of the average cost curve. Though in practice that positioning would occur merely by chance, placing it there will facilitate comparison between the behavior of a monopoly firm and a perfect competitor.

A Likelihood of Lower Output, Higher Costs, and Higher Prices

A profit-maximizing monopoly is likely to produce less and charge a higher price than will the firms in a competitive industry. In Figure 7.8, the monopoly's profits are maximized at quantity Q_m.

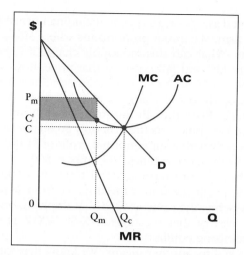

Figure 7.8. The disadvantages of monopoly. Several potential disadvantages of monopoly can be viewed on the diagram. These include lower quantities, higher prices, higher production costs, and monopoly profits.

What will happen if the monopoly is suddenly faced with perfectly competitive conditions? (Perhaps this happened because the monopoly's country has joined in a common market with neighboring countries that have many firms in this industry.) Now the overall demand for the product will be much greater, and each firm will face a horizontal demand curve. If costs are the same for all producers, then following adjustment to the competitive pressures the horizontal demand curve will be located at price C. The competitive pressures will eliminate super-normal profit and will cause production to occur at the quantity that minimizes cost per unit. This is at quantity Q_c, where average cost equals price at level C. Left to itself, however, the monopoly will maximize profit at the lower quantity Q_m.

Because the monopoly firm chooses to produce a smaller quantity than it would under perfect competition, its costs will be higher. Under competitive conditions, the firm will be forced to produce at the lowest point on its average cost curve, but the monopoly will be higher up on that curve. See how the monopoly's choice of a lower quantity of production causes its costs to be C', higher than the C under perfect competition.

Finally, by reducing output, the monopoly can charge a higher price. In a perfectly competitive industry the price is C. Under monopoly, with production of the lesser amount Q_m the price charged will be higher (P_m). Note that the degree to which a monopoly finds it profitable to raise its price is governed by the price elasticity of demand. If the demand for a monopoly's product is less elastic, then consumers will pay a higher price without cutting back their purchases very much. In such a case, the monopoly with a less elastic demand curve can charge a price higher than if its demand curve were more elastic, with profits consequently greater than the shaded area in Figure 7.8.

We would have to modify these conclusions if the output of a monopoly firm were large enough so that the firm realized significant economies of scale, perhaps even qualifying it as a natural monopoly. With the average cost curve continuing to decline at higher levels of production, our predictions that the monopoly would produce less at a higher cost and higher price might not hold true. Equilibrium could *conceivably* occur at a higher quantity of output and lower price than under competition. (We will return to this question later.)

The Monopoly's Retention of Super-Normal Profits

As Figure 7.8 shows, the monopoly will maximize profit by producing quantity Q_m. If the firm were suddenly faced with a perfectly competitive situation, it would be forced to alter its level of output, because new firms would enter the industry to share in the super-normal profit being earned by the monopoly. In the long run, that profit would be eliminated by the forces of competition. Because a monopoly is protected by barriers to entry, it does not have to concern itself with competing firms, which cannot enter to share the profit. The monopoly's above-normal profitability could continue even in the long run.

The Allocation of Resources and the Distribution of Income under Monopoly

As we have seen, a monopoly will operate at a lower level of output than a competitive industry with many firms; consequently, its employment of factors of production will be lower. Moreover, the higher price it charges means that other industries using its output as input are likely to purchase less of it than they otherwise would. All this implies a nonoptimal allocation of society's resources.

This misallocation will probably cause the distribution of income to be different from what it would be under competitive conditions. A monopoly extracts its super-normal profits from the pockets of consumers and deposits them in the pockets of its owners (stockholders) and managers. If the consumers have lower average incomes than these owners and managers, as is often the case, income is transferred from poorer to richer. In any case, income is being redistributed from losers (consumers) to gainers (the monopolists). That leads to the likelihood that "rent-seeking activity" will arise, as we will see in the next section.

Rent-Seeking Activity

Monopoly profits are often called "rents." (The reason for the use of this term is explored in Chapter 12.) These profits or rents may be so attractive that a firm will devote resources to capturing them in the first place and to assuring that they will continue to flow. For example, the monopoly may hire lobbyists to promote tariffs against imports, to guard against government regulation, or to ensure that existing regulations are not altered in an unfavorable way. Moves to secure and protect such advantages and the resulting profit or rent is called "rent-seeking activity." The monopoly decides to devote *some* of its super-normal profit to safeguard or enlarge what remains. Rent-seeking activities include illegal bribery and corruption as well as legal lobbying and other political action.

Inefficiency of Production

The monopoly has little motivation to modernize its plant or to eliminate inefficiencies in production. Because profits are above normal anyway, it may prefer to allow the firm's old equipment to wear out before replacing it, even if more efficient designs become available. With the spur of competition absent, a stagnant "don't rock the boat" mentality may set in at all levels of management. Harvey Leibenstein of Harvard University has used the term "X-inefficiency" to describe this slacking off of managerial effort, which is a type of inefficiency in production. Under competition, inefficient firms are driven out of business, but under monopoly they may well continue to operate.

Allocative Inefficiency (Deadweight Loss)

Finally, the monopoly is subject to allocative inefficiency, or deadweight loss. In Figure 7.9, the marginal revenue curve must cut the marginal cost curve to the left of the point where the downward-sloping demand curve crosses the marginal cost curve.

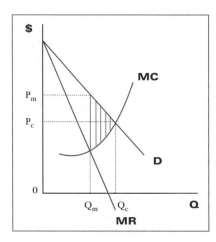

Figure 7.9. Allocative inefficiency (deadweight loss) of the monopoly. When a monopoly reduces its production to raise its prices, it introduces an allocative inefficiency. Consumers are willing to pay more for the output between Q_m and Q_c than it costs the monopoly to produce these units. The allocative inefficiency can be seen as a shaded triangle between the demand and marginal cost curves.

That being so, society suffers a loss in output. Had this industry been competitive, the quantity produced would have been higher at Q_c. There, price P_c is equal to marginal cost, the equilibrium condition under perfect competition. Because the industry is a monopoly, it will produce only Q_m where MC = MR, the equilibrium condition under monopoly.

The lost output results in an allocative inefficiency or deadweight loss. The cost in resources of producing one more unit is shown by the marginal cost curve; but consumers would be willing to pay a price as shown on the demand curve. Another unit beyond output Q_m, and yet others all the way to quantity Q_c, could be produced at a cost less than what consumers would be willing to pay. The resulting triangle of allocative inefficiency will be present even if the monopoly commands large economies of scale. Remember, however, that in the case of a natural monopoly with large economies of scale the relevant comparison is not between the allocative inefficiency of a monopoly and the efficiency of perfect competition. If an industry is characterized by decreasing costs, then it may be a monopoly *because* of free-market forces, and restoring perfect competition in these circumstances would not be possible. This outcome of natural monopoly must be compared to regulated monopoly or government ownership rather than to the results under perfect competition.

EMPIRICAL ESTIMATES OF ALLOCATIVE INEFFICIENCY

The actual size of the allocative inefficiency or deadweight loss in an economy is a difficult empirical problem, and the range of estimates is wide, from well under 1% of U.S. national income annually to as much as 7%. (These figures include the allocative inefficiency of firms that have some market power but are not monopolies.) The pioneering estimates of Arnold Harberger (University of Chicago and UCLA) yielded the low figure of under 1%; D.R. Kamerschen of the University of Georgia has given a much larger figure of about 6%, while the high of 7% has been advanced by Keith Cowling of Warwick University and Dennis Mueller of the University of Maryland. The figures are all relatively small; even the largest, though certainly important, does not appear as overwhelming as implied by a long tradition of anti-monopoly invective. One view might be that the costs of imperfect competition are not actually all that important. Another view might be that foreign trade, the difficulty in obtaining and holding a monopoly position, regulation, and antitrust law have combined to keep the problem under control. Deterrence to monopoly power is the subject of Chapter 9.

Conclusion

All the disadvantages that we have discussed constitute a serious indictment of monopoly. They explain why many countries have adopted antitrust laws that provide for government regulation of monopolies and make some forms of monopoly illegal. They also explain why most economists are opposed to erecting barriers to foreign trade. Keeping one's borders open to imports may be one of the most effective ways to foster competition and discourage monopoly.

PRICE DISCRIMINATION

So far, we have assumed that a monopoly charges the same price to all buyers. Under certain circumstances, however, it may be more profitable to practice **price discrimination** by charging different prices to different buyers. Say two groups, adults and children, exhibit different demand curves for movie tickets. For children, demand is likely to be elastic; moderate price reductions will probably lead to large increases in movie attendance, and higher prices will cut back attendance sharply. (Children as a group are poorer than adults, and as a result are likely to be more sensitive to price changes.) Adults will be less sensitive to changes in ticket prices, and rises or falls in the price will not alter their attendance as much. Their demand is less elastic, as Figure 7.10 shows.

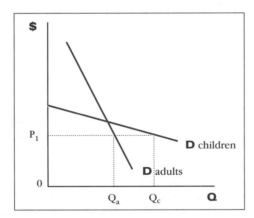

Figure 7.10. Elasticity of demand and price discrimination. The price elasticity of demand for movie tickets of children and adults differs. So it is profitable to undertake price discrimination. Lower prices for children and higher prices for adults will maximize profits.

So a single given price, such as P_1, would result in a quantity of tickets sold Q_a to adults and Q_c to children. This price will not maximize profits. A higher price for adults would increase total revenue from that segment of the market; adults' demand is inelastic (on the lower half of the demand curve) at price P_1. A lower price for children would increase total revenue from that segment; children's demand is elastic (on the upper half of the demand curve) at price P_1. In short, the monopoly can maximize profits within each age group, and thus its total profits as well, by charging higher prices for adults and lower prices for children.

Relatively few sellers are able to engage in price discrimination. Airlines can charge youth fares and sell cheaper tickets to those who purchase in advance with a Saturday-night stopover; electric utilities charge different rates depending on consumption; motels may set reduced off-season rates; and restaurants offer lower prices for the same item at lunch as at dinner. More broadly, a firm may sell the same product for a higher price in one country than in another.

Firms that engage in price discrimination must be in a position to segregate a market into independent groups by one means or another. In the examples just given, the segregation was based on age for the cinema and the airline with its youth fares; the sudden need for travel by business people and their unwillingness to be away on the weekend, as in airlines' rules for advance reservations and Saturday night layovers for the cheapest tickets; amount purchased for the electric company charging different rates depending on measured consumption; time of the year for the motel with off-season rates; time of day for the restaurant with lower lunch prices; and geographical location whenever national markets are separated by high barriers to trade.[14] Even the "cents off" coupons that companies put in their newspaper and magazine ads follow the same rule: they segregate on the basis of the greater sensitivity to price on the part of those willing to clip the coupons and take them to the store.

PRICE DIFFERENCES MAY REFLECT COST DIFFERENCES RATHER THAN PRICE DISCRIMINATION

Care must be taken when attempting to identify cases of price discrimination. If the cost of providing the product or service to the groups involved is different, then the price differential simply reflects the cost differential and does not represent price discrimination. For example, a motel in Vermont that closes down half its rooms in the off-season and a restaurant that closes one of its dining rooms for lunch may both have lower costs, and if so they are not discriminating when they charge a lower price for a night's stay or for lunch. It is not always easy to distinguish between price discrimination and cost differences.

If the ability to compartmentalize a market is lacking, however, price discrimination cannot work. If the children who buy cheap movie tickets could sell them to adults at a slightly higher price, these little entrepreneurs could turn a tidy profit.[15] They cannot do so because the adults, recognizable by the movie management, would be stopped at the door. The rule, then, is that where resale is difficult or impossible, price discrimination can be practiced. Otherwise it cannot. Perhaps the main reason price discrimination does not cause greater public uproar is that less elastic demand is usually exhibited by consumers with higher income, who are fewer in number than the lower-income consumers with the more elastic demand. In many cases, the few rather than the many are the ones who pay the higher price when discrimination is practiced.

CONCLUSION

Perfectly competitive markets are not often encountered in developed countries. (In less-developed countries, low opportunity costs often lead to many more competing firms and much greater competition in some markets.) Unadulterated monopolies are rare as well. The conditions leading to monopoly do not often occur, government regulation and antitrust law are frequently applied when they do occur, and foreign trade acts as a deterrent to them. Even so, the lessons learned in the last two chapters on perfect competition and monopoly have considerable relevance in the study of microeconomics, because many aspects of these polar models can be

---

14.   The price discrimination can be substantial. The same airlines frequently charge undiscounted fares 2½ to 4 times greater than those where the deepest discounts apply. Pharmaceutical firms operating in different countries are known to charge 10 times or more for exactly the same drugs. In this case, the differences can arise for either of two reasons: (1) because a multinational firm is the sole seller of a patented pharmaceutical, thus faces no competition and can charge different profit-maximizing prices; or (2) because trade barriers restrict competition and permit a higher price to be charged in the protected market.

15.   The practice of buying a good at a low price and selling it again at a high price is known as *arbitrage*. For the majority of goods where resale cannot be prevented, price discrimination would immediately cause arbitrage to spring up, which would work to eliminate the discrimination.

applied with advantage to the other forms of industrial organization that lie between them. These other forms, which actually characterize most markets in most developed countries, are the subject of the next chapter.

SUMMARY

1) Imperfectly competitive firms face a downward-sloping demand curve; for them, a greater quantity sold causes the price received to fall, while a smaller quantity causes prices to rise.

2) Reasons why markets may be imperfect include imperfect information among buyers, high transactions costs in interfirm trade, economies of scale, government regulation, patents and copyrights, tariffs and quotas, superior management, control of an essential resource, and high entry costs.

3) A profit-maximizing monopoly will choose to produce the quantity of output where marginal revenue equals marginal cost. It will charge a price as indicated by the demand curve directly above the output level where MR = MC. This price is predictably higher than it would be if the firm were perfectly competitive.

4) Unless economies of scale are particularly strong, monopolies are likely to have some damaging consequences for the public. These include lower output, higher production costs, higher prices, greater profits, a less equal distribution of income, a rise in rent-seeking activity, and greater productive and allocative inefficiency.

5) Price discrimination can be profitable if a firm finds it possible to charge a higher price to those whose demand is less elastic and a lower price to those whose demand is more elastic. But price discrimination can occur only if the seller is able to compartmentalize the market, identifying its customers by category and preventing resale of the item from those who have been charged a low price to those who have been charged a high price.

Chapter Key Words

Copyrights: Exclusive rights to publish or issue books and articles, photographs, plays, music, and now (increasingly) computer software, for 28 years in the United States, renewable for another 28 years. Protects writers, etc., but is also a means by which some firms gain market power in an industry. Also see *patents*.

Economies of scale: The condition wherein average costs fall as plant size increases.

Exclusive dealerships: The practice of limiting dealers to the sale of one firm's product. Often an effective way to raise costs for competing firms, who are thus forced to set up their own dealerships.

Imperfect information: The lack of complete information about potential competition that can be a reason why a market is imperfect.

Marginal revenue (MR): The extra revenue from selling one more unit of output.

Monopoly: One seller. Monopolies can result in higher prices for the consumer, less output, higher costs of production, long-lasting super-normal profits, income distribution problems, rent-seeking activity, stagnant operation, and allocative inefficiency. Also see *natural monopoly*.

Natural monopoly: The condition where a monopoly exists because the optimum size of a firm is too large or the size of the market is too limited to allow for more than one firm.

Patents: Exclusive rights to utilize an invention, for 17 years in the United States. Protects inventors, but also is a means by which some firms gain market power in an industry. Also see *copyrights*.

Price discrimination: The idea that profits can be maximized by charging individual groups of consumers different prices. Possible only where resale is prevented and where consumer groups can be segregated.

Transactions costs: A firm's costs of carrying on its transactions, which are likely to differ depending on whether the firm makes or buys its inputs. One reason why markets may be imperfect.

Chapter Questions

1) Chen's Rice Company is a major wholesale rice distributor in Taipei, Taiwan. Its brand name is widely respected in the city, although in truth its product is of no higher quality than its competitors. When Taiwan was a poorer country, rice was a large part of its citizens' budgets, but now Taiwan is better off and rice is a less important item on the shopping list. Chen's management hires you to explain how this change will affect the company. Draw the demand curves for Chen's Rice in the past and today. Justify their slopes using the concept of imperfect information.

2) In Figure 7.3, it was shown that sometimes there is no room for two firms in an industry, provided that the two split the total demand equally. Prove that if this is true, then there would be no room for two firms no matter how they split the output. Hint: Remember that the demand curves of the two firms must add to the total market demand. Think about the demand curve of the smaller of the two firms. Could that firm exist?

3) You receive a copyright on your word processing program called Slowwrite. As a promotion you give away copies of Slowwrite and find that people take 100 copies per day. Suppose your demand curve is straight and downward-sloping. After the promotion ends, how many copies should you produce if you want your price elasticity of demand to be equal to 1? Use the marginal revenue curve in determining your answer.

4) You have been hired by Furters Hot Dogs, the only hot dog stand on Twenty Mile Beach. Frank, the owner of the stand, says, "Even though we have a monopoly, we're losing money. We had an economist out from your school's big rival, and she said to set marginal revenue equal to marginal cost. So we sell 40 hot dogs a day, and we sell them for 20 cents, because 20 cents is the marginal revenue of the 40th dog. Every day there is a long line and we have to turn people away, but we're still losing money. How come?" Tell Frank what he is doing wrong, and explain why that long line of people is there.

5) Suppose a monopoly determines its profit maximizing quantity and price as described in this chapter. Can it still lose money? Draw demand and marginal revenue curves for a monopoly. Then draw the marginal and average cost curves in such a way that even when profits are maximized, the monopoly loses money.

6) A spokesperson for Amalgamated Tricycle, a childrens' transportation monopoly, makes the following statement: "We are against regulation of our company because the market already regulates us. If we restricted output (as we have been accused of doing) our average costs would rise, and thus our profits would fall. Therefore we do not restrict output but instead produce at an efficient level." Suppose that Amalgamated's marginal cost, average cost, and demand curves all intersect at the same point. This would be the competitive equilibrium. Would the company restrict output below the competitive equilibrium if it were not regulated?

7) A Congressional committee is considering regulation of Amalgamated Tricycle. A Congresswoman on the committee says to you, "I was elected to get rid of inefficiency. Show me a picture of the inefficiency caused by Amalgamated's monopoly." Draw such a diagram and explain your reasoning.

8) Suppose you own a convenience store. You notice that small changes in price have little effect on the number of candy bars adults buy, but a large effect on the number bought by children. Assuming you could price-discriminate, what is your profit-maximizing strategy? Could you really implement this strategy?

Imperfect Markets II:

Monopolistic

Competition

and

Oligopoly

OVERALL OBJECTIVE: To examine the forms of industrial organization known as monopolistic competition and oligopoly.

MORE SPECIFICALLY:

- To show that the equilibrium under monopolistic competition involves a tangency solution, with the demand curve just touching the side of the average cost curve.

- To discuss the difficulties in constructing a general theory of oligopoly. Some oligopolies are loose, generally not very concentrated, with little or no collusion, considerable effective competition, and contestable markets. Some oligopolies are tight, with high concentration, collusion, price leadership, more market power, and higher super-normal profits.

- To emphasize the mutual dependence of oligopolies; the behavior of oligopolistic firms depends to a considerable degree on the behavior of their rivals.

- To establish that both monopolistically competitive firms and oligopolies engage in product differentiation, particularly in the form of quality change and advertising.

Both perfect competition and unregulated monopoly are now relatively rare in developed countries. Industrial organization usually lies somewhere in between. Near one end of the spectrum, we find industries in which there are numerous highly but not perfectly competitive firms. In the 1930s, Professor E. H. Chamberlin of Harvard coined the term **monopolistic competition** to describe such industries.[1] Near the other end of the spectrum we find industries in which there are only a limited number of firms, often large and sometimes possessing substantial market power. An industry in this position is called an **oligopoly**, from the Greek *oligos polein*, meaning a few sellers. In this chapter we examine both forms of industrial organization.

MONOPOLISTIC COMPETITION

When an industry is monopolistically competitive it will have numerous firms. Entry to and exit from the industry will be relatively easy, and **product differentiation** will be a primary mechanism by which the firms try to attract customers. This means that firms will try to set their products apart from those of their competitors by improving quality, providing information to prospective customers, advertising distinctive features, promoting brand names, and packaging their products in an eye-catching way. The location of their stores or factories; the selection of inventory so that buyers can find the model, color, size, features, and quantity that they want; credit and delivery policies; the courtesy of their sales staff; their service and warranty arrangements; their guarantee of refunds "with a smile" to dissatisfied buyers; and their other forms of customer service all contribute to product differentiation.

Monopolistic competition is common in retailing. We see good examples in supermarkets, convenience stores, gasoline stations and garages, lawn and garden centers, and in stores selling building supplies, home appliances, hardware, auto parts, video items, clothing, shoes, drugs, and liquor. Many motels, restaurants, pizza shops, beauty parlors and barber shops, construction companies, and plumbing and electrical contractors also fit the description of monopolistic competition, along with a considerable number of other small-scale service activities. In manufacturing, monopolistic competition was once very common, but the rise of big business has reduced its scope. Current examples include many bakeries, dairies, local producers of furniture, and the like.

The effect of a rise in price under monopolistic competition is similar to that under a monopoly but unlike what happens under perfect competition. As Figure 8.1 shows, a rise in price will reduce the quantity demanded (from Q_1 to Q_2) but will not eliminate it entirely, as would be true along a perfectly elastic demand curve.

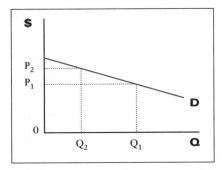

Figure 8.1. Less than perfectly elastic demand under monopolistic competition. A monopolistically competitive firm will retain some of its demand if it raises price, so it faces a downward-sloping demand curve. But there are many competing firms, so the slope of the curve is likely to be shallow.

---

1.   Arguably this is not the clearest term that could have been used—the first word, "monopolistic," gives a misleading impression of the degree of market power involved—but it has become established. Joan Robinson of Cambridge University had much the same insights at about the same time.

Because firms possess a limited degree of market power in monopolistic competition, prices are relatively uniform, though usually not identical, across the market for competing goods and services.

In the short run, the monopolistically competitive firm's price and quantity decisions resemble those of a monopoly. The firm maximizes profit at the price and quantity where MC = MR. We see this at P_{mc} and Q_{mc} in Figure 8.2. (Here and below the subscript *mc* stands for monopolistic competition). This position is the profit-maximizing equilibrium.

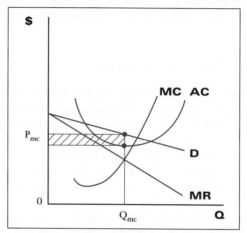

Figure 8.2. Short-run equilibrium under monopolistic competition. A monopolistically competitive firm will maximize profits if it produces the quantity where marginal cost equals marginal revenue. Given the circumstances in the figure, there will be a temporary super-normal profit.

The equilibrium shown here will not survive for long, however. The rectangle in the figure indicates that an attractive super-normal profit is being earned. Because entry and exit are easy, firms that are earning only a normal profit elsewhere will be attracted into the industry. Faced with the competition from these new entrants, a firm that has been enjoying demand D_1 for its product, as shown in Figure 8.3, is likely to find its demand reduced to, say, D_2. Here, too, a super-normal profit is being earned, although it is smaller than before. More new firms are attracted into the industry, with the result that the demand curve facing a single firm pushes even further to the left, say to D_3.

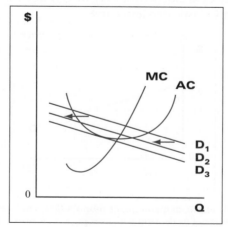

Figure 8.3. Demand facing a single firm falls as new firms enter. The super-normal profit will attract new entrants, causing the demand curve facing an individual firm to retreat to the left.

When that happens, no combination of output and price will yield a super-normal profit, so the motive for new firms to enter the industry disappears.

Perhaps so many new firms have entered that the demand curve has been pushed as far leftward as D_4 in Figure 8.4. In that case, price read from demand curve D_4 is always below average cost. Once the firms in the industry begin to suffer a loss, some of these firms—the weakest, perhaps, or those whose managers are quick to perceive profit opportunities elsewhere—will exit the industry. The firms that remain find the demand for their product rising again, as shown in the movement from D_4 to D_5 in the figure.

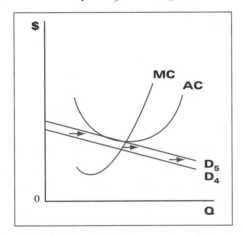

Figure 8.4. Demand facing a single firm rises as firms exit. If firms are earning losses, some will exit the industry, causing the demand curve facing an individual firm to move to the right.

Entry by new firms seeking high profit, and exit by old firms to avoid losses, will cease only when the firms in the industry are earning no more than normal profit, just sufficient to keep them in business. As Figure 8.5 shows, that occurs when the demand curve (D_{mc}) is tangent to the AC curve, so that neither super-normal profits nor losses are being incurred. The firm is producing quantity Q_{mc} and is selling each unit at a price of P_{mc}, which is equal to the cost per unit (including normal profit). This long-run equilibrium under monopolistic competition is known as the *tangency solution*.

As an example of the push toward equilibrium, consider the pizza shops clustered in the neighborhood of a large university. If profits are good, new shops keep springing up. Equilibrium is constantly upset by dollar-off sales, coupons in the university newspaper, free pizza if delivery is tardy, and so forth. Although the *overall* demand for pizza might be quite constant, the shops are in hot competition.

These kinds of competition mean that the equilibrium is inherently unstable, and the tangency solution is unlikely to hold in the long run. At any time, firms can try to increase their profits by launching new advertising campaigns, by improving the quality of their product, or by any other tactic that might have a positive effect. If they succeed, they will have changed the position of their own demand curves, pushing them to the right. The whole process of competing away these profits by means of the entry of new firms will begin anew. Rather than finding a long-run equilibrium in monopolistic competition, we find instead a *tendency toward equilibrium* that is continuously upset by profit-seeking entrepreneurs trying to increase the demand for their product.

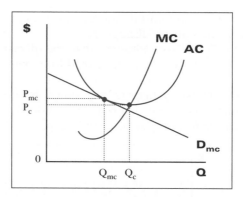

Figure 8.5. Long-run equilibrium in monopolistic competition. If demand is just sufficient so that price will cover average costs, there is no motive for new firms to enter the industry or old ones to leave it. The point at which the demand curve just touches the average cost curve is thus the point of equilibrium under monopolistic competition. This is the "tangency solution."

THE PROS AND CONS OF MONOPOLISTIC COMPETITION

How does the tangency solution for a firm under monopolistic competition compare with the equilibrium for a firm in a perfectly competitive industry? In both models, super-normal profits are eliminated and the selling price is just equal to average cost. But there are differences: In the long run, the perfectly competitive firm will be forced to produce the quantity and charge the price that will minimize cost per unit. If the perfectly competitive firm had the same cost curves as the one in Figure 8.5, then its horizontal demand curve positioned at price P_c would just touch the bottom of the average cost curve. The equilibrium would be at quantity Q_c and price P_c per unit.

A monopolistically competitive firm, however, reaches equilibrium at a lower quantity Q_{mc} and a higher price P_{mc}. Furthermore, output Q_{mc} is lower than the quantity Q_c that would minimize average cost. Average cost is at P_{mc}, reflecting that higher cost per unit. This tendency to produce a quantity lower than that which would minimize average cost is called the *excess capacity theorem*. Notice that the equilibrium price P_{mc} is higher than the equilibrium price P_c under perfect competition. In the long run, price is higher and output is lower under monopolistic competition than under perfect competition.

Monopolistic competition imposes a number of other costs on society. One cost is the waste occasioned by the entry and subsequent exit of firms in and out of an industry. When super-normal profit causes too many firms to move into an industry, profit turns into loss. One gas station can thrive at a busy intersection, but when four open up—one on each corner—some of them may fail. The "closed" signs on their empty buildings testify to the waste accompanying the movement toward equilibrium under monopolistic competition.

The efforts of monopolistically competitive firms to differentiate their products also may impose a cost on society. If, for example, a firm resorts to trivial changes in quality or packaging, or if it engages in misleading advertising, or if it uses other marketing tactics that raise costs, these costs will have to be borne by the consuming public until the public learns its lesson. (Both quality change and advertising are discussed more fully later in the chapter.)

On the positive side, monopolistic competition can lead to substantial benefits. Competing firms are eager to develop new goods and services and to offer consumers a wider range of product variety. Consumers can choose among a large selection of slightly different products. Brand names produce trust and confidence, it is said. "Variety is the spice of life"; living in a world where almost all cars are painted black, where different features and models are unavailable, and where firms do not struggle to innovate would be less satisfying. Readers who agree with these sentiments are likely to be the more approving of monopolistic competition.

OLIGOPOLY

When people speak of big business, large corporations, or multinational enterprise, they usually have oligopolies in mind. An oligopoly, as we have seen, is an industry in which there are only a few sellers. Oligopolies are a powerful presence in business life throughout the world. In the United States, for example, more than 85% of all U.S. industrial output is produced by only about one-tenth of 1% of all the firms. Over 98% of all manufacturing firms are small (with assets of under $10 million), but these small firms earn only about 10% of the profits in manufacturing (1991 figure). For this to be the case, a significant number of industries must be oligopolies— though there is no hard and fast line dividing oligopoly from monopolistic competition.[2]

TIGHT AND LOOSE OLIGOPOLIES

Knowing that an industry is oligopolistic does not, however, mean that the firms in the industry face little effective competition. There may be low barriers to entry so that new firms would quickly enter if profits rose by much; the existing firms might engage in considerable price competition; imports from other countries may be exerting competitive pressure. An industry so characterized is a **loose oligopoly**, and profits for its firms may be no greater than if the industry were monopolistically competitive. But if there are only a very few firms, protected from new competition by high costs of entry and high trade barriers, and little in the way of price competition, then we have a tight oligopoly. In a **tight oligopoly**, super-normal profits can be significant.

The Concentration Ratio

One way to determine whether an industry is a tight oligopoly, with potential market power, is to check its concentration ratio. This indicates the percentage of total industry output produced by the four largest sellers. Some sample U.S. four-firm **concentration ratios** from the U.S. *Census of Manufactures* are shown in the accompanying box.[3]

U.S. CONCENTRATION RATIOS AND THEIR TREND OVER TIME

U.S. concentration ratios include aluminum 74% (down from 100% in 1966, when all the aluminum in the United States was manufactured by the four biggest firms in the industry), aircraft 72%, automobiles 90%, cigarettes 92%, electric light bulbs 91%, soaps and detergents 65%, synthetic fibers 76%, and tires 69%. Despite the merger fever of recent years, the trend has been downward. Among all U.S. industries in 1900, about one-third had four-firm concentration ratios above 50%. That was still true in 1963. But during the 1970s and early 1980s the proportion fell to about one-fourth. The reduced concentration among industries contrasts with the *increased* importance of the country's 100 largest firms. These firms produced only

---

2.   For the data see *the Statistical Abstract of the United States 1993*, Table 883, and the *New Palgrave Dictionary*, Vol. 1, p. 353. The world's top 15 nonbank firms in order by market value in 1992 were Royal Dutch Shell, Exxon*, Nippon Telephone and Telegraph, Philip Morris*, GE*, Wal-Mart Stores*, AT&T*, Merck*, IBM*, Coca-Cola*, Toyota, British Telecom, Glaxo Holdings, Bristol-Myers Squibb*, and DuPont*. Those marked * are American. See the *Wall Street Journal*, September 24, 1992.

3.   The *Census of Manufactures* also reports concentration ratios for the largest eight and the largest 20 sellers. The ratios cited in the box are from 1987.

23% of total U.S. output in 1947, but 33% in 1972 and again in 1982. The degree to which the 1980s merger mania will affect these statistics remains to be seen.

The industries with the highest concentration ratios in the United States also appear to have the highest concentration ratios in other countries as well. This is in spite of the different conditions under which these industries developed and the differing degree of government regulation involved. Apparently, the technology used in an industry has much to do with the degree of concentration.

We must be careful in interpreting concentration ratios. When imports are a significant factor in the market, the ratios tend to overstate the real degree of market power held by the leading firms because the imports are not included in the count. For example, Japanese auto imports have provided heavy competition to the U.S. car industry, even though U.S. firms are highly concentrated. When concentration is high in one geographical area but not in the country as a whole, the ratios tend to understate the degree of market power. The local concentration ratio for newspapers is often 100%, although the U.S. national ratio is only 14%. Moreover, the ratios give no indication of the relative sizes of the four biggest firms in an industry. They may all be about the same size, or very dissimilar. Consequently, concentration ratios do not always indicate the actual level of market power that exists in an oligopolistic industry.

Even so, a high degree of concentration of 60% or more usually means that the firms in an industry are large and probably enjoy substantial economies of scale in production. The heavy financing required by a newcomer hoping to enter a highly concentrated industry is likely to pose a substantial barrier to entry. Considerable use of advertising and a slower pace of technical innovation (because of the smaller number of competitors) often characterize highly concentrated industries. All in all, tight oligopolies with market power usually are highly concentrated—though it is fair to say that another industry with exactly the same concentration ratio might for other reasons be a loose oligopoly with little power to fix prices.

MODELS OF OLIGOPOLY

The economic models of oligopoly are less precise in their predictions than the models of perfect competition, monopolistic competition, and monopoly. Because oligopoly can take several forms, no completely acceptable general theory of oligopoly has ever been devised. For example, an oligopoly may consist of as few as two firms (a *duopoly*) or as many as two dozen or more—as already noted, there is no set number of firms dividing oligopoly from monopolistic competition. An industry made up of only two firms is likely to behave very differently from one made up of many firms. Moreover, some oligopolies have a "price leader" or a "dominant firm"; others do not. Entry into some oligopolistic industries is relatively easy, into others more difficult. If entry is easy, the market power of the existing firms will be limited because super-normal profits would attract new entrants. Markets with easy entry are said to be **contestable markets**. This means that the market power of established firms can be challenged, or contested, by new competition. In a contestable market even a small number of firms might have to behave *as if* they were facing substantial competition. An oligopoly can be a loose one even if its concentration ratio is high.

WHAT MAKES A MARKET CONTESTABLE?

A market will be more contestable if potential newcomers do not have to run the risk of plunging a large amount of capital into the effort only to find it is difficult to withdraw again. Large-scale steel making is not very contestable. To compete in that industry, substantial sums must be expended on building mills, and the capital is sunk in the sense that, if the venture fails, there will not be much of a market for the sale of the used plant and equipment if they have to be disposed of. (Technical change can, however, make a difference. Nowadays, mini-mills that use electric arc technology to obtain steel from scrap metal can be erected relatively cheaply, making the steel industry more contestable than it used to be.)

Airline routes are a good example of the logic of contestability. Such routes even when monopolized can be highly contestable. If a monopolist tried to raise price much above a competitive level on some route, another airline could transfer a spare aircraft or two to that route, thus providing competition very easily. Hardly any sunk costs would be involved. (Again, appearances may be deceiving. If landing rights at crowded airports cannot be obtained, then a particular route might not be very contestable after all.)

Historical Development of Oligopolies

A further obstacle to a general theory of oligopoly is that, historically, this form of industrial organization emerged through two distinct developments. Starting in the latter half of the nineteenth century, many industries became increasingly *concentrated* by exploiting economies of scale. Concentration is visible in pure form in industries such as cement or steel where the product is almost completely standard, or homogeneous, but where scale economies have led to firms of large size. Such a situation is sometimes referred to as *perfect oligopoly*. Here, only a dozen or so firms may provide sufficient competition to prevent large super-normal profits from accruing.

Later, mostly during the twentieth century, firms in many industries engaged in greater *product proliferation and differentiation* by introducing and advertising variations in the quality of what were basically the same products. Examples are brand-name clothing, soft drinks, beer, cigarettes, and canned foods. Such a situation is sometimes referred to as *imperfect oligopoly*. It often proved easy for a firm to introduce yet another variety of the same product, utilizing its existing plant, equipment, organizational structure, and advertising so that several products could be produced together at a cost lower than if they were produced separately. (For example, it is cheaper to advertise two models of the same car in a magazine ad than to advertise them separately with two ads.) These **economies of scope** made it more likely that oligopolies would result.

Many firms shared in *both* developments, realizing economies of scale while at the same time engaging more actively in product proliferation and differentiation giving economies of scope. Examples include producers of durable goods such as automobiles, household appliances, television sets, VCRs, and computers, and manufacturers of petroleum products and pharmaceuticals. Some service industries, including banking and insurance, have developed along much the same lines. In the 1970s and 1980s it appeared that product differentiation was becoming the dominant force in the tendency toward oligopoly, whereas at an earlier time economies of scale had predominated. The growing sophistication of consumers' knowledge and the fickleness of their tastes was the most reasonable explanation of why this was so. (We will look more closely at product differentiation later in the chapter.) The distinct causes of the tendency toward oligopoly, first because of scale economies and second because of product proliferation and differentiation, are further reasons why a general theory of oligopoly has proven difficult to develop.

Finally, in any given oligopolistic industry there may be **collusion** between firms—a world of so-called cartels, pools, trusts, and "gentlemen's agreements" with their agreed-on prices and quantities—or again there may be no collusion.

For all these reasons, the theory of oligopoly is neither neat nor sharply defined. Even so, economists have devised a number of useful models with which to analyze discrete aspects of oligopolistic behavior.

THE MUTUAL DEPENDENCE OF OLIGOPOLIES

In the absence of collusive agreements between firms to set price and quantity, many oligopolies do have one noticeable characteristic in common. Entrepreneurs never know exactly how rival firms will react to changes in price or output that they initiate. In fact, one good definition of oligopoly is an industry in which the number of firms is so small that each firm must take into account the reaction of the industry's other firms when it makes a marketing decision. Economists refer to this situation as the **mutual dependence**, or interdependence, of oligopolies. For example, if one firm's manager unilaterally raises the selling price, and the other ten firms in the oligopoly fail to follow suit, that firm is likely to lose a significant share of its market. Alternatively, what if a manager decides to lower the price of the firm's product in the hope that consumers will purchase more of it at the reduced price? If the other firms all decide to lower their prices as well, rather than lose market share, then the firm initiating the price reduction is not likely to gain much in sales. Either way, the manager of a firm would succeed or fail depending on whether the rival firms follow or do not follow price changes. For that manager, making an accurate forecast of rivals' behavior may turn out to be a matter of survival.

Such conditions of mutual dependence have been incorporated into several models that analyze how prices are determined under oligopoly.

The Edgeworth Model

One of the first models of oligopoly pricing was fashioned by the English economist Francis Edgeworth at the turn of the century. According to the Edgeworth model, when one firm in an oligopoly cuts its prices in order to obtain a larger share of the market and increase its profit, the other firms will cut their own prices by even more in order to win back their customers. The first firm responds in kind and a "price war" breaks out. The market continues to be unstable and never reaches equilibrium. The Edgeworth model reflected the initial behavior of such newly concentrated industries as steel, tobacco, meat packing, railroads, and oil. Fearing the consequences of instability, and expecting that profits would be higher if price wars could be avoided, many of the leaders of those industries engaged in explicit or implicit collusion and set up a variety of cartels and "gentlemen's agreements."

The Kinked Demand Curve

The **kinked demand curve** model of oligopoly pricing suggests that mutual dependence may lead to price stability even *without* collusion. This model was independently conceived by the British economists R.L. Hall and C.J. Hitch, and the U.S. economist Paul Sweezy, in 1939.

Figure 8.6 shows a kinked demand curve for a single firm in an oligopolistic industry. The shape of the curve implies that the firm will hesitate to provoke its rivals by changing price. If the firm decides to raise its price above P_0, and if the competing firms do not go along with the price increase, the firm runs the risk of reduced sales and lower total revenue. This risk is reflected by the highly elastic portion of the demand curve above the kink. Conversely, if the firm decides to lower its price and the competing firms go along with the price cut in order to retain their market share, the firm's sales may increase very little. Along the inelastic portion of the demand curve below the kink, total revenue will fall off quickly. The main implication of the model is that each firm in an oligopoly acts as if it had a vested interest in market stability and consequently is reluctant to initiate a price change.

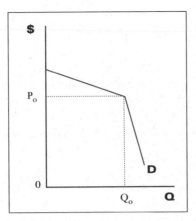

Figure 8.6. The kinked demand curve facing a firm in an oligopolistic industry. The kinked demand curve points to the risk facing the managers of oligopolistic firms. If they are the first to raise price and other firms do not follow, the quantity demanded will decline sharply. If they cut price and other firms match the cut, the quantity demanded will not increase by much.

THE KINKED DEMAND CURVE AND COST CHANGES

The model of the kinked demand curve can also be used to show that a firm may resist altering its prices even when it experiences a change in its costs. Figure 8.7 duplicates the kinked demand curve of Figure 8.6. We know that when the demand curve is a straight line, the marginal revenue curve will also be a straight line lying halfway between the demand curve and the vertical (Y) axis.

Here the marginal revenue curve has two segments to it, both following the "halfway rule." The top segment runs to a point directly under the kink and applies to the flat portion of the demand curve. The bottom segment of the marginal revenue curve starts directly under the kink and applies to the steeper portion of the demand curve.

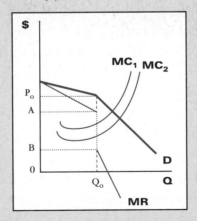

Figure 8.7. The kinked demand curve and cost changes. The marginal revenue curve associated with a kinked demand curve contains a gap. So a change in marginal cost can occur without triggering a price change; profits will still be maximized at price P_0 and quantity Q_0.

The two segments of the marginal revenue curve are separated by a gap of AB, shown by a dotted line. Assume that a fall in production costs changes the position of the marginal cost curve from MC_1 to MC_2 (or that a rise moves the marginal cost curve from MC_2 to MC_1). Marginal cost would still equal marginal revenue (and hence profits would be maximized) at output Q_0. Indeed, a change in MC *anywhere* within the gap AB would still leave MC equal to MR at price P_0 and quantity Q_0. So given the existence of a kinked demand curve, even a cost change might not persuade the firm to alter its price.

Many microeconomists today regard the kinked demand curve model with some skepticism. Admittedly, the assumptions it makes about behavior are somewhat simplistic, and there is little empirical evidence that oligopolistic firms will follow a price cut but will not follow a price rise. Perhaps the major weakness of the model is its inability to explain why the kink occurs precisely where it does. Why not at some higher price and lower output, or vice versa? The answer may reflect what transpired during the industry's development—the debates, negotiations, price wars, peace treaties, personal friendships and animosities, and other factors that bind rival firms together in a pattern of mutual dependence.

Still, the model does suggest why managers fearing a "worst case" outcome might have a strong preference for price stability in an oligopolistic industry. The logic of the model could well exert an influence on managerial behavior, perhaps toward collusion in one form or another, even though the predicted events rarely happen. This is probably the main reason why the kinked demand curve survives.

Sticky Prices

Recent studies suggest that all types of oligopolies show a preference for adjusting quantity rather than price, whether they are heavily concentrated or not. They prefer **sticky prices**, keeping prices relatively constant to avoid price wars while responding to economic events by adjusting quantity and engaging heavily in product differentiation.

Yet we all know that oligopolies *do* change their prices, especially during periods of inflation. Although an individual firm is reluctant to raise or lower its prices on its own, firms are quite willing to alter their prices when a change in costs hits them all at the same time. A new labor contract might raise wages throughout an industry. Tax rates or interest rates might rise. Price increases for some essential raw material (oil, for example) might occur. Faced with such events, all the firms in the industry are likely to raise their prices simultaneously. They may even lower their prices if tax rates or interest rates go down, or oil prices fall generally, or if imports threaten to eat into their market share. Even then, however, the price decreases often come in the form of discounts and rebates from list prices rather than in the form of direct price reductions. The discounts and rebates confirm the unwillingness of the firms in an oligopoly to compete in terms of price. Before imports of autos from Japan were limited in 1981, all U.S. car manufacturers were giving rebates, sometimes large, off the sticker price; when imports rose again in 1985–1986, the rebates resurfaced.

General cost changes will, perhaps after some delay, cause firms to adjust their prices. They commonly do so at discrete intervals, and in rather large steps, instead of making small adjustments on a daily basis. One reason is that it is expensive for a large firm to alter all its price lists. Another is that when one firm in an oligopoly changes its prices frequently while its rivals are changing theirs infrequently, the danger arises that price competition will break out.

GAME THEORY TO PREDICT RIVALS' REACTIONS

Being able to predict what another firm will do is a key part of the decision-making process in oligopoly. In recent years, a field of mathematics known as **game theory** has been applied to this problem. By using the mathematics of probability in conflict situations, game theory puts prediction on a more scientific basis. The theory was developed by John von Neumann and Oskar Morgenstern, whose influential book, *The Theory of Games and Economic Behavior*, was published in 1944. (Von Neumann had written a preliminary article in 1928 in which he described a rational strategy for matching pennies.) Since then, the theory has been used in analyzing war and politics as well as in analyzing the behavior of firms in an oligopolistic industry. The result of such analysis is to assign probabilities to what rivals may or may not do as a result of some initial move. Game theorists may have a bright future on the staffs of the large corporations, although application of the theory has proven more difficult than anticipated. The "game" becomes very complex as the number of participants increases, and the results are sometimes both ambiguous and uncertain. Yet the influence of game theory continues to grow among students of oligopoly, and it is currently being employed in the search for more general models of oligopoly behavior. Specialists indicate that some (limited) hope exists that a more general theory may in the course of time emerge.

STRATEGIES FOR DEALING WITH INSTABILITY AND UNCERTAINTY IN OLIGOPOLIES

Over time, oligopolists have devised many strategies for dealing with the instability and uncertainty that threaten their profits. Such strategies are easiest to implement and execute in tight oligopolies with few competitors and concentration ratios in the range of about 60% or more. (In loose oligopolies, with concentration ratios of only about 40% or less, the cohesion needed to support a common strategy is more difficult to achieve.) It has been estimated that about 21% of U.S. output is produced under conditions of tight oligopoly.[4]

Collusion

Firms have often entered into collusion by means of formal or informal agreements in an effort to achieve the market power of a monopoly. They may agree to form a *cartel* in which they act as if they were one firm. The cartel then searches for the monopoly price and quantity that will maximize profits for the group as a whole. Sometimes a cartel will pool revenues rather than allow member firms individually to keep the revenue they earn, so reducing the likelihood of cheating. Cartels commonly maintain excess production capacity which enables them to expand production any time they wish. This ability to drive prices down by stepping up production serves to deter potential new entrants from entering the industry.

In his *Wealth of Nations*, Adam Smith spoke of the danger to the public posed by collusive behavior:

> People of the same trade seldom meet together, even for merriment and diversion, but the conversation ends in a conspiracy against the public, or in some contrivance to raise prices.

---

4.   Estimate for 1980 by William G. Shepherd in his "Causes of Increased Competition in the U.S. Economy, 1939-1980," *Review of Economics and Statistics*, Vol. 64, No. 4, November 1982, p. 618. Tight oligopoly is defined here to include dominant firm price leadership, discussed later in the chapter. Shepherd makes them two separate categories.

Private cartels were especially important in Germany from about 1900 until the end of the Second World War.[5] They were also widespread throughout the rest of Europe and in Japan. In the United States and Great Britain cartels have been illegal for many years and consequently have been less common. (A secret cartel of producers of industrial electric equipment, mainly GE and Westinghouse, operated in the United States in the 1940s and 1950s before it was broken by the federal government.)

If cartelization or other tight collusion does occur, but some of the colluding firms have relatively high costs while others have lower costs, then problems tend to arise. To keep their arrangement intact, they may agree to deviate from their respective profit-maximization positions. Perhaps the low-cost firms will make side payments to the high-cost firms as an inducement for them to cut back their output, leaving the low-cost firms free to expand and leading to greater profits on the whole. The money transfers may leave a "paper trail," however, so increasing the risk of detection.

Constant tension is always present in collusive arrangements. All the firms appreciate that they will gain from working together as a monopoly, but each firm also knows that it could enjoy greater gains by cheating. By selling at a price below the agreed-upon price, a cheater can increase its market share and enhance its profits at the expense of the other colluding firms. This explains the eventual breakup of many cartels.

Public cartels created by the government appear to be more common, or at least more visible, than private cartels at the present time. The purpose of some public cartels is to limit output (OPEC in oil, for example, or government control of farm production by means of quotas). By allocating radio and television licenses, the U.S. Federal Communications Commission has in effect cartelized broadcasting. For many years the Civil Aeronautics Board cartelized U.S. airlines by allocating routes, and this remains standard practice in many other countries. The European Community has set up a multinational steel cartel ostensibly to phase out that high-cost industry in a rational way, but so far it has accomplished little beyond keeping output low and prices high.[6] Like private cartels, public cartels that place quotas on production are vulnerable to the problem of cheating by members who may increase output and sell it at the high cartel price.

Price Leadership

Private cartels and other types of explicit collusion are illegal in the United States and many other countries, though admittedly conversations in a restaurant or on a golf course that result in price-fixing are hard to police. To be legal, collusion among firms must be tacit. One example of tacit collusion is **price leadership**, in which the lowest-cost or largest or most influential firm in an industry makes its price decisions independently and the other firms follow its lead. As a result of experience, the price leader has a good idea of what its rivals will do and acts to maximize its own profits. The courts usually hold price leadership to be legal so long as it is truly tacit and not embodied in any formal agreement. The practice is especially common in the steel, gasoline, and airline industries. For homogeneous products, prices arrived at in this way are likely to be nearly identical. For products that are differentiated, prices tend to be different from firm to firm, but when they change they usually move in the same direction and by roughly the same proportion.

Price Leadership by a Low-Cost Firm. If all the firms in an industry face essentially the same costs and the same demand curves, the firms that follow the price leader will maximize profits along with the leader. If the price leader is a low-cost firm, however, the firms with

5.   The classic case was I.G. Farben, the German chemical giant. It was not owned by any Herr Farben. Its name was derived from **Interessen Gemeinschaft Farben**industrie, which means "Community of Interest in the Dye [German: *farben*] Industry." I.G. Farben was a cartel of eight firms that merged into one in 1925.

6.   The Japanese government's policy of "recession cartels" encourages private firms to agree on market shares during business down-turns. As long as these cartels are temporary, they are less harmful than permanent ones and have the advantage that in a recession firms that might go under through no fault of their own are enabled to survive. The United States permitted much the same thing in the Great Depression of the 1930s.

higher costs will have to sacrifice some of their profits when they follow the leader. (Because their production is more costly, they would have maximized their own profits with a higher price.) Despite that sacrifice, the high-cost firms follow the leader because they want to avoid entering into price competition.

"Barometric" Price Leadership. A "barometric" price leader is a firm with a good track record in predicting how the market will move. Other firms have come to trust its market sense and regularly follow its lead, just as weather forecasters follow their barometers. The barometric price leader is not necessarily either a low-cost firm or a large firm, and it may even be in a different industry. For example, U.S. Steel, now USX, has sometimes been regarded as a barometric price leader for the firms in the automobile industry, with the latter altering car prices as steel prices changed. Barometric price leadership is perhaps most likely when an oligopoly has several big firms of about equal importance, so that even tacit agreement on who is to act as leader poses difficulties.

Price Leadership by a Dominant Firm. When a large firm dominates an industry with a fringe of many smaller producers, *dominant firm* price leadership may occur. The dominant firm is free to choose a price and quantity that will maximize its profits, but it knows it cannot set a price higher than the fringe firms would charge if the dominator did not exist. In the left-hand panel of Figure 8.8, the demand curve D_i shows the entire market demand for the industry's product and the supply curve S_f shows what the fringe firms will supply to the market at various prices. In the absence of the dominant firm, the fringe firms would charge the equilibrium price P_f. If the dominant firm charged a price *higher* than that, its sales would be zero. Consumers would simply buy what they wanted from the fringe firms. If the dominant firm charged a price *lower* than P_f—say P_1—it would attract consumers away from the fringe firms. At price P_1 the quantity demanded would exceed the quantity supplied by the fringe firms by the amount **AB**, and that quantity would be supplied by the dominant firm, as shown by the distance **AB** in the right-hand panel.

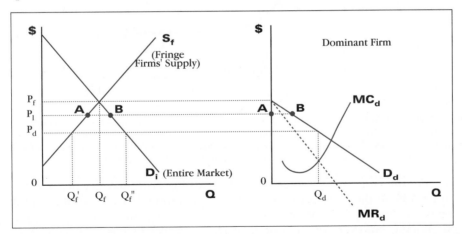

Figure 8.8. Price leadership by a dominant firm. Here the dominant firm is shown on the right, and the entire industry's demand curve and the supply curve of the other firms are on the left. If the dominant firm selects a price of P_d, it will have sales of Q_d, which equals $Q_f'Q_f''$ on the right-hand diagram. The fringe firms will command what remains of the total quantity demanded, or Q_f'. The dominant firm has selected the price that maximizes its profit; the fringe firms follow the price leader.

The demand curve faced by the dominant firm is thus the excess demand that the fringe firms are unable to satisfy at any price below their equilibrium price. That is, the position of the right panel's demand curve at any price is always equal to the gap between the supply and the demand curves in the left panel. The dominant firm, knowing the position of its demand curve and thus its MR curve, and knowing the position of its MC curve, can choose the price and quantity that will equate MC and MR, thus maximizing its profit. Here that combination is P_d and quantity Q_d. At that price, the fringe firms will supply Q_f', and the dominant firm will capture the rest of the market $Q_f'Q_f''$ ($= Q_d$).

Good examples of price leadership by a dominant firm are U.S. Steel in the American steel market earlier in this century and Saudi Arabia's paramount position in the oil industry. It is estimated that about 13% of U.S. output produced under conditions of tight oligopoly comes from industries with a dominant firm.[7]

The Limit Price

Setting a so-called **limit price** is a strategy sometimes used by firms in an oligopolistic industry to discourage potential rivals from entering that industry. Through tacit collusion (perhaps by means of price leadership) the firms decide to forgo maximum profits in the short run in order to maximize profits in the long run. In Figure 8.9 several oligopolistic firms facing a demand curve D_o might choose to set their price at P_o. They would thereby earn considerable profit, because average cost for the quantity Q_o that would be sold at that price is C_o, well below the price P_o. But if some potential rival entered the market and managed to capture enough demand (D^*) at price P_o so that it could cover its costs, it could establish a foothold in the industry and survive. At price P_o the new firm could sell quantity Q_n, just enough to cover its long-run average costs (LRAC).

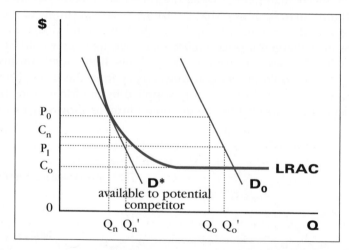

Figure 8.9. The limit price. Here a limit price of P_l charged by the existing firms keeps a potential competitor from entering the market. The competitor cannot cover its costs at the limit price. But if the existing firms charged the higher price P_o, that *would* allow the potential competitor to gain a foothold in the industry. The limit price is thus a means to prevent the entry of new firms.

To prevent the entry of such interlopers, the existing firms may decide to keep their price low—say at level P_l. At this limit price, they will sacrifice some but not all of the profit they are currently enjoying. Price P_l is still above the cost per unit C_o of producing quantity Q_o'. That price is not high enough, however, for the potential rival to cover its costs. At price P_l it could sell quantity Q_n', but the price would be less than the cost C_n of producing that quantity. So the potential rival, condemned to losses by the existing firms' strategy, cannot gain a foothold and the existing firms have closed off entry by means of a limit price. (A monopoly firm might also employ a limit price to stave off potential entrants.)

Predatory Pricing

For many years **predatory pricing** has been viewed as a strategy for driving competitors out of the market by lowering prices dramatically, perhaps even below average cost. The predatory firm

---

7.   Estimate for 1980 by William G. Shepherd as cited in footnote 4. A primary part of Shepherd's definition of a dominant firm is a "market share of 50% to over 90%, with no close rival."

or firms could then raise its price to monopoly levels. Predatory pricing was one of the methods allegedly employed by John D. Rockefeller's Standard Oil Company. By the 1960s and 1970s many economists had begun to doubt that such a strategy would be effective. They pointed out that the price cutting would mean substantial losses for the firms that resorted to it and that the hoped-for monopoly profits might never materialize because they would act as a stimulus to the entry of new competitors.[8]

In the 1980s a modified view of predatory pricing gained attention. According to this view, predatory pricing is not intended to drive competitors out of the market, but merely to deter them from trying to expand their market share or from making new investment and undertaking new product development. If judicious price cutting can lower the profit expectations of one's rivals, it can also protect one's own profits.

A case in support of this modified view of predatory pricing involves the response of Maxwell House Coffee when Folgers attempted to enter the midwest market. Price cutting by Maxwell House certainly did not deliver a mortal wound to Folgers, but it *did* apparently cause Folgers to abandon its further plans to enlarge its market share in eastern markets, especially in New York City. Predatory tactics to lower the profit expectations of rivals are alleged to exist in the market for microchips. In 1990 the Justice Department opened an investigation of the interlinked airlines reservation network; some airlines were suspected of using the data network to signal proposed price changes that would be damaging to a competitor in response to a competitor's proposed fare cut. The intention, it was alleged, was to make the competitor back off.

PEACE OR WAR?

Under certain circumstances, an oligopolistic industry may enjoy a peaceful existence for prolonged periods of time. In the absence of those circumstances, it may find itself plunged into periods of competitive warfare.

Among the factors contributing to peace and cooperation are the following: (1) A price leader that is both the lowest-cost firm *and* the dominant firm has substantial power to impose prices on the rest of the industry, which, fearful of the leader, is then likely to be more peaceful. If, however, the price leader loses its cost advantage or a significant portion of its market share, it may also lose its position as price leader. In that event, instability may prevail until a new price leader emerges. (2) When there are only a few firms in the industry, gains made by one firm at the expense of the others are highly visible. That may lead to dissension. (3) If the products produced by an industry embody little product differentiation, then it is more difficult for any single firm to expand its market share through advertising and quality change, and the more peaceful the industry will be. (4) If an industry's sales are expanding, a firm may be able to increase its sales without provoking other firms. (5) High barriers to the entry of new firms lessen the danger that price competition will break out. (6) Foreign trade stimulates competition, while trade barriers decrease it.

The outcome for an oligopoly that maintains the peace with explicit collusion, tacit collusion, price leadership, a limit price, threats of predatory pricing, or any other method is likely to be more profits in the long run for all the firms involved. The profit motive is a reasonable explanation why modern oligopolies exhibit more of peace than of war. Yet the lure of profit beckoning a firm that can get away with cheating on some arrangement also explains why collusion so often proves impermanent. The wide range of possible outcomes justifies the conclusion by F.M. Scherer that with oligopoly, virtually anything is possible.

▶ PRODUCT DIFFERENTIATION

Monopolistic competition and oligopoly are often characterized by firms' attempts to differentiate their product from that of their rivals. Product differentiation takes many forms, as

---

8.   Even the evidence on the predatory behavior of Standard Oil at the turn of the century proved questionable.

we saw at the beginning of this chapter, but, of these, quality change and advertising are especially significant. Firms introduce variations in their products (quality change) to influence consumers' views of the firms' output, and they incur selling costs (advertise) in an attempt to increase consumer demand for these products.

QUALITY CHANGE

As a competitive technique, quality change has considerable advantages. Price changes are conspicuous; competitors notice them at once and may match them. Price cuts may be hard to withdraw once they have been put in place. Nonprice competition by means of quality change is, however, difficult to monitor even when the firms in an industry are engaging in collusion to fix prices. The most tightly controlled cartels seldom make much effort to restrict it. Moreover, it takes rivals far longer to retaliate against a firm that competes on the basis of quality change than it takes to retaliate against a firm competing on the basis of price. It may even be impossible for rival firms to take action against a firm whose products are developed and modified by uncommonly gifted designers. The technology underlying a quality change may not be available to other firms, or it may be difficult to transfer because of obstacles to bundling it as one package and in finding the personnel able to operate and repair it. At best, imitations take time to market. So a firm that makes a practice of regularly and frequently introducing new and improved products may be able to establish a lead over its competitors. Though such concentration on quality change may raise the firm's costs, it will also deter potential rivals from entering the market.

How Much Should Be Spent on Quality Change?

How much should a firm spend on quality change? The amount is dictated by the already familiar rule for profit maximization. It should spend on quality change up to the point where the marginal cost of the change is equal to the marginal revenue the change generates. At that point, the profits from the quality change will be maximized. Estimating how much quality change adds to the cost of a particular item is not easy, because a firm's research and development (R&D) expenditure is usually spread over several products. The contribution of quality change to the firm's revenue is even harder to predict.[9] Still, the firm must make the best estimates that it can. Generally, the greater the predicted consumer response to a given quality change, and the higher the profit per unit sold, the more the firm is likely to spend on quality change. (Because of the difficulties of estimation, many firms arbitrarily budget a certain percentage of these firms' sales revenues for R&D.)

To What Extent Are Large Oligopolies Responsible for R&D Effort?

Few would doubt the trend toward quality change in oligopolies. It is possible, however, to debate whether the oligopolies themselves are the initial source of the technical improvements. The research departments of large corporations with over 5000 employees account for over 85% of private research and development spending in the United States. It was once common, however, to hear the argument that the degree to which this R&D activity overshadowed the efforts of small research institutions and independent inventors was exaggerated. Thus, three decades ago, the report of a U.S. government advisory group headed by Robert A. Charpie of Union Carbide cited several studies showing that small companies and independent inventors were "responsible for a remarkable percent of the important inventions and innovations of this century—a much larger percent than their relative investment in these activities suggest."

For example, the following list of inventions were not developed by the R&D staffs of large corporations: air conditioning, power steering, the Xerox process, cyclotrons, cotton-pickers, helicopters, FM radio circuitry, automatic transmissions, zippers, shrink-proof knitwear, the kodachrome process, the Polaroid camera, cellophane, continuous hot strip rolling of steel, oxygen steel making, and major processes for refining and cracking petroleum. Each of these

---

9. The outcome of a firm's R&D spending is especially difficult to anticipate. Inventions come at very odd times and in very odd ways.

came from independent inventors or small firms. Donald Schon, in *Technology and Change* (1967), suggested that many large companies owed their success more to their ability to carry out market and engineering development of inventions derived from other sources than to their own research output. In this view, the crucial factors were marketing and technical service resources and skills, not R&D.

More recently, the balance appears to have tipped toward recognizing the impact of the large research establishments. There are several reasons for the shift. Small companies cannot usually afford the cost of developing such high-tech products as aircraft, biotechnology, pharmaceuticals, computer hardware, microchips, VCRs, and compact discs. When technology is being tailored to a specific product, in-house R&D efforts hold advantages because the creators of the technology can work directly with the manufacturers of the product. The direct dealing speeds up the flow of information. Moreover, the accelerated pace of innovation means that patents become obsolete more quickly. The 17-year life of a patent (in the United States) has ceased to have as much value as before. In many industries, a firm's general research effort—which may indeed involve a continuing *flow* of patents—is more important than any individual patent. Head starts and lead times and learning-by-doing appear to be more important now than formerly. Finally, many technical advances are unpatentable, which means that the inventor cannot directly receive the returns. When the in-house research lab of a large firm makes an unpatentable technical advance, that firm may be able to incorporate it into several of its products or even conceal it in one of its many patented products. But an independent inventor may have nothing to show for an effort but the unpatentable invention, as noted in the accompanying box.

GREAT ADVANCES MAY PROVE TO BE UNPATENTABLE

A good example of an unpatentable technical advance is the principle of maneuvering an aircraft. The Wright brothers believed that their patent was comprehensive, but the courts disagreed, holding that their method—wing warping—was just one of many possibilities, all of which could not be encompassed by a single patent. In fact, competitors quickly developed the aileron, and the Wright brothers derived little profit from their pioneering efforts in aircraft design.

Having said all that in favor of the research effort of large establishments, even today numerous economists doubt whether the most significant innovations are very closely connected either with firm size or market concentration.

Conclusion

Few would doubt the strong evidence that oligopolistic enterprises have swiftly adopted many major inventions and marketed them with ability, even if the paramount role of oligopolies in discovering the original inventions can be exaggerated. The large-scale R&D efforts of oligopolistic firms exercise a powerful influence on how marketing is accomplished. Arguably, the widespread introduction of quality change by those firms outweighs the allocative inefficiency that they may inflict on the public through their pricing policies.

ADVERTISING

Advertising is often a very effective nonprice method for improving a firm's position. About 3% of all spending in the United States is devoted to that activity. Advertising serves as a major source of product information and a powerful agency for product differentiation.[10]

Informative Advertising Versus Uninformative Advertising

Advertising that calls attention to price differences, the appearance of new firms, and the development of new products is called **informative advertising**. It serves an important purpose in a world of imperfect knowledge, and brings more competition to a market. Classified ads and supermarket inserts in newspapers, for example, are mostly in the informative category; 25% of all advertising as measured by its cost appears in newspapers. Specialized catalogs that list books, office supplies, clothing, boats, and hundreds of other products, along with some direct mail pieces, also often qualify as informative; 20% of all advertising takes these forms. It is certainly much less costly for firms to advertise their products than for consumers to devote the time necessary to search out the same information for themselves. By reducing the effort consumers must devote to that search, informative advertising serves to promote competition on the basis of both price and quality. But even advertising that conveys some useful information is always slanted in favor of the advertised product. That is why "neutral" buyers' guides such as *Consumer Reports* flourish. It also explains why many countries have passed truth-in-advertising legislation.

A considerable amount of advertising is designed simply to catch the consumer's attention and makes no attempt to provide useful information: tuneful jingles, attractive people using the product, frequent repetitions of a 15-second commercial. Such **uninformative** or **competitive advertising**, as this is called, appears most often on television (which accounts for 22% of all spending on ads), on radio (7%), in magazines (5%), and on billboards (1%). Even though such ads provide little useful information, they do serve as a signal to consumers that a firm is willing to commit substantial resources to promote its products—money that will be lost if consumers do not like the product. If repeat sales are possible, then arguably a firm with a high-quality item will utilize more advertising than will a firm selling a low-quality item.

The repetitive nature of uninformative ads, seen over and over again hundreds of times by viewers and readers, often has a more sophisticated purpose than might be imagined. The repetition is intended to have a cumulative effect, giving consumers a sense of familiarity with a product. Just as meeting an old acquaintance is easier than meeting a stranger, so a familiar product can give a momentary feeling of being at home in a supermarket aisle.

Uninformative advertising is usually more effective with nondurable goods such as soap powder, beer, soft drinks, snack foods, cold medications, and so forth, than with durable goods such as cars, computers, refrigerators, and the like. It does not pay consumers to go from store to store searching for the lowest-priced box of detergent, but when they are buying a new refrigerator they are willing to extend their search.

Whether advertising brings useful information or merely increases familiarity with the product, it is certainly much employed as a device to obtain a mass market. In many industries, it seems necessary to advertise in order to succeed in gaining national attention. Perhaps this activity will grow even more important as technical change comes faster than before and the time between introduction of a product and its obsolescence grows shorter. To the extent that advertising does lead to mass markets, it would thus share in the credit for the attainment of economies of scale. To the extent that it facilitates the more rapid introduction of valuable technical changes, it should share in the credit for that, too.

---

10.   The total bill for advertising in the United States in 1990 was $130.1 billion. According to the U.S. Federal Trade Commission, advertising costs in an industry can reach as much as 20% of sales revenue (over-the-counter drugs). Other high figures are 14% for toys and 10% for nonalcoholic beverages. The national average for all consumer goods is about 4%.

Effect of Advertising on Competition

Overall, does advertising *decrease* competition by making entry into an industry more expensive and thus more difficult? Or does it *increase* competition by increasing the amount of information available to the public, bringing awareness that some firms charge lower prices or offer better quality than others do? The evidence is mixed, and the results appear to vary by industry. Eyeglasses seem a compelling case. Their price is 25 to 30% lower in states where advertising glasses is permitted than in the states where it is not. The 1970 ban on radio and television advertising of cigarettes provides evidence that advertising stimulates competition among brands. As a result of that ban, it became more difficult to establish new brands in the market; consequently, competition declined and profits rose. In the beer industry, however, an *increase* in advertising, by forcing smaller breweries to merge or close down, seems to have had the same effect of reducing competition and raising profits. In the market for pharmaceutical drugs, well-advertised brands sell at a much higher price than generic drugs that are identical in every way. A supermarket in my Maine college town charges $5.89 for 100 tablets of Bayer aspirin, whereas 100 tablets of the store's own brand, exactly the same chemical compound, are priced at $1.19. Notice, however, that a finding of higher profits in an industry that employs considerable advertising may not indicate a cause-and-effect relationship between the advertising and the profits. The relationship may possibly be in the reverse direction, with advertising more prominent in an industry *because* its profits are high.

Advertising certainly has the capacity to change market share for particular brands. It seems to have much less impact, however, on the *total* demand for a given product. A successful Pepsi ad, for example, has far more impact on the sales of Coke than it does on the total sales of soft drinks. Furthermore, advertising apparently has little effect on the percentage of income that consumers spend on all goods and services. Empirical studies show that changes in advertising spending typically lag behind changes in consumer spending. For example, early in the century, when the advertising industry was growing faster than the economy as a whole, the proportion of consumers' income spent on goods and services (rather than being saved) was quite stable. The proportion of income used for spending in other countries also appears to be little affected by the differing levels of advertising expenditure in those countries.

How Much Should Be Spent on Advertising?

As with expenditures on quality change, the amount a firm should spend on advertising involves the principle for profit maximization. In accordance with the profit-maximization rule, the firm has an economic motive to spend on advertising up to the point where the marginal cost of the ads equals the estimated marginal revenue generated by them. Again, however, though the costs of an advertising campaign can be estimated accurately, the effect of the ads on the firm's revenue is difficult to predict. One complicating factor in determining how much to spend on advertising is that sometimes ads have a capital-like effect; a campaign this week may have some residual effect next year on consumers who remember. Still, some estimate will have to be made. In general, the greater the predicted consumer response to advertising, and the higher the profit on each unit sold, the more the firm is likely to spend on ad campaigns. Given the difficulty of estimating marginal revenue, many firms arbitrarily base their advertising budget on a percentage of sales. This is similar to the rule often adopted by firms for their R&D spending.[11]

►► ADVANTAGES AND DISADVANTAGES OF OLIGOPOLY

What are the advantages and disadvantages of oligopoly as a form of industrial organization? Defenders point out that oligopolies achieve economies of scale that reduce production costs and

---

11.   It should be noted that if oligopolistic rivals are battling for market share, then advertising costs for all the firms may considerably exceed the profit-maximizing figure for these firms if they engaged in collusion and fixed prices.

consumer prices to levels that could not be reached under perfect competition. Further, they use the profits they earn to finance research on product development that competitive firms could not afford to undertake. The potential for profits from a quality change gives an incentive to use innovations at once. If the results *do* turn out to be profitable, the higher profit could last a long time because of the difficulties facing new firms that want to enter the industry, and because rivals might not be able to match the quality change right away. If rivals do match the quality change, then consumers will benefit.

Critics of the oligopolistic form of organization suggest that the economies of scale argument is not altogether convincing. They note evidence that the level of concentration in many U.S. oligopolistic industries is higher than is necessary to reach the minimum efficient scale of production. Research findings on this point in the 1970s by F. M. Scherer and others confirmed the broad thrust of the pioneering studies conducted by Joe S. Bain in the 1950s.[12] To the extent that Scherer, Bain, and other critics are correct, the advantages bestowed on society by the large size of oligopolistic firms are reduced.

Furthermore, the critics argue that even the achievement of lower production costs does not necessarily mean lower prices for consumers. The scale economies may be more than offset by the costs of advertising and instituting quality changes, which must be paid for by consumers. These costs occur more frequently in oligopoly than in any other market situation, and most frequently in the most concentrated industries. Moreover, the critics claim that oligopolies, like monopolies, increase their profits by raising prices and by reducing output below the levels required to minimize average costs. The cost advantages that might potentially emerge from oligopolies' large scale of production might not be fully realized if prices are kept high and output low in an attempt to boost their total profits.

There is, in fact, consistent evidence that the rate of profit is higher in the tighter and more concentrated oligopolies. Whether this is due to economies of scale, with the lower costs allowing the higher profit while consumers pay a reduced or at least the same price, or whether the higher profits are simply due to the higher prices, is debatable. Recently, indications have emerged that prices do rise as the level of concentration increases.[13] Yet the effect does not seem to be great, with major increases in concentration resulting in rather small price increases. Possibly enforcement of the antitrust laws has suppressed a natural tendency for firms in concentrated oligopolies to raise their prices.

OLIGOPOLY AS A COMPROMISE

A reasonable judgment of oligopoly is that it involves a compromise. We must recognize the possibility of higher prices and some allocative inefficiency, especially in tight oligopolies. Against this we must weigh the benefits of nonprice competition, especially the innovation, product variety, and development of new goods and services that oligopoly provides. It would be satisfying if lower prices for consumers and allocative efficiency in competitive markets were always completely compatible with dynamic nonprice competition. Because they are not, oligopoly as a compromise between the two positions may well be a reasonable outcome as long as cartels and price fixing do not come to dominate markets.

CONCLUSION

Between the polar cases of perfect competition and monopoly lie monopolistic competition and oligopoly, the forms of organization most common in developed economies. The level of

---

12.   Studies over a broad range of countries typically reveal mixed results, with scale economies important in some industries, but not in others where they might logically be anticipated. Pan A. Yotopoulos and Jeffrey B. Nugent have surveyed seven studies containing a large number of estimates. These showed the greatest economies of scale in industrial gases (oxygen, chlorine, ethylene) and in some food processing (beer, fruit and vegetable canning, sugar refining). But economies were, perhaps surprisingly, far less important in some other areas such as autos, computers, diesel engines, generators, machine tools, rubber goods, shoes, and fish canning.

13.   "[D]ozens of empirical studies now firmly establish that increases in market concentration and price levels are positively correlated." *Journal of Economic Literature,* Vol. 28, No. 4, December 1990, p. 1755.

effective competition in monopolistic competition and loose oligopoly is usually sufficient to protect the public from collusion and price fixing. But sometimes, especially in the tight oligopolies, it is not. That is why most governments have antitrust regulations in one form or another. Antitrust regulation is the subject of the next chapter.

SUMMARY

1) Most industries are characterized either by monopolistic competition or oligopoly.

2) Under monopolistic competition, the easy entry and exit leads to a tangency solution with the demand curve tangent to the average cost curve. Super-normal profits are eliminated and price is equal to average cost.

3) A general theory of oligopoly is difficult to construct. Some oligopolies are loose, meaning that they are generally not very concentrated, engage in little or no collusion, and face considerable effective competition in markets that are contestable. Some oligopolies are tight, however, with high concentration, collusion, price leadership, more market power, and higher super-normal profits.

4) Oligopolies exhibit considerable mutual dependence, meaning that the behavior of a given firm depends to a large extent on what its rivals do.

5) Both monopolistically competitive firms and oligopolies engage in product differentiation, including especially quality change and advertising. Oligopolies often prefer to engage in these forms of competition rather than run the risk of a price war that may break out if they compete by means of price.

APPENDIX
MODELS THAT DO NOT
ASSUME PROFIT MAXIMIZATION

The models we have discussed so far are all based on the assumption that the goal of firms is to maximize their profits. The assumption of profit maximization leads to many precise predictions and is extremely useful in the mathematical modeling that predominates in higher-level economics. Without it, the predictions of many microeconomic models would be less certain than they are.

The assumption of profit maximization is based on more than the convenience of model makers, however. Economists have generally accepted that firms actually *do* want to maximize profits in a broad sense. A number of arguments make this acceptance appear reasonable. One such argument is that perfectly competitive and monopolistically competitive firms *must* maximize profits in the long run, for any deviation from that goal will lead to a loss. (In both cases, competition ensures that at long-run equilibrium, only normal profit is being earned. Anything less means a loss.)

Oligopolists and monopolists, who possess more market power, have greater leeway. But even in these situations the assumption of profit maximization appears reasonable. If the managers of oligopolies and monopolies decide to seek some other goal (a quiet life or community service, for example), they are likely to find themselves in difficulty with their stockholders. Other firms that do earn higher profits will be held up for unfavorable comparisonat the annual stockholders' meeting. Continued failure to maximize profit will invite attempts by outsiders to buy the firm and transform it into a profit maximizer. Managers will thus be pushed toward profit maximization even if initially that was not their primary aim.

► TAKEOVERS AND BUYOUTS AS EXAMPLES OF PROFIT-MAXIMIZING BEHAVIOR

During the 1980s, especially in the United States and Great Britain (though less so in other major economies such as Germany, Japan, and France), a wave of **takeovers** and **buyouts** hit the business community. The perception that some firms were not full profit maximizers was a major motive behind the acquisitions. Many sorts of companies attracted attention as not being profit maximizers. Sometimes firms were being poorly managed or were paying their workers higher wages than necessary. Some had many subsidiaries that produced unrelated products, and those attempting the takeover suspected that these subsidiaries could be sold off at a higher price than had been paid for them. The implication was that these subsidiaries, if sold and managed separately, would be more efficient than previously. Other takeover targets were believed to be holding overly large cash reserves; perhaps they had invested little in capital improvements or had paid low dividends. In most of these cases, those who initiated the takeovers were confident that they could increase the profitability of the firms they acquired. (Explanations based on profits are not necessarily the only ones. Empire building and a lust for power may have been important as well.)

Most takeovers are accomplished by purchasing enough of a company's common stock to gain control over its operations. Several corporate raiders—among them Carl Icahn, T. Boone Pickens, Donald Trump, and James Goldsmith—acquired reputations reminiscent of the industrial robber barons of the nineteenth century.

► THE CASE THAT PROFITS ARE NOT MAXIMIZED

Even accepting that a broad thrust toward profit maximization does exist, a number of pointed questions concerning the maximizing principle deserve discussion, and it is possible to make a case that firms do not always maximize profits in actual practice.

LACK OF FAMILIARITY AMONG MANAGERS WITH THE CONCEPTS OF MARGINAL COST AND MARGINAL REVENUE

It is unrealistic to assume the all managers are familiar with the marginal cost and marginal revenue curves employed by economists in the calculation of maximum profits. Many of them have never even *seen* such curves. How then, can we assume that they are motivated by a desire to maximize profit? This challenge is, however, not a serious one. The model of profit-maximization predicts only that firms will behave in a certain way. It does not specify the manner in which that behavior comes about. The behavior may be the result of trial and error, canny judgment, or just plain luck—or it may involve the tools of marginal analysis.

FAILURE TO MAXIMIZE PROFITS IN THE SHORT RUN

Firms often put other goals ahead of immediate profit maximization. They may spend substantial sums to foster good will in the community. They may avoid what appear to be profitable undertakings because of negative public reaction. Some movie theaters will not show X-rated films; some manufacturers will not produce napalm. Firms may also choose not to maximize short-run profits in order to ward off government antitrust action, or to prevent the entry of new competitors into the industry (remember the limit price), or to avoid provoking wage demands from labor unions.

These examples of behavior appear reasonably common. Yet none of them is necessarily evidence that firms are not broadly committed to profit maximization. Contrary behavior might dissipate good will, lead to an antitrust charge, attract new entrants, and provoke labor unions. Each could have a negative effect on the firm's *future* profits. Behavior that sacrifices some short-run profit may actually involve profit maximization in the long run.

Unfortunately, it is often difficult to show empirically whether settling for less immediate profit is a real deviation from profit maximization, or whether it is a case of long-run maximization.

MARK-UP PRICING, SALES MAXIMIZATION, AND "SATISFICING"

More fundamentally, objections to the idea that firms maximize profit involve alternative views on how firms actually make and carry out their decisions. A number of managerial economists, principally William J. Baumol of Princeton University and Herbert Simon of Carnegie-Mellon University, have developed models of oligopoly behavior based on assumptions other than profit maximization. The principal areas treated by these models are **mark-up pricing**, **sales maximization**, and **satisficing**.

Baumol suggests that, though profit maximization may once have been the aim of many large oligopolistic firms, the push to maximize profits may now be somewhat weaker. Models such as the kinked demand curve and the limit price, and mathematical analysis such as game theory, may be too sophisticated for day-to-day decision-making. Baumol argues that many managerial decisions take little or no account of the possible reaction of rivals. Speculation about other firms' countermoves may figure only slightly in important judgments concerning inventory size, transport patterns, the line of products marketed, and the size of the R&D effort.

The main reason, according to Baumol, is that large corporations have grown more complex than they once were, somewhat clumsier and slower moving than suggested by the standard models of oligopoly behavior. Routine decisions made by one firm may be ignored by its competitors. Even if these rivals do decide to make a countermove, lengthy discussions in committee meetings may delay action for long periods of time. Moreover, Baumol suggests that the managers of many firms may be too busy and their skills too limited for them to make use of complicated formulas for profit maximization. That is especially true of managers in firms that market hundreds of different products. Even if this problem could easily be overcome, firms have learned and relearned an old lesson: very flexible prices are an annoyance to consumers, whose good will it is important to retain. Day-to-day ups and downs in prices are more upsetting to consumers than is stability.

Mark-up Pricing

To simplify their decision making, oligopolistic firms often resort to rules of thumb. For example, they may set prices by adding a standard percentage markup to average costs at some target level of capacity utilization and may devote a fixed percentage of total revenue to their advertising and R&D budgets. A recent sample survey of managers showed that 75% believed they were using average costs rather than marginal costs in determining prices, and 25% of that group were using a rigid markup.[14] When managers are asked how they determine the size of such markups, many reply that they base it on an estimate of how high they could push the price without prompting competitors to follow suit. Prices change in this model when costs change, or when the markup is altered to reflect new assessments of "what the market will bear."

These rules of thumb may originally have led to implicit profit maximization, but Baumol argues that the rules must be simple to be useful, and to be simple they cannot take explicit day-to-day account of what other firms do. Price cuts by rivals may not be matched if the competing firms are all using a system of mark-up pricing. This result differs appreciably from the orthodox theory of oligopoly behavior.

---

14.   See Gerald R. Faulhaber and William J. Baumol, "Economists as Innovators: Practical Products of Theoretical Research," *Journal of Economic Literature*, Vol. 26, No. 2, June 1988, p. 593.

Sales Maximization

Baumol also advances an alternative hypothesis to explain the *goals* of oligopolistic firms. There is some evidence, he suggests, that sheer size of operations may have superseded profit as the prime objective of modern corporations. Why would this be so? One reason is that larger firms can often obtain a lower interest rate on bank loans and bond issues than smaller but highly profitable firms can. Moreover, a certain glamour seems to be associated with large size in the corporate world. The salaries and perquisites of middle and top managers appear, according to Baumol, to be correlated more closely with sales volume than with profit levels. Often the vice president of a large but only moderately profitable firm is paid much more than the vice president of a small but highly profitable firm, travels in a corporate jet instead of economy class on an airliner, and gets many more lucrative benefits.[15]

This suggests that there may be a motive to maximize the firm's sales rather than its profits. Not maximizing profit is quite different from ignoring it, however. The managers must observe some minimum "profit constraint"—some level below which profit cannot dip if the stockholders are to be kept satisfied, takeover bids are to be avoided, and the firm is to earn enough to reinvest in new plant and equipment.

Satisficing

Herbert Simon (winner of the 1978 Nobel Prize in Economics) has emphasized that the managers of many large corporations may develop goals quite separate from that of the owners—that is, the stockholders. They may tend to behave in ways that are "satisfactory" to the stockholders rather than profit maximizing.

An argument that the managers of corporations might pursue goals different from those of the stockholders dates as far back as Adam Smith and *The Wealth of Nations*. It was developed and expanded by Adolf A. Berle and Gardiner C. Means in the 1930s. Berle and Means noted how personal profit maximization by the managers of corporations, including high salaries, perquisites, and the like, might supersede profit maximizing for the owners (stockholders). The difficulty in motivating managers to behave in the way owners would has come to be called the **principal-agent problem**. Various ways to deal with it include giving managers a stake in firms' earnings by means of stock-ownership plans, profit-sharing schemes, and incentive pay that is linked to profitability. These ideas are considered further in Chapter 25.

Perhaps the managers can generate returns satisfactory to their stockholders even though they do not maximize profits. So long as the stockholders remain unaware of the possibility of greater returns, the managers might keep their positions indefinitely. Such practices have been called **satisficing**. A management that engages in satisficing could choose from a range of possible output and prices instead of being bound to the output and price required by profit maximization. In Figure 8A.1, so long as the cost curves do not change position, that range would occur within the limits where the demand curve lies above the average cost curve, with output somewhere between Q_1 and Q_2 and with price somewhere between P_1 and P_2.

The price could thus be lower or higher than the profit-maximizing price P_m, and the quantity higher or lower than Q_m. If the firm's goal is to maximize sales rather than profit, it would presumably choose a price in the lower range, from P_m to P_2. Even if the firm did not try to maximize sales, why would it want to look bad to the public by charging a price *higher* than P_m when it could earn the same profit with a price *lower* than P_m? Following this logic one step further, note that a monopoly firm that is a sales maximizer rather than a profit maximizer would produce a greater quantity at lower prices, so negating the usual monopoly results discussed in Chapter 7.

15.　Baumol notes that the requirements for membership in the Young Presidents Organization include being under 40 and president of a company whose annual sales volume is over a million dollars. No mention is made of profit.

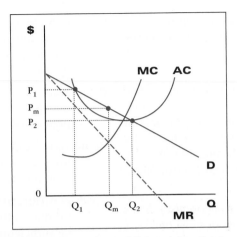

Figure 8A.1. The range of price and output under satisficing. A firm that is a satisficer rather than a profit maximizer might charge any price from P_1 to P_2 and produce quantities from Q_1 to Q_2. This range of prices and quantities would allow average costs to be covered.

▶ USE OF THE PROFIT-MAXIMIZING ASSUMPTION IS LIKELY TO CONTINUE

The analyses of Baumol, Simon, and many others investigating these topics are a stimulating addition to the debate on oligopoly behavior. Studies are continuing in this area, but empirical evidence is obviously difficult to acquire because firms' pricing strategies are usually closely guarded commercial secrets. Largely anecdotal evidence indicates that the degree of satisficing differs significantly among industries, and perhaps even more among countries. Even so, additional evidence with which to test the traditional theory is in time bound to surface and will provide further insights into behavior under imperfect competition. When it comes, that evidence is unlikely to show that profit maximization as a working assumption is so misleading as to cause significant damage. A reasonable guess is that several decades hence, models incorporating this vital assumption will still be the standard in microeconomics. The majority opinion that the large gains from precise prediction and mathematical tractability outweigh the small loss in accuracy will probably continue to hold sway.

Chapter Key Words

Collusion: Agreements between oligopolistic firms to fix prices. Usually illegal in the United States.

Concentration ratio: The percentage of an industry's total output produced by the industry's four largest firms.

Contestable markets: Markets in which the market power of established firms can be easily challenged, or contested, by new competition. In such markets even though the number of existing firms is small, these firms might be forced to behave *as if* they were competitive.

Economies of scope: The idea that additional varieties or models of some basic product (cigarettes, clothing) can be introduced and marketed at a cost lower than if they were produced separately.

Game theory: A mathematical technique for predicting the reaction of others. It is useful in analyzing how an oligopolistic firm's competitors will respond to its marketing policies, and so in choosing one's own strategy .

Informative advertising: Advertising, usually in newspapers, catalogs, and direct mailings, that presents useful information (especially the price) of a product.

Kinked demand curve: A model suggesting that the demand curve for oligopolistic firms is kinked, indicating the dangers of unilateral price changes not followed by competitors and explaining the absence of price competition in many oligopolistic industries.

Limit price: The price set by oligopolistic firms to discourage the entry of newcomers. A limit price below the average cost of a new entrant would condemn that new entrant to losses and discourage it from making the attempt.

Loose oligopoly: An oligopoly characterized by a relatively low concentration ratio, low costs of entry, and low trade barriers, and considerable competition by means of price. The firms in loose oligopolies may face sufficient effective competition so that significant super-normal profits do not appear.

Mark-up pricing: Pricing by means of adding a standard percentage markup to average costs.

Monopolistic competition: A market structure with many sellers, a small degree of control over price, and easy entry and exit. Results in the elimination of abnormal profits and a high degree of product differentiation.

Mutual dependence: A situation in oligopoly where firms find that the impact on profits of a price change made by them depends largely on the action taken by competing firms. Provides the basis for the kinked demand curve and suggests a reluctance to compete by means of price.

Oligopoly: A market structure with a few firms that may or may not collude, each of which must take into account the reaction of competitors when making marketing decisions. Oligopoly is usually what is meant when "big business" is referred to. See "*loose oligopoly*" and "*tight oligopoly*."

Predatory pricing: Price-cutting designed to drive competitors out of the market, after which prices can be raised to levels involving super-normal profits.

Price leadership: Informal collusion between oligopolistic firms that follow the pricing policies of one firm in the industry.

Principal-agent problem: The problem involved in motivating hired managers to seek profits in the way owners would.

Product differentiation: The attempt to make a product sufficiently different, or appear to be sufficiently different, so that demand is increased at the expense of other producers of the same good. A standard practice in both monopolistic competition and oligopoly.

Sales maximization: Pricing to maximize the quantity sold while still covering average costs.

Satisficing: Managers of a firm may develop goals separate from that of the owners (stockholders); they may aim to earn a level of profit "satisfactory" to the owners rather than maximizing the profit, leaving them free to pursue other goals.

Takeover: The acquisition of a company by outsiders, often associated with a perception that the company was not previously maximizing its profits.

Tight oligopoly: An oligopoly characterized by a high concentration ratio, high costs of entry, high trade barriers, and little price competition. Firms in a tight oligopoly may be earning significant super-normal profits.

Uninformative (or competitive) advertising: Advertising that makes little or no attempt to give information of value. Designed to catch attention in one way or another.

Chapter Questions

1) Mario's Pizza was the first pizzeria to locate near the campus of City University, and Mario has been making large profits. Armetta is considering opening her own pizzeria. She says, "A pizza is a pizza. The market is perfectly competitive, and if I sell at a lower price than Mario, everyone will buy from me." Is her statement correct? Explain what will happen to the quantity of pizza Mario makes if Armetta does enter the market?

2) Neighborhood laundromats are monopolistic competitors. Suppose the market is initially in long run equilibrium, and then 5th Street Laundry installs newer washing machines. As a result more people do their laundry there. Describe how this change affects the demand curve for the whole market, the demand curve of 5th Street Laundry, and the demand curve of a representative competitor, 6th Street Laundry. Draw diagrams showing the short run profits or losses for both laundries. What do you guess might happen to restore long run equilibrium?

3) A small airport in western Kansas is served by only three airlines. What is the 4-firm concentration ratio at this airport? The airport's board is concerned because there are two unused gates at the airport. Most board members argue that the airlines form a tight oligopoly, but a skeptical member notes that they offer competitive discounts against one another. Is it possible that the three airlines form a loose, rather than tight, oligopoly?

4) You are the manager of Pacific Writing Instruments, one of the companies in the oligopolistic pen industry. You believe that your competitors would never follow your firm's price increase, but they would always follow your price decrease. Suppose a new local tax increases your costs. Would you be more likely to increase your price to make up for the tax or simply pay it out of your profits at the current price? Use the kinked demand curve model in your answer.

5) Initially the steel industry was characterized by price leadership by a dominant firm (USX). Technological advances led to the development of the "mini-mill," so many new fringe firms entered the industry. Show how to derive USX's demand curve before and after the increase in fringe firm supply (assume the position but not the slope of the supply curve changes). Will USX produce more or less steel than before?

6) You are president of a company that produces road atlases. There are only two other major road atlas producers in the country. You have two options available. You can reduce the price of your atlases or you can improve the quality of your maps. Either course of action is expected to increase your market share by 10%, and likewise each is expected to increase profits by 10% (before any response by your competitors). Which option do you choose and why?

7) Coca-Cola operates in a tight oligopolistic industry and has considerable market power. Nonetheless it spends a great deal on uninformative advertising. Suppose you are told that a recent Coke TV campaign cost more than the revenue obtained from people who watched the commercials. You are also told that the initial investment needed to begin producing soft drinks is quite low. Based on this information, do you think that the Coca-Cola Company followed the profit maximizing rule?

APPENDIX

8) You have a very large amount of money to invest, and you also can sell "junk" bonds to raise even more money. As you look over data on companies, you find one large corporation in an oligopolistic industry that does not equate marginal cost and marginal revenue. Instead it sets its price very close to average cost, making only a small profit. What is the term for this behavior and why does it occur? What might you do next?

CHAPTER 9

Controlling Market Power:

Government

Regulation

and Antitrust

Law

OVERALL OBJECTIVE: To examine attempts to control market power by means of government regulation of industry and antitrust law.

MORE SPECIFICALLY:

- To show that natural monopolies and certain other industries may be regulated by means of "fair rate of return" or average-cost pricing, or marginal-cost pricing, and to explain the logic behind each of these, including their advantages and disadvantages.

- To discuss the development and present stance of antitrust law in the United States, including the two major pieces of legislation, the Sherman Act and the Clayton Act, and the most important court decisions that make up U.S. case law on the subject.

- To explain the differences between horizontal, vertical, and conglomerate mergers and assess the state of the law with respect to these.

- To show why economists generally believe that under modern conditions, some relaxation of antitrust law might be beneficial.

- To assess the different antitrust stance in Europe and Japan, explain why vertical coordination in Japan is currently attracting attention in the United States, and query whether a worldwide convergence in antitrust policy may be taking place and is sensible.

In the past few chapters, we have seen that monopoly and oligopoly create serious costs of various sorts and also carry offsetting advantages. Governments have viewed the balance between these costs and benefits in quite different ways. In most countries, natural monopolies such as electricity and water supplies are given special treatment. Where an activity is a natural monopoly, enforcing competition would lead to a wasteful duplication of capital. Governments usually decide either to regulate such natural monopolies or to own them outright.

Oligopolies are not usually treated in this way. Some countries appear to believe that the benefits of oligopoly are considerably greater than the costs, even including the dangers of collusive action, and so they make little or no direct effort to limit private-market power over pricing and output. Japan and South Korea are good examples, although in both countries there is considerable consultation between the government and private firms, which does provide some indirect policing of monopolizing activity. Another group of countries, the 12 nations of the European Community, or Common Market, sometimes blocks monopolistic combinations, but on the whole takes a rather lenient view of oligopolistic behavior. Finally, the United States has a long tradition of government supervision by means of antitrust law. This tradition is currently bending, partly because of the more permissive rules in other countries, but is still relatively strict. This chapter traces the impact of government regulation and surveys the differing views of government attempts to control market power.

▶ REGULATED INDUSTRIES

When an activity is a natural monopoly, such as the delivery of electric power, water, and natural gas, government can supervise the activity through regulatory commissions. In many instances, **regulated industries** are also called **public utilities**, but the term is somewhat misleading because the utilities are actually private firms. Furthermore, government regulation ranges beyond natural monopolies, for example, to trucking, airlines, and broadcasting. Regulation is common in the United States, and this system is also growing in importance abroad. The government regulatory commissions that do the supervising usually must grant approval for changes in price and output. Some industries (electric power, natural gas) are subject to stricter regulation than others (trucking, cable television).[1] Each state has its own commissions to regulate intrastate business, while various federal commissions regulate interstate business. The federal Interstate Commerce Commission supervises railroads and trucking, and the Federal Communications Commission oversees radio and TV broadcasting.

Because regulated industries are often monopolies, we can use the monopoly model to analyze their regulation. We begin with a monopoly that is unregulated, shown in Figure 9.1. The equilibrium price and quantity of this monopoly are P_1 and Q_1. It is earning a super-normal profit, as shown by the shaded rectangle AP_1VB. Allocative inefficiency is apparent because consumers would be willing to pay more than the marginal cost for each unit of output between Q_1 and Q_3. The total amount of allocative inefficiency is equal to the triangular area WVZ. Due to the lower quantity of output and the higher price chosen by the monopoly in comparison with the competitive outcome, resources are being misallocated and income distribution may become less equal. These are the reasons that government undertakes the regulation.

---

1.   It is worth pointing out that views of what is a natural monopoly and what is not can often diverge widely, with politics playing a major role in determining which industries are made subject to regulation.

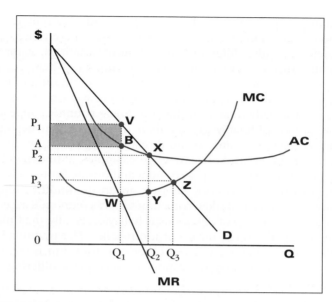

Figure 9.1. A regulated industry. An unregulated monopoly would maximize its profits with a price of P_1. The average-cost price, or fair rate of return in this situation, would be P_2. Here the price just covers the average cost of production and super-normal profit is eliminated, but there would still be some allocative inefficiency. The marginal-cost price, P_3, would eliminate the allocative inefficiency but it would require a subsidy from the government.

AVERAGE-COST OR "FAIR RATE OF RETURN" PRICING

The government might choose to regulate this monopoly by imposing a price that would wipe out its super-normal profit of AP_1VB. That price, which would be just equal to the average cost of production including a normal profit, would be at the point where the demand curve intersects the average cost curve. Price P_2 would just cover average cost. Any lower price would mean that the monopoly would incur a loss; any higher price would result in super-normal profit.

Would this form of regulation benefit society? In some respects it would. For example, once the monopoly has been subjected to regulation it will produce more output (Q_2) at a lower price (P_2) than it would if left unregulated. Because the super-normal profit is eliminated, the distribution of income will probably become more equal. With the larger output at Q_2, the firm will slide down its cost curve from A to P_2. The gap between price and marginal cost will be reduced from VW to XY, thus shrinking the triangle of allocative inefficiency from WVZ to YXZ.

Such **average-cost pricing**, often called a **fair rate of return**, is widely used by state regulatory commissions as a means of regulation. Even though it eliminates the monopoly profit, it does create some serious problems. For example, it invites disagreement between the regulated industry and regulatory commissions over what costs are legitimate. Without the spur of competition, a privately owned regulated industry has less incentive to try to minimize costs. An electric power company is unlikely to spend long hours searching for the cheapest coal to run its power plant if there is a good chance that the regulatory commission will approve a price for electricity based on the use of higher-cost coal. Even more intractable problems may arise. For example, is it legitimate for the regulated industry to spend money on ads to persuade voters to approve the building of a hydroelectric dam in a wilderness area? Consumers, including the environmentalists among them, will have to pay for such ads if the regulatory commission decides they can be included in the industry's costs.

Regulated industries sometimes overstate their costs, including generous fringe benefits, elegant board rooms, company cars, country club memberships, and other expenses that can be hidden in the costs of production. Similarly, they may over-invest in plant and equipment in order to expand the cost base on which the return on investment is calculated.[2] For outsiders to calculate the firm's costs rather than to take a firm's word for it introduces complex problems for the regulators. Finally, regulated industries have little incentive to cut costs through innovation and technological change. The regulators often pass cost reductions on to consumers in the form of a lower price, so the firm does not benefit. Even temporary profits may not accrue because public utilities commissions are often empowered to order rebates to be made.

To overcome these problems, in 1989 the Federal Communications Commission introduced an experimental regulatory approach that deviates significantly from average-cost pricing. It ruled that AT&T, though still subject to a regulated price ceiling, would be permitted to retain any profits resulting from keeping costs below the costs used in calculating the ceiling.[3] Such *price-cap regulation* does not put a cap on the firm's rate of return, so encouraging cost-cutting. A 1992 review indicates that under the new form of regulation, AT&T's prices fell while the its rate of return increased. This was an indication that the new policy is successful. Further favorable results may cause the government's regulatory policies to undergo substantial revision, at least in certain industries.

MARGINAL-COST PRICING

Another type of regulation, called **marginal-cost pricing**, is less common than average-cost pricing. Under this form of regulation, it is possible to eliminate allocative inefficiency altogether by setting price equal to marginal cost. In Figure 9.1, the marginal cost price would be P_3, determined by the intersection of the MC curve and the demand curve, and the quantity produced would be Q_3. That price and quantity would mean no one is willing to pay more for another unit of the good than the cost of producing that unit. The allocative inefficiency, WVZ in an unregulated monopoly and YXZ under average-cost pricing, would disappear.

One difficulty with marginal-cost pricing, as with average-cost pricing, is that the regulated firm has no incentive to reduce costs. Another difficulty, unique to this method, is that a price based on marginal cost may be below average cost. Consequently, the regulated firm would be faced with a continuing loss on its operations and the government would have to grant it a permanent subsidy, paid for out of taxes, to keep it going. (The collection of these taxes, if it introduces distortions into factor use, will carry costs of its own. Any gains from marginal-cost pricing would thus have to be large enough to offset the costs of misallocation caused by the tax system and its associated bureaucracy in order to justify the payment of the permanent subsidy.) Marginal-cost pricing was once a popular regulatory policy in Europe, but rising government budget deficits in recent years have led most European countries to go back to average-cost pricing.

Marginal-Cost Pricing under Conditions of Overload and Congestion

Despite its shortcomings, marginal-cost pricing is an appropriate policy for regulation under conditions of frequent overload or congestion—an electric power plant with inadequate capacity to handle the load from summer air conditioners, for example, or a toll road that approaches gridlock at certain hours.

In Figure 9.2, production can be expanded with no increase in either average or marginal costs up to Q_a. To the left of Q_a there is adequate capacity to generate more electricity or to provide room for more cars on the road. Over this range both the AC curve and the MC curve are horizontal. Beyond Q_a, however, additional air conditioners in use or cars on the road inflict extra costs. The power plant may have to call an old backup generator into service, and traffic will slow during rush hours. The additional cost (MC) is reflected in higher electricity bills and extra time spent in commuting.

---

2.   This is the "Averch-Johnson Effect," named for its formulators, H. A. Averch and L. L. Johnson. It applies when the "fair rate of return" is above the interest rate that must be paid to acquire new capital. (If the fair rate of return is below that figure, there will be underinvestment.)

3.   The idea received its initial trial in 1984 when the British government applied it to British Telecom, which operates the telephone system.

The marginal cost caused by the overload is higher than the average cost. An additional air conditioner may raise electricity charges to each user only 10¢ per month but the $100,000 rise in *overall* costs was due to just the one more machine. An extra car may raise commuting time by one minute for each driver, but that can be 100 hours for *all* drivers due to the extra car.[4]

In Figure 9.2, an average-cost price P_{ac} will reflect only the slight increase in costs from the overload spread over all users, and quantity will be at the high level Q_{ac}. A marginal-cost price P_{mc}, however, will reflect the high costs imposed on other users by an *additional* air conditioner or car, and that higher price will cause a lower quantity Q_{mc} to be demanded.

Using marginal cost pricing to address overload or congestion problems would clearly encourage conservation and the use of alternatives. Air conditioning would be set at higher temperatures with price P_{mc} than with price P_{ac}; commuters would be more enthusiastic about carpooling and staggered office hours. Moreover, no subsidy will be required.

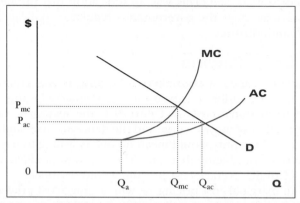

Figure 9.2. Marginal-cost pricing to address overload and congestion. Under conditions of overload and congestion, regulation by means of an average-cost price would not limit quantity as much as would a marginal-cost price. In this case, because the marginal-cost price is above average cost, no subsidy from the government would be necessary.

THE MOVE TOWARD DEREGULATION

Over the years, many U.S. state and federal regulatory commissions were accused of favoring the firms they are supposed to regulate rather than serving the interests of the consuming public. Many economists argued that this "capture of the regulators" had extended to the point that the regulatory agencies were weakening competition and permitting regulated firms to charge unjustifiably high prices. They also suggested that deregulation would increase flexibility and efficiency. The regulated airlines could not compete by means of price, could not establish new routes, could not give up unprofitable ones. Regulated trucking firms were constrained to follow fixed routes and sometimes prohibited from carrying particular cargoes. Regulated railroads were not able to adjust rates or consolidate lines.

Eventually under the Carter administration and then the Reagan administration, a number of industries were wholly or partially decontrolled. Trucking rates and routes, and railways were largely deregulated in 1980. New entry was permitted into the airline industry from 1982, while fares were deregulated in 1983. Restrictions on entry into long-distance telephone service were lifted in 1982, and freedom to set charges was granted at that time. Other areas of telecommunications, including cable television, have been deregulated as well. The deregulating activity has brought the current proportion of total U.S. output produced by regulated industries

---

4.   Columbia University economist William Vickrey has estimated that an extra driver at rush hour can impose a marginal cost ten times greater than the average cost faced by that driver.

down to about 7%, less than half of what it was when Jimmy Carter assumed office in 1976. For the most part, economists appear to have welcomed the decontrol measures, especially those involving transport. Further deregulation is on the horizon, as in the proposals to allow telephone companies to bring cable TV and interactive shopping and banking into homes. (But note that some reaction has recently set in. For example, cable television companies in the United States during the 1980s were granted franchises that allowed them to operate as local monopolies, but without control of their rates. Amid growing public outcry, Congress reregulated cable TV rates in 1992.)

GOVERNMENT OWNERSHIP

Many regulated industries are owned and operated by the government. Throughout the world, and especially in Europe, almost all postal services, most railroads, many telephone, water, sewage, electricity, and gas systems, and local transport, such as buses and subways, are owned by the government. Short of outright ownership, the government sometimes purchases a portion of firms' stock large enough to give it some control over its performance, including price setting. This is common practice in Sweden and was at one time in Britain and France as well.

During the 1980s, government ownership of firms declined steadily, most notably in Great Britain. Government leaders either decided that certain industries would operate more efficiently in an unregulated competitive framework or that government involvement could be scaled back to supervision of a monopoly firm's pricing policy. Not incidentally, the sale of government-owned firms into private ownership brought substantial revenues to the national treasuries.

THE BRITISH RETREAT FROM STATE OWNERSHIP

Great Britain was noted for a high percentage of state ownership of firms until Margaret Thatcher's government began to sell them off after 1979. Included in the rather long list of privatized firms are British Aerospace (the aircraft manufacturer), British Telecom (the phone system), British Gas (most homes in Britain are heated by natural gas), the National Freight Company (road haulage), Rolls-Royce Aero Engines, Sealink (the nationalized ferry company), Associated British Ports (the docks were nationalized), Jaguar motor cars, and many council houses and flats (public housing). Even the provision of water is being privatized, and London's Heathrow and Gatwick airports are now privately owned and operated. It has been a most remarkable turnaround for Britain, once known as one of the more "socialized" of the market economies. There is concern, however. The privatizing has been carried out in a context of weaker government regulation of monopoly practices than is true in the United States, with accompanying fears of output restriction and price gouging.

▶ ANTITRUST LAW

Since the time of Adam Smith, economists have been concerned that under a market system firms might try to engage in collusive behavior or mergers that create monopoly power. To ensure that some degree of competition continues, governments frequently make the attempt to police monopoly or monopolizing behavior among oligopolistic firms. This is done by means of **antitrust law**.[5]

ANTITRUST LAWS IN THE UNITED STATES

Many countries have resorted to antitrust laws to protect the public from firms that possess market power, but the movement has been especially strong in the United States. Courts have played a major role in the development of these laws in the United States, far more so than in other countries.

The Robber Barons

The late nineteenth century was the time of the so-called "robber barons of industry," whose firms exercised considerable monopoly power. John D. Rockefeller, founder of the Standard Oil Company, is one of the best-known examples. Rockefeller is said to have employed predatory pricing tactics to seize control of the oil industry. By setting its prices below the costs of its competitors, Standard Oil forced one company after another to agree to mergers until at last it was in a position to charge monopoly prices. (The main product was kerosene for cooking and lighting. It was the 1870s, before the days of automobiles and gasoline.) The company became so strong that it was able to extract rebates from the railroads on its shipments, and even on the shipments of its *competitors*. The railroads themselves, in effect acting as spies for Standard Oil to keep Standard's large volume of business, secretly supplied information on the size of competitors' shipments. By 1879, nine years after its founding, Standard Oil controlled between 90 and 95% of the nation's output of petroleum products. Its ability to set prices made it one of the world's most lucrative monopolies.[6]

The Robber Barons made no apologies for their monopolizing behavior. "What do I care about the law? Hain't I got the power?" asked Cornelius Vanderbilt, the shipping magnate, when told a step he was about to take was illegal. His son William was equally straightforward about the right of the public to police monopoly practices: "The public be damned," he said.

It is no coincidence that such unabashed exercise of monopoly power coincided with a period of extremely high tariffs in the United States. Free trade usually provides very effective control over monopolizing behavior because the world is a large place with many competitors. Trade barriers, by preventing foreigners from competing, make domestic monopolies more powerful.

The Sherman Act of 1890

During the 1880s a populist antimonopoly movement arose in the United States. The movement was particularly strong in the Midwest, and the first antitrust law was passed in Kansas in 1889. By 1893 15 states had antitrust laws. These state laws were largely ineffectual, however, because they violated the constitutional ban against interference with interstate commerce.

The first federal antitrust law was the **Sherman Antitrust Act of 1890**, named for Senator John Sherman of Ohio. The act was loosely worded and full of loopholes, apparently by design. It declared that any *combination or conspiracy in restraint of trade or commerce is illegal*, but its definition of these terms was inadequate. It made no provision for an enforcement agency. (The Antitrust Division of the Justice Department was not established until 13 years later.) Moreover, the Supreme Court was hostile to the act. The Court's 1895 ruling in the *U.S. v. E. C. Knight Co.* that "commerce is not manufacture," illogical as that seems today, weakened the act

---

5. The word "trust" has a meaning involving collusive behavior by firms, as when the stockholders of several corporations turn their stock over to a board of trustees that manages the corporations as one entity. Hence "antitrust law."

6. Allan Nevins wrote of Standard's predatory strategy of buying out its competitors with "or else" price wars, that "of all the devices for the extinction of competition, this was the cruelest and most deadly yet conceived by any group of American industrialists." Remember from Chapter 8, however, that the evidence concerning Standard Oil's tactics has proved to be controversial. Nevins also points out that many of Standard's competitors hardly had to be forced into agreement. The potential for monopoly profits was vast, and large numbers of them sold out quite willingly on generous terms to Rockefeller's firm. Some competitors even took the lead in proposing a buyout. However, the charges that Standard's tactics were predatory were certainly believed at the time and strongly influenced public attitudes.

for years with regard to manufacturing.[7] During the McKinley administration (1897–1901) only five prosecutions were made under the Sherman Act, although 146 major industrial combinations were formed between 1899 and 1901.

Theodore Roosevelt changed all that. Thrust into the White House by McKinley's assassination in 1901, Roosevelt was a populist opposed to monopoly practices. Over the years, as he named justices to the Supreme Court, his view came to prevail. In the innocently named Northern Securities Company case of 1904, the court, by a 5-to-4 vote, blocked a plan to establish a transcontinental railroad monopoly. (The Northern Securities Company, in spite of its inoffensive title, was a cover to merge the railway empires controlled by E.H. Harriman, J.P. Morgan, and James J. Hill. This would have put four of the six transcontinental railroads into a holding company under the same management.) In the following year, 1905, in *Swift and Co. v. U.S.*, the court broke up the beef monopoly. All this even though in that year only five federal attorneys were at work on antitrust cases.

The most famous year for the government "trust-busters" was 1911, when the Supreme Court broke Rockefeller's huge Standard Oil Company into several smaller companies. These include today's Exxon (Standard Oil of New Jersey), Mobil (Standard Oil of New York), Chevron (Standard Oil of California), Sohio (Standard Oil of Ohio, now the American branch of BP), Amoco (Standard Oil of Indiana), Conoco (Continental Oil), and Atlantic (now part of Sun Oil). In 1911, the Supreme Court also forced the reorganization of the tobacco trust in *U.S. v. American Tobacco Company*. But there was a catch to these antimonopoly victories. The wording of the Sherman Act did not make it clear whether monopoly *itself* was illegal. The Court concluded that some monopolies were worse than others and held that only undue or unreasonable restraint of trade was illegal under the Sherman Act. It confirmed this so-called **rule of reason** in 1920 when it refused to convict J.P. Morgan's U.S. Steel Company, of restraint of trade, even though for many years the company had produced over 60% of the country's steel and had considerable monopoly power. The Court declared that it was not enough to show bigness: "The law does not make mere size an offense. It … requires overt acts." The justices held that the very existence of a conspiracy to fix prices proved that U.S. Steel did not have actual monopoly power, for if it did it would not have resorted to price fixing. (U.S. Steel had been remarkably tolerant of new competition and had allowed its market share to drift well below 50% by the year the case was decided. In large measure this tolerance was a tactic to avoid an antitrust defeat, and as such it was entirely successful.) The Court backed up its U.S. Steel decision in 1927, in *U.S. v. International Harvester*, declaring that there is no evidence of crime "however impressive is the existence of unexerted power." The rule of reason was to hinder the prosecution of antitrust cases for many years to come.

The Clayton Act of 1914

In 1914, during Woodrow Wilson's administration, Congress passed the **Clayton Antitrust Act**, which strengthened the Sherman Act in several areas. The Clayton Act outlawed price discrimination that tends to create monopoly—as, for example, when producers give each other discounts in order to undercut and eliminate competitors. The Act also made illegal contracts in which the contracting parties agree not to buy or sell the products of competitors. It prohibited companies from acquiring shares in competing companies when that would tend to lessen competition. (This clause was used to force DuPont to divest itself of large holdings of General Motors stock in 1957.) It forbade interlocking directorates where one or more individuals serve simultaneously on the boards of competing firms. Finally, it provided that corporate officials could be held personally responsible for monopoly practices. Under the Sherman Act, only the corporation, and not its managers, could be penalized following conviction. (It was under

---

7.   The case concerned sugar refining, 98% of which was controlled by the company. A century later, interpretation had changed greatly. "Commerce" now included even the activity of nonprofit organizations such as colleges and universities, which had to face challenges on occasion. Some select private colleges and universities were astounded in 1989-1992 to find themselves the targets of a federal antitrust investigation.

the Clayton Act that several high G.E. and Westinghouse officials were sentenced to prison for price fixing in 1961.) The Clayton Act also excluded trade unions from its antitrust provisions, an important development that we will discuss in Chapter 12.

To help police the Clayton Act, the Federal Trade Commission Act was also passed in 1914. It established the FTC to consider complaints of unfair competitive practices, including false advertising.[8]

Subsequent Antitrust Legislation

During the Great Depression of the 1930s, Congress passed several laws that had the curious effect of discouraging competition.[9] But a turnaround toward more energetic use of the antitrust laws took place just before World War II, when the "rule of reason" came under attack. In 1940, the Socony-Vacuum decision ruled price fixing illegal, whether it was reasonable or not. Five years later, in the famous Alcoa Case of 1945, Justice Learned Hand of the New York Court of Appeals overturned the rule of reason, holding that excessive market power could be an offense in itself. Because the Supreme Court declined to review the case, Justice Hand's decision stood. Though the Court seemed for some years to back away from that decision, it reaffirmed Hand's basic logic in *U.S. v. Grinnell Corporation* (1966) in which it held that monopoly power could be illegal *per se*. (The Court also held, however, that if the monopoly was the result of a superior product, business acumen, or historical accident, it was not illegal under the Sherman Act.)

In 1946 the Supreme Court enlarged the grounds for policing oligopoly behavior. Under the Sherman Act, overt price-fixing agreements had always been held illegal. But when no outright price-fixing agreement could be presented as evidence, no convictions had been obtained even when firms had been behaving *as if* they were fixing prices. In *American Tobacco Co. v. U.S.* (1946), the Court ruled that illegal agreement could be inferred. The three major U.S. tobacco companies—American, Liggett and Myers, and R. J. Reynolds—had priced their products and had paid tobacco growers in such a similar fashion that price fixing could be inferred, the court declared. Prosecution of oligopolistic behavior seemed set to expand substantially.

More recent court decisions did not sustain this trend, and the direct frontal assault on oligopoly lost force. Some flank attacks on oligopoly behavior still continue, however, and after a hiatus during the Reagan administration they have even gained somewhat in intensity. In 1992 the government charged that three infant formula makers were carrying on conduct that might facilitate price fixing and market sharing, as when they lobbied states for bidding procedures to their liking and established codes to restrict their advertising. That, alleged the government, limited both their competition for state welfare contracts and their willingness to advertise. In another 1992 case, suit was brought against Eastman-Kodak because of alleged "tie-ins" locking the buyers of its copying machines into servicing and repair contracts. Though the machines themselves were purchased in a relatively competitive market, the government charged that, in effect, Eastman-Kodak was enforcing a monopoly on the servicing and repair work.

---

8. The agency had a powerful weapon in the first five years of its life—the ability to issue "cease and desist" orders without being subject to judicial review. This was overturned by court decision in 1919. Many observers have mixed feelings about this. The long delays involved in judicial review can allow exploitative practices to continue unchecked for months or years. On the other hand, the unhindered use of cease and desist orders is no doubt open to abuse.

9. The short-lived National Recovery Administration established so-called fair competition codes under which firms agreed to avoid price cutting. In some cases, firms were encouraged to raise prices by reducing output. These codes were enforceable by law and exempt from antitrust action. They affected 500 industries with 22 million workers. Fair competition codes were declared unconstitutional in *Schechter Poultry Corp. v. U.S.* (1935).

THE SHERMAN AND CLAYTON ACTS REMAIN THE IMPORTANT ONES

Congress has not passed any major antitrust laws since the Clayton Act of 1914. The Sherman and Clayton Acts remain the important legislation. Congress did, however, pass a measure in 1950 to fill a loophole in the Clayton Act. Under the Clayton Act, acquiring ownership of a competing firm could clearly be illegal. But a 1926 decision, *Thatcher Manufacturing Co. v. F.T.C.*, held that the merger of companies by acquiring assets was legal. This meant that the Clayton Act could not be used to prevent mergers. To rectify the situation, the Celler-Kefauver Act was passed in 1950. This declared illegal any acquisition or merger that "substantially lessens competition or tends to create a monopoly." Originally, only corporations could be prosecuted with Celler-Kefauver, but Congress extended that act to partnerships (large accounting or law firms, for example) with the Hart-Scott-Rodino Antitrust Procedural Improvements Act of 1980.

HORIZONTAL AND VERTICAL MERGERS

How mergers between firms will be treated has become one of the most important questions for antitrust law. There are three basic sorts of merger. **Horizontal mergers** are between sellers of the same good, for example, between two steel makers. **Vertical mergers** are between the producer and the user of a certain input, for example, between a copper-mining company and a firm that makes copper pipe. **Conglomerate mergers** are between firms that neither compete with one another nor supply one another, such as between a motion-picture producer and a book publisher.

Horizontal Mergers

Horizontal mergers were once most prevalent, particularly during the early years of the century, when U.S. Steel, General Motors, and many other large firms were formed. As late as 1940–1947, 62% of all mergers were still horizontal. Since the early 1960s, however, horizontal mergers have made up only some 10% of all mergers. One reason for the decline is that the rules controlling such mergers have been made increasingly precise. In 1968 the Justice Department adopted a standard of "75-10-2," which meant that it would challenge any merger in an industry with a concentration ratio of 75 or more in which a firm with at least 10% of the market was trying to acquire a firm with at least 2% of the market.[10]

In the early 1980s the 75-10-2 rule came under attack from critics who realized that it sometimes sent odd signals. For example, four firms each with 15% of the market and 40 firms each with 1% of the market would give the same concentration ratio of 60 as would *one* firm with 57% of the market and 43 firms with 1% each.[11] Obviously the market power in these two markets would be very different, but the concentration ratio of 60 would be identical.

A new method of measurement, the so-called *Herfindahl index*, (sometimes this is called a Herfindahl-Hirschman index, or HHI) was introduced during the Reagan administration. The Herfindahl index is the square of the market share of all the firms it is practicable to count. The larger the index number, the greater is the degree of concentration in an industry. In our first example above, the Herfindahl index number would be 940, because [4 x (15 x 15)] + [40 x (1 x 1)] = 940. In our second example, the Herfindahl index would be 3,292, because [1 x (57 x 57)] + [43 x (1 x 1)] = 3,292.

---

10.   The rule had many gradations. Thus if an acquiring firm were bigger, with as much as 15% of the market, then it would be challenged if it tried to buy out a firm holding only 1% of the market. "75-15-1."

11.   Remember that only the three largest of the 43 firms would figure in the calculation, as we are dealing with a four-firm ratio. The numbers would be 57+1+1+1 = 60.

Under the new guidelines, the government is unlikely to challenge a merger in an industry where the index number is below 1000. Between 1000 and 1800 the government will show some concern about concentration; if a proposed merger threatens to raise the index more than 100 points, the government will issue a challenge. If the index is over 1800, concentration will be considered high and a challenge will be forthcoming if a proposed merger will cause the index to rise by 50 points or more. Horizontal mergers that were prevented by the Reagan and Bush antitrust authorities included a merger of Schlitz with Heilemann (beer) and a merger of Mobil with Marathon (oil). These administrations clearly took a stronger line with these measures than with any other type, although the total number of challenges was down compared to previous administrations.

Vertical Mergers

Until recently, *vertical mergers* that seemed to carry a tendency toward monopoly were opposed by the government. For example, the merger of Bethlehem Steel with the Youngstown Sheet and Tube Corporation in 1958 was prevented on the grounds that it would lessen competition. In recent years, however, the government has usually not opposed such mergers unless it could be shown that strategically important monopoly advantage would result.

The view that vertical integration is undesirable has been largely abandoned by the government and by many economists as well, in part because of the excellent performance demonstrated by many vertically integrated Japanese companies such as auto and auto-parts makers. It is now more widely accepted that vertical mergers can reduce the costs of transacting business, thus making it possible to lower prices for consumers. Among the potential advantages are increased dependability of supplies, more complete information available within a vertically merged company, and the greater access to capital, manufacturing capacity, and distribution systems that ensue when new specialist firms merge with established ones. Above all are the greater opportunities for cooperation, including better protection of proprietary knowledge obtained from research and development because such knowledge can be kept within the merged company. Texas Instruments' vertical integration of its microchip manufacturing and its production of electronic equipment is a good case in point.

Questions still arise. Vertical mergers may sacrifice the benefits of competition and may cause a loss of economies of scale if sales are not permitted outside of the merged enterprise. The free flow of information back from many buyers may be lost as commercial secrecy comes to predominate. In spite of that, the case for vertical mergers is viewed as more persuasive than it was, say, before the 1970s. It is thus ironic that vertical mergers, like horizontal ones, have fallen sharply in importance, to about 10% of all mergers in the last 25 years.

CONGLOMERATE MERGERS

Since the late 1960s, *conglomerate mergers* have become by far the most common type of merger. For example, ITT (International Telephone and Telegraph) has acquired various insurance companies, the largest bakery in the United States, and the largest hotel chain; Paramount Communication (formerly Gulf & Western) has acquired companies that produce sugar, tobacco, steel, paper, banking services, insurance, motion pictures, and books (including this one).

Some 80% of all mergers since 1966 have been conglomerate mergers. Whether these mergers should be welcome or worrisome has posed a puzzle both for economists and antitrust lawyers. They do not obviously lessen competition because the firms are largely unrelated in form and function. They have, in fact, been credited with a number of advantages. For example, their R&D expenditures and patent holdings may have spin-off uses, as when an innovation at a sugar mill proves useful to an affiliated paper producer. There may be economies of scope, as when several products are advertised together, or when improved methods of financial management spread among the branches of the firm. Capital costs may be lower if lenders believe risks are reduced by the greater earnings stability of the unrelated units of the conglomerate.

Even so, the wave of conglomerate mergers in recent years has made some observers uneasy. One fear is that the members of a conglomerate will be inclined to buy their inputs from one another, to the detriment of competition. Another blow to competition might occur if conglomerate firms are loathe to challenge each other in one product line for fear of stirring up trouble in other areas of their business. Furthermore, predatory tactics might appear if one arm of the conglomerate could draw on profits from other branches to subsidize price wars. Even the possibility of such tactics might deter new entrants to a given industry.

Though there has been little empirical support for such misgivings, several prosecutions were undertaken during the Carter administration. The antitrust authorities tried to prove that there was some overlap in the activities of the member companies in certain conglomerates, but the courts usually found the argument too trivial to warrant action. Attempts were made to show that one of the merged firms might, if it had remained independent, have provided competition for another of the conglomerate's firms. But this line of argument failed in its biggest test to date, the Anaconda/Atlantic Richfield case, which had to do with a merger between a mining company and a petroleum company.

In one case, however, the U.S. Supreme Court did take a stand. *F.T.C. v. Procter & Gamble* (1967) overturned the 1957 purchase by Procter & Gamble of Clorox, the producer of laundry bleach. Justice William Douglas, speaking for a unanimous court, pointed out that Procter & Gamble's advertising budget was larger than Clorox's total sales. It commonly sponsored network TV programs during which it advertised several products, enabling it to give each product network exposure at a fraction of the cost per product that a firm with only one product to advertise would incur. The court concluded that Procter & Gamble's "huge advertising advantages" might impair competition in the bleach industry.

By and large, though, the courts have rarely ruled against a conglomerate merger. In 1970 the principle was established that mergers would be allowed if a big conglomerate on the outside of an industry looking in acquired a smaller firm and thus gained a competitive toehold in the industry (*F.T.C. v. the Bendix Corporation*, 1970). After that, attempts to halt conglomerate mergers lost headway—all government attacks on them have failed since 1973.

PATENTS AND ANTITRUST LAW

Taking out a patent on a new invention or manufacturing process is a legal way of acquiring market power. Most people would agree that inventors should be rewarded for their time and effort, but these same people might also agree that monopoly power should be controlled to protect the consumer. One possible compromise would be to require the holder of a patent to license it to anyone who is willing to pay a fixed percentage of the profits earned from its use. Current U.S. law allows patent holders to be very restrictive in deciding how their inventions are to be used. In fact, they can see to it that their inventions are not used at all, even by themselves. *Hartford-Empire Co. v. U.S.* (1945) established the principle that patent holders may suppress entirely the use of their discoveries for the full 17 years a patent is in effect. We have already noted the success of the United Shoe Machinery Company in tying up important patents. G.E. protected its light-bulb business by using only 20 of its 300 patents. (Great Britain and most other European countries require compulsory licensing by the patent holder after an extended period of nonuse.) Patent holders also have the right to place severe conditions on license recipients who pay for the privilege of using a patent.

In recent years the Supreme Court has sometimes ruled against companies that carry on monopoly practices involving patent arrangements. For example, it has declared illegal some cases of cross-licensing, whereby firms share patents with one another in order to gain a market advantage. In any event, the power of patents to protect against imitations is weaker than it once was, as we saw in the preceding chapter. Legal imitation in many fields may not cost much—often being cheaper than the innovation itself—and may not take long. Numerous firms have thus turned toward more reliance on commercial secrecy (proprietary knowledge) and on lead-time and learning advantages than on patents.

CHANGING ATTITUDES TOWARD ANTITRUST PROSECUTION

For a time in the 1970s it seemed that the federal government was about to step up its enforcement of antitrust legislation. There was talk in Congress of passing new laws that would make market dominance grounds for breaking up large firms. During these years the FTC was either considering or was actually involved in suits against tire companies, IBM, Xerox, the oil industry, and the cereal industry. In the cereal case it was charged that brand proliferation was being undertaken so that new entrants to the market would find it ever harder to have their advertising heard over the din of competing claims.

But as time passed, many economists and even the antitrust authorities themselves revised their views. One reason was that antitrust cases were consuming an enormous amount of time, running an average of eight years in the courts. The IBM suit, launched in 1969, was the most complex ever, with tens of thousands of pages of documents and depositions assembled before the government abandoned it in 1982. Many felt that the high cost to taxpayers could not be justified by the limited success of the prosecutions. By 1984 the government had terminated all the major antitrust actions just mentioned.

Another and more important reason for this change was the growing conviction that economies of scale and distribution, and the technical superiority and efficiency that give rise to market power, should be promoted. It was argued that mergers make it easier to shut down inefficient and underutilized plants, and that industries facing stiff foreign competition should be exempted from the antitrust laws. Foreign trade is a major procompetitive force, and in its strong presence antitrust enforcement is less necessary. (A firm that is obliged to compete with imports is unlikely to exercise monopoly power even if that firm is a country's only producer of a product. To constrain that firm would merely lessen its ability to compete in what is a world, and not a national, market.)

The government has continued to oppose price fixing by competitors who produce the same product. Horizontal mergers are still policed, though less actively than before. The relaxation has been due to the belief that if a firm is inefficient, merger may help to make it less so, and growing confidence that most markets are contestable.[12] Many economists believe, however, that the contestability argument is being overused. This argument, we recall, requires that barriers to entry be insignificant, and that the contestability of markets actually does constrain the behavior of firms in their pursuit of market power.

---

12.   More exceptions have been allowed in recent years even to the weaker horizontal merger rules. For example, the government has recently given permission for several such mergers when it believed that one of the companies would otherwise fail. Texas Airlines' acquisitions of People Express and Frontier were cases in point.

A more lenient attitude has been displayed toward vertical mergers and conglomerate mergers. For every 100 mergers opposed by antitrust authorities during the Carter administration, only 28 were opposed during the period 1980–1988. The wave of conglomerate mergers that set in during the 1960s continued into the 1980s, and the 18 largest mergers in U.S. history have all occurred since 1980. Eventually, however, many conglomerates began to sell off unrelated subsidiaries.

The initial evidence suggested that profitability and productivity in the merged firms did not improve significantly after buyouts, at least in the short run. Many mergers, it was suspected, were being undertaken for reasons of corporate finance rather than for reasons of efficiency. More recent studies, however, have suggested that with the passage of time, higher levels of efficiency are being attained by many merged firms. There seem to be several reasons involving more efficient use of inputs and heightened management effort. They include a closer link between quality of performance and financial rewards and penalties, closer monitoring of managers by investors, and a reduction in the ratio of nonproduction workers to production workers. Moreover, merged firms have shown a tendency to rid themselves of activities that are not related to their main line of business. The proportion of single-industry companies is growing again after years of decline, and the effect appears to have been a rise in the efficiency of their operations.

For many years there were few suits other than those initiated by the federal government. But relaxation of antitrust enforcement was followed by an understandable rise in the number of *state* antitrust suits undertaken by state governments, and *private* antitrust suits brought by companies complaining that they had been harmed by restraint of trade. From 1976, states were permitted to file suits in federal court, and to cooperate with the federal authorities in the prosecutions. Some states, including New York, California, Texas, and Florida, are now major players in antitrust prosecutions. Private suits have been permitted ever since the passage of the Clayton Act, which calls for the payment of treble damages (three times the actual proven damages) to a victorious litigant that proves harm from restraint of trade. Recently, an average of over a thousand private suits has been filed each year, twenty times the number of government antitrust prosecutions. Earlier in the century the numbers were about equal. When Texaco lost a private suit in a Texas court, the multibillion dollar damage award seemed astounding. (Many economists argue that private litigation is a poor way to control monopoly behavior. The awards are wildly inconsistent, subject to the whims of judges and juries. A surer method would be consistent government enforcement of revitalized, but also liberalized, antitrust laws.)

An Assessment of the U.S. Antitrust Stance

What effect have the antitrust laws had, and where is policy going? As we mentioned in Chapters 7 and 8, monopoly profit has been kept to a relatively low proportion of total U.S. income and output, and the prevalence of monopoly and tight oligopoly appears to have fallen appreciably. The share of all assets held by the 200 largest U.S. (nonfinancial) corporations has declined slightly, from 38% in 1970 and 1975 to 36% in 1980 and 34% in 1984.[13]

Just before the congressional elections of 1986, the Reagan administration was urging changes in the antitrust laws that would have made interlocking directorates legal, would have granted complete exemption to firms facing substantial competition from imports, and would have done away with treble damages in private suits. It was also calling for a weakening of the Clayton Act by removing the clause that allows prosecutions if the possibility of reduced competition exists. (Under a proposed amendment, the reduced competition must actually have occurred.) But public unease concerning the wave of mergers sweeping across the economy at that time, combined with the Democratic Party's congressional victories in the 1986 and 1988 elections, led to the defeat of all those proposals.

---

13.   See Golbe and White's Table 9.4 , in Alan J. Auerbach, ed., *Corporate Takeovers, NBER, 1988.*

Under the Clinton administration, a debate is being conducted between elements in the administration that favor strong enforcement of the existing laws and those that favor relaxation of the laws. Which policy will eventually predominate will become clearer when the administration decides whether to encourage high-tech mergers, especially between telephone and cable TV companies. Future government attitudes will also be important in the proposed mergers among firms that depend on defense contracts, occurring because defense spending is declining. The number of mergers was up sharply in 1993–1994, reaching levels not far short of the mid-1980s, so there are plenty of cases that could be made into tests. One harbinger concerned resale price maintenance, the term used when a manufacturer instructs retailers to charge a specific price or not to undercut some minimum price. In 1985 the Reagan administration decided not to challenge such arrangements, but in 1993 the Clinton antitrust authorities changed the interpretation, announcing that it might prosecute manufacturers who engage in resale price maintenance.

The Importance of Foreign Trade in Assessing Policy

However the debate transpires, it is unlikely that the antitrust authorities will launch any new frontal attack on the oligopolies in the near future. Whether this retreat will lead to increased market power in the long run depends to a large extent on what happens in foreign trade. So long as trade barriers are low and foreign trade is encouraged, competition will exist and monopoly power will be constrained even in the absence of strong antitrust enforcement. That is why manufacturing firms in small countries such as Belgium and the Netherlands most often are in a very competitive environment even if, as often happens, they are the only domestic producer of the product. High barriers to trade coupled with a relaxation of antitrust enforcement would, on the other hand, be worrisome. In that event, further mergers might strengthen market power, giving rise to monopoly profits, higher prices for consumers, and less nimble, less efficient management. It follows that oligopolistic firms should not be given the freedom to merge while at the same time being granted protection against foreign competition. Because numerous industries in the United States and other large countries *are* relatively free from foreign competition, continuing government restraint of monopoly power seems advisable.

In other U.S. industries, however, the level of foreign competition is sufficient to guarantee adequate restraint of market power. U.S. imports as a percentage of the nation's total output rose from 4.3% in 1950 to 12.9% in 1990. That trend suggests that certain aspects of antitrust legislation might be relaxed. It might be desirable, for example, to dispel the antitrust uncertainty surrounding joint-production, joint-marketing, and joint-research programs among U.S. firms. Japanese and European firms are much freer to enter into such arrangements. Greater joint activity along these lines in the United States could, if permitted, allow more effective coverage of a research area and reduce some of the wasted duplicative effort when firms attempt to "reinvent the wheel." It could build on the advantages of vertical coordination by establishing a network of up and down flow among many participants. It could also lead to a stronger U.S. effort as new markets open worldwide in the former Communist countries, and as the Japanese and European economies grow. The U.S. antitrust restrictions could advantageously be lifted, at least in part, as long as trade barriers against imports are kept low. Some steps have already been taken, as examined in the accompanying box.

THE LOOSENING OF THE ANTITRUST LAWS IN CASES OF JOINT RESEARCH AND JOINT PRODUCTION

Partial antitrust exemption for joint-research ventures was granted in 1984, allowing firms to pool R&D resources. The National Cooperative Research Act of that year requires the courts to consider the benefits of such ventures before finding that they would lessen competition. That act also lowers the damages that can be awarded in a private suit from treble to actual. (As already noted, in normal suits under the antitrust laws, treble damages are the rule.) By 1989, 134 such joint-research ventures had been established. One of the biggest is USCAR (United States Council for Automotive Research) established in 1992 by Ford, GM, and Chrysler to develop improved plastics for use in automobile bodies. Another is the joint research on the Power PC microchip undertaken by IBM, Apple, and Motorola.

A further loosening of the antitrust laws, to cover joint-production ventures, took place in 1993. In that year a new law removed the treble damages provision from production in joint ventures if the courts find that the competitive climate (including foreign competition) warrants the removal. The joint ventures' production must be in the United States for the new rule to apply. It remains the case, however, that joint manufacturing and marketing in the United States continues to run up against the antitrust laws. It is actually much easier for U.S. firms to collaborate with foreign ones than with each other.

Not all economists favor these relaxations of the antitrust laws to permit more joint research and production. The doubters warn that the joint projects may lead to price rigging for the products involved, and that incentives to introduce innovations may be fatally compromised if oligopolistic firms fear to upset the status quo. These economists warn that innovation usually brings most benefits when competitive rivalry is strong.

ANTITRUST LAWS IN EUROPE

Most European countries have had antitrust and antimerger laws in effect for many years, though the severity of the laws varied greatly depending on the country. After World War II, for example, the West German government was rather stern in its enforcement, but only Britain and France in addition to Germany had separate agencies to supervise antitrust enforcement. Italy had no antitrust laws at all.

With the emergence of the European Community (EC or Common Market), major aspects of antitrust enforcement have been assigned to a supranational authority. At present, the EC Commission possesses the sole power to halt corporate mergers and takeovers above a certain size as determined by sales revenue. (Below that size, the 12 national governments retain antitrust authority.) The EC Commission is permitted to judge mergers solely on the grounds of their effects on competition, which means that it looks only at horizontal and vertical mergers rather than conglomerate ones. It is also empowered to make exceptions to the antitrust laws when enforcement would hinder economic and technical progress. The most important antitrust instrument in the EC has not, however, been laws concerning monopoly. Instead, it has been the powerful stimulus to competition that resulted from the elimination of trade barriers among member countries. The rising level of trade among the members has overwhelmed many former centers of monopoly power. (Some government policies favoring monopoly still survive, however, and the EC is currently working on reforms to introduce further competition. The year 1992 was set as the date for the implementation of these reforms, but the process has been difficult, delays have been encountered, and the target date was not met.)

THE JAPANESE VIEW

Japan has followed very different policies. It has *encouraged* the formation of large combinations, and its antitrust laws are little-used survivals of the American occupation after the Second World War. Before that war, the Japanese economy was dominated by *zaibatsus*, large enterprises based on conglomerate mergers that had taken place over the years without opposition from the government. As Japan began to recover in the 1950s, its new and powerful Ministry of Trade and Industry (MITI) encouraged the rise of successors to the old *zaibatsus*, which had been broken up by the American authorities, and which MITI believed could succeed in international trade. On MITI's advice, the Ministry of Finance lent these new firms substantial funds at below-market interest rates. MITI hired the best graduates of the best universities, and many of its bureaucrats (who usually retired at a relatively young age) moved on to top positions in the very firms MITI was attempting to nurture.

Japan reserved part of its domestic market for these new large enterprises by means of trade restrictions that until 1960 covered about 60% of the country's imports. The profits generated by the higher prices paid by consumers—Japan's TV sets sold for $2\frac{1}{2}$ times more at home than in the United States, for example—served as a sort of tax to promote investment and development. Cartelization was permitted, leading to further profits that were used to finance massive marketing expenditures and heavy research and development spending. The R&D was supplemented by modest government subsidies. To ease the ill effects suffered by Japanese consumers, MITI insisted that the firms receiving its support undertake at least some competition with one another.

In the 1950s, MITI's administrative guidance contributed to Japan's advances in steel making and ship building; in the 1960s to advances in machine tools, some electronic goods, and perhaps autos; and in the 1970s to advances in high-tech electronics. Japan's economic growth set records year after year.

As early as the 1970s, the government lost its ability to allocate loans as the private capital market grew and prosperous companies turned to self-financing. Administrative guidance and cartelization receded as the new prosperity allowed firms to opt for more independence. In Japan today, the vigorous competition for technological breakthroughs through R&D bears a strong resemblance to the model of competition for market share through quality change discussed in the preceding chapter. Consumer prices, however, are on the whole higher than in the United States, averaging 42% more for a large market basket of goods and services according to a 1989 study.

WHY JAPAN'S HOME-MARKET PRICES ARE HIGHER

A major reason why Japan's home-market prices are higher than those of the United States is without doubt the market power of oligopolistic industries. Many producers run their own retail distribution systems. This, together with an "old-boy" network of long-term links between producers and distributors, makes it difficult for new firms, whether foreign or Japanese, to break into many markets. Interestingly, however, another reason is that for social and legal reasons large firms have to some degree not been *allowed* to compete. Japan's complex wholesale and retail distribution system has several more layers of suppliers (on average about four) than are encountered in Europe and the United States (about two). Approximately 80% of Japan's wholesale establishments employed fewer than ten workers in 1985. These feed a huge number of small "mom and pop" stores. This fits with the tastes of most Japanese, whose kitchen storage space is limited, and who mostly walk to the stores daily. But it also means there are twice as many stores per capita as in the United States, and so distribution costs are raised. Further, Japanese law allows small storekeepers, who are a force in politics, a say in the granting of site permits for supermarkets. One result is that Japan's largest retailers account for a relatively small proportion of total retail sales. Japan has committed itself to a reform of this inefficient system. The reform will presumably introduce a greater degree of oligopoly presence. To economists, the next few years will present a remarkable test case. Prices may fall rapidly because of scale economies in the reformed distribution system; or they may not, if oligopoly power leads to continued price fixing.

Vertical Coordination: the Keiretsu

Among economists the view has surfaced that vertical cooperation and coordination among firms that supply inputs and those that use them are a major factor in Japanese economic life. The lack of antitrust hindrance to these vertical relations, and the government's tacit or explicit support for them, are being seen as Japanese advantages.

Keiretsu means "system" in Japanese. Vertical keiretsu relationships involve manufacturers and their networks with suppliers, wherein users of technology work in close relationships with the providers of that technology. There are about 40 major keiretsu organizations, most importantly in autos, steel, and electronics, and including many of Japan's most famous firms. A good example is the close liaison between Kawasaki, which first licensed robot technology from the United States, and Nissan, one of Japan's largest users of robotic equipment. Information flows constantly, up and down between user (Nissan) and provider (Kawasaki). Often the impetus for change comes from the *user's* suggestions made during the many consultations held to consider improvements.

Vertical coordination appears to have positive results for quality control, interchange of ideas for quality improvement, and smooth supply of components. When innovation is hindered because the innovating firm is uncertain whether it can market its work, vertical relationships may give the assurance. Vertical coordination of separate firms may well be preferable to vertical merger, because keeping the firms separate retains the benefits of competition and the free interchange of information with other buyers and sellers outside the relationship. All of this has led economists to raise their estimate of the value of vertical coordination among suppliers and users. Some even believe that coordination is as important, or even more so, than the amount of R&D that is carried on.[14]

---

14.   But in 1992, the U.S. Department of Justice announced that the close *keiretsu* relations among Japanese firms could hurt U.S. exporting firms and could be considered a violation of U.S. antitrust laws. It decided that these laws in the future could be used to penalize the branches of Japanese firms in the United States for practices carried out in Japan.

THE SOUTH KOREAN VARIANT

South Korea's policy toward oligopoly is very similar to the early Japanese policy. The Koreans are clearly imitating the Japanese, with much the same results thus far. Korea has its own MITI, maintains trade barriers to preserve the domestic market for Korean firms, and encourages exports by making low-interest credit available.

Great family enterprises, conglomerates called *chaebols*, such as Samsung, Hyundai, Goldstar, Lucky, and Daewoo, are all still run by the families that founded them. The ten biggest conglomerates produce about 33%

of Korea's total manufacturing output, and concentration is increasing. The Korean president himself chairs monthly meetings attended by representatives of the firms and Korea's MITI. Although Korean consumers suffer from the oligopolistic pricing policies of the *chaebols*, the remarkable success of these conglomerates in exporting goods has contributed significantly to the nation's rapid economic growth. That growth has eclipsed even Japan's, with national income rising $6\frac{1}{2}$ times in real terms from 1953 to 1987.

CONVERGENCE IN THE TREATMENT OF OLIGOPOLY?

Oligopolies can command substantial super-normal profits by engaging in predatory practices, by colluding tacitly or explicitly, by merging to decrease competition, by suborning regulators, or by forcing the levying of tariffs and quotas against imports. To guard against such behavior and to preserve some measure of price competition, governments pass and enforce antitrust laws. It would also appear that oligopolies should be encouraged to achieve economies of scale and compete with the nonprice methods including quality improvement and improved marketing at which they excel. If a judgment may be rendered, the United States in the past has paid too little attention to the benefits of scale and nonprice competition, while Europe and Japan underestimated the degree to which combinations in restraint of trade could gouge the public with higher prices.

Something of a convergence can be identified in the way national governments of the United States and Europe view the costs and benefits of the oligopoly form of organization. In the United States, the movement over the past decade has been toward less rigorous enforcement of the antitrust laws. This appears to reflect a conviction that valuable technical progress is furthered by the R&D activities of oligopolies, that other countries' looser rules have given them an advantage in this regard, and that international trade if kept free provides effective police power over oligopoly behavior. In Europe, however, the new European Community rules on mergers and monopolizing reflect *increased* awareness that unregulated oligopoly behavior behind foreign trade barriers can have substantial negative consequences. The meeting of the minds has progressed so far that the United States and the EC concluded a new agreement in 1991 for coordinated antitrust enforcement. The consultations and information exchanges provided for in the treaty would have been unthinkable only a few years ago.

In Japan (and Korea), less convergence with the United States has taken place, and their systems still largely encourage rather than discourage the growth of oligopolistic organization. Government has not shown much recognition of the negative effects of monopolizing behavior on consumers. Movements toward freer trade in both countries, now pronounced in Japan, will eventually increase competitive pressure, however, and Japan's MITI for a number of years appears to have been altering its advice and guidance away from cartelization and toward more competition. In what may signal a policy change, Japanese officials have stated that that country's Fair Trade Commission (equivalent to the U.S. FTC) would receive enhanced powers to deal with price fixing and other anticompetitive behavior. In 1992 the maximum fine for an antitrust violation was raised by twenty times, though the new level of about $750,000 is still very low by international standards. One reason for the change was a study by the U.S. Department of Justice that considered whether the scope of America's own antitrust laws should be expanded to cover collusion that excludes U.S. exports. This radical suggestion, if adopted, could mean large fines including treble damages against the U.S. subsidiaries of Japanese firms.

The contrast in Japanese and U.S. government attitudes toward the control of market power is nevertheless still pronounced, reflecting continued differences in assessment of the oligopolistic form of organization. Further research on the economic costs of oligopoly versus the benefits from scale economies and quality change thus has the potential to influence government policy in a major way. A convergence in Japanese and U.S. antitrust policy is perhaps the most likely outcome, though that judgment is not at all certain.

SUMMARY

1) When industries are, or are thought to be, natural monopolies, governments often regulate the prices they are permitted to charge and much else as well. When regulation is by means of a "fair rate of return" or average-cost pricing, the government requires the regulated firm to charge a price that just covers average costs.

2) Because some allocative inefficiency remains under average-cost pricing, a government may instead utilize marginal-cost pricing. Under this form of regulation, the price may be below average costs, so requiring a government subsidy.

3) The two major pieces of U.S. antitrust legislation are the Sherman Act of 1890 and the Clayton Act of 1914. Several important court decisions have modified the application of these laws and demonstrate how important the courts have been in the development of U.S. antitrust law.

4) The antitrust laws are most stringent in the case of horizontal mergers between producers of the same product, less so in the case of vertical mergers between a producer of output and a producer of input, and most permissive in the case of conglomerate mergers where the merging firms are unrelated to one another.

5) Economists would generally support some relaxation of the antitrust laws in cases where the level of foreign trade is high, and some steps have already been taken in the area of joint-research ventures and joint production.

6) In Europe and Japan, governments have typically enforced less stringent antitrust policies, seeing more advantage from the oligopoly form of industrial organization than has been true of government in the United States. But the harm to consumers from price fixing in these areas is now attracting more attention, just as U.S. authorities seem to be realizing that more vertical coordination along the lines of the Japanese *keiretsu* might be beneficial. A convergence in antitrust policies may be taking place.

Chapter Key Words

Antitrust law: Legislation and court decisions to control monopoly power. The most important laws in the United States are the Sherman Act of 1890 and the Clayton Act of 1914.

Average-cost pricing: See *"fair rate of return."*

Clayton Antitrust Act: The law of 1914 that filled loopholes in the Sherman Act.

Conglomerate mergers: Mergers between firms that are unrelated either horizontally (see *horizontal mergers*) or vertically (see *vertical mergers*). Came to be the most common form of merger in the United States, peaking in the 1980s.

Fair rate of return: Average-cost pricing in a regulated industry. The price is set at the point where the demand curve crosses the average cost curve, so that all costs of production are covered.

Horizontal mergers: Mergers between firms that produce the same product. Most likely form of merger to be challenged under the U.S. antitrust laws.

Keiretsu: Japanese word for "system." Refers to the coordination and cooperation of vertically related firms; believed to enhance the quality of inputs and the pace of technical change.

Marginal-cost pricing: A pricing method for a regulated industry. The price is set at the point where the demand curve crosses the marginal-cost curve, so avoiding allocative inefficiency. Requires a subsidy if average costs are not covered. Useful in treating problems of congestion and overload.

Public utilities: Private firms subject to government regulation, usually applied to the delivery of some item such as water, gas, and electricity where conditions of natural monopoly prevail.

Regulated industries: Industries, often natural monopolies, in which prices and business practices are supervised by government regulatory commissions. Also see *public utilities.*

Rule of reason: Interpretation of antitrust law made by the Supreme Court in 1910 and reinforced in 1920, holding that monopoly itself is not illegal, but only the overt acts that bring a monopoly into being. Caused serious harm to antitrust enforcement until overturned in 1945.

Sherman Antitrust Act of 1890: Important as the first federal antitrust law (1890); declared illegal combination or conspiracy in restraint of trade or commerce.

Vertical mergers: Mergers between suppliers of input and the users of those inputs.

Chapter Questions

1a) It is 1912 and the electric company in your Midwestern city is not regulated. The state imposes average cost pricing on the company. Draw a diagram showing the allocative inefficiency before and after regulation.

1b) As the years go by, the electric utility reports that its average costs are increasing. Do you think the average costs would have increased if there were no regulation? Short of deregulation, what might you propose to bring costs down again?

2) Marginal-cost pricing can be the best form of regulation of natural monopolies because it completely eliminates allocative inefficiency. However, many countries have moved away from this practice because they have been running persistent government budget deficits, with their spending outpacing their revenues. Use a diagram to show why government budget deficits have anything to do with marginal cost pricing.

3) On Friday evenings during the summer, New Jersey's Garden State Parkway (a toll highway) becomes very crowded as people living in New York head for the beach. However, tolls on the parkway are set at a flat rate which reflects the average cost of an additional car on a normal day. The following diagram shows how the flat rate is below the average cost on a Friday evening, and the average cost is below the marginal cost:

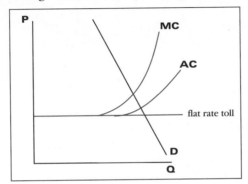

Compared with the rigid flat rate, even average-cost pricing would be an improvement. Show the allocative inefficiency under the flat rate toll and under average-cost pricing. (Notice that quantity is too high, so the triangles of allocative inefficiency are to the right of the demand curve.) Can you give an explanation of why the marginal cost of an additional car might be so much higher than the average cost?

4) It is the year 1900, and you are a robber baron of industry! Through ruthless attacks on smaller companies, your firm has grown to have a near-monopoly in coal production. In order to drive out the few remaining competitors, you practice predatory pricing. That is, you give special discounts to the customers of your competitors to cause them to switch to your coal, and so drive your competitors out of business. How would each of the following affect your position of market dominance: the existence of the Sherman Act, the accession of Theodore Roosevelt to the Presidency, the passage of Clayton act?

5) National Pencil Company is already the largest producer of pencils. The company has extra cash, and is considering buying one of the following three companies:
   a) United Pencil Company, the second-largest pencil producer.
   b) Southwestern Rubber Corp., a maker of rubber products including pencil erasers.
   c) Boise Potato Chip Company, a snack food firm.
   For each potential merger, identify whether it is horizontal, vertical, or conglomerate. Which of the mergers is most likely to be challenged by the government? Which is most likely to result in lower prices for consumers of pencils? What gains might there be from the remaining merger?

6) Suppose that Canadian authorities were pursuing an antitrust case against a monopoly in that country. Then the North American Free Trade Agreement was signed, removing trade barriers with the United States (which has many firms similar to the Canadian monopoly). Not long after, the Canadian government announced that it was dropping the case. Was this a reasonable decision? Would it still have been reasonable if it had been the U.S. authorities bringing a case against a U.S. monopoly?

7) With Japan's rise to industrial prominence, two terms have become current in the U.S. business community: zaibatsu and keiretsu. What type of merger or coordination (conglomerate, vertical, or horizontal) does each of these terms represent? Which form of industrial organization is having an influence on U.S. antitrust law and why?

CHAPTER 10

Externalities

When Private and Social Costs and Benefits Diverge

OVERALL OBJECTIVE: To assess the economic consequences of nonmarket externalities caused by the divergence between private and social costs and benefits.

MORE SPECIFICALLY:

- To demonstrate that nonmarket externalities can be negative (as with pollution) or positive (as with education), and to show how these externalities can be illustrated diagrammatically.
- To discuss why the private market is often unable to correct for externalities, so giving rise to public goods, that is, items that the private market is unable to supply in adequate quantity.
- To explain how social costs and benefits can be measured and the difficulties involved in doing so.
- To assess what steps might be taken to cause the private market to take account of externalities, including command-and-control measures, taxes, subsidies, and emissions trading.
- To analyze how much pollution it would be sensible to allow, given that eliminating *all* pollution would require damagingly large cuts in total production.
- To note how difficult it is to determine proper policy for the very long run with problems such as global warming, the consequences of which are highly uncertain but possibly catastrophic.

Up to this point in our study of the market economy, we have concentrated on how producers respond to market signals as they answer the universal economic questions of what to produce, how to produce it, and how to distribute it. In a market system, the answers to these questions are determined by the private market decisions made by buyers and sellers.

Yet many of those decisions have effects—either negative or positive—on people who have had no part in making them. Such nonmarket effects are called **externalities**. They may accompany any sort of exchange, including both production and consumption, in any setting from perfect competition to monopoly. Some externalities are relatively insignificant. If your neighbor hires someone to mow the lawn at 7 a.m. on Sunday morning, and the noise wakes you up, the lawn mowing has caused a **negative externality**, however trivial.[1] The neatly mowed lawn may also provide some pleasure later in the day, and you may realize that your neighbor's attention to the yard adds to the value of your own property. Thus the early-morning lawn mowing also creates a **positive externality**.[2] Both are unintended nonmarket consequences of the market transaction between your neighbor and the person hired to mow the lawn.

Obviously, the externalities of market transactions can involve matters much more vital than the noise from lawn mowing. Pollution of the environment, national defense, and education are all topics where the analysis of externalities applies. The subject represents a significant enlargement of the themes that applied economists are called upon to investigate. We look first at negative externalities and then turn to positive externalities.

NEGATIVE EXTERNALITIES: SOCIAL COSTS EXCEED PRIVATE COSTS

The Paul Lewter Lumber and Paper Company of Makesmee, Ill. carries on timber and sawmill operations. It has several competitors, so Mr. Lewter works diligently to minimize his production costs. But he considers as costs only items that represent an outlay to him personally—his **private costs**. There are, however, several other costs that do not affect his pocketbook and hence do not enter into his reckoning of profit. For example, his loggers have stripped the timber from the shores of the Makesmee River, causing runoff that has eroded neighboring farms and flooded property downstream. The waste products his mill dumps into the river have killed all the fish, and fishermen are never seen on the banks of the Makesmee these days. On calm days the noxious fumes from the paper-making plant blanket the area with a stench like that of rotten eggs, and the whine of the power saws is heard all night long. The personal cost to Lewter of these negative externalities is $0. He pays nothing for the air, water, and noise pollution he is causing. Yet he is inflicting real hardship on the residents of Makesmee and the surrounding area.

In the presence of negative externalities, the **social costs** of a transaction are higher than the private costs by themselves. Social costs include all private costs plus the costs occasioned by the negative externalities. For Lewter himself, treating the environmental damage he causes as costless is quite rational. The market system gives no direct signal that he is inflicting social costs on the public. The lesson applies to any sort of negative externality. There is no essential difference between the failure of the market to signal the social costs inflicted by the Paul Lewter Company and the failure of the market to signal social costs of any sort.

The Failure of the Market to Reflect Externalities Is the Cause of Pollution

The divergence between private costs and social costs is the fundamental cause of all types of pollution. It represents what economists call a "market failure." In defense of the market system, there is no reason to expect that the divergence in most economic activity will be more than trivial. Decisions based on private costs alone are often acceptable from a social point of view

---

1.   Negative externalities are also called external diseconomies, or negative (unfavorable) spillovers, third-party effects, or neighborhood effects.

2.   Positive externalities are also called external economies, or positive (favorable) spillovers, third-party effects, or neighborhood effects.

as well. Even when they are not, as long as the difference is not very great, accepting the resulting inefficiency may be preferable to government controls administered by a cumbersome and expensive bureaucracy.

Nevertheless, private market decisions of many sorts can involve negative externalities too large to ignore. The price of automobiles does not reflect the smog that blankets Los Angeles, Denver, and Athens. The price of electricity does not reflect the smokestack emissions, most prominently from the sulfur-containing coal burned by many power plants, that cause the acid rain many scientists believe to be responsible for widespread damage to forests and lakes. (The damage is especially severe in Germany, where *waldsterben* or forest death is visible in many areas. Only 8% of Europe's trees showed damage from acid rain in 1982; by 1986 the figure had reached 50%.) The price of cigarettes does not reflect the social costs of diseases associated with smoking and the potential for early death. Industrial wastes dumped "for free" can kill rivers, as in the celebrated case when flammable pollutants in the Cuyuhoga River at Cleveland caught fire and burned for several days. Much larger bodies of water may be affected by pollution. Swimming is now banned for health reasons in the northern Adriatic. Naturalists visiting lonely Pitcairn Island in the remote southeast Pacific have cataloged a dismaying variety of debris that has washed ashore, even though Pitcairn is about as far from the major sources of pollution as one can get. The world-scale environmental problems such as global warming and ozone depletion have the same essential cause as the more local problems: the failure of the market to reflect externalities.

It is appropriate to point out that recently the public has become so aware of environmental issues that almost any new use of a natural resource is bound to arouse opposition. Healthy concern for the environment is certainly justified, but if carried to extremes it may reduce standards of living by curtailing production and reducing income. Some environmental issues that were viewed with alarm 20 years ago failed to materialize, including, for example, the world food crisis, dying oceans, and the threat of airplane contrails to the ozone layer. There is no substitute for intelligent assessment of individual problems.

A society's view of social costs depends to a large extent on how well-off its members are. Obviously, poorer people are relatively less interested in protecting the environment and more interested in acquiring material goods. Tourists visiting scenic areas polluted by odors from a nearby paper mill have been told by the mill workers that the stench is "the smell of money." Less-developed countries usually are willing to accept higher social costs in exchange for higher money incomes. Brazil, India, South Korea, Taiwan, and many others have shown themselves much more tolerant of serious pollution than have richer nations such those of North America and northern Europe.[3]

---

3.   It is understandable that the residents of a poor country might treat a clean environment as a luxury good. On occasion, however, decisions about the environment in these countries are being taken by government leaders who have not been democratically chosen. For example, countries with laws against the dumping of toxic wastes have shipped their wastes to countries without such laws, whose leaders have imposed the decision on their subject peoples. Guinea-Bissau, a poor West African nation, was once paid $40 per metric ton to accept dangerous materials from the United States and Europe. This payment bore no relation to the potential damage to the residents of that country, but it brought in revenues that totaled more than half the government's budget. The nearby Republic of Bénin accepted just $4 a ton to dispose of some toxic shipments, a great bargain for those who made the decision without bearing the costs, but incomprehensible when the externalities were considered. The political leaders of these countries apparently made no plans at all to protect their citizens from the dangerous materials.

EXTERNALITIES HAVE A LONG HISTORY, AND THEY ALSO OCCUR IN PLANNED ECONOMIES

We tend to associate negative externalities with modern large-scale production, forgetting that they were often immense at an earlier period. Societies that are poorer and less technically advanced may have little choice but to put up with the costs as best they can. Consider the problems of a large city around the year 1900, when transportation was provided by horses. It has been estimated that *every day* in New York, horses were responsible for depositing $2\frac{1}{2}$ million pounds of manure and 60,000 gallons of urine on the streets.[4]

Externalities occur in planned economies as well as in market economies. When a ministry in a Communist country instructed a mill to maximize its annual output by using the most abundant fuel available, the mill then burned dirty coal that caused thick smog. In fact, the focus on heavy industry and output targets in the former USSR and eastern Europe led to some of the planet's most serious pollution problems. In one monumental environmental blunder, the Soviet authorities diverted the Amu-Darya and Syr-Darya rivers to irrigate Uzbekistan's cotton and rice fields. The Aral Sea into which these rivers flow has lost 60% of its water. Almost all the fish have disappeared, and the sea has retreated about 45 miles from some of the fishing ports. Around the badly shrunken Aral Sea and nearby Lake Balkhash, salty deserts now stretch to the horizon. Far to the north in the Arctic, vast stretches of tundra have been destroyed, and the nickel-mining areas on the Kola Peninsula and the oil fields of Yamal have been transformed into wastelands. Damage from radioactivity has been far worse in the planned economy of the old USSR than in the market economies of the west. The meltdown of the Chernobyl reactor was a world-famous disaster, while nuclear testing in Kazakhstan and on Novaya Zemlya has seriously affected the health of the people who live in the area.

In Poland, immense pollution problems emerged under central planning. In China, the potential for pollution to be worse than in any other country increases year by year as industrial production accelerates in that very poor nation of over a billion people.

POSITIVE EXTERNALITIES: SOCIAL BENEFITS EXCEED PRIVATE BENEFITS

Some externalities are positive, so that market transactions will have nonmarket beneficial effects on people not involved in the original exchange. In the presence of positive externalities, the **social benefits** associated with a market transaction are greater than the **private benefits** alone. Social benefits consist of the private benefits plus the external benefits associated with a market transaction. One of the earliest examples used in economics was that of a beekeeper and the owner of a neighboring apple orchard. In the spring, the beekeeper's bees leave their hives, fly to the apple trees, pollinate the blossoms, and ensure a good harvest of apples. Because the services of the bees are free, the owner of the orchard enjoys a positive externality in addition to the private benefit the beekeeper realizes from the sale of honey.[5]

---

4.   See James J. Flink, *The Car Culture*, Cambridge, MA, 1975, p. 34.

5.   Unless, as actually often occurs, the orchard is big enough and the bees essential enough so that the orchard-owner is willing to pay to have the hives moved close by.

Similar logic explains how social benefits can arise when a new railroad or subway line is put into service. The owners of the line receive a private benefit through the sale of tickets. On a social basis, the benefit to the public may be much greater, in the form of reduced congestion on nearby highways and increased property values in communities served by the line. (Though any social costs, such as noise, fumes, or degradation of scenery, would, of course, have to be subtracted to obtain the net social benefits.) When social benefits exceed the private benefits to the entrepreneurs who build the lines, the market system will not signal accurately the optimum amount of railway building.[6]

The social benefits that flow from education are noteworthy. Schooling to make a child a good citizen instead of an unemployable illiterate will make life better for everyone. At the very least, it lets you know that I can read a traffic sign well enough to stop my car at the intersection you are approaching. You are likely to be more productive on the job because I, working beside you, am adequately trained. You will experience less crime if my training enables me to earn enough to buy a car rather than stealing yours. You are likely to experience higher-quality government if your public officials are reasonably educated. More interesting movies and TV fare, well-designed buildings, and handsome landscaping are other examples of education's social benefits.

Though we tend to focus on negative externalities and social costs, we are all recipients of social benefits as well. Indeed, the positive externalities may outweigh the negative ones.

DIAGRAMMING EXTERNALITIES

Economic analysis of externalities and what might be done to correct them utilizes the basic framework of demand and supply. In this section we will show how to diagram private costs and benefits, and then explore what happens when we introduce social costs and benefits. Finally, we will consider the economic implications that arise when private costs and social costs, and private and social benefits, differ from one another.

Ordinary Demand and Supply Curves Reveal the Private Costs and Benefits

Ordinary demand and supply curves show the additional private cost of producing one more item, and the additional private benefit of consuming one more of that same item. Figure 10.1 presents the demand and supply curves for the wood products produced by the Lewter Company and the other firms in that industry when only private costs and benefits are taken into account. Consider first the supply curve S_p. As we recall from Chapter 4, the supply curve of each firm is identical to its private marginal-cost curve, down to a price level so low that the firm will decide to shut down. Moreover, an industry supply curve is the horizontal summation of the supply curves of all the firms in the industry at each price. Thus, the supply curve S_p for an industry must be the same as that industry's private marginal-cost (PMC) curve, which in turn is the horizontal summation of the private marginal-cost curves of all the firms in the industry. So in the figure we can write S_p = PMC.

The demand curve D_p in Figure 10.1 reflects only the private benefits to buyers. The discussion of consumer surplus in Chapter 4 showed that along a demand curve, each point lying above the market price reflects that some consumers would have been willing to pay a higher sum for an item than they actually had to pay for it. They receive a consumer surplus. Their willingness to pay is a measure of the private benefit they receive, because we would not expect people to pay a price for something higher than the benefit they receive from making the purchase. Thus, the private demand curve (D_p) for a product is identical to the private marginal-benefit curve (PMB) for that product. In the figure, we write D_p = PMB.

---

6.   On occasion the social benefits might, however, be appropriable by the builder of the line. When the Los Angeles street car system was constructed before World War II, some of the branch lines were profitable not because of the revenue paid in by passengers but because the company owned land along the route that it was able to sell for development. At an earlier time, U.S. railroad building in the midwestern and western states was financed by federal land grants. The existence of the railroads served to raise the price of the land, which was sold to finance construction and pay off loans.

With only private costs and benefits taken into account, equilibrium is at the intersection of the supply curve and the demand curve, that is, where PMC = PMB. The equilibrium price is P$_e$, and the equilibrium quantity is Q$_e$. The existence of externalities is not reflected by the position of either the demand curve or the supply curve.

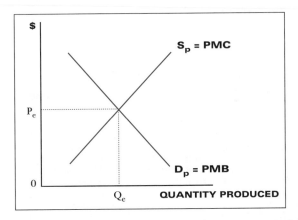

Figure 10.1. Private costs and benefits. A supply curve reflects the private marginal costs of production, while a demand curve reflects the private marginal benefits of consumption. At the equilibrium, private marginal costs equal private marginal benefits.

Negative Externalities in Production

If there are no externalities of any kind, then the private demand and supply curves showing private costs and benefits also reflect the social costs and benefits. If there is an externality present, either negative or positive, it can be illustrated by drawing new curves to reflect the social costs and benefits. First, consider *negative externalities in production*—for example, the harm to the public caused by the fumes emitted from the Lewter Company's smokestacks. (We are assuming that there are no externalities in the *consumption* of the product, so the demand curve measures both private benefits and social benefits, as shown in Figure 10.2.) The negative externalities raise the cost to society of any level of output; that cost may consist of respiratory ailments requiring expensive medical treatment, heightened laundry and dry-cleaning expenses, or just the discomfort that people would pay to avoid if they could. Reflecting that social cost is higher than private cost, in Figure 10.2 the curve for *social* marginal costs (SMC = S$_s$) lies above the curve for *private* marginal costs (PMC = S$_p$) all along its length. The smokestacks belch more fumes at higher quantities of output, so the negative externalities are greater as more is produced. That explains why SMC rises further above PMC as quantity increases.

If the Lewter Company and the other firms were forced to take into account the negative externalities of their output, then any given quantity of production would have to bear a higher price. To supply the former equilibrium quantity Q$_e$, for example, firms would have to charge a higher price P$_h$ to reflect the additional social costs. But that would not be an equilibrium price and quantity. Because of excess supply, neither price nor quantity could remain at that level. They would settle at P$_1$ and Q$_1$. In short, when firms are held responsible for the negative externalities they create, they produce less and charge a higher price.

If the firms continued to make their decisions solely on the basis of private costs and benefits and persisted in producing Q$_e$, then the total pollution damage would be the area between curves S$_p$ and S$_s$ up to Q$_e$ (the entire shaded area in the figure). The first unit of output would carry social costs higher than private costs equal to the distance S$_p$S$_s$. The second unit would carry additional costs shown by the slightly greater vertical distance between S$_p$ and S$_s$, and so on. The total damage from the negative externalities (the fumes) would be much greater than the net *economic* damage, however. Consider that one consumer would have been willing to purchase the first unit of output at the high price indicated by the intersection of the demand

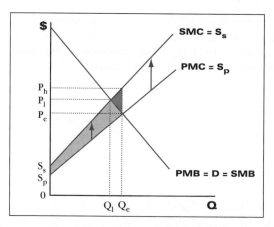

Figure 10.2. Negative externalities in production. Negative externalities in production mean that social marginal costs (SMC) are higher than private marginal costs (PMC), and hence that the supply curve reflecting the externalities (S_s) is higher than the supply curve reflecting only private considerations (S_p). The two curves diverge because the negative externalities connected with low levels of production are likely to be less than they would be at higher levels of production.

curve with the vertical (price) axis. That high price is a measure of the benefit the consumer derived from the purchase. (If the benefit were any less, the consumer would not have paid that price.) The benefit from consuming the good is much larger than the cost of producing the good, including the cost occasioned by the fumes emitted in its manufacture. Producing just that one unit brings a clear net benefit to society. The same logic holds all the way out to quantity Q_1. Every additional unit produced up to that point brings society benefits greater than the cost of producing it, including the cost caused by the fumes. Only to the right of Q_1 do costs, including the damaging fumes, outweigh benefits. At quantity Q_e, for example, the cost of the last unit produced including the fumes (P_h) is higher than the benefit realized by its purchaser (P_e). If a total quantity Q_e were produced, the net economic cost (allocative inefficiency or deadweight loss) would be the area of the heavily shaded triangle in Figure 10.2.

Negative Externalities in Consumption

Negative externalities may also accompany the *consumption* of goods. For example, additions to the number of cars driven by the residents of Denver adds to the smog and congestion in that city. So the private benefits (PMB) derived from the purchase of an additional car must be reduced by the amount of the damage caused by the negative externalities. Consequently, the *social* benefit (SMB) is less than the private benefit, and for that reason in Figure 10.3 SMB lies below PMB all along its length. The damage caused by the first car is equal to the vertical distance D_pD_s, the second car causes slightly more damage than the first because of the cumulative effect of the smog and congestion, and so on. Thus, SMB falls further below PMB as more cars are purchased.

If car buyers had taken into account the social cost of their actions, they would have purchased fewer cars. The demand curve would have fallen to D_s and they would have been willing to pay only the low price P_1 for the former equilibrium quantity Q_e. But that would not be an equilibrium. Price would settle at a new equilibrium P_2, and quantity would be Q_2.

If buyers did *not* consider the damage they were causing by their private consumption decisions, the total damage caused would be the area between curves D_s and D_p up to Q_e (that is, the entire shaded area in the figure). The first unit of output would carry social benefits lower than private benefits by the distance D_sD_p. The second unit would bring a slightly greater reduction of benefit because the damage is cumulative. The total reduction in benefits resulting from the negative externalities in consumption would be much greater than the net economic damage, however. Up to quantity Q_2 the benefit from an additional unit of consumption is

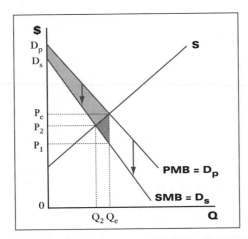

Figure 10.3. Negative externalities in consumption. Negative externalities in consumption mean that social marginal benefits are lower than private marginal benefits, and hence that the demand curve reflecting the externalities is lower than the demand curve reflecting only private considerations. The two curves diverge because the negative externalities connected with low levels of consumption are likely to be less than they would be at higher levels of consumption.

larger than the cost to society of producing an additional unit, even when the negative externalities in consumption are taken into account. Only beyond Q_2 does the cost of producing an additional item outweigh the benefits from that item, including the negative externalities from consumption. At quantity Q_e, for example, the cost of producing the last unit is P_e, higher than the (reduced) benefit realized by its purchaser (P_1). At that quantity the net economic cost (allocative inefficiency or deadweight loss) would be the area of the heavily shaded triangle in Figure 10.3.

Positive Externalities in Production

When production gives rise to positive externalities—that is, when it generates social benefits—the situation is reversed. Assume, for example, that you are the beekeeper whose bees pollinate your neighbor's apple trees while producing honey that you sell. In Figure 10.4, the demand curve for honey, D, measures both the private and social marginal benefit. The private supply curve, S_p, measures the private marginal cost of producing honey. The resulting equilibrium, with the positive externality ignored, occurs at price P_e and quantity Q_e.

If the social benefit of the pollinated trees could somehow be made to accrue to the honey producer, the private cost of producing the honey would decline and would result in a new supply curve S_s. That curve would be lower than S_p all along its length, indicating that the social marginal cost (SMC) was lower than the private marginal cost (PMC). The more honey that is produced, the more bees that fly into the neighbor's apple trees, and the lower the social marginal cost of honey production will be. So SMC lies further below PMC at higher quantities of output than it does at lower quantities; SMC rises less steeply than PMC.

At the new equilibrium, output Q_h would be higher and price P_1 would be lower. If you ignored the positive externality and continued to produce quantity Q_e, society would suffer a net economic loss (allocative inefficiency or deadweight loss) equal to the shaded triangle in the figure. Each additional unit of output between Q_e and Q_h would confer a benefit to society greater than the cost to society of producing it.

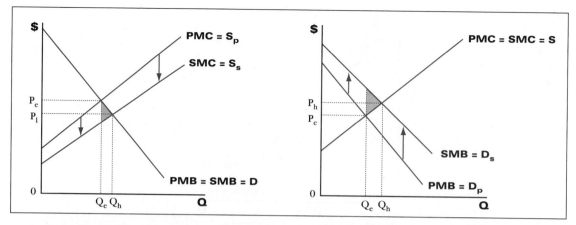

Figure 10.4. Positive externalities in production.
Positive externalities in production mean that social marginal costs are lower than private marginal costs, and hence that the supply curve reflecting the externalities is lower than the supply curve reflecting only private considerations. The two curves diverge because the positive externalities connected with low levels of production are likely to be less than they would be at higher levels of production.

Figure 10.5. Positive externalities in consumption.
Positive externalities in consumption mean that social marginal benefits are higher than private marginal benefits, and hence that the demand curve reflecting the externalities is higher than the demand curve reflecting only private considerations. The two curves diverge because the positive externalities connected with low levels of consumption are likely to be less than they would be at higher levels of consumption.

Positive Externalities in Consumption

Social benefits may flow from consumption as well as from production. You just played your newly purchased CD of a Beethoven symphony and convinced your roommates that listening to classical music can bring great pleasure. The social marginal benefit (SMB) from the purchase of the CD is greater than the private marginal benefit (PMB). The more CDs of the symphony that consumers buy, the greater number of other people who are affected positively and the more social benefit exceeds private benefit. Thus, SMB lies further above PMB at higher quantities of output than it does at lower quantities; PMB falls more steeply than SMB.

The demand curve D_s in Figure 10.5, which reflects the social benefits, lies above the demand curve D_p, which reflects only the private benefits. With the positive externality taken into account, at equilibrium both the price and the quantity would be higher at P_h and Q_h, reflecting the stronger demand. If the externality were ignored, society would suffer a net economic loss (allocative inefficiency or deadweight loss) equal to the shaded triangle. Each unit between Q_e and Q_h will bring a greater benefit to society than the cost to society of producing it.

CONCLUSION

To summarize: when there are negative externalities in either production or consumption, the forces of the private-market economy cause too much to be produced. Where there are positive externalities in either production or consumption, those forces cause too little to be produced. Unless this situation is properly measured and corrected, the predicted advantages of the market system will be overstated, and too many or too few resources will be allocated to the production of the item concerned. If the externalities are small, as in the case of the early morning lawn mowing or the playing of the Beethoven symphony, typically little or nothing needs to be done. If the externalities are large, however, the consequences could be quite important. Negative externalities such as air and water pollution may cause governments to take corrective steps. Positive externalities, such as the nonmarket effects of education and research, may lead governments to encourage these activities. We turn now to the measurement of externalities and what to do about them.

WHY DOESN'T THE PRIVATE MARKET CORRECT FOR EXTERNALITIES?

We have seen how the market system acts to move prices and quantities to equilibrium, so correcting for shortages and surpluses. Why, then, is the private market apparently unable to correct for externalities? Why could not those who suffer (the townspeople of Makesmee, Ill. for example) and those who gain from negative externalities (Mr. Lewter) enter into some financial arrangement that would be beneficial to both? The townspeople might get together and pay Mr. Lewter to stop polluting the water and air, or Mr. Lewter might compensate the townspeople for the damage he is causing. Market solutions of this sort are not easy to arrange, however, for a number of reasons.

Inadequate Definition of Property Rights

If the townspeople believe that the law entitles them to live free from Lewter's pollution, they will probably be unwilling to pay him anything for desisting. Instead, they may turn to the courts to pursue what they see as their rights. If Lewter believes that the law entitles him to run his mill as he pleases, he will have no interest in compensating the townspeople for the damage he causes. The problem here is that the law is unclear on who holds the property rights to the air and the water. Does society have an obligation to keep these resources clean, or can a polluting firm behave in any fashion it wishes regarding them? The lack of a clear answer to these questions has often prevented a market solution to the problem.

Transactions Costs

Another difficulty is that the transactions costs involved in arranging a financial solution to the problem may be prohibitive. The parties to the problem may regard the time spent in meetings and the cost of lawyers more onerous than living with the pollution. The greater the number of people who take part in the bargaining, and the more difficult it is to measure the damage and define the property rights, the higher the transactions costs will be.

Free Riders

Free riders are people who might like to see pollution eliminated, or have certain social benefits made available, but who are unwilling to pay their share of the cost. They are confident that others *will* pay, and that they will enjoy the advantages for free. For example, one of the families in Makesmee dislikes the pollution caused by the Lewter plant but refuses to join in a private arrangement to pay Lewter to desist from polluting. The family knows the pollution will stop in any case once an arrangement has been negotiated. It gets a "free ride." The more people that become free riders, the greater the financial pressure on those that remain.

THE FREE-RIDER PROBLEM AND PUBLIC GOODS

The free-rider problem applies to all **public goods**. These are goods and services that the government provides because the private market is unlikely to provide them. Say a town's police force were to be marketed on a subscription basis, whereby you would pay an annual fee for protection. (That was indeed the practice in London up to 1829, when Sir Robert Peel established the London Metropolitan Police. The "bobbies" are named after him.) If a private police force were run efficiently, everyone would benefit from the lower crime rate whether they were subscribers or not. A private protection company would find it hard to attract paying clients. The same is true of national defense. Defense can be marketed as a product—in medieval times wealthy guilds in Italian and Flemish city-states hired mercenary soldiers. But all residents of the city were protected by the soldiers manning the walls, even those who contributed nothing to the cost. Street lighting, flood control, rapid transit that reduces highway congestion, public radio and television, and the elimination of pollution in general are further cases in which the market system does not work well because no one can be excluded from enjoying the benefits. This is called the property of "nonexcludability." Such activities are also marked by "nondepletability," sometimes called "nonrival consumption," meaning that observers do not notice the greater use when additional consumers of the good or service appear. I do not get less street lighting because a nonpayer is standing under the lamp post. The free-rider problem is the main reason why some goods cannot successfully be provided by the private market.

It should be noted that not all goods provided by government are public goods. Education is an example. The private market could provide education quite successfully. Government does so because primary education conveys positive externalities, not because it is a public good.

Undesirability of Excluding Nonpayers

A final reason why the private market sometimes fails to correct for externalities is that it would be undesirable or dangerous to exclude nonpayers from certain services. Take fire departments, for example. In the eighteenth and nineteenth centuries, private fire-fighting companies were common in both Great Britain and America. Subscribers were careful to display their company's medallion prominently on their premises.[7] The trouble was that when a fire broke out in unprotected buildings they could easily spread to protected ones. The possibility of extreme negative externalities during a fire was too great to ignore, and so in most places, fire protection became a municipal service. (Private fire protection can and sometimes does still spring up, but nowadays only in suburbs and rural areas where the houses are widely scattered.[8]) Similarly, if inoculations, vaccinations, water purification, or similar activities were left to the private market, there would be a serious risk that some contagious disease might arise among the untreated population. This could lead to high costs that a charitable public or the taxpayer would have to bear.

If the private market cannot be trusted to cope with externalities, what recourse is possible? Government action is the path taken by most countries.

---

7.   One of the world's great fortunes was founded on private fire protection. Marcus Licinius Crassus, one of the triumvirs along with Caesar and Pompey, organized Rome's first fire department. Rather than accepting prepaid fees for protection, however, Crassus and his slave firemen either bargained at the scene of the fire or purchased the property from its anxious owner at, literally, fire-sale prices. Hundreds of valuable city houses and tenements ended up as part of Crassus' commercial empire.

8.   Usually the private fire companies require a fee to join the service and a fee if the service comes to your property to put out a fire (say $60 to join and $500 every time the company is called to your property.) In the United States, private fire companies are currently most important in Arizona.

▶ NARROWING THE GAP BETWEEN PRIVATE AND SOCIAL COSTS AND BENEFITS

Government can take various corrective actions when private costs and benefits differ from social costs and benefits. In this section, we will examine government command-and-control regulation of externalities, taxes and subsidies to counter them, private lawsuits in the courts to discourage them, and emissions trading to limit them to a desired level. The first task, however, is to determine how in practice the differences between private and social costs and benefits are measured.

ESTIMATING SOCIAL COSTS

To measure the impact of externalities on society we must find some way of assigning a market value to something for which there is no market. Both in theory and in day-to-day planning, one of the greatest hurdles in modern economics is the lack of accurate techniques for estimating the money value of externalities. Only a small proportion of them can be measured with any degree of precision.

In Makesmee, Ill., it would be rather easy to establish some of the direct costs imposed by the Lewter Company's pollution. Houses have to be painted every three years instead of every ten, clothing has to be replaced because of frequent laundering, more eyedrops and air conditioners are sold, commercial fishermen lose income, the water purification plant must buy special filters, and many people purchase bottled water. All of these can be valued. In New York City such costs (primarily for painting, washing, and laundry) were estimated to be $200 per person per year during the 1970s. One difficulty with this method of measurement is knowing whether the cost was really due to the pollution. For example, you bought the air conditioner partly to filter out the pollutants, but partly because you are richer now and prefer a cooler house. You drink bottled water partly because the town water doesn't taste very good, but partly because you think it is prestigious to do so.

Estimation by Means of Property Values and Questionnaires

Other costs, just as or more burdensome for the community, are much harder to estimate. What is the dollar value of not being able to go swimming or boating in the Makesmee River, of being deprived of peace and quiet by the noisy operations at the Lewter plant, of not being able to breathe clean air because of the fumes from the plant, of not seeing the stars at night because the haze blots them out, of rarely seeing wild animals and birds in the surrounding area, of stinging eyes and scratchy throats? We are sure these are costs, but in dollar terms how large are they?

Several methods of estimation have been developed. One is to compare property values in polluted Makesmee with property values in similar communities that do not suffer from pollution. The difference might approximate the social costs involved. Similarly, we could look at wages to see how much higher they have to be in order to attract workers to the polluted city.

Another method is to distribute questionnaires asking citizens how much they would be willing to pay to reduce a particular type of pollution. Answers to an air-pollution questionnaire, for example, would differ from respondent to respondent, ranging perhaps from Mrs. A's $20 through Mr. B's $10, Ms. C's $7.50, and Mr. Lewter's $0.00. By adding up the figures volunteered by all the respondents in town we would have an estimate of the dollar value the community ascribes to clean air. We would then know where to position the supply curve in Figure 10.2 to reflect the fact that social costs are larger than private costs.[9]

A major problem with such surveys is that the respondents may not be telling the truth. Some may assume that they will actually be charged for pollution control in proportion to their answers, and they may thus make very low estimates. Others may make very high estimates, on the assumption that a high figure will motivate the government to do something about the

---

9.   Similar methods can be used to estimate the value of indirect benefits, such as preserving scenic areas that you may visit sometime (Yellowstone) or preserving the habitat of those things that you probably will never see (okapis in Central Africa, Bachman's warblers in North Carolina, spotted owls in the Pacific Northwest). These "nonuse values" are especially hard to measure.

pollution. One way to guard against such untrustworthy responses is to disguise the purpose of the survey by mixing in questions on other topics. Another much used approach is to ask a yes/no question: "are you willing to pay at least $X" to preserve some amenity? Then, by finding the proportion of a sample that will pay over $100, the proportion that will pay more than $1000, and so forth, useful generalizations can be made. (This type of questionnaire is believed to be more reliable than the open-ended kind because it requires less careful analysis by the person questioned.)

In any case, care has to be exercised in assessing survey results because polluting firms may mount larger advertising programs to influence public opinion more than conservation groups are able to do. (Though as concern for the environment grows, this becomes less of an issue.) Furthermore, a decision has to be made about whether to mention in the questionnaire anything about the possibility of increasing unemployment or a decline in wages following the elimination of a negative externality, say the closing of a polluting factory. Such information is likely to influence the answers.[10] A further problem is that the person questioned may never have experienced what you're talking about and has difficulty in deciding on a value. For example, imagine inquiring about the value of the stars at night to someone who lives in a big city and has never seen stars in a dark sky.

One curiosity with the questionnaire method has been noticed. People usually appear willing to pay a much smaller amount to obtain an environmental amenity that they do not have than they are willing to take to give up exactly the same amenity if they already have it. This may reflect a strong "if I've got it I don't want to lose it" attitude, or it may reflect a declining marginal utility of environmental gains (that is, the more you obtain of something the less you value further increments). Perhaps it reflects both.

Estimation by Travel Costs When An Amenity Has to Be Visited

A different technique can be used to put a dollar value on the protection of amenities such as national parks that have to be visited.[11] A value can be estimated by ascertaining what people are willing to pay for transportation to a certain site. For example, a Bostonian pays $600 to visit Yosemite, an Iowan pays $300, and a Californian pays $100. A net benefit (or consumer surplus) exists when the visitor would have been willing to pay more than the trip actually cost. Here is a sample calculation: Say that 10% of Bostonians, 20% of Iowans, and 30% of Californians have visited Yosemite. From that we might infer that 10% of *Californians* (like Bostonians) would also be willing to pay at least $600 for the privilege, while another 10% (like Iowans) would have been willing to pay at least $300. Each group of Californians paid only $100, however. So we can estimate that 10% of all Californians receive a net benefit of at least $500 ($600 – $100), while another 10% receive a net benefit of at least $200 ($300 – $100). Similarly, we can estimate that 10% of all Iowans receive a net benefit of at least $300 ($600 – $300), and so on. With this technique, we can approximate a minimum value for keeping Yosemite undeveloped. Some difficulties with the technique include differences in income (Bostonians richer than Iowans, for example) and innate enthusiasm (there may be more, or fewer, strong environmentalists in California than in the other areas). Income differences can be allowed for, but different degrees of enthusiasm are difficult to pin down.

Not surprisingly, these various measurement techniques are likely to yield different results. The signals that reach politicians are inconsistent, encouraging them to pick those that favor their cause. Yet substantial progress in measuring the value of externalities has been made over the past two decades, and coherent estimates are now often available. This is in contrast to the complete guesswork that used to characterize the debates on the subject.

---

10.   This entire discussion of how to value social costs is relevant to the earlier section of the chapter on why private agreements to eliminate externalities may be difficult to forge. Any attempt to engineer a private financial arrangement between Lewter and the townspeople would have to involve some reasonably precise valuation of the costs imposed by the pollution. In the absence of government participation or some existing academic study, the participants to the private agreement would have to fund the studies themselves. Though this is increasingly being done, it is yet another, and a potentially serious, transaction cost.

11.   The example here is taken from *The Economist*, March 3, 1990, citing work by Per-Olov Johansson in the *Oxford Review of Economic Policy*.

DEALING WITH EXTERNALITIES

Once the difficulties of measurement are overcome, the next question is, what to do with the figures obtained? Several steps can be taken to make the private market take account of externalities. Whether to do so is one of today's most significant economic debates.

One radical school of thought argues that economic growth should be halted, or at least cut back. Note, however, that this method would only stop or slow the *increase* of pollution, not reduce it. Alternative methods, though imperfect, have already done much better than that.

In practice, the most common way to deal with externalities is government regulation through "command-and-control" measures. The government prohibits some things (such as very high compression engines in automobiles and certain chemicals such as DDT) and makes other things mandatory (like seat belts, catalytic converters, and public education). Clearly, government regulation of this type will always be necessary where certainty is needed, for example the strict prohibition against the release of toxic strontium-90 into the atmosphere. Like all government regulations, however, regulations dealing with externalities are managed by bureaucracies. As we all know, bureaucracies tend to be cumbersome and slow-moving, often lacking energy and imagination. Moreover, the information available to a bureaucracy may be inadequate, and the regulation it is responsible for administering may be so broad that it cannot accommodate regional differences. To avoid complication, the government often sets standards that are rigidly uniform. Yet exhaust emissions that contribute to pollution in downtown Los Angeles or Denver are not noticed on roads in northern Maine or Minnesota; a toilet every five acres for farmworkers is reasonable for New Jersey truck farms but is hardly needed on a 2000-acre cattle spread in Montana.

If the government's regulations attempted to allow for any number of conceivable situations, its rule books would run to thousands of pages. Even as it is, a company that is subject to the U.S. Clean Air Act must somehow try to observe over a hundred specific limits. Often the government agencies involved are understaffed, faced with the overwhelming task of policing more than 60,000 firms that are classified by the U.S. government as "major polluters." Perhaps these complications could be avoided by leaving the control of pollution to be determined locally, but that leads to problems of its own. Businesses would face a maze of differing regulations; polluting firms could play off one locality against another to soften their regulations when a new plant is built.

Even when a company abides by a specific command-and-control standard, it has no incentive to do better than the regulation requires. A law that calls for a 25% reduction of waste disposal into the Makesmee River gives a polluting firm no reason to search for ways to eliminate the problem altogether, or to reduce its pollution by 50%, or even by 26%. In fact, the incentives are perverted: if the law requires industry to use "the best technology available" for pollution control and a firm *did* develop a better way, then the government would just force you to install the new technology, perhaps at considerable expense. Why go to the trouble of innovating? Furthermore, if the law requires new capital equipment to be less polluting than old capital, that also creates a negative incentive to keep the old and dirtier equipment in use for a longer period of time.

Taxes on Negative Externalities

Because of all these difficulties, many economists favor working through the market mechanism, utilizing taxes and subsidies to cope with externalities. In the United States, taxes on negative externalities (often called "effluent charges" when the externality involves pollution) are now widely discussed and some are already in place. Taxing negative externalities holds advantages: for example, if a country taxes income, it is always possible that its taxpayers will choose to work fewer hours and save less. If that country chooses instead to tax negatives such as carbon emissions and highway travel, the same principle of reducing the taxed activity would apply, but in this instance the country would obtain cleaner air and less congestion on the roads. The revenue obtained could even be used to reduce income taxes, potentially allowing a country's economy to become more productive while at the same time it becomes a nicer place to live. No wonder that taxes on negative externalities have considerable appeal.

A tax imposed on each unit of pollution would shift the supply curve upward, just as did the sales taxes we discussed in Chapter 4. In Figure 10.6, firms willing to supply the quantities shown along the supply curve S would now be willing to supply those amounts only if they are paid the former price plus the amount of the tax (equal to the distance AB shown by the arrows). The supply curve S shifts up to S_t, resulting in a new equilibrium with a higher price and lower output (P_t and Q_t instead of P_e and Q_e). Private marginal costs would be forced up to the level of social marginal costs, and the allocative inefficiency (deadweight loss) would be eliminated.[12]

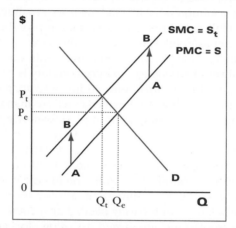

Figure 10.6. **Taxing negative externalities.** A tax on the production of items with negative externalities would shift the supply curve upward, resulting in a higher price and a lower output.

When it taxes pollution, government will not need to engage in specialized research to determine how to cut the pollution (though it *will* need the equipment to monitor pollution). That is because a pollution tax would give firms that are knowledgeable about their own operations a financial incentive to search for the most efficient means of reducing their emissions, perhaps by means of joint projects that would yield economies of scale.

Another advantage of taxation over command and control has to do with the fine-tuning of the results. At present, government regulation by command and control means that the same exhaust device is required on a big car that gets 15 miles to a gallon as on a small one that gets 30. A tax on gasoline would shift new car sales toward those that consume less fuel, and all things being equal, pollute less. The tax could be adjusted up or down depending on its effectiveness in controlling pollution. Notice also that the tax revenues can be directed if desired to specific antipollution projects, for example technical development of more efficient engines and nonpolluting energy sources, so that a doubly beneficial effect can be expected. Currently, however, the government favors command-and-control regulations rather than taxes as a means for controlling social costs. (The notable exceptions are the taxes on liquor and cigarettes, designed in some part to limit the consumption of these products and thus restrict their damage.)

The Effects of Education and Information

Effective educational and informational programs would induce consumers voluntarily to reduce their demand for products marketed by firms that cause pollution. Then the demand curve would shift leftward, say from D_1 to D_2 in Figure 10.7. That would cause a polluting firm's output to decline from Q_1 to Q_2, with a resulting reduction in the quantity of pollutants released into the

---

12.   As well as taxing a firm to force it to clean up, that firm could be paid a government subsidy to persuade it not to pollute. Although a policy of taxation and one of subsidization have similarities, there is also a major difference. A subsidy would tend to increase profits, and hence, as new firms are attracted into the industry the production of the polluting item would tend to increase. That might keep the level of pollution undesirably high, and explains why pollution-reduction subsidies receive less support from economists than do taxes on polluters.

environment. (Note that a decline in demand would also cause a decline in price, from P_1 to P_2 in the figure, and not an increase in price as would be true of taxes that move the supply curve upward.)

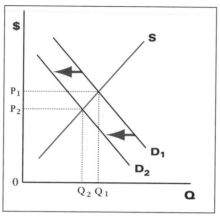

Figure 10.7. Effect of education on the output of a polluting firm. If education concerning pollution causes less of a polluting product to be demanded, then like a tax the quantity produced would fall, but unlike a tax the price would fall as well.

LAWSUITS AS A SUBSTITUTE FOR TAXES IN POLLUTION CONTROL

Another approach for controlling pollution is for those who are damaged to sue in the courts. Here there is neither a command-and-control mechanism nor a tax mechanism. If polluters are made legally liable for the damage they inflict, then they are exposed to a stick wielded by judges and juries. Enforcing legal liability to make polluters bear the financial burden of the damage they have caused works something like a tax, with the major difference that direct compensation goes to those who are harmed. A legal doctrine of "joint and several liability" has been embodied in some environmental legislation that has changed the situation when pollution is created jointly, as when five different companies each dump some effluent into a river. This doctrine makes each defendant liable for *all* the damages, no matter what their share of the contribution to the damages. It clearly makes wealthy polluters much more careful about what they do because they will obviously be targeted by litigants.

Major problems exist when lawsuits are relied upon to police pollution. One is that damage awards may be haphazard, dependent on the variable moods of judges and juries. The same behavior may lead to a small judgment in one state or locality, and a large one in another, depending on how the wind blows at the moment. There is also a motive for those instigating the lawsuits to overstate their damages, the certainty of large extra costs of lawyers and consultants, and overload on the judicial system.

Subsidies in the Presence of Positive Externalities

When the production of a product generates positive externalities, then the market mechanism will result in too little output of that product. The government, therefore, sometimes uses subsidies to lead firms to increase their output. Unfortunately, however, government subsidies have often been associated with questionable purposes, inefficient use of the funds by the recipients, and high taxation to finance them. Thus, in the 1980s their popularity declined substantially. But subsidies do stimulate firms to increase their output, as Figure 10.8 shows. Firms that are willing to supply various quantities at the market prices along the supply curve will be willing to supply the same quantities at a lower price when they receive a subsidy that makes up the difference. If the money value of the subsidy is equal to AB per unit, the supply curve will shift from S to S_s. A new equilibrium will occur at the greater quantity Q_s (rather than Q_e) and the lower price P_s (rather than P_e). Most states subsidize poor school districts in recognition of the positive externalities that accompany education; public subsidies are commonly accorded to recreational facilities, museums, and parks because of the aesthetic and educational benefits they make available to the public. But the case for subsidies is easily abused. Government support for public golf courses when few taxpayers play golf, or for building stadiums for professional teams when many taxpayers never go to the games, seems a blatant misuse of the positive externalities argument.

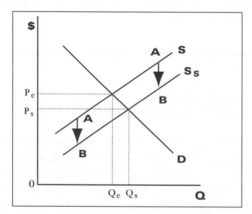

Figure 10.8. Subsidies and positive externalities. A subsidy on the production of items with positive externalities would shift the supply curve downward, resulting in a lower price and a higher output.

HOW MUCH SHOULD WE CUT POLLUTION?

As we have seen, taxation is sometimes used as a means for reducing negative externalities such as pollution. This leads to an extremely important question. How much *should* we cut pollution? Some would say, "eliminate it completely," but that would not be wise because it would involve an inefficient use of resources. In Figure 10.9 the vertical axis shows dollars and the horizontal axis measures the quantity of pollution emitted. (Notice that this is a change in the diagramming. Up to now, the horizontal axis has shown the quantity of output produced.) To the far left at the origin, 0, pollution control is at a maximum and no pollution is being emitted. To the far right, at quantity Q_3, no pollution control is being undertaken and pollution is at a maximum.

Now start at the origin, with maximum control and no pollution, and ask what the damage from pollution would be if control were relaxed just a little bit. The cost of the damage caused by the first ton of effluent might be represented by point A, a small cost. A tiny amount of smoke in the air might not even be noticed; the atmosphere has a great deal of self-cleansing capacity. The cost of the damage caused by a second ton might be greater as indicated by point B; and so on. We expect that the *marginal cost of damage* (MCD) from pollution will rise as exhaust fumes begin to cause smog, or as water pollution begins to affect the fish. The MCD curve might eventually rise steeply as the air pollution affects human health, or as water pollution causes massive fish kills. This sharp rise is apparent on the right-hand side of the diagram, where MCD is almost vertical.

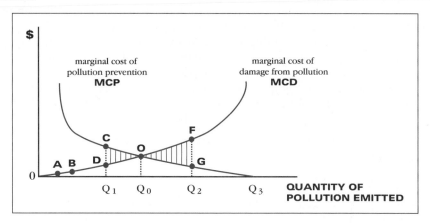

Figure 10.9. The economics of pollution reduction. The marginal cost of damage from pollution is higher at large quantities of pollution than when the level of pollution is small. The marginal cost of pollution prevention is low when large amounts of pollution are emitted, but high when most pollution has already been eliminated. The curves allow the determination of the optimum level of pollution (at the level where the curves cross).

The marginal cost of pollution prevention, MCP, has a different shape. At Q_3 where no attempt is being made to control pollution, pollution is at a maximum and no cost of prevention is being incurred. There it would be inexpensive to be rid of some of it. When attacking pollution, the first steps are cheap and easy. A $20 screen added to a smokestack might prevent some of the clinkers and ash from entering the atmosphere. Getting rid of larger amounts becomes more costly, however, because the marginal cost of cleanup increases. Notice that as pollution is reduced leftward from Q_3, MCP rises.

Examples of rising marginal cost of pollution prevention are abundant. A recent report to the U.S. Environmental Protection Agency noted that the cost of removing 90% of the pollutants stemming from carbon steel production is 26¢ per kilogram of pollutant. To remove 97%, the cost rises to $4.98 per kilogram, and to remove 99% the cost is $32.20 per kilogram. In petroleum refining, nearly 70% of the polluting discharge can be eliminated for about 7¢ per pound of discharge. To eliminate 80% costs 14¢ to 15¢ per pound, and to eliminate 90% costs over 20¢ per pound. A much broader estimate covering reduction of U.S. carbon emissions suggests a cost of $8.55 per ton for a reduction of 8%, $16.96 per ton for 14%, and $60.09 per ton for 32%.[13]

Attempts to achieve some very low level of pollution (by using a high level of pollution control), say level Q_1 in Figure 10.9, will be very costly. To clean up the last unit of pollution at Q_1 would cost much more (at point C) than the cost of the damage inflicted by that unit (at point D). That would be true of all other units of pollution to the right of Q_1, all the way to point O (the "O" standing for "optimum"). To the left of point O society would suffer a net economic loss (allocative inefficiency or deadweight loss), equal to the shaded triangle OCD.

The bargain is also bad when too little effort is made to reduce pollution and too much pollution is emitted, as for example at Q_2. At Q_2, the cost of cleaning up the last unit of pollution (at point G) would be much less than the cost of the damage caused by that last unit of pollution (at point F). That is true of all other units of pollution between Q_0 and Q_2. The damage from each of these units is greater than the cost of cleaning it up. A decision to allow an amount of

13.   See Dale W. Jorgenson and Peter J. Wilcoxen, "Reducing U.S. Carbon Emissions," in John R. Moroney, *Advances in the Economics of Energy and Resources*, Vol. 7, Greenwich, CT, 1992, pp. 125–128.

pollution Q_2 thus causes a net economic loss (allocative inefficiency or deadweight loss) equal to the shaded triangle OFG located to the right of O.

From this analysis emerges an "optimal level" of pollution. That optimal level is Q_O in Figure 10.9. At that point, where the cost of the damage inflicted by the last unit of pollution emitted is exactly equal to the cost of cleaning it up, the combined total cost associated with pollution and its control is minimized. In Figure 10.10, that combined cost consists of area A, the cost of the damage caused by the pollution remaining at Q_O, and area B, the cost of the cleanup that has been undertaken. This combined cost A+B is lower than the combined cost at any other level of pollution. To the right of Q_O a lessened effort at pollution control increases the damage from pollution faster than the rise in savings from reduced pollution prevention. To the left of Q_O, a greater effort at pollution control raises the cost of the prevention faster than the fall in the cost of the damage. The solution at Q_O is economically efficient.

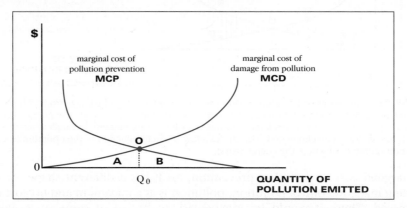

Figure 10.10. The optimal amount of pollution control. The most efficient level of pollution reduction would be to establish the quantity of pollution emitted where the marginal cost of damage from pollution is equal to the marginal cost of pollution prevention. That level of pollution inflicts the least cost on society.

Achieving the Efficient Level of Pollution Control Through Taxation

If the government were to impose a tax on each unit of pollution emitted (say "$50 per ton of solid discharge"), market forces would push firms to limit their polluting emissions to the efficient quantity Q_O. In Figure 10.11, the government has established such a tax at level T. Now, polluting firms have to choose between paying the tax for the pollution they emit, or reducing their pollution. Consider a firm that is currently polluting at level Q_1. What would it do when a tax is established? If the firm wants to minimize its costs, its decision is clear. At Q_1 the cost of paying the tax T on the last unit of pollution emitted (the distance from Q_1 to line T) is *less than* the cost of cleaning up that last unit (shown by distance Q_1A). The firm would prefer to pay the tax on that last unit than to clean it up. That would be true of any other unit of pollution all the way rightward to Q_O.

What about a firm that is emitting quantity Q_2 of pollution? There the cost of paying the tax T on the last unit of pollution would be *greater than* the cost of cleaning it up, shown by distance Q_2B. This firm would prefer to clean up that last unit instead of paying the tax. (A firm that was extremely dirty might even decide to close down rather than making the payment.) The same logic would hold for any quantity of pollution between Q_2 and Q_O. The rational response of firms to the tax would move them toward Q_O. Firms would, advantageously, have a strong incentive to adopt new technologies for the control of pollution whenever that would save the firm money.

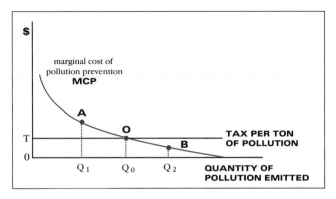

Figure 10.11. A pollution tax. Requiring firms to pay a tax on the pollution they emit gives government a tool for regulating the amount emitted. In the figure, firms would prefer to clean up rather than pay the tax if they are emitting more than Q_0, but if they are emitting less than Q_0 it is cheaper to pay the tax. So the quantity of pollution emitted tends toward Q_0.

Quantity Q_0 in Figure 10.11 need not represent the optimal amount of pollution, however. Perhaps the optimum would involve a greater or lesser amount. By raising or lowering the pollution tax, the government could promote movement toward *whatever* level of pollution control it deemed desirable.

When Should Command-and-Control Measures Be Preferred to Taxation?

The analysis just completed allows us to suggest the conditions under which government command-and-control requirements to reduce pollution would be preferred to taxes on polluting activity. If there is a threshold beyond which it would be dangerous to go in terms of the marginal costs of damage from pollution (technically, a steep MCD curve), then a mistake that caused too much pollution to be emitted might have disastrous consequences. Therefore, close control over the level of pollution emitted is essential, and command-and-control measures are the more desirable.

If, on the contrary, the marginal cost of preventing pollution fell very rapidly (a steep MCP curve), and if the government tried to set a command-and-control limit on pollution that was a little too strict, the cost of complying would be very great. A pollution tax would be better because firms would be able to pay the tax rather than meet the over-optimistic target.[14]

EMISSIONS TRADING

Taxes on pollution are not the only recent idea. Another concept contributed by economists is called **emissions trading**. This is the idea of making pollution control more cost effective by allowing firms to buy and sell emissions-reduction credits on an open market. The idea is based on the fact that some firms can clean up pollution much more cheaply than others. Usually the ease of the cleanup is related to the differing age or sophistication of the technology, plant, and equipment that firms are using. Figure 10.12 shows the MCP curves for two firms, A and B. Firm A is the same one shown in Figure 10.11, with its MCP curve rising as the quantity of pollution emitted falls from its maximum of 20. The MCP curve of Firm B has the same basic shape; pollution is cheaper per unit to clean up when more of it is emitted. To make the diagram more useful we have placed the origin for Firm B's curve at the lower *right* corner, with B's emissions running from the B origin *leftward* to its maximum, which is also 20.

---

14.   The principle that the steepness of MCP and MCD will determine when command-and-control measures are preferred to taxation is the "Weitzman Proposition," named for Martin Weitzman of Harvard University, who formulated it.

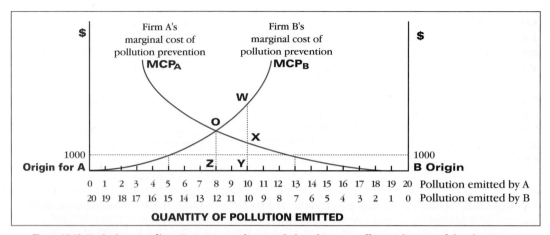

Figure 10.12. Emissions trading. Emissions trading can help achieve an efficient division of the cleanup effort. In the figure, Firm A can clean up more cheaply than Firm B. For any given amount of cleaning up, it would be sensible for A to do more of it and B to do less. A could sell to B emissions credits earned from the cleanup. The end result is a lower total bill for cleaning up, compared to the situation where each firm had to cut its emissions by the same percentage.

The figure shows that Firm A can clean up more cheaply than Firm B. Notice how A's marginal costs of pollution prevention (MCP_A) rise rather slowly as cleanup proceeds from the maximum pollution level of 20 at the far right. Firm B's curve (MCP_B) rises more rapidly from *its* maximum pollution level of 20 at the far left. Cleanup is more expensive for B than for A. For the same amount of money ($1000, shown on both vertical axes) Firm A can clean up 7 units of pollution (from 20 down to 13) while B can clean up only 5 (from 20 to 15).

In the absence of government regulation, assume that both firms are polluting at their maximum level of 20 units, for a total of 40 units. Now view the situation if the government decides to cut total pollution by half to 20 units. It might require each firm to reduce its pollution from 20 units to 10 units. That solution would not be efficient, however. Firm A could do it cheaply. A's cleanup cost for its last unit (10th) of pollution would be just XY. Firm B's pollution control is expensive, however. The cleanup cost of B's last (10th) unit of pollution would be WY. The net cost of pollution control to society could have been *reduced* if Firm A had cleaned up another unit (lowering its pollution to 9 units), and if Firm B had accomplished *less* cleanup (increasing its pollution to 11 units). Even if that were done, another unit of pollution control is still cheaper for Firm A than it is for Firm B; further cost reduction could be achieved if A reduced its emissions to 8 units and if B increased its emissions to 12 units. Only at O is the marginal cost of pollution prevention (OZ at that point) equal for the two firms. At that point, Firm A would emit only 8 units of pollution while Firm B is allowed to emit 12 units. The government would achieve its goal of reducing pollution by a total of 20 units, while avoiding an allocative inefficiency (deadweight loss) equal to OWX. Point O, therefore, is the optimal (efficient) division of cleanup effort between the two firms.[15]

If the government simply ordered Firms A and B to cut their level of polluting emissions to 10 units each (at point Y), it would be cheap for firm A but expensive for firm B. So the U.S. Environmental Protection Agency (EPA), and the similar agencies of several European governments, have instituted a new policy, allowing firms to buy and sell "emissions credits." In the U.S. program, the EPA's Emissions Trading Program first establishes a target for the reduction of some type of pollution. It then allows firms in a position to clean up cheaply (such as Firm A

15.　　Another way to put it: in this example the total cost of pollution control is the combined total cost to both A and B of their cleanup activity. Firm A's total cost is the cost of cleaning up *its* 20th unit of pollution, plus the cost of cleaning up its 19th unit, and so forth, all the way back to point O (with 8 units of pollution still being emitted). Firm A's total cleanup cost is thus the triangular area OZB. Firm B's total cost is similarly the cost of cleaning up *its* 20th unit, plus its 19th, and so on, back to O (with 12 units of pollution still being emitted). Firm B's total cleanup cost is thus the triangular area OZA. The combined total cost for firms A and B, the area AOB obtained from adding together areas OZA and OZB, is the smallest possible total cost given the shape of the curves in Figure 10.11.

in our example) to reduce their emissions below their fair share. They can then claim emissions reduction credits that they can sell to firms (such as Firm B above) that find it cheaper to buy some credits rather than to clean up as much as would otherwise be required. The end result is to reduce the total amount of pollution to the desired level in the most efficient, least-cost way.

This innovative idea, first utilized in the United States in 1977, had led to the creation of approximately 10,000 emissions credits by 1989. Many of the trades have concerned the lead permitted in gasoline. Emissions trading for sulfur dioxide (SO_2) was included in the 1990 Clean Air Act Amendments. The present plan is to reduce sulfur dioxide by a little more than half by the year 2000. Starting in 1995, utilities will receive allowances to emit SO_2 at their 1985 level, and there will be an annual auction of emissions permits. Each firm will be charged a 2.8% deduction that will be awarded to newcomers. There is little doubt that emissions credit can save society money. The plan for SO_2 emissions credits is expected to cost some $3.6 billion annually compared to the $5 billion that cleanup by means of command and control would cost. The box shows the cost-saving arithmetic of a simple case.

AN EXAMPLE OF HOW EMISSIONS CREDITS SAVE MONEY

That emissions credits can save money can be made clear with some simple arithmetic. Say Firm A can reduce polluting emissions by one ton for $300, while it costs Firm B $500 to reduce emissions by one ton. If the government wants to reduce emissions by 100 tons and assigns a command-and-control cleanup quota of 50 tons each to the two firms, the total cost of pollution reduction is ($300 x 50) + ($500 x 50) = $40,000. If the government instead issued 50 tons of tradable emissions credits to each of the firms, then Firm A could sell its 50 credits to Firm B, say for $400 per ton. Firm B, where the cleanup would be expen-

sive, goes on polluting; Firm A cleans up by 100 tons. The cost to A is $300 x 100 = $30,000, less the $400 x 50 = $20,000 it received from the sale of the credits to B, for a net cost to Firm A of $10,000. Firm B pays $20,000 for the emissions credits it purchased from A, but saves $5,000 because a cleanup of 50 tons would have cost it 500 x 50 = $25,000. The total cost of the 100 ton reduction in pollution is the $10,000 net cost to Firm A and the $20,000 payment by Firm B for the emissions credits, for a total of $30,000 rather than the $40,000 a uniform rollback would have required.[16]

The U.S. Emissions Trading Program has grown rather slowly, however, and few trades are taking place in the area of air pollution. Business leaders object to the imposition of what they see as yet another type of tax, forgetting the money-saving implications explored in the box. Environmentalists oppose the idea that a private firm might make money by selling to some other firm the right to pollute, or that a polluter might get away with the damage by callously buying that right. To some environmentalists, emissions trading violates the sanctity of the environment. Neither group seems particularly impressed by the argument that emissions trading could *lower the cost* to society of reducing pollution.

WHEN NEGATIVE EXTERNALITIES ARE UNCERTAIN BUT POTENTIALLY CATASTROPHIC

A good way to conclude this chapter is to see how its lessons can be applied to negative externalities the impact of which is uncertain and debatable, the correction of which would be

---

16.   The example is from Donald A. Hanson, "The 1990 Clean Air Act," *Economic Perspectives*, Vol. 16, No. 3, May/June 1992, p. 8.

expensive, but the results of which might possibly be catastrophic. Global warming and the depletion of the ozone layer are international environmental problems in this category.

Global Warming

Global warming is the term used to describe the possible rise in world temperatures resulting from a "greenhouse effect" [17] The potential increase, if it occurs, would be a nonmarket externality of private market decisions. Most releases of carbon dioxide attributable to human activity are from the consumption of fossil fuels in industry and transportation. A smaller proportion comes from the clearing of land by cutting down tropical rain forest and the burning of the resulting slash. The destruction of the forests reduces the absorption of carbon dioxide while the burning of the slash produces more of that gas. The atmospheric emission of carbon dioxide is currently increasing at about $\frac{1}{2}$ of 1% per year.[18] A large rise in CO_2 emissions could create a greenhouse effect, acting in effect like an extra blanket that retains heat. If there were general agreement that global warming is a certainty and its results highly damaging, then policy recommendations—even if painful—would be easier to make.

But considerable uncertainty surrounds the problem. First, any warming will be long delayed because it will take decades to change ocean temperatures. So the full effects of greenhouse gases emitted now will not be fully felt for many years. Second, it is very difficult to forecast the future emissions of CO_2, which will depend largely on economic growth and technical change. The quantity of emissions will in large part determine how much warming occurs, so the predicted warming differs greatly depending on the assumptions employed. The estimates of warming from 1900 to the year 2100 range from about 2°C to about 10°C. Third, there is widespread disagreement on how great the costs would be if nothing were done. (The estimates run from nil to about 16% of world output). Fourth, the costs of treating the problem also involve considerable uncertainty. (Stabilizing the world emissions of carbon dioxide at 1990 levels would carry an annual cost of less than 1% to about 4% of total world output, depending on the estimate.)

One body of opinion holds that the possibility of catastrophe exists, so immediate action must be taken even if it is expensive. In this view, higher average world temperatures could disrupt food supplies, depriving fertile areas (like the American Midwest) of rainfall and reducing their output. They could also cause melting of the polar ice caps. The melting would result in further warming as the polar regions fail to reflect as much sunlight as before, and would raise the sea level as the polar ice turns to water. A 1°–2°C warming might therefore render uninhabitable many low-lying coastal areas and islands (including much of Bangladesh, for example) and cause some island republics (the Maldives and Tuvalu) to disappear. This school of thought demands immediate steps to limit greenhouse gas emissions by controls and taxes, on the grounds that failing to act now might lead to irreversible consequences.

Other experts are skeptical. They point out that temperatures have risen about 0.6°C in the century after 1880, but that most of this rise occurred before 1940 whereas most of the greenhouse gas emissions occurred after that date. Weather records show little temperature change in the 1980s, whereas most models predicted at least some warming during this period. Some recent models of sea-level changes show increases nowhere near the 15–25 feet suggested in the early 1980s; a few models even predict a decrease. These skeptics emphasize the modest and uncertain nature of the damage from global warming, and argue that only when the climate change actually starts to occur will it be known how much actually has to be done.

---

17.   In particular I used the "Symposium on Global Climate Change," especially the articles by Richard Schmalensee and William D. Nordhaus, in the *Journal of Economic Perspectives*, Vol. 7, No. 4, Fall 1993, pp. 3–86, and William Cline, *The Economics of Global Warming*, Washington, D.C., 1992.

18.   The United States is responsible for about 20% of the present increase, but less-developed countries, especially China and India, are expected to be the major source of future increases.

To supporters of this view, gradual adaptation to the warming is the best strategy. For them, the proper course is to encourage economic growth and then use the resources that growing economies can eventually mobilize to support sea defenses and drought resistance in plants. In this view no international agreement will be needed. Yale University economist William Nordhaus is a believer in relatively modest action, on the grounds that the benefits of controlling the problem are long term and dubious while the costs come now and may be considerable. The respected *Economist* magazine has recently joined the skeptics, arguing that global warming does not deserve the very high priority that many would give it.

> Water pollution kills more people than global warming is likely to do; soil erosion leaves more people hungry;…deforestation has locally (and perhaps internationally) dramatic effects on climate. The world has only so much wealth to devote to solving environmental problems. Any one of these deserves greater priority than global warming.[19]

The Economist argues that if evidence does in time emerge that warming is substantial, then large reductions in emissions can be made as needed.

Given the great uncertainty as to how severe the problem is, and the potential for catastrophe, economists face obvious difficulties in recommending optimal policy. But then many decisions, including military spending, exploration for oil and minerals, and research and development spending have to be made without complete information. As with these, the sensible course is to obtain the best available information on the consequences and their costs, to weigh the probabilities of the various possible outcomes—likely, possible, highly implausible—and take the course that appears to be most reasonable.

EMISSIONS TRADING, CARBON TAXES, AND GLOBAL WARMING

If the decision *is* taken to move soon against global warming, many economists would recommend that the tools discussed in this chapter should be put to use. International quotas on greenhouse gases could be established. (Actually, all of the major industrial countries except Turkey and the United States already have targets for carbon dioxide emissions). Once these quotas were in place, they could be bought and sold in an extension of the emissions trading already discussed.

Yet there is a considerable problem. The world's less-developed countries, especially China, India, and the former Communist countries, burn more carbon (coal, largely for electric power) as a proportion of their total energy use than do the developed countries. What will the quota share of these countries be? They currently emit rather small amounts of the greenhouse gases, but with economic growth their emissions are expected to triple by the year 2025. These countries are understandably reluctant to harm their industrialization unless the already developed countries take the lead. If the quotas were distributed by population they would go mostly to the poor countries, and it would be very expensive for the rich to buy the transferable permits they would need. (The World Bank estimates that it would cost the rich countries $70 billion to buy the permits for one year's total emissions.) If, on the other hand, the quotas were distributed by income level, then the rich would receive most of them, which would be very unfair. In any case, there are as yet no examples at all of international emissions trading.

At the 1992 Earth Summit held at Rio de Janeiro, some European countries advocated a carbon tax, and a few, including the Netherlands, Finland, and Sweden, already have one. Such a tax would be applied to fuels that contain carbon. But a carbon tax would be especially disadvantageous for China, Russia, the United States, Canada, and OPEC—the nations involved that have most of the coal, oil, and natural gas. The revenues from a carbon tax could be shared with the countries hurt the most, but this would involve huge international transfers, and in any case several of these countries are very rich.

Following the logic developed in this chapter, any international plan should aim to reduce emissions most in countries where it costs the least to do so. This will, however, require some sharing of the burden. Otherwise, countries will have an incentive to stay out of an agreement or cheat.

The controversy is a momentous one, which will doubtless be with us for a long time to come. A mistake in assessment and failure to take timely action could lead to very serious consequences, but so could an approach of premature panic. Constant monitoring of the situation and careful planning for contingencies would seem clearly called for.

Ozone Depletion

In 1985, British scientists revealed that the ozone layer of the atmosphere is shrinking and that a vast hole is opening up over Antarctica. Because the ozone layer provides protection against the harmful effects of sunlight, the incidence of skin cancer is likely to increase as time passes. The private market decision responsible for this development is the use of chlorofluorocarbons (CFCs) as propellants in aerosol cans, as a coolant in air conditioners and refrigerators, and for insulation. Because of the long delay before the escaping CFCs destroy atmospheric ozone, the damage being seen at the start of the 1990s was due only to the releases that had occurred up to the early 1980s.

There is considerably more agreement on the existence of an ozone problem than on global warming. Moreover, the steps to correct it are universally acknowledged to be less expensive than what would be needed to control the emission of the greenhouse gases. So it proved possible to attack ozone depletion through international agreement. At Montreal in 1987, the major industrial nations signed an accord to limit CFC production in 1989 to the level reached in 1986, and to roll it back 50% from that level by 1998. Recent evidence that the depletion is occurring at a rate faster than predicted may cause a speed-up in this timetable.

CONCLUSION

For years a lively debate has surrounded the study of externalities and how to correct for them. The inability of private market decisions to reflect fully social costs and benefits is one of the great areas (the others being monopoly power and the problem of persistent poverty among an "under-class") where the market does not always provide a completely acceptable outcome. Many externalities *can* be insignificant, but damage to the environment has rapidly moved the debate beyond lively to critical. How to bring the problems under control is likely to become more contentious, rather than less so, because actions that involve low costs of pollution reduction and high benefits from the reduction are obviously the ones that will be taken first. After the cheap successes, the subsequent steps will be more difficult. The future will surely bring many proposals to adopt environmental regulations that impose more costs on society than the benefits conveyed, and economists will be involved in the measurements and analysis of the costs and benefits.

SUMMARY

1) Nonmarket externalities can be negative (as with pollution) or positive (as with education). Externalities are caused by the difference between private and social costs and benefits.

2) Private costs are illustrated diagrammatically by the supply curve, and private benefits by the demand curve. When negative externalities (social costs) in production are present, they can be illustrated diagrammatically by a supply curve upward and to the left of the supply curve that reflects private costs alone. When negative externalities (social costs) in consumption are present, they can be illustrated diagrammatically by a demand curve downward and to the left of the demand curve that reflects private benefits alone. Positive externalities (social benefits) in production are illustrated by a supply curve downward and to the right of the supply curve that reflects private costs alone. Positive externalities (social benefits) in consumption are illustrated by a demand curve upward and to the right of the demand curve that reflects private benefits alone.

3) Public goods are goods the government must supply because the private market will not do so in sufficient quantity. If private producers made the attempt, they would face the free-rider problem that some people will not pay because they will benefit anyway, as with street lighting, and so making the activity privately unprofitable.

4) Social costs are difficult to assess, but new methods for measurement are emerging. Property values, questionnaires, and estimation by travel costs are all cases in point.

5) Externalities can be dealt with by means of command-and-control measures, taxes and subsidies, suits in the courts, and emissions credits.

6) Economic analysis helps to determine the optimum level of pollution, which is the quantity where the marginal cost of pollution prevention is equal to the marginal cost of the damage from pollution.

7) It is especially difficult to determine proper policy for very long-run problems such as global warming. The existence and degree of the warming is debatable, and the costs are uncertain. But there is a possibility that its results could be catastrophic, so the uncertainty surrounding the issue is worrisome. Vigilance and contingency planning are called for.

Chapter Key Words

Emissions trading: An idea to reduce the costs of pollution control. Allows the purchase and sale on an open market of emissions credits that convey permission to emit a certain quantity of pollution.

External diseconomy: See *negative externality*.

External economy: See *positive externality*.

Externalities: Nonmarket effects of economic transactions on people not directly concerned with these transactions, as in pollution from a factory or the rise in house prices caused by building a subway line into the neighborhood. Social costs and social benefits are externalities.

Free riders: Those who benefit from an act without paying for it. The free-rider problem makes it unprofitable to provide some services (street lighting, police, flood control) by means of private enterprise. These are *public goods*, which see.

Global warming: A term used to describe a rise in world temperatures caused by the blanketing effect of greenhouse gases, especially carbon dioxide.

Negative externality: Cost not conveyed through the market mechanism. Incurred by people not directly concerned with the economic transaction that gave rise to the cost. Industrial pollution is an example. Can be associated either with production or consumption. Also known as social cost.

Positive externality: Benefit not conveyed through the market mechanism. Received by people not directly concerned with the economic transaction that gave rise to the benefit. The effect on property values of improved transportation is an example. Can be associated either with production or consumption. Also known as social benefit.

Private benefits: Measured by the profit or income earned on economic transactions. Private benefits are conveyed through the market mechanism.

Private costs: Measured by the dollar costs of producing output, and conveyed through the market mechanism.

Public goods: Output that will not be provided in adequate quantity or at all by private firms because users cannot be excluded from the benefit. Also see *free riders*.

Social benefits: See *positive externality*.

Social costs: See *negative externality*.

Chapter Questions

1) Diefast Chemical Company makes dangerous products including poisons. Its discharge into the air causes health problems in the town of Badod, Oregon, where the company is located. Rank the following ownership arrangements from worst to best in terms of the size of the pollution externality. Explain your ranking using the definition of externalities.

    a)   Diefast is an employee-owned company and most employees live in Badod.

    b)   Diefast is owned by one of the leading families of Badod.

    c) Diefast is owned by two wealthy industrialists from Portland, Oregon.

    d) Diefast is owned by the city of Badod and managed by a city council appointee.

2) Nuclear power stations are typically required to build parks and an education center in the communities in which they locate. One might argue that the private benefit of these facilities is small, while the social benefit is large, and that therefore the facilities represent a positive externality. Is it possible, however, that the private benefit is actually as large as the social benefit? Does your answer depend on how receptive the community is to having a nuclear reactor nearby?

3) Draw demand and supply curves for gasoline. There is a negative externality in the consumption of gasoline because it causes pollution. Draw a new curve to reflect this externality. Assuming that the market does not account for the externality, show the allocative inefficiency.

4) Sometimes a positive and a negative externality can cancel one another out. Suppose that book binderies release polluting chemicals, but that book consumption raises literacy rates. Draw the demand and supply curves for books. Then draw the new demand and supply curves taking account of the externalities. (Assume that the externalities are the same size for any given quantity.) Is there any allocative inefficiency?

5) Flowerton is home to the famous Elite Bulb Company, a seller of tulip bulbs. Everyone in town enjoys looking at the magnificent fields of tulips, and the scenery raises their property values. Use a diagram to show why the townspeople would be better off if Elite produced more bulbs. Flowerton once took up a subscription drive to pay Elite to plant more tulips, but few people signed up. Can you explain why?

6) In a city where a park was going to be turned over to a developer, surveyors went door to door. They asked, "How much is it worth to you to keep the park undeveloped? Don't worry, you won't actually have to pay any money." The total amount was $400,000. A pro-development city counselor claimed that this method did not measure anything. She sent around surveyors who asked, "How much is it worth to you to keep the park undeveloped? Your answer is a pledge to pay that much in increased taxes." Now the total was $2,500. Do you believe either figure is correct? How would you improve the survey to find a better estimate of the true value?

7) Let us return to Badod, Oregon, and the Diefast Chemical Company. Assume that the company is owned by out-of-town industrialists. The Badod city government decides to pass some measure against Diefast in order to reduce its pollution. Assume further that Diefast is an oligopolistic firm with upward sloping supply and downward sloping demand. Show the new supply curve if the Badod city government simply sets a limit on Diefast's output. Show the new supply curve if Diefast is taxed for its pollution. In the long run, what positive steps might Diefast take under the tax that it would not take under the strict control?

8) Suppose that emissions of a carcinogen were set at what was thought to be the optimal level of pollution. A new study finds that it only takes half the level of the carcinogen to cause the same amount of damage. Show on a diagram how the optimal level of pollution changes. If the government had been using a tax to control the pollution, is there any reason to consider shifting to command and control?

9) For many years, environmentalists targeted Ace Mills and Leroy Mills, two polluters on the same river. Ace is the older mill and strenuously resisted regulation because of the high cost to reconfigure its old machinery. The environmentalists finally persuaded the state to limit Ace and Leroy to the same amount of pollution. But then Ace's manager said, "Let us pay Leroy to pollute even less, and we'll pollute more. The total level of pollution will be the same, and fewer jobs will be lost because the cleanup will be cheaper." Do you buy this argument? Use a diagram to explain your reasoning.

CHAPTER 11

Factor Productivity and Income

OVERALL OBJECTIVE: To appreciate that the productivity of the factors of production and their supply determine the incomes of the factors of production.

MORE SPECIFICALLY:

■ To explain that the marginal physical product (MPP) of a factor is the extra physical output obtained from employing another unit of that factor, while the marginal revenue product (MRP) of a factor is the extra revenue a firm earns from employing another unit of that factor.

■ To show that the least-cost combination of the factors of production requires that the last dollar spent on each of the factors brings the same amount of additional output (MPP).

■ To demonstrate how the marginal revenue productivity of a factor is obtained by multiplying the factor's marginal physical productivity by the price of the product and how a profit-maximizing competitive firm will hire factors up to the point where MRP = price.

■ To understand that the MRP curve for a factor is therefore the (derived) demand curve for that factor.

■ To investigate whether factor markets are "fair."

■ To show how monopsony (a single buyer), monopoly (a single seller), and bilateral monopoly (a single buyer facing a single seller) alter the predictions of the competitive model of factor markets.

We have seen how microeconomics addresses the questions of what to produce and how to produce it. Now we turn to the question of how to distribute the production. In Chapter 2 we saw that incomes, and hence ability to purchase, go to those who embody, own, or control labor, which earns income in the form of wages and salaries; land (including natural resources), the income to which is called rent; capital, which earns interest; and entrepreneurship, which earns profit.

Income determination mirrors the analysis of how products are priced in a market system, so we are already familiar with most of the analytical tools necessary to understand how factor incomes are established. Essentially, the returns to the factors of production are determined by the forces of supply and demand. Individuals who have at their command factors that are scarce or much in demand (for example, labor involving substantial training and skills, great athletic ability, entrepreneurial talents, or productive oil wells) will earn relatively high incomes (wages, rent, and so on). Those with factors that are abundant or are not much in demand (labor with little education, few skills, or unmotivated to work, or the factors employed in declining industries) will earn relatively low incomes.

When factor incomes are very different over time, important consequences will ensue. The differing incomes will mean that ownership of a country's assets (its wealth in the form of factories, mines, houses, stocks, bonds, bank deposits, and so forth), will vary greatly. Higher incomes enable their earners to acquire more assets, and larger assets generate higher incomes for their holders. In Chapter 13 we will discuss the disparities in income and wealth that arise in a market system.

The next two chapters address how factor incomes are determined, with the general analysis and a focus on wages and salaries in the remainder of this chapter. In the following one, we examine the modifications that must be made in the general theory when wages are influenced by labor unions and comparable worth laws, and the adjustments needed to cover the cases of rent, interest, and profit .

► FACTOR INCOMES IN A MARKET ECONOMY

How are the incomes of the factors of production determined in a market economy? As with goods and services in product markets, the answer involves supply and demand. Figure 11.1 shows the supply and demand curves for a particular grade of labor in a particular industry. (We might also have chosen land, capital, technology, or entrepreneurship to make the example.) The point where the curves intersect shows an equilibrium price (wage) of W_e, while the equilibrium quantity is Q_e. The total income earned by the workers in this occupation is the wage times the quantity employed, or the area of the rectangle $0W_eEQ_e$.

Of these curves, the supply curve is relatively straightforward. The position of the curve, and shifts in it, will be due to all the determinants of labor supply. We adopt the usual maximizing assumption that people will want to maximize their returns from a given amount of effort, so the wage or salary paid is important. Given a constant wage, a general determinant of labor supply is the size of the population able and willing to work. This in turn is determined by net result of birth rates and death rates, health, the net outcome of immigration and emigration, and details such as child labor laws, requirements for retirement, and the degree of mobility within a country. For specific occupations, occupational requirements such as innate ability, education, training, and skills will make a major difference in the labor supply. So will changes in wages in other jobs that a person could take, any change in the desire for leisure rather than work, and expectations of future changes in the economy—including government policies toward those who are not working. Changes in these determinants will alter the position of the labor supply curve.

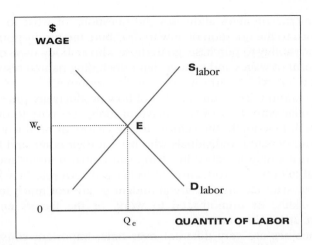

Figure 11.1. The supply and demand for a particular grade of labor. Wages and the quantity of employment in labor markets are an outcome of supply and demand relationships. Usually we would expect the curves to have their standard slopes. Demand is, however, a derived demand that stems from an employer's desire to use labor to make a profit.

Holding all determinants of labor supply constant except for the rate of pay allows us to draw a supply curve. We would expect the supply curve to slope upward on the assumption that higher wages will attract more labor to a particular occupation.[1]

The demand curve's downward slope requires considerably more analysis, however. There is a major difference between the demand for a product and the demand for the services of a factor of production. The demand for a product is direct: Consumers want the product in order to consume it themselves. The demand for a factor of production is not direct. It derives from the desire of a producer to use the factor in the production of a product that can be sold for profit. Consequently, the demand for a factor of production is referred to as a **derived demand**.

Our task now is to explore what determines a firm's demand for the various factors. In essence, a profit-maximizing firm will want to hire the quantity of each factor that, in combination with the other factors, enables it to earn the greatest possible profit.

▶ THE CONCEPT OF MARGINAL PRODUCTIVITY

In order to discover this profit-maximizing combination, the firm needs to know what the impact will be if the firm adds additional units of a factor. To judge this impact, economists utilize the concept of the **marginal productivity** of a factor, which is an essential determinant of income. Marginal productivity is a concept that has wide-ranging practical applications. For example, most readers of this book will find that the incomes they earn throughout their lives will depend to a large extent on how productive their employers find them to be.

The concept of marginal productivity allows us to explore what will happen to a firm's profitability if the firm uses a greater amount of a factor. For example, what if it hires additional labor? Assume that the other factors used by the firm are fixed in quantity: so many acres of land, so many machines and buildings, and so forth. Labor, however, is a variable factor. In Table 11.1, the first column shows the various quantities of labor a pizza shop could hire to work with fixed quantities of land, capital, technology, and entrepreneurship. The firm could hire any number of workers up to six, beyond which there would be no space behind the counter of the shop.

---

1.   Wages are not the only reward for labor, of course. Nonmonetary rewards include an interesting type of work, pleasant working conditions, and nonwage fringe benefits. We can either adjust the supply curve to reflect these (even though some may be difficult to measure), or we can adopt a *ceteris paribus* assumption and hold them constant in our analysis.

TABLE 11.1
Determining physical productivity.

Units of Variable Factor (Workers) (Other Factors Fixed)	Total Physical Product (TPP) (pizzas per hour)	Marginal Physical Product (MPP) (additional pizzas per hour)
0	0	
		14
1	14	
		15
2	29	
		14
3	43	
		10
4	53	
		4
5	57	
		-5
6	52	

To make its hiring decisions, the firm must know how much output will be forthcoming from the various quantities of labor. The second column shows that the pizza shop will obtain greater output as more workers are hired. The output produced by all the workers during any given time period is called the *total physical product* (TPP) of labor. Notice from the numbers that TPP climbs rapidly as the first workers are hired, then increases more slowly as additional workers are added, and even declines when the sixth worker is hired.

MARGINAL PHYSICAL PRODUCT (MPP)

The third column shows the result of adding each *additional* worker. That result is called the **marginal physical product (MPP)** of labor.[2] Adding a third worker, for example, raises total output from 29 to 43 pizzas. So the marginal increase in output resulting from the hiring of that one additional worker is 14 pizzas. All the other entries for MPP in the right-hand column of Table 11.1 are derived in the same manner. The MPP of labor is shown diagrammatically in Figure 11.2.

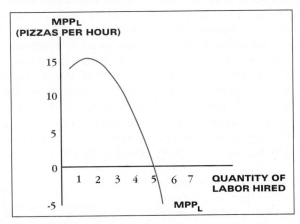

Figure 11.2. **The marginal physical product of labor.** Adding units of labor to a fixed quantity of other factors would eventually cause diminishing returns to labor; that is, each new worker would add a smaller quantity of output than the last one did, so marginal physical product declines.

2.　For simplicity we could call this the marginal product of labor, but we shall use the longer term MPP so as never to confuse it with another productivity concept, MRP, described later.

The pattern here follows a very familiar economic rule: increasing and then diminishing returns to a variable factor of production. The initial increasing returns, seen as the MPP curve rises, could result from the more effective division of labor that can be accomplished as more workers are hired. The eventual diminishing returns might result from the congestion that arises in the workplace as too many workers try to use the available capital. There will be overcrowding around the pizza ovens (or, in other industries, on the land or assembly line) as workers get in each other's way.

One of the most widely reported phenomena in economics is diminishing returns as any variable factor is added to a fixed quantity of other factors. This ties closely to our earlier discussion of a firm's short-run costs. The increasing returns as additions are made to a small quantity of a variable factor help explain why total costs may rise slowly at low levels of output. Conversely, the decreasing returns that accompany additions to a variable factor when a large quantity of that factor is already in use help to explain the rapid increase in total costs at high levels of output.

The concept of MPP is useful: First, it enables the firm to identify the least-cost, most efficient combination of factors for the production of any given quantity of output. (See the box.) Moreover, it enables the firm to calculate the quantity of each factor that it should actually hire.

USING MPP TO FIND THE LEAST-COST COMBINATION OF FACTORS

To produce any given amount of output, a firm could use various combinations of the factors—a little capital and a lot of labor, perhaps, or a lot of capital and just a little labor. How can a firm achieve the *least-cost combination* of factors to produce some given quantity of output? There is a convenient method for making the calculation.

Take an example. Assume that you can hire a unit of capital and a unit of labor for $1 each. Assume further that in producing a given quantity of a good, the last unit of capital used has an MPP of 2, and the last unit of labor used has an MPP of 1. In that case, the last dollar you spend on capital must be yielding 2 units of output, while the last dollar you spend on labor is yielding only 1 unit of output. If you are a profit-maximizing manager, you would choose to use less labor and more capital.

Clearly it makes sense to substitute a factor (capital in this case) that yields more output per dollar spent for a factor (labor) that yields less output per dollar spent. Remember, however, that using a greater amount of capital will cause its MPP to fall (see Figure 11.2), while using less labor will raise its MPP. So the MPPs of the two factors move toward one another. *Only when the last dollar spent on capital and the last dollar spent on labor yield exactly the same amount of additional output (MPP) has the most efficient, least-cost, combination of capital and labor been attained.*

In the real world, the prices of capital and labor are not likely to be the same. The price of a day's hire of a machine may be far more than a day's hire of a worker. We take account of this by using the following formula, in which L stands for labor and K for capital. The formula identifies the least-cost combination of the factors by indicating the additional output obtained per dollar spent on each factor.

$$\frac{MPP_L}{P_L} = \frac{MPP_K}{P_K}$$

Consider the insights made possible by this formula. In China, labor is very cheap compared to capital. The formula tells us that to produce a given output of a product, it would be economically sensible to employ a large quantity of cheap labor, thus bringing the MPP of labor quite low, and a small quantity of expensive capital, meaning that the MPP of capital will be quite high. The entrepreneur's task will be to substitute labor for capital, or capital for labor, until the MPPs per dollar spent on these factors are equal. Here to maximize output per dollar spent, production must be "labor intensive."

In the United States, by contrast, labor is relatively expensive and capital is relatively cheap. It would be economically sensible to produce the same output of the same product in a different way. With P_L high and P_K low, MPP_L will have to be high and MPP_K low to bring about equality in the formula. So U.S. employers would use a relatively large quantity of capital, resulting in a low MPP_K, and a relatively small quantity of labor, resulting in a high MPP_L. To maximize output per dollar spent, production must be "capital intensive." Just as it would be silly to

build a dam in China with capital-intensive methods, so it would be silly to build the same thing in the United States with gangs of high-paid workers carrying wicker baskets of dirt on their backs.

What if there are more than two factors of production, say land and entrepreneurship in addition to labor and capital, or perhaps different grades of labor or types of capital? The analysis remains the same: obtain the greatest quantity of output per dollar spent. We simply expand the formula to accommodate the additional factors:

$$\frac{MPP_A}{P_A} = \frac{MPP_B}{P_B} = \frac{MPP_C}{P_C} = \cdots = \frac{MPP_N}{P_N}$$

We have been making implicit use of this least-cost rule in our microeconomic analysis for several chapters now. Every average cost curve drawn in the diagrams from Chapter 6 on has actually been a least-cost curve. Had we drawn any one of these AC curves to reflect an inefficient combination of the factors of production, the curve would have moved up to a higher position showing increased average costs at any level of output.

MARGINAL REVENUE PRODUCT

The least-cost rule explored in the box applies to *any* level of output. But a firm needs to know more than this. It will have to calculate the actual quantity of factors that it should hire in order to maximize its profits, and the information conveyed by marginal physical product is too limited to determine this. The firm must have information on the extra profits it will earn by hiring more units of a factor, not just the amount of new output that will result. Only then can it determine the quantity of factors to hire. To make the calculation, the firm will need to know the price at which it will sell the new output. In a perfectly competitive industry, other things being equal, the market price will be constant whatever the amount sold. In the third column of Table 11.2, the market price of the product is assumed to be $2 per unit. We can now multiply the marginal physical product of adding one more unit of labor by the price at which the product can be sold. This establishes the extra revenue earned by employing the additional unit of labor. The result is called the **marginal revenue product (MRP)** of a factor. Thus:

$$MPP_{factor} \times P_{product} = MRP_{factor}$$

TABLE 11.2
Determining marginal revenue product (MRP).

Number of Workers Hired	Marginal Physical Product (MPP)	Selling Price of Product (Pizzas)	Marginal Revenue Product (MRP)
0			
	14	$2	$28
1			
	15	$2	$30
2			
	14	$2	$28
3			
	10	$2	$20
4			
	4	$2	$8
5			
	–5	$2	–$10
6			

Not surprisingly, since we have multiplied MPP by a constant, MRP shows the same increasing and then diminishing values as does the original MPP curve, as shown in Figure 11.3.

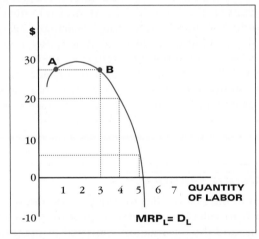

Figure 11.3. **The marginal revenue product of labor.** The marginal revenue product of labor is the marginal physical product times the price at which the product can be sold. If that price stays the same as more is sold, then the MRP curve has the same shape as the MPP curve.

With this information, the firm needs to know only the cost of labor in order to determine how much labor it should hire. If the wage rate is $20 per hour, a manager who wants to maximize profits will hire an additional (marginal) worker only if that worker's MRP is at least $20 worth of output per hour. If the MRP of the last worker who might be hired is *less* than $20, the firm will not pay out $20 to hire that worker. Conversely, if the MRP of a last worker seeking a job is *greater* than $20, the firm will have a definite incentive to hire that worker. The firm will add workers when MRP is greater than the wage paid, but will not if MRP is lower than the wage. Equality between the wage and the MRP thus determines the quantity of labor that will be employed by the firm. (This example assumes that the labor market is competitive, and that the firm's decision to hire or not to hire will not affect the market wage rate. Later in the chapter we will consider the case where the firm's hiring decisions *do* affect the level of wages.)

In Figure 11.3, the MRP drops below the $20 wage paid immediately after the fourth worker has been hired. So the firm has an economic motive to hire the fourth worker, but not the fifth. If the wage rate had been $8 per hour, the firm would have hired five workers, but not six. At $28 per hour it would have hired three workers but not four. But notice a complication if the wage had been $28 per hour. The $28 wage equals the MRP at two different points, **A** and **B**. In this situation the firm would always hire the larger number of workers (three at point **B**) rather than the smaller number shown at point **A** because at **A** the MRP_L curve is rising. That means that another worker will always bring more MRP than was brought by the last worker hired, even though the addition to cost is the same. A profit-maximizing firm would not stop hiring as long as it can increase its earnings by adding another worker. Thus, the rising portion of the MRP_L curve is not relevant for the firm's hiring decisions, and that rising portion will be omitted from our subsequent diagramming.

It follows that a firm's MRP_L curve is identical to its demand curve for labor below the point where the curve begins to fall. If the going wage is $20 per hour, the firm will choose to hire four workers. As mentioned earlier, the demand for a factor of production is a *derived demand*, with the factor not wanted for its own sake but for what it will contribute to a firm's profits. Thus the demand curve in Figure 11.3 is known as a *derived demand curve*.

What Might Cause a Firm to Alter Its Hiring Decisions

The analysis allows us to predict the circumstances under which a firm will alter its decision to hire a given number of workers.

1) If the marginal physical productivity of labor (MPP_L) rises, then the marginal revenue product of labor (MRP_L) will rise as well. That is because MPP is a component of MRP; $MRP_L = MPP_L \times P_{product}$. Therefore, the MRP curve will shift upward, from MRP_L to MRP_L' in Figure 11.4. The firm will increase its hiring of workers (at a wage of $20 per hour from four to six workers in the figure).

2) If the market price of the product rises, again the MRP curve will shift upward as in Figure 11.4, and the firm will increase its hiring.

3) If the wage rate falls but MRP_L remains unchanged, the firm will increase its hiring. In Figure 11.4, with labor productivity shown by the curve MRP_L', a decline in the wage rate from $20 to $10 per hour prompts the firm to hire seven workers instead of six. Note that this involves a movement along a stationary curve rather than a shift of the curve to a new position, as in the first two examples.

4) If the productivity of labor falls, or if the market price of the product falls, or if the wage rate rises, the firm will cut back on its hiring of workers.[3]

These are the considerations that determine what quantities of the factors of production a profit-maximizing firm will hire. We have used labor as our example, but the analysis would be similar for any other factor of production. Like the derived demand for labor, the derived demand for the other factors is also based on the value of the output that these factors will yield.

---

3.   Other events that would alter a firm's hiring decision include changes in the supply of all factors and changes in the productivity of the other factors.

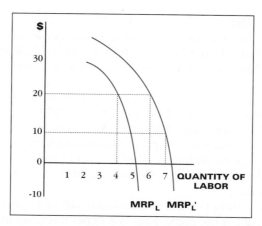

Figure 11.4. An increase in MPP$_L$, an increase in the price of the product, or a decrease in the wage rate lead to more hiring. Because the firm equates the wage and the MRP to determine the quantity of labor to hire, hiring will be increased if the MRP rises (due either to an increase in MPP or in the price of the product) or if the wage rate falls.

How Are Wage Rates Determined in the Market?

Why are wage rates sometimes $6, sometimes $10, and sometimes $20 per hour? We can answer that question by using marginal revenue product analysis. In general, wages are determined by the total supply of and total demand for labor in a given occupation. The supply curve S$_L$ for labor (or other factors of production) is usually upward-sloping, as in panel **a** of Figure 11.5, an indication that higher wages (or interest or rent) will call forth a greater quantity of labor (or capital or land). The total demand for any factor of production is the sum total of the demands of all the firms that want to employ the factor. The demand curve of each firm is that firm's MRP curve, as in panel **b**. (Notice that the horizontal scale of panel **b** is different from that of panel **a**.) As we saw back in Chapter 3's Figure 3.3, the market demand curve for goods is the result of the horizontal summation of individuals' demand curves in that market. In panel **c**, the market demand curve for a factor is also the horizontal summation of the MRP curves of all the separate firms that demand the factor. With factor demand, however, the horizontal summation must be adjusted because it is a little more complicated than it is in the market for a product. Consider what would happen if a decline in the price of a factor (say in the wage rate because of an increase in labor supply) caused *all* firms in the market to expand their hiring and therefore their output. We would expect the price of the product to decline. Thus in the formula MPP x P = MRP, the "P" for price of the product would fall, whereas the product price would not decline if just one firm too small to affect the market expanded its hiring and output. As a result, the demand curve for labor (D$_L$ in panel **c**) will be somewhat steeper than the ΣMRP$_L$ arrived at by horizontal summation.

In panel **c**, the intersection of the demand curve for labor (D$_L$=ΣMRP$_L$) and the supply curve for labor (S$_L$) at a level of $20 per hour determines what the wage rate will be in this occupation.

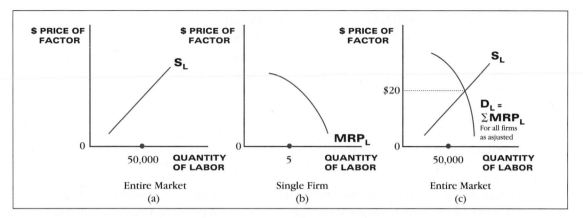

Figure 11.5. Determination of wages in the labor market. Panel **a** shows the supply curve for labor in the entire market. Panel **b** shows the MRP curve for labor for a single firm. This curve is the same as the firm's demand curve for labor. Panel **c** puts the market supply curve together with the summation of all the demand curves for labor of the individual firms. (The summed demand curves have to be adjusted, however, as explained in the text.) These two curves together show how wages are determined in the labor market as a whole.

Using the MRP of Labor to Find the Income of Labor and the Other Factors

The demand curve for labor ($D_L = \Sigma MRP_L$) can also be used to determine the income of the factors of production, including labor and the others as well. In Figure 11.6, the number of workers hired by a firm at wage W_L is Q_L. Multiplying the number of workers by the wage rate gives a rectangle labeled "wage income." This is the wage bill the firm pays to its workers. But the MRP_L curve tells us more than that. Hiring one additional worker adds to the firm's revenue an amount equal to the entire distance from the horizontal axis up to MRP_L. Part of this distance, from the horizontal axis to W_L, is paid as wages to the worker. The rest of the distance, from W_L up to MRP_L, is the revenue to the firm from the additional hire that was not paid out as wages. It must therefore be the income (interest, rent, and profit) that accrues to all other factors because of the employment of one more worker. What is true of one worker is true of all. So the income earned by all the factors of production other than labor utilized by the firm is represented by the area between W_L and MRP_L. The division of income shown in Figure 11.6 is about average for a U.S. firm, because wages constitute approximately three-quarters of all income.

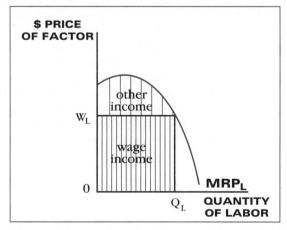

Figure 11.6. Finding the income of factors other than labor. An MRP curve for labor allows us to view the wages of labor together with the income earned by the other factors that work with the labor.

ADVANTAGES AND DISADVANTAGES OF PERFECT COMPETITION IN FACTOR MARKETS

The market mechanism that determines factor incomes is flexible, just as is the market mechanism for distributing products. Income is high or low as supply and demand dictate. In an area or an industry where the supply of a factor is abundant, or the demand for it is limited, its income will be low. The market will then give an incentive for that factor to move to an area or an industry where it will command higher income. This helps explain why so many immigrants came to the Americas in the late nineteenth and early twentieth centuries, why great numbers of blacks moved from the Deep South to northern cities, why Mexicans are flocking to the United States, why young people leave rural areas and inner cities, and why huge tracts of good farmland are being sold to developers.

Though the model predicts that, other things being equal, competition tends to move wages and other factor incomes toward the same level over a range of uses, often all things are not equal. For example, if auto mechanics earn $15 per hour while shoe workers earn $6 per hour for work that is approximately equivalent in terms of the skills and training required, we would expect that more people (including shoe workers) will seek jobs in auto repair shops, while fewer will seek jobs in shoe factories. What if, however, one job is far more pleasant than the other, or less risky? In that case a "compensating wage differential" sufficient to attract labor into the less pleasant or more risky job is likely to emerge. Moreover, special requirements of education, skill, or talent may limit entry into certain jobs. For example, retail clerks and computer programmers may be "noncompeting groups," just as janitors and surgeons do not compete with one another. For these reasons factor incomes may not move toward equality. (Other kinds of differences may arise in labor markets. For example, spouses may be willing to work at much lower-than-market wages, given their skills, if they are thereby able to continue living in the same household. In small college towns, often only one spouse is able to get a "professional" job at the college, while the other spouse must accept something in the local labor market that does not measure up to his or her training.)

The market mechanism for factor incomes also serves as a regulating device. Changes in supply and demand in factor markets cause factor incomes and quantities to move to new equilibria, thereby eliminating the shortages and surpluses that would otherwise develop just as they do in the markets for goods. Knowledge of supply and demand conditions in factor markets can yield penetrating insights. Economic historians posit that the main reason for the sharp wage increases that occurred in fourteenth-century Europe was that the bubonic plague reduced the labor supply. Geologists can understand why their discovery of an ore containing the element ytterbium (Yb, atomic number 70) has been ignored—ytterbium has no known uses in the production of anything, and although this element is by no means abundant, demand is *extremely* limited. Yet their other discovery, a mile away, of an yttrium deposit (Y, atomic number 39) has made them rich—yttrium is the key material in warm superconductors, invented in 1987. Supply is low but demand is high.[4] Telephone operators replaced by automated phone systems, Linotype operators whose jobs disappeared with computerized typesetting, steel makers whose product is being replaced by plastics, autoworkers facing foreign competition and automation—all have something in common. Demand for their labor is declining, and therefore so are their incomes. In short, the model of supply and demand in factor markets explains a great deal about factor incomes.

---

4.   Both elements were discovered, nearly a hundred years apart, in ore near the Swedish town of Ytterby. The scientist who discovered the superconductivity of yttrium deliberately concealed it "by misprinting it as ytterbium...in early drafts of a paper he knew would leak." *The Economist,* September 8, 1990.

Chapter 11 ■ Factor Productivity and Income

IS THE FACTOR MARKET FAIR?

Does the market mechanism distribute factor income fairly? Should economists be paid more than English teachers? Should Kevin Costner make several times more from one film than a manual laborer earns in a lifetime? Should Mike Tyson earn (as he once did earn) $21 million for two months' training and a 45-minute bout, while small-town pugilists battle for $100 in a club fight? Should Madonna make more from one release than a great symphony orchestra earns in a decade?

In a market system, rewards are high or low due to the interaction of supply and demand, not because of some abstract or philosophical concept of usefulness or fairness. Because the supply of certain types of labor (unskilled, undereducated) is high and the supply of other types of labor (basketball players who can perform like Shaquille O'Neal, singers who can pull in crowds like Michael Jackson) is extremely low, supply curves differ greatly. The demand for any type of labor is based on its productivity, which in turn depends on how much people are willing to pay for whatever it produces. If attendance rises 20% when a baseball team's best pitcher is on the mound, that pitcher has a high MRP—higher than that of other pitchers on the team—and should be able to negotiate a correspondingly higher salary. If Madonna brings in larger gate receipts than a famous symphony orchestra, then Madonna has a higher MRP than the orchestra and will earn more money.

In a market system, inequalities in the way income is distributed are unavoidable. We shall see in Chapter 13 how such inequalities are measured, and what can be done to deal compassionately with the poor and the underprivileged. Although the market system does well in directing factors into their most productive use, it does not rule out the emergence of an underclass of poorly educated and poorly motivated people. The social fabric is a delicate garment easily torn, and treating this problem is best seen not just as a civic or moral obligation, but involving a useful insurance policy against the possible disruption of society.

► MARKET IMPERFECTIONS AND FACTOR INCOME: MONOPOLY, MONOPSONY, AND "BILATERAL MONOPOLY"

So far in our discussion of income distribution, we have assumed that perfect competition prevails among both the producers of output and the suppliers of factors of production. Yet just as markets for goods and services are seldom perfectly competitive, so, too, the markets for factors may show evidence of power held by sellers of factors, or power held by buyers, with attendant inefficiencies and deadweight loss. We now look at four cases that involve imperfections in the market. Each alters to some degree the predictions of the basic model.

MONOPOLY IN THE PRODUCT MARKET

If the firm hiring labor or some other factor of production is a monopoly or an imperfect competitor of any other type, additional workers will be hired up to the point where the wage equals the marginal revenue product. Whether or not to hire an additional unit of labor or of any other factor will be determined by comparing the cost of that unit to its MRP. But we must adjust our method of computing the marginal revenue product of the factors hired by a monopoly seller. The reason is that a firm in a competitive market can always sell more of its output without affecting market price. A monopoly or other imperfect competitor, however, faces a downward-sloping demand curve for its output and it cannot increase sales without causing the price of the product to decline. The marginal *physical* product of different quantities of labor will be the same as it is under perfect competition because a monopolist and a perfect competitor both face the same technical relationships in obtaining physical output from factor inputs. But the marginal *revenue* product will be different.

Table 11.3 shows what would happen if 100 competitive firms similar to the one shown in Table 11.2 were to be combined in a monopoly. The data in columns 1 and 2 have therefore been multiplied by 100. Column 3 shows that when the monopoly tries to increase its output, the market price of its product falls.

TABLE 11.3
Productivity when the producer is a monopoly.

Units of Variable Factor (labor) Added to the Fixed Factors	Total Physical Product (TPP) Available for Sale	Selling Price of Product (P)	Total Revenue Product (TRP = TPP × P)	Marginal Revenue Product (MRP)*
0	0	$3.00	$0	
				$3,850
100	1,400	$2.75	$3,850	
				$3,400
200	2,900	$2.50	$7,250	
				$2,200
300	4,300	$2.25	$9,675	
				$925
400	5,300	$2.00	$10,600	
				-$625
500	5,700	$1.75	$9,975	

*Notice that this MRP is obtained from adding a group of 100 workers rather than 1. As individual workers are added between the intervals shown, small falls in MRP will occur.

When a monopolist hires more units of labor, or of any other factor of production, the marginal revenue product of the added input will reflect the increase in revenue gained from selling more output minus the loss in revenue caused by the fall in product price. Notice what happens when the monopoly decides to hire 400 workers instead of 300. The 300 workers produced 4,300 units which sold at $2.25 each, for a total revenue product (TRP) of $9,675. The 400 workers will produce 5,300 units. The 1000 additional units sold at the new lower price of $2.00 each would seem to add 1000 x $2.00 = $2,000 of marginal revenue product. However, the price has not only dropped to $2.00 on the extra 1,000 units, but also on the original 4,300 units. That means 4300 x 25¢ = $1,075 in revenue must be deducted from the $2,000 gained from selling the additional units. In short, the result of adding 100 new workers can be shown as:

Gain from selling 1000 new units @ $2.00 each	+$2,000
Loss from reducing price $0.25 on 4300 units	−$1,075
Net change in total revenue product (= MRP)	+$925

Hiring 400 workers instead of 300 would result in marginal revenue product of $925 (the amount by which TRP rose), which is less than it would have been had the price stayed the same.

Consequently, the monopolist's MRP curve has to be calculated differently from that of a perfect competitor. For the monopolist, the MRP of the last unit of labor hired is equal to the physical output that unit produced (MPP), times the price at which the output is sold, minus the loss occasioned by the lower price of *all* units of output sold.

There is a general rule for making this calculation. In the example just given, when we say that the sale of one more unit of output brings the firm $x we are saying that the *marginal revenue* (MR) derived from selling the additional unit was $x. This concept of marginal revenue allows us to construct a general formula:

$$MRP_{factor} = MPP_{factor} \times MR_{product}$$

The formula is general and does not depend on the degree of competition in product markets. It can be used for monopolies and perfect competitors alike. That is because, as we saw earlier, marginal revenue is the same as price under perfect competition. The MRP curve for a factor of production is the same as the demand curve for that factor under both imperfect competition and perfect competition. The difference is that the imperfect competitor's curve will move, shifting to the left in panel **c** of Figure 11.5. Other things being equal, MRP for an imperfect competitor is less than for a perfect competitor.[5]

In general, whether the hiring firm is a perfect competitor or a monopoly, the prediction is the same: The productivity of a factor, together with its supply, will determine the income earned by that factor. The price of the factor (say the wage of a particular type of worker) is determined in the market as a whole, as in panel **a** of Figure 11.7, whereas the quantity of the factor hired by an individual firm is found by comparing the price (wage) to the MRP curve of the factor, as in panel **b**. (Note that the horizontal axes of these two diagrams are drawn to different scales.)

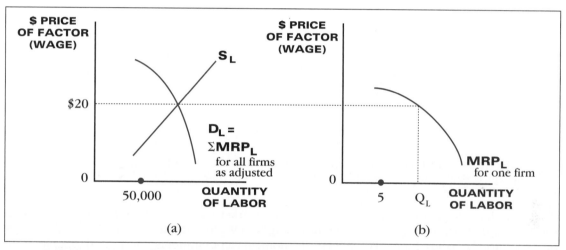

Figure 11.7. **MRP and wage determination.** When there is a monopoly in the product market, the price of the good produced declines as more is sold. The MRP of labor must therefore be adjusted accordingly. Otherwise the model is the same as when the firm hiring labor is a perfect competitor.

The only difference between the cases where the firm hiring labor is a monopoly seller rather than a perfect competitor is that the MRP of the labor hired by the monopoly must be calculated differently.

MONOPSONY IN THE FACTOR MARKET

It is possible for the sellers of the factors of production to suffer from ignorance of alternative opportunities, or from inability to transfer easily into other occupations or uses. Under these circumstances a condition called **monopsony** may arise. The Greek *monos opsonein* means single buyer; a monopsonistic firm is the only buyer of factors in a particular market. (When a small number of firms are the only buyers, the situation is known as *oligopsony*.) The presence of monopsony power will alter the predictions of the perfect-competition model.

Say there is just one employer of labor in an isolated community of northern Michigan—it may be one firm, or it may be an association of producers acting collusively. The workers in the community are loath to move, either because they have no information on job opportunities

---

5   Once more, however, all things may not be equal. We have seen in our discussions of monopoly and oligopoly that imperfect competitors may enjoy large scale economies that will counterbalance the fall in product prices as production increases. Conceivably, their labor may be especially productive, with a higher-than-ordinary MPP and thus a higher MRP, even though the price received by the firm declines with greater output.

elsewhere or because they are held back by tradition, inertia, or family ties. Perhaps they just like living in northern Michigan. Whatever the reason, the monopsonistic firm's demand curve for labor will be, like any other firm's, identical to its marginal revenue product curve. Its supply curve of labor, however, will not resemble that facing a firm in a competitive labor market. In a competitive market, the labor supply would be very large in relation to the firm's demand. Consequently, the firm would be able to hire any quantity of labor at the going wage rate, because the supply of labor in a perfectly competitive market is perfectly elastic—the supply curve is a horizontal line.

With no competition for the labor, however, the labor supply curve facing a monopsonistic firm is the supply curve for the entire market, as in Figure 11.8.

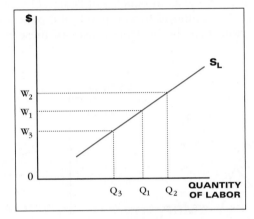

Figure 11.8. The supply curve of labor for a monopsony. A monopsony's labor supply curve slopes upward. Its decision to hire more labor will cause wages to rise, while a decision to hire less will cause wages to fall.

If the firm hires a quantity of labor Q_1, it pays the market wage W_1. Should it decide to hire a larger quantity of labor Q_2, it will have to raise wages to W_2 in order to attract additional workers (Q_1Q_2) into the labor force. These may be homemakers, students, or retired people from within the community, or newcomers attracted from outside the community. Conversely, if the monopsonistic firm decides to lay off some of its workers (Q_1Q_3), those unemployed workers— who still want to work, but who will not or cannot move out of the community—will cause the going wage to fall to W_3.

All this poses a cost problem for the monopsonist that wants to hire more workers. Unlike a competitive firm, to hire more labor a monopsonist must raise wages for the new workers and also for the workers it is already employing.[6] This means that the marginal cost of hiring more labor will be greater than the wage paid to the additional labor. For example, if the monopsonist is employing 1000 workers, and if it has to increase wages from $10 per hour to $12 in order to hire another 100 workers, the increase in labor costs is not just $12 x 100 = $1200, but ($12 x 100) + ($2 x 1000) = $3200. It must pay $2 more per hour to both the new workers and to the already employed workers.

Figure 11.9 indicates this by the position of the marginal cost of labor curve MC_L. That curve lies above the supply curve for labor S_L because it costs the firm more to hire an additional worker than the wage paid to that worker.[7]

---

6.   The monopsonist firm could attempt to operate a two-tier wage system, with the new workers paid more for the same job than the workers already employed, but such schemes generate hostility among the most experienced part of the labor force and have proved generally unpopular with both labor and management.

7   If these two curves are straight lines, the convenient geometric property we encountered with the marginal revenue and demand curves of a monopoly holds true here as well: The straight-line marginal cost curve will bisect the horizontal distance between the vertical axis and the supply curve. The same analysis would apply to other factors of production as well.

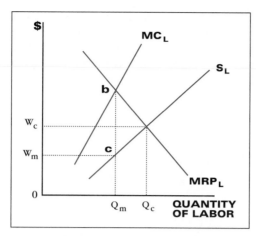

Figure 11.9. Equilibrium for a monopsony. A monopsony will hire labor up to the point where the marginal cost of an additional worker equals the marginal revenue product that worker will bring in. As seen, the wage paid is below labor's marginal revenue product.

The number of workers hired and the wage paid by a profit-maximizing monopsony (that is, the monopsony's equilibrium in its factor market for labor) will thus have to be looked at in a modified way. A monopsony's demand curve for labor, like that of any other firm, is the same as its marginal revenue product of labor curve, MRP_L in Figure 11.9. It will not pay the firm to hire an additional worker whose MRP_L is less than the cost of hiring that worker. This cost, however, is more than just the wage paid to that worker; it must also include the wage increases that have to be paid to everybody else. These two costs together comprise the marginal cost of labor (MC_L).

The monopsony will *not* achieve equilibrium where the wage equals MRP_L at W_c and Q_c, but instead at point **b** where the marginal cost of labor (MC_L) equals MRP_L. The quantity hired is Q_m. For each additional worker hired beyond Q_m, the marginal cost of hiring that worker (MC_L) would be greater than the marginal revenue product (MRP_L) each new worker would bring to the firm. Move a little to the right of Q_m along the quantity axis to see that this is so.

What wage will the monopsonistic firm have to pay in order to hire the quantity of labor Q_m? The supply curve of labor S_L gives this information. Quantity Q_m would require a wage of W_m and no more; that wage is less than MRP_L by the amount **bc**. (The term "exploitation," much used by the general public to describe wages that are low, is usually avoided by economists. But it can accurately be applied to this situation because wages are lower than justified by productivity. If the firm were not a monopsony, competitive pressures would oblige it to pay a wage equal to, not less than, the MRP of labor.)

It needs to be said that many examples of low pay, such as in restaurants, gas stations, convenience stores, and supermarkets, are almost always a sign of low productivity rather than a sign of monopsony power. Generally, low-wage workers have many alternatives for other low-wage work. The waiter can get a job at a 7–11 store, and it is hard to imagine employers colluding to rig wages in such jobs. Monopsony is a special case of market power that does not appear very often. One plausible case is hospitals' relations with nurses in communities where there is only one hospital at which the nurses can work. The hospital may have sufficient market power so that it can pay a wage lower than the nurses' MRP.

MONOPOLY IN THE FACTOR MARKET

The predictions of the perfect competition model will also not hold when the seller of factors has monopoly power in the factor market. Examples of a factor monopoly include: a strong labor union bargaining with competitive employers, a landowners' association negotiating rental contracts with tenant farmers, or a banking cartel that has rigged the loan market. Analytically, factor monopolies are akin to cases in product markets when a monopolist controls the output of a good. There is no need to duplicate that discussion, beyond a short review. In Figure 11.10, a strong union with monopoly power over labor has succeeded in unionizing a competitive labor market. (Under competitive conditions the wage level would be at W_c where the supply of labor S_L is equal to the demand for labor, which is the same as its MRP, or $S_L = D_L = MRP_L$. The quantity of labor employed is Q_c.)

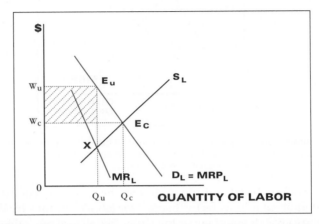

Figure 11.10. Monopoly in the labor market. If a monopoly seller of labor restricts the supply of labor, the effect is to raise wages and increase the total earnings of those who remain employed.

Figure 11.10 is identical to that for a product monopoly—for example, Chapter 7's Figure 7.7. From the union's point of view, every additional worker hired causes a decrease in the wages for all other workers, just as a product monopoly's decision to increase output causes a decrease in price on all units sold. Like the marginal revenue curve for the monopoly seller of goods that takes into account the need to lower price when more is produced, a marginal revenue curve (MR_L) for the monopoly seller of labor takes into account the need for lower wages if more workers are hired. The curve is located in accord with the usual rule—halfway between the vertical axis and the demand curve.

The union can maximize the total wages of its members by forcing wages up to W_u and allowing employment to fall to Q_u. The striped area represents the increase in total wages accruing to those union members who still have jobs. The workers who can no longer find employment in this industry (Q_uQ_c) must seek employment elsewhere. Their productivity in the unionized industry would have been higher than the cost of employing them; the demand curve for labor (MRP_L) is well above the supply curve (S_L). The output lost to society as a result of their exclusion equals the area of the triangle XE_uE_c. This area represents the allocative inefficiency or deadweight loss associated with a factor monopoly.

LABOR UNIONS MAY DIFFER FROM MONOPOLY PRODUCERS

A labor union may differ from a monopoly producer in one major respect. A reduction in employment caused by the higher wage rate might have little influence on the union if the industry is a growing one, because the reduction in employment will take the form of fewer new hires rather than layoffs among present union members. Also, if the union has a "last-in-first-out" contract, the most junior workers are always the first to be laid off, and the senior workers might agree to the job loss, knowing they will receive the higher wages and keep their jobs as well. Under these conditions, we cannot say exactly what wage rate a union might aim to achieve.

FACTOR MONOPOLY AND FACTOR MONOPSONY: THE CASE OF "BILATERAL MONOPOLY"

The term **bilateral monopoly** is shorthand for the situation in which a single seller of a factor (factor monopoly) and a single buyer of that same factor (factor monopsony) face each other—for example, when a powerful labor union that controls a specific type of labor bargains with a large corporation that is the only user of that type of labor. Economic theory does not allow us to determine what the outcome of the bargaining will be, but it does establish the range within which the outcome will lie. In Figure 11.9, where a monopsony firm is hiring in a competitive labor market, the wage will be W_m and the quantity of labor hired will be Q_m. If a monopoly union appears on the scene and manages to win the bargaining completely, it will seek a wage W_u and a quantity of employment Q_u as shown in Figure 11.10.

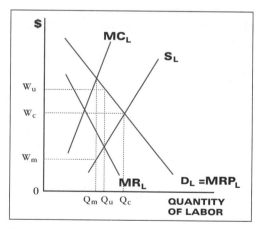

Figure 11.11. The case of "bilateral monopoly." When a monopoly seller of labor faces a monopsonistic employer, we cannot determine the resulting wage except to say that it will lie between the levels W_m and W_u.

In Figure 11.11 we superimpose the two cases. Notice that the wage sought by the monopoly union (W_u, with the associated level of employment Q_u) is higher than that sought by the monopsony firm (W_m, with employment level Q_m). Depending on the strength of the parties and their skill in negotiation, the bargained wage may be anywhere between the goals of the monopolist and the monopsonist. Under bilateral monopoly the wage and the quantity of labor hired are both indeterminate. (The mathematical theory of games, encountered in Chapter 8 when we discussed oligopoly, is a potentially useful tool for analyzing bargaining power under bilateral monopoly.)

The charge that union activity leads to a curtailment of employment and less efficiency in the use of resources, illustrated in Figure 11.10, may not hold when a union bargains against a monopsony. If the union can negotiate a fixed wage some distance above W_m in Figure 11.11, perhaps W_c, the monopsony firm would find that its marginal cost of hiring more workers was always that fixed wage W_c. (Once the union has negotiated a fixed wage, the supply curve for labor becomes a horizontal line and wages are equal to the marginal cost of labor.) It will then be willing to hire the larger quantity of workers Q_c, because at that level of employment the wage will be equal to MRP. The result of the union's bargaining would be more employment rather than less. Moreover, the rise in wages and the simultaneous creation of new jobs in the monopsony industry would reduce the size of the allocative efficiency or deadweight loss shown by triangle XE_uE_c in Figure 11.10. Minimum wage laws, which we criticized in Chapter 5 as causing unemployment to develop, will not do so in the presence of monopsony. If increased wages (say to W_c) are required by law, employment will rise (to Q_c) rather than fall. If wages are pushed beyond W_c, however, a decline in employment will again set in.

CONCLUSION

The income earned by a factor of production is determined by the factor's productivity and by its supply. Market forces working through supply and demand determine the prices of factors and thus their income just as they determine the prices of goods and services. In a market system, however, the distribution of income is likely to exhibit significant inequality. Some factors will be abundant in supply, but will be little demanded; others will be scarce and much wanted. A central lesson of the analysis is that nations wishing to raise their income must increase the productivity of their factors—that is, move the position of the MRP curves of their factors of production to the right.

The theory of how rewards are distributed among the factors of production is a general one, though in this chapter labor markets have provided most of the lessons. In the next chapter, we look at certain special cases of factor rewards—wages in the presence of labor unions and comparable-worth laws, along with rent, interest, and profit, all of which deserve enhanced treatment.

SUMMARY

1) The marginal physical product (MPP) of a factor is the extra physical output obtained from employing another unit of that factor, while the marginal revenue product (MRP) of a factor is the extra revenue a firm earns from employing another unit of that factor.

2) The least-cost combination of the factors of production requires that the last dollar spent on each of the factors brings the same amount of additional output (MPP).

3) The demand for a factor of production is a derived demand; the demand curve is the same as the curve for the marginal revenue product of that factor. Marginal revenue product is found by multiplying the factor's marginal physical productivity by the price of the product. A profit-maximizing competitive firm will hire factors up to the point where MRP = price.

4) Wages determined by supply and MRP do not reflect any abstract concept of fairness. They differ substantially in the same activity when one individual's MRP is much greater than another's.

5) When factor markets involve monopsony (a single buyer), monopoly (a single seller), or bilateral monopoly (a single buyer facing a single seller), the diagramming must be altered to reflect these conditions. Monopsonies pay their factors less than their marginal revenue product; factor monopolies restrict the sale of factors under their control; while the outcome of bilateral monopoly is indeterminate.

Chapter Key Words

Bilateral monopoly: A situation in which a monopoly seller of factors faces a monopsony buyer of factors. Illustrated by a large labor union bargaining against a big corporation. Actual wage is indeterminate in the case of bilateral monopoly, and will depend on the bargaining power of the two contestants.

Derived demand: The demand for a factor of production wanted not in its own right but because it will contribute to the production of goods that can be sold.

Monopsony: A single buyer of factors of production. Monopsony can result in lower earnings for the factors of production employed, and a smaller quantity hired.

Marginal physical product (MPP): A measure of how much extra physical output (bushels, tons, etc.) will be produced by an additional unit of a given factor of production in combination with a fixed quantity of other factors.

Marginal revenue product (MRP): A measure of the extra revenue brought to a firm by hiring another unit of a given factor in combination with a fixed quantity of other factors.

Chapter Questions

1) New Sharon Tractor Repair is a small firm in Iowa. Assuming no new tools or garage space are added, the following table gives the number of mechanics needed to repair various quantities of tractors:

Mechanics	Tractors Repaired
0	0
1	2
2	5
3	7
4	8
5	8

What is the marginal physical product of each mechanic? Draw the MPP curve.

2) Suppose a small factory is a perfect competitor in the factor market. The price of capital is $100, and the MPP of capital is 1000 units of output. Labor costs $80 per day, and its MPP is also 1000 units. Should the factory's manger hire more labor and sell some capital, lay off some labor and add capital, or do nothing?

3) Use the data from question 1 to answer this question. Suppose that New Sharon Tractor Repair charges $50 for each repair of a tractor. What is the marginal revenue product of each mechanic? Draw the MRP curve. How would this curve shift if the mechanics suddenly became more productive? How would it shift if the price of tractor repairs rose?

4) The MRP curve found in question 3 is an individual firm's demand curve for labor. If there are many such firms that make up the market, explain how the slope of the market demand curve differs from the slope of the individual firm's demand curve.

5) Ships' pilots are people who specialize in steering ships into ports they know well. They work with other factors of production such as navigation equipment, deck hands, lighthouses, and so on. At the port of Savannah, Georgia, there are 10 pilots who earn an equilibrium wage of $40,000 per year. The demand curve for pilots is a straight line that intercepts the y-axis at the wage of $100,000. What is the total income of the pilots? What is the total income of the other factors that help guide ships into Savannah's port? (It will help you to remember that the area of a triangle is one half the length of the base times the height.)

6) In 1955 there was a 10% increase in the wages of telephone assemblers. At that time, all phones were produced by the AT&T monopoly. In 1989 there was again a 10% increase in the wages of telephone assemblers. By then, antitrust proceedings had forced AT&T to become a nearly perfect competitor in phone production. In response to both wage increases, AT&T moved up and left along its MRP curve, laying off some workers. All other things being equal, were more workers laid off (on a percentage basis) when AT&T was a monopoly or when it was a nearly perfect competitor?

7) You are the manager of Southern Electric, a producer of electronic components. Your company has two plants. At the Charlotte, North Carolina plant, you are a perfect competitor in the labor market (that is, you face a flat labor supply curve). At your Baxley, Georgia plant, you have a labor market monopsony. It so happens that your MRP curves are the same at both plants. Furthermore, the market equilibrium wage happens to be W_C in Charlotte and also would have been W_C in Baxley if a free labor market had existed in that town. Draw diagrams of both labor markets. In which plant do you employ fewer workers? In which plant do you pay lower wages? Why?

8) You are a union organizer in the mushroom farming industry. The labor supply curve of mushroom farm workers is approximately a 45° line. Mushroom farms are small and use a great deal of labor, so MRP falls quickly as labor is added. Thus the straight-line labor demand curve is very steep. Wages are low, and your union would like to raise them to the income-maximizing level. Show the quantity of labor currently employed and the quantity employed when income is maximized. Can you explain why the mushroom workers will be difficult to organize if you tell them you plan to maximize income?

9) Classic examples of labor market monopsony could be found in early twentieth-century coal mining towns in West Virginia. In these towns, the company ran every business, and labor conditions were deplorable. After sometimes bloody struggles with the mine owners, the miners organized strong unions. Show on a diagram the miners' wages before unionization. What is the highest wage the unions might have obtained by bargaining with the owners? Where did the wage actually end up?

Wages, Rent, Interest, and Profit

OVERALL OBJECTIVE: To introduce modifications to the analysis of factor incomes covering the cases of wages when unions and comparable-worth laws are present, and the incomes to the other factors in the form of rent, interest, and profit.

MORE SPECIFICALLY:

- To assess how labor unions attempt to raise wages by increasing the demand for labor, decreasing its supply, or establishing a negotiated wage above the market equilibrium; and to discuss the institutional framework that labor law provides for labor unions.
- To examine comparable-worth laws.
- To show that rent is the return to any factor of production greater than needed to supply it.
- To explain how rents can be capitalized into the purchase price of an asset by means of the formula for net present value.
- To discuss the concept of interest, showing how the word interest is used to describe both the price of loans and the return to capital, and how these two concepts are related.
- To assess the role of profit as the return to entrepreneurship, the reward for initiation, innovation, and risk taking.

In Chapter 11 we developed a general model of how rewards to factors of production are determined. That model applies to *all* factors of production. But some forms of reward to the factors possess special attributes that require economists to enlarge and modify their treatment. The task of this chapter is to consider wages when unions are present or comparable-worth laws have been passed, and then to examine incomes in the form of rent, interest, and profit.

▶ LABOR UNIONS

Labor markets and the wages paid in these markets can be significantly affected by the presence of labor unions. Labor unions first arose in the United States early in the nineteenth century. They were local and small-scale, however, not surprising in a country that was still basically agricultural. The first national union, the Knights of Labor, was prominent in the 1880s. Though it ultimately collapsed, it was the pioneer industrial union, the type that attempts to organize all workers, skilled or unskilled, under the same umbrella. That is the practice followed today by the unions that make up the CIO (Congress of Industrial Organization), which was founded in 1935. Meanwhile, another type of union was emerging in the 1880s. This was the craft union, in which membership is limited to practitioners of a particular trade—plumbers, electricians, painters, locomotive engineers. A number of craft unions united in 1886 as the AFL (American Federation of Labor). Though the AFL and the CIO merged in 1955, the distinction between craft unions and industrial unions survives.

Significant changes in the status of labor unions took place soon after the turn of the century. A section of the Clayton Act of 1914 that is still in force declared that labor is not a commodity or an article of commerce, and therefore that unions cannot be prosecuted as monopolies in restraint of trade. (In the Danbury, Connecticut, Hatters Strike of 1902, the Sherman Antitrust Act had been used against the strikers. The Clayton Act made this impossible.)

Other major steps were taken in the 1930s. The passage of the Norris-La Guardia Act of 1932 restricted the use of court injunctions as a weapon against strikes. **The Wagner Act** of 1935 went further. It outlawed so-called yellow-dog contracts, the agreements whereby workers could be fired for joining a union. It also prohibited the use of threats, force, and other sorts of influence by companies against unions. The Wagner Act also made illegal the hiring of replacement workers in a strike involving employer practices.[1] In its most important provisions, still in effect, the Wagner Act required management to bargain in good faith with unions, and guaranteed that a union could become sole bargaining agent by majority vote of the workers in a plant. Elections are supervised by the National Labor Relations Board (NLRB), which can issue cease-and-desist orders to stop unfair election practices and which polices the observance of this and other labor acts.

Congress, convinced that the law had tilted too far toward the unions, passed the **Taft-Hartley Act** of 1947 over President Truman's veto. This act, described in the accompanying box, is still central to labor law. The unions were strongly opposed to this legislation, though later they came to live rather comfortably with it.

The most recent labor laws of importance were the Landrum-Griffen Act of 1959, aimed at racketeering and corruption in labor unions, and certain legal modifications in the 1960s that permitted unions to expand in the public sector. No significant changes have occurred since that time.

---

1.   Replacement workers *can* be hired, however, when a strike is limited to economic issues, and in *Belknap v. Hale,* 1983, the Supreme Court held that they do not have to be bumped by strikers who return to work. The 1980s saw more use of replacement workers by management, and more union bitterness on the issue.

THE TAFT-HARTLEY ACT

The Taft-Hartley Act has three main provisions.

1. It bans the **closed shop**, in which only union members can be hired. Unless state law is more restrictive, it permits the **union shop** in which workers are required to join the union shortly after being hired. Finally, it authorizes states to pass **right-to-work** laws permitting the **open shop**, under which workers do not have to join a union to obtain or keep a job. Presently, 20 states have right-to-work laws, most of them in the south. The last state to pass such a law was Wyoming in 1968.

2. Taft-Hartley requires that a union must give 60 days' notice before going out on strike. If the President declares a state of emergency, he can order a further 80-day "cooling-off period" during which a strike is illegal. At the end of the 80 days, union members must vote by secret ballot to approve the strike. Use of the cooling-off period has been fairly successful. It was imposed on average once a year during the first 32 years after its authorization, and only about a quarter of the strikes failed to be settled during the 80-day period. About half of these were settled within a few days thereafter.

3. Taft-Hartley makes several labor practices illegal. Among these "unfair labor practices" are the following: compelling workers to join unions; calling a strike because of a jurisdictional dispute over which union will represent the workers; **featherbedding**, defined as payment for work not performed; charging excessively high dues to restrict union membership; and waging secondary boycotts in which a union forces an employer to boycott the products of another firm that is involved in a labor dispute.[2]

UNION STRATEGIES FOR RAISING WAGES

Labor unions use three main strategies in their efforts to raise wages: increasing the demand for labor, decreasing the supply of labor, and interfering with the market mechanism by means of a negotiated wage above the market equilibrium.

1) *Increasing the demand for labor.* As Figure 12.1 shows, if a union can somehow engineer an increase in the demand for labor from D_1 to D_2, market forces will cause wages to rise from W_c to W_u. The demand for labor depends on the productivity of labor (MPP_L) and on the price at which the output produced by labor is sold. If the union can increase either of these, the demand for labor will grow and wages will rise.

To increase labor productivity, unions can urge members to work harder, and they can encourage and assist employers to establish training and attitude programs. Such strategies work best when union members have a strong motive to comply—in wartime, for example, or during some other national emergency, or when their employer is threatened by new competition, foreign or domestic. Unions can also support the enactment of tariffs, quotas, or other restraints on foreign trade, as they did in the 1980s in an effort to reduce the number of cars imported from Japan. By stimulating sales of

---

2.   Unlike secondary boycotts, direct product boycotts by union members are legal. This tactic involves "informational picketing" and public relations campaigns to persuade consumers of a product to refrain from buying it. California grapes were a well-known example. Labor activist Cesar Chavez received substantial support from consumers, including many union members, in a dispute concerning the wages of agricultural workers.

their employer's product, they boost the demand for their labor. Unions can also sponsor advertising campaigns to persuade the public to "look for the union label," as with women's clothing. If people do so, the demand for the product is correspondingly increased and the demand for labor rises.

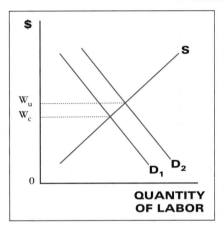

Figure 12.1. Increasing the demand for labor. A union can cause the wages paid to its members to rise if it can achieve an increased demand for labor.

Finally, unions can devise featherbedding arrangements, not the sort illegal in the United States under Taft-Hartley where *no* work is done, but by contriving work rules that artificially stimulate the need for workers. For example, they might require railroads to hire a fireman on their engine crews, even though locomotives have had no fireboxes to attend in about 40 years; they might require airlines to hire a third crew member on the flight deck when only two are needed; they might force newspapers to hire manual type-setters even when type is being set by computer; or theaters to hire live musicians even when recorded music is played. Some unions set quota limits on production, as when house painters are forbidden to use brushes that exceed a certain width or to use rollers—rules that were judged legal by the Supreme Court in 1969.

Unions defend such practices by claiming that they contribute to safety, health, or high-quality work. The truth is not always easy to spot amid the competing claims of unions and employers, though higher prices resulting from unnecessary labor costs are sometimes obvious to the consuming public.

2) *Decreasing the supply of labor.* As Figure 12.2 shows, if a union can somehow shift the supply curve for labor from S_1 to S_2, market forces will cause wages to rise from W_c to W_u. Unions try to accomplish this by urging the government to impose restrictions on labor supply or by imposing certain rules and regulations of their own.

For example, unions have frequently lobbied the government to pass strict immigration laws that will limit the number of foreigners entering the country. There is indeed evidence that immigration during the 1980s adversely affected the earnings of U.S. blue-collar workers by increasing the supply of such workers, so cutting that supply is an understandable tactic. Unions have been enthusiastic supporters of child labor laws and compulsory retirement schemes. (In the United States, many states at the turn of the century passed laws limiting *women's* work, and perhaps this, too, was partly a ploy to increase demand for male labor.) They have endorsed moves toward a shorter work week and supported limitations on the number of hours truck drivers can spend in the cab or airline pilots in the cockpit. They succeeded in persuading Congress to pass the Davis-Bacon Act, a 1933 law still in effect that requires the pay for labor on federal construction projects to equal the highest wage being paid in a given area, rather than the average wage. They have warmly supported successful moves to require state licensing of plumbers, electricians, cab drivers, and other service workers.[3]

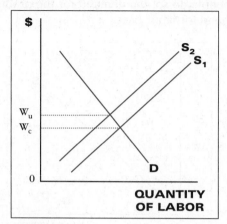

Figure 12.2. Decreasing the supply of labor. A union can raise the wages paid to its members if it is able to decrease the supply of labor.

Many of the government regulations we have mentioned may be socially useful, and the consequences of *not* having such regulations might, in some cases, be severe. Yet they also serve the economic self-interest of the unions involved. Their usefulness must be weighed against the higher costs they impose on the public.

Craft unions have strategies of their own for reducing the supply of labor. For example, unions of painters, plumbers, and printers may restrict membership by means of stiff entrance requirements, high initiation fees and annual dues, quotas on new members, exclusive aptitude and intelligence examinations, and long apprenticeships. (Prejudice against minority groups, though illegal, sometimes serves the same purpose.) The higher wages that result from the reduction in labor supply may make this "exclusive unionism" very attractive to those who meet the requirements.

Such strategies are effective, however, only if the demand for labor is sufficiently inelastic. In Figure 12.3, when demand is elastic, as with curve D_e, reducing the labor supply from S_1 to S_2 will merely cause a decrease in the employment of union members, with very little gain in hourly wages (which rise only from W_c to W_e). Here the union has succeeded in undercutting itself. Total earnings of union members fall from $0W_cE_cQ_c$ to $0W_eE_eQ_e$. When demand is inelastic, however, as with curve D_i, hourly wages rise significantly (from W_c to W_i), and total earnings of union members increase to $0W_iE_iQ_i$. In practice, unions have clearly had the greatest effect on wages where the demand for a type of labor is inelastic.

3.   Professionals, even when not unionized, often use similar tactics to reduce the labor supply. For example, doctors and dentists try to ensure that licensed medical and dental schools do not increase the number of applicants they accept and that few new schools open up. Lawyers support the requirement of a rigorous bar exam that must be passed as a condition for practicing. Even barbers and beauticians must be licensed in most states. To obtain a license they may have to demonstrate that they can locate the sphenoid bone and do finger waves, to satisfy some dubious argument having to do with public safety or some other public interest.

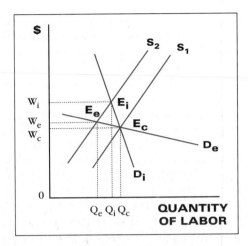

Figure 12.3. **The effects of elastic and inelastic demand on wages and the employment of union members.** If the demand for labor is inelastic, union efforts to raise wages are more likely to succeed, and the amount of labor hired will not fall off sharply. Conversely, if the demand for labor is elastic, union efforts to raise wages are likely to have less success and result in a considerable drop in employment.

3) *Establishing a negotiated wage above the market equilibrium.* Industrial unions of the CIO type, which have both semiskilled and skilled workers as members, find it difficult to influence labor supply by restricting membership because there is no good way to exclude new applicants. So instead of trying to shift the supply curve of labor, they may attempt to negotiate an agreement for a fixed wage above the equilibrium wage. In Figure 12.4 the equilibrium wage under competitive conditions would be W_c. If a union managed to negotiate a fixed wage of W_u, then union members who kept their jobs would receive that higher wage, but the firm would cut the number of workers employed to Q_u. Distance Q_uQ_c represents the number of workers who lose their jobs.

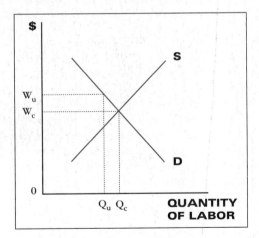

Figure 12.4. **A "negotiated minimum wage" above equilibrium.** A union might choose to negotiate an above-equilibrium wage with an employer, knowing that the members who have a job will benefit but that the number of jobs available will fall.

The more inelastic the demand curve, the fewer the number of jobs that will be lost as a result of the above-equilibrium wage. The firm will not cut employment drastically if it is difficult to substitute machines for workers, or if labor is only a small part of production costs, or if the higher labor cost can easily be passed on to consumers by way of price hikes on the product sold.

Even when the ultimate reduction in employment threatens to be substantial, the union may still fight for the wage increase. The union knows that most firms, eager to maintain good public relations, are reluctant to lay off large numbers of workers all at once. Instead, they prefer to reduce their labor force slowly through attrition, not replacing workers who retire or change jobs. So, at least temporarily, employment may remain higher than is indicated by the firm's demand curve for labor.

The United Mine Workers took just that course. That union succeeded in winning much higher wages, but in the process it brought about a sharp reduction in the number of jobs in the coal industry. Wages had been low for many years, but a momentous agreement reached in 1950 raised them substantially. Today they are about 25% above the national average wage in manufacturing. The high wages prompted mine owners to substitute machines for workers, and output per miner tripled over the two decades. The number of jobs, however, fell by almost half in the five years after the agreement. (With the increase in the demand for coal in the OPEC era, the number of miners rose again, but to a figure still very much lower than it had been in 1950 even though all-time production records were set successively in 1987, 1988, 1989, and 1990.)

THE EFFECTS OF UNIONS ON EMPLOYMENT AND WAGES

As just discussed, the negotiation of an above-equilibrium wage by a union generally leads to a decline in the number of jobs available. Under certain circumstances, however, this may not happen.

If the industry is a monopsony or an oligopsony that has not been paying wages equal to the workers' full marginal revenue product, the union may actually be able to increase employment. As seen in the preceding chapter, it could do so by using its bargaining strength against the monopsony to establish a wage floor.

If the MRP curve—the demand for labor—is shifted upward by a rise in the productivity of labor or by a higher market price received by the employing firm from the sale of its output, employment will not necessarily decline. The very existence of the union and the wage advantages it brings may boost worker morale enough to increase productivity. Workers in unionized firms tend to quit less often, which means that essential skills are retained longer and on-the-job learning is enhanced. Better labor-management communication, greater cooperation, and fewer disputes may also result from unionization.[4] Moreover, if the economy is strong, so that the demand for the product rises, or if the firm has enough market power to pass on a wage increase in the form of higher prices, the selling price for output may rise. Wage increases (and antilayoff clauses) are much more easily negotiated in a booming economy and when the firm commands some measure of monopoly power. A firm with monopoly power usually has some profits (rents) that it can use as it sees fit, and labor and management can bargain over who will receive them. In the extreme case a wage increase will not require a change in the firm's output, or in the price that it charges, or in the number of workers that are hired—the only difference will be the division of the profits.

---

4.   Evidence that in some circumstances these conclusions are correct is provided by Richard Freeman and James Medoff, *What Do Unions Do?* New York, 1984. It should be noted, however, that if these benefits are real, employers would presumably welcome the formation of unions—which traditionally they do not. In fact, share prices of firms going through unionization typically *fall* a little rather than rising. Barry Hirsch cites corroborating evidence in his book *The Economic Analysis of Unions,* Boston, 1986, that unionization lowers firms' profits to some degree, and also cuts into their reinvestment and R&D activity.

It is difficult to determine the effect unions have on wages. Changes in the supply and demand for labor may be occurring for reasons not connected with unionization, and these are not easily isolated. Another problem is that the wages for some jobs were already high before unionization took place. Nonetheless, the gap between the pay of unionized workers and the lower pay of the nonunionized is substantial, near the historic high reached at the beginning of the 1980s. According to the U.S. Bureau of Labor Statistics, the median earnings of union members in 1992 were 32% greater than the earnings of nonmembers.

The effect of union/management wage bargains on workers in firms and industries that are *not* unionized is debatable. Hypothetically, unionization might cause a decline in the wages of nonunionized workers because workers excluded from the unionized sector would have to seek jobs elsewhere. Alternatively, nonunionized firms might pay wages higher than they otherwise would in order to keep unions out. Both results are often reported, but the empirical evidence is limited. All told, the first of the two possibilities is probably the more likely one.

THE RECENT DECLINE IN UNION MEMBERSHIP

During the 1980s and 1990s, union membership in the United States declined sharply in response to a combination of influences. Serious recessions hit the country in the early '80s and early '90s; the economy was shifting toward service industries where unions are less strong; foreign competition was intensifying in many sectors; attitudes toward regimentation seemed to be shifting, with workers apparently believing that union membership was less desirable; and employers were increasingly inclined to resist unionization. The percentage of the labor force belonging to unions was down to 16% in 1992, compared to 24% in 1977 and a high of about 35% in the mid-1940s and mid-1950s.[5] In the private, nonagricultural sector, union membership has fallen even lower, to only 11.5% of the labor force in 1992, well down from the 22% of 1977. Only in the public sector have unions been showing strength. Government workers were 37% unionized in 1992, an increase on the 33% of 1977, and they now make up 41% of all union members, compared to only 26% in 1977.[6]

EXPERIENCE DIFFERS WIDELY AMONG COUNTRIES

It is fair to say that the economic, social, and political effects of unions have been very different among countries. Experience ranges from strongly disruptive to quite positive, as exemplified by the cases of Britain and Japan explored in the box.

A comparison of union activity in the United States, Britain, and Japan suggests that the structure of labor unions may have substantial economic implications. When union bargaining is at the level of the firm (common in the United States), unions will probably have relatively little ability to affect national wage levels. One firm alone cannot easily raise its prices, so unions will have difficulties in negotiating higher wages as well. When bargaining is at the national level (Germany, and effectively Japan where the company unions all bargain with their employers at the same time of the year), unions often behave rather responsibly because they know that irresponsibility on their part may trigger an inflation. Furthermore, national unions may face national organizations of employers. When bargaining is at the industry level (as in Britain), a problem may ensue. Unions might then have the power to affect wages, but may not accept the responsibility for the resulting inflation.

---

5.   The overall figure for union membership in Great Britain has been as high as 50+%, and it has reached over 90% in Scandinavia.

6.   Strikes by public employees—the armed forces, police, firemen, sanitation workers, water departments, air traffic controllers—often present grave problems of safety and public health, and are generally illegal. Sometimes they occur anyway, presenting the government with a dilemma. President Reagan ordered the replacement of all the striking air traffic controllers when their union, PATCO, called a walkout early in his administration. Chaos at airports was only narrowly avoided.

BRITISH AND JAPANESE UNIONS: TWO ENDS OF A SPECTRUM

The British Experience

The British experience with labor unions has been considerably more disruptive than the experience of the United States. A crippling general strike—a strike by many unions in many industries—took place in 1926 and left bitter memories that lasted for a generation. (No general strike has ever occurred in the United States.) Unions helped found the British Labour Party, and its influence was reflected in a succession of permissive labor laws passed by Parliament over the years. These laws were much more tolerant of militant union behavior than was legislation in the United States.

Collective bargaining agreements, for example, were for decades not enforceable under British law. Thus, if a union broke a labor contract with a firm, the firm could not sue for damages. Wildcat strikes, unannounced and unforeseeable, became common. Because unions were not liable for the unlawful actions of their members, rowdy behavior and property damage often went unchecked by the union leadership. Secondary boycotts were legal, which meant that a strike might spread quickly as a union's allies joined in support. The closed shop was legal, so in many firms workers could not be employed at all unless they were union members. Union leaders, who were often quite radical, did not have to stand for election. Finally, the government was unable to prevent strikes against itself in key nationalized sectors, and so the country suffered through frequent electricity strikes, coal strikes, and strikes by the garbage collectors. The government almost always caved in to the workers' demands, thus setting a precedent for the future.

Margaret Thatcher's election in 1979 together with large Conservative Party majorities throughout the 1980s, led to a sweeping reform of the labor laws. Secondary boycotts were made illegal in 1980, and in 1984 Parliament required that strikes had to be approved by secret ballot. Union leaders now have to be elected every five years. Although by U.S. standards British law is still lenient toward unions, the number of strikes there has declined dramatically. The 1990 walkout total was the lowest in 55 years, and less than 25% of the annual average in the 1970s. Union membership has dropped by about one-fifth. Though not broken, the once-powerful British unions have been somewhat tamed.

Japanese Labor Unions

Japanese labor unions exhibit considerable cooperation with employers and flexibility in their response to economic change. Because unions in Japan are not organized around crafts or occupations, but instead around the company, they rarely become embroiled in jurisdictional disputes. Job security is not viewed as lifetime tenure in the same activity, as is true in Britain. Instead, it is more a guarantee of employment, though not necessarily in the same occupation or even in the same industry. Consequently, workers are more willing to shift from plant to plant and from one job to another. Such mobility is made easier because large Japanese firms provide privately financed retraining, in keeping with the Japanese tradition of "lifetime employment." Most firms maintain union-management consultation committees that share information and foster cooperation between workers and managers. The good labor-management relations that prevail in Japan seem to be present as well in most Japanese-owned companies in the United States.

THE FUTURE FOR STRIKES

The economic rationality of a union's major weapon—the strike—is open to question. Of course, many strikes have very little effect on the public. But others may have a very serious impact. The direct cost of a walkout in a key industry—say trucking, railroads, airlines, or electricity—may be far exceeded by the social cost incurred by businesses and consumers not involved in the strike. Throughout the economy schedules are disrupted, plants are shut down, workers are laid off, and, in extreme cases, public inconvenience becomes public danger. The amount a major union gains by winning a strike or forgoes by losing one may be small in comparison to the losses suffered in the economy at large. Even local strikes with little impact on consumers tend to poison social relations within a community, especially if the firm that is struck hires replacement workers and keeps operating.

Some observers have proposed that nationally important strikes be settled by compulsory arbitration involving a neutral third party. The arbitrator would then impose a solution, usually by selecting one of the two final proposals made by the contending parties. The U.S. Congress imposed this sort of arbitration in the national railroad strike of 1992, and the "winner-take-all" principle also finds current use in major league baseball for settling salary disputes between individual players and management.

Arbitration could also be required for strikes of lesser magnitude after some time has passed, perhaps seven days. Opponents of the idea argue that unless a union is free to call a strike, no one can judge what settlement might have been reached through collective bargaining. Arbitration, insist the critics, substitutes a solution by a fallible human for a market solution. This argument is correct to a point, but most strikes of national importance usually pit big unions against big corporations or against the government, so a market solution would not occur in any case. Opponents also claim that compulsory arbitration would lead to bitterness and hostility. That has not been true of Switzerland, however, where arbitration has virtually eliminated strikes. It is doubtful in any case that the bitterness and hostility caused by compulsory arbitration would be any greater than that caused by a walkout. Given the vast potential for social cost involved in strikes, it is surprising that compulsory arbitration has not attracted more public support.

► COMPARABLE WORTH

One other unusual feature of labor markets, the recent development of a wage policy known as comparable worth, deserves careful attention. Comparable-worth legislation arises from the view that for many women, labor markets do not work in an acceptable way. The belief that labor markets are failing is based on the fact that, traditionally, the average hourly earnings of women in the United States have been only two-thirds that of men. (Though by 1992 the average had risen to 75%, and the pay of never-married women is quite close to that of men. Marriage and children obviously constrain women's earnings.)

Paying women less than men for doing the same job was made illegal by Title VII of the U.S. Civil Rights Act of 1964—and cases are brought frequently under that law. But advocates of a comparable-worth policy go further. They seek equal pay for jobs that require equivalent skills, that call for equivalent risk or effort, and that involve equivalent responsibilities. They argue that certain occupations have for many years been carried on almost exclusively by women, and that wages in those occupations are lower than the wages in occupations dominated by males even though the requirements of education and skills are essentially the same. (For example, in recent years women have made up 94% of all nurses, 98% of kindergarten and nursery school teachers, and 99% of secretaries.)

Judgments on what constitutes comparable worth have to be made by a board or a panel set up under government auspices. Involving the government in pricing policy is a controversial issue, however, and the movement for comparable-worth policy has met with strong opposition.

OBJECTIONS TO A COMPARABLE-WORTH POLICY

Opponents of comparable worth insist that a job is worth only what employers are willing to pay to have it done. They argue that wages are determined by supply and demand, and that comparable worth fails to take into account the different levels of demand for various types of labor. They use the same logic that is customarily advanced by opponents of any kind of minimum wage: A minimum wage set at or below the equilibrium wage will have no economic effect, and a minimum wage set above equilibrium will reduce the quantity of labor demanded. They argue that comparable-worth policy would amount to a selective minimum wage covering only the occupations treated by the government agency that determines comparable worth.

Furthermore, they say, the fact that a lower wage is being paid for job A than is being paid for job B may not reflect a labor market failure at all. Job A may be less physically demanding, or may involve a safer working environment, or may offer greater flexibility in working hours. To the extent that women prefer these conditions, it is reasonable to expect that they will be drawn to that job, and that the abundant supply of labor there will keep wages low. In occupations where these conditions do not prevail, the wage gap will tend to disappear. In this view, lower wages reflect a market failure only when the barriers that keep women from transferring to other occupations are not self-imposed. Opponents conclude that the attempt to peg wages to some artificial measure of comparable worth will destroy the economic incentives for women working in these jobs to move on to other employment where supply and demand conditions result in higher wages.

The Rebuttal

In rebuttal, supporters of comparable-worth policy claim that the lower wages prevailing in female-dominated occupations are often due to monopsony behavior—hospitals deciding on wage scales for nurses, for example—and that a comparable-worth policy would increase efficiency and would at the same time correct inequity. They also note that wage scales sometimes reflect institutional attitudes not closely related to labor productivity. The wages paid to middle-level managers in large corporations, for example, or to government employees, may bear little comparison to comparable employment elsewhere in the economy. In such cases, say the supporters, the market may be failing to work, and comparable-worth policy may be the way to eliminate it.

In any case, the controversy continues. On the federal level, the U.S. Civil Rights Commission, in a report dated April 11, 1985, rejected the policy of comparable worth, and there the matter rests, at least for the moment. On the state level, some form of comparable-worth legislation has been adopted by California, Iowa, Minnesota, Montana, and Washington, and is being considered by many other states as well. Forty-eight of the 50 states and more than 1,000 local governments are making or have already made adjustments to raise wages in jobs that have traditionally been regarded as women's jobs. Minnesota has already raised the wages in such occupations by an average of $2,200. So far, these laws have required adjustment only in wages paid by government, and not by the much larger private sector (although there are indirect effects beyond the public sector, because employers may voluntarily alter wage scales).

Perhaps the most comprehensive comparable-worth law now in effect is that of the Canadian province of Ontario, which also includes the private sector. Under Ontario's equal-pay-for-equal-work provisions, firms employing over 500 workers had to file plans for achieving this goal by January 1, 1990. By 1994, all firms employing over 10 workers are to have filed plans. Most of the firms are setting point totals for skills, effort, working conditions, and responsibility, and many of them have already adjusted wages accordingly. The Ontario experiment is being watched closely by economists and policymakers.

THE WASHINGTON AND MINNESOTA PLANS

State government in Washington classifies its jobs by point totals. The points are awarded in four categories: knowledge and skills required, mental demands made by the work, accountability and need for decision making, and the difficulty and unpleasantness of working conditions. The occupation of registered nurse is ranked at 573 points, compared to 197 for an electrician and 97 for a truck driver. Such methods take into account some, but not all, of the determinants of labor supply and do not take into account at all the demand for labor.

The award of points in job-evaluation studies has been widely emulated by many state and local governments. In Minnesota, consultants evaluate exactly what a job entails, in some cases with a set of up to a thousand questions, and then assign points. The Minnesota system has been criticized for a high degree of politicization. The rewards are high for "working the system." Those who have done so most effectively—librarians, for example, who presented their evidence well and were especially articulate—have made considerable gains, while others less skillful in making their case have ended up disgruntled.

CONCLUSION

The existence of trade unions and comparable-worth laws are aspects of labor markets that require specific treatment. Both lead to interesting analysis and conclusions different in significant respects from the general theory of rewards to factors in competitive markets explored in the previous chapter. In the remainder of the chapter, we will see that several qualifications to the general theory must also be made in analyzing the rewards to the other factors as well.

▶ RENT

Economists use the term **rent** to describe the return to any factor of production greater than what is needed to supply it. Such a situation is most obvious when a factor cannot easily be reproduced (that is, a factor that is inelastic in supply). Land is a good example of an irreproducible factor, though as we shall see, the concept has much wider application than that. Analysis of what gives rise to land rent is one of the oldest subject areas in economics. We begin with the explanation advanced by the English economist David Ricardo between 1815 and 1821, an explanation that still has validity.

DIFFERENTIAL, OR RICARDIAN, RENT

Ricardo was curious about why the rental value of one acre of farmland (or house lot, or forested parcel, or mine—the logic is the same whatever the type or use of the land) is sometimes higher than that of another acre that is being put to the same use. He called this phenomenon **differential rent** (it is also called after him **"Ricardian" rent**), and he suggested that it arises from disparities in what can be earned from farming the two properties. These disparities may stem from any attribute that influences earnings, such as differences in fertility or location.

For example, acre A and acre B are both used to grow corn, but acre B is more fertile than acre A. The same resources (labor, equipment, seed) applied to acre B will yield a larger crop, and hence greater earnings, than if they were applied to acre A. Consequently, farmers will be willing to pay a higher rent for the use of acre B because of its higher productivity. How high will these differential, or Ricardian, rents be? If a farmer could earn $50 more from farming acre B than from farming acre A, a contract requiring him to pay $10 more rent for B would be a bargain. So would a contract to pay a rent differential of $20, $30, or $40. But a differential of $60 would exceed the $50 margin of higher earnings. So using Ricardo's logic, we can predict that in a competitive market the rent on acre B will be bid up to $50 above the rent on acre A. Not less, because someone will always be willing to pay a little more to garner the $50 in increased earnings that come from renting acre B. Not more, because any rental payment above $50 would more than wipe out the increase in earnings.

The same logic holds whenever an entire category of apparently identical items command quite different rents. For example, the rental payment for a given office in New York City, San Francisco, London, or Tokyo is higher than the rental payment for an identical office in Albany or Fresno or Birmingham or Osaka, even if the vacancy rate is the same in all the cities. The reason is that the greater commercial opportunities (hence the higher productivity) in the larger cities raises the willingness to pay (the demand) for offices there.[7]

Ricardo declared that rents are *price-determined*, rather than *price-determining*. The professionals who rent expensive offices in New York may argue that they must charge a high price for their services because of the high rent they have to pay. Not so, according to Ricardo's analysis; the rent is high because their rates are high. Because lawyers can charge clients high fees in the commercial environment of New York City, the rental price of office space in that city will be bid up. Or, as Ricardo put it, the rental price of land is high because the price of corn is high, not the other way around.[8] In short, Ricardian, or differential rent arises when the quality of the things rented differs.

ECONOMIC RENT
AS A RETURN TO IRREPRODUCIBLE FACTORS

Ricardo viewed rent as a return to land. Broadly speaking, however, **economic rent** is a return to any factor greater than the payment needed to supply it. As we have noted, rent will arise in particular when the factor is limited in supply and cannot easily be reproduced. Figure 12.5 shows the supply and demand curves for a scarce, irreproducible factor. That factor might be the half-acre of land at the corner of a city's main intersection, or the services of a famous athlete, or the music of a Madonna or a Pavarotti. In each case, the factor that is scarce and impossible to reproduce receives a return greater than necessary to keep the factor employed in its best use.

Such a factor will continue to serve in its best use (as the site of an office building, playing baseball, performing music) at any price above P_t. Depending on the demand (which equals MRP) for the factor's services, the equilibrium price may be very high, or it may be quite close to P_t. Any payment to the factor above P_t will keep the factor employed in its present use, as shown by the vertical (perfectly inelastic) portion of the supply curve. The amount by which the price (or wage) exceeds P_t represents economic rent. Here, it is $P_t P_e$ per unit, for a total rent equal to the area $P_t P_e EA$. If the price (or wage) paid falls *below* P_t, however, that will cause the services of the factor to be transferred into its best alternative use, so the quantity supplied falls to 0. The supply curve is the L-shaped figure SAP_t.

---

7.   We are assuming that all other things are held constant. Overbuilding of offices or the onset of a local business recession may reduce office rents sharply. When Houston, Texas, went through an oil boom in the 1970s, many new office buildings were constructed. With the end of the boom in the 1980s, a surplus of office space caused rents, and hence property values, to decline. That led to many bankruptcies among developers, and distress among the banks that held the mortgages.

8.   The question had immense practical importance in nineteenth-century England. Farmers were protected against foreign competition by the "corn laws" that prohibited the importation of grain (the English called all grain "corn" in those days). When accused of selling their grain at exorbitant prices, the farmers argued that they had to charge high prices because renting agricultural land was expensive. Ricardo destroyed their case, and eventually the Corn Laws as well, by showing that rents were high because grain prices were high, rather than the reverse. The Corn Laws were repealed in 1846.

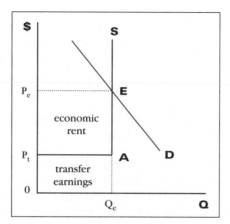

Figure 12.5. Economic rent and transfer earnings. At any wage below P_t, the factor will transfer to other uses. A wage above P_t involves economic rent, because a wage of P_t is already enough to keep the factor fully employed in its present use.

The part of earnings that comprises the area $0P_tAQ_e$ is not economic rent, but is called the *transfer earnings* of the factor. If the factor has *no* alternative uses, the supply curve for its current use extends down to the horizontal axis, at Q_e. In that case, the entire payment to the factor is rent—"pure economic rent," so-called, and there are no transfer earnings.

For those who prefer actual cases we might consider the example of the (former) boxer Mike Tyson. Mr. Tyson earned an estimated $29 million in 1990. In any other occupation but boxing, it is unlikely (or so we shall postulate) that he could have earned more than a small fraction of that figure. Assume that in his best alternative occupation he could have earned a wage P_t in Figure 12.5 for a year's worth of work Q_e, for a total of $0P_tAQ_e$. Perhaps that is $30,000 a year. Every dollar earned beyond that up to the $29 million he actually earned would be economic rent arising from his unique boxing talents.[9] In short, the combination of very high demand (because of exceptional ability to generate revenue) and very low supply of such ability results in very high earnings.

Why were Mr. Tyson's earnings so astronomical when other sports figures, supreme in their own fields, were earning far less? Because sports fans will pay more to watch heavyweight boxing championship bouts than they will to watch other sports events. Ringside seats for the Tyson-Spinks heavyweight championship bout in 1988 went for $5,000. Tennis fans are not nearly so generous with their money: Boris Becker, the highest-paid tennis player in 1990, earned only about $7 million for his year's work. Table tennis fans will pay hardly anything to see their heroes perform: Dan Seemiller, a top American player, earned just $3,415 from his sport (in 1988).[10]

The economic rent of an individual player in a team sport is more complicated to establish, because it is determined jointly with that of the other team members. Shaquille O'Neal is paid several million dollars a year for playing basketball, but he would presumably be worth less to his employers if the other Orlando players were inept. Long losing streaks repel the fans even when a player of O'Neal's caliber is working his magic on the court.

9.   For some sports heroes, the best alternative occupation might not be very lucrative. The occupation of the New York Yankee's famous Babe Ruth before he took up baseball was rolling and lifting beer barrels, which was very low-paid work. The Babe, according to his biographers, was not very intelligent, but he had considerable physical strength. He was also extremely resentful of what he perceived as insults, so perhaps the author should add that still-very-much-alive Mr. Tyson may, once he is released, have alternative opportunities in which he could earn well beyond the posited $30,000.

10.   The information is from *Forbes Magazine's* annual list of athletes ranked by income, and Jon Fowler, "Rents, Ricardo, and Mike Tyson," *The Margin*, Vol. 5, No. 4, March/April 1990, pp. 25–26.

Economic Rent as Marginal Analysis

We can generalize analysis of economic rent to an entire market for many units of a factor. Figure 12.6 shows supply and demand curves for young new professors of economics. (The curves would serve equally well for farmland, or for any other factor). Nine people with the qualifications to be economics professors are shown along the horizontal axis. The equilibrium salary is W_e. Notice, however, that at least one dedicated professor would work for a salary of only W_a. Professor no. 2 could be hired for a little more, no. 3 for still a little more, and so on. All are paid the equilibrium market salary W_e, however, because competition bids wages up to that level.

Hence professor no. 1 receives economic rent equal to the distance **ab**, and professors 2 through 6 also earn economic rent equal to the vertical distance from the supply curve to the equilibrium wage that is actually paid. Professor no. 7 earns no economic rent. At a level of pay any less than W_e, that professor, who has other opportunities, would immediately find employment elsewhere. Persons 8 and 9 are fully qualified and would have taken employment as professors if the salary had been higher, but they had better alternatives elsewhere. So the striped area W_aW_eE is the total economic rent earned. (Now we can repeat a point made in Chapter 4. The concept of economic rent is the same as that of producer surplus discussed in that chapter—a return to factors above the opportunity costs of the factors represented by a triangular area above the supply curve and below the price. Economic rent and producer surplus are the same thing.)

The more elastic the supply curve, the less the total economic rent will be—until, with perfect elasticity of supply, there is no economic rent at all. In the case of a horizontal supply curve, any decline in price will cause the entire supply of the factor to transfer to other uses.

The idea that economic rent is a return to a factor of production that exceeds that factor's opportunity cost has wide application. For example, the price of copper will be determined by supply and demand in the copper market as a whole, as in Figure 12.6 (which can do double duty). The position of the supply curve indicates that some mines, those near E, are expensive to operate either because their ore is of low quality or because conditions make mining difficult. Alternative uses for the land are nearly as lucrative as mining it. Other mines have high-quality ore or ore that is cheap to bring to the surface. Low costs (as for the tonnage produced near point **a** in Figure 12.6) combined with sales at the market price (as at point **b**) give an economic rent of **ab** for that portion of production.

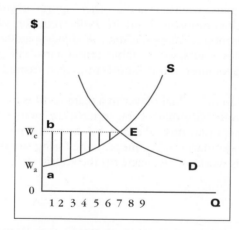

Figure 12.6. Economic rent in a factor market. Economic rent can be seen in marginal terms. The first professor would work for a salary W_a, but actually receives the market salary W_e. That professor earns an economic rent equal to the distance **ab**. The next professor receives a slightly smaller amount of rent, and the next a smaller amount yet. The total economic rent of all professors hired is equal to the striped area in the figure.

More broadly yet, any profit earned by a monopoly firm in excess of its normal profit represents earnings greater than the opportunity cost of the factors employed. So super-normal monopoly profit is also an economic rent. Economists often use the terms "monopoly profit" and "monopoly rent" interchangeably. In this case, the economic rent accrues to whatever it is that bars the entry of competing firms—perhaps a favorable location, or a patented technology, or a government license, or superior management.[11]

ECONOMIC RENT AND EXECUTIVE SALARIES

A timely question in considering economic rent is whether high executive salaries that prevail in many oligopolistic industries are truly a return to scarce managerial talents. If they are, the market is working properly and our analysis in this section applies. Skeptics suggest, however, that it may often be otherwise, especially in the United States. The average pay plus benefits of the chief executive officers of large U.S. firms in 1960 was 41 times the average pay of a factory worker, while by 1988 that multiple had risen to 93. Annual salaries of well over a million dollars are widely reported; median total annual salary plus compensation for the CEOs of a sample of 136 large U.S. companies was $1,050,000 in 1992. Executive compensation in the United States is considerably higher than that for comparable positions in Europe and Japan. In Britain, the pay of chief executives is just 35 times that of an average worker; in France and Germany, only 23 to 25 times; in Japan, only 17 to 24 times. American executives at the vice-presidential level and up earn about 5 times more than Japanese executives at the same level, and Japanese salaries are much more likely to be cut if the company's profits decline.[12] Critics note that the pay of U.S. chief executives rose 2.6 times between 1980 and 1989 while corporate profits were virtually unchanged in that period, and workers' wages rose by just 1.4 times. CEOs' pay rose 7% in 1990, a recession year during which corporate share values plus dividends actually fell by 9%. The critics also point out that the boards of directors of firms, which usually have direct control over management salaries, are mostly (60% or so) made up of executives from other firms. The stockholders may have little say in setting executive salaries.

Firms that enjoy a degree of monopoly power can treat the high management salaries as an above-normal cost that is tolerable because prices can be kept above competitive levels. This would be an example of X-inefficiency, to use the terminology of Chapter 7. High executive salaries that result from back-scratching among directors or from the exercise of monopoly power still constitute an "economic rent," but they cannot be said to accrue to scarce entrepreneurial talent.

Little research has been carried out on whether scarce talent or monopoly power more closely characterizes the market for top managers. The question is difficult to investigate because, like that to a top basketball player, the return is determined jointly in combination with other members of the management "team" and by other factors owned or controlled by the firm. Moreover, it might be hard to find corporations willing to fund such research.

---

11.   The grocery store or bank in a remote rural community enjoys some degree of monopoly power as a result of its locational advantage. Patented technologies confer advantage, especially in high-tech industries such as electronics and computers. Government licensing of broadcast wavelengths and channels conveys monopoly power to the owners of radio and television stations.

12.   See Steven Kaplan, "Top Executive Rewards and Firm Performance: A Comparison of Japan and the United States," *NBER Working Paper No. 4065*, 1992.

HENRY GEORGE AND THE SINGLE TAX

Henry George (1839–1897), a nineteenth-century American economist, used the concept of economic rent in an influential book, *Progress and Poverty* (1879), that was widely read for many years.[13] George proposed a simple plan for a **single tax** on economic rent. Because factors will continue in their current use so long as they earn economic rent, George suggested that part of the rent be taxed away, with the tax revenue used to finance government expenditures. (George specified a land tax, but a tax on any form of economic rent would serve the same purpose.) So long as the amount of the tax did not exceed the amount of the economic rent, the tax would not distort factor use—that is, it would not cause the factor to be withdrawn from its current use. A high tax on your *income* might cause you to work less, thus distorting the supply of labor; but a high tax on a building that you own would not cause you to take the building out of use until the tax absorbed all of the economic rent.

Accurate measurement of economic rent is, however, very difficult, so administering such a tax would be a nightmare. Furthermore, there are cases when application of capital investment can augment the amount of land and its productivity—landfills that expand seaside cities, Dutch dikes, mining, and so forth. In such cases, taxation of the land's economic rent would surely reduce the motive for land-augmenting capital investment. It is often extremely challenging to distinguish between factors whose supply is completely inelastic and factors whose supply can be increased by applying capital. It remains true, however, that a tax on economic rent would have less effect on factor use than other forms of taxation.

Ramsey Taxes

Henry George's idea still lives on in a modified and more sophisticated form that focuses on demand as well as supply. Modern economists agree that taxes on *any* item that is inelastic in supply (land) or inelastic in demand (liquor, cigarettes) distort production and consumer welfare less than other forms of taxes. The land will stay in use even if it is taxed; taxing the liquor and cigarettes will generate revenue but will not cut consumption that much. Such nondistortionary taxes on items inelastic in demand or supply are sometimes called **Ramsey taxes**, after the Cambridge University economist and mathematician Frank Ramsey (1903–1930) who pioneered in modeling them. But if demand is inelastic because a good is a necessity such as home heating oil, the poor would spend a larger proportion of their income on that good. In this case, a Ramsey tax would force the poor to pay a larger proportion of their income in tax than the well-to-do. A nondistortionary policy is not always a fair one.

QUASI-RENTS

Economic rent, the result of factors of production earning returns greater than their opportunity cost, sometimes appears and then vanishes after a short time. A firm that finds increasing demand for its product is able to raise its price. The factors employed by the firm will share in the bounty, earning higher returns. But in time, new competition will arise, shifting the supply curve. The lower price will erode the higher returns to the firm's machines, its skilled labor, and its management. The economic rent disappears. *Temporarily,* however, the factors will have earned a rent higher than their opportunity cost, and they will continue to do so until the gains are wiped out by competition. Economists use the term **quasi-rent**, meaning "like a rent," to describe these temporary returns.

CAPITALIZING RENTS:
THE CONCEPT OF NET PRESENT VALUE

When a factor of production is earning economic rent or quasi-rent, the price of the factor is ultimately bid up. The rent is then said to be "capitalized"—that is, it is embodied in the purchase

---

13.   Translated into many languages, it is still the best-selling book ever written on economic theory and policy, according to the *New Palgrave Dictionary*, New York, 1987.

price of the factor. For example, the price of a productive plot of land that earns high returns will be reflected by a high selling price. The owners of a copper mine that taps better-quality ore will be able to charge a higher price for the mine if they put it up for sale. A monopoly that is generating a rich flow of profit for its owners will sell for a high price. That the existence of economic rent will lead to higher values comes as no surprise. But how do we determine exactly how much higher that value will be? The calculation involves the concept called **net present value**, which we explore in this section.

Let's say we want to *purchase* an asset—a copper mine, or an oil well, or a new technology and the patents that go with it. What price would be rationally justifiable? Of course we know the answer involves supply and demand, but what causes the demand curve to be positioned where it is? To answer that question we calculate a *discounted value* for the asset that will be pouring out a stream of income over time. The idea behind discounting is that a dollar in hand is worth more than a dollar that will be received a year from now. With the dollar in hand, we can buy an interest-bearing security that at the end of the year would be worth $1 plus whatever interest it had earned during the year.

This principle of discounting lets us estimate the value of any income-earning asset, as follows. Assume that we expect a copper mine to yield a return (economic rent) of $100,000 per year as far into the future as we can estimate. The amount we are willing to pay for that mine depends on the prevailing rate of interest. If the interest rate is 8%, and if we expect it to remain at 8% in the future, we can calculate how much money we would need to put into interest-bearing securities in order to earn $100,000 per year for as long as we can foresee. The formula for calculating that sum is

$$\$NPV = \frac{\$N}{r}$$

where $\$NPV$ = the net present (capitalized) value of the asset, $\$N$ = the perpetual annual return from the asset, and r = the rate of interest. To earn a perpetual $100,000 per year at 8% interest, we would need to put $1,250,000 into an interest-bearing account, because $1,250,000 at 8% a year will earn $100,000 per year. ($1,250,000 × .08 = $100,000.) The formula above then appears as

$$\$1,250,000 = \frac{\$100000}{.08}$$

We would not rationally offer more than $1,250,000 for a mine that yields $100,000 per year. Nor would the owners expect us to offer more, because they know we could earn $100,000 annually if we just put our $1,250,000 into an account earning the going interest rate of 8%. Nor could we buy the mine for less than $1,250,000 under competitive conditions because the owners could earn more from holding on to it than they could by selling it to us and investing the proceeds. In any event, if we were to offer less than $1,250,000, some competing buyer would appear and outbid us.

We can make the matter a bit more complicated by allowing for the possibility that revenues from the mine will decline as time passes—perhaps we believe that ore production will start to fall off in about 5 years as the vein of metal is depleted, and that output will cease altogether in 25 years. We cannot be certain of what will happen, of course, but we can make the best possible estimate and use it in a somewhat more complex formula for net present value.

That formula is

$$\$NPV = \frac{\$N_1}{1+r} + \frac{\$N_2}{(1+r)^2} + \frac{\$N_3}{(1+r)^3} + \dots + \frac{\$N_n}{(1+r)^n}$$

Its derivation is explained in the accompanying box. Obtaining an answer used to be tedious, but business calculators now have a key programmed to do the calculation swiftly.

THE FORMULA FOR NET PRESENT VALUE

What sum (X) would you pay today for a contract to receive $1 a year from now? This is the same as asking what sum (X), plus the amount that sum could earn in interest over a year at the going rate (rX), would equal $1:

$$X + rX = \$1$$

This can be rewritten $X(1 + r) = \$1$, or, by rearrangement,

$$X = \frac{\$1}{(1+r)} \, ,$$

which would be the net present value after one year. If you were obliged to wait two years before receiving the $1, then the amount you would pay (X) would be less, because that sum would be earning interest for two years, not one. That is, the sum X would be worth X + rX after one year, and then that sum would earn interest for another year, or r[X + rX]. Thus, for a two-year period we must solve for X when

$$X + rX + r[X + rX] = \$1$$

By rearrangement, $X + 2rX + r^2x = \$1$, and in turn $X(1 + 2r + r^2) = \$1$. This can be written $X(1+r)(1+r) = \$1$, and further rearranged as $X(1+r)2 = \$1$. After one last rearrangement,

$$X = \frac{\$1}{(1+r)^2} \, ,$$

which is the net present value after two years. Thus, if the rate of interest is 8%, the net present value of $1 to be received in two years is $0.86.

The net present value formula is used routinely in financial transactions of all sorts. In primitive form it was first employed in fourteenth-century Italy for discounting loans, but it was not until 1907 that the American economist Irving Fisher applied the principle to cash flows and valuations of any capital project. Greater complexity is introduced if we allow for changing interest rates—perhaps we expect interest rates to rise over the next few years. That, too, can be accomplished algebraically. To see how, the interested student can consult more advanced texts.

Though net present value is introduced here as a subject connected with economic rent, it is certainly not limited to that. Exactly the same formula is used to establish bond values, and to determine how much investors should spend on a new machine or factory. Historically, its general idea even had a place on the plantation, as owners calculated how much should be spent to acquire an indentured servant or a slave.

▶ INTEREST

Two main meanings of the word **interest** are the price of loans and the return to capital. These meanings are related, as we explore in this section.

INTEREST AS THE PRICE OF LOANABLE FUNDS

Most people know the word **interest** as the price of loanable funds, that is, funds which people, businesses, and governments want to borrow and that lenders make available as loans. When we pay 8% a year for a loan to buy a new car, 10% for a personal loan, and so forth, we are paying the price for loanable funds. The annual percentage rate of interest is the price we must pay annually to get the loan. If the interest rate is 10% and we borrow $10,000, we must pay $1000 per year to the lender. In general, the price of loanable funds (that is, the interest rate) is determined by the supply and demand for these funds, just as supply and demand also determines the prices of goods, services, and the more tangible factors of production.

In Chapter 19 we will see that interest rates are influenced by government monetary policies to affect the supply of money generally. Governments use monetary policy in an attempt to avoid inflation or recession by manipulating interest rates; this tactic is an important area of macroeconomics. Here, rather than dealing with the macroeconomics of the issue, we will concentrate on a micro issue: the price of loans in one specific market for loanable funds. There are many such markets. For example, we could discuss the interest rate on loans to businesses that want to finance their capital investment, or to households that want to finance consumer spending and mortgage payments, or to federal, state, and local governments that borrow to finance their spending.

Let us take bank loans for the purchase of new factory equipment as our example. Consider first the demand for such loans. All other things being equal, high interest rates would tend to discourage borrowing for the purchase of new equipment, and lower interest rates would tend to stimulate it. Your firm will be much more likely to seek a loan when the going interest rate is 2% than when it is 12%. Thus, the demand curve for loanable funds in Figure 12.7 has a downward slope.

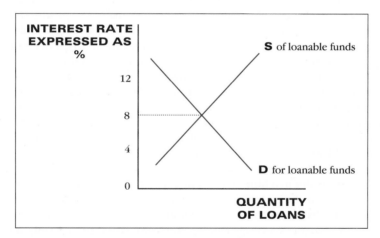

Figure 12.7. Determination of interest rates. The rate of interest can be seen as the price of loanable funds, determined by supply and demand.

Now consider the supply of loanable funds from banks. The supply curve in Figure 12.7 is upward-sloping, reflecting that the higher the rate of interest the bank receives for loans on new equipment, the greater the quantity of loanable funds that banks will want to make available for this purpose. The reasoning is that at low interest rates on loans for equipment, banks will prefer to use their funds for other purposes such as lending to consumers or buying government bonds. At high interest rates for loans on equipment, however, banks are being well compensated and will prefer such loans to other uses of their funds. In Figure 12.7, interest rates below 8% will cause the quantity demanded of such loans to exceed the quantity supplied, and the interest rate will tend to rise. Interest rates above 8% cause the quantity supplied to exceed the quantity demanded, so the interest rate will fall. Here, the equilibrium rate of interest is 8%.

Many different rates of interest exist at the same time even when the matter is so seemingly simple as loans for new equipment. There is one rate for long-term loans to customers, and another rate for short-term loans to the same customers; one rate for equipment that is easily resellable if the firm fails to make its payments on the loan and the bank has to foreclose, and another if the equipment would be hard to resell; one rate for risky firms and another for dependable firms. Indeed, a wide variety of possible rates is likely to exist for the very same equipment, depending on the bank's perceptions of risk and time to maturity.

INTEREST AS THE RETURN TO CAPITAL

As described in the last section, one meaning of the term interest rate is the price of loanable funds. Like the word rent, however, interest has a broader significance for economists, who also use the term interest to refer to the return to capital. The two uses of the term are connected. Consider the items of physical capital a firm has acquired through its past investment—buildings, machinery, vehicles, and so forth. Each of these items of capital has been purchased either with borrowed funds, or with funds the firm had on hand. If the funds were borrowed, the annual cost of the physical capital can be expressed as the annual interest rate paid on the loan. If the funds were already on hand, the result is the same. These funds are thereafter tied up in capital goods; instead of $1000 that could have been put into an interest-bearing account, the firm has $1000 worth of machinery. So we can regard the annual cost of owning an item of capital as the interest that could have been earned if the funds used to purchase it had been put instead into an interest-bearing account.

We can also express the *earnings* from acquiring a new machine as a percentage rate of return. Actually, where capital goods are concerned, we must usually do exactly this. Why is this so? Because there is a complication in determining the demand for capital. Like the demand for any other factor of production, the demand for capital is a derived demand, derived from the earnings that the new machine will engender when it is used for production. Like the other factors, the demand for capital depends on the capital's marginal revenue product, so the analysis of factor income in Chapter 11 applies. The complication arises because capital does not yield its return all in one time period, but does so over an extended time. Hire labor for a year, and the labor yields its returns in the same year. Buy a machine this year, however, and the lengthy nature of the returns must be taken into account. A $1000 machine that lasts 50 years will yield only $\frac{1}{50}$ of its lifetime earnings this year.[14] That is why when discussing the productivity of capital, economists tend to speak of rates of return rather than the marginal revenue product of capital.

So the productivity of capital is expressed as a rate of return per year. If a $1000 machine yields net income of $100 per year, the annual rate of return from operating the machine is 10% per year. Comparing the annual interest costs incurred from acquiring the machine to the annual rate of return from the machine determines whether we should purchase it. This is true if we use borrowed money for the purchase or if we use our own money. If the annual interest cost is 8%, but the earnings from owning the machine are 10%, we are better off if we buy it. If interest costs are 8%, but the earnings from owning the machine are only 6%, then we would lose money if we buy it.

Firms will therefore purchase an item of capital when they can obtain an annual rate of return on the capital higher than the going rate of interest. This will have two effects in the capital market as a whole. The increased demand for loanable funds to finance the purchase of machines will raise the interest rate on loans. (The demand curve for loanable funds in Figure 12.7 will shift to the right.) Moreover, the additional purchases of capital will reduce the return on capital through the process of diminishing returns. In a competitive market, the annual rate of return from owning capital will be pushed to equality with the rate of interest. Therefore, the market rate of interest will be the same as the percentage rate of return to capital.

---

14.   But remember the formula for net present value discussed earlier in the chapter. A dollar received 30 or 40 or 50 years from now is not worth as much to you as a dollar received this year. Assessment of rates of return on capital assets must usually involve "discounting." We return to the subject in Chapters 16 and 19.

If the rate of return on capital remains greater over time than the going rate of interest, the situation must be due to some imperfection in the market (superior technology that cannot be duplicated, government intervention including patents, slow adjustment to competitive pressures, and so forth). The extra return to capital over and above the going interest rate is in this case properly seen as a rent or quasi-rent. Rents, as we have discussed, can be earned on capital just as on any other factor of production.

► PROFIT

Profit, as we have discussed, is the return to the entrepreneur. It is what remains after the costs of a firm's operations have been subtracted from its revenues. Profit plays the major role of directing the output of a market economy, as entrepreneurs shift production toward items that are most profitable. Yet much of what business people call profit in the everyday world of commerce would not be called profit by economists. For example, store owners who spend some of their time serving as clerks are acting in the role of labor and are earning implicit wages that should not be regarded as profit. Part of the earnings of owners of machines or factories is an implicit interest return on the funds tied up when the capital was purchased and also does not constitute profit in the economist's sense.

Two outstanding writers on the meaning and significance of profit were Frank Knight (1885–1962) of the University of Chicago and Joseph Schumpeter (1883–1950) of Harvard. Knight viewed profit as a reward to entrepreneurs for risk-taking in an uncertain world. Every commercial project carries a prospect of gain and a risk of loss or even failure. Entrepreneurs who accurately calculate demand, costs, government policy, and the odds of success reap a reward in the form of profit. Those who fail to do so lose out and suffer negative profits (losses). Another type of risk that entrepreneurs may have to take involves unstable earnings. In some businesses, weather is the cause of the instability. A wet summer reduces the income of tourist resorts; a dry summer cuts into farmers' earnings; a winter with little snow hurts ski resorts. Risk also resides in the business cycle: auto sales rise and fall with consumer income, for example. Finally, risk accompanies changes in the rate of interest: residential construction is especially dependent on interest rates, because many house buyers finance their purchases with mortgage loans. In short, profit and risk taking are intimately related. (Studies suggest that about 3 to 6 percentage points of the profit rates earned by firms are associated with risk borne by the entrepreneurs.)

Joseph Schumpeter explored the relationship between profit and the entrepreneur's success as an initiator and innovator. In any commercial project, someone must hatch new ideas and commence new activities (the role of initiation). Profit rises, even if only temporarily, when new operating methods make possible reductions in costs, entry into untapped markets, the marketing of new products, or the alteration of existing products (innovation). In a sense, Schumpeter pointed out, profit is a return to the entrepreneur's ability to initiate and innovate. Taken together, the notions of Knight and Schumpeter have formed the modern view of the entrepreneurial function: initiation, innovation, and risk-taking, with profit as the reward.

Profit is thus the return to entrepreneurial effort. Ordinarily, competition will limit that return to a normal profit just sufficient to keep entrepreneurs in their present employment (as we discussed in Chapters 6 and 7), but sometimes it does not. Some entrepreneurs have skills that cannot be reproduced and continue to perform well above the average throughout their careers. Just as a substantial part of the return to boxer Mike Tyson was an economic rent, so the return to auto pioneer Henry Ford and software creator Bill Gates was also in large measure an economic rent. Moreover, much of the "profit" of a monopoly may not be a reward to risk taking or innovation, but an economic rent that accrues because the monopoly is able to use its market power to maintain its position. In such cases, the concepts of profit and economic rent merge, which is why economists treat the terms super-normal profit and economic rent as synonyms.

CONCLUSION

The main purpose of this chapter has been to extend to wages in unionized industries and in the presence of comparable-worth laws, to rent, to interest, and to profit the general model describing how returns to the factors of production are determined. In each case, the supply of the factor and its productivity determine the factor's reward, but the special attributes discussed in this chapter make necessary some modification and enlargement of the basic model.

SUMMARY

1) Labor unions attempt to raise wages by increasing the demand for labor, decreasing its supply, or establishing a negotiated wage above the market equilibrium. Their success in doing so depends significantly on the elasticity of the demand for labor.

2) Comparable-worth laws, which require that people should receive equal pay for jobs that are equivalent, are controversial. Typically they take into account only some of the determinants of labor supply and do not take into account the demand for labor.

3) Economic rent is the return to any factor of production greater than necessary to keep it employed in its present use. Ricardo introduced the idea of differential (or "Ricardian") rent, where differences in economic rent arise from differences in the quality of the things rented.

4) Quasi-rents are temporary returns over and above opportunity cost that accrue to factors of production because a rise in the price of the product has taken place. Quasi-rents are eroded in the long run.

5) Rents can be capitalized into the purchase price of an asset by means of the discounting formula that allows the calculation of the asset's net present value. This formula has wide use in many areas of economics.

6) The word interest is used to describe the price of loanable funds and also the return to capital. These two concepts are related because the interest cost of loanable funds determines how much a capital good will cost on an annual basis. Comparing this interest cost to the rate of return on the capital determines whether it is economically sensible to make the purchase.

7) In a competitive market, the rate of return on capital is pushed to equality with the rate of interest.

8) Profit is the return to entrepreneurship. It is the reward for entrepreneurs' initiating activities, innovation, and risk taking.

Chapter Key Words

Differential rent: Differences in economic rent arising from differences in the quality of the things rented. Also called *Ricardian rent*.

Economic rent: The return to any factor of production greater than what is needed to keep it employed in its present use. Can apply to land, natural resources, personal skills, and entrepreneurial ability. See also *profit*.

Featherbedding: Union rules requiring labor to be employed when the employer would not voluntarily do so.

Interest: The price of borrowed funds; the return to capital.

Net present value: The discounted value of a flow of returns accruing over time.

Open shop: An employment arrangement where workers need not join a union. The only type of shop permitted in states that have a right-to-work law.

Profit: The return to entrepreneurship; the reward for initiation, innovation, and risk taking. Super-normal profit is an economic rent.

Quasi-rent: The temporary return over and above opportunity cost that accrues to a factor of production because of a rise in the price of the product produced. Quasi-rents are eroded in the long run.

Ramsey taxes: Nondistortionary taxes, named after British economist and mathematician Frank Ramsey, who first modeled them. They embody the idea that taxes on items inelastic in supply (such as land) or inelastic in demand (such as liquor or cigarettes) will distort production and consumer welfare less than will other forms of taxes.

Rent: The return to any factor of production greater than what is necessary to supply it. Most obvious when the factor cannot be reproduced. See *differential* or *Ricardian rent* and *economic rent*.

"Ricardian" rent: See *differential rent*.

Right-to-work laws: Under the Taft-Hartley Act, individual states may ban the union shop by passing specific legislation.

Single tax: The proposal by Henry George to tax economic rent on the ground that doing so would not alter production decisions.

Taft-Hartley Act: The law passed in 1947 that banned the closed shop, permitted the union shop except where states have a right-to-work law, provided for an 80-day cooling-off period in strikes, and established several unfair labor practices that were henceforth illegal.

Union shop: An employment arrangement where workers need not belong to a union to be hired, but must join one shortly thereafter. Legal under the Taft-Hartley Act in states without a right-to-work law.

Wagner Act: A major piece of labor law passed in 1935. Requires management to bargain in good faith with unions and guarantees that a union can become sole bargaining agent by majority vote of the workers in a plant.

Chapter Questions

1) It is 1946 and you are skilled at sewing. You would like to work at the local garment factory. The factory is a closed shop, and you are not a member of the garment-makers union. Do you favor the Taft-Hartley Act? Why?

2) The National Union of Ditch-Diggers is proposing an extensive battery of tests for those who want to become licensed ditch-diggers. How would the following people feel about this plan:
    a) a farmer who needs a ditch dug?
    b) a ditch-digger who knows that demand for ditch-diggers is elastic?
    c) a ditch-digger who know that demand for ditch-diggers is inelastic?

3) When a union negotiates an above-equilibrium wage, those who receive the wage gain. Identify who loses when the industry in question is perfectly competitive in the goods market. Do the same groups necessarily lose if the industry is a monopoly?

4) Secretaries are mostly women, and they tend to earn low wages. Comparable-worth legislation would raise those wages. Would such legislation be a good idea if wages are low because the supply of secretaries is high? What if it was found that companies behave as oligopsonists, following a "wage leader" firm in setting secretarial wages?

5) "Simple" Simon develops office buildings. Rather than hire an expensive consultant, Simon threw darts at a U.S. map to pick office complex locations. The two randomly selected locations he picked were the corner of 6th and Arch Streets in Philadelphia and land along U.S. Route 83 near Brownlee, Nebraska. Simon says, "I charge a higher rent in Philadelphia than in Brownlee because the land cost more in Philadelphia." Is this really why Simon charges a higher rent in Philadelphia?

6) Four men are willing to be rock musicians if they are paid enough money. John must be paid at least £10,000; Paul must be paid at least £8,000; George must be paid at least £6,000; Ringo must be paid at least £4,000. Draw the supply curve of musicians (it looks like stair steps, but there are no more than four people, so it becomes vertical at the quantity of 4). Demand for these musicians is relatively strong, so the equilibrium wage is £2,000,000. Show the rents and transfer earnings earned by each musician.

7) Why did Henry George feel that there was an advantage in a single tax on economic rent? Why not just tax income or consumption?

8) One day your broker calls you on the phone. She says, "I have a great deal for you. The government is issuing a bond that pays $1,000 a year forever. All it costs is $10,000. I recommend that you buy it." Your other investments are paying a return of 9% per year, and you do not expect that to change in the future. Should you buy the bond?

9) The market for loanable funds is perfectly competitive. Loans to businesses to buy capital equipment currently have an interest rate of 6%. You work at a management consulting firm. Your research shows that there have been some sudden increases in the productivity of capital in recent months. You expect the return on capital to run at 10% for the foreseeable future. What is your best forecast of the future interest rate on business loans? How will the market move to this interest rate?

Income Distribution and Poverty

OVERALL OBJECTIVE: To explain why substantial differences in income distribution are usual in market economies, why persistent poverty is a growing concern, and what might be done about it.

MORE SPECIFICALLY:

- ■ To explain the methods for measuring income distribution, including the income earned by quintiles, Lorenz curves, and Gini coefficients.
- ■ To discuss the causes of unequal income distribution.
- ■ To assess discrimination in labor markets, discussing when and how discriminatory practices increase income inequality.
- ■ To define poverty and assess why it persists.
- ■ To consider whether a culture of poverty has arisen and suggest what economic policies might help to counter this situation.
- ■ To query whether the problems in inner cities have grown so massive that economic improvement for the populations there will require multifaceted and interdisciplinary solutions.

A market system carries no guarantee that incomes will become more equal over time. The supply of some factors is scarce, of others, abundant, while productivity differences among individuals can be substantial and sometimes huge. The first part of the chapter examines the causes of income (and wealth) inequality and how to measure it. Then it goes on to look at the question of persistent poverty. That the market system has been an effective instrument for raising levels of living is generally acknowledged. But it is also acknowledged that wealth and poverty coexist in advanced market economies, particularly in the United States. A significant number of people endure *underclass* status, the manifestations of which include long-lasting poverty, welfare dependence, and homelessness, and from which many find it difficult to escape.

▶ THE DISTRIBUTION OF INCOME

The distribution of income can differ substantially within and among the world's market economies. In some of these, incomes are rather equally distributed, but in others, a large proportion of the population is very poor and earns very little of the income, while a small group of the well-to-do earns most of it. How to measure a country's distribution of income is the topic of this section.

MEASURING INCOME DISTRIBUTION

A common means for measuring the distribution of income in a country is to establish the percentage of the income earned by all households by quintiles, that is, the percentage of income earned by the poorest 20% of the population, the next 20%, …, the richest 20%. The 1991 figures for the United States are shown in Table 13.1. Line A shows the distribution before taxes and government transfers. Line B shows the distribution after government taxes and transfer payments in cash or kind.

TABLE 13.1
Percentage share of U.S. household income, 1991:
by percentile groups of households.

	Lowest 20% (To $17,000)	Second 20% (To $29,111)	Third 20% (To $43,000)	Fourth 20% (To $62,991)	Highest 20% (Above $62,991)
A.	1.1	8.0	15.9	25.3	49.6
B.	5.1	11.1	16.7	24.0	43.0

Source: U.S. Bureau of the Census. See *Statistical Abstract of the United States 1993*, Table 750. Wages and salaries are the most important component of income. Other items include interest on bonds and bank accounts, stock dividends, royalties, rental income, business profits, and the like.

Thus the poorest 20% of the population earned only 5.1% of U.S. income after taxes and transfers, while the richest 20% earned 43.0% of all income earned. Compare this to the data for Brazil, a country with one of the world's most unequal income distributions, and Sweden with one of the most equal, as shown in Table 13.2. The political impact of differences as great as Brazil's is likely to be substantial, and many observers believe that Brazil's economic inequality is a major cause of the underlying crime and violence in that troubled society. (Of course, levels of living differ greatly between these countries even in the same percentile grouping. For many, life is considerably closer to the margin of subsistence, or below it, in Brazil than it is in Sweden.)

TABLE 13.2
Percentage share of household income
by percentile groups of households, Brazil and Sweden.

	Lowest 20%	Second 20%	Third 20%	Fourth 20%	Highest 20%
Brazil	2.1	4.9	8.9	16.8	67.5
Sweden	8.0	13.2	17.4	24.5	36.9

Source: World Bank, *World Development Report 1993,* Table 30. After taxes and transfers.

The Lorenz Curve of Income Distribution

Data on income distribution can be presented in a graph, using a Lorenz curve as in Figure 13.1. Named for its inventor, the American statistician Max Otto Lorenz, a **Lorenz curve** puts the accumulated percentage of all income earned in a country on the vertical axis and the accumulated percentage of the population on the horizontal axis. Zero percent of the population obviously earns 0% of a country's income, and 100% of the population earns 100% of its income. If every quintile earned 20% of all income, so that 40% of the population earned 40% of the income, 60% earned 60%, and so on, income would be distributed with complete equality, and the series of points tracing this would be a straight 45° line "Lorenz curve" as on the diagram. If the poorest 20% earned only 5.1% of income (the U.S. figure), that would give a coordinate point at X in the diagram. The next 20% earning 11.1% would mean that the poorest 40% of the population earns 16.2% of the income, which gives another point Y, and so on. The resulting bowed Lorenz curve measures the degree of income inequality.

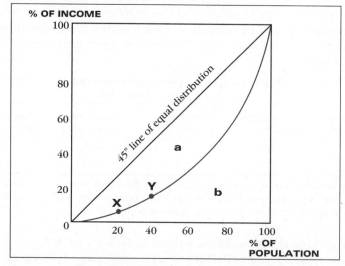

Figure 13.1. A Lorenz Curve. A Lorenz Curve shows the degree of income inequality. If the curve lies along the 45° line, income is distributed with complete equality. The deeper the bend, the greater the degree of inequality. Areas **a** and **b** are used to calculate the Gini coefficient, a numerical measure of income inequality.

The Gini Coefficient

The distribution of income can conveniently be expressed as a single number derived from the shape of the Lorenz curve. Use the letter **a** to indicate the area between the Lorenz curve and the 45° line, and the letter **b** to indicate the area under the Lorenz curve. Then the ratio **a/(a+b)** in the diagram is known as the **Gini coefficient**, named after Corrado Gini, the Italian statistician who first formulated it. The Gini coefficient would be 0.00 if income were distributed with complete equality; this is because the Lorenz curve would be a 45° line, so the area of **a** would be 0. If one person had all the income and the rest had none, so that the Lorenz curve looked like a reversed letter L running horizontally from 0 to 100 and then vertically from 100, area **b** would disappear, and **a/(a+b)** would equal 1. Gini coefficients must therefore lie between 0 and 1. The coefficient is 0.38 for the United States, somewhat higher than it was 15 years ago. It is above 0.60 in a number of less-developed countries with highly unequal income distribution. Some selected Gini coefficients are shown in Table 13.3.

TABLE 13.3
Gini coefficients for selected countries.

Jamaica	0.66	India	0.42
Honduras	0.62	United States	0.38
Brazil	0.57	South Korea	0.36
Mexico	0.50	Taiwan	0.32
Thailand	0.47	Canada	0.32
Chile	0.46	United Kingdom	0.32
Philippines	0.45	Indonesia	0.31
Colombia	0.45	Japan	0.31

Source: Taken where available from United Nations Development Program, *Human Development Report 1993*, New York, 1993, Table 18. The U.S. figure is from the *Statistical Abstract of the United States, 1993*, Table 750. For many countries, data limitations mean that Gini coefficients are calculated infrequently; the data from *HDR 1993*, for example, are for various years, 1975 to 1988. The U.S. figure is for 1991.

IS THERE A "RIGHT" TO ECONOMIC EQUALITY?

Great debates have been conducted on the question of whether there is a "right" to economic equality. Almost everyone would agree on a normative position that there ought to be *some* type of economic equality. But there are many ways to define and interpret economic equality, as explored in the accompanying box.

THE DEBATE ON ECONOMIC EQUALITY

The debate on economic equality is highly normative, involving value judgments. Most economists in the market economies would undoubtedly declare themselves *against* "equal incomes for all." Equality of income was the position taken by the "Levellers" of the seventeenth century, and Karl Marx's famous Communist rubric "to each according to his need" conveys the same message. Socialist economists and political parties, especially in Europe, have often adopted a less rigorous version of the same idea, namely that government should deliberately use its tax and spending policy to move the distribution of income toward substantially more equality. But achievement of equal incomes for all would obviously vitiate the market's ability to move factors of production into more productive uses and would therefore cause enormous economic inefficiency. Moreover, the achievement of equality of income would require an extreme degree of government intervention. In any case, a significant amount of income inequality is voluntary; some people prefer leisure to income or less-intense work to more intense.

The conservative economists called "Libertarians" would interpret economic equality in a different way. Some of these would favor equality among individuals in allowing them to have the maximum amount of liberty to pursue economic ends. Other economists find such a position worrisome, however, to the extent that it implies maximum liberty to construct monopolies, or monopsonies, or enterprises with negative externalities such as pollution. These critics of the Libertarian position would, however, often accept the idea of an equality of liberty to pursue economic goals—but not maximum liberty to do so.

There is much agreement among economists of all stripes that economic equality before the law ought to be a right. This implies that the giant corporation and the average citizen should be treated equally by the law and the courts where economic regulations are concerned. Little state intervention is needed to achieve this goal,

which merely requires that the government be fair in its dealings.

Many people would declare themselves in favor of "equality of economic opportunity," though on closer examination the realization of this idea of equality is more problematic. In practice, inequality of economic opportunity is pronounced, and achieving it would require much more extensive state intervention than is now practiced. Consider that, taken literally, equalization of economic opportunity would mean limits on inheritances, and at the outer bound would require equality in education. Probably most people really mean equality before the law and equality in pursuance of economic goals when they use the words "equal opportunity."

WHAT CAUSES UNEQUAL INCOME DISTRIBUTION?

Inequalities in income distribution in a market system can usually be traced to one or more of several underlying economic causes. The fundamental ones are discussed in the following sections.

THE OPERATION OF MARKETS FOR FACTORS OF PRODUCTION

In a market system, high incomes (often including significant economic rent) accrue to those who own or control factors that are in limited supply and are much demanded. That is, those whose contribution is not easily duplicated, who work hard, and whose marginal revenue product is high will receive larger incomes than those whose contribution is neither scarce, nor very advantageous to anybody, nor marked by hard work.

The economics of the issue are illustrated in Figure 13.2, which shows the demand and supply for the labor in two different occupations having to do with telecommunications. In panel **a**, we see that the demand for trained computer technicians who can repair the computerized telephonic transmission links is high. The job is essential; if not repaired immediately, breakdowns can be very costly—the marginal revenue product of those able to do the job is high. But the supply of such workers is limited. Thorough training and considerable experience are necessary, and the number of workers who can do the job is limited. Wages set by the high demand and the low supply are accordingly elevated, at W_h.

In panel **b**, we see the demand and supply for telephone operators. Because of computerization, the demand for operators has decreased greatly over the years. The supply of workers able to do the job is high, however, because the educational requirements for this employment are modest and few skills are required. Wages set by the small demand and the large supply are therefore low, at W_l.

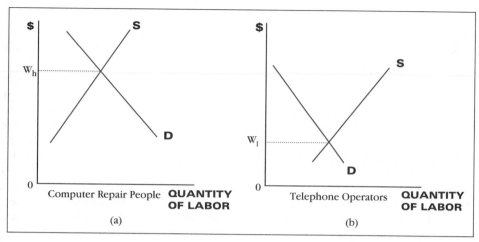

Figure 13.2. **Wages may differ greatly because of demand and supply.** In panel **a**, the high demand for trained computer repair personnel together with the low supply leads to a high wage. In panel **b**, the low demand and high supply for telephone operators leads to a much lower wage than for the computer-repair personnel.

Low Demand for Unskilled Labor

In general, the position of the demand curve for a particular type of labor is straightforward. As discussed in Chapter 11, it is established by the worker's marginal revenue product, that is, the value of the worker to the employer. But in recent years, increasing technical sophistication in production has been a major driving force in changing the demand for labor. In industrial countries, that demand has been shifting against unskilled labor (leftward in panel **b**) and toward labor that embodies more skill, training, and education (rightward in panel **a**). Wages have been rising for the skilled, while falling for the least skilled, as we shall see.

Another contributor is the relatively free importation of goods produced abroad by unskilled workers. In the world as a whole, there is plenty of cheap, unskilled labor willing to work for very low wages, below $1.00 per hour in some of the least-developed countries. America cannot compete in making the low-tech, unsophisticated products exported from these countries. (Indeed why would it want to try? Later, when we explore international trade, we will see that it is not economically sensible for the United States to try to make items that can be produced more cheaply abroad.) The future for the United States clearly lies in technologically skilled, professional-grade labor. Workers who do not possess enough general education to communicate effectively, or use a computer, or otherwise compensate for their lack of education, training, and skill tend to suffer inordinately from this falling demand for their labor.

High Supply of Unskilled Labor

The elements that play a role in the supply of labor have already been discussed in Chapter 11. Here, we emphasize several aspects of labor supply that tend to enhance the availability of *unskilled* labor. For reasons discussed below, the supply curve in Figure 13.2's panel **b** is positioned out to the right. There are also signs that it is shifting further in that direction, with negative effects on the wages of unskilled workers.

1) Just as firms invest in machines (capital) to increase their future profits, so workers invest in education and training (human capital) to increase their future earnings. But acquiring education and training can be a lengthy and costly process, and many people do not have the money, or the energy, or the innate ability to see it through. The supply of unskilled labor is large. Distress in the public educational system is making the problem more intractable.

2) Population growth increases the proportion of young people in the population. This is likely to decrease income equality because young people on the whole make less money either from wages and salaries, or from income derived from wealth, than do older people. This tendency toward inequality is exacerbated because birth rates are higher among the part of the population that earns lower incomes. The children in this group on average acquire less education than do the children of higher-income parents. The result is a larger increase in the supply of unskilled labor than would otherwise be true.

3) Immigration now accounts for over a third of U.S. population increase and over a quarter of the new entrants to the U.S. labor force. The skill and educational level of recent immigrants has fallen and is below the average for the population as a whole, so augmenting the supply of unskilled labor.

4) Social factors have worked to increase the supply of labor that prefers part-time employment, where skill levels (and wages) are often low. A major contributor is the large increase in the number of single parents (mostly mothers, many of whom have not continued their schooling) attempting to raise children while also holding a job.

All of these demand and supply considerations have contributed to a growing gap between the wages paid in labor markets for skilled and unskilled workers. For example, from after World War II until the early 1970s, income growth averaged 2.5–3% a year, and the growth was approximately the same among lower-paid and higher-paid workers. But in the 1970s and 1980s this changed. During this period, the income of better-paid workers continued to rise, at about 0.9% a year, but the income of the lower-paid workers *dropped*, by about 0.7% per year. In addition, the earnings differential between college graduates and high school graduates has been steadily widening, and the incomes of those who only finished the eighth grade have been falling.

THE INEQUALITY IN THE DISTRIBUTION OF WEALTH

Inequality of incomes is also caused by underlying inequalities in the distribution of wealth. Wealth consists of the ownership of companies, buildings, houses, land, natural resources, bonds, stocks, bank deposits, and other such assets. Income in the form of rent, interest, and profit depends on ownership of wealth. That ownership is determined by the income earned in the past, together with the economic and social system in operation at the time the wealth was being acquired. Wealth is far less equally distributed than is income itself. In the United States, for example, the richest 20% of families by net worth own 78.7% of all private assets (1983 figure). By contrast, the poorest 20% of the population by net worth of assets have *negative* assets. In that group, accumulated debts are greater than whatever wealth is held.[1] The disparities in wealth among social groups is pronounced, much greater than the disparities in income. While the median white household owned assets worth $44,408 in 1991, the median black household owned $4,604, and Hispanic household $5,345.

Certain *forms* of wealth are distributed even less equally. In 1983 the top 1% of U.S. wealth holders owned 49% of the "capital wealth" held mainly for the financial gain it provides (for example, stocks, bonds, real estate other than owner-occupied housing, and equity in unincorporated businesses). The top 5% of wealth holders owned 75% of this capital wealth.[2]

---

1.   The data on wealth ownership in the text is when the population is arrayed by wealth holding; that is, the wealthiest 20%, and so on. If the population is instead arrayed by income earned rather than by wealth owned, the poorest 20% in terms of income own 5.1% of the wealth, while the richest 20% own 58.6% of the wealth.

2.   These figures are calculated by Edward N. Wolff, "Estimates of Household Wealth Inequality in the U.S.," *Review of Income and Wealth,* Vol. 33, No. 231, September, 1987, pp. 231–256. The wealthiest 10% owned 71% of all the corporate stock owned by individuals and 70% of all corporation and government bonds, according to figures cited by Kevin Phillips, *The Politics of Rich and Poor,* New York, 1990, p. 79.

Because capital wealth on average produces considerable income for its holders, its unequal distribution is an important cause of the underlying inequality in the distribution of U.S. income.

IMPERFECTIONS IN THE MARKETS FOR THE FACTORS OF PRODUCTION

Another explanation of unequal income distribution involves imperfections in factor markets. Wages and salaries can be boosted by institutional factors such as the labor unions discussed in the previous chapter. Unionized firms pay more than the nonunionized, so it appears that the decline of union membership among low-wage workers has contributed to the low growth or even decline in wages for such workers. (One reason has been greater employer resistance to unionization; another has probably been the growth of competition foreign and domestic that has eroded the profitability of tight oligopolies and made it less likely that they would pay enhanced wages to their workers.)

Another market imperfection that may lead to income differentials is discrimination based on race, sex, class, religion, or anything else. Every form of income, including rents, interest, and profit, as well as wages and salaries, may be higher for some and lower for others in the presence of discrimination that results in lower economic opportunities for a portion of the population.

Discrimination in Labor Markets

The tools of supply and demand enable us to investigate the economics of discrimination, and to predict in general terms when the impact of discrimination in labor markets is likely to increase income inequality. First, let us consider the case of *limited discrimination within an industry*, as when one individual firm's managers refuse to hire certain people, or employees refuse to work alongside people who are the subject of their prejudice. This case is not as economically harmful as it might be, because the market works to penalize the discriminating firm. Consider Figure 13.3, where the firm in panel **a** discriminates against some minority group, while the firms in the rest of the industry do not. In this case, the discriminating firm's labor supply will decrease, from S_A to S_A', as in panel **a**, with the result that wages there rise from W_A to W_A'. Meanwhile, as the workers who are discriminated against seek jobs at the other firms in the industry, labor supply for these firms will increase from S_B to S_B', as in panel **b**, with the result that wages fall from W_B to W_B'.

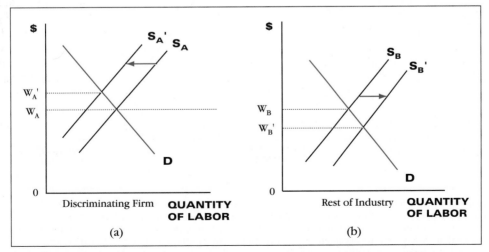

Figure 13.3. **Limited discrimination.** Here, discrimination harms its perpetrators. In panel **a**, discrimination drives away part of a firm's work force, so the firm has to pay a higher wage. When those discriminated against try to find work at firms where they are accepted, the greater supply (panel **b**) causes wages to decline. The lower costs in market B put the firm that discriminates at a competitive disadvantage.

In a competitive market, the firms that do not discriminate in their hiring will therefore have lower costs than the firms that do. The nondiscriminating firms, with their lower costs, will be able to undersell the discriminators, who will either have to follow suit or "go bust." The ability of this type of discrimination to increase income inequality is therefore more limited than would otherwise be the case.

Now assume that the managers and the employees in an entire industry engage in *broad-based discrimination*. Several results are possible. One result can be segregation in the work space. Another might be a compensating wage differential, with extra pay provided to the prejudiced workers to overcome their antipathy. Below, we consider a case in which income distribution is made less equal because all the workers that are discriminated against are driven out of an industry and have to find employment in an industry where their skills are superfluous.

To make this argument, assume that there are two job markets: Market A, in which higher-than-average education and skills are required for employment; and Market B, in which the education and skills required are below those for A. Assume further that the population is evenly divided between a group that is prejudiced and another group that is discriminated against. Finally, assume that each group possesses the same average ability, skills, and education (that is, each group has the same proportion of individuals eligible for employment in Market A and in Market B).

If no discrimination in hiring is being carried on, half the workers in each market will be prejudiced workers and half will be the object of prejudice. If the demand for labor is approximately the same in both markets, wages will be higher in Market A (W_A in panel **a** of Figure 13.4) than in Market B (W_B in panel **b**). That is because the supply of labor in Market A will be relatively low because the labor in that market must be above average in skills. Now assume that discrimination is imposed in Market A, with the workers who are discriminated against excluded from all jobs in that market. The labor supply will be cut at once and those excluded will have to move to Market B, increasing the labor supply there. The discrimination, by reducing the labor supply in Market A from S_A to S_A', raises wages there, from W_A to W_A'. Meanwhile, wages fall in Market B from W_B to W_B' as labor supply rises from S_B to S_B'.

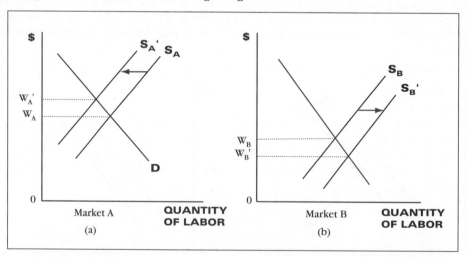

Figure 13.4. Broad-based discrimination. Unfortunately, under certain circumstances discrimination can pay its perpetrators. In panel **a**, discrimination drives away part of the work force, resulting in a higher wage for those employed in that industry. When those discriminated against try to find work in occupations where they are accepted, the higher supply causes wages to decline in those other occupations. Income inequality increases.

Under the circumstances described, discrimination can reward its perpetrators while harming both the target of the discrimination and the nation. The workers in Market B receive lower wages, and national income will fall because labor has been transferred from a market in which it is more productive to a market in which it is less productive. By contrast, the prejudiced workers who were responsible for the discrimination in the first place have succeeded in eliminating the objects of their discrimination from their work space and have achieved higher wages as well. These gains to the discriminators increase the difficulty of eradicating discrimination from labor markets. They also foster its spread because the influx of workers into Market B will lower wages there and arouse animosity against the newcomers. For this reason, history has often seen one group of immigrants (Irish, Italian, Slav) resenting the next group to arrive, resentment with an economic base because of the competition for unskilled ("Market B") jobs. Similarly, Hispanic-Americans and blacks today sometimes compete for the same entry-level jobs with results not always harmonious.

When discrimination in labor markets pays the discriminators, it is harder to eradicate than it would be if no pecuniary gain were involved. As a result, such discrimination can contribute to increasing income inequality. Fortunately, however, the more competition that takes place among firms, the more difficult it is to carry out discriminatory practices, as we have seen.

Discrimination May Have an Effect in Other Factor Markets as Well

Just as discrimination may alter the market equilibrium in the labor market and increase income inequality, it may do so in other factor markets as well. Because of ethnic, or age, or sex discrimination, an irreproducible talent may not be able to earn economic rent, or a property may not be freely rentable by anyone who can afford it, or loans may not be available to certain groups, or entrepreneurs may find some activities closed to them. Discrimination arising from government controls on credit, or from zoning laws on property, may also impair the working of market forces. Consequently, the income to the individuals discriminated against may be lower than otherwise, with income less equal as a result.

GEOGRAPHY

Geographical location plays a significant role in the distribution of income. Average annual pay in the United States was $24,600 in 1991, but it was over $27,000 in six states and under $19,000 in eight others. Except in the Northeast, those who live in rural areas have median incomes far below those who live in metropolitan areas. Of course, cost of living and the level of amenities also differ among areas, but geographical location can make a significant difference in earnings even when these are taken into account.

The basic reason for the lower income in certain geographical areas is that low productivity frequently has a distinct regional focus. A combination of declining industries, which throws many inadequately educated people whose training is suddenly made obsolete on to the job market, together with an unwillingness or inability to move out of the declining area, can bring long-term distress.

In the United States, West Virginia and the upper peninsula of Michigan are cases where declining deposits of and/or demand for labor in the mining of coal and ore have left pockets of poverty. On occasion, monopsony power on the part of firms may contribute. Rural blight can be found, especially in Maine, the "border states" of Kentucky, Tennessee, and Arkansas, and right across the deep South. Further cases in point are Wales and northern England, parts of Ireland's west and north, and the southern "Mezzogiorno" of Italy.

It might be expected that the differences would disappear as people move from low-income to high-income areas. They do not, however, because many barriers to moving exist even in a country where labor is as mobile as it is in the United States. Limited knowledge of job openings elsewhere, skills specific to a regional industry, strong ties to relatives and friends, home ownership in places where sale would be at a loss, climatic preference, general dislike of uprooting tight-knit families, regional accents, prejudice, and other sociological factors all may play a part in keeping many people in geographical areas where economic performance is well below average.

The Massive Problems of the Inner Cities

The effect of geographical location on income distribution is clearly most negative for the residents of the inner cities. Even though the great majority of those who live in the run-down inner cities are honest, peaceable, and industrious, nevertheless homelessness, poor housing, poor schools, endemic violence, drug addiction, and teenage pregnancy are facts of everyday life. The dilapidated buildings, sometimes stretching on for miles, and the unsafe conditions are not conducive to investment and economic health. Many of the good jobs have long since moved away from these weakening inner-city economies to more favorable locations, and many of the better educated and more motivated (the best equipped to bring about change) have understandably left with the jobs. Long periods of welfare and extended episodes of joblessness are common.

Why such conditions exist crosses the discipline's boundaries into sociology, anthropology, and psychology, taking economics back to its roots as a social science. One attempt at an explanation by a distinguished economist is traced in the accompanying box.

THE EASTERLIN HYPOTHESIS OF INNER-CITY CROWDING

The crowding of masses of disadvantaged people in blighted inner-city neighborhoods is the main cause of the low income in these areas, according to Richard Easterlin of the University of Southern California. The Easterlin Hypothesis suggests detrimental economic and social effects from the crowding of the poor into the inner cities. Inner cities are and always have been a magnet for the poor. It is a worldwide phenomenon. Immigrants from other countries or minority groups within a country seek out places where their religion or language or skin color is not held against them in finding employment, housing, and social contacts. Like attracts like, and if relatives or acquaintances have already gone to the inner city, that is where the newcomers go as well, pushing down wages because of high supply.

A crowded population may have to pay severe penalties. The high supply of unskilled labor combined with the low productivity (MRP = demand) of that labor means that wages will be correspondingly low—and falling as the demand for labor turns against the unskilled. A surge of new entrants into the schools increases the number of students per teacher, reduces space, and is likely to reduce academic attainment. Many pressures may be associated with inadequate income: more drugs, greater alcoholism, more mental depression, more suicides. The disappointment, frustration, bitterness, and rage lead to much more crime and unsafe streets. The low income also makes it harder to support a family, so pregnancies often lead to unmarried mothers rather than marriage.

DATA ON THE DIFFERENCES IN INCOMES

The operation of the basic market forces of demand and supply as just discussed, together with any imperfections in these markets, is the major cause of the differences in wages and salaries in market economies. Table 13.4 presents data showing some of the disparities that exist in wage and salary income in the United States. Wages and salaries clearly differ greatly depending on occupation, and they also differ substantially depending on family status, race, and education.

TABLE 13.4
Median pay, full-time U.S. workers, 1990.

Executives, administrators, and managers	$34,284
Sales workers	$24,673
Less skilled blue-collar workers	$17,499
Service workers	$15,369
Farming, forestry, and fishing	$13,617
Male heads of households, no spouse present	$26,827
Female heads of households, no spouse present	$15,346
White families	$33,915
Hispanic families	$21,769
Black families	$19,329
Households headed by a college or university graduate	$49,180
Households headed by a high school graduate	$28,060
Households headed by an eighth grade graduate	$12,696

Source: Statistical Abstract of the United States.

The Government Can Play an Important Role in the Distribution of Income

Government's views of income inequality can have an important impact on the distribution of income. Taxes and transfers can be designed to increase equality, and indeed they do so as seen in Table 13.1 earlier in the chapter. Progressive taxes collect a greater percentage of the income of the rich than of the poor, and so tend to limit the gaps in income. Welfare benefits that increase the income of the poor have the same effect of limiting inequality, a redoubled one if they are financed by progressive taxes. Conversely, making taxes less progressive or cutting transfers to the poor can decrease income equality. The establishment of government policies such as price controls with rationing when the poor have no access to the rationed goods, controls over foreign trade designed to protect the owners and workers of some given industry, or commercial regulations that promote monopoly power can also decrease income equality.

One reason why the distribution of income in the United States became less equal during the 1980s was the elimination of much progression in personal income taxes and a reining back of transfer programs that supplement the incomes of the poor. Some increase in the income tax rates for the highest income groups was, however, reintroduced in 1990 and 1993.

▶ THE ECONOMICS OF PERSISTENT POVERTY

If the rise in income inequality meant only that the rich were getting richer a little faster than the poor were rising out of poverty, then there might be little cause for concern. But for a portion of the poor, poverty may prove to be persistent and difficult to escape. The result might be **underclass** status for a part of the population.[3] A permanent underclass with membership

---

3.   The term underclass was apparently brought into common English usage by the Swedish economist Gunnar Myrdal, winner of the 1974 Nobel Prize. Some scholars prefer not to use the term. "Urban poor" or "ghetto poor" are among the synonyms.

extending across generations from parents to their children, and on to their grandchildren, would be a concern of the utmost importance. Because the term underclass does not have a precise meaning, estimates of the number of people in underclass status vary widely, though a figure of 3% of the U.S. population often appears in the press. In this section, we take up the question of persistent poverty.

THE MARKET IS SUPPOSED TO WORK TOWARD ELIMINATING PERSISTENT POVERTY

In a market system, the mechanism of supply and demand is supposed to work toward the elimination of poverty, as follows: People responding to the signals of the market move by sheer necessity out of poverty, and they do so by their own efforts. Because poverty is uncomfortable, the motivation to escape from it contributes to the supply of labor. That, with the demand for labor, determines wages. The highest wages attainable given a person's capabilities provides the greatest attraction; people voluntarily acquire training and education to improve their chances for better jobs; workers shift among jobs to raise their incomes; persistent poverty is escaped.

Though there is a highly optimistic gloss to this description, plenty of evidence exists that markets were and remain a powerful force to eliminate poverty. Movement to the cities all over the world, and emigration to countries like Australia, Canada, and the United States, can be seen as attempts at economic improvement. The tremendous rise in the number of people finishing primary and secondary school, and going on to college as well, can all be looked at in the light of people bettering their prospects by investing in human capital. Yet in market economies, experience shows that even when people are generally free to try to improve their economic position, a problem of an underclass has developed. Some able-bodied and mentally competent people stay poor despite the incentives provided by the market system, even in periods of business prosperity. Our task in the remainder of the chapter is to explore this topic in detail.

DEFINING POVERTY

Let us first attempt to define what poverty means. The United States and most other governments have established formal definitions of poverty and regularly publish figures based on these definitions. In the United States, a calculation of the percentage of the population living in poverty began in the early 1960s. The level was established by use of the following method. First, it was observed that a family that had to spend as much as one-third of its income on food to obtain an adequate diet was about at the margin of poverty. From that observation, a family was considered needy if its income was less than three times the cost of a nutritionally adequate calorie intake. By this standard, U.S. poverty was worse in the 1980s than it was in the 1970s, with the 14.2% in poverty in 1991 well above the 11–12% of the 1970s. The modern peak of 15.2% was, however, reached some years ago, in 1983. The poverty line in 1991 for a family of four was at an income level of $13,924. This is an average; the figure varies by geographic area and size of community. Table 13.5 shows further details.

TABLE 13.5
Percentage in poverty, 1991.

Total population	14.2
Whites	11.3
Hispanics	28.7
Blacks	32.7
Families headed by a female, no husband present	39.7
Families headed by a black female, no husband present	51.2

Source: U.S. Bureau of the Census. In calculating the figures, noncash government transfers such as food stamps, school lunches, provision of medical care through Medicaid, and low-cost housing are not included. If such in-kind assistance is included, the number of people below the poverty line drops by about one-fifth.

Many other measures mirror the effect of incomes below the poverty line. In general, the poor live shorter lives, eat a less nutritious diet, suffer from more sickness, acquire less schooling, and own few houses. They seldom accumulate savings; on average they are in debt and their savings are negative. Though any abstract concept of "satisfaction" is difficult to assess, the deprivation and the limited opportunities of the poor mean that from many aspects they are less satisfied with their lives. Money may not buy happiness, but it certainly increases the range of choices concerning what to do about *un*happiness.

A Further Look at the Data

Further conclusions can be drawn from the existing data (which are voluminous). Young people under 18 make up 40% of those in poverty; they are affected out of proportion to their numbers in the population. About 40% of the poor live in areas of concentrated poverty, mostly inner cities. Studies that put poverty figures on the same basis, adjusting for different methods of measurement, show U.S. poverty rates to be two to five times greater than they are in the other major industrial countries. (Canada is in second place, with about 7% of its population in poverty compared to the 14% in the United States. By comparison, the figure is 5% in Britain, 4% in France and Sweden, and 3% in Germany and the Netherlands.)

Note that the poverty figures in Table 13.5 do not indicate the degree of deprivation. That is, it cannot be determined from these percentages whether most of those in poverty are very poor, far below the threshold, or just under it. In fact, about 38% of those below the poverty line have less than half the poverty level of income. This segment of the very poor is growing—the figure was only 30% in 1975.

The data also contain some surprises: 62% of all poor households have a car, nearly half have air conditioning; 31% have microwave ovens.[4] As we have already noted, those in poverty in the United States are not on average as poor as the lowest income groups are in the world's least-developed countries.

WHY WORRY ABOUT THE ECONOMICS OF POVERTY?

It is fair to ask why it matters. Why should persistent poverty be of concern to society? Just as much of the debate on economic equality is normative, so is the debate on why persistent poverty should be a major concern of economics.

There is indeed a compelling pragmatic argument that societies should make the effort through their collective action to eliminate persistent poverty if they can. An acceptable social "safety net" reflecting some standard of economic justice for all segments of society can be seen as an insurance policy that the political framework within which a market system operates will remain reasonably calm. As Jacob Viner of Princeton University put it, great advantages flow from keeping all parts of society "tolerably content" so that peace, quiet, law and order reign, and the business of everyday life can go forward.[5] Respect for the market can, as history shows, be bruised, certainly among the underclass in poverty, and also among others more fortunate who for moral reasons are concerned with such developments.[6] The erosion of law and order creates uncertainty, so cutting profits, hindering investment, interfering with education, and eliminating growth.

---

4.   *Wall Street Journal,* April 14, 1992, citing the Heritage Foundation.

5.   See Jacob Viner, "The Intellectual History of Laissez Faire,"*Journal of Law and Economics,* Vol. 3, October, 1960, pp. 45–69.

6.   Neither Karl Marx nor Friedrich Engels, the great intellectuals of Communism and enemies of the market, were born into poor families (in fact, Engels was a rich man). Many other communists, socialists, and other "ists" were not poor either. They took up their cudgels against the market not because of their own poverty, but because they believed that the market system did not give sufficient guarantee against persistent poverty for many.

In effect, social action against persistent poverty can be seen as insurance that the economic system will continue to work. However, a warning is in order. A genuine concern for a problem is no guarantee that government action to rectify it will make things better. There is plenty of evidence that antipoverty policies can make matters worse if they are not carefully thought out, as we shall see.

WHY DOES POVERTY PERSIST?

The basic question that has to be answered is, "why does poverty perpetuate itself among certain families, and why does it too often pass from generation to generation?" Three major alternatives present themselves from our earlier discussion of income distribution. The cause could be systemic in that the productivity of a portion of the population is very low because of inadequate capabilities including limited education and training, so low as to mean long-term poverty for many. It could be a product of pervasive discrimination that reduces opportunities and results in an underclass. It could also occur because unwise government policy offsets the incentives of the market system, causing people to decide that welfare is preferable to work. Of course, it could also be a combination of all these reasons. This question is discussed in the remainder of the chapter.

A "CULTURE OF POVERTY?"

Mounting evidence indicates that the most serious problems associated with long-term poverty in the United States are homelessness, welfare dependency, and the difficulty in improving conditions in the inner cities. We address each of these in turn, providing a description of the situation and some analysis of what form improvements might take.

Homelessness

A much studied recent topic has been the cause of the homelessness so noticeable in large cities. The number of homeless people is uncertain. The 1990 U.S. Census figure of 229,000 is widely agreed to be an underestimate because of difficulties in contacting the homeless. Private groups place the number at 600,000 to 2 million; 750,000 to 1 million is perhaps a reasonable estimate. The majority are believed to be white males. Surveys of the homeless reveal that about half have a drug and/or alcohol problem, while about another third of the homeless are mentally ill but do not qualify for institutionalization, largely because of recent cuts in spending on mental institutions. Homelessness may also be the outcome for people who have lost their jobs and cannot find another, or who do not want to work, and whose welfare payments are not enough to rent decent housing. Some are affected by more than one of these causes.

Economics figures importantly in all of them. Rent controls in cities matter because they lead to housing shortages; so do widespread cuts in federal and state funding for mental institutions and low-income housing; so do zoning laws that prohibit what use to be called "flophouses." As they now are, homeless shelters in cities are usually Spartan, and at worst they can be both dehumanizing and dangerous. What to do? Many of the homeless receive some forms of government assistance, mainly food stamps, but the assistance has done little to provide more affordable low-cost housing or enhance their employability and self-respect. Given the large numbers of homeless who are involved in substance abuse or who are mentally ill, the problem will be difficult to solve.

Welfare Dependency

Much debate surrounds the degree to which the economics of poverty reflect the influence of family and community background in establishing a dependency on government welfare programs linking the fates of parents and children. All observers point to a long history of low productivity and discrimination, and to the effects of ill-designed government programs considered below. But it is also true that the economics of poverty are affected by cultural and psychological influences of family and community. These influences, downplayed in earlier statistical analyses, are now receiving much more attention and recent data tend to confirm their importance.[7] It is still unclear exactly what the links are between a cultural environment and welfare dependency, and how large is the independent influence of discrimination and previous deprivation in closing off opportunities.

In some cases, it appears that children who grow up poor remain poor because their parents' low income damaged the children through some mechanism involving malnutrition or inadequate health or educational deprivation. In these cases, programs to provide the children with nutritious meals, monitor their health, and provide them with preschool experience would be of value in ending the cycle of poverty. The child development program called Head Start tries to do exactly this for children up to age 5. Head Start dates from 1965 and has worked well. For an annual cost of $2.2 billion (1992), it enrolls over 600,000 children 3–5 years old. Eligibility depends on family income; currently a little over a quarter of the number of children who are eligible are actually enrolled. Studies comparing siblings in the program with those who were not show a general improvement in health and nutrition. Head Start also has brought an overall improvement in academic achievement, though much less so for inner-city children where the magnitude of social problems is intense.

Strong statistical evidence exists that there is a problem when single parents (overwhelmingly mothers) receive assistance from the **Aid to Families with Dependent Children (AFDC)** program. AFDC is the biggest single U.S. welfare program, now (1992) costing about $23 billion per year, a rise of 25% since 1990. (The rise was propelled by the early-1990s recession and the rapid increase in illegitimate births.) AFDC's costs are about half the total budget for welfare spending for the poor, which also includes such items as food stamps, benefits for the disabled, medical care through the Medicaid program, housing subsidies, grants for winter fuel, and the small amount of "general assistance" administered by local governments. AFDC is a joint federal-state program. States set their own benefit levels and eligibility requirements, while the federal government pays from 50% to 80% of the benefits. AFDC supports about 5 million families; one out of every seven children in the United States is in an AFDC family. About half the families leave the program within two years, but from 1.5 to 2 million of them stay in it for an average eight years or more.

The fact that many people stay on AFDC for a very long time has attracted considerable attention. Authors such as Charles Murray emphasize that parents' views as to whether there is a stigma associated with accepting welfare are often passed on to their children.[8] Murray argues that this stigma, which was at one time widely felt, has broken down to a significant degree. He states that the economic assistance to the mother does little to take the children off the welfare rolls in later years. Indeed, evidence does indicate that even controlling for income, it is more likely that daughters from families on AFDC will also eventually be in the AFDC program themselves.[9] The younger recipients are when they enter, the longer they stay in. According to the Manpower Development Research Corporation of New York City, mothers who received AFDC payments before they were 22 years old are on welfare for an average of 8.8 years.

Moreover, wide disparities in welfare benefits means that the poor get far different treatment depending on the state where they live. For example, California starts AFDC payments to a family of three if its gross income falls below $1284 per month, and the maximum grant is $663 per month. In Missouri the payments to the same family would not start unless gross income fell below $577, and the maximum grant would be $292.[10] If you were poor and living in Missouri, what thought would cross your mind? Promoting more coordination among the states would undoubtedly be difficult politically, but it could solve this sort of problem.

---

7.   I made use of a thorough survey by Robert Moffitt, "Incentive Effects of the U.S. Welfare System: A Review," *Journal of Economic Literature*, Vol. 30, No. 1, March, 1992, pp. 1–61, and also Mary Corcoran, Roger Gordon, Deborah Laren, and Gary Solon, "Effects of Family and Community Background on Economic Status," *American Economic Review*, Vol. 80, No. 2, May 1990, pp. 362–366.

8.   See Charles Murray, *Losing Ground*, New York, 1984.

9.   See Peter Gottschalk, "AFDC Participation Across Generations," *American Economic Review*, Vol. 80, No. 2, May 1990, pp. 367–371.

10.   For the figures, see Committee on Ways and Means, U.S. House of Representatives, *1992 Green Book*, pp. 636–637.

▶ **WHAT TO DO?**
THE ECONOMICS OF WELFARE REFORM

Generally, politicians, the general public, and many economists have come to recognize that some of the most important incentives in the U.S. welfare system are perverse, even extremely so. Leaving welfare to take a job often means medical coverage is lost; Medicaid covers welfare recipients, but many low-paid jobs do not include health insurance. AFDC has also been much criticized because benefits are cut off if the father remains with the mother and the children. About half the states have a rule that if the father is living with the family, then the family is ineligible to receive AFDC. In any case, marriage means loss of AFDC benefits. If young welfare recipients save to go to trade school or college, their savings are called an asset that results in a reduction of benefits. Welfare often pays better than a minimum-wage job. Because benefits are calculated according to family size, the present system may actually encourage women to have more children.

The widespread dissatisfaction with the U.S. system has sparked an extended debate on what should be done. Most would agree that the structure of the system should encourage welfare recipients to leave the welfare rolls, take a job, and keep their children from following in their footsteps, rather than becoming a permanent underclass living on government grants.

BASIC EDUCATION,
TRAINING, AND WORK EXPERIENCE

An unskilled mother who did not finish high school, started receiving AFDC payments when she dropped out, and who has been in the program for eight years or so is unlikely to be an especially good candidate for employment.[11] This and similar observations have led to a growing consensus that more must be done to provide welfare recipients with adequate general education, training for specific jobs, and work experience.

Indeed, major changes involving expanded education, training, and work appear to be in the offing for the AFDC program. Considerable support has developed for **workfare** requirements that require the able-bodied welfare-dependent to take public employment if private jobs cannot be found. Such requirements are becoming common. They are a means for screening the really needy from those who are not, for encouraging those who prefer leisure to work to take private sector jobs, for delivering work experience, and for providing some on-the-job training.

A federal law of 1988, the Family Support Act, already imposes training and work requirements on welfare mothers with children above three years of age. (Mothers with children under three, who make up more than a third of AFDC recipients, are exempted from the requirements.) The act provides child care and health insurance for a year after leaving welfare. The idea behind this federal-state program of training and work, called JOBS for Jobs and Basic Skills, is laudable, but so far, unfortunately, it has not worked well. It has proved to be rather expensive, and compliance has been spotty and underfunded. The program is financed partly by contributions from the states, which have been unwilling to provide enough funding, so the training could not be made compulsory. Furthermore, overloaded state welfare agencies have done poorly at making available information on the programs, and many welfare recipients know nothing about JOBS. Thus in 1992 that program was just 20% of the size that had originally been envisaged in the legislation. Only about a sixth of all welfare mothers have been accepted for training; these were the ones who volunteered.

A number of states are also pursuing their own ideas for education, training, work requirements, and pursuing fathers for child support, as explored in the box.

---

11.   According to Robert Moffitt ("Incentive Effects of the U.S. Welfare System," p. 11), the percentage of women who leave AFDC to take paid employment in a given year is very low, only 6% in 1987.

RECENT STATE REFORMS TO AFDC

The U.S. government has granted waivers to about a third of the states to allow modifications in standard AFDC practice. New Jersey gives no additional aid to mothers who have children while on welfare, but gives a bonus to those who take job training or take a job. Wisconsin imposed a two-year welfare limit in two counties beginning in 1994. Welfare recipients must start training within the first month. After the two years, food stamps and housing vouchers are all that are left.

Other reforms aim to force the parent who is not at home (fathers usually) to take some responsibility for maintaining the family's income. When a family is receiving AFDC, Wyoming forces the parent not at home to enter the state JOBS program and help with child support. Some states are now providing additional child allowances where a parent has obtained a child support order from a court. This allows fathers to be identified and pursued for payment. In New York's new Child Assistance Program, women must have court-ordered child support from their children's fathers in order to obtain benefits; Arkansas, California, Massachusetts, and Montana are using their tax collection agencies to enforce delinquent child-support payments. Other states, presently including Florida, Illinois, Maine, and North Dakota, deny drivers' licenses to parents who fail to meet their child-support obligations. On the federal level, the Clinton administration has announced that it plans to emulate these state efforts by pursuing fathers who do not pay child support.

WELFARE AND INCENTIVES TO WORK

Evidence from Europe indicates that the level of welfare assistance can be set so close to the wage that could be earned from working that the incentive to work is seriously eroded. An obvious problem exists if some recipients come to see being on welfare as preferable to working. Any such difficulty is diminished in the United States, where assistance to poor families from welfare payments and food stamps is below the officially defined poverty line in every state except Alaska. Even in the United States, however, welfare programs such as AFDC (though not food stamps) have historically been administered in such a way that assistance falls by one dollar for each dollar earned when the recipient takes a job. A first reaction might be, this is only fair. But consider the situation facing a single mother on welfare receiving, say, $8,000 per year in benefits. If she took a job paying $8,000 and as a result lost her benefits, her gain of $8,000 would be counterbalanced by the same amount of loss. The implicit tax on her labor would be a confiscatory 100%. There would be no economic motive to take the job, surely not what was intended by the policymakers.

The strong evidence that the financial incentives embodied in the welfare system have not been able to diminish the numbers receiving assistance has led the Clinton administration to support a new idea: placing a time limit on welfare of two years for able-bodied adults, after which those capable of doing so must work. The argument is that cutting poor people loose from welfare after some time period will give them an increased motive to take a job. Proponents of this step contend that it would interrupt the culture of welfare dependence.

Critics point out that such a plan would be expensive, actually more so than the present system of welfare benefits, because of the need to fund job training and day care for the children involved. It is estimated that the training requirement would cost about $2,000–$5,000 per welfare mother per year, not counting any cash allowance to her. The costs for day care, transport, and supervision would be an additional $4,000–$5,000 a year. Many of the welfare mothers are among the least prepared people in the economy to find a private-sector job, so after the training, government public service jobs or employment subsidies paid to private employers would presumably have to be provided. The current estimate that 1.2 million jobs, and perhaps even more than that, would have to be created by new public funding is daunting, because that would cost about $10 billion per year and would involve nearly twice as many jobs as in any government employment program since World War II. Yet after all, perhaps these political and economic barriers will be hurdled. Republicans in the U.S. House of Representatives, formerly critical of government jobs program, are now actually calling for an even bigger and more costly approach that would extend work requirements to fathers of AFDC children.

Concerning a cutoff of benefits after two years, numerous questions arise. Would a cycle emerge with mothers on welfare for two years, then in a community service job for two or three more years, then back on welfare for two more? Who would be exempted? People addicted to drugs, or those with emotional problems, or learning disabilities? There would no doubt have to be an exemption for mothers with infant children, but what age limit would be enforced? Using present state standards for workfare, about half of all welfare mothers would be exempted because of preschool-age children, their own age, or disability.

More difficult is the problem of what to do if a mother about to reach the time limit has another baby. New Jersey and Wisconsin do not give increased benefits to women who have additional children while still on welfare, taking a tougher position than in the recent past and reflecting an attempt to alter the behavior of welfare recipients more directly than before. Some authorities, such as Charles Murray, would take a harder line yet, forcing a mother who wanted to keep a child to fall back on her own or family resources. If she cannot subsist in this way, the child would be privately adopted or placed in an orphanage. Others advocate compulsory use of Norplant, the chemical contraceptive, in such cases.

CUTTING COSTS BY SELECTIVE TARGETING

In an era of large budget deficits, a general requirement for training and placement in a job, including the accompanying child care, would be so expensive that this reform might be fatally compromised. That has led to ideas for targeting programs toward specific groups where the most could be accomplished per dollar spent. In terms of saving money, many have been attracted to the local programs (especially Ohio's) that target teenagers rather than everybody. Ohio does so by requiring teenage welfare mothers to stay in school. If they do not, their welfare payments are reduced by $62 per month, but if they do, they receive a bonus of the same amount. If national targeting of teenagers is adopted, it might be sensible to adopt an additional requirement that single mothers (or, more rarely, fathers if the children remain with them) must live with their own parents to qualify for payments. Teenagers could no longer go on welfare to gain their "freedom and independence."

After graduation from high school or reaching the age of 20, the welfare recipient could be required to take work. The costs of the public-service or subsidized jobs would be supportable because the number of teenage parents on AFDC (about 400,000) is much lower than the *total* number on AFDC. Jobs could be provided for about $500 million per year. Some critics argue that teenage targeting would simply cause women to wait until they are 20 to go on welfare. But even if this is the case, at least many would have a high school diploma and a better chance to escape the permanent poverty trap. To the extent that costs are an issue—as indeed they are—targeting seems to be a good idea.

TAX CREDITS FOR THE POOR

Many economists have long recommended that cash subsidies for the working poor administered through the tax mechanism would be an improvement on the present system of welfare, rent supplements, food stamps, and the like. A federal **earned-income tax credit** is now in place that can be claimed on the IRS income tax return. As presently constructed, it is tantamount to a 17% subsidy to working heads of families with annual earnings of $8,000. The subsidy is greater below that level of income, and less above it. The subsidy starts to phase out at an income level of $11,840, and disappears completely at $22,570. The Clinton administration strongly supports these tax credits, and in 1993 working poor with no children were made eligible for them.

Though relatively small in size, such tax credits possess several advantages. The payments preserve the incentive to work because a welfare recipient who would otherwise have no reason to take a job receives a subsidy to do so. Under the tax credit plan, there is no motive for fathers to abandon their families, as is true of the AFDC program and much else in the present welfare system.

States have also moved to establish a greater incentive to take work. Among many examples of recent reform, New York's Child Assistance Program scales its benefit reductions to mothers who go to work in order to increase incentives to take a job. It also has substituted cash benefits for food stamps in order to reduce the stigma of poverty and introduce an element of choice. Minnesota allows welfare recipients to earn 120% of the welfare level before any benefits are phased out.

Opposition to money subsidies for the poor comes from those who doubt the wisdom of handing over cash to the disadvantaged. In an outspoken way of putting it, the money might be used for beer or lottery tickets or junk food rather than for a nutritious diet, housing, and clothing, which would make the destitution worse than before. The objection amounts to charging that if the poor had the initiative and ability to manage properly the cash given to them, then they would already have taken the necessary steps to escape from poverty. At least food stamps must go for food, while cash need not. (Also, without question, those who supply the food and the housing much prefer direct allocation of these by means of food stamps and direct provision of housing.) Others argue that the major aim should be to wean people from government grants altogether.

Yet the concept of persuading the indigent to take a job in order to qualify for the subsidy, and then to decide for themselves how they will allocate their benefits, has undoubted appeal. By providing incentives for them to take paid work, it increases the odds that poverty will be an episode rather than a culture. By forcing them to be responsible in their spending, it gives a form of training valuable in itself. By reducing the direct provision to the poor of food, housing, and so forth, it improves the odds that the system will be judged on its merits rather than for the "welfare benefits" it brings to farmers, supermarkets, building contractors, and landlords.

SPECIFIC PROGRAMS FOR CHILDREN

Economists have recently been active in recommending that specific measures must be directed at the children growing up in a situation of welfare dependency. Presently one of the best indicators of whether a child will be on welfare later in life is whether the single parent raising the child is on welfare now. This cycle is an unfortunate one, and a focus on children could help to break it.

What policies oriented toward children would have the best economic results? The following are the recommendations of University of Wisconsin economists Robert Haveman and Barbara Wolfe.[12] (1) Lengthen the amount of time children stay in school. Adopting policies that reduce high school dropout rates and increase post high school training will improve the employment prospects of young people and help to break the dependency cycle. (2) Recognize the evidence that children in welfare families are seldom harmed in any measurable way when

---

mothers take jobs (perhaps under the workfare arrangements discussed previously). In fact, the reverse seems to be true. Moreover, the children can be considerably influenced by growing up with an expectation that income cannot permanently be obtained from staying on welfare. (3) Increase child support payments from fathers (or mothers). (4) Ensure that health care coverage is provided for children on welfare. That would decrease the incidence of disease, encourage the entry of their mothers into the labor force, and increase the mobility of labor.

▶ THE MASSIVE PROBLEMS OF THE INNER CITIES

Almost all observers would agree that persistent poverty is most difficult to combat in the inner cities. In the inner cities, health is worse—black infants in those surroundings are more than twice as likely to die before they reach the age of 1 as white babies in the suburbs. Two out of three of black inner-city children have been born to unmarried mothers, compared to one out of four in the 1960s. Over 60% of black households (1991) are headed by mothers with the father not present, compared to 28% in 1959. These mothers and their children have a median income only one-third that of black households where both parents are present.[13] The life expectancy of a black male in Harlem is no better than that of a black male in an underdeveloped country in Africa. Black men are six times more likely to be murdered than white men; blacks, most from the inner cities, make up 40% of the U.S. prison population but only 12% of the total population.[14] Those who serve a jail term are far less likely to be employed at a later time than those who don't. Disturbingly, earnings from crime, mostly drug dealing, are higher than for low-paid unskilled work.

Unemployment is exceedingly high: 40% of young blacks aged 16–19 are currently (1992) unemployed, and 24% of those aged 20–24. Each of these figures is more than double those for the white population. To a lesser extent, all of these problems are shared by Hispanics, particularly Puerto Ricans, in the inner cities. The result is that overall unemployment in cities such as Detroit, Los Angeles, Miami, and New York is 8% or 9%, well above the national average.

These conditions have had serious economic results. At the start of the 1990s, the median income of blacks was only 57% of median income of whites. In 1991, as we have already seen, just 11.3% of the white population was below the poverty line, while that figure was 32.7% for blacks and 28.7% for Hispanics. (It should, however, be pointed out that because there are far more whites in all, the total number of whites in poverty exceeds the total for the minority groups.)

SPECIAL PROGRAMS FOR THE INNER CITIES

The situation in America's inner cities is much worse than elsewhere in the country. Many observers now believe that an attack on a broad front will be necessary, because the individual problems are interconnected and reinforce one another to such a degree that piecemeal measures to improve the situation may have little effect. Multifaceted intervention may be required. Many current suggestions go beyond economics. Prominent among them are the reinstitution of law and order with more police, federal marshalls, and bootcamp incarceration for criminals; reduced access to Saturday-night specials (that is, cheap handguns), and bans on semiautomatic and automatic weapons with large-capacity magazines; the establishment of residential schools; and dispersal programs that help inner-city residents to move out of blighted neighborhoods.[15]

---

13.   It should be pointed out that white illegitimacy rates (22% of all births, 44% of births to mothers below the poverty line) are now higher than these rates were for black mothers 30 years ago.

14.   From *The Economist,* March 3, 1990. In 1989, 20% of all black men aged 16–34 were either in prison, on parole, or on probation (whites: 7%). Some three-quarters of black high school dropouts aged 25–34 have criminal records. For these details see Richard Freeman, "Crime and the Employment of Disadvantaged Youths," *NBER Working Paper No. 3875,* 1992.

15.   A small program called Moving to Opportunity was passed by Congress in 1992. When operational it will give rent support and assistance in finding housing to 1500 families in six cities. The program will allow these inner-city families to move to low-poverty areas in the suburbs, where jobs are more easily obtained.

The most prominent suggestion directly involving a standard economic tool is that economic development subsidies could be established for the inner cities. Development subsidies were a major idea of the Bush administration that has been taken up by President Clinton. The 1993 budget contains $3.5 billion for nine empowerment zones and 95 enterprise communities. About two-thirds of both zones will be in urban areas, mostly inner cities. The other one-third are classified as "rural." The empowerment zones will be getting up to $100 million each, while the enterprise communities will be getting up to $3 million each, all spread over two years. Tax advantages and grants will be made available to stimulate investment in blighted areas. Applicants will be judged for their plans to attract state, local, and private investment. The major incentives aside from federal aid will be tax incentives for hiring, and exemption from the capital gains tax. A number of nonprofit community development banks will also be established under a Clinton plan for bringing credit to these areas.

Critics worry, however, that tax credits and loans to lure entrepreneurs run up against the problem that the inner cities lack the skilled labor, the infrastructure of public utilities, the transportation, the law and order, the education, and the housing that are required. Even if these deficiencies are overcome, tax credits may do nothing more than shift investment from some area outside the enterprise zones into them. There is a risk that the firms given the credits will end up employing people from outside the inner cities and will depart when the benefits end.

IMPROVEMENT OF THE INNER CITIES WILL BE HARD

Whatever the programs adopted, improving conditions in the inner cities will be terribly hard. There is a golden rule that those who live there are determined to leave, and at the first opportunity they *do* leave. Many use the military to make their escape. Sometimes parents scrimp to pay for a parochial school education with its far better discipline and educational results, which is another common method for escape. Note what the military and parochial schools have in common: strict rules and requirements, and high expectations, neither of which are remotely present in most inner-city public schools. The out-migration of the most talented from the inner cities is especially bad for education. The middle-class families leave; the student body loses good role models; the remaining parents may be mostly single mothers; parent involvement with the schools collapses as the most active parents depart; the gangs' influence grows; the drugs are heavier; weapons are carried into the schools. More generally in the inner cities, the poor left behind have lost their leadership and their employment as well. The depths of these problems explain why the scholars who study the issue often recommend a massive and multipronged approach that goes beyond economics.

CONCLUSION

All in all, the battle against the development of a permanent underclass outside the mainstream of the economy is a great economic challenge still to be overcome. It will take skill and perseverance to rectify the situation. Since the causes of persistent poverty are partly cultural as well as economic, the struggle to end it is likely to be difficult, and to take a long time. That being the case, it would seem sensible to view antipoverty programs as a cost of a reasonable life for the majority, in effect an insurance policy against urban violence, a way to "buy" safer cities and a stronger national fabric. Poverty programs are at least a partial substitute for the additional police forces, prisons, and courts that are always needed when people are poor.

SUMMARY

1) Income distribution can be measured in several ways, including the percentage of income earned by quintiles (lowest 20% of the population by income, next 20%, etc.), Lorenz curves, and Gini coefficients. Lorenz curves are a graphic method. If income were equally shared among an entire population, the Lorenz curve of income distribution would be a 45° line, while the more unequal the distribution, the more bowed below the 45° line the Lorenz curve will be. A Gini coefficient is a numerical way to measure income distribution, with 0.0 meaning complete equality (everyone having the same income) and 1.0 complete inequality (one person having all the income and the rest having none). However measured, wide differences in income exist within and among the market economies.

2) The major causes of unequal income distribution are the operation of markets for factors of production, inequality in the distribution of wealth, and the existence of imperfections in the markets for these factors. Government policies toward income distribution can have a major impact as well.

3) Discrimination in labor markets is relatively self-limiting in a competitive framework where one firm attempts to discriminate while the others in its industry do not. In certain circumstances, though, discriminatory practice may raise the income of its perpetrators and lower that of those discriminated against.

4) Measures of the poverty line are typically based on the amount of income needed to purchase an adequate diet. In the United States, poverty measured in this manner is now higher than it was in the 1970s, though below its early-1980s maximum.

5) A major reason why poverty persists appears to involve a cycle wherein children follow parents on to the welfare rolls. This cycle of welfare dependence appears pronounced in the large AFDC (Aid to Families with Dependent Children) program. To break the cycle, many observers recommend compulsory training and work experience (workfare), and possibly a cutoff from AFDC benefits after two years. But the training and the provision of public service jobs or employment subsidies would be expensive, so reforms along these lines are difficult to implement. It is especially important to ensure that benefits are calibrated in such a way that the incentive to take paid work is preserved. Hence the earned-income tax credit for low-income workers.

6) The massive problems of the inner cities appear intractable. Many observers now contend that multipronged interdisciplinary approaches involving law and order, schools, and housing will be needed, as well as more standard economic approaches such as economic development subsidies and tax credits.

Chapter Key Words

Aid to Families with Dependent Children (AFDC): A major U.S. government program to aid single parents (usually mothers) and their children.

Earned-income tax credit: A system of federal subsidies paid to people who are willing to take low-paid work. Being expanded by the Clinton administration.

Easterlin hypothesis: The idea that the crowding of population, as in inner cities, is detrimental to economic and social welfare.

Gini coefficient: A numerical way to measure income distribution, with 0.0 meaning complete equality (everyone having the same income) and 1.0 complete inequality (one person having all the income and the rest having none).

Lorenz curve: A graphic method to present the data on income distribution. If income were equally shared among an entire population, then the Lorenz curve of income distribution would be a 45° line. The more unequal the distribution, the more bowed below the 45° line the Lorenz curve will be.

Underclass: Urban poor or ghetto poor. Poses a problem, especially for the United States, because persistent poverty among an underclass has worsened even though the economy has been growing, and a cycle of welfare dependence appears to have emerged.

Workfare: The requirement that people receiving welfare assistance must also look for work, or actually work, or take educational courses, or take job training (state regulations vary greatly).

CHAPTER QUESTIONS

1) The kingdom of Pecunia has evenly distributed income except for the king who is very rich. The lowest earning quintile of households receives 10% of all income. The second quintile also receives 10%, as does the third, fourth, and fifth. The king (who is also king of Graustark, where he lives, and so is not included in any quintile) earns the other 50% of Pecunia's income. Draw the Lorenz curve for Pecunia. What is Pecunia's Gini coefficient? (Hint: remember that the area of a triangle is one half the length of the base times the height.)

2) If you were at the lower end of the income distribution, would you prefer to live in a country with a Gini coefficient of .38 or one with a coefficient of .57? Why?

3) In response to concerns about low wages for unskilled labor, Congress authorizes a new program that increases demand for workers in low-skill occupations. As a result the demand curve for unskilled labor becomes identical to the demand curve for high-skilled labor. However, wages of unskilled workers continue to be lower than for skilled workers. Explain.

4) East-West Freight is a large trucking company that only hires men to drive its trucks. An interview with the president reveals why: He says, "Women aren't strong enough to be truck drivers, so we don't want them." However, the data show that other trucking companies do hire women drivers. What do you predict will happen to East-West freight?

5) New data on the trucking industry become available. As it turns out, all trucking companies discriminate against women. What is the effect on wages and employment in the trucking industry? In alternative industries? Is the economy hurt in any way?

6) Suppose that the official poverty level in a rural area is $12,000 and in an urban area it is $15,000. Explain how such a difference arises. If 20% of the rural people and 10% of the urban people are below the poverty level, are you certain that there is more suffering and deprivation in the rural area?

7) A city planning board passes the following three-part plan to improve the housing situation of low-income people:

   a) Rent ceilings will be imposed in order to prevent landlords from charging exorbitant rents.

   b) Dirty and unsafe boarding houses will be razed.

   c) Unused school buildings will be made into shelters for those who cannot find housing.

   Do you think this plan will tend to increase or decrease homelessness?

8) The following is a simple welfare scheme: All whose incomes are below $10,000 will have their income supplemented so that it is equal to $10,000. Note that a full-time job paying $5 per hour results in a yearly income of $10,000. How would someone who does not work feel about:

   a) A part-time job paying $5 per hour?

   b) A full-time job paying $5 per hour?

   c) A full-time job paying $6 per hour?

   Does your answer depend on how people value their leisure time?

An Introduction to Macroeconomics

OVERALL OBJECTIVE: To indicate that market economies are often subject to contractions called recessions and expansions so rapid that they cause inflations, and to explain that recessions and inflations can cause serious economic damage.

MORE SPECIFICALLY:

- To show that recessions and inflations have historically been very common.
- To explain that the damage from recessions includes unemployment, lost output, domino effects on other countries, and serious political consequences.
- To discuss the damage from inflation: To creditors and those on fixed incomes and holders of assets earning fixed interest rates when it is unexpected, and the menu costs and shoe-leather costs even when it is expected.
- To view the much greater damage from hyperinflation, which is caused by extreme government overissue of new money.

Macroeconomics is the study of the whole economy's behavior rather than the behavior in individual markets. What determines the size and growth rate of a nation's output and income? What causes output and income to fluctuate? An economy's growth can slow down, or stop, or even become negative. When an economy contracts, the decreases in production and accompanying high unemployment are called **recessions**, or **depressions** when they are more severe.[1] An economy can also expand so rapidly that it overheats with general price rises called **inflation**. Great national issues such as the level of taxes, government spending, national debts, and budget deficits are all tied to these topics. All are branches of macroeconomics, and all are surveyed in this part of the book.

Macroeconomic instability has afflicted the market system not only recently but for centuries. Whether a "business cycle" of major economic fluctuations is inevitable, and whether government action can succeed in smoothing these swings, are questions in which everyone has a stake. Unpredictable oscillations in the macro economy are even more damaging than the unemployment and inflation that commonly accompany them. They bring the risk that decisions taken by businesses (such as new capital investment) and households (such as purchase of a home or car) at the *micro* level will be postponed or wrong. They certainly can cause major political overturns. Conversely, a stable macro economy with steady growth will suffer little damage from unemployment and inflation and will provide the setting for correct micro decision making by households and firms.

Understanding what *causes* the repetitive cycles of boom and slump requires a basic knowledge of macroeconomics, so it is premature to take up that question now. Investigation of this question is pursued in most chapters of this half of the book, and it is addressed specifically in Chapter 18. Here at the outset, our task is the simpler one of establishing that recurrent macroeconomic instability has been a fact of life in the market economies.

▶ RECURRENT RECESSION AND INFLATION

All the major market economies of Europe and North America exhibit a cyclical growth pattern with slowdowns or declines in economic activity following rapid expansions that often include inflationary price movements. Such fluctuations are not new; they occurred even in the time of Adam Smith, over 200 years ago. The timing and severity of these cycles are not fully predictable, and they have not always affected all countries simultaneously. But they do occur, for reasons we must examine.

Figure 14.1 shows the experience between 1900 and 1992 in a format that shows the long-term ups and downs in the nation's total output. The measure of output used is **gross domestic product**, or GDP, which is the standard way to count the total value of all goods and services produced in an economy in a given year. (How to calculate GDP is addressed in the next chapter.)

On the figure you can easily identify the booms, where the blue line extends above the horizontal line drawn at 0%, and the slumps below that line. When economic historians view earlier booms and slumps along with those of the twentieth century, they are able to identify 91 separate periods of expansion and contraction in the U.S. economy between 1790 and 1990. The duration of the individual episodes have been as short as a few month and as long as eight or nine years.

---

1.   The word recession has a conventional meaning among economists: a decline in production lasting six months or more. The word "depression" has no technical meaning beyond "bad recession." "The Great Depression" refers to the severe economic slump during the 1930s, which is discussed later in the chapter.

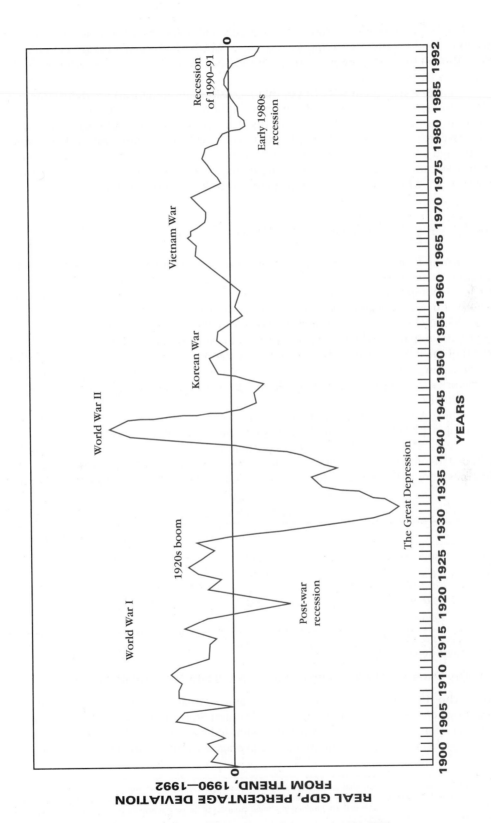

Figure 14.1. Real GDP, Percentage Deviation from trend, 1900-1992.

Cyclical behavior has plainly been a consistent fact of economic life—though with the favorable development that contractions since World War II have been generally shorter than before then (11-month average, compared to about double that in the earlier period), while the expansions have been longer.

Though it may seem self-evident that recessions and inflations are damaging, only when we get to know them intimately can we appreciate how serious that damage can be, and has been. Indeed, it is not too fanciful to consider that bad recessions and bad inflations have some of the same results as thefts and embezzlements in the world of business. All of them cause economic loss, though a bad recession or inflation robs the majority, not just a minority, of the population. The next section looks at the extent of the damage. Once we have established that the injury can be severe, we will recognize how important it is to keep it from occurring.

▶ THE DAMAGE FROM RECESSION

Downturns in economic activity have the obvious consequences that fewer goods and services are produced as businesses operate at less than their full capacity, joblessness increases, and people have less income to buy what is produced. A rule of thumb is that each 1 percentage point rise in the rate of unemployment, say from 6% of the labor force to 7%, means over a million addition-al people out of work, and an annual loss of about $100 billion in output, over $400 per person.[2] A detailed estimate for 1980–1983 states that if unemployment had held at 6% during those years instead of the 8.5% actually registered, the U.S. economy would have produced additional goods and services worth $654 billion. Some of this lost output would be capital goods such as machines and factories, the absence of which will be felt far into the future because the economy will be less productive.

Table 14.1 shows the figures for unemployment and for capacity utilization (that is, the proportion of productive industrial capacity currently in use) in the two worst recession years of the past 20 years, 1975 and 1982. It compares them to the worst figures from the Great Depression of the 1930s, long-term averages in the 1970s, and the current figures. (The details of how unemployment and capacity utilization are calculated are considered in the following chapter.)

TABLE 14.1
The damage from recession.

	Unemployment, %	Capacity utilization, %
1930s (worst)	24.9?	40?
1975	8.5	74.6
1970–1979 average	6.2	81.8
1982	9.2*	75.0†
Current	6.0 (June 1994)	83.5 (May 1994)

*Worst, December 1982, 10.8%.
†Worst, November 1982, 68.8%.

The Damage May Be Concentrated on Certain Individuals and Groups

Those who lose their jobs face considerable damage on a personal and family level. Unemployment benefits help, though in the United States they are limited to six months after a job is lost. (But that time period is usually extended by Congress during serious downturns.) Yet the average benefit is only about 40% of the average earnings of the employed, and thus the drop

---

2.   The real output loss is somewhat overstated, however, because the unemployed use some of their otherwise idle time to produce output at home such as painting, small repairs, tuning up the car, and so forth. As we shall see in Chapter 15, such home-produced output is mostly not counted in the statistics for national production. Some estimates of the output gain from the home-produced output of the unem-ployed run up to 25% of the reported loss.

in income for the out-of-work is very substantial. In Europe, the benefits are generally higher—over 80% of the beneficiary's working wage in a few countries—and are paid for a longer period. The U.S. public seems little interested in paying the taxes that would be needed to finance greater benefits, however. In any case, the European generosity has been blamed for making it easier to remain on the dole.

Many of the U.S. jobless do not receive benefits. Those just entering the labor force, those who haven't worked long enough to qualify, those who quit rather than being laid off, seasonal farm workers, students who would like to work, part-time employees, and the self-employed are all ineligible. The states administer unemployment compensation, and state laws vary greatly. Because of tightening up of the criteria, benefits have been paid to less than half of U.S. unemployed in recent years (42% in 1991 compared to more than three-quarters in the 1975 recession). In Massachusetts, 50% of the unemployed qualify for benefits; in Virginia, only 20%.

The unemployment that accompanies recessions hits certain groups harder than others. Teenagers as a whole have considerably higher unemployment than do adults, often at least double in both North America and Europe. (The U.S. figure for those aged 16–19 was 17.8% in December 1993, compared to 6.4% for all workers.) In the United States, blacks in every age group face more unemployment (12.9% in 1993) than the national average, six times more for black teenagers (40.1% in 1993). Certain industries are more affected than others by recessions, construction for example. In recession when the jobless figures rise nationally, they almost always rise faster in construction (17% in 1992). The number of part-time workers rises considerably in a slump. Part-timers who would prefer full-time jobs but cannot find them are "under-employed," true of some 6 million people in the recession year 1991, or about 5% of the labor force. A little more than half of these had had their workday cut, while the rest could only find part-time work. Furthermore, the longer a recession lasts, the longer it is likely to take an individual to find a new job. In the recession of the early 1980s, the length of time the average unemployed individual stayed jobless nearly doubled from 11 weeks in 1979 to 20 weeks in 1983. (The figure was still high, 18 weeks, in 1993.) In prosperous 1973 only 8% of the unemployed did not find a new job within 26 weeks; in the recession year 1982 the figure was 17%. As economic conditions worsened after 1989, the figure doubled from 10% in that year to 20% in 1993.[3]

The longer the episode of unemployment, the more discouraged some out-of-work people will become. These **discouraged workers** may stop looking for jobs. In early 1993 there were about 1.2 million of these individuals, about 1% of the labor force.[4] Unfortunately, the longer people stay unemployed, the greater the danger that skills will atrophy and that work habits will decay. Employers show strong preference for hiring those who have not been out of work for a long time.

Human Costs

Some of the human consequences of unemployment go beyond the economic effects. Tensions rise in families, and divorces increase. A 1% increase in U.S. unemployment is associated with 650 more murders, 920 more suicides, 20,000 more heart attacks, 4,000 more admissions to mental institutions, and 3,300 more inmates added to the population in state prisons.[5]

Globalization Means That Recessions May Spread

If a serious recession gets started in some major country, there is a likelihood that it will spread to other countries as well. The world's economies are more globalized than they used to be, with international trade and international finance linking them more than ever before. If in a

---

3.   It might be noted that a surprising amount of "churning"—changes in status—takes place not only among the unemployed but in the labor force as a whole. For example, each month in the United States about 20% of the unemployed leave the labor force, while in the same month, nearly three-quarters of those who obtain employment were not in the labor force during the preceding month.

4.   At the height of the early 1980s recession, there were 1.8 million discouraged workers, about 1.8% of the labor force.

5.   See Barry Bluestone and Bennett Harrison, *The Deindustrialization of America*, New York, 1982, Chapter 3.

recession income falls in the United States, then U.S. buyers will purchase fewer goods from foreigners. This fall in U.S. imports means a fall in foreign exports, less favorable business conditions abroad for firms that export, and perhaps developing unemployment. (That, in turn, can reinforce the recession in the United States, as foreigners reduce their purchases of U.S. exports.) In a recession, the lower income for U.S. firms may reduce their willingness to build new plants in foreign countries, another reason why business activity in other countries may show signs of "imported" recession. The closer connections forged by international trade and finance are in many ways a highly favorable development, but they do increase the risk that when one country catches a cold, others will get the sniffles too.

The Political Fallout

The political fallout from recession can be considerable. An Eisenhower-era slump in the 1950s was a major factor in the election of John F. Kennedy as president in 1960. A slump helped Jimmy Carter defeat Gerald Ford in 1976, while a major inflation in the late 1970s caused in part by attempts to end that slump contributed to Carter's defeat at the hands of Ronald Reagan in 1980. Finally, another downturn in 1990–1991 was a major factor in Bill Clinton's defeat of George Bush in 1992. In other countries the political effects have sometimes been catastrophic. For example, the Great Depression of the 1930s was particularly severe in Germany, helping to sweep Hitler and the Nazis into power. The recent reawakening of a nationalist and perhaps even fascist right wing in Russia is associated with the severe fall in output in that country.

In sum, the costs of recessions and depressions lie in the associated unemployment, the lost output, including the lost capital that means an economy has less productive capacity than otherwise, the domino effect on other countries, and the potential political upheaval.

HOW BAD CAN A DOWNTURN BECOME?

The United States had seen bad times in the nineteenth century. The Panic or Depression of 1837–1841 was a grim period during which business, manufacturing, and shipping all stagnated. Another severe recession beginning in 1873 was the longest to that time, with recovery delayed until about 1880. Following a revival that was not all that strong, recession recurred from 1893 to about 1898, when economic historians estimate that unemployment reached 18% of the labor force, and one-third of the nation's railways went bankrupt.

Yet these early recessions and their associated unemployment in the United States and elsewhere were more mild in their effects than what later came to be true. With the significant exception of Great Britain, most families in most economies were farm families late into the nineteenth century. A downturn in business conditions would have less effect when a household produced much of its own consumption, because this "domestic farm economy" would be little influenced by a commercial crisis. Even for people without farms, the frontier in the United States, Canada, and Australia provided an opportunity for acquiring one. The westward movement was like a giant safety valve that allowed an escape from an economic slump.[6]

The Great Depression of the 1930s

These nineteenth-century experiences were pale compared to the Great Depression of the 1930s, which was an unprecedented economic calamity. Nor has any subsequent slump been so steep, and so in large degree we have lost touch with how serious a recession can actually become. That period provides striking evidence on how severe the damage can be. To guard against any such future devastation, it becomes all the more important to understand the proper conduct of macroeconomic policy by governments. Such policy, as we shall see, is the economy's major defense against any recurrence of the disastrous 1930s.

---

6.   We should note, however, that the view of the frontier as safety valve has undoubtedly been exaggerated to some degree. Factory workers in a mill town of New England were not always very likely candidates for carving out farms on the frontier.

The production lost because of the Great Depression of the 1930s was equal to almost 3.5 years' output at that time; or more dramatically, equivalent to the sacrifice of civilian output devoted to fighting World War II. Just from 1929 to 1933, the U.S. economy's physical quantity of output fell by about 25%. Capacity utilization (the proportion of productive industrial capacity in use) fell to about 40% compared to normal figures of 80% or more. Nearly 44% of all U.S. banks failed between 1929 and 1934, meaning a whole or partial loss of the accumulated savings by those who had deposits in these banks. Business profits sank to zero. Construction activity fell to only 5% of its 1929 level. On average, $100 in corporate stock in 1929 was worth $26.63 in 1932. Unemployment had been only 3.2% of the labor force in 1929, but it reached 15.9% in 1931 and 23.6% in 1932 before peaking at 24.9% in 1933. Five years later, in 1938, unemployment was still 19%, and even by 1940 it had not fallen below 14%. Due to unprecedented difficulties in gathering data from people constantly moving about the country looking for work, even the peak of 24.9% may be an underestimate. Consumer spending fell from nearly $80 billion in 1929 to just over $46 billion in 1933. Prices fell, too, by about a quarter, but not nearly enough to counteract the halving of spending.[7]

For many of those who lost their jobs, living conditions during the Great Depression were appalling. Under *normal* circumstances, unemployment was not nearly so distressing because the existing social structure of families and churches could accommodate it. In the crisis of the 1930s, that structure failed to do so. The situation was made far worse by the absence of any system of government unemployment benefits.

There have been no further downturns as serious as the Great Depression in the world's major economies. Ensuring that there will be no repetition is one of the most important goals of macroeconomic policy and, indeed, the policies now available to lessen the severity of depressions would almost certainly have enabled the United States to avoid most of the rigors of the 1930s. Unfortunately, during that period, serious though unwitting macroeconomic errors were committed by government, errors that probably deepened the slump.

► THE DAMAGE FROM INFLATION

Market economies are also susceptible to inflation. Inflation is defined as a rise in the average level of prices as measured by a price index. (A sample price index is calculated in Chapter 15.) Since U.S. prices rose by an average of 3.3% in 1992, it follows that the rate of inflation in that year was 3.3%. In the United States, the peak years for inflation in the last two decades were 1974 (11.0%) and 1980 (13.5%). Inflation fell to 3.9% in 1982 and 1.9% in 1986, and has since been moderate (4.8% in 1989, 5.4% in 1990, 4.2% in 1991, 3.3% in 1992).

In comparison to the damage from a full-scale slump, inflation, especially when it is mild, is generally not as injurious as recession, and its consequences are often exaggerated. Many people believe that inflation will harm workers, but as all prices rise, wages usually rise as well. If, however, the inflation is serious, and there is a lag between price increases and wage increases, wage earners can suffer. Many also believe that inflation harms the elderly by eroding the value of their savings and pensions. This is now less true than in the past because governments generally tie their retirement programs to some index of the cost of living. (The U.S. Congress did so with the Social Security System in 1974.) Some private pension plans are also indexed to price changes. Yet damage from inflation can still be significant, especially when it is unexpected, and the analysis is somewhat more subtle than it was for recessions and unemployment.

DAMAGE WHEN THE INFLATION IS UNEXPECTED

Major losers in inflations, even mild ones, are those who did not anticipate it and are surprised. These are the people living in countries that have had little recent experience with inflation and

---

7.   For an excellent examination of the period, see Charles P. Kindleberger, *The World in Depression, 1929-1939*, Berkeley, 1975.

who, if they had known, could have taken steps to defend themselves. People with fixed incomes are particularly vulnerable. This group includes those dependent upon unadjustable insurance payments, or those receiving an unalterable rate of interest on bonds, or those being paid a fixed amount under a private pension. Salary earners with long-term contracts may find it difficult to get their salaries adjusted upward in time to keep up with steadily rising prices. School teachers, for example, usually receive a salary adjustment once a year, which in a moderate inflation could cause significant income loss as a result. (If prices double in a year, at the end of that year a given salary will buy only half as much as before.) In all these cases, if the inflation had been properly anticipated, people would not have put their savings into assets yielding fixed returns or have signed long-term salary agreements that could not be adjusted.

In the United States, poor people receiving welfare payments from their state or local government also suffer from inflation because welfare, unlike social security, is not tied to the rate of price increases. Many other countries *do* automatically raise their welfare payments as prices rise.

During unexpected inflations, lenders of money will lose and borrowers will gain until interest rates adjust to reflect the price rises. Consider the plight of a lender who did not foresee an inflation, and who loaned $1000 to you on your promise to repay $1050 a year from now. This means that the **nominal interest rate**, uncorrected for inflation, is 5%, since $50 is 5% of $1000. If prices remain stable, the lender will have a real gain of $50. But if inflation suddenly sets in so that prices rise by 10% during the year, the situation looks very different. It will now take $1100 to buy what $1000 would have purchased at the start of the year. The lender has lost on the transaction, because the interest payment of $50 is not enough to cover the losses from the inflation. That is, the lender can purchase less with the $1050 today than could have been purchased with the $1000 lent to you at the start of the year. In fact, for the lender just to break even, the interest payment would have to be $100, for then the repayment by the borrower would be $1100, exactly what $1000 could buy when the money was first lent. This means that to get back what was lent, the lender would have had to charge a nominal interest rate of at least 10%.

If inflation is correctly foreseen, lenders will demand to be compensated for it, and borrowers will consent. The result is that a correction for the expected rate of inflation will be built in to the nominal rate of interest. Lenders and borrowers must agree on a reasonable **real interest rate**—that is, a reasonable nominal interest rate corrected for anticipated inflation. Let us say they settle on a 3% real rate, which more or less has been the level of real interest rates in the United States for a long time. To obtain a real interest rate of 3% after taking expectations of 10% inflation into account, the repayment of the $1000 loan will have to be $1133, or a nominal rate of 13.3%. The numbers may seem a bit strange, but they are easily explained. The $1133 would be made up of $1000 to repay the loan's principal sum that you borrowed, $100 to compensate for the 10% inflation's effect on the $1000 principal; and a further $33 in interest, made up of $30 which is the agreed-upon 3% of $1000, plus another $3 to compensate for the effect of 10% inflation on the $30 interest payment. (Information on calculating real rates is provided in the accompanying box.) So, when inflation is foreseen, the nominal rate of interest will be higher than the real rate. In all the areas of economics where interest rates play a part—and there are many—it is important to keep in view that the real rate corrected for the expected rate of inflation is usually the one that counts.

If the inflation is *not* foreseen, then lenders will lose and borrowers will gain until interest rates adjust. For example, when inflation set in during the late 1970s, banks and other financial institutions suffered losses because many of their loans had been made at fixed interest rates. When a 30-year mortgage on a house is at a fixed rate, the interest payment is unchanged over the whole 30-year life of the loan; banks found they had lent at, say, 8% but inflation was

CALCULATING REAL INTEREST RATES

The interest rate corrected for inflation, called the real interest rate, can be calculated as:

$$\frac{1 + \text{nominal interest rate}}{1 + \text{rate of inflation}} = 1 + \text{real interest rate}$$

If the anticipated rate of inflation is 100% and the nominal interest rate is 110%, the calculation would be:

$$\frac{1 + 1.10}{1 + 1.00} = \frac{2.1}{2} = 1.05.$$

Thus the real rate of interest is 5%. If the expected rate of inflation is not too high, say no more than about 15 to 20%, a simplified version of this formula works reasonably well.

nominal interest rate – expected rate of inflation = real interest rate

Thus an expected 10% rate of inflation and a nominal interest rate of 12% would mean a real interest rate of 2%. The calculation is not as exact as it is with the extended formula above, but it is close enough to use for ordinary purposes.

running at 10%. That meant they were receiving a negative real rate of –2%. Borrowers gained considerably from the situation.[8]

An unexpected inflation causes obvious losses for those whose wealth is held in unindexed bonds or currency. For instance, the $1000 in currency that your grandparents put in their wall safe for you in 1979 would in 1994 (when they gave it to you as an "off to college" present) buy only a little less than half the goods that could have been purchased with the currency in 1979, because of the price increases that have occurred in the intervening years. Inflation does not have to proceed at a very fast rate to make a significant difference. Arithmetically, an annual rate of price increase (inflation) of 5% will cut the purchasing power of a dollar down to 50¢ in just slightly more than 14 years. Once they are familiar with this loss of purchasing power, grandma and grandpa will be sure to put their cash into interest-bearing securities or tangible assets such as property, antiques, art works, or anything else that they expect to rise in value along with the general price level. Hedging, as this is called, is always common when periods of significant inflation are expected to occur.

Finally, unexpected inflation can change the distribution of income. Firms have trouble reading price, so prices cease to be accurate guideposts for what should be produced. The confusion and lack of knowledge about prices is damaging for rational decisions concerning long-term contracts. Among these are investment decisions, retirement planning choices, and insuring against long-term disability. Such decisions become very difficult; some will guess better than others, gaining wealth and income from the inflation while the unlucky lose.[9] At the very

8.   As these institutions learned from their experience, many loans came to be at variable interest rates, with rates changing during the life of the loan to reflect the amount of inflation occurring or expected, rather than at fixed rates. Banks did not move entirely to variable-rate lending; in mild inflations, fixed rates will still exist, but they come to include a premium for the risk of future inflation. That risk premium explains why, in all modern economies, long-term fixed-rate mortgages on houses carry higher interest rates than do variable-rate mortgages.

9.   Theoretically, if all contracts of all kinds were fully indexed this problem could be avoided. In practice, however, some are more successful than others in obtaining full indexing even when inflation is widely anticipated. The former gain at the expense of the latter.

least, a country's long-term investment is likely to suffer. If the losses to the unlucky are large enough, the perceived injustice of the forced changes in the distribution of income may weaken people's support for existing institutions and the government. The social fabric may be torn by political upheaval.

DAMAGE WHEN THE INFLATION IS EXPECTED

When inflation is more intense, further consequences emerge even when it is *expected* and no one is surprised. The greater the price changes, the more serious these consequences are.

Menu Costs

In stronger inflations, a variety of problems, called **menu costs**, accompany the rapid price changes even when they are fully anticipated. Inconvenience and expense are associated with these menu costs. Typically, existing coins become far less useful than they used to be. First, the lowest-value coins become obsolete and just a nuisance; next, vending machines, pay telephones, subway turnstiles, and parking meters have to be changed to take coins of higher value; later, full pockets of coins have to be carried as prices rise. The labor costs to count huge bags full of coins may not be sensible, yet the government may find it too expensive to withdraw the existing coins for replacement with new ones of higher denomination. Finally, with continued inflation, coins are no longer used at all, and the machines that take them have to be adjusted to take bills or tokens.

If inflation becomes significant within a period of a month or so, it makes sense for consumers to charge their purchases. When the credit card bill is paid off at the end of the month, it will be paid in money that has lost some of its value. The buyer gains. Sellers learn the same lesson. It therefore becomes harder to find businesses that will accept credit cards, or if they do, the credit card price may be higher than the cash price. During a rapid inflation this problem may mean that cards become unacceptable to merchants.

With rapid inflation of, say, 50% or 100% per year, people cease to have very accurate information about prices. During Israel's severe inflation during the mid-1980s, surveys showed consumer knowledge concerning products they bought infrequently, such as shoes, could be so obsolete that they were often wrong in their estimates by a magnitude of ten times. The labor in simply changing prices on a weekly or daily basis becomes burdensome. (This is where the term "menu costs" comes from.) In inflationary Argentina, supermarkets in one chain were getting new price lists from headquarters every 1.3 days, and stamping new prices over old ones became a major chore.

Shoe-Leather Costs

Another sort of repercussion from inflation, even when it is correctly anticipated, is the so-called **shoe-leather cost**. The term is derived from the frequent trips to banks or stores made to avoid holding depreciating cash balances. In severe inflation, all segments of the economy from households to corporations to banks themselves must pay careful attention to managing their money balances held in cash, bank accounts, bonds, and so forth. Money must be put to earning interest at a rate at least equal to the rate of inflation, or used to buy goods. Otherwise, money will lose its value. The shoe-leather syndrome sets in even during quite mild inflations; a U.S. study of some years ago (1977) shows that each percentage point rise in inflation causes about $1 billion more per year to be spent on activities to restrict the size of money balances.

Returns from finding ways to use company cash to keep up with the inflation may become greater than those from investing in plant and equipment. For example, in Brazil during the 1989 inflation, 80% of the profits of the automobile companies were coming from shrewd decisions in putting out at interest the companies' cash reserves. In such circumstances, plant expansion and even maintenance may be neglected.

In sum, even relatively mild inflations that are anticipated will carry menu and shoe-leather costs that divert activity away from production to defense against the inflation.

HYPERINFLATION

There is the possibility that inflation will accelerate out of control, reaching the very damaging stage called *hyperinflation*. A standard definition of **hyperinflation** is price increases of at least 50% per month which, because of the powerful effects of compounding, corresponds to an annual rate of almost 13,000%. At that rate, money loses over 99% of its purchasing power within a year.[10] Its harmful effects are much more obvious than when the inflation is mild or moderate. As we shall see, hyperinflations are always caused by extreme government overissue of new money, and they end when the currency growth is brought under control.[11]

In the nineteenth century, money supplies were largely based on precious metals, so that great increases in the quantity of money were unlikely. Experiences with inflations were thus limited to countries that encountered gold and silver shortages and resorted to the undisciplined printing of paper money. Often this happened during periods of war. Though the United States has never suffered from a true hyperinflation, overissue of paper notes by the Continental Congress did cause U.S. prices to rise by about 2,000% in the six-year period up to 1781.[12] The Southern Confederacy had a similar experience, with about 1,100% inflation covering the three-year period from 1863 to 1865.

In the twentieth century, hyperinflations became much more common, and several are going on at this moment. Anecdotes about them are often memorable. In the German hyperinflation of 1923, still the most famous of them all, the postage stamps for one ordinary letter rose in price to several billion Deutsche marks, far greater than the total quantity of the whole German money supply in existence just ten years before. (As in other countries where hyperinflations are in progress, it was thought necessary to leave blank spaces in the center of postage stamps, so that postmasters could write in the requisite large number of zeroes as prices rose.) About four trillion marks were equal in value to one American dollar. Bank accounts in which people had been depositing their savings for a lifetime did not, because of inflation, contain enough purchasing power to buy a candy bar. Holders of corporate bonds, mortgages, and any other fixed-interest assets lost everything. Before the capital markets broke down, annual interest rates on new loans rose to over 900%, but anyone imprudent enough to lend at this figure was ruined because the inflation was far in excess of that. (That is, *real* interest rates were for a period negative in the extreme).

Though it is hard to believe, the German inflation is not the most extreme example. Hungary set all records in 1946 with a hyperinflation that averaged 19,800% per month between August 1945 and July 1946. During that July, prices went up 42 quadrillion percent, an amount almost impossible to imagine. In the final stages, one U.S. dollar equaled 30 quintillion Hungarian pengöes (that's 30 followed by 18 zeros). In a cafe, customers would order two or three glasses of wine because they knew the price would go up before they finished their first. Waiters would pass out new price lists while diners were still eating. On a train, the price of the ticket would go up in the middle of a journey and the conductor would come around to collect the surcharge.

Various consequences are inevitable. Menu and shoe-leather costs become a great burden throughout society. Long-term activities like saving for college or old age, and investment in new machines or factories, break down completely. Even printing new money becomes costly because so much of it must be provided. (In Bolivia during 1985, newly printed peso notes became the third-largest import after grain and mining equipment.) A common result is flight from the local

---

10.   The definition is Philip Cagan's, from his classic essay, "The Monetary Dynamics of Hyperinflation," in Milton Friedman, ed., *Studies in the Quantity Theory of Money,* Chicago, 1956. Many students of hyperinflation also add to the definition the proviso that the inflation is accelerating.

11.   Even with considerable overissue of money, price increases (inflation) might be suppressed by government price controls. The results, as sketched in Chapter 5, are shortages, queues, and perhaps a system of rationing. The Soviet Union, Poland, and other Communist countries did this for years. When the price controls were removed, inflation immediately broke out.

12.   The notes were called Continentals. "Not worth a Continental" was the saying at the time.

currency into some stable foreign money such as the U.S. dollar. In a sort of grass-roots monetary reform, prices even come to be quoted in dollars, with the daily exchange rate posted in shops and stores. In Bolivia, Peru, and Uruguay, all recent victims of hyperinflation, dollars in circulation were estimated to be over 50% of the value of the domestic currency in circulation. In Germany in 1923, the value of foreign currency circulating was at least equal in value to the circulating domestic currency. Though governments usually try to limit or prohibit such currency substitution, that just causes people to hide their illegal foreign exchange transactions.

During the 1960s and 1970s the world was largely spared from further bouts of hyperinflation, but there are now additional vivid examples to discuss, some of them in countries that are neither small nor obscure. A selection is presented in Table 14.2.

TABLE 14.2
Recent hyperinflations and near-hyperinflations.

Country	Year	Annual rate of inflation (%)
Bolivia	1985	23,000
Israel	1985	400
Argentina	1989	3,100
Nicaragua	1990	11,000
Peru	1990	7,650
Brazil	1993	2,000
Russia	1992	2,500

The most serious current inflations have been in Ukraine and Yugoslavia (Serbia and Montenegro). Yugoslav inflation in August 1993 was 1,880%, which is an annualized rate of 363 quadrillion percent. In November it was 20,190%, an annualized rate of 45 octillion percent and close to the highest monthly rate in the 1923 German hyperinflation. Yugoslavia printed 500 billion dinar currency notes toward the end of its inflation. A currency-stabilization program in January–February 1994 put an end to the money creation and the hyperinflation—whether temporarily or permanently remains to be seen.

How Do Hyperinflations Come About?

How do hyperinflations come about? The mechanism is well understood, and the preventative medicine is simply not to make the initial policy mistakes.

1) The hyperinflation begins because governments finance their spending needs by the creation of additional money, for example through printing new currency notes and using them to make purchases. Usually some event triggers the need for new revenues. In the Germany of 1923 it was the need to finance the strikers who were protesting the Versailles treaty. In Latin America, it was usually some shock to the economy such as victories by militant trade unions (Argentina), or oil price rises, or political instability that cuts off foreign investment (Bolivia). Sometimes the cause is economic disruption associated with a war or rebellion (Nicaragua, Yugoslavia). The money is very cheap to create, for paper notes just the paper and printing costs, but it can be spent by government at its face value. The difference between the cost of the money creation and the government's new purchasing power is in effect a substitute for direct taxation, employed because the tax mechanism is poorly developed, or ruined by war, or because higher taxes face overwhelming political obstacles.

2) The high inflation cuts the effectiveness of whatever tax system *had* been operating, because tax collections lag behind the price rises. The income tax, for example, is paid on *last* year's income, not this year's. (This was the reason that the Bolivian government's tax revenue as a percentage of the country's total income fell from 9.5% in the period 1979–1981 to 1.3% in 1985.) The fall in tax revenue makes money creation even more necessary than before.

3) The inflation worsens as holders of money attempt to shift to real assets, bidding up their prices, and switch to foreign currencies and barter for their day-to-day transactions.

The end of giant hyperinflations often appears almost miraculous. The German and Serbian (Yugoslav) hyperinflation died away in weeks, the Bolivian in ten days. Why? Because the emergency is critical enough so that the government adopts a wholesale currency reform and halts the issue of new money. These drastic steps are often easier simply *because* a country is suffering from almost complete breakdown. New directions are then obviously imperative, and the public is eager to accept the reform.

THE TASK AHEAD

Steady economic growth is highly desirable; the social and economic consequences of both recession and inflation are potentially severe. Whether they can be avoided, and how that might be accomplished, are subjects of intense interest.

Given this background, our task in the remaining chapters of this book's second part will be to examine how macroeconomists measure and analyze growth, recession, and inflation. In doing so, we will find that the micro model of supply and demand studied in Part 1 provides the foundation for a considerable amount of the macro analysis. That is why we follow a sequence of micro first and macro afterward.

In our analysis we will devote considerable attention to the policies that can be recommended to promote steady economic growth, and what the successes and failures of these policies have been. These ideas and their development generate some of the most important political debates of our time, and a basic understanding of them is necessary if citizens are to make informed decisions that will affect them throughout their lives.

SUMMARY

1) Contractions in output called recessions and expansions that lead to general price rises called inflations are common in the history of market economies, and these cycles still continue.

2) The damage from recession lies in unemployment, the reduced output including fewer capital goods so that future economic growth is harmed, the tendency for recession to spread to other countries, and the political consequences.

3) The unemployment caused by recession is often focused on certain specific groups such as teenagers and minorities, and certain industries that are particularly susceptible to changing incomes. The human costs, including discouraged workers who cease looking for work and deteriorating physical and mental health, can be appreciable.

4) The Great Depression of the 1930s was unprecedented, with unemployment reaching about a quarter of the labor force and the lost output equivalent to the sacrifice of civilian output devoted to fighting World War II.

5) The damage from inflation differs according to whether the inflation is unexpected or expected. When it is unexpected, creditors lose and debtors gain; those on fixed incomes and owners of assets earning fixed interest rates will suffer. Even if the inflation is expected and people are able to protect themselves by renegotiating contracts and putting their assets in variable interest rate securities, there will still be menu costs and shoe-leather costs. Menu costs involve the inconvenience and expense of living with the price increases, as when menus must be constantly reprinted. Shoe-leather costs involve the considerable work that must go into the avoidance of holding assets at fixed interest rates or in cash.

6) Hyperinflation is much more damaging than mild inflation, as redistributions of income, menu costs, and shoe-leather costs become intense and eventually intolerable. They typically begin when governments attempt to pay their bills by creating new money. Commonly, the inflation worsens as the tax system is undermined and as holders of money shift into real assets and switch to foreign currencies and barter. Hyperinflations often end suddenly, when the government ceases to finance its spending by means of the over-issue of money.

Chapter Key Words

Depression: A general term meaning a serious decline in production accompanied by substantial unemployment of labor and other factors of production. Unlike the term *recession* (which see), the word depression has no technical meaning. The Great Depression of the 1930s was the worst of modern times.

Discouraged workers: Workers so discouraged at the prospect of ever finding a new job that they stop looking for work.

Hyperinflation: The special case of inflation in which governments print very large quantities of new money, causing price increases to reach an extreme. Famous cases include Germany in 1923, Hungary in 1946, various Latin American countries in the 1980s, and Ukraine and Yugoslavia at the time of writing.

Inflation: A rise in the general level of prices, resulting in hardships for those whose income is fixed or does not advance sufficiently to keep up with the inflation. *Menu costs* and *shoe-leather costs* (which see), and income redistributions accompany serious inflations.

Menu cost: One of the costs of inflation. The term is taken from the time and expense of updating restaurant menus when inflation is rapid.

Nominal interest rate: The interest rate uncorrected for inflation.

Real interest rate: The interest rate corrected for inflation.

Recession: In general, a decline in production accompanied by higher unemployment. Recession also has a conventional meaning among economists: a decline in production lasting six months or more.

Shoe-leather cost: One of the costs of inflation, the name taken from the frequent trips to banks or stores necessary if the erosion of money's purchasing power is to be avoided.

CHAPTER QUESTIONS

1) Look again at Figures 14.1 and 14.2. What is its lesson for those who live in market economies? According to the historical experience, what is the effect of wars?

2) Recessions do more than just reduce output. How might a recession affect each of the following people?
    a) An experienced worker who has had her job for 10 years.
    b) A high school graduate who has just entered the labor force.
    c) A person suffering from psychological depression.
    d) Workers in a foreign country.
    e) The President of the United States.

3) The Great Depression of the 1930s is the most recent example of a very long economic downturn. However, long downturns occurred before that time. Why did these earlier downturns not cause as much damage as did the Great Depression?

4) It is often said that governments hate anything that causes harm to "widows and orphans." Such damage causes terrible reports in the press and can destroy political careers. Does surprise inflation hurt "widows and orphans" disproportionately? Why or why not?

5) Suppose the inflation rate is running at 6% annually and the nominal interest rate is 9%. Calculate the real interest rate exactly and by using the simplified formula.

6) You own a small convenience store. The items you sell off your shelves have their prices marked on them. In addition, you have a couple of vending machines and a pay telephone. Every few days you take the cash you have earned out of your safe and bring it to your bank. Some of your customers prefer to pay using credit cards, which is fine with you since it increases your business. What costs would you face if there were an inflation that you expected?

7) In your country inflation has been accelerating rapidly. A few months ago it was running at 240% per month, but more recently it was 5,400% per month. Now it is running at 16,000% per month. Doing business has become almost impossible, and the economy is breaking down. There are constant demonstrations against the government. Which of the following do you think is most likely to happen to inflation next month?
    a) It will increase to 20,000% per month.
    b) It will remain at 16,000% per month.
    c) It will fall to a low level and remain stable.

CHAPTER 15

Measuring Economic Performance

OVERALL OBJECTIVE: To explain that a system of economic measurement is essential for judging an economy's performance and for making sensible economic decisions.

MORE SPECIFICALLY:

- To demonstrate that total output as measured by gross domestic product is total consumption spending plus investment spending plus government purchases plus net exports.
- To show that, in principle, a country's total output is the same as the total income earned in the production of that output.
- To investigate how the national accounts are constructed and to discuss the problems involved in calculating them.
- To introduce and interpret other measures of economic performance including the figures for unemployment and capacity utilization, the data for inflation, the leading indicators, and the misery index.
- To show how a price index can be used to deflate nominal numbers in order to obtain real numbers, corrected for inflation, and to discuss how to adjust nominal GDP to allow for inflation.

We have seen that long-term economic growth is not a steady process. Market systems are subject to recessions and inflations, and each brings the possibility of substantial economic damage. To analyze why these fluctuations occur and to formulate preventive policies, we must first be able to measure the economy's performance. Accurate measurement provides data on the current condition of the economy and the means for identifying the turning points toward recession or inflation. If we can identify the start of a slump or inflationary boom before it becomes too serious, we may be able to take steps to prevent a further move into dangerous ground. This is important because both recession and inflation can become more intractable once they become entrenched. Thus a system of measuring economic performance is a kind of early-warning radar that allows economists to conduct analysis, businesses to plan, and governments to formulate policy responses *before* serious adverse effects set in. Without proper tools for measurement, we would be working in the dark.

Economists have developed a battery of instruments for measuring economic growth, recession, and inflation. The main yardsticks are the **national accounts** that measure a country's total output (product) and its total earnings (income). Other important measurements are unemployment data, capacity utilization figures, and price indices. An "index of leading indicators" brings together other information that allows trends in the economy to be identified. This chapter will examine how these measurements are made and how they can be used.

▶ MEASURING OUTPUT AND INCOME

The national accounts of total output and total income are central to economic measurement in all market economies. Though the discussion following emphasizes the experience of the United States, the fundamentals are the same everywhere, even in the former Communist countries that have rapidly adopted the measurement tools of the market systems. It is important to have a reasonable understanding of the national accounts. Without these primary tools of measurement, information concerning economic growth could only be obtained by impressions and guesses, and that would be troublesome as explained in the accompanying box. Macroeconomic analysis could have made little progress without reasonably accurate measures of what was taking place in the economy.

ABSENCE OF PROPER MEASUREMENT CAUSED GREAT DIFFICULTIES

The use of national accounts dates from only about a half century ago, spun off from the Great Depression and World War II. Before the 1930s, measurements of output and income were infrequent, were based on scattered information, and appeared long after the time to which they applied. The lack of information about economic conditions was a tremendous handicap.

How damaging this handicap can be is exemplified by the poor U.S. record in the First World War. Knowledge about the economy being limited, productive potential was overestimated and the government's targets for output were too ambitious. Airplane and tank production were cases in point. Due mostly to supply bottlenecks caused by overoptimistic predictions, not one American-made combat aircraft or tank reached the front lines during the year and a half that the United States was at war. If, using the production possibilities curve model from Chapter 1, we draw a curve for the United States in 1917–1918, the planned point of production is located far beyond its boundaries. (Germany also suffered because of a lack of timely data in World War I. No wartime information on total output was available even after several years of hostilities. Germany had to plan its production on the basis of pre-war data that were several years out of date.)

Absence of data also brought serious problems during the Great Depression. In the United States, output and income were obviously in sharp decline, but the government was incapable of determining how steep the fall actually was. Only in 1934 were the official product and income

figures for 1929–1932 made available. The government was becoming aware that its spending and tax policies had a significant impact on total economic activity. It needed to plan what to do, but it was not getting current data on which to base its policies.

The approach of World War II enhanced the frustration. Governments everywhere had to assess how much total output was available and how much was possible. Knowing what had happened in the First World War, they accelerated their efforts to develop systems for timely measurement of output.

TOTAL OUTPUT

We begin with the measurement of total output. The total output of a country is measured with the product and income accounts, and the mechanism is basically the same for all market economies.[1]

The first and most common measure of total output is **gross domestic product,** or **GDP**. (Until 1991, the United States emphasized a related measure, gross national product or GNP, a name that is still very familiar. The rather slight difference is explored later in the chapter.) Gross domestic product represents the value of the nation's yearly production of goods and services. Goods are tangible items, such as autos, food, and clothing. Services are intangible items, like haircuts, the work of an insurance agent, the transport of goods by ship, railway, or trucking company, a stay in a motel, or a visit to the dentist. There is only one meaningful way in which all these diverse items can be brought together—through money values, which serve as the common denominator. The money value of a good or service produced during a given year is its *market price*. So gross domestic product is the money value at market prices of total output of the goods and services produced within a country during one year.

There are two ways to measure this total value. The first is to assess the value of all output sold. The second is to count the total amount of spending devoted to the purchase of output. The methods yield the same result—that is, total output and total spending on that output are exactly the same—as long as goods added to inventory are counted as being "sold to their producer," which is the standard practice. (See the following box for an explanation.)

---

1.   Prior to the 1960s, great differences existed among countries in the way the measurements were made. The United Nations has taken the lead, however, in standardizing most of the rules.

THE IMPORTANT ROLE OF INVENTORIES IN MACROECONOMIC ANALYSIS

The stocks of unsold goods held at any given time by businesses—called their **inventories**, and usually amounting to about three months' worth of sales in the United States—play an important role in macroeconomic analysis. The value of a country's output will not be the same as the spending made to buy that output if the output added to inventory is considered to be unsold. For purposes of measuring the domestic product, it is standard practice to classify production added to inventory as "sold to its producer." Economists do so because the goal is to measure all production, rather than all sales or all consumption.

If additions to inventory are *planned*, they indicate that firms believe they can operate more smoothly with a larger stock of goods in the storeroom. If they are *unplanned* and *undesired*, however, the additional inventory may signal that an economy is producing more that it can sell. The firms that produce 1000 units when the public is willing to buy only 900 will find that, whatever their inventory was previously, it has now risen by 100 in an unplanned addition. The owners and managers of these firms will not approve; storing unwanted accumulations of unsold goods is expensive and ties up resources that could be better employed elsewhere. Similarly, falling inventories may signal that an economy is producing less output than buyers want to purchase. We shall see in later chapters that changes in inventories are central in business decisions to raise or lower their output.

Dividing GDP into Its Component Parts

Economists often analyze the macroeconomy by examining the component parts of GDP. Some of the production that makes up the GDP goes to consumers; this is called *consumption* or *C*. Some is *investment* or *I*. Investment is, as we have seen, the creation of capital, the production of goods not for current consumption but which are intended to raise future production. Examples of investment might include construction of a factory building or a new machine, building a railroad, or putting goods into inventory. (Why additions to inventory are classified as investment, which is a point of some importance, is explained later.) Further output is for the *government*, labeled *G*. This might include a warship, a new school, or the services of the post office. Foreign trade is the final category in the gross domestic product. Goods and services produced in the United States but sold abroad are *exports*, or *X*. Exports are clearly part of America's total output. Goods and services produced abroad but sold in the United States are *imports*, or *M*. Imports are not part of American annual output, and they should *not* be counted in U.S. GDP.

To summarize, gross domestic product measures the value of the goods and services produced in a country—its consumption output, investment output, government output, and its exports.

It would thus seem logical to view gross domestic product in the following form: GDP = C+I+G+X. Because of the way the national accounting data are collected, however, it is necessary to go through another step. The problem is that when consumption is counted at retail outlets, and investment at the firms that, say, purchase a machine, there is no convenient way to exclude imported items from the tally. The managers of firms ordinarily do not have complete information on what is imported and what is not among the items that they buy or sell. Thus imported consumer and capital goods are (inadvertently) counted in the figures for both consumption and investment along with domestically produced goods. These imports must be subtracted to obtain an accurate figure for GDP. Fortunately, the figure for total imports is easily available from another source—the trade data collected when the imported items enter the country. Thus in the published statistics for GDP, imports (M) are subtracted from C+I+G+X, giving us:

$$GDP = C+I+G+X-M.$$

The X–M term shows the net contribution of foreign trade to GDP, and is called "net exports." The dollar figures for U.S. GDP in 1992 are shown in Table 15.1:

TABLE 15.1
U.S. GDP (billion dollars), 1992*.

Personal consumption expenditure (C)	4096
Gross private domestic investment (I)	770
Government purchases of goods and services (G)	1115
Net exports (X–M)	-30
Total GDP	5951

* Figures are rounded off to the nearest billion. Note that the figure for net exports is negative. That is because imports exceeded exports in 1992.

PROBLEMS OF MEASURING THE GDP

When estimating the GDP we must be very careful to recognize and deal with certain ticklish problems. These include what is called "double counting," how to treat investment, and how to deal with the output of government.

Double Counting

The first and perhaps the greatest potential error is called **double counting**. An example of double counting would be to include in GDP all the wood pulp produced, all the paper produced, and all the books and newspapers produced. This would mean including the value of the wood pulp three times. The value of the wood pulp is part of the value of the paper, and of the books too.

The solution is to count only the item that includes the value of all the intermediate items that go into the finished good; that is, count only the final product, in this case the book or newspaper. So, if a book costs $40, it would be a mistake to argue that GDP should include $2 for the wood pulp, $6 for the paper, $36 for the book when sold at the publisher's warehouse, and finally $40 for the book when sold by the local retail bookseller. Summing these intermediate stages together with the final price gives $2 + $6 + $36 + $40 = $84 in all. This would be mistaken because the wood pulp, the paper, and the price of the book at the publisher are *already included* in the final price of the book at the bookstore. Thus GDP is not the total of *all* production in a year, but the production of final (or finished) goods and services. If we count only the value of the final good, such as the book but not the paper or wood pulp, we avoid the double counting.

Double counting can also be avoided by a second method, counting the value added at each stage of output. In the case of a book that would be $2 for the wood pulp, $4 for the paper, $30 for the book at the warehouse, and $4 for the book sold at retail = $40 in all. This **value-added approach** to GDP has special importance in modern economics. First, it allows economists to assess the contribution made to GDP by specific industries and sectors of the economy. Second, the principle of value added is extremely important for taxation. Many countries, including all but one in Europe, Japan since 1988, and Canada since 1991, levy a tax on the value added at each stage of production. The United States is one of the three remaining industrial countries without a value-added tax, or VAT. (The others are Australia and Switzerland.) Adoption of a U.S. VAT is presently being much discussed.

The logic of avoiding double counting also extends to used or traded items, or goods sold out of inventory. Neither of these represents current production, which is what we are trying to measure. Any second-hand goods already sold once ought not to be valued in the national accounts, because if something has already been sold then it has at some former time, either this year or in some past year, been included. In measuring this year's production, we would not want to count the 1989 Plymouth you bought today. That used car was already included in 1989's output, and although its ownership has just changed, no additional production has occurred. The same logic holds if this year you buy a car that the dealer held over in inventory from last year; the car has already been counted in last year's GDP. In either case, to include the items again in the value of this year's output would be double counting. Nor should transfers be included. Gifts do not represent new production but simply a transfer of something to a new owner. If your parents give you their old computer, its value should not go into GDP because it was already included in the nation's output when it was produced. Its transfer as a gift adds nothing to that output. What if the gift is a *new* good? Even in this case, it will have already been included in the national accounts when produced and sold, and must not be included again when transferred from one person to another.

The Treatment of Investment

Another problem in measuring the GDP involves the treatment of investment. Some investment is for new capital such as an additional industrial plant or equipment. Other investment, new though it may be, is meant as replacement for the old capital that has worn out and been retired from service. The two types taken together are called **gross investment**, which is used in determining the gross domestic product. The word gross is the reason for the "G" in GDP. When only *additions* to capital are included, not counting replacement of worn-out capital that just maintains the capital stock, this is termed **net investment**. (If domestic product is calculated with investment defined in this way, the result is termed **net domestic product**, or **NDP**.)

Figure 15.1 shows the relationship between investment and the capital stock.

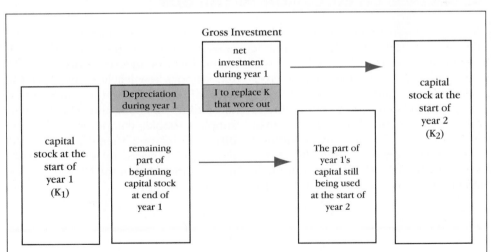

Figure 15.1. **The relationship between investment and the capital stock.** A portion of investment replaces worn-out capital while another portion is a net addition to the stock of capital. Both forms of investment taken together are called gross investment, while the portion that is a net addition is called net investment. The figure shows the relationship.

Remember the definition of capital: production not for current consumption but to raise future production. The definition helps to classify certain activities. The construction of new housing is considered to be investment, on the argument that housing delivers most of its services in the future. Goods produced and put into inventory rather than being sold are also counted as investment. This is because unsold goods that have been produced during the year must be counted somewhere, and they can be considered as investment since they will eventually add to future consumption. The "double counting" logic developed earlier applies also to investment: the sale and transfer of used plant and equipment would be double counting and thus should not be included in this year's total output as measured by GDP.

The Treatment of Government

The treatment of government output involves yet further problems of measurement. Some of the government's output is destined for consumers and some is for investment purposes. But by convention no division is made here, as was done with consumption (C) and investment (I) in the private sector of the economy. Government output, whether for consumption purposes or investment goods, is lumped together under the term G. As before, the sale of second-hand government goods must be excluded.[2]

Another problem with the counting of government activity is the difficulty of valuing the output of an employee such as a policeman, teacher, or clerk in a licensing office. If that output were sold on a market, it would simply be counted at its market price. Since their output is *not* sold on a market, by convention the output is valued at the cost of hiring the employee. Though this makes the problem manageable, it also tends to understate government output when productivity changes take place. So a clerk with a new computer may process double the number of licenses as a year ago, but the measured output of government does not change unless hiring costs for the clerk change.

HOW A SCHOOL'S OUTPUT IS ASSESSED FOR INCLUSION IN THE GDP

To illustrate the treatment of government output in the GDP, consider the public school you went to as a child. When it was built in, say, 1950, the construction costs were included in the GDP for that year. Ever since it has been turning out a flow of young people who are more educated than when they entered. Valuing the education (human capital) imparted annually to the students, which is the school's real output, is so difficult that it is not attempted. Instead, the school's contribution to output is considered to be the value of the factor inputs involved in a year's operation. Thus if the school's ten teachers are paid $30,000 each ($300,000 in all), the principal $45,000, the janitor $20,000, and $35,000 worth of supplies (books, computers, electricity, fuel oil) are purchased, then the total "output" of the school is stated to be $400,000. That is the sum included in the GDP.

This completes our initial look at the components of GDP: consumption, investment, government, and net exports, or, as already noted,

$$\text{Gross Domestic Product} = C + I + G + X - M$$

---

2.   Some economists contend that many government activities involve double counting. They view the Internal Revenue Service as akin to a battery on a new car, an intermediate good included in the car's purchase price and not a final product. Though this position has some logic to it, the reasoning has not been persuasive to the national accounts statisticians.

We will now investigate several variations in how to measure a nation's output. But no matter what method is used, the point of the analysis is that a modern economy has the ability to measure its economic output, and hence to measure the fluctuations in its growth. This ability allows us to conduct economic analysis and formulate economic policy with an accuracy that would be impossible without them.

GROSS AND NET DOMESTIC PRODUCT

We saw earlier that in addition to gross domestic product, or GDP, there is another measure, net domestic product or NDP. The difference between the GDP and NDP involves the definition of investment. Remember that investment can be considered gross (including the value of replaced or worn-out machines and other capital) or net (including only net additions to the stock of capital). Gross domestic product includes gross investment. The 1992 U.S. GDP was $5,951 billion. Net domestic product (NDP) differs from GDP in that it includes only net investment, omitting the value of replaced or worn-out capital goods. So, to the extent that capital goods do wear out, or undergo **depreciation**, GDP differs from NDP.

$$\text{GDP} - \text{depreciation} = \text{NDP.}$$

The annual figure for depreciation (often called the *capital consumption allowance*) and hence the difference between gross and net domestic product, is usually about 10% of GDP. In 1992 it was $653 billion, so NDP was $5,951 – $653 = $5,298 billion.

TOTAL OUTPUT IS THE SAME AS TOTAL INCOME

In addition to the total value of output, and its equivalent, the total spending on that output, there is another way to look at the nation's product. Consider that one person's spending is another person's income. Every dollar of spending on new output must be equal to the income earned somewhere in the production of that output. Consider a TV set. The value of the set is clearly counted as part of the nation's product if it was produced this year. Say its market price is $300 and that is what the purchaser paid. Then people somewhere must have earned $300 in new income. If the expense of producing the TV is $150 for labor (wages and salaries), $125 for the expenses of using machines and other capital and purchasing raw materials (interest and rental costs), then total production costs are $275. But the item was sold for $300, creating a profit of $25. Profit is defined as whatever remains after all other costs are paid out, and it is also income to someone. Thus the income earned from the sale of the item is identical to the market price at which the item is sold. When this example is repeated for all goods and services produced in an economy, then it becomes clear that the value of all output in a year is equal to the income generated by the production process. So in concept, another way to measure a nation's total output is to measure the total of all incomes earned by the factors involved in producing that output.

The total income earned during the production of one year's goods and services would be the earnings of an economy's factors of production: labor, land, capital, and entrepreneurial ability. All these factors earn income when a good is produced; this includes wages and salaries, rent, interest, and finally the profit that accrues when the goods are sold.

When these forms of income are added together, their sum is the national income, the total income earned in a given year by the factors of production. The size of the U.S. **national income** in 1992 was $4,743 billion, as seen in Table 15.2.

TABLE 15.2
U.S. national income (billion dollars), 1992.*

Wages and salaries	3525
Rental income	5
Interest	415
Profit (comprising corporate profit plus proprietors' income)	798
National Income	4743
(which, after adding depreciation, indirect business taxes, receipts of factor income from the rest of the world and payments of factor incomes to the rest of the world)	1208
Equals: **Gross Domestic Product**	5951

* Figures are rounded off to the nearest billion.

COMPLICATIONS IN THE CALCULATION OF NATIONAL INCOME

The published figure for national income in Table 15.2 involves four complications.

First, in adding up the total income resulting from the production of output, we must once more be careful to avoid double counting. We must not include cash flows that do not stem from actual production. One such item is transfer payments. Government transfers (relief payments, veterans' benefits, Social Security payments, and so on) do not represent current production of any goods or services, and thus ought not to be included in the nation's output or income. Private transfers must also be kept out of the national accounts. If Joan gives Lesley a Christmas gift of cash, a real transfer of purchasing power has taken place, but the gift does not represent current income or output. When Joan earned the money, it was of course included, but it would be mistaken to include it again when she gave it away. Similarly, if Pierpont sells Morgan a share of common stock in a corporation, a transfer takes place—Morgan gets the stock and Pierpont gets his money. But because there is no current production nor income earned, the transaction is not valued in the national accounts. The exception would be if they do business through a stockbroker who makes a living by facilitating such transactions. The broker's activity would be classed as a service, and thus would be part of the nation's output, and the broker's earnings (typically a percentage of the sale price) would be part of the nation's income. The full price of the share would not be included, however; only the broker's commission that represents the value of the service. The same logic applies to bonds, the sale of houses, land, and so forth. Only the dealer or agent commission would be included in output and income, not the total value of the transaction.

A second complication in calculating the national income involves the definition of profit. Corporate profits are not ambiguous and are included in the national income. But "unincorporated enterprises," a term encompassing most businesses, farms, and professionals, often do not report their "proprietors' income" in a way economists would find most convenient. For example, farmers' net incomes may well include some profit, but these also include what would otherwise be counted as wages for their labor and interest on their investments. The data do not allow these components to be identified separately. Thus the figure for "profit" in Table 15.2 actually appears in the detailed accounts in two segments, "corporate profit" and as a part of "proprietors' income," that is, the income of unincorporated enterprises.

A third complication also involves profit and has to do with the valuation of business inventories. How would you handle a rise in the value of your company's inventory between the time a good was put into stock and the time of its sale to a consumer? Say an item was produced in November and put into inventory, though it was not sold to a final consumer. As we have already seen, the item was counted in that year's GDP (as an addition to inventory, an investment). Now assume that the item is sold the following February at a higher price than it carried in November because some inflation has occurred. What would you call the markup? If you called it profit, then you would be saying that part of the calculated figure for profit is inflation on inventory. But inflation does not represent new production or the income earned from that production, so you would not want to do this. Thus the effect of inflation on goods held in stock is countered by applying an "inventory valuation adjustment." This adjustment wrings out the inflation's effect on goods sold out of inventory.

A final complication in measuring the national income involves rental income, which as seen in Table 15.2 was extremely low in 1992. How could this be? The answer is that rental income in the national accounts is not the same as the economic rent, defined as the return to a factor beyond its opportunity cost, that we discussed in Chapter 12. A much narrower definition, the contract rental income of persons, is used. This would include the contract rental income to landlords from renting apartments to tenants, or to farmers renting land to other farmers, but it would not include most economic rent. If rental income is received by an unincorporated business, it appears as part of "proprietors' income," that is, the income of unincorporated enterprises. If rental income is received by a corporation, it is included in the calculation of "corporate profits." The rather small amount of rent that remains as "rental income of persons" is further reduced because rental properties depreciate. After subtracting depreciation, the figure for rental income was actually negative in 1990 and 1991.

The Figures for GDP and National Income Differ Somewhat

The actual calculated figure for national income is somewhat less than gross domestic product even though in theory the value of all output is equal to the value of the incomes generated in the production of that output. There are three reasons why the measured figures for GDP and national income differ.

1) Depreciation is included in GDP but no income is earned because of it. Because it is not income to anybody, depreciation is therefore not included in the national income. We have already seen that in 1992, depreciation was $653 billion.

2) Firms pay certain taxes (called **indirect business taxes**) that are not income to anyone. These indirect business taxes include state sales taxes and any other indirect (or excise) taxes. Take, for example, an item selling for $1 without tax. With a 5% sales tax a retail firm will collect $1.05 when the good changes hands. The 5¢ must be paid directly to the state's government, but it is no one's income nor is it income to the government either. No factors of production were furnished (land, labor, capital, or entrepreneurial ability) in return for the 5¢. No product has been produced directly and no income has been generated directly. Yet the 5¢ *is* part of the net (and gross) domestic product; it is included in the market price at which the good was sold. Because it does not represent income to anyone, however, it cannot be counted in the figure for national income.[3] In 1992 net indirect business taxes amounted to $531 billion.[4]

3) Finally, as the word "national" in national income indicates, the income of a country's residents (its nationals) is being counted. National income is equal to the income earned by the factors of production owned or controlled by a country's residents. This measure includes the wages of an American working in Britain or the profits American firms earn from operating in Mexico, or the interest and dividends paid to Americans by foreign companies. These are all income to American residents. But note that this portion of national income was not the result of the production of output domestically within the borders of the United States. To find U.S. national income, it is thus necessary to add to GDP the receipts of factor income paid to Americans by the rest of the world.

---

3. Of course, the 5¢ in taxes does help to *finance* many incomes (of government employees), but it is not in itself part of the national income; rather, it is a transfer from taxpayers to government.

4. The term "net indirect business taxes" is used because the government also pays some subsidies per unit sold, as well as levying taxes per unit sold. Logic compels the national accountants to *add* the amount of the subsidy to GDP in order to find national income. Both cases of tax and subsidy can be comprehended by *net* indirect business taxes.

Part 3 ■ Macroeconomics

(The amount added was $129 billion in 1992). Conversely, you would *not* want to count wages earned by a Mexican citizen working in Texas as part of U.S. national income. These wages are not income earned by a U.S. national, even though it *is* income generated by production that occurs in the United States. Similarly, you would not want to count profits earned by a Mexican firm operating in the United States, or interest and dividends paid by U.S. firms to Mexicans. To find U.S. national income, all these payments of factor income to the rest of the world have to be subtracted from U.S. GDP. (The amount subtracted was $118 billion in 1992.)

Thus the figures for GDP and national income do indeed differ somewhat. To obtain national income from GDP, we must subtract depreciation and indirect business taxes and add factor income paid by foreigners minus factor income paid to foreigners. U.S. national income was $4,743 billion in 1992.

GDP AND GNP

In 1991 the U.S. government made a significant change in the U.S. national accounts. It decided to emphasize the measure called gross domestic product (GDP), rather than the **gross national product (GNP)** that had previously received almost all of the attention. The difference is relatively slight for the United States, though it is large for some other countries.

The difference between the two lies in what you are trying to measure: the economic activity of a country's *residents*, or the economic activity within a country's *territory*. They are not the same. The old measure, gross *national* product, assessed the activity of a country's residents. It included the profits earned by American firms operating in Canada, but not the profits earned by Canadian firms operating in the United States. Gross *domestic* product (GDP) differs because it is based on geography. It does count the profit earned by a Canadian firm in the United States (because it was part of the value of output produced on U.S. territory), but not the profit earned by a U.S. firm operating in Canada (because that was *not* part of the value of output produced on U.S. territory).

Some countries' GDPs differ significantly from their GNPs. For example, the GDPs of Egypt, Jordan, and North Yemen are lower than their GNPs (In 1989, they were lower by 2, 3, and 16% respectively.) This occurs because many workers from these countries took jobs in the oil-producing states of the Persian Gulf. Switzerland has many profitable investments abroad; its GDP is lower than its GNP by 5%.

The presence of many foreign firms in a country may boost GDP above GNP. That is the situation in Canada, Brazil, Mexico, Malaysia, and Jamaica, where in 1989 GDPs were higher than GNPs by 3, 4, 5, 5, and 12% respectively. U.S. GDP and GNP are virtually identical, as are those of Britain and Japan. However, foreigners are currently purchasing U.S. businesses, agricultural land, real estate, and other assets in quantities greater than U.S. purchases of assets abroad. Since the profits of foreign operations in the United States *are* included in the GDP, while the profits of U.S. operations abroad are not, continuation of the trend will mean that eventually U.S. GDP will exceed GNP.

Most countries emphasize GDP in their accounting. Their reasoning is that GDP gives the most accurate reflection of domestic production within a country, and therefore of the macro pressures set up in that country. The U.S. decision of 1991 to join most other nations in putting the main focus on GDP means that GDP data is now available two months before GNP data. Only Germany and Japan among the major western countries continue to give primary emphasis to GNP.

In summary:

GDP + net factor receipts from and payments to the rest of the world = GNP

DISPOSABLE PERSONAL INCOME

In order to assess the outlook for business sales, it helps to have more accurate measures of earned income that the public actually has available for spending purposes. That need has led to further refinements of the national accounts. The underlying problem is that some of the total income earned in an economy is never actually received by the public. Corporate profits provide an example. Some of this profit is clearly paid to shareholders as dividends. When corporations pay dividends, they are "dividing" their profits among those who own the shares, just as that name implies. Other portions of corporate profit, however, are not paid as dividends, for example the income taxes eventually paid by corporations and the earnings that companies keep to plow back into the business, called "undistributed corporate profits." The public does not share these two portions of corporate profit.

Another example is Social Security taxes, deducted from paychecks before they are cashed. Your earned income must be reduced by that amount to find how much usable, or "disposable," income is left for you. Finally, there are various personal taxes that must be paid and are not available for your own use—the federal income tax being by far the largest. Thus from national income we must subtract corporate taxes, undistributed corporate profit, Social Security taxes, and personal taxes to find what is actually retained.

On the other side, some of the moneys available to an individual do not represent earned income as we have defined it, but they are nonetheless at one's disposal. Examples include such items as Social Security retirement benefits, other welfare and pension funds and payments, veterans' benefits, and any other government transfer payments that do not involve income earned from the production of goods and services. When these are added to national income, and after undistributed corporate profits, corporate taxes, Social Security taxes, and personal taxes are all subtracted, the result is a figure that is defined to reflect, more accurately than does national income, the amount available for actual spending or saving by the public. This figure is called **disposable personal income**. (It was $4,431 billion in 1992.)[5] This figure is eagerly watched, and its publication tends to command wide attention. The attention is warranted because changes in it are an especially good signal of future economic performance. For example, household consumption and personal saving are closely correlated with this measure, as we shall see.

Our discussion is summarized in Table 15.3. At the top of the table is gross domestic product, the measure of all new production of final goods in the economy. In the middle we see the relationship between gross domestic product and national income. At the bottom we see how national income is not the same as the income available to the public—the disposable personal income that the public can actually spend.

---

5.   When personal taxes are not subtracted, the resulting figure is called personal income, as distinct from disposable personal income. The figures for personal income used to be made available more frequently than those for disposable personal income, once a month instead of once a quarter, because it was difficult to estimate accurately personal tax collections (such as from the income tax) in periods as short as one month. The monthly announcements of personal income thus attracted considerable notice in the press. Changes in withholding rules and improvements in interpreting the data have made it more feasible to estimate personal tax collections on a monthly basis, however, and from 1990 both personal income and disposable personal income are being released at the same time.

TABLE 15.3
Summary of the National Accounts.

Where C = consumption, I = investment, G = government, X = exports, and M = imports, then:

1)   Gross Domestic Product = C+I+G+X–M

         – Depreciation

      = Net Domestic Product

2)   Net Domestic Product

         – Indirect Business Taxes

         + receipts of factor income from rest of world

         – payments of factor income to rest of world

      = National Income

3)   National Income

         – Corporate taxes

         – Undistributed Corporate Profits

         – Social Security Taxes

         + Government Transfer Payments

         – Personal Taxes

      = Disposable Personal Income

How the National Accounts Are Constructed

We have now discussed the concept of the nation's product and income. In practice, however, the measurement of these values involves a process of informed estimation; the national accountants build the numbers piece upon piece. Data come from a wide variety of sources relating to specific portions of the economy or certain types of transactions.

What are the important sources used for estimation? On the side of national income, the most widely used and comprehensive are government tax records. This includes Internal Revenue Service data on the income tax and the corporate tax, and information on Social Security payroll taxes. Wages and salaries, rent, interest, and profits all receive coverage through these tax data. Supplemental evidence from agricultural censuses, sample surveys, and so on, help to fill the gaps.

Far different methods are used in estimating the nation's product. In particular, periodic censuses of industry give reasonable estimates of the output of goods.[6] Services are much more difficult to cover; there are private surveys by trade groups, a census of business, surveys of education, sampling data, and various other bits of information to draw on. A recurring census of government provides comprehensive coverage of that sector.

Sometimes data are available giving an accurate estimate of a sector for a particular year because some relevant census was taken in that year. If that census will not be repeated for five years, then to find the GDP in the intervening years estimates can be made on the basis of the two "benchmark years." For example, if a census was taken in 1987 and 1992 but will not be taken again until 1997, this means finding the amount of increase (or decrease) in output between the

---

6.   The first U.S. Census of Manufactures covered the year 1809. This census now is taken every five years, in the years ending with a "2" and a "7." A sample census of about a quarter of all manufacturing establishments is taken annually in the other years.

two years 1987 and 1992, then applying that rate as an estimate for the GDP of 1993–94–95–96. Errors in estimation can then be corrected retrospectively, in 1997. The benchmark technique is always supplemented by any additional data that might be available, thus providing both a check on accuracy and further opportunities for revising the statistics that have already appeared.[7]

THE NATIONAL ACCOUNTS: AN IMPERFECT MEASURING ROD

We are dependent on the national accounts to measure economic performance. But these accounts are imperfect in a number of ways, and economists who use them need to be aware of what these defects involve. Failure to appreciate them may give a biased picture of an economy, or possibly lead to bad planning and bad policy.

INACCURACIES IN THE STATISTICS THEMSELVES

First, the statistics themselves are not entirely accurate because some production is hidden, because some data sources disagree with others, and because some production is very hard to value at market prices. This section explores how reliable the national accounts really are.

The Underground Economy

Evidence suggests that substantial income and production are not reported in the national accounts. This involves the so-called **underground economy**. Some of this activity will be legal but not reported for tax purposes: the plumber who repairs your sink, but asks for cash; the waitress who receives tips but does not report that income to the IRS, and so on. Moonlighting without reporting the income and off-the-books transactions to avoid taxes are other examples. Bartering may also be a way to avoid taxes. A dentist may trade a root canal to a carpenter for a new roof, or a physician may take several cords of firewood in payment for treatment. In such cases it is likely that neither the income earned nor the value of the service produced will be counted. The activity itself may also be illegal. Growing marijuana, illegal gambling, fencing stolen goods, or engaging in loan sharking, drug dealing, or prostitution all produce income and output that will not be counted. (Unreliable estimates suggest a "legal" underground economy in a range from about the same size as the illegal sector to twice as large.)

In the developed countries, Greece, Italy, and Spain are believed to have the largest underground economies as a proportion of their GDP (20–30%), while Switzerland and Japan have the smallest (about 4%). There is a wide range of alternative informed guesses for the size of the U.S. underground economy, with a generally cited range between about 5% and 15% of GDP. A likely figure of 8% would be equivalent to a concealed economy the size of Canada's.

Whatever the size of the underground economy, there is wide agreement that it has grown during the past decade or two in practically all developed countries. As a result, an economy's capacity to produce and its actual output are both likely to be higher than the orthodox estimates, and its government's tax revenues and its rate of unemployment are both likely to be lower.

The Statistical Discrepancy

Recall that product and income, which in concept should be identical, are actually measured using very different sources of information. Tax data is more likely to be used in estimating income, and census of business data in estimating product. So a large discrepancy between national income and GDP could indicate that at least one of the estimates was erroneous,

---

7.   Many research papers have been spoiled because their writers failed to appreciate that the product or income data employed in them were original and unrevised. The latest sources should be used for past national accounts, because these include the latest revisions. The first and second revisions to each month's data actually occur in the second and third month after their original publication; the process continues for years.

whereas a small discrepancy should indicate a reasonably high degree of accuracy. In actual experience, the **statistical discrepancy** showing the margin of error between GDP and national income is always quite small in the United States, usually less than 1%. Even though it is small, the statistical discrepancy usually increases as revisions are made. It was infinitesimal when the 1988 data were first published, but it has now grown to about one-half of 1%. The last period of large gaps between measured income and product was during World War II, when black markets were operating to evade government price controls. (Note that the statistical discrepancy fails as a check on accuracy when both the output and the income generated from it are missed.)

Production Not Sold on the Market

Some production is definitely output and is not hidden, but it is not sold on the market and so is not included in the national accounts. The most common and controversial example of this is the provision of services by homemakers. The services include cooking, cleaning, taking care of children, and so on. This would be valued in the GDP if it were done by a salaried cook, house cleaner, or worker in a day-care center. But the Department of Commerce believes that the difficulties and ambiguities of measurement are too great to include homemakers' services in the GDP. It is thought that several hundred billion dollars worth of product, which in concept should be valued, is omitted because of this decision. Thus GDP rose significantly in the United States and Europe when women entered the paid labor force in larger numbers, not only because the women were now holding paid jobs, but because of the expansion of support services they utilized, including day-care, laundry firms, and greater sales of semiprepared and prepared foods. Even home entertainment products such as VCRs were produced in much greater quantity as a result of this phenomenon. (Nonmarketed production, that is, homemakers' services, presumably fell at the same time, but this is not recorded in the national accounts.)

There are some similar exclusions concerning output that are very difficult to estimate because the output is not sold on the market and hence is not counted. A major example is do-it-yourself work in the home, such as carpentry, house painting, or plumbing, and voluntary labor of all kinds. Student "work" related to their studies, as when a student types a paper, is in this category. The work is not included in any of the accounts, whereas if the job had been done by a typing service it would have been included.

Some items not sold on markets are, however, estimated and included, in apparent contradiction to the cases cited. Examples are food home-grown and consumed by farmers, and the value of the services rendered by owner-occupied housing. (It would indeed not be sensible if the services rendered by your house built many years ago were entirely measured by the building cost that went into the GDP in the year it was built.) Other examples are "free" financial services, such as checking accounts and investment counseling, and payments in kind. The reason for counting these items but not the others appears to be a not-very-sophisticated one: for these the measurement is relatively easy, while for the others it is not.

THE NATIONAL ACCOUNTS MEASURE TOTAL OUTPUT AND INCOME, WHICH IS NOT NECESSARILY THE SAME AS LEVELS OF LIVING

The national accounts are intended to measure output and income. Sometimes, however, they are used to draw conclusions about welfare or the level of living. Consider such statements as, "U.S. GDP has doubled in recent years, so the United States is twice as well off as it was." Or, "U.S. GDP is larger than Britain's; therefore the U.S. population has a higher level of welfare and well-being." In a sense, there is plenty of justification for doing this: low output and income are consonant with low living standards. Yet comparisons of this sort are fraught with difficulty and attempts to do so must be treated with care for a variety of reasons explored here.

Per Capita

If you want to use the national accounts to estimate the level of a nation's well-being, you must account for differences in the size of the population. It would be senseless to contrast U.S. and British levels of living by looking at their total GDPs because the United States has many more people. The solution to this problem is to calculate the product or income per person, known as **per capita GDP or income**. This is obtained by dividing the total product or income figure by the size of the population. For the United States, the $5,600 billion GDP of 1991 is more than five times greater than Britain's $877 billion (when converted into dollars). The United States has 253 million people, however, compared to Britain's 58 million, so their per capita GDPs are much closer: about $22,200 per person in the United States, and $16,500 per person in Britain. The adjustments can make a huge difference: Switzerland's total output is small by world standards, but its per capita GDP was over $33,000 in 1991. China's total output is quite large, but its per capita GDP was only $370 in that year.

Leisure

Most people value their leisure time, but it is not output and so is not included in national income or GDP. In the United States, the work week has declined to about 60% of what it was in the 1920s. But recently, the trend has been reversed: average leisure time per person in the United States was estimated to be 26.2 hours per week in 1973; by 1987 this figure had fallen to 16.6 hours. Leisure also figures in comparisons of levels of living across countries. The average American worked 1,957 hours per year in 1989, well under the Japanese figure of 2,159 hours per year but well above the average German's 1,638 hours. Germans have 40 days off in holidays and vacation, no European country has less than 30 except Ireland (28), whereas Americans take only 20 days off per year and the Japanese 15. All this presumably makes a difference in how well we live, but no sign of it appears in the national accounts.

What Goods?

Levels of living are certainly affected by the choice of goods to produce. The GDP makes no distinctions between mink coats for dogs and cloth coats for people, or abdominal surgery that saves your life and plastic surgery that just tucks your tummy. They are treated alike no matter what the benefits for humanity. A country paradoxically appears better off if there is an increase in travel to work. A new subway goes into GDP even though it would not have been necessary except for the growing congestion in the city; the congestion is *not* counted as a negative in the national accounts. Disasters such as floods, hurricanes, and earthquakes are in fact usually good for the GDP. Though the lost capital is subtracted as depreciation, personal property losses are not considered depreciation. Thus when cars, furniture, appliances, and so forth are replaced, GDP goes up. (The logic does not apply to housing, which is classified as capital.)

The long-term damage from production at rates that cannot be sustained because the forests are being cut down, or soils eroded, or fisheries exhausted, is counted the same as production that *is* sustainable, and the exhaustion and erosion does not affect the measured accounts. Similarly, products that carry with them costs to society such as polluted streams and air are counted along with the clean-up effort and the equipment that abates the pollution. In short, the product mix chosen will certainly affect levels of well-being, but this will not be reflected in the totals of the national accounts, which take a neutral view that all production should be counted whether that reflects increased or diminished welfare.

Attempts to Adjust GDP to Reflect Social Welfare

Recent years have seen substantial efforts made to develop modifications in the national accounts to reflect the "leisure" and "what goods" problems. One attempt to make GDP more accurate is the measure called Net Economic Welfare (NEW) proposed by William Nordhaus and James Tobin of Yale University, which subtracts an economy's "bads" and adds nonmarket activities plus leisure. In the United States during the 1970s and '80s, NEW was rising more slowly than GDP because leisure was falling, as we have seen, and because of the increase in pollution problems. The United Nations is recommending a less ambitious concept called "resource accounting," in which countries would subtract from GDP a sum representing natural resource depletion. Though this adjustment would be small for most advanced countries, it would be large for many less-developed ones. When resource accounting was applied retrospectively to Indonesia's GDP growth between 1971 and 1984, the adjusted annual increase fell from 7.1% to only 4%. The U.S. Congress

voted along these lines in 1989 that the Department of Commerce must publish a "gross sustainable productivity" measure.

Other scholars have pursued proxy measures such as the "human development index" published by the United Nations Development Program. The HDI is an index of life expectancy, years of schooling, adult literacy, and real GDP. Its use for ranking countries can lead to radical rearrangement. China and India have almost exactly the same per capita GDP. But China's HDI is twice as high as India's. Mauritania's GDP per capita is double that of Sri Lanka, but due to unsatisfactory performance in health and education its HDI is only one-fifth as great as Sri Lanka's. Such innovations are intended to be an improvement over GDP in their ability to provide an objective measure of human welfare, though they have been little noticed up to now compared to the figures for GDP and national income.

Psychic Income

Psychic income is a term used by economists. It means that some output carries with it psychological or "inner" satisfaction—work as a nurse, doctor, teacher, for example—that is not reflected in the national accounting. Conversely, other output—coal mining, employment in a slaughterhouse, garbage disposal, repetitious assembly-line work—may bring psychic dissatisfaction to those employed in these occupations. This dissatisfaction *per se* is similarly ignored in the national accounting, where the output of these occupations and the income earned from them are included only at their dollar values and without reference to any underlying psychic considerations.

Quality

GDP does not reflect improvements in the quality of a product, except insofar as its price changes. Per dollar spent, many items from television sets to calculators to automobile tires and batteries to synthetic fabrics have better performance and more reliability than they did in decades past. A $7.95 pocket calculator of today has more power than one costing $200 twenty years ago. New goods such as personal computers come into use that previously weren't available at all. Consider that GDP did not fully reflect the change in the level of living (for better or worse) when television was introduced, since the new spending in that industry was counterbalanced to some extent by relative reductions in spending on the movie industry, book publishing, and other forms of recreation. Whatever the case, quality enters the GDP only indirectly as reflected in price, even though it surely has a great influence on welfare.

Distribution

A further problem with using the national accounts to measure welfare is that of distribution of the product or income. It is obvious that there is a difference in satisfaction depending on who gets the goods. An observer would expect a far different general level of well-being in a country with a few very rich citizens and many who are very poor, in comparison with a country where the distribution of income, that is the sharing in the goods and services produced, is more or less equal.[8]

Inflation

Finally, the national accounts are subject to the problem of inflation. What appears to be a rise in measured GDP may not be due to any increase in the quantity of production, but may be caused entirely by a rise in the prices of the goods being produced. Fortunately, this difficulty can be overcome by the use of statistics corrected for inflation by means of price indices. How to construct such indices, and how to apply them to the national accounts, is explored toward the end of the following section.

► UNEMPLOYMENT, CAPACITY UTILIZATION, INFLATION, THE LEADING INDICATORS, AND THE MISERY INDEX

We have examined how the national accounts are calculated and some of the difficulties of measurement. Now we examine the other major tools of economic measurement, including the unemployment statistics, capacity utilization figures, price index data for assessing inflation, the so-called "leading indicators" that attempt to give some forewarning of downturns or upturns in the economy, and the "misery index" used by many politicians.

THE MEASUREMENT OF UNEMPLOYMENT

There are two major methods for measuring unemployment. Most of Europe obtains the data by counting those who register at unemployment offices. The United States, Canada, Sweden, and Japan use sample surveys of households. In the United States, for example, the Bureau of Labor Statistics samples randomly some 70,000 households per month, asking the following question to an adult member of each household: are you or anyone else over the age of 16 in your family now not working, and (a) have you actively looked for work in the last four weeks; or (b) are you laid off but know that you are being recalled; or (c) are you waiting to report to a new job in the next month? A "yes" answer means one more person counted as unemployed.

---

8.   The methods for measuring income distribution, and the causes and results of income inequalities, have already been discussed in Chapter 13.

COMPARISONS OF UNEMPLOYMENT AMONG COUNTRIES ARE DIFFICULT

The differences among countries in methods of counting do not affect the measurement of unemployment over time in a single nation, but they do make comparisons among countries difficult. The European method of enumerating those who register will mean that some people are uncounted because they didn't register—people whose spouses are employed, for instance, because these people are not eligible for unemployment benefits. The method may, however, count some people as unemployed who have registered to claim benefits but are not really looking for work. In Britain, those claiming benefits for over a year were recently called in for an interview concerning their job search. An appreciable number failed to report and ceased claiming benefits, presumably in part because they were not looking for work. Based on annual household surveys, it is believed that on balance the number of people who register but do not seek work exceeds those who do not register because they are not eligible for benefits. As a result, European statistics for unemployment must be adjusted downward for comparability with American

figures. The Organization for Economic Cooperation and Development (OECD) now publishes a standardized unemployment rate for 16 countries based on annual household surveys. Recently, for comparability with the United States, unemployment in Belgium and Germany had to be adjusted downward by two percentage points, Italy –3, and the Netherlands –5.

Some countries not only measure unemployment by different means, but they also define the labor force differently. The United States and Canada, for example, exclude the armed forces, whereas several European countries do not make this exclusion. The OECD standardized rate adjusts for this as well. Japan's unemployment rate presents particular difficulties because of the common Japanese practice among major firms of providing lifetime employment. Some workers may thus be employed, but they may be assigned to low-productivity make-work jobs, given extended holidays, and the like. While technically in the work force, they may be making only a very small contribution to the nation's total output.

Interpreting the Unemployment Data

The overall unemployment figure receives considerable media attention when it is published each month. But the overall figure is limited and can be misleading in a number of ways. In the previous chapter, we saw that it does not reveal the very dissimilar rates of unemployment among different races and age groups, nor changes that have been occurring in the average length of an episode of unemployment. It misses shifts in the number of discouraged workers. It fails to identify the numbers of people who, unwillingly, have had to take part-time work, a reduction in working hours, or involuntary loss of overtime. (If all workers involuntarily went to a short four-hour day rather than a regular eight hours, then logically, but not officially in the statistics, unemployment should be 50%.) In the 1990s, adding in the discouraged workers and the part-timers wanting full-time jobs would give a U.S. unemployment rate nearly double the official rate.

The overall unemployment figure also fails to pick up geographical differences within a country, which can be large. In the United States, for several years in the 1980s unemployment was much higher in Texas and Louisiana than it was in New England. More recently, unemployment in Massachusetts has been over a quarter higher than the U.S. average. In Italy, unemployment is much more a problem in the southern part of the country than it is in the north.

In Britain, unemployment is much higher in the north than in the south. The overall unemployment rate also misses the significant differences among industries.

Finally, the total figure does not take into account "displaced workers," those who are currently employed but whose training, work experience, and skills have become obsolete as their former jobs disappeared due to changing economic conditions. Displaced workers are largely re-employed, but at wages often lower than they had previously earned. (Between 1983 and 1988, of those workers whose jobs disappeared and were re-employed in some other job, over 40% took a pay cut of at least one-fifth.) Regularly published data are actually available on most of these categories of unemployment. But the public and the press continue to focus their entire attention on the overall rate of unemployment.

Zero Unemployment Is Practically Not Attainable

One interesting aspect of the unemployment data is that a zero or near-zero rate of unemployment, which would seem highly desirable, is practically impossible except in a "pressure cooker" atmosphere of wartime or other great emergency. Even if no one at all were ever laid off, at any given moment new workers are entering the labor market looking for jobs, and some workers are quitting old jobs and searching for new ones. In the United States, an unemployment rate of 3% to 4% is recorded for these "frictional" reasons alone. ("Frictional unemployment" is the term applied by economists to this temporary joblessness.) Thus whenever U.S. unemployment drops below about 5% of the labor force, concern mounts among economists that the economy is reaching a condition of labor shortage with the danger that inflation will follow.[9]

MEASURING CAPACITY UTILIZATION

Capacity utilization is the amount produced divided by what could be produced.[10] The calculation of "what could be produced" is more complex than it appears. The figure is calculated on the basis of the maximum level of production that would reasonably be sustainable if existing work schedules were maintained, if manpower and materials were added as needed to reach maximum output, but with no change in the machinery and equipment currently in place. The overall capacity utilization figure faces certain difficulties of interpretation. For example, it differs substantially both geographically and across industries—in mid-1993, it was 81.2% for all U.S. industry, but 67.9% in the U.S. aerospace industry and 91.3% in the paper industry. The same plant, were it to move to a different conventional work schedule or to production of a greater number of models involving more "down time" for retooling, would report different capacity utilization. It is also suspected that the "what could be produced" element in the data may be slow to pick up technical changes such as computerization, robotics on assembly lines, new methods to economize on inventories, and managerial improvements. These, if fully factored in, might mean that actual capacity utilization is below the published estimates.

Even so, movements in capacity utilization are significant, and the monthly announcement of the figure is closely watched. A U.S. figure for capacity utilization rising over about 85% is worrisome, for it is thought to be an important sign that inflation will increase. At that level, bottlenecks in supply are expected to become frequent, with price-boosting results. Conversely, capacity utilization below about 80% leads to concern about recession.

---

9.   The difference between the 3 or 4% frictional unemployment and the 5% figure where concern mounts can be considered "structural unemployment." The structurally unemployed are those whose skills are obsolete or whose training is inadequate for the available jobs. The condition is explored in detail in Chapter 24.

10.   Various different measures of capacity utilization are in use. The figures cited in the text are those of the Federal Reserve Board, which have been published continuously since 1966.

DEBATES ON CAPACITY UTILIZATION

Some economists believe a lower figure of 81% or 82% is the turning point beyond which inflation will increase, though the experience of the late 1980s suggests that these numbers are on the low side. Other economists have recently been critical of the idea that 85% capacity utilization represents a turning point. The computerization, robotics, and improvements in inventory management mentioned in the text may mean that capacity in some industries can expand well beyond 85% before encountering bottlenecks. In a few industries, the figure is now believed to be at least 90%. Many economists would no doubt prefer to see the present method of measuring capacity utilization replaced by an economic definition, where full capacity would be defined as the low point on the U-shaped short-run average-cost curve. See Chapter 6 for the appearance of these curves.

MEASURING INFLATION BY MEANS OF A PRICE INDEX

A **price index** allows inflation to be measured accurately, and so price indices are a key tool of macroeconomics. With such indices, corrections can be made for the price changes that would otherwise make year-to-year GDP comparisons inaccurate. For example, GDP might be $2,000 billion this year and $4,000 billion next year. But if the average price of all items has doubled in the meantime, the real change in output has been zero and the doubling in GDP has not indicated real growth but only a price rise.

Correcting for inflation is carried out with a price index. Consider the following simple example. If all prices have doubled, then prices have increased by two times. We can divide the nominal (or current, or money) GDP figure by the amount of the price increase, in this case $4,000 billion ÷ 2, to obtain the so-called real or constant-dollar GDP, based on the price level in some previous year. The actual measurement is carried out a little differently, as we will see, but this simple example captures the idea. In newspapers you will often come across figures such as "1995 GDP based on 1987 prices." The writer of the article is attempting to report what happened to real output by cancelling the effect of changes in the general price level over time.

The three major price indices now used in most countries are the consumer price index (CPI), the producer price index (PPI), and the GDP deflator. The CPI concentrates on prices paid by consumers. The PPI measures prices at the wholesale level and thus signals future changes in the CPI. The GDP deflator is a more general way to measure inflation in the prices of the entire range of goods and services included in the GDP, as we shall see.

Of these, the CPI traditionally commands the greatest attention, in large part because it is the measure to which in recent years many incomes have been linked, or "indexed." In the United States, Social Security benefits, postal salaries, food stamps, military and federal civil service pensions are all tied to it. Some union wage contracts are also tied to the CPI by means of cost of living adjustment (COLA) escalators, the first U.S. example being a 1948 United Auto Workers contract with General Motors. During inflationary periods the bigger and stronger unions bargain hard for COLA agreements. Even more indexing exists in Europe.

In the United States the CPI is computed monthly as a sample survey of 400 items sold by 19,000 establishments in 91 locations. Obviously it would not do simply to average one item with another, as in the statement "movie tickets went up in price 50%, apartment rental prices went up 10%, thus average prices went up

$$\frac{(50 + 10)}{2} = 30\%.\text{"}$$

The problem is that apartment rentals are far more important in the consumer budget than are movie tickets. It is thus necessary to assign a "weight" to the items according to their importance in the average consumer's budget. The weighting is obtained from diaries that families in selected areas around the country are asked to keep. (The identity of the households, as well as the businesses and the items surveyed mentioned at the start of the paragraph, are kept confidential.) A major change in weights is made once every ten years; the present ones based on the years 1982–1984 are seen in Table 15.6. They sum to 100 because 100% of consumer spending is covered.

TABLE 15.6
Present weights in the U.S. consumer price index.

Food, beverages	17.6
Housing	42.5
Apparel	6.3
Transportation	17.5
Medical care	5.8
Entertainment	4.4
Other goods, services	5.9

There are problems with any system of weighting. What will you do with new products introduced since the weights were established? How will the changes in the quality of goods be picked up? (Failure of the index to reflect the rapidly increasing power of computers is said to have meant that U.S. GDP was about 1% lower than it would have been had the index been kept current. The procedure for computers was changed in 1986.)[11] What if changes in preferences cause consumers to spend a different proportion of their income on these categories than is indicated by the weights? Such substitution will be especially important during an inflation, as consumers protect themselves against its effects by shifting to goods where the price rises have been relatively lower. None of this will register, however, until the weights are officially changed, and inflation may therefore seem worse than it really is.

The mechanics of a price index can be seen in Table 15.7, which shows two goods, A and B. A's price increased by 50% during the year, B's by 10%. The increase in prices when expressed on a base of 100 is called the relative. For example, a 2% price increase would give a relative of 102, or 2% above the base of 100. The relative when prices increase by 10% is 110; with a 50% increase it is 150. These are the figures entered in the table under the column heading "relative." Now consider the weighting of the index. Good A is very important in consumers' spending, making up 80% of purchases, while good B is less important at 20%. These percentages are the weights.

TABLE 15.7
Constructing a weighted price index.

	1994 price	1995 price	Relative	Weight	R x W
Good A	10	15	150	80	12000
Good B	0.90	0.99	110	20	2200
				sum of R x W	14200

11.   It has been estimated that overall, U.S. inflation as measured by the CPI for 1947 to 1983 would have been lower by 1.5 to 2 percentage points if better adjustment had been made for the improved quality of consumer goods. This is important as we shall see later in the book. It means that a measured rate of inflation of 1.5 to 2% might mean that, adjusted for quality, prices did not increase at all.

The next step is to multiply the relative (R) by the weight (W) for each item, sum the results, and then divide that sum by 100 to obtain a *weighted price index*. In this example, the sum of

$$R \times W \div 100 \ = \ \frac{14200}{100} = 142.$$

The average weighted price increase was not 30%, which is the unweighted figure, but 42%, because good A is the more important and its price rose faster.

If you know the weighted price index for two years running, both figures based on an earlier year, it is a simple matter of conversion to find the rate of inflation between the two years. The formula is:

$$\frac{\text{(This period's price index)} \ - \ \text{(last period's price index)}}{\text{(last period's price index)}}$$

If, hypothetically, 1994 = 130 and 1995 = 142, then we know that inflation between 1994 and 1995 is:

$$\frac{142 - 130}{130} \ = \ 9.2\%$$

A weighted price index can be used to correct for the effect of inflation on any nominal number such as new car prices, or the contents of your saving account, or your annual salary. The technique for deflating nominal numbers to obtain real numbers adjusted for inflation is one of the most commonly used statistical exercises in all of economics. Without it, any economic comparisons over time would be much more difficult to make.

Let us deflate the value of a basket of consumer goods worth $300 in 1995 to reflect hypothetical inflation of 9% in the prices of these goods between 1994 and 1995. The method involves dividing the nominal 1995 value by the weighted price index and multiplying the result by 100, as in the formula:

$$\frac{\text{nominal 1995 value}}{\text{weighted price index}} \ \times \ 100 = \text{real 1995 value at 1994 prices}$$

Because prices, properly weighted, rose during the period by 9%, the weighted price index is 109. The calculation is as follows:

$$\$300/109 \times 100 = \$275.22$$

The basket of goods worth $300 in 1995 was worth in real terms at 1994 prices only $275.22.

Correcting the Nominal GDP to Obtain Real GDP

A standard procedure of economics is to adjust **nominal GDP** to obtain **real (or constant dollar) GDP** corrected for inflation. The Department of Commerce uses a method to ascertain real GDP that requires more data than does simple correction by means of a price index. Here we trace the means by which the nominal 1992 gross domestic product for the United States was corrected ("deflated") for the inflation that had occurred since 1987.

First, the statisticians valued 1992's output at 1992's prices, giving them the nominal GDP for that year. They determined that nominal 1992 GDP was $5,951 billion. Next, they once again valued 1992's output, using 1987's prices. The use of 1987 prices indicates that 1987 was the "base year" for the calculation.12 The value of 1992's output valued at 1987's prices was $4923 billion. This is the real GDP for 1992 at 1987 prices.

The rate of inflation between 1987 and 1992 is therefore easily calculated. It is the quotient when 1992 output at 1992 prices (nominal GDP) is divided by 1992 output at 1987 prices (real GDP). The rate of inflation calculated by this method is called the **GDP deflator**. Algebraically,

$$\frac{\text{nominal GDP}}{\text{real GDP}} = \text{GDP deflator.}$$

Using the actual data for 1992,

$$\frac{5951}{4923} = 1.208.$$

As measured by the GDP deflator, prices rose by 20.8% between 1987 and 1992.[13]

The real GDP data also allow us to analyze the rate of economic growth. Back in 1987, that year's nominal GDP (at 1987 prices) was $4,524 billion. The difference between that and the real GDP for 1992 at 1987 prices ($4,923 billion) was small; economic growth was slow in real terms, less than 2% per year. Of the increase from $4,524 billion to $5,951 billion in the nominal value of the GDP between 1987 and 1992, most ($1,028 billion or 72% of the increase) was due to inflation.

THE LEADING INDICATORS

The national accounts, unemployment data, capacity utilization, and price indices are the main methods of measuring an economy's performance. Many other types of data have importance for macroeconomics, however. The identification of the turning points in an economy's growth is clearly so important that any early warning would be of great value to the business community and to policymakers alike. For many years, the Department of Commerce has searched for measures other than the large aggregates that would indicate that a downturn or upturn in the economy was in the offing. Numerous **leading indicators** are now published. They possess the significant trait of usually turning downward before production itself starts to decline, and turning upward before production increases. That is, they "lead." On the current list are (1) average weekly hours on the job in manufacturing, (2) average weekly claims of unemployment benefits, (3) new orders for consumer goods, (4) vendor performance, which is an index of the speed of deliveries from suppliers, (5) contracts and orders for plant and equipment, (6) new building permits, (7) changes in manufacturers' unfilled orders for durable goods, (8) changes in the prices of sensitive crude materials, (9) stock market prices, (10) changes in the money supply, and (11) an index of consumer sentiment. The "index of leading indicators" gives a value to each of these 11 measures. These values are weighted and then distilled into a single number that is published on a monthly basis. It attracts wide attention in the press.

Unfortunately, the ability of the index of leading indicators to foretell the economy's future performance has declined in recent years. Of seven recessions in the period 1962–1988 predicted by the indicators, four of these recessions failed to materialize. Mistakes have been made in forecasting upturns as well. The worsened performance in foreseeing turning points was

---

12. Every few years, the base year is advanced. A 1982 base was used until November 1991. The choice of base years ending with 2 or 7 is due to the careful studies of the economy carried out by the Bureau of the Census for those years. The price data for those years are comprehensive.

13. The GDP deflator differs in several respects from the consumer price index (CPI) discussed earlier. It is an implicit figure obtained by dividing nominal GDP by real GDP, rather than an explicit figure based on actual prices as is the CPI. The CPI includes only the prices of the goods and services bought by domestic consumers. The GDP deflator is broader, implicitly including the prices of all goods and services that are *produced* domestically. In practice, the major differences are that the CPI includes import prices and excludes export prices, while the GDP deflator includes export prices but excludes import prices; and also that the CPI excludes the prices of investment goods and government goods and services while the GDP deflator includes them.

most noticeable during the 1980s. Among the reasons three stand out: (1) A rather heavy weight is given in the index to stock market prices, but program trading of stock in which large transactions in the market are signaled by computers when stock prices hit a certain level, together with corporate takeovers that have also greatly affected these prices, have loosened the connection between share values and the economy's performance. (2) Changes in the money supply affect the index in a major way, but as we shall see, innovations in money markets have made "the money supply" harder to define. (3) The importance of international trade has been growing, especially in the United States, and the index does not reflect the global influences on the economy particularly well. It might be added that even if the leading indicators are predicting accurately, actions by economic policymakers to counter the predicted upturns or downturns might succeed. If so, the forecast would appear to be less accurate than would have been the case in the absence of a policy change.

THE MISERY INDEX

Unemployment and inflation can and do exist at the same time, though their joint occurrence has been a rather recent development. It has become common among politicians to cite a **misery index** that adds together the percentage rate of unemployment and the percentage rate of inflation. In the United States, Jimmy Carter used the idea in 1976, and Ronald Reagan turned it against him in 1980. By current standards, a "misery index" of 5 would reflect excellent macroeconomic performance, while one of 20 would be very bad. In early 1994 the misery index for Japan was 3.9, for the United States 9.5, for Italy 15.9, for Spain 28.1. Sometimes unemployment is given a double weight in these calculations, on the reasonable presumption that unemployment is more damaging for society than is inflation. On that measure, in early 1994 the misery index for Japan was 6.8, for the United States 16.1, for Italy 27.6, for Spain 51.2. (Some scholars would give unemployment an even greater weight—as much as four times.) The very existence of the misery index shows that macroeconomic conditions have changed over the years. How it is that considerable unemployment and inflation can coexist will require careful treatment in the chapters that follow.

We have now completed our study of how economic performance is measured. Though we have presented caveats concerning the methods used, we should understand that these data are the best available, that there has now been nearly a half-century's experience in interpreting them, and that they serve reasonably well as the benchmarks for the economic policy decisions of all major countries. Conducting macroeconomic policy without such data might still be possible, but it would be exceedingly difficult.

With an understanding of the methods available, we can now move to the discussion and analysis of what factors affect a country's economic performance. The questions to be addressed are: why does economic growth occur, what are the causes of unemployment and inflation, can a battle against them be waged, and if so, how? To these fundamental topics of macroeconomics we now turn.

SUMMARY

1) In the absence of a reasonably accurate system of measuring economic performance, many private and public economic decisions would be mere guesswork. The absence of proper data during World War I and the Great Depression, which caused serious problems, was a major catalyst in the establishment of our present system of national accounts.

2) An economy's total annual output can be measured as the total amount of consumption spending plus investment spending plus government purchases plus net exports. Together, these equal gross domestic product, or GDP; GDP = C+I+G+X–M. In assessing the total, it is essential to avoid the double counting of intermediate products such as the paper included in a book.

3) In principle, every dollar of output generates a dollar of income in the form of wages, salaries, interest, rent, or profit. So a nation's GDP is approximately equal to its national income. "Approximately" because allowance must be made for depreciation (the wearing out of capital goods) and indirect business taxes such as sales taxes, which are included in the price of output but are not income to anyone.

4) The national accounts are an imperfect measuring rod. There are problems in the accuracy of the statistics, in deciding exactly what to measure (housework?), and in using them to assess levels of living and progress over time.

5) Unemployment data and the figures for capacity utilization are useful measures of economic performance, but they also involve several problems of interpretation.

6) It is possible to factor out the effects of inflation on any nominal price or value by "deflating" the nominal figures by means of a weighted price index. When nominal numbers are deflated in this way, the resulting numbers are known as "real," that is, adjusted for inflation. The standard formula for doing so is: real number = nominal number ÷ weighted price index x 100. A country's nominal total output (GDP) is usually deflated by a different and more data-intensive method. The statisticians measure the nominal GDP for a given year, and then recalculate that GDP at the prices prevailing in some base year. The rate of inflation (GDP deflator) is equal to nominal GDP ÷ real GDP.

Chapter Key Words

Capacity utilization: The ratio of the amount actually produced divided by what could be produced. An important economic indicator.

Depreciation: The wearing out of capital, subtracted from GDP to obtain NDP.

Disposable personal income: Income actually received by an economy's individuals. Different from national income in that corporate profits and taxes are subtracted as are income, social security, and other personal taxes, while government transfer payments are added.

Double counting: The impermissible practice of counting items twice in valuing a nation's output. Avoided by counting only final sales, or using the *value-added approach,* which see.

GDP deflator: The rate of inflation obtained by dividing a given year's nominal GDP by that year's real GDP valued at some base year's prices. Nominal U.S. GDP in 1992 was $5,951 billion, while real GDP at 1987 prices was $4,923 billion. Hence, prices as measured by the GDP deflator increased by 5951/4923 = 1.208, or 20.8%, between 1987 and 1992.

Gross domestic product (GDP): The money value at market prices of a country's total output of final goods and services produced during one year. The measure of total output that includes *gross investment,* which see. GDP = C+I+G+X−M.

Gross national product (GNP): The total output produced by a country's residents, as opposed to GDP which is the total output produced within a country's borders. In the United States, now mostly superseded by GDP. GDP + net factor receipts from and payments to the rest of the world = GNP.

Gross investment: New additions to capital together with the replacement of worn-out capital.

Indirect business taxes: Sales and value-added taxes which, though included in the price of goods, are not anyone's income. Because indirect taxes are part of market prices but are not incomes to anyone, in practice, national product (which includes them) is always slightly larger than national income.

Inventories: Stocks of goods produced but not yet sold to final users. Unplanned rises or falls in inventories are an important signal of macroeconomic performance.

Leading indicators: A collection of measures of economic performance that usually turn downward before production itself starts to decline, and upward before production increases. That is, they "lead."

Misery index: An index number used mainly by politicians that adds together the rate of unemployment and the annual rate of inflation.

National accounts: The system of measurement for a country's total output and income.

National income: The measure of all income earned in the production of output. Equal to wages and salaries plus rental income plus interest plus profit.

Net domestic product (NDP): The measure of total output that does not include the replacement of worn-out capital. NDP = GDP − depreciation.

Net investment: New additions to capital; does not include the replacement of worn-out capital.

Nominal GDP: Total output at current market prices, as in "1995 GDP at 1995's prices." Uncorrected for inflation. See *real* (or constant dollar) *GDP.*

Per capita GDP or income: The figure obtained by dividing national product or income by population size, thus allowing for more accurate comparison between the economies of different countries.

Price index: The tool that allows inflation to be measured and corrected for inflation.

Real (or constant dollar) GDP: Nominal GDP corrected for inflation and so providing a more accurate comparison of how output has changed over time.

Statistical discrepancy: The difference between measured output and income that springs up because reliance is put on different types of data.

Underground economy: Economic activity, both illegal and legal in itself but not reported in order to evade taxes. Not reflected in the national accounts.

Value-added approach: A country's total output can be measured by counting the value added at each stage of production. A value-added tax, or VAT, is levied on these stages by most advanced countries, though not the United States.

CHAPTER QUESTIONS

1) In the Pacific Northwest a large log is cut and sold to a woodworker for $200. The woodworker makes the wood into five tables. Three of the tables are sold to regular customers, and one is sold to a school library. The woodworker is not able to sell the other table, so he stores it in his shop waiting for a customer. The tables sell for $300 apiece. How much has GDP increased? Under which component of GDP is each table counted?

2) You are given data on domestic consumption, domestic investment, domestic government expenditure, and exports. Is it still correct to calculate GDP as C+I+G+X–M? Why or why not?

3) You buy from a friend a 1990 Toyota that originally cost $15,000. The price is $9,000, which includes $2,000 of repairs done by your friend. How much did this car add to GDP in 1990? How much did it add when you bought it from your friend?

4) In the country of Weartearia, consumption every year is $1,000 million. Government expenditure is always $500 million. Weartearians invest $300 million per year in machinery with a 12-month life span. What is Weartearia's GDP? What is its NDP?

5) This year, a very small country has a GDP of $1,000. Depreciation is $100, and net factor income to and from the rest of the world is $50. National income is $800. What is the amount of indirect business taxes? How do you know this?

6) You invite a friend from Argentina to visit you. When she comes, your neighbor learns that she is a gifted violinist, so he pays her $100 for several lessons. How do the lessons change the difference between U.S. GDP and GNP?

7) You take a job as a receptionist in a rather quiet office. In real terms, your pay is somewhat lower than what your great-grandfather made as a coal miner in the early part of the century. Therefore your contribution to real GDP is lower than your great-grandfather's was. Does this mean your level of living is lower? Give reasons why or why not.

8) A survey of households in the Chicago area finds that only 5% of them contain people who are not working but are looking for a job or waiting to report to one. Therefore the authorities decide that unemployment is not a problem in Chicago. Is it possible that despite the low figure, unemployment actually is a problem? Why?

9) The following table gives data on the price of two goods in three different years and the weight of each good in the consumer's budget:

Good	1987 price	1995 price	1996 price	Weight
Lettuce	.40	.80	1.00	40
Cars	10,000	14,000	15,000	60

Use this data to construct a price index for 1995 and an index for 1996 (both should be based on 1987 prices). Then use the two indexes to find the rate of inflation between 1995 and 1996.

10) In 1990, Brazil had a nominal GDP of 32,646 million cruzeiros. In 1991, nominal GDP rose to 164,486 million cruzeiros. Taking 1990 as the base year, the GDP deflator for 1991 was 4.98. How much did prices increase from 1990 to 1991 according to the GDP deflator? What was the real GDP in 1991 at 1990 prices? What was the rate of growth of Brazil's real economy between 1990 and 1991?

How the Level of Output Is Determined

The

Concept of

Macroeconomic

Equilibrium

OVERALL OBJECTIVE: To show how the level of economic activity is determined in a market system, exploring the concept of a macroeconomic equilibrium between total output and total spending.

MORE SPECIFICALLY:

■ To illustrate that the concepts of demand and supply provide a microeconomic foundation to macroeconomics.

■ To view an economy's total output and its total spending as a circular flow from households to businesses and back again, with saving a leakage from the flow and investment an injection into the flow.

■ To define macroeconomic equilibrium as the level of economic activity where the country's total output (C+S) is equal to its total spending (C+I), and to show that this is true whether we use a fixed-price (Keynesian) model or a flexible-price (or flexprice) model.

■ To demonstrate that when total output exceeds total spending, inventories will accumulate and output will fall (in the fixed-price model), or both output and prices will fall (in the flexprice model); and that when total spending exceeds total output, inventories will fall and output will rise (in the fixed-price model), or both output and prices will rise (in the flexprice model);

■ To explain the income and nonincome determinants of consumption and saving, and to diagram these.

■ To analyze the average and marginal propensities to consume and save.

■ To analyze how the expected net rate of return and the rate of interest determine the amount of investment, and to introduce the accelerator model.

In this chapter we begin our analysis of why market economies do not always exhibit steady growth, but instead show significant fluctuations in total output and total income. Recessions and inflations are the great enemies of steady economic growth and they bring heavy human costs. What causes them? Once we have a basic understanding of the causes, we can assess in subsequent chapters what, if anything, government policies can do to smooth the swings.

▶ MICROECONOMIC FOUNDATIONS TO MACROECONOMICS

In this chapter and those to come, we will find that certain elements of microeconomics—especially the model of demand and supply—provide a foundation for the most important macro theories. In practical terms that is the reason why this book takes up macro after first studying micro. (Readers who have not taken microeconomics will find an introduction to demand and supply in the brief concluding section to Chapter 2, "The Elements of Price Determination." Those who need a review should read that section now.)

We will find that much of the discussion on the severity of recessions and inflations has to do with our knowledge of how prices as determined by demand and supply behave in the microeconomy. In macroeconomics, our concern is not only with the prices of goods and services but also the wages of labor in labor markets and the interest on loans in financial markets. All are determined by demand and supply. This section surveys three areas where microeconomics serves as a foundation for macroeconomics.

MICROECONOMICS AND THE DEBATE ON THE SEVERITY OF UNEMPLOYMENT

The debate on the severity and longevity of unemployment in a recession illustrates well the essential contribution of microeconomics to understanding the macroeconomy. Why does unemployment sometimes reach damaging levels for long periods? The answer turns on micro modeling of the behavior of the markets for labor. One group of economists believes that the structure of labor markets *does not* contribute to severe bouts of unemployment, while another group *does* believe that labor markets are a cause of the problem.

Wage Flexibility and Unemployment

Economists who believe that the structure of labor markets is not a cause of long-lasting severe unemployment draw on microeconomics to make their case. In their view, shifts in the demand or supply of labor lead to a rapid return to equilibrium at a new wage level. Look at Figure 16.1, which shows demand and supply curves for the labor market and the resulting price of labor (wage rate) and level of employment determined by these curves. Similar diagrams showing prices (including wages, which are the price of labor) as the outcome of demand and supply were first introduced in Chapter 2.

Here the initial equilibrium is at an average market wage of W_1. If the labor market consists of L_3 potential workers, then L_1L_3 of these would choose not to take work; these people prefer nonpaid activities including leisure to employment at the current wage of W_1. To attract all of these potential workers into paid employment, wages would have to reach the high level W_3. At that higher wage, the supply curve shows that the remaining potential workers L_1L_3 would decide to enter the labor market.

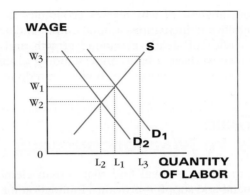

Figure 16.1. Demand and supply curves in the labor market. A great debate in macroeconomics on the question of the severity and longevity of unemployment turns on whether labor markets move rapidly to equilibrium. The initial equilibrium is at wage W_1 and employment level L_1. All who are willing to work at this wage find employment. Others (the quantity L_1L_3) voluntarily stay out of the labor force; they prefer nonpaid activities including leisure to working at wage W_1, and a wage of W_3 would be needed to attract them into paid work. In the figure, a recession causes the demand for labor to fall from D_1 to D_2. If the labor market adjusts rapidly, moving to its new equilibrium, then wages will drop from W_1 to W_2 and employment will drop from L_1 to L_2. Those who want to work at wage W_2 will have a job; those for whom the wage is now too low will prefer to do other things outside the paid labor force.

Now say a recession ensues. Businesses find their sales dropping, so they reduce the demand for labor from the demand curve D_1 to the lower one D_2. Wages would fall (to W_2) and employment would sink to L_2.[1] At the lower wage rate, workers in the range L_1L_2 prefer not to work because the lower wages do not compensate them for the nonpaid activities including leisure that they lose. All who wanted to work at the going wage W_2 would, however, have a job. Because of the **wage flexibility**, the structure of labor markets could not be a cause of long-lasting and severe unemployment. Economists who hold this position claim that government policy mistakes are often the main cause of long-lasting and severe unemployment.

Wage Rigidity and Unemployment

Another group of economists looks at labor markets in a different way. This group believes that labor markets exhibit some **wage rigidity or stickiness** in a downward direction, with wages not easily falling to reflect the new equilibrium. In that case, involuntary unemployment *could* develop and be long lasting. The relative rigidity might have a number of causes. The working public dislikes wage cuts in the extreme, and strikes are likely when they are made. Governments react politically to this dislike of wage cuts by enforcing minimum-wage legislation. A substantial portion of the unionized labor force in the United States works under contracts of one to three years in duration, with three years usual. Some contracts are even longer. Many nonunionized workers also work under contract; these, too, have legal protection against wage cuts for the life of the contract.

 Even workers with no contract at all often appear to have informal understandings with their employers that their wages will not be cut. For many years, ever since about the turn of the century, managers of firms have seen that it is a poor idea to cut wages in a slump. For one thing, workers' morale will suffer. With less to gain from applying themselves and less to lose if they are let go, "shirking" may increase, in which case firms will have to increase the supervision of their labor.[2] Furthermore, wage cuts carry the risk that workers with skills specific to the firm will

---

1. We assume that the fall in wages is in real terms. That is, prices elsewhere in the economy did not fall, or did not fall enough, to match the fall in wages. Later we will have to discuss the difference it makes if the recession causes prices elsewhere in the economy to fall by as much or even more than the decline in wages (in which case, real wages would be unchanged or even rise).

2. As we shall see, the practice of not cutting wages because that would cause workers to be less diligent, even in the face of unemployment in labor markets, means firms are paying an *efficiency wage*.

depart, perhaps taking with them lengthy training too costly to lose and which would be vital when conditions improve. As a result, firms have often preferred to avoid wage cuts as long as they can, making sure that their experienced workers are retained. The term "hoarding labor" is sometimes applied to employers' decisions to keep on more workers than necessary to maintain output. Labor hoarding is a type of insurance that necessary skills will be available when times improve.

If firms believe they *must* reduce their labor force, they may decide to lay off the newest, most recently hired workers, rather than cut the wages of their experienced employees. The experienced workers, following their own self-interest, would usually approve.[3] In recent U.S. recessions, even though downward pressure on wages was present, a solid floor to wages involving "no cuts" was widely respected by most employers. Wage cuts are rare by comparison to the large number of new contracts that keep wages unchanged. Reluctance to cut wages extends far down in the labor markets; even the local car wash or convenience store seldom resorts to pay cuts in a recession. As Arthur Okun put it, employment now seems more governed by an "invisible handshake" than by an invisible hand.

To this group of economists, a major factor in explaining unemployment is a "market failure on a grand scale," involving delays in wage reductions or even complete absence of them as the demand for labor falls.[4] The consequence is that wages during a recession may not be in equilibrium, but above it, as at W_h in Figure 16.2. Now there are people willing to work at wage W_h (L_4L_5 in the diagram) but who cannot find jobs. They are involuntarily unemployed. Lack of complete flexibility in wages can thus be a cause of long-lasting involuntary unemployment.

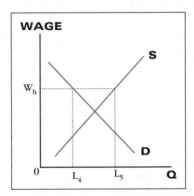

Figure 16.2. **Inflexible wages as an explanation for involuntary unemployment.** If wages do not fall, or only fall slowly, to equilibrium, then involuntary unemployment might be severe and might continue for a considerable time. If wages stay at W_h rather than falling to equilibrium, the quantity of labor demanded by employers (L_4) falls short of the quantity supplied (L_5).

In short, debates on the microeconomics of labor markets underlie much of the recent controversy concerning why involuntary unemployment can be long lasting.

---

3.   Two-tier wage systems that would avoid wage cuts for long-time experienced employees by establishing new, lower wage scales for the most recently hired, have proved highly unpopular with workers. Dissatisfied labor being unproductive labor, two-tier wage scales have never made much headway.

4.   The quotation is from N. Gregory Mankiw, "A Quick Refresher Course in Macroeconomics," *Journal of Economic Literature*, Vol. 28, December 1990, pp. 1645–1660.

WAGE CUTTING IN THE GREAT DEPRESSION

A similar debate surrounds the question whether wage inflexibility was a major cause of the Great Depression's heavy unemployment. One school of thought suggests that because wages actually fell substantially in the United States during the early 1930s, the rigidity or stickiness of wages could not have been the major cause of the unemployment. Indeed, wages *did* fall to a substantial degree, 21% from 1929 to 1933 according to Wesleyan University's Stanley Lebergott. At that time there was no government minimum wage, and the lack of unemployment insurance meant that laid-off workers were more desperate to take any job offer, even one involving a large pay cut. (By contrast, Britain *did* have a minimum wage at the time, a welfare system called the "dole," stronger labor unions than in the United States, and even a Socialist prime minister. For Britain and other European countries, the case for rigid wages is stronger.)

The argument thus can be made for the United States that rigid wages inflexible downward could not have been a cause of the heavy unemployment of the 1930s. By way of reply, however, the theory of wage inflexibility leading to unemployment does not require that wages be static, only that their fall lags behind the fall in prices. (That is, wages could fall in nominal terms but could rise in real terms.) The process of wage decreases during the 1930s took years to accomplish, and was hardly begun until

1931. It is fully plausible that falling wages lagged behind falling prices sufficiently always to generate unemployment at any given moment. In terms of Figure 16.1, a fall in the demand for labor would push wages downward, but the process took time. Meanwhile, the demand for labor fell again, and then fell some more. Arguably, the actual wage always remained above the changing (falling) equilibrium. The question is not settled, though hardly anyone would doubt that wages are less flexible downward now than they were in the 1930s.

More Flexible Wages in the Years to Come?

Recent developments raise the prospect that in the years to come, wages may become *more* flexible after a long period of relative rigidity. In Chapter 11 we noted that profit-sharing schemes and lump-sum bonuses became much more common in the 1980s in the United States, and in Europe as well. (Bonuses were already traditional practice in Japan.) Because these new methods of compensating employees both result in lower wage income when the economy enters a recession, more flexibility would be introduced into what up to now has been a relatively rigid system. Wage stickiness as a cause of long-term unemployment could, if these developments persist, conceivably become less important.

MICROECONOMICS AND THE CAUSE OF INFLATION

Microeconomic models are of great assistance in understanding the causes of inflation as well as unemployment. The underlying cause of serious inflations is universally understood to be government creation of new money to pay its bills. The mechanism by which the money creation raises prices has its roots in microeconomics. Think of the creation of money as involving government use of its printing presses to run off new paper notes that it then spends. The additional money basically increases the demand for goods and services that the government buys. The higher demand raises the prices of these goods and services. Consumers, finding the prices of the items the government purchases now higher, substitute other items, so the demand for these rises too. As long as the supply curves for the various goods and services are elastic—

that is, as long as suppliers are prepared to increase their output as prices rise—the inflation does not become acute. But as the point is approached where firms have no more capacity to produce greater amounts, the increased demand will cause prices to rise. Essentially, the money creation pushes demand in the individual markets for goods and services beyond the point where more can be supplied in these markets, leading to inflation.

In hyperinflations, the price rises reach rates that cause consumers to want to spend their money immediately. If they do not, prices will rise in the meantime and their money will lose some of its value. That, too, causes the demand for individual goods and services to rise. But firms neglect their maintenance and their investment in hyperinflations, and spend much time finding safe havens for their cash rather than concentrating their efforts on production. Supply of many individual products is likely to fall. The combination of higher demand and lower supply for many individual goods and services, and therefore higher prices for them, is the microeconomic result of inflation caused by the creation of new money.

DEMAND AND SUPPLY IN THE MACROECONOMY

The link between micro and macro can be carried one step further. The overall performance of the macroeconomy can be looked at as being the outcome of forces of demand and supply in the economy as a whole. In general we can think of all the annual output of an economy as being that economy's total (or aggregate as we shall call it) supply, and all the spending made on that output as being the total (or aggregate) demand of buyers. As we shall discuss in Chapter 18, curves of aggregate demand and aggregate supply can be drawn that relate the economy's total output to its average price level, as in Figure 16.3.

In appearance, the curves resemble the demand and supply curves for a single good. Overall behavior in the macro model of aggregate demand and aggregate supply is similar to behavior in the micro model of demand and supply for a single good. We will find that an economy is pushed toward an equilibrium price level (P_e) and quantity of total output (Q_e) where the two curves intersect. Anywhere away from that intersection at **E**, forces are set up that move the average price level and the quantity produced to the equilibrium, and changes in the position of either curve will lead to a *new* equilibrium. This model of aggregate demand and aggregate supply is the central model of current macroeconomics. But we must keep firmly in mind that, for all their resemblance to the micro curves, the macro curves for aggregate demand and aggregate supply are more complex than the demand and supply curves for a single good. The explanations for their position and slope is not the same as it was for the micro curves, and the subject will require careful explanation before we can put these macro curves to work. These explanations occupy much of the next three chapters.

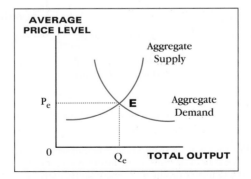

Figure 16.3. Macroeconomics has a microeconomic foundation. The most important model of macroeconomics, aggregate demand and aggregate supply, discussed in Chapter 18, involves a diagram with much the same appearance as the micro model of demand and supply. Just as in the micro model, the intersection of the curves represents equilibrium (E), and anywhere away from that intersection forces are set up that move the average price level and the quantity of total output produced *to* the equilibrium. But as we shall see in Chapter 18, the explanation of the aggregate curves is considerably different from the demand and supply curves of microeconomics.

In short, macroeconomics is deeply rooted in microeconomics, and a basic knowledge of microeconomics is extremely useful for studying all branches of macro.

WHAT DETERMINES TOTAL OUTPUT AND TOTAL SPENDING?

A SIMPLE MODEL OF THE CIRCULAR FLOW

We now begin to investigate what determines an economy's overall level of output. The key determining relationship is between the amount of *output produced* and the amount of *spending available* to purchase that output. The basic question: Is everything sold that has been produced? This relation between total output and total spending governs whether an economy is stable in a position of **macroeconomic equilibrium**, or whether it is under pressure to grow or contract. In the second half of the chapter, armed with the knowledge of why the relationship between output and spending determines equilibrium, we turn to the analysis of the separate *components* of output and spending.

THE CIRCULAR FLOW MODEL

A simple model called a **circular flow** diagram helps us to visualize the relationship between output and spending, and so understand how the level of output is determined. The circular flow diagram in Figure 16.4 is an elementary model of an operating economy. The diagram is drawn on the basic premise that all production in an economy is carried on by firms in the business sector, while all consumption is carried on by households, the members of which also receive all the incomes earned. To keep the model very understandable, two assumptions are made to ease the task. First, we will ignore government as an economic actor, leaving a discussion of its taxes and spending until the next chapter. Second, we shall also ignore foreign trade until the next chapter. For now, the discussion will concern only the macroeconomic conditions within the domestic, private economy.

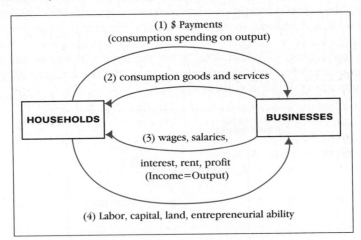

Figure 16.4. The circular flow between households and businesses. This circular flow diagram assumes that production is carried out by firms in the business sector of the economy, which pay income to households for the factors of production. These households carry on the economy's consumption of what is produced. Income and spending comprise a circular flow between the household sector and the business sector.

In the model, households spend all their income on consumption by purchasing output from the firms in the business sector. This money flow is shown at (1) on the top of the figure. The counterpart of this money flow is a flow of consumption goods and services from the business sector to households, shown at (2) in the figure. If the entire output of goods and services is sold, so that no unsold goods accumulate in inventory, then the value of these goods and services produced must be exactly equal to the value of the spending on them.

All the spending business receives is paid out to households, which own all the factors of production. Firms make payments to cover the costs of hiring the factors of production. Payments from firms to households can be wages and salaries for labor, rent for land, interest on capital, or the profit earned by entrepreneurs. (Entrepreneurs own and manage the firms in the business sector but, as recipients of income, they are by definition in the household sector.) The money flow of incomes to households is shown at (3). Total income must be exactly equal to the value of the factor services that flow from households to the business sector, shown at (4) in the figure. As long as all production is sold, and all income is spent, each of the flows on the diagram must be the same size.

In this simple model, *the value of the output produced in the business sector must exactly equal the value of the income earned by households.* Households spend all that income on consumption, buying the output of goods and services produced by the same firms. Firms find that total spending on their output is just sufficient to buy all that output. A circular flow exists. From this point on, as we build on the circular flow model we will not include the flows (2) and (4). They exactly equal their counterparts, and omitting them from further diagrams reduces clutter and allows us to concentrate on the dollar flows (1) and (3).

The circular flow can be traced numerically. If firms produce goods and services valued at $1000 per year, then they pay out $1000 as income to the owners of the factors of production in the household sector. Perhaps the payment is $900 for land, labor, and capital, with $100 left over as profit for entrepreneurs. These payments are at (3) in Figure 16.4. With their income of $1000 per year, these same households carry on consumer spending of $1000. This total spending on output is at (1) in the figure. As long as all output is sold, then in this simple case all these magnitudes in the circular flow—the value of output, incomes earned, and the consumer spending on that output—must be identical. There are no leakages of spending or income to any destination outside the circular flow, nor any injections of spending or income from any outside source into the circular flow. Whatever amount firms pay out to the household sector as costs of production including profit, these firms receive back in the form of consumer spending by the households.

ALLOWING FOR SAVING AND INVESTMENT

To begin making the model more useful, let us allow for **saving** and **investment** to occur. Saving is that part of this year's income not spent by households for this year's consumption. We assume for now that all saving is done by households. Investment is this year's spending not made on consumption, but on the output of capital goods. We assume that investment is carried on by the firms in the business sector of the economy. Saving and investment add new routes to the circular flow, included in Figure 16.5 and 16.6.

Saving

In a world of no government or foreign trade, any part of household income not spent on consumption (C) must be saved (S). (Note that in this model, households do not invest. Investment is spending to increase output, and output is carried on in the business sector.) Household income is as before equal to the value of the output produced by firms. It may either be consumed (C), in which case the income flows back to firms as spending, or it may be saved (S). Thus total income earned by households = C+S. The value of firms' output is the same as the income earned from producing that output, so C+S represents total output too. This is seen at the bottom of the circular flow in Figure 16.5.

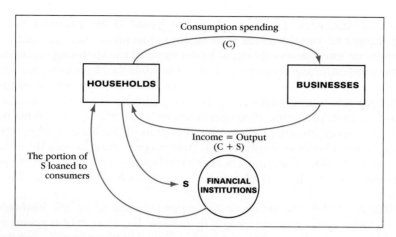

Figure 16.5. **Saving and the circular flow.** Saving is a withdrawal from the circular flow. In the model it is deposited with financial institutions. Some of it flows back to households in the form of consumer loans.

The portion of household income that is saved (S) and not spent for consumption is a leakage out of the circular flow. Most of this saving will find its way into banks and other financial institutions.[5] These institutions thus acquire the financial resources with which they can make loans. Part of these resources flow directly back into the household sector as banks lend to consumers (shown on the left of Figure 16.5). Another part is loaned by financial institutions to firms, which use the funds for investment.

Investment

Firms invest by creating new capital (plant, equipment, and so on). The financial means for investment spending is represented as a flow of funds from financial institutions. These loans are an injection of new spending into the circular flow, moving the savings of households to the firms that do the investing. (See Figure 16.6.)

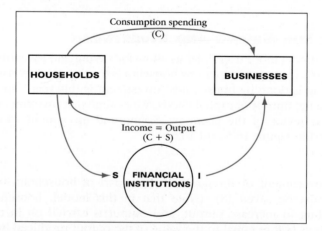

Figure 16.6. **Consumption, saving, and investment in the circular flow.** Saving is a withdrawal from the circular flow, while investment is an injection back into it. In the model, if all saving is invested, then total output and hence income earned in the economy (C+S) is matched by a flow of total spending (C+I), so that all that is produced is sold.

---

5.   Some of the saving will be done directly by business firms that put aside "undistributed profits" for future use. We could, if we wished, lead a stream of saving from the business sector to financial institutions, meaning that less would be paid out to households as incomes by firms, and thereby diminishing the flow from businesses to households. The logic is the same, however, and the diagram is neater, if the undistributed profits are treated as belonging to the entrepreneurs who own the firms. Since these entrepreneurs are part of the household sector, business saving can be treated as flowing first to households and then to banks and other financial institutions.

Total spending in an economy is now represented by the sum of consumption spending (C) plus investment spending (I).

EQUILIBRIUM BETWEEN TOTAL OUTPUT AND TOTAL SPENDING

The relationship presented in a simple model of the circular flow prepares us to examine central questions of macroeconomics. Will there be sufficient total spending available in the economy to purchase the total output of firms in the business sector? If not, what will happen to the economy?

The total output of the economy is equal to the economy's total income. Knowing that output equals income, we can therefore think of output as the way income is utilized. Income can be utilized either for consumption or saving, C+S. Thus **C+S = total output**.

The total *spending* of the economy can be expressed symbolically as spending for consumption plus spending for investment, or C+I. That is, **C+I = total spending**. The relationship between total output and total spending is a central one in macroeconomics. When the two are equal, there is enough spending to purchase all that is produced. But when they are not, there will be either too much or too little spending to purchase the economy's output, and economic consequences will ensue.

EQUILIBRIUM: WHEN TOTAL OUTPUT IS EQUAL TO TOTAL SPENDING

Consider an economy in which firms taken together find that the value of their output (C+S) exactly equals the amount of spending that they receive (C+I) for that output. In that case, firms will be under no special pressures to adjust their production. They are selling all they are producing; and they are producing a sufficient quantity so that no general shortage or surplus of goods occurs. This situation, where total output and the income paid out to produce this output (C+S) equals total spending (C+I), is one of **macroeconomic equilibrium**. There is no general tendency for firms to alter their level of activity, and the economy stays stable. The equilibrium condition can be summarized as follows.

Equilibrium:

Total Output = Total Spending

$$C+S = C+I$$

DISEQUILIBRIUM: WHEN TOTAL OUTPUT DIFFERS FROM TOTAL SPENDING

What happens if the total level of the nation's output and the spending on that output are not equal? For example, spending may fall because households decide to save more of their income, while firms continue to invest at the same level. Because households have raised their saving (S) and therefore reduced their consumption (C) by the same amount, the total spending on firms' output (C+I) must fall below the value of that output (C+S). A lower C plus a constant I is less than a lower C and a higher S, as in the following box.

Disequilibrium:

Total Output ≠ Total Spending

$$C{\downarrow}+S{\uparrow} \neq C{\downarrow}+I$$

In this case, the total value of the output of firms (C+S) is greater than the total spending being received back by these same firms (C+I).

Because they are not selling all they produce, firms will find inventories of unsold goods accumulating in stores, shops, and showrooms. The firms will have to respond to this situation. *How* they respond makes a significant difference for the analysis of the macroeconomy.

FIXED-PRICE AND FLEXIBLE-PRICE MODELS

Economists have two different conceptions of how firms will react to the accumulation of unsold goods. What distinguishes the two concepts is different assumptions concerning the role of prices in the determination of output and income. One assumption is that prices are fixed. In these **fixed-price models**, as changes in total output and income take place, the average price level in the economy is assumed not to change. The other competing assumption is that prices are flexible. In **flexible-price (or flexprice) models**, the average price level in the economy varies as fluctuations occur in total output and income. The path to macroeconomic equilibrium must be modeled differently depending on whether a fixed-price or flexprice view is taken. Each of the assumptions and the models based on them is the more useful depending on the prevailing economic circumstances. The better predictor in one setting may be the worse in a different one.

In the material that follows we shall explore an economy's path to equilibrium verbally and in the form of diagrams, using each of the two assumptions, fixed prices and flexible prices. The fixed-price model is chosen as the starting point because it is generally the easier of the two, and because some of the apparatus acquired and methods developed in its construction are applicable to the flexible-price model. In addition, examining equilibrium first in one model and then in the other is an excellent illustration of how economists practice their craft. As more and more empirical testing is applied to competing theories, the necessary evidence accumulates with which the models can be judged.

THE KEYNESIAN FIXED-PRICE MODEL

The fixed-price model was created by John Maynard Keynes. In 1936, Keynes published *The General Theory of Employment, Interest, and Money*. That book considered the causes of the Great Depression which at that time was ravaging all of the world's advanced market economies. It spawned an intellectual revolution that brought into being the fixed-price models of macroeconomic analysis.

JOHN MAYNARD KEYNES

Keynes (1883–1946) was a professor at England's Cambridge University. The name is pronounced "Kanes." He first came to prominence at the close of World War I, when he wrote a book entitled *Economic Consequences of the Peace*, a scathing and deserved attack on the harsh conditions imposed on Germany by the Treaty of Versailles. His stellar academic reputation, combined with his social station as an aristocrat in an aristocratic society, meant that a book by him on the causes of the Great Depression was likely to have a profound effect. It did. He was also a major player in the setting up of the great international economic agencies such as the World Bank and the International Monetary Fund after the end of World War II. He was made Lord Keynes six years after the appearance of *The General Theory*. Though gone from the scene for nearly 50 years, Keynes remains a redoubtable figure in macroeconomics, and he started the great debate over fixed-price versus flexprice modeling that still goes on.

Keynes' view of economic equilibrium, heavily influenced by the depression conditions during the time he was writing his book, presumed that economies operated with substantial excess capacity. In Keynes' view, unemployed resources were available in quantity. Thus a large expansion in output could occur just through putting these unemployed resources back to work. There was no need in this view to be concerned with a significant upward movement in the price level.[6] In terms of any given individual good or service, production could be expanded by hiring unemployed workers and starting up existing but unused machines. No wage increases or new investment seemed necessary to accomplish this. Thus the supply curves for individual goods and services could be looked at as quite elastic (flat); price stability would be the rule.

This "Keynesian" fixed-price view was understandable for the times in which it was formulated, and it remains of considerable interest and importance in economies attempting to deal with deep recessions. For economies at or near full employment, however, the Keynesian fixed-price assumption is not as helpful. For these circumstances, economists now prefer to use flexprice models, as we shall examine.

WHEN TOTAL OUTPUT IS GREATER THAN TOTAL SPENDING IN A FIXED-PRICE MODEL

Given a fixed-price assumption, let us pursue the problem of what happens when a nation's output is greater than its spending, and stocks of unsold inventories accumulate. The question is, what will happen to the macroeconomy as firms attempt to stop accumulating unwanted goods? In a Keynesian fixed-price framework, the logical decision of firms would be to cut back on their orders for new goods, and hence to reduce the level of total output. (If you were tempted to say that rather than reducing output firms might instead cut prices, then remind yourself of the fixed-price assumption.)

This reduction in total output would mean an equivalent reduction in income. This, in turn, means that consumption and saving must fall. Total spending would not fall so far, however, if we continue to assume that investment spending is constant. C is reduced, but I stays the same. As long as output exceeds spending, firms will reduce their orders and output will continue to decline. The decline comes to an end when total output (C+S) has fallen to the point where there is sufficient total spending (C+I) available to buy all the goods and services offered for sale in the market. In that case, once again C+S = C+I and the economy returns to an equilibrium.

Equilibrium Again:

Total Output = Total Spending

C+S = C+I

Inventories do not change

---

6.   Keynes also assumed that prices would exhibit some fixity in a *downward* direction as well. The reasons for this stickiness are examined in Chapter 18.

INVESTMENT AS TREATED HERE IS DEFINED AS DESIRED OR PLANNED INVESTMENT

It is important to understand that the investment component (I) of total spending (C+I) discussed here is *desired* or *planned* investment. It is the amount that firms *want* to invest. Our analysis has shown that when output is greater than spending, then C+S > C+I, and since C = C, therefore S > I. Yet in the hands of a statistician measuring the country's saving and investment, *S and I are always equal*. This could be confusing, but the difference is only a semantic one. The statistician considers additions to inventory to be investment, and subtractions from inventory to be negative investment. The economist, however, defines any difference between S and I to be an inventory change. In an economy with no government or foreign trade to consider, *actual* measured S and I would thus always be equal, while *desired* or *planned* S and I could differ substantially because of unexpected inventory changes. All our analysis in the text has been conducted in terms of *desired* or *planned* investment, and that will continue to be the case. Spotting the difference between planned and actual investment was an important early contribution to the development of ideas about macroeconomic equilibrium.

WHEN TOTAL OUTPUT IS LESS THAN TOTAL SPENDING IN A FIXED-PRICE MODEL

What would happen if starting from a position of equilibrium, for some reason total spending is higher than firms' total output? Spending might rise because households decide to save less of their income and consume more of it. Assume that investment stays the same. Because households have raised their consumption (C), and lowered their saving (S) by the same amount, they will now spend more on the output of firms than they did before. Total spending (C+I) rises above the value of total output (C+S), and we have a situation of disequilibrium.

Disequilibrium:

Total Output < Total Spending

C↑+S↓ < C↑+I

Inventories fall

The result is the opposite of the earlier case. With more spending than output, firms would notice a depletion of their inventories. To remedy this and to cash in on the potential for increased earnings, the managers of firms would place new orders with the result that total output increases. The pressure for growth in output will continue up to the point where a growing C+S will once more equal a growing C but a constant I. Then, with total output C+S equal to total spending C+I, there is no reason to expect inventories to be further depleted. There is now a sufficient amount of spending to purchase the output of the economy. Again an equilibrium is reached, with the economy no longer under pressure to expand.

Equilibrium Again:

Total Output = Total Spending

C+S = C+I

Inventories do not change

The essential point is that when total output and hence income (C+S) are not equal to total spending (C+I), inventories will change. The reaction of firms' managers to the inventory change will mean a movement in total output. The adjustment in output will continue until an equilibrium is reached where inventories cease to expand or contract. These ideas are central to macroeconomics.

FIXED-PRICE EQUILIBRIUM EXPLAINED NUMERICALLY

The path toward equilibrium in a fixed-price setting can also be illustrated with some simple arithmetic. Table 16.1 presents seven columns of data. Column 1 shows five different hypothetical levels of total output running from a low of $2,000 billion to a high of $4,000 billion.

Columns 2 and 3 show the consumption and the saving associated with each level of output. Because output is equal to income and because, given our assumptions, all income must be consumed or saved, then column 2 plus column 3 equals the total shown in column 1.

Column 4 shows the level of investment by firms. The assumption in the table is that investment is a constant figure, $300 billion.[7]

TABLE 16.1
A numerical example of fixed-price equilibrium.
(all in billions of dollars)

(1)	(2)	(3)	(4)	(5) (=1)	(6) (=2+4)	(7) (=5–6)
Total Output	Consumption	Saving	Investment	Payments Made by Business (Income=Output)	Spending on Output of Business = Business Receipts	Change in Inventory
2000	1800	200	300	2000	2100	–100
2500	2250	250	300	2500	2550	–50
3000	2700	300	300	3000	3000	0
3500	3150	350	300	3500	3450	+50
4000	3600	400	300	4000	3900	+100

Column 5 shows the payments made by firms in producing the nation's output. Remember that this figure must be the same as the income received by the factors of production engaged in producing the output. So, business expense to produce the national product is equal to income earned (column 5) and is in turn equal to the nation's output shown in column 1.

Column 6 is spending on the output of business (business receipts). That spending is the sum of consumption spending (column 2) plus investment spending (column 4).

Table 16.1 allows us to see how much of the total income paid out by business (column 5) will flow back to business as spending on output (column 6). Examine carefully the situation where total spending (column 6) is greater than total output (column 1). For example, at output level 2000 and spending level 2100, purchases are greater than production and inventories must decline by 100 (column 7). As a result, firms will expand their level of output. Note how this also holds true at the higher output level, 2500. Again, spending on production is greater than the production itself, again the outcome must be a decline in business inventories, this time by 50, and there is again a tendency for firms to increase output as in the first case.

Now examine higher total output levels: 3500 or 4000, for example. These high levels of output in both cases exceed the amount of spending on the output. The result will be that a portion of production will remain unsold, inventories will increase, and the business sector will be under pressure to reduce its production.

---

7. This assumption of a constant amount of investment is, by the way, only a simplifying convenience that can be altered with no major change in the analysis, as we shall see later.

Only at a level of total output equal to 3000 is there a sufficient amount of spending so that there is neither a general shortage nor a general surplus of goods. At this point, total output C+S equals total spending C+I. At this level, inventories will neither expand nor contract, and it follows that in this case there will be no overall tendency for firms to increase or decrease their total output.

Whether traced in circular flow diagrams or by means of numerical examples, the concept of macroeconomic equilibrium between total output and total spending is central to the analysis of an economy's behavior. The next section delves further into the individual components of these broad aggregates.

APPENDIX:
CONSUMPTION, SAVING, AND
INVESTMENT: KEY MACROECONOMIC VARIABLES

We have seen that the relationship between total output (C+S) and total spending (C+I) determines whether an economy will be in equilibrium. Consumption, saving, and investment are the components of output and spending, and so our study of the path to equilibrium must turn to an examination of what determines the size of each of these components. The tools developed in the analysis of consumption, saving, and investment are essential in understanding the functioning of the macroeconomy. Though the fixed-price assumption is used in the diagramming and much of the discussion that follows, the information is also essential in the construction of flexible-price models as well, as we take up in the next chapter.

 ## CONSUMPTION

In modern market economies, by far the largest of the components of total output and total spending is consumption, usually amounting to two-thirds or more of the total even when government spending and foreign trade are included in the analysis. (For the time being, we continue to exclude them.)

A very important factor determining the level of consumption is the level of income that people have available to spend. The measure called disposable personal income, discussed in Chapter 15, shows exactly that. In the remainder of this section, the word income means disposable personal income, the best predictor of the level of consumption.

The relationship between income and consumption is not straightforward, however. Transitory shifts in income (unexpected or "windfall" gains and losses, for example) have far less effect on consumption than shifts that are expected to be permanent. The consumer who receives an unexpected $100 windfall this month may well save most of it, whereas the consumer who expects to receive an extra $100 *every* month is very likely to end up consuming a large part of it. Conversely, the consumer who suffers a loss of $100 this month may well maintain spending by drawing down savings or borrowing, while a permanent loss of $100 per month will probably lead to a permanent decline in spending. The most recent estimates by economists suggest that permanent changes in income may have an effect twice as large as temporary changes. Older estimates point to an even greater margin of about three to five times.

THE PERMANENT-INCOME AND LIFE-CYCLE HYPOTHESES

The lesson that permanent changes in income have a greater effect than temporary changes is one of the aspects of the **permanent-income hypothesis** elaborated by long-time University of Chicago professor Milton Friedman. A related theory, the "life-cycle" hypothesis of MIT's Franco Modigliani, yields similar results. If present income is low, but it is anticipated that future income will be high, as with a group of medical students, for example, then present consumption will be relatively high. Both the Friedman and the Modigliani formulations emphasize that long-run changes in income influence consumption considerably more than short-run changes do.

Because of the permanent or lifetime income-hypotheses, some economists believe that short-run temporary changes in income have no major effect on consumption. Yet a considerable amount of statistical research does confirm the basic idea that changes in consumption track changes in current income rather well.[8] One problem with spreading out consumption over a lifetime, higher than justified by income in young adulthood, lower at a more advanced age—which is what these hypotheses predict will happen—may be the difficulties involved in obtaining sufficient credit on reasonable terms to boost consumption when income is low. Furthermore, adjusting consumption to a permanent income change may be rather slow even when it does occur. Research suggests that perhaps one-fourth to one-half of all income earned accrues to consumers who do not change their consumption as predicted by permanent-income and life-cycle theories. These consumers react to income changes only as they occur, and hence temporary changes in their income may have considerable impact. Even so, few would doubt that permanent changes in income have a greater effect than temporary changes. Henceforth, when income changes are discussed they should be considered to be permanent changes unless otherwise noted.

Table 16.2 helps to illustrate the relationship between (permanent) income changes and changes in consumption for a nation as a whole. Presume that disposable income for the aggregate of all individuals in the country can vary over a range from low to high, perhaps from $1,000 billion up to a figure of $4,000 billion. Disposable income could be anywhere within this range (column 1 of Table 16.2 shows seven arbitrary levels). Economists can estimate what people would spend on consumption at these various income levels. Such information can be informed by time-series and cross-section data concerning what actually occurs. Time-series data gives the measured income and consumption in different years; cross-section data are built up from information about consumption among various income groups in the same year.

---

8. "A consensus seems to be emerging ... that consumption is too sensitive to current income to be consistent with a lifetime conception of permanent income .... Numerous authors have studied the shape of consumption profiles over the life cycle and have concluded that they resemble income profiles too much to be consistent with ... life-cycle theory." Richard H. Thaler, "Anomalies: Saving, Fungibility, and Mental Accounts," *Journal of Economic Perspectives,* Vol. 4, No. 1, Winter 1990, pp. 193–205.

TABLE 16.2
Income, consumption, and saving.

(1) Disposable Income	(2) Consumption (All in billions of dollars)	(3) Saving
1000	1100	-100
1500	1500	0
2000	1900	100
2500	2300	200
3000	2700	300
3500	3100	400
4000	3500	500

The figures in the second column show possible levels of consumption at various given incomes. As is to be expected, where the level of income is very low, the level of consumption is also low. So low in the case of the second figure, $1,500 billion, that people feel too poor to want to save anything. They feel even worse off when disposable income is $1,000 billion. At this level, they are actually consuming more than they earn in income—living off their savings at the rate of $100 billion per year, so that saving is negative. (Historically, negative saving actually occurred during some years of the Great Depression.) Conversely, at higher levels of disposable income, the level of consumption is also greater. Furthermore, at higher incomes people feel they can afford to save something. Their saving rises with income, as is shown by the figures past the second line of the table.

CONSUMPTION AND SAVING RELATED

If we leave aside government and foreign trade, then the part of income that is not consumed must be saved. When income is $1,500 billion, people consume $1,500 billion worth of goods and services, and saving must be zero. At $2,000 billion income, consumption is $1,900 billion and saving is $100 billion. At the high level of income $4,000 billion, the difference between income and consumption is much greater; saving is $500 billion. Using the letter Y to stand for output and its equivalent, income, we can write $Y = C + S$. With this formula we can calculate any column in Table 16.2 as long as the figures for the other two columns are known.

The Average Propensities to Consume and Save

In order to conduct macroeconomic analysis of a market economy's fluctuations, we need to develop some measures of the behavior of consumption and saving. Several useful measures involving simple algebra can indeed be calculated when the data for Y, C, and S are available.

The first of these is the proportion of income used for consumption at any level of income. This measure, C/Y, is called the **average propensity to consume** (or **APC**). At an income level of $1,500 billion, the average propensity to consume would be:

$$APC = C/Y$$

$$= 1500/1500$$

$$= 1$$

At higher incomes, the APC is lower than 1 because some income is saved, and it is above 1 whenever consumption exceeds income.

Similarly, the **average propensity to save** (or **APS**) is S/Y, the proportion of income used for saving. At an income level of $1,500 billion, the average propensity to save would be $APS = S/Y = 0/1500 = 0$. Since by definition all income is either consumed or saved, $APC + APS = 1$. The algebraic proof of this is as follows:

$$Y = C + S$$

Dividing by Y, $$Y/Y = C/Y + S/Y$$

Therefore, $$1 = APC + APS$$

APS is known when APC is known. That is because $1 - APC = APS$. APC is also known when APS is known, because $1 - APS = APC$.

The Marginal Propensities to Consume and Save

In analyzing how the macroeconomy behaves, it is often important to find the *extra* C and *extra* S that occur from each *additional* dollar of income. Note in Table 16.2 that an additional $500 billion of income causes an additional $400 billion of consumption and an additional $100 billion of saving. These concepts involve $\Delta C/\Delta Y$ (here .80), which is called the **marginal propensity to consume (MPC)**, and $\Delta S/\Delta Y$ (here .20), which is the **marginal propensity to save (MPS)**. Since the whole increment from any addition to income must be either consumed or saved, then MPC + MPS = 1.

The algebra involves dividing by ΔY, as in the following formula:

$$\Delta Y = \Delta C + \Delta S$$

Dividing by ΔY, $$\Delta Y/\Delta Y = \Delta C/\Delta Y + \Delta S/\Delta Y$$

Therefore $$1 = MPC + MPS$$

Diagramming Consumption and Saving

We can now begin to construct diagrams of consumption and saving, diagrams that eventually will contribute further to our knowledge of how the macroeconomy behaves and what policies might be useful in addressing its fluctuations. Our first effort will be to show the relationship between disposable income and consumption. In Figure 16.7, the dollar level of disposable income is on the horizontal axis. Total income equals total output. We use $Y to stand for both income and output. (In our further diagramming, we will simplify by using just the letter Y and the explaining phrase total output, understanding this to mean the dollar value of both income and output.) On the vertical axis is consumption, also measured in dollars and labeled as $C. (In our further diagramming, the vertical axis can be used to measure *any* component of income and output, not only consumption but also saving, investment, government activity, and foreign trade. It greatly simplifies the labeling simply to call the vertical axis "$", understanding that the dollar value of all the various components of income and output can be measured there. That is what we do henceforth.)

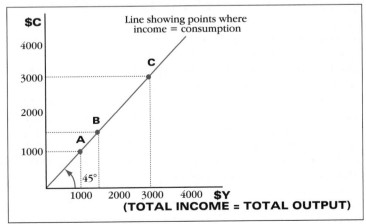

Figure 16.7. **Diagramming income and consumption.** Dollar levels of income and output are on the horizontal axis, while dollar levels of consumption are on the vertical. The 45° line shows all the points where all of income is used for consumption.

Notice the 45° line running out from the origin. This line defines a boundary in how income is used: it is the series of points along which all income would always be used for consumption. If income is $1,000 billion, and the public consumes the entire $1,000 billion, that would give a coordinate point "A" on the diagram, with the point equidistant from each axis. At the higher income level of $1,500 billion, then if all income were consumed, consumption also would be $1,500 billion. The point showing this would be at B. Similarly, income $3,000 billion and consumption $3,000 billion would give a point C.

The Consumption Function

The data contained in Table 16.2 is pictured diagrammatically in Figure 16.8. The figure shows consumption at different levels of disposable income. Consider $1,000 billion of income. Consumption is $1,100 billion, with a coordinate point at V. At $1,500 billion of income consumption is $1,500 billion, with a coordinate point at W. At $2,000 billion, consumption is $1,900 billion, with a coordinate point at X—and similarly up to an income of $4,000 billion where consumption is $3,500 billion, with a coordinate point at Z. Connecting the points V, W, X, and Z gives a line showing consumption at different levels of income. Economists call this line a **consumption function**; it is marked here as C. The vertical distance from any given income level along the horizontal axis up to the consumption function C thus measures the amount of consumption at that level of income.

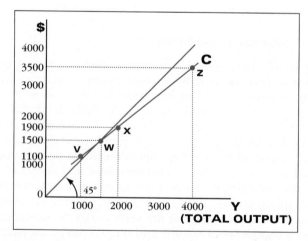

Figure 16.8. The consumption function. Line C is a consumption function relating the level of consumption to the level of income. At point Z, $3500 billion is consumed out of a total income of $4000 billion.

Where does saving appear on the diagram? The 45° line helps us find it. As pointed out earlier, whatever income is not consumed must be saved. (Y = C + S). Recall that the vertical distance up from the horizontal axis to the consumption function represents the dollar amount of consumption. Remember also that if all income earned is used for consumption, then the vertical distance showing this consumption will reach up to the 45° line. The vertical difference between the 45° line and the C line must then represent that portion of income not consumed, the income that is saved. For example, the consumption function (C) of Figure 16.9 shows that at an income level of $3,000 billion, the level of consumption is $2,700 billion. The distance between C and the 45° line must be whatever is left over. It amounts to $300 billion, which is the amount of saving that Table 16.2 told us to expect.

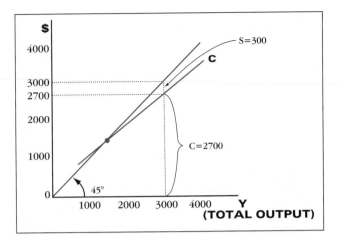

Figure 16.9. Diagramming consumption and saving. Consider income level $3000 billion. Since saving is that part of income not consumed, and $2700 billion is consumed at that income level, then saving must be $300 billion, the vertical distance from $2700 billion to $3000 billion.

The Savings Function

Saving can also be diagrammed directly, as in Figure 16.10. Here income (output) is on the horizontal axis, and saving measured in dollars is on the vertical. (As before, we label the vertical axis $ because in time we will be measuring a number of other variables along this axis as well as saving.) Notice that at low levels of income, saving is negative. The **savings function** runs up and to the right, showing higher levels of saving at higher levels of income.

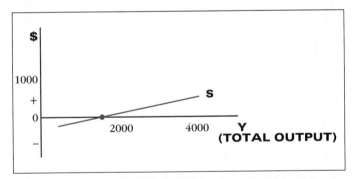

Figure 16.10. The savings function. Line S is a savings function relating the level of saving to the level of income. At the point where S crosses the horizontal axis, all income is consumed and there is no saving.

The Average Propensities to Consume and Save

With these diagrams and the use of some geometry, it becomes possible to identify the propensities to consume and save discussed earlier. Knowing how to find these measures on a diagram will later be useful in tracing the forces that work to expand or contract an economy. The average propensity to consume (APC) is, we recall, the proportion of income consumed at any level of income, or C/Y. The APC is easily shown on the consumption function in Figure 16.11.

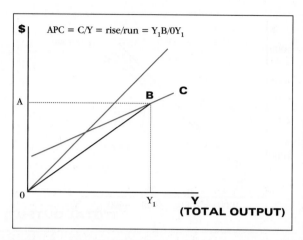

Figure 16.11. **Finding the average propensity to consume.** The APC is calculated as C/Y, or $Y_1B/0Y_1$. Since this is the rise over the run of a right triangle, the result is the slope of the line 0B, which is the APC.

At income level $0Y_1$, for example, consumption (C) is measured vertically ($0A = Y_1B$). Since $C/Y = APC$, therefore $Y_1B/0Y_1 = APC$. Some geometry is useful here: Y_1B is the vertical side of a right triangular figure, while $0Y_1$ is the horizontal side of the same figure. Dividing the length of the vertical side of a right triangle by the length of the horizontal gives the slope of a line from the origin to the point B on the consumption function. Thus, if $Y_1B = 1000$ and $0Y_1 = 2000$, then the slope of 0B is $1000/2000 = 0.5$. This slope is the APC.

The **average propensity to save (APS)** is the proportion of income saved at any level of income. Once the APC is known, the APS is easily determined because $1 - APC = APS$. The APS can also be diagrammed directly, as in Figure 16.12, by finding the slope of a line from the origin to a point on a savings function. Here, $Y_1V/0Y1_1 = $ the slope of 0V, which is the average propensity to save.

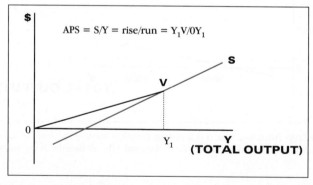

Figure 16.12. **Finding the average propensity to save.** The APS is calculated as S/Y, or $Y_1V/0Y_1$. That yields the slope of the line 0V, which is the APS.

The Marginal Propensities to Consume and Save

The **marginal propensity to consume (MPC)** is, we recall, the proportion of any *increase* in income that is consumed, or $\Delta C/\Delta Y$. The technique for identifying the MPC on a diagram is similar to that for the APC. On the consumption function, how much does consumption rise as income rises? Start at point B in Figure 16.13.

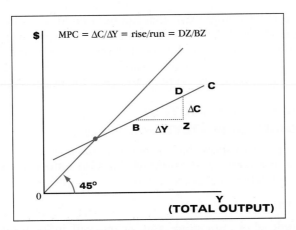

Figure 16.13. **Finding the marginal propensity to consume.** The MPC is calculated as $\Delta C/\Delta Y$, or DZ/BZ. That yields the slope of the line BD, which is the MPC.

If income increases by BZ, then consumption rises by DZ. Since the marginal propensity to consume is $\Delta C/\Delta Y$, then MPC = DZ/BZ. DZ and BZ are the two sides to a right-angled triangle, so the result is the slope of a line BD. This is identical to the slope of the consumption function. When that function is a straight line, the MPC is constant; when the line curves, the MPC varies. If the consumption function is shallower at higher incomes to the right, it follows that the MPC is lower to the right. (Empirically, short-run studies are generally consistent with straight-line consumption functions.) In recent years the U.S. MPC has been .9 or more.

The **marginal propensity to save (MPS)** is, as we have already seen, the proportion of any *increase* in income that is saved, or $\Delta S/\Delta Y$. Once the MPC is known, the MPS is known too because 1 – MPC = MPS. The MPS can also be obtained geometrically with a savings function. In Figure 16.14, WX/VX gives the value of the slope of the savings function VW, which is the MPS.

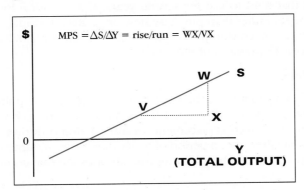

Figure 16.14. **Finding the marginal propensity to save.** The MPS is calculated as $\Delta S/\Delta Y$, or WX/VX. That yields the slope of the line VW, which is the MPS.

These marginal propensities to consume and save are especially important in macroeconomics. We will make much use of them in the next chapter.

In the Long Run, Dissaving Could Not Occur

The relationship between income, consumption, and saving just discussed must be modified to cover long-run situations, because in the long run, negative saving (dissaving) cannot occur. Look back to Figure 16.13: at low levels of income, to the left of the intersection of the consumption function and the 45° line, consumption exceeds income. Similarly, in Figure 16.14 to the left of the point where S intersects the horizontal axis, saving is negative. The dissaving (negative saving) at low levels of income could continue only over a relatively short period of time, only as long as a stock of savings exists that can be used for consumption or lenders willing to make loans can be found. Eventually, the dissaving would have to stop. Because consumption cannot continue indefinitely to be above income, the consumption and savings functions in the long run would have to be drawn to show no negative saving. In Figure 16.13, no part of C could lie above the 45° line; in Figure 6.14, S could not start below the origin of the diagram.

THE CONSUMPTION FUNCTION AND THE NONINCOME DETERMINANTS

Although we have taken pains to show that income is a major determinant of consumption and saving, there are some **nonincome determinants** that also influence consumption and saving. Five important nonincome determinants are noted.

Cultural Attitudes

First, the public's attitude about spending and saving will influence consumption. In some cultures and at some time periods, saving is emphasized over spending, while at other times and places more weight is placed on consumption. For example, in recent years Americans have been very consumption-oriented, while the Japanese for various reasons have been oriented toward saving. Attitudes may also depend on one's *former* level of income, as when a family that has suffered a fall in income attempts to maintain its level of consumption for reasons of habit and status.

Expectations (Confidence)

Expectations about prices and incomes help determine consumption. If people believe that prices will rise sharply in the near future, or that their incomes are due to increase, they tend to purchase more goods now. If there is an expectation of falling prices or reduced incomes, consumers will decide to postpone some of their purchases. Sales of "big ticket" durable goods are especially vulnerable to pessimistic expectations. This includes items such as cars, computers, VCRs, and appliances that tend to last for several years. If a recession looms, people will drive their old cars a little longer rather than purchase new ones. Recent studies indicate that the effect of consumer confidence on consumption spending is relatively small, though it was more considerable in the Great Depression of the 1930s.[9]

Stock of Durables

A third determinant of consumption is the stock of durable goods the public holds. Purchases of these will increase during a period of economic boom, or perhaps following a war when many durables have worn out and need replacement, or after a slump during which purchases have been postponed. For some time after a period of heavy purchases of durables, however, there may be no pressing need to replace them, lessening consumption on that account.

Wealth

A fourth nonincome determinant is the public's wealth held in accessible form—its holdings of stocks, bonds, insurance policies, bank accounts, and so on. The greater these holdings, the better off people will believe themselves, and the more inclined to consume. A decline in such wealth holding, for example a stock market crash, would be expected, conversely, to lower consumption at any given level of income. People who feel worse off will consume less.[10]

---

9.   One cause of the Great Depression was the great uncertainty generated by the collapse of stock market prices in late 1929. Then the subsequent banking collapse led to unprecedented pessimism. The effects on consumption (and investment, as we discuss later) led Franklin D. Roosevelt to say "The only thing we have to fear is fear itself."

10.   Though probably not by much. The rule of thumb before the stock market crash of October 1987 was that each $1 of paper loss in the stock market cuts consumption by only 3–5¢. The 1987 crash appears to have had even less effect on consumption than that; saving actually fell a little.

Changes in the price level can also work through wealth holdings to influence consumption and saving. For example, if prices rise, holders of wealth will discover that their cash, bonds, and bank accounts will purchase less than before. Disappointed, they can be expected to reduce their consumption as a result of this **real balances effect**. The reverse is also true. If prices fall in a recession, the purchasing power of assets will increase, working to restore consumption spending. (Note, however, that the strength of the real balances effect is reduced by the existence of debt. If prices rise, debtors get to repay debt with cheaper dollars and accordingly may *increase* their spending. If prices fall, debt must be repaid with more expensive dollars, so debtors may *decrease* their spending. Debt, which works against the real balances effect, is a much larger proportion of the nation's income now than it was 20 or 30 years ago.)

Credit Conditions, Interest Rates

A fifth nonincome determinant of consumption has to do with the availability of credit and the level of interest rates. Easy credit terms and low interest rates encourage consumption. A shortage of credit, considerable indebtedness, and high interest rates discourage it. Interest rates can also be affected by inflation, which may increase the burden of repaying loans that carry variable rates—variable-rate mortgages on houses, for instance. Those who must increase their repayments have less left over for consumption.

CHANGES IN THE NONINCOME DETERMINANTS SHIFT THE CONSUMPTION FUNCTION

Whenever any one of the nonincome determinants just discussed is altered, then at any level of income the desire to consume and save changes and the position of the consumption function is affected. Say more credit is available, or buyer confidence improves. If as a result, people decide to consume more than formerly, then whether their income is relatively low, as at A in Figure 16.15, or high as at B, or indeed at *any* level of income, the whole consumption function will shift vertically upward all along its length to C_1.

What if the changes are in the opposite direction? Say less credit is available, or people feel pessimistic about the future. Then at any level of income, people will consume *less* than formerly. The consumption function will fall vertically to C_2 in Figure 16.15.[11]

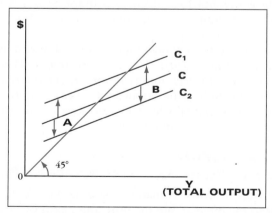

Figure 16.15. **Shifts in the consumption function.** If a change occurs in one or more of the nonincome determinants of consumption, the consumption function will shift upward or downward.

---

11.   Note that in this and most following examples, the new "C" line is drawn parallel to the old one. This will not always reflect the relationships exhibited in the real world. For example, an attitude of "keeping up with the Joneses" might become more entrenched as a society grows richer, in which case the new C line must be drawn with a steeper slope than the old one. It is simple and handsomely symmetrical to make parallel shifts, however, and henceforth that is usually what we do. Readers can alter the slopes to take account of special cases as necessary.

There is one final point, an important one, to make on this topic. Many years of investigation on the public's spending and saving patterns indicate that the consumption and savings functions do not rise or fall very rapidly. Changes generally take a considerable amount of time. Perhaps this is because spending and saving habits are ingrained and difficult to change, or perhaps because the nonincome determinants of consumption may not all shift in the same direction. For instance, determinant #1 might move in the direction of more consumption while at the same time determinant #5 might alter in the direction of more saving. In this case, the two effects might cancel each other out, leaving the consumption function about where it had been before.

Table 16.3 shows the year-to-year changes in saving as a percentage of income during the years 1983 to 1987, a period when the figures for the United States were more-than-usually volatile. Note that even so, the changes were slight. The table does, however, also make clear that savings behavior differs substantially among countries, with effects on economic growth that we shall examine later. Saving has also moved significantly in the long run. In the United States, it averaged 8% of disposable personal income in the early 1970s, but has been in a slow decline for many years until a slight upturn set in from 1988. (U.S. household saving was 4.8% of disposable income in 1992.)

TABLE 16.3
Household saving as a percent of disposable income.

	1983	1984	1985	1986	1987
United States	5.4	6.1	4.4	4.1	2.9
Japan	16.3	16.0	16.0	16.4	16.1
Seven Major Industrial Countries	10.5	10.8	9.7	9.5	8.9

INVESTMENT

We recall that the relationship between total output (C+S) and total spending (C+I) determines whether an economy will be in equilibrium. Having discussed consumption and saving, we now move on to investment. In the previous chapter we defined investment as the creation of capital, the production of goods not for current consumption but which are intended to raise future production. New equipment, new machines, and new buildings are all examples of investment made to increase future output.

What are the factors that determine how much firms will invest in a given time period? The answer involves the anticipated *net return* from the investment. This is the expected revenue earned from carrying out the new project, minus all the expected costs of the project. If, after all costs are taken into account (including the opportunity cost of capital and management), a firm still presumes that an addition to capital will yield a positive net return, then that firm will have an economic motive to carry out its investment plans.

INVESTMENT DETERMINED BY
EXPECTED NET RETURN AND THE INTEREST RATE

The decision to invest or not to invest is made by comparing the expected percentage rate of return on the investment to the interest rate the firm could earn on alternative uses of its money, such as keeping it in bonds or bank accounts.[12]

Say a firm is trying to decide whether to purchase a $100,000 machine. What would it need to know in addition to the $100,000 purchase price? First, it would want to ascertain the net return per year from operating the machine. To find this, it would have to discover the

---

12.   This percentage rate of return on investment can be called the marginal productivity of investment, but this is a little misleading as already explained in Chapter 12. Unlike other factors, the returns to capital may come not at once but in future years.

expected gross return from selling the output produced by the machine. Say the firm's managers expect that to be $20,000. It would also need to know the annual cost of operation (fuel, hiring labor, a minimum return to keep the firm's entrepreneurs from moving on, insurance, repair, maintenance, and so on). There would also have to be an allowance for depreciation to cover the machine's eventual wearing out, but to simplify the example we shall assume that the machine is so long lasting that depreciation is of no concern. If all costs add up to $5,000, then the expected annual net return from the machine will be $20,000 − $5,000 = $15,000. Expressed as a percentage of the original purchase price of $100,000, the net return is 15%.

Assuming that 15% is the predicted rate of return, under what circumstances will the firm make the investment? If the firm's managers have to borrow the $100,000 from a bank, to go ahead with the project they will clearly have to expect greater earnings from the investment than the interest they must pay on the loan. It would not make sense to pay 16% interest ($16,000) per year when the project is expected to yield only 15% ($15,000) per year. The general rule is that there is an economic incentive to borrow when the expected net rate of return on an investment exceeds the rate of interest.[13]

What if the firm already possessed the $100,000 and did not need to borrow it? Does this alter the rule? No, because the same logic will apply even if the funds are already on hand. If the expected rate of return on the investment is less than the interest rate, the firm could clearly earn more on its funds held in bonds or bank accounts than it could from making the investment. Thus whether the funds are borrowed or already in hand, an expected rate of return higher than the rate of interest provides the motive for the investment to take place.

It is important to understand that the percentage rate of net return (15% in our example) is a prediction but not a certainty. It is based on a firm's *expected* revenues earned from a new machine and the *expected* costs of operating it. The uncertainty of the final outcome is important. Any entrepreneur with investments risks funds for some period of time. If economic conditions worsen, actual returns will be lower than expected returns. Many economic and psychological factors affect business expectations, including announcements of changes in major economic indicators, movements in interest rates, stock market booms and crashes,[14] changes in government regulation of business, price controls, taxes, oil shocks, wars, revolutions, weather (in agriculture and tourism), strikes, elections, technical change—anything at all that influences business confidence. A bleaker economic outlook would lead to scaling back of the expected rate of return; a prediction of a prosperous future would mean a higher expected return. It is not surprising that with so many different factors to consider, expectations sometimes lend a volatility to investment decisions that make these decisions difficult to predict.

The three variables in this model of investment are the cost of capital goods, the rate of interest, and the expected rate of return from the new investment. The model predicts that higher real interest rates will curtail investment, while lower rates will stimulate it.[15] This relationship can be seen in Figure 16.13, which shows a "demand for investment" function. The demand for investment is shown with a steep slope, indicating that the response by businesses to changes in the real interest rate appears to be relatively small (that is, inelastic).

---

13. In the presence of inflation, both the expected rate of return and the interest rate ought to be in real terms, corrected for the inflation.

14. Changes in stock market values can have important effects on business confidence and thus on investment, just as on consumer confidence and consumption. This was amply demonstrated in the crash of 1929 and the ensuing Great Depression. The repercussions on investment of the 1987 stock market crash were, to the contrary, hardly noticed.

15. And indeed the high real rates of the early 1980s in the United States did cause a great decline in U.S. investment in that period, while the lower real rates of the later '80s caused an increase in investment.

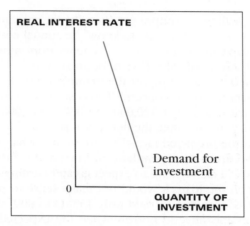

Figure 16.16. The model of investment determined by real rates of interest. This model of investment suggests that high real rates of interest discourage investment while low rates encourage it.

INVESTMENT CAN BE IRREVERSIBLE, WHICH INCREASES RISK

In the discussion above, the roles of interest rates and expected net returns in determining the amount of investment were relatively straightforward. The process is more complex, however, when—as is common—firms face irreversibility together with uncertainty. Irreversibility means that once an investment is made, the funds are committed and cannot easily be recovered. A machine may possibly have no other use at all except to the firm that built it. If this is the case, the firm could sell it only for its scrap value. Even if the machine can be sold to some other firm in the same industry, or to a firm in another industry, its resale value may be considerably less than the price of the investment itself, just as the price of a new car declines greatly once it is driven a few miles. When an investment is made, the firm that does the investing gives up the possibility of using its funds in some other way, such as investing in something else or holding funds in interest-bearing bonds. There is a risk that economic conditions will deteriorate, or that new government tax policies will encroach on earnings. A mistaken investment once made cannot easily be modified or withdrawn.

So, comparing the rate of interest to the expected net return from an investment will have to be evaluated carefully for risk, and the outcome will have to be favorable enough to offset the advantages of keeping options open. Any given investment can usually be postponed; firms that consider irreversibility and uncertainty to be serious problems may therefore delay their investment plans. This outcome is common when talk of recession is in the air. It also is common in inflation to find firms fearful of investing, because they know that mistakes in forecasting the rate of inflation could spoil their prediction that an investment will be profitable.[16]

16.   For a thorough account, see Robert S. Pindyck, "Irreversibility, Uncertainty, and Investment," *Journal of Economic Literature*, Vol. 29, September 1991, pp. 1110–1148.

INVESTMENT DETERMINED BY CHANGES IN INCOME (THE ACCELERATOR)

Another model is also in use to explain the level of investment. It is the **accelerator**. This theory suggests that investment is related to changes in output and income (ΔY). It is written as a functional relationship, $I = f(\Delta Y)$. As an example, consider a company with 10 shoe-making machines. Each year, one of the machines wears out and is replaced, so gross investment equals one machine. Assume that each machine turns out 1,000 pairs of shoes, for a total of 10,000. Then consider the outcome if demand grows 10%. Customers will want to buy 11,000 pairs. Two new machines will be needed this year, one for replacement and one for expansion, instead of just the one for replacement. So, total investment rises 100%, from one machine to two, because of a 10% increase in output. In this model investment depends on ΔY, and the coefficient linking them, α in $I = \alpha(\Delta Y)$, is the accelerator. In our example, $\alpha = 10$; that is, investment was accelerated by 10 times the rise in income.

The accelerator will not operate, and there will be no investment caused by the growth in income, if there is excess capacity in the industry. If unutilized machines can simply be brought back into operation as demand increases, then no new investment need occur. This means that during a recovery from a recession investment is likely to be weak, and growth will be slower than otherwise because new investment will not be necessary as output increases. In an economy without excess capacity, however, rising income and output are likely to cause an increase in investment because of the accelerator.

The accelerator now receives less attention from economists than formerly for a number of reasons. Once the accelerator process starts to operate, there may be considerable time lags involved. New capital cannot be put into place instantly, so investment started when the economy is expanding may continue for a time even after the expansion has slowed down. The planning of investment may also take some time to accomplish. All in all, a link between investment and changes in income as direct as that just described seldom appears in the empirical data. Furthermore, in the crude form presented here the accelerator is undoubtedly a simplistic model. It says nothing about expectations concerning future demand, business conditions, or prices. Investors are perhaps better at anticipating ups and downs in demand than the accelerator theory suggests, and the time horizon of investors often appears to be longer than the short-run demand changes emphasized by it. Yet the accelerator model does have the advantage of directing attention to a "snowball effect" in modern economics. In general, it is correct that once downturns and upturns get underway, they tend to be strengthened because of the mercurial response of investment to changes in income.

The models of investment just discussed (I depends on the relation between the expected net rate of return and the rate of interest, I depends upon ΔY) are not mutually exclusive. These relationships might exert an effect at the same time.

THE NEXT STEP

The concept of an equilibrium involving equality between total output (C+S) and total spending (C+I) is central to macroeconomics. Following on the discussion of consumption, saving, and investment in this chapter, the next chapter shows how these three variables combine to determine an economy's equilibrium level of output. It then adds government and foreign trade to the analysis.

SUMMARY

1) Macroeconomics is built on a foundation of microeconomic models, especially the model of demand and supply. One of the greatest of economic issues, a defining one for modern macro modeling, is whether labor markets tend to move to an equilibrium as readily as do most product markets. If they do not, then an economy might have to bear significant long-lasting unemployment in recessions.

2) An economy's total output and its total spending can be seen as a circular flow of income (which is equal to output) to households as businesses pay for the factors of production they use, and a flow of spending from households to businesses as households consume the output of business. Saving is a withdrawal from that flow, income that is not used for consumption. Investment is an injection of spending into the circular flow, additional to consumption spending.

3) At equilibrium, the value of an economy's total output (C+S) and its total spending (C+I) are equal. If output is greater than spending, then inventories of unsold goods must be accumulating, while if spending is greater than output, inventories of unsold goods must be falling. Managers of firms will respond by changing their orders for output, or by changing their prices, or both. In the fixed-price modeling pioneered by John Maynard Keynes during the Great Depression of the 1930s, the assumption is that only output changes. In flexible-price (or flexprice) modeling, both output and prices change. This chapter and the next utilize the fixed-price assumption, while Chapter 18 moves on to the flexprice case. Either way, equilibrium results when total output equals total spending, while inequality between them results in disequilibrium.

4) Two key macroeconomic variables are consumption and saving. Consumption and saving both vary as disposable income changes, and as certain "nonincome determinants" change as well. Holding all determinants constant except for income allows us to draw functions for consumption and saving showing how they rise with higher levels of income and fall with lower levels of income. These functions shift with any changes in the nonincome determinants. Useful measures involving consumption and saving are the average propensity to consume (C/Y) and save (S/Y), and the marginal propensity to consume $\Delta C/\Delta Y$ and save ($\Delta S/\Delta Y$).

5) How investment is determined can be looked at in two ways: as the outcome when the expected net rate of return from investment is compared to the rate of interest, and as determined by an accelerator where the level of investment depends on changes in the level of income and output.

Chapter Key Words

Accelerator: The idea that changes in output will affect the level of investment.

Average propensity to consume (APC): The proportion of income devoted to consumption, C/Y.

Average propensity to save (APS): The proportion of income devoted to saving, S/Y.

Circular flow: A way of looking at economic relationships that treats income and spending as a circular flow between the household sector and the business sector. Helps in explaining how total output is determined.

Consumption function: A line relating the level of consumption to the level of income. In drawing such a line, it is assumed that there is no change in any of the *nonincome determinants of consumption*, which see.

Efficiency wage: The term used to describe the practice of not cutting wages even in the face of unemployment in labor markets because that might reduce workers' productivity.

Fixed-price models: Macroeconomic models in the Keynesian tradition. Changes in total output and income take place with little or no change in the average level of prices.

Flexible-price (flexprice) models: Macroeconomic models where changes in total output and income take place along with changes in the average level of prices.

Investment: Spending not made on consumption but on the creation of new capital goods.

Macroeconomic equilibrium: The condition in which the relationship between total output and total spending gives the economy no cause to grow or contract.

Marginal propensity to consume (MPC): The proportion of an addition to income devoted to saving, $\Delta C/\Delta Y$.

Marginal propensity to save (MPS): The proportion of an addition to income devoted to saving, $\Delta S/\Delta Y$.

Nonincome determinants of consumption and saving: Factors other than income that determine the level of consumption and saving. These include cultural attitudes, expectations, stocks of durable goods, wealth, credit conditions, and the rate of interest. All are held constant when drawing a consumption function. Changes in them result in a movement of the consumption function itself.

Permanent-income hypothesis: The theory elaborated by Milton Friedman, one aspect of which is that permanent changes in income have a greater effect on consumption than temporary changes.

Real balances effect: The idea that a decline in prices during a recession would raise the purchasing power of assets such as cash, bank deposits, and bonds, thus restoring spending by consumers and reviving employment.

Saving: The part of income not used for consumption, tax payments, or imports.

Savings function: A line relating the level of saving to the level of income. In drawing such a line, it is assumed that there is no change in any of the *nonincome determinants of consumption and saving*, which see. Also see *consumption function*.

Wage flexibility: The idea that unemployment will reduce wages and thus reduce the number of unemployed people because some will not be willing to work at the lower wage. If wages are highly flexible, unemployment could not be expected to be severe or long lasting. Also see *wage rigidity or stickiness*.

Wage rigidity or stickiness: If social, legal, and economic barriers to wage reductions cause wages to be rigid or sticky, especially in a downward direction, then unemployment might be severe or long lasting. Also see *wage flexibility*.

CHAPTER QUESTIONS

1) There is a recession, and demand for goods falls. As a result the derived demand for labor also falls. Show on a diagram what happens if wages are flexible and what happens if they are rigid. In which model does employment fall more? In which model is there involuntary unemployment?

2) Draw a circular flow diagram showing households, businesses, and financial institutions. You know from the reading that income = output = C+S is a flow from businesses to households. Suppose that this flow is $100, of which $80 is C and $20 is S. Draw the flows back from households to business and give the amount of each flow, assuming the economy is in equilibrium.

3) Suppose there is some bad news for the economy of question 2. As a precaution, consumers reduce their consumption to $70 and increase their saving to $30. Businesses do not change the amount of investment. Draw the new circular flow diagram, again labeling the amounts of each flow. How much is total spending? How much is total output?

4) Suppose, as in question 3, that saving is $30 and firms want to invest $20. At the end of the year, how much will firms actually invest? (Hint: actual saving always equals actual investment). Since firms only planned to invest $20, how does this additional investment come about?

5) The economy in question 3 is not in equilibrium. C = $70, S = $30, and I = $20. Thus C+S = $100 and C+I = $90, so total output is more than total spending. Assume that this is a fixed-price, Keynesian model. How will firms react to the disequilibrium? What will happen to total output and to total spending? Where will the process end?

6) Suppose Britain has a fixed-price, Keynesian economy that is in equilibrium with C+S = C+I. Oil is discovered under the North Sea, but it requires a great deal of investment to pump it out. Therefore investment rises considerably, but consumption and savings are initially unchanged. How does the economy adjust to the increase in investment?

7) Assume that the permanent-income hypothesis is correct. Suppose in one year most workers receive a one-time bonus, while in another year most of them receive permanent raises. In which year will the marginal propensity to consume be higher, all other things equal? In which year will the marginal propensity to save be higher?

8) Draw a diagram showing a 45° line and a consumption function. Show a level of output where there is dissaving, one where there is neither saving nor dissaving, and one where saving is quite high. If consumer confidence suddenly falls, show how the consumption function shifts. What happens to saving at any level of income when consumer confidence falls?

9) We know that investment will rise, all other things being equal, when interest rates fall. This is because it is less expensive to borrow money. But suppose that firms have enough cash on hand that they do not need to borrow money to invest. How does that affect the relationship between interest rates and investment?

Pursuing the Fixed-Price Analysis

OVERALL OBJECTIVE: To investigate the fixed-price equilibrium where total output (C+S) = total spending (C+I), and then to introduce government activity and foreign trade to the analysis.

MORE SPECIFICALLY:

- To show how investment can be added to consumption to give a function for total spending (C+I), and to demonstrate that the point where (C+I) crosses the 45° line is the equilibrium level of output and income.

- To explore the multiplier effect, wherein an increase in total spending initiated by new consumption or investment results in a greater increase in total output and income.

- To show that in the Keynesian fixed-price model, equilibrium need not be at the full employment level of output, and how recessionary and inflationary gaps may therefore exist.

- To add government economic activity (including its spending on output of goods and services, its transfer payments, and its taxes) to the analysis, and to show that changes in any of these also have a multiplier effect on total output and income.

- To explore the balanced-budget multiplier, the principle that changes in government spending on output have a somewhat greater effect on the economy than changes in taxes (or transfer payments).

- To introduce foreign trade to the analysis, and to show that changes in exports and imports also have a multiplied effect on an economy's total output and income.

Pivotal to macroeconomics is the concept of an equilibrium between total output and total spending. As we have seen, when output and spending differ, changes in firms' inventories cause these firms to alter their behavior. As a result, the economy moves toward equilibrium, where output equals spending. The movement to equilibrium can be looked at in a fixed-price (Keynesian) setting, where inventory rises or falls cause firms to change only their output, or in a flexible-price setting, where both output and prices change. This chapter pursues the fixed-price analysis, while the next goes on to consider the case of flexible prices.

In a simple model of macro equilibrium, total output is C+S and total spending is C+I. In the previous chapter we developed diagrams of consumption and saving. We can build on these diagrams by adding investment to them, thus allowing us to consider all the components of output and spending needed to portray equilibrium. (Neither government nor foreign trade will be allowed to affect this equilibrium for a little while yet.) This analysis is valuable not only for understanding equilibrium, but for tracing why macroeconomic fluctuations might occur and what might be done about them.

FIXED-PRICE EQUILIBRIUM WITH FUNCTIONS OF CONSUMPTION AND INVESTMENT

The conventional diagram illustrating equilibrium in the fixed-price case begins with the consumption function developed in Chapter 16. The consumption function in Figure 17.1 shows consumption (measured in dollars on the vertical axis) rising as total output and income (Y) increase. For example, if total output and income (Y) are $1000 as measured on the horizontal axis, then consumption is seen to be $800 on the vertical axis. Changes in C and Y are in real terms; prices do not rise or fall in this analysis. This is in keeping with the fixed-price assumption that abundant unemployed resources are available. Throughout this chapter, the horizontal and vertical axes of the diagrams show real dollars unaffected by price changes.

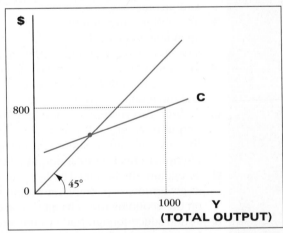

Figure 17.1. A consumption function in the fixed-price case. The consumption function C indicates that at a level of output (and income) of $1000 as read on the horizontal axis, consumption would be $800 as read on the vertical.

Adding Investment to the Diagram

The next step is to add investment to the diagram, as in Figure 17.2. We assume that the level of investment by firms is always equal to a fixed amount (here $300) no matter what the level of total output. In order to find the total level of spending in the economy at any level of output, the vertical distance $300 must be added atop the consumption function at every point along it, so giving a new function that reflects consumption plus investment, or C+I. We can now view total spending (C+I) on the vertical axis at any level of total output (income) on the horizontal axis. For example, at output $1600, consumption (C) on the vertical axis is $1000, while total spending (C+I) is $1300.

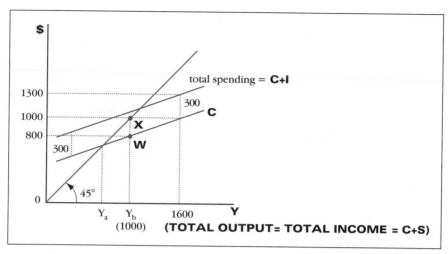

Figure 17.2. **Adding investment to consumption.** Assuming that investment is a constant $300 at any level of output (C+S), then total spending (C+I) can be indicated by a line $300 higher than the consumption function C.

The 45° line is a reference line that allows us to trace out the same amounts of output on the vertical axis that are shown at each point along the horizontal axis. By means of the 45° line, any number representing output on the horizontal axis can now be made to appear on the vertical axis as well. For example, an output of Y_b ($1000) can also be read as output of $1000 on the vertical axis to the left of point X, which is on the 45° line.

As we know, the value of output is identical to the value of income generated in producing that output, and income is either consumed (C) or saved (S). So total output can be written as C+S, as is indicated along the horizontal axis.

In Chapter 16 we saw that at any level of income shown on the horizontal axis, the vertical difference between the consumption function C and the 45° line represents the portion of income that people do not use for consumption. This is saving. For instance, at income level Y_b in Figure 17.2 people want to consume an amount equal to Y_bW, which is $800. Out of their income of $1000, the amount WX, or $200, is not spent. It is saving.

At income level Y_a, however, people do not want to save anything; their earnings are too low. Since the distance from the horizontal axis to the 45° line is total income C+S, and all of it is consumed, there can be no saving. At any income below Y_a, there is *dis*saving; people will draw down their level of accumulated past savings. National dissaving is rare, but it did occur during the Great Depression of the 1930s.

To summarize: (1) Total spending (C+I) can be read on the vertical axis. (2) Total output and income (C+S) shown on the horizontal axis can, because of the 45° line, be shown on the vertical axis as well.

Equilibrium on the Diagram

This diagram shows, for any given level of total output, whether the amount of total spending is too little, too great, or just sufficient to purchase that output. Macroeconomic equilibrium can be viewed directly as the point where total output equals total spending. In Figure 17.3, equilibrium is at point E, where the C+I line crosses the 45° line. Only there will business inventories neither increase nor decrease, with no resulting pressure for changes in total output. Thus in Figure 17.3 the output level at which total spending (C+I) is equal to total output (C+S) is Y_e, say $1200. The "e" stands for equilibrium.

Take a moment to trace it through. See how at Y_a on the horizontal axis total output is $700. This output level of $700 is also identifiable on the vertical axis because of the 45° line. Total spending (C+I) at the output level of $700 is higher than $700, however. Let your eye run vertically upward to the total spending line C+I, and you can see that spending is $1000 as measured on the vertical axis. Because total spending (C+I) exceeds total output (C+S), inventories will be depleted, and production will be expanded by the actions of firms. Conversely, if total output (C+S) is at a higher level Y_b ($1600 on the horizontal axis, also indicated on the vertical axis by means of the 45° line), then that output of $1600 exceeds total spending (C+I) which is only $1300. Total output greater than total spending means rising inventories and pressure to contract total output. Changes in inventory and pressures to expand or contract production cease when the economy reaches an output level Y_e. At that level of total output ($1200 on the horizontal axis, also read as $1200 on the vertical axis), total spending C+I on the vertical axis is exactly the same amount ($1200). Spending is equal to output. The economy is in macroeconomic equilibrium.

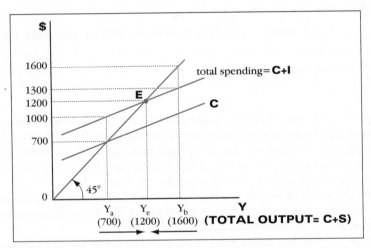

Figure 17.3. Equilibrium. Macroeconomic equilibrium occurs where the amount of total spending in the economy (C+I) is just sufficient to purchase the total output that is produced (C+S). In the diagram, the equilibrium level of output is $1200; at that level of output total spending is also equal to $1200.

EQUILIBRIUM WITH FUNCTIONS OF SAVING AND INVESTMENT

The analysis just undertaken can be duplicated with a second type of diagram that, though it shows the same result, is easier to use in conducting some of the analysis later in the chapter.

This second sort of diagram, shown in Figure 17.4, starts with the savings function already encountered in Chapter 16. (See Figure 16.10.) We have added an investment function (I), and continue to assume that firms invest the same amount regardless of the current level of income and output.

The task is to show that total output moves toward an equilibrium level Y_e, where the savings function and the investment function intersect. The intersection is marked with an "E." Three cases present themselves, just as they did before:

1) *At* E, saving is equal to investment. We know that income and output are equal to C+S, while spending on that output is C+I. On the diagram S = I; therefore, C+S = C+I. All goods produced are sold; inventories neither accumulate nor decline. The managers of firms are under no particular pressure to change their level of business activity.

2) Say that the nation's income and output are *above* E, so that people save more than firms plan to invest. If S > I, then C+S > C+I, meaning that total output is greater than total spending. Firms must not be selling all they produce; inventories are accumulating. In response, firms cut back their orders, and total output declines toward E. The process

continues as long as total output is above E. Only at the level of output E are there no pressures to alter the level of production.

3) If total output in Figure 17.4 is *below* E, then people save less than firms invest. With S less than I, C+S must be less than C+I, and therefore output is less than spending. This means that inventories must be falling. Firms will be under pressure to increase their output toward E, a pressure that continues until E is reached.

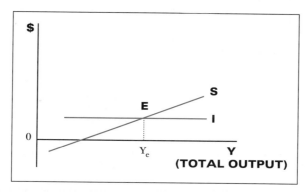

Figure 17.4. Saving and investment. Functions for saving and investment can be used to portray equilibrium. Though the curves have a different appearance from those in Figure 17.3, the explanation for the equilibrium is the same. Because S = I where the curves intersect, then C+S = C+I and total output equals total spending.

This completes our study of how the economy moves toward equilibrium in a simple fixed-price economy with no government economic activity or foreign trade to consider.

▶ MOVEMENTS IN THE FIXED-PRICE EQUILIBRIUM

In analyzing the behavior of the macroeconomy, any changes in consumption, saving, or investment will have important effects. Such changes will, as we see in this section, alter the position of the equilibrium. The economy therefore moves to a new level of output and spending.

CHANGES IN C OR S MOVE THE EQUILIBRIUM

Chapter 16 discussed several nonincome determinants that could affect the level of consumption and saving. These included the public's attitude toward thrift, expectations concerning movements of prices and incomes, the quantity of durable goods held by the public, stocks of liquid assets, credit conditions including the level of debt, and interest rates.

When any of these underlying conditions changes, spending and saving behavior will change. If people find that a stock market crash has wiped out some of their wealth, or if they become more concerned with old age (to give two examples), they may decide to consume less now and save more from their earnings. These changes can be pictured as a shift in the consumption function.

Figure 17.5 shows decreases in consumption (and thus increases in saving) caused by a change in one or more of the nonincome determinants. The consumption function shifts vertically downward. The reduction in C automatically lowers C+I, to C'+I. Now at output level Y_a, total spending C'+I is less than total output (as shown on the 45° line). Inventories will accumulate, firms will reduce their orders, and output (income) will fall to a new equilibrium E', at a lower level of total output Y_b.

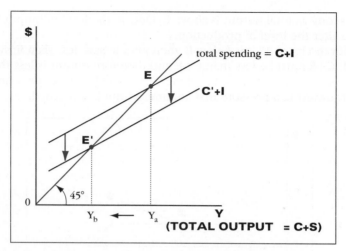

Figure 17.5. A fall in C+I results in a new equilibrium. A reduction in total spending from C+I to C'+I results in a new equilibrium at E'. Total output falls from Y_a to Y_b.

An increase in consumption (decrease in saving) would have the opposite effect.

CHANGES IN I MOVE THE EQUILIBRIUM

Investment might also be subject to changing conditions not associated with the present level of national income. For example, a decline in the rate of interest could lead to more investment, and a rise to less investment. In addition, expectations of the future may change. A belief that business will boom is likely to cause an increase in investment at any level of income. When expectations are gloomy, we can expect a decline in the amount of investment. Changes in investment are shown in the same way as changes in consumption: by moving the C+I function vertically upward or downward all along its length. Figure 17.6 shows a rise in investment that moves C+I to C+I', which also moves the equilibrium from E to E' and raises output (income) from Y_a to Y_b. A decrease in investment would have the opposite effect.

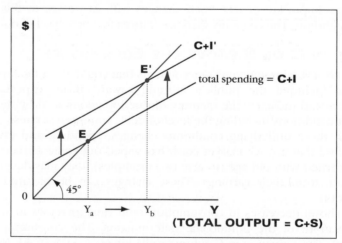

Figure 17.6. A rise in C+I results in a new equilibrium. An increase in total spending from C+I to C+I' results in a new equilibrium at E'. Total output rises from Y_a to Y_b.

CONCLUSION

Changes in the desire to consume or save, or in firms' plans to invest, create a new C+I function that crosses the 45° line at a different point. Because that crossing place is the point of equilibrium, then equilibrium will also change.

For example, a desire to consume less and save more is shown on a diagram as a decline in total spending C+I, as in Figure 17.5. The downward movement in the C+I function will change the equilibrium to a new point where the reduced C+I crosses the 45° line. Only at that new position will total spending C+I be equal to total output C+S. The same result would follow if, for any reason, firms decided to invest less at any given level of national income.

The logic is similar when the case is reversed. Suppose that consumption increases and saving decreases for any reason independent of the level of income (perhaps a belief that prices will rise, or attempts to "keep up with the Joneses"), or that investment increases, or both. In these cases, total spending C+I will rise as in Figure 17.6, with a resulting increase in the equilibrium level of total output.

In short, movements in C (or S), or movements in I, cause changes in the equilibrium level of output and income.

▶ THE FIXED-PRICE (KEYNESIAN) MULTIPLIER

Look again at Figures 17.5 and 17.6. Notice that the changes in consumption (or saving) or investment, shown on these diagrams as movements in C+I, cause changes in total output greater than the original movements in C+I. In Figure 17.5 the fall in output measured horizontally from Y_a to Y_b is plainly greater than the reduction in C+I as measured vertically. Similarly, in Figure 17.6 the rise in output Y_a to Y_b is greater than the increase in C+I. This phenomenon is called the **multiplier effect**. Any initial change in spending is multiplied in its effect on total output and income.

WHAT IS THE MULTIPLIER?

The multiplier is caused by the spending of the income earned as a result of new consumption or investment. Take the case where an investor purchases a new $1000 machine.[1] The purchase of the new machine reflects $1000 worth of output, for which people must have received $1000 in new income from their labor, raw materials, and so on. So the country's output and income must rise by at least $1000. The recipients of this new income will spend part of it on consumption and save part of it. The amount they devote to consumption will be determined by their collective marginal propensity to consume. The MPC, as we recall from the previous chapter, is the proportion of new income devoted to consumption. For example, if the nation's MPC is .80, then on average the amount the recipients of $1000 in new income will spend on new consumption is $800. They will save the rest, $200. The $800 that they spend also becomes new income for some group of people and is also an addition to the country's income. (The $200 that they save does not become new income to someone else; it is a leakage that is not multiplied further.)

The process continues in successive rounds. Recipients of the $800 will spend a large portion of it as determined by their MPC. With an MPC of .80, further consumption will be .80 x $800 = $640, with $160 being a leakage into saving. The $640, too, is new income. At this point, an initial investment of $1000 has already generated new income of $1000 + $800 + $640. The process has not yet ended, though. In the next round, .80 x 640 = $512 of new consumption will be generated, and so on in smaller and smaller amounts as shown in Table 17.1.

---

1.   The choice of new investment to make this case is due to the fact that consumption and saving are ordinarily more stable than investment.

TABLE 17.1
Successive rounds of new spending in a multiplier process.

Initial New Investment = $1000, MPC = .80	
$1000	$210 x .80 = $168
$1000 x .80 = $800	$168 x .80 = $134
$800 x .80 = $640	$134 x .80 = $107
$640 x .80 = $512	$107 x .80 = $86
$512 x .80 = $409	$86 x .80 = $69
$409 x .80 = $328	$69 x .80 = $55
$328 x .80 = $262	**Total so far: $4780**
$262 x .80 = $210	**Ever smaller rounds of additional spending will bring the total to $5000.**

The Multiplier Formula

There is a convenient formula available to measure the outcome of an infinite geometric progression of this sort. That formula is:

$$\Delta Y = \Delta I \times \frac{1}{1 - MPC}$$

We can also write the formula in an alternative way, because as we have already discussed, $1 - MPC = MPS$. Therefore:

$$\Delta Y = \Delta I \times \frac{1}{MPS}$$

The multiplier is the last term in the formula; it is the number by which a change in investment is multiplied to find the resulting change in total output and income. When the MPC is .80 (and the MPS is thus .20), the multiplier is 5, since

$$\frac{1}{1 - .80} = \frac{1}{.20} = 5.$$

A new investment of $1000 would therefore have an eventual effect on total output and income of $5000. Notice that the formula calculates the result including the initial new investment of $1000. This $1000 generated another $4000 of additional spending.

Practice with multiplier calculations can be helpful. If the MPC had been .60, the multiplier would have been

$$\frac{1}{1 - .60} = \frac{1}{.40} = 2.5,$$

and a new investment of $1000 would have resulted in a total change in national income of $2500. Alternatively, an MPC of .66 would mean a multiplier of

$$\frac{1}{1 - .66} = \frac{1}{.33} = 3$$

and a change in national income of $3000 following a new investment of $1000.

Considerations Concerning the Multiplier

The lesson of the multiplier is that an increase in investment spending (or an original increase in consumption spending, for the same logic applies to that case as well) will raise national income by more than the original increase in spending. Economists have long noted that the multiplier process requires time. Little effect from the multiplier would be expected within just two or three months of an injection of new investment; those receiving the new incomes will take time to raise their consumption. Generally, we expect that a year or more will pass before the major impact of the multiplier process is felt.

Another consideration is whether the injection of $1000 in new investment spending this year is just a one-time event, or whether it continues in subsequent years as well. If it is just a one-time event, with only one injection of $1000 in new investment that is not repeated next year, then next year's income will eventually sink back to its former level. If the $1000 in new investment is continued in subsequent years, however, then this permanent injection leads to a permanent rise in income.

The multiplier effect of a temporary injection of new investment is also likely to be smaller for another reason. Temporary rises in income are more likely to be saved. (That is, the MPC will be smaller for such temporary changes.) So, for any given change in investment, the value of the multiplier is likely to be higher if the change is a long-run one rather than taking place only in the short run.

It is important to note that the multiplier also works in reverse. That is, any reduction in spending will reduce national income by more than the original change. The logic is the same as for an increase in spending. Say investment (or consumption) falls by $1000. In that case, someone or some group will receive $1000 less in income. Depending on the MPC, they will cut their own consumption by $800 if the MPC is .8. After the multiplier process works itself out, national income will have fallen by $5000, as calculated by the multiplier formula.

DIAGRAMMING
THE FIXED-PRICE (KEYNESIAN) MULTIPLIER

The multiplier can be traced on the already familiar diagram of saving and investment. Figure 17.7 shows an initial equilibrium at E and a rise in investment from I to I'.

We start with knowledge that a rise in investment (ΔI) equal to the distance E'Z has caused a rise in total output and income (ΔY) from Y_e to Y_e', equal to the distance EZ. We know further that dividing the vertical leg of a right-angled triangle by its horizontal leg yields the slope of that triangle's hypotenuse. Thus,

$$\frac{E'Z}{EZ} = \text{slope of EE'}.$$

We also know, from Chapter 16, that the slope of the savings function (EE') *is* the marginal propensity to save, showing how much saving rises as income rises. Therefore,

$$\frac{\Delta I}{\Delta Y} = \text{MPS}.$$

By transposition,

$$\Delta Y = \frac{\Delta I}{\text{MPS}}, \quad \text{and } \Delta Y = \Delta I \times \frac{1}{\text{MPS}}$$

which is the multiplier formula.

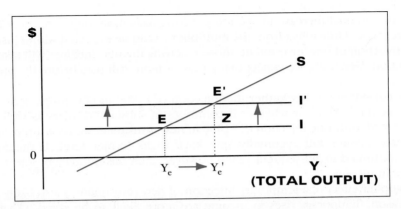

Figure 17.7. The multiplier when investment increases. The multiplier can be derived from an S and I diagram. If investment rises by E'Z, then income rises by the greater amount EZ. Since E'Z/EZ = slope of EE', then $\Delta I/\Delta Y$ = MPS, and by transposition, $\Delta Y = \Delta I \times \frac{1}{MPS}$.

As we know, the multiplier also works in reverse. An initial fall in investment would mean less income for those who produce capital goods and less consumption spending by them in a continuing progression. Figure 17.8 shows the downward movement in total output (which, we recall, is equal to total income) from Y_e to Y_e' as investment falls from I to I'.

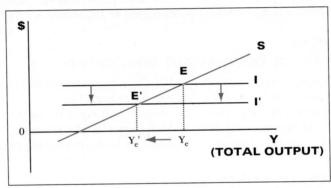

Figure 17.8. The multiplier when investment decreases. The multiplier effect works in reverse when investment falls.

A High MPS Means a Low Multiplier, and a Low MPS a High Multiplier

Note how a high MPS leads to a low multiplier (1/.25 would be a multiplier of 4) while a low MPS results in a high multiplier (1/.10 would be a multiplier of 10). This can be verified from Figure 17.9. The steep slope (high MPS) of the savings function in Panel **a** means that an investment increase will cause only a small rise in total output to occur, from Y_1 to Y_2. The shallow slope (low MPS) of S in Panel **b** means a large increase in total output from Y_1 to Y_3 following the same rise in investment.

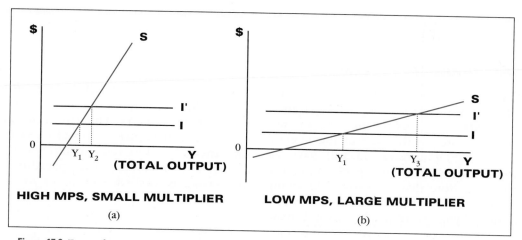

Figure 17.9. **Examples of a small and a large multiplier.** When the MPS is high, the savings function is steep and the multiplier effect is small. When MPS is low, the savings function is shallow and the multiplier effect is large.

A Multiplier Effect Flows from Any Change in Total Spending

A multiplier effect flows not just from new investment, but from *any* new increase or reduction in total spending. For example, a shift in any one of the determinants of consumption and saving could initiate a multiplier effect. Such a shift is pictured in Figure 17.10, where an increase in consumption (decrease in saving) at any level of output leads to a downward movement from S_1 to S_2 in the savings function, and to a multiplied impact on output, which rises from Y_1 to Y_2.

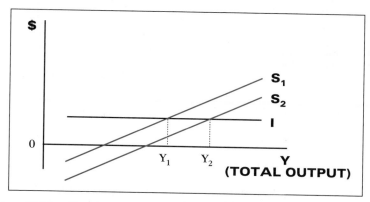

Figure 17.10. **A multiplier effect flows from *any* change in total spending.** Here we see a multiplied impact from an increase in consumption (decrease in saving).

THE PARADOX OF THRIFT

Keynesian economists use the multiplier effect to explore what they call a **paradox of thrift**. They argue that an attempt to save more on the part of the general public during a recession will have an unexpected and damaging effect on the economy. Note that an increase in saving (a cut in consumption) that moves the savings function vertically upward from S_1 to S_2 in Figure 17.11 will cause *a fall in the equilibrium level of output and income* from Y_1 to Y_2. This fall in income would in turn reduce the level of saving (because of the close relationship between saving and income). The paradox is that saving is pushed back to its former level by the fall in income.

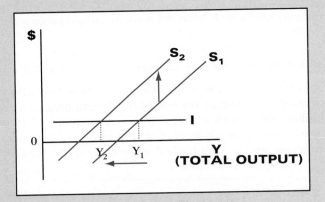

Figure 17.11. The paradox of thrift. Attempts to save more cause output and income to fall, so that the total amount of saving does not rise after all.

FINDING THE MULTIPLIER ON THE C+I AND 45° LINE DIAGRAM

The multiplier is somewhat less visible on a diagram showing C+I and the 45° line, but it is certainly there. In Figure 17.12, the original equilibrium is the point where C+I = C+S (total spending = total output), labeled E. If investment rises by an amount AB, moving the function from C+I to C+I', total output increases by XZ. The multiplier effect is visible because the distance XZ is greater than the distance AB.

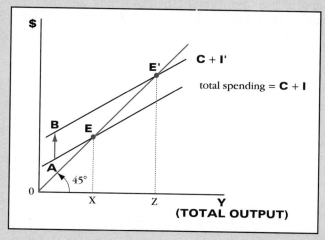

Figure 17.12. The multiplier on a diagram showing C+I. The multiplier on a diagram showing C+I is visible because the distance XZ, which is the change in output and income, is greater than the distance AB, which is the change in investment. The size of the multiplier depends on the slope of the C+I function.

To calculate the multiplier in Figure 17.12, we can utilize the standard formula: which is

$$\Delta Y = \Delta I \times \frac{1}{1 - MPC}$$

with $\dfrac{1}{1 - MPC}$ being the multiplier. By transposition,

$$\frac{1}{1 - MPC} = \frac{\Delta Y}{\Delta I}$$

Since in the diagram $\Delta Y = XZ$ and $\Delta I = AB$, the multiplier must be XZ/AB.

FIXED-PRICE (KEYNESIAN) EQUILIBRIUM AND FULL EMPLOYMENT

We can now assess where recession and unemployment fit into the Keynesian model (which, after all, are the conditions for which it was constructed).

The discussion thus far has dealt with the tendency for output and income to move toward an equilibrium, *not* whether there would be full employment at that equilibrium. Somewhere along the horizontal axis of Figure 17.13 there must be a level of output and income sufficiently large so that the economy's factors of production are fully employed.[2] Any level of output lower than that will not involve enough production to prevent unemployment and will mean that factories, machines, and so forth are running beneath their optimal capacity. Total output and income much below the full employment level on the diagram would reflect recession.[3]

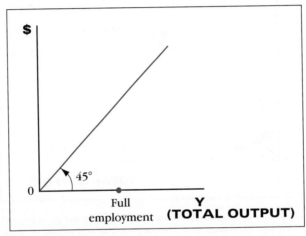

Figure 17.13. Full employment on a Keynesian diagram. Some level of total output must be just high enough to provide full employment for the economy's factors of production. To the left of that point, output is too low for full employment; unemployment of the factors will exist.

The original Keynesian fixed-price model was intended to explain recession conditions, and it paid little attention to inflation. The Keynesian model's horizontal axis was, for practical purposes, output and income in real terms. At full employment it would not be possible to obtain more real goods and services unless the economy's productive capacity were to change, not something that could ordinarily be accomplished in a short period of time. In effect, then, the outer bound to real output in the fixed-price Keynesian model is the point of full employment. In real terms, the area to the right would be unattainable given the available productive capacity, while the area to the left shows output lower than the output that would bring full employment. Any level of output much to the left of the point of full employment is associated with recession conditions.

Thus, depending on where the C+I function intersects the 45° line, the position of equilibrium could be to the left of the full employment point (as at Y_a in Figure 17.14), which is well below full employment. Or it could be just at the full employment level of output, as at Y_f. The key point is that the existence of an equilibrium (C+S = C+I) does not guarantee that the economy will be positioned *at* the level of noninflationary full employment.

---

2.   In Chapter 18 we shall see that the concept of full employment must be treated with care—in that chapter we shall not define it as zero unemployment, but instead as that level of employment that cannot be exceeded without causing prices to rise.

3.   The word recession is used here not in its technical meaning of a decline in GDP lasting six months or more, but in its meaning as "hard times" with reduced economic activity and high unemployment. It is worth pointing out that these two slightly different uses of the word recession have become part of politics. High unemployment and low production would technically not qualify as a recession if GDP were rising, even if only slightly. In such circumstances, some politicians will emphasize the first meaning, "no recession if growth is occurring" (as did President Bush in 1991–1992), while others will prefer the second meaning, "hard times," as did the Democrats in 1991–1992. At this point in the text we are using the "hard times" definition.

Keynes and his followers believed that there is no *necessary* relation between full employment and equilibrium, certainly in the short run and even over longer periods. In particular, their claim was based on the ten-year Great Depression of the 1930s, which, as Keynesians argued, confirmed that equilibrium could involve recession or depression even over periods as long as a decade or more. This position was widely held among economists of the 1950s and 1960s. More recently it has become the subject of considerable further modeling by macroeconomists, with results explored in the next chapter.

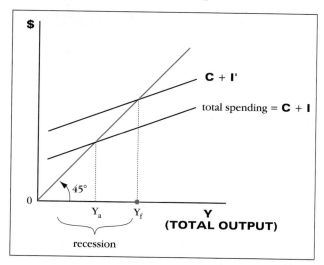

Figure 17.14. In the Keynesian model, equilibrium does not necessarily mean full employment. The equilibrium where total output (C+S) equals total spending (C+I) can occur at the full employment level of output, but it can also occur at output levels such as Y_a, which is below the full employment level.

RECESSIONARY AND INFLATIONARY GAPS

The Keynesian fixed-price model allowed analysis of situations where the equilibrium level of t' tal output and income was below the level that would give full employment without inflation. ⸝ the hands of Keynesian economists, the analysis suggested that government policy might help tu counter the effects of recessions and inflations. Later, some attempt was also made to analyze inflation within this model, although in the Keynesian analysis, recession was the central focus.

The Recessionary Gap (GDP Gap)

First, consider the case where total output is in equilibrium at a point well below the full employment level. Figure 17.15 shows an equilibrium at E_r ("r" for recession) where C+I crosses the 45° line. Total output at Y_r is low compared to that which would bring full employment; the greater amount of output needed to reach full employment is a **GDP gap**.[4]

Notice at this equilibrium that a deficiency in total spending exists that will have to be rectified in order to bring total output up to the full employment level. That is, some measurable rise in the total spending (C+I) function would bring C+I to a new intersection with the 45° line at a new equilibrium, E_f, and thus move the economy to the full employment level of output and income, Y_f. This hypothetical rise is the distance between the old C+I that resulted in equilibrium below full employment, and new C+I that would result in noninflationary full employment. It can be marked off on the diagram as a vertical distance between the recession level of C+I and C+I at full employment. Keynesian economists called this the "deflationary gap," although more recently the term **recessionary gap** has become standard.

4.   Originally and still commonly known as the GNP gap, as the theory was formulated before emphasis was placed on GDP rather than GNP.

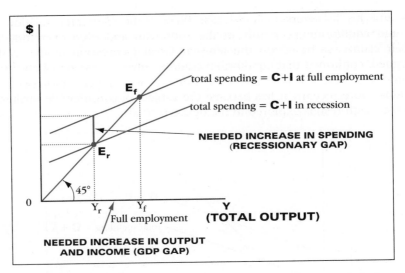

Figure 17.15. The Keynesian recessionary gap and GDP gap. The recessionary gap is the increase in total spending needed to bring total output to the full employment level. The GDP gap is the increase in total output and income needed to reach full employment.

Okun's Law and the Recessionary Gap

Empirical data on how much growth in total output and income would be needed to reduce unemployment was contributed by Arthur Okun (1929–1980). In the early 1960s he formulated **Okun's Law**, the principle that under the conditions prevailing in the United States, a one percentage-point reduction in unemployment is associated with an increase of two to three percentage points in real output and income.[5] So in order for the level of unemployment to fall by one percentage point per year (say from 6% to 5%), the annual rate of growth in real output and income must rise by two or three percentage points (say from 1% to 3–4%).

Okun's Law allowed for an extension of recessionary gap analysis. That analysis had originally applied to static situations where current spending was less than current output. Okun and other economists working in the Keynesian tradition realized that Okun's Law had implications for the recessionary gap. The full-employment point in the preceding diagrams has been at a fixed position. That point will, however, move if some augmentation of the factors of production raises productive capacity. For example, if the labor force is growing, then the full-employment level of output and income will push slowly to the right. The economy would *have* to grow in order for the additional workers to find employment. Okun's Law implied that as the labor force expands, real output and income must grow at about 2–3% a year in order to keep unemployment from rising. If economic growth were slower than this, the increasing size of the labor force would cause unemployment to increase, and a recessionary gap to open.

The Inflationary Gap

Rather obviously, given its central assumption of fixed prices, the Keynesian model's focus was not on inflation. Yet some useful insights can be made nevertheless. What if equilibrium (E_{in}) occurs at a level of total output and income higher than the point of noninflationary full employment, such as Y_{in} in Figure 17.16? We know that the point of full employment at Y_f is the level of output in real terms that cannot be exceeded because there is no productive capacity left to utilize. The only way the value of output could rise past this point is if prices increase. So if total

---

5.   The actual numbers depend on several factors such as labor force growth and the efficiency with which an economy's resources are used. For example, if employment were already high in an economy, then a rise in income would presumably take the form of longer hours worked by some. The numbers cited for Okun's Law are not constants, and specialists in the subject suggest that 2% is now more credible than the 3% emphasized by Okun and usually cited for the 1980s. It is the relationships that matter.

spending C+I should equilibrate with total output C+S to the right of the full employment point, then total output would rise, but not because a greater real quantity of goods and services was being produced. Instead it would rise because of inflationary price increases.

This being so, there must be some measurable fall in total spending C+I that would result in a new equilibrium marked E_f *at* the noninflationary full employment level of total output Y_f. This hypothetical fall, which is the vertical distance between the old function for total spending, C+I in inflation and some new function C+I at full employment, is known as the **inflationary gap**.

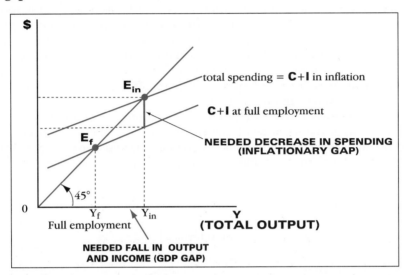

Figure 17.16. The Keynesian inflationary gap. The inflationary gaps was the decrease in total spending needed to bring total output down to the full employment level. In this case, the GDP gap is the decrease in total output and income needed to reach full employment.

The existence of recessionary and inflationary gaps were treated by the Keynesian economists as a challenge. They believed that judicious use of government policy to manage the economy could lead to the elimination of these gaps. How successful this effort was, or could be, is a major question of macroeconomics. We begin the study of this question in the next section by introducing government and foreign trade to the Keynesian analysis.

▶ INTRODUCING GOVERNMENT AND FOREIGN TRADE

To this point, the model by assumption has not taken into account the economic effects of government or foreign trade. These are extremely important sectors for the macroeconomy, much more so than a half century ago. Government economic activity has grown considerably, and governments conduct economic policy to try to counter economic fluctuations. Simultaneously, foreign trade has expanded greatly and the world's investment and financial flows have been globalized. In macroeconomics, international factors could once be almost ignored, but no longer. The remainder of the chapter introduces government and foreign trade to the analysis.

INTRODUCING GOVERNMENT

Governments have become major actors in macroeconomics, their outlays amounting to about one-fifth to one-third of the total output of a modern economy (23.7% in the United States in 1993). Even as late as 1929, the U.S. figure had been less than 3%. In Figure 17.17, we examine how government economic activity affects macroeconomic equilibrium. This figure is a diagram of the circular flow. It shows that the government takes a portion of all incomes earned by households, mostly in the form of taxation. In addition to taxes, some income goes for government fees such as tuition at public universities, permits for logging, or admission to national park campgrounds. Because taxes and fees have the same economic effect, we will lump them together under the term taxes, or T. In the circular flow, government taxes, T, are another use for income in addition to consumption or saving. Income earned is equal to the ways in which the income is disposed of, including consumption plus saving plus the government taxes. Since income is equal to output, total output can now be written C+S+T.[6]

Government also gives some of this revenue back to households, in the form of transfer payments such as Social Security, unemployment compensation, agricultural price supports, and veteran's benefits. These transfer payments back to households mean that the flow of consumption and saving does not fall as far as it would if none of the taxation was transferred back to households. In effect, the gross outflow from households in the form of taxes is larger than the net outflow of taxes, because transfer payments offset some of the taxation. The "T" in the C+S+T of the previous paragraph is net taxes.

Figure 17.17 also shows a stream of government spending on output labeled G flowing into the business sector. This government purchasing of goods and services produced by the business sector of the economy is spending additional to consumption and investment. Therefore, total spending in the economy now includes consumption, plus investment, plus government purchases, or C+I+G.

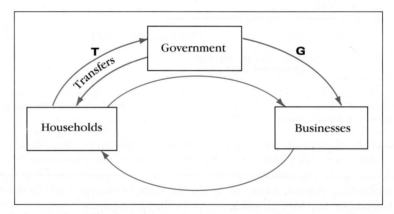

Figure 17.17. Government in the circular flow. Government taxes (T) represent a leakage out of the circular flow, that is, a portion of income that is used neither for consumption nor for saving. Some of the tax revenue is, however, returned to households in the form of transfer payments. The remainder of the tax revenue is used by government to purchase business output (G). The purchases represent an injection into the circular flow, serving to increase the amount of total spending in the economy.

The addition of government taxes and transfers and government purchases of output affects the definition of the equilibrium level of output (income), though fortunately the basic rule still holds. Equilibrium will occur, as before, where there is sufficient total spending to purchase the total output produced. Thus the equilibrium condition is C+S+T = C+I+G, as shown below.

Equilibrium with Government Included:

Total Output = Total Spending

C+S+T = C+I+G

Inventories do not change

6.   Government also taxes the business sector as well. If we wished to make the diagram more complex, we could lead another stream of taxation T from business to government to show this. Fewer profits would then be paid out by firms, diminishing the flow of income from business to households at the bottom of Figure 17.17. It does not, however, change the logic of the presentation if all taxes are treated as paid by households, and for simplicity that is done in the figure.

The effect of government spending on output can be shown readily on the standard diagram by adding one more line. If government spending on output G is added to all other spending C+I, we get a new function for total spending, C+I+G. (See Figure 17.18.) The vertical distance between this function and the old C+I is the amount of government spending at each level of income (output). Government taxes and transfer payments are diagrammed differently from government purchases. When taxes are collected and transfers are made, households will have a different amount of disposable income available for consumption C than they did before. The consumption function C will not be at the same level it would have reached in the absence of the taxes and transfers. (Unless these two are exactly the same. But in practice, taxes are always higher than transfer payments, so the net effect of government taxes and transfers is to lower the position of C.[7])

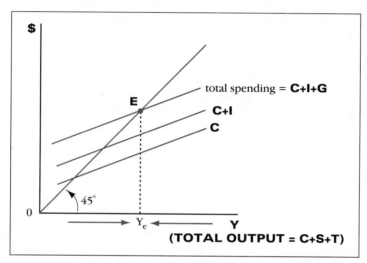

Figure 17.18. Equilibrium with government. Government spending on output is added to consumption plus investment spending in order to find the function for total spending, C+I+G. At any given level of output (income), total spending equals total output where C+I+G crosses the 45° line.

This "Keynesian cross" diagram shows that any level of total output (income) is equal to total spending only at the unique series of positions along the 45° line. To the right of the equilibrium E, total spending C+I+G is less than total output C+S+T; to the left spending exceeds output. As in the simple model without government, if total spending does not equal total output then inventories will change. Managers will take remedial steps, increasing their orders for new output if inventories decline (when spending exceeds output), or reducing their orders if inventories accumulate (when spending is less than output). In either case, they will be under pressure to change production decisions. Overall, this will change the value of total output and income toward the equilibrium position Y_e in Figure 17.18.

Government Policies to Influence Economic Performance: A Brief Introduction

A major and contentious question in macroeconomics is the degree to which government policies can be used to influence total spending and thus total output and income. If such policies are effective, then governments will have some power to dampen the business cycle of inflation and recession that affects market economies. If they are not effective, or worse yet if they are counter-productive, then governments should leave well enough alone.

With government now present in the model, we can provide a brief introduction to what government policies for influencing macroeconomic performance might involve. We should

---

7.   Taxes and transfers can also affect investment, but to keep the analysis simple we shall assume for now that the entire impact is on consumption. Later we shall relax this assumption.

understand that this is our initial introduction to a subject that is complex, controversial, and vigorously debated by economists. In later chapters, we will consider frequently what the role of government should be in dealing with economic fluctuations.

Persuasion and Exhortation By Government

One way government could try to influence total spending is by attempting to alter private-sector consumption and saving patterns through policies of persuasion and exhortation. Long experience has shown, however, that people's desires to consume and save are not very open to government manipulation. There seem to be only a few exceptions to this. One such exception is during major wars that have widespread popular support, such as World Wars I and II. In such periods, it has been possible to achieve some shift in consumption and saving by means of a widespread propaganda effort: for example, a campaign to persuade people to buy war bonds. When effective, this sort of effort will shift the consumption function downward, causing less consumption and more saving at any level of income.

Patriotic messages of this type can be employed at other times as well, though usually with considerably less success. For example, during an economic slowdown in 1970, various U.S. government officials urged the public to raise its consumption. Conversely, in the late 1970s officials responded to inflation by urging the public to save more and consume less. Both attempts were unsuccessful, largely because the public ignored them.

Monetary Policy

More hope for the government to influence total spending stems from the possibility that it can alter the interest rate on loans.[8] As we have seen, the interest rate is among the determining factors that establish how much investment will be undertaken. Low (real) interest rates tend to encourage investment and high rates to discourage it. Thus if government policy actions could reduce interest rates, firms might decide to undertake more investment. Conversely, higher interest rates might discourage new investment. Some consumption will also be sensitive to interest rate changes, especially big ticket items such as cars and appliances that are often purchased on credit. Falling interest rates will encourage their sales, while rising interest rates will discourage them. Government attempts to manipulate interest rates are a major part of what is called **monetary policy**. How monetary policy might be carried out in practice is examined in Chapters 20 and 21. For now, it will suffice to say that if monetary policy can change interest rates, then that could cause changes in investment and consumption that would shift C+I+G upward or downward, as in Figure 17.19. The shift in total spending would move the equilibrium to E' or E" and exert a multiplied effect on the nation's output and income, which would rise to Y_e' or fall to Y_e''.

---

8.   The actual mechanism for altering interest rates usually involves the government's official or central bank—the Bank of England, the Bank of France, or, in the United States, the U.S. Federal Reserve System. Central banking is examined in Chapters 19-21.

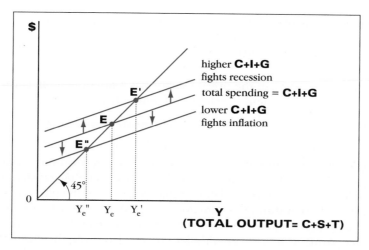

Figure 17.19. The effects of government monetary and fiscal policies. If monetary policy can alter real interest rates, then investment and some consumption might change as a result. The function of total spending C+I+G would therefore shift, with a multiplied effect on the nation's output. A fiscal policy of changing the government's spending on output, transfers, or taxes could also serve to move C+I+G; changes in government spending on output move the function directly, while changes in taxes and transfers mean more or less is available for consumption.

FISCAL POLICY

Governments might also attempt to influence the level of total output and income in an economy by changing their levels of spending on output, transfers, and taxes. Purposeful changes in government spending and taxes carried out to influence economic activity are called **fiscal policy**.

A Fiscal Policy of Changing Government Purchases of Goods and Services

If government raised or lowered its own expenditures on the nation's output, G, without altering the level of taxation, that would move the function of total spending C+I+G up or down as in Figure 17.19. That in turn would move the equilibrium to E' or E" with a multiplied change in output from Y_e' or $Y_e"$, giving the possibility of counteracting recessions or inflations. The government spending changes could affect any portion of the budget involving purchases of goods and services, including its outlays on roads, medical research, education, defense, and so on.[9] (About one-third of the federal budget consists of government purchases of goods and services. The rest is transfer payments such as Social Security, Medicare, veteran's benefits, income support for farmers, welfare, and so forth.)

The Multiplier for Changes in Government Purchases of Goods and Services

Just as with changes in investment, or C, or S, changes in government purchases of goods and services have a multiplier effect, with the government spending spent again according to the MPC of its recipients. Any given increase in government purchases of $1000, say for road building, would become $1000 of new income to others. Much of that (depending on the MPC) would be spent in a multiplier process. The multiplier formula for a change in government purchases of goods and services (G) is:

$$\Delta Y = \Delta G \times \frac{1}{1 - MPC} .$$

---

9.   Changing government spending without changing taxes would of course mean that the government's budget would move toward surplus or deficit—less spending than revenue means a surplus, more spending than revenue means a deficit. This unbalancing of the budget, an integral part of fiscal policy, will receive careful examination when we study fiscal policy in more detail.

If MPC = .80, and ΔG = $1000, then

$$\$1000 \times \frac{1}{1 - .80} = \$5000.$$

Just as new investment spending in the private sector has a multiplied effect on the economy, so increases or decreases in government purchases are multiplied as well.

A Fiscal Policy of Changes in Government Transfer Payments

Any change in government transfer payments such as Social Security, Medicare, veteran's benefits, unemployment compensation, or welfare, will also have an effect on the economy. The process works differently from a shift in government purchases. A change in transfers means a different amount of disposable income is now available to the recipients of the payments. So on a diagram such as Figure 17.19, the consumption function C will shift, upward when transfers increase, downward when they are reduced. Like new government spending on output, a change in government transfer payments sets off a multiplier process. However, the effect of a rise in transfer payments will be less than it would be for the same amount of government spending on output.

Let us trace a decision to pay $1000 more in Social Security benefits. Consumption will rise because purchasing power has been increased, but it will *not* rise by the entire $1000. Some of the $1000 will be saved. Exactly how much depends on the marginal propensity to consume, MPC. If the MPC = .80, then $1000 in new benefits will cause an $800 initial increase in C; the remaining $200 is a rise in *saving*. (In Figure 17.19, C+I+G moves up, but not as far is it did when government spending on output was increased by $1000.) Decreases in government transfer payments work the same way, but in the reverse direction. The salient point is that a change in government transfers of $X affects the economy *less strongly* than a change of $X in government spending on output. A rise in government spending of $1000 would have moved the total spending function upward by the full $1000, as in Figure 17.19. A rise in government transfers moves the total spending function upward by less than that, only $800.

The Multiplier for Changes in Government Transfers

Now trace through an increase in government transfers (GT) of $1000 to find the multiplier effect. The transfer increase means that more is available for consumption, which will thus rise. Since the MPC = .80, the $1000 in new transfers will initially increase consumption by $800. (The rest of the transfer payment will be added to saving.) The initial rise in consumption caused by the transfer increase is labeled C_{GT} in the formula that follows. This rise of $800 will have a multiplier effect; consumption will increase by $800 \times .80 = $640 in a first round, $640 \times .80 = $512 in a second round, and so forth. The end result can be calculated in the usual way:

$$\Delta Y = \Delta C_{GT} \times \frac{1}{1 - MPC}$$

which with the numbers above is

$$\$800 \times \frac{1}{1 - .80} = \$4000.$$

The basic Keynesian argument is that raising government spending and transfer payments increases a country's total output (income) and fights recession; lowering spending and transfers constricts a country's output (income) and combats inflation. (Though, as we have seen, a given change in government spending on output has a somewhat greater impact on total spending than does a change in government transfers.) Keynesians therefore believe that governments can combat booms and slumps through a fiscal policy involving government spending on output or transfer payments. Major controversies surround this analysis, however, and some of these controversies will be examined in the next chapter.

A Fiscal Policy of Tax Changes

Finally, Keynesians suggest that governments can use their power of taxation as a tool of policy. If a government raises taxes without changing its spending on output or transfers, there will be less disposable income left to households for consumption (and also less to firms for investment, though our focus here is on consumption). The higher taxes push C+I+G down, lowering the equilibrium level of total output and income by a multiple. If government instead *reduces* taxes while keeping constant its own spending on output and transfers, then there would be more disposable income left to households for consumption and more to firms for investment. In that case, C+I+G would rise, also raising the equilibrium level of total output (income) by a multiple.[10]

Tax Changes Not Fully Equivalent to Government Spending Changes in the Keynesian Model

The effect of tax changes is not entirely the same as that of changing government spending in the Keynesian model. The logic is the same as that just presented when showing the difference between government spending on output and government transfer payments. Follow through a decision to raise taxes (applying to household incomes only) so that the government collects an additional $1000. In that case, consumption at any level of income will fall because purchasing power has been reduced, but it will *not* fall by the entire $1000. It depends on the marginal propensity to consume, MPC. If the MPC = .80, then $1000 in new taxes will cause an $800 direct reduction in C; the remaining $200 is a reduction in *saving*. (See Figure 17.20, where C+I+G moves to C'+I+G.)[11] Tax decreases have the same effect, but in the reverse direction. So a tax change of $X that affects consumption is (like a government transfer payment) *less powerful* in its effect on an economy than a change of $X in government spending on output. A cut in government spending of $1000 would have moved the total spending function downward by the full $1000, from C+I+G to C+I+G', rather than by $800 when taxes were raised.

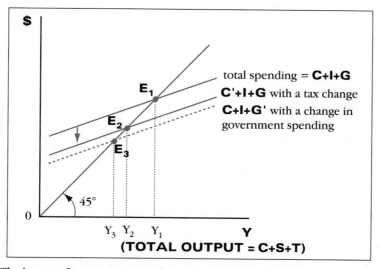

Figure 17.20. **The impact of government taxation and spending is different.** A cut in government spending on output of $1000 would lower the position of C+I+G by that amount, but a tax increase (like a transfer decrease) would not lower C+I+G by so much. With an MPC = .8, a tax increase of $1000 would cause an initial fall in C of only $800.

---

10. Notice that a tax change without an offsetting change in government spending and transfers would push the government's budget toward imbalance. The deliberate engineering of budget surpluses and deficits is part of fiscal policy, as already noted and as we will examine at a later point.

11. A tax that applied only to investment would avoid this difficulty. Taxes levied on *both* consumption and investment would require more complicated analysis.

A tax change will have a multiplied impact on output, but that impact will be less than when government spending on output changes. In Figure 17.20 you can see that the tax increase moved the equilibrium from E_1 to E_2, thereby lowering total output from Y_1 to Y_2, whereas a decrease in government spending of $1000 moved the equilibrium from E_1 to E_3, lowering total output from Y_1 to Y_3.

THE BALANCED-BUDGET MULTIPLIER

The realization that changes in government spending on output and changes in taxation were not fully equivalent in their macroeconomic impact was a late development of the Keynesian economics. Years ago it was believed that an increase in government outlays for output financed by a tax increase of the same amount would be *completely* offsetting, with a neutral macroeconomic effect on the economy. Eventually, economists concluded that this was not so. The increased spending component delivers a somewhat stronger multiplied expansionary impact than the multiplied contractionary effect of the tax increase used to pay for it. The asymmetrical effect of tax and spending changes received the name **balanced-budget multiplier**. The name comes from the fact that using tax increases to finance spending increases does not cause the government's budget to go out of balance, even though the multiplier impact of these increases is different.

The balanced-budget multiplier uses the reasoning that changes in government spending on output generate income directly, while changes in taxes affect saving as well as consumption. Assume that government spending on output rises by $1000 to pay bills connected with a new highway project. A multiplier effect will ensue as the new income is spent:

$$\Delta Y = \Delta G \times \frac{1}{1 - MPC}$$

If MPC = .80, and ΔG = $1000, then

$$\$1000 \times \frac{1}{1 - .80} = \$5000$$

An initial injection of $1000 in new government spending resulted first in $800 of new consumption, and then $640 in a second round, and so on, with the multiplied impact totaling $4000 in new consumption, making in all a total rise in the nation's output and income of $5000.

Now trace through a tax increase of $1000 to pay for the new spending. The tax increase means that less is available for consumption, which falls. With the MPC = .80, the imposition of $1000 in taxes will initially reduce consumption by $800. (The rest of the tax is paid out of saving.) The initial fall in consumption caused by the tax increase is labeled C_T in the following formula. This fall of $800 will have a multiplier effect; consumption will decline $640 in a first round, $512 in a second round, and so forth. The end result is:

$$\Delta Y = \Delta C_T \times \frac{1}{1 - MPC}$$

which with the numbers above is

$$-\$800 \times \frac{1}{1 - .80} = -\$4000.$$

The increase in government spending on output exerted a stronger influence than did the increase in taxation; total output and income ended up $1000 higher after both multipliers had worked themselves out. In this simple case, the balanced budget multiplier of new government spending is 1; that is, the new spending of $1000 eventually raised total output and income by that same amount. Obviously, the stimulus is weak compared to a situation where government spending on output rises by $1000 but no tax increase is made—in that case, total output and income would then have risen by five times as much, to $5000. But there is still a stimulus when both spending and taxes are raised by the same amount. (Readers can check their understanding by reversing the example. A spending cut and simultaneous tax reduction would not be completely neutral; total output and income would fall by the amount of the initial cut in spending if the numbers above were used.)

THE MULTIPLIER WITH GOVERNMENT TAXES

A government's tax revenues will usually rise as taxpayers' income grows. This means that the slope of the consumption function, and hence C+I+G, must be somewhat flatter than it otherwise would be; some of the increases in income that would otherwise be consumed leak into taxation. The multiplier formula has to be altered accordingly. An accurate derivation of the multiplier when tax collections rise as income increases must be done algebraically, and is rather more complicated than is appropriate for first-year economics, but the method discussed here is close and adequate for most purposes.

The task is to find the result for total output (ΔY) following a change in any of the components of total spending: investment (ΔI), consumption (ΔC), or government spending on output (ΔG). As always, new spending of, say, $100 would become new income to recipients—but the government would take some of it, say 10% or $10, as taxes. That means recipients would have only $90 in new *disposable* income to spend or save in the first round of the multiplier. Assuming recipients save 10% of new income (that is, MPS = .10), then they would save $9 and spend $81. In the second round of the multiplier, new recipients would receive $81 but would have to give up 10% of this, or $8.10, as taxes. Of the remaining $72.90 of disposable income, they would save 10% or $7.29, and spend $65.61. The

multiplier formula allowing the calculation of the final outcome takes into consideration that the rounds of spending in the multiplier process are reduced by the presence of both saving and taxation. The saving and the taxes are both leakages that cannot be multiplied further. In the simplest model, the multiplier was

$$\frac{1}{MPS}.$$

When taxes rise with increasing income we must also include the marginal propensity to pay taxes from a dollar of additional income (MPT).[12] Thus the multiplier is

$$\frac{1}{MPS + MPT}.$$

The entire multiplier formula in the presence of taxes that rise with income then becomes: the overall change in disposable income equals an initial change in total spending times the multiplier. In symbols,

$$\Delta Y = (\Delta I + \Delta C + \Delta G) \times \frac{1}{MPS + MPT}$$

So if MPS = .10 and MPT = .10, new investment of $100 would result in a final change in total output of $500. As we stated above, this formula is only an approximation, though it is adequate for most purposes.[13]

---

12. Admittedly, the term marginal propensity to pay taxes may make it appear that tax payments are as voluntary as marginal decisions to consume or save. Even though taxes ultimately do reflect the preference of voters, perhaps we ought to think of MPT as the "marginal prerequisite to pay taxes."

13. With the figures given, the difference between the approximation and the actual result with the more complex formula found in upper-level texts is slight. The more complex multiplier is: 1/[MPS + MPT + (MPC x MPT)]. With MPS = .10, MPT = .10, and MPC = .80, the result with the more complex formula is new total output of $481, very close to the $500 obtained with the approximation.

INCLUDING FOREIGN TRADE

The major economies are becoming globalized, with international trade and international financial flows of all kinds increasingly important. Worldwide, the proportion of exports in total output is now about 20%. The figure can reach 50% or more in countries such as the Netherlands and Belgium, though it is only about 11% in the United States and Japan. The figure has at least doubled in many countries during the last 30 years. Economic fluctuations in a large economy now typically affect other countries around the world, and macro policy decisions nowadays are taken in the full knowledge that they may have serious repercussions on foreign countries.

To see the Keynesian fixed-price model in its fullest form, we now consider the "open economy," as macroeconomists say, which includes foreign trade. With the experience already obtained with the model, this last step is not particularly complicated.

Consider a country that exports (X) everything that it produces ($1000 worth of sales abroad) and imports (M) everything that is bought by domestic households ($1000 worth). Assume that there is no consumption of domestically produced goods, no investment, no saving, and no government sector. In that case, $1000 of exported output will generate $1000 in income to the factors of production, and all of that income is used to buy imports. Output (= income) can be written as M. All spending flowing to businesses is on exports (also = $1000) and comes from foreigners. Total spending can thus be written as X. Total output = total spending; M = X. The economy is in equilibrium.

What if foreigners increase their spending on exports, but no change in output of these exports occurs? The result is a familiar one: more is being sold than is being produced, inventories decline, new orders for production are placed, and the economy expands toward a higher equilibrium. Conversely, what if the country's total output rises but foreigners do not increase their spending on it? Then less is being sold than is being produced. Inventories swell and firms reduce their orders for output. The economy contracts toward a lower equilibrium.

Now let us include all the usual domestic flows, C, I, S, G, and T in addition to exports and imports. The last two paragraphs have shown how to allow for the macroeconomic impact of foreign trade. Exports are an addition to the spending of an economy by foreigners who purchase the goods that are exported. Total spending includes X and can thus be written as C+I+G+X. Similarly, all output produced in a country, and hence all income earned, must now include imports because importing is another way in which income can be used, along with consumption, saving, and tax payments. Thus the economy's total output (income) is equal in value to C+S+T+M.[14] Equilibrium is, as before, where total output equals total spending.

Equilibrium With Government and Foreign Trade Included:

Total Output = Total Spending

C+S+T+M = C+I+G+X

Inventories do not change

That equilibrium E, giving a level of total output and income Y_e, is shown diagrammatically in Figure 17.21. The inclusion of foreign trade requires only the addition of export spending atop C+I+G, and a realization that imports are now a permissible way to utilize income earned from the production of output. (In the presence of foreign trade, domestic C and I will be somewhat lower than they would otherwise be because some income is used to buy imports rather than to buy domestically produced consumer and investment goods.)

---

14.   Remember from Chapter 15 a real-world statistical complication. In the measured national accounts, convenience dictates that imports are included with consumption. Here we use a purer form of analysis, with C defined as domestic consumption only, that allows a clearer focus on the principles involved.

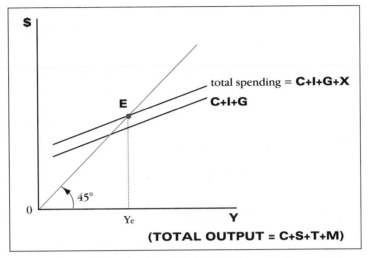

Figure 17.21. Equilibrium with government and foreign trade. Exports (X) are another form of spending, and they must be added to obtain the full function for total spending, C+I+G+X. Imports (M) are another use for income, so income (= output) can be written C+S+T+M. As in the simpler models, equilibrium is where total output equals total spending. All that is produced is sold, and inventories do not change.

THE MULTIPLIER WITH FOREIGN TRADE

Changes in the value of exports and imports have the usual multiplier effects. Exports are an injection into the system (just as ΔI or ΔG), while imports are a leakage that cuts into the multiplied rises in C. This being so, and assuming that taxes do not increase with income, the denominator in the multiplier becomes MPS+MPM. MPM is the marginal propensity to import, the amount of any additional dollar of income that is used to buy imports. The entire multiplier formula can now be written

$$\Delta Y = (\Delta I + \Delta C + \Delta G + \Delta X) \times \frac{1}{MPS + MPM}$$

Any addition to spending is multiplied, but the eventual amount of multiplication is limited by the leakage of some of each dollar received into saving or imports.[15] (How to treat the further leakage of tax payments that rise with income was discussed in the previous box.) It is these considerable leakages, taken all together, that limit the multiplier to a rather low figure, usually estimated to be about 1.5 in the United States, rather than the high 4 or 5 often used in textbooks (including this book). In countries such as France or Germany, with a larger tax burden and a greater propensity to save and import than in the United States, the multiplier is somewhat lower yet.

---

15.   More compactly, let ΔE be any change in spending, and let $\Delta E/\Delta Y$ be the marginal propensity to spend in any form. Then $1 - \frac{\Delta E}{\Delta Y}$ represents the marginal propensity *not* to spend, including savings and imports. If we let $m = 1 - \frac{\Delta E}{\Delta Y}$, then the multiplier formula may be written $\Delta Y = \Delta E \times \frac{1}{m}$. If government taxes rise with income, the problem is more complex, but the formula in this note still gives a reasonable approximation of the final multiplied impact on output and income.

Since from the macroeconomic point of view, exports and imports behave much like investment and saving, Keynesian economists see opportunities for including foreign trade in a strategy of economic management. Though we postpone a full-scale discussion until a later chapter, Keynesians might advocate policies to raise exports and lower imports in order to stimulate the economy, whereas the reverse would deliver a contractional impulse. Several policies are available to influence the level of exports and imports independently of other actions. These include subsidies, tariffs, quotas, "voluntary restraints," and the like, all of which will eventually receive due consideration. At this early point, we might note that lowering imports through barriers to trade, though that would indeed tend to raise domestic employment, would do so at the expense of lower employment abroad, while exports would decline if only because foreigners retaliate with their own barriers.

▶ THE EVOLUTION OF MACRO POLICY

The Keynesian model of economic management through monetary and fiscal policy (with the emphasis definitely on the latter because the Keynesians believed that monetary policy was the weaker of the two tools) made steady progress in the 1940s, 1950s, and 1960s. The Keynesian position that without government intervention, recessions might not correct themselves in any short period of time proved immensely influential. Eventually, large numbers of public officials and informed voters came to believe that the design of macroeconomic policies to counter instability was centrally important for governments. In the 1970s, however, a major reaction set in against the Keynesian position. Though the debate is by no means fully settled, it is clear that the Keynesian model is most insightful in analyzing deep slumps in the economy, and in understanding how governments can cause inflation with their tax and spending policies. Most economists would now agree, however, that the Keynesian model is less penetrating in its analysis of economies near full employment, and many believe that in such circumstances, Keynesian policies can be counterproductive.

These points must receive further consideration. Our next task is to examine an alternative macroeconomic model that arose in response to the growing belief that the Keynesian analysis was not appropriate for promoting growth and stability, especially in an economy at or near full employment.

SUMMARY

1) Investment when added atop consumption gives a function for total spending (C+I). The point where C+I crosses the 45° line is the equilibrium where total output (C+S) equals total spending (C+I). Any level of output and income different from the equilibrium will trigger a change in inventories, and thus a movement toward the equilibrium level of output. Changes in consumption, saving, or investment will change the position of the equilibrium.

2) An increase in spending (for example, a rise in consumption or investment) has a multiplied impact on total output and income. This multiplier effect stems from the fact that new spending becomes new income to the recipients of the spending, who then raise their consumption according to the marginal propensity to consume. That additional consumption becomes new income to yet more recipients, continuing the multiplier process. The formula for the total expansion caused by an increase in investment is $\Delta Y = \Delta I \times 1/1 - MPC$.

3) In the Keynesian fixed-price model, equilibrium need not be at the full employment level of output. If the equilibrium is below full employment, there is a recessionary gap—an amount by which total spending would have to be raised in order to reach the full employment level of output. If the equilibrium is above full employment, there is an inflationary gap—an amount by which total spending would have to be reduced in order to reach the full employment level of output.

4) Government economic activity affects the economy. Government spending on output is a direct addition to the flow of spending and has a multiplier effect. Government transfer payments (such as Social Security benefits) and taxation also have an effect because they alter disposable income and therefore change the level of consumption. They, too, have a multiplied impact, though the end result is slightly less than that for government spending on output—a principle illustrated by the balanced-budget multiplier.

5) Exports and imports also affect the economy. Exports are like investment and government spending, a flow of additional spending on an economy's output. Imports are like saving and taxes, a portion of a country's income not spent on domestic consumption. Changes in exports and imports also have a multiplier effect.

Chapter Key Words

Balanced-budget multiplier: The concept that a rise (or fall) in government spending balanced by a fall (or rise) in government taxes will have a small net expansionary (contractionary) effect on an economy because government spending is slightly more powerful in its effect than is taxation.

Fiscal policy: Government action to stimulate or restrict the economy by changing government spending on output, government transfer payments, and/or taxes.

GDP gap: See *recessionary gap*.

Inflationary gap: The situation where an economy is at equilibrium somewhere above full employment, and hence suffers from inflation. The gap measures the distance by which actual total spending would have to fall to give a noninflationary full employment equilibrium.

Monetary policy: Government action to change the money supply, which affects the level of total spending and so alters total spending and total output.

Multiplier effect: The phenomenon whereby a one-dollar change in total spending has an effect on total output greater than one dollar. Important in that some given change in total spending will have extra leverage in its resulting effect on economic performance.

Okun's Law: The principle contributed by Arthur Okun that under the conditions prevailing in the United States, a one percentage-point reduction in unemployment is associated with an increase of two to three percentage points in real output and income. It follows that if the labor force increases by one percentage point, then real output and income must grow by two or three percentage points in order to avoid an increase in unemployment.

Paradox of thrift: The paradox that an attempt to save more by the general public during a recession would have a damaging effect on economic performance, so that saving does not rise after all.

Recessionary gap (GDP gap): The situation where an economy is at equilibrium below full employment. The gap measures the distance by which actual total spending would have to rise to give a full employment equilibrium. The related GDP gap is the rise in output necessary to reach the full employment level of output.

CHAPTER QUESTIONS

1) Draw a basic "Keynesian Cross" diagram with a 45° line and a line for total spending (C+I). Find a high level of output to the right of where the two lines cross. Could the economy stay at this high level of output for long? Explain what would happen over time.

2) In the 1980s, consumers decided to save less of their income and to consume more of it. Perhaps this change was a shift in cultural attitudes toward saving. How would the decreased desire to save affect the equilibrium level of output? Show the process on a Keynesian cross diagram.

3) In the State of the Union Address, the President says, "My fellow Americans, our economy is doing poorly. We as a country consume 75 cents of each new dollar that we earn, but we simply must spend more in order to raise output. I have spoken with the heads of major corporations, and they have agreed to add to investment. The new investment will increase output by 200 billion dollars." That night, a junior reporter at your newspaper writes a scathing attack on the President. He notes that the corporate leaders only promised $50 billion of new investment. Do you publish this piece?

4) Japan and the United States are both in recession. Their governments rewrite regulations pertaining to investment, and as a result investment in the two countries increases by the same amount. Draw savings and investment diagrams for both countries, showing the change in investment. Remember that the MPS is much higher in Japan. Which country has the greater multiplier?

5) Sometimes the macroeconomic equilibrium lies below full employment output. On a Keynesian cross diagram, show such a situation. Identify the GDP gap and the recessionary gap. One of these gaps is always smaller than the other. Which one and why?

6) In the simplest form of the equilibrium condition, total output = total spending is written C+S = C+I. It follows that in equilibrium, S = I. If we add government and taxes, total output = total spending becomes C+S+T = C+I+G. Now suppose that S<I, but the economy is in equilibrium nonetheless. How can investment be higher than saving? Is the government doing some saving of its own?

7) When Ronald Reagan became president, he stimulated the economy by raising government spending and cutting taxes at the same time. Suppose for the sake of simplicity that the tax cut and the increase in spending were both equal to $40 billion. Also assume that the MPC was .5. How much did output increase because of the higher government spending? How much did it increase because of the tax cut?

8) Refer back to question 7. Suppose everything was the same except that Reagan raised taxes by $40 billion instead of cutting them. This course of action would not have increased the deficit. Would it have increased output? If so, by how much?

9) If foreign trade becomes a major component of output and spending, then government cannot use fiscal policy as effectively as before. Imagine that the governments of the United States and the Netherlands each increase spending by $1,000. In both countries the MPC is .75. However, the Netherlands is tightly linked to its neighbors, so its MPM is .5. The much larger United States has an MPM of only .083. How much does the change in government spending increase output in both countries?

A Contemporary Model of Aggregate Demand and Aggregate Supply

OVERALL OBJECTIVE: To present a contemporary model of aggregate demand and aggregate supply that not only determines output but also allows for changes in the price level.

MORE SPECIFICALLY:

■ To show that aggregate demand and aggregate supply curves, though they appear to resemble the demand and supply curves of microeconomics, have to be explained in very different ways.

■ To explain the slope of aggregate demand and aggregate supply, and consider why movements in these curves may occur.

■ To discuss how the passage of time may make a significant difference for the shape of the aggregate supply curve.

■ To assess the position of the long-run aggregate supply curve, and explain its relationship to the potential level of output beyond which prices will rise.

■ To show that the natural rate of unemployment, below which price rises will break out, is associated with the potential level of output.

■ To explain that in the long run, actual output moves toward the potential level, and actual unemployment toward the associated natural rate.

■ To query why economic fluctuations in market economies occur with such frequency, and to suggest that business cycles of expansion and contraction are caused by a combination of real factors and confidence factors.

The macroeconomic forces that determine an economy's total output and its overall price level are the same forces that determine whether and when that economy will suffer from unemployment and inflation. Understanding these forces is obviously central to designing policies for fighting back. This chapter develops a contemporary model of the macroeconomy that allows us to consider a wider range of economic conditions than does the Keynesian fixed-price model of the past two chapters.

The fixed-price model was spawned in the Great Depression of the 1930s and is still useful in analyzing economies beset with substantial unemployment and excess capacity. Beginning in the 1960s and 1970s, however, a different set of economic problems emerged, and one of the problems was rather widespread inflation that seemed harder to understand and control than in the past. This period saw the development of a new set of models that could be used to analyze macroeconomic behavior from the point of view of relatively full employment. The new modeling uses the concepts of aggregate demand (AD) and aggregate supply (AS) already mentioned in Chapter 16. Curves of aggregate demand and supply bear a resemblance to the demand and supply curves of microeconomics, but it must be emphasized that the explanations underlying the macro curves are quite different.

► THE BASIC AGGREGATE DEMAND/AGGREGATE SUPPLY MODEL

The AD/AS model allows for an explicit discussion of price changes, which is not as easy in the Keynesian framework discussed in the past two chapters. The AD/AS model can also accommodate different employment and inflation conditions, ranging from deep recession to high inflation, on the same diagram. These are considerable advantages.

On Figure 18.1, the horizontal axis shows the economy's total quantity of commodities. Here we can measure both total real spending and total real output (equal to income). The vertical axis shows the average price level expressed as an index number. (See Chapter 15 for a discussion of price indices.) The curve that shows the relationship between total spending in the economy and the price level is called the **aggregate demand curve**, or **AD**. It slopes downward, showing more total spending at lower price levels. But as we explore subsequently, the reasons for the slope differ from the explanation that applies to the demand curve for a single product. The question is examined in the next section.

The curve that relates the economy's total output and the price level is called the **aggregate supply curve**, or **AS**. The time period described in Figure 18.1 is short run, so we have labeled the curve *SRAS*. As you can see, the SRAS curve slopes upward, but the reasons for this upward slope are not the same as for a single product's supply curve. These reasons are discussed later in the chapter.

The point where the two curves cross is the equilibrium, E, associated with the price level P_e and the quantity of output Y_e. Economic forces work to move the price level and quantity of output toward this equilibrium. The reasoning involves inventory changes, just as it does in the fixed-price model. At any prevailing price level above E, say at P', total output at B would be greater than total spending at A. An excess supply (surplus) of goods would be accumulating in inventory. Firms would respond by reducing their orders and cutting their prices, until equilibrium is reached at E. At any price level *below* P_e, say at P'', total output at W would be less than total spending at X. An excess demand (shortage) would develop, and inventories would decline. Firms would respond by increasing their orders and raising their prices, until equilibrium is reached at E.

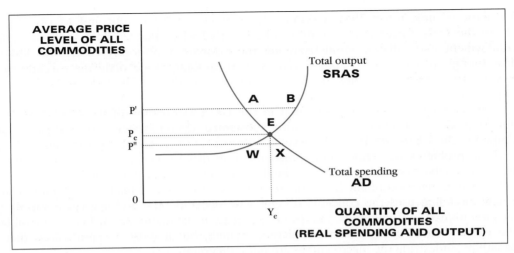

Figure 18.1. Aggregate demand and aggregate supply. Where AD and SRAS cross, total spending equals total output and inventories will not change. Where AD ≠ SRAS, inventories will either increase or decrease, causing changes in the quantity produced.

As we have noted, however, the slopes of the curves shown in Figure 18.1 require careful explanation. Though the diagram certainly resembles one showing demand and supply for a single good, the logic behind the downward slope of aggregate demand and the upward slope of aggregate supply is different. We look at each in turn.

THE SLOPE OF THE AGGREGATE DEMAND CURVE

An aggregate demand curve shows the relationship between total spending in the economy and the price level. It slopes downward. A major reason why the demand curve for *just one good* slopes downward is because as price rises, many people buy cheaper substitutes. But the slope of aggregate demand cannot be explained with this logic. When the vertical axis shows the average price of *all* goods, not just one, then consumers cannot substitute cheaper goods for the more expensive the way they could if the price of just one good rose.

Why does the aggregate demand curve slope downward? The key explanation involves interest rates. When the average price level rises, firms and households will need a larger amount of money to pay their bills. Many will borrow to meet this need. If the overall quantity of money available in the economy remains the same while the demand for money increases, then interest rates (the price of borrowing money) will rise. When interest rates are higher, people are less likely to purchase items that require credit. This includes auto sales, the housing market, installment buying of consumer durables, state and local government spending involving borrowed funds, bank-financed small business activity, and investment projects of all kinds that depend on credit. Thus the higher interest rates caused by a higher average price level can lead to a lower quantity of aggregate demand, with a movement up the AD curve.

The higher interest rates affect aggregate demand even in situations where a firm or individual does not have to borrow. This is because the opportunity cost of spending rises as interest rates increase. If you can earn a relatively high rate of interest by leaving your money in the bank or by putting it in bonds, you may be less likely to purchase goods and services with it.

Independently, two other possible reasons can explain the downward slope of AD. The first is that prices may have risen more in one country, say the United States, than in others. Spending on U.S. exports will decline. At the same time, domestic consumption of U.S. goods may be replaced in part by less expensive imports.[1] Either way, the country will move up along its AD curve, with a lower quantity of aggregate demand as prices rise. The final reason for the downward slope of AD is that at higher average price levels, existing stocks of wealth (bonds,

1.   This effect will be present when, as frequently happens, exchange rates among currencies do not move sufficiently to offset the price changes. The topic is discussed in more detail in Chapter 28.

dollars in a savings account) will appear less valuable. Consumers might then reduce their spending and increase their saving to restore their former level of real balances.[2]

The logic explaining the slope of AD applies equally well to the case of *lower* prices. The fall in prices means less money is necessary to finance transactions, and the demand for borrowed funds falls. The resulting lower interest rates stimulate investment and any consumption dependent on credit. Furthermore, exports may rise and imports may decline (raising domestic consumption); both increase the quantity of aggregate demand, with a move down the AD curve. Finally, the effect on people's real balances suggests that at lower prices, wealth appears greater. Consumers, thinking themselves better off, spend more. All these examples are consistent with an AD curve that slopes downward and to the right.

MOVEMENTS IN THE AGGREGATE DEMAND CURVE

The position of the aggregate demand curve will alter as any underlying component of AD changes. Remember that aggregate demand consists of all the spending in the economy, for consumption, for investment, government spending, or spending on imports. Any increase in these will shift the AD curve rightward as shown in Figure 18.2; at any given price level such as P_1 there would be more spending, at Y' instead of Y. Conversely, a reduction in any component of total spending will shift the AD curve to the left.

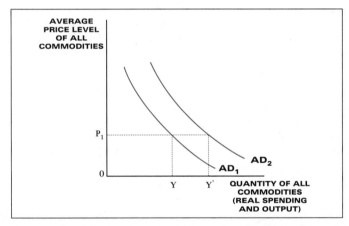

Figure 18.2. The AD curve can shift. Any change in total spending shifts the position of the AD curve. For example, if investment increases because of a fall in interest rates, then at price level P_1 there might be Y' in aggregate demand instead of Y.

In this and following chapters we will encounter many examples of shifting aggregate demand. For example, a consumption increase because of greater consumer confidence would move AD to the right. A cut in interest rates may stimulate investment and also move AD to the right. Increased government spending, as in the Vietnam War from 1966, or a tax cut, such as John Kennedy's 1963 proposal, passed in 1964, and Ronald Reagan's in 1981, would raise the level of total spending, again moving AD to the right. Reverse all these examples to see why AD would move to the left.

THE SLOPE OF THE AGGREGATE SUPPLY CURVE

As you can see in Figure 18.3, the short-run aggregate supply curve (SRAS) exhibits different slopes along its length. These different slopes occur because the underlying economic conditions change.[3]

---

2.   In Chapter 16 we called this the real-balances effect. This reason is the weakest of the three because the burden of debt works in the opposite direction, as that chapter pointed out.

3.   The slope of the aggregate supply curve is a question surrounded by great theoretical and empirical debates. Here we take a position that draws from both the Keynesian (recession) and the more modern "full employment" traditions, and occupies what many economists consider to be reasonable middle ground.

In a period of recession, for example, unemployed resources and unutilized capacity are likely to be abundant. Firms could therefore expand output over a wide range without much upward pressure on prices, or perhaps without any such pressure. This situation is portrayed on Figure 18.2 by the flat portion of SRAS, from 0 to Y_1. Here firms have plenty of productive capacity readily available, and no price change is necessary to draw forth increases in output. (This situation is consistent with the Keynesian fixed-price model of the previous two chapters.)

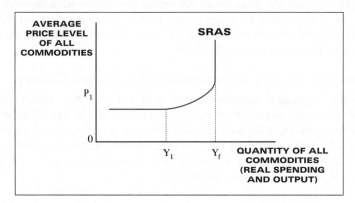

Figure 18.3. **The slope of the aggregate supply curve.** SRAS starts as a flat line, then rises, then goes vertical. The flat segment indicates the existence of large quantities of unutilized resources and unemployment, while the vertical segment indicates that no spare production capacity exists in the economy.

When output moves into the area to the right of Y_1, toward Y_f, more goods and services can still be produced, but obtaining them involves higher prices. Prices rise because, compared to the recession case to the left of Y_1, the degree of excess capacity or "slack" in the economy is now reduced. Because of the limited remaining capacity to produce, an output increase in this area causes supply bottlenecks to develop in the industries that have the least remaining capacity to increase output. In these industries, specific shortages lead to price rises there before they break out elsewhere. For example, as the economy grows toward full employment at Y_f, a shortage of some raw material or some necessary skill may occur in industry A. In that case, prices may increase first in industry A, and only later in industries B, C, and D as further output increases lead to supply bottlenecks in these industries as well. Yet the price rises do not break out all at once; output can still rise for a considerable time toward Y_f without any very large increase in prices.

The aggregate supply curve will have a third segment that is vertical. In Figure 18.3, this occurs at output level Y_f, a high level of economic activity with full employment (hence the "f" in Y_f). Here there is no remaining excess capacity, and it is not feasible to obtain more output regardless of the prices that are offered.[4]

THE IMPORTANCE OF PRICE RIGIDITY
AND WAGE STICKINESS FOR THE SHAPE OF SRAS

The shape of the aggregate supply curve is pivotally related to the speed with which prices and wages change in the markets for goods, services, and labor. To the degree that they exist, price rigidities in the markets for goods and services and wage stickiness in labor markets are of great

---

4.   We neglect abnormal possibilities such as forced labor working 18-hour days or ruinous overstressing of machinery; and a little more output, no matter how small, can usually be squeezed out of even the most tightly wound economy. Even so, in the short run with a fixed resource stock there must *effectively* be an upper limit to output.

consequence. Indeed, the slowness of prices and wages to move when market conditions change helps explain both the flat portion and the upward-rising portion of the SRAS curve.

Rigid Pricing By Imperfect Competitors

The flat part of SRAS, and to some degree the upward-rising portion, both indicate that in some economic circumstances consumers can demand and get more output from producers without setting off a price rise. Part of the explanation is that oligopolistic firms are very important in modern economies. As discussed in Chapter 8, such firms may generally avoid price changes when they can. Fear of being left out on a limb by a price increase that others do not follow may cause an individual firm to avoid being the first to move.

Furthermore, small changes in prices bring both money costs and annoyance. There are menu costs of printing new catalogs (and, of course, menus); of changing price tags; of altering signs; of informing potential buyers. If price-making firms do decide to change prices, these firms have to spend time and effort estimating the new profit-maximizing price, which runs up the costs. Customers are easily alienated by price increases and may defect to firms that are more willing to choose a price and stick to it. At the least, the firm that increases its prices stands to lose some good will.

Sellers are well aware of all this. If they have the choice of increasing output rather than increasing prices, as is the case to the left of Y_1 in Figure 18.3 and partly true between Y_1 and Y_f, then they may opt for price stability. As their output grows from left to right, they may hold the line on prices, produce more, and hire more labor to make it possible. Even when prices do change, they change slowly.[5]

Wage Stickiness in Labor Markets

In assessing any tendency toward rigid pricing by imperfect competitors, it is important to examine what is going on in labor markets. Consider that in order to raise production, firms will hire more labor. If that causes large wage increases, it might then be impossible for firms to hold the line on the prices of what they produce. If, on the contrary, wages are sticky, slow to rise as more labor is hired, that reduces the pressure on firms to mark up their prices as output rises. Price rigidities on output are more logical if wages are slow to change.

Wage stickiness, with wages slow to adjust as labor market conditions change, has an additional effect when wages move upward more slowly than the prices of goods. Along SRAS between Y_1 and Y_f in Figure 18.3, notice that goods prices do rise in some degree as output increases. But ask this question: Why would suppliers be willing to produce a larger quantity as prices rise *if all their costs rise at the same time by the same amount?* Wouldn't an increase in the economy's average price level mean that the prices of the factors of production were pushed up as well? Indeed it would. With their costs now higher, presumably firms would *not* have an incentive to boost production. But if some business costs rise more slowly than the general price level, firms could profit from the increased production. That is where wage stickiness in labor markets fits in: When firms' wage bills rise more slowly than the prices for their output, there is a motive to increase output. That being the case, the aggregate supply curve slopes upward.

Why would wages be sticky in an upward direction? Workers may have agreed to long-term labor contracts that cannot be adjusted for one to three years or more. (Other input costs such as those for raw materials may also be fixed in price by contract for relatively long periods, which has the same effect as wage stickiness.) In addition, firms may already have included a premium in wages so that workers have better morale, do not need as much supervision, and are less inclined to "jump ship" to another firm. A firm is said to be paying an **efficiency wage** if it pays

---

5.   A research project being carried out by Alan Blinder of Princeton University is compiling evidence confirming that the prices charged by oligopolistic firms tend toward rigidity. After a change in demand or in costs, most firms wait three or four months before a price change occurs. More than half of the firms surveyed by Blinder change their prices no more than once per year. In many cases a firm is unable to judge right away whether a change in demand or costs is unique to it or is economy-wide. It will take time to acquire the information and make a decision, adding to the rigidity of prices in imperfect markets.

more than the market price for labor in order to gain these advantages. In addition, senior workers with skills specific to a firm may consider it risky to leave in search of higher wages and so may be less forward in pushing for wage gains. In that case, firms can ask workers to extend their working hours without incurring higher costs per hour. Since there is slack in the economy to the left of Y_f, it is also probable that new workers can be hired who would otherwise be unemployed. They can be paid the same wages as the present workers.

Wages may also rise more slowly than prices because of **money illusion**. This term is used when workers take some time to recognize that their wages are falling behind increasing prices, and so do not press for wage gains large enough to stay even. Money illusion is more likely to occur after an extended period of price stability when workers have no immediate experience with inflation.

To summarize: As prices rise, firms will be willing to produce more. They will do so because important elements in their costs, including wages, salaries, and some other input costs, may not increase as fast as the prices of the goods and services that the firms sell.

THE IMPORTANCE OF THE SHAPE OF THE AGGREGATE SUPPLY CURVE

The shape of the aggregate supply curve displayed in Figure 18.3 suggests that additional output can be obtained with no increase in production costs from 0 to Y_1, a range over which recession conditions exist. More output can be obtained though only at higher cost between Y_1 and Y_f, which is an area of some but lessening slack in the economy. At Y_f, full capacity has been reached; no further increase in real output is possible given the fixed stock of resources. Attempts to raise production will affect only the price level.

The economic effect of any shift in aggregate demand brought about by new investment, or a government policy of expansionary spending increases or tax cuts, or any other reason, will be very different depending on the shape of the aggregate supply curve. For example, in Figure 18.4 we see a rightward movement from AD_1 to AD_2. (Perhaps firms have decided to raise their level of investment.) The outcome is a new equilibrium, with a rise in output from Y_1 to Y_2, but that rise does not affect prices which stay unchanged at P. A similar movement in aggregate demand along the middle segment of SRAS, say from AD_3 to AD_4, increases both output (from Y_3 to Y_4) and prices (from P_3 to P_4). Finally, a movement from AD_5 to AD_6 yields no additions to real output (which remains at Y_5) but only a price rise (from P_5 to P_6). What the impact of a rise in AD will be depends on the shape of SRAS.

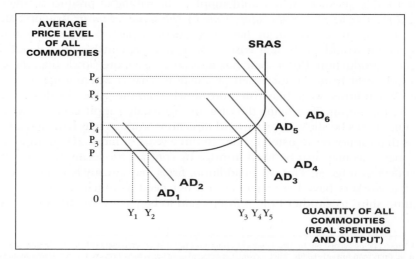

Figure 18.4. The effect of changes in AD depends on the slope of SRAS. An increase in aggregate demand results in higher output but not prices when SRAS is flat, raises both output and prices when SRAS is upward-sloping, and raises prices but not output when SRAS is vertical.

PRICE AND WAGE RIGIDITIES

The discussion to this point has been pitched toward increases in AD and growing output. What happens when AD *falls* and output *declines*? Firms may be even more reluctant to cut prices than they are to raise them. Managers will see cuts as an admission of defeat. Start cutting prices, they will reason, and other firms will match us so we won't sell much more. Also, a price cut may lead customers to believe that further decreases by the firm or by the competition will follow, so they don't buy much more. Managers know that lower prices but little or no increase in output mean reduced profits that threaten their salaries. Considering all the risks, no one wants to be the first to make the cut.

It is noteworthy that in modern recessions, the average price level hardly ever falls. It may increase more slowly; it may even stay the same for a time, but general price reductions seem noticeably absent. Even in the depths of the Great Depression of the 1930s, it took two years for serious price cutting to make an appearance. So the price rigidities we saw with an increase in AD may be even more pronounced when AD falls.

Managers' unwillingness to cut prices is reinforced by their knowledge of how difficult it is to cut wages. If wages cannot easily be cut as output declines, then it will not be practical for firms to reduce prices either. Rather, workers will have to be laid off as output declines. We have already discussed the strong forces that make wages more sticky downward than upward. Firms know that wage cuts will be very unpopular among workers and the public at large, and strikes may break out. Firms may be unwilling to make wage cuts because doing so would lower morale, risk the loss of essential workers with skills specific to the firm, and increase the need for supervision. Furthermore, long-term labor contracts, often one to three years or more in duration, are an impediment to wage cuts. Finally, minimum-wage laws and notions of comparability of pay, fairness, and social responsibility may inhibit any fall in wages. Even when wage cuts occur, they may be slow and tentative.[6]

The reluctance to accept wage cuts, and the resulting difficulty facing firms that might otherwise lower their prices, may lead to a so-called ratchet effect. The **ratchet effect** implies that there is a wage/price floor below which it is difficult to go. This floor rises (ratcheting upward) whenever the economy expands.

Consider an economy that is first expanding, with AD increasing along its SRAS curve. In Figure 18.5, average prices rise from P_1 to P_2 after a movement from AD_1 to AD_2 shifts the equilibrium from E_1 to E_2. The presence of a ratchet would mean that the price level would *remain* higher if aggregate demand were to decline again, say to AD_3. Prices and wages will not go back down as easily as they rose. The ratchet appears as a shift in the horizontal portion of the aggregate supply curve up to a new position, shown by the dotted line leading leftward from E_2 to P_2 in the figure. The fall in demand to AD_3 leads to an equilibrium at E_3, bringing a decline in output to Y_3, further than would have occurred if prices had not been rigid. In that case, the equilibrium would have been at $E_3{}^*$, and the fall in output would have been to $Y_3{}^*$. When a ratchet is present, the current price level, whatever it is, becomes a floor marked by the horizontal portion of the SRAS curve. Ratchet effects involving firms' reluctance to cut prices are usually stronger when recessions are not very deep or when experience with them has faded. Many months into a recession, any ratchet is likely to be substantially weaker as firms finally decide they cannot resist price cuts and workers decide they must tolerate wage decreases rather than accept more layoffs.

---

6.   It was not always so. Economists debate when wages became more sticky in a downward direction, some arguing that it was just before the beginning of the twentieth century and others that it occurred later, in the years just before the start of the Great Depression. An important development was the move to hiring labor on contract rather than on a day-to-day basis. When hiring was day-to-day, at hiring halls, street corners, or at a firm's front gate, cutting wages was much easier. Another development was the increased willingness of workers to go out on strike to protest a grievance. Until quite late in the nineteenth century, strikes were relatively rare.

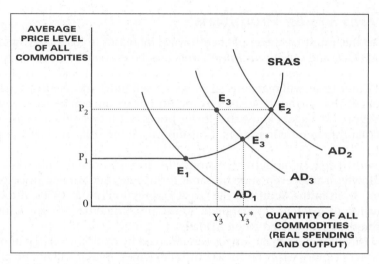

Figure 18.5. The ratchet effect. Strong forces working to prevent declines in prices and wages may cause a ratchet effect to emerge. In the diagram, if AD rises to AD_2 causing prices to rise to P_2, then prices may not fall below this level even though AD sinks back to AD_3.

Notice that the rigidities that cause a ratchet effect make the most difference when the aggregate supply curve is steep. In Figure 18.6, if aggregate demand falls from AD_1 to AD_2 but prices do not fall (because of a ratchet), then output declines all the way from Y_1 to Y_3, rather than just Y_2.

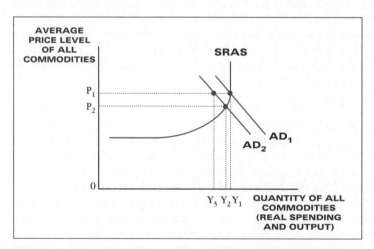

Figure 18.6. Rigidities make the most difference when the aggregate supply curve is steep. When SRAS is steep and prices are flexible, a decline in AD will cause a major fall in prices (P_1 to P_2) and only a slight fall in output (Y_1 to Y_2). If prices are rigid at P_1, however, the fall in output will be much greater, from Y_1 to Y_3.

The rigidities that cause a ratchet effect make much less difference if the SRAS curve is relatively flat, as in Figure 18.7. Here prices will not fall below price level P_3. In this case, a decline in aggregate demand from AD_3 to AD_4 will cause total output to decline only a little more (to Y_6) than it would have (to Y_5) if prices had been free to fall.

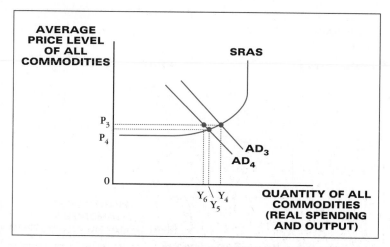

Figure 18.7. **Rigidities make less difference when the aggregate supply curve is flat.** When SRAS is flatter and prices are flexible, a decline in AD will cause only a slight fall in prices (P_3 to P_4) along with a large fall in output (Y_4 to Y_5). If prices do not fall below P_3, however, the fall in output will only be a little more, from Y_4 to Y_6.

So the existence of price rigidities is of much greater consequence to an economy when that economy finds itself along the steep portion of the aggregate supply curve.

MOVEMENTS IN THE AGGREGATE SUPPLY CURVE

The position of the short-run aggregate supply curve can move, and such movements illustrate the impact of some of the momentous events of recent economic history. The oil shocks of 1973–74 and 1979–80, and another one that appeared likely for a time in 1990–91, can be portrayed particularly well. In the first two crises, OPEC boosted oil prices, and in the third, Iraqi and Kuwaiti oil was embargoed. This raised the cost of producing everything that required petroleum as a raw material. Almost half the energy used in the United States is oil, about 40% of which is imported. Real oil prices rose nearly five times during the OPEC price hikes, and that pulled other energy costs up as well. The cost of energy used per dollar of U.S. GDP rose from about 5¢ in 1973 to 19¢ in 1982. Even with a 17% decline during that period in the physical amount of energy (barrels of oil and so forth) used per dollar of GDP, the effect was profound. Any given quantity of output shown on the horizontal axis now cost more than before to produce. The cost of supplying commodities, as shown by the position of the aggregate supply curve, rose. Figure 18.8 shows that.

The movement from SRAS to SRAS' has obvious unpleasant effects. Notice that the shift in equilibrium from E to E' involves a rise in prices from P to P' at the same time that total output is falling from Y to Y'. This combination of rising prices and falling output has come to be known as **stagflation**. Though we used oil shocks for this example, a rise in the price of *any* input, including the wages of labor, would move SRAS in the same direction, while a decline in such prices would move SRAS vertically downward. Changes in the available quantities of the factors of production, or in their productivity (including technology), will also move SRAS. (For example, if labor costs fall because unions become less aggressive or if a new cost-reducing technology becomes available, then any quantity of real output could be produced at a lower price—SRAS moves downward.)

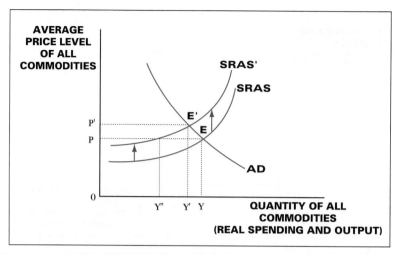

Figure 18.8. Movements in SRAS may be detrimental. Events that raise the costs of producing output, such as the OPEC oil shocks of the 1970s, raise the SRAS curve. At the new equilibrium E', prices are higher and output is lower, a combination called stagflation.

In some other circumstances, the movement in SRAS is better described as leftward or rightward, rather than up or down. For example, a war or natural disaster that destroyed some of a country's productive capacity would mean a reduced aggregate supply at any given price level, for example Y" instead of Y at price level P. Here, too, equilibrium would shift, from E to E', with resulting stagflation. Conversely, a greater quantity or higher quality of capital, or more labor or harder-working labor, at the same price level as before would move the SRAS curve to the right. That, too, would change the equilibrium.

► THE LONG RUN

The predictions of the model of aggregate demand and aggregate supply depend to a considerable degree on the time horizon employed. With the passage of enough time, some of the conclusions reached earlier in the chapter have to be modified, particularly those relating to aggregate supply.

THE LONG-RUN AGGREGATE SUPPLY CURVE

The upward slope of the aggregate supply curve, such as shown in Figure 18.8, is credible in the short run, but not over long time periods. The reasoning behind SRAS is heavily dependent on the slowness with which firms change their prices, and the even more sluggish behavior of wages, salaries, and other inputs whose costs are fixed by long-term contract. These input costs may be quite slow to adjust as an economy's average price level changes.

Thus in the short run, firms see an opportunity for profits when some costs, especially labor costs, are sticky for a time, while the selling prices of the goods they produce are rising. With the passage of enough time, however, *all* these costs—including wages and any other costs that are slow to change—*also* rise along with average prices. When this occurs, *higher prices give firms no incentive to increase production,* since their costs have risen along with their revenues. Nor will lower prices lead to less output, because wages and other input costs fixed in the short run will fall along with the average price level. In the long run, therefore, no motive exists for firms to alter their output as the price level changes, and the long-run AS curve (LRAS) will therefore assume an unusual shape, *vertical* as in Figure 18.9.

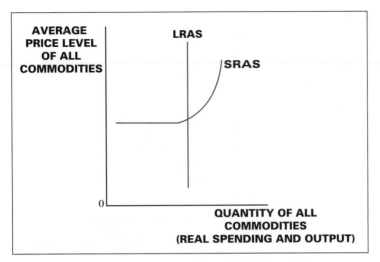

Figure 18.9. The long-run aggregate supply curve (LRAS) is vertical. In the long run, wages will eventually rise or fall along with goods prices. If wages and prices both rise or fall together, firms will have no incentive to raise their output in response to a price change. The vertical LRAS curve shows an unchanged quantity at higher or lower prices.

EXPLAINING THE POSITION OF LRAS

In the last section we saw why LRAS is expected to be vertical. If sufficient time is allowed to elapse, a change in the average price of output will cause the costs of production to change as well. Even costs such as wages which are slowest to adjust will change, though the adjustment could take as long as several years. In this section we see that in the long run, the aggregate supply curve (LRAS) is positioned precisely at the output level where any increase in output would cause overall increases in wages and other costs to set in. Let us examine why this is so.

Begin in Figure 18.10 with the aggregate demand curve AD_1 and the short-run aggregate supply curve $SRAS_1$. Output is in equilibrium at Y_1, and the average price level of all commodities is P^*. Now suppose a rise in aggregate demand takes place. Any decision resulting in greater total spending could have this effect: for example, consumers choosing to consume more, or firms deciding to raise their investment, or an increase in government spending or cut in taxes.

Aggregate demand shifts rightward, say to AD_2. Notice that this will raise output to a greater level Y_2, but it will not trigger an inflation; the economy is still on the horizontal portion of its aggregate supply curve $SRAS_1$, and the price level remains at P^*. If aggregate demand increases to AD_3, we reach the level of output Y^* where any *further* increase in AD will cause the average price level to rise. At any level of total output to the right of Y^*, prices start to climb rapidly, which will eventually trigger rises in wages and other costs. An increase in aggregate demand (to AD_4) will have this effect. The equilibrium shown at the dot involves a higher average level of prices. If enough time is allowed to pass (the long run), wages and other input costs that are slow to change will also increase. The greater demand for these inputs, which are needed to produce the larger quantity of output, will eventually cause even long-term contracts to be renegotiated. An increase in wages and other costs will cause a vertical rise in the short-run aggregate supply curve, as shown by the shift from $SRAS_1$ to $SRAS_2$. As we shall now see, this triggering of a change in the position of the SRAS curve is central in explaining why the long run curve (LRAS) is located where it is.

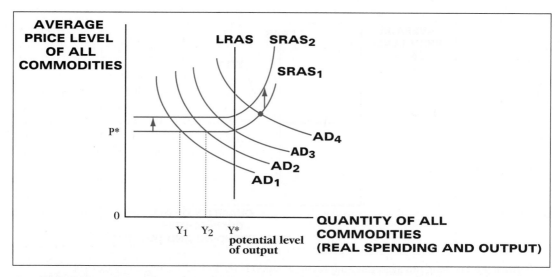

Figure 18.10. In the long run, a level of output greater than Y* will trigger an upward move in SRAS. In the figure, an increase in AD has no effect on the price level until AD rises beyond AD_3. After that, however, prices rise. In time the higher prices will boost wages as well. Because wages are a cost of output, SRAS will rise vertically, from $SRAS_1$ to $SRAS_2$.

A FURTHER NOTE ON THE POSITION OF THE LRAS CURVE

We have positioned LRAS in Figure 18.10 just to the right of the point where SRAS starts to turn upward. Doing so implies that not every small rise in the economy's price level will necessarily cause wages and other business costs to increase as well. SRAS stops being horizontal and starts to slope upward because production bottlenecks are encountered in some industries as expansion occurs. In the short run, these bottlenecks cannot be avoided, but in the long run, capital and labor may flow from where it is available to the bottleneck sectors. For example, an expanding economy might first encounter a bottleneck in the computer industry, and prices start to rise in that sector. But with plenty of slack elsewhere in the economy, some capital and labor may be able to transfer into computer making, halting the price rise without ill effects on overall wages and costs, or perhaps even bringing computer prices back down. Since the effects of these adjustments may not have been serious enough to trigger general wage and other cost increases, then SRAS will not yet start to shift upward. Beyond Y^*, any further growth in output will lead to more general price rises that *do* trigger wage and cost increases. Thus we see that the position of the vertical LRAS curve at Y^* will probably be somewhat to the right of the point where SRAS begins its upward slope. The key idea is that LRAS is positioned at just that level of output beyond which wage and other cost increases occur.

The Potential Level of Output

The **potential level of output** is the term economists use to describe the level of production beyond which wages and other input costs will increase, thereby causing a rise in the SRAS curve. In Figure 18.10, that potential level of output is shown as Y^*. This concept must be fully understood to comprehend much of modern macroeconomics. The basic principle is that when the potential level of output is exceeded, the price of output will increase sufficiently to trigger a general cost inflation. In the long run, wages and any other costs that are not fully flexible in the short run will rise along with prices. That will shift a given SRAS curve vertically upward, reflecting firms' higher costs of production. The upward shift from $SRAS_1$ to $SRAS_2$ in Figure 18.10 is an example of this.

The Natural Rate of Unemployment Is Associated with the Potential Level of Output

Back in Chapter 15 when we discussed unemployment, we noted that for practical purposes the level of unemployment cannot be pushed down to zero or near zero without inflation breaking out. This observation lies behind the idea of a **natural rate of unemployment**, the percentage rate of unemployment below which inflation would be triggered. The natural rate of unemployment is connected directly to the potential level of real output beyond which inflation would occur. For example, if the potential level of output were $5 trillion, and if, given the size of the labor force, $5 trillion in output would be accompanied by 5% unemployment, then 5% is the natural rate of unemployment. Attempts to reduce unemployment below 5% would necessitate raising output beyond $5 trillion; that in turn would trigger eventual wage and other cost increases and cause the short-run aggregate supply curve (SRAS) to rise. (The natural rate of unemployment is not shown directly on Figure 18.10; it is the unemployment *associated with* the potential level of output, which *is* shown.)[7]

So the natural rate of unemployment can be seen as a barrier below which it would be difficult to reduce unemployment through increases in aggregate demand without sparking off inflationary increases in costs. It is thought that in the United States, the natural rate of unemployment is in the area of 5 to 6%—a subject discussed in Chapter 24.[8]

Actual Output Falls Toward Its Potential Level

Now let us develop further the logic involved in the potential level of output and the associated natural rate of unemployment, using Figure 18.11. Here the initial equilibrium is at E_1 where AD_1 crosses $SRAS_1$. Assume that aggregate demand rises to AD_2, perhaps because of additional investment in the economy. At the new equilibrium E_2, the actual level of output Y_2 is higher than the potential level of output Y^* (and the associated rate of unemployment must be lower than the natural rate). The average price level will rise, and increases in wages and other input costs will eventually follow. SRAS will thus move upward, shown here as a vertical shift from $SRAS_1$ to $SRAS_2$. Yet the new equilibrium at E' still results in a level of output Y' that is above the potential level of output Y^*. Therefore, price rises will continue, eventually causing wage and other cost increases and thus a further upward movement in the aggregate supply curve to $SRAS_3$. At the next equilibrium, which is E^*, actual output is no longer above the potential level. So the pressures for further wage increases have been removed. The general point is that in the long run,

---

7.   The same idea can be expressed as the "nonaccelerating inflation rate of unemployment," or NAIRU for short. Some writers are now using a variant term, "noninflation-accelerating rate of unemployment," or NIARU. These cumbersome terms actually convey more information than does "natural rate," though that usage would now be hard to change.

8.   Though 5% seems high, under current conditions unemployment of 3 to 4% would be registered even if no one were ever to be laid off. That 3–4% would be made up of new entrants to the labor force searching for work, and people who have given up old jobs in order to look for or transfer to new ones. This "frictional unemployment," in the apt older phrase that is now somewhat out of fashion, accounts for most of the natural rate. The remainder of the 5% can be considered the "structurally unemployed," those whose skills are obsolete or whose training is inadequate for the available jobs. This brief account will be expanded in Chapter 24.

if an economy's actual level of output moves above its potential level, a process of price increases followed by wage increases sets in, eventually causing actual output to fall to its potential level Y*.

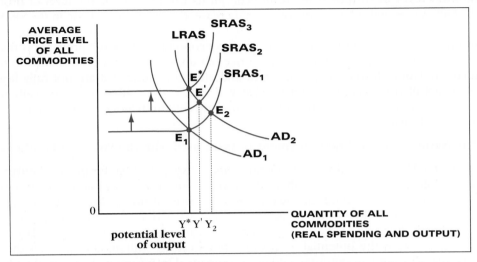

Figure 18.11. In the long run, actual output falls to the potential level. If output rises above the potential level, to Y_2, that causes the average level of prices to rise. Unemployment is now below the natural rate, and eventually this causes wages and other input costs to rise as well, so moving SRAS vertically upward to a new equilibrium at E'. But if that equilibrium is still above the potential level of output, then further price rises and eventually wage and other cost increases will be triggered, moving SRAS upward yet again and resulting in a new equilibrium at E*. Since E* is at the potential level of output, further wage increases will not occur and SRAS ceases its upward movement. Output has fallen to its potential level.

Actual Output Rises Toward Its Potential Level, but More Slowly

Now consider an actual output level *below* the potential level Y*, as in Figure 18.12. This situation will trigger a process of adjustment the reverse of that explained in the last paragraph, involving an output rise to its potential level. The process is likely to be slow, however. Because the delay can be pronounced, the diagramming needs to be interpreted somewhat differently than the case of the output fall described in the last section. Initially, AD_1 crosses $SRAS_1$ at the equilibrium E_1; total output is at its potential level Y*, and unemployment is at the natural rate. Now say aggregate demand falls to AD_2, perhaps because fears that a recession is coming causes investment to fall. That results in a new equilibrium E_2, and a decline in actual output to Y_2, which is below the potential level of output. (Therefore, unemployment will be above its natural rate.)

Remember that the SRAS curve is short-run. In the short run, prices do not decline as easily as they increase. That is why the SRAS curve is shown as horizontal to the left of the equilibrium E_1. Yet output at Y_2 is now low, well below the potential level. If the recession is long lasting, pressures toward price cutting are likely to develop after all as some firms begin to sacrifice profits to keep from having to close their doors. (In effect, SRAS may slowly develop some downward slope to the left of E_1 rather than staying completely flat.)

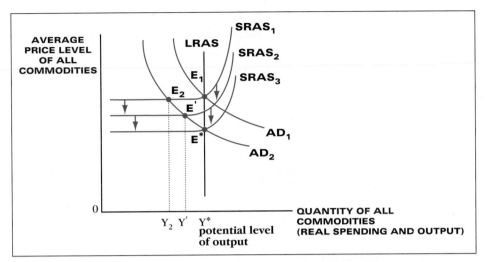

Figure 18.12. In the long run, actual output rises to the potential level. Say AD falls, causing actual output to decline to Y_2, which is below its potential level at Y^*. If output remains below the potential level long enough, then the average level of prices may fall. Eventually, wages and other input costs will fall as well, so moving SRAS vertically downward, with a new equilibrium at E'. But if that equilibrium is still below the potential level of output, then further wage and other cost decreases will be triggered, moving SRAS downward yet again and resulting in a new equilibrium at E*. Since E* is at the potential level of output, further wage decreases will not occur and SRAS ceases its downward movement. Output has risen to its potential level.

In labor markets, as a recession lengthens, some firms lose their reluctance to pursue wage cuts, and some workers may be more willing to accept lower wages if the alternative is to lose their jobs. If the recession is mild, this process may not occur, and even if it does it may take a long time. If the recession is long and severe, however, then eventually wages and other input costs will begin to drop. We can see the results in Figure 18.12. $SRAS_1$ will shift down, say to $SRAS_2$. Notice, however, that at the resulting equilibrium at E', the higher actual output at Y' is still below the potential level of output. Further wage declines will (or at least may) ensue, causing the aggregate supply curve to fall again, say to $SRAS_3$. Now at the equilibrium E*, actual output has risen to the potential level, Y^*, and there is no further pressure to move SRAS. From this we see that in the long run, if an economy's actual level of output is below its potential level, a process of wage decreases may begin, eventually causing actual output to rise to its potential level Y^*. This process is more likely to happen if the recession is deep and long-lasting.

In this model, if actual output is above or below the potential level Y^*, it will adjust over time to that potential level. It follows that the long run aggregate supply curve—which shows total output after sufficient time for adjustment has elapsed—must be vertical at that output Y^*.

THE LONG-RUN TENDENCY
FOR SELF-CORRECTION IN AN ECONOMY

The adjustment process just discussed has substantial implications for the macroeconomy. It suggests that self-induced changes may occur whenever an economy's actual output deviates from its potential level of output. Figure 18.13 illustrates this mechanism for self-correction. On the left, Panel **a** shows that a gap has opened, with total output Y *higher* than the economy's potential output Y^*. (Perhaps AD has risen due to a government tax cut or some other increase in total spending.) In Panel **b** a similar gap appears, with total output Y *below* potential output Y^*. (Perhaps AD has fallen because of a rise in taxes or some other decrease in total spending.)

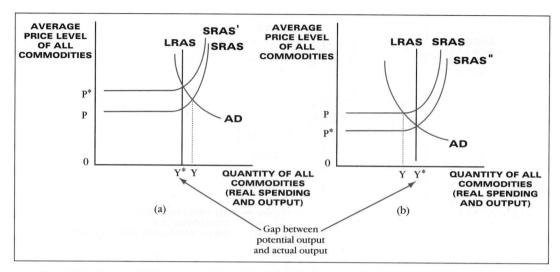

Figure 18.13. **In the long run, economies have some built-in tendency for self-correction.** In panel **a**, output above the potential level at Y leads to rising wages and other costs, shifting SRAS upward to SRAS', and moving the equilibrium level of output back to the potential level Y*. In panel **b**, output below the potential level at Y may after some considerable time lead to falling wages and other costs, shifting SRAS downward to SRAS", and moving the equilibrium level of output up to the potential level Y*.

Consider first the gap that has opened up in Panel **a**, the left-hand diagram. The fact that actual output is above its potential level will eventually raise wages and other lagging costs, and will thus push SRAS upward to SRAS'. In the absence of any further change in AD, we can expect prices to rise from P to P*, and real output to fall from Y to Y*. This is a stagflationary combination of rising prices and falling output. As long as input costs continue to rise, the gap between potential and actual output will become smaller until finally it is eliminated at Y*.

A similar process might be discerned when the economy is below its potential output, as in Panel **b**. If a recession is severe and long lasting, wages and other lagging costs in time may fall, thus moving the SRAS curve downward to SRAS". Here we would expect prices to fall from P to P* and real output to rise from Y to Y*, in a reversal of stagflation. As long as firms' costs continue to fall, the gap between potential and actual output will become smaller until finally it is eliminated at Y*. This can be a much slower process, however, as the ten-year Great Depression of the 1930s suggests.

In both cases, if all input prices, especially wages, were flexible enough both up and down, then any gap between actual and potential output would eventually disappear, and long-run aggregate supply would be a vertical line at Y*. Much of the debate in modern macroeconomics centers on this very issue: how much less flexible *are* wages than other prices, and how rapidly do adjustments of this type take place?

LRAS CAN SHIFT
OVER TIME AS AN ECONOMY GROWS

Over time, we might expect the position of LRAS and hence the level of potential output to shift to the right (to LRAS' and Y*' in Figure 18.14) as capital accumulation occurs, technological change takes place, population expands and the labor force grows, educational improvements are registered, and the like. Each of these additions to resources makes it possible to produce more output at any given price level. With more capacity to produce, inflationary pressures will not be encountered until greater levels of output are reached.

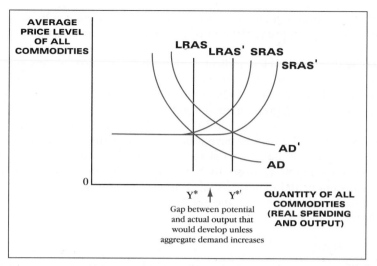

Figure 18.14. **In the long run, growth shifts the position of LRAS and changes the potential level of output.** Additions to the quantity and quality of the factors of production mean that more can be produced without triggering inflation. The potential level of output moves rightward to a higher total at $Y^{*'}$. Because the LRAS curve is positioned at the potential level of output, it also shifts rightward, from LRAS to LRAS'.

This involves the same principle we encountered in the previous chapter under the name Okun's Law. The idea is that a growing productive capacity will require an increase in actual production and spending. Otherwise, unemployment of workers and other factors of production will develop. Okun's Law suggests that real output and income in the United States must grow at about 2–3% a year to keep this from happening. In Figure 18.14 unless wages fall, lowering the SRAS curve, or aggregate demand increases from AD to AD', a gap would open between the new potential level of output $Y^{*'}$ and the unchanged actual level of output (and the former potential level) Y^*. The problem is less serious, however, to the degree that changes in aggregate supply and aggregate demand are linked. For example, a larger population causes consumption to rise, any capital accumulation means more investment spending, and technical change may lower costs and also cause a rise in investment. In these cases, LRAS and AD move rightward together. But there is no certainty, and given Okun's Law, wages may have to drop or governments may have to resort to expansionary macro policy to keep unemployment from developing.

CONCLUSION

The AD/AS model has become central to modern macroeconomists' efforts to explain economic behavior. An essential contribution of that model is the clarity with which it shows how price increases may be expected to set in before full employment (defined as no excess capacity remaining in the economy) is reached, how wage and other cost increases will follow, and how an economy's total output will adjust as a result. For all that the flexprice AD/AS model looks quite different from the fixed-price "Keynesian cross" with its 45° line, they do share some common ground. Those interested in tracing the links between these two models can pursue the subject in this chapter's appendix.

▶ THE BUSINESS CYCLE IN MARKET ECONOMIES

We have now completed our examination of the main models of macroeconomic equilibrium. Through the whole analysis, it has been clear that in the market economies, economic fluctuations are frequent and expected. Booms and slumps, like death and taxes, seem always with us. Here we examine the underlying causes of the unsteadiness in economic performance, asking why market economies seem so susceptible to a **business cycle** of expansion (boom) up to a peak, followed by contraction (slump, recession) to a trough that is, in turn, followed by another rise.

Experience with these cycles indicates that they are not of any set length, though historically a period of three to five years from peak to peak or trough to trough has encompassed most cycles. (The Great Depression of 1929–1940 and the long period of expansion from 1982 to 1990 are notable exceptions.) A great many different reasons have been advanced explaining why business upturns and downturns occur, and the proliferation of reasons signals that indeed no two business cycles in recorded history have followed exactly the same course.

Even so, most cycles do appear to share some attributes that account for the instability. "Real" causes involving tangible changes in economies, together with confidence factors based on the mood of consumers and producers, appear to provide the most reasonable explanations for the cyclical behavior. Both the real and the confidence elements can and usually do have a simultaneous effect.

REAL FACTORS

After a long period of economic expansion, certain real factors can cause a downturn. To see how, consider what the situation was like early in an expansion. At that time, firms were attempting to build up their stocks of inventory to meet the greater demand from consumers. Because sales to consumers were rising at the same time, however, the build-up of inventories was slow and firms therefore continued to place new orders. A multiplier process raised incomes, and when the economy's idle plant and equipment was put to work, then further new orders caused an investment-raising accelerator process to begin as well. (The accelerator model was discussed in Chapter 16.) In turn, the accelerated investment generated new income and an additional multiplier effect. This "accelerator-multiplier" process delivered yet more thrust to the expansion.

Eventually, firms do attain their target figures for inventories, or they may even overshoot their targets if for any reason the growth of consumer demand slows, even if slightly. In that case, firms will cease to order as much for addition to their inventories. This drop in orders for new inventories has been a typical factor in almost all recent recessions. The multiplier effects on the country's output and income therefore go into reverse, with less new spending by firms meaning reduced income and less spending by consumers. Furthermore, the initial decline in orders will have a negative effect on investment through the accelerator process. The reduced investment causes a further multiplier effect on income, decreasing it even more.

Investment by firms may decline for other reasons as well. During the expansion, costs (of labor, raw materials, and capital) may have risen and credit may have become harder to obtain from banks because the demand for loans has been high. That alone might be discouraging for some investment projects, which do not go forward. Any slowing in the growth of consumer demand would have the same effect. Again, the multiplier and accelerator impacts on the economy's performance are negative; a downturn may begin.

The real effects extend to consumers, too. Consumers may have been acquiring durable goods at a brisk pace during the expansion phase of the cycle, but then comes a time when, temporarily, most people have amassed the durables they desire. For example, after a few years of boom there may come a time when sales of VCRs slow somewhat because so many families have already purchased them. If few of the VCRs or other durables acquired during the boom have yet worn out, there is no need to replace them. Technical improvements might lead consumers to buy new items before the old ones are worn out, but perhaps no major improvement has been made recently.

Decline in the growth of consumer demand will affect producers through their inventories. Firms will add less to their stock, or even change over from building it up to running it down. The decline in the growth of consumer demand may also cause firms to reduce their new investment in plant and equipment. In time, replacement needs will arise. For now, however, firms face declining demand and find that they are accumulating unsold stocks of goods. That causes them to cut back on both their new orders for the goods they produce, and on their investment. Though durable goods and investment in plant and equipment make up well under a quarter of all output, changes in these sectors usually account for 80% or more of a typical economic downturn. Layoffs in these industries will contribute to a contraction in consumer spending generally.

The decline in income and output may convince banks that firms have overinvested; they will become more conservative in their lending. If property values fall, even the banks may find themselves in difficulty. Their loans for new office buildings and condominiums may look insecure if the prices of these assets decline and the developers who borrowed to build them start to allow the banks to foreclose on them rather than continue paying interest on the loans. Perhaps even some bank failures result, as in the late 1980s.

Government policies can also generate real effects that result in a "political" business cycle. A country's politicians may attempt to ensure that a boom always precedes an election. If they are willing to employ expansionary monetary and fiscal policy a few months before the campaign, they may be rewarded with increasing national prosperity, and therefore increasing popularity for themselves, just before the voters go to the polls. If the boom becomes inflationary, the politicians may likewise dictate that the contractionary monetary and fiscal measures be administered a long time before the next poll. (The political nature of business cycles will likely be more pronounced when legislatures and the chief executive are of the same political party, and if the central bank is directly under the government's control, rather than having an autonomous voice.)

CONFIDENCE FACTORS

A loss of confidence by consumers and/or firms may have an independent effect. The erosion of confidence can come in many forms:

1) It could be triggered by the danger of a war somewhere (Iraq, Kuwait in 1990).
2) An oil price shock (OPEC, 1973, 1979; the embargo of Iraq, 1990) or a food shock (the world food shortage of 1973) could cause it.
3) A stock market crash (1929, though the crash of 1987 caused little harm) or financial failure (banks in 1929–1933 and in almost all pre-1929 recessions; savings and loan institutions in the late 1980s) could be the cause.
4) Pessimism may stem from some inability to govern (the U.S. budget deficit impasse in recent years) or a loss of confidence in politicians and the financial community (the savings and loan disaster, the junk bond scandal). All of these are explored later.

Whatever the cause, if consumers lose confidence, they may figuratively tighten their belts, purchasing fewer goods and services, especially homes and big ticket consumer durables. If producers lose confidence, then acting on their declining confidence, they place fewer orders for machinery and equipment, and they run down their stocks of inventory. Production is reduced directly and, through the multiplier and accelerator effects, income and output fall elsewhere in the economy. It should be noted that the horrendous drop in confidence among *both* consumers and producers in 1929–1931 and its failure to improve much for a long time thereafter made the Great Depression much worse than can be explained by the real factors. To an important degree, Franklin D. Roosevelt was right when he declaimed that "the only thing we have to fear is fear itself."

CYCLES TEND TO SPREAD TO OTHER COUNTRIES

The booms and slumps tend to spread around the world because markets are interlinked by foreign trade and capital movements. In expansions, a country imports more; by generating exports in other countries, the expansion spreads abroad. Conversely, a slump causes a country to import less; the decline in exports in foreign countries can trigger slumps there, too. Obviously, the linkage is more likely to be from major economies to minor ones. "If the United States (or Japan, or Germany) coughs, the world catches cold," as the saying goes.

CYCLES MAY BECOME LESS PRONOUNCED

Business cycles may become less pronounced, and may even have become so already, because of certain fundamental changes that have occurred in many market economies. First, in all advanced economies a shift in demand has been taking place away from manufactured goods and toward services. The reason is basically that a richer economy wants more services. Consumers want more and better entertainment, restaurant meals, higher-quality vacations, improved medical care, and so forth. Businesses want more insurance, better consultants, higher-powered attorneys, and the like. Services are not durable and cannot be stored, so the cyclical nature of declining and increasing inventories of them does not occur. It is thus significant for the cyclical behavior of market economies that while only 28% of all jobs in the United States were in the service sector at the start of this century, the figure is about 70% now.

Several other aspects of modern economies may diminish the severity of cycles. First is the rising importance of government spending. Such spending in the industrial countries was 28% of GDP in 1960, but is 41% now. Government spending typically does not fall in a recession; it is counter-cyclical. Second, the unwanted inventory accumulation that traditionally accompanies a slump may in the future become less sizable. Computers allow much better control to be maintained over the size of inventories and permit more frequent ordering of smaller quantities "just-in-time" for these stocks to be used as input or sold. Just-in-time inventory management may eventually reduce the average size of inventories, lessening the prospects of inventory accumulation in a slump and rundowns in a boom. Finally, though not permanently, the business cycle in the period 1982–1990 was partly damped by a fortuitous fall in oil prices that extended through most of the period even as the economic expansion occurring at the same time began to grow rather old by historical standards. Avoidance of future oil shocks would certainly help to smooth fluctuations.

THE SLOW RECOVERY OF 1992–1993

The most recent U.S. downturn, from July 1990 to April 1991, was matched by recessions in Canada, Europe, and Japan. In none of these countries did the recessions end with as vigorous a recovery as has usually been true. For example, in the United States the 1990–1991 recession was actually rather mild. Only two of the previous eight recessions dating back to 1948 were shorter in duration. The country's output dropped by less than half as much (1.2%) as the average of the earlier eight (2.6%), and the highest rate of unemployment reached (7.1%) was under their 7.8% average. But the rate of growth during the subsequent two years of recovery was very slow. One reason may be that economizing on inventories was playing a role. Inventory restocking during the 1992–1993 recovery appeared to be weaker than in the past, and the ongoing transition to "lean management" of inventory may well have been the cause. Disturbingly, unemployment rose for some time even after recovery was underway. Since 1948, only once before had unemployment increased after output began to grow following a recession's end. Furthermore, it appears that most of the increase in unemployment during and after the 1990–1991 recession involved permanent job losses rather than temporary layoffs. These were worrisome developments. A number of possible causes, including rapid technological change, structural problems, and government policies, will be discussed in Chapters 24 and 25. Fortunately, the U.S. recovery seemed stronger in 1994, though very slow growth still lingered in most of Europe and Japan.

Cycles in market systems are likely to continue. They cannot, given the present state of knowledge, be eradicated. Their recurrence will put a premium on the search for macroeconomic policies adequate to counter these cycles while reducing the costs that accompany the stabilizing policies. The changing nature of what economists believe *is* proper macroeconomic policy, and the broad disagreements that still exist among the various schools of thought, will be emphasized in the chapters just ahead. When these debates within the discipline are sorted out, and when policies are improved—and with the passage of time and the accumulation of more empirical evidence, greater proficiency in policy management will surely follow—then further progress in damping the business cycles of modern economies can be anticipated. Until then, the ups and downs, booms and slumps that have been part of the history of market economies will continue to be part of their future as well.

SUMMARY

1) The contemporary model of aggregate demand and aggregate supply allows for analysis of both the level of output and for changes in the price level. Though these curves appear to resemble the demand and supply curves of microeconomics, they have to be explained in very different ways.

2) Aggregate demand slopes downward because of the rise in interest rates as the average price level rises, the effect of price changes on exports, and the real-balances effect of prices on wealth. The aggregate demand curve will shift its position with any change in one or more of the components of total spending, such as consumption, investment, government spending, or spending on exports.

3) The short-run aggregate supply curve (SRAS) exhibits different slopes depending on economic conditions. We can model it as follows: SRAS starts as a flat line, indicating the existence of large quantities of unutilized resources and unemployment. It then begins to turn upward, indicating bottlenecks in supply and higher costs. Finally, it goes vertical, indicating that no spare production capacity exists in the economy. Wage stickiness is important in explaining why firms will produce more as the average level of prices rises; without the stickiness, wages would rise simultaneously with the price increases on goods, and firms would have no motive to increase their production.

4) Firms do not resist price increases as much as they resist decreases, resulting in a "ratchet effect" whereby once average prices rise in a boom, they do not tend to decline in a slump, or do so very slowly.

5) Events that raise the costs of producing output, such as the OPEC oil shocks of the 1970s, raise the position of the SRAS curve.

6) The passage of time may make a significant difference for the shape of the aggregate supply curve. For example, a rise in aggregate demand may push actual output above the "potential level" at which prices start to rise. With unemployment now below the "natural rate" associated with the potential level of output, in time wages will start to rise as well, shifting SRAS upward. A new equilibrium of AD and SRAS will occur at a higher price level and lower level of output. The economy is pushed toward the potential level of output, and unemployment toward its natural rate. Because in the long run the country's output is pushed to the potential level of output, the long-run AS curve (LRAS) is a vertical line positioned at the potential level of output.

7) Conversely, a fall in aggregate demand may cause actual output to fall below the potential level, and unemployment to rise above the natural rate. In that case, there may be a slow adjustment as labor costs and other input costs fall. The lower costs would mean a fall in the position of the SRAS curve. A new equilibrium of AD and SRAS will occur at a lower price level and higher level of output. Here, too, the economy is pushed toward the potential level of output, and unemployment toward its natural rate. Again, the adjustment means that the long-run AS curve (LRAS) is a vertical line positioned at the potential level of output. But cost declines may take a long time to transpire, and so the process is likely to be longer than the one discussed in the last paragraph.

8) In the long run, growth shifts the LRAS to the right and raises the potential level of output. Additions to the quantity and quality of the factors of production mean that more can be produced without triggering inflation.

9) Economic fluctuations occur with frequency in market economies, with a business cycle of expansion following contraction. This cycle is caused by a combination of real factors, especially changes in inventories, and confidence factors that trigger changes in spending. Recovery from the early-1990s recession though now underway has been surprisingly slow, giving economists some cause for concern.

APPENDIX
LINKAGES BETWEEN THE KEYNESIAN DIAGRAM
AND THE AD/AS DIAGRAM

The Keynesian fixed-price diagramming and the AD/AS diagramming have a very different appearance. Yet a number of revealing linkages exist between these two methods of graphical analysis that improve our understanding of both. We focus here on equilibrium, the multiplier, and the recessionary and GDP gaps.

EQUILIBRIUM IN THE TWO DIAGRAMS

First, consider the position of equilibrium in the two diagrams. The equilibrium in both is the point where total output equals total spending, as in Figure 18A.1. Total output moves to Y_e. The bottom diagram (AD and SRAS) shows the average price level specifically; the top diagram (Keynesian cross with 45° line) does not.

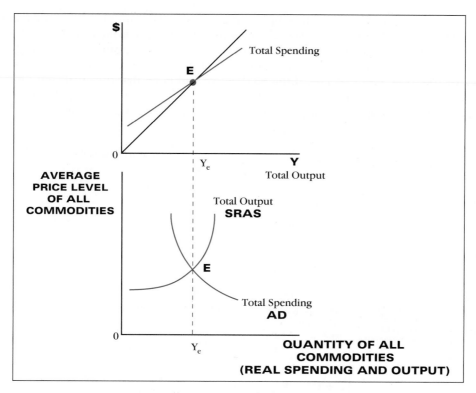

Figure 18A.1. Equilibrium in the two diagrams. The equilibrium in both diagrams is where total output and total spending are equal. The bottom diagram (AD and SRAS) shows the average price level specifically; the top diagram (Keynesian cross with 45° line) does not.

THE MULTIPLIER AND THE AD/AS DIAGRAM

The Keynesian diagram abstracts from the price level, but in the diagram of aggregate demand and aggregate supply, price changes take place explicitly. When using AD and SRAS curves, any underlying changes in the level of C (and S, T, or M that affect C), I, G, or X have the potential to change *both* the equilibrium level of output and the price level at the same time. As a result, the Keynesian multiplier must be reconsidered to allow for the price changes.

To demonstrate the point, assume that the Keynesian multiplier is 5. In that case, a new investment of $10 billion would lead to $50 billion in new output, as in the top part of Figure 18.16. See how C+I+G has risen by $10 billion to C+I'+G, moving the equilibrium from E to E' and raising output by a multiple from $1,000 billion to $1,050 billion. That is a standard Keynesian fixed-price case with the economy below full employment.

The bottom part of Figure 18.16 shows exactly the same situation, still assuming a fixed-price environment, with aggregate demand and aggregate supply curves. A flat SRAS curve (dashed line) indicates that output can rise without causing an increase in prices, reflecting the Keynesian assumption of fixed prices. In that case, a rise in investment of $10 billion, a multiplier of 5, and no price change would raise the economy's total spending by $50 billion. Hence aggregate demand would move to the right by $50 billion. (Note particularly that the multiplier effect can be traced directly in the Keynesian top part of Figure 18A.2, whereas in the AD/AS construct in the bottom part of the figure the movement of AD *includes* the multiplier effect.) At the new equilibrium E' along the horizontal aggregate supply curve, total output is $1,050 just as in the Keynesian case at the top of the figure.

What if, however, the aggregate supply curve is upward sloping? Let us say that an increase in aggregate demand from AD_1 to AD_2 changes the equilibrium from E to E". Real growth in output is only $40 billion. See how at the equilibrium E", real output has risen by $40 billion rather than $50 billion. See also that the rise in output involves a price increase; prices rise from an index of 100 to an index of 120. If the SRAS curve had been flat, the "real" multiplier would have been 50/10 = 5 and prices would not have changed. With an upward-rising SRAS curve, however, the "real" multiplier is smaller, only 40/10 = 4, and prices *do* change.

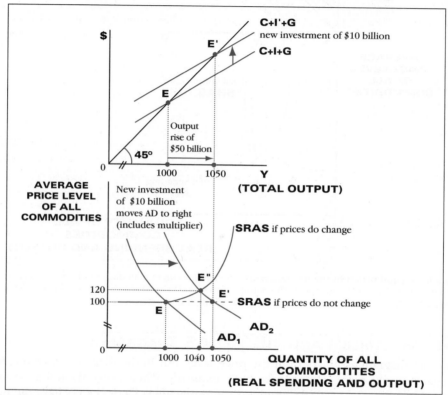

Figure 18A.2. The multiplier in the AD/AS diagram. On an AD/AS diagram, an increase in AD raises output but it also raises the average price level. The "real" multiplier is smaller than the Keynesian multiplier unless SRAS is flat.

How large the real multiplier will be and how much prices will change depends on how steeply the aggregate supply curve slopes upward. Where SRAS turns vertical, no further increase in real output can occur because the economy's factors of production are fully employed. The value of total output can still increase, and there can still be a multiplier effect, but only in nominal terms, reflecting that the same real quantity of goods is being sold at higher prices.

THE RECESSIONARY AND GDP GAPS IN THE TWO DIAGRAMS

The concepts of recessionary gaps and GDP gaps are important in the Keynesian fixed-price analysis. These gaps can be illustrated with both the 45° line diagram, as at the top of Figure 18A.3, and with aggregate demand and supply curves, as at the bottom of that figure. Doing so emphasizes the different ways in which the concept of full employment may be defined, and how important it is to have a consistent definition. If we designate full employment output as the output level $Y_e"$ at which no spare capacity remains in the economy, then in the bottom diagram of the figure the short-run aggregate supply curve must be vertical at that point. No further real increase in total output can be obtained. Now consider an economy in a deep recession, at equilibrium E where AD and SRAS intersect, and a low level of output Y_e. That initial position involves heavy unemployment and excess capacity. Moving to a new equilibrium at E" where output at $Y_e"$ is sufficiently high that all the excess capacity is put to use, can be achieved by shifting the aggregate demand curve from AD to AD", perhaps by increasing investment. Thus the GDP gap marked with an asterisk (GDP gap*) has been filled. On the Keynesian diagram at the top of Figure 18A.3, the same idea of an expansionary investment increase would involve a rise in total spending from C+I+G to C+I"+G. That will close the recessionary gap marked with the asterisk (the movement in the total spending schedule being vertically upward from E to B). That in turn moves the equilibrium from E to E". Output increases by a multiple, and the GDP gap between actual output Y_e and the full employment level of output (defined as no spare capacity) $Y_e"$ is closed.

Yet it is also possible to define the full employment level of output not as the level where all spare capacity to produce is exhausted, but instead as the potential level which, if exceeded, would trigger price and wage increases. At that potential level of output, unemployment would be at its natural rate. If this definition of full-employment output is used, then the GDP gap is smaller, between Y_e and Y_e'. In the bottom part of the diagram, closing this smaller GDP gap can be achieved by increasing aggregate demand from AD to AD', thus moving the equilibrium from E to E'. In the Keynesian top part of the figure, the same idea is seen as a move in total spending from the original C+I+G to a new C+I'+G, a vertical distance from to E to A. Filling this recessionary gap and so moving in the equilibrium from E to E' means a multiplied increase in total output from Y_e to Y_e'. The whole exercise underscores the importance of a careful definition of full employment.

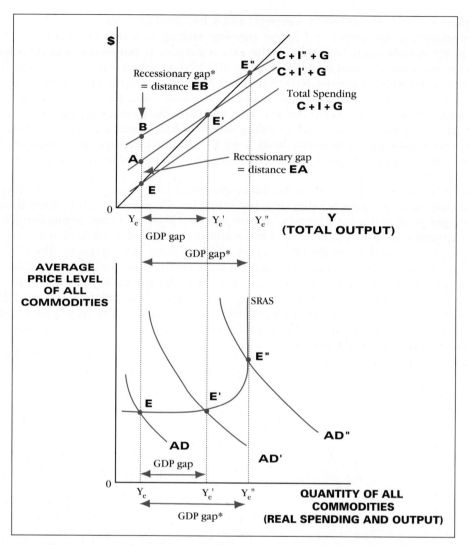

Figure 18A.3. Recessionary and GDP gaps in the Keynesian and AD/AS diagrams. The two diagrams are useful in defining full employment. If it is defined as no spare capacity to increase production, then the full employment level of output is Y_e''. If it is defined as the unemployment that would exist at the potential level of output (the natural rate of unemployment), then the full employment level of output is Y_e'. In the first case, the recessionary gap is EB and the GDP gap is Y_eY_e''. In the second case, the recessionary gap is EA and the GDP gap is Y_eY_e'.

Chapter Key Words

Aggregate demand curve, or AD: The curve relating an economy's total spending to its average price level.

Aggregate supply curve, or AS: The curve relating an economy's total output to its average price level. Can be short run (SRAS) or long run (LRAS).

Business cycle: A characteristic of market systems, which experience cycles of economic expansion (boom) up to a peak, followed by contraction (slump, recession) to a trough in a pattern that then repeats itself. Caused by "real" and "confidence" factors.

Efficiency wage: Payment to labor of a wage higher than the market price because that brings better morale, less need for supervision, and less risk that workers will "jump ship" to another firm.

Long-Run Aggregate Supply Curve (LRAS): The curve located at the *potential level of output* (which see). Indicates a long-run tendency for an economy's actual output to revert to its potential level because of adjustments in wages and other costs.

Money illusion: The idea that workers may take time to recognize that their wages are falling behind increasing prices. An explanation why pressures for higher wages may not develop until some time after prices have begun to rise in an economy.

Natural rate of unemployment: The percentage rate of unemployment associated with the *potential level of output* (which see). If the actual rate of unemployment falls below the natural rate, wages and other costs will increase, causing the short-run aggregate supply curve to rise. If the actual rate of unemployment rises above the natural rate, wages and other costs may eventually decline, causing the short-run aggregate supply curve to fall.

Potential level of output: The level of production which, if exceeded, will push unemployment below the *natural rate* (which see), triggering wage and other cost increases and thus an upward movement in the short-run aggregate supply curve. If actual output falls short of the potential level, that would push unemployment above the natural rate, possibly causing wages and other costs to decrease and thus meaning a fall in the short-run aggregate supply curve.

Ratchet effect: The tendency for the prevailing price level to become a "floor," due to the reluctance of firms to cut prices and wages and workers to accept wage cuts.

Stagflation: The combination of rising prices and falling total output.

Wage stickiness: The idea that wages may be relatively slow to change. When labor markets become tighter, wages may rise slowly because of long-term labor contracts, because a premium (*efficiency wage*, which see) is already being paid, or because of *money illusion* (which see). When demand for labor weakens, wages may not fall fast or far because of long-term contracts, minimum-wage laws, considerations of fairness, and the unpopularity that attaches to the firm making the cuts.

CHAPTER QUESTIONS

1) Which of the following events describe a movement along the AD curve? Which describe a shift of the AD curve?
   a) Business optimism causes investment to increase.
   b) Investment increases because a falling price level leads to lower interest rates.
   c) Inflation causes U.S. exports to become more expensive, so foreigners buy fewer of them.
   d) U.S. firms do not improve the quality of their products, so foreigners buy fewer of them.

2) Along the upward-sloping portion of the SRAS curve, the rising price level induces firms to supply more output. But it is not just the price of the firms' products that are rising. The prices of inputs are going up along with product prices. Why are firms willing to supply more output anyway?

3) An economy starts at a low level of output, with AD intersecting the horizontal portion of SRAS . Increased consumer confidence shifts AD to the right, so that it intersects SRAS along the rising portion of the curve. Draw and describe how the economy moves from the old equilibrium to the new one.

4) Imagine an economy that is very overheated, with AD intersecting the vertical portion of the SRAS curve. The government decides that fighting inflation will be painless and easy. If it just reduces spending, AD will shift down. Price will fall, but output will not decline. Show on a diagram what the government would like to happen. What do you think will really happen?

5) Some economists believe that a major cause of the Great Depression was bank failures. When many banks fail, the close relationships between borrowers and lenders are destroyed. The result is that doing business is more costly. If costs of production suddenly rise across the economy, how does this shift the SRAS curve? Suppose that bank failures also affected AD because consumers lost confidence (and lost wealth too). How would the AD curve shift? Assuming that equilibrium had been on the upward-sloping portion of SRAS, how would output and the price level respond to the wave of bank failures?

6) Governments often get carried away with expansionary fiscal policy. Imagine that the government expanded AD so far that the intersection of AD and SRAS was to the right of LRAS. What would happen next? What would have been a better way to conduct fiscal policy?

7) Imagine that in the next presidential election, the winning candidate promises "the biggest tax increase in history" in order to eliminate the deficit. (Imagine hard!) The huge tax increase will shift AD considerably to the left, pushing the country into recession. If no more shocks come along, what will happen to end the recession?

8) German reunification can be looked at as an addition of East Germany's economy to West Germany's. The additional labor and capital shifted the West German SRAS and LRAS to the right. However, East Germany was relatively poor, so its inclusion did not shift AD very far to the right. Show on a diagram what this meant for Germany. What did the German government do about the situation?

9) When the economy is booming along, you may receive a phone call from a broker wanting you to buy stocks. "The economy is going nowhere but up," she may say. What signs would cause you to believe otherwise?

Money and the Banking System

OVERALL OBJECTIVE: To explain how changes in the money supply affect the economy, and illustrate how these changes come about primarily through increases or decreases in banks' reserves.

MORE SPECIFICALLY:

- To define the money supply in its basic form as demand deposits plus coins and paper currency, to discuss how the demand for money is determined, and to realize that the interest rate (which is the price of money) equilibrates the quantity of money that is supplied and the quantity of money that is demanded.

- To explore the link between interest rates and economic performance, showing that higher interest rates tend to restrict investment, some consumption, some government spending, and net exports, so causing a multiplier effect on total output.

- To see the quantity theory of money (MV = PY) as an alternative way to analyze the impact of money supply changes on an economy.

- To understand the difference between private, commercial banks, and the government's official or central bank (the Federal Reserve System in the United States).

- To show that when banks acquire additional reserves, the lending of these reserves and their redeposit in the banking system results in the creation of new money.

The money and banking system is of great importance in explaining the behavior of the macroeconomy. We take it for granted that money and banks exist. Without money we would live in a world of barter, where we would have to find someone not only willing to take what we had to trade, but who had something we wanted to acquire. Without banks we would be dependent on strongboxes and cash hoards. Life would be far less convenient and far less safe. Undoubtedly, money and banks are enormous facilitators to trade and all other commercial activity.

It is now time to see how money and banks fit into the discussion of the past few chapters, where we have worked to identify the forces that cause an economy to expand or contract. Governments' monetary authorities (their official or central banks) often attempt to influence this process through monetary policy. By adjusting the money supply, they try to affect nations' output and income. Optimally, such a tool could be used to brake the economy in inflationary periods and boost it in recession. Yet to a significant degree, money and the banking system are influences in their own right, and governments cannot always fully control either of them. This chapter begins a three-chapter investigation of money, banking, and monetary policy. Chapters 22 and 23 then move on to look at fiscal policy, the alteration of government taxes and spending.

▶ WHAT IS THE MONEY SUPPLY?

Before we begin a detailed exploration of our monetary system, we should define what we mean by the "supply of money" (M_S). This is not so simple as it sounds. Take a poll on the street that asks the question, "What is money?" Though there would doubtless be a certain amount of agreement, the differences in opinion would probably be substantial. Everyone would agree that cash in the form of coins and paper currency are money. But most transactions are not carried out with coins and paper money. Over 40 billion checks are written every year in the United States, and these make up 97% of all U.S. transactions by value.[1] These checks are drawn on checking accounts in banks, which are called **demand deposits** by economists since they are payable to the holder on demand.[2] Because checking accounts are the main method for transacting business, they must be serving as money and hence must be included in any measurement of the money supply—as indeed they have been for many years. In fact, in the United States nearly three-quarters of the basic money supply is made up of checking accounts, with only a little more than the remaining quarter comprising coins and paper money. This basic measure of the money supply, which is called **M1** by economists, is summarized in Figure 19.1.

---

1.   The figures are for 1984. Though cash is unimportant in value terms, it is used for most individual transactions, well over 80% of them according to best estimate. You often buy candy and chips and pizza with cash, but you buy clothes, cars, and houses by writing a check. Anytime you use a credit card, you pay the balance due by writing a check as well. In any given year, the value of the infrequent large purchases is immensely greater than the value of the frequent small ones, explaining why the value of payments made by check is so substantial.

2.   Many demand deposits are called NOW accounts. The name, standing for "negotiable orders of withdrawal," originated with the first interest-bearing checking accounts in New England in March 1976; the rest of the country was permitted to have them only in 1981. Before that date, U.S. law had prohibited interest on checking accounts since 1935. Many countries abroad never banned interest on demand deposits, however.

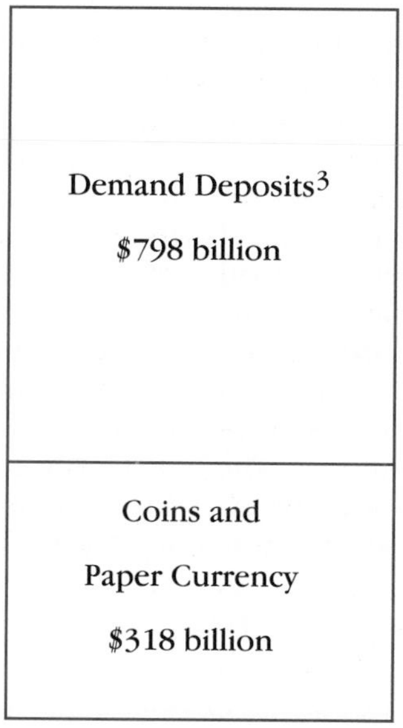

Figure 19.1. U.S. basic money supply (M1) as of October 1993. (Total = $1116 billion)

MONEY HAS BECOME HARDER TO DEFINE

The definition of the money supply has become much more complex in recent years because of innovation in financial markets and the banking system. In this chapter, we will continue to use the M1 definition of the money supply. Once we have understood the basic issues involved, we will be in a better position to expand our analysis to include additional components of the money supply, which we do in the next two chapters.

MONEY FUNCTIONS, MONEY WORDS

A suitable money is expected to serve as a medium of exchange (for carrying on transactions), as a store of value (so that wealth can be held in the form of money), and as a unit of account (so that transactions can be measured in money terms—your marble can be valued at 6¢, my stick of gum at 8¢; after our trade you owe me 2¢). Historically, many items that have filled one role have not been able to fill all. In nineteenth-century Africa, the cowrie shells that served adequately as a medium of exchange and unit of account were too small in value to serve as a store of wealth; slaves were better for this purpose, though an inconvenient unit of account and a poor means for transactions involving small values. A dollar, pound, mark, yen, or any of a hundred others serve all three purposes.

Substantial human interest attaches to the study of money, with currency names and words relating to money and finance often telling a fascinating story little known to the public and even to many economists.

---

3.   Also included in M1's total for demand deposits are automatic transfer service (ATS) facilities where the bank moves money as needed into your checking account, and travelers' checks.

The words "pecuniary" and "impecunious" date back to the curious use of cows (*pecus* means cow in Latin) as money early in the Roman republic. The word "coin" comes from *cuneus*, a wedge. Early coins were mere bits or slices of metal. (The word cuneiform to describe the wedge-shaped writing of the ancient Babylonians has the same root.) The word "estimate" also has ties to the early history of money: in Latin, *aes tumare* means to value copper, lumps of which also served as an early currency. The British pound and the Italian lira (which means pound in Italian) are easy: these currency units were originally a pound of precious metal. The German mark also started out as a weight, as did the Greek drachma (the weight "dram" used by druggists comes from the same root.) Peso means weight in Spanish. The word dollar has a more obscure origin. It comes from the *Joachimsthal* (German: Joachim's valley), a valley in the present-day Czech Republic whose German-speaking lords in centuries past minted a coin named the *Joachimsthaler*. The coin was called *thaler* for short, and this word was (and is) pronounced "taler" in German. The Joachimsthal has one other distinction. It produced the ore in which uranium was first discovered.

▶ HOW CHANGES IN THE MONEY SUPPLY AFFECT THE ECONOMY

The belief that changes in the money supply affect the economy is very old, dating back at least to the sixteenth century. The idea that such changes might be engineered by a government's monetary authorities to obtain a macroeconomic result dates from actions taken by the Bank of England in the nineteenth century, and similar U.S. actions just before and after World War I. How does a change in the money supply influence the economy? What monetary policies are appropriate for carrying this out? These are controversial topics, the subject of much debate among economists and politicians. We examine them in this chapter and the following two.

Money Supply, Money Demand, and Interest Rates

A basic proposition is that changes in the money supply affect interest rates, and variations in interest rates will affect the overall level of spending in an economy. Interest rates are believed to have special significance for investors in plant, equipment, and other forms of capital, house buyers, and consumers of durable goods purchased with borrowed funds. Government spending, too, will be affected by interest rates because many units of government borrow in order to spend. More generally, all spending of any kind may be influenced by the interest rate, because spending always carries an opportunity cost. That is, choosing to spend means forgoing the interest you would have earned on your savings.

The price of borrowed money (credit), which is the interest rate, is established by the supply and demand for money. The determinants of the supply and demand for money are discussed below.

THE MONEY SUPPLY IS ESTABLISHED BY THE GOVERNMENT'S MONETARY AUTHORITIES

The money supply (M_S) is fixed by a country's monetary authorities, who usually have the power to alter the size of that supply, as we discuss in Chapter 20.[4] At any given time, government

---

4.   But not always—some small countries including Liberia and Panama use the U.S. dollar; some Pacific island nations use the Australian dollar; some states of the old USSR use the Russian ruble. Their governments have little control over their money supplies.

provides a stock of money limited to a certain amount. This amount does not depend on the interest rate. Reflecting this, Figure 19.2's panel **a** shows the M_S curve as a vertical line; the quantity of money is fixed as shown along the horizontal axis.

The Determinants of Money Demand

Money demand (M_D) is made up of three different components. *Transactions demand* refers to money needed for carrying out purchases on a day-to-day basis; this demand is largely synchronized with the growth of the economy and how frequently one's wage or salary is paid. As an economy grows richer, it will require more money for use in daily transactions. The increase in the country's income causes consumption to rise, and individuals will need more money to facilitate their increased purchases of goods and services. So the demand for money rises as income grows. How frequently one is paid also affects the demand for money. People who buy groceries every day, but are paid once a month, need a greater average stock of money (including bank deposits) than people who are paid once a week and thus get more frequent replenishment.

Another component of the demand for money is a *precautionary demand* for money available to meet unexpected needs or emergencies. A wealthy family with large holdings of stocks and bonds and ten different credit cards can still find itself in trouble if it has neglected to hold sufficient precautionary balances of money. What if the car breaks down on a weekend when wallets are thin, someone forgot to top up the checking account, and the wrecker crew won't take credit cards?

Finally, there is a *speculative demand* for money. A family would not want to hold all its spare resources in stocks and bonds if it thought that stock and bond markets were due for a sharp fall. Better to hedge by holding deposits until the danger was past.

The transactions, precautionary, and speculative demands for money have a major point in common. The higher the rate of interest, the more costly to hold cash bearing no interest, or checking accounts bearing only a low rate.[5] Thus the quantity of money people desire to hold can be portrayed as in Figure 19.2's panel **b**, falling at high interest rates (r) and rising as rates fall. The resulting demand for money (M_D) is sometimes called liquidity preference.

Expressing the demand for money as a demand for transactions, precautionary, and speculative balances is in the Keynesian tradition. An alternative view of the demand for money is favored by non-Keynesians such as Milton Friedman. This view emphasizes that money is the most liquid of all assets, valued for the flow of services it yields to its holders. More of it will be demanded as society's wealth increases. Holding money also carries an opportunity cost, however—the interest forgone from not earning interest, or only low interest, on cash or checking accounts. Higher interest rates will thus reduce the demand for money, and lower interest rates will increase it. For our purposes it does not matter which view of the demand for money is taken. Both involve a downward-sloping demand curve as in panel **b**.

The point at which M_S and M_D cross, as at point r_e in Figure 19.3, is the equilibrium price of money. The price of money is the rate of interest that must be paid to borrow it. The behavior of the market for loans is similar to the markets for goods and services; surpluses and shortages will occur at interest rates that differ from the equilibrium. With curves M_S and M_D, an interest rate higher than r_e will mean an excess of money supply over money demand and the interest rate will fall. An interest rate below r_e means the demand for money exceeds the supply, causing the interest rate to rise.

---

5.   The rate of interest here is the *nominal* rate, not corrected for inflation. If nominal rates are 8%, inflation is 8%, and the real rate of interest is 0%, your sacrifice when you hold cash instead of a deposit is the 8% nominal interest you could have earned.

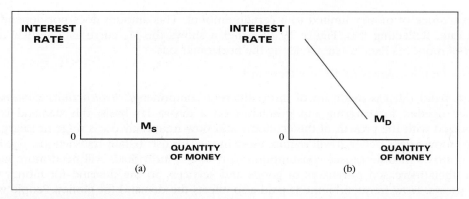

Figure 19.2. Money supply and money demand. The money supply curve M_S is vertical at some given quantity of money determined by the monetary authorities. The money demand curve is downward-sloping because at high interest rates, people will economize on their money holdings in cash and checking accounts that earn low or no interest.

A decision by a government's monetary authorities to increase the supply of money to M_S' is likely to cause a decrease in the interest rate that must be paid to borrow it. This is because a greater amount of money M_S' causes the money supply to exceed the demand for money at interest rate r_e, pushing the interest rate down to a new equilibrium, r'. If government reduces the money supply, say to M_S'', that causes an excess of demand over supply at interest rate r_e, and the interest rate will rise to r''. These lower or higher interest rates have particular importance for an economy's spending, as we examine in the next section.

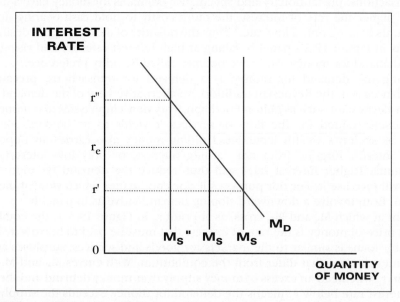

Figure 19.3. The equilibrium rate of interest. An increase in the money supply from M_S to M_S' will lower the rate of interest to r'; a decrease in the money supply from M_S to M_S'' will raise the rate of interest to r''.

INTEREST RATES AND BOND PRICES

The mechanism in these supply-and-demand terms seems simple enough, but economists have traced through the steps in the process in much more detail. The means by which a greater quantity of money actually affects the interest rate can be seen in the bond market. If the government makes more money available, then firms and individuals find themselves holding greater amounts of money than can be justified by their needs for day-to-day transactions. Rather than hold these excess balances in cash or low-interest checking accounts, corporate treasurers will seek to purchase bonds and securities to park the funds. The increased purchase of bonds by these same treasurers will bid up the price of bonds, so that a bond selling for $99 today may sell for $102 tomorrow. Traditionally, bond prices vary according to supply and demand even when they have a fixed face (or "par") value such as $100. If a bond is a U.S. Government $100 par value 6% security coming due in 1996, it will pay its owner a fixed return of .06 x $100 = $6 per year. But if today's price for this bond is $99, then $6 is *greater* than 6% of $99. (Actually, it is 6.06%.) If the price of the bond rises to $102 tomorrow, $6 is *less* than 6% of $102 (actually 5.88%). A cardinal rule of the financial markets is that more purchases of bonds in the market raises bond prices, which has the effect of lowering the general rate of interest.

The relationship between interest rates and bond prices is important in our later work—and it is also a key piece of information for people who own bonds.

THE LINK BETWEEN INTEREST RATES AND ECONOMIC PERFORMANCE

What will happen to a country's economic performance if interest rates change? We have seen that interest rates will affect the level of total spending, and therefore the level of total output. If interest rates fall, there will be more spending and the effect is expansionary.[6] A rise in interest rates works in the opposite way to contract the economy. (The interest rate changes we refer to here are real, adjusted for inflation. Nominal interest rate changes can be offset by price changes; nominal rate changes are not what the managers and consumers in an economy react to.) We now look at the process in greater detail.

Investment

Investment (I) in plant and equipment is very dependent on interest costs, as we saw in Chapter 18. Lower interest rates mean that more projects are profitable than before, and firms will decide to increase their investment. Lower interest rates also encourage home building, which is another form of investment. In 1993 mortgage loans were more affordable (averaging about 7.5% at midyear) than at any time since the early 1970s, and the construction of new housing was increasing rapidly. Lower interest rates will also mean that firms' inventories do not have to be monitored so closely. The inventory of new cars on the car dealer's lot do not cost the dealer so much when interest rates are low. A *rise* in interest rates will *discourage* new investment, including home building and the holding of inventory. Of course, many factors other than interest rates affect investment. The strength of demand for products, the level of profits,

---

6.   A feedback mechanism is involved to a degree. A money supply increase if it lowers interest rates and raises income will thereby cause some increase in the demand for money. In Figure 19.3, the rightward move of the M_S curve may in time cause the M_D curve to move to the right as well, so interest rates do not end up as low as they otherwise would have.

business confidence, and the amount of capacity utilized would all be expected to exert an influence. In a deep recession, the business outlook may be so poor and firms so pessimistic that lower interest rates may stimulate little new investment. Nevertheless, interest rates have a very important effect on investment.[7]

Consumption

Changes in interest rates may have a major effect on some elements of consumption (C), particularly durable goods purchases, sales of which will expand. Big ticket durables such as cars and appliances will appear more attractive when interest rates are low. Consumption will also increase when interest rates fall because the burden of debt is reduced. If people have borrowed anything at variable interest rates, or if they refinance their fixed-rate mortgages at lower rates, they have more to spend on consumption. A *rise* in interest rates will *curtail* borrowing for durables purchases and increase the burden of debt.[8] Interest rate changes will also affect prices of bonds and stocks, following the logic contained in the previous box. If lower rates raise their prices, then consumers may feel more wealthy and may increase their consumption. Higher rates would reduce bond and stock prices, and if this made people feel less wealthy, consumption may fall.

Government Spending

Changes in interest rates will also affect some government spending (G). Governments that borrow to finance their spending find that lower rates make the borrowing more affordable. For example, your local government might be contemplating taking out a loan to finance the construction of a new school. Low interest rates would encourage it to go ahead. *Rising* interest rates will *discourage* new government spending.

Foreign Trade

Finally, a change in interest rates will affect both exports and imports. That happens because interest rate changes tend to alter the exchange rate between the dollar and other currencies. To see this, consider what happens when U.S. interest rates fall in comparison to those in other countries. Some Americans will take dollars out of U.S. banks and will deposit them at the higher interest rates paid by foreign banks, or they will buy foreign bonds and securities. Some foreigners holding U.S. dollars will do the same thing. To make deposits abroad, holders of dollars must buy foreign currencies on the foreign exchange market. Like the markets for goods and services, that market, too, is subject to the principles of supply and demand as we saw in Chapter 4. Just as a rising supply of wheat decreases the wheat price, so a rising supply of dollars lowers the price of dollars. If one U.S. dollar cost 110 Japanese yen (¥) on the foreign exchange market yesterday, the new supply of dollars may bring the price of dollars to a lower ¥100 today. The dollar has "depreciated." If, on the other hand, interest rates *rise*, the dollar will *gain* value, or "appreciate."

A lower value (depreciation) of the dollar or a higher value (appreciation) have a macroeconomic effect. If the dollar depreciates, imports now are more expensive; a dollar buys fewer yen than before, and therefore fewer Japanese goods. Because of the decreased imports, sales of American goods rise, meaning an increase in domestic consumption and therefore a rise in total output as well. The lower value of the dollar also means that the Japanese buyers of American goods now find these goods are less expensive; a U.S. export item priced at $1 now

---

7.   James Tobin of Yale University sees another route through which lower interest rates increase investment. His *portfolio theory* suggests that lower interest rates will increase the demand for stock as people shift out of interest-bearing deposits and into the stock market. The new demand will serve to bid up stock prices. Corporations will then want to sell more stock, the proceeds of which can be used for investment. The sale of stock finances only a relatively small share of investment, however.

8.   Working to some degree in the opposite direction is the change in consumption because consumers earn interest as well as pay it. When interest rates fall, people with assets such as bank deposits and bonds will have less to spend for consumption. When interest rates rise, people have more to spend.

costs the Japanese buyer ¥100 instead of ¥110. U.S. exports, now priced more competitively, rise. Conversely, if the dollar appreciates, Japanese buyers of American goods will find these goods more expensive, and U.S. consumers will find that imports from Japan are a better bargain. U.S. exports fall and U.S. sales of goods that compete with imports will weaken. So total U.S. output declines.

In short, if lower interest rates decrease the value of the dollar, that will cause a fall in U.S. imports, a rise in American consumption of U.S.-made goods, and a rise in U.S. exports to foreign countries. From mid-1991 to early 1992, a major fall in U.S. interest rates to a point lower than Japan's and only about half what they were in Germany caused the dollar to depreciate significantly against the yen (by 11%) and the mark (14%). As predicted, exports strengthened and imports weakened. The effect was to increase total spending on U.S. output.

Conversely, if higher interest rates increase the value of the dollar, then imports will rise because they are now cheaper, consumers will buy fewer domestic goods, and consumption falls. Exports, now priced expensively, will decline. The effect is to decrease total spending on U.S. output. In the mid-1980s, high U.S. interest rates appreciated the dollar to unprecedented levels against some currencies. At the dollar's peak in 1985, one dollar could buy almost exactly one British pound, an all-time record. Predictably, U.S. exports fell and imports increased, with the effect of decreasing total spending on U.S. output.

The Spending Increases Will Be Multiplied

We have seen that a decrease in the real interest rate will begin a process that leads to a rise in total spending. It does so by stimulating investment, domestic consumption, some government spending, and exports. A fall in the interest rate also discourages imports, which is another reason for a rise in the consumption of domestically produced goods. In the other direction, a rise in real interest rates cuts total spending by decreasing investment, domestic consumption, some government spending, and exports. It also encourages imports, which helps to lower the consumption of domestically produced goods. Symbolically, with r standing for the real rate of interest,

$$\Delta r \rightarrow \Delta I + \Delta C + \Delta G + \Delta X \rightarrow \Delta GDP.$$

Each of these changes in spending will have a *multiplied* impact on the nation's output. Each will be subject to the multiplier effect traced in Chapter 17.

The economic effect of lower real interest rates is illustrated in Figure 19.4, with a movement in total spending (C+I+G+X) in panel **a**'s Keynesian diagram or in aggregate demand (AD) in panel **b**'s diagram of the contemporary model. In both panels, equilibrium shifts from E_1 to E_2, raising the level of output and income from Y_1 to a higher level, Y_2 in panel **a** and Y_3 in panel **b**. (The difference in the increases in income is because in panel **b**, prices rose.) To see the effect of an interest rate increase, reverse all the movements. Output and income will fall.

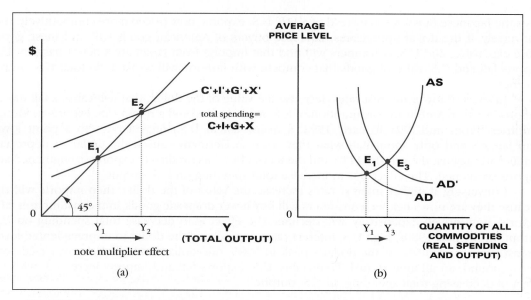

Figure 19.4. The effect of lower interest rates. A fall in real interest rates will increase some consumption, investment, government spending, and export spending. In the Keynesian model, total spending rises, equilibrium shifts from E_1 to E_2, and total real output rises by a multiple to Y_2. In the contemporary model, aggregate demand rises, equilibrium shifts from E_1 to E_3, and total output rises to Y_3. To see the effect of higher interest rates, reverse all the movements.

INTRODUCING MONETARY POLICY

The idea that interest rates can affect total spending and hence total output leads to a dramatic possibility. A country's monetary authorities might take advantage of this relationship by using their control over the supply of money (M_S) to alter interest rates (r). That would give them some ability to manipulate total spending and could result in a multiplied impact on output. The mechanism is as follows:

$$\Delta M_S \rightarrow \Delta r \rightarrow \Delta I + \Delta C + \Delta G + \Delta X \rightarrow \Delta GDP$$

But remember that when government alters the supply of money, the resulting change in interest rates is *nominal*. As we have emphasized, only a *real* interest rate change will have a substantial effect on economic activity. Inflation or price decreases may possibly upset the policy apple cart, as we shall see.

Now let us trace what type of monetary policy the monetary authorities would use to combat a recession, and what sort could be utilized to do battle with inflation.

Monetary Policy During Recession and Inflation

During a recession, government would like to engineer an increase in output. If the government's monetary authorities could arrange an *increase in the growth of the money supply* (**easy money** or **monetary ease**), then more funds will be available for lending. That would cause interest rates to fall, total spending to increase, and the nation's output to rise by a multiple.

What if the monetary authorities wished to combat an inflationary boom? Here, too, the link between interest rates and output can be utilized. If a *slowdown in the growth of the money supply*, or even a contraction (**tight money** or **monetary tightness**) can be engineered, then interest rates could be expected to rise. The higher interest rates will cause total spending to fall, and therefore cause a multiplied decrease in the nation's output. The pressure for prices to rise will ease.

THE QUANTITY THEORY OF MONEY: AN ALTERNATIVE VIEW OF THE IMPACT OF MONEY SUPPLY CHANGES

The last section viewed monetary policy as working because changes in the money supply alter the rate of interest. The quantity theory of money, first advanced by Professor Irving Fisher (1867–1947) of Yale in the 1920s, provides another way to conceptualize the impact of money supply changes on an economy. The Fisher equation (often called the equation of exchange) states that

$$MV = PY$$

where $\quad$ M = the supply of money

V = the velocity of money's circulation

P = the average price level

Y = the quantity of real final output

The money supply and the average price level are already familiar terms. PY is the nominal value of all final output, made up of P, the average price level, times Y, the real quantity of output. For example, if total output is 500 widgets and 500 gizmos, and widget price is $2 each while the gizmo price is $4 each, then P = $3, Y = 1000, and PY = $3,000. The **velocity of circulation**, V, is a term we have not yet encountered. It is the number of times the money supply changes hands annually. For example, if the total money supply in the country is a $1 bill and that $1 bill changes hands just once during the year, then the velocity of circulation is 1.

The quantity theory states that the money supply times the velocity with which this money circulates equals the nominal value of all final output. An example will clarify how the formula works. If the only money in existence consists of just the one dollar bill mentioned, and the total value of all final output sold this year is $5, then the dollar bill used to purchase that output must have changed hands five times; that is, its velocity of circulation is 5. The relationship is actually an identity that is always true, so it can be written $MV \equiv PY$.[9]

As long as V is reasonably stable, the value of output PY following a change in the money supply can be predicted with some degree of certainty. A school of economists known as the *monetarists*, whose influence was strong in the late 1970s and early 1980s, believed that V was stable. They made detailed forecasts of PY based on changes in the money supply. If V rises or falls, however, it upsets the ability of the model to forecast the impact of changes in M. Many economists believe that as the money supply changes, there are indeed reasons to expect changes in V, predictably in a direction opposite to the money supply change. This belief is based on the link between the money supply and interest rates. When interest rates decline, the opportunity cost of holding money in low-interest demand deposits is reduced. For any given level of spending, there is less need to keep these deposits small and turn them over rapidly. Instead, these low-interest deposits can be allowed to grow and they do not have to be "worked" as hard. That is the same as saying that velocity falls.

Unfortunately for monetarists who attempted to forecast economic performance from money movements, velocity *did* become less stable, at least for periods shorter than a year or two. For example, during a few months of 1979, velocity rose by over 2% in the United States, whereas during another short period of time in 1982 it fell more than 5%. During the 1980s, velocity fluctuated in most other advanced countries as well. These alterations were unexpected,

---

9.　There is a complication involving velocity that should be noted. Many transactions involving money do not represent the purchase of final output, but instead involve purchases of secondhand goods or intermediate inputs. So money actually changes hands more often than the figure for V implies. That is, V for *all* transactions is higher than V for the purchase of final output. In our discussion, V is always defined as the velocity of money used for the purchase of final output.

damaging to the position that velocity is stable, and made it more difficult to predict the results of changes in the quantity of money. (Why velocity changes take place is discussed at greater length in the next chapter.)

The Quantity Theory Is Useful for Analyzing Hyperinflation

In spite of the debates on the quantity theory, almost every economist would agree that that theory is a useful and even essential tool for analyzing a hyperinflation. Vast increases in M are sure to drive PY to the point where Y (real output) reaches the full employment level. With no extra capacity remaining in the economy, any further increase in M would be inflationary unless, inexplicably, V were to decline. On the contrary, with inflation setting in, V is likely to rise, perhaps substantially. With M and V both pushing ever upward in a fully employed economy, inflation is the certain result.

In severe inflations (or deep recessions), changes in velocity are more or less inevitable. Velocity rose 30 times in the German hyperinflation of 1923.[10] Another way of saying this is that the German money supply rose by a considerably smaller percentage than did German prices during the period of the hyperinflation. Velocity surged because money not spent quickly was money that lost purchasing power. (Remember Chapter 14's tale of the customers in cafes who bought two or three glasses of wine all at once, rather than one at a time, to protect themselves against a price rise while they were at their tables? That is a velocity increase with a vengeance.) Even in moderate or mild inflations, holders of money must pay the penalty of eroded value, so velocity is likely to rise. Conversely, a cooling of inflation is likely to slow velocity because people will not be in such a hurry to spend. Velocity will also probably be lower in a recession because of the reduced level of economic activity.

It should be noted that the quantity theory (MV = PY) and the theory that monetary changes affect an economy by altering its total spending and output ($\Delta M_S \rightarrow \Delta r \rightarrow \Delta I + \Delta C + \Delta G + \Delta X \rightarrow \Delta GDP$) are not in serious conflict. An important prediction of both these models is that the impact of a money supply increase is expansionary and a decrease is contractionary. In the quantity theory, an increase in the money supply gives a higher nominal value of final output. In the alternative view, an expansion in the money supply will raise output through a lower interest rate and greater level of total spending. The main debate between monetarists and nonmonetarist economists does not concern the overall impact of money supply changes, which both camps agree will expand or contract the economy, but the degree to which the output change involves a real change in quantity, or a nominal change involving price levels. That question is treated in the accompanying box.

---

10.   This probably represents something of a ceiling to the velocity of circulation no matter how dizzy the hyperinflation becomes. It is extremely difficult to spend money even faster once its turnover has reached 25 to 30 times normal levels.

HOW ACTIVE SHOULD MONETARY POLICY BE?

Some economists (called "new classical" economists) and members of the financial community believe that monetary policy may have far less influence on economic activity than has been suggested by our analysis so far. The debate is on the question of how quickly the economy returns to its potential level of output, as discussed in the previous chapter. The new classicists assert that the economy moves rapidly to its potential level of output and natural rate of unemployment. Recall how that process involves price increases if the economy starts from a position above the potential level of output, and price decreases if the starting position is below the potential level of output. The price movements will mean that nominal interest rate changes will not be the same as real interest rate changes. If the monetary authorities raise the money supply, nominal interest rates may indeed fall, but real interest rates may not. In this reading of the new classicists, an activist monetary policy will not work because it is always being overtaken by price changes. Stimulative policies will quickly bring on inflation. That being the case, these economists would prefer a policy of nonintervention by the monetary authorities. Make steady increments to the money supply to accommodate economic growth, they would say; an activist strategy is doomed to fail.

Many (probably most) economists argue differently. They see a nation's adjustment to the potential level of output as occurring more slowly. Businesses are tardy in changing prices; and wages respond even more sluggishly. Small shifts in total spending brought about by monetary policy might not lead to higher prices at all, but instead to higher real output. Large shifts in total spending will cause prices to change in time, but probably not right away. There is room to maneuver. Those who study the timing of monetary policy suggest that while monetary policy starts to affect the level of economic output in about 6 months or so, it actually takes 18–24 months before a change in the money supply affects the rate of inflation. In this case, a nominal change in interest rates caused by an alteration in M_S will be a real change as well. The link between money, interest rates, and the nation's output *can* in this reading be utilized by the monetary authorities. Certainly that is the view of the monetary authorities themselves, who fought the early 1990s recession with all of the tools at their command. Chapters 21–24 return to these arguments in more detail.

CHANGING THE MONEY SUPPLY INVOLVES COMMERCIAL BANKS AND THE CENTRAL BANK

Large changes in the money supply will have substantial economic consequences for a country. Through their monetary authorities, most governments have direct control over the volume of currency (coins and paper) they can issue, but as seen earlier in the chapter currency is not a very large part of the money supply. The major element in the money supply is actually the volume of bank deposits, and the major means to *alter* the money supply involves the ability of a country's monetary authorities to control the size of these deposits.

COMMERCIAL BANKS

Because bank deposits are so significant in determining the size of the money supply, the role of **commercial banks** must be fully understood in order for the analysis to proceed. Commercial banks are privately owned banks in business for profit, supervised in most countries by a government central bank. They take deposits *from* the public and lend money *to* the public.

By world standards, the United States is atypical, one of the few remaining countries with many separate, individual banking firms.[11] There were about 12,000 commercial (private) banks in 1993, though there were many more, well over 20,000, before the Great Depression of the 1930s caused thousands to close their doors. Their range in size is enormous, much greater than is usual in other countries. A giant such as Citicorp in New York has assets of over 200 billion dollars, ten thousand times larger than many hundreds of small-town banks that still exist.

Of the 12,000 American banks, about one-third are national banks, meaning that they have obtained their charters of incorporation from the federal government. The other two-thirds are state banks, having acquired their charters from the state in which they were incorporated.

The situation as regards size is very different elsewhere. In most countries, a few large banks with hundreds of branch offices dominate the banking industry. In Japan, for instance, a few banks reach enormous size, with Dai-Ichi Kangyo now the largest in the world, and six more of Japan's banks ranking in the world's largest 10 when size is measured by value of assets. In England, the Midland, Barclay's, Lloyd's, and National Westminster are seen everywhere, and there are few others. The same is true of Canada, where the Royal Bank of Canada, the Imperial Bank of Commerce, and the Bank of Montreal are of overwhelming importance. In Germany, the Deutsche Bank, the Dresdner Bank, and the Commerzbank command the financial scene. In many countries the largest banks surpass the smallest by only a small margin. This concentration of power often makes for closer relations between the government and the handful of very large banks than is true in the United States.

CENTRAL BANKS

The monetary authority of most countries is an official government bank known as a **central bank**. Central banks supervise and regulate the private banking system. They act as "lender of last resort," standing ready to make loans to commercial banks in times of financial crisis. (Central banks are usually *not* permitted to lend to private nonbank businesses or individuals, however.) Of great importance, central banks carry out monetary policy, engineering changes in the money supply in order to affect their nations' output and income levels.

The U.S. central bank is the **Federal Reserve System**, called the **Fed**. It was created by Congress in 1913 and is a latecomer among central banks. Most of the other developed countries established theirs decades or even centuries before the Fed was founded.[12]

---

11.   U.S. law was once very restrictive, with many states requiring unit banking (that is, a banking firm could have only one office) and prohibiting banks from other states from opening an office. The states now permit as many separate offices as a bank wishes to open, and all states except Hawaii now allow interstate bank holding companies. Thus, banks under the same management umbrella can operate in several states. Eight states permit full interstate banking (six of them only reciprocally with states that grant the same privilege). The new trend has led to many mergers and is moving U.S. banking in the direction taken by Japan, Britain, Germany, and many others. The concentration of deposits in the United States has been growing as a result; the 100 largest U.S. banks now hold 64% of all U.S. banking assets compared to 50% in 1960, and the largest 10 hold 25% of total banking assets compared to 20% in 1960. Over 20% of all banking assets are held by out-of-state organizations. It is worth noting that the historical reluctance to allow branch banking in the United States made the banking business more risky. When banks were tied to a single community, the risk was enhanced that a crop failure or factory closing could cause them major damage.

12.   The Sveriges Rijksbank, the central bank of Sweden and the world's first, was founded in 1668. The Bank of England is indeed the "Old Lady of Threadneedle Street," dating from 1694. The Banque de France was founded by Napoleon in 1800. Other well-known central banks are Nihon Ginko (the Bank of Japan), Germany's Deutsche Bundesbank, and the Bank of Canada.

THE EARLY U.S. ATTEMPT TO ESTABLISH A CENTRAL BANK

An early attempt to establish an American central bank failed. The Bank of the United States, located in Philadelphia, operated during 1791–1811 and then again from 1816 to 1836. It was a mixture of private and government enterprise; of its 25 directors, only 5 were appointed by the U.S. government; the other 20 were elected by the private investors in the bank. The Bank of the United States was the largest U.S. corporation of its time, the repository of the public funds, and the source of some government regulatory power over what was otherwise a chaotic private banking system. The most famous head of the bank, Nicholas Biddle, believed that the institution's policies should be independent of the government's and should aim for financial stability, a view of central banks widely held today by economists all over the world. Biddle and the Bank eventually ran afoul of President Andrew Jackson, a populist who opposed "Eastern financial dominance."

Jackson ordered the government's deposits withdrawn from the Bank of the United States in 1833, disrupting the country's finances and helping to plunge the economy into a depression. The Bank lost its charter in 1836 and with that its national role. (In private hands it eventually went bankrupt in 1839.) A period of unregulated banking followed, with crooked banking practices and damage to the economy as a whole. Private banks issued their own paper currency, and travelers needed little books to tell them whether some given bank's notes were unsafe. The concerns over "financial dominance" continued, however, lasting long after the demise of the Bank of the United States. When a U.S. central bank was established in the second decade of this century it was thought necessary to truncate its power somewhat by giving it a curious structure as we see in the following section.

The Fed

The U.S. Federal Reserve System consists of 12 banks, one in each of the 12 Federal Reserve Districts.13 A map of the districts is shown in Figure 19.5.

All 12 banks have their own boards of directors and presidents, but the real power resides in the seven members of the Federal Reserve's Board of Governors, with headquarters in Washington, D.C. (The Fed Board of Governors has veto power over the choice of the district bank presidents.) The members of the Board of Governors are appointed by the President for terms of 14 years. Appointments must be confirmed by the Senate. The terms are long enough to assure considerable independence for the Fed, especially since they are staggered so no President is able to appoint a block of members to the Board of Governors at the same time.[14] The divorce of banking matters from immediate political control is thought to be highly desirable by economists concerned that governments would be tempted to buy elections with more spending. (In other countries there appears to be considerable correlation between direct control of central banks by government and high rates of inflation.)

---

13. The Deutsche Bundesbank has a similarity in that its board of directors is made up of representatives of the länder, or state governments.

14. For some in Congress, the independence of the Fed is too great. Various ideas considered from time to time are that the chairman's term should end with the President's; that the individual bank presidents should be appointed by Congress; or that the Secretary of the Treasury should be a member of the Fed's Board of Governors (which was true from 1913 to 1935). Many economists, concerned that Congress would allow politics rather than prudent finance to dictate Fed decisions, would be troubled to see more Congressional or presidential control of the Fed.

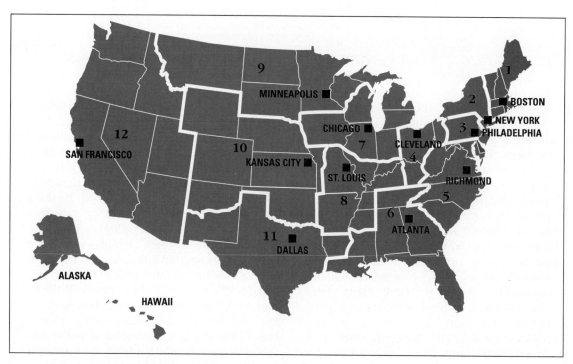

Figure 19.5. The Federal Reserve system. The twelve Federal Reserve Districts, and the location of the twelve Federal Reserve Banks, are as shown.

The most important member of the Fed's Board of Governors is its chairman (there has not yet been a woman in the post, though women have served on the Board of Governors). The chairman, also appointed by the President, serves for four-year terms and can be reappointed. The current holder of the post is Alan Greenspan, who shoulders the prime responsibility for announcing and explaining the management of the U.S. money supply. Because the U.S. economy is the planet's largest, the Fed's role as manager of monetary policy and lender of last resort for the banking system make it one of the world's most important institutions.

With this background concerning private commercial banks and government central banks, we can begin our study of how a change in the money supply might actually be accomplished.

How Banks Participate in Creating Money

Under certain circumstances, commercial banks have the capacity to create or destroy money. This capacity—which usually comes as a surprise to those who have not studied the banking system—is what central banks manipulate in their efforts to control a country's money supply.[15]

To see how the principle of money creation works in practice, look at the stylized balance sheet for a commercial bank shown in Figure 19.6. On the left-hand side of this *T-account*, so-called because of the T-shape of the dividing lines, are shown the assets of the commercial bank. Assets are simply the holdings of a bank, that is, the property or money that it holds, owns, or controls. On the right-hand side are the liabilities of the bank, that is, what the bank owes to others.

---

15.   Governments have an alternative to working through the banking system. They can simply roll the printing presses and run off new paper notes, as is done in Russia, Ukraine, Yugoslavia, and some less-developed countries. Printing new notes is a slow process, however, and the monetary authorities of modern industrial countries have a much faster way to create money, as we shall see.

```
              ASSETS │ LIABILITIES
                     │
                     │
                     │
                     │
                     │
                     │
                     │
                     │
                     │
                     │
```

Figure 19.6. A T-account. Resembling the letter T, a T-account puts assets (what is owned or controlled) on the left side and liabilities (what is owed) on the right.

Due to the nature of double-entry bookkeeping, assets and liabilities must always be equal. Whatever is held under the control of any institution (including banks) is automatically owed to someone. For example, if an institution has $1000 worth of cash and buildings on hand, then some of this $1000 (the institution's assets) must be owed to those who have lent money to it, or to those to whom the institution owes unpaid bills. The remainder of the $1000 that is not owed in this fashion must automatically represent a claim by the owners (the stockholders if the institution is a corporation). So any sum of assets must always be represented by an equal sum of liabilities, because what is held or owned by an institution must by definition be owed to or claimed by someone, even if that someone is the owner. In short, assets always equal liabilities.[16]

In the case of a commercial bank, by far the largest liability will be what is owed to those who have made deposits in the bank. If $1000 in cash has been placed by depositors in demand deposits, then we can show this $1000 as a liability on a T-account (see Figure 19.7). Those who make the bank's policy must now decide what to do with this $1000 in cash. They might decide to keep the entire $1000 as cash in the vault. That would be reflected on the asset side of the T-account in Figure 19.7. (Other kinds of banking assets, for example buildings, furniture, and fixtures, and other kinds of liabilities such as bills payable, are not considered here. To understand the principles involved in money creation, these other assets and liabilities can safely be ignored.)

```
              ASSETS │ LIABILITIES
                     │
        cash in vault │ demand deposits
                     │
              $1000  │     $1000
                     │
                     │
                     │
                     │
                     │
                     │
```

Figure 19.7. Assets match liabilities on a T-account. For each liability there must be matching assets. Here, depositors have placed $1000 on deposit and are owed that amount as a liability. The matching asset is the $1000 in cash that now sits in the vault.

16.　　In our simple T-account, we do not make a separate accounting for the equity of the bank, that is, its capital stock held by its stockholders. To accountants, this equity is the bank's "net worth" rather than a liability. Thus, it is technically proper to say "assets equal liabilities plus net worth," but in our simplified presentation we include net worth with liabilities. In any case, our treatment does not need to consider net worth.

If we retain as cash in our vault all the deposits we take in, we will soon discover that the bank is not obtaining any earnings. Better to put the money in our vaults to work by lending it to suitable borrowers and charging interest, which in practice is indeed banks' major source of earnings. When making these loans it will, of course, be necessary to keep sufficient reserves of cash on hand to meet the needs of day-to-day withdrawals, but it is not necessary to keep large amounts of cash because (unless there is a banking panic) only a small proportion of our depositors will ever wish to withdraw their deposits in a given period of time. That is why only a tiny fraction of a bank's deposits are kept as cash; by far the greater proportion is loaned out to the bank's customers.[17]

THE MULTIPLE EXPANSION OF BANK DEPOSITS

How do banks create or destroy money? Take a bank into which someone puts $1000 in cash as a demand deposit, that $1000 not having been in the banking system before. Perhaps the paper notes had been in a strong box for many years. Figure 19.8 shows that $1000 has been added to demand deposits.

The new demand deposit is an additional liability of the bank, but the bank also has a new asset, the $1000 in paper notes with which the depositor opened a new account and which is now "cash in the vault."

ASSETS	LIABILITIES
cash in vault	demand deposits
+$1000	+$1000

Figure 19.8. A new deposit of $1000 starts an expansion. The process of money creation begins with a new deposit that provides the bank with additional cash in its vault (reserves).

Let us assume that bankers believe it is necessary to keep 20% of the cash deposited to meet the average day-to-day demand for withdrawals. This cash-in-vault is called the bank's **reserves**. The remaining 80% can be loaned out at interest. As you can see in Figure 19.9, $200 is kept as reserves and the remaining $800 is lent to customers.

Under normal conditions, bankers unregulated by the state would choose to keep as reserves far less than 20% of their deposits. In nineteenth-century Great Britain, conservative bankers traditionally retained 10% of deposits, later reducing this to 8%. It is usually safe practice for day-to-day operations to keep as little as only 2%. (As we shall see in the next chapter, many countries have laws that require a certain portion of deposits to be retained as reserves.)

---

17.   That is also why one Canadian bank achieved a certain immortality by surviving for 40 years before the banking authorities discovered that it did not have enough healthy assets to cover its liabilities. The bank had made a number of very bad loans four decades previously. It did, however, have enough cash on hand to cover customers' day-to-day withdrawals. So, though technically it could not cover its liabilities, it continued to operate successfully until, decades later, bank examiners finally penetrated its doctored books.

THE SAFETY AND SOLVENCY OF BANKS

Twenty percent of demand deposits held as reserves is far more than reasonable banking practice would ever dictate, but not nearly enough if customers *en masse* begin to fear for their deposits, make large withdrawals, and cause a "run on the bank." Because loans and bonds cannot be liquidated immediately in response to customers pulling out their deposits, the bank might have to suspend payment and close its doors. Worse, in a recession a bank's loans might go bad. Farmland or condominiums serving as the collateral for mortgages may have dropped sharply in value, or factories may have shut down and may be unsellable even if the bank forecloses. These were common occurrences in the Great Depression, and the experience has been repeated to a lesser degree in the recessions since that time. In the 1980s, for example, many banks in Texas and Louisiana were hard-hit by changes in the economy; in 1990–91, New England's banks suffered severe damage. These are the reasons why government insurance schemes, such as the Federal Deposit Insurance Corporation (FDIC) in the United States, are important.

The FDIC was established as a result of the Great Depression of the 1930s. It now insures deposits up to $100,000, financed by a small premium paid by banks. Should the accumulated fund fail to cover the insurance payments, Congress would be expected to make up the difference. The FDIC had a rather quiet existence for many years, but it became more important as bank failures rose from only about 4 per year in the period 1956–1960 to 48 in 1983, reached the 100 mark in 1985, and passed 200 in 1988.

The savings and loan industry in the United States, recently much distressed, was insured by a different organization and had to be bailed out. Its situation was much more precarious than the commercial banking industry. One reason is that Congress prohibited S&Ls from offering adjustable-rate mortgages in the 1970s. The steady rise in interest rates in the 1980s meant that the S&Ls had to pay high interest rates to depositors even while most of its money was lent out to borrowers at fixed, lower rates of interest. That led to imprudent behavior as some S&Ls made risky loans at higher rates to try to keep up. Many of the loans went bad, leading to failure on the part of some institutions. Another factor contributing to the distress of the industry, as has been widely reported, was that some managers and owners of S&Ls turned out to be crooks.

Numerous economists now believe that deposit insurance needs reform. The failure of many savings and loan associations stands as a warning that bankers have been less prudent in their lending than would likely have been true in the absence of the insurance. Ideas being discussed include varying insurance premiums according to the degree of riskiness of a bank's loans as reported by its auditors; imposing a "deductible" on the amount of money that would be paid to the depositors of a failed bank; cutting back on the amount of each deposit insured (currently $100,000 per account, as already noted); and requiring the banks' investors (stockholders) to put up more of their own capital funds than they currently do.

Money Creation with 20% Kept as Reserves

The fact that commercial banks keep in reserve against their deposits an amount that is only a fraction of these deposits is important in understanding how money can be created or destroyed. In the following examples we will assume that banks keep 20% of their deposits as a reserve against those deposits. In that case, a bank that receives a new deposit of $1000 is required to keep $200 as reserves, but it will lend the remaining $800 to customers. That situation is shown in Figure 19.9.

ASSETS	LIABILITIES
cash in vault (reserves) +200	demand deposits +1000
loans +800	

Figure 19.9. Reserves and loans following a new deposit. A new deposit of $1000 increases cash in the vault (reserves) by $1000, but the bank does not need to hold that much as a reserve. If it keeps 20% for a reserve, it will hold only $200 and can lend out the remaining $800 to customers.

Now we must ask what happens to the $800 loan. Presumably it is spent immediately by the borrower, or it would not have been borrowed in the first place. Recipients of this spending will deposit their earnings in their own bank or banks. So once the initial $800 loan is spent, it will find its way into another bank, or group of banks. Any bank into which the proceeds of the loan are redeposited is called a "second-generation bank." Figure 19.10 shows, on the right, that the $800 spent by the borrower has been redeposited in a second-generation bank by the recipient of the spending. At this point, $800 in new money has been created because the $800 loan has become a new demand deposit. Demand deposits are, of course, counted as part of the nation's money supply.

1st GENERATION

ASSETS	LIABILITIES
reserves +200	demand deposits +1000
loans +800	

2nd GENERATION

ASSETS	LIABILITIES
reserves +160	demand deposits +800
loans +640	

Figure 19.10. Money creation. The initial loan has been deposited in a second-generation bank. The new $800 deposit is an addition to the money supply. Just as did the first bank, the second-generation bank keeps only 20% as a reserve and lends the remainder.

This process continues. If the second-generation banks keep 20% of the deposit in cash as reserves, they will loan 80% of $800, or $640, which will eventually find its way once again back into the banking system. When the loan is spent, recipients of the spending make deposits in their own banks, which can be called third-generation banks. Thus more new money is created in the amount of $640. In turn, 80% of this, or $512, will be loaned. On and on go the lending, spending, depositing, and relending, in ever smaller amounts, until they finally die away.

Calculating the Multiple Expansion of Bank Deposits

There is a simple formula for the **multiple expansion of bank deposits**, or "money multiplier" as it is sometimes called. With this formula, after enough time has elapsed to allow the process of lending, spending, and redepositing to exhaust itself, the exact increase in total deposits can be calculated. Because the multiple expansion of money involves a geometric progression, the formula looks similar to the national income multiplier of the previous two chapters. The two should never be confused.

The formula for the multiple expansion of bank deposits is:

$$\text{Final change in deposits} = \text{original new deposit} \times \frac{1}{\text{reserves kept (\%)}}$$

$$\text{In the example used above, } \Delta DD = \$1000 \times \frac{1}{.20} = \$5000.$$

Note that the *net* creation of new money is only $4000, because the formula includes the initial deposit of $1000, which was already part of the money supply when it was brought into the bank.

Thus deposits have been created over and above the initial deposit. The process will work, we should remind ourselves, only if the public is willing to keep its money in banks; if the banks are willing to loan these deposits with only a fraction retained as cash in the vault; and if people and businesses are willing to borrow from banks. (We might note that the multiple expansion of money does not create any new private wealth for bankers, beyond their increased income earned because the interest charged on their larger quantity of loans exceeds the interest paid on their larger quantity of deposits. The money creation means that assets are larger, but these are matched by larger liabilities.)

MULTIPLE CONTRACTION OF DEPOSITS

The process also works in reverse. Say $1000 is withdrawn from a bank and is buried in a tin can so that it does not reenter the banking system. The bank must pay $1000 to its (former) depositor from its cash-in-vault, that is, its reserves. T-account (**a**) on the left of Figure 19.11 displays the bank's total position—monetary contraction is easiest to grasp when looking at *total* deposits. Assume the bank had a total of $10,000 in demand deposits before the withdrawal, and that it was retaining $2000 as reserves while loaning the remaining $8000. In this case, following the $1000 withdrawal it will now have only $9000 in deposits, and since it paid the depositor out of its vault cash, cash on reserve has now decreased to $1000. See the middle T-account, (**b**), in the figure. But that amount of reserves is not 20% of $9000; it is only one-ninth, or 11%. So if our bank wants to keep 20% reserves, it must hike its reserve holdings to $1800, which is 20% of $9000. It can do this if it reduces its loans to $7200, as in the right-hand T-account, (**c**). Many a beginner sees this in mind's eye as urgent messages from the bank to borrowers aghast to find their loans have been called in. But this would be imprudent as well as illegal for most loans, because loans are advanced for fixed time periods. (A few loans really are "callable," as the term is, but they make up only a small proportion of total lending.) Instead, the bank simply does not make new loans when old ones are paid off, accomplishing the same end.

ASSETS	LIABILITIES	ASSETS	LIABILITIES	ASSETS	LIABILITIES
reserves $2000	demand deposits $10,000	reserves $1000	demand deposits $9000	reserves $1800	demand deposits $9000
loans $8000		loans $8000		loans $7200	
(a)		(b)		(c)	

Figure 19.11. The multiple contraction of money. Here we see that a withdrawal from a demand deposit begins a process of multiple contraction of the money supply that is a mirror image of the expansion process discussed above.

Necessarily the $800 must be withdrawn from banks somewhere—second-generation banks—for it is from bank accounts that borrowers obtain the funds to pay off old loans. So second-generation banks lose $800 in deposits. They, too, will have to cut back their loans if they are to maintain their level of cash in reserve at 20% of demand deposits. In turn, demand deposits will decline at other (third-generation) banks, and so on. The same formula applies to the multiple contraction of money as it did to multiple expansion, with reversed sign.[18]

With a $1000 withdrawal and a 20% reserve requirement, the multiple contraction would amount to

$$\Delta DD = -\$1000 \ \times \ \frac{1}{.20} \ = -\$5000$$

EXCESS RESERVES

With an amendment, the formula for multiple expansion and contraction can be made more accurate. Return to the example where $1000 is brought into the banking system as a new deposit. Banks might slow the expansion process if they decide, perhaps because of recession conditions, to hold **excess reserves** above the 20% that they had formerly chosen to hold, or were required to keep. If banks retain 5% more as excess reserves, they will hold $250 rather than $200, and they will lend not $800 but only $750. That means $50 which would have become a deposit in a second-generation bank does not do so, limiting the multiple expansion. The alteration needed to incorporate this braking element into the formula for expansion or contraction is to put it into the denominator of the fraction, as follows:

$$\text{Final change in deposits} = \text{original demand deposit} \ \times \ \frac{1}{RR + ER}$$

where RR = required reserves in percent, and ER = the percentage of excess reserves retained.

Here, if the original demand deposit = $1000, RR = .20 and ER = .05, then:

$$\$4000 = \$1000 \ \times \ \frac{1}{.20 + .05}$$

18. William Baumol and Alan Blinder tell a fine tale of student radicals in the late 1960s who, having assimilated this lesson in their economics courses, urged the public to protest (the Vietnam War? the capitalist system? both?) by withdrawing their bank deposits all on the same day. Up to a point these radicals knew their economics. Massive simultaneous withdrawals would indeed have been disruptive, at least until the Fed intervened with the tools to be explored in the next chapter. The student radicals did not, however, know their political science so well, and few people—or at least few people with major deposits—were listening.

The $4000 result is made up of $3000 in new money plus the $1000 original addition to bank deposits that began the expansion in the first place.[19]

CONCLUSION

This, then, is the analysis of the process by which money is created and destroyed within the banking system. The practice of keeping only a fraction of banks' deposits as reserves and lending the rest is the centerpiece of the mechanism. Banks create money when they make loans with their excess reserves. Changes in reserves have a greatly leveraged ability to change the level of deposits and hence the money supply. That is why bank reserves are often called high-powered money.[20]

The next chapter will employ this information to examine what a nation's central bank might do to control the creation and destruction process so as to bring about changes in the money supply—in other words, to carry out monetary policy. We will see that its method for doing so is to raise or lower the amount of reserves available to banks, thus altering the amount of high-powered money in the system. The chapter after that will survey the record of monetary policy in recent years, and the problems currently facing it.

SUMMARY

1) The money supply in its basic form is demand deposits (checking accounts) plus coins and paper currency. Checking accounts are much the largest of the three. Money demand is made up of a transactions demand for money to make purchases, a precautionary demand for money to meet emergencies, and a speculative demand to hedge against a fall in asset prices such as stocks and bonds. Given the demand for money, changes in the money supply can influence the economy by raising or lowering interest rates. Nations' monetary authorities (their official or central bank) have various tools with which they can influence the size of the money supply and thus interest rates. Attempts to do so are called "monetary policy."

2) Changes in interest rates can affect economic performance. Higher rates tend to restrict investment, some consumption, and some government spending. They also cause foreigners to purchase a country's currency to earn interest on it, thus raising the price (appreciating) and the value of the currency, so making exports more expensive and causing them to fall, and making imports cheaper and thus raising them and reducing consumption of domestic goods. As a result, higher interest rates lower total spending. Conversely, lower interest rates raise total spending. In each case there is a multiplier effect on total output.

---

19.   At one further level of sophistication, we can take into account that as the process of lending and spending is working itself out, the public might decide to hold some of the loan proceeds as cash for use in hand-to-hand circulation. This leakage into circulation, or "cash drain," stays out of the banking system and so cannot be used to create new deposits. If we assume that on average 5% of every loan is leakage into hand-to-hand circulation, then a new $1000 deposit leading to a new $800 loan will result in only a $760 deposit in a second-generation bank, with $40 representing the cash drain. This $40 is an addition to the money supply, but because it remains outside the banking system it will not trigger further expansion. A formula derived in more advanced texts can be used to calculate the change in the money supply in the presence of a cash drain. If CD = the percentage cash drain into hand-to-hand circulation, that formula is as follows:

$$\text{Final change in money supply} = \text{original demand deposit} \times \frac{1 + CD}{RR + ER + CD}$$

The formula indicates that the greater the leakage into hand-to-hand circulation, the smaller will be the expansion in the money supply from some initial new deposit in the banking system.

20.   Reserves share this trait with currency. As we shall see, additions to or subtractions from currency in circulation will also cause multiplied changes in the level of deposits. Currency is thus high-powered money as well. The term "monetary base" is sometimes used to mean the same thing as high-powered money—currency plus reserves.

3) An alternative way to analyze the impact of money supply changes on an economy is the quantity theory of money (MV = PY). It is much used by the so-called monetarist economists. The money supply (M) times the velocity of circulation of money (V) must equal the total value of transactions, that is the average price level (P) times the total real quantity of output (Y). The quantity theory is especially valuable as a tool for analyzing hyperinflation.

4) The banking system consists of many private, or commercial, banks, together with the government's official or central bank. In the United States, the central bank is the Federal Reserve System.

5) Commercial banks can create money. They can do so because they hold as reserves only a fraction of their total deposits. If a new deposit enters the banking system, a bank holds only a part of it as reserves and lends the remainder to customers. When spent, the loans become new deposits in the banking system, so expanding the money supply. The banks that have received the new deposits also hold only a fraction of their new deposits as reserves, and lend the rest, so continuing the expansion process. The multiple expansion can be determined by the "money multiplier," which is:

$$\text{final change in demand deposits} = \text{original new deposit} \times \frac{1}{\% \text{ reserves kept}}$$

If a deposit is removed from the banking system, the process works in reverse and the money supply contracts.

Chapter Key Words

Central bank: The government bank in charge of monetary policy and the supervision of commercial banks. In the United States, the Federal Reserve System.

Commercial banks: Privately owned banks in business for profit, supervised in most countries by a government central bank. Commercial banks take deposits from and lend money to the public.

Demand deposits: Checking accounts in banks, called demand deposits by economists since they are payable to the holder on demand. The largest component of the money supply defined as *M1*, which see.

Easy money or monetary ease: Central bank policy of expanding the growth of the money supply in order to lower interest rates and stimulate economic activity. A weapon against recession.

Excess reserves: Bank reserves in addition to those legally required by government.

Federal Reserve System (Fed): The U.S. central bank, unusual in that it consists of 12 regional banks instead of just one. In charge of supervising U.S. commercial banks and carrying out U.S. monetary policy.

High-powered money: The name sometimes used for bank reserves (and currency as well) because changes in their amounts will cause deposits, and hence the money supply, to change by a multiple.

Fisher Equation: MV = PY. See *Quantity theory of money*.

M1: The basic measure of the money supply, consisting of demand deposits plus coins and paper currency.

Monetarists: Economists who support the view that changes in the money supply are a good predictor of movements in final output.

Multiple expansion and contraction of money: The phenomenon whereby the money supply is raised or lowered by the action of commercial banks who receive deposits and then lend these deposits to borrowers. Explains how banks can create or destroy money. Can be managed through monetary policy to affect the size of the national income.

Quantity theory of money: A way to view the impact of money supply changes on an economy. Utilizes the Fisher equation MV = PY, where M is the money supply, V is the *velocity of circulation* (which see), P is the average price level, and Y is the quantity of real final output.

Reserves: That portion of a bank's deposits which are not loaned out to borrowers. Banks may be required to hold reserves by law (in which case they are subject to a "reserve requirement," but they may also choose to hold excess reserves.

Tight money or monetary tightness: Central bank policy of slowing the growth of the money supply or actually contracting it in order to raise interest rates and restrict economic activity. A weapon against inflation.

Velocity of circulation: The V in the quantity theory of money, MV = PY. The number of times the money supply changes hands annually.

CHAPTER QUESTIONS

1) Which of the following represent a movement along the money demand curve? Which represent a shift of that curve?
    a) A fall in consumers' disposable income reduces the transactions demand for money.
    b) Consumers hold less money because a rise in interest rates makes holding cash more expensive.
    c) Forecasts of severe winter weather increase the precautionary demand for money.
2) Suppose an economy is recovering from recession. As income increases, the transactions demand for money also increases. Show this change on a diagram of money demand and supply. How does the increased demand for money affect the quantity of money and the interest rate?
3) In 1979, the then chairman of the Fed, Paul Volker, began a policy of reducing the money supply. What was the effect of this policy on interest rates? How would you have expected the change in interest rates to affect investment, consumption, local government spending, and foreign trade?

4) Recall from the previous chapter that the long-run aggregate supply curve is vertical. Suppose the economy is in long run equilibrium at the intersection of AD and LRAS. If the central bank expands the money supply, what will happen to output and the price level in the long run?

5) (This question is a restatement of question 4 in terms of the quantity theory of money.) Suppose that in the long run Y is fixed at the potential level of output. Assume that V, the velocity of money, is fairly constant, but tends to increase somewhat during inflations. What will be the long run result of an increase in M?

6) You have been offered your choice of jobs: president of the Chase Manhattan Bank or president of the Federal Reserve Bank of New York. Which job would you do best at if your experience was in

    a)   Commercial loans to major corporations?
    b)   Regulating banks?
    c)   Determining the optimal monetary policy?
    d)   Marketing different types of accounts to consumers?
    e)   Evaluating when to bail out troubled banks?

7) Farmville is a small North Dakota town with only one bank, Farmville Savings. This bank keeps 10% of deposits as reserves, and lends the rest to local residents. These residents only shop at Farmville businesses, and the businesses keep their accounts at Farmville Savings. A new resident moves to town and deposits $1,000 in the bank. The bank lends out 90% of this money. Show the bank's T-account. Now the townsperson who received the loan spends it at a Farmville business, which re-deposits the money. How does the T-account look after this second round? Eventually, how much new money (including the original $1,000) will be created in Farmville?

8) One night in your dorm you order a pizza. You write a check for $10 on your local bank. Suppose your bank keeps five percent of deposits as reserves. Your bank clears the check by paying $10 out of its reserves. Five percent of this fall in reserves ($0.50) poses no problem, because deposits are lower by $10. But the other 95% ($9.50) is too large a reduction in reserves. Show on a T-account how your bank reacts to the withdrawal. By how much will your check eventually reduce the money supply?

The Tools of Monetary Policy

OVERALL OBJECTIVE: To demonstrate the tools of monetary policy—the reserve requirement, the discount rate, and open market operations—and discuss why various disadvantages with the first two of these have made open market operations the favored instrument.

MORE SPECIFICALLY:

- To explain the reserve requirement and show why changes in it are now seldom made.
- To introduce and discuss the discount rate charged on central bank loans to commercial banks, showing that sometimes it is a useful signaling device but sometimes just a follower of the financial markets.
- To consider open market operations, the primary weapon of monetary policy, demonstrating that central bank sales of securities on the open market work to restrict the money supply and the economy, while purchases work to expand the money supply and stimulate the economy.

In Chapter 19 we saw that increases or decreases in the amount of deposits held in the banking system can change the quantity of money, and so affect an economy's total spending and output. This chapter describes how central banks use this mechanism to initiate the enlargement or contraction of the nation's money supply. Chapter 21 will look at monetary policy in action and the problems in conducting it.

Central banks have in their possession three main weapons with which they can influence the supply of money. These are *reserve requirements*, the *discount rate*, and *open market operations*. Both the reserve requirement and the discount rate are now of less significance than formerly, but they are also the easier to understand. So we begin with them, rather than the present main weapon in the United States, the more complicated open market operations undertaken by the Fed.

► THE RESERVE REQUIREMENT

The first of the weapons is the **reserve requirement**. In Chapter 19 we noted that commercial bankers will always retain a certain percentage of their demand deposits as reserves. They do so to ensure that their banks have sufficient funds in the vault to pay off depositors who wish to withdraw their money. As only a small number of depositors will want to do this during any given day or week, the reserves dictated by a banker's own ideas of safety can be kept quite low; 6 to 8% would be far more than adequate under any normal conditions.

In most countries, governments determine how much banks must keep in reserve.[1] They require banks to hold reserves additional to what they would choose to keep as cash in the vault, usually as a deposit at the central bank. In the United States, the deposits are at the nearest Federal Reserve Bank. Banks failing to meet the requirement must pay a penalty to the Fed. Therefore banks commonly keep much less cash on hand than the legal required reserves the government compels them to keep. (But the proportion of banks' reserves made up of vault cash has been steadily rising in recent years, partly due to the need to hold cash for automatic transfer machines. Vault cash now makes up slightly more than half of all reserves.) It is important to note that whether banks keep their reserves as cash in the vault or as deposits in the Fed, they do not earn interest on them—the Fed pays no interest on its deposits.

The reasons for government reserve requirements are twofold. First, establishing a legal required reserve helps to guard against imprudent banking practices. More importantly, it allows the authorities to vary the requirements with monetary management in mind. The present U.S. law covering bank reserves, the Monetary Control Act of 1980, states explicitly that reserve requirements are a device for monetary policy. The requirements apply to a wide range of institutions including mutual savings banks, savings and loan associations, and credit unions.

Reserves required to be retained against demand deposits may be set by the Fed within a range of 8% to 14%. (The current U.S. reserve requirement is 10%.[2]) The Fed has the power to change the reserve requirement within the permitted limits. This gives it a tool with which it can influence the level of demand deposits.

The United States was the first country to use reserve requirement changes for policy purposes (in 1935), but the tool has considerably more leverage in some other countries.

---

1.   Some countries do not do so, however. Australia and Switzerland have no legal reserve requirements, and Great Britain's requirement, dating only from 1971, has little or no effect.

2.   The first $3.8 million of deposits is exempt from reserve requirements. Well over half the financial institutions covered (some 19,000 in 1990) are too small, with deposits below $3.8 million, to have to keep reserves. For institutions that have to keep reserves, the requirement is 3% for deposits between $0 and $46.8 million. The break points for the exemption and for the low 3% rate are recalculated annually, based on the total of all deposits. Those shown are for 1993. The Fed can also impose an additional requirement of 4 more percentage points on top of the ordinary 14% maximum (that is, 14% + 4 percentage points = 18%) if the Fed believes special measures are needed to halt monetary expansion. The Fed's permitted range before 1980 was larger, 7% to 22%. Reserve requirements against savings deposits used to exist, but are now abolished.

Germany can legally go to 30%, and Sweden has the highest permitted maximum of 50%. (At present, however, these countries' actual requirements are similar to those of other countries that have much narrower ranges.) For reasons we will explore, reserve requirement changes have become far less frequent in most countries, including the United States.

REDUCING AND RAISING RESERVE REQUIREMENTS

Though changes in reserve requirements to fight recession or inflation can be a powerful weapon of monetary policy, in recent years the policy has been used very sparingly for a number of reasons. To understand why, let us examine how such changes affect the money supply.

Reducing the Reserve Requirement

Consider first a reduction in the reserve requirement. Assume that banks are operating under a legal 20% requirement. (This is much higher than the current figure of 10%, and is beyond the legal limit in the United States, but it will simplify the arithmetic.) With a 20% requirement, we can set up a T-account for an individual bank such as the one in Figure 20.1.

ASSETS	LIABILITIES
reserves $2000	demand deposits $10,000
loans $8000	

Figure 20.1. A 20% reserve requirement. With deposits of $10,000 and a reserve requirement of 20%, a bank needs to hold $2000 as reserves, whether vault cash or as a deposit with the central bank. It can lend the remaining $8000.

The bank holds demand deposits of $10,000. It is required by law to keep minimum reserves of $2000 against these deposits. So the bank is free to lend that portion of its deposits not required for reserves, or $8000. When checks are written against these loans, the $8000 flows to other banks.

If the Fed lowers the reserve requirement to 10% (Figure 20.2), the bank is obligated to retain only $1000 in reserves against the $10,000 in deposits. This frees an extra $1000 from reserves and allows that sum to be used for lending to the bank's customers. Under normal economic circumstances the bank will be eager to find borrowers for these funds because it can earn commercial interest rates on the money loaned but not on its reserves. (Recall that money held as vault cash earns no interest and that the Fed pays no interest to commercial banks on reserve deposits.)

ASSETS	LIABILITIES
reserves $1000	demand deposits $10,000
loans $9000	

Figure 20.2. **A reduction in the reserve requirement to 10%.** If the reserve requirement is lowered to 10%, only $1000 rather than $2000 needs to be held as reserves against $10,000 in deposits. The excess reserves of $1000 can be lent, so loans rise to $9000.

If the $1000 freed up by the reduction in the reserve requirement is loaned, the process is not yet ended. The new $1000 in loans will rapidly be spent by the borrower (else the money would not have been borrowed in the first place). When the money is spent, it comes into the hands of other firms and households, which will deposit their receipts into their own bank or banks. The banking system will now have acquired $1000 in additional deposits. Under the new 10% reserve requirement, second-generation banks, whose combined T-account is shown in Figure 20.3, are legally obligated to keep in reserve $100. They are free to loan the remaining $900 to customers.

SECOND-GENERATION BANKS

ASSETS	LIABILITIES
reserves +$100	demand deposits +$1000
loans +$900	

Figure 20.3. **Monetary expansion with a reduction in the reserve requirement.** Second-generation banks that receive $1000 in new deposits will, with a 10% reserve requirement, keep $100 as reserves and lend the remaining $900.

The expansion continues, because the $900 in new loans when spent will come into the hands of recipients who will deposit the funds in their (third-generation) banks. These banks, their reserve requirement also lower than before, will hold 10% of their deposits as reserves, and are free to loan the remainder. So it goes, round after round. The effect of lowering the reserve requirement is thus to permit an expansion in the nation's money supply.

Raising the Reserve Requirement

The converse policy of raising the reserve requirement is a tool for reducing the money supply. If the reserve requirement is 10%, then a single bank's T-account might appear as follows: demand deposits are $10,000, required reserves are $1000, and the individual bank in this position can loan $9000.

If the requirement is raised to 20%, a bank with $10,000 in demand deposits will now be legally obligated to boost its reserves. It could do this either by increasing the cash held in its vault to $2000, or by raising its deposits placed in the central bank to the same figure, or by some combination of the two. In order to get the extra $1000 for its reserves, the bank will have to lower its total lending from the former figure of $9000 to a new level of $8000. To accomplish this, the bank will not renew some old loans that come due. On any given business day, some old loans made in the past will be repaid by customers. Ordinarily, the bank would take these funds as they come in and then lend them out again to new borrowers. But to reduce its level of lending, the bank can choose not to make new loans of $1000 that day with the funds obtained as the old loans are paid off. The $1000 can be used to build up the bank's reserves.

The process does not end at this point. The customers who have paid off the $1000 in old loans very likely obtained the funds from a demand deposit in a bank. So wherever the borrowers withdrew the money—it may be the same bank that made the loan, or another bank, or several others in the second generation—$1000 in demand deposits is lost. These second-generation banks must then build up their reserve accounts, which were depleted when they paid out the $1000. They will reduce their level of lending, resulting in further withdrawals of deposits from third-generation banks, and so forth. Thus, a reduction in the money supply can be achieved.

RESERVE REQUIREMENT CHANGES IN THE PAST

Though the Fed has become reluctant to use reserve requirement changes for monetary management, historically the weapon was used with some frequency. In the period 1958–1960, for example, signs of recession were appearing and the Fed attempted to expand the money supply. The reserve requirement started at a high point of $19\frac{1}{2}\%$, but the Fed, adopting an easy money policy, cut the ratio to $16\frac{1}{2}\%$ in five separate steps. With inflation a problem during the Vietnam War, the Fed adopted a tight money policy, raising the reserve requirement from $16\frac{1}{2}\%$ in early 1968 in three steps to 18% in July 1973. Deepening recession and Fed desires to expand the money supply in the mid-1970s brought two cuts in 1975 and 1976 that took the ratio from $17\frac{1}{2}\%$ to $16\frac{1}{4}\%$. The lowest ever (most expansionary) reserve requirement has been 10%, reached during the Great Depression and again in 1992. The highest (most restrictive) was 22% in 1948 during the post-World War II inflation. In the 1930s, some of the individual changes were very large, reaching as high as 4 percentage points at a time. (In the 10 months from August 1936 to May 1937, the Fed *raised* the reserve requirement from 10% to 20%, even though economic recovery from the Depression was just getting underway. It proved to be one of the great mistakes ever of monetary policy and contributed to halting the revival.)

PROBLEMS WITH CHANGING THE RESERVE REQUIREMENT

Though changing the reserve requirement is a potentially powerful instrument, it shares a problem with the other forms of monetary policy. During a recession, when the policy is to expand the money supply, the central bank can always provide the banking system with plenty of additional reserves so that banks will be able to increase their lending. The worse the recession, however, the less likely that more lending will appeal to commercial banks. From their point of view, lending to firms is bad business when borrowers are defaulting. Reacting conservatively, bankers may decide simply to hold more reserves than are legally required, and these **excess reserves** cannot then stimulate the economy. Central banks have no power to compel banks to lend, nor to compel businesses to borrow. So during a serious recession, providing reserves to the banking system may not have the desired effect.

There is also the possibility of a destabilizing "announcement effect." A reserve requirement change is very visible, one of the most dramatic steps a central bank can take. When firms and financial markets hear that a change has been made in the requirement, say a cut to fight recession, they may react perversely. The manager of a firm picks up the morning paper and reads: "Fed lowers reserve requirement." That manager might in the next few minutes reach for the phone and cancel the firm's upcoming investment plans on the ground that the Fed has just confirmed the fear that the economic outlook is grim. This was certainly not what the Fed intended. Furthermore, the high visibility of the step presents an obvious target for anyone in politics who opposes it. If a quieter and less ostentatious method were available, the Fed might well want to use it.

For 12 years after President Carter signed the Monetary Control Act of 1980, there were no further changes in the conventional reserve requirements, and some commentators claimed that this particular weapon was obsolete.[3] In April 1992, however, the Fed surprised these commentators by cutting the reserve requirement from 12% to 10% as part of its campaign to stimulate the economy. There was still some life left in this once prominent tool of monetary policy.

There is a school of thought that calls for the abolition of reserve requirements on the grounds that the Fed's nonpayment of interest on the reserves it holds amounts to an unfair tax on commercial banks. (This is apparently a reason why the Bank of Canada is eliminating reserve requirements during 1994.) Though U.S. commercial banks do complain loudly about this cost, about three-quarters of all banks meet their reserve requirements with their vault cash alone; for them the nonpayment of interest on deposits at the Fed is costless. Even for the others, the cost is relatively modest. Still, complaints from commercial banks and early-1990s Fed fears that banking profits had fallen substantially persuaded the Fed to take the position that interest should be paid on reserve deposits. It argues that paying interest would be a better outcome than ending reserve requirements. Thus far Congress has not agreed because it would be costly to do so. The 1992 reduction in the reserve requirement from 12% to 10% was widely reported to be another attempt by the Fed to raise commercial bank profitability, so making banks more willing to undertake risks and make loans.

▶ THE DISCOUNT RATE

The next form of monetary policy to be taken up is changing the **discount rate**. This is the interest rate charged to commercial banks that want to borrow from the central bank.[4] When the U.S. Federal Reserve system was first set up in 1913, based on European experience it was expected that the discount rate would be the major means of controlling the growth and size of the nation's money supply. Until the 1920s this was the case, and it still is in numerous foreign

---

3.   In late 1990, with concern about recession growing, the Fed did eliminate the 3% reserve requirement on corporate certificates of deposit. There have also been some extensions of the requirement, such as to Eurodollar accounts (described later in the book).

4.   At an earlier time, this was called the rediscount rate.

countries. Banks, finding themselves low on reserves, may borrow funds for their reserve accounts and so meet their legal obligations. These legal obligations must be met at the close of business on Wednesdays as it happens, since reserves are computed as a weekly average from each Thursday until the next Wednesday against the weekly average of deposits during the same period.[5] Since loans from the Fed to banks ordinarily involve very little risk, the rate of interest charged can be kept lower than the rates charged by banks to private borrowers.

The Fed can change this discount rate. For instance, when inflation threatens, the Fed can be expected to raise the discount rate, thereby deterring banks from borrowing from it. Banks that might have been able to expand their own loans by borrowing from the Fed will be discouraged from doing so.

When recession looms, the Fed will probably lower the discount rate. The lower rate will encourage banks to borrow from the Fed. This may enable them to avoid reducing their loans to businesses and consumers, or even to raise their level of lending. This role, lender to banks that might otherwise be in trouble in a recession, has caused the Fed and other central banks around the world to be called lenders of last resort, as mentioned in the previous chapter. Central banks always have funds to lend in time of need because, as we shall see, they can create them.

The mechanism can be illustrated with a set of T-accounts as in Figure 20.4. To illustrate how discounting is designed to work, we will need a separate T-account for the Federal Reserve System, shown in the middle of the figure. In reality, the Federal Reserve System has many items in its assets and liabilities columns, and the Fed's T-account could be complicated a great deal if all were to be shown. Fortunately, this is not necessary, and we can simplify by concentrating on only those assets and liabilities that play a role in discounting. That tactic is followed in Figure 20.4.

The liability of the Fed most important for this analysis is the reserve deposits of commercial banks with the Federal Reserve System. Recall that banks keep a significant proportion of their legal required reserves on deposit with the Fed. To the Fed, these are a deposit owed, a liability. To a commercial bank, these same required reserves are a deposit owned, an asset. Therefore the same reserves appear in two places in the T-accounts. See how at (3a) and (3b) in the T-accounts, commercial bank reserves of $200 held on deposit at the Fed are a liability to the Fed and an asset to the banks. On the asset side of the Federal Reserve T-account, the item essential for an understanding of discounting is "loans and discounts" (2). Like commercial banks, the Fed's loans are an asset.

Now let us use these T-accounts to trace the discounting procedure. Say that a commercial bank finds its reserves have fallen below the required level by $200, as in (1) on the left. This bank is legally required to add $200 to its reserves. The bank can contact the "discount window" of its district's Federal Reserve bank and negotiate a loan.[6] The loan shows up on the Fed's books (2) as an asset with a corresponding deposit added to the commercial bank's reserves (3a). These new reserves are an additional asset to the commercial bank (3b), balanced by a new liability in the form of the loan itself which is a "bill (loan) payable" (4).

The end result is that the commercial bank has acquired the $200 in reserves that was needed to avoid reducing its loans. The entire mechanism also works in reverse, with a rise in the discount rate making such loans more expensive and so discouraging them.

---

5.   Since 1984, required reserves have been calculated against present deposits. Before that, for some time they were determined on the basis of deposits as they had been two weeks earlier. The result is that banks have much less time to adjust their portfolios and rearrange loans than they once did.

6.   The term discount window is founded on historical experience. In the Federal Reserve banks, some of them at any rate, there was a counter window to which bankers could bring commercial paper (loan documents, bonds, and so forth) for "rediscounting." In effect, this commercial paper provided the collateral for loans by the Fed to commercial banks. The system has changed, but the term discount window has not.

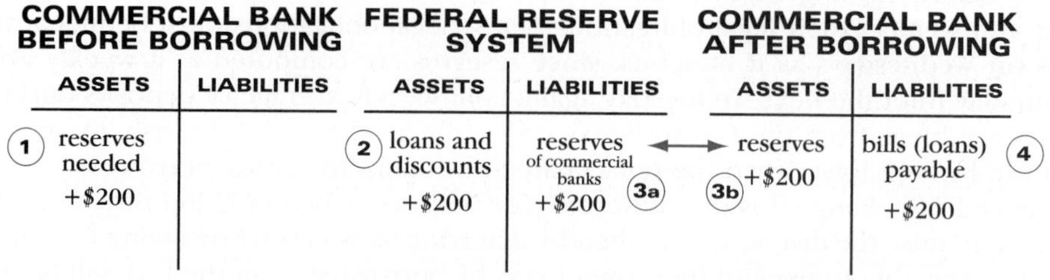

COMMERCIAL BANK BEFORE BORROWING		FEDERAL RESERVE SYSTEM		COMMERCIAL BANK AFTER BORROWING	
ASSETS	**LIABILITIES**	**ASSETS**	**LIABILITIES**	**ASSETS**	**LIABILITIES**
① reserves needed +$200		② loans and discounts +$200	reserves of commercial banks +$200 ③a	③b reserves +$200	bills (loans) payable +$200 ④

Figure 20.4. Borrowing from the Fed can provide banks with additional reserves. On the left is a commercial bank that needs reserves. It can obtain what it needs by negotiating a loan at the Fed, which credits the reserve account of the commercial bank.

DIFFICULTIES WITH THE DISCOUNT RATE

There are some specific difficulties involved in using the discount rate as a policy instrument. Though this device has been important in many countries and still retains a major role in some (Japan, for example, and Britain to a degree[7]), in the United States it faces a barrier. On the whole, American bankers do not like to borrow from the Fed. Many bankers never borrow at all from that source, and a large substitute market called the "federal funds market" has developed among commercial banks themselves. In this market, bankers who wish to borrow can find other bankers who wish to lend at the so-called "federal funds rate,"[8] thereby avoiding the Fed and its discount rate policies altogether. One reason for avoiding the Fed is bankers' fears that borrowing will be taken as a sign of financial weakness, and their reluctance to subject themselves to the examinations of the books that are part of the borrowing process.

This "reluctance theory" exerts a strong influence. Discounts now rarely reach even 5% of total reserves in the United States, and 2 to 3% is typical. (Early in the Fed's history they furnished 30–40% of reserves.) As a result, changes in the discount rate now have a very small actual impact on the size of the nation's money supply.

THE DISCOUNT RATE AS A SIGNAL

Perhaps *because* of the small impact on the money supply, the discount rate has been used to some extent as a signaling device by the Fed. Should the monetary authorities believe that recession threatens, they can announce, with appropriate fanfare, that the discount rate has been lowered. The result may be minute in the way of direct influence on the money supply. It will be clear, however, that the Fed's position about the threat of recession is serious, and that it could bring to bear its more powerful weapons. In many cases, the Fed says as much when it makes its press release. A release might begin "In the light of continuing declines in retail sales and rising unemployment, the Fed today announced a decrease in the discount rate...." Similarly, if inflation threatens the discount rate can be *raised* as a signal that further action is being contemplated by the Fed.

Even in its role as a signaling device with little direct effect on the money supply, discount rate changes are not free from controversy. The same type of adverse "announcement effect" that afflicts reserve requirement changes may attach to discount rate changes as well, with the public reacting perversely to an announcement of a rise or a fall.

---

7.   Britain in 1981 abolished its discount rate, called in that country the minimum lending rate. On Treasury instructions, the Bank of England still does intervene in credit markets, however, making it harder or easier for commercial banks to borrow funds on their own.

8.   In Britain this is called the "Lombard rate." The name has a nice derivation. Commercial banking first arose in Italy during the Middle Ages, particularly in the region of Italy known as Lombardy. A London street where many early banks established themselves accordingly received the name Lombard Street, and from that name came the term Lombard rate, the interest rate charged when one bank borrows from another. Some other countries use the same term.

FOLLOWING RATHER THAN LEADING

For some time during the inflationary 1970s, the Fed came to be a follower with the discount rate, rather than a leader. It appeared to be changing the rate in response to changes in other interest rates, rather than as a policy measure.[9] As inflation drove commercial bank interest rates up, the Fed was forced to raise the discount rate. If it had not done so, then banks would have greatly increased their borrowing of reserves from the Fed at the lower discount rate, so stimulating bank loans when that was not desirable. Even as it was, in some months of the early 1980s borrowed reserves rose to 6–8% of all reserves.

The same argument can be made for recessions. If an economy's market rates of interest fall, but no change is made in the discount rate, banks will borrow fewer reserves. Their managers will be reluctant to pay the Fed a relatively high rate while the earnings from their loans are falling. The Fed may then feel it has to reduce the discount rate just to keep in step, or else the decline in borrowed reserves will act to reduce the money supply. Here again, the Fed may be following rather than leading.

A LOOK AT HOW THE FED HAS CHANGED THE DISCOUNT RATE

The lowest discount rate in the Fed's history was just $\frac{1}{2}$ of 1% for several years in the 1940s, and in 1954 it was still only $1\frac{1}{2}$%. The highest discount rate was 14% in 1981. Starting from 5% in January, 1973, the rate advanced in seven steps to 8% by mid-1974. At that time the figure was the highest in the Fed's history. The 8% figure of 1974 was just a beginning, however. The rate was boosted again during the late-1970s inflation, this time in earnest, with 12 changes in a long climb that reached 13% in February 1980. It slipped back to 10% before rising once again to its all-time peak of 14% in May 1981. In the early-1980s battle against inflation, the discount rate was kept high for a long time even as recession set in, but a steady decline then ensued, to $5\frac{1}{2}$% in August 1987. With fears of inflation recurring from late in 1987, the rate was moved up again in three steps, to 7% in February 1989, where it remained until December 1990. At that time, growing concern for recession caused the Fed to lower the rate in five steps to $3\frac{1}{2}$% in December 1991. The last cut of 1991 was one full percentage point, the largest since 1981, and the $3\frac{1}{2}$% rate was the lowest since 1964. The Fed cut the discount rate again, to 3%, in July 1992. The 3% nominal rate was about zero in real terms. In February 1994, the Fed raised the rate to $3\frac{1}{4}$% in recognition that the slow economic recovery from the early-'90s recession was speeding up.

The Fed appears to have been using the discount rate as a signaling device in the 1990s, whereas the many changes dating back to the late 1970s probably involved a mixture of following the financial markets and trying to send signals to them.

---

9.   The same process has taken place in Japan, where from 1988 the Bank of Japan's discount rate has tended to follow events rather than lead them.

For years there has been a school of thought that the discount rate should be permanently changed to a market rate plus a penalty to discourage banks from borrowing from the Fed. This step would be tantamount to abandoning the discount rate as a policy tool.

Changes in both the reserve requirement and the discount rate are highly visible. For the Fed, that visibility is not an advantage. Changing them can have adverse political repercussions, and there could be a perverse announcement effect as well. Furthermore, in the United States the reserve requirement has become caught up in institutional changes within the Fed, and the discount rate, relatively ineffectual anyway, has for long periods proved to be more follower of market conditions than leader. So we turn next to what is the Fed's most powerful tool, open market operations.

▶ OPEN MARKET OPERATIONS

Open market operations involve the purchase and sale of U.S. government securities by the Fed in order to influence money and credit markets. These operations can be adjusted with the utmost delicacy while, at the same time, they attract little public attention. They are a major device of money management for most large-country central banks, and they are by a considerable margin the chief instrument in the United States.

To illustrate how open market operations affect the banking system and the money supply, we can once more view a T-account for a commercial bank. Because these operations alter the Fed's holdings of U.S. government securities, we will also need to include a T-account for the Fed.

The assets and liabilities that play a role in open market operations are shown in Figure 20.5.

FEDERAL RESERVE SYSTEM		COMMERCIAL BANKS	
ASSETS	**LIABILITIES**	**ASSETS**	**LIABILITIES**
U.S. gov't securities	reserves of commercial banks	reserves	demand deposits

Figure 20.5. Beginning the analysis of open market operations. Open market operations undertaken by the Fed involve it in the purchase or sale of U.S. government securities. These operations are intended to alter the level of reserves and deposits in the commercial banking system, and hence the size of the money supply.

Recall that the reserve deposits of commercial banks with the Federal Reserve appear in two places on the T-accounts. To the Fed they are a deposit owed, a liability; to a commercial bank they are a deposit owned, an asset.

On the asset side of the Federal Reserve T-account we see holdings by the Fed of U.S. government securities. U.S. government securities are all the various sorts of U.S. Treasury bills, notes, and bonds that have been sold by the Treasury to finance government spending in excess of tax revenues. The total amount outstanding of all these securities held by firms, banks, private citizens, and governments both foreign and domestic is the amount the U.S. government has borrowed. It is the U.S. "national debt." The different names—bills, notes, and bonds—indicate the different maturities; Treasury bills (T-bills) are short-term, some maturing in 90 days, others in six months or a year. Notes are intermediate. Bonds are long-term, some maturing in 10 years, others in 30 years. These securities earn interest, recently about $11 billion, which pays the Fed's operating expenses and provides a substantial balance that is transferred back to the Treasury.

Open market operations by the Fed consist mainly of buying or selling the short-term issues—long-term Treasury bonds figure little in these transactions—on the "open market" for government securities in New York City.

INCREASING THE MONEY SUPPLY WITH OPEN MARKET OPERATIONS

The Fed's decision to buy or sell these U.S. government securities will have an effect on the nation's money supply. For example, the Fed can pump additional dollars into the private banking system by purchasing securities on the open market. By doing so, the Fed is transferring dollars into the banking system that can be used as a basis for an expansion of loans. In turn this increases the level of demand deposits and expands the money supply. Let us trace such a transaction in detail.

The Fed Makes an Open-Market Purchase from a Commercial Bank

The Fed begins by buying U.S. government securities on the open market. The T-accounts for both the Fed and for a single commercial bank are provided to illustrate the transaction. The securities could be purchased from commercial banks, which own very many of them, or from the general public. In this first case we assume the purchase by the Fed in the amount of $1000 is from one commercial bank. (See Figure 20.6.)

First of all, the Fed is now the owner of $1000 worth of U.S. government securities that it did not have before. So on the asset side of the Fed's T-account, at (1a), we see an entry of +$1000. On the asset side of the commercial bank that made the sale, at (1b), we see –$1000, showing that the commercial bank no longer owns the security. When the Fed buys a security from a bank, it will ordinarily pay by adding to that bank's reserve account, shown here at (2a) and (2b) as an addition of +$1000 to the Fed's liabilities and to the commercial bank's assets. No cash changes hands, of course. The addition will be a computer entry of +$1000 to the commercial bank's reserves.

As the commercial bank's demand deposits are unchanged so far, the entire $1000 added to reserves is excess to requirements. This allows the bank to seek out higher earnings by lending out the entire $1000. This is lost to reserves (3a) and becomes a new loan (3b). When that loan is spent, the proceeds become a new demand deposit in the banking system (4). So begins a monetary expansion that leads to yet more loans and more deposits.

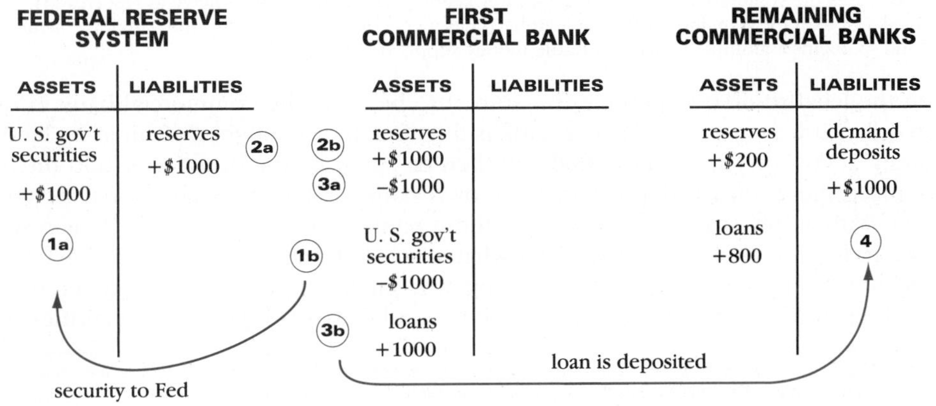

Figure 20.6. A Fed open market purchase from a bank starts an expansion of M. The Fed's purchase of a security from a commercial bank (1a and 1b) adds to that bank's reserves (2a and 2b). These are excess reserves, and we can expect the commercial bank to loan the funds (3b), thus removing them from reserves (3a). The loan becomes a new demand deposit in the banking system (4), and so begins a multiple expansion of the money supply.

The formula for the multiple expansion of money can predict the size of the expansion. If the legal reserve requirement is 20%, then the calculation is

$$\Delta DD \times \frac{1}{.20} = \$1000 \times \frac{1}{.20} = \$1000 \times 5 = \$5000.$$

Note that the entire $5000 is new money, because the expansion process started not with $1000 in existing money brought into the banking system, but instead as a new $1000 demand deposit made possible by the Fed's purchase of the security.[10]

The Fed Makes an Open Market Purchase from a Private Individual

The Fed might also purchase the security from a private individual, rather than from a commercial bank. In that case, it would add the security to its assets shown at (1) in Figure 20.7 and pay the individual by check. It is essential to discover what happens to this check. The individual who sold the securities to the Fed now has it and will deposit it in a commercial bank. Here it becomes a new demand deposit of $1000, shown at (2) in the middle T-account below. Notice that this is a new net addition to the banking system's sum total of deposits.

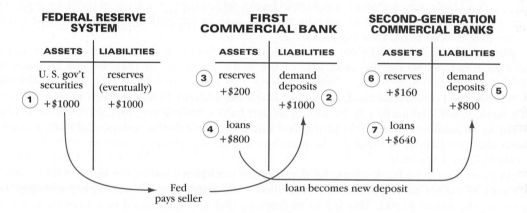

Figure 20.7. A Fed open market purchase from an individual starts an expansion of M. The Fed's purchase of a security from a private individual (1) leads to a new deposit in the seller's account (2). That increases the commercial bank's reserves. After keeping the required percentage as reserves (3), the bank can loan the remainder (4). The loan becomes a new demand deposit in the banking system (5), and so begins a multiple expansion of the money supply (6 and 7).

With the legal reserve requirement assumed to be 20%, the commercial bank in question must keep only $200 as reserves (3). The bank is thus free to seek higher earnings by lending out the remaining $800 (4). The loan of $800 will then be spent by the borrowers, and the eventual recipients place the $800 on deposit in their own bank or banks as additional new demand deposits (5). With a 20% reserve requirement, these banks must retain only $160 as reserves (6) and are free to lend to their own customers whatever is left over after meeting this figure. That comes to $640 (7). The process goes on, growing ever smaller, until no further repercussions are felt. The end result of the multiple expansion of demand deposits following a securities purchase

---

10.   The $5000 figure assumes that banks are "loaned up" so that no excess reserves are retained, and no leakage into hand-to-hand circulation occurs. In the last chapter, the full formula for the multiple expansion of money was shown to be:

$$\text{final change in money supply} = \text{original demand deposit} \times \frac{1 + CD}{RR + ER + CD}$$

where RR = required reserves, ER = excess reserves, and CD = cash drain (leakage into hand-to-hand circulation). So if excess reserves of 2% are retained and leakage into hand-to-hand circulation is 3%, then the calculation would be

$$\$1000 \times \frac{1 + .03}{.20 + .02 + .03} = \$4120.$$

from a private individual eventually works out to the same amount as in the case where the Fed buys the security from a commercial bank—$5000.

The general principle is that the Fed can buy securities on the open market whenever it wishes to start a multiple expansion of bank deposits. In this way it can engineer an expansion of the money supply. There is no restriction on the use of this mechanism, and its unlimited potential for monetary expansion, beyond the rationality of those who manage the Fed.[11]

The Fed's open market operations to increase the money supply are subject to the same difficulties already discussed with regard to the other types of monetary policy. To expand the money supply in a recession the Fed can flood the banking system with new reserves, thus providing a large pool of excess reserves available for lending. Yet even if a high level of excess reserves is pumped into the system, there is no guarantee that firms or individuals will want to borrow. They may very well decide *not* to do so when business conditions look very bad. At the same time there is no guarantee that banks will want to lend. Ordinarily they would wish to, in order to earn market interest rates on their excess reserves; but in bad times, they may prefer to park their money in low-yield government securities, or even hold excess reserves, rather than lending to firms under depressed economic conditions. Of course they will lose the better interest rate they would otherwise earn on their loans, but they may prefer this to the much higher losses if firms begin to fail and default on their repayments. In short, if banks follow a conservative policy, they may foil the intent of the Fed's expansionary open market operations.

RESTRICTING THE MONEY SUPPLY WITH OPEN MARKET OPERATIONS

What will the Fed's open market policy be if it wishes to *restrict* the money supply? In this case the Fed will want to *sell* U.S. government securities on the open market. The Fed thereby takes dollars away from the private banking system, reducing bank reserves and initiating a contraction in the money supply.

Trace the effect if the sale is to a commercial bank. If the Fed sells $1000 in securities, shown at (1) in Figure 20.8, then a commercial bank now has an extra asset (2). The Fed would receive payment simply by debiting the reserve account of the bank, (3a) and (3b) in the figure.

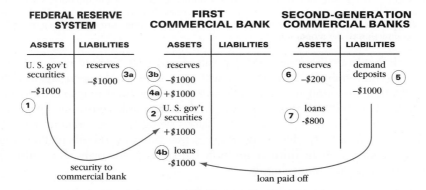

Figure 20.8. A Fed open market sale to a bank starts a contraction of M. The Fed's sale of a security to a commercial bank (1 and 2) causes a reduction in that bank's reserves (3a and 3b). With reserves now below the required level, we can expect the commercial bank to reduce its lending (4b), using the funds so acquired to build up its reserves (4a). Those who paid off the loans (4b) took the funds out of demand deposits in second-generation banks (5), so beginning a multiple contraction of the money supply (6 and 7).

---

11.   The Fed's powers to expand the money supply were formerly limited by a link to government holdings of gold. As an asset, the Fed was required to hold 35% of the value of its bank reserve accounts in gold, stored at Fort Knox, Tennessee, and in the basement of the Federal Reserve Bank of New York. In the 1940s this requirement was impinging on the Fed's ability to expand reserves, so Congress quietly reduced the gold percentage to 25%. Economists long suspected that if the 25% figure posed problems for further expansion, it too would be lowered, and indeed in 1965 it was simply abolished. A requirement for similar percentages of gold to be held against the value of Federal Reserve notes was abolished in 1968. This was the last tie between gold and U.S. money, a tie that some businesspeople, but few economists, would like to see restored.

No change has occurred in demand deposits. Unless this bank was holding excess reserves, it must add $1000 to its reserves (4a) by calling in loans (4b). Borrowers repay the loans by writing checks on deposits in second-generation banks, which will cause a fall in demand deposits in these banks (5). That would cause a decline of *their* reserves and loans as well (6) and (7). A process of multiple contraction in the money supply sets in, measured by the usual formula, this time with the signs negative. No monetary contraction would occur, however, as long as excess reserves exist; if they are present, they will have to be absorbed first before the contraction gets underway.

If instead the Fed sells $1000 in government securities to the general public, rather than to a bank, the T-accounts have a somewhat different appearance. They would show the Fed's ownership of securities declining by $1000 at (1) on the left of Figure 20.9. At the same time, the buyer has to pay the Fed, and assuming the $1000 in payment comes by means of a check, then the buyer's demand deposit in a commercial bank will decline by that amount, as shown at (2) in the middle of the figure.

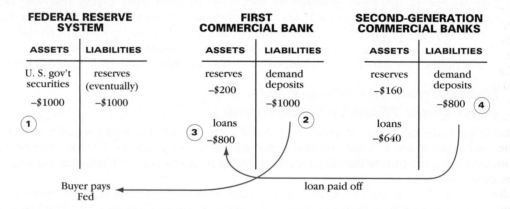

Figure 20.9. A Fed open market sale to a private individual starts a contraction of M. The Fed's sale of a security to a private individual (1) leads to a reduction in deposits in the buyer's account (2). That decreases the commercial bank's reserves. The bank must therefore call in loans (3). The funds to pay off the loans comes from demand deposits in second-generation banks (4), so beginning a multiple contraction of the money supply.

If the bank that loses these demand deposits is currently "loaned up," and again assuming that the reserve requirement is 20%, then it will have kept as a reserve against that $1000 of deposits only $200. It must find an extra $800, and the means for doing so is to reduce the bank's own level of lending by $800.[12] If this occurs at (3), then the bank's customers paying off old loans must obtain $800 themselves, the source of the funds being the second-generation banks. Here, in turn, deposits are down (4), depleting reserves that must be rebuilt to their required level, meaning further contraction in third-generation banks, and so forth. The entire process is a multiple contraction of the money supply.

A SUMMARY OF OPEN MARKET OPERATIONS

A short summary statement about open market operations may be helpful. Fed purchases and sales of U.S. government securities (Treasury bills, notes, and bonds) will alter bank reserves and will therefore initiate a multiple expansion or contraction of the money supply. The Fed *adds* to bank reserves by *buying* securities on the open market. Deposit expansion follows, though this

---

12. Perhaps the bank might build up its reserves in another way, by selling $800 worth of U.S. government securities that it owned. This would not avoid the contraction, however. Since the Fed is not buying, the sale would be to the general public, with the payment from demand deposits. So these deposits decrease and the multiple contraction is generated anyway.

depends on the reaction of commercial banks and their customers. The former must be willing to lend, the latter to borrow. When the Fed reduces bank reserves by *selling* securities on the open market, then deposit contraction occurs because banks are legally obligated to meet the reserve requirements for demand deposits. There will be some delay in the contraction process if banks are holding excess reserves. If this is so, sales of securities must continue until the excess reserves are eliminated, for only then will banks find themselves under the necessity of reducing their loans and hence the level of demand deposits in the banking system.

HOW THE FED CAN OVERCOME PUBLIC RELUCTANCE TO BUY OR SELL SECURITIES

A question might arise as to how open market operations could be conducted if banks and individuals were reluctant to buy or sell securities. For example, in a period of recession, why would holders of government securities want to sell them when these securities are safe and earning interest, and profits elsewhere are low? The Fed might want to buy securities on the open market to stimulate the economy, but who then would sell these securities? Or perhaps the Fed is concerned about the danger of inflation. In that case of boom times, profits are probably high, lending opportunities are good, and interest rates on government securities may temporarily not be competitive with these other uses of funds. The Fed might want to sell securities on the open market to cool off the boom, but who would buy the securities? Indeed, the Fed has no powers to *force* people or banks either to buy or to sell.

The answer to the question lies in the fact that the Fed's bond purchases and sales are on a free market. If it wishes to buy securities, but if sellers are not abundant at the going price for bonds, it can offer a higher price through its brokers. Recall from the previous chapter the connection between the prices of securities and interest rates—when the prices of securities rise, that means the interest rate on those securities falls. Some banks and individuals, seeing the price of the securities they own rising, but the interest rate on them falling, would change their opinion—sellers materialize. If the Fed wishes to *sell* but encounters difficulties in finding *buyers* at the going price for bonds, it offers large enough lots for sale so that securities prices fall and the interest rates on these securities rise. A security that can be acquired cheaply but which bears a high interest rate is attractive. Buyers appear. Presumably only some very unusual event—war, revolution, economic debacle of some sort, or, as in some countries, a government decision to fix the price of bonds and so peg interest rates—would interfere with the Fed's ability to conduct open market operations.

AN INHERENT CONFLICT BETWEEN THE FED AND THE U.S. TREASURY

There is a potential problem concerning the securities markets, in that open market operations may make U.S. Treasury financing more difficult. Say that the Treasury is attempting to sell new securities to the general public to finance government spending over and above the level of tax collections. In other words, a budget deficit is being financed. The Treasury understands that its sales of new securities, by increasing the supply of these securities, will lower securities prices and raise interest rates. That will boost the costs of its financing. It would prefer the Fed to keep interest rates *low* through its monetary policy. Similarly, when old securities come due, the Treasury will want to replace them at no *higher* interest rate than before. If the Fed complies, keeping interest rates low by creating new money, that could be inflationary. Fighting inflation would require higher interest rates, not lower ones. The goals of the Treasury and the Fed would then be in conflict.

This was a dispute that had to be settled. During World War II and up to 1951, the Fed was restricted from fighting inflation because it had agreed to ease the task of financing Treasury security issues. The Fed chafed under this restriction; President Truman negotiated a famous "Accord"; and the Fed has been free to pursue monetary policy ever since. Nonetheless, an inherent conflict of interest exists between inflation-fighting by the Fed and easy Treasury financing, a conflict often reported on in the financial press.

Nowadays another aspect of conflicting interests is apparent. Unemployment tends to offend voters more than inflation does, and the Treasury represents the administration. The Treasury therefore usually desires a more expansionary monetary policy than does the Fed. Thus far, the Fed has been able to maintain its independence on these issues, and as long as that independence is maintained, inflation fighting will still be carried on.

Arguably the most important advantages open market operations have over the other forms of monetary policy are quietness and flexibility. At the time a policy change is put into motion, there will be very little publicity, and no awkward announcement effects. Open market operations eventually do become known, but unless they are extremely large by then it is old news and no one will pay much attention. The announcement effect is diluted to almost nothing, as distinct from changes in the reserve requirement and the discount rate, which immediately become public knowledge. Furthermore, open market operations can be used at greatly differing levels of intensity, from the sale or purchase of a few securities on a day-to-day basis for some careful and gradual adjustment, or for operations of very large size that will deliver a powerful impact. Open market operations are by far the Fed's most important tool of monetary control, and the buying and selling of securities by the Fed is carried on during every business day. (During much of 1991–1993, the Fed was actively engaged in securities purchases to stimulate the economy.) It might be noted that one of the monetary policy mistakes of the Great Depression was the unwillingness of the Fed to make sufficient use of stimulative open market operations. It is likely that the fall in the money supply by about one-third between 1929 and 1933 would have been less sharp if the Fed had pursued easy money with more diligence.

OPEN MARKET OPERATIONS IN OTHER COUNTRIES

Though no other country's central bank uses open market operations so intensively as the Fed, such operations are usually important in other developed countries, and they are increasing in size. One reason for the intensity of use in the United States is that the U.S. market for government securities is much larger than it is in many other major countries. For example, these markets in Germany, France, and Britain are all less than 10% the size of the U.S. market (1989 figures). Japan's market is larger, in size about 44% of the U.S. market; thus open market operations *could* be carried out, and the Bank of Japan in fact does so. Even so, the market for government securities in that country is not organized in such a way as to make these operations as easy as they are in the United States. In less-developed countries, domestic bond markets are often much too small for the central banks of these countries to conduct open market operations effectively.

HOW OPEN MARKET OPERATIONS ARE ACTUALLY CONDUCTED

U.S. open market operations are directed by the Fed through a separate committee, the **Federal Open Market Committee (FOMC)**.[13] The FOMC meets at Washington, D.C. eight to ten times a year, usually on a Tuesday, with additional telephone conferences as needed. At these meetings the FOMC decides the direction of open market operations, and thus the direction of U.S. monetary policy. The committee's work is out of the spotlight, ensured by its secrecy. The decisions made are not published until five or six weeks later, following the next meeting. Information on the views of individual FOMC members is contained in twice-a-year reports to Congress, fresh when delivered but 26 weeks out of date just before the next updating.

The FOMC directs its agent for open market operations, the Federal Reserve Bank of New York, to undertake either the buying or selling of U.S. government short-term securities. The transactions are channeled through a small number of private dealers (recently 42) located in New York City.[14] The buy or sell orders are placed directly by telephone, and so the operations can be accomplished very quickly whenever desired. The scope of these transactions is huge: in 1992 the Fed bought and sold almost one and a half trillion dollars' worth of securities. Because a very large amount of both buying and selling is carried on during the year, the Fed's actual ownership of securities (about $300 billion in 1992) and the net change in Fed holdings (about $21 billion in the same year) are both much smaller.

---

13.   The FOMC has 19 members, including the 7 members of the Board of Governors and the presidents of the 12 regional banks. At any one time only 12 of the 19 vote: all the governors, the President of the New York Fed, and 4 of the 11 other presidents on a rotating basis. A bill in Congress in 1991 would have removed the district bank presidents from the open market committee, on the argument that they are not appointed by elected officials but by the Fed's Board of Governors. In recent years the district presidents have taken a more anti-inflationary position than the board of governors.

14.   The firms are subject to limits on how much of a particular operation can be handled by any single firm. Breach of these rules in 1991 by a large broker, Salomon Brothers, caused a major scandal.

CHECK CLEARING

Once we have some familiarity with the reserve accounts that commercial banks keep at the Fed, it is possible to investigate another topic: the clearing of checks through the financial system, which involves the use of these reserve accounts. Check clearing is an important topic, even though few people are aware how one bank pays another. If such a mechanism did not exist, it would presumably be necessary to transport huge amounts of cash from bank to bank, increasing the cost of doing business, the risk of loss, and the need for expensive security measures.

The Fed provides an important conduit through which checks are cleared, as can be seen if we trace a check in its sometimes-lengthy travels. Say a firm in Portland, Maine, receives a $1000 check written on a San Diego, California, bank to pay for a piece of computer hardware purchased by a San Diego company. The Maine firm will place the funds in a demand deposit in its Portland bank, shown at (1) on the far left of Figure 20.10. The Portland bank now has a piece of paper ordering payment, nothing more. It then sends the check for collection, using in this case the Fed's check-clearing mechanism. Portland is in the district of the Federal Reserve Bank of Boston, where the check goes by mail. At the Boston Fed, $1000 is credited to the Portland bank's reserve account (2a), also (2b), and the check is sent on to the Federal Reserve Bank in which San Diego is located. That bank is in San Francisco. When the check arrives at the San Francisco Fed, its clerks debit the reserve account of the San Diego bank (3a), also (3b), which in turn debits the account of the company that wrote the check in the first place (4).

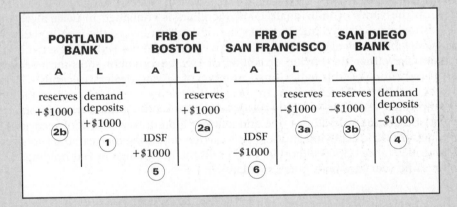

Figure 20.10. Check clearing through the Fed. When a check is cleared through the Fed, the transaction involves subtracting from the reserve account of the commercial bank making payment, and adding to the reserve account of the bank receiving payment.

At this point the Portland firm has been paid, the San Diego firm has had its deposits reduced, and the banks in the two cities have had their reserve accounts adjusted accordingly. It appears, however, that the San Francisco Fed owes $1000 to the Boston Fed. That seeming imbalance is settled by a daily adjustment (5) and (6) in the accounts of the so-called "Interdistrict Settlement Fund" at Washington, D.C.

Note the great safety and convenience of the mechanism. No cash ever needs to change hands between the banks involved in check clearing, because the transactions are handled through the reserve accounts of the Federal Reserve System. Access to the mechanism was formerly free for member banks, but the Fed now (since 1981) makes a charge. As a result, competition has sprung up, especially for local big-city clearing, with a number of private clearinghouse systems now in operation. Recently, the checks cleared by the New York Fed have dropped from about 9 million checks a day to 8 million. (The total number of checks cleared by the Fed, 17.6 billion in 1988, is now less than half the total written annually in the United States.)

It used to be the case that clearing by mail meant that checks were credited to the reserve accounts of recipient banks some days before they were debited to paying banks. As a result, net extra reserves were created within the banking system. This "float," as it was called, was subject to change, as when bad weather closed airports and delayed the mails. The Fed introduced regional check-processing centers in 1972, which cut the float almost in half. Later, the initiation of the computer-based Automatic Clearing House (ACH) network speeded up the crediting and debiting still further, and by 1985 the float had almost been eliminated, down to only about a half-a-billion dollar daily average compared to over $6 billion in 1979. A float still exists because even with the improvement, the clearing is not instantaneous, and in any case computers can break down temporarily. A power outage on Wall Street in August 1990 led to a sudden float so large that interest rates were affected. An internal software problem at the Bank of New York in November 1985 led to another massive float. The Fed, however, is now required to charge for any reserves added to a bank's assets by means of the float.

THE NONMONETARY WEAPONS OF THE CENTRAL BANK

Central banks, including the U.S. Fed, have a number of less well-known and less important tools that do not directly affect the money supply, but can nonetheless have a macroeconomic impact.

MORAL SUASION

The first of these is **moral suasion**. Suasion means exactly the same thing as persuasion; the term is a traditional one dating from the nineteenth century. When inflation or recession threatens, a central bank (or any other branch of government) can use its persuasive powers in an attempt to avert it. It might be able to exert its influence, for instance, to try to control the behavior of commercial banks' lending policies. Warnings, pleadings, propaganda, personal phone calls, fax messages, letters, and meetings between bankers and officials might all play a role.

There is perhaps no reason *not* to try a policy of this sort, but experience reveals little success. The only exceptions appear to be during wartime or other national crises, when appeals to patriotism can be relied upon; or in countries with a sufficient tradition of respect for the central bank or government involvement in the economy (for example, Britain, Japan, France, Italy) to touch a chord of obedience. The bank of Japan, Nihon Ginko, is not as independent as the Fed is in the United States, and it has been known frequently to put heavy pressure on commercial banks to conform to the government's desires concerning lending policies. Normally, however, in countries where governments' wishes carry less weight, moral suasion is not likely to be very effective unless used in combination with more overt measures of monetary and fiscal policy. For example, in the United States during the inflation that accompanied the Vietnam War, exhortation by the Fed, the Treasury, and President Johnson himself accomplished little. A later campaign by President Ford called WIN ("Whip Inflation Now") became something of a national joke. The Fed was, however, much more effective in persuading U.S. banks to continue lending to less-developed countries in the debt crisis (discussed further in Chapter 30) that hit these countries in the 1980s.

SELECTIVE CONTROLS

Certain *selective controls* are important in some foreign countries, prominently in Great Britain, France, Sweden, and Japan. In the United States, only a few such controls exist.

For many years the Fed had the power to set limits on private consumer credit, such as that obtained for purchasing a new car or a refrigerator. The Fed was able to establish a down payment minimum percentage, for example 25% down, and a time-period maximum, for instance five years to pay. If the Fed wanted to slow the economy, it could establish a new regulation such as 75% down, only one year to pay, thus lowering the level of consumer spending fairly directly. This selective control was eliminated by Congress in 1952–1953, and it has not been restored even though the Fed argues periodically that it should regain this power. An argument often made against its restoration is that controls on consumer credit are likely to have a far greater impact on low-income groups than on the rich.

Selective controls on consumer credit are important in Britain, where they are called hire-purchase regulations. Japan sets time limits and minimum down payments on loans for some consumer goods. For many years the Bank of Japan actually set quotas on lending, known as "window guidance."[15] The French government is also an avid allocator of credit. Sweden carries the idea furthest, with an "annual credit agreement" negotiated between the Swedish Central Bank and the country's commercial banks as to the types of loans that should be made and avoided during the coming year. Especially in less-developed countries, central banks and/or governments sometimes establish rules for lending targets, for example "20% of all loans this year must go to agriculture." Going so far as this is clearly risky if the government is not as efficient at allocating credit as are the financial markets—and in many Third World countries, there is much evidence to confirm this fear.

THE MARGIN REQUIREMENT

A form of control over conditions in the stock market is the **margin requirement**. It is well known that one of the elements associated with the onset of the Great Depression of the 1930s was the stock market crash of October 1929. That memorable event contributed to a collapse in business confidence, with massive postponements and cutbacks in investment plans. One reason for the crisis in the stock market was the practice of buying on margin. When stock is purchased on margin, the buyer pays by putting a certain percentage of the purchase price down (say 10%), and finances the remainder of the purchase (say 90%) with a loan from a broker. The stock itself is used as collateral for the loan. The reason for doing this is the hope that the price of the stock will rise after it is purchased, eventually allowing the buyer to sell, pay back the loan, and realize a gain. Buying on margin is a means to engage in stock speculation without using large amounts of one's own money.

---

15   These quotas on bank lending are no longer very effective, because of the gigantic growth in Japanese capital markets and the ability of firms to finance their own capital needs by reinvesting their profits.

What happens, however, if the stock market breaks suddenly and prices decline sharply as in 1929? Then the scheme has failed, and the buyer takes a loss. The loan must be repaid, and to do so ready money must be found. If buyers have speculated heavily with funds borrowed on margin, the loans will be difficult to repay. The stock must be dumped on the market for whatever it will bring; the effect will be further declines in stock market prices as the enforced selling occurs; and the final result might then be a deepening crisis of confidence.

The margin requirement was instituted during the Great Depression as a device to control such speculation. A requirement of 50% means that one-half the purchase price of the stock must be paid for immediately, while only the remaining 50% can be financed by loans on margin, instead of the 90% or more that was common just before the Depression. If the Fed is concerned about possible adverse effects on business confidence because of speculation in the stock market, it can attempt to cool the market by raising the margin requirement. The legal ceiling being a full 100%, buying on margin can actually be stopped altogether.

No move has been made in the margin requirement since 1974, when it was lowered from 65% to 50%.[16] New controversy has arisen concerning it, however. A market in stock options in which not the stock itself but options to purchase the stock for future delivery has recently been developed. In that market, stock purchases are subject only to a 10% margin requirement. This was thought to be a factor associated with the sharp drop of the stock market in 1987, one that numerous economists believe needs correcting.

CONCLUSION

This chapter has introduced and analyzed central banks' instruments of monetary policy: the reserve requirement, the discount rate, the preeminent open market operations, and a few other tools that do not directly affect the money supply. In actual practice, however, the carrying out of monetary policy has not been smooth, has revealed numerous elements of unpredictability, and has generated enduring controversies among economists. Chapter 21 addresses these issues.

SUMMARY

1) Central banks often establish a reserve requirement, setting a legal minimum level of reserves that commercial banks must hold either as cash in their vaults or as deposits with the central bank. The current figure in the United States is 10%. Raising the reserve requirement acts to reduce the money supply and constrict the economy, while lowering it raises the money supply and stimulates the economy. In recent years, changes in the requirement have seldom been made, one reason being the substantial "announcement effect" of the change and another being that an increase in reserves—on which the Fed pays no interest—acts as a tax on banks, which complain loudly.

2) The discount rate is the interest rate charged on loans from the central bank to commercial banks. A high rate discourages banks from borrowing, and so means that borrowed reserves are less likely to be the base for new loans and an expanded money supply. A low rate encourages banks to borrow, which, by adding to their reserves, allows them to lend more freely. In recent years, the Fed has used the discount rate more as a signaling device to indicate its policy than as an actual weapon of monetary management. Also, sometimes the Fed has followed rather than led in changing the discount rate, altering it to reflect market conditions rather than to influence them.

16.   A school of thought within the Fed would prefer to see the margin requirement abolished altogether, the view being that the requirement is an unwarranted interference with free markets. Congress did not, however, agree with a 1985 proposal to do so.

3) Open market operations are the main weapon of monetary policy in the United States. They involve purchases and sales of U.S. government short-term securities. To increase the money supply, the Fed would purchase securities on the open market. The payment by the Fed adds to bank reserves and begins a multiple expansion of deposits. To decrease the money supply, the Fed would sell securities on the open market. The payment by the buyers to the Fed subtracts from bank reserves and begins a multiple contraction of deposits.

4) Check clearing through the Fed involves subtracting from the reserve account of the commercial bank making payment, and adding to the reserve account of the bank receiving payment. When checks are cleared, no cash needs to change hands.

5) A number of nonmonetary weapons are available to central banks, including moral suasion, selective credit controls, and margin requirements. Moral suasion involves efforts to persuade banks to change their levels of lending. Selective credit controls include maximum rates of interest, down payments, and length of time allowed for payment. Margin requirements limit the ability of buyers of stock to make the purchase on credit. Moral suasion and selective credit controls are generally more important in certain other countries than they are in the United States.

Chapter Key Words

Discount rate: The interest rate charged by central banks on loans made to banks. Can be raised to counter inflation and lowered to counter recession. A tool of monetary policy, still important in Japan and some other countries, though much less so in the United States.

Excess reserves: Holdings of reserves by commercial banks over and above the level required by law. The possibility that banks will hold excess reserves increases during bad recessions; banks may hesitate to make loans when they fear borrowers will default on repayments.

Federal Open Market Committee (FOMC): An important committee within the Federal Reserve System that directs open market operations. Meets at Washington, D.C., usually 8 to 10 times a year, to decide on policy.

Margin requirement: The legal limit on the amount of stock that can be used as collateral for loans financing the purchase of that stock. A 100% margin requirement means that no such loans can be made. Raising the requirement discourages stock purchases and is a tool used against inflation; lowering the requirement encourages stock purchases.

Moral suasion: Central bank exhortation of commercial banks to follow expansionary or contractionary lending policies. Not notably successful in the United States; more important in some other countries.

Open market operations: The main tool of U.S. monetary policy, involving the purchase or sale by the central bank of short-term government securities. Open market sales decrease the money supply or slow its growth and have a contractionary effect on the economy. Open market purchases increase the money supply and have an expansionary effect on the economy. Less important in countries with small markets for government securities.

Reserve requirement: The legal requirement administered by central banks requiring some minimum percentage of commercial banks' deposits to be kept as reserves, either as cash in the vault or as a deposit with the central bank. Can be raised to counter inflation and lowered to counter recession. A tool of monetary policy, though changes in the requirement have been rare in recent years.

CHAPTER QUESTIONS

1) Suppose that the total amount of bank deposits is $1,000 billion, and the reserve requirement is 10%. The Fed decides that inflation is a problem, so it raises the reserve requirement to 20%. By how much do banks have to raise their reserves? How large is the resulting reduction in the money supply?

2) The Fed is concerned that the economy is slipping into recession. To provide some stimulus, it lowers the reserve requirement. But statistics soon show that banks are now lending less money, and investment is falling. How can this be?

3) Suppose you manage a commercial bank. A large firm closes out its account with your bank, and as a result you need to replenish your reserves. How does the discount rate affect the way you build up your reserves again? How does your decision affect the money supply?

4) If the Fed believes inflationary pressure is building it may raise the discount rate.
   a) Does this mean that discounts drop off from a high percentage of reserves?
   b) Does this mean the money supply is significantly reduced?
   c) In light of your answers to a) and b), why does the Fed raise the discount rate in inflations?

5) The basic principle of open market operations is that the Fed can create or destroy money by buying or selling things. Suppose the San Francisco Fed purchases $50,000 in computer equipment from Apple Computer. It does this by writing a check to Apple and then crediting the reserve account of Apple's bank when Apple cashes the check. If the reserve requirement is 10%, how much has the money supply changed?

6) Being a generous relative, you want to buy a $1,000 T-bill for your cousin's graduation present. You call a broker, and it turns out the Fed is conducting open market operations. You write a check to the Fed and receive the T-bill in return. Assume the reserve requirement is 10%. Show this transaction on your bank's T-account and the Fed's T-account. Is the money supply reduced or increased?

7) In the midst of an inflation the Fed decides to brake the economy by selling Treasury securities. However, the Fed wants to sell a huge amount of securities, and not enough people want to buy them at the going price. What happens? The Treasury is also selling Treasury securities in order to raise money for the government. How does it feel about the Fed's actions?

8) Suppose that the Fed had had a margin requirement prior to the stock market crash of 1929. If it had raised the margin requirement to 100% in that year, would the crash have been more or less damaging? Why?

The Conduct of Monetary Policy

OVERALL OBJECTIVE: To examine the conduct of monetary policy in recent years, emphasizing that it is the primary means for stabilizing an economy, but also to point out the difficulties in applying it, some of which are new.

MORE SPECIFICALLY:

- To understand that currently, monetary policy is the first line of defense against recession and inflation.
- To explore the problems of monetary policy, including its selective impact, its long lags, its weakness in major recessions, its vulnerability to expectations, the growing reluctance to use it because of international factors, and rapid innovation in financial markets.
- To appreciate the Fed's strategy of countering unwanted changes in the money supply (defensive monetary policy) while at the same time carrying on dynamic monetary policy to fight recession and inflation.
- To consider what difference it makes when the Fed targets interest rates or monetary growth.
- To see that changes in the velocity of circulation have had a significant impact on central banks around the world.

Central banks have both the authority and the means to respond to the changing economic fortunes of nations, and the monetary policy of these institutions is a rampart against the ravages of recession and inflation. This chapter considers whether the past conduct of monetary policy has been judicious, what the present view of that policy is, and what the future may hold in store.

Looking back at the conduct of monetary policy over the past half-century is a humbling exercise. Serious mistakes of management have occurred, and those charged with carrying out monetary policy are all too aware that it is not an easy task. How a central bank should properly address the management of the money supply is one of the greatest economic and political issues of our times. Changing economic circumstances have made monetary policy more difficult to conduct now than it was, say, three or four decades ago, but it still remains the first line of defense against recession and inflation. Its recent record in the United States has continued to be reasonably successful; the curbing of U.S. inflation in 1980–1982 gave special cause for satisfaction at the Fed. The period of expansion with reasonably low inflation from 1983 to 1990 was the second longest in the country's history, and monetary policy worked effectively to keep it going. Then the Fed moved, rather slowly, to respond to the recession of 1990–1991. Influenced by monetary policy, nominal interest rates fell significantly, with short-term rates down by 3.5 percentage points in the 12 months to January 1992, and another half a percent by mid-1993. Real interest rates also fell. By 1993, economic data indicated that the U.S. economy was finally recovering, though at first the recovery was very gradual. In 1994, an upturn seemed to be well underway, and the Fed took steps to slow the speed of the expansion.

As the difficulties in the conduct of monetary policy have become more apparent, however, they have become a source of growing apprehension. Like a doctor aware that modern medicine cannot cure every disease, so the managers of central banks must have a thorough understanding of monetary policy's shortcomings as they respond to the expansions and contractions of the economies they are trying to manage.

▶ PROBLEMS WITH THE CONDUCT OF MONETARY POLICY

The pivotal importance of monetary policy is recognized not just in the United States, but around the world. Yet as a policy instrument it is by no means perfect. Problems are associated with its use, similar to those that often accompany the use of powerful modern medicines. There may be significant unwanted side-effects on patients; doctors debate when to administer the medicine and what the size of dose should be; some minority critics charge that the powerful medicine will actually worsen the eventual outcome. This section looks at the caveats and criticisms of monetary policy's conduct.

SELECTIVE IMPACT

The first of the problems has to do with the selective impact of monetary policy. Experience has shown that some types of capital investment are far more sensitive than others to changes in the (real) interest rate. For example, house construction is drastically affected by the cost of borrowed funds, because that cost is such a high percentage of the total. When interest rates rose to unprecedented levels in the 1980s, "housing starts" (start-ups in the construction of new homes) plummeted from 1.2 million in 1979 to 852,000 in 1980, 705,000 in 1981, and 663,000 in 1982. In 1973–75, another episode of tight money cut housing starts by more than half. The move by banks from the late 1970s toward adjustable floating-rate mortgages whose interest rates move up or down as credit becomes tighter or easier has led to a stronger link between interest rates, housing, and consumption. Formerly, with higher interest rates on fixed-rate mortgages, only the sales of new homes were curtailed. Nowadays, a rise in interest rates affects existing homeowners as well, because the increase in their interest payments means they will restrict their consumption.[1]

Higher interest rates will also have a chilling effect on the sale of certain consumer goods such as autos and other durables that are often bought on credit. In addition, investment of small businesses may depend heavily on borrowed funds. Small businesses have less access to nonbank forms of credit, such as bond markets, than do large ones. The failure rate of small businesses increases substantially when interest rates rise.[2] Higher interest rates also influence some government spending, especially that of state and local governments for roads, bridges, and schools, because such projects are often financed by borrowed funds. (The borrowing of the federal government in the United States, and national governments overseas, are less dependent on the level of interest rates. Even so, the increased costs of national borrowing at higher interest rates seem more and more a liability to politicians running for office. In the longer run, that would work to curtail the borrowing.)

CREDIT RATIONING MAY ALSO OCCUR

The selective impact may come in quite a different way, and be felt mostly by firms that the banks perceive to be the more risky ones. As money tightens, banks may suspect that if they raise their interest rates, the best, least risky borrowers will turn to other alternatives for financing their investment needs. For example, large corporations often have internally generated profits or can sell stock or bonds if bank loans become more expensive. As these low-risk customers turn elsewhere, that may leave a larger proportion of more risky firms in the customer pool, firms that banks may believe are willing to run greater risks. So the banks, knowing that a higher number of defaults will reduce their return on loans, may choose not to raise interest rates as high as they otherwise would. Instead they may engage in "credit rationing," keeping rates at moderate levels but lending selectively to the better risks while freezing out the firms perceived to be the poorer risks. If the Fed decreased the money supply under conditions of credit rationing, the limit on loans rather than the higher rate of interest would cause a decline in investment. The firms affected are more likely to be new ones and small ones, rather than established ones with a long credit history.

SLOWNESS IN RAISING RATES

In periods of increasing inflation, when conventional analysis calls for tighter money and higher interest rates, the monetary authorities have sometimes exhibited reluctance to take these steps. An inflationary expansion in the economy was well underway during the Vietnam War years from

---

1.   Currently, the rates on about half of U.S. mortgages float. The proportion is much greater than this in a number of other countries, such as Britain, where almost all mortgages are at floating rates. Some recent research indicates that rising interest rates may increase earnings on variable-rate *assets* such as money market funds sufficiently to offset much of the contractionary impact of variable-rate debt such as mortgages. This question is currently receiving considerable attention.

2.   Some countries (but never the United States) have laws permitting specific lower reserve requirements when loans are made in sectors that may be specially harmed by higher interest rates. Cases in point are housing and small businesses. Whereas the normal reserve requirement against deposits might be 10%, it might be only 6% if the 4% freed up is used for mortgage loans and loans to small businesses. These laws also may extend to lending to export industries, agriculture, and depressed regions. In effect, the lower requirements are a way to deliver a government subsidy. Germany, Italy, Japan, and the Netherlands are among the developed countries that have done this. The practice is common among Third World central banks.

1967 to 1969, but significant moves toward monetary restraint were too long delayed.[3] Similarly, during the late 1970s the Fed's response to mushrooming inflation as the economy recovered from the 1973-1974 OPEC oil shock was initially inadequate. The tight money was eventually administered in 1979–1981, but the country had to endure several years of inflation before the necessary steps were taken.

Concerns about the selective impact on certain sectors of the economy explain part of this, but more broadly the Fed's sluggishness reflects politics. Large portions of the general public tend to favor low interest rates. There are far fewer lobbyists for high rates. The lesson appears clear that tight money is politically not palatable, and Fed officials read the newspapers, too. It takes courage and determination to turn down the steam. Election years are particularly sensitive, with hardly any politicians ever in favor of raising interest rates. If mistakes of monetary ease are to be made, they are often made then—and the party that wins the election might even argue that the resulting inflation was, from its partisan point of view, not really a mistake!

WEAKEST DURING RECESSION

Another problem, potentially major, was introduced in Chapter 20. Monetary policy may be weakest during serious recessions. In such periods, expectations might be so dismal that even a very low rate of interest, near to zero, would result in little borrowing by firms or consumers. Businesses may see new investment as unprofitable and risky, while consumers worried about being laid off are unlikely car buyers even if interest rates are low. Banks might not lend, either, because of pessimism concerning the safety of loans made during a recession. "You can't push on a string" as the old saying goes. Or, "You can lead a horse to water, but you can't make him drink." Added to that, the central bank's monetary policy might have little ability to bring about lower interest rates if the rates are already very low. Monetary policy might lose considerable effectiveness under these conditions. During the Great Depression of the 1930s, these weaknesses surfaced to an alarming degree. Interest rates charged to borrowers did decrease, but the lower rates did not indicate a stimulative monetary policy. They only indicated the sharp decline in the demand for money as economic activity slowed down.

Fed Bungling in the 1930s

In fact, the Fed bungled by allowing the money supply to fall by about one-third between 1929 and 1933. This was partly due to the unwillingness in the private sector of banks to lend and businesses to borrow, as discussed in the last section. Partly it was due to the failure of thousands of banks and the loss of a large proportion of their deposits. But partly it was also due to the Fed's unwillingness to pursue an easy-money policy. The reluctance was due to the unwarranted fear that feverish stock market speculation à la 1928 might recur, to indecision, and to the Fed's desire to support the value of the dollar on international markets as we shall see. Because of the last of these reasons, the Fed even resorted to *tighter* money at the end of 1931. As a result, (nominal) interest rates charged by banks on short-term business loans in 1931–1933 (3–5%) were actually no lower than they were in the early 1950s, a time of prosperity. Making matters worse, prices of goods and services were falling in 1931–1933, so that the *real* interest rate on short-term business loans was a prohibitive 10% or more during these crucial years of the Depression. By hindsight, the Fed's failure to pursue easy money at this time was extremely poor judgment, ranking as one of the great all-time blunders of economic policy. (But the great loosening of monetary policy after 1933, not only in the United States but in other advanced countries as well, was a major source of eventual recovery from the Great Depression. The Fed and other central banks should at least have the credit for that.)

---

3.   Nominal interest rates increased during this period, but the rise served only to reflect the inflation and *real* rates fell. So, in real terms, for many investors the rate of return on investment came to exceed the prevailing rate of interest. As a consequence, investment and output continued to expand.

Banks' Reluctance to Increase Loans in the Early 1990s

A reflection of these difficulties surfaced in the recession of 1990–1991, with the Fed encountering difficulties in raising the money supply. Banks had suffered from poor performance and high losses on loans in the 1980s. Loans for real estate, to the oil and gas industry in the southwest, and to less-developed countries such as Argentina, Brazil, and Mexico, were all in jeopardy. The damage to banks was particularly great in New England, Texas, Louisiana, and California. Confidence was further shaken by the savings and loan crisis discussed in Chapter 19, with fears that the rot would spread to the commercial banking industry. Dozens of commercial banks failed in an echo, however faint, of the Great Depression. The closings caused some further reduction in deposits and tightness in the money supply. Concerned about bank safety, U.S. bank regulators posted new rules that in effect required banks' stockholders to put up more money and bear more of the risk of losses than previously. (These new risk-based capital requirements took full effect at the end of 1992. Banks must now hold more capital against loans than against securities, which evidence indicates has swung banks' preferences toward U.S. government securities and away from commercial loans.)

The commercial banks were clearly skittish about the economy, troubled about the high level of debt that borrowers had accumulated, concerned about the risk of default from stressed businesses, and worried about the soundness of federal deposit insurance. Many simply refused to renew old loans, exercised great care in making new ones, toughened collateral requirements, put new limits on the size and maturity of their lending, and increased their holdings of U.S. government bonds. On their part, borrowers behaved in a way that seemed to mirror the banks' conduct. Eager to reduce their level of debt, they cut back on their demand for credit.

So as old loans were paid off, deposits fell, and the effect of that was to reduce money supply growth. In some months, the money supply actually shrank. Once again the Fed faced the fact that falling interest rates do not necessarily indicate a stimulative monetary policy, but may merely reflect declining demand for money as economic activity slows down. The old lesson that monetary policy may be less effective in a recession seemed to have been reconfirmed.

LONG TIME LAGS

Another problem with monetary policy is the possibility of a long time lag before the policy is effective. Lags of one sort or another affect every policy of every conceivable sort. There will be some time between the recognition that the economy is facing difficulties and the decision to implement a policy change. This is called the **recognition lag**. Any policy will also require that some time elapses between the recognition that a new policy is needed and the implementation of the new policy. This is the **implementation lag**. Finally, time will pass before the implementation of a new policy has an effect on the economy. This period of time receives the name **response lag**.[4]

Clearly, the recognition and implementation lags of monetary policy are short. New data on GDP are available every month (although these are preliminary and are often adjusted in the next month or two, so in practice perhaps three months is a reasonable estimate for the recognition lag). The decision to implement a new monetary stance takes only a few hours, at a meeting of the Fed's Open Market Committee; the mechanism is in place and the implementation of the policy can start at once. The response lag of monetary policy is a different story. Milton Friedman, the most influential of the monetarist economists, argues that the response lag of monetary policy is "long and variable," and the argument appears to be sound. If a decision to expand is made, it will take time for the multiple expansion of money to proceed, and time for the general structure of interest rates to reflect the changes in rates on U.S. government securities, which are the rates immediately affected by open-market operations. For example, changes in the prime rate that commercial banks charge their best customers, and most other rates as well, almost always lag behind changes in the rate on Treasury bills, which are affected almost at once by money

---

4.   The names are not standardized. The recognition lag is also called the decision lag. That plus the implementation lag have also been called inside or policy lags. Response lags also carry the names outside or expenditure or execution lags.

supply changes. The delay is partly because many rates are set administratively by commercial banks, with decisions having to be made to change them, and partly because alterations in the expectations of borrowers and lenders may take time to accomplish. It then takes even more time for spending to increase because firms and households do not change their plans at once. After this, more time will pass before the multiplier effect from increased spending works itself out. A range of 6 to 18 months is frequently cited in the debate, which is not at all settled. Recent evidence suggests that 9–12 months is reasonably likely.

In the case of monetary contraction, many loan commitments have already been made months in advance by banks, and they have to go through with these contractual arrangements even if the Fed tightens money. Furthermore, if an episode of inflation has altered expectations so that people *expect* the inflation to continue, then tight money's impact might even be more delayed until these expectations are removed. Money was relatively tight, and sometimes very much so, for two full years from the end of 1979, but the stubborn late-1970s inflation was not finally damped until 1982.

The Effect Might Come Too Late

If the effect of monetary policy is not felt for many months, it is possible that policy action might come too late to help, and might even destabilize the situation. Say that an economy is swinging through to the trough of a recession, as at point A in Figure 21.1. Probably most mild recessions would not last much more than a year if left untreated; the economy has some considerable capacity for self-correction, as we saw in Chapter 18. The path of the dotted line in Figure 21.1 shows that the recession eventually eases even without the Fed's intervention. If stimulative monetary action were taken at A, and the impact of that action were felt at B, then monetary policy could be stabilizing. GDP would make an early recovery from the recession along the path back to the full employment level of GDP indicated by the solid line. What if, however, the stimulative action taken at A does not have an effect on the economy until after a considerable lag? If the monetary policy's expansionary effect is delayed until GDP has reached point C, then the stimulus comes too late. In that case, the economy might overshoot as along the path indicated by the rising arrow, with GDP pushed to inflationary levels. Friedman and others have argued that attempts to manage the economy with monetary policy should thus be abandoned and replaced with an undertaking to plan for a steady increase in the money supply just great enough to support a reasonable amount of real economic growth. Many economists continue to believe otherwise. The controversy does suggest, however, that as and when forecasting improves, targeting GDP some months ahead may have a promising future.

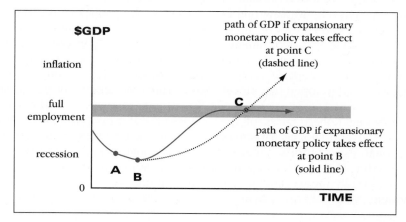

Figure 21.1. **The lags of monetary policy may be damaging.** Because it takes time for expansionary monetary policy to have an effect, the result of the policy may cause the economy to overshoot into an inflation.

EXPECTATIONS

A further problem involves expectations. When the money supply is expanded in a recession, the public may conclude that the new money will eventually cause inflation. These expectations can change economic behavior. Lenders and borrowers might both be convinced that as inflation develops, nominal interest rates will rise. Acting on their expectations, lenders may charge and borrowers may be willing to pay higher nominal interest rates than before, especially on long-term loans. Just such a development seemed to explain why in 1992–1993, U.S. short-term interest rates were very low, but long-term rates were staying high. The high long-term rates were disappointing to the Fed because they are the ones that affect most new investment and housing construction. The public was apparently showing its expectation that the low short-term rates were possible harbingers of inflation, and, acting on their belief, they bid up long-term rates.

The reverse case of tight money leading to expectations of reduced inflation, and hence a decline rather than an increase in interest rates, might also occur. If borrowers and lenders become convinced that inflation will decline, they will agree to lower nominal rates reflecting the lower inflation. Real rates may not rise after all. In these instances, money supply changes would have an outcome opposite to the conventional wisdom, perhaps frustrating the goal of monetary policy. **Rational expectations** arguments that borrowers and lenders will act in this way have eroded confidence that the impact of money supply changes will always have the results predicted by the conventional analysis. (See the accompanying box for a more detailed discussion.)

It is fair to point out, however, that the rational expectations position is controversial and subject to extensive debate. Furthermore, because of the Fed's secrecy, neither the general public nor experts on Wall Street can be entirely sure what the stance of monetary policy is or is going to be at a given time. Even if they did know, the subject is a sophisticated one, and few people are likely to act because most are aware that their understanding of the subject is poor. Still, the point remains that people acting on expectations can potentially alter the output the Fed predicts will flow from some given dose of monetary policy.

RATIONAL EXPECTATIONS

Economists have long agreed that expectations about the future are a determinant of present economic behavior. We saw this in Chapter 16, where people's views of future prices and incomes were two determinants of the present level of consumption. From the 1970s, however, a concept of rational expectations has been developed that moves beyond the earlier view. Led by a group of economists including Robert Lucas of the University of Chicago and Thomas Sargent of Stanford, rational expectations theorists have built a structure of models that assume people understand fully the working of the economy and alter their behavior whenever new government economic policies are put in place. In this view, people anticipate the effects of new policies, and their accurate knowledge together with their change in behavior can result in the policy having no effect, or an effect that is the reverse of what was intended. The example in the text concerning monetary policy suggested that a Fed attempt to lower interest rates might not be successful if people expected inflation to be the result and acted on those expectations.

The position is controversial, partly because some proponents of a rational expectations approach have carried their modeling to an extreme that requires everyone to possess and use efficiently all relevant knowledge. In spite of the controversy, rational expectations modeling has helped to explain why in a more educated society, equipped with more knowledge of the economic consequences of government action, policies may work with less effectiveness than before. No forecasting model nowadays is complete without some attention to the consequences for the economy if the forecast is widely believed, leading people rapidly to change their behavior. Further applications of rational expectations arguments will be encountered in the remaining macro chapters of the book.

There May Be an Expectation That the Central Bank Will Give Up the Fight

If a central bank is closely connected with the rest of government and has little independence, people may reasonably expect that the fight against inflation will not be carried out with much enthusiasm. Inflation fighting tends to boost unemployment, at least for a time, and politicians may fear the job losses more than price rises. When subject to such political pressures, central banks may lose credibility. This complicates their ability to carry out monetary policy against inflation. People may simply not believe that the monetary authorities have the courage to finish the task and act as if the inflation will continue. In fact, countries with the least independent central banks often have the least effective monetary policies and suffer from the most severe inflation problems. Italy, Spain, and New Zealand have all found themselves in this situation in recent years; Third World countries frequently face the same difficulty. On the contrary, central banks most independent of government tend to have the lowest rates of inflation. Germany and Switzerland are two examples.[5]

RULES VERSUS DISCRETION

Some economists believe that central banks should abandon discretionary monetary policy, where judgment is used to determine policy actions, and move to strict rules of behavior. A rules-based policy might be "if inflation rises one percentage point, the Fed will cut money supply growth by one percentage point." Rules of that sort certainly make a central bank more credible, but they also remove any ability to react flexibly. It seems clear that a central bank that has already acquired a reputation for credibility and commitment will be believed. That bank can afford to be more flexible in its monetary policies. If a central bank has, however, lost its reputation for commitment, it may have to adopt specific rules and follow them carefully for some years in order to regain its credibility. The New Zealand central bank is presently attempting just that. It has been made subject to a rule that its governor must meet targets for halting inflation or be dismissed. The adoption of a target for inflation has become something of a fad, with such targets now adopted by Britain, Canada, Finland, and Sweden, as well as New Zealand.

---

5.   But German inflation has recently been abnormally high for that country because of financial problems concerning the unification of West and East Germany. Germany's economy is closely tied with Switzerland's, and lately Swiss inflation has also been much higher than normal for that country. Without care, even the strongest reputations for inflation fighting can be lost in a hurry.

The problem of credibility loss affected the U.S. Fed in the late 1970s, when for a time the Fed was seen as "soft" on inflation. From 1979 it took a much harder line, eventually regaining its credibility. Appointments to the Board of Governors during the Reagan and Bush years included a number of bankers who were strongly anti-inflation. Some of these new appointees held the view that inflation should be reduced to zero. As one result, expectations of inflation in the United States have declined significantly in recent years. (More recently, the district presidents have been more anti-inflation than the Board of Governors.)

THE GREATER SIGNIFICANCE OF INTERNATIONAL FACTORS

The much greater significance of international economic relations in recent years has undoubtedly affected the ability of the Fed to carry out monetary policy. Smaller "open" economies heavily dependent on international trade and capital movements have always found their monetary policy options to be limited. Foreigners could easily move bank deposits into or out of the country depending on the level of interest rates there. So a small economy's central bank always has to keep a weather eye on the holders of these deposits and interest rates in other countries, knowing that if it engineers slight changes, significant flows of funds into or out of the country could occur.

In the United States, the Fed now increasingly shares this problem. If it tries to lower interest rates to counter recession, deposits may flow abroad. Americans and foreigners alike will understandably prefer to earn, say, 8% on deposits held in a foreign country if interest rates on accounts held in the United States are only 3%. The movement may be in the other direction if the Fed attempts to raise interest rates in an attack on inflation. Deposits flow in from countries where the rates are lower. Such seeking for high interest rates was far less common during the long period from the 1930s to the 1960s, when there was less confidence in a harmony of interest among the major economies and the risk of shifting among currencies was seen as being larger. Now, however, investors tend to treat bonds, securities, and deposits in their home currency and those in the major foreign currencies as much the same thing.

The Effect of Interest Rate Changes on Currency Values

Important consequences follow from the outward or inward flow of funds. In Chapter 19, we saw that they affect the exchange rate between the dollar and other currencies, which can affect the country's level of spending and output. Recall that when U.S. interest rates move up, foreign funds flow in for deposit in U.S. banks or for the purchase of U.S. bonds and securities. Foreigners wanting to earn the higher rates must buy dollars with their own currencies on the foreign exchange market. The rising demand for the dollar increases its value.

The higher value of the dollar makes imports cheaper; a dollar buys more foreign currency than before, and therefore more foreign goods. Imports rise, while sales of American-made goods fall. This decline in domestic consumption means that total output declines as well. The higher value of the dollar also means that the foreign buyers of American exports will now find these American-made goods more expensive, and so U.S. exports will fall. In short, a monetary policy of higher interest rates that increases the value of the dollar can cause a rise in imports (thus reducing the consumption of domestically produced goods) and a fall in exports. The resulting fall in total spending may indeed have been what the Fed was trying to bring about with a contractionary monetary policy, but here the cost is borne inordinately by the producers who face foreign competition or who export. Calls may ensue for tariffs and other barriers to trade, both to keep out imports and to punish foreigners for refusing to buy American goods; relations with governments abroad may deteriorate.

The early 1980s provided an excellent example of just such an international repercussion from monetary policy. U.S. interest rates (in real terms) were above those in most foreign countries, partly due to the Fed's monetary tightness during those years. In Japan, however, interest rates were relatively low. Just as theory would predict, the dollar appreciated from $1 = ¥194 in 1978 to $1 = ¥251 in 1984.[6] That made U.S. exports a poor buy for the Japanese and caused a great increase in U.S. imports from Japan. Before long, the strong dollar had caused a very large imbalance of trade between the United States and Japan. (We will look at that in more detail in the chapters on international economics.) The U.S.–Japan trade imbalance continues to cause a great deal of political trouble.

In 1991–1992, as an antirecession measure the Fed drove down U.S. real short-term interest rates to levels well below those of Germany. Germany's central bank was less concerned with unemployment, and more with the possibility of future inflation. The German government had underestimated the costs of unification with the East and had borrowed heavily to finance these costs, so the German central bank felt it had to move strongly toward tight money to control the inflationary potential of this deficit spending. The heavy borrowing plus the tight money drove up German interest rates and slowed growth. Other European countries had to raise their interest rates too; otherwise their citizens would have purchased marks to hold at the high German interest rates. Thus at a time when the U.S. discount rate was just 3%, the German discount rate was 8%, highest in half a century. The dollar fell sharply against the mark; the central banks of both countries expressed concern as to how far the change in currency values should be allowed to go.

Clearly, the increasing financial flows among nations had repercussions for monetary policy. The effect of monetary supply changes on interest rates was working more through foreign exchange rates and trade flows in the manner just described than had been true even in the quite recent past. The Fed, as indeed the world's other central banks, became aware that monetary policy is increasingly becoming less national and more international.

Interest Rates and the International Demand and Supply for Loans

Monetary policy can be complicated by changes in the international demand and supply for loans. If the Fed engineers lower interest rates to fight recession, that may stimulate more borrowing in U.S. markets by foreigners who find money cheaper in the United States than at home. This additional demand for loans makes it harder for the Fed to push interest rates—especially long-term rates—down by increasing the money supply. (To understand why, think of what would happen in the wheat market. A bumper crop might cause wheat prices to fall sharply, but the price fall will be cushioned if in response to the lower price foreign buyers increase the quantity of wheat they purchase.) Similarly, if the Fed boosts interest rates to counter inflation, foreign borrowers of dollars will turn away. The reduced demand for loans means that interest rates, particularly long-term rates, rise by less than would otherwise be true.

The connection between monetary policy and international financial flows can be seen in the Fed's attempt in 1990–1991 to counter a developing recession by lowering U.S. interest rates. Within a short time it was apparent that both short-term and long-term interest rates were falling. But the fall in long-term rates ended abruptly even though short-term rates continued to decline. What apparently happened was that, simultaneous with the Fed's action, German investors were raising their demand for dollar loans. (This was because of the unification of East and West Germany, as mentioned in the last section.) In Japan, meanwhile, interest rates were rising because of certain government policy changes, and that increased the Japanese demand for dollar loans as well. The initially lower long-term U.S. interest rates were attractive to both German and Japanese borrowers, who deflected their demand for loans to the United States, away

---

6.   The theory is more complicated than implied by a straight comparison of interest rates, however. Anyone contemplating the purchase of dollars with yen in order to hold the dollars at higher interest rates than could be earned on yen has to make some estimate of what will happen to exchange rates. For example, if you see a U.S. bond with an interest rate 3% above the rate paid on a Japanese bond, but you think that during the year the dollar will decline by 4% against the yen, then you must conclude that you would lose if you bought the dollar bond. The higher interest rate on your dollar bond will be more than offset by the decline in the value of your dollars.

from the more expensive credit available to them at home. This increased foreign demand for loans worked to keep U.S. long-term rates high even as short-term rates fell. The Fed's monetary policy was thus partly offset by new foreign demand for credit. (Recall that expectations of eventually higher inflation also probably contributed to the large spread between U.S. short-term and long-term interest rates.)

International Factors Have Made Monetary Policy Tougher to Manage

International considerations have made it harder for central banks to alter interest rates. They have also introduced important side-effects on currency valuation and hence on exports and imports when interest rates *do* change. The United States and most other economies are now more "open" to trade and financial flows than formerly, that is, more foreigners utilize their loan markets and a greater proportion of their GDP is represented by exports and imports. The days when the Fed or other large central banks could ignore the international impact of monetary policy are over. Attempting to counter these trends with government controls over trade and capital movements would cause serious economic damage. So countries have little alternative but to live as best they can within these international constraints on the effectiveness of monetary policy.

The difficulties monetary policy faces because of the globalization of trade and finance ought not to be overemphasized, however. National long-term interest rates certainly have not converged completely. This would happen only if there were *no* reluctance to hold foreign exchange instead of domestic currency. Moreover, the loss of control over interest rates is balanced to a degree by the influence gained over the exchange rate. So, creation of new money by the Fed might not lower interest rates as much as before, but it does lead to more dollars on the foreign exchange market, a fall (depreciation) in the dollar's value, and a resulting rise in U.S. exports, which foreigners now find cheaper, and a rise in U.S. output of consumer goods as imports become more expensive. As a result, the U.S. economy is stimulated—the goal of the money creation in the first place.

RAPID INNOVATION IN FINANCIAL MARKETS HAS MADE MONETARY POLICY MORE DIFFICULT TO MANAGE

Another difficulty with monetary policy stems from the rapid innovations occurring in financial markets. These innovations have weakened the Fed's ability to contract reserves and thus reduce the money supply as a weapon against inflation.

The problem has to do with a proliferation of new types of deposits. Thirty years ago it was easy to define money. Coins, paper currency, and checking accounts (demand deposits) were indisputably money, and that was it. Their distinguishing factor was that they bore no interest. Depositors could also opt for bank savings accounts ("passbook savings" with their little bank books) that did bear interest. The bank would, at your request, write a "cashier's check" drawn on these deposits. This was much like a personal check on a demand deposit except that you had to visit the bank to have the check written by a cashier. Because of the inconvenience, deposits in savings accounts were not quite so easy to spend (liquid) as regular checking accounts. Furthermore, banks were permitted by law to delay payment when depositors wanted to make withdrawals. (Thirty days was the usual legal delay—though banks seldom chose to exercise this right.) These savings accounts were thus known to economists as *near-money*; they had many of the attributes of demand deposits, but they took a little longer to convert to cash. Also classed as near-money were U.S. savings bonds and short-term U.S. securities. These were somewhat less liquid than savings accounts, but could still be cashed quickly by means of a trip to the bank or by working through a broker.

M2, M3, and L

Now much has changed. Coins, paper notes, and checking accounts (demand deposits) are certainly still money. This is the definition known as M1 introduced in Chapter 19. As explained in that chapter, most checking accounts now bear an interest rate, like the savings accounts of old, even if the rate is a low one. (The total for M1 was $1,116 billion in October 1993.)

Several other types of deposits have arisen, however. These are almost as liquid as demand deposits, but usually carry higher interest rates. For example, savings deposits bear higher interest rates than demand deposits, but personal checks can now often be written on them. New forms of deposits including bank savings certificates and money market mutual funds also bear higher rates than do demand deposits, and checks can be written on many of the money market funds. These deposits have some restrictions: the bank or financial institution may be permitted to delay payment following a request for withdrawal, or may establish limits on the number of checks that can be written in a given time period. Because of this, they are slightly different from money in its M1 definition. When added to M1, these various deposits give a much greater figure called **M2**. (In October 1993, M2 totaled $3,534 billion, more than three times greater than M1.)

Another banking innovation has been large certificates of deposits, CDs, issued in denominations of $100,000 or more. These are somewhat less liquid, involving slightly more delay or possible delay in cashing. Adding the large CDs to M2 gives a resulting **M3**, $4,184 billion in October 1993. Still less liquid, but much like money nevertheless, are the U.S. savings bonds and short-term U.S. securities that require a trip to the bank or working through a broker for cashing. These, when added to M3, are now classified as **L**, which totaled $5,073 billion in September 1993. (Publication of this figure lags behind the other money measures.[7])

Switching Among Money Forms

The innovation of new types of accounts and securities in the financial markets reflects the relaxation of government regulation over banking in recent years. It has brought difficulties of analysis for economists and has made management of the money supply more problematical. Let us examine why.

First, frequent switching among types of deposits takes place. In the days when only M1's cash and noninterest-bearing demand deposits were of concern to the Fed, tightening the money supply and resulting higher interest rates caused holders of money to switch from checking accounts (demand deposits) to interest-bearing bonds. The switching sped the contraction of the money supply. Now, however, if interest rates are rising, other shifts are likely to occur. Depositors will move out of M1's demand deposits, on which the rates are low and are changed sluggishly by banks, into deposits such as money market funds (included in M2). These accounts not only bear higher rates than do demand deposits, but their rates also respond quite rapidly to changing market conditions, moving on a daily basis. Such movements are reinforced because many people now keep some part of their savings in their checking accounts, and stay on the lookout for higher rates. This reduces the inclination to switch out of money, as broadly defined, and into bonds. Rather, as interest rates rise, people tend to move their funds from one form of money (M1) to another (M2). Thus M1 can fall at the same time that M2 (which includes money market accounts) rises.

Conversely, with falling interest rates from the mid-1980s, the interest rates paid on M1 demand deposits have come closer to the rates paid on M2 and M3 deposits. Under these circumstances, the convenience of M1's checking accounts are more attractive than other types of deposits, and holding them involves a lower opportunity cost in forgone interest. So people switched their deposits back into checking accounts.[8] The money supply as measured by M1 may therefore rise substantially, but this movement does not necessarily reflect an underlying rise in the money supply as measured by, say, M2; depositors may simply have moved funds from money

---

7.   The monthly U.S. *Federal Reserve Bulletin* gives the exact definitions of M1, M2, M3, and L, which include some more minor or obscure items. Recently, the Federal Reserve in the United States was calculating a range of money supply measures from M1 to M29, but M1, M2, M3, and L are fully adequate for our purpose.

8.   The payment of interest on many forms of M1 was itself largely due to the flow of demand deposits in the 1970s into the money market funds included in M2 but not in M1. This flow was instrumental in prompting Congress to remove the regulations against paying interest on checking accounts.

market accounts into demand deposits. The large variations in the quantity of M1 due to these factors caused the Fed to conclude that financial deregulation and innovation had fundamentally changed the behavior of the M1 measure of the money supply. It ceased issuing pronouncements on the annual growth of M1 after 1986 and shifted its focus to the M2 and M3 definitions.[9]

A further development occurred in 1991–1993. As the Fed eased money to fight recession, short-term interest rates fell for bank demand deposits, money market funds, and CDs. Not only did rates fall because of the easy monetary policy, but also because, apparently, banks were no longer having to compete as aggressively for deposits with savings and loan institutions, which had encountered severe financial problems. The low interest rates led people to shift large sums from demand deposits (included in M1), money market funds (included in M2), and CDs (included in M3) into the stock market and into bond mutual funds where returns were higher. (Deposits in mutual funds, some of which even carry check-writing privileges, are *not* included in these measures of the money supply.)

Because of these outward shifts, the Fed was having difficulty in raising the M2 and M3 money supply by means of monetary policy. For example, during the last half of 1991 the M2 money supply grew only about 1.5%, well below the growth rate of at least 2.5% that the Fed wanted to achieve for that year. In some months of 1991 and 1992, M2 even declined (by 1.9% in April, 1992) for the first time in the 33 years that this measure had been calculated. With M2 falling, people "worked" their deposits harder, and M2's velocity rose to well above the long-term average of 1.6, reaching about 1.72 in several months of late 1992. That was a surprise: in the past a *fall* in velocity was predicted when interest rates on demand deposits declined, because lower interest rates had always made it less costly to hold cash balances. A vicious circle may even have developed: (1) The Fed tries to increase growth in M2 by open market operations. (2) The new money causes interest rates to fall further. (3) Depositors, looking for better rates, take even more M2 and put it into stock and bond funds.

These flows out of the money supply have caused a number of knowledgeable observers to suggest adoption of a new money supply definition that adds stock and bond mutual funds to M2. Such a measure would seem to track the historical relationships between money, interest rates, and output better than M2 or M3 alone.

CHANGES IN FIRMS' FINANCING MAY ALSO HELP TO EXPLAIN THE RECENT SLUGGISH GROWTH IN THE MONEY SUPPLY

The recent anemic expansion of the money supply may also be due to changes in firms' financing decisions. During the 1980s' boom times, many firms had borrowed heavily from banks at high interest rates. They now found they could issue commercial paper such as bonds and securities and then use the proceeds to pay off their high-cost bank loans. Commercial paper has become easier to market because credit-rating firms like Moody's and Standard & Poor's make available information and monitoring that used to be available only to banks. Furthermore, commercial finance companies now provide more credit to borrowers than formerly: just 10% of short-term business loans in the late 1960s were from this source, but 20% now. Part of this money was also used to repay the firms' high-cost bank loans. The reduction in bank loans tended to cause a monetary contraction. These developments were limited: bond issues are possible only for large well-established firms, and finance companies lend only on good collateral. So their effect, though it was important for some firms, was nil for many others, especially small and medium-sized ones. But the new types of financing did apparently lead to a lower level of bank lending.

---

9.   Wall Street still pays inordinate attention to movements in M1, even though this once-reliable indicator of monetary policy can now be highly misleading as a signal of how the money supply is changing.

SUMMING UP THE PROBLEM

Traditionally, the Fed attempts to counter recession with an easy-money policy, and inflation with tight money. But the conduct of monetary policy has become more difficult. Great discrepancies and great volatility have sprung up in the growth rates of money as variously defined, and the amount of money the public wishes to hold can vary substantially depending on whether interest rates are high or not. Furthermore, there are no reserve requirements on some of the M2 and most of the M3 components, which also weakens the impact of monetary policy. It is not that the impact has disappeared, since higher interest rates will certainly not cause holders of M1 to shift only into M2 and M3 money and vice versa. Yet the process of tightening or easing the money supply may now take longer and be less predictable. All this has suddenly introduced new problems of monetary management for the Fed, and no solution is immediately apparent. In the present political climate, the greater regulation of M2 and M3 that would ease the difficulty does not seem at all likely.

▶ THE FED'S STRATEGY

We can think of the Fed, or the central bank of any major country, as a medical community seeking to conquer a disease. The doctors who spot the first signs of trouble with cardiac monitors or X-rays or CAT scans are the economists and statisticians inside and outside the Fed who examine the economy for the first symptoms of recession and inflation. The specialists at the hospital are the Chairman, the Board of Governors, and the members of the Open Market Committee. These specialists decide when and whether to begin treatment. The three main medications are the rather outdated reserve requirement, the rather ineffective discount rate, and the efficacious and dependable open market operations. The doctors' medications do not work quite so well as they used to, and there are some critics who believe that the treatment will be ineffective or even cause harm. Yet this treatment is the first line of defense for the economy's good health, and how the Fed plans its therapy is vital to every citizen. This last section of the chapter surveys how the Fed's monetary policy treatments have evolved, and the present stance of monetary policy.

COUNTERING UNWANTED CHANGES IN THE MONEY SUPPLY

Until now we have focused on the Fed's role in countering recession or inflation with central bank actions to change the money supply. This is called **dynamic monetary policy**. However, certain events in the economy not connected with recession or inflation also work to change the size of the money supply. Often these changes are unwanted and could even bring on an economic crisis unless they are corrected. So, on a day-to-day basis, a little-noticed but important mission of the Fed is to minimize the damage from temporary shortages of currency and unwanted changes in the money supply with **defensive monetary policy**. Such damage was great in the nineteenth century, before the United States had a central bank, and its virtual elimination with defensive monetary policy has been a major accomplishment of the Fed.

Year-in, year-out, as often as several times a week, the Fed conducts defensive monetary policy aimed at stabilizing unwanted changes. A large proportion of open market operations are for this purpose. What is the cause of these unwanted changes?

Holiday Demand for Cash

A good example of an unwanted change in the money supply can be found during the Christmas season. At that time many depositors will want to hold greater amounts of cash for shopping. Assume a depositor withdraws $100 in currency from a bank to carry in a wallet. The bank has no trouble obtaining sufficient paper notes as needed. Indeed, one of the great innovations of the Federal Reserve System was that it overcame the prior problem of seasonal currency shortages that could develop in just this way. The mechanism is as follows in Figure 21.2. The customer withdraws $100 from demand deposits, seen on the right of the diagram. The $100 is paid out of vault cash, seen on the left.

COMMERCIAL BANK

ASSETS	LIABILITIES
vault cash (reserves) −$100	demand deposits −$100

Figure 21.2. Currency (vault cash) is depleted by withdrawals. At holiday seasons people want to carry more cash. They therefore make withdrawals from their demand deposits, so depleting bank reserves. At such times a bank may run low on vault cash.

Now what if the bank is running low on Federal Reserve Notes? A solution is at hand, as seen in Figure 21.3. The bank phones the Fed and asks for a replenishment. Crisp newly printed notes (see 1a) arrive rapidly by armored car, and are added to the commercial bank's vault cash (1b). The bank makes payment to the Fed through a debiting of its reserve account, which is reduced by $100 on both the left and right (2a and 2b) of the figure.

FEDERAL RESERVE SYSTEM **COMMERCIAL BANK**

ASSETS	LIABILITIES	ASSETS	LIABILITIES
	reserves −$100 (2a) Federal Reserve (1a) notes +$100	reserves (2b) −$100 (1b) vault cash +$100	GENERATES MULTIPLE CONTRACTION

Figure 21.3. Currency (vault cash) is replenished by debiting reserves. A bank's holding of currency (vault cash) can be replenished by debiting that bank's reserve account at the Fed. But the loss of reserves starts a multiple contraction of bank deposits, to avoid which the Fed will have to engage in open market operations.

Note, however, that although the replenishing of vault cash has been accomplished smoothly, there is an unwanted side-effect. The original loss of demand deposits, shown in Figure 21.2, will engender a multiple contraction in the money supply because the bank must build up its reserves. That leads to a reduction in lending and in deposits at other banks in a process already discussed in Chapter 19. The contraction of the money supply must be counteracted if an impact on the economy is to be avoided. The Fed will thus engage in open market purchases as an offset.

Later the currency comes back into the banks because, with the Christmas season passed, stores deposit the currency spent by shoppers and people reduce the amount of cash they desire to carry. The entire process will go into reverse. The Fed must then offset this flow also, with open market sales, to avoid changes in the money supply and an unwanted effect on the economy.

The Money Supply Can Change If Certain Deposits Are Shifted

Several other occurrences can affect the money supply unless they are negated by central bank action. For example, the U.S. Treasury is free to keep its own deposits either in the Federal Reserve System or in commercial bank accounts. Foreign governments are able to do the same. If the U.S. Treasury or the finance ministry of a foreign government makes payments within the United States from its account at the Fed, that will feed demand deposits in the commercial banking system and initiate a multiple expansion of the money supply. If payments are made *to* the U.S. Treasury, perhaps by taxpayers in April when income tax payments are due, or if foreign governments are paid by U.S. citizens, the payments will come out of demand deposits. If the receipts are placed in the Treasury or foreign government accounts at the Fed, then a multiple contraction is stimulated. The Fed may want to take steps to offset either occurrence with open market operations.[10]

Movements of Deposits Into and Out of the Country Also Make a Difference

Transfers into deposits in the United States from foreign countries, and out of deposits to foreign countries, are also often made both by U.S. citizens and by foreigners. These, too, will either swell or diminish demand deposits, and generate an expansion or contraction unless the movements are "sterilized," a term much-used where foreign flows are concerned. The **sterilization**—that is, canceling the effect of the inflow or outflow on bank reserves and therefore on the money supply—once again would be by means of open market operations.

THE FED'S DEBATES ON WHAT TO CONTROL

The Fed's experience during the last decade has been educational in a number of ways. The Fed's "doctors" learned valuable lessons, and as a result there have been significant changes in the Fed's strategic decisions on what to control, or target, in its management of the money supply. The debates on what to target give insights into the theory and practice of monetary policy, insights that for the most part have become available only recently.

Recall that monetary policy is expected to influence the money supply, hence interest rates, and GDP. In previous years, it appeared that the choice of which of these variables to adopt as a target for monetary policy made no difference. The Fed could decide to raise the money supply; or it could decide to decrease interest rates; or it could decide to bring about growth in GDP. These were one and the same, according to the initial view. Each of these policies could serve as the strategic target for the Fed, because each was linked to the other. However, as economists came to appreciate in the 1970s, the original Fed policy of stabilizing interest rates could *destabilize* the economy.

Targeting Interest Rates

In 1951, the Fed began a long period of targeting interest rates. It decided what their level should be and then used monetary policy to push and keep them there. Short-term interest rates were the Fed's main "instrumental variable."[11] In time, the specific interest rate that became the target was the federal funds rate at which commercial banks borrow from one another. The Fed could influence this rate quite directly by money supply changes, and movements in this rate were

---

10. Alternatively, changes in U.S. Treasury deposits could be allowed to affect the money supply, thus giving the same results as a change in monetary policy carried out by open market operations. Using this principle, the Fed sometimes achieves an effect identical to contractionary open market operations by managing the maturity dates in its portfolio of securities. Let us assume that today a certain number of securities held by the Fed come due (mature). Their face value will be paid to the Fed by the Treasury. If the Fed does not buy new securities to replace them, then net Treasury deposits in commercial banks will fall as the payment is made, and, as described in the text, commercial bank reserves will decline and a multiple contraction is initiated. These tactics might even be agreed upon between the Fed and the Treasury. They would not be secret, however, because the Treasury announces its transactions with the Fed.

11. Before the "Accord" of 1951 negotiated between the Treasury and the Fed by President Truman and mentioned in the last chapter, the Fed had not been free to conduct monetary policy since World War II. Its efforts during that period were directed toward making it easier to finance Treasury bond sales.

expected to affect all other interest rates as well. If the economy slowed, the Fed pursued monetary ease to lower the federal funds rate, and thus to lower interest rates generally. If it believed economic growth was becoming too rapid, it tightened money to raise interest rates. Some said the Fed in doing this was "leaning against the wind."

That strategy seemed acceptable for a long time, but later it came to be seen as flawed. Small mistakes could have important consequences. Suppose the Fed, seeking stability, mistakenly established a nominal interest rate target at a level a little below the expected rate of return on many new capital investment projects. That would cause an increase in investment, and a growth in total output and income. In turn, the higher output and income would raise the demand for money and credit, causing an increase in interest rates. Recall, however, that the Fed was attempting to keep interest rates fixed at some given target level. To keep them from rising, the Fed would have to use its policy tools to increase the money supply, but that would start another round of higher output and income, higher demand for money, higher interest rates, and more money creation to keep rates stable. Eventually, inflation would set in; lenders would insist on an inflation premium in interest rates to protect them against the erosion in the value of what they had lent; the Fed would have to create even more money to keep interest rates stable. The opposite could also occur—interest rates kept just above the rate of return on many possible new investment projects; declining investment and hence output and income; a reduced demand for money leading to a fall in interest rates; and finally Fed tightening of money to keep rates stable.

The result was that choosing an interest rate target for policymaking could be destabilizing, with a snowballing movement toward inflation or recession. The situation is illustrated in Figure 21.4. Here a rise in the demand for money from M_D to M_D' takes place. If the Fed does not intervene, interest rates rise from r to r'. If it does intervene to keep interest rates stable, it must increase the supply of money from M_S to M_S'. It can stabilize *either* the interest rate or the money supply, but it cannot stabilize both.

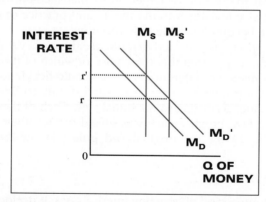

Figure 21.4. **Either the interest rate or the money supply can be stabilized, but not both.** If the Fed tries to keep interest rates fixed, it must change the money supply. If it tries to keep the money supply fixed, then interest rates will vary.

Targeting Monetary Growth

Perceptions that these unfortunate effects were unacceptable might have led to more frequent shifts in the interest rate target. It does not, in fact, seem very wise to set such a target and simply leave it there through all the events just described. Instead, partly due to the persuasive debating skills of the monetarist economists, partly to their intellectual dominance, and partly to the psychology of the times, moves were made to adopt money supply targeting as a new strategy. Congress first called on the Fed in 1975 to set money supply targets in the form of announced growth rates. Such targets were required by law in 1978. The Chairman of the Board of Governors was ordered to appear before Congress twice a year to report what they were, a requirement that still continues. (Similar debates took place in most major countries, many of which established targets for money supply growth from the early 1980s.)

In October 1979 the newly appointed Fed chairman, Paul Volcker, announced a complete shift to money measures as the Fed's "instrumental variable." Typically, targets were announced as ranges of permitted annual growth of M1, M2, and M3. The targets for 1979 were 1%–4.5% for M1, 5%–8% for M2, and 6%–9% for M3. Because of the large shifting among deposits discussed earlier, the M2 and M3 targets proved to be the most important; the Fed stopped setting targets for M1 in 1986. In recent years the M2 and M3 targets have crept downward as the Fed worked to bring down inflation. Table 21.1 shows them during the period 1986-1994.

TABLE 21.1
The Fed's targets for growth in the money supply, percent, 1986–1994.

	1986	1987	1988	1989	1990	1991	1992	1993	1994
M2	6.0–9.0	5.5–8.5	4.0–8.0	3.0–7.0	3.0–7.0	2.5–6.5	2.5–6.5	1.0–5.0	1.0–5.0
M3	6.0–9.0	5.5–8.5	4.0–8.0	3.5–7.5	2.5–6.5	1.0–5.0	1.0–5.0	0.0–4.0	0.0–4.0

Source: Federal Reserve System.

A targeted figure for growth in a monetary measure did have the advantage that, even if it led to some inflation or deflation, these effects would not be so cumulative as had been true of interest rate targeting. Just as was predicted in Figure 21.4, however, if the demand for money rose to M_D', then steadiness in the money supply at M_S meant far more variability in interest rates (to r' in the figure) than ever before. Such proved to be the case almost immediately. The prime rate charged by banks to their best customers went from 11.75% in January 1979 to 15.25% a year later, 19.77% in April 1980, 11.12% in August 1980, 21.5% in December 1980, and 13.5% in September 1981.[12]

Such high variability in interest rates over short time periods was unprecedented in this century, and brought other problems. It made investment more difficult to plan and was especially painful to borrowers who had negotiated loans with variable rates. It was a major cause of the debt crisis in less-developed countries, which had borrowed large amounts in the late 1970s and early 1980s at variable rates and now found themselves facing unexpectedly massive interest costs. And it had an effect on the exchange rate between the dollar and other currencies, with major repercussions on U.S. exports and imports, as already discussed.

Unstable "V"

During the years when the Fed's strategy involved strict targets for monetary growth, the Fed discovered that the effectiveness of the strategy was being eroded by changes in the velocity of circulation, the V in MV = PY. During "normal" times, V had been believed by economists of almost all persuasions to be relatively stable. Monetarist economists went further: *they* believed V to be *very* stable. Yet in 1982, the velocity of all measures of money, however defined, declined sharply, and continued to fall for several more years. (For example, the velocity of M2 was almost 1.8 at its 1982 peak, but only about 1.6 in 1983, a difference of well over 10% in a number that was believed to be almost a constant. It has continued to be variable, rising a bit before dropping to about 1.55 in 1987, and then rising again to 1.65 in 1991 and as high as 1.72 in several months of late 1992.) *Why* velocity has proven to be so variable appeared to be connected with the ability of people and firms to economize on cash balances, making their deposits "work harder" by turning them over faster. By doing so, they could exchange some of their deposits for securities that paid higher rates of interest, or put them into the stock market.

---

12.   Not only were these rates quite variable, but they were higher than for many, many years. It took time for the financial community to appreciate that these high rates were nominal ones. Much of the climb in the nominal figure was only a reflection of the inflation, and, at least at first, *real* rates were still fairly low. The high nominal rates were *not* initially a sign of much tighter monetary policy.

The mere fact that V *was* variable caused severe problems for the Fed's strategy of influencing the economy through targeting the growth of the money supply. If velocity (V) changes—as it did unexpectedly in 1982 and subsequent years—then any given money supply change (M) can have very different effects on nominal GDP (PY). For example, 1982's fall in velocity meant that the money supply growth for that year did not support nearly as much growth in GDP as was anticipated. The relationship between the money supply and nominal (or real) GDP had clearly weakened.[13] This episode, extending over several years and apparently still going on, was damaging to strict monetarist models, some of whose predictions of imminent inflation went badly awry as a result.

The experience led to a change in targeting strategy. From about the fall of 1982, the Fed began to use a more discretionary, more eclectic approach. Exactly what the targets were was not so clear as formerly. Money growth goals continued to be announced, as required by Congress, but in effect the Fed was not attaching much meaning to these goals. Instead, the Fed appeared to be targeting the level of nominal GDP—or in an alternative way of saying this, the money supply and velocity—if not publicly, then implicitly at any rate.[14] With GDP now a concern to the Fed, more attention was paid to interest rates when setting the targets for money growth. The effect was that both interest rates *and* reserves (hence the money supply) were allowed to vary. Within a few years, it was apparent that interest rates had become more stable than they were after 1979, but less stable than they had been before that time. Reserves, and therefore the money supply, were *less* stable than they were in the Volcker period from 1979 to 1982, when monetarism was in flower. Many economists, though not all, thought that the Fed had absorbed valuable lessons from these episodes of targeting, and that the new strategy was a sensible one.

One of the more visible results of the changes since 1982 has been the widening of the Fed's targets for the money supply to cover a greater permitted range. The 1988 through 1993 targets, for example, ranged over four percentage points for M2 and M3, respectively, compared to only three percentage points before that time. The larger range allows for more Fed flexibility in its monetary decisions.[15]

 ## CONCLUSION

This completes our analysis of monetary policy, the first line of defense against recession and inflation. Monetary policy will surely remain important through the 1990s and beyond, and will remain reasonably effective, though carrying it out is both more difficult and more complex than it was in the recent past. In spite of the greater complexity, valuable lessons about how to plan monetary strategy have been learned, some of the lessons at the expense of the then-prevailing

---

13.   According to Fed Chairman Alan Greenspan, "The historical relationships between money and income, and between money and the price level, have largely broken down, depriving the aggregates of much of their usefulness as guides to policy." (Alan Greenspan, "The Fed Aims for Price Stability," *Challenge,* Vol. 36, No. 5, September/October 1993, p. 8.) In almost every other advanced economy, evidence has mounted that the link between the money supply and nominal and real GDP has weakened in these countries too. It might be said that velocity is still *relatively* stable; in the United States; the velocity of M2 was never more than 1.8 or less than 1.5 during the entire period 1959-1991, with an annual average of 1.6. But that still means that with the same money supply, PY or nominal GDP could have changed by about 20%.

14.   Remember that targeting nominal GDP (PY) as well as the money supply (M) means that velocity in MV = PY is being estimated. A problem with targeting nominal GDP is that the information about GDP is always at least a month old. A target of *future* nominal GDP as *forecast* would avoid this problem—except that forecasting is an uncertain business with a mixed record of success. Without making much of it, the Fed probably does alter its monetary policy stance in part because of changes in forecasts of future GDP performance. Targeting nominal GDP growth has also been tantamount to targeting the rate of inflation in recent years, because real growth in the economy has been relatively steady at around 2.5% per year. That stability cannot be depended upon, however, and over the years real growth in GDP has been even harder to predict with accuracy than nominal growth. That is why adoption of a real growth rate target is seldom suggested.

15.   One new Fed indicator called "P*" deserves brief attention. We know that MV = PY. If Y is defined as the potential level of output (that level beyond which inflation would accelerate), if velocity V is relatively stable, and if the money supply M is given, then P is the price level toward which the economy will move. That price level is defined as P*. But the persistent rise in velocity makes the P* model more difficult to use as well. In 1993-1994 there has been talk that the Fed might introduce a real interest rate target. This idea has had something of a rough ride from economists, however. The major objection has been the great difficulty in using real interest rates as a target when the rate of inflation at the moment is not knowable.

wisdom. Probably there will be no return to any single indicator or target. "Seat-of-the-pants" monetary management seems now the sensible order of the day, with all relevant information about where the economy is moving forming the basis for Fed policy decisions.[16] Furthermore, the small month-to-month movements in the money supply to "lean against the wind," characteristic of monetary policy until the early 1980s, is most likely a thing of the past. There is now less confidence that these small changes are useful, and more conviction that monetary policy should be directed only at serious economic problems. Nonmonetary policies of the Fed such as moral suasion and selective credit controls are unlikely to grow in importance or even regain the ground they have lost. These conclusions will surely benefit the Fed in its management of future battles against recession and inflation.

The next chapter turns to the study of fiscal policy: the macroeconomic effect of governments' taxation and spending. The topic has special significance for U.S. monetary policy, because as that chapter will indicate, in recent years for reasons of domestic politics the annual U.S. federal budget has constantly shown large deficits. To a significant degree, deliberate movements in taxes and spending to stabilize the booms and slumps of the economy have been suspended in the face of these deficits. As a result, monetary policy has emerged with even greater importance than before, and for now at least, fiscal policy is in retreat.

SUMMARY

1) Monetary policy is currently the primary means for stabilizing an economy against recession and inflation, but it has its weaknesses, some of which are new.

2) The major problems of monetary policy include its selective impact on certain sectors of the economy, the long time lag before it affects economic performance, its weakness in major recessions, its vulnerability to expectations, the growing reluctance to use it because of international repercussions, and the rapid innovation in financial markets that has made it more difficult to manage.

3) When the Fed uses its policy tools to counter recessions and inflations, the action is known as dynamic monetary policy. But it engages much more frequently in defensive monetary policy, which involves attempts to counter unwanted changes in the money supply such as would otherwise occur at holidays.

4) Over the years the Fed has several times changed its views on what the primary target of monetary policy should be. At first, it targeted interest rates, but under certain circumstances this proved to be destabilizing. It moved to targets for monetary growth (which are still published), but unexpected changes in the velocity of circulation meant that such targets lost much of their usefulness. Presently, more eclectic "seat-of-the-pants" monetary management rather than adherence to fixed targets seems to be the rule.

---

16.   For those unfamiliar with the term "seat-of-the pants," it comes from the early days of flying when airplanes did not have a turn-and-bank indicator. Pilots flying in clouds could best tell from the reduced pressure on their posteriors whether they were flying upside down. It amounts to reading all the signs as best you can in the absence of complete instrumentation.

Chapter Key Words

Defensive monetary policy: Monetary policy to counter unintended shifts, seasonal or otherwise, in the money supply.

Dynamic monetary policy: Monetary policy to counter recession or inflation.

Implementation lag: The time between the recognition that an economy is facing difficulties and the decision to implement a policy change. The implementation lag is short for monetary policy.

L: The definition of the money supply consisting of *M3* (which see) plus U.S. savings bonds and short-term U.S. securities that require a trip to the bank or working through a broker for cashing.

M2: The definition of the money supply, including M1 (coins and paper notes plus demand deposits), savings deposits, bank savings certificates, and money-market mutual funds.

M3: The definition of the money supply consisting of *M2* (which see) plus large certificates of deposits.

Rational expectations: The idea that people understand the working of the economy and alter their behavior whenever new government economic policies are put in place, anticipating the effects of new policies. The change in behavior might then result in the policy having no effect, or an effect that is the reverse of what was intended.

Recognition lag: The time between the recognition that the economy is facing difficulties and the decision to implement a policy change. The recognition lag is short for monetary policy.

Response lag: The time between the implementation of a new policy and its effect on the economy. The response lag is long for monetary policy.

Sterilization: A central bank action, usually involving open market operations, to ensure that inflows into deposits from foreign countries and outflows to foreign countries do not affect the money supply in an unwanted way.

CHAPTER QUESTIONS

1) Explain the degree to which monetary policy influences the following:
   a) Consumption of gasoline
   b) Consumption of refrigerators
   c) Government expenditure on roads
   d) Government expenditure on national defense
   e) Investment by major corporations
   f) Investment by small businesses

2) You are the Fed chairman. You receive the following report: "The economy has moved beyond full employment. Inflation is already breaking out and will intensify over the next few months." Your first response is to tighten the money supply as quickly as possible. Is there a potential problem with that course of action?

3) Some members of Congress would like to see direct Congressional control over the Fed. Suppose they obtained such control in a period of inflation. If the Fed then announced that inflation was too high and raised the discount rate, would the inflation lessen?

4) The Ford Motor Company competes with Japanese imports in the U.S. car market. It is also trying to make inroads into the Japanese market. If interest rates in the United States were lower than in Japan, how would Ford's sales in both countries be affected?

5) Suppose the Fed raises interest rates in order to cool off the economy. The Fed normally expects that M1 will fall. Why? Consumers like to earn a high rate of return on their money by investing in stocks and bonds, but they do not like to take risks. How could this behavior lead M1 to rise instead of fall?

6) Very successful marketing by greeting card companies and toy manufacturers causes Groundhog Day to become a gift-giving extravaganza. However, Fed officials have no children and do not realize the increased significance of the holiday. What they do notice is a sudden rise in interest rates beginning in February and lasting for some weeks. Why did this happen?

7) The rate of return on investment currently averages about 10%. However, the Fed is targeting interest rates at 11%. The Fed could respond to the downward pressure by lowering interest rates, but instead it holds to its target. Show what happens on a money supply and demand diagram. How can this policy lead to recession?

8) Suppose the Fed is targeting money supply growth while the economy is in recession. The Fed decides to increase the rate of money growth in order to stimulate the economy. But neither the price level nor output increases. How can this be? What can the Fed do about it?

Fiscal Policy

Taxation

and

Spending

OVERALL OBJECTIVE: To show that government's taxes and spending (in the form of government transfers and government spending on output of goods and services) affect the economy, and to trace the advantages and disadvantages of a fiscal policy involving such changes.

MORE SPECIFICALLY:

- To explain that a fiscal policy of government tax changes and spending changes involves budget deficits and surpluses.
- To discuss how tax reductions stimulate the economy, and are thus effective fiscal policy for combatting a recession, while tax increases constrict the economy, and are thus effective fiscal policy in combatting an inflation.
- To show that tax increases, when used as fiscal policy against inflation, are far more difficult to enact than are tax decreases against recession, and that the public reacts differently to temporary and permanent tax changes.
- To consider the effects of changes in government transfers and spending on output, including especially entitlements, public works, and public employment, and to note the political difficulties involved in using such changes for fiscal policy purposes.
- To point out that the federal budget deficit has in large measure hobbled expansionary fiscal policy.

We have seen the ways in which a government's monetary policy can affect an economy's performance. Now we turn to the government's taxes, transfers, and spending on output of goods and services. Of course, *most* government taxation and the transfers and spending on output financed from it is undertaken for public purposes—schools, highways, Social Security, the military, and so on—quite independently of any need to stimulate an economy during a recession or to restrict it during an inflation. But government's taxes and outlays have the potential to speed or slow a country's economy. By changing their levels, governments can utilize **fiscal policy** to influence the direction of the macroeconomy. In Chapter 17, we saw that in the Keynesian fixed-price model, lowering taxes, raising transfers, and increasing government spending on output is a stimulative policy, while raising taxes and lowering transfers and spending on output is restrictive. Contemporary economists are engaged in a lively debate on the accuracy of this claim, and most would accept that the original Keynesian position overemphasizes the amount of stimulation and restriction that would actually occur and misses some of the adverse side-effects of such policy. Yet many and probably most economists would still accept the central thesis that, subject to certain conditions, lowering taxes and raising government outlays stimulates the economy, while raising taxes and lowering government outlays brakes it.

In any case, it helps the learning process if we first view fiscal policy from the original Keynesian perspective, and then in the next chapter add to that perspective by taking up the contemporary critique of the Keynesian position. Following that plan, this chapter treats fiscal policy in three parts: tax changes in the first section; changes in government outlays (including both its transfers and its spending on output) in the second; and in the third, how the politics of both taxes and government outlays have in large degree served to hobble fiscal policy in recent years.

FISCAL POLICY INVOLVES BUDGET DEFICITS AND SURPLUSES

Fiscal policy involves changing taxes and government spending (including transfers) so that the government's accounts move toward a **budget deficit** with spending exceeding revenue or toward a **budget surplus** with revenue exceeding spending. For example, the stimulative effect of greater government spending assumes that there is no matching increase in taxes, and thus the government's budget has turned toward deficit. The reason for this is that if greater spending were combined with high taxes to pay for that spending, then the stimulative effect would be largely lost because raising taxes tends to contract the economy.[1]

The same comment applies to all the other possible combinations of policy. Cutting government spending but matching that with a tax decrease; raising taxes and then using the new revenues to pay for more spending; reducing taxes and then cutting government spending—all of these involve largely offsetting macroeconomic effects. Expansion through fiscal policy is obtained only when government spending rises relative to tax revenues, by means of a spending increase, a tax cut, or both. All represent a move toward deficit in the budget. Contractionary fiscal policy involves the opposite. It is the result of tax revenues rising relative to government spending, by means of a tax increase, spending decrease, or both. These represent a move toward surplus in the budget.

➤ TAXES AS AN INSTRUMENT OF FISCAL POLICY

A general awareness that changing taxes could affect an economy's performance dates from early in the nineteenth century. Careful modeling of exactly how the alterations in taxes exerted their influence was a major contribution of the Keynesian analysis.

---

1.   Largely, but not completely offsetting as we saw in Chapter 17 when we studied the principle called the balanced-budget multiplier. Recall that the multiplier effects of taxes and government transfers (such as Social Security payments and subsidies to farmers) are slightly smaller than the multiplier from government spending on output such as new highways, new schools, and so forth.

HOW TAX CHANGES AFFECT THE ECONOMY

If taxes are lowered there will be more income available for households to spend on the consumption of goods and services. Investment might also respond, both to the higher consumption and to the increased availability of funds for investment if corporate taxes are cut. Figure 22.1's panel **a** shows the diagramming in the Keynesian tradition. Here a tax cut raises consumption and investment, and hence total spending, from C+I+G to C'+I'+G, moving the equilibrium from E to E', and increasing the nation's total output from Y to Y'. Panel **a** shows clearly that the tax decrease has a multiplier effect. That is, a cut of $100 in taxes increases total output by *more* than $100; total output Y moves further than the initial movement in C+I+G.

Panel **b**'s contemporary AD/AS model allows, as we recall, for price changes along the vertical axis. Here the tax reduction causes a rise in aggregate demand (in which consumption and investment are included) from AD to AD', thereby causing a rise in total real output from Y to Y' (less than in panel **a** because a price change also occurred). This analysis suggests that **tax reductions are effective fiscal policy for combatting a recession**.

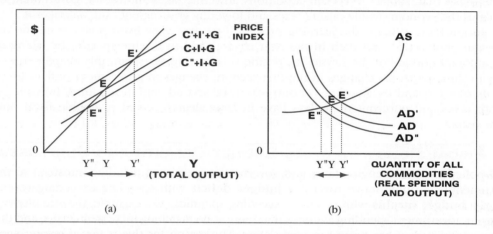

Figure 22.1. The effects of tax changes. A tax reduction will leave the public more for its own spending. In panel **a**'s Keynesian diagram, total spending (C+I+G) will rise. In panel **b**'s contemporary AD/AS model, aggregate demand will increase. Either way, the result of a tax cut is to increase total output. Tax increases have the opposite result. In either model, they reduce total output.

What effect would a tax *increase* have? A greater tax bite would leave less for consumption, meaning a decline in total spending to C"+I+G in Figure 22.1's panel **a**. The equilibrium would move from E to E", and the country's total output would decrease by a multiple, from Y to Y". Alternatively, the effect of a tax increase in a situation where prices vary can be pictured as a decline in aggregate demand from AD to AD" in the figure's panel **b**. In either case, the consequences will be even more contractionary if the reduced consumption leads firms to constrict their investment plans, or if corporate tax increases leave less for investment purposes. This analysis suggests that **tax increases are effective fiscal policy in combatting an inflation**.

The ease with which a fiscal policy of tax changes can be used quite evidently differs according to whether taxes are cut or raised. Taxation tends to be extremely unpopular with the public, so cutting is welcomed but raising them is politically risky. Walter Mondale's landslide defeat in the U.S. presidential elections of 1984 is ascribed in part to his insistence that taxes should be raised, compared to Ronald Reagan's insistence that he would never do so. In 1988, George Bush continued in the Reagan tradition by promising that he would never raise taxes. Later, in 1990, he did agree to raise them, and in the 1992 elections the broken promise was used against him.

The economics of tax changes are complicated by the fact that taxes have economic effects additional to their impact on spending. First, some taxes—most importantly the corporate income tax, excise and sales taxes, and value-added taxes—are at least partially shifted forward to consumers in the form of higher prices. So a tax increase is likely to mean a direct, though temporary, addition to inflation that will have to be taken into account. Second, taxes cost money to administer. An increase in taxes will probably raise the administrative costs of collecting them, especially when new types of taxation are introduced. "Compliance costs" may also be high because people and businesses have to engage in time-consuming recordkeeping. (For the United States, the administrative costs of the personal income tax are estimated to be as much as 2–3% of the revenue raised, and compliance costs as much as 5–7%.) Third, a tax increase might tend to decrease the supply of inputs to production. For example, labor will see that the income from work (which is taxed) is penalized compared to the alternatives, leisure and uncompensated activities in the home (which are not taxed). The impact of the reduced incentives might be pronounced on several groups, such as married women, the young, and elderly workers, who might prefer to follow untaxed pursuits rather than taking paid work. Finally, a tax increase is likely to stimulate activity in the illegal "underground economy" where income is not reported to the tax authorities.

The result is not only that tax increases are unpopular with the public, but that fuller appreciation of their negative side has made them less desirable to economists and policymakers as well. Leaders in congresses and parliaments have to keep these new factors in mind. Tax *decreases*, it should be noted, do not share in these difficulties. They are enormously popular politically, have a welcome deflationary impact if the tax cuts are shifted forward in the form of lower prices, tend to increase the supply of labor, and discourage the underground economy.

TYPES OF TAXATION

Before discussing the experience of tax alterations as a tool of fiscal policy, it is useful to discuss what types of taxation are encountered in practice. In the United States, the most important ones are the federal personal income, Social Security, sales-type, and corporate income taxes. (We ignore state and local taxes in what follows. These are important, collecting about 82% as much as federal tax revenue in 1991. But state and local governments almost never attempt to alter their taxes in counter-cyclical ways. The entire burden of managing U.S. tax policy lies with Congress and the president.[2] In most other countries as well, only the national taxes and not the local ones are available for fiscal policy purposes.)

Income Taxes

In 1913, the 16th Amendment to the U.S. Constitution made income taxes legal.[3] The federal personal income tax, by far the largest tax in the United States, collected $510 billion in 1993. A fundamental point about income taxes is that they are tied directly to income and hence production. Tax revenues will thus fluctuate with changing business conditions.

The U.S. personal income tax is a **progressive tax**, that is, the percentage of income each person must pay in taxes rises as taxable personal income rises. (Taxes that collect the same percentage of income as income rises are called proportional, while taxes that collect a smaller percentage of income as income rises are regressive.)

---

2. Using U.S. state and local taxes for fiscal policy purposes would be very difficult to organize among the 50 state governments and 86,743 (in 1992) local governments. Legal issues also interfere: states and municipalities are often limited by law as to the amount by which taxation can be varied, and attempts to cut taxes while holding spending constant are constrained by legal limits on the size of state and city debt, and how that debt can be held and spent. Forty-nine of the 50 state governments have subjected themselves to balanced-budget requirements. The result is that these governments do not participate in fiscal policy. If anything, the expectation is that state and local governments might even raise tax rates in a recession to keep revenues and hence services from declining. State tax increases when recession set in during fiscal 1990 totaled about $10 billion, and further tax increases were imposed in 1991-92.

3. Income taxes were first levied by Great Britain under William Pitt the Younger in 1799. In the United States their short use during the Civil War was ruled unconstitutional by the Supreme Court.

The fact that with a progressive income tax collections rise as people's incomes increase has an interesting economic result. It brings an automatic quality to fiscal policy. Remember the idea that tax increases will counter inflation, and tax decreases work to offset recession. When inflation sets in, personal incomes rise, so the amount people must pay in income taxes rises too. All other things being equal, the inflation is slowed. The opposite is true as well: the reduction in incomes during a recession means a lower amount of tax is collected, so making more funds available for private spending. In both cases the tax system is counter-cyclical. The feature of taxation that it collects more or less as income rises or falls came to be known as an **automatic stabilizer**, or alternatively a **built-in stabilizer**. (Federal spending also has automatic stabilizing aspects, as we shall see later in the chapter.) Because growth in output and income bring their own increased tax bill, tending to brake the growth, the name **fiscal drag** came to be much used.

Indexing the Brackets

The tendency for income taxes to collect more as income rises used to be stronger than it is now. Until quite recently, when people's income rose, they were pushed into a higher tax bracket, where higher percentage rates applied, so their taxes rose not only because their income went up, but because the percentage rate they paid had gone up too.[4] The opposite was true in recessions. Tax collections fell in any case as incomes declined, but people were also pushed into a lower tax bracket where they paid a lower percentage of their incomes.

A specific case will illustrate how this happened. Say the income tax laws required you to pay 10% of your income up to $20,000 and 15% of any income above that figure. If your annual wage was $20,000, you paid $2000 in tax. Now assume that all prices (including your wages) increased by 20%. In that case your extra earnings of $4000 pushed you into the higher 15% tax bracket. You had to pay 15% of the extra $4000, or $600, in extra tax. But your wage increase was not a real gain, only a nominal one. To leave you in the same position as before, you should have paid $2400, which is 10% of $24,000. Because you were pushed into the higher bracket, you had to pay $2600. Your real tax bill went up while your real purchasing power stayed the same. Congress did not vote to raise your tax bill, but it went up anyway because of the effect of inflation.

Economists generally appreciated the built-in counter-cyclical aspects of taxation. But in the 1960s and '70s, legislatures in the United States and abroad seemed to appreciate the built-in aspects even more. If economic growth raised tax receipts, then those new receipts might permit more federal spending without any painful necessity for raising tax rates. To a politician, this was a **fiscal dividend**, akin to manna from heaven. The notion that taxes brought a fiscal dividend was based on the same principle that taxes served as an automatic stabilizer with a fiscal drag, namely that taxes rise as incomes rise. The difference is that with fiscal dividend, legislators spent the tax receipts.

As inflation set in during the 1970s, the fiscal dividend became ever larger. The higher incomes led to higher tax revenues, extra cash that did not require the legislators to raise tax rates and was available to finance new government spending. Very widely, the legislators did indeed spend the revenues.

Voters' protests against this situation grew louder. A movement to limit the increase in taxes caused by "bracket creep" from inflation grew stronger from the late 1970s. That led to "tax indexing," that is, raising the range of the tax brackets each year so that inflation would not lead to higher tax bills. Tax indexing was adopted in the United States (from 1985), Australia, Canada, the Netherlands, Sweden, and numerous other countries as well. In our example just given, the old 10% tax bracket would be extended to the higher nominal level of income ($24,000) reached because of the inflation. With inflation of 20% this year, the 10% income tax bracket would now apply to the first $24,000 of income ($20,000 + 20%) rather than to the original $20,000. Your tax bill would then be $24,000 x 10% = $2400, rather than the $2600 with "bracket creep." True,

---

4.   Technically, one result of the movement into higher brackets was to lower the size of the multiplier. Higher incomes brought a higher marginal propensity to pay tax, the "MPT" of Chapter 17.

your taxes in real terms have been kept stable, which was the intent of the indexing, but the automatic stabilizing effect of the income tax has been reduced by the $200 in lost tax revenue. Tax collections still do rise, so the procedure does work to contain the inflation, but because of the indexing they do not rise by as much as they would have.

Economists who see merit in the stabilizing aspect of income taxes are often of two minds on the issue of tax indexing. They recognize that if legislators will not allow the automatic stabilization to work, but instead spend the revenues as a fiscal dividend, this does indeed seem a case of "taxation without representation." Taxpayers pay a higher tax bill that their representatives did not vote for. Many would also insist, however, that weakening the principle of stabilization through indexing was a mistake. Repeal of indexing would, however, face the usual obstacle of public resistance to any scheme that smacks of a tax increase.

THE TAXATION OF CAPITAL GAINS

One further element of the personal income tax deserves discussion: the taxation of capital gains by means of a **capital-gains** tax. Income may accrue when stocks, bonds, real estate, paintings, antiques, and the like are sold by their owners at prices higher than their original purchase price. How is such income treated? Is it personal income just as wages and salaries, or is it something special? In the United States, the tradition has been to consider capital gains a form of income, and therefore fair prey for the tax authorities. Capital gains are not, however, taxed in some countries, including Japan, Germany, Austria, Belgium, the Netherlands, and Italy.

Since 1986, capital gains have been taxed at 28% in the United States, which at that time was the same as the highest rate of income tax.[5] From 1988 to 1992 there was intense lobbying to reduce the capital gains tax to 15%. Proponents of this move (including most notably President Bush) contended that it would raise investment and economic growth. They argued that tax revenues would rise over five years because people would cash in their holdings to reap capital gains. Opponents argued that revenue would fall greatly in the long run (from 1997) and that the rich would garner most of the benefits.

Two-thirds of capital gains accrue to people with incomes over $200,000. The U.S. Treasury states that tax revenues would increase through 1996 because of increased selling of assets, but would fall greatly from 1997. About 70% of the capital gains tax cut proposed by President Bush in 1992 would go to those with incomes over $100,000 per year, according to the Congressional Joint Committee on Taxation. The average tax saving for those whose income is over $200,000 per year would be $8,478; for those with income between $30,000 and $40,000 it would be $297.

Opponents argued further that capital gains are received from the sale of many sorts of property (especially real estate and collectibles) that have little to do with the capital investment that makes an economy more productive. Of all reported capital gains in 1985, 42% was from sale of corporate stock, 16% from residential real estate, 13% from business real estate, and 10% from farm and other land. Selling a gambling casino gives rise to capital gains, but why should that necessarily justify a lower rate of tax? Indeed, reducing the tax on capital gains is decidedly not the same thing as reducing the tax on productive investment.

---

5.   Originally, 50% of capital gains were exempt from tax; this was raised to 60% in 1978. The remaining 50%, later 40%, was taxed at a rate of 28% until 1981, when the rate was cut to 20%. In the 1986 tax act, the capital gains exclusion was eliminated (that is, all such gains were made subject to tax), and the rate returned to 28%.

Some who oppose cutting the capital gains tax would, however, agree that it should be indexed to eliminate the effect of inflation on capital assets. A rise of 100% in the price of a house is not, of course, a real gain if inflation has been 100% since the house was purchased. In some periods, inflation has meant that the effective tax rate on the real gains from an investment has been much higher than 28%, and has even been above 100% for many investments made before the rapid inflation of the 1970s. Limiting the tax to real capital gains is done in a number of countries, for example Great Britain, and this seems a reasonable approach.

Yet it should also be remembered that the present capital gains tax *already* gives preferential treatment to capital gains even if it is collected at the same rate as the tax on other income. That is because the tax on the gains is deferred until they are realized. In effect, government makes a long-term loan to the taxpayer of the revenue that would have been paid had the tax been collected on the annual gain. For example, assume that the capital gains tax and income tax rates are the same. Then consider an investor who reaps a capital gain of $X every year on, say, a building, then 20 years down the road sells the building and pays the capital gains tax. Given recent tax and interest rates, that investor would end up with about two-thirds more money than another investor who bought a bond that yields interest of $X annually, which is taxed annually.[6]

Following his election, President Clinton proposed a much more limited reduction in the capital gains tax that applied only to small businesses. In 1993, Congress agreed to halve (to 14%) the capital gains tax rate for investors in small firms that are just starting up.

Other Types of Taxation

Other national taxes besides the personal income tax are (or could be) available for fiscal purposes. Many countries have a separate tax on corporate profits. In the United States, it has been 35% since 1993; in that year it collected about 11% of all federal revenue. Corporate income tax receipts, like personal income tax collections, rise and fall during booms and slumps, but the corporate tax is not graduated beyond quite a low level. One long-standing criticism of the corporate income tax is that it represents double taxation: The corporation must pay tax on its profits, but when these profits are paid out as dividends, the dividends are considered taxable income under the personal income tax laws. This means corporations' investments must be profitable enough to cover the double tax, which tends to reduce the amount of new investment by corporations. A proposal not yet adopted is to eliminate the double taxation by allowing recipients of dividends to receive credits for the corporate income tax already paid. Eliminating the corporate income tax entirely would probably not be a good idea for revenue reasons; it does allow some taxation of foreign-owned assets that would otherwise escape.

In the developed countries, a national sales-type tax called the **value-added tax**, or VAT, is almost universal. We explained in Chapter 15 how VATs are collected on the value added by firms at each stage of a good's manufacture and sale, as when tax is charged on the producer of wood pulp, the paper-maker, the printer, and the final seller of a book. Only the United States, Australia, and Switzerland are currently without a VAT. The last countries to come on board were Japan in

---

6.   For the arithmetic see William Vickrey, "An Updated Agenda for Progressive Taxation," *American Economic Review*, Vol. 82, No. 2, May 1992, p. 257.

1988 and Canada in 1991.[7] Worldwide, 64 countries had one in 1992, usually collecting 15–25% of total tax revenue. Although a VAT has been discussed in the United States, adoption is barely on the horizon. All such sales-type taxes could also be altered as a weapon of fiscal policy, although in Europe the European Community's rules standardizing VAT rates among countries has made this next to impossible.

VATs AND EXCISE TAX CONSIDERATIONS

A VAT raises prices, but only in a once-for-all change. The charge that VATs are regressive (that is, weighing more heavily on the poor than the rich), can be met by excluding food, fuel, housing, medical care, and children's clothing (as in Britain), and by using other parts of the budget such as welfare spending and income tax rebates to offset remaining regressivity. It is hard to avoid paying VAT; the tax is in part self-policing, because producers at later stages of production are motivated to ensure that the tax has been paid by firms at earlier stages. Otherwise, they may be stuck with the bill themselves. (A sales tax such as that charged by most U.S. states is easier to avoid, since it is paid only at the final point of sale. Only one person need be involved in the tax avoidance; there are no links in a chain of production, and therefore no self-policing by other firms.) A further advantage of a VAT is that it would not tax saving. The U.S. income tax is levied on all income earned whether the income is used for consumption or for saving; a VAT is levied only on consumption. That would be helpful in encouraging a higher savings rate in the United States. Alternatively, one could allow savings to be subtracted from income to determine a taxpayer's total expenditure,

and then tax just this expenditure. The idea has some support, but would involve much more onerous bookkeeping than is necessary at present.

The United States has a few federal excise (sales) taxes that are a tax on final sales rather than a VAT, but they *are* a direct tax on consumption. They collect about 5% of federal revenue. Among the small number of items that have been subject to federal excise taxes for many years are gasoline, tires, batteries, cigarettes, alcoholic beverages, long-distance telephone calls, airline tickets, pistols and revolvers, and slot machines. A 10% luxury tax was imposed in 1990 on the purchase price above $10,000 of furs and jewelry, above $30,000 for cars, above $100,000 for boats, and above $250,000 for airplanes. Critics complained that the industries producing these items were seriously harmed, with sales down and jobs lost, and indeed the elasticity of demand for these items did prove to be higher than anticipated. All these taxes except the one on cars were dropped in 1993. Some economists argued that the decline in sales of the taxed items was due much more to the ongoing recession's effect on sales than it was to the price-enhancing effect of the taxes.

Inheritance or "estate" taxes are another type of taxation. They collect little in the United States, only 1% of federal revenue in 1993, one reason being that the first $600,000 of an inheritance is exempt from tax. Inheritance taxes are far more important in some other countries, especially Great Britain. The famous nineteenth-century economist John Stuart Mill spent a lifetime arguing that taxes on inheritances should become the most important source of government revenue. He suggested that they carry less costs to society than other taxes because the

---

7.   France and Germany adopted their VATs in 1968. The British and Italian VATs date from 1973. Their rates are all currently in the 17–18% range, compared to Canada's 7% and Japan's world low of 3%. The *highest* rates of VAT in the western countries in 1992 were 24.5% in Iceland and 21% in Ireland; the world high standard rate is currently Malawi's 35%. Even the former Communist countries have adopted them, Russia and Ukraine in 1992 (both 28%).

incentive to work and enjoy one's own income is not affected in one's lifetime. He believed that inheritance taxes were preferable to other types of taxes because they discouraged the creation of a permanent aristocracy of wealth. Many economists today find Mill's position persuasive, but the public does not appear to agree.

The final type of tax in the United States is the Social Security payroll tax, earmarked for the financing of the Social Security system. A special tax for this purpose is common in many countries. The U.S. Social Security tax has a number of unusual features. It is the fastest-growing federal tax, now (1993) the source of 37% of all federal revenue. It collected less than one-third as much as the federal income tax in 1957, reaching one-half by 1967 and over 85% today. It is levied as a flat percentage of income (15.3% in 1993, compared to only 6% in 1960). Half is paid by the employer and half by the employee, up to a certain income level ($57,600 in 1993). The portion of people's incomes higher than that figure is not taxed. Nor does the tax apply to interest, dividends, or capital gains earned in addition to wages and salaries. Because the poor thus pay a much higher percentage of their income for this tax than the well-to-do, the Social Security payroll tax is the most regressive of the federal taxes. Essentially, it makes labor more expensive and encourages firms to keep employment down. This is hardly a desirable outcome. Many argue that some or all of the Social Security tax should be abolished, and the funds made up from the general income tax revenues. This would both reduce the regressive element in the present tax structure and lessen the constraint on employment.

CHANGING TAXES AS A TOOL OF MACROECONOMIC MANAGEMENT

The major principles of a fiscal policy involving tax changes become clear if we examine U.S. tax policy during the last 30 years. Changes in tax rates became a staple of counter-cyclical fiscal policy in the 1960s and 1970s. The Kennedy administration proposed the first major tax reduction in American history designed to stimulate the economy, then coming out of a recession. The proposal led to a long and acrimonious debate, and it was not adopted until early in the Johnson administration. Known as the Revenue Act of 1964, it cut personal income tax rates by about one-quarter. Combined with spending increases occurring at the same time, the federal budget was driven into what then seemed a substantial deficit. Thus the U.S. government embraced a major principle of fiscal policy: **tax reductions stimulate the economy, while tax increases constrict it**. (During the Great Depression, these principles had been violated in the extreme. In 1932, the federal government was finding it difficult to pay its bills as tax revenues decreased. That year's Tax Revenue Act increased income tax rates to nearly double their previous level.)

At the time, most economists and politicians agreed that the 1964 tax cut provided a healthy stimulus, helping to lower unemployment by one percentage point from its 1962–63 average, and to raise the annual real growth rate of output from $2\frac{1}{2}$% in 1959–60 to 6% in 1965. Inflation stayed low at less than 3%. Tax change as an agent of fiscal policy had apparently passed its first trial with flying colors.

The colors were soon flying in a very different way, however, as the United States became embroiled in Vietnam. With a large rise in defense spending between the middle of 1965 and the end of 1966, tacked on to even more spending for Lyndon Johnson's "Great Society" programs that provided assistance to the poor, the economy began to overheat. The inflation statistics showed a 3% rise in the consumer price index between 1966 and 1967, 4% from 1967 to 1968, over 5% in 1968 to 1969. The trend was unmistakable.

Economists called for a reversal of the tax cuts as the needed fiscal response, but the process took much longer than the tax cut had taken. President Johnson did not agree to propose an increase until early in 1967, and he did so with little enthusiasm. Congress procrastinated for a long time. With action so long delayed, it was thought necessary to increase the contractionary dose, and the original proposal for a 6% surcharge (percentage added to tax bills) on the personal income tax and corporate tax became a 10% surcharge. Widely believed by economists to be still too little and definitely too late, the 10% surcharge was finally passed in June 1968.

An important economic lesson was immediately obvious: **tax increases, when used as fiscal policy against inflation, are far more difficult to enact than are tax decreases against recession**. For tax increases, the implementation lag is long.[8]

THE LAG OF TAX INCREASES IS SHORTER FOR MANY OTHER COUNTRIES

The long implementation lag for tax increases was and is a problem that to some degree is specific to the United States, where the Constitution gives Congress a largely independent voice in tax policy. A difference of opinion with the executive branch can easily delay, or even stymie, a tax change, in particular a tax increase. In the parliamentary systems of Canada, Japan, and most of Europe, the difficulty hardly exists because the prime minister usually belongs to the ruling party and commands a parliamentary majority. (Usually, because in some cases a coalition of parties has formed the government. No party to the coalition may be willing to take the political heat for unpopular policy changes. In such countries—recently including Belgium, Denmark, Ireland, Italy, and Sweden—a tax increase may be just as difficult to engineer as it is in the United States.)

Where a single party governs, a tax increase may still be rejected as overly unpopular, but at least the structure of government does not add to the problem. (One federal system with a separation of powers, Germany, has a "Law of Stability and Growth" dating from 1967 that permits the executive branch to pass a tax change within certain limits, 10% in most circumstances, without submitting the measure to the legislature.)

A second problem with the 1968 tax increase came as a surprise to most economists. The 10% surcharge of that year was *temporary* and not a permanent change in taxes. The results helped to make it clear that **the public reacts differently to temporary and permanent tax changes**. The reason is related to the permanent-income, or life-cycle hypothesis of consumption spending that we studied in Chapter 16. This is the principle that permanent changes in income are likely to have a greater effect on the amount consumed than are changes that are not permanent. This theory of consumption behavior implies that temporary tax changes have more modest effects than those that are permanent. If taxes are increased temporarily, a large proportion of the bill might be paid out of savings to avoid the discomfort of a temporary dip in consumption. If the increase were permanent, that alternative could not be followed, because savings would dip too far. So consumption would be restricted more than in the case of the temporary increase. Conversely, a temporary tax reduction would result in additions to savings greater than if the change had been permanent. In effect, the C+I+G function in the Keynesian model, or the aggregate demand curve in the contemporary model, does not move as far following a temporary tax change as it does after a permanent one.

---

8.   The implementation lag—the time between the recognition of a problem and the decision to implement a new policy—is familiar from the previous chapter. The response lag, the time from adopting a new policy to its having its effect, is considered to be *shorter* for fiscal than for monetary policy because households and firms immediately have more or less purchasing power as soon as less or more is taken out of their incomes by government. The process is not instantaneous, because it takes some time for households and firms to alter their spending plans, and for firms to alter their level of dividends, but it is still shorter than for monetary policy. Even so, the longer implementation lag of tax changes—specifically tax increases—mean that the combined lag of such changes are usually longer (at best a year or more) than for monetary policy.

The conviction that temporary tax changes have less effect than permanent ones was heightened during the next episode of tax alteration. A tax cut was made in 1975 to counter the growing recession that stemmed from the first OPEC maneuvers in 1973 to raise the price of oil. A portion of taxes already withheld was returned to taxpayers as a rebate, but once more the impact on the economy seemed to be less than had been anticipated.

Economists working with data concerning the impact of the temporary 1968 surcharge and the 1975 rebate concluded that the eventual effect on consumption, and hence on output, was at most only about one-half of what could be expected from an identical but permanent change in taxes. The knowledge was important and implied that if tax changes are to be used in one-time doses to counter a developing inflation or recession, with a subsequent restoration to original levels, they may have to be larger than originally believed. This makes it even less likely that a temporary tax increase for fiscal policy purposes can be passed within a reasonable amount of time.[9]

"INVESTMENT TAX CREDITS": A TEMPORARY TAX CUT THAT MAY BE MORE EFFECTIVE

One temporary tax cut that appears to be more effective than the others is an **investment tax credit** involving a tax reduction on new investment. Thus if a firm made a new investment of $1000 this year, and an investment tax credit of 10% were in place, that firm could claim a $100 rebate from the government. A 7% investment tax credit was passed in 1962 and suspended in 1966. Restored in 1967, it was eliminated in 1969, reinstated in 1971, and increased to 10% in 1975 before being eliminated again in 1986. (Following his election, President Clinton proposed a new investment tax credit retroactive to December 3, 1992, but Congress would not agree.) Investment tax credits do introduce an artificial bias in favor of investment, but if they are kept temporary they can deliver a strong stimulus to an economy. Here is a temporary tax cut that can actually be greater in its impact than a permanent one. The reason is that companies may speed up their investment plans to take advantage of the credit they know will be temporary. Because the increase in investment now may be at the expense of a temporary decrease later, the policy would have to be carefully managed.

To obtain the maximum effect, it may be best to make a temporary investment tax credit incremental in nature, applying only to new investment over some base line. Thus a firm that had been making a million dollars' worth of investment every year would get no tax credit for investing another million next year. The credit would apply only to investment next year that was over $1 million.

THE ERTA TAX CUTS

The substantial tax cuts of the Reagan era will be controversial for many years. During the campaigning for the 1980 election, President-to-be Reagan promised to cut taxes. In August 1981, Congress passed the Economic Recovery Tax Act, or **ERTA**. The new law cut the personal income tax in three annual installments of 5%, 10%, and 10%. Taxes were also reduced on savings through tax deductions of $2000 for income contributed to individual retirement accounts, or IRAs.

---

9.   If a tax change is adopted as permanent, but government then makes yet another "permanent" change, and then another, and so on, the public will probably come to treat these as if they were temporary. Each "permanent" change is likely to have less effect. A policy announcement itself, before a tax change is actually made, is likely to have an even smaller impact. One reason may be that for many taxpayers it may take some time for the news to sink in. Others may face a "liquidity constraint"—they know that their taxes will decline, but they have few resources they can call on to increase their spending until the tax cut really takes place.

It was generally believed that tax cuts to encourage investment were likely to work faster, and probably would be more effective, than tax cuts to stimulate work effort and personal saving. So the ERTA also cut corporate taxes by allowing faster depreciation of capital investment. Firms can take a tax deduction to allow for the wearing out of their capital, so speeding up the deductions (say spacing them over 10 years rather than 15) permitted more business expenses to be deducted from income. That lowered the tax bill. Tax credits for research and development expenditures were also introduced. The decline in corporate taxes was so sharp that they collected only about 8% of federal revenue in 1985 compared to as much as 28% in the 1950s.

The purpose of the ERTA tax cut was not that of Keynesian fiscal policy. President Reagan and his supporters believed that high taxation was harmful, and growth in the economy would be enhanced by unshackling entrepreneurs who would increase their effort and their investment. The tax cuts were not intended as temporary counter-cyclical fiscal policy, but as a permanent stimulus to the economy's total output. As effort was stimulated and as investment increased, more output would be forthcoming at any given price level. The result would be a change in the position of the aggregate supply curve, as from AS_1 to AS_2 in Figure 22.2. Because of this, Reagan's tax cuts were called a "supply-side" policy. Consumers, now paying less in taxes, would use the income left in their hands to purchase the new output, seen as a movement from AD_1 to AD_2. The hoped-for result was economic growth without inflation. That is, after the two curves shift, output has grown from Y_1 to Y_2, while the price index remains unchanged at P_1.

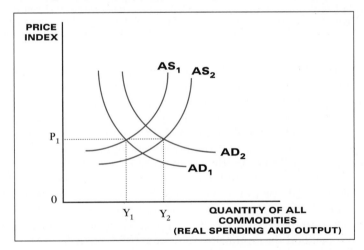

Figure 22.2. **The hoped-for effect of the ERTA tax cut.** Its proponents hoped that the Reagan tax cuts of the 1980s would unleash effort and enhance capital investment, so moving the aggregate supply curve to the right. At the same time, consumers would have more income available, so aggregate demand would move to the right as well. Output would grow, but without inflation.

By hindsight, several results of the 1980s supply-side tax cutting are now apparent. First, the favorable changes in aggregate supply were slow to develop, while the shift in aggregate demand was rapid. Under different circumstances, that would have posed inflationary dangers, but with the economy depressed at the time of the cuts, the stimulus was welcome. Second, the way taxes were cut, the rich gained considerably more than did the poor and the middle classes. Many observers criticized the cuts as allowing the rich to pay less than their fair share of the costs of government. Finally and most importantly, taxes were cut well below the level of government spending. A large budget deficit therefore developed, with significant adverse consequences that we shall have to examine and that are with us yet.

Could the Tax Cuts Finance Themselves?

At the time of the tax cuts, a small band of economists led by Arthur Laffer at the University of Southern California denied that the tax cuts would cause a budget deficit to develop. They insisted that *cuts would finance themselves* by generating so much more income to be taxed that tax revenues would rise even with a sharp fall in tax rates. According to this theory, U.S. taxes were so high that they diminished work effort, and lower tax rates would stimulate effort. During lunch, so it is said, Laffer sketched what became known as the **Laffer Curve** on a napkin. Shown in Figure 22.3, it depicts the tax rate on the horizontal (X) axis and tax revenues on the vertical (Y) axis. In this model, tax revenues will rise with increases in the tax rate only to a certain point, beyond which further increases in the rate will diminish revenues because taxpayers reduce their work effort.

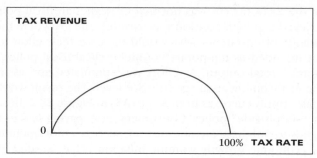

Figure 22.3. The Laffer Curve. A curve showing tax revenues rising as the tax rate increases up to a point beyond which further increases in the rate will diminish revenues. The argument was widely made that the United States was positioned on the right side of the curve. Thus cutting taxes would increase tax revenues. This view was influential in attracting support for the Reagan tax cuts of the early 1980s.

The Laffer idea never received much of a welcome in the economics profession. The inhospitable reception was not based on the conviction that the idea was necessarily wrong—very high (confiscatory) taxes certainly *can* diminish effort—nor on any lack of desire to have it be true. Economists like everyone else would be the beneficiaries if lower taxes really did collect more tax revenue, and would be as enthusiastic as Laffer and his supporters if events had proved the model correct. The great majority of economists took the position that the stimulative effect on effort would be far too small to offset the fall in tax rates. Earlier studies covering a number of countries and time periods had suggested that the recovery of tax revenues following a large cut in tax rates, of 25% or so, might be as low as 5%. It did seem reasonable that high tax rates might deter a marriage partner from taking a paid job, and that lower taxes would therefore bring more people (and taxpayers) into the labor force. But no serious empirical study, or indeed persuasive evidence of any kind, justified the optimistic view of a 100% recovery. The major problem with the theory was that for at least the last two decades, tax rates in the United States have not appeared to be high enough so that cutting them would have the desired large effect on effort. Last-ditch defenders of the Laffer principle can still be found, arguing that later rises in U.S. taxes took place before the increased effort was unleashed, but see the box that follows for evidence that U.S. tax rates, even after the ERTA rates were raised somewhat, are actually *low* by international standards.

It should also be noted that the viewpoint that lower taxes unleash effort appears to be in direct contradiction to Swedish and other Scandinavian experience, where some of the world's highest tax rates seem to have propelled married women **into**, not out of, the labor force, in an attempt to maintain disposable income levels. The annual average rate of real per capita economic growth in high-tax Scandinavia was above American levels in 1965–1989 in spite of the low U.S. taxes. In fact, *all* the countries shown in Figure 22.4 registered growth greater than the 1.6% per year in the United States during that period, even though their tax burdens were higher. The next lowest growth, 1.7%, was in Australia, the country with the second lowest taxes. No persuasive evidence exists that economic growth is closely correlated with low taxation, for the understandable reason that taxes can pay for things the government provides that stimulate growth and productivity—better education, health, highways, bridges, and so forth. The subject of economic growth is surveyed in Chapter 26.

TO WHAT DEGREE DO U.S. TAXES DISTORT ECONOMIC BEHAVIOR?

In the 1960s and early 1970s, economists believed that the effect of taxes on people's economic behavior, especially the amount of labor they were willing to supply, was relatively modest. Later the pendulum swung far in the other direction. A common view held in the early 1980s was that taxes had large effects on economic behavior. An emerging position based on the evidence available is that labor supply is not very sensitive to tax policy, and especially that moderate tax increases would not lead to a severe decline in work effort in any but the world's highest-tax countries. As Figure 22.4 shows, the United States is not one of these. Even in 1982, the year the first and smallest of the ERTA cuts was phased in, U.S. tax revenues as a percent of total output and income were still well below that of many other countries. By 1990, the United States had the lowest taxes as a percent of GNP of all the major industrial countries, and also the least-progressive tax system as well.

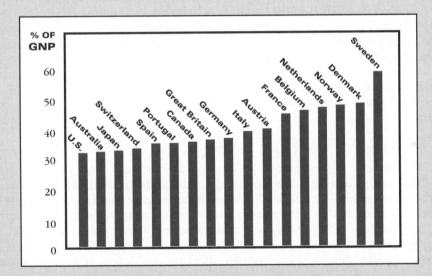

Figure 22.4 Tax revenues at all levels of government, percent of GNP, 1990.
Source: OECD data for 1990, as presented in *The Economist,* September 21, 1991.

There was a time in the period after World War II when U.S. marginal income tax rates charged by the federal government alone were as high as 90¢ on a dollar of additional earnings. This 90% marginal rate was certainly high enough to have strong disincentive effects. Under ERTA, however, the marginal rate for the highest income bracket at the national level was 28% for the United States, the lowest of any major industrial country. The highest marginal rate in Britain is 40%, in Japan 50%, Germany 53%, and France 57%. Recent increases in the U.S. marginal rate for high-income taxpayers still leaves that rate below these figures, though Canada, New Zealand, Norway, Sweden, and Switzerland are now lower. (Sweden's low rate represents a considerable change from the percentage in the figure—marginal rates there used to be among the highest in the world.)

The Effects of the ERTA Tax Cuts on the Economy

Many economists argued that the ERTA tax cuts had stimulative effects on the economy, though the Reagan administration had undertaken them for other reasons. At the time they were enacted, the stimulus was welcome. The Fed's anti-inflationary tight-money policy beginning in late 1979 clearly had had a powerful impact, suppressing the inflation of the time but with serious side effects. The rise in real interest rates caused by slower growth in the money supply penalized investment and those parts of consumption and of government spending that are dependent on interest rates. A sharp recession followed. The large ERTA tax cuts were therefore sensible given the conditions, bringing a timely delivery of stimulative fiscal policy whatever the original motive for the cuts.

But the ERTA tax cuts had a very significant negative effect as well. They contributed substantially to the creation of a large federal budget deficit during the years after 1981, a deficit that has become an almost permanent fixture of the economy.[10] Permanent large deficits are not a good thing for an economy, as we discuss later in this chapter and in the next.

Who should be blamed for this adverse outcome? It could be seen as the fault of the Reagan administration, which proposed a big tax cut but not enough spending cuts to pay for these. In fact, for the fiscal years 1981–1985, President Reagan asked Congress to approve $4,307 billion in spending, while Congress actually approved $4,342 billion, an addition of just 8/10 of 1% to the president's budgets. It could be seen as the fault of Congress for going along, for allowing tax cuts to be too large and even adding to them, and for not cutting spending further. Perhaps the public should be blamed for its unwillingness to pay the full price for what it gets from government, and its practice of electing presidents from one party and legislators from another, so allowing party disagreements to stymie policy. Perhaps economists should shoulder a share of the blame as well. They should have taken a stronger position early in the battle. Complete innocence seems in short supply.

THE ATTEMPTS TO TAKE BACK SOME OF THE CUTS

The 1981 ERTA tax cut was eventually recognized as too large, and the Bush and Clinton Administrations have been taking back some of the reductions. In 1990, President Bush—at great political cost as it transpired—acquiesced in a budget agreement that raised the highest marginal rate of income tax from 28% to 31%, phased out many exemptions for upper-income taxpayers, raised "sin taxes" on beer (16¢ per six-pack) and cigarettes (8¢ per pack), raised the gasoline tax by 5¢, and imposed the luxury taxes on autos, boats, jewelry, furs, and aircraft mentioned earlier in the chapter. Though this had little enough effect on the deficit, it angered voters and left politicians even more aware than before that raising taxes is dangerous business.

When President Clinton took office, he nevertheless pushed for further takebacks from the ERTA of the 1980s. The 1993 bill doing so was a close-run thing (218–216 in the House, Vice President Gore breaking a tie in the Senate). Taxes were raised on upper-income individuals, to a marginal rate of 36% on those with incomes above $140,000 and 39.6% on those with incomes above $250,000, though this top rate is still rather low among the major countries. The corporation tax was raised from 34% to 35%, and an additional 4.3¢ tax was placed on gasoline.[11]

Still, these tax changes were not only rather small, but they were very painfully achieved. It was proof positive that a fiscal policy involving tax increases is very difficult. The present situation

---

10.   Whether the actual managers of the tax cut, right up to the President himself, believed that they would create a deficit is not clear. These actors in the drama were trying diligently but unsuccessfully to cut government spending at the same time. Whether they believed that a deficit would be stimulative is also unclear. Budget Director David Stockman's autobiography indicates that at least some in the administration were aware that these would be the results. See David Stockman, *The Triumph of Politics,* New York, 1986.

11.   A broad-based energy tax would have been better at reducing the social costs of pollution and would have raised more revenue, but it proved politically impossible to pass this. Other changes that were made included taxing 85% of Social Security benefits, rather than just 50%, on those with incomes above $44,000; denying the right of corporations to deduct as a business cost the portion of executive salaries over $1 million; and limiting the deductibility on meals and entertainment to 50% rather than 80%. Other tax-like features included the raising of grazing fees raised on western lands, and the introduction of competitive bidding for telecommunications wave lengths.

is that politics impedes tax increases to control booms, while the large federal budget deficit makes tax decreases to fight slumps less desirable and even dangerous. Given these difficulties, it is little wonder that attention shifted to the other branch of fiscal policy, the management of government spending discussed in the next section.

► FISCAL POLICY: SPENDING

Changing taxes is one type of fiscal policy. The other type is changing government spending, defined as transfer payments and government spending on output of goods and services. In the Keynesian model, increases in government spending have an expansionary impact on the economy, while decreases have a contractionary effect. The effect can be viewed as a rise or fall of G in total spending C+I+G in Figure 22.5's panel **a**, or as a rise or fall in aggregate demand (which includes government spending) in panel **b**. In either case, an increase in government spending moves the equilibrium from E to E' and has a multiplier effect on total output, which rises from Y to Y'. If government spending is reduced, the equilibrium moves from E to E" and lowers total output by a multiple from Y to Y". (Remember that, as explained in Chapter 17, the multiplier effect of a change in government transfer payments will be slightly less than the effect of a change in government spending on output of goods and services.)

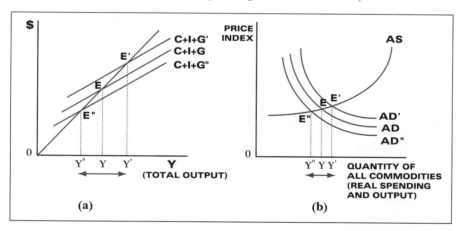

Figure 22.5. **The effects of government spending changes.** An increase in government spending will stimulate the economy. In panel **a**'s Keynesian diagram, the rise in G causes total spending (C+I+G) to rise. In panel **b**'s contemporary AD/AS model, aggregate demand shifts to the right. Either way, the result of an increase in government spending is to raise real total output. (The increase is greater in panel **a** than in **b**, because in panel **b** a price change has occurred.) Decreases in government spending have the opposite result. In either model, they reduce total output.

SOME FORMS OF GOVERNMENT SPENDING ARE AUTOMATIC STABILIZERS

We have already noted that taxation acts to a degree as an automatic stabilizer of the macroeconomy, collecting more revenue as income rises and hence cooling booms, and less as income falls, so limiting slumps. Some forms of government spending—mostly those involving transfer payments to the public—also have desirable automatic aspects. Unemployment compensation and welfare expenditures rise in recessions and fall with the return of prosperity. Spending on farm aid programs mounts when agricultural prices fall and recedes as those prices recover.

Taking government taxes and transfer payments together, how powerful are the automatic stabilizers? In the United States, statistical analysis suggests that every $1 decrease in GDP tends to decrease taxes and increase transfer payments by about 22¢. In effect, a significant portion of any given change in the nation's output is offset by the action of the automatic stabilizers.

THE STRUCTURE OF GOVERNMENT SPENDING

About two-thirds of the federal government's budget outlays involve transfer payments and interest payments, which are conceptually similar to transfers. Spending on the output of goods and services accounts for the remaining third of the budget. Of the spending on goods and services, some 34% is for the wages and salaries of federal employees, while the rest is for the government's purchases.

The major problem with using a fiscal policy involving changes in government spending, either in the form of transfers or the purchase of goods and services, is that for political and institutional reasons the changes may be difficult to bring about. Inflation fighting by means of spending cuts raises stormy political seas; those who were receiving the spending will object. Raising spending to fight recession used to be politically easy, but no more. The public and the politicians in the United States and numerous other countries are well aware that large and potentially damaging budget deficits have become an annual occurrence. They hesitate to increase these deficits even in a good cause.

In the United States, the federal budget for the fiscal year 1993 (October 1, 1992, to September 30, 1993) was $1,408 billion. That figure is about 23.7% of GDP, compared to only 3% in 1929.[12] The first two columns of data in Table 22.1 show U.S. government budget outlays by category in fiscal 1993, both in dollars and as a percent of the total, starting with the largest. The next two columns show the Clinton administration's projections of the budget for fiscal 1997 when the total outlays are planned to be $1,691 billion. In the last column, the percent of total government spending in the last year of the Carter administration, fiscal 1980, can be used to gauge the later changes in the budget.

TABLE 22.1
U.S. government budget outlays, fiscal 1993, and projections for 1997.

Category of Spending	1993 Billion $	1993 Percent	1997 Billion $	1997 Percent	1980 Percent
Social Security and Medicare	435.1	31	568.5	34	26
National Defense	290.6	21	256.4	15	23
Income Security (Welfare, Unemployment Insurance)	208.0	15	242.5	14	15
Interest on Debt	198.9	14	234.0	14	9
Health, Education, and Training	148.1	11	237.9	14	9
Veterans' Benefits	35.7	3	41.5	2	3
Natural Resources, Environment, Energy	24.5	2	27.0	2	4
Commerce, Housing, Transport, Community and Regional Development	22.1*	2	49.2	3	5
Agriculture	20.3	1	13.1	1	1
International Affairs	17.2	1	17.7	1	2
Science, Space, Technology	17.1	1	17.1	1	1
Other	28.0	2	32.0	2	5

Source: U.S. Office of Management and Budget. Includes "on-budget" and "off-budget" items. Does not add to 100% because of rounding and a quasi-revenue item (offsetting receipts) not included in the table.
*Temporarily low because of large repayments of housing loans in 1993. The 1992 figure was $50.3 billion.

---

12.   For some historical perspective, government spending was only about $1 billion during the entire 60 years from 1789 to 1849; $15 billion from 1850 to 1899; and about $3 billion per year as late as the 1920s. (These figures are not corrected for inflation, but government spending has expanded enormously by any measure.)

The table, together with the data on total government spending, allows for a review of the difficulties that lie in wait for budget-cutters. (The actual process of changing government spending is discussed in the accompanying box.) After more than a decade during which exceptional attention was given to cuts in government spending, federal spending of 23.7% of GDP in 1993 was actually higher than the 22.0% of 1980. Big government got a little bigger in spite of all the rhetoric. One major reason for the spending increase between 1980 and 1993 was growth in transfers such as Social Security and Medicare spending on the elderly, a trend projected to continue well into the future and clear in the 1997 budget. Another reason was the increase in interest on the national debt, which rose from $53 billion in 1980 to $199 billion in 1993; this item registered the largest percentage increase. The interest payments reflected the constant federal budget deficits during the period.[13] Both the social transfer payments and the spending on interest are very difficult to cut, as we examine below in more detail.

Several major *decreases* have recently occurred as well. Defense spending is now being cut back after having undergone temporary growth of over 6% per year between 1980 and 1986. (It had decreased by 2.5% per year during the 1970s.) Spending on agriculture has also fallen, after having risen greatly, from only $8 billion in 1980 to $31 billion in 1986. Federal revenue sharing with state and local governments, wherein a part of federal tax revenues were turned over to these governments for various uses, has been considerably curtailed. This explains much of the decline in the "other" category in Table 22.1. (Grants-in-aid are still made to states and local governments to fund specific programs—these grants make up about 12% of the federal budget and are mixed in among the various items in the table. But the aid is not nearly great enough to fund the numerous federally mandated programs Congress has imposed on state and local governments in recent years, so a substantial shifting of financial responsibility has occurred.) In percentage terms, significant cuts have also been made in the spending on welfare, foreign aid, and energy and the environment.

The Reagan administration complained for years that Congress failed to cut spending in tandem with the deep tax cuts of 1981, causing the resulting budget deficits that set in during the 1980s. Some saw this as a lost gamble, the administration's gamble being that if taxes were cut, total government spending would have to be cut too. The spending cuts did not happen, but the tax cuts were retained. Thus politics caused an outcome that few, if any, economists would have suspected or endorsed.

THE BUDGET PROCESS

Presently, new U.S. government spending involves the following process: the Senate and House each has a budget committee. These committees agree on a single (joint) budget resolution that must be passed by both houses. This resolution includes both actual "outlays" and future "authorizations"; since at this stage only a resolution has been passed, no presidential signature is necessary. Following the joint budget resolution comes appropriation bills in both houses, and then reconciliation bills so that House and Senate are in agreement. The president's signature, or passage over his veto, makes them law. When there is an irreconcilable disagreement between the two houses of Congress, or between Congress and the president, a "continuing resolution" may be necessary. This allows government spending to proceed at the same level as in the previous year. Continuing resolutions have become commonplace in recent years.

---

13.   If interest on the national debt is excluded, however, a spending cut of about 2% of GDP has been achieved since 1980. Interest on the debt was only 1.2% of GDP in the late 1950s, but it has been 3% or more (3.3% in 1993) since 1984. It had grown to over $1/7$ of the federal budget by 1989. The additional 2 percentage points of GDP going to pay interest obviously crowds out other possible types of government spending. Accurate calculation of interest on the debt is more complicated than might appear. When prices are rising, some part of interest payments just compensates bondholders for the lower real value of the repayment that will eventually come to them. Counting all interest as a net burden on government fails to consider the lower burden of the debt, the repayment of which will be in cheaper dollars. It would be proper, in determining the real value of government interest payments, to adjust these payments by subtracting the interest premium due to inflation. That is not done in the conventional budget, however, and so interest payments are actually overstated.

State and Local Government Spending

In the United States, there are other forms of government spending in addition to that at the federal level. State and local government spending are important, contributing 45% to the grand total, with the federal government responsible for the remainder, 55% (1991 figures). The largest items in state spending are highways and education; by far the greatest amount in local spending is for education. As with taxes, state and local spending are not likely to be altered as part of any plan for macroeconomic management—many state and local governments are in fact required to balance their budgets. It is much more probable that these forms of spending will be pro-cyclical, rising in prosperity and falling in recession. In the early 1990s recession, many states and local governments were cutting their spending. That together with tax increases led to a swing of state budgets toward surplus by $32 billion in the two fiscal years 1990–1991. It might seem reasonable that some form of federal revenue sharing be adopted to counter unwanted macro-economic trends. The federal government might transfer revenues to states and local governments during recessions and cut back this assistance in inflations. That could neutralize the present unhelpful swings in state and local budgets. At present this is not done.

THE POTENTIAL SCOPE FOR FISCAL POLICY

A government intent on carrying out fiscal policy by altering its spending can choose to make *any* change in that spending. In a recession, three basic sorts of policy usually receive the most attention. The first is to raise the size and scope of transfer payments, including, for example, revenue sharing with states, local governments, and school districts; Social Security, welfare, and unemployment compensation; payments to veterans and farmers; and any similar sort of transfer. The second method is to undertake government spending on projects, called **public works** spending. The third method is direct or indirect government employment of the jobless, along the lines of the employment schemes of the Great Depression or the related efforts of the 1970s.

In the Roosevelt administration during the 1930s, substantial enthusiasm grew up around the concept of "pump-priming" as a major type of fiscal policy to combat recessions. On the farms of the day, a little water added to a pump's mechanism would permit large amounts of water to flow from the well when the handle was pumped. Pump-priming of the economy was a similar idea: a small dose of government spending, working through the multiplier, would restore confidence and lead to a recovery of private spending. It was a nice image, but experience in the Great Depression showed that pump-priming was not effective against a slump so deep. For fiscal policy to work under these conditions, it had to be sustained. One-time injections of government spending, though they might increase the public's confidence during a mild recession, were not enough to cope with the Great Depression.

Programs of government spending on a greater scale face a number of difficulties. Transfer payments to individuals and groups can often be arranged rapidly, so that the resulting macroeconomic impact is relatively swift. When carried out in a serious recession, the expectation would be that the marginal propensity to consume from the new income is high, and hence the multiplier effect is likely to be high also. (Recall, however, that *some* of the new income will be saved; an increase in transfer payments, like a decrease in taxes, has a less powerful impact on the economy than does an increase in government spending on new output.)

Once Spending Is Raised, Cutting It Back Is Difficult

Probably the greatest objection to such transfers is the tendency for the grants to become institutionalized. The usual practice is to make increases in transfers open-ended, so that any reduction later on does not follow automatically, but only with the passage of new legislation. It will then be politically difficult to cut back these payments when, from the point of view of fiscal policy, the need for them has passed.

The basic problem is that political constituencies grow up and solidify around their so-called **entitlements**. (The word entitlement identifies the government transfer payments that *must* be paid to those who qualify.) Under the laws as they stand, they are an obligation. Senior citizens, farmers, veterans' organizations, and associations of welfare recipients rapidly become accustomed to the higher level of benefits and are adamant in refusing to see them cut. Entitlements made up only about a tenth of the budget in the early 1960s, but about half now. During 1970–1990, they grew at more than twice the rate of the economy.

Social Security and Medicare are the most important. Few politicians who want to stay in office are willing to argue that fiscal policy should ever require cuts in these programs. Actually, there are ways in which these entitlements could be cut back. Incentives to early retirement might be reduced; cost-of-living increases could be trimmed (most workers are not similarly protected); some sort of income or "means" test could limit payments to those whose income levels are high; benefits could be made fully taxable when received by high- and middle-income recipients. But even in inflationary booms, when cutting transfer payments would be a highly beneficial fiscal tactic, no one wants to give up an entitlement.

One economic aspect of government spending makes it even more difficult to achieve success in making cuts. An attempt to reduce government spending, say by $10 billion, would actually require Congress to find *more* than $10 billion in cuts. This is so because of the automatic stabilizer aspect of spending for unemployment compensation, welfare, support programs for farmers, and so on, all of which tend to rise as GDP falls. An initial $10 billion reduction in government spending would tend to reduce GDP, and as a result some government spending would automatically rise as GDP falls. Achievement of a $10 billion *net* fall in spending would therefore require more than $10 billion in initial spending cuts.

PUBLIC WORKS

Public works spending can be enlarged to expand the economy and reduced to restrain it. There is no question that public works can pump large amounts of new spending into an economy, and the idea has long been understood. The pharaohs of ancient Egypt carried on the construction of their pyramids in the dry season when peasant farmers were unable to grow crops, no doubt mostly to guarantee their place in the afterlife, but partly to absorb the temporary unemployment.

In the United States, the Roosevelt administration used public works as a major weapon to combat the Great Depression in one of its major, though still inadequate, accomplishments. Public works projects during this period included the construction of new federal highways, farm-to-market roads, rural electrification, dams for power and flood control including the Grand Coulee dam and the Tennessee Valley Authority, river and harbor improvements, public parks, sidewalks, airports, and a wide variety of other schemes. Two government agencies conducted most of these projects, the Works Projects Administration (WPA) and the Civilian Conservation Corps (CCC). During its eight years of existence, the WPA undertook over 1.4 million projects, including 650,000 miles of road, 125,000 public buildings, 124,000 bridges, 8000 parks, and 1000 libraries.

Public works also have some decided disadvantages, however. One most often pointed out by conservatives is that big government per se is to be shunned as an unwelcome intruder. Another is that public works might be caught up in politics, with projects located for their political impact in areas where votes are needed rather than where they would do the most good for the economy. A third is the general problem of waste, inefficiency, and misuse of funds that can surround government spending of all types. Therefore, conservatives typically prefer a fiscal policy of tax cuts rather than government spending on public works, because this avoids further enhancement of government activity. Even when public works give a large stimulative effect and are efficiently managed, they can still result in "boondoggles" such as a useless road from beyond Blue Horizon to Nowhereville. Certainly when public works are undertaken, how much the better if the results are socially beneficial. Thus a power project or school is to be preferred to a pyramid or "digging holes and then filling them in," as the story went in the Great Depression among those who opposed public works.

A second problem is that the lags in initiating public works can be long. The response lag is not a problem—the new government spending is directly included in the GDP. Once the paychecks begin, the spending and multiplier effects will come swiftly. But the steps leading up to the stage—that is, the implementation lag—may take months or years. First, there must be a consensus about the need for policy action involving public works. Then a bill must be approved by Congress. It will take time to draw up detailed plans and blueprints for each project. Land may have to be obtained through negotiation and even condemnation proceedings. Then contracts must be negotiated with builders and suppliers. These in turn must make arrangements with the workers and managers who will do the actual work.

With bad luck, the public works spending may start to flow in quantity just about the time the need for it has passed. The spending may then prove overly stimulative, perhaps even inflationary, but a large public works program may politically be very difficult to reverse. Consider the massive interstate highway program. The enabling act for these highways was passed in 1956. Major outlays on the interstates were being made by the time of the recession year 1958 and provided useful economic stimulus. Before long, however, the United States was battling inflation, and the need for stimulus had passed. It eventually proved possible to slow construction, and later to speed it again, but in both cases the lags were understandably long.

The problem of lags has never been addressed in detail in the United States, but certain other countries have done so. For many years, Sweden has had a "shelf" of public works projects, planned and ready to go on a few months' notice. In recession, Swedish governments turn to the shelf and choose those programs that combine the best timing with the highest social priority. If public works are to be used as fiscal policy, it does seem reasonable to engage in advanced planning of this nature. (The civil functions branch of the U.S. Army Corps of Engineers does, however, have a considerable back list or "shelf" that may come up for consideration in a counter-cyclical way.)

A further problem with public works involves the possibility of direct competition with the private sector. Conceivably, the government's hydroelectric dam or airport might discourage private investors, who would have undertaken the project but are shouldered aside by the government's competition. This is certainly conceivable, though several factors mitigate the problem. First, program designers can be alert to the possibility, and can seek to avoid it by careful project choice. Second, the chance of competition with private investment will be reduced the more severe a recession is. In a major slump, investment of all kinds will be much lower anyway.

In spite of the real disadvantages, there is still support for public works as a measure to counter adverse economic conditions. Schools, highways, national parks, slum clearance, and so forth are generally needed and can be provided as federal public works at times when state and local governments cannot fund such projects. (In 1994, Senators Simon of Illinois and Boren of Oklahoma were calling publicly for a new WPA to do these things.) But it is also true that even in inflationary booms, projects such as new schools or highways remain desirable. Cutting back on such spending may be politically difficult, or even morally unacceptable. This fact makes it more difficult to use public works cutbacks in fighting inflations.

PUBLIC EMPLOYMENT IN THE UNITED STATES

The WPA and the CCC of the Great Depression were in large measure agencies designed to provide **public employment** as well as to undertake public works. The CCC reached a maximum size of about half a million young people aged 18–25, while the WPA employed as many as 3.4 million people in 1936. These depression-era agencies were popular both with voters and with economists. The idea of public employment for the jobless was neglected for nearly three decades after the Great Depression, but since the 1960s it has been resurrected several times, as shown in Table 22.2.[14] President Nixon's modest PEP of the early 1970s was the first to emphasize

---

14.   This section has benefitted from the work of Peter Gottschalk of Boston College. The scope of federal employment programs has been highly cyclical, with pronounced variations in spending on them. In 1964, for example, only 0.01% of GDP was being spent to finance federal employment of the jobless. Ten years later, that figure was 0.21%; it hit a high of 0.52% in 1978 but by 1982 had fallen far, to 0.19%.

public service employment rather than employment on public works. (PEP eventually filled 200,000 state and local government jobs with new firefighters, police, hospital workers, street cleaners, teachers' aids, maintenance workers, clerks, and recreation assistants.)

TABLE 22.2
Major U.S. public employment programs since World War II.

Program	Principal Years of Operation	Total Outlay	Peak Outlay (in $ billions)
Accelerated Public Works Program	1963–65	3.2	1.3 (1964)
Public Employment Program (PEP)	1972–74	6.1	2.8 (1973)
CETA	1975–81	55.1*	17.0 (1978)
Emergency Jobs Act	1983–86	5.8	2.3 (1984)

Source: Sar A. Levitan and Frank Gallo, "Wanted: Federal Public Service Program," *Challenge,* Vol. 34, No. 3, May/June 1991, p. 34.

*Includes CETA public service employment, Job Opportunities Program, and Local Public Works Program. It may be pointed out that at present, with no large-scale public employment program in operation, federal, state, and local governments in the United States nonetheless employ about 16% of the labor force.

Confidence in the effectiveness of public employment programs has declined, however, with questions arising over what they actually were intended to achieve. Were they expected merely to decrease unemployment during a slump? Were they to be permanent or temporary? Were they to emphasize training and job experience so that after being part of a program, "graduates" would be more productive workers and hence more employable in the private sector? It is also fair to point out that organized labor and contractors in the private sector can generally be counted on to oppose federal jobs programs because they fear that their own chances for work will be reduced and their wages undercut.

THE PROBLEM OF PUBLIC EMPLOYMENT AS SEEN IN THE CETA PROGRAM AND ITS DEMISE

Though all the programs in Table 22.2 were broadly similar in outline, the Comprehensive Employment and Training Act (CETA) was by far the largest. It had grown by 1978 to $17 billion in funding for 752,000 public service jobs. The general problems encountered by public employment schemes are nicely illustrated by the rise and fall of CETA.

Early in CETA's life, the emphasis was on public service employment for the jobless, without regard for need or background. The relatively high level of education and income of CETA participants, who were neither the poorest nor the least educated of the unemployed, led to claims of "creaming."

Three-quarters of the jobs went to high school graduates, and more than half to people who did not come from low-income households; those in both categories were more likely to find new jobs even if no program existed. Creaming made management of the program easier, but it also meant that many of those who could have benefited most were not being enrolled.

Another problem was that state and local governments receiving CETA money reduced considerably the number of workers hired with their own budget dollars. Sometimes the states and municipalities even managed to bring their regular workers under CETA funding. More fundamental criticism was that many participants received no useful training, and had little success in acquiring private-sector jobs once they left the program.

In the end, CETA's high budget costs and relatively low ability to increase net employment caused a withdrawal of political support, and in 1981 it was allowed to die. In the United States, public employment has found no favor since. (The existing U.S. programs emphasize education and training rather than direct employment, as we shall see in Chapter 25.) While it lasted, however, CETA did give work experience and cash income to many who would otherwise have been jobless, and who would have run up the bills for unemployment compensation and welfare benefits. And a good deal of useful work was actually performed.

Though public employment has largely expired in the United States, and was not renewed even during the recession and slow recovery of 1990–1992, some programs of this type *were* underway at the time of writing in Great Britain, France, Sweden, and Germany. A new $4.5-billion program was announced by Canada's Liberal Government just two weeks after its election in 1993. They all involve training as well as employment. If unemployment were to take a serious turn for the worse in the United States, even a conservative administration might find some merit in public employment programs because they can be used as a direct assault on joblessness. Furthermore, if they include education and training, they can be made to reach the least advantaged portion of the labor force.

▶ THE HOBBLING OF EXPANSIONARY FISCAL POLICY BY THE FEDERAL BUDGET DEFICIT

It must be emphasized once again that the examples of fiscal policy discussed in this chapter all involve movements in a government's budget toward deficit or surplus. As we have seen, a movement toward large annual deficits in the federal budget occurred during the 1980s. The growth of the U.S. federal budget deficit—and budget deficits in Canada and most of Europe as well—was caused by major changes in taxation and spending. This striking feature of the world economy holds great importance not only for fiscal policy, but for macroeconomic conditions in general.

Economists identify four major reasons why the U.S. federal budget moved so deeply into deficit during the 1980s. (1) The great cut in tax rates made in the early 1980s did not raise government revenues and lead the budget toward balance. Instead, the tax cut caused tax revenues to fall until 1984. Estimates are that about a third of the shift toward deficit was due to this cause. The decline in tax revenues due to the recession and the tax cuts was dramatic, from 21% of GDP in 1981 to 18% in 1984. Even by 1993, federal revenues as a percentage of GDP (19.4%) were still well below their 1981 levels. (2) The early 1980s battle against inflation, conducted with monetary policy by Paul Volcker at the Fed, brought high real rates of interest that led to very slow growth. Thus tax collections did not rise as much as had been predicted, and some government programs (unemployment benefits, welfare) paid out more money than expected. It is estimated that in the mid-1980s the slow growth was the cause of about a quarter of the resulting budget deficit. Slow growth in the 1990s continues to limit tax receipts. (3) Defense spending was boosted in the early 1980s, explaining perhaps another tenth of the deficit. Finally, (4) about a fifth of the shift was due to the higher interest payments the government had to make on the debt it was running up. Partly the higher interest payments were due to the larger debt, and partly to the rise in interest rates on that debt.

The large U.S. federal budget deficit can be viewed in Figure 22.6, where it is shown as a percentage of GDP. (Note that measuring by percent of GDP is far more meaningful than simply using a dollar figure. Inflation can cause the dollar amount of deficits to rise greatly, but a doubled deficit is fiscally neutral if the price level doubled also.) In the figure, the deficit is the difference between federal government spending as a percentage of GDP, and federal government revenue as a percentage of GDP. The gap between the two lines was greatest in 1983, at almost 6%, but it has stayed high by historical standards ever since, always above 2% and back to nearly 5% ($290.3 billion) in fiscal 1992.

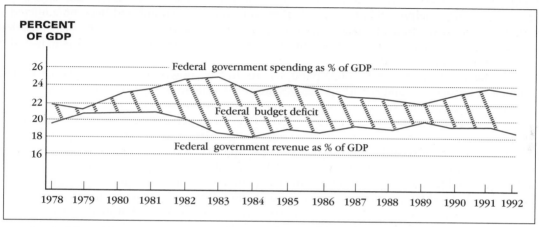

Source: Office of Management and Budget data, updated by the author from a graph in *The Economist,* January 21, 1989. The figures are for fiscal years.

Figure 22.6. The U.S. budget deficit, 1978–1992. The tax cuts of the early 1980s combined with an inability to make significant reductions in government spending caused the appearance of large federal budget deficits that are with us yet.

Even with 1993's deficit reduction bill, which provided for a total of $496 billion in total deficit reduction over five years (that is, an average of about $99 billion in each of five years), the federal budget deficit is expected to stay around $200 billion, over 3% of GDP, for years to come. Table 22.3 shows the deficit to fiscal year 1996, with the 1992 and 1993 figures the actual ones and the 1994–1996 figures the projections of the Clinton administration.

TABLE 22.3
Projected U.S. federal budget deficit, fiscal 1992 to fiscal 1996.

(Billion Dollars)	
1992*	290
1993*	255
1994†	235
1995†	242
1996†	205

Source: Office of Management and Budget.

*Actual figure.

†Projected figure. The projections are based on current plans for taxes and spending, and estimates of economic growth during the period. Stronger than expected economic growth could cut the size of the deficit somewhat. President Clinton has called for spending reductions that would reduce the 1995 and 1996 figures.

As Figure 22.6 and Table 22.3 show, the United States is well into its second decade of consistently large federal budget deficits, which are likely to continue for years to come. No school of economic thought advocates large deficits irrespective of whether the economy is in boom or slump. Indeed, there is considerable cause for worry about the effects of prolonged deficits, as the next chapter will discuss. But politicians' ability to raise taxes and cut spending has clearly not been adequate to the task, up to now at any rate. The result has been that fiscal policy is largely immobilized in the United States. In booms, the government's fiscal stance contributes unwanted stimulus. In slumps, the ability to expand the deficit is hindered by fears of the unwelcome or dangerous side effects from many years of the same thing—just as doctors would distrust the effects of otherwise helpful pharmaceutical stimulants after the patient had become addicted to them over many years. Fear of further expanding the deficit was the major reason why President Clinton's rather modest $13 billion program for increased government spending was defeated by Congress in the summer of 1993.

Similar problems of fiscal policy paralysis are, in fact, now worldwide, including Canada and much of Europe. Tax and spending changes are very visible to the general public, tax increases are difficult to make, and spending increases are hard to reverse. Some of these countries have developed long-term budget deficits that are even larger as a percentage of GDP than that of the United States, as seen in Table 22.4. The average budget deficit for the seven biggest industrial economies was 1% of GDP in 1989, but it was 2% in 1991. Whatever its difficulties, monetary policy has recently been far easier to manage than fiscal policy. (Japan is an exception. It has usually registered budget surpluses in recent years, and so has been able to make effective use of fiscal policy. Four different doses of government spending and tax cuts are delivering over $400 billion of stimulus to combat Japan's current recession. In 1993 that pushed the Japanese budget into significant deficit for the first time since 1987.)

TABLE 22.4
Government budget deficits, selected countries, percent of GDP.

Belgium	5.2 (1991)		Germany	2.6 (1991)
Britain	1.3 (1991)		Italy	10.4 (1991)
Canada	5.1 (1992)		Sweden	3.2 (1990)
France	1.4 (1991)		United States	4.9 (1992)

Source: IMF, *International Financial Statistics,* October 1993, for all countries except the United States. The years are the latest shown in that publication. The U.S. figure is from Office of Management and Budget data.

This chapter has reached the conclusion that, to a considerable degree, fiscal policy is now paralyzed in the United States and several other major economies. For some time, the paralysis seemed not to matter very much. U.S. economic performance was relatively good from the early 1980s to 1990, with the economy able to avoid recession even with fiscal policy hobbled. During this period, the ability of the Fed to obtain macroeconomic stability with monetary policy was significantly better than many economists would have expected, and some of these doubtless came to believe that fiscal policy was simply not as necessary as before in the control of modest fluctuations.

Yet the great budget deficits in the United States and other countries are now more clearly an unfortunate legacy. When the U.S., Canadian, and European economies turned down in 1990–1991, and when their recovery was very slow thereafter, it was frustrating to realize that budget deficits had made anti-recession fiscal policy very difficult to use. Governments simply cannot risk great depressions, and fiscal policy remains a weapon that could be available to prevent them if budget deficits had been better managed. Economists and politicians wished they could emulate the Japanese with stimulative policy, but the dangers were too great, as we explore in the next chapter.

SUMMARY

1) Fiscal policy involves government tax changes and spending changes (defined as government transfers such as Social Security payments and government spending on output of goods and services) to influence the level of economic activity. Tax cuts and spending increases, which push the budget toward deficit, are expansionary, while tax increases and spending cuts, which push the budget toward surplus, are contractionary. The effect of changing government spending on output is, however, slightly stronger than the effect of changes in taxes or transfers. All of these conclusions involve controversies, however; these will be considered in the next chapter.

2) Tax increases used to counter inflation are clearly much more difficult to enact than are tax decreases against recession.

3) The public reacts differently to temporary and permanent tax changes. For example, following a temporary tax increase, the public might keep its consumption at its old level by dipping into saving, while a permanent increase in taxes is much more likely to result in a curtailment of consumption.

4) Changes in government spending, either transfer payments (including "entitlements") or spending on the output of goods and services (including public works and public employment), can be an effective way to alter the level of economic activity. A difficulty with this approach is that once spending has been raised (say for entitlements such as Social Security benefits), then cutting it back may be politically difficult. Another is that public works projects may take a long time to plan and implement, so that their expansionary economic effect comes too late to have a favorable impact. A third is that public employment projects to hire the unemployed may do little to make its "graduates" more employable in the private sector after their participation comes to an end.

5) A massive federal budget deficit has existed for over a decade, and this deficit has in large measure hobbled expansionary fiscal policy. The deficit came into being because taxes were reduced in the early 1980s (the ERTA tax cuts), but government spending was not. Deficits can be damaging, as the next chapter discusses, so both economically and politically it has not been possible to make much use of fiscal expansion in recent years.

Chapter Key Words

Automatic stabilizer: A feature sometimes seen in the tax and spending mechanism that raises an economy's total spending in recession and lowers it in inflation. Two examples are the federal income tax and unemployment compensation. The automatic stabilizers are useful in that economic swings are to some extent countered automatically, without the need for difficult political decisions involving long delays. Also known as built-in stabilizers.

Budget deficit: A situation when government spending exceeds government revenues; a tool of fiscal policy that can be used against recession. Deficits can be increased by raising government spending, cutting taxes, or both.

Budget surplus: A situation when government spending is less than government revenues; a tool of fiscal policy that can be used against inflation. A surplus may be increased by cutting spending, raising taxes, or both.

Built-in stabilizer: See *automatic stabilizer*.

Capital-gains tax: A tax on the increase in the value of items such as stocks, bonds, real estate, and the like, realized when the item is sold.

Entitlements: Government payments that must be paid to those who qualify. Examples include Social Security, assistance to farmers, veterans' benefits, and so forth.

ERTA: Economic Recovery Tax Act, an act that ushered in a major period of tax cuts beginning in 1981 during the Reagan administration. Controversial because of the effect on the federal budget deficit.

Fiscal dividend: The idea that a growing economy will cause an increase in tax revenues that the government can use for increased spending.

Fiscal drag: The idea that a growing economy will cause an increase in tax revenues and hence a braking effect on the economy's growth.

Investment tax credit: A tax policy in which a company's taxes are reduced by a certain percentage of the capital investment it undertakes.

Laffer curve: The curve purporting to show higher tax rates resulting in lower tax revenues. Used to justify the ERTA tax cuts early in the Reagan administration. Although it is widely agreed that taxes can rise so high that tax revenues will indeed decline, U.S. taxes are actually not high by international standards.

Progressive tax: A tax that collects a greater percentage from higher incomes than from lower.

Public employment: A government provision of jobs to reduce unemployment in a recession. Well-known and popular in the Great Depression, but worked imperfectly in the 1970s.

Public works: New spending on public projects such as schools, parks, roads, and the like. Effective in raising total spending, but only after a long time lag.

Tax indexing: The practice of altering the income tax brackets so that inflation does not result in a higher tax bill. Significant in reducing the automatic stabilizing aspect of the tax system.

Value-added tax (VAT): A tax levied on the value added at each stage of production by most advanced countries, though not the United States.

CHAPTER QUESTIONS

1) Show equilibrium on an AD-AS diagram. If the government lowers taxes, how does the AD curve shift? Why does it shift? What are the effects on output and the price level? Now suppose that the lower taxes lead many women and elderly people to enter the labor force. Show this change in the labor market equilibrium on the AD-AS diagram. Now what happens to output and the price level?

2) To what degree do each of the following taxes have an automatic stabilizing effect?
    a) The pre-1985, unindexed personal income tax
    b) The post-1985, indexed personal income tax
    c) The Social Security payroll tax

3) Following the collapse of communism, two political parties emerged on the Animal Farm. They are the Pork Party and the Squirrel Party. When there is extra money in the government treasury, the Pork Party spends it on public works projects. In the same situation the Squirrel Party runs a budget surplus because it saves the money for a rainy day. Suppose that taxes are progressive, and that Animal Farm's output increases. What is the effect of each political party's policy?

4) You run the North American Toothpick Company with one plant in the United States and one plant in Canada. The company has fallen on hard times, so you are willing to bend the rules on paying taxes. The U.S. supplier of lumber to your Vermont plant offers to sell you logs under the table so that both of you can understate your profits and pay less in U.S. corporate income tax. At about the same time the Canadian supplier of your New Brunswick plant says that he will not report sales to you in order to avoid the Canadian VAT. Given that you are a profit maximizer and not very scrupulous, which offer is it safest to accept? Why?

5) The President's advisors disagree about whether the economy is above or below full employment. They offer the President four possible courses of action with regard to tax policy:
   a) Permanently decrease taxes.
   b) Offer a tax rebate this year.
   c) Institute an extra surcharge on this year's taxes.
   d) Permanently raise taxes.

   One year after the President first proposes one of the policies, the advisors plan to measure the magnitude (not the direction) of the tax policies' effect on the economy. Which of the policies would you expect to have a large effect, and which would have a smaller effect?

6) When Ronald Reagan cut taxes in 1981, his supporters believed that lower taxes would increase tax revenue. Democrats in Congress disagreed. Draw the Laffer curve as estimated by the Republicans and by the Democrats.

7) Suppose that during a serious recession, people try to save electricity, and reading becomes more popular than watching TV. The government is concerned that the TV networks may go out of business. The FCC comes up with two plans to save the industry. Plan 1 involves buying American families a new, energy-efficient state-of-the-art TV set every five years. Plan 2 involves a special government program that will produce two seasons of TV shows. Which program is likely to have a greater effect shortly after it is announced? Will either program cause problems in the long run?

8) Imagine that the government cuts spending on all its program and procurements. The cuts are large enough that spending on everything other than debt payments just equals taxes. However, the budget is still in deficit because of the debt payments. If the government continues in this way for many years, will the debt rise, fall, or stay the same?

Deficits and Debt in a Modern Economy

OVERALL OBJECTIVE: To explain how budget deficits increase the national debt, and explore the economic consequences of deficits and debt.

MORE SPECIFICALLY:

■ To show that a country's national debt is the sum total of outstanding government bonds issued to finance the deficits in the government budget.

■ To analyze the crowding out of private investment and exports by the higher interest rates that follow from budget deficits.

■ To see what difference it makes when budget deficits are financed by the creation of new money and when they are not.

■ To consider certain arguments that actual budget deficits do not matter that much, including Ricardian equivalence, measurement problems, and structural deficits.

■ To assess the dangers of a national debt.

During the 1980s and 1990s, the U.S. government and the governments of many other countries consistently spent more than they were willing to tax, thereby running up budget deficits that came to seem almost permanent. Previous generations did not have to cope with the effects of deficits year after year, largely because of politicians' and voters' long-standing belief in financial rectitude. The prevailing mood for generations was that a country should pay for what it gets from government.

With the Keynesian economics, this position was modified to allow for budget deficits to stimulate an economy in a recession. Keynes and his followers never called for permanent deficits, however, and neither did any other school of economists—but that is basically what happened. The financial rectitude of voters and politicians had clearly weakened considerably. Late-1970s deficits became an early-'80s flood of red ink.[1] Understandably, economists began to look much more closely at the effects of deficits than they had in the 1950s and '60s. Though there was rather general agreement on the disadvantages and even dangers from long-standing deficits, several of the questions explored in this chapter are not finally settled and are the subject of ongoing debate.

One aspect of constant deficits was that the red ink was running up the **national debt**. The connection between budget deficits and the nation's debt is a direct one, and understanding the link is fundamental for macroeconomics. Anytime the government spends more than it taxes, it has to find some way to obtain revenue over and above its tax receipts. The standard way to do this is to borrow the money from the public. For example, if the government spends $10, but its tax revenue is only $9, then the resulting budget deficit of $1 can be financed by the government's sale of a new $1 bond to the public. The bond is a promise to repay $1 in the future, so it is part of a nation's debt. The national debt is the sum total of the outstanding government bonds issued over the years to finance the deficit spending. In our example, if a deficit of $1 per year (a flow) were run for five straight years and financed by bond sales, then the national debt (a stock) would rise by $5. The second part of this chapter considers whether the sheer size and growth in the national debt has negative effects on the economy.

Then the chapter assesses what might be done about the budget deficit and the associated rise in the national debt. Finally, it concludes with a reminder that, unless deficits are brought under control, fiscal policy will remain difficult to implement.

▶ ISSUES CONCERNING BUDGET DEFICITS

The view that the consequences of budget deficits are more adverse than originally believed is now widely accepted. One reason is that under some circumstances deficits tend to raise interest rates. The effect of the higher rates is felt not only by the individual countries that run the deficits, but by the entire world as the higher rates are transmitted internationally. Under other circumstances, deficits can pose an extra danger of triggering inflation. Yet there is also a debate on how much deficits matter. Are they measured properly? Why, if they are so damaging, do we still seem to be doing reasonably well? These are the topics of this section.

CROWDING OUT

In the 1970s an objection to the traditional use of fiscal policy gathered force. Economists noted that changes in government spending or taxation might affect the level of *interest rates*, and that in turn might offset some of the impact of the spending or taxes. Consider a rise in government spending or cut in taxes, perhaps intended to counter an economic downturn, as depicted in Figure 23.1's panel **a**. Here an increase in aggregate demand from AD to AD' along the horizontal (recession) portion of the aggregate supply curve moves the equilibrium from E to E' and pushes up total output (income) from Y to Y'. As real output rises, however, changes take

---

1.   A nice term coming from the practice of accountants, who used red ink in their ledgers to indicate negative balances.

place in the markets for credit. The higher output causes the demand for money to carry on transactions to increase, perhaps from M_D to M_D' in Figure 23.1's panel **b**.

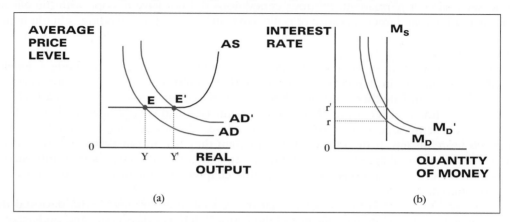

Figure 23.1. Changes in the level of output can affect interest rates. In panel **a**, a fiscal policy of increased government spending or reduced taxes raises aggregate demand and therefore total output and income. The greater economic activity increases the demand for money in panel **b**, so forcing a rise in interest rates.

For the purposes of this discussion, let us assume that the monetary authorities make no change in the money supply. (That would involve monetary policy, and here we are investigating the independent effects of fiscal policy.) With a fixed supply of money, the higher demand for money will raise the level of interest rates, from r to r'. Because prices do not move, the interest rate change is in real terms.

The higher real interest rates will have an effect of their own. They will serve to reduce private investment to some extent, curtail that part of consumption most dependent on interest rates (consumer durables such as automobiles), perhaps restrict government spending, particularly that financed by state and local government bond issues, and, through the foreign exchange rate, reduce exports and raise imports. These reductions in total spending on the country's output will mean that the expansionary effect transmitted by the original rise in government spending (or tax cut) will be less than otherwise, in what is called a **crowding-out effect**. The term is apt: the higher interest rates resulting from the expansionary fiscal policy crowd out, or eliminate, some other forms of spending. The consequences are seen in Figure 23.2. An increase in government spending or tax cut that *would* have moved aggregate demand from AD to AD' in the absence of crowding out actually moves it only to AD" in the presence of crowding out. Total output, which would otherwise have risen to Y', rises by a smaller amount to Y" because of the crowding out effect.

Whether crowding out is, in reality, large or small is the subject of vigorous debate. Monetarist economists usually believe crowding out is large, adding further weight to their argument that fiscal policy is ineffective. Modern Keynesians believe it is small, in which case fiscal policy has a strong impact. The Keynesians argue forcefully that the presence of crowding out is less likely under recession conditions, and least likely in a full-scale depression when private investment and consumption are already low. Especially in the latter case it is more appropriate to suggest that some stimulation of private spending will occur as investors and consumers are encouraged by higher national output and income to go ahead with their spending plans. Even close to full employment, a government deficit that leads to new capital might improve the economy's efficiency, as when new roads or port facilities are built. In that case, too, the private sector may see expanded profit opportunities and may increase investment, rather than decreasing it as predicted by the crowding-out effect. Yet the analysis does suggest that during a period of expansion, with the economy closer to full employment, the demand for money and credit will be high and a rise in the government budget deficit will increase that demand. Higher interest rates would seem to be an understandable outcome, and private spending may be curtailed as a result.

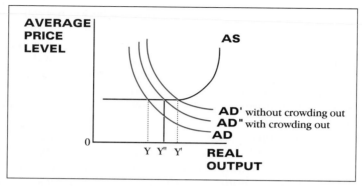

Figure 23.2. The crowding-out effect. In the absence of the crowding-out effect, a rise in government spending or fall in taxes would have moved the aggregate demand from AD to AD', so raising real output from Y to Y'. Because of the rise in interest rates, however, crowding out of some private spending occurs, so aggregate demand curve rises only to AD", and real output only to Y".

Many economists now argue that during periods of reasonably high employment and capacity utilization, fiscal stimulus transmitted through budget deficits may indeed be mostly crowded out—that is, largely cancelled by the effects of higher interest rates—within about three or four years. This points to a problem with U.S. economic policies in the 1980s. Large fiscal deficits were present during this period even though employment was high. To counter the resulting fiscal stimulus, the Fed maintained a stance of tight money and high interest rates. Both the crowding out from the fiscal deficits and the tight monetary policy meant that real interest rates were much higher, with adverse effects on the country's investment and economic growth.

The crowding-out process can be looked at in reverse to explain the case of reduced government spending or rising taxation. As the government's budget moves toward surplus, the resulting reduction in aggregate demand (from AD' to AD in Figure 23.1's panel **a**) will lower total output (from Y' to Y). That in turn will reduce the demand for money (from MD' to MD in panel **b**), causing interest rates to fall (from r' to r) and increasing private investment. This repercussion may in part offset the contractionary effects of the budget surplus, so that aggregate demand does not fall all the way to AD in Figure 23.2, but only to AD". Total output declines, but only to Y", not to Y.

Crowding Out and the Rest of the World

The crowding-out effect from an expansionary fiscal policy also exerts an influence on other countries. The international implications have come to be a central issue for U.S. policy. An expansionary fiscal deficit may raise real interest rates, which is the principle of crowding out just discussed. Those higher interest rates may affect both the foreign exchange markets and the capital markets in a negative way. The effect of interest rates on exchange rates has already been described in Chapter 21. The higher real rates proved attractive to foreigners. As foreigners became aware of them, some of them bought dollars for deposit in the United States.[2]

That higher demand for dollars had the effect of making the dollar more valuable, appreciating it on foreign exchange markets. This made U.S. exports more expensive, so causing them to fall. In fact, exports dropped by 14% between 1980 and 1982, when interest rates were very high. Thus a rise in interest rates caused by a fiscal deficit may not only reduce (crowd out) investment, but may also reduce a country's exports. The initial expansionary impulse of a deficit

2.   If foreigners had *not* done this, U.S. interest rates would have risen much further because of the expansionary fiscal policy. In effect, the savings of foreigners was financing a significant part of the U.S. deficit, nearly ⅓ of it by 1985 by comparison to negligible amounts before the 1980s.

will still be there, and total output and income will still rise, but the increase is scaled back even further because of the export fall alongside some crowding out of investment. At the same time, the fall in exports due to the currency appreciation is joined to a rise in imports as foreign goods now are cheaper for U.S. consumers. (Imports climbed 9% between 1980 and 1982.) Jobs are lost both because of the reduced exports and because the increased imports provide heavy competition for domestic industries; consumption of domestically produced goods and services falls.

When we examine how higher U.S. interest rates affect the rest of the world, we must also allow for the fact that capital markets are interconnected. Borrowers who found loans more expensive in U.S. markets borrowed more in foreign markets, so causing interest rates to increase in other countries as well. Unfortunately, in the 1980s and early '90s, investment slowed worldwide as a result of this process.

In addition to U.S. economic policy, several other factors worked to raise interest rates abroad. These included a demand for funds to develop former East Germany and Eastern Europe, Middle East reconstruction from the Gulf War, Japan's large investments in roads, railways, ports, and other infrastructure, and the budget deficits in most other major industrial countries. The German deficit, incurred to maintain East German consumption levels, and to keep afloat a number of the East's industries, was an especial contributor to the problem. But the U.S. budget deficit, usually over $200 billion per year in the decade after 1983, must receive a large share of the blame. According to the World Bank, a $100-billion increase in annual demand for capital tends to raise real interest rates about one percentage point unless the supply of capital (savings available for lending) increases. In general, world savings have *not* increased in recent years. The world slowdown in investment will probably be the most obvious long-run legacy of the fiscal deficits, tight money, and high interest rates. (It should be noted that even in the midst of the 1990–1991 U.S. recession, which temporarily reduced the demand for credit, U.S. long-term real interest rates were still high by past standards.)

DIFFERENCES BETWEEN EXPANSIONARY FISCAL POLICY AND EXPANSIONARY MONETARY POLICY

Expansionary fiscal deficits can have dramatic international repercussions. Notice, however, that the rest of the world is affected quite differently by an expansionary *monetary* policy. We assume that the increase in the supply of money will reduce the real rate of interest. That should cause foreigners to buy fewer dollars, and Americans to buy foreign currencies for deposit abroad. The resulting fall in value (depreciation) of the dollar will make American goods cheaper to foreign buyers, and therefore *raises* U.S. exports (and cuts U.S. imports as well). The greater quantity of exports caused by the monetary expansion increases total output and income *more* than if there had been no international repercussion, opposite to what would have occurred with an expansionary fiscal policy.

These asymmetric effects of government policy were important in the early 1980s, because the U.S. fought inflation with tight (contractionary) monetary policy, but for political reasons had an easy (expansionary) fiscal policy with large budget deficits. The monetary contraction worked to raise interest rates, and so did the expansionary fiscal policy. The double-barreled effect on interest rates was long-lasting and started the great rise in U.S. imports and fall in exports that still has to be corrected. The harm caused to U.S. domestic producers by imports led to a serious rise in protection by means of trade barriers.

The discussion of crowding out serves as a warning that the outcome of a stimulative fiscal policy involving deficits may be weaker and more perilous than anticipated by the Keynesian economists who first analyzed these effects.

THE DANGER WHEN DEFICITS ARE FINANCED BY THE CREATION OF NEW MONEY

How damaging deficits are for an economy depends to a large degree on how the government chooses to finance its deficit. This involves the connection between deficits and money. There has to be such a connection: Governments would be unable to spend more than they receive in tax revenues unless they were able to acquire the necessary cash balances for doing so. Several different possibilities exist for financing deficits. It is important to understand them, because their consequences can vary substantially from virtually neutral to very damaging, depending on which method is adopted.

Methods for Financing a Deficit

The main distinction in financing a budget deficit is between the ways that do not involve the creation of new money and those that *do* involve the creation of new money. There are four actual methods for financing deficits. In what follows, we will see which ones result in the creation of new money and which do not.

Borrowing the Money from the Public. The most conservative policy is for the Treasury to borrow savings from the private sector of the economy, without any action by the monetary authorities. The Treasury issues new federal government bonds and securities, the sale of which brings in the money the Treasury needs to carry out the deficit spending. Two polar macroeconomic effects of this borrowing can be identified. First, buyers of the bonds may reduce their level of bank deposits or hoarded cash in order to make the purchase. If the banks have been holding substantial excess reserves because of recession conditions, and the government rapidly spends the proceeds of the bond sales, the effect will be expansionary. If, however, the new bondholders finance their purchase by reducing their current consumption and investment by the full amount of the government deficit, then aggregate demand will not change, and no macroeconomic stimulation will follow. (We do not expect this to happen because people who own the new bonds will probably consider them as additions to their wealth, leading them to increase their spending. Nor will it happen if foreigners buy the bonds.)

Monetarist economists may prefer to view the same events through the Fisher equation (or equation of exchange), $MV = PY$. Bond sales to finance a deficit in this case are accompanied by no change in the money supply. Assuming a rise in aggregate demand follows from the deficit, there will be an increase in total output and price levels, hence an enlargement in the transactions demand for money, and therefore a rise in the level of interest rates. Holders of money will react to higher interest rates by using and reusing their cash balances more rapidly, the same as saying that the velocity of circulation, V, will rise. Some strict monetarists may argue that V is stable even so, in which case fiscal policy loses its power to affect income and output. Such economists believe that fiscal policy has little impact. Most economists appear to believe that deficits do raise interest rates. All other things being equal, that would increase V, and thereby give fiscal policy an independent influence over the economy even if the deficit leads to no creation of new money. The changes in velocity registered during the 1980s seems to have given this latter argument the lead in the controversy. But it would be premature to say that the debate is a settled one; much remains unexplained about velocity changes.

Borrowing from Commercial Banks. A method that involves *limited* creation of new money is bond sales by the Treasury to commercial banks. If these banks had been holding large amounts of excess reserves in the vault or as deposits in the Fed, the bond sales will allow the excess reserves to be mobilized for spending by the government. This is akin to what would have happened if the banks had used their excess reserves to make loans to private investors. If the banks devote all their excess reserves to bond purchases, the creation of new money would be the same as if the funds had been lent to the private sector by the banks themselves.

Creation of New Bank Reserves. A far more powerful means to finance the deficit is the creation of new reserves by the central bank. This enables commercial banks to purchase more bonds than would otherwise have been possible. The main method for providing additional reserves to the banking system is open market purchases by the monetary authorities. In effect, the central bank creates reserves, which from the standpoint of the commercial banks are excess reserves. These banks choose to use part of their reserves to purchase bonds, so financing the deficit, the spending from which boosts aggregate demand.

This method is ordinarily the one used when a central bank creates new money to finance the deficit. In a recession, it is an effective way to finance government's deficit spending. If the economy is closer to full employment, however, it runs the risk of an inflationary expansion fueled by the creation of new money.

Borrowing Directly from the Central Bank. If all else fails, the Treasury may borrow directly from the central bank. This is the complete equivalent of printing new paper notes except that it is far more efficient and can be done as a relatively simple accounting transaction. Printing huge quantities of new paper money is traditionally associated with the early hyperinflations (the 13 American colonies, the Confederate States, Germany in 1923) and with less-developed countries (Bolivia in 1985, Serbia and Ukraine now). But it is an inconvenient and old-fashioned way to finance a budget deficit. It takes too long and involves far too much paper, ink, guards, armored cars, and storage space.[3]

Money creation takes only a few hours if the Federal Reserve System purchases $50 billion in bonds from the Treasury. To compensate the Treasury for the bonds, the Fed adds to Treasury deposits in the Fed an additional $50 billion, on which the Treasury can then write checks as it pleases. This very simple way to enlarge Treasury deposits is depicted in Figure 23.3 as a consolidated T-account of the Federal Reserve System. No printing press, however modern, could ever keep up with this method. It was last used on any scale in World War II. After that, the Fed decided that it would purchase new bonds directly from the Treasury only to "roll over" or refinance maturing securities it already owned. Though such purchases were carried out from time to time, their amounts were small. Since 1981, the Fed has not bought any bonds at all directly from the Treasury. If, however, during some national emergency the Treasury ever encountered serious difficulty in marketing new securities to the public, one could make a confident wager: the present practice would be quickly changed, and the Fed would buy the bonds directly from the Treasury.

**FEDERAL RESERVE
SYSTEM**

ASSETS	LIABILITIES
Bonds +50 bil.	Treasury Deposits +50 bil.

Figure 23.3. Treasury bond sales direct to the Fed. Here a budget deficit is financed by Treasury sales of bonds to the Federal Reserve System, which pays for the bonds by creating new deposits that the Treasury can spend.

---

3.   It takes a long time just to print the paper notes. Say you started the presses at noon today intending to print $50 billion in $20 bills. If you print ten bills per second, you would reach almost $18 million by the end of the first day, but you wouldn't reach $1 billion for more than a month and a half, and it will take you over seven years to finish the job! To finance a deficit, the money is needed now, not later.

Financing Deficits by Money Creation Is Potentially Damaging

Of the four methods by which a government can finance a budget deficit, the first and possibly the second do not involve the creation of new money, while the last two definitely do. This difference is a central one. When new money is not created, the major damage inflicted by a deficit is likely to be the run-up in interest rates that comes from the crowding-out effect, as discussed in the previous section. But deficits that are financed by the creation of new money can cause much more damage than that, because they hold the potential for high inflation. The reason is that fiscal deficits are expansionary in any case, but so is monetary expansion. In any country suffering from a serious inflation, it is actually quite likely that the government is using expansionary fiscal policy and financing the resulting deficit with expansionary monetary policy carried on by the central bank. In deep recession this might be acceptable for a time. But closer to full employment, the combination of deficits and new money is dangerous.

Analysis of "Monetizing" the Deficit

When a budget deficit is financed by central bank creation of new money, we say the government is **monetizing the deficit**. Alternatively, the money creation is sometimes called an **accommodating monetary policy**, the term accommodation used because the money creation makes it easier to accomplish the financing of the deficit. A major difference between a fiscal deficit that is monetized (accommodated) and one that is not is the effect on interest rates, as seen in Figure 23.4.

Panel **a** shows a fiscal policy of increased government spending or decreased taxes that raises aggregate demand rightward from AD. The result is a rise in total output and income from Y to Y'. Following our analysis of the crowding-out effect earlier in the chapter, the higher income raises the demand for money in the economy, seen in panel **b** as a rise from M_D to M_D'. The rise in interest rates from r to r' means that aggregate demand at AD' has not pushed out so far to the right as it would have if crowding out had not occurred. In panel **c** the situation is different. Here the central bank has monetized the deficit by creating money. The increase in the money supply from M_S to M_S' keeps the interest rate from rising, or from rising as much. Aggregate demand is therefore not restricted by the higher interest rates and pushes out further, to AD". The equilibrium at E" means that output and income, at Y", are higher than they would be if new money had not been created. In short, **deficits that are monetized are more expansionary than those that are not**.

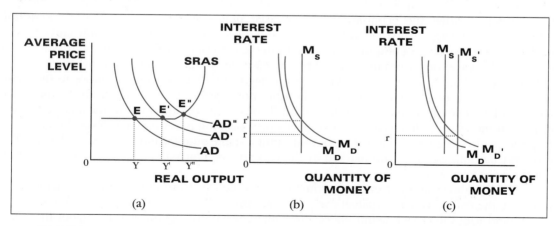

Figure 23.4. **Monetized deficits are more expansionary than those that are not.** In panel **a**, a fiscal policy of increased government spending or lower taxes raises aggregate demand and therefore total output and income. The greater economic activity increases the demand for money in panel **b**, so forcing a rise in interest rates. But in panel **c**, the central bank monetizes the deficit by creating new money, so keeping interest rates lower than they would otherwise be. The crowding-out effect is avoided, and the monetized deficit results in greater aggregate demand (AD" in panel **a**) than would otherwise be the case.

Analysis of the Potential for Inflation When the Deficit Is Monetized

In Figure 23.5 we utilize the concept of a potential level of output beyond which inflation will break out, already developed in Chapter 18. Figure 23.5's panels **a** and **b** show the difference between a deficit that is monetized and the other methods for financing deficits that leave the money supply unchanged. Because monetized deficits are more expansionary than deficits that are not, they contain a greater potential for inflation when the economy is near to the potential level of output. (When the economy is in a deep recession, then the extra stimulus from a monetized deficit might be quite welcome.)

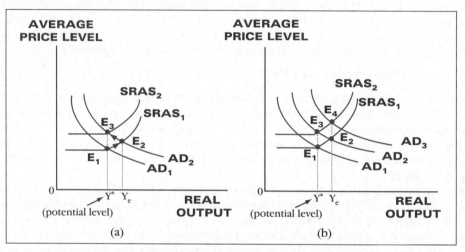

Figure 23.5. The danger that monetized deficits will cause an inflationary spiral. The diagram shows the greater danger of inflationary consequences when a budget deficit is monetized (that is, financed with new money creation). We start at E_1 in panel **a**. A tax decrease or government spending increase unaccompanied by any change in the money supply would raise aggregate demand (to AD_2). If output is pushed above the potential level (to Y_e), costs will rise, pushing the SRAS curve upward. The economy returns to its potential level of output Y^*, but at a higher price level. In panel **b**, the government finances the deficit with new money, which raises aggregate demand further (to AD_3) than would be the case with no money creation. Output stays higher (at Y_e). But this is above the potential level of output, so costs are likely to continue rising, with the potential for an inflationary spiral.

Panel **a** shows the economy before a fiscal policy change. Equilibrium E_1 is at the intersection of the aggregate demand curve AD_1 and the short-run aggregate supply curve $SRAS_1$, just at the potential level of output Y^* that results in the natural rate of unemployment. Now imagine a tax decrease, or government spending increase, or both, leading to an increased budget deficit. The additional spending would cause the aggregate demand curve to move to the right, say to AD_2. At the new equilibrium E_2, total output now rises from Y^* to Y_e, above the potential level and high enough so that unemployment falls below the natural rate. In the absence of any change in monetary policy, wages will begin to rise, pushing SRAS up to $SRAS_2$. The economy responds with rising prices and falling output, until a stable equilibrium E_3 is reached at Y^*. The economy has followed the path marked by the two arrows. Output is back at its potential level, but the price level is higher.

Panel **b** shows another option for financing the deficit. Here the central bank chooses to monetize the deficit with an expansionary monetary policy. Because interest rates do not rise, as they would with the crowding-out effect, investment and consumption will be higher than they otherwise would be, and aggregate demand is pushed further to the right, say to AD_3 with an eventual equilibrium at E_4. This keeps total output at the higher level Y_e rather than the level Y^*, which is the outcome in panel **a**, but the policy has a cost. Output remains above the potential level, the price rise that was caused by the first move from AD_1 to AD_2 now continues, SRAS will shift again, and sustained inflation will set in. The lesson is that **deficits that are monetized are**

potentially more inflationary than those that are not. All this is of great importance. Because the U.S. budget deficits of the 1980s were *not* financed by the printing of new money, inflation did not increase even though the size of the deficits continued to be large. Had the deficit been monetized, the danger of inflation would have been much greater.

Do Deficits Matter That Much?

Up to this point we have been discussing the damage caused by budget deficits, including their crowding out of private spending and their potential for inflation when they are monetized. Yet there is a group of economists that holds another position, that deficits don't matter that much, and unless they are accompanied by considerable creation of new money, their adverse effects are overemphasized. These arguments are controversial and appear to be a minority view, but they deserve consideration. Most of them apply to the national budget deficits not only of the United States, but of *any* country. Let us review them.

"Armageddon Never Came"

The first argument is that disaster never arrived, even though the U.S. budget deficit is still high (over 5% of GDP in the fiscal year 1992, having, however, declined from its historic peacetime record of almost 6% of GDP in the period 1983–1986). This argument that the budget deficit is benign seems to overlook the fact that serious damage has already been done. Until 1982, U.S. deficits in peacetime had never reached even 3% of GDP with the single exception of the 1975 recession. The deficit continues to absorb over half of U.S. savings, and investment is very low by the standards of the past (on a net basis it averaged an annual 6.7% of GDP in the 1970s, but only 4.7% in the 1980s). Investment is also well below the percentage of GDP invested by many other countries. Productivity growth has been very low, lowest among the world's major economies (though some turnaround occurred in 1992, as we shall discuss). These adverse effects may be largely the result of how the deficit affects interest rates. Higher real interest rates make *long-term* investment, including any long-lived plant and equipment, particularly unattractive. Such capital, if financed by borrowing, may involve excessive costs when interest rates are high, or excessive interest forgone if a firm's own cash is used. As a result, the composition of GDP is likely to shift toward short-lived consumption goods and services where high interest rates on borrowed funds are of less concern. This means reduced investment in capital that could make an economy more productive.

THE SHORTER SERVICE LIFE OF NEW INVESTMENT WHEN REAL INTEREST RATES ARE HIGH

Empirical evidence does support the claim that as the real rate of interest rises, firms' investment shifts toward items that are not as long lasting. That is, the service life of new investment goods shortens. When service life falls, depreciation rises because the capital item wears out over a shorter period of time. Thus gross investment, which includes depreciation, has recently been higher than it would otherwise have been. The U.S. figure for gross investment through the 1980s ($674 billion in 1990, 13.0% of GDP) therefore appears more satisfactory than the figure for net investment ($120 billion, 2% of GDP) and is thus deceptively high. Real-life negative manifestations of this shorter service life can be seen in such diverse areas as a lower level of housing starts, continued deterioration of central cities, and erosion of productivity in old-line manufacturing industries. The flip side is the rapid growth of short-term investments in service-oriented firms such as pizza parlors, one-hour photo-developing firms, copy centers, video rentals, and hundreds of others.

The resulting damage may take years to become completely apparent, especially if any factors serve to conceal it. One such concealing factor does appear to have been operative. The high real interest rates of the 1980s attracted foreign funds—in effect, foreigners were transferring their savings to the United States to an unprecedented degree, the flow reaching about 4% of GDP in 1986. This moderated the rise in interest rates, which otherwise would have been much greater, and therefore kept investment from declining as much as it would have. Since then, the flow of foreign savings to the United States has slowed, with the result that real interest rates have tended to stay at a high level by the standards of the fairly recent past.

Furthermore, whenever U.S. unemployment falls, the danger grows that the continuing deficit will prove to be inflationary. An expansionary budget deficit that is welcome at a time of unemployed resources would do damage at a time of full employment. A large deficit of 6% of GDP brought advantages in 1983. With lower unemployment, a deficit of only half that could well have serious consequences if monetary policy does not offset it.

Both borrowers and lenders now appear to be well aware that continuing large government budget deficit poses two unpalatable choices. The first of these is that massive government borrowing of the country's private domestic saving will continue at a time when foreigners are indicating less desire to purchase U.S. securities. That would serve to keep real interest rates high. Alternatively, there is a danger that whenever economic growth is weak, the Fed at some point might adopt an easy monetary policy in an attempt to lower interest rates. In that case, monetary stimulus would be added to the large fiscal deficit. A perception that inflation would be ignited because of the combination of easy money and a stimulative deficit might, however, serve actually to push up interest rates.

Both arguments lead to the conclusion that real interest rates might be abnormally high in the foreseeable future. Even when slow growth in 1990–1993 reduced the demand for credit in the private sector and caused short-term interest rates to fall sharply, long-term rates—the ones of most concern to investors—stayed high. Thus short-term interest rates in 1992 (3.46% on U.S. Treasury Bills) were about the same as they had been back in the early 1960s (an average of 3.55%, 1963–1965), but long-term rates on government bonds and bank loans remain much higher, by 2.5 to 3 percentage points. (The rate on long-term government bonds was 7.01% in 1992, but the average was only 4.16% in 1963–1965.) The high long-term rates cause direct harm by reducing investment and that part of consumption where buyers finance their purchases over several years.

Our conclusion must therefore be that deficits do matter, and that though Armageddon didn't come, substantial damage did, damage that still continues.

Ricardian Equivalence

The school of thought that believes in rational expectations views deficits quite differently from most economists. Building on an argument first advanced by David Ricardo in the nineteenth century, this school suggests that the macroeconomic effect of a budget deficit is no different from what would have occurred if taxes had been raised to prevent a deficit from developing. This phenomenon, of larger deficits and higher taxes having the same effect, is called **Ricardian equivalence**.

The argument holds that taxpayers are forward-looking. They foresee that a deficit will require higher taxes in the future to pay the interest on the bonds sold to finance the deficit, and to pay the principal when the bonds mature. Knowing this, they increase their saving—for without a pool of savings that they can tap in the future, their consumption will have to be reduced by an uncomfortably large amount to pay the necessary new taxes. A general rise in saving is contractionary for the economy as a whole. If instead of running a deficit, however, taxes had been raised at once to pay the government's bills, that too would have been contractionary. Believers in Ricardian equivalence thus maintain that deficits do not stimulate, and that their effect is the same as if taxes had been increased.

This seems logical enough, so long as taxpayers are truly forward-looking and act on their "rational expectations." For various theoretical and empirical reasons, however, most economists doubt that Ricardian equivalence is very strong in practice. They believe that many people don't pay much attention to fiscal policy decisions, and that taxpayers' time horizons are short enough that they prefer to consume now rather than worrying about taxes in the future. Also, the prospect of future taxes may be distant enough so that taxpayers believe a later generation can deal with it.[4]

Evidence of an actual positive connection between government budget deficits and private saving is not abundant. It does appear to be rather pronounced in the data for Belgium and Italy. This may be significant, because both countries have been running large deficits, increases in which might seem to require higher future taxes. No Ricardian equivalence has been found, however, in Japan, Britain, and France where deficits have been under more control, and very little in the United States, Canada, and Germany. In fact, for years U.S. household savings *fell* in the face of large budget deficits, contrary to the prediction of Ricardian equivalence. It is probably fair to judge that Ricardian equivalence can occur, with a government's budget deficit to some extent offset by a rise in private saving, but that the effect is not generally very large.

The Argument That the Deficit Is Smaller Than Generally Believed

Another argument made by those who argue that the damage from deficits has been overstated involves how they are measured. A case can be made that the size of deficits is usually exaggerated. *Some* government spending goes for capital that remains as an asset. One could logically argue that the capital should be treated as a partial offset to the deficit. (We return to this topic later in the chapter when we discuss the national debt.) Furthermore, inflation will cause any given nominal deficit to rise, but without altering the size of the *real* deficit. The real figure is the one that matters, but it is not the figure that attracts attention.[5]

Each of these points makes sense, and they do indeed add up to saying that the deficit is smaller than generally believed. They do not, however, negate the fact that the U.S. federal government borrows large amounts or that this borrowing will absorb savings and raise interest rates, with damaging effects on private investment and on foreign trade.

The Actual Budget Deficit May Not Be a Very Good Measure of Fiscal Policy

At this point in our study of budget deficits we take up the concept that the size of any given deficit will depend upon the state of the economy at that moment. The reason why is related to the previous chapter's discussion of the automatic stabilizing aspects of taxes and government spending. That analysis made the point that, when otherwise left alone, budgets move toward deficit whenever an economy contracts and toward surplus as it expands. Let us recall why. Assume that with any given federal budget, a recession sets in. What is the result for the budget? As total output and income sink, tax collections will fall because personal income taxes, Social Security taxes, and corporate taxes are levied on the amount of income earned. Simultaneously, government spending will rise because unemployment and welfare benefits will increase. Without any conscious decision, tax collections fall and government spending rises, moving the budget toward deficit.

This effect makes itself felt in every country where the government's taxes are based on income, and its spending is in part tied to economic conditions. The link is strong: A rise in unemployment of one percentage point in the mid-1980s would have cost the U.S. Treasury about

---

4.   A more complex reason is that individuals almost always face higher interest rates than do governments. Thus the discounted present value (see Chapter 13) of a tax increase in the perhaps-distant future may be much less than the discounted present value of increased consumption in the immediate future. If, as a result, consumption increases, then Ricardian equivalence will not hold.

5.   A leader in making these arguments is Northwestern University professor Robert Eisner, who has written frequently on the subject. Another argument, that in the United States, state and local governments run surpluses that offset in part the federal government's deficits, is now obsolete. State and local government budgets ceased to be in surplus after 1986. The burden sharing currently being placed on these governments for such spending as Medicaid and their needs in education, law enforcement, infrastructure, and the like, make it unlikely that state and local surpluses will reappear in the near future.

$35 billion in lost taxes and increased unemployment benefits. (The tax loss is far the larger of the two, comprising more than three-quarters of the total.)

This pattern to deficits is shown in Figure 23.6. Here, a *budget function* shows the position of the budget (whether it is in deficit, balanced, or in surplus) given an existing structure of spending and tax laws. That is, we assume that the government makes no deliberate changes in its spending and taxes, so only changes in the country's economic conditions affect tax collections and spending. Say that today the government's budget is balanced, with government tax revenue just equal to government spending, giving a point on the budget function at zero on the vertical axis. (Higher points would indicate a budget surplus; lower ones a deficit.) The point showing a balanced budget is associated with a level of total output at Y_b along the horizontal axis. Now say the country's total output rises to the higher level Y_h. In that case, tax collections will grow and some items of spending will fall, thus pushing the budget into surplus. The budget function shows that at output level Y_h, a budget surplus would develop equal to the distance AY_h. All other things being equal, a growing economy tends to push the government's budget toward surplus.

Now consider what would happen if, starting with a balanced budget at Y_b, the economy enters a recession and output declines to the lower level Y_l. In that case, tax collections will fall and some forms of government spending will rise. The budget is driven into deficit of the size Y_lB. All other things being equal, a declining economy tends to push the government's budget toward deficit. The key fact is that the same structure of taxes and spending could mean a large deficit, a small one, a balanced budget, or a small or large budget surplus, depending on the economy's level of output.

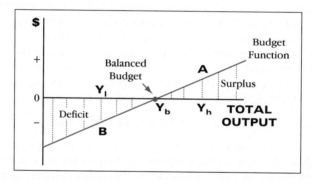

Figure 23.6. A budget function. By generating more tax revenues and causing some forms of government spending to fall, economic growth causes the federal budget to move toward surplus. A slowing economy causes deficits to develop.

Therefore, the size of a country's actual budget deficit is not a good indication of how stimulative its fiscal policy is. In the cases cited, fiscal policy was entirely unchanged, and the budget was being altered only by changes in the country's level of output.

This exposes the common fallacy that a large budget deficit indicates an expansionary fiscal policy. In fact, **a large budget deficit does not necessarily indicate that fiscal policy is stimulative**.

Structural Deficits and Surpluses Are a Better Measure of the Stimulus

Economists came to see that actual budgets have to be adjusted to reflect the state of the economy if conclusions are to be drawn on how stimulative or restrictive these budgets are. Figure 23.7 shows how such an adjustment can be made. Consider an economy at output level Y in that figure. The tax collections and government spending at this output level cause the budget to be in surplus by the amount AY. This is the **actual (or current) surplus**. Changes in the budget would take place, of course, if the economy moved toward recession with output dropping to Y_1. The fall in output would cause an actual deficit to develop, shown by the vertical distance Y_1B.

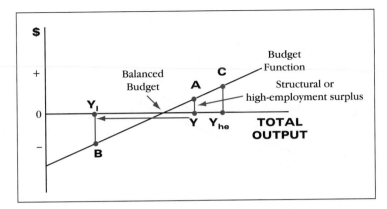

Figure 23.7. Actual deficit, structural surplus. With an unchanged fiscal stance of taxes and spending, the deficit of Y_1B at output level Y_1 would have been a surplus of CY_{he} at the level of output Y_{he}. The structural or high employment budget measures what the budget would be like at the high employment level. Here it would be in surplus, so the actual deficit registered at output level Y_1 is not very stimulative.

But consider how differently this all would have looked if the economy had been healthier and had not entered a recession. Assume that instead of declining, the economy had grown, say to Y_{he}. At that greater level of output Y_{he}, tax collections would have been higher and some forms of government spending would have been lower, and the budget would have shown a surplus of CY_{he}.

To ascertain whether a given budget is stimulative, we need to ask how high the level of output would have to be to give the highest level of employment possible without triggering an inflation. Let us say that level is Y_{he}, the "he" standing for high employment.[6] With this amount of output, exactly the same budget pattern that gave us an actual deficit at Y_1 now gives us a *surplus*. This **structural or high-employment surplus** *does not change* as the country's total output changes, as long as the stance of fiscal policy remains the same. Whatever the level of output actually is (at Y or Y_1 for example), the budget *would* have been in surplus if output had been as high as Y_{he}. Budget surpluses are contractionary, so the fiscal policy stance is contractionary at output level Y_{he}. There is a *structural surplus* even though at output levels Y or Y_1 there are deficits in the *actual* budget.

The actual deficit accompanying the recession-level of output Y_1 in Figure 23.7 is thus not really very stimulating, since at high employment there would have been a surplus. To change this fiscal policy stance, the government could either lower taxes, or raise spending, or both. The budget function would fall as in Figure 23.8, perhaps from BF_1 to BF_2; the budget would be moved toward deficit at any level of output. Here the change has been large enough so that the structural (high-employment) surplus disappears; if output were at Y_{he}, the budget would be balanced.

A structural (or high-employment) balanced budget in a recession thus has a very different meaning than an actual balanced budget. Some economists recommend a policy of eliminating structural surpluses and deficits, that is, balancing the structural budget every year, or even running a moderate surplus. In that case, most economic downturns would not drive the actual budget into deficit, or not a very serious one at any rate. Others economists suggest that the government could utilize structural deficits against recessions, and conversely structural surpluses against an overheated economy—the rationale in both cases being the greater fiscal effect.[7] In that case the structural budget could be balanced "over the cycle" as the saying goes. None of these ideas is very familiar to the public because budget deficits (both actual and structural) have become such a permanent feature of U.S. fiscal policy.

---

6. This high-employment level of output is technically the same as the potential level of output, Y^*, that was introduced in Chapter 18.

7. Obviously, economists who take this view do not believe that budget deficits are fully crowded out by higher interest rates.

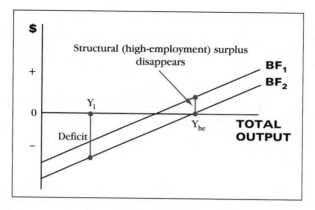

Figure 23.8. A change in the position of the budget function. To increase the degree of stimulus imparted by the budget, the government could lower tax rates and increase spending independent of the level of output. That would push the actual budget toward deficit at any level of output, moving the budget function down from BF$_1$ to BF$_2$.

The Great Structural Deficit of the 1980s

In fact, the structural (high-employment) budget was driven into unprecedented deficits during the 1980s. Never between 1958 and 1982 did the budget so defined differ from balance by more than 2% of GDP except in just one year (1960), and that by only 2.3%. There was a structural surplus or balance in every year from 1958 to 1966, but ever since, structural deficits have reigned, except for a surplus in 1969 and balance in 1974. (The last time the *actual* budget was in surplus was also 1969.) But after 1982, structural deficits became chronically large because of the tax and spending decisions already analyzed in the preceding chapter. High and rising as seen in Table 23.1, these structural deficits were a new force in American politics and economics alike. Though by 1989–90 they had fallen back somewhat, the structural deficit in 1993 was still 3.3% of GDP, larger than in any year from the end of World War II until the Reagan administration. (U.S. structural deficits are projected to stay at about 2.2–2.3% through the late 1990s.) The same problem of structural budget deficits affects Canada and Europe as well. Of all the major economies, only Japan has registered a significant structural budget surplus in recent years.

TABLE 23.1
Federal structural budget deficits, percent of GDP, 1983–1993.

1983	2.9	1989	3.2
1984	4.4	1990	3.2
1985	5.2	1991	3.2
1986	4.4	1992	3.4
1987	3.4	1993	3.3
1988	3.4		

Source: Dept. of Commerce until 1990, and Congressional Budget Office thereafter. Figures are for the calendar year until 1990, and fiscal year thereafter. The CBO uses the name "standardized employment budget."

▶ A NATION'S DEBT

In the first part of this chapter, we made the case that budget deficits can be damaging for an economy. Now we must assess the link between budget deficits and a nation's debt, and weigh the consequences of continuous growth in the national debt.

The most common way for a government to finance a budget deficit is through the sale of new bonds. As we have seen, the total of a country's bond issues outstanding makes up that nation's debt.[8] Large U.S. budget deficits have been run up in every fiscal year of the 1980s and 1990s to date. (See Table 23.2 for the figures from 1985 to 1993. The figures are actual, not structural, because the actual deficit is what has to be financed.) The financing of these deficits with bond sales caused the national debt to mount steadily. That debt was $4,411 billion at the end of the fiscal year 1993.[9]

TABLE 23.2
Actual U.S. federal budget deficit, billion dollars, fiscal 1985–1992.

1985	212.1	1990	218.1
1986	212.6	1991	272.5
1987	147.5	1992	290.3
1988	155.5	1993	254.9
1989	143.8		

Source: IMF, *International Financial Statistics Yearbook 1993*, p. 727, for 1985-1991. Office of Management and Budget data for 1992-1993.

A clock on 42nd Street just east of Times Square keeps New Yorkers informed with a constantly updated figure on what a family of four owes as its share of the national debt: In 1994, passersby could see that the figure was above $60,000. Does a continuously growing national debt pose an economic danger to an economy? If so, and if the danger is serious, then economists will obviously be less likely to recommend monetary and fiscal policies involving budget deficits, because these would run up the national debt.

WEAK ARGUMENTS THAT A NATIONAL DEBT IS DANGEROUS

Although there is a temptation to view them as such, national debts are not like a private debt that must be paid off. There is no legal, economic, or political requirement that the national debt ever be paid off. Old bonds mature, of course, but new ones can be sold to take their place. As long as the public demands the new bonds, the debt can be "rolled over" forever. A major distinction between a public, national debt, and private, personal, or corporate debt, is that a nation's government has the power to tax—fully backed by the force of law—to meet the interest payments and pay off the principal on its bond issues. That means a government's bond issues will usually be considered far more secure than a corporation's bonds, or an individual's IOUs, where no such coercive power exists.[10] That in turn means that government bonds are typically much demanded by those persons (including bank managers, supervisors of pension funds, corporate treasurers, ministers of finance in other countries, and investors in the general public) who want to earn interest on the safest possible securities.

The country that manages to retire its whole national debt by paying off all its bonds would discover some unpalatable consequences. The safest category of bonds will now have disappeared; commercial banks, private pension funds, corporations, and citizens generally would have to purchase other securities that even at best would carry some greater degree of risk. Once upon a time, in 1835 during Andrew Jackson's administration, the United States did indeed succeed in eliminating its entire national debt. It soon found that wisdom dictated its recreation, and today no informed person would seriously argue otherwise.

---

8.   National debts were invented during the Middle Ages. The Roman Empire and the other ancient empires did not have them.

9.   This is the "gross national debt." Some of the national debt is held by the government itself, as with the bonds that are the assets of the Federal Reserve System and by the social security system. The "net national debt" held by the public at the end of fiscal 1993 was almost one-third less than the gross debt.

10.   A national debt is indeed an exceptionally difficult problem when a country does not have the power to tax. The United States was in this position under the Articles of Confederation during and after the Revolutionary War. The power to tax was gained by the federal government only in 1789.

What about the argument that the burden of a national debt is transferred to future generations? This *can* be true, but only under certain circumstances. Consider wartime financing during World War II. Much of the war's costs in most of the participating nations was financed by bond sales, for the perfectly understandable reason that to finance the war on a "pay-as-you-go" basis entirely from taxation would have pushed taxes to an undesirably high level. Bond sales made good sense, because patriotic buyers could appreciate that their purchases did not just disappear, as tax payments did, but would continue to earn interest for years. In 10 or 20 years' time, when the bond matured, its full face value (original cost plus interest) would be repaid. Bond sales did not erode the incentive to work and invest in the way confiscatory taxes would have.

Who then bore the burden of the debt financing? Certainly the bondholders bore it initially, because they were the ones who voluntarily turned their purchasing power over to the government instead of spending it on consumption. In a sense, these people were buying tanks and army barracks for their government instead of automobiles and houses for themselves. The sacrifice was made by the initial buyers, who reduced their consumption and accepted a lower standard of living in order to buy the bonds that paid for the war. In this simple sense, it is not accurate to say that future generations bear the burden of a national debt.

What then *is* the role of future generations where the debt is concerned? Clearly, the country's future citizens will be responsible for paying the interest on the debt, and also for paying the principal when the bonds mature. The government must tax these citizens, or sell new bonds to them, in order to make these payments. Yet the category called "citizen" includes both those who own the bonds and those who pay the taxes to finance the interest and principal payments. The burden of the debt is not, in this reading, a net burden, because the society that pays the taxes is the same society that receives the payments. Funds move, to be sure, from taxpayer to bondholder, but the movement itself does not mean a net loss of either output or purchasing power. As Abraham Lincoln saw it, a nation owes its national debt to itself, unlike an individual's or corporation's debt, which is owed to others. For the most part, he was correct.

STRONGER ARGUMENTS THAT A HIGH LEVEL OF NATIONAL DEBT IS DANGEROUS

Several popular arguments that the sheer size of the national debt poses dangers are therefore mostly wrong or at best misleading. But a number of legitimate issues remain concerning a high and rising debt.

The Distribution of Income

Abraham Lincoln viewed a nation's debt as owed to itself, but there may still be an income distribution problem. Think of an economy divided into two groups, the rich and the poor, and then assume that the rich originally purchased many bonds while the poor bought few. In this not unrealistic case, the taxes to pay the interest on the debt and the principal payments at maturity (called "debt service") will be levied on all. But these payments will go mostly to the rich group. If the tax system is regressive, or not very progressive, then a transfer of income will occur from poor to rich. The country's income will become less equally distributed. People who believe that this development would be the cause of social and political problems will presumably prefer tax financing to debt financing. The reply that the rich made the initial sacrifices by buying the bonds, while the poor did not make that sacrifice, may or may not be comforting, depending on one's political outlook.[11]

If the Debt Is Held Abroad

Another argument that a high level of national debt causes trouble concerns how much of the debt is held by foreigners. If foreigners have purchased a large portion of the nation's debt, then the debt service payments flow outside the country, and not to the citizens of that country. This

---

11. In World War II, much effort was directed at persuading all income groups to purchase bonds, mostly of course to raise more revenue, but partly to avoid later income distribution problems. Every week even first and second grade students came to school with 10¢ (which was then enough for a candy bar and soft drink) to buy a savings stamp. These stamps eventually filled a book that could be traded in for a war bond.

debt service is thus a net flow of purchasing power beyond the country's borders, and represents a greater sacrifice as people in the country are taxed to pay people outside the country rather than paying themselves. Historically, some of the old British dominions (Canada, Australia, and New Zealand) had this problem, having sold many bond issues in Great Britain. The British had to sell large quantities of bonds abroad earlier in this century, many of the sales connected to the two great wars. Imperial Russia also sold a large portion of its debt abroad (much to France). In all these cases, servicing the foreign-held debt eventually posed difficulties of high taxation and net financial flows to the outside world. In the 1970s and early 1980s, dozens of less-developed countries sold their bonds to foreign banks and then found themselves in serious debt-service difficulties as the payments proved too large to make. The resulting hardships both to themselves and to the banks that had done the lending is known as the "debt crisis."

For many years, only a small part of the national debt of the United States was held by foreigners. The figure was 2.3% of the total in 1950 and 4.0% in 1970. The high interest rates of the 1980s changed that. When rates rose, U.S. government bonds and securities became more and more attractive abroad. By 1993, $568 billion, or 19% of the U.S. national debt owed to the public, was owned by foreigners, with the Japanese the largest holders.

It is important to remember, however, that foreigners made a sacrifice in consumption in order to buy the bonds, while one's own citizens did not. So, while payments of interest and principal on a large foreign-held debt do represent a burden on future generations within the country, there is a compensating gain in that one's domestic forebears did not have to sacrifice, as they would have done had the bonds all been sold domestically.

How Were the Borrowed Funds Used?

How damaging a high level of debt might be depends on the way the borrowed money was used. Future generations might be less likely to complain about servicing a large debt if their forebears had used the funds acquired by selling debt to finance government building of bridges, roads, and schools, and for the creation of other physical and human capital. Society in later years would then presumably be more productive and enjoy a higher income from which to service the debt. But if the spending is for the tanks and planes to fight a war, then in a few years these will be junked. Future generations will *not* have an enhanced stock of capital and will be poorer as a result. (Of course the war may have enabled future generations to live free of Fascism or slavery, for example, which might count for much more than the lost capital.) Private investment may be affected as well. Continuous growth in the national debt implies continuous deficit spending. As we are already aware, government budget deficits can drive up interest rates through the crowding-out phenomenon. In that case, private investment will be reduced.

In short, a real problem with a high and rising national debt is that future generations may be endowed with less capital than otherwise, unless the borrowed funds were used for the purpose of creating capital.[12] This point is clearly relevant for the American deficit of the 1980s and (thus far) of the 1990s, when investment did not rise as a percent of national income. The borrowed funds were used for purposes other than investment.

The Tax Burden from Debt Service May Distort Economic Performance

A debt *could* grow so high that the taxes needed to finance the interest payments begin to have unpleasant side-effects. Taxes may rise to the point that they reduce the supply of effort and encourage people to enter the underground economy. At a further stage, servicing the debt with taxes may become very difficult, or even impossible, bringing a threat of default and collapse of the government's credit. Rather than face this problem, a government might be tempted to turn

---

12.   Because of this reasoning, some scholars—Robert Eisner prominent among them—believe that national debt figures should take into account the net worth of the assets held by the government. For example, a government that owes $x billion in debt but owns neither capital nor natural resources is surely in a worse position than its neighbor that owes $x billion also, but has a huge infrastructure of government-owned capital and sits on an ocean of government-owned oil reserves. Such adjustments to the debt figures appear sensible, though they are not generally made. If the U.S. government's holdings of cash, foreign currency, shareholding in companies, and loans to the private sector are subtracted from the U.S. national debt, that debt is reduced by about 40%.

to inflationary financing so as to erode the real value of the debt. (Your $1000 bond would in real terms be worth only $500 if prices doubled.) Hyperinflations can effectively wipe out the national debt, and some less-developed countries have turned to this alternative for eliminating their debt.

To judge whether the size of the U.S. national debt is now so large as to pose financing difficulties, it is instructive to compare the present circumstances to various periods of the past, and to the debt situation elsewhere. We have already noted that a debt's size should be measured as a percentage of a nation's income. For example, a private debt of $1 million would be small and give no problems to the Rockefeller family, whereas a debt of $100,000 might be a serious burden to a young teacher in a public school. So it is with countries. A debt is large or small only in relation to the size of a nation's income. Similarly, the interest payments on that debt can be termed large or small only after considering the size of the national income that can be taxed to pay that interest.

Table 23.3 shows the U.S. national debt in six selected years in the first column, the interest payments on that debt in the second column, and the national income in the third. Two results stand out. As a percentage of national income, past debts have been much higher than they are at present in the United States. In Great Britain, debt as a percentage of national income was two or three times higher than the current U.S. figure at some periods during the century of its greatest prosperity. (Several developed countries, including Ireland, Italy, and Belgium, now have national debts of approximately 100% of national income.) By historical standards, interest payments are now very high in the United States, but still well below the levels that have been reached in Britain during long periods.[13]

TABLE 23.3
The burden of the national debt: the United States and Great Britain.

Year	(1) National Debt	(2) Interest Payments on National Debt	(3) National Income	(4) Size of Debt as % of National Income	(5) Interest Payments on Debt as % of National Income
			United States		
	(billion $)	(billion $)	(billion $)		
1868	2.6	0.13	6.8	40%	1.9%
1939	47.6	0.95	72.6	70%	1.3%
1945	278.7	3.66	181.5	150%	2.0%
1975	303.2	19.3	1549.0	20%	1.2%
1985	1816.9	129.4	3234.0	56%	4.0%
1990	3397.3	185.8	4417.5	77%	4.2%
			Great Britain		
	(billion £)	(billion £)	(billion £)		
1818	0.8	0.031	0.4	210%	7.7%
1923	7.7	0.325	3.95	190%	8.2%
1946	24.0	0.5	8.1	300%	6.2%
1975	46.4	2.79	105.7	40%	2.6%
1983	127.9	11.3	283.4	50%	4.0%

Source: U.S. Department of Commerce, U.S. Treasury, *Statistical Abstract of the United Kingdom*, IMF, *International Financial Statistics Yearbook 1993.*

Both the U.S. debt and interest on that debt still appear a long way from *crisis* levels. The acid test—can government bonds be sold at reasonable rates of interest—is still being passed, which must imply that the bond markets believe the present levels of U.S. debt and debt service

---

13.   It is worth reminding the reader that the interest payments on a national debt (as on other debt as well) are usually exaggerated because no account is taken of any erosion of the value of the debt due to inflation. If inflation is present, part of the nominal interest payments just compensates bondholders for the erosion of the real value of their bonds. It would be proper to count only the real portion of the interest payments, but this is not done in practice.

THE HIGH LEVEL OF PRIVATE DEBT

To assess whether a large national debt is supportable, we might notice that the level of private debt is far higher than the national debt. The U.S. private debt of households and corporations was about 60% of the national debt in 1946, larger than the national debt by 1950, and four times larger by 1973. The national debt has recently been catching up to private debt: the latter was only a little more than $2\frac{1}{2}$ times as large as the former in 1993. Japanese private debt is greater than it is in the United States as a percentage of national income. In that country, households borrow much less, but corporations borrow much more than do their U.S. counterparts.

remain supportable. Yet the rate of growth of the U.S. debt has been high, unprecedented except in wartime, interest payments on the debt have reached record levels by any measure, and the debt has grown very significantly as a percentage of national income. One would not want to count forever on the willingness of the credit markets to absorb ever-vaster quantities of U.S. debt.

To the time of writing, then, the macroeconomic damage caused by the sheer size and growth of the U.S. national debt has been limited. But the endless repetition of large budget deficits is causing continual growth in that debt as a percentage of national income. It would not be prudent to allow this to go on indefinitely. If the federal budget deficit can be brought under control, then a much slower-growing debt would not rise as a percentage of national income and should be manageable, at least by past standards. Whether and how that will happen is our next subject.

WHAT CAN BE DONE ABOUT THE DEFICIT?

We have seen that large deficits affect both domestic and international economic conditions. Now we must ask, what can be done about them? Any deficit can be addressed by enhancing revenues, by reducing spending, or by doing both. The methods may be broadly automatic, as when the legislature adopts some compulsory rule binding future governments to limit spending or match new spending with new tax revenue. Or they may involve an activist approach, as when the legislature decides to raise taxes or cut a spending program.

"AUTO-PILOT" METHODS

Automatic devices to contain the budget deficit have attracted much attention. For many years, Congress has placed a legal limit on the size of the national debt. This limit, if enforced, would clearly restrict the size of federal budget deficits, requiring their entire elimination when the debt is at the legal limit. In fact, such legal limits have proved to be a charade acted out every few months by Congress. When the debt presses near the legal limit, Congress raises the limit! The statutory ceiling has been increased regularly, as Table 23.4 shows. It is not easy to see how the situation would have differed if there had been no legal ceiling at all, beyond several hundred fewer pages in the Congressional Record. It is mere "window-dressing."

TABLE 23.4
Changes in the statutory limits on the national debt, 1986–1993 (billion dollars).

Third quarter 1986	2111	Fourth quarter 1989	3123
Fourth quarter 1986	2300	Third quarter 1990	3195
Second quarter 1987	2320	Fourth quarter 1990	4145
Third quarter 1987	2800	Second quarter 1993	4370
Third quarter 1988	2870	Third quarter 1993	4900

Source: U.S. Federal Reserve Bulletin, Table 1.40. The quarters shown were the ones during which the statutory limit was changed.

A Balanced-Budget Amendment to the U.S. Constitution

Many politicians have suggested a constitutional amendment to balance the federal budget in the United States, in essence requiring the government to collect sufficient tax revenues every year to cover spending in that year. The popular arguments in favor of such an amendment are aimed entirely at deficits, and are often simplistic. Families must earn as much as they spend, so it is said, or bankruptcy ensues, and the same is true of the national government. "Bankruptcy" is seen to follow from the large and growing national debt that accompanies continual deficits in the annual budget. The appeal of this argument is undeniable: Public support for a balanced-budget amendment is substantial, with polls usually recording about two-thirds of the public in favor and fewer than one out of eight people willing to say they oppose the proposal.

Criticism of a Balanced-Budget Amendment

To the extent that a budget deficit is stimulative and a surplus contractionary (with the crowding-out effect therefore small), the consequences of a balanced-budget amendment on fiscal policy would be unwelcome. Consider what would happen as the country entered a recession. We have already seen that recessions push the budget toward deficit because tax collections fall and certain types of government spending (especially unemployment and welfare payments) rise. If the authorities feel compelled to move the budget back toward balance, or are required to do so by a balanced-budget amendment, then they will have to raise taxes or cut government spending, or both. Either action, or a combination of the two, will reduce aggregate demand, with a multiplied negative effect on total output and income. On this score, the initial recession is made worse.

Far from being just a theoretical issue, it was balanced-budget thinking that caused President Hoover to support a tax increase right in the middle of the Great Depression, in 1932, and the incoming President Roosevelt to endorse the idea. At the same time, both the old and the new president curtailed many spending items, defense and highways for example. The outcome of this fiscal perversity, which ranks as one of the country's greatest mistakes of economic policy, caused considerable damage to an already reeling economy.

A similar pro-cyclical effect can be found when attempts are made to push the budget toward balance during periods of inflation. An economic expansion will cause tax receipts to rise and leads to a decline in some forms of spending. The budget moves toward surplus. Attempts to balance the budget in an overheating economy will then require either a tax decrease, or a spending increase, or both. Either action, or the two together, is stimulative, and total output and income will increase by a multiplier. The move toward a balanced budget has stoked the inflationary fires yet further.

This is not the same as saying that a balanced budget is *never* desirable. If by happenstance all the private-sector macroeconomic factors (C, S, I, X, and M) combine to leave an economy at or near the lowest level of unemployment that can be reached without setting off inflation, then a neutral fiscal stance by a country's government is suitable. Balanced budgets are appropriate when neither fiscal stimulus nor fiscal restraint is called for. Such a situation of perfect order would be rare, and perhaps would not last long, but even so it could happen.

The Political Advantage of a Balanced-Budget Amendment

In spite of the criticisms, a balanced-budget amendment possesses a political advantage that is quite overwhelming. Because a constitutional amendment would take a long time to pass, discussions of unhealthy fiscal policy can be focused on some indefinite future. In the 1980s and 1990s, a time of constant, large, and damaging budget deficits, it was possible for politicians to advocate a balanced-budget amendment, and yet continue voting for tax cuts and increasingly high levels of government spending. The problem was present even at the presidential level. Presidents Reagan and Bush both called for a balanced-budget amendment at the same time that their budget proposals to Congress embodied deficits at historic highs. (Congress usually made the deficit worse by adding a little more spending to these presidents' proposals.)

Five times since 1982 a balanced-budget amendment has come to a vote in Congress—the last time in 1994—and five times it has failed to get the necessary two-thirds vote. Once, in 1986, the margin in the Senate was just one vote; in 1990, the House missed passing it by seven votes, while in 1994, the margin in the Senate was four votes. But new opposition had developed. Some conservatives now argue that passage of the amendment will lead to large tax increases; some liberals believe that sharp cuts in spending on entitlements would be required. People of all persuasions worry that making the issue into a constitutional one will inevitably involve the Supreme Court in what to now has been essentially a political question.

Meanwhile, another route to an amendment, an unusual one, was being tried. At last count, 32 U.S. states had voted to call for a constitutional convention to consider a balanced-budget amendment.[14] To call a convention, only 34 states (two-thirds of the total) are required. If a constitutional convention is indeed ever called, that would represent the first use of this rusty 200-year-old tool. Three-quarters of the states (38) would have to approve the amendment after the convention presented it. Legally it is not clear whether a constitutional convention called to debate a balanced-budget amendment could consider other issues as well.

CONGRESSIONAL ACTION TO CONTROL THE SIZE OF THE BUDGET DEFICIT

Though a balanced-budget amendment to the Constitution has not been successful, concern over the size of U.S. deficits has led Congress to take a number of steps. (It should be noted that in fiscal policy terms, the steps taken were contractionary.) In 1985 it passed a law embodying a new approach to public finance, the Gramm-Rudman-Hollings bill. (The bill was often called simply Gramm-Rudman; here it is abbreviated as GRH.) If Congress could not concur on the ways to cut the deficit by an agreed-on annual amount, then the president would be empowered to make across-the-board spending cuts.

GRH was superseded by new 1990 and 1993 budget agreements between Congress and the president. Under their rules, money for any new spending must be raised either by increasing taxes or by cutting an existing program. Any new entitlement program, such as a new health care bill, must be offset by a decline in spending on another entitlement program or by a tax increase. Any tax cut unless balanced by specific spending cuts will trigger automatic across-the-board spending cuts. These are the "pay-as-you-go" provisions. Revenue from tax increases cannot be used to pay for additional discretionary expenditures, but only for increases in mandatory entitlement spending (like Social Security) or deficit reduction. Separate caps were established for various categories of discretionary spending that lasted until 1993. Now there is an overall spending ceiling on discretionary spending, called the "flexible freeze." Should this rigid cap be exceeded, an automatic sequestration goes into effect. This cuts spending on other programs by an equal percentage, so that total spending does not change. The rules require that these

---

14.   Two of these states, Alabama and Florida, rescinded their call in 1988, representing a constitutional question in itself.

sequesters occur almost immediately, and several have already been imposed. They make the new budget agreements harder to violate than was GRH.

AN ASSESSMENT OF THE AUTO-PILOT SCHEMES

Many inside and outside the economics profession have been dubious about the automatic-pilot schemes. They question whether Congress will have the fortitude to let the mechanical process work. All the mandated limits could be changed at any time by congressional vote, just as the GRH law was eventually scrapped. Even if the auto-pilot schemes do work, should Congress abdicate its responsibility for establishing spending priorities, cutting programs with high benefits along with the wasteful ones with low benefits? For example, presidents intent on cutting spending are more likely to get their way than before, because if Congress did pass a tax increase to pay for some new spending, the President could veto it and then look on as the compensating spending cuts mandated by law took effect. Should Congress have gone this far in making it so difficult to use expansionary fiscal policy against recessions?[15] Former President Ford has called the whole process a mindless "parliamentary robot."

For all that, it is fair to point out that the situation might be far worse without the idea of automatic limits, however flawed it is. The limits can be seen as embodying the pessimistic assumption that Congress is unlikely to agree on what can be cut from the spending side of the federal budget, and that further tax increases to control the deficit are unachievable. Automatic limits are not a good substitute for responsible policy choices that weigh the legitimate needs for government spending against the difficult task of raising revenue, but arguably they *are* a good substitute for fiscal paralysis.

RAISING REVENUES AND CUTTING SPENDING

Rather than using auto-pilot schemes, Congress could bite a bullet by raising revenues and cutting spending. Doing so is, however, extremely difficult because voters tend to oppose both tax increases and any spending cuts that affect them personally. Experience has taught that the only tactic with much of a promise of success is to spread the pain widely, so that the voters believe the sacrifice is being shared.

Enhancing Revenues

Revenues could be raised, with the understanding that Congress should not *spend* the new revenue collected from taxes if it wants to reduce the deficit. But enhancing revenues has until now been a political minefield. The income tax increases of 1993, which affected only a tiny minority of high-income taxpayers, passed the Senate by just one vote. However impossible further increases might be politically, they are not impossible economics unless a country is in a recession. The United States still has the lowest tax rate on high incomes of any major country except Canada. As a rule of thumb, a one percentage-point increase in individual and corporate income tax rates brings new revenue of about $30 billion.

In addition, the myriad of tax deductions in the U.S. tax code could be limited, which would also raise considerable revenue. For many years Congress has awarded tax breaks for various interests, but every dollar of reduced tax revenue expands the deficit, just as does every dollar of government spending. This is why the term "tax expenditure" is sometimes used to describe the tax breaks. Some have suggested that if the major federal income tax deductions for home mortgages, local property taxes, medical expenses, and pensions were disallowed, well over $200 billion would be raised—thus eliminating the deficit. Certainly mortgage deductions for second homes seem to subsidize the well-to-do. Alice Rivlin, White House budget director and former Director of the Congressional Budget Office, has suggested that for every

---

15.   There are, however, certain rules that allow the caps to be waived during a significant recession, and the President can also declare an emergency that allows a waiver.

"tax expenditure" awarded by Congress there be a requirement for raised revenue from other sources or a spending cut.

Alternatively, a national value-added tax could be adopted. A 5% U.S. VAT (a low rate by international standards even if added atop state sales taxes) would collect a considerable amount, perhaps $70 billion, or about $40 billion if food, housing, and medical care were excluded from the tax. A rather moderate reform in the very limited U.S. inheritance tax could easily raise $10 billion or more.

Imposing environmental charges such as energy taxes, further gasoline taxes, pollution charges of various kinds, and taxes on cigarettes and alcohol have a growing constituency. Such taxes would have the decided advantage of working to correct major environmental and health problems while collecting a substantial amount of revenue. By comparison, taxes on income may reduce effort, while those on payrolls may reduce hiring, as we have seen elsewhere in the book.

To take one example of what might be accomplished, higher taxes on cigarettes and alcohol could easily raise $10 billion while at the same time cutting the country's health care costs significantly. For another example, every 1¢ increase in the tax on gasoline would raise almost $1 billion. U.S. gasoline taxes are among the world's lowest, even after a small rise in 1993. All gasoline taxes, including state ones, averaged less than 40¢ per gallon in 1993, as compared to the tax in Japan and most of Europe running between about $1.40 per gallon to a little over $3.00. One result of cheap fuel has been that the average miles obtained per gallon by new cars sold in the United States peaked in 1988 and has fallen since then as people turned to bigger and more luxurious cars that have poorer gas mileage. Not only would significant new revenues be collected by raising the federal tax on gasoline, but also the tax would decrease consumption with useful results in reducing highway congestion, lessening pollution from auto exhausts, and enhancing national security because domestic petroleum reserves could be preserved against future emergencies. A tax would be more effective than new-car fuel efficiency standards because it hits at older cars right away. Because the United States depends on auto transport more than most other developed countries, and because the poor tend to drive old gas guzzlers, a new gasoline tax would presumably require some kind of rebate in the federal income tax to avoid having the greatest burden fall on those of lowest income.[16]

More limited schemes have attracted a following among politicians because they do not involve a general and unpopular tax increase, while still raising revenues. Sometimes the schemes have a rather hopeless ring to them: for example, raising revenues through tax amnesties to collect backlogs of taxes. Yet some of the schemes seem practical enough. More revenues could be collected by charging user fees for free or low-cost public services. (Some of many such examples include charges for Coast Guard rescues, fees for flying private planes from federally funded airports, higher royalties for logging in national forests, charging farmers and ranches prices for water that are closer to the government's cost of providing it, and instituting or raising admission fees to national parks.) Finally, the tax on Social Security benefits could be raised from the present 85% to 100%. One hundred percent of Social Security benefits is subject to income tax in most other countries, and in these countries as well as the United States, private pensions are fully taxed as well. There seems no coherent reason not to take this step, which would reintroduce some further progression to the income tax by affecting the retired rich more than the retired poor.

Cutting Spending

Could spending be reduced to eliminate the budget deficit? No doubt, but consensus is lacking on what spending to cut, and the political will to do the cutting is in short supply. Reviewing ground covered in Chapter 22, some of the items in the budget have already been pruned sharply—welfare, commerce-housing-transport, education, funds for community development,

---

16.   More futuristic, a national system of urban road tolls and tolls on congested highways could be adopted, with the tolls assessed by scanners operating much like those at supermarket checkouts and with the bills charged automatically to credit cards. Such a system could have favorable effects on congestion and pollution while at the same time raising considerable revenue.

the environment, and the federal transfers to states and cities called revenue sharing. Further decreases would be very difficult politically. One item, interest on the debt, is a legal liability, and Congress has no power short of an unthinkable repudiation to avoid this form of spending—though, helpfully, deficit reduction ought to cut interest rates, and therefore lead to lower payments to bondholders.

The entitlement programs such as Social Security, Medicare, and veterans' benefits have had overwhelming political support, and large and militant groups always figuratively man the barricades when the suggestion is made to cut them. Other areas of spending have arguments so strong in their favor that Congress has been unwilling to make cuts when the administration has requested them—health, international affairs, science and technology, justice.

Further Cuts in Defense Spending and Agriculture?

Obvious areas for attention are defense spending and agriculture. Defense offers great opportunities for a "peace dividend" as mentioned in Chapter 1. Cuts are indeed being made, with the defense budget slated to go from $291 billion in fiscal 1993 to $265 billion in fiscal 1996. But there is arguably room for deeper cuts, especially in the weaponry designed to lob missiles or drop bombs on Soviet cities and to hunt down Soviet submarines. To many, such expensive hardware now seems superfluous. A hindrance is that reducing defense spending means a direct cut in employment in defense industries that will, at least locally, cause considerable protest.

Spending on agricultural subsidies is on the way down as well, with present plans calling for a reduction from $20 billion in 1993 to $12 billion in 1996. As Chapter 5 discussed, these subsidies as they are now constituted are questionable public policy, and support for them, though still strong in the farm states, seems to have weakened somewhat in the face of the budget deficit. Increasingly popular in Congress (and among economists) is the idea of making agricultural support dependent on farmers' willingness to follow environmentally sound conservation practices. Then the spending on agriculture would deliver wider benefits than it does when it merely supplements farmers' income.

"Reinventing Government" by Cutting Waste and Privatizing

The Clinton administration's National Performance Review, undertaken by Vice President Gore, has received the name "reinventing government." The plan would cut government spending $108 billion over five years and reduce federal employment by 252,000 workers. Among the hundreds of proposals in the Gore initiative are items such as privatizing air traffic control, government printing, and property management. It also would establish performance targets for the federal agencies and make it possible to fire workers for poor performance.

Reforming the Spending Process

Observers of the congressional budget process have suggested several reforms. Moving from a one-year to a two-year appropriation period would allow for longer, more informed consideration of sensitive questions such as social grant programs and more careful judgments on issues such as weapons procurement. The frequent consideration presently undertaken is arguably both wasteful of time, and subject to hasty "pork-barrel" deals where members of Congress trade expensive favors in support of one another's spending bills. The Clinton administration wants to move to a two-year budget cycle as of fiscal 1997. (Twenty-one U.S. states and numerous foreign countries already budget on a biennial basis.)

A more major reform would be to establish a separate budget for government capital investment. All items in the budget, whether immediately consumed or expected to last for hundreds of years, are now treated as current spending, even though about 11% of all government spending in the United States goes for capital outlays (fiscal 1991 figures, 7% at the federal level, 12% for state and local governments). Most U.S. states (37 at last count), many other countries, and many private businesses have separate capital budgets where the financing of long-term capital assets is treated differently from current spending. A deficit in the capital budget, created as the government borrows to fund productive public investment, could be treated more leniently than a deficit in the rest of the budget, which could be put on a pay-as-you-go basis. The mere existence of a U.S. capital budget would force Congress and the president to consider more carefully which spending will contribute to a more productive future and which will not. It would be useful in teaching the public that government spending is not all of a kind, and that some of it is vital to an economy's long-term growth. (We return to this issue in Chapter 26.) Capital budgeting would seem a sensible reform for the United States, and the Clinton administration is currently pushing the idea. Critics contend, however, that politicians might abuse a capital budget by terming spending "capital" when it really is not.

Capital budgeting might also be combined with a general "sunset law" which would require *any* program involving government spending to be reapproved on a regular basis. That way, programs could not simply continue to exist year after year without the regular scrutiny of the legislature.

Further ideas to put a lid on spending involve presidential action. What if the president were free to impound budgeted funds—that is, not spend them even if they were appropriated by Congress? Or what if a "line-item veto" were available—that is, power to veto single items in an appropriations bill? Impoundment was, however, ruled unconstitutional by the courts when President Nixon tried it in the 1970s, and in 1974 Congress strengthened the ban by passing an Impoundment Containment Act. A line-item veto would need the agreement of Congress, which has not been forthcoming even though the governors of 43 states presently have this power over state appropriations bills.[17]

A REMINDER THAT DEFICITS HAVE HOBBLED FISCAL POLICY

Reducing the budget deficit implies an ever-*tighter* fiscal policy. The resulting lessened stimulus imparted to the economy is proper in inflation, but damaging during a recession. That is why the recession of 1990–1991 and the slow recovery of 1992–1993 were intellectually as well as economically painful. Fiscal policy, which could have been of use, was hobbled by the fears that already large and long-lasting deficits should not be further increased.

Finding a proper role for fiscal policy is therefore now difficult. Toward the end of the 1990–1991 recession, many economists were calling on the president and Congress for $50 billion in temporary deficit spending for building the economy's infrastructure. But as we have seen, Congress in 1993 refused to pass President Clinton's much more modest $13 billion package, a bill that would presumably have had easy passage in the years before budget deficits hobbled expansionary fiscal policy.

CONCLUSION

It is certainly possible that economic history classes 50 years from now will study in detail the decline and fall of fiscal policy. If they do, it will be because the consequences were damaging. If they do not, it will be because today's generation of politicians at last showed more fortitude in raising revenues and constraining spending so that government spends only what can be afforded.

---

17.   Line-item veto power was, interestingly, granted constitutionally to the president of the Confederate States. President Jefferson Davis had budget problems far too large to be solved by this device, however useful it potentially was.

SUMMARY

1) A country's national debt is the sum total of outstanding government bonds issued over the years to finance the deficits in the government's budget.

2) The increase in aggregate demand caused by a rise in a government's budget deficit will probably increase the demand for money, which in turn will lead to a rise in interest rates. The higher interest rates will mean a lower level of private investment; the investment has been crowded out. This penalty in reduced capital investment is likely to be one of the most serious consequences of long-term deficits.

3) The higher interest rates will also cause foreigners to buy the local currency in order to earn the high rates, causing the currency to increase in value (appreciate). That will reduce exports and increase imports.

4) When budget deficits are financed by the creation of new money (that is, when they are monetized), they are more expansionary than when the deficits are financed by bond sales not involving the creation of new money.

5) A number of arguments can be made that actual budget deficits do not matter that much. One such is Ricardian equivalence—the idea that people will save more when deficits develop in order to build up savings with which to pay the higher taxes needed in the future. Another is measurement problems that mean the deficit is smaller than generally believed. A third is that the actual deficit is not as accurate an indicator of fiscal policy as the structural deficit that factors out the effects of booms and slumps from the actual deficit. Each of these arguments has some merit, so modifying the economic impact of budget deficits—but only in degree and not in kind.

6) Arguments that a high and rising national debt holds disadvantages include the resulting shift in income distribution, the damage if the debt is held abroad, the long-term harm if the borrowed money is used in ways that do not increase the productive potential of the economy, and the possibility that the debt might grow so large that the tax burden for debt service becomes unsupportable.

7) A major proposal to control the deficit is the balanced-budget constitutional amendment. Such an amendment holds advantages to politicians, who can support passage of the amendment at some future time while not making the painful choices needed to raise revenues and reduce expenditures. More credible has been the congressional attempt to control the size of the deficit by means of enforceable spending ceilings and requirements for new tax revenues to finance new spending. The Gramm-Rudman-Hollings Law was the first of these. It is now superseded by the budget agreements between Congress and the president of 1990 and 1993.

Chapter Key Words

Accommodating monetary policy: See *monetizing the deficit.*

Actual surplus or deficit: Government budget deficit unadjusted for inflation or recession. See *structural deficit.*

Balanced-budget amendment: A proposed constitutional change requiring equality between U.S. government spending and revenues. Has wide support, but could make inflations and recessions worse. Because ratification would take considerable time, provides politicians with a way to postpone hard decisions on the U.S. budget deficit.

Crowding-out effect: The principle that government budget deficits increase real interest rates and thus "crowd out" private investment, lessening the expansionary impulse of the deficit.

Current surplus or deficit: See *actual surplus or deficit*.

Gramm-Rudman-Hollings Bill (GRH): An "auto-pilot" scheme to cope with the large U.S. government budget deficit. Dates from 1985; superseded by the 1990 budget agreement.

High-employment budget: See *structural budget*.

Monetizing the deficit: The situation in which the central bank provides new money to finance a government's budget deficit. Provides for more expansion than is true of deficits not financed with new money, and potentially inflationary.

National debt: The total of government bond issues outstanding; arises as governments finance periods of budget deficits that occur when their spending exceeds their revenues.

Ricardian equivalence: The argument that the public will respond to government budget deficits by raising their level of saving. If accurate, means that expansionary fiscal policy will be nullified by the higher saving.

Structural (high-employment) budget: The concept whereby government spending and tax revenues are judged by what they would have been at the high-employment level of output.

CHAPTER QUESTIONS

1) Though the economy is at full employment, the government decides to run a deficit. It increases spending (G) without raising taxes. What would you expect to happen to investment and to net exports over the next few years? Why?

2) You are the prime minister of Japan. Because of political difficulties, you are currently unable to change your country's monetary or fiscal policy. However, you know that the United States is in recession. Its government is deciding between stimulative fiscal and monetary policy. Assuming your only goal is to maximize Japanese output over the next few years, which policy do you hope the United States will choose?

3) After graduation you take a job in the Ministry of Finance of the developing nation of Debitania. Debitania has always financed its budget deficits by selling bonds to its poor but thrifty citizens. This year however, Debitanians and foreigners alike have lost confidence in the government. They will only buy bonds at exorbitant interest rates. One day the minister walks into your office and says, "I have a great idea! We'll order the Central Bank of Debitania to buy the bonds. They won't have any trouble coming up with the money, and we'll be able to finance the deficit." Do you think this is such a great idea?

4) For many years now the U.S. government has been running large budget deficits. However, the 1980s were a decade of strong economic expansion, and the nation is now in recovery from the early-1990s recession. Since the economy is doing quite well, there was obviously no damage from the deficits. Comment on this statement.

5) When Ronald Reagan came to office in 1981, he cut taxes considerably, but did not cut spending. The cuts stimulated consumption, and the economy boomed for many years. Does this experience tend to support or refute the principle of Ricardian equivalence?

6) Suppose a president is elected who promises "to take us back to the 1800s." This president eliminates all welfare and Social Security and also gets rid of the income tax. Instead he raises revenue through a flat head tax on each citizen. Draw the budget function before and after these changes.

7) Assume that in some future year the United States and Japan happen to run actual budget deficits of exactly the same size. However, the United States has a structural budget deficit, while Japan has a structural budget surplus. Draw budget functions for both countries. Can you say for sure whether each country is in a recession or a boom?

8) Many years from now, an aging member of "Generation X" complains, "I have to pay high taxes because of the high national debt. My generation didn't run up this debt; the baby boomers did. We didn't benefit from the initial spending, and we certainly don't benefit as the debt is paid off now." Comment on the validity of the various parts of this complaint.

9) Imagine that a balanced budget amendment has been passed. What would happen if the country entered a recession?

The Long Run

Stagflation
and
Long-Term
Unemployment

OVERALL OBJECTIVE: To discuss how the long-run effects of macroeconomic policy may differ from the short-run effects; to analyze how supply shocks, entrenched expectations of inflation, and rises in the natural rate of unemployment might lead in the long run to a condition of stagflation—that is, a simultaneous increase in prices and fall in output—and to explore the reasons why long-term unemployment has been rising.

MORE SPECIFICALLY:

■ To show the changing view of the relationship between inflation and unemployment, as indicated by position of the so-called Phillips Curve that relates these two variables.

■ To explore why the shape of the Phillips Curve differs in the short run and the long run.

■ To define stagflation as the simultaneous increase in average prices and fall in output, to show how a supply shock such as a major increase in oil prices or entrenched expectations of inflation can cause stagflation, and to discuss how accommodating monetary or fiscal policy to offset this stagflation can make the situation worse.

■ To assess the costs of reducing inflation to zero.

■ To discuss the reasons why over time the natural rate of unemployment might change, including changes in the levels of frictional and structural unemployment and the emergence of long-term unemployment caused by government regulations and other factors that keep real wages above the market equilibrium.

Not so long ago macroeconomists had rather easy solutions for the big macro problems, and little conception that the passage of time might alter the effectiveness of their prescriptions. In a recession, easy money and a stimulative fiscal policy would surely work to reduce unemployment and bring an economy smoothly to noninflationary full employment. In an inflation, tight money and a restrictive fiscal policy would serve to control the price rises and carry the economy to a safe landing at noninflationary full employment.

The situation has now changed considerably. Economists see more complexity in these issues. They realize that the short-run effects of macro policy may differ greatly from the long-run effects. The trade-offs between inflation and unemployment that may exist in the short run might not be present in the long run, with macroeconomic policy therefore less able to influence events. Because policymakers for some time did not realize this difference between short-run and long-run consequences, policy mistakes have been committed and bad situations have been made worse. Moreover, experience has demonstrated that various "shocks" to the economy can cause **stagflation**, that is, a simultaneous rise in prices and increase in unemployment. This disagreeable condition was not anticipated by economists of an earlier era.

▶ THE RELATIONSHIP BETWEEN CHANGING OUTPUT AND THE PRICE LEVEL

Exactly what is the relationship between changing output and the price level? That question has been the subject of considerable study, and economists' views have recently been altered, as we explore in this section.

THE CHANGING VIEW OF THE RELATIONSHIP

Until the late 1950s, the relationship between prices and output was understood to be as shown in Figure 24.1. Real output (on the horizontal or x axis) could rise, reducing unemployment without changing prices, until the point of full employment was reached at Y_f. Beyond that point, the models suggested that any rise in output would be in nominal terms only, resulting in price rises (inflation). No further fall in unemployment was possible because full employment had already been reached. Reversing the example, if an inflation were in progress, with prices rising, then a fall in (nominal) output would have the effect of reducing the inflation until it was completely wrung out—again at point Y_f. Any further reduction in output would have the effect of raising unemployment.

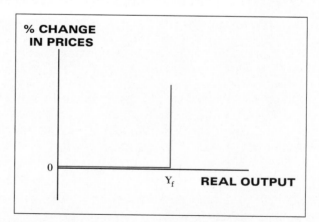

Figure 24.1. Earlier view of the relationship between prices and output. The earlier and simpler view was that real output could rise until the full employment level of output was reached, but after that, no more real output could be obtained. Any attempt to raise output beyond that point would cause prices to rise.

From the late 1950s, economists began to appreciate that in an economic expansion prices would begin to rise before full employment was reached, as pictured in Figure 24.2.

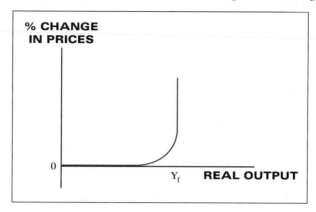

Figure 24.2. Later view of the relationship between prices and output. Later experience indicated that rising output would cause rising prices before full employment was reached.

This seemed to be the case because full employment arrives in uneven fashion, industry by industry. Steel mills or microchip producers might reach their full capacities before other industries do, or specific skills (trained engineers, for example) or specialized capital equipment may become scarce as the economy approaches full employment. If these resources specific to an industry could be duplicated at short notice, there would be no problem, but often they cannot be. Thus shortages and bottlenecks start to develop in some industries and markets before they do in others, with the potential to cause some price increases before the entire economy comes to full employment. Though the price increases may be limited to just the sectors of the economy where bottlenecks occur, the average level of all prices will go up. Inflation may also rise indirectly if any of the output of these industries is used as input by other industries; the higher costs for those who use the input will be translated into increased prices for their output. Under these circumstances, a trade-off arises: When higher output occurs, it leads to higher prices, as seen in the curved area of Figure 24.2.

THE PHILLIPS CURVE

At the London School of Economics in 1958 an economist from New Zealand, A.W. Phillips, was studying empirical data for Britain. Phillips (1914–1975) thought he saw in those data a relationship between prices and unemployment that confirmed the developing view that both could change at the same time. He believed he had found a *trade-off* between inflation and unemployment, in the sense that reducing one tended to increase the other, much as pushing in at one place on a balloon pushes it out somewhere else.

Phillips constructed a curve that presented this trade-off between inflation and unemployment. It soon came to be known as a **Phillips Curve**. In Figure 24.3, various rates of inflation (percentage changes in prices) are shown on the vertical axis, while rates of unemployment are shown on the horizontal axis. According to Phillips, a reduction in the level of unemployment, say from 4% in year 1 to 3% in year 2, would be accompanied by an increase in the rate of inflation, say from 2% in year 1 to 3% in year 2.

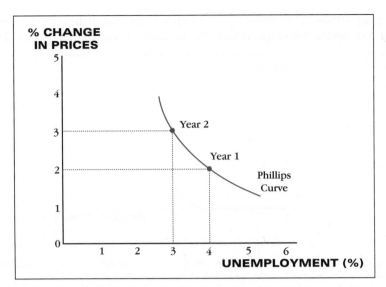

Figure 24.3. A Phillips Curve. A Phillips Curve shows a trade-off between inflation and unemployment. Higher rates of inflation are accompanied by lower levels of unemployment, and vice versa.

Phillips Curves were rapidly constructed for all the major countries, and year by year new points were added to the diagrams. For a long period, the results conformed closely to the original model. Lower rates of unemployment did indeed seem to be accompanied by higher rates of inflation, and vice versa. This brought an end to the original optimistic notion that inflation and unemployment could simultaneously be brought to low levels by means of economic policy, a belief that was characteristic of Keynesianism up to the 1950s. The concept of a macro trade-off even became embedded in politics. The more liberal or labor-leaning groups—Democrats in the United States and the Labour Party in Britain—came to advocate a somewhat lower level of unemployment, understanding that would mean somewhat higher rates of inflation. The more right-wing, business-oriented groups—Republicans in the United States, the Conservative Party in Britain—preferred keeping inflation low, even if the result was higher unemployment.

Figure 24.4 below shows how convincing the relationship was in the United States for the period between 1958 and 1969.[1]

The decade of the 1970s brought a chastening experience for those who had come to depend on a stable Phillips Curve. Something was clearly awry. Those years revealed points of inflation and unemployment far above and to the right of the 1958–1969 relationship. The curve in Figure 24.5 shows that somehow the Phillips Curve had shifted substantially; more inflation and more unemployment were now coexisting at the same time.

---

1.   The data for this and the following figure are from the *Economic Report of the President*, various years. The change in prices is measured from December to December.

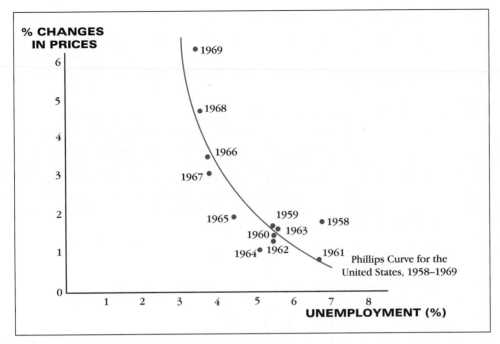

Figure 24.4. The Phillips Curve for the United States, 1958–1969. The figure shows a curve fitted to the data for inflation and unemployment during the years shown.

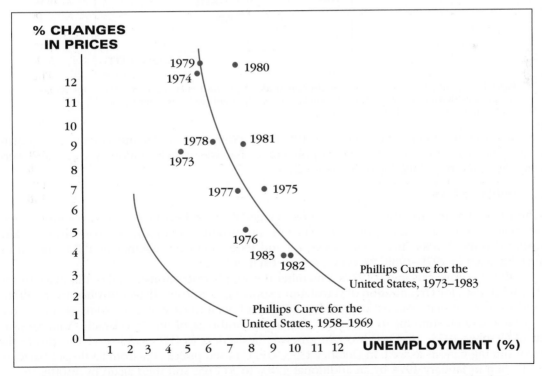

Figure 24.5. The shift of the Phillips Curve to a less favorable position, 1973–1983. A curve fitted to coordinate points of inflation and unemployment in the period 1973–1983 is upward and to the right of the curve for the years 1958 to 1969. This was an unfavorable development because it meant more inflation and more unemployment were occurring at the same time.

THE ARRIVAL OF STAGFLATION

What had caused the shift? The first of the explanations emphasized the "supply shocks" that hit many of the world's economies in the 1970s. The original Phillips Curve model envisaged a trade-off between inflation and unemployment, but did *not* suggest that both would worsen at the same time. To understand this development, economists turned to the aggregate demand/aggregate supply model.

Consider how the Phillips Curve trade-off as it appeared in the 1950s and 1960s can be pictured on an AD/AS diagram. In Figure 24.6, an initial equilibrium is given by the curves AD_1 and $SRAS_1$. If aggregate demand were raised from AD_1 to AD_2, then inflation would occur. The rate of inflation can be calculated by comparing the original price index P_1 to the higher level at P_2. At the same time, the rise in output from Y_1 to Y_2 would result in lower unemployment, because higher output will mean more jobs. If, however, aggregate demand were to fall from AD_1 to AD_3, then inflation would fall—the price index declines from P_1 to P_3—while output also falls (from Y_1 to Y_3), leading to a rise in unemployment.

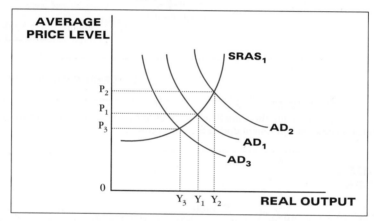

Figure 24.6. An AD/AS hypothesis explaining the trade-off in the 1950s and 1960s. Here movements in aggregate demand along a stationary short-run aggregate supply curve were giving the different points shown along the Phillips Curve in Figure 24.4.

In effect, the Phillips trade-off of the 1950s and 1960s implied that movements in aggregate demand along a short-run aggregate supply curve that was largely stationary over time were giving the different points shown in Figure 24.4.

Supply Shocks

In the 1970s, new macroeconomic conditions changed the position of the aggregate supply curve. The reason was that the prices of certain important commodities rose dramatically, causing **supply shocks**. Two such shocks, oil and food, occurred together in 1973, and an oil shock hit again in 1979–1980. We now examine each of these.

All who drove cars in the 1970s remember the supply restrictions on oil put in place by the oil cartel (OPEC, for Organization of Petroleum Exporting Countries) that controlled over half the world's supply of that essential commodity. OPEC had been in existence for some years when it received a sudden stimulus to its morale due to the outbreak of the Arab-Israeli "Yom Kippur" war of October 1973. That war brought a new cohesiveness to OPEC and served to divide the oil-consuming nations as well. In October 1973, OPEC raised prices 70% from $3.00 per barrel to $5.11; then in January 1974 by an additional 128% to $11.65, and then again by another 6% in October 1975, leaving oil in the range of $12–$13 per barrel where it stayed for some time. The further disruption in oil markets in 1979–1980 caused by the outbreak of the Iran/Iraq war brought the price up to $34 per barrel.

Price rises of this magnitude for a commodity as essential as oil were bound to have a large impact. At that time, in the United States about 10% of the country's total consumption went either directly or indirectly for the purchase of energy. One would thus expect roughly 10% inflation to ensue from a 100% rise in energy prices. The cost of products that used energy, even if only because the products had to be transported, rose appreciably.[2]

In Figure 24.7 we see the consequences of an increase in the oil price as an upward movement in the short-run aggregate supply curve from $SRAS_1$ to $SRAS_2$. The new short-run aggregate supply curve means that any given quantity of output, whether lower as at Y' or higher as at Y", now costs more to produce as seen along the vertical axis of the diagram.[3] The oil shocks showed how monopoly power in input markets could move the aggregate supply curve. (Producers of a number of other commodities thought they had monopoly power, too, and they tried to emulate OPEC by restricting the output of coffee, sugar, tin, copper, bauxite, uranium, and other commodities. But they did not have OPEC's unity, and consumers turned to substitutes, so the tactics failed. No major supply shocks came from these other sources.)

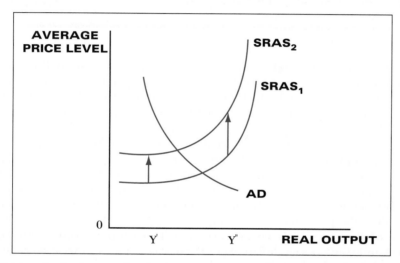

Figure 24.7. A supply shock moves the short-run aggregate supply curve upward. The supply shocks involving oil and food shifted the SRAS curve vertically upward, signifying that each level of real output now costs more to produce.

2.   It might be argued that a supply shock will not be inflationary because any higher price for the item subject to the shock would cause less spending on other items, and therefore lower prices for these items. But the downward movements in the prices of the many other items will be slow if prices are sticky, especially in the downward direction. Not all supply shocks are so immediately powerful as the oil shock was. Some, such as the rising costs of medical care, may occur gradually over many years. A shock that, like health-care costs, is slow to develop means that other relative prices can adjust, falling as health care costs rise. In that case there is a good chance that general inflation may not follow.

3.   The term "cost-push" is often applied to this situation. The concept has an interesting history. Evidence accumulated in the late 1950s that prices were rising in the absence of any increase in aggregate demand. Economists of that era hypothesized that something must be boosting costs in the absence of any macroeconomic stimulus. Their original explanation was that strong labor unions with some monopoly power in labor markets were succeeding in raising wages by exerting market power over employers. These employers, some of whom also possessed market power in oligopolistic markets, could pass these increases on to consumers by raising prices. This original explanation for cost-push inflation is now largely obsolete, having failed to receive much empirical verification.

THE DECLINING IMPORTANCE OF OIL SHOCKS

It should be pointed out that rises in the price of oil imports are less likely to shock the U.S. and other economies now than used to be the case. Substantial progress has been made in energy conservation. Much oil is now produced by countries that are outside the OPEC framework. The United States has put in place a large oil reserve of half a billion barrels to be used in high-price emergencies. The industrial countries have a mechanism to share supplies in a crisis. For these reasons it is now believed that the macroeconomic effect of an oil price increase is only about half what it was 10 to 15 years ago. Saudi Arabia, the world's largest producer by far, was at the time of writing a committed ally of the United States and unlikely to lead a renewed OPEC charge. All this has calmed oil markets and reduced the risk of further oil supply shocks.

The other incident, the food shock, showed how nature could deliver the same results because of a temporary scarcity. Bad Soviet harvests led that country to purchase large quantities of grain on world markets in 1972. Much of it came from the United States, which nevertheless kept in place its supply restrictions on output for 1973. Unfortunately, in that year a blight hit the U.S. corn crop. Other events contributed to the food shock: In several less-developed countries of Africa and Asia, bad harvests related to devastating droughts increased the demand for imported grain, and a poor fish catch in the western Pacific meant that agricultural products were substituted. All combined to give a rise of two-thirds in farm prices between 1971 and 1974.

A look at Figure 24.8 shows how fundamental the consequences of an upward movement in the SRAS curve can be. Comparing the new equilibrium E_2 to the old one E_1 reveals an output level Y_2 *lower* than the previous level of output Y_1, while at the same time prices have *risen* from an index of P_1 to P_2. This coexistence of falling output (with accompanying greater unemployment) and rising prices (inflation) is, as we have seen, known as stagflation.

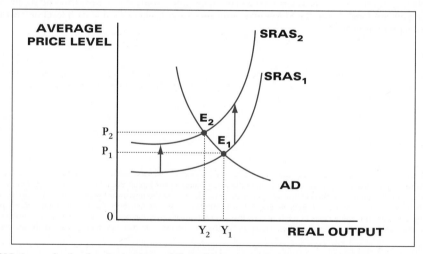

Figure 24.8. A supply shock raises prices while reducing output. The upward shift in the short-run aggregate supply curve moves the equilibrium from E_1 to E_2, with the result that output falls at the same time that the average price level rises. This is known as stagflation.

Inflations Continue If Supply Shocks Are Accommodated

As long as a supply shock keeps moving the aggregate supply curve upward, the rise in prices will continue. But when the shocks stop, then SRAS ceases to rise, and the inflationary price increase comes to an end. Policymakers may not be satisfied with that, however. They see the fall in output (from Y_1 to Y_2 in Figure 24.8) and the accompanying rise in unemployment, and they may want to act.

The central bank, for example, might employ stimulative monetary policy to drive up aggregate demand. A movement from AD_1 to AD_2, seen in Figure 24.9, would succeed in regaining all the lost output and eliminating the unemployment that developed, returning the economy from Y_2 to Y_1. Alternatively, an expansionary fiscal policy could be used. Such actions are called **accommodating monetary or fiscal policies**. (There is a basic similarity in purpose between accommodating policy to offset a supply shock and the monetization or accommodation of a budget deficit to avoid the eventual consequences of the crowding-out effect.) An accommodating policy has a decidedly unwanted side-effect, however. To be sure, the boost in AD reduces the unemployment, but it also causes inflation to break out again. See how the index of prices in Figure 24.9 rises from P_2 to P_3.

This creates a dilemma for economic policy in the face of a supply shock. Letting it run its course yields stagflation; accommodating it by means of policy recaptures the lost output, but reignites the inflation. Because of supply shocks, economic policymaking became considerably more difficult, and the old Keynesian and monetarist prescriptions became less effective.

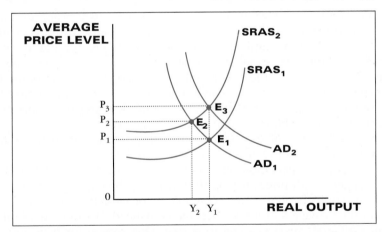

Figure 24.9. Accommodating a supply shock. Here the government attempts to offset the stagflation caused by a supply shock by accommodating policy that increases aggregate demand. The equilibrium is at E_3 rather than E_2. Output is higher, but prices rise.

Recessions Worsen If the Inflation Caused By Supply Shocks Is Extinguished

The analysis of accommodating policy can be turned around to view what a government would do if it wanted to avoid the price rises from a supply shock, rather than avoiding the loss of output and the greater unemployment. A country such as Germany, which has a long tradition of inflation fighting, might prefer this. So might those economists and bankers in the United States who argue that inflation should always be held to zero. To trace the results, look at Figure 24.10. Here a supply shock has moved the aggregate supply curve from $SRAS_1$ to $SRAS_2$, and the equilibrium from E_1 to E_2. What policy action would roll back the price increase? That would happen if the government used its monetary or fiscal policy to *lower* aggregate demand to less than AD_1. Here the movement caused by that contractionary policy is to AD_2. Now the equilibrium is at E_3. The policy extinguishes the inflation (the average price level stays at P_1), but it makes the recession worse because output falls to Y_3 rather than to Y_2.

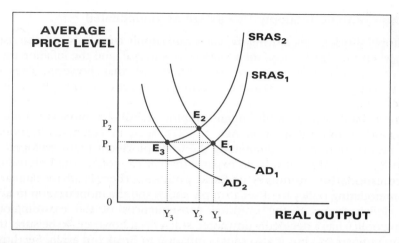

Figure 24.10. Extinguishing the inflation that follows a supply shock. Rather than preventing the lost output and unemployment that follows from a supply shock, a government may choose to prevent the inflation that accompanies it. Doing so would involve contractionary monetary or fiscal policy, but the result would be to increase the loss in output and the amount of unemployment.

THE ROLE OF EXPECTATIONS

The realization that supply shocks were a cause of stagflation was a major advance in macroeconomic analysis. It provided a reasonable explanation for the outward movement of the Phillips Curve in Figure 24.5. At about the same time, economists were also coming to see that in addition to supply shocks, the collective *expectations* of individuals in the economy were affecting aggregate supply. That, too, had a role in explaining the changed position of the Phillips Curve.

People's expectations about macroeconomic conditions originally played little part in the modeling of the Phillips Curve, or in explaining movements in aggregate supply. After several years of late-1970s stagflation, however, it became clear that the economic behavior of both firms and workers was changing *because* of the stagflation. Incorporating expectations into the Phillips Curve and aggregate supply was the next major change in macro modeling.

To see how changing expectations can alter a macroeconomic model, look again at Figure 24.9. We left that diagram with prices having risen from P_1 through P_2, and finally arriving at P_3. Now consider what would happen if all economic actors—including workers and their trade union leaders, and the managers of firms—become convinced that the rate of inflation shown in the figure (say it is 10% per year) is going to persist. One reason for believing so may be their opinion that supply shocks are going to continue (further OPEC price increases, for example), and that they will be accommodated because of government's fear of unemployment. In effect, people will have become accustomed to that rate of inflation. In the next round of wage bargaining, labor will insist on a wage increase of *at least* 10% to make up for the wages lost to inflation. Employers would, of course, resist such a large increase if it were a real one, but because they expect their *prices* to rise by 10% during the year, they will acquiesce. The surges in wages in the late 1960s and 1970s do appear to have been amplified by expectations of inflation. They were especially strong in Britain, Germany, and Japan but also occurred in the United States; they were more in evidence in unionized industries than in the nonunionized. The following box examines how **wage drift** works to spread wage increases among industries.

In Figure 24.11, wage increases induced by expectations of inflation appear as a *further* upward movement in the short-run aggregate supply curve, to $SRAS_3$. It is another kind of supply shock, an internal one, and as a result an additional dose of stagflation hits the economy. Equilibrium shifts from E_3 to E_3', with real output falling from Y_1 to Y_1' and prices rising from P_3 to P_3'. Expectations have thus caused the stagflation to continue, even though the other underlying causes of it — the supply shocks and the accommodation—have ceased.[4]

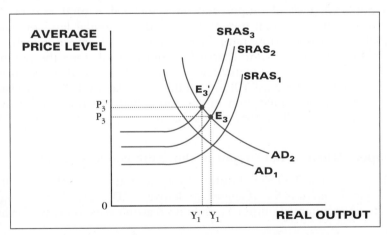

Figure 24.11. Expectations and stagflation. Expectations 0f further inflation cause economic actors to change their behavior. Their demands for higher incomes to offset the inflation cause the short-run aggregate supply curve to move upward, in another type of supply shock, causing the stagflation to worsen.

Once more the government must decide whether to allow the fall in output, and hence the rise in unemployment. Once more it may accommodate the shift in SRAS with monetary or fiscal policy. Once more, if it does so, AD will shift outward and the process continues. Supply shocks can be even more destructive than they initially appear if they set off round after round of shifts

4.   Difficulty in predicting how expectations might change is a significant reason why large computer-driven macroeconomic models that forecast an economy's performance are now somewhat less in fashion than they were a few years ago.

in aggregate supply because of individuals' changes in expectations and government accommodation to offset the rise in unemployment. That can be a route to a prolonged inflationary spiral.

A corollary of these considerations is that the adverse results of supply shocks will die away rapidly after the shocks stop if expectations adapt promptly. If the shocks do not stop, however, their legacy may be long lasting. Another corollary is that a government shift to monetary and fiscal *constriction* to halt the ill-effects of accommodation will have more favorable results if the expectations of individuals immediately shift to anticipating restrictive action. If expectations change only slowly, however, then the continuing rise in aggregate supply will have further stagflationary consequences. For example, the effect on the expectations of the U.S. public caused by oil price rises in the 1970s appears to have been about twice as strong as it became in the 1980s.[5] The lower expectational effects of the 1980s probably reflected people's beliefs that the Fed would not be accommodating, that is, would not try to offset the contractionary impact by expanding the money supply. With growing certainty among the public that the Fed would hold the line, the danger of a wage-price spiral receded.

Finally, we should note that the events portrayed in Figures 24.8, 24.9, and 24.11 give points on a Phillips Curve that reflect *both* higher inflation and higher unemployment, just as happened after 1973 as pictured earlier in Figure 24.5. When expectations are built in to the Phillips Curve model, the damaging outward shift in the curve that originally appeared inexplicable can find a satisfactory explanation.

WHY SOME COMBINATIONS OF INFLATION AND UNEMPLOYMENT ARE UNSUSTAINABLE

A realization took hold during the 1970s that the damaging shift in the Phillips Curve may have had another cause in addition to supply shocks. The combinations of inflation and unemployment shown along the original curve of Figure 24.4 may not have been stable, and if so they would not have been sustainable in the long run. To understand why, we must once more consider the idea that there is a potential level of output and an associated natural rate of unemployment. In Chapter 18 we saw that if actual output exceeds the potential level of output (that is, if unemployment falls below the natural rate), increases in wage costs are triggered. The potential level of output defines an equilibrium. If actual output is lower than the potential level, then actual output will rise toward the potential level. Conversely, if actual output is higher than the potential level, then actual output will fall toward the potential level. The associated natural rate of unemployment is also an equilibrium in the sense that if actual unemployment is lower than the natural rate then it will rise toward the natural rate, or if higher it will fall toward the natural rate.

What Happens When Actual Output Is Above the Potential Level?

In Figure 24.12, assume that the level of output Y_1 is the potential level, and that the associated natural rate of unemployment is 5%. If aggregate demand (AD_1) and short-run aggregate supply ($SRAS_1$) intersect just at potential output Y_1, then no reason exists to expect further adjustments in the economy.

What if aggregate demand is higher than that? Perhaps the government's budget moves into deficit, so AD rises to AD_2. In that case, output is at Y_2, larger than potential output Y_1. Unemployment will be *lower* than the natural rate. When this is true, wages will rise because of a labor shortage. Rising wages result in an upward shift of the short-run aggregate supply curve to $SRAS_2$. The rising SRAS curve will begin to cut back the level of output leftward toward the potential level Y_1 and thus will increase unemployment until its natural rate is restored. At that point, the wage rises that caused the upward movement in SRAS will cease.

---

5.   It is estimated that in the 1970s, the indirect effect on prices of inflationary expectations brought about by oil price rises contributed about one-third as much to inflation as did the direct effects of the increased oil prices. The expectational consequences reached their peak about three years following the initial shock.

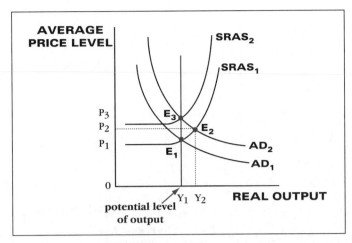

Figure 24.12. Adjustment when actual output is higher than the potential level. When actual output is higher than the potential level, the short-run aggregate supply curve rises and the economy eventually returns to its potential level of output.

Consider again what has happened here. First we have an equilibrium at E_1 in Figure 24.12 with an associated price index of P_1 and an output level of Y_1. The rate of inflation can be calculated by comparing the price index P_1 to the price index in the previous year, while a given amount of unemployment will be associated with a given level of output. Knowing both the rate of inflation and level of unemployment in Year 1, we can identify a point for that year on a Phillips Curve. Again referring to Figure 24.12, we see a change in aggregate demand (to AD_2) that moves the economy in Year 2 to a new equilibrium E_2 with a higher price index P_2 (allowing us to calculate the new rate of inflation) and a higher level of output Y_2 (hence less unemployment). This allows us to identify another point, for Year 2, on a Phillips Curve. The two points together with other observations for other years would show exactly what the original model of the Phillips Curve predicted: a trade-off between inflation and unemployment.

In the long run, however, SRAS shifts upward (to $SRAS_2$), causing an even *higher* rate of inflation (the price index having risen to P_3) and *lower* output Y_1, hence *higher unemployment*, at the equilibrium E_3 in Year 3. Worsened inflation and unemployment at the same time mean that the entire position of the Phillips Curve must have changed, just as appears to have been the case in the 1970s. In short, on a Phillips Curve such as Figure 24.4, given points showing annual inflation and unemployment data may not be sustainable in the long run. If the observed unemployment level is below the natural rate, then adjustments are triggered. In time aggregate supply rises; output falls, and unemployment increases toward the natural rate.

The Wringing Out of Inflationary Expectations: When Actual Output Is Below the Potential Level

The opposite case, when actual output is below the potential level, helps us to illustrate how expectations of inflation may eventually be suppressed, or "wrung out" of an economy. To consider the effects of expectations we use Figure 24.13, which starts where Figure 24.12 left off. Equilibrium is at E_3 and output is back at the level Y_1 where unemployment stands again at its natural rate. Prices have risen to P_3.

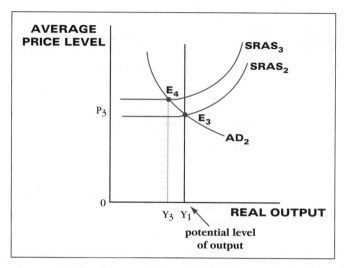

Figure 24.13. Actual output drifts back to the potential level. If inflationary expectations have caused a rise in the SRAS curve, actual output may fall below the potential level. In that case, unemployment may rise, wages may fall, and actual output drifts back to its potential level. The inflationary expectations may be extinguished.

Now assume that expectations of further inflation cause workers to push for higher wage gains than they would otherwise seek. Assume also that these expectations, shared by employers who expect that they can raise their own prices, weaken resistance to granting the wage increases. That upward push to costs would mean a further upward movement in the aggregate supply curve, perhaps to SRAS$_3$ in Figure 24.13. At the resulting new equilibrium E$_4$, real output has fallen to Y$_3$, and at that lower output, unemployment will now exceed the natural rate.

Expectations might not adjust right away. SRAS may even move further upward than SRAS$_3$, with unemployment now well above the natural rate. Prices do indeed continue to rise, but the growing unemployment will be putting downward pressure on wages. Wage cuts may occur in some industries before others (perhaps those most affected by technical change or foreign competition), they may happen slowly, they may not even happen at all for a very long time. Eventually, though, with unemployment higher than the natural rate, labor costs will start to fall. As they do so, however haltingly, the earlier movements in aggregate supply reverse direction; SRAS falls. The inflationary expectations on the part of labor and employers are now being wrung out of the economy. SRAS continues its slow decline until output is raised again to Y$_1$, the level that gives the natural rate of unemployment. At that point, no further pressures exist to change SRAS, and the adjustment process comes to an end.

Admittedly, a difficult part of this analysis at present is that the amount of time necessary for wringing out inflationary expectations is not known with any degree of certainty. When the Fed used tight money in and after 1979 to halt the late-1970s inflation, it took some time to eliminate the inflationary expectation, which had become entrenched. The job took at least three years to accomplish.

THE VERTICAL LONG-RUN PHILLIPS CURVE

The analysis in the past few paragraphs indicates that when unemployment is either below or above the natural rate, adjustments in short-run aggregate supply will move it toward that rate. That has a major implication for the diagramming of the Phillips Curve, as seen in Figure 24.14. Remember that the Phillips Curve plots the percentage change of prices against the rate of unemployment. With enough time for adjustment, the rate of unemployment tends toward a given figure no matter what the rate of inflation is. In that case, the Phillips Curve will be vertical, signifying that in the long run a given natural rate of unemployment is consistent with any rate of inflation. Points off the vertical long-run curve (including some of those shown in Figure 24.4 at the start of the chapter) cannot maintain themselves, and a Phillips Curve drawn through these may be good for the short run only. The vertical Phillips Curve can certainly move, however, if anything arises to change the natural rate itself, as we shall discuss later in the chapter.

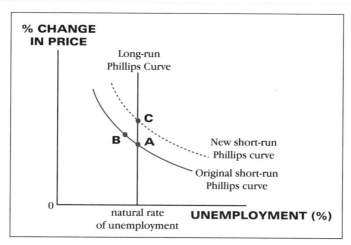

Figure 24.14. The vertical long-run Phillips Curve. Actual output tends to move to the potential level, and actual unemployment to the natural rate. Because in the long run, unemployment is at the natural rate, then a long-run Phillips Curve is vertical at the natural rate.

In Figure 24.14, assume that the economy starts at Point A, with a given degree of inflation read from the vertical axis and a level of unemployment equal to the natural rate. A short-run Phillips Curve runs through Point A, signifying that macro policy (tight money, cuts in government spending, tax increases) could be used to reduce inflation at the cost of some increased unemployment, or to lower the unemployment figure but at the cost of some heating up of inflation. If policymakers choose the second alternative, higher inflation but lower unemployment, then the economy moves from Point A to Point B. Unemployment is now below the natural rate, however; behind the scenes, wages start to rise and short-run aggregate supply begins to shift up, bringing increased inflation and reduced output.[6] The lower output raises unemployment toward the natural rate, so that in the long run the economy moves off its former short-run Phillips Curve to Point C where the adjustments come to a halt. Notice that Point C is directly above Point A. A new short-run Phillips Curve will now run through point C. In the long run, according to this model, the Phillips Curve is vertical at the natural rate of unemployment.

What if policymakers instead decide to fight inflation? We can see what happens by once again considering the policy choices made in the United States early in the Reagan administration. Tight monetary policy was used to choke the late-1970s inflation, and indeed by 1982 inflation *was* much reduced. That pushed the economy down its short-run Phillips Curve, however, with a trade-off as shown in Figure 24.15. The reduced inflation came at the cost of falling output and an associated large increase in unemployment, seen on the Phillips Curve in the figure here as a movement from Point A to Point B.

---

6.   Here, too, the timing of these events is hard to pin down, although most economists would probably agree that the process is fairly slow. Simulations by the Federal Reserve Bank of San Francisco suggest that a permanent gap of one percentage point between a lower actual and higher natural rate of unemployment will cause inflation to increase by something under one-half of a percentage point per year.

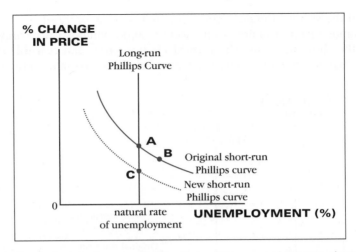

Figure 24.15. A further look at the long-run Phillips Curve. When unemployment is above its natural rate, falling labor costs set in, pushing unemployment back to its natural rate. Again, the long-run Phillips Curve is vertical at the natural rate.

Unemployment was now, however, well above its natural rate, and thus began an adjustment process of falling labor costs and a resulting downward movement in the aggregate supply curve. The effect of the falling aggregate supply curve was the reverse of stagflation, yielding a simultaneous rise in output and cooling of inflation. The rise in output also reduced unemployment; that, together with the reduced inflation, appears in the Phillips Curve of Figure 24.15 as a movement from Point B to C. The economy has been pushed back to a position on the long-run Phillips Curve, and the natural rate of unemployment is sustained, though the process takes considerable time. A new short-run Phillips Curve will now run through Point C.

Let us summarize: In the short run, policymakers will see a trade-off between inflation and unemployment. In a longer time period, however, the economy gravitates to some point along its long-run Phillips Curve. Attempts to reduce unemployment permanently below its natural rate will thus require ever larger doses of accommodating monetary or fiscal policy, and this continuing stimulus to aggregate demand will result in an inflationary spiral. Thus the only long-run choice is the natural rate of unemployment with greater inflation or less.

A point concerning the natural rate of unemployment should be made clear. Calling some amount of joblessness "natural" does not mean that that amount of unemployment is in every way optimal for an economy. If unemployment could be brought below that rate, the economy would enjoy additional output and many more people would have work. Unfortunately, inflation would increase.

POLICY IMPLICATIONS

The scope for macro policy is therefore less than the original Keynesian macroeconomics seemed to promise. In conducting its battle against the joint enemies, inflation and unemployment, a country cannot keep unemployment permanently below (or above) its natural rate.

A great many economists take the position that policy alternatives are still available in the short run. They argue that monetary and fiscal policies can and should be used to stimulate the economy during slumps and cool it during inflationary booms. Consider first what can be done if unemployment is high, above the natural rate. An economy in recession will eventually experience a fall in its short-run aggregate supply curve as wages adjust downward, working to end the recession. The evidence of economic history shows, however, that the process is slow. A policy of stimulating aggregate demand with monetary and fiscal measures can be used to speed the adjustment, even though some increase in inflation may result. In this view, the essential role of government policy is to hasten the return to full employment.

Reducing unemployment at the expense of more inflation, moving up a short-run Phillips Curve, is relatively easy to accomplish. Expansionary monetary and fiscal policy will be the more desirable the greater the damage inflicted by unemployment, in comparison to that levied by inflation. Recall from Chapter 14 the strong case that inflation, as long as it is not explosive, is most often not as damaging to an economy as is recession and unemployment. The consequences of the lost output and lost jobs are socially more hurtful than is adjusting to price rises. Stimulating aggregate demand will also appeal if the resulting inflation is mild but a great deal of unemployment is eliminated. It will become even more attractive when the operation of the economy's self-adjustment process is slow.

High inflation can be attacked as well, with contractionary monetary and fiscal policy. This will cut output and push unemployment temporarily above the natural rate. Generally it is thought that this movement downward along a Phillips Curve is more difficult because it takes time to alter the public's entrenched expectations of further inflation. These inflationary expectations may change slowly because the public may doubt the government's will to carry out its contractionary program. Experience indicates that when governments are weak, these public doubts have been well founded.

If expectations of inflation remain entrenched, then the costs of inflation fighting will be high because unemployment will rise quickly while the benefits of reduced inflation are registered only slowly. U.S. experience in the early 1980s more or less confirmed this pessimism, as it took several years to halt the serious inflation that began in the late 1970s. The time taken to do so was not as long as some economists predicted it would be, however, arguably because the Fed's strong stance caused people to change their expectations. Here, too, macro policy to stabilize the economy is useful.

HOW COSTLY IS IT TO REDUCE INFLATION?

Experience indicates that bringing down the rate of inflation does carry costs of reduced output. There appear to be few cases where inflation has been brought down in a completely costless way. How costly is it? One recent study by Laurence Ball of Princeton University indicates that on average in the United States, a one percentage-point reduction in the rate of inflation spread over several years costs about 2.4 percentage points in lost total output (GDP).[7]

There is a debate on whether a rapid reduction in inflation by means of contractionary policies carries less costs in lost output than does a slow reduction. A slow reduction has the advantage that it gives time for prices and wages to adjust, whereas such adjustment may not immediately accompany a fast reduction. Any lack of adjustment could cause involuntary unemployment to develop. However, a rapid reduction in inflation has the advantage that it might be able to alter inflationary expectations. Gradualism invites skepticism about government willingness to stay the course; firms may change prices and workers may accept lower wages in response to major changes but not minor ones. Laurence Ball's work suggests that the second alternative, fast reduction, is the less costly one. He estimates the costs of inflation reduction over a period of one year and three months costs only about a third as much lost output as a reduction in inflation of the same amount occurring over five years.

Estimates of this sort tend to stimulate considerable controversy. The main reason for the differences is inability to agree on how

---

7.   Taken from Laurence Ball, "How Costly is Disinflation: The Historical Evidence," Federal Reserve Bank of Philadelphia *Business Review,* November/December 1993, pp. 17–28.

fast inflationary expectations would adjust. The debate has been undertaken using the concept of point years, a point year being unemployment above the natural rate by one percentage point for one year. Benjamin Friedman of Harvard calculates that it would take 3.5 to 4 times more point years of unemployment to bring inflation down to 2% than does Martin Feldstein of Harvard. Friedman's estimate would mean that inflation reduction is very expensive, costing four to five times more in lost output than is implied by Feldstein's estimate. As empirical evidence mounts as to which position is correct, economists will be better able to judge whether moving rapidly to zero inflation is an overly costly idea or not.

One finding from Laurence Ball's study is that the costs from reducing inflation in the United States may be higher than in some other countries because U.S. wages are less flexible. The United States has many three-year contracts, while in Japan the contracts are for only one year. That differential helps to explain why Japan's costs are estimated by Ball to be 0.9 of a percentage point in lost total output for a one percentage-point reduction in the rate of inflation compared to the much higher U.S. cost of 2.4 percentage points. He suggests that if the United States moved away from long-term labor contracts, the costs of reducing inflation could be lessened.

Reducing Inflation to Zero?

Several presidents of the twelve Federal Reserve Banks have recently called for a rollback of inflation to zero. If "zero inflation" were interpreted to mean no inflation at all (rather than, say, 2% or so as has been widely assumed), then difficulties might surface in addition to the costs of lost output just described. Negative real interest rates can never be achieved if inflation is zero, but negative real rates can be quite stimulative for economic activity. A firm that has borrowed at a 2% nominal rate while inflation is 3% finds at the end of the year that its cost of borrowing in real terms has been negative. The real interest rate is −1%, and that firm's creditors have effectively paid it to borrow. Negative real rates are thus very encouraging for business investment and are usefully engineered by monetary policy in a slump. Achievement of a zero rate of inflation means, however, that this possibility is unavailable.

A second reason explaining why zero inflation might not be a good idea is that price indices as presently constructed may overstate inflation. That would be so, for example, when the quality of products improves, for then a higher price may be associated with higher quality, leaving consumers no worse off or even better off. Also the weights in the price index might be old (they are from 1982–84 in the United States). People might be substituting cheaper goods for more expensive ones as prices rise, offsetting some of the effect of the inflation. Robert Gordon of Northwestern University estimates that for these reasons a reported U.S. inflation rate of 1.5% is implicitly equivalent to zero inflation, and a reported rate of zero inflation would imply implicit price reductions, which would result in difficulties. Debtors would lose to lenders, and consumers would postpone purchases in expectation that prices would soon be lower. All in all, no inflation at all might not be as good as it sounds.

▶ A FURTHER CAUSE OF STAGFLATION: THE RISE IN THE NATURAL RATE OF UNEMPLOYMENT

Until now, we have been discussing the natural rate of unemployment as if it never changed. With the passage of time, however, the natural rate *may* change. Indeed, the battle against stagflation in the 1970s was complicated by the fact that the natural rate rose. From the standpoint of macroeconomic policy, any rise in the natural rate is bad news, because of the inflationary consequences that ensue from attempts to reduce actual unemployment below the natural rate.

Calculating the natural rate is always an exercise in approximation. Until the late 1950s, economists believed that the natural rate in the United States was about $3\frac{1}{2}$%. In the early 1960s, 4% was the accepted figure. By the end of that decade, a range of 4–5% was being quoted. A middle-1970s estimate of 5% had advanced to $6\frac{1}{2}$% by 1981–1983, and some even suggested 7%. (This figure was used by the Chairman of the Council of Economic Advisors, Martin Feldstein, in 1982.) These rises in the natural rate meant that the level of unemployment below which inflation would break out was, unfortunately, higher than before. (But read on for evidence that after years of increases in the natural rate, it has now probably declined somewhat.)

Not only did the natural rate change over time, but large differences are thought to exist among countries. At the very time when $6\frac{1}{2}$% was believed to be the U.S. natural rate, higher figures of 8% in Germany and France, 9% in Britain, and $10\frac{1}{2}$% in the Netherlands were believed to exist, and a much lower one of 2% in Japan. Most probably these differences are related to the differing structure of the economies concerned. In the remainder of the chapter, we examine why changes in the natural rate have occurred and why they differ from country to country.

FRICTIONAL UNEMPLOYMENT

Economists have long recognized that two specific types of unemployment, *frictional* and *structural*, are very difficult to reduce. An increase in either of these would raise the natural rate. **Frictional unemployment** describes people who are just entering the job market and are thus still looking for work, or people who are in the process of changing jobs.[8] A graduating senior who does not find a job until the fall, and a professor moving from one university in June to another in September are both counted among the jobless because it takes time to acquire and move into a new position. If a worker quits, or a person enters the labor force, but has not yet found a new job, the term "involuntary frictional unemployment" applies. If, however, jobs are available but a worker is considering alternatives and searching for a *better* job, the term is "voluntary frictional unemployment," or alternatively, "search unemployment." Both types of frictional unemployment would be virtually impossible to eliminate. Even in the most efficient economy imaginable there would still be frictional unemployment. For example, during World War II when every effort was being made to squeeze all possible production out of the economy, frictional unemployment still existed, and probably even increased for a time, as people deserted small towns and rural areas to take work in shipyards, munitions plants, and factories. The existence of frictional unemployment reflects the flexibility of market economies.

Frictional unemployment has typically been higher in the United States (at some 3 to 4% of the labor force) than it is in other countries, because the U.S. population is historically very mobile; people change jobs and residences more frequently than the citizens of other industrial economies. Strong evidence supports the case that U.S. workers are more mobile than those of most other advanced countries. For example, per hundred workers, only about half as many British or Germans left their jobs as did Americans in the mid-1980s. In 1980, 3.3% of Americans moved from one state to another, compared to 1.3% of Germans moving between *lands* (states) and 1.1% of the British between regions. The U.S. figure for annual labor force mobility of about 3% has changed little for many years, but British and German mobility have fallen in recent years by about a quarter.

In the 1970s the level of frictional unemployment grew for several reasons. First, women entered the labor force in much larger numbers. Females aged 25 and over made up 27.3% of the U.S. labor force in 1965, but 29.0% in 1975 and 31.6% in 1980.[9] Furthermore, as the "baby

---

8. The term frictional unemployment is considered to be old-fashioned by some economists now, but the concept is a useful one, and we utilize it here.

9. The trend was pronounced among married women. In 1890, fewer than 5% of married women were in the labor force.

boomers" (those born between 1945 and 1965 when birth rates were temporarily high) began to leave school, the proportion of young people aged 16–24 in the labor force rose from 19.0% in 1965 to 24.1% in 1975 before dropping back slightly (to 23.6%) in 1980.

Both groups had to go through the search process, and as new entrants to the labor force, they changed jobs often. (Over half of all first jobs last less than one year; when workers are 50 years old or more, nearly three-quarters of them have been in the same job for five years or longer.) Women moved into and out of the labor force more on average than men did, while the young people, especially the teenagers among them, often took jobs that lasted only a few months before they took another or returned to school. This extra mobility raised the level of U.S. frictional unemployment, and that also meant a rise in the natural rate since frictional unemployment cannot be much reduced by stimulating the economy.

In Europe, the influx of women occurred to a lesser extent, and the "baby boom" was much less pronounced. To that degree, European frictional unemployment has been lower. Working in the other direction, however, has been the greater generosity of European jobless benefits, which make it easier for the unemployed to search longer for work.

Finally, frictional unemployment will rise in any economy where rapid changes in technology or in the flows of foreign trade cause more rapid industrial adjustment and thus more job switching. All modern economies have been more subject to changes of this sort in recent years than was true of the 1950s and 1960s.

STRUCTURAL UNEMPLOYMENT

Another type of joblessness is called **structural unemployment**. Some people without the proper skills or education will not be able to acquire jobs even when vacancies exist, because the available jobs require a certain minimum of skill or training. The lack of skill or training might be due to social conditions—poor people with fewer opportunities to obtain it, minorities who encounter various prejudices in their education, women just joining the labor force after years in the home, workers in industries that are declining and who must look for jobs in technically different fields. Other people may have the training, but may be locked into a depressed geographical region by family ties, or because they find it hard to sell their houses. Well-known examples of depressed areas include Appalachia, the "Rust Belt,"[10] Northeast England, Scotland, and southern Italy.

The geographical depression may also be due to the changing structure of industry, as some decline and others expand. Textiles, shoes, steel, automobiles, and industries related to national defense are all examples of industries that have been downsizing their labor force in recent years. In general, a shift away from manufacturing and toward services is occurring in all advanced countries. Rapid technical developments and intensified competition through foreign trade accelerate the changing structure of employment. The effects of poor education and declining industries are very likely to make the problem of structural unemployment more severe. Indeed the number of structurally unemployed in the United States rose on the order of one to two percentage points in the late 1970s and early 1980s.[11]

REAL-WAGE STRUCTURAL UNEMPLOYMENT

High and inflexible real wages could also result in a type of unemployment called **real-wage structural unemployment**. This is thought to be a key reason for the elevated natural rates in some European countries, though less so in the United States. The reasoning is that wages held above a supply-and-demand equilibrium will cause unemployment. The causes could be high

---

10. A rather loose term that includes (at least) the industrial areas of Illinois, Indiana, Michigan, Ohio, and Pennsylvania, where old-line industries have been facing problems of obsolescence and foreign competition.

11. Notice that both frictional and structural unemployment can exist even when jobs are otherwise readily available in the economy. With frictional unemployment, a person either has not found a correctly matched job that exists, or has found it but has not started work yet. With structural unemployment, the job that exists does not match the worker's training or location.

minimum wages brought about either by legislation or collective bargaining, and high Social Security payments by firms. Because labor is more costly, fewer people are hired.

This reasoning is logically sound. It is difficult, however, to make a convincing case that above-equilibrium wages are anywhere near as important as other structural causes of unemployment. For example, in most countries of Europe and North America during the last decade, union strength was diminishing, though the 28% reduction in U.S. union membership and 20% decline in Britain since 1980 have been large compared to the experience of most countries. Furthermore, minimum wages were falling in real terms (especially in the United States). It is therefore less likely that wages were being pushed above a free-market equilibrium compared to what had been true in the 1960s and 1970s. The movement was rather in the other direction. The inflexibility of wages held above equilibrium would not therefore explain the worsening unemployment of recent years.

A second argument, that the economic structure, especially in Europe, makes employers reluctant to hire additional labor even if wages fall, is more persuasive. Several reasons are said to account for this purported structural impediment. One is that contract terms, especially as they relate to layoffs, discourage new hiring. If the legal framework makes layoffs expensive for employers, these employers will be reluctant to add to their labor force if in a recession that labor force cannot easily be reduced. To that degree, the demand for labor falls.

The high cost of layoffs in Europe is widely associated with government action to promote job security. Laws to this effect are widespread, often dating from the late 1960s. In Britain, for example, legislation requires 90-days' notice against large layoffs and also contains strong unfair dismissal rules, both often toughened in private agreements between firms and unions. The German laws are the most comprehensive, with workers very hard to dismiss, and with the burden of proof on the firm to show that a dismissal is "socially justified."[12] European business-people are said to conceive of these laws as guarantees of payment for so many more weeks or months of employment of workers who would otherwise be laid off in a slump. That raises the cost of labor and leads to lower hiring in general. (Because firms then substitute capital for labor, the remaining workers become more productive and are paid even higher wages—the "insiders" gain while the "outsiders" lose out.) In short, so goes this case, layoffs are costly and firms will not lightly hire more workers. Unemployment becomes entrenched, or structural, explaining why Europe's unemployment is now nearly double that of the United States and why the number of new jobs has grown so slowly there—only 6% since 1960 compared to 84% in the United States and 46% in Japan.

In earlier years, laws that make it expensive to lay off labor were of only academic interest in the United States, but Congress adopted a plant-closing provision in 1988 (60 days' notice). The new U.S. law has numerous limitations, however, and it is very mild by comparison to the European laws.[13]

The structural arguments relate to rules and regulations, mostly government but some private, that have an effect on the demand for labor. Labor *supply* can also be affected, with further structural considerations that might lead the unemployed to make a less avid search for

---

12.   One such justification is "urgent economic need" on the part of the firm, but the labor courts have been restrictive in their interpretation, and even then six months' notice is required for long-service workers, who are a high proportion of the whole. The Labor Office can stop dismissals for two more months even if it finds the layoffs justified by a firm's need and has used the power frequently. In many industries, collective bargaining makes it impossible to lay off long-service workers. The Worker Participation Law of 1972 means management may have to pay compensation to those laid off, or to those whose work hours have been reduced. In the United States, impediments to layoffs are far less rigorous, but they do exist. Federal and state civil service employees commonly possess much the same degree of job security found widely in Europe.

13.   The view that layoff notification laws contribute to higher labor costs and thus increase structural unemployment is criticized as not taking into account several factors. First, informed workers will search more efficiently as they switch to other jobs; second, their morale and productivity may accordingly be higher than before; and finally they will avoid wasteful investment in training and skill acquisition specific to a firm that, had the workers only known, was about to lay them off. They could have sought other training instead. Empirical evidence on this question is mixed. Knowledge is limited on whether the costs of such acts are large, or passed on to consumers, or offset by higher productivity. It is clear enough that Europe in moving to ease the layoff laws, which was done as we shall see in the next chapter, has taken a conservative position.

new jobs. Again, the chief problem appears to be in Europe, where high jobless benefits and few requirements for benefit recipients act as an enticement to keep people on the dole. Unemployment benefits in the United States, though state-determined and not entirely uniform, usually last for only 26 weeks, and average just under half the previous wage earned. (In the recession of 1990–1991, over a million people exhausted their unemployment benefits. In November 1991, unemployment compensation was therefore extended by 13 to 20 weeks, depending on how high unemployment was in a particular state.) Japan's benefits also are short-term, lasting just six months. In Britain and Germany, however, the figure is about three-quarters of the previous wage for a year, and in Britain minimum-wage jobs until very recently paid only 4% more than usual unemployment benefits, which give indefinite support above an officially defined poverty line. Elsewhere in Europe, unemployment benefits can be virtually permanent. So it probably does not come as a surprise that the jobless in America make many more job applications than do the European unemployed, for example four times more per person compared to Britain. In the Netherlands, benefits are between 75 and 80% of the previously earned wage for three years, and the unemployed need not accept a job at less than the former wage. The Dutch were recently paying a benefit of 80% of the previous wage for life in the case of disability, and (suspiciously) the number of totally disabled workers was rising at 10% a year in the 1970s.[14]

Most troubling of all is the growing evidence, again mostly from Europe, that extended periods out of work may make people less employable in the long run. Employers may come to mistrust the commitment to work of the long-term unemployed, to worry about their eroded work habits and loss of skills, and to avoid offering jobs to them. The ex-workers may think of *themselves* as not likely to work again—indeed, their "human capital" of skills and education *may* be declining—and as a result they might stop competing for jobs. Thus the longer people are jobless, the worse the chances that they will work again.[15] This is thought to explain at least in part why many people are unemployed for much longer periods in Europe (in 1989, 40–50% without a job for more than a year in Britain, France, and Germany, over 50% in Belgium, Ireland, Italy, the Netherlands, and Spain) than in the United States (and Canada), where the 1989 figure was just 6–7%. (The U.S. figure is rising, however; it was 11% in 1992.)

The outcome is that severe long-term unemployment can exist side by side with job vacancies and rising wages. Major metropolitan areas in many countries exhibit the results: help-wanted signs in the windows of numerous businesses and unemployed people standing on the street corners. Vacancies exist, but firms do not hire the long-term jobless. Unions, caught in a conflict of interest between their own membership and the jobless, press for the usual wage gains just as if these unemployed workers were complete outsiders—which in an economic sense they are. In a sort of vicious circle, labor appears in shorter supply than before, wages rise, and the chances for the long-term unemployed to obtain a new job become worse yet. The longer a worker is out of a job, the more likely it is that the worker will stay jobless. In effect, the natural rate of unemployment moves upward toward the actual rate.

Economists have adopted an old word from the physical sciences, **hysteresis**, to describe the situation.[16] Hysteresis means that present high unemployment leads to the maintenance of high unemployment in the future, thus ratcheting up the natural rate of unemployment. It also leads to the possibility that where hysteresis is present, a boost in aggregate demand that lowers

14.   Independent investigations by European economists claim that a third to a half of these workers were not really disabled, thus explaining perhaps a quarter of Dutch unemployment. Though it is now commonplace to blame overly generous benefits, a revisionist case can be made that such benefits did not grow as a percentage of average earnings, and even fell in a number of countries in the 1980s. Yet unemployment increased.

15.   A British Department of Employment study (of 1986) estimated that for those losing a job today, the probability of being rehired within three months is 40%. But if unemployment has lasted for six to nine months, the chance is only about half that, 22%, and if three years, a very low 6%.

16.   The word is used, for example, to describe the persistence for a time of an electromagnetic field even after the electricity is shut off.

actual unemployment below the natural rate might reduce the natural rate itself, permanently. The timing of any such development would likely be very slow, but if it did transpire, it would be a welcome reversal of the stagflation of recent years.

A Decline in the Natural Rate of Unemployment?

Frictional and structural unemployment in all their forms when added together determine the natural rate of unemployment, the minimum level of unemployment that cannot be reduced without raising the rate of inflation. Any additional unemployment beyond that figure is due to a lack of sufficient aggregate demand in the economy. With frictional plus structural unemployment rising in the 1970s and early 1980s, the stagflation dilemma grew more serious.

Fortunately, some of the damaging changes just discussed are reversing themselves. The effects of the baby boom in the United States eventually came to a halt, with the result that between 1980 and 1985, the percentage of young people aged 16–24 fell from 23.6% of the labor force to 20.5%. Though the percentage of females 25 or older in the labor force has continued to rise (31.6% in 1980, 34.5% in 1985), unemployment is not now higher in this group than it is for adult males. The demographic factors that led to an increase in the natural rate of unemployment appear to have gone into reverse.

As a result, the Congressional Budget Office began to announce figures for the natural rate that were under the 6% or more used earlier in the 1980s. Its announced figure for 1986–88 was 5.7%; for 1989–91, 5.6%; while for 1992 it was 5.5%. Experience with inflation in the late 1980s and early '90s seemed to confirm that the natural rate had indeed fallen somewhat. (The Department of Commerce still uses a higher figure than the CBO in making its calculations and policy recommendations, however, and Harvard's Martin Feldstein believes the natural rate is still above 6%. Some economists argue that defense industry cutbacks, high immigration of unskilled labor, and the growing need for greater worker sophistication in high-tech jobs will eventually raise the natural rate once again. If these economists are correct, the risk of eventual inflation may be greater than generally believed.)

Important steps have been taken in Europe to lower the natural rate. Many European governments have perceived that their own policies, or lack of them, were contributing to structural unemployment and have implemented changes. A number of governments, especially Great Britain's, have attacked union power, while others have cut back on their benefits for the unemployed, as noted in the accompanying box. Policies such as this may be effective, but they are also politically very contentious.

EUROPE CHANGES TACK

The British government has greatly reduced unemployment benefits; the unemployed now receive less than 20% of the average wage, well under half the figure of a few years ago (and well below the U.S. figure of 36%). The profligate Dutch welfare system has also been cut back. New rules require work in three of the past five years in order to become eligible for long-term benefits, and benefits have been stopped for 16- and 17-year-olds to encourage them to remain in school. From 1994, people under 21 are ineligible for social assistance unless they are single parents. The Netherlands has also cut the minimum wage for those under age 23 by 15% for each year of age, and as a result of these changes youth unemployment is at last shrinking in the Netherlands.

The British government's assault on the unions has been dramatic, as already discussed in Chapter 11. Since 1982, the Conservative Party has pushed through new legislation requiring union leadership to be elected every five years, the immunity against breach of contract suits has been removed by Parliament in the case of strikes in support of another union, and immunity does not apply even to strikes against one's own employer unless a majority has voted to strike in secret ballot. Of the 77 injunctions sought on these matters, 1984 to 1987, 73 were granted by the courts. The number of strikes was quickly cut in half, partly because of the laws, though partly by the economic recession that hit Britain during this period. Union membership has dropped by about one-fifth. If not broken, the once-powerful British unions have been somewhat tamed.

CONCLUSION

The futility of attempting to lower unemployment below the natural rate in the long run, the slowness of long-run adjustment, and growing long-term unemployment have all been frustrating aspects of macroeconomics that make the long run different from the short run. These aspects pose a challenge to standard monetary and fiscal policy. Whether approaches are available that could treat them specifically while still being acceptable across the political spectrum is the subject of the next chapter.

SUMMARY

1) Economists' original beliefs that inflation and unemployment would not occur at the same time was succeeded in the 1960s by a belief that there was a so-called Phillips Curve involving a trade-off between inflation and unemployment. The Phillips Curve as first conceived suggested that reductions in inflation would lead to increases in unemployment, and vice versa.

2) Disturbing empirical evidence in the 1970s indicated that more inflation and more unemployment were occurring at the same time, contrary to the prediction of the original Phillips Curve model. The simultaneous increase in prices and fall in output that caused greater unemployment received the name stagflation.

3) One explanation of stagflation is that supply shocks, such as major rises in the price of oil and food in the 1970s, shift the short-run aggregate supply curve vertically upward, signifying that each level of real output now costs more to produce. That causes output to fall at the same time that the average price level rises.

4) Governments may attempt to offset the stagflation caused by a supply shock by accommodating monetary or fiscal policy that increases aggregate demand. As a result, output is higher, but prices rise. If instead governments use contractionary monetary or fiscal policy to prevent the inflation that accompanies supply shocks, the result is to increase the loss in output and the amount of unemployment.

5) Expectations further inflation cause economic actors to change their behavior. Their demands for higher incomes to offset the inflation cause the short-run aggregate supply curve to move upward, in another type of supply shock, causing the stagflation to worsen.

6) Some combinations of inflation and unemployment may be unsustainable in the long run, causing adjustments in output and prices to occur. When actual output is higher than the potential level, the short-run aggregate supply curve rises and the economy eventually returns to its potential level of output. Because actual output tends to move to the potential level, and actual unemployment to the natural rate, the long-run Phillips Curve is vertical at the natural rate.

7) The costs of reducing inflation are the subject of current debate. Though economic logic does not give a clear answer, as to whether fast reduction is to be preferred to slow reduction, some empirical evidence suggests that a fast reduction in inflation may be less costly than a slow reduction.

8) For several reasons, the natural rate of unemployment apparently rose during the 1970s and early 1980s. The baby boom and the entry of women into the paid labor force raised the level of frictional unemployment because new workers change jobs more often; changing patterns in world trade made some training and skills superfluous and so caused structural unemployment to rise; government labor market policies that raised the cost of hiring labor or put unemployment benefits near the wage that could be earned caused real-wage structural unemployment, particularly in Europe. The slowdown in the baby boom and the entry of women into labor markets, and reforms of labor laws, have all tended to counteract the rise in the natural rate of unemployment, which is thought to have fallen back somewhat in recent years.

Chapter Key Words

Accommodating monetary or fiscal policy: Policy designed to offset a fall in output, for example in response to a supply shock.

Frictional unemployment: That portion of unemployment caused by people being temporarily out of work while changing jobs.

Hysteresis: The concept that present high unemployment leads to the maintenance of high unemployment in the future because those with a record of joblessness may lose some skills and may be distrusted by employers. The effect is to ratchet up the natural rate of unemployment below which inflation will increase.

Phillips Curve: Named for New Zealand economist A.W. Phillips, a curve describing the trade-off between inflation and unemployment. The short-run Phillips Curve for the United States shifted outward during the 1970s and early 1980s, meaning greater problems of macroeconomic management than before. If in the long term, unemployment gravitates to its natural rate, then the long run Phillips Curve is vertical.

Real-wage structural unemployment: A type of structural unemployment caused by high and inflexible real wages that remain above equilibrium.

Stagflation: A simultaneous rise in prices and fall in output (and therefore increase in unemployment).

Structural unemployment: That portion of unemployment caused by a lack of skills and education. Difficult to eliminate by normal fiscal and monetary policy, even when aggregate demand is pushed to high levels, because qualifications are not properly matched to job requirements. Can apply to the underprivileged or to workers whose occupations are in decline.

Supply shocks: Upward movement of the short-run aggregate supply curve, indicating that a given quantity of output costs more to produce. OPEC's price-raising activities and the sudden higher prices for food in the 1970s are both examples of supply shocks.

CHAPTER QUESTIONS

1) In Chapter 18 we saw that the short-run AS curve has a horizontal, an upward-sloping, and a vertical section. When the economy recovers from a severe recession, the AD curve shifts far to the right over time. Equilibrium moves along the AS curve as output increases. Show this process in two ways: on the AD-AS diagram as described and on a Phillips Curve.

2) The island nation of Terraminima has always been limited by its small size. Over the course of a year, there is a series of gigantic volcano eruptions, and the government declares a state of emergency. However, by a great stroke of luck the volcanoes cause no damage and the lava flows add 100 square miles to this small country. This new land rapidly becomes arable. Show what has happened to Terraminima's economy using both an AD-AS diagram and a Philips curve.

3) Following an oil price shock, output will fall and inflation will rise. The government could increase output again by employing stimulative policies. What are the advantage and disadvantage of such policies?

4) The government makes the following announcement: "We will not tolerate unemployment. In the event of a supply shock, we will use all policy tools in order to prevent unemployment from developing." People widely believe the statement. Suppose there is, in fact, a supply shock. Describe what will happen and illustrate with a diagram.

5) An advisor presents the President a diagram of the U.S. Phillips Curve. The President says, "The economy is running smoothly right now, but I think we could tolerate a little more inflation in order to get the unemployment rate down. I see here that I can make that trade-off." If the President carries out this policy, what will happen over time?

6) The advisor in question 5 is chastened by the inflation that results from the policy she helped construct. The President is also upset, so the advisor brings him another diagram, this time showing a vertical long-run Phillips Curve. The President says, "Phew, I thought things were bad, but I see there's no problem. We can quickly decrease inflation without increasing unemployment. All we have to do is move down along this curve!"
If the President carries out this new policy, what will happen over time?

7) A government program aims to reduce all types of unemployment to zero. If the program were successful, in what ways would it be a good thing and in what ways would it be bad?

8) In 1998, the U.S. government makes a surprising discovery. There has been an accounting error, and the last ten years' worth of deficits were actually surpluses. A rebate is made to the public over a five-year period, during which time each citizen receives an annual payment of 150% of the income earned by a minimum wage worker. Obviously during the rebate period fewer unemployed people hunt for new jobs. After the five years is over, what do you expect will happen to structural unemployment?

Macroeconomic Innovation

OVERALL OBJECTIVE: To explore the "heterodox" methods (as opposed to orthodox monetary and fiscal policy) for influencing the macroeconomy, including labor market policies, wage-price controls and indexing, and supply-side policies.

MORE SPECIFICALLY:

- To explain that while heterodox methods are no substitute for reasonable, orthodox monetary and fiscal policies, they do provide innovations that may under some circumstances help to promote economic stability.
- To discuss labor-market policies that may assist in lowering the level of long-term unemployment, such as training programs, national service, and the provision of better information to the unemployed.
- To assess why dealing with inflation by means of wage-price controls and indexing is now often believed to be counterproductive.
- To consider supply-side reforms that might reduce the costs of any given level of output or, alternatively, increase output at some given price level.

During the 1970s and 1980s economists had to reconsider their views on what macroeconomic policy can accomplish. The tools of economic management, if employed intelligently, could cope with serious inflations and deep recessions. But smaller doses of inflation and unemployment, especially when they are becoming worse at the same time, seemed less manageable. This chapter discusses innovations, some old and some new, in macroeconomic policy. In the word recently adopted by economists, they are the **heterodox policies**. Some have been tried, and empirical evidence is available for evaluating them. Others remain untested ideas, and we can only speculate on their possible efficacy. The goal of our exploration is not to provide a final judgment on the heterodox policies. Rather, it is to present a set of options beyond the **orthodox policies**, both monetary and fiscal, that we have been discussing up to now.

Let us be clear that there are no proper alternatives to reasonable, orthodox monetary and fiscal policies, and this chapter does not suggest the contrary. The heterodox ideas are unlikely to make much headway against the general macroeconomic imbalances that follow from errors in the orthodox monetary and fiscal policy stance. Thus heterodox methods are not substitutes for orthodox policies. Instead, they give the possibility that in particular circumstances the results of orthodox policies might be assisted and improved.

The policies discussed in this chapter are diverse. They include attacking unemployment with labor-market policies, attacking inflation with incomes policies, innovations in taxation, profit sharing and worker participation in management, and, finally, supply-side reforms to increase output and efficiency. In the discussion, both pros and cons will be discussed.

► ATTACKING UNEMPLOYMENT WITH LABOR-MARKET POLICIES

If a government finds that structural unemployment cannot be brought down by standard monetary and fiscal policy without starting an inflation, it may attempt to make labor more employable by means of labor-market policies. Supporters of this position argue that broad-based reform is needed to cope with long-run structural unemployment. A work force liberally educated to higher levels, and a much more advanced program of education and retraining of adults, would help give workers the ability to cope with rapid obsolescence of skills in societies that are growing technologically more sophisticated. Economic progress will be fastest when a labor force is flexible, adaptable, and retrainable. A less flexible workforce is increasingly less employable, a substantial disadvantage as economic change becomes more rapid and more consistent.

Key features of the heterodox labor-market policies are reduced taxation on employment, education and training focused on long-term and youth unemployment, better job information (including information on how to search for a job), attempts to make labor more mobile, and wage subsidies to persuade firms to hire the graduates of the programs.

REDUCING TAXES ON EMPLOYMENT

Those who believe in a heterodox public role suggest that Social Security taxes are a particular problem in many countries. Typically they tax payrolls, so introducing a "wedge" between the higher amount that firms must pay and the lower amount that workers actually receive. From the point of view of firms, they raise the cost of employment. The situation is of special concern in Europe, where the tax wedge is about 40% in France and Italy and about 30% in Germany. The wedge is less but still appreciable in the United States, at about 14%. If Social Security could be financed by means other than a payroll tax (income or value-added taxation, for example), then the cost of hiring would not be increased by the taxation.[1] Employment would be raised because it would be less expensive for firms to hire workers.

---

1.   It might be noted that if the supply curve for labor is very inelastic, then most of the tax bill that employers have to pay will be passed on to workers in the form of reduction in the wage paid to them. The logic is the same as explored in Chapter 4 when we asked "who pays the sales tax?" When the supply curve for a product is very inelastic, the consumer pays most of it.

TRAINING OF WORKERS IN GOVERNMENT PROGRAMS

The old idea that unemployment could just be absorbed by the government, with the jobless given some sort of public-service work, is now in disfavor. Though public-service employment might be useful during a severe recession, it does nothing at all to raise the productivity of workers and make them more employable. Because of this shortcoming, it is now far more fashionable to recommend a labor-market policy of greatly expanded training for workers.

There is reason to believe that unless governments participate in the training of workers, the amount of training undertaken by private firms may be inadequate. Firms that train workers may find that they then jump to other firms that can pay them more because they did not have to shoulder the costs of the training. As a result, government programs to train young people and the long-term unemployed are universal in the developed countries. They have now become a major addition to macro policy, though far more so in Europe than in the United States.

One criticism often heard is that reforms emphasizing training and worker mobility, especially those that include wage subsidies, cost a great deal of money. That is true; as we shall see, the advanced Swedish employment schemes make up 8% of the government's budget and about 2% of GDP. Several points about the expense of labor-market policies may be made, however. First, the cost is a net cost, not a gross one. Unemployment compensation for large numbers of people is also expensive, and if it is reduced because of the employment programs, the saving can be deducted from the costs. If long-term unemployment can be reduced, the net cost of the programs is lower yet. This is because spending made *now* on reforms potentially means much less spending on the unemployed in the *future*. Budgeting for training, mobility, and wage subsidies can be included whenever a more stimulative fiscal policy is in order—that is, when unemployment is partly due to lack of aggregate demand. In that case, the new spending on employment reforms could be part of an increased budget deficit, and it would thus do double duty in the fight against recession. By making workers more employable, heterodox policy could make orthodox monetary and fiscal policy work more effectively. Countries with a large budget deficit (including the United States) would find it difficult to finance reforms in this way, however.

Sweden: World Leader in Training Programs

A number of European countries, including Great Britain, have advanced programs for training workers. Of these, the Swedish training scheme dating from the late 1940s is the world's largest, most famous, and oldest. The training is funded by government grants to municipalities, with the greater amounts going to the more depressed areas. These municipalities decide who is to provide the training—schools, companies, or the government's official training board. Sweden's current annual spending on these activities is almost 2% of GDP, much greater than that of other countries where the figure seldom exceeds 1%. (See Figure 25.1.) Indeed, Sweden is the only major developed country to spend more on retraining than on straight unemployment benefits. That country follows the precept that money spent on getting people jobs is preferable to paying them jobless benefits.

Sweden has adopted a hard approach: if you are unemployed, you will either be offered a job through the national employment service or be given a spot in a training program. If you do not agree to take the training, the generous benefits are halted. (This is called **workfare** in the United States, but U.S. training schemes are far less comprehensive.) Most people take one of the offers.[2] Following graduation, the all-computerized Swedish employment information system makes data on jobs widely available, and 60% of the unemployed get their next job through this system. Unwillingness to relocate, or to dispose of one's house in a depressed market, is counteracted with moving grants and housing allowances. Labor mobility is as high as in the United States' free market. For many years, over 90% of Swedish trainees found new jobs within the year, and Sweden's unemployment was in the range of about 2%.

---

2.   Another program supports graduates for a few months if they wish to become entrepreneurs.

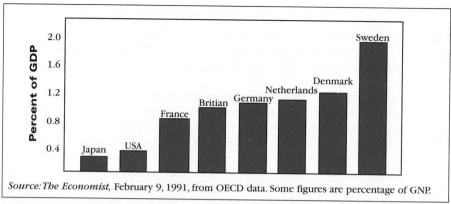

Source: *The Economist*, February 9, 1991, from OECD data. Some figures are percentage of GNP.

Figure 25.1. Government spending on training as a percentage of GDP, 1987.

SWEDEN'S LABOR POLICIES FOCUS ON LONG-TERM UNEMPLOYMENT

Swedish policy focuses on coping with the problem of long-term unemployment. For many years, the country was quite successful at this, with only 1 in 10 of Sweden's unemployed out of work for a year or more compared to about half in the rest of Europe. Those who cannot find a job after completing the normal training courses enter a 24-week special course combining more vocational training with counseling and job-search information. Graduates are awarded priority status with the national employment service. The training courses are good. A wage subsidy of about 60% to 100% of wages is paid to firms for six months or a year to encourage the hiring of graduates of the scheme who have been unemployed for six months or more.[3] These grants have been criticized on the ground that the hiring would have occurred anyway, so that the money is wasted. That line of argument appears weak, however, because the workers involved have already been unemployed for a long time.

Recently, Sweden has encountered serious economic problems, and its recent experience shows convincingly that even well-designed labor-market policies cannot overcome large macro and microeconomic distortions. On the macro side, inflation, linked to government monetary and fiscal ease and to foreign trade problems, was running at nearly 11% in 1991. A new government then adopted very tight policies to defeat the inflation—but at the price of the worst recession in many years. GDP fell by 2% in 1992 and by 4% in 1993. As a consequence, unemployment mounted alarmingly, to over 8% in 1993. On the micro side, Sweden's powerful trade unions have traditionally supported wage equalization among all types of work. As a result of their success in achieving considerable wage equality, wages have been pushed above equilibrium in many low-tech occupations, contributing to the growing unemployment. Even so, Sweden's labor market policies have been retained intact by the new and much more

---

3.   Alternatively, a government could award a tax deduction or credit to firms that hire unemployed workers. France has done so since 1977. Britain also uses the idea to a degree. An argument sometimes made by proponents of employment subsidies is that output will be higher than otherwise, so that the inflationary impact of the higher government spending to finance them will to that degree be reduced.

conservative government committed to free-market principles. These policies continue to work remarkably well at keeping the long-term unemployed searching for jobs rather than dropping out.

To be sure, the Swedish economy is much more specialized than that of the United States. One of the biggest difficulties in assessing how this heterodox policy would work in the United States is the degree to which it would be compatible with the giant, decentralized, U.S. economy.

Government Training Programs in the United States[4]

By contrast to Europe, less has been done in the United States to promote training under government auspices (though it should be remembered that the large U.S. military carries out considerable job training that later is useful in civilian life). The Manpower Development and Training Act of 1962 was originally a training program for workers displaced by structural changes in industry. With Lyndon Johnson's War on Poverty of 1964, the focus of the training shifted to disadvantaged minorities. A small Job Corps dating from that period still exists, enrolling 60–70,000 young people aged 16–21 every year and currently operating at 108 centers around the country. More than two-thirds of the Job Corp's members are blacks and Hispanics, most of them high-school dropouts who have never worked full time. In an average stay of about eight months in a boot camp atmosphere, they get basic education classes, vocational training, and work experience, along with health care and counseling. A little more than half the members who complete the program move into a job, and another 15% into further education outside the Job Corps.

CETA. Mostly, however, the training aspect in government programs was superseded in the early 1970s by the public service employment discussed in Chapter 22. Training was present only to a small degree in the Comprehensive Employment and Training Act (CETA) of 1973. Just 20% of CETA participants received classroom instruction. Studies did indicate that CETA training schemes, especially those with classroom instruction, increased the participants' chances for private-sector employment and were cost-effective. These training programs were far from perfect, however, as numerous anecdotes attest. Problems included putting people who could not pass a basic math test or use a calculator into courses that required such skills; cramming a year of training into 20 weeks; protecting instructors' reputations with inflated grades; unrealistic expectations; and little or no help in finding a job upon completion of the training. The general unpopularity of CETA's public-service employment, especially among conservatives, reached such a pitch that the entire program, including the training, was scrapped early in the Reagan administration.

JTPA. CETA was succeeded by a Jobs Training Partnership Act (JTPA) in 1982, but JTPA has been small and underfunded. JTPA did, however, introduce a turn toward retraining the structurally unemployed. For the first time in U.S. experience, the training was linked to the actual needs of employers in a given locality, so the program targeted current jobs rather than potential future jobs. (Failure to have done so was a fundamental flaw in CETA.) The idea of training tailored to existing openings had been pioneered in other countries, particularly Germany, Sweden, and Japan, but it has now spread around the world, even in newly industrializing countries such as Brazil and Singapore. There is a negative side to JTPA, however. According to its critics, the program has focused on training the jobless with good prospects for future employment to the neglect of the long-term, hard-core unemployed.

Recent Developments. A new advance in U.S. use of training took place in 1988 as part of that year's Trade Bill. Congress voted much enlarged funding for retraining, the training to be available to all workers who were out of work as a result of plant closures. Cash assistance was included in the benefits provided by the bill, but for the first time in U.S. practice, workers had to take the training in order to be eligible for the cash. The states are responsible for 80% of the organization. Unfortunately, because of the continuing crisis over the U.S. budget deficit the new

---

4.   This section has benefited from the work of Peter Gottschalk of Boston College.

training program had still not been fully implemented by 1994.[5] The Clinton administration, convinced that government must improve workers' ability to change jobs, wants to implement a new "reemployment system" that would combine career advice, retraining, and job search assistance. The centerpiece is a "dislocated-worker" training program for those who have been permanently laid off because of factory closures, corporate restructuring, and competition from imports. This would combine six existing programs and would double the total funding to $3 billion.

National Service. Many find attractive the idea of national community service with the service resulting in grants to pay for subsequent training and education. One advantage of a program of this type is that workers would be available for various labor-intensive public services that are at present understaffed, underfinanced, or not done at all. Community service workers might include teachers' aides, illiteracy workers, hospital, mental hospital, nursing home, and child care helpers, assistants for the elderly confined to their homes, and staff for homeless shelters. It might provide aides and counselors for crime victims and drug addicts. Its workers could tidy the highways, streets, and subways, clean and maintain parks, pick up beaches, and help rehabilitate slums.

President Clinton supported the idea during his campaign, and a new bill enacted in 1993 established a corps for national service called AmeriCorps. A high school diploma is a requirement for participation. Because of budget constraints ($300 million in fiscal 1994, rising to $700 million in fiscal 1996), enrollment will at first be limited to 20,000 young people, mostly aged 17–25. Each volunteer will earn $8,000 plus health and child care benefits in a program that lasts for 12 months. Graduates will get a grant of up to $4,725 that can be used for expenses connected with higher education. All states will have a community service commission to administer the program.[6]

State Programs. A number of U.S. states have fashioned European-style employment programs of their own, some of which emphasize training, and some of which do not. California and Delaware use state revenues to fund worker training. The subsidy helps to overcome the resistance of private firms to financing the training themselves. As we have noted, firms often do not want to do so because of the substantial risk that they might lose their newly trained workers to competitors who did not share in the training cost. Minnesota currently uses tax funds to subsidize a firm's employment (by $5 per hour per worker for six months) if that employment is larger than in the past year. The Minnesota plan parallels closely the wage subsidies of the Swedish program.

Concerns about Government Training

Though considerable emphasis has recently been given to government programs for training workers, a number of concerns have also arisen. One is macroeconomic in nature. If the training schemes are very expensive, then the higher taxes needed to finance them may have a sufficient contractionary effect on the economy so that fewer jobs in the private sector are available for

---

5   The training was intended to be funded by an across-the-board import fee (tariff) of 0.15%. A rise in tariffs violates (though rather mildly) many U.S. commitments made in trade negotiations over the years, other governments protested this method of financing, and in the end the tariff plan was dropped. That has left the retraining programs chronically underfunded.

6   There will also be a smaller (800 student) Civilian Community Corps. Its students will be housed at military bases, and unlike AmeriCorps, a high school diploma is not necessary for membership. The CCC will work on green spaces, tree planting, and erosion control. VISTA (Volunteers in Service to America), dating from 1964, is being folded into the new program. Its 3,400 volunteers earn the same as AmeriCorps members and do much the same work. This is an area where local initiatives were taken well before the federal government acted. The City Year program in Boston accepts students aged 17–23 who are trying to pass high school equivalency tests or are high school graduates or college students. Members receive $100 per week and a $5000 grant at graduation. The program emphasizes racial harmony as well as useful community improvement. The National Service Corps for the City of New York has operated since 1984. Service Corps members are paid two-thirds of the minimum wage, with the other one-third usually paid as a tuition voucher at the end of the year. The Wisconsin Conservation Corps dates from 1985. It is open to all unemployed in the age group 18 to 25, who are paid the minimum wage, get some educational training, and are awarded a $1,500 tuition voucher after 12 months in the Corps. Eleven other states have similar schemes.

the graduates of the program. The deficit spending that might avoid this problem is less likely for the many governments that have been running up chronic large budget deficits during the 1980s and '90s.

Another concern is that in a world of rapid economic change, specific training may become obsolete in a fairly short time. In this view, improvements in general education will provide the flexibility needed to better cope with change, and attention to liberal learning rather than specific training is the course to follow. (Improvements in general education are addressed in the next chapter.)

Finally, it must be repeated that no training scheme of any kind will perform very well if governments pursue contractionary monetary and fiscal policies for long periods. These will push the economy toward high interest rates, tight money, recession, and unemployment, and the absorption of unemployed workers will be more difficult no matter how well trained they are. In that sense, predictions of a training program's good performance must involve predictions about an economy's good performance as well, for without the latter, the former will be much more difficult to achieve. Reasonable macroeconomic policies of an *orthodox* type make it possible for heterodox policies to assist.

GERMANY'S APPRENTICESHIPS

Germany approaches training in another way, through its national apprenticeship program. This system for vocational training differs from government training programs in that it is largely privately managed by firms and trade unions rather than being run by the government. The government's role is indirectly to provide much of the funding—all the costs of the program can be taken as a tax deduction. Almost 70% of German students, two out of five of them female, enter the national apprenticeship program at age 15. For three years they attend a training school for one day a week and undergo four days of on-the-job training, sometimes in replicas of real factories. Students are trained for many service jobs as well as for jobs in manufacturing. Apprentices are paid about a third of a full salary. After a period of final exams, the students are awarded certificates of competency in the skills for which they have trained. Only 10% of young people, aside from those who go on to university, do not take the training. The very large numbers involved (recently 1.7 million) have kept youth unemployment low in Germany, though the apprenticeship scheme has done little to attack that country's *long-term* jobless problem.

By contrast, in the United States there are only about 300,000 apprenticeships, about one-twentieth the number that Germany has on a per capita basis. U.S. apprenticeship schemes are often run by trade unions for their own workers and are not intended to deal with national issues unless these issues correspond directly to a union's own concerns. Fewer than 1% of U.S. companies spend money on training programs, and most of this is for managers and executives rather than for workers. The training of workers that does occur in the United States is still mostly on-the-job, sometimes known as "following Joe around."

Because of the limited scope of U.S. apprenticeships, the German program and other lesser-known ones in Europe are currently receiving considerable favorable attention in the United States. There are critics, however, who worry that the apprenticeships are very job-specific in a world of rapid change where generalists, not specialists, are increasingly useful. These critics also note the high costs of apprenticeships and point out that most new jobs will be in services and not in manufacturing where apprenticing works best.

DEFICIENCIES IN INFORMATION

One of the largest U.S. problems in dealing with structural unemployment is lack of information about job openings beyond a state's borders. A fair number of states do have reasonably sophisticated job information and employment services. Many localities—mostly cities but sometimes counties as well—also provide these services. By and large, they appear to work well within their limited geographical scope.

Little is done, however, to spread information about job availability in *other* states. Knowledge concerning openings on a national basis is not collected and publicized systematically, as is done by numerous other countries. (The national employment service approach was pioneered by Sweden.) Current U.S. practice is haphazard, including such time-honored practices as phoning relatives or visiting the local library to read out-of-town papers or scan phone books. For years economists have recommended that the United States should establish a computerized job bank that is easy to access, with up-to-date information on available jobs. A national job bank has been in the planning stage for some time, but the only present result is a rudimentary job-clearing center in Albany, N.Y., to which only about half the states mail their lists of job vacancies. Even these lists are not very detailed, either because employers do not adequately register their job openings or because the states are not entirely willing to share information with one another. Those who could benefit from knowledge about new jobs thus may not get it for several weeks (by which time the job may have been filled), or they may not get it at all. The imperfect data concerning job openings beyond the limits of a locality or state appears to be a failure of U.S. public policy.

JOB SHARING

Another idea for dealing with rising unemployment is **job sharing** (also called work sharing). Legislation might require that, rather than laying off workers, firms may shorten the work week but must spread the work around among all the job holders. The incidence of job sharing rose substantially during the early 1980s recession. In the United States, California, Arizona, Oregon, Washington, and Florida were among the states adopting such laws. Usually the losses of the workers who went to short time were partly made up by paying them some unemployment compensation, on the grounds that if they had been completely without a job, even more public funds would otherwise have had to be used. Canada adopted job sharing in 1982 and ran a large-scale national program. During that year and the next, similar schemes were in use in Britain, France, the Netherlands, and West Germany. France and Germany were both considering mandatory four-day work weeks in 1994 to cope with their still-high unemployment; Germany now pays partial unemployment benefits to workers who voluntary accept a shorter work week.

Job sharing is hardly the most innovative assault on unemployment. From the economy's point of view, if two workers are involuntarily forced to work four-hour days, that means the output that could be produced by one full-time worker is being lost. Job sharing is perhaps better than nothing, however. Arguably it is more acceptable to women and teen-agers, a larger proportion of whom are said to prefer part-time work because of family circumstances. (In Europe, job sharing schemes have been more effective whenever employees with shortened schedules could choose what hours they would work.) For all that it is only a stop-gap measure, job sharing certainly provides a useful safeguard against an outbreak of the hysteresis problem described in the previous chapter.

► ATTACKING INFLATION WITH INCOMES POLICIES

Historically, a number of heterodox measures have been used against inflation, and others have been discussed though not yet adopted. Taken together, these heterodox measures are often called **incomes policies**. They are intended to attack inflation without reducing aggregate demand. The oldest, and among the most controversial of these, are controls on wage and price increases.

WAGE-PRICE CONTROLS

In a stagflationary economy, it might appear possible to fight unemployment with standard monetary and fiscal policy, while controlling or even freezing the inflation with laws prohibiting wage increases, price hikes, or both. **Wage-price controls** are hardly new; both were established in the ancient Babylonian Empire under the Code of Hammurabi about 2100 BC. In Rome, an edict of 301 AD issued by Emperor Diocletian involved comprehensive controls. All the major belligerent countries in World War II operated widespread control systems involving rationing of many products. U.S. controls were first introduced in April 1942, at which time inflation had vaulted to 12% in just a few months following the outbreak of the war. The controls lasted until November 1946. In January 1951, during the Korean War, some controls were reintroduced, being finally removed by President Eisenhower in 1953. Huge bureaucracies administered these programs—the Office of Price Administration, OPA, during World War II, and the Office of Price Stabilization, OPS, during the Korean conflict.

Jawboning and Guidelines

In most developed countries, controls were not used again until the early 1960s, at which point they slowly began to make a comeback in a much milder form. In the United States, President Kennedy attacked the steel industry for what he believed to be an unwarranted rise in steel prices in 1962. The persuasion of firms to hold the line on prices came to be called "jawboning." Democratic presidents have been most active in using jawboning, and President Lyndon Johnson above all. The Nixon administration moved to outright controls, as we shall see, but President Carter returned to jawboning in 1978. It did not work well against the entrenched inflation of the late 1970s, and after his election in 1980, President Reagan halted use of the tactic.

Jawboning came to involve more than just persuasive efforts. Voluntary wage-price "guideposts" or "guidelines" were established, first in the Johnson administration. Typically these called for price increases not to exceed a target rate of inflation, and for wage increases not to exceed that same target rate of inflation plus the rate of productivity growth. (Thus if labor became 2% more productive, it was permissible to reflect that in 2% higher pay.) Productivity change is difficult to ascertain in short periods of time, however. Even if it were easy, these guideposts and guidelines were voluntary, and they could not be policed except by bringing to bear the jawboning power of the president and other government officials. The Johnson efforts were not effective, losing what little clout they had as inflation picked up in 1967. When President Carter returned to guideposts in 1978, he too set a target rate of inflation. Wage hikes beyond this would be frowned upon, unless they were accompanied by productivity increases. Again the voluntary nature of the guideposts and the lack of policing limited compliance, although the Carter administration did in some instances direct government contracts away from firms that did not comply.

The lesson learned by economists and politicians was that jawboning and voluntary guideposts are unlikely to be effective unless they are backed by strong public support. Such support has not been sufficiently forthcoming in the U.S. experience.

The Legally Binding U.S. Controls of 1971–1974

Legally binding wage-price controls had never before been used in peacetime in the United States until President Nixon imposed them on almost all economic activity in 1971. The controls were far more comprehensive than anything that had received serious discussion up to that point. (The details of the U.S. controls, and the resort to controls by many other governments during this period, are explored in the accompanying box.)

THE PERIOD OF LEGAL WAGE-PRICE CONTROLS

The U.S. experience with controls involved four "phases" that lasted from 1971 to 1974. Phase One, announced on August 14, 1971, was a three-month freeze on most prices, rents, wages, and salaries. The intent of the freeze was to administer a shock to reduce inflationary expectations. Certainly the freeze did slow price and wage increases; consumer prices rose at an annual rate of only 1.9% and wages at a rate of under 2%, instead of the 8% rate just before the freeze was imposed.

Phase Two was instituted when the freeze ended on November 14, 1971. It lasted until January 11, 1973. During this period, legally binding guidelines limited most price increases to 2.5% per year, and most wage increases to 5.5% per year. Inflation was contained somewhat (3.6% annually during Phase Two), but aggregate demand and aggregate supply changes would have caused higher price increases in the absence of the controls, so suppressed inflationary pressure was building up. The understaffed price commission given the administrative duties—it had a staff of less than 1,000, supplemented by about 3,000 Internal Revenue Service agents who aided in policing the regulations—was swamped by the magnitude of the job. As one example, if just the Dow Chemical Company had refused to cooperate during Phase Two, then the Price Commission would have had to police nearly 100,000 separate prices for that company alone.

Phase Three (January 11 to June 12, 1973) consisted of voluntary as opposed to mandatory guidelines. The percentages remained the same, 2.5% for prices and 5.5% for wages. This short period was a disaster for the advocates of voluntary price controls, as consumer prices jumped up immediately (8.3% annual rate) while wholesale prices soared (24.4%). The incident demonstrated how mandatory price controls in place for a long period may serve only to suppress the inflation temporarily, rather than stopping it. The underlying macroeconomic policies at the time remained expansionary, with the government's budget seriously in deficit. Further, the first great supply shock on oil supplies was hitting home in 1973. The move to voluntarism allowed the pent-up inflation to run free. The experience left little doubt that when underlying economic forces are expansionary, relaxing mandatory wage-price controls will cause a burst of inflation.

Phase Four (June 13, 1973 to May 1, 1974) started with a 60-day freeze to rein in the inflation once again. It continued with government powers to roll back price or wage increases on a case-by-case basis. During 1974, the U.S. government obtained voluntary agreements with a number of major industries, including autos, rubber, and cement, as well as with many retailers, to hold prices down and expand their productive capacity in exchange for freedom from the controls.

The consensus was that Phase Four was less effective than Phase One had been, because it proved almost useless against supply shocks. To the extent that controls were directed against the rising food and fuel costs, the inevitable shortages (especially of beef, pork, and poultry) soon proved embarrassing to the controllers. Fearing to exacerbate these shortages, the controllers failed to assault many price increases, and during Phase Four consumer and wholesale prices rose at an annual rate of 9.6% and 14.3% respectively. In February 1974, President Nixon announced that price controls would end on May 1 (except for petroleum and health care), and few tears were shed. Once the controls were lifted, the shortages they caused rapidly disappeared—but until they did, the shortages probably made the inflation even worse.

Controls Elsewhere

During approximately the same time period as the U.S. curbs, mandatory wage-price controls were in use in numerous other market economies (though neither Germany nor Japan adopted them). In the Netherlands, a freeze followed by legal restraints covered the period 1969 to 1971, were lifted for a year, and were then reintroduced. Initially efficiently managed, the Dutch controls soon achieved general unpopularity. France froze prices in 1969, reinforced controls in 1971, and removed them in 1972. A long Swedish price freeze was in force through the period from October 1970 until the end of 1971. Great Britain adopted control measures that closely paralleled those of the United States, with a wage-price freeze late in 1972 that lasted six months, strong legal price and wage restraint until October 1973, and looser controls thereafter. The British even called these policies by their American names, Phase One, Two, and Three. Like the U.S. experience, the earlier British measures were more favorably thought of than were those of the later period, when the controls were thoroughly breached. The episode ended with a famous miners' strike, with electrical power interrupted, with an election called, and with Edward Heath's Conservative government defeated. The following period of Labour Party rule under Prime Ministers Harold Wilson and James Callaghan brought a period (1975–1978) of "Social Contract," essentially a series of agreements with trade unions to abide by certain guidelines concerning wage increases. The Social Contract collapsed in 1978 amid a welter of union/government disagreements; the next year brought the election of a Conservative parliament under Margaret Thatcher, and British incomes policy disappeared.

THE DECLINE OF CONTROLS

Since about 1980, controls on wages and prices have generally been out of favor. An episode in France involving a four-month freeze and New Zealand's year-long wage-price freeze starting in June 1982 are among the few recent examples. More and more, the problem with controls became all too apparent. They can serve, and even serve well, if employed as a short and sharp psychological shock to break entrenched expectations. That may catch the public's imagination and mobilize support, giving a government credibility if the public takes the shock as a serious revelation of new purpose, and a breathing space to introduce other measures, orthodox or heterodox, to carry on the fight. But if a price freeze is in effect when the weather turns bad (agriculture) or a foreign cartel restricts supply (OPEC's oil), then inexorably the frozen price will be below the free-market equilibrium, the quantity demanded will exceed the quantity supplied, and a shortage will develop. That last judgment would be widely accepted by anyone who lived through the 1979–1980 oil crisis. In those years, OPEC cut oil supplies at a time when U.S. price controls on gasoline were still in force. The resulting gasoline shortage brought closed gas stations, long lines at the pumps, and disrupted lives for all who depended on motor vehicles for transport. The distortions to an economy caused by these scarcities can easily bring more acute problems, including lower economic growth, than would have been caused by a rise in price.

Thus few economists can now be found who believe that wage-price controls or guideposts hold much promise except in the very short run as an attempt to break expectations of chronic high inflation or during a major national emergency such as a war that commands wide public support. Those that do favor them would usually insist that when used, they must be combined with orthodox fiscal and monetary policy. There seems considerable agreement that controls will not be of much help if the inflation to be fought is relatively low. Nor will they work when inflation is extremely *high*, for hyperinflation is always due to government creation of money to fund budget deficits. In that case, monetary and fiscal restraint is the proper prescription, and without that, the controls will either be ineffective or damaging.

Indexing

Indexing is an attempt to render inflation harmless by adjusting wages and salaries, pensions, taxes, or any other money figure, to reflect the amount of inflation. For example, if full indexing of wages is in place and monthly inflation of 10% is registered in this month's consumer price index, then the government will require that employers raise wages by 10% at the end of the month. The purchasing power of wages (the real wage) is thus restored to where it was at the start of the month. In effect, indexing assimilates the inflation without attacking the causes. The principle involved is "if you can't beat 'em, then join 'em."

Iceland, a very small economy, pioneered the idea in 1939, with Finland following in 1944. Israel was also an early convert, adopting indexing shortly after independence. Little notice was taken, however, until Brazil's comprehensive indexing was established from the mid-1960s. With Brazilian inflation running at over 90% in 1964, economists in that country felt that standard monetary and fiscal solutions would reduce growth too drastically. Their solution was to incorporate escalator clauses (known in the United States as COLAs or Cost of Living Adjustments) into most areas of Brazilian economic activity. By 1967 these clauses covered cost of living adjustments for wages, interest rates on bank deposits and bonds, taxes, and rents. The principle was later extended to the adjustment of asset values. Eventually the value of corporate stocks and bonds, government bonds and securities, savings accounts, and even legal judgments were adjusted upward according to the most recent price index.

Visiting economists heard Brazilians argue that their nation could tolerate a much higher degree of inflation than could an unindexed country while maintaining fast growth in real GNP, and they saw evidence to support this claim. The 1970–1977 Brazilian average real increase in GNP, an excellent 9.8% a year, had few competitors (the figure was three times the U.S. average during those years). The implication was that Brazil's 1970–1977 annual average inflation of 29% was doing little damage because of the widespread indexing, whereas expansionary monetary and fiscal policies could be used to promote growth and lower unemployment to minimal levels. The causes of inflation could be ignored and the fight against it simply abandoned, all because of the remarkable new talisman: indexing.

When the economist Milton Friedman of the University of Chicago returned from Brazil in 1974, he was widely quoted as favoring some form of indexing for the United States. Though no U.S. national policy has ever been close to adoption, the practice did spread widely in certain sectors. COLA agreements in union/management wage contracts dated from as far back as 1948 in the United States, but until the late 1960s they were not very important. But COLAs then began to spread. The percentage of union workers covered by indexed contracts rose from approximately one-fourth in the early 1970s to about three-fifths in the late 1970s. In the government sector, Social Security benefits were tied to the cost of living in 1975, and pensions for government workers received similar treatment. Canada and many European and South American countries went further than this. Some of them—Argentina, Chile—introduced systems that approximated the Brazilian example in their wide coverage.

Hard Times for Indexing

Within 10 years, however, the reputation of indexing in the countries that adopted some version of the scheme had been much diminished. Two sorts of problems arose. First, even with careful attention to design, such systems did not work perfectly. For example, Brazil's original plan indexed according to an *expected* rate of inflation, but the estimates were often too low so some groups fell behind the inflation. At various periods the system was somewhat more effective for protecting holders of capital than for wage earners, and the poor were disadvantaged because they tend to hold unindexed cash rather than indexed assets of other kinds.

Another serious consequence was the extension of inflation when it was caused by outside supply shocks, such as the OPEC oil crisis. Brazil found that when a whole nation becomes poorer, as was the case when oil prices rose so greatly, then indexing can make the situation worse. In an unindexed country a shock of this nature has only a temporary inflationary impact before its effect dies away. No upward spiral of prices results, unless the government employs accommodating monetary or fiscal policy. Where indexing is widespread, however, a price rise triggers a wage rise, which the government is forced to accommodate with increases in the money supply. That in turn is followed by another price rise, and another wage increase, in a vicious circle. As hyperinflation begins to appear, people with indexed incomes cannot now afford to have their wages fall behind prices even by as little as a month. The likelihood thus increases that indexing will not maintain incomes equally for all segments of society. Furthermore, even if adverse effects on income distribution can be avoided, the high levels of unfought inflation begin to bring the menu and shoe-leather costs discussed in Chapter 14. In short, the realization grew that since indexing meant the abandonment of the fight against inflation, that would make inflation relentlessly worse. The more indexing solved problems, the more the problems that were created.

A reaction set in against this surrender, as indexing came to be viewed as a cause of inflation rather than as a solution. As a result, numerous governments retreated. The pioneer, Iceland, suspended its comprehensive indexing in 1983; Finland, the second country to employ it, had already given up in 1967. The roll of the defectors is steadily lengthening, with many other abandonments or backward steps having occurred. These include Australia after 1977, much of Belgium's and Luxembourg's programs in 1980, Denmark and Chile in 1982, and Italy in 1985. Even in Brazil, though indexing still survives, the government has lost much of its enthusiasm for it. In the United States, COLA agreements in labor/management contracts are becoming less common, and even the politically sacrosanct indexing of Social Security benefits has been under recent attack. All in all, it is now far more common to find *de-indexing* proposed as a solution to inflation than the reverse.

INNOVATIVE APPROACHES USING THE TAX SYSTEM

Certain types of tax policy are close to the boundary between the heterodox approaches and orthodox fiscal policy. Some are intended to make countercyclical tax changes more or less automatic; others link firms' tax bills to evidence that they are willing to fight inflation.

Automatic Variations in Taxes

Several countries have a tax policy where a government can make certain rapid changes without having to fight these changes through a legislature. In Great Britain, the Chancellor of the Exchequer (equivalent to a Minister of Finance, or U.S. Treasury Secretary) has the power to raise or reduce British excise taxes by up to 10% as a type of semiautomatic fiscal policy. In Germany, the "Law of Stability and Growth" of 1967 allows the executive branch to alter tax rates within certain limits. During inflation, taxes can be raised by 10% for one year with the receipts deposited in a special account to be refunded to taxpayers when the inflation has passed. Conversely, in a recession, income and corporate taxes can be cut for one year by 10%, and a temporary 7½% investment tax credit can be established. (At the time the law was passed, it was believed that its effect would be larger than actually transpired: remember the principle that temporary tax changes have considerably less effect on consumers' behavior than do permanent changes.)

An interesting tax device in Sweden is the "tax-free investment reserve" that dates from 1955. Under this plan, Swedish firms may be informed during an inflation that they are now allowed to set aside up to 40% of their profits in a tax-free fund. This revenue is not spent by the government, but is kept in special deposits so that the fiscal impact is to cool the inflation. Later, if recession strikes, the government can release the funds back to the firms for the purpose of investment. Utilization of funds from the reserve took place in 1958, 1962, 1967, and 1971. In some of these Swedish recessions as much as a quarter of private investment was from the tax-free reserve, and the cyclical nature of investment had to a large extent been countered.[7]

---

7.   By 1975, however, the reserve was being used essentially as a permanent boost to investment rather than as stimulant during recessions, so its countercyclical nature has essentially been lost. During the present Swedish economic crisis, with the government trying to counter stagflation by eliminating a large budget deficit, the reserve is an inappropriate tool to push down unemployment.

Germany has a somewhat similar system in which a maximum of 3% of the previous year's government tax receipts can be allotted to an antirecession reserve held in the central bank, to be unfrozen and spent once the inflation has passed. Although such ideas seem generally sensible, efforts to promote anything of the kind in the United States have never succeeded.

THE TIP SCHEME

In the early 1970s, Professors Henry Wallich of Yale and Sidney Weintraub of the University of Pennsylvania proposed an anti-inflation policy that utilized the tax mechanism to ensure that firms paid wage increases close to some national norm. The proposal received the name "Tax-Based Incomes Policy," or **TIP**. Many TIP variations have been discussed. The original one would have penalized firms paying more than some norm. Say a firm exceeded a 5% norm for wage increases by paying 7%. It might then find 1% added to its tax bill. In Arthur Okun's variation, rewards would be given for compliance with some standard. Thus, for example, a firm holding the line at 5% increases might be awarded a tax rate 2% less than the established rate. Either way, the result would be the generation of resistance to inflationary expectations and cost-push forces that would not otherwise have been present.

The objection that the amount of red tape involved would be intolerable could be countered by limiting application of the TIP to large firms, say those employing at least 500 workers. Increases in the productivity of labor could be allowed for, so that the TIP penalty would not kick in until wage increases exceeded the national norm plus any gains in labor productivity registered during the year.

Other objections proved more difficult to deal with, however. The national norms would have to be policed, bringing yet more government intervention atop the bureaucracy that would be needed to run the program. (To the Reagan administration, that flaw was a fatal one.) Labor unions objected because of the TIP scheme's focus on wages. They, with numerous economists, argued that a limit on wage increases in expanding sectors of the economy would have the effect of limiting the incentive for labor to move into those industries. In any case, the unions argued that it was unfair to single out labor as the sole cause of inflation. Many questions remained unanswered. Would firms hit with a TIP penalty pass that penalty forward as a price increase? Would TIP be calculated on a plant-by-plant basis or by looking at an entire firm? Would it not be easy to avoid the regulation by manipulating overtime and working conditions? Might not the exemption of small firms eventually lead to a gap in wages between them and the corporate sector, with resulting inefficiencies?

To the time of writing, the questions have not been answered because a TIP scheme has not been tried in the United States. The Carter administration expended some effort in trying to implement one, but ultimately it failed. The Reagan administration had no interest in expanding the role of government in this manner, and neither the Bush nor the Clinton administrations have (so far) revived the idea. In spite of this neglect, the TIP principle survives and thrives elsewhere in the world. Recently it has been adopted in a number of the eastern European countries that are converting their economies from command systems to the market.

▶ COMBATTING SUPPLY SHOCKS WITH SUPPLY-SIDE REFORMS

Modern macroeconomics emphasizes that supply shocks that move the aggregate supply curve vertically upward are a major cause of stagflation. As seen in Figure 25.2, the movement from $SRAS_1$ to $SRAS_2$ causes both a rise in prices (P_1 to P_2) and a decline in output (Y_1 to Y_2), hence more unemployment. A strategy to combat the resulting stagflation is obvious enough. If government action could push the aggregate supply curve back down from $SRAS_2$ to $SRAS_1$, the process would reverse itself. The ground lost to stagflation could be reclaimed as inflation falls back, and as output grows, so decreasing unemployment. Hence the name **supply-side reforms** to describe measures that would have this effect.

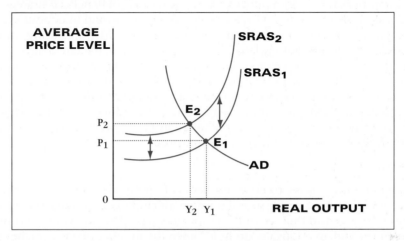

Figure 25.2. Supply-side reforms to counter stagflation. If government action could reduce the cost of output, stagflation would be attacked by the downward movement of the SRAS curve.

What supply-side steps *can* be taken to push the aggregate supply curve downward? The question involves a searching analysis of government policies and programs to see if any of them have the effect of propping up costs without sufficient compensating benefits for society. The range of possibilities is wide. We discuss them alphabetically.

Agricultural Policies

As we have already seen in Chapter 5, price supports and acreage restrictions are both common in farming, especially in the United States, the EC, and Japan. Both policies have a price-boosting impact. Reducing the supports and lifting the restrictions would work to lower the average price level of any given quantity of output and would appear as a movement from $SRAS_2$ to $SRAS_1$ in Figure 25.2. In the dry American west, government controls over water use mean that farmers pay an extremely low price for irrigation, in California just $10 per acre-foot of water. That is only about 10% of the true cost. Food prices are doubtless lowered somewhat by the cheap water, but because farmers use about 85% of California's total water consumption, the cost for any other industry that uses water is raised considerably. Eliminating this practice would reduce the cost of water to industries outside of agriculture and on balance would probably lower the position of the aggregate supply curve.

Government Buying

Many countries favor domestic production when governments purchase goods and services. The U.S. "Buy American" Act is one of many such pieces of legislation found around the world. Even states and provinces have their own laws giving preference to local purchasing by governments— 20 U.S. states and all the Canadian provinces have such laws. To the extent that they have an effect, they cause governments to buy more expensively than is necessary. Eradicating these laws would probably lower costs.

Investment in Physical and Human Capital

Benefits are expected to flow from investment in physical and human capital. Poor government policies might, however, prevent these benefits from being realized. For example, a country's tax laws could cause neglect of private investment in plant and equipment. Built-in impediments to effective research and development programs might exist. Declining educational standards and a decaying infrastructure of highways, bridges, and other forms of public capital will push up costs and reduce output growth (in effect, a detrimental movement in the aggregate supply curve from $SRAS_1$ to $SRAS_2$ in Figure 25.2). In such cases, tax reform to increase investment and raise R&D spending, plus appropriately chosen public investments, can be a beneficial strategy. The situation is not hypothetical: Statistics show the United States dropping behind in educational quality, ranking last among major nations in the ratio of public investment to GDP, still facing antitrust laws that prevent joint research consortia among large firms, and dead last in the rate of productivity growth.[8]

The need to increase investment in physical and human capital is surely the most compelling item on our list. Much of the next chapter is devoted specifically to this topic. There we shall also posit that some role may exist for a government "industrial policy"—seed money or low-interest loans for R&D in areas of high potential productivity and profitability. Though debatable, this concept was (and is, in a more limited way) important in Japan, and has also been adopted by South Korea and some other newly industrializing countries.

Labor Costs

Several government policies serve to boost the costs of hiring labor above what would be true in a free market. Social Security taxes in some countries (including the United States) are charged in part to employers as a tax on their payrolls; employers pass these costs on to consumers in the form of higher prices and are motivated to hold down the number of workers they hire. Funding Social Security out of general income tax revenues would avoid these cost-boosting by-products of social policy. The cost of medical care facing American firms is very high, as we saw in Chapter 5. Every additional worker hired boosts these costs further, so like Social Security taxes they, too, act as a tax on employment. A redesigned system could avoid this levy on hiring. Health-care costs appear to be a major reason explaining the move toward the employment of temporary workers in the United States, and the rise in overtime among full-time workers. (One-fifth of all full-time workers now work longer hours than the normal 40-hour week, a significantly higher proportion than was formerly true.) These developments clearly reflect a desire by employers to cut their labor costs by economizing on the hiring of full-time workers. The downside of this is that on-the-job training is less effective when employment is temporary, and untrained workers have less commitment to their firm and leave their jobs more often in a kind of vicious circle.

Similarly, minimum-wage laws that push wages above a free-market equilibrium may also increase labor costs and discourage employment. Other methods to assist low-income workers, such as cash allowances financed by the tax system, would avoid this problem. The Davis-Bacon Act, a Great Depression measure dating from 1933 and still in effect, requires that labor on U.S. government construction projects be paid the highest wage available in a given locality, rather than the average wage. That, too, boosts the costs of hiring labor. Reforms in these areas would cause a downward movement in the position of the aggregate supply curve.

Protectionism in Foreign Trade

Tariffs, quotas, "voluntary restraints," and many other barriers to international trade all serve to raise prices. As we discuss in Chapter 27, tariffs, being a tax, raise prices directly, while quotas and

---

8.   Presently in the United States, net federal civilian fixed investment as a percentage of GNP is about $\frac{1}{3}$ of 1%, compared to about $1\frac{1}{2}$% in Canada, 2% in Britain and Italy, over 2% in France and Germany, and over 5% in Japan. U.S. productivity growth is far down the list, a little over $\frac{1}{2}$ of 1% in 1973-1985, well below the nearest important rival (Canada, about $1\frac{1}{2}$%). Antitrust uncertainty still surrounds U.S. joint research and production ventures, even though Congress has now twice liberalized the law in this area, as we discussed in Chapter 9.

restraints that limit the supply of imports do so indirectly. Several important manufacturing sectors are heavily protected in many countries, including steel, automobiles, clothing, and textiles.

Breaking down trade barriers, politically difficult as it is, would be an effective weapon against inflation.[9] In particular, if an industry is inefficient and cannot meet the competition from abroad, it is socially expensive to keep that industry alive. The economy as a whole will be better off if resources shift into industries that *can* compete effectively. This principle of "comparative advantage" is analyzed in detail in Chapter 27.

Services

Many countries impose controls on services such as banking, broadcasting, and insurance. Most often the controls limit competition from foreign sources, but it is not unknown for regulations of this type to apply even within a country. Canada, for example, has many provincial controls, while numerous U.S. states have laws prejudicial to out-of-state banking firms and insurance companies. Sometimes out-of-state banks are banned altogether, as we saw in Chapter 19. Reform in all these cases would arguably bring lower costs, which again would serve to lower the position of the SRAS curve in Figure 25.2.

Transportation and communications are often regulated, and although competition in airlines, trucking, and telephones has been allowed to intensify in recent years, especially in the United States but less so in Europe, cost-boosting regulations still exist. For instance, though the U.S. trucking industry was largely deregulated in 1980 as far as the federal government is concerned, 43 states at last count still restrict entry into that business and regulate rates. That means less price competition than would otherwise occur, and boosts costs generally for all goods that are transported in trucks. The Interstate Commerce Commission still regulates some railroad rates, and the Federal Maritime Commission imposes similar controls over shipping. Both have price-boosting effects. In merchant shipping, the U.S. Jones Act requires all cargoes shipped between American ports to go on American-flag ships, costing consumers about a billion dollars a year. Tankers carrying oil for the U.S. strategic petroleum reserve must also carry the U.S. flag. Per ton-mile these ships cost about four times more to operate than foreign-flag vessels. Worldwide, the rigging of airline and shipping rates is extensive. In all these cases, new policies could reduce costs, shifting the aggregate supply curve downward.[10]

Taxes

Another supply-side tax consideration concerns sales taxes (or the value-added taxes used in Europe). These have an impact on prices already analyzed in Chapter 4, tending to push them up. A fall in sales taxes works in the reverse direction. If sales taxes were to be replaced in whole or part by income taxes, then we could expect that the aggregate supply curve would accordingly move downward all along its length. Yet if income tax rates are overly high, that can limit effort, cause misallocation of resources, and lead to tax evasion. Carefully designed tax policies— perhaps including a revival of federal revenue-sharing with the states—can attempt to hew to a middle way between these two obstacles, jointly minimizing the adverse side-effects of taxation while maximizing the creation of physical and human capital by government and the private sector. To the extent that present policies can be improved upon, the aggregate supply curve will move downward.

---

9.   Sometimes the importance of this element is missed. Consider that in the United States, unemployment in some areas (for example, all of New England and New Jersey) was well below the national average, at only 3 or 4% during the mid- and late-1980s. Yet inflation in these states was not noticeably worse during this period, except in housing, than in the other states. How could this be? The major reason is the unimpeded trade among the states. Similarly, the countries in the EC that have in effect linked their currencies together also find that trade serves to keep the rate of inflation similar, even though some of these countries have much lower levels of unemployment than others.

10.   In the United States, the lower prices and improved service from the 1982–1983 airlines deregulation, the federal railway and trucking deregulation of 1980, and the telecommunications deregulation of 1982 added perhaps 8% to the value of the output of the sectors producing these items. That was equivalent to about 1% of GDP.

Summary

To summarize, some government policies have a cost-raising side to them that, if removed, would make an effective weapon against stagflation. There may well be other reasons to favor the policies anyway, justifications sufficiently strong so that any given restriction or regulation might in the end be retained. Yet it is still proper for an economist to recommend that such policies receive frequent, searching examinations to ensure that their price-boosting aspects are warranted by the good that they do. Many of these policies, it seems clear enough, could not pass such a test.

LONG-RUN CONSEQUENCES

The supply-side reforms just discussed are not all of a kind. *Some* of them hold a promise that the capacity of the economy to produce might be enlarged. The two reforms most likely to have this effect are measures to raise the level of investment and modifications in the tax system that can increase the supply of saving, which is then available for investment and can also stimulate effort. In these happy cases, the greater productive capacity would mean that the potential level of output increases and that the associated natural rate of unemployment falls. Such highly favorable circumstances are seen in Figure 25.3, with the long-run aggregate supply curve (vertical, as we recall) marching steadily to the right as the economy's capacity to produce grows. In the figure, greater productive capacity of the economy means that a higher output level Y_3 can be reached before inflation is triggered. See how the new short-run aggregate supply curve $SRAS_3$ reflects the situation that more can be produced at any level of prices, and how this curve begins its upward turn further to the right than before. Because the potential level of output is higher at Y_3, it follows that a new long-run aggregate supply curve, $LRAS_3$, is positioned at Y_3. Output can now grow to a greater quantity before inflation sets in. The natural rate of unemployment is lower than before.[11]

The tax cuts starting in 1982 were the centerpiece of this type of policy in the United States. The cuts, especially large for those in the highest income brackets, were intended to encourage investment by raising the level of savings, and to raise investment directly because taxes on business were cut as well. The United States did not, however, adopt programs to boost investment through government activity, as has been true of a number of European economies and Japan. Some of these policies are explored in the following chapter on economic growth.

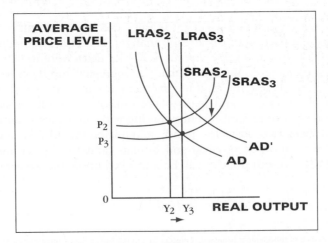

Figure 25.3. Some supply-side reforms may increase the economy's long-run capacity to produce. Some supply-side measures, especially those that raise the level of investment and those that increase the supply of saving, may move LRAS to the right. This indicates a larger capacity to produce. Output can grow to a greater quantity before inflation sets in, and the natural rate of unemployment is lower than before.

---

11.   We have drawn $SRAS_3$ in Figure 25.3 to show a decrease in costs together with an increase in capacity compared to $SRAS_2$. If new investment increased capacity but did not lower production costs, then SRAS would be shifted rightward but its position would not be lowered.

A program of supply-side reforms that aims to increase an economy's productive capacity has to take into account a further ramification. Investment that raises the stock of physical or human capital, or tax cuts that increase the supply of effort, will have the effect of raising aggregate demand.[12] In Figure 25.3, the movement in AD is visible as a rightward shift to the new position AD'. This "Keynesian" result is very likely to be discerned *before* the effect on the capacity of the economy is felt; capacity increases take time to bring about, perhaps several years, whereas the higher spending occurs right away. Many economists believe that the major consequences of the Reagan administration's supply-side policies in the 1980s were actually delivered through an increase in aggregate demand. If this is the case—and the interpretation seems a likely one—then the so-called Reaganomics would be much closer to a standard Keynesian policy than its perpetrators intended. The policy was an odd Keynesian one, however. A smaller budget deficit, with easier money and lower interest rates, would have led to more private capital formation and would have delivered similar economic stimulus without the adverse side-effects. (It should be noted that for long periods in the Reagan administration, and at the start of the Bush administration, many officials in the executive branch were calling for easier monetary policy in the presence of the large federal budget deficit. Fortunately, that inflationary prescription was not tried.)

Any major *supply-side* results for the U.S. economy were still difficult to discern years after the 1982 tax cuts had taken effect. Rather than increasing, saving as a percentage of personal disposable income actually fell.[13] Gross private investment did not rise. Arguably, the reason the tax cuts did not engineer the looked-for supply-side response is that the large U.S. government budget deficit of the 1980s was absorbing the economy's savings. That deficit, 4.1% of U.S. GDP during the period 1980–1986, absorbed over half of U.S. savings in those years. (Net private saving was 6.2% of GDP, while the saving of state and local governments added another 1.3% of GDP, making 7.5%. The 4.1% federal budget deficit is more than half of the 7.5% that was saved.) The resulting higher real interest rates kept the growth in investment from taking place.

A REVIEW

Informed citizens who seek to understand the economies in which they live will find that those economies are at once more manageable than pessimists believe, but less tractable and less certain than optimists hope. *More manageable* in that serious inflations or hyperinflations can be controlled by sensible contractionary monetary and fiscal policies, while deep 1930s-style depressions can be fought with sensible expansionary monetary and fiscal policies. *Less tractable* in that monetary and fiscal policy are unable to eliminate the short-run trade-off between unemployment and inflation, while in the long run lowering unemployment below the natural rate sets in motion a process of increasing costs that eventually raises unemployment once again. *Less certain* in that neither monetary nor fiscal policy have effects entirely as predictable as once believed.

However embarrassing these obstacles are for modern economists, and however difficult they are to solve, they do represent a great advance over the old helplessness in the face of the great depressions and inflations of the past. Perhaps some of the heterodox measures discussed in this chapter will eventually become useful additions to orthodox monetary and fiscal policy, or perhaps further experience with them will find them wanting. The only certainty is that much remains to be done to ensure that full employment, price stability, growth, and satisfactory international economic relations can be achieved at the same time.

---

12.   Investment is part of aggregate demand, so increasing it would raise AD directly. A tax cut, depending on its design, would raise consumption, or investment, or both, and so again AD would move to the right.

13.   Saving was 7.5% of personal disposable income in 1981, but only 3.9% in 1986. As a counterpart of this fall in savings, consumption rose, from 62.8% of GDP in 1979 to 65.8% in 1986.

SUMMARY

1) Heterodox methods are not a substitute for orthodox monetary and fiscal policies in combatting recession and inflation. Under some circumstances, however, they might provide a useful way to combat unemployment without adverse effects on inflation or combat inflation without causing worse unemployment. For example, this might allow a heterodox method to be used to attack unemployment while orthodox policy is used to restrain inflation.

2) Labor-market policies may make it possible to bring down the level of long-term structural unemployment. Examples of such policies include reducing taxes that boost the costs of labor, and programs to train labor and increase its mobility. Well-known examples include the German apprenticeship program and the Swedish emphasis on training for the unemployed. By contrast, the United States has made less use of such programs, and government has been lax in coordinating information about job openings. Yet there is also a school of thought that the U.S. emphasis on general education may be a better way to cope with rapid economic change, which tends to make specific training obsolete.

3) Inflation can be attacked by incomes policies including wage-price controls or lived with by means of indexing of wages. But neither policy has as much support among economists as formerly because of the damaging side effects that accompany their use.

4) Supply-side reforms that reduce the cost of output can be used to counter inflation. Among the possibilities for reducing costs are agricultural reform, abandoning preferences in government purchases, reconsidering government actions that boost labor costs, reducing trade barriers, freeing markets for services, lowering taxes, and raising the investment in physical and human capital.

5) Some supply-side measures, particularly those that raise the level of investment and those that increase the supply of saving, may move the long-run aggregate supply curve to the right, reflecting a larger capacity to produce. Output can grow to a greater quantity before inflation sets in, and the natural rate of unemployment is lower than before.

Chapter Key Words

Heterodox policies: Unorthodox methods for achieving macroeconomic stability, as distinct from orthodox monetary and fiscal policy. The major example used against inflation is wage-price controls. The major example used against unemployment involves government labor-market policies.

Incomes policies: A heterodox policy to control rises in incomes without reducing aggregate demand, sometimes used to combat inflation.

Indexing: An attempt to render inflation harmless by adjusting wages and salaries, pensions, taxes, and so forth, to reflect the amount of inflation. Pioneered by Brazil. Has lost popularity, even in Brazil, because restraining inflation becomes more difficult.

Job sharing: The concept that rather than laying off workers, firms might shorten the work week and spread the work around among all the job holders.

Orthodox policies: Monetary and fiscal policy, as distinct from *heterodox policies*, which see.

Supply-side reforms: The term used to describe measures that would lessen the cost of output by pushing down the position of the aggregate supply curve. Examples include agricultural reform, deregulation of services, investment in physical and human capital, measures to reduce labor costs, tax reform, and the elimination of protectionism in foreign trade. Important for economic growth.

TIP: "Tax-Based Incomes Policy," rewarding firms that stay within some norm for wage increases with a lower tax bill.

Wage-price controls: A heterodox measure to control inflation by legal controls on wage and price increases. Have lost allure because shortages and other distortions are likely to result, but potentially useful in countering expectations of inflation. Used in the United States during 1971–1974.

Workfare: The requirement that recipients of welfare benefits must take training or a job.

CHAPTER QUESTIONS

1) Supporters of a government training program claim that the increased productivity of the graduates justifies the cost of the program. If this is true, why do firms not undertake the training on their own?

2) Arguing against government training, a Senator claims, "An expensive government training program can lead to one of two results: higher interest rates and less investment, or a full-blown contraction in output." Is this comment just political grandstanding, or does the Senator have a point?

3) A supply shock has hit the economy, and the President has imposed wage and price controls for a few months. The time is fast approaching to lift the controls. Discuss the inflation-fighting effectiveness of each of the following policies that could be implemented after the controls are lifted:
   a) Doing nothing.
   b) Jawboning.
   c) Instituting contractionary monetary policy.

4) During the recovery from the 1992 recession, inflation was very low for a long time. However, there were some months in which it picked up a bit. How do you think things would have been different if the U.S. economy were as heavily indexed as Brazil's once was?

5) The government is considering three policies to fight a negative supply shock. They are:
   a) increasing investment in infrastructure,
   b) reducing agricultural subsidies, and
   c) repealing the minimum-wage law. Draw AS-AD diagrams showing how each policy would affect the economy.

6) Suppose the government begins a massive program to improve education. The idea is to increase the quality of labor and shift the AS curve down. After a few years, however, inflation has actually risen. How can this be?

Economic Growth in Market Economies

OVERALL OBJECTIVE: To explore the causes of long-run economic growth and assess what might be done about the recent slowdown in growth.

MORE SPECIFICALLY:

■ To present a production function that ties growth in output to changes in the factors of production, emphasizing that the efficiency with which the factors of production are used (intensive growth) is more important than additions to their physical quantity (extensive growth).

■ To emphasize the great importance of technical change and education as causes of economic growth.

■ To call attention to the recent slowing of productivity gains and decline of long-term economic growth in all major countries—a decline that has been pronounced in the United States—to explore the causes of the slowdown, and to suggest what might be done about it.

■ To consider whether a national industrial policy such as that utilized by Japan might be useful for the United States.

Economic growth, the major question addressed in this chapter, is central to the study of market economies. In the long run, a slowdown in the rate of growth would reduce the ultimate ability of the market system to satisfy those who live and work under it. That could ultimately be more important than the short-run ebb and flow of recessions and inflations that have occupied us thus far.

What are the causes of long-run economic growth? Why has it slowed down in recent years? The answers to these questions are not entirely certain. Even an approach to them requires a general knowledge of the principles of macro, which is the reason we come to them so far along in the book.

▶ WHAT ARE THE CAUSES OF ECONOMIC GROWTH?

Growth involves the economy's supply-side, as introduced in the preceding chapter— the determinants of how much an economy is physically capable of producing. Let us define economic growth as an increase over time in a country's productive capacity (which would involve an outward shift in the production possibilities curve of Chapter 1). Greater productive capacity is the key to higher levels of living because it allows for greater real output (GDP) per person.[1] Countries unable to deliver better living conditions, like the former communist countries, run the risk of political upheaval.

Economists who study economic growth view it as the outcome of changes in a "production function" relating growth to the factors of production. There is wide agreement that improvement in any of the following categories promotes growth:

1) The amount and quality of labor, including skills, education, training, and other forms of learning, health, and the length of the work week. Population growth and the willingness of people to become members of the labor force govern the amount of labor, while **human capital** formation—that is, the amount of investment in education, training, and so forth—governs its quality.
2) The amount and quality of land, including natural resources and climate. New discoveries of natural resources and more efficient use of existing natural resources are included here.
3) The amount and quality of physical capital (plant and equipment), and the **infrastructure** of transportation, communications, power, and marketing facilities.
4) Technical change, including the improvements that flow from research and development activity. Technical change increases the productivity of the other factors of production.
5) The amount and quality of entrepreneurial input. This includes an ability and willingness of entrepreneurs to innovate and to transfer resources away from less effective uses and into more effective ones.
6) Economies of scale and specialization as the size of the market grows.
7) Psychological, cultural, and social changes that lead to growth. These include providing a structure of commercial law, maintaining order and good government, developing attitudes favorable to work, containing prejudice, and the like.

Growth can occur because the quantity of factor inputs rises, as when more labor, more land and natural resources, more capital, and more entrepreneurship become available. This is **extensive growth**, occurring because the economy is becoming larger. For many centuries, extensive growth predominated. By the twentieth century, it was apparent that **intensive growth**—that is, increases in the quality of the existing factors and the way they are combined—

---

1.   The greater capacity will permit a country to achieve higher output without triggering inflation. In recent chapters we have been discussing movements of actual output around the potential level; here we focus on a rise in the potential level itself. For a discussion of how output is measured and the dangers involved in equating GDP with levels of living, see chapter 15.

was becoming the predominant contributor to overall progress. Intensive growth serves to increase the output from a given amount of factor input, which most economists now believe is the key to better levels of living.

Whether extensive or intensive, growth is obviously subject to market influences. For example, if workers see that they can raise their incomes by acquiring more training and education, then the market system provides an economic incentive for them to take the training or return to school. The lure of profit leads to the development of new supplies of natural resources. Potential profit also provides the motive for firms to invest in new capital and to search for technical improvements. Profit leads aspiring entrepreneurs to business school, to innovate, and to shift resources under their control from less productive to more productive uses. Finally, profit gives an incentive for exploiting economies of scale. To the extent that these motivations are operating, the market system will be oriented toward economic growth.

THE EFFICIENCY OF THE PRODUCTIVE FACTORS IS MORE IMPORTANT THAN THEIR PHYSICAL QUANTITY

Early attempts at measuring the importance of each category of inputs in the growth process, made in the 1950s and 1960s, yielded surprising results. Growth theorists studying the U.S. economy agreed that the *physical quantity* of the factors of production were less important than the *productivity* of those factors. These studies revealed that much in the growth process is not explained by physical accumulation.

We are already familiar (from Chapter 11) with the concept of productivity as it relates to the determination of incomes. The standard measure is labor productivity, that is, the efficiency with which a quantity of output is obtained from a given quantity of labor input. So, if L = annual input of labor in quantitative terms (hours worked), while Y = a nation's annual quantity (real value) of output, then labor productivity is measured by the fraction Y/L. If labor productivity improves, then the economy will be able to obtain more output (Y) per year from a given annual amount of labor input (L) and the value of Y/L rises. Broadly, labor productivity reflects the efficiency of production, and increases in it are the key to economic growth.

STATISTICAL INVESTIGATION OF THE CAUSES OF INCOME GROWTH

The work of Edward Denison is prominent among the economists who study the causes of economic growth. It shows how important efficiency is.[2] Denison's pioneering study of 1962 utilized statistical methods to break down the contribution of separate productive factors to the growth in real income per worker in the United States during the period 1929 to 1957. Denison demonstrated that most of the increase in real income per worker in those years was due to qualitative change in the economy's inputs, and not to the physical quantity of those inputs. Table 26.1 summarizes Denison's work, which identifies the proportion of growth contributed by each of the listed items during the periods shown.

Notice the critical importance of education. Less than 5% of all Americans had a college education in 1940, and only a quarter had a high school diploma, whereas in 1992, 21% had a college degree and nearly four-fifths had completed high school. Recent studies with identical twins indicate that one year of additional schooling raises average earnings per person by 16%.[3] The enlargement of human capital through education has made it possible to increase productivity by establishing more specialized jobs requiring a greater degree of learning. At the turn of this century, a few hundred types of machinery could be built, operated, and repaired with a

---

2.   Denison's work was built on a foundation laid by Robert Solow of MIT, who won the 1987 Nobel Prize largely for his work on economic growth.

3   Orley Ashenfelter and Alan Krueger, "Estimates of the Economic Return to Schooling from a New Sample of Twins," *NBER Working Paper No. 4143,* 1992.

few hundred skills and specialties in the labor force. But today the various types of machinery, equipment, and electronic hardware number close to a million; this requires a commensurate increase in the skills and training of workers. The industrial "proletariat" of unskilled workers has given way to a work force in which skills and education rather than muscle power are the predominate determinants of labor productivity.

During the 1929–1957 period first studied by Denison, technical progress was almost equal to education in its contribution to the growth in income per worker. Technical progress involves better knowledge about production, better management, and more specialized and productive equipment. Technical change made it possible to design and build for greater specialization, and the higher levels of human capital were a major factor in making the technical change possible.

Other important aspects of income growth were the higher productivity of labor associated with fewer hours worked, and the impact of scale economies. Together with the human capital added through education and skills, and rapid technical change, these explained the bulk of the increases in real income. In total they were large enough to offset some reduction in hours worked per person as the work week was reduced.

When Denison's research methods were applied to the periods of 1909–1929 and 1948–1973, the basic conclusions remained the same. From 1909–1929, the significance of the quantity of capital was substantially higher, but still far behind other factors in explanatory power. The years 1948–1973 showed much the same results, with technical change rising in importance to a point where it explained more about the growth in income per worker than all the other determinants together. The findings did not support the view generally held by earlier economists that the physical volume of the factors of production was the pivotal determinant of economic growth, and that remains a fundamental conclusion of growth theory.

It should be noted that a large stock of natural resources has been central to the growth of some countries. Saudi Arabia and Libya without oil would doubtless be poor, and in U.S. and Canadian history resource extraction was important. Yet it should also be pointed out that some of the world's fastest-growing countries have very few natural resources (Japan, South Korea, Taiwan) or none at all (Singapore, Hong Kong).

TABLE 26.1
Contribution to growth in real income per worker, 1909–1973.
(Calculated as percentage contributed to growth of income during the period indicated)

	1909–1929	1929–1957	1948–1973
Volume of capital	29	9	15
Reduction in hours worked	-19	-33	-8
Education	29	42	19
Effect of fewer hours on labor quality	19	21	—
Change in age and sex composition of labor force	—	—	-8
Technical progress (knowledge)	20	36	54
Economies of scale	23	21	15
Improved allocation of resources	—	—	15

Sources: E.F. Denison, *The Sources of Economic Growth in the United States and the Alternatives Before Us,* New York, 1962; *Why Growth Rates Differ,* Washington D.C., 1967; *Accounting for United States Economic Growth,* 1929-1969, Washington D.C., 1974; and *Trends in American Economic Growth,* 1929-1982, Washington D.C., 1985. Column totals do not add to 100% due to rounding and omission of several minor items. Where numbers do not appear, they were not calculated or were negligible for the years in question.

HOW SUCH FIGURES ARE OBTAINED

The method involved in assessing the contributions made by the various factors of production to output growth is as follows: Say that output (GDP) grows 9% over five years. Say also that employment (labor hours) grew by 5% during this period while the capital stock grew by 10%. Finally, say that labor receives 70% of total income as wages and salaries while capital receives 30%, in the form of interest and profit. Labor's weight in total income is thus 70%, while capital's is 30%. The 5% growth in employment, weighted at 70%, can be interpreted to mean that labor contributed 5% x 70% = 3.5 percentage points to the total output growth of 9%. Similarly, we can estimate that capital contributed 10% x 30% = 3.0 percentage points. So labor and capital together contributed 6.5 percentage points to the total growth of 9%. There is then a residual of 2.5 percentage points that must be due to technological improvement and other factors. Similar methods can be used to break down the contribution of educated and skilled labor versus uneducated and unskilled, and so on.[4]

**The Small Contribution
of the Volume of Capital in
These Studies May Be Misleading**

As a country acquires a greater capital stock, it is reasonable to posit that diminishing returns will set in, with the marginal productivity of new investment tending to fall. That would seem to explain the substantial decline in the contribution to growth made by additions to the physical volume of capital, seen in the first line of Table 26.1. Yet such a view might be misleading. Consider that capital investment is decidedly more productive in most rich countries than in most poor ones. That immediately gives rise to doubts about diminishing returns to capital investment. A recent view is that accumulation of physical capital may be subject to increasing returns rather than the reverse. New investment in physical capital allows technological change and research and development to be put in place and have an effect. Otherwise the technical R&D successes may be "disembodied," possessing no way to empower greater productivity. In this light, investment in physical capital can be seen as enabling knowledge to be put to use and, in turn, making the investment more effective.

Why Productivity Increases Are So Important

That productivity has grown historically is a point of exceptional significance for levels of living. Consider what would happen if no productivity increases ever occurred. If population grew but the physical quantity of capital (tools, machinery) did not, then each worker would have less and less capital to work with. All things being equal, there would be diminishing returns to labor which would become *less* productive, and therefore income per worker would fall. If population grew and the physical quantity of capital grew at the same rate, then labor would maintain its productivity; average wages and levels of living would stay the same. If labor's productivity were to grow, however, then average wages and levels of living would improve. Consider the example in Table 26.2: If at age 22 you were to take a job paying $20,000, depending on how fast productivity has grown your annual wage at retirement (65) would be as follows :

---

4.   This explanation is based on Charles L. Schultze, *Memos to the President,* Washington D.C., 1992, p. 234.

TABLE 26.2
Income growth depends upon productivity growth.

If the growth rate of productivity is:	then your income at age 65 will be:
0.5%	$24,784
1.0%	$30,679
1.5%	$37,937
2.0%	$46,863
3.0%	$71,290
3.5%	$87,794
5.0%	$162,993

Virtually all economists now agree that changes in the productivity of the factors of production (intensive growth), and not simply the available quantity of these factors (extensive growth), are a central feature in improving the level of living. Unfortunately, the great variety of elements that contribute to productivity change—technical progress, human capital formation, gains from more efficient resource allocation—are complex, and studying the effects of changes in them is very difficult. Yet such analysis is absolutely essential: Comparisons among countries reveal that the effectiveness (productivity) of the factors of production can be dramatically different. For example, from a given amount of capital investment some nations are able to obtain a rise in output *four times* higher than some other countries.

The U.S. Growth Record

Measured by annual changes in real GNP in the century following the Civil War, U.S. economic growth was an excellent 3.6% per year, exceeded among major market economies only by Japan's 3.8% and far ahead of Germany's 2.8%, Britain's 1.9%, and France's 1.7%. During that hundred-year period, growth became increasingly more intensive, that is, dependent on productivity increases. Since the 1960s, U.S. growth has not been nearly so satisfactory. Annually it averaged only 1.7% in real terms between 1965 and 1990. That figure is last on the list of the major western industrial countries, as Table 26.3 shows. Among the smaller industrial market economies, real growth from 1965–1990 was lower than that of the United States only in New Zealand (1.1% per year).

TABLE 26.3
Average annual growth in real GNP, 1965–1990, in percent.

Japan	4.1
Italy	3.0
Canada	2.7
Germany (West)	2.4
France	2.4
Britain	2.0
Netherlands	1.8
United States	1.7

Source: World Bank, *World Development Report 1992*, p. 219.

THE SLOWING OF PRODUCTIVITY GAINS AND THE DECLINE IN ECONOMIC GROWTH

Adam Smith believed that growth would take care of itself through the operations of the "invisible hand." Later classical economists such as David Ricardo and John Stuart Mill were concerned that growth would present a significant long-term problem for market systems. They suggested that as the demand for food increased with population and income growth, food prices would rise, forcing up wages and rents. These higher costs for business would diminish the rate of profit, inexorably, until growth ceased in what they called the "stationary state." Nearly two centuries of virtually uninterrupted growth proved them wrong.

Yet, worrisomely, economic growth *has* declined noticeably during the most recent quarter-century. This interruption to a long trend calls for explanation. There is wide agreement that *the proximate cause of the decline in U.S. economic growth is the slowdown in the growth of U.S. productivity*. Table 26.4 shows how dramatic this slowdown has been, after years of steady increase during the century after 1870.

TABLE 26.4
The slowdown in the growth of U.S. productivity, 1870–1990.

Years	U.S. Productivity Growth, Percent
1870–1913	2.0
1913–1950	2.4
1950–1973	2.5
1973–1984	1.0
1985–1990	0.6

Source: Angus Maddison, "Growth and Slowdown in Advanced Capitalist Economies," *Journal of Economic Literature,* Vol. 25, No. 2, June 1987, p. 650, for 1870-1984, and *Economic Report to the President,* Washington, D.C., 1993, Table B-45, for 1985-1990. The definition used is labor productivity computed as GDP ÷ hours worked.

The slowdown has affected other advanced countries as well, as Table 26.5 shows, although the U.S. decline has been deeper and to a lower level than that of the others.

TABLE 26.5
The productivity decline has affected most countries.
(annual rate of productivity growth, percent)

	France	Germany (West)	Japan	Britain	United States
1950–1973	5.1	6.0	7.7	3.2	2.5
1973–1984	3.4	3.0	3.2	2.4	1.0

Source: See Table 26.4.

It has been a damaging development; had U.S. productivity kept up the pace even of its slower advance in the late 1960s and early 1970s, U.S. GDP would now be about 50% higher than it is. Indeed, *many* economic problems of the present—including the budget deficit, tax questions, spending for defense, education, transport, medical care, the elderly—could be much more easily addressed if productivity were to resume its earlier growth path.[5]

5.   Recently, U.S. labor productivity has started to rise again. From a tiny increase of 0.1% in 1990, it was up by 1.4% in 1991 and 2.8% in 1992. But heartening as these figures are, they do not necessarily indicate that the long-run decline in productivity has been arrested. These were years of recession and the beginning of recovery, and labor productivity almost always rises under these conditions. That is because in a business slump, firms tend to lay off their least productive workers and keep their most productive. Output does not fall by as much as would have been the case if all the workers had equal productivity. Then when recovery begins it is usually possible for firms to increase their output by utilizing their existing workforce more intensively. Whether the productivity gains will continue after the recovery is well underway was, at the time of writing, not yet clear. There are reasons to expect that perhaps the gains will indeed continue. First, the average age of the population is rising as the baby boom slows, so the experience level in the workforce is rising. Second, the higher cost of labor due to labor scarcity will probably stimulate capital investment and raise labor productivity. Third, the lower real interest rates of recent years, partly due to Federal Reserve credibility in keeping inflation under control and partly to the lower federal budget deficit, should stimulate capital investment.

WHY HAS PRODUCTIVITY GROWTH SLOWED DOWN?

The reasons for the falling off in productivity growth are much debated and cannot be explained in a fully satisfactory way. The following reasons are, however, probably most significant, though agreement is lacking on their relative importance.

A Decline in Saving and a Decrease in the Growth of Capital per Worker

Inadequate national saving has probably played a central role in the decline of productivity. National saving is important because low saving leads to low investment, further cuts in productivity because labor has less capital to work with, falling output, and lower levels of living. If, conversely, a country can save more, it can increase its investment, so raising the amount of capital per worker and increasing labor productivity.[6]

Figure 26.1 below shows the sharp decline in U.S. national saving from the 1960s to 1990.

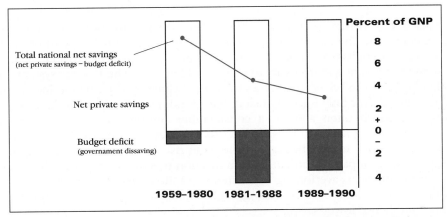

Source: Congressional Budget Office data. See Charles L. Schultze, *Memos to the President,* Washington D.C., 1992, pp. 46–47, 50. The graphical method is taken from *The Economist,* March 25, 1989.

Figure 26.1. U.S. net national saving as a percentage of national income, 1959–1990. Total net national saving, shown by the black dots, has fallen because net private saving has declined while the federal budget deficit has increased.

U.S. total net national saving, shown by the black dots, was over 8% of national income in 1959–1980, but had fallen to just 3% in 1989–1990.[7] Total net saving is less than private net saving because the government's budget deficit absorbs some of the saving. Though the deficit explains part of the fall in total saving, more than half of the decline is due to the reduction in *private* saving from 9.6% of national income in 1959–1980 to 6.6% in 1989–1990.[8]

Saving has also declined elsewhere, but the fall in the United States has been to levels lower than in most other developed countries. Table 26.6 makes the comparisons.

---

6.   Notice, however, that given Denison's calculations just discussed, simply raising saving to boost the stock of capital while doing nothing else would presumably be a slow way to increase economic growth.

7.   Total net national saving is defined as follows: household saving plus business saving plus government saving = gross saving. Gross saving - depreciation = net saving. Net saving ÷ national income = the net saving rate.

8.   The complete figures, taken from Schultze, *Memos to the President,* pp. 46–47, are as follows. U.S. net national saving as a percentage of national income: 1959-1980, 8.2%; 1981-88, 4.2%; 1989-90, 3.0%. U.S. private saving as a percentage of national income: 1959-80, 9.6%; 1981-88, 8.7%; 1989-1990, 6.6%. Government budget deficit: 1959-80, -1.4%; 1981-88, -4.5%; 1989-90, -3.6%.

TABLE 26.6
Net national saving by country as a percent of income, 1990

Canada	7.0
France	9.8
Germany	14.9
Great Britain	5.1
Japan	23.6
United States	2.5

Source: Charles Horioka, "Japan's Consumption and Saving in International Perspective," *Economic Development and Cultural Change,* Vol. 42, No. 2, January 1994, p. 311. There are some measurement biases (mostly having to do with the treatment of depreciation and consumer durables) that exaggerate Japan's saving by perhaps 2 to 3 percentage points and underestimate U.S. saving by another 2 to 3 percentage points, but they do not alter the general case that the United States is a low saver.

What has caused U.S. private saving to decline? The reasons are not entirely certain. Some possibilities include: (a) The baby boom generation is at an age of high spending, so inhibiting saving. Increasing materialism and high housing costs play a role. (b) Improvements in the Social Security system have meant less necessity to save for old age. (c) The U.S. tax system, unlike that of many other countries, gives no incentives to saving, which is taxed by the income tax just as consumption is taxed. Not only is saving taxed, but spending in the form of the interest paid on home mortgages, which often absorbs a considerable amount of a family's income, is tax deductible. Less therefore needs to be saved in order to buy a home. (d) In the years shown in Figure 26.1, a great stock market boom and the large rise in the value of housing made many people richer, at least on paper, and cut their motivation to save. At the same time, easier credit terms reduced the need to save for big ticket items. (e) Slow growth has cut into the ability to save, creating a vicious circle of lower saving, higher interest rates, reduced capital investment, lower income, and hence lower saving.

Private saving is hard to raise by means of economic policy, as experience shows. Private saving is rather insensitive to increases in interest rates, perhaps because people saving for retirement need to save less as interest rates rise. So though higher rates do increase the reward for saving, they also lower the necessity for doing so.

Saving is the only source of investment. The decline in U.S. national saving has thus meant a decline in the level of investment. For example, in the period 1959–1980, U.S. national saving of 8.2% of national income was enough to finance a high level of domestic investment (7.8%) with a little left over for U.S. investment abroad (0.5%). In 1989–1990 investment was much diminished, to 4.9% of national income. Of that figure, 3.0% came from national saving. Foreigners were willing to lend to the United States, and this foreign saving equal to 1.9% of U.S. national income boosted U.S. investment to the reported 4.9% of national income.[9] This slippage in the amount of investment meant U.S. workers had to make do with fewer machines in older factories than would have been the case if investment had been maintained.

The Erosion of the Public Infrastructure

The decrease in U.S. investment has been pronounced in the public sector, with erosion in the infrastructure of education and transport. The reason is largely political. During the Reagan administration, there was a revolt against "big government" and a general unwillingness to pay

---

9.   From Charles L. Schultze, *Memos to the President,* Washington D.C., 1992, pp. 46–47, 50. On average in the 1980s, a decline of $1.00 in domestic saving caused a fall in investment of about 79¢. The figure used to be about 90¢ before the appearance of much foreign lending to the United States. Such foreign lending has recently gone into decline, however. See Martin Feldstein and Philippe Bacchetta, "National Saving and International Investment," NBER Working Paper No. 3164, 1990.

more taxes. As a result, the stock of public capital in the United States grew less than 20% as much in the 1980s as it did in the 1950s. Public sector investment is very low in comparison to other major countries: In net terms, U.S. federal civilian fixed investment as a percentage of GNP is currently about one-third of 1%, compared to 1.5% in Canada, about 2% in Britain and Italy, over 2% in France and Germany, and over 5% in Japan.

Growth theorists claim that educational and technical progress are the most important factors in the growth of real income per worker during this entire century. Americans are, however, now used to hearing bad news about their educational system. Americans are in school as long as they used to be, so any decline in productivity because of educational deficiencies must be due to changes in educational quality, not quantity. For example, the SAT scores of U.S. high school seniors fell from 958 verbal plus math in 1967 to 899 in 1992.[10] Though perhaps half of this decline is due simply to a larger proportion of students taking the test, the trend is nonetheless disturbing. Studies by John Bishop of Cornell University indicate that productivity was almost 4% lower than it would have been without the decline.[11]

Over a quarter of the students in U.S. high schools simply drop out. The *average* Japanese 12th grader has better math scores than 95% of American 12th graders. U.S. students were last among those of the major industrial countries in separate testing of knowledge in math and geography. Two-thirds of the physics teachers in U.S. high schools have never taken a college course in physics.

According to the *National Assessment of Educational Progress,* national testing in the United States in 1986 and 1988 revealed that only 6% of 17-year-olds were able to use basic algebra or to solve problems that required multiple steps. Just 8% knew how to draw conclusions and infer relationships based on scientific knowledge; only 5% were able to interpret and use specialized reading materials. Tests in 1988 that compared the results in six major industrialized countries showed U.S. students least qualified in mathematics and next to last in science. No wonder why: American high school students spend just $3\frac{1}{2}$ hours per week studying compared to 24 hours watching television. Japanese students on average study 19 hours per week and watch TV for less than 4 hours.[12]

If the only repercussions of all this were that Americans are becoming a little less intelligent than they used to be, and than foreigners are, it might simply be ignored as too bad but not important. But it is important because there is plenty of evidence that living standards will eventually fall as a result. A survey by the National Association of Manufacturers that included 400 of its member firms revealed that one-third of the companies regularly turn down applicants because they cannot read properly, while one-fourth reject them because of their poor communications skills and inadequacies in their basic mathematics.[13]

It is unlikely that capital will be redesigned, especially in any short time period, to accommodate the "dumbing down" of the labor force. Therefore the situation is hindering attempts to raise productivity. Of the firms surveyed by the NAM, 30% said they could not

---

10.   But the 1992 figure represented a slight rise over 1991, the first in years. See *Statistical Abstract of the United States 1993,* Table 265.

11.   John Bishop, "Is the Test Score Decline Responsible for the Productivity Decline?" *American Economic Review,* Vol. 79, March 1989, pp. 178–197.

12.   The data are from Timothy Tregarthen in *The Margin,* Vol. 7, Fall, 1991, p. 26. The schools should receive only part of the blame. Attitudes toward learning and toward work are, of course, formed partly in the home and in the streets. The high divorce rate that has led to many broken homes, the lessening of the cultural and religious ethic that prizes personal industry and deprecates idleness, and the fear prevalent in the school-age population of many cities have all contributed to the problem.

13.   Superficially, reading ability does not seem that much of a problem: the U.S. literacy rate is 99%, the same as for the other highly developed countries. But this figure is for reading at a quite elementary level. Examining more closely, one finds that about 40% of those who can read do not in general choose to, and 60% of all American families do not buy as much as one book a year. See *The Economist,* February 29, 1992.

reorganize work activities because the employees lacked the skills to learn new jobs, while 25% said they could not improve the quality of their product because the workers were unable to learn the skills that would be necessary. A quarter of the companies made the disconcerting admission that they had been forced to cut their entry-level standards. They had no choice, they said, even though they realized that the lower standards would result in reduced product quality. The NAM report concludes by stating that 60% of the new jobs in the United States will require education beyond high school, while 70% of the new entrants to the labor force will not meet that standard. The report speaks of the decline in educational quality as sowing the "seeds of a new underclass."

Education is not the only area of decline. The advancing and sometimes alarming disrepair of streets, highways, bridges, railroads, docks, dams, water and sewage systems, mass transit, airport facilities, and the like create extra costs for the private firms that utilize this infrastructure as an input. Such firms will be less productive, and less competitive with producers in countries where the decay has not occurred. David Aschauer of Bates College, a critic of infrastructure decline, asserts that the lower efficiency of the public sector causes the private sector to be less efficient as well. Trucks go more slowly and wear out faster on poor road surfaces, tracks and ties in poor repair keep speeds low on the railroads, and so forth. Aschauer estimates that if public investment had stayed at its level for 1953–1969, then during 1970–1988 the rate of return to private capital investment would have been higher by about 22%, while productivity in the private sector would have been greater by about half again.

Many economists have taken the position that these numbers are exaggerated.[14] These skeptics argue that if the years covered are altered, the Aschauer results are modified, indicating a lower efficacy of public investment. Also, critics point out that some public investments, such as dams for irrigation, supersonic transport aircraft, and the supercollider, do not promise very high benefits. Both critics and supporters would agree that not all public investment needs to be enhanced. Moreover, even if Aschauer is correct, we must recall that if increased public investment is funded by running up the budget deficit, there could be a crowding-out effect on private investment. In that case, the return to the public investment would have to be considerably higher than the return to private investment to make deficit spending for capital investment a safe course of action.

The decay in the infrastructure of education and transport has other causes besides the neglect of public investment in these areas, but that neglect is certainly one important cause. It is also fair to add that the inadequacy of public infrastructure is sometimes due to damaging pricing policies, with prices set well below equilibrium. Take highways as a prime example. The fees paid by heavy trucks do not cover the cost of the damage they do to highways; tolls are not charged on crowded portions of the interstate system; time-of-day pricing is seldom used on toll roads; gasoline is not priced to cover the environmental costs of the automobile. With the pricing as questionable as this, it is important to "get the prices right" as well as to increase investment in the system.

The Switch from Manufacturing to Services

As countries have grown richer, manufacturing (as well as mining and agriculture) has been losing ground to services. In the United States, for instance, an average of 46% of the population was employed in the service sector, 1913–1950, but the figure was 80% in 1992. This happens because a richer society wants more medical care, education, transportation, vacations, communications, insurance, banking, brokerage, restaurant meals, and so forth. That would be unremarkable, except that historically productivity growth has been greater in manufacturing jobs than in service jobs. For example, it has been easy to increase the productivity of steel and auto workers with improved machinery and more advanced technology. The workers in these industries

---

14.   A volume investigating the extent of the "infrastructure crisis," Alicia H. Munnell, ed., *Is There a Shortfall in Public Capital Investment?* Boston, 1990, also suggests a high return on public investment. For criticisms of the Aschauer/Munnell position, and a rebuttal to them, see Alicia H. Munnell, "Infrastructure Investment and Economic Growth," *Journal of Economic Perspectives,* Vol. 6, No. 4, Fall 1992, pp. 189–198.

then produce larger quantities than before of valuable output. In service industries it is more difficult to raise productivity. It is doubtful whether faster-talking professors would cause their students to learn more; nurses cannot easily raise the number of hospital patients they can care for in an hour; waiters and waitresses have to walk and cannot very well run.

Similarly, it is hard to raise productivity in a wide range of services including health care, postal delivery, legal advising, day care, street cleaning, finance and insurance, management of government and business, and the like. As the prices of these services rise they will appear more important in the national product, and their stagnant productivity will bias downward the entire nation's productivity. Avoiding the problem looks difficult or impossible.

Corporate Policies

A case can be made that corporate policies in the 1980s caused capital investment to receive less attention than "paper" activities such as speculation, mergers, corporate raiding, and hostile takeovers. The popularity of "leveraged buy-outs" with borrowed money meant that many firms incurred very large interest bills. These bills arguably limited managers' time horizons as they aimed for short-run rather than long-run profitability, another aspect of the continuing separation between ownership and management discussed in the appendix to Chapter 8. They were doing so because the stock market pays careful attention to companies' quarterly earnings reports. Indeed, managerial pay and perquisites *are* frequently linked to share value, and hence to firms' profits in the short run. As a result, long-term investment may have been neglected to some degree.

Neglect also overtook research and development (R&D) spending and the training of workers, which as the venue for introducing technical change are certainly important in the determination of productivity. F.M. Scherer of the University of Pennsylvania argues that a major problem with R&D has been the failure of U.S. firms to react to technical challenges from abroad, with firms often cutting back on their R&D outlays rather than increasing them as they face greater competition from imports. U.S. R&D at 1.8% of GNP now lags considerably behind Germany's 2.5% and Japan's 2.7%. To be sure, the United States does relatively well in government support for basic research, but not so well in government support for commercial applications of the research. This is the sort of R&D that applies basic discoveries to products. The U.S. government support for research is heavily concentrated in the areas of health, environment, and space (59% of government support went for this purpose in 1987, with only 41% for other purposes). But in Germany, the figures were 13% and 87% respectively, while in France, 15% and 85%, and in Japan, 9% and 91%.[15]

The Inexperienced Worker Problem

The proportion of inexperienced workers in the labor force grew as "baby boomers" and housewives entered the labor force. Large numbers of young and inexperienced workers dilute the impact of the older and more experienced workers and cause a decline in productivity. This development has already been discussed in Chapter 24. It is ultimately self-correcting, and much correction has in fact already occurred, but it nonetheless has had and still has an effect.

Higher Costs of Energy and Regulation

Finally, the economy was affected by higher costs because of the oil cartel's restrictions on oil supplies, and to a lesser extent because of government regulation, such as occupational and safety standards, environmental controls, and product liability laws. For example, crude oil prices were approximately $3 per barrel in 1972, and over $30 per barrel in 1979. The rise in energy costs in the 1970s meant that large quantities of energy-using plant and equipment became obsolete and had to be replaced. This higher depreciation meant that the net growth of the capital stock slowed. The costs of government regulation have also increased, although it must be

---

15.   Schultze, *Memos to the President,* Washington D.C., 1992, p. 304.

remembered that regulations often were adopted to reduce the even greater costs of environmental deterioration. To that degree, the decline in measured productivity occurred only because the statisticians did not include environmental improvement in their calculation of the economy's output.

▶ WHAT TO DO ABOUT THE DECLINE IN PRODUCTIVITY

Numerous ideas have been advanced for addressing the decline in productivity in the United States. Some would involve changes in government policy, most of which could be implemented rather quickly if voters wanted to do so. Others would involve more fundamental changes in the conduct of the economy and could presumably occur only in the long run.

GOVERNMENT POLICY CHANGES TO ADDRESS THE DECLINE IN PRODUCTIVITY

Several government policy measures could be used to reverse the damaging fall in net saving and investment. Decreasing the budget deficit would lower real interest rates and therefore promote investment. Investment might also be encouraged by giving a tax credit to firms undertaking new investment. (Though President Clinton favors this approach, an investment tax credit was dropped from the 1993 budget bill.) Giving a tax advantage to saving would also contribute to decreased interest rates. Lowering the income tax and adopting a national VAT would likely have this effect, while raising the marginal rate of income tax and creating a large deduction for saving could have similar results. (But again, remember Edward Denison's studies. Raising investment is unlikely to be a complete answer to the decline in productivity because capital is not the main contributor to economic growth. Growth from that source is well worth having, but for more major gains, the infrastructure, education, and technical change will have to be addressed.)

Other measures could address the decay of the infrastructure. Some spending could be transferred away from the military, agricultural subsidies, and Social Security payments to those who are not in need of them. That could fund additional spending on education, transport, and communications. These recommendations might also require higher taxes, which is politically difficult. Furthermore, if the economy is in recession, higher taxes would do fiscal damage. In that case, the new infrastructure investment could instead be accomplished by means of some additional deficit spending, which would deliver welcome fiscal stimulus along with the improved infrastructure. Unfortunately, the giant deficits of recent years limit this course of action—although perhaps a modest increase in the deficit of, say, $50 billion, for capital investment might be permissible in a long-extended recession. As recovery from recession is achieved, the investment could be continued, not by running up the deficit (which should be cut) but instead by reductions in defense spending and some of the entitlement programs, together with a dose of higher taxation.

In education and training, more spending without thorough reform is unlikely to be a complete solution. It would, however, allow a rise in teacher pay, now averaging about $30,000 per year, to a point closer to the Japanese and German figure of about $50,000. Some of the pay could be awarded for merit and for better teacher credentials. Money could also buy more equality between poor school districts and rich ones. Most funds for education are raised locally; the federal government spends only 6% of the country's total spending on this activity. Poor school districts understandably often provide poor schools. (A portion of the money could come from cuts in the swollen educational bureaucracy.)

Money would also buy smaller class sizes, preschool for all and full-day kindergartens, a longer school day and year, and state and national examinations that would set some standards for proficiency. (Most of the countries the United States competes with already have adopted these educational reforms.) At present, entry-level wages paid by the U.S. business sector do not reflect school performance to any significant degree, so there is little incentive to perform better in schools. In any case, high school records are difficult to compare. Better testing would allow for such comparisons; employers could reward better performance; students would have an incentive to greater achievement.[16]

Another attractive possibility might be to establish apprenticeship programs in the schools in cooperation with local firms, so drawing on Germany's good experience. Requiring firms to spend 1% or 2% of their annual payroll on training, as a number of European countries already do, might be useful. Another idea is financial assistance for college paid in return for a year or two of national service. As we saw in Chapter 25, a Clinton administration proposal to this end was enacted in 1993; students are now eligible to receive up to $4,725 in education benefits in exchange for a year of community service. Some have proposed the broader approach of granting an investment tax credit to those who pay for their own higher education.

Improvements in education and training would be an appropriate response to the shift in labor demand away from unskilled workers. In 1989 only 2.2% of U.S. college graduates were unemployed compared to 9.1% among those who did not complete high school. The problem is getting worse: average unemployment among the lowest-paid 10% of the male U.S. workforce was 15% in 1967–1969, but more than double that, 31%, in 1987–1988.[17] For those *with* jobs, the balance is tilting in the same direction: greater educational attainment is needed. For example, the proportion of 25- to 34-year-old males who did not go to college but earned more than $20,000 was 57% in 1979 but was down to only 46% by 1987.[18] The advantages from increased education and training appear clear enough. More and more, "what you earn depends on what you learn." In 1990, 18% of the functions in a typical Ford auto plant involved a computer. The 1994 figure is 82%. Every year of postsecondary school education increases earnings by about 5–10%.

Research and development spending has positive externalities in that the social returns to the nation are often higher than the private returns to the firms that use the R&D. That is because many firms other than the investing one could make profitable use of a patented or proprietary technology. This suggests that government assistance for R&D could be beneficial. Research and development could be encouraged by relaxing the antitrust laws prohibiting cooperative R&D activities and by giving R&D tax credits to firms that raise their spending on these activities. President Clinton has advocated both; one outcome is a program to encourage research partnerships between firms and government labs, while another program will lead to the establishment of 100 national technology centers to help small businesses adopt new technologies. Defense Department funds are also being spent to develop "dual-use" technologies that can contribute to private-sector output. It would help if greater international safeguards could be provided for intellectual property. The United States still has inadequate treaties or no treaties at all with some countries to police the copying of technical advances. Providing more protection for the fruits of R&D expenditure would encourage increased investment in technical progress.

Finally, government regulations that carry costs to society greater than their benefits, such as barriers to international trade, controls on agricultural output, regulation of trucking, and other like regulations discussed in Chapter 25, should be reduced or eliminated whenever their costs cannot be justified. That would increase the efficiency of the economy and help to arrest the productivity decline.

16. Several of these points are from Schultze, *Memos to the President*, pp. 294, 297.

17. See Chinhui Juhn, Kevin M. Murphy, and Robert H. Topel, "Why Has the Natural Rate of Unemployment Increased Over Time," *Brookings Papers on Economic Activity,* No. 2, 1991, pp. 75–126.

18. See Frank Levy and Richard J. Murnane, "U.S. Earnings Levels and Earnings Inequality: A Review of Recent Trends and Proposed Explanations," *Journal of Economic Literature,* Vol. 30, No. 3, September 1992, p. 1371.

IMPROVING LABOR PRODUCTIVITY
THROUGH COOPERATIVE MEANS

Other proposals for reversing the fall in productivity are more fundamental and involve worker incentives, morale, and dedication to the job. Profit sharing and worker participation in decision making are two such areas.

Profit Sharing

Profit sharing for workers is a very old idea; the journeymen workers of early capitalism in effect shared profits, and for centuries so have sharecroppers in farming. Under profit sharing, instead of receiving just a fixed wage, employees are paid in part by sharing in the firm's revenues. Usually such plans combine wages with profit sharing, but at the far end of the spectrum a firm might choose to pay no wages at all and reward its workers entirely with profit sharing. (In the United States, Martin Weitzman of MIT has proposed a large-scale reform along these lines which he has called a "share economy.") Economists often approve of profit sharing, at least in the abstract, because making profits important to workers would seem to foster labor/management cooperation.

Profit sharing can be seen as holding some advantages both for management and workers. Arguably, greater incentives would exist for learning and efficiency on the part of labor. Workers might see that they will gain from contributing ideas that increase profits. Managers might appreciate that workers will, to a larger extent, monitor each other. Risks for both labor and management could be reduced because labor costs would now be more flexible over the business cycle. Up to now the general rule in the market economies has been to pay fixed wages, even though that means reduced security against layoffs in a slump. A firm's payments to its labor would decline as its profits fell, unlike the present system where in recessions wages are typically not reduced, but some workers are laid off. Many trade unions oppose profit sharing for exactly that reason: It means more of the risks of business will fall on workers' incomes. Even when adequate unemployment benefits are paid to the jobless, there is an economic sacrifice to consider in this arrangement. Layoffs allow job-specific skills and training to be lost to the firm, and to atrophy from the point of view of the worker. An economy will thus suffer damage every time a laid-off worker has to change jobs, especially when it is a different job. The greater flexibility of labor costs under widespread profit sharing could help release this brake on a country's productivity.

In the United States, profit sharing for workers was unimportant prior to the 1980s, though it is now rather common. Contracts involving some form of bonus linked to profit rather than a straight wage increase covered about 22% of the full-time employees of medium and large U.S. firms by 1986–87. Such agreements are found in nonunionized firms as well as unionized ones, though more so in the latter, where in 1986 they were specified in 51% of major union/management contracts. Profit sharing is even more widespread in Europe, but its present bastion is Japan. In that country a semiannual bonus is paid to workers, its size depending upon the profitability of the firm making the payments. As much as 50% of workers' income can be in the form of these bonuses, much larger than in the United States.[19] The transplant Japanese auto plants now established in the United States pay annual or semiannual bonuses to workers, just as they do at home.

Empirical conclusions are thus far rather sparse. In the United States, there is evidence to indicate that profit sharing has meant slower growth in labor costs, with a 10 percentage point increase in profit sharing contributing to a 0.3 percentage point fall in wage inflation. Worker productivity is on average slightly higher (3%) in the U.S. firms that utilize profit sharing than in

---

19.   Japan's semiannual bonus has another effect on productivity. Liquid funds accumulate in the banking system as firms save to make the payments. After they are made, workers have swollen bank accounts for some time as they slowly spend their bonuses. The net result is a boost to net savings deposits in banks, compared to countries that pay wages and salaries on a weekly or monthly basis. In turn, investment is promoted.

those that do not, and there is also some modest positive effects on firms' profits.[20] (German data show similar results; British data yield little evidence of improvement compared to firms that pay straight wages.)

In spite of the scanty evidence, persuading workers that they can gain directly from their contribution to a firm's higher profits would appear to be worthwhile. It seems inherently logical that giving workers a greater stake in the success of their firm will increase labor productivity.

Worker Participation in Management

Another innovation that may lead to more employee/employer harmony is labor **co-determination** with management. This system involves participation by workers in the management of firms. The European Community has embraced this model, with an EC-wide requirement that worker directors have seats on corporate or management boards.

The idea of systematically appointing workers as members of boards of directors first arose in Germany. The German system called "governing together" [German: *mitbestimmung*] is the most developed of the EC's various national plans. In that country labor representatives have served on management boards in the coal and steel industries since 1951. The system has since been expanded so that all corporations with over 500 employees must by law give a third of their board seats to worker representatives (in coal and steel the proportion is 50–50), and the majority rules in making decisions. In the United States, the idea is still rare. Only 4% of the firms that have employee stock ownership plans allow employee representatives to sit on their board of directors.[21]

According to supporters of the idea, the addition of worker representatives to management boards makes it more likely that workers will be interested in the success of the firm, with positive effects on labor productivity. When workers have a say in how work is organized, labor may be personally more pleasant and rewarding, so improving morale. When workers have access to "inside information" about the prospects for the firm, they may take a longer view of investment and engage in fewer conflicts with management.

The system has its critics, who argue that worker participation in management introduces another layer of complexity, and that lower-level managers lose some of their authority and some of their confidence. Though worker participation might improve the situation at the start, conflict can certainly reappear. The difference of opinion between employed and unemployed workers might be striking. Workers could become even more interested in protecting their own position at the expense of the unemployed. Finally, and contrary to a point mentioned in the last paragraph, workers might display some unwillingness to invest, preferring instead to be paid higher wages.

Further along the spectrum is complete employee ownership and management of firms, which is in effect a combination of the two principles, profit sharing and worker codetermination. About 1,500 firms in the United States are currently owned by their employees, mostly small but including the appliance manufacturer Amana, Avis Rental Cars, and Weirton Steel as noteworthy larger examples. The idea is spreading in the airline industry, where Northwest, TWA, and United are either partly or wholly employee-owned. Zeiss in Germany, John Lewis in Britain, and Mondragon in Spain are important European examples of this still uncommon arrangement.

---

20. Linda Bell and David Neumark, "Lump-Sum Payments Lower Wages in the 1980s," NBER Working Paper No. 3630, 1991; Douglas L. Kruse, "Profit Sharing and Productivity: Microeconomic Evidence from the United States," *Economic Journal*, Vol. 102, No. 410, January 1992, pp. 24–36.

21. There are about 10,000 employee stock ownership plans in all, involving about 12% of U.S. workers and about 4% of all corporate stock. These plans could have increased the voice of workers in management, but most of the stock (80–85%) consists of nonvoting shares, and most stock ownership plans do not involve greater worker participation in management decisions. So the effect of U.S. employee stock ownership plans on productivity does not appear to be very significant.

Experience suggests that on the whole, worker ownership may possess an inherent flaw—the short-term interest of the workers may consistently receive priority over the long-term growth of the firm. This would be so, for example, if workers always chose to pay themselves higher incomes rather than provide for long-term capital investment. Older workers nearing retirement, or younger workers considering a change of jobs, might always choose to do so. This is said to have been the experience of what was Yugoslavia, where firms were managed by their workers since shortly after World War II, and also of Hungary, where the history of worker management has been shorter.[22] These may not be necessary flaws of such a system—in both countries, workers had no claims on firms' assets and could only reward themselves with wages—but they will clearly have to be faced by any country that experiments further with worker management.

Yet the alienation of workers that too often characterizes relations when management and labor are entirely separate may be largely eliminated when the workers take the profits and are themselves the managers. If a guess may be made, worker ownership and management are likely to become more common in the market economies in the years to come. It is also fair to say that there may be costs from such cooperation of which we are as yet only dimly aware.

IMPROVING MANAGERIAL QUALITY

The separation of ownership and management and the short-term time horizons for profitability have been noted as problems contributing to the decline in productivity. A long-standing German policy, and a somewhat similar system in place in Japan, hold the potential to improve management at the level of the firm. Many observers believe the policy has actually done so. Historically, the German supervisory board [*aufsichtsrat*] came into being to give more power to shareholders of a firm. It is a standing committee that supervises corporate managers much more closely than an annual meeting of stockholders. The big German banking houses such as Deutsche Bank, Dresdner Bank, and Commerzbank are influential on these boards because of the German practice [known as *depotstimmrecht*] whereby small shareholders usually deposit their shares with their bank, giving the bank a proxy to vote these shares at companies' annual meetings. The representatives of the banks have a unique opportunity to compare efficiency and management among industries and among firms within an industry. It is common for banks' representatives on the supervisory boards of poorly run firms to give advice informed by their simultaneous membership on the boards of efficiently run firms in the same industry. The interchange of information does appear to be significant in improving the general level of entrepreneurship. Because attention to improved management quality can pay off in the form of more dividends for shareholders, the banks have a motive as well as the means to monitor managers' behavior. In particular, they generally insist that executive salaries be linked to firms' profitability.

Data from Japan, with its similar system, also indicate that advantages may flow from bank participation in management. They show that firms whose shares are owned mostly by financial institutions perform better than firms whose shares are owned by individuals or other institutions. As in Germany, the banks monitor performance with care and intervene aggressively to turn around poor performance. In the United States, however, there is little of this because of restrictions on banks and pension funds.

Even if such managerial reforms would be too drastic a change for the United States, it may be possible to tie managers' rewards more closely to the long-run performance of the firms under

---

22.   In former Yugoslavia, and in the Hungarian enterprises that follow the same principles, the firms are not strictly owned by the workers, but they are worker-managed to such a considerable degree that the problem of limited investment has become clear. The Yugoslav workers' councils had considerable authority. They had the power to appoint managers, fix pay, and allocate a firm's earnings between investment and wages. At first, labor productivity rose substantially, but in the mid-1970s a trend set in toward bureaucratic management of firms more like that in use elsewhere in eastern Europe. Admittedly, Yugoslavia did not provide the optimal test of worker-management because the government frequently engaged in agreements with firms to limit or increase their wage distributions. These agreements often limited wages for the firms where earnings were high and increased them where they were low, apparently in an attempt to maintain a more equitable income distribution in the country as a whole. Yugoslavia had just embarked on new reform in 1988–1991 that moved it toward a market system when in 1991–1994 a civil war unconnected with these reforms plunged the country into economic chaos.

their control. European and Japanese managers ordinarily do not see their compensation continue to rise if their companies perform poorly. It is plausible that when salaries are tied to profitability, managers are more motivated to focus their energies on the improvement of long-range performance. One means for doing so would be to pay top managers much more moderate salaries than at present, but to add in company shares that cannot be sold for five years. If a firm is managed profitably over this relatively long time period, the share values will increase and the managers will glean their reward. If the performance of the company is poor, then the shares will be worth less. Salary penalties for poor performance are another option. Such reforms should probably be a task for stockholders rather than for government. Government could, however, assist by passing legislation making it easier for stockholder resolutions on compensation to have some influence on corporate boards of directors. Presently such resolutions are often completely banned by company bylaws.

NATIONAL STRATEGIES FOR INDUSTRIAL POLICY

Finally, we come to the recent debate on whether to adopt a **national industrial strategy** of government encouragement for certain firms by means of government subsidies. Such a policy involves some form of collaboration and cooperation between firms and governments to change, more rapidly than the market would, the existing pattern of a nation's economy.

Elements of such strategic planning by governments were visible in the nineteenth century; Germany's long campaign to acquire and develop the technologies needed for new industries is the outstanding example. The strategy has come to be associated primarily with Japan since the 1950s. South Korea, Taiwan, Brazil, and France are also thought to be countries that stress these methods. In the United States, a number of economists influential in politics have advocated a U.S. industrial policy. The theme has been taken up by some Democrats who have suggested national measures to increase research and development expenditures in "targeted" industries. The ideas have also attracted considerable support in the EC.

Two main rationales are advanced in support of industrial targeting: the existence of positive externalities and the need to achieve learning and scale effects. These arguments are examined in turn.

Positive Externalities

If research and development spending is a key to economic growth, then the existence of positive externalities may mean that government subsidies to support the R&D are justified. A free market would lead to an appropriate amount of private spending on R&D only if externalities were absent or if they could be completely appropriated (or "internalized") by the firm undertaking the spending. An example of an inappropriate amount of expenditure on R&D might involve a firm that believes its expensive R&D will become available to competitors if its employees who know about its discoveries are hired by those competitors. Or it might believe that other firms will disassemble and copy products embodying the new technology without paying for it. These losses might mean that the firm will not undertake the R&D spending in the first place. So, where R&D is important but the resulting knowledge may leak to others, it may be sensible for government to make up for the reduced level of activity by subsidizing it. (A similar argument is used to justify training subsidies: A firm may train its skilled labor at great expense, only to find that the value of the training is transferred to competitors who hire away the skilled labor at a wage that does not include any premium for the training costs.)

These arguments for a national industrial policy are persuasive but they are also narrow. Neither governments nor firms can know at the beginning what the proper level of subsidization would be. Firms would unquestionably lobby for large amounts of taxpayer money to be devoted to these subsidies, and monitoring the use of the funding might be difficult. It would be much cheaper to permit research consortia of a country's own producers to pursue joint projects, and in the United States, some steps to permit this were taken in 1984 and 1993, as already discussed in Chapter 9.

The Effects of Learning and Scale

Learning by doing and scale economies can also explain economic growth. Knowledge makes labor more efficient while large-scale production lowers costs per unit of output. A country wishing to exploit these possibilities might decide to give an initial push by providing subsidies as an impetus to gain competitive strength in some new industry. But this policy needs to be treated with caution. Why would the private capital markets not be able to anticipate these possibilities as well, or even better, than government can? Loans from banks, repaid with interest from the subsequent profits of the firm doing the borrowing, would mean that the capital markets were voting that the project would succeed and would avoid the drain on the government's budget. In spite of the warnings, the argument has been persuasive to many.

SEMICONDUCTORS (MICROCHIPS) AS AN EXAMPLE OF AN INDUSTRY WITH POSITIVE EXTERNALITIES

Of the industries where positive externalities, learning, and scale have been used to justify a national industrial strategy, semiconductors (microchips) stand out. These tiny silicon wafers used in computers and many other electronic devices with a memory involve enormous R&D expenditure, with learning and economies of large-scale production both important in lowering costs per unit of output. (Much of this, it should be noted, is not accepted by all economists, and the information needed for a full assessment of the arguments will, because of commercial secrecy, probably be unavailable for many years.)

The argument has been made that Japanese government R&D subsidies allowed that country to begin manufacturing its own 16K DRAM (dynamic random access memory) chips, an activity that would not otherwise have been profitable, in the years 1979 to 1983. The subsidies were not especially large, but it is said that they enabled Japanese industry to become established in a market that had been dominated by the Americans. As a result of the Japanese competition, both prices and profits fell. American firms withdrew from the competition until only Texas Instruments and a small firm, Micron Technology, remained.

The Japanese strategy had apparently worked well. These microchip developments emphasize that a national industrial policy may have its losers, too—the firms in a country without a strategy, put under pressure by the success of another country's programs. Obviously subsidies could be used in a predatory way, designed to seize markets at the expense of firms in other nations. Recently U.S. chip makers have regained considerable momentum, taking the lead in the development and production of advanced microprocessors; these processing chips are much more sophisticated and profitable than DRAMs. A number of joint development agreements have been made by U.S. and Japanese chip makers. The collaboration plus the better U.S. performance has lowered the level of tension.

REASONS FOR REJECTING A POLICY OF SUBSIDIES

Despite the possible advantages, many economists are nonetheless most reluctant to recommend an activist industrial policy of subsidies to promote growth. They make two basic objections: the subsidies would be high in cost, and they would be open to political manipulation.

The High Costs of Subsidies

Opponents of an active industrial policy warn that governments are not competent to make the necessary choices, because the knowledge of the hidden costs involved is far too limited. They note the difficulty of identifying profitable investments in the first place. They point to the possibility that subsidies might attract other entrants into the market, leading to unconstrained expense for the government. Consumers would pay the higher costs if subsidies divert resources away from other products. (Factor costs might rise if greater output in the subsidized industry causes resources to be attracted away from other industries. That would raise costs in these other industries as well.) The budget deficits or higher taxes resulting from the subsidies could be more damaging than any good that would flow from an active strategy. The unknown size of all of these is indeed a cause for unease.

The Political Dangers of a Policy of Subsidies

An industrial strategy involving subsidies also brings high risks of political manipulation and corruption. Any tub-thumping politician promising government subsidies would at once have an enormous following among business people. But small firms would surely be less likely to get the subsidies than large ones. Subsidies would perhaps be made available to influence a closely contested election—certainly past experience with subsidies for any number of purposes has indicated that often they are used in just this way. With politicians doling out the public funds being major gainers from a policy of subsidies, how would the outlays be controlled? Further, if a program *did* grow large, who would put a stop to it if it did not work as well as expected? Concern that an industrial policy would be captured by special interests seems all too justified.

JAPAN'S INDUSTRIAL STRATEGY AND ITS IMITATORS

Japan is the nation most closely associated with the idea of a national industrial strategy. In the 1950s, as Japan began to recover from World War II, its new and influential Ministry of Trade and Industry (**MITI**) instituted a policy of encouraging industrial winners, especially those that could be leaders in international trade. Low-interest loans were guided by the Ministry of Finance, which directed scarce credit in this period to large firms in industrial sectors that it favored. MITI's advice was usually followed; it employed the finest graduates of the most prestigious universities, and when its bureaucrats retired (at a relatively young age), they often obtained senior management posts with the very firms they had been attempting to influence. Others who retired took senior positions in business research organizations and industry trade groups where their influence was felt strongly. (It is noteworthy that about 90% of Japanese managers have a college or university degree compared to just under 50% in the United States.)

Cartelization was permitted, and favorable tax treatment was granted, thus boosting profits that eventually financed massive marketing costs and large R&D spending. The R&D was supplemented by modest government subsidies. MITI's guidance is thought to have been significant for shipbuilding and steel in the 1950s; in the 1960s for machine tools, some electronic goods, and autos; and in the 1970s for high-tech electronic goods. Japan's economic growth set records during this period.

It may well be true that the strategy was partly responsible for the success. At least the effectiveness of the strategy cannot be *disproved*. Unfortunately, however, the lessons are not that plain, and the significance of the government's strategy is debatable. Much of Japan's educated and highly motivated labor was available for industrialization because it was employed in low-productivity agriculture. Japan's energetic and innovative managers, and its impressive national rates of saving and investment, would surely have brought rapid growth even if MITI had not existed. There is actually no way of knowing whether a free market would have led to the same or a different outcome, especially since the government was allocating credit. It *is* fair to say that seldom did MITI attempt to buck market forces in its identification of winners, but it is also fair to suggest that results in an even freer market *might* have been better yet. It is not possible to tell.

In the 1970s, the government lost its ability to allocate loans because of the growth of the private capital market, as profitable companies turned to internal self-financing. Administrative guidance faded as the firms' new prosperity allowed them to choose more independence. The guidance and the cartelization to some degree deterred the technical breakthroughs that come from the competitive, even duplicative, R&D spending by rival firms. Winners became much more difficult to choose, and experience showed several early choices had been completely mistaken. Autos were not originally given preference. The choice of steel was arguably a mistake, because steel making had few positive externalities. In fact, that industry's profits were well below the Japanese average. Shipbuilding was profitable only for a short time. The earlier encouragement of computers had poor results, though more recently the record has been better. The choice of petrochemicals and aluminum was a blunder because the energy crisis made it impossible for Japan to compete against countries with cheap energy.

Though Japanese industrial strategy helped the country to recover from World War II and assisted in bringing about high economic growth, that strategy is now much less important. Government still utilizes modest subsidies, now directed toward several high-tech areas. But as a percent of GDP, these are only slightly higher than the subsidies provided by the U.S. government, though they are more concentrated. The Japanese government's encouragement of joint public-private research projects has probably been more important than the subsidies. It has attempted to promote technological advance in industries where large-scale R&D is an advantage. The government activities are innovative and important, but they have moved a long way from the old policy of widespread industrial targeting. The major recent developments in Japan—including competitive practices such as robotic techniques and computerized measures to economize on the size of inventories—had little to do with the government. By and large, Japanese industry, however much it cooperates, now receives little explicit support from government.

In short, the Japanese did indeed employ a national industrial strategy involving subsidies and cheap credit, and it appears to have been reasonably successful. But, contrary to widespread perception, these tools are now little used. These tactics belong to Japan's past when winners were easy to choose, but they count for much less today when winners are not nearly so obvious.

Japanese Flexibility Is Important

Japanese adjustment to the pressures of changing economic conditions has been an especially successful part of that country's industrial policy. The flexibility within the Japanese economy is marked by a willingness to move resources from declining industries to areas of greater promise. More declining industries exist in Japan than might be expected, first because of the rise in energy costs, and later as the result of the increasing value of the yen. Though supply and demand are the main instruments of change, the Ministry of Trade and Industry (MITI) helps firms to shift their resources to other industries. As we have just seen, MITI is famous in the United States for its early attempts to target winners. But it deserves more credit for its coordination of programs to purchase and scrap the excess stock of declining industries.

Let us consider the decisions taken to run down several industries. By 1991, over half of Japan's shipbuilding capacity, more than a third of ethylene capacity, and over two-thirds of aluminum capacity had been scrapped. Further downsizing is underway in pulp and paper, steel, and coal. Many of the firms involved have diversified production into other and more profitable output. Workers have been moved to affiliates, especially service companies that have prospered as income grows. In textiles and clothing, massive readjustment occurred earlier, mostly in the 1970s. The textile industry received some modernization subsidies for new plant and equipment, moved into higher value items, and was bolstered by large R&D expenditure on robotic techniques.

Up to now, Japanese workers seem to have been more willing than those of the United States and the EC to move among jobs. One reason is the "lifetime employment" system, with firms willing to shift workers to other branches of the same firm if reverses strike.[23] Another reason is that Japanese unions are based on companies and industries and do not defend particular crafts. The security so obtained and the higher level of union cooperation have greatly reduced the resistance of Japanese workers to technical change. In addition, many union-management joint consultation committees promote knowledge sharing; firms and local governments cooperate closely; and firms sponsor a considerable amount of vocational training for new jobs. All of these help to stimulate Japan's labor's productivity, the growth in which is easily the highest of any major industrial country.

Other Countries' National Strategies

South Korea's national industrial strategy shows a remarkable similarity to the early Japanese policy. One can safely conclude that the Koreans are explicitly attempting to imitate the Japanese—with much the same results so far. Korea has targeted autos, steel, shipbuilding, and consumer electronics, all with great success. French experience with a national industrial strategy leads to more pessimistic conclusions. France has a limited policy of attempting to target "national champions," with the decisions buttressed by some administrative guidance, some subsidies, and some use of discriminatory government purchases to encourage the favored industries. Thus far the results have been discouraging, with the computer development program moving slowly, the sales of nuclear plants disappointing, the Airbus series of airliners not profitable enough to repay its development costs, and the Concorde supersonic airliner an economic white elephant. This is not necessarily an indictment of the strategy as a whole, but it certainly indicates that French targeting so far has not been very effective. Brazil is also a celebrated user of industrial policy (including aircraft, computer hardware and software, pharmaceuticals, etc.) but that country's huge budget deficits and hyperinflation led in 1990 to sweeping cutbacks in the subsidies used to support the policy.

U.S. Possibilities?

Although President Clinton's Chair of the Council of Economic Advisors, Laura D'Andrea Tyson, was known as a supporter of industrial policy when she was appointed, few steps have yet been taken. Clinton in the 1992 campaign called for "microenterprise" banks to provide credit for small businesses which otherwise would not be able to get it, and a number of these banks have been included in President Clinton's budgets. The president has also proposed a new civilian research agency that would be funded with some of the moneys currently spent on military research, and a program to convert defense industries and their workers to civilian production. Some industrial-policy advocates in the United States have called for a federal development bank to assist targeted industries. Yet any move toward a U.S. industrial policy has so far been modest, and many economists continue to counsel caution.

WILLINGNESS TO DISINVEST IS IMPORTANT

A major lesson concerning adjustments to economic change is that some countries are much more willing than others to *disinvest*. Efficient economies must be willing to run down industries that are losing competitive strength. Of the world's major economies, Japan has shown greater ability to do so than have the United States and the EC. Too often, industries in decline are able to persuade governments to protect them against foreign competition with trade barriers against imports. In such cases, capitalism is not being allowed to work. Many economists (but only a few politicians) would insist that a country willing to close down its loss-making industries will become stronger and more productive.

---

23. Lifetime employment affects about a third of the economy. It is a relatively recent idea, developing mostly in the 1950s and 1960s when labor was scarce and a stable labor force was highly desired. (Japanese workers receive more on-the-job training than do U.S. workers, so a mutual attraction between labor and management is understandable.) Japan is currently in a recession, and the longer it lasts, the more likely that layoffs and unemployment will mount in that country. (The Japanese government has started up an employment subsidy fund that pays half the wage bill of workers either furloughed or put into training, rather than being laid off.)

Of course, if the market does not work smoothly to provide alternative jobs for the workers so displaced, the social costs of unemployment would have to be weighed against the increased efficiency from running down the losers. That gives particular importance to the careful management of monetary and fiscal policies to promote full employment, and to the retraining programs that can make workers more employable in other jobs.

CONCLUSION

Whether the world's developed economies will be able to return to higher rates of growth that will provide more rapid improvement in levels of living is one of the greatest of all the questions of macroeconomics. To obtain that result, it is essential that the reasons for the decline in productivity be more adequately diagnosed, so that the decline can be halted and eventually reversed. Though some recent evidence gives cause for hope, the decline has been both steep and damaging.

SUMMARY

1) Economic growth can be analyzed by means of a production function that ties changes in output to changes in the factors of production. One important consideration is that the efficiency with which the factors of production are used (intensive growth) is more important than additions to their physical quantity (extensive growth).

2) Students of the causes of economic growth such as Edward Denison emphasize that technical change and education are major causes of modern economic growth.

3) In recent years, productivity gains and long-term economic growth have slowed in all major countries. The slowdown has been pronounced in the United States. Though the causes of the slowdown are not entirely clear, they appear to include a decrease in the growth of capital per worker and a decline in national saving, erosion of the public infrastructure, a switch from manufacturing to services, damaging corporate policies, worker inexperience, and the higher costs of energy and regulation.

4) Government policies toward education and technology have an important role to play in reversing the decline in productivity, with a considerable body of evidence pointing to the truth of the statement that "what you earn depends on what you learn."

5) Other possibilities for improving productivity include corporate reforms such as more worker-manager cooperation and profit sharing. At the outer bound are national strategies for industrial policy such as those used by Japan and South Korea that rely on the concepts of positive externalities, learning, and scale—though many economists are wary of such national policies because of their costs and their proneness to political manipulation. A national industrial strategy of "picking winners" worked well in the development of Japan (and Korea), but it is questionable that it offers much to rich countries that are already industrialized. Government support for running down declining industries, especially assistance for the retraining and relocation of their workers, appears to promise more, as does facilitating private R&D efforts through changes in antitrust law.

Chapter Key Words

Codetermination: Worker participation in management decisions. The European Community has a requirement that worker directors have seats on corporate or management boards. May reduce the alienation of workers, but controversial.

Extensive growth: Growth that occurs because the quantity of factor inputs rises, as when more labor, more land and natural resources, more capital, and more entrepreneurship become available.

Human capital: Education, training, experience, and skills that make labor more productive. Called human capital because, like physical capital, investment is needed to create it.

Infrastructure: An economy's stock of transportation, communications, power, education, and marketing facilities. Its creation and maintenance often involve a government role. Neglect of investment in infrastructure can reduce the economy's productivity.

Intensive growth: Growth that occurs because of increases in the quality of the existing factors and the way they are combined, so that the output from a given amount of factor input rises.

MITI: Japan's Ministry of Trade and Industry, important in Japan's national industrial strategy.

National industrial strategy: A national policy to "pick winners" by targeting and developing selected industries. Often advocated as a way to gain an advantage in international trade. Associated especially with Japan (see *MITI*) and South Korea. May work well in some circumstances, but also may be costly and politically dangerous.

Profit sharing: Use of bonuses and stock acquisition, so that workers and managers share in firms' profits. Firms with considerable profit sharing are less motivated to lay off workers in a recession. Appears to increase (slightly) worker productivity.

CHAPTER QUESTIONS

1) Technoland and Computa are two growing countries. You are told that they both have experienced rapid economic growth in the past decade, and that the growth has been due to the use of computers in business. You are also told that Technoland has experienced intensive growth, while Computa has experienced extensive growth. Give a description of the way computers have contributed to growth in both countries.

2) While walking down a city street, you see a former economics student holding a sign reading "Abandon all hope, America." You pause to read the fine print which says, "We have no new natural resources to use, our population growth has slowed, and we are not adding to our capital stock. Therefore we will never get any richer." Assuming that the sign-holder is correct that no new factors will be added, is it true that we can never expand output?

3) Give some reasons for the low rate of saving in the United States. How can lower saving now lead to lower saving in the future?

4) Suppose there are two similar countries with low productivity. Each country follows all the proper policies to increase productivity. However, one country has a manufacturing economy, while the other produces mostly services. Which country will have the higher growth rate of productivity?

5) The Boom, Bust, and Western Railroad became employee-owned about twenty years ago. At first the workers worked extra hard and the railroad seemed to be doing very well. After some years however, the locomotives and rolling stock began to decay and the track became worn and uneven. Explain what may have caused this to happen.

6) Suppose the United States institutes a comprehensive industrial policy, with government targeting certain industries with subsidies. What positive effects could this policy have? What problems would likely arise?

International Trade

OVERALL OBJECTIVE: To explore the gains from international trade and assess the consequences of barriers to trade.

MORE SPECIFICALLY:

■ To discuss and diagram the principle of comparative advantage, showing that international trade can increase world production and consumption of output even though the world's stock of resources stays the same.

■ To consider the dynamic gains from trade, including the greater efficiency that flows from increased competition, the spread of knowledge, and the diffusion of technology.

■ To assess the reasons for protectionist trade barriers and discuss the consequences of such barriers.

■ To explore the similarities and differences in the effects of tariffs, quotas, and voluntary export restraints (VERs).

■ To discuss the development of trade policy, particularly in the United States, from the disastrous Smoot-Hawley Tariff of the 1930s to the NAFTA and GATT agreements of 1993-1994.

Should countries trade with one another? What goods will they trade? Would levels of living be increased by buying only from a country's own producers? These questions have been debated as long as there have been nations, and they remain contentious political topics. Economists agree widely that trade is beneficial and tends to raise a country's level of living, and that of its trading partners as well. But many politicians and a considerable number of voters believe that trade must be restricted by protectionist measures such as tariffs and quotas. In the 1990s, the calls for protection have become louder. This chapter explores these issues.

For some goods, the desirability of international trade is plain and no one contests the point. One country may have an advantage of very low cost in producing a particular good; it will export that good. Another country either produces that good at very high cost or cannot produce it at all; it will import that good. It is perfectly reasonable that the United States imports bananas from Honduras instead of trying to grow them at home, and equally reasonable that Honduras imports computers from the United States where they are relatively cheap instead of manufacturing them domestically at great expense.

When one country's resources (factors of production) are more productive than another country's in the output of some given product, the first country will use fewer resources to produce that good than does the second. An **absolute advantage** is said to exist when a country uses fewer resources to produce a product than does another country. In the case of Honduras and the United States, Honduras has the absolute advantage in the production of bananas, and the United States has the absolute advantage in the production of computers. Absolute advantage in the production of a good or group of goods can come about for a variety of reasons, including natural resource availability, positive endowments of climate and soil, the cheapness of labor, the price and quality of capital and human capital (including education and technology), the vigor of entrepreneurs, the presence of economies of scale and specialization, and favorable political conditions in the countries concerned.

▶ THE THEORY OF COMPARATIVE ADVANTAGE

The question of whether to trade is often not so simple to evaluate, however. Say two countries are the same size and have the same quantities of the factors of production, but these factors are more productive in one of the countries (Beavaria) than in the other (Lazyria) in every line of production. That is, Beavaria can produce *any* good with fewer resources than can Lazyria. (Therefore, Beavaria has an absolute advantage in all goods.) Would trade occur between these two countries? Would it be advantageous to Beavaria, which is more productive in everything? And what about Lazyria, which has nothing to offer for Beavaria's goods but items that the Beavarians could make more productively for themselves?

To answer these questions we turn to the work of the English economist, David Ricardo. Ricardo (1772–1823) formulated the theory of **comparative advantage** in 1817. Stated as simply as possible, the theory says that even if a country can produce *everything* more productively than any other country (and so has an absolute advantage in everything), it can better its position by concentrating on the products it produces at relatively less cost and buying from a trading partner the goods it otherwise would have to produce at relatively greater cost. (The reasons why one product may be produced with relatively greater or less cost than another are the same as those given when we discussed absolute advantage—lower price or higher quality of land and natural resources, labor, capital and human capital, and entrepreneurship; opportunities for economies of scale and specialization; and favorable political conditions.) A **comparative advantage** is said to exist when one country can produce a product at lower cost in terms of opportunities foregone than can another country.

The theory of comparative advantage can be illustrated by taking an example from the everyday life of a highly paid professional person. Consider the case of Lawyer Mason at work in the city. Mason is the most successful attorney in the state, fast, efficient, and intelligent.

Moreover, no secretary is a match in keeping the files organized, scanning the mail, or in typing. Should Mason then also do the secretarial work? The answer is no. The time Mason spends on cases and legal precedents is much more lucrative than time spent on filing and typing. People should be hired to do these tasks, even though they cannot work as quickly. Mason's excellent earnings from the practice of law make the opportunity costs of Mason's time very high. Even if it takes five secretaries to accomplish what Mason could in a day, this accomplished lawyer is better off hiring the secretaries. True, Mason alone could have done all that secretarial work and saved the cost of the five secretaries, but that would mean diverting time and losing lucrative earnings— much greater than the wages of the five secretaries, whose opportunity costs are much lower—from that day's legal work. In short, Mason has a large *comparative advantage* in law as compared to secretarial work. (The instructive Billy Rose story, which carries the example further, is related in the accompanying box.)

THE BILLY ROSE STORY

An unusual case of this situation carried to an instructive extreme was noted by Charles Kindleberger of M.I.T. some years ago. In the 1930s and '40s, a certain Mr. Billy Rose became a noted "impresario of stage and screen," making millions in musicals, plays, and films. But that same Mr. Rose also had a unique talent—he was immensely fast at secretarial work. In fact, he held the world title for speed and accuracy, won in championship competition. The question for him is obvious. Should he do his own typing? Of course not, because the reward for spending his time on staging musicals is much greater than for secretarial work.

Diagramming Comparative Advantage

The logic followed by Lawyer Mason and Billy Rose is the same as the logic underlying the model of comparative advantage in international trade. Here we examine how comparative advantage applies to countries engaging in international trade. The model first formulated by Ricardo is still used today. Assume that the two countries mentioned earlier, Beavaria and Lazyria, each produce the same two commodities. In his famous discussion, Ricardo called the two products wine and cloth, and we shall do likewise. Ricardo's striking conclusion was that even if Beavaria can produce both wine and cloth with fewer resources than can Lazyria, trade will nevertheless take place between the two countries and it will be beneficial to both.

Beavaria has all the advantages. Its good climate allows for a large wine output, and its prolific sheep give so much wool that cloth, too, is easy to make. Meanwhile, Lazyria's vines produce fewer grapes because the climate is less favorable, and its sheep produce less wool. Furthermore, Lazyria's workers are rather clumsy. Because of all these disadvantages, they produce less wine per hour of labor, and also less cloth per hour of labor, than do the industrious workers of Beavaria. Beavaria has an absolute advantage in production of both goods, and Lazyria has an absolute disadvantage in both.

Let us establish some production data to make the case. Beavaria is, as we have seen, the most efficient producer of both products. If Beavaria puts all its factors of production to work making cloth, it can produce 40 yards of cloth per day. Should it transfer all available resources to wine production, then Beavaria could produce 40 quarts per day. In Lazyria, if that country specialized in cloth it could obtain only 12 yards per day. Should Lazyria transfer all available resources to wine production, it would obtain 36 quarts per day. Clearly Beavaria has the absolute advantage in both commodities, and the implication is that Lazyria would be overwhelmed by Beavaria if trade opened up between them.

In Chapter 1 we used production possibilities curves to illustrate the economic choices facing an economy. Two such curves, one for each country, are constructed here in Figure 27.1. In panel **a**, Beavaria's is a line connecting 40 cloth and 40 wine; while in panel **b**, Lazyria's line runs between 12 cloth and 36 wine. The lines show the combination of cloth and wine that could be produced by each of the two countries. For simplicity, straight lines are used, which means we are assuming constant costs of production. (A more conventional increasing-cost assumption, with a bowed-out production possibilities curve, would yield the same results, but the diagrams would become more complicated. It will conserve time and effort if we limit ourselves to constant costs.[1])

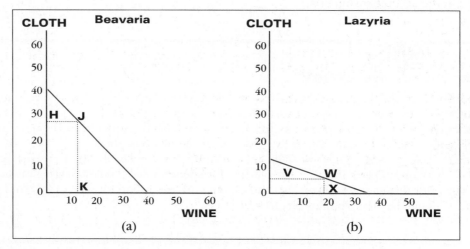

Figure 27.1. Production possibilities curves for Beavaria and Lazyria. These production possibilities curves show that Beavaria has an absolute advantage in the production of both cloth and wine, but a comparative advantage in the production of cloth. Lazyria has an absolute disadvantage in the production of both cloth and wine, but a comparative advantage in the production of wine.

In Beavaria, the opportunity cost of a quart of wine is a yard of cloth. That is, Beavarians can obtain another quart of wine by transferring resources from the production of a yard of cloth to the production of a quart of wine. In Lazyria, the opportunity cost of a quart of wine is $\frac{1}{3}$ of a yard of cloth. That is, the resources to make a quart of wine can be obtained by transferring to wine making the resources used to produce a third of a yard of cloth. Now we need to postulate how much wine and how much cloth each country decides to produce. Say Beavaria wants more cloth than wine (point J, with 0H cloth and 0K wine). Lazyria consumes more wine than cloth (point W with 0V cloth and 0X wine).

What will happen if trade now begins between Beavaria and Lazyria? Recall that in Lazyria, it takes three quarts of wine to obtain a yard of its expensive cloth, while in Beavaria only one quart of wine is needed to obtain a yard of cloth. Put yourself in the place of a Lazyrian merchant. Having heard about these different relative prices, the merchant quickly calculates that one quart of wine, which will buy only $\frac{1}{3}$ of a yard of cloth at home, can be exchanged for a full yard of cloth in Beavaria. Clearly, the Lazyrian merchant can gain from trade. Now look at the situation from the point of view of a Beavarian merchant. That merchant, too, will see advantages from trade. In this case, a yard of Beavarian cloth at home exchanges for a quart of wine, but if the yard of cloth is carried to Lazyria it will exchange for three quarts of wine.

---

1.   The concept of production possibilities curves can be reviewed in Chapter 1. A basic underlying assumption of Ricardo's theory deserves mention. The factors of production (labor, land, capital) are mobile within a country but not between countries. That is, goods will move across borders but labor and other factors of production will not.

Here is the great revelation of the principle of comparative advantage. It makes no difference to the merchants of either country that Beavaria is the more efficient producer of both commodities. All that interests them is how much wine they can obtain for their cloth and vice versa. The Beavarian merchant could hire a ship and take cloth to Lazyria where wine is relatively cheap; the Lazyrian could hire a ship (perhaps the same one) for a voyage in the opposite direction, taking wine to Beavaria. Each can obtain more abroad than at home. No matter that Lazyria is not as efficient in producing either product as Beavaria is. The differing opportunity costs mean that Lazyria can get more cloth for its wine by exporting wine and importing cloth; Beavaria gets more wine for its cloth by exporting cloth and importing wine. Beavaria has a comparative advantage in cloth production while Lazyria has a comparative advantage in wine.

The theory of supply and demand now permits predictions to be made about the actual prices charged in the cloth and wine markets in the two countries. The good that is exported (cloth from Beavaria and wine from Lazyria) will become more expensive than before as Beavarians find less cloth in their home market and Lazyrians discover less wine in their shops. The good that is imported (wine into Beavaria, cloth into Lazyria) will become cheaper as larger supplies come onto the market of the importing countries. To what degree will prices change? Because there will always be an incentive to take goods from the country where they are cheap to the country where they are expensive, trade will continue until the prices are equal in the two countries, barring only a difference caused by transport costs. Except for transport costs (and tariffs if they are present), international trade would equalize prices of a particular good among all countries that trade with one another.

Without knowledge of demand conditions in Lazyria and Beavaria, the level at which prices will equalize cannot be known exactly. The price *range* can be identified, however. Before trade, in Lazyria one unit of wine brought $\frac{1}{3}$ of a unit of cloth. There is no chance that after trade wine will bring even less cloth. No one in Lazyria would trade wine at a price of *less* than the 1:$\frac{1}{3}$ that could be obtained domestically. Actually, as Lazyria imports cloth, cloth will become cheaper, and as it exports wine, wine will become more expensive. After trade, one wine will exchange for *more* than $\frac{1}{3}$ cloth. In Beavaria before trade, one unit of cloth exchanged for one unit of wine. After trade, the new price level will settle at a point where a unit of cloth brings *more* than a unit of wine. Let us assume that the final price in both countries settles at the level of 2:3, that is, two yards of cloth will exchange for three quarts of wine in both Lazyria and Beavaria.

At this point, diagrams are useful in demonstrating that both countries will gain from trade. Look first at Beavaria's production possibilities curve (panel **a** of Figure 27.2), running from 40 yards of cloth to 40 quarts of wine. Before trade, Beavaria produced and consumed 0H cloth and 0K wine, shown by point J on its curve. Now, however, cloth and wine can be exchanged in trade with Lazyria at the new price ratio of 2:3, so that two cloth now bring three wine. This after-trade price ratio is shown running from 40 cloth to 60 wine (40:60 = 2:3) as a dashed line in the figure. Note the advantage reaped by the Beavarians if they specialize in cloth production, producing only cloth (40 yards, or 0C). They can easily better their before-trade position by retaining only 0L cloth and exporting the rest of their output (LC) to Lazyria. At the price ratio of 2:3, Beavaria will receive LM wine in payment from Lazyria, equal to 0N along the horizontal axis. Beavaria ends up producing 0C cloth, and consuming 0L of that. Consumption is at point M with both more cloth and more wine than when it was self-sufficient at point J.

Now consider Lazyria. Before trade it produced 0V cloth and 0X wine, shown by point W on its production possibilities curve (panel **b** of Figure 27.2). Lazyria will gain substantially if it decides to specialize in wine, producing its potential maximum (36 wine, or 0D). For then it can trade with Beavaria at the new 2:3 price ratio, shown by a dashed line running from 24 cloth to 36 wine (24:36 = 2:3). See the results if Lazyria retains 0U wine for its own use and exports the remainder of its output, UD. Trading this at the 2:3 price ratio allows it to obtain UT cloth from Beavaria, shown along the vertical axis as 0S. By specializing in wine production, keeping 0U, and trading UD wine for 0S cloth, Lazyria ends up at point T. This situation is one of more consumption for the Lazyrians, who end up with more wine *and* more cloth than they did before trade started. (Point W was their position before trade opened.)

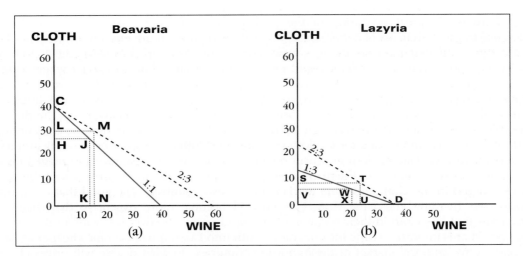

Figure 27.2. **Trade allows for more consumption in both countries.** Because international trade allows countries to specialize in what they do best, total "world" production can increase. Each trading partner can consume more than what was possible when all production was undertaken at home. International trade allows a country to consume at a point outside its production possibilities curve.

Several similarities link the two diagrams in Figure 27.2. Beavaria's exports of cloth must equal Lazyria's imports of this good, there being only two countries in the model. Thus the distance LC in Figure 27.2's panel **a** must be exactly equal to the distance 0S in panel **b**. Furthermore, since Beavarian imports of wine are the same as Lazyria's exports, then 0N in panel **a** is identical to UD in panel **b**. Lastly, the price ratio being the same in both countries at 2:3, the dashed line in both diagrams has the same slope. (Economists call this price ratio the **terms of trade**.)

In this model, the different opportunity costs of production in Beavaria and Lazyria originally caused relative prices to be different in the two countries and led to trade. Even if costs were exactly the same in Beavaria and Lazyria, however, trade would still take place if prices were driven to different levels for other reasons. One way this could occur would be sharp differences in demand leading to dissimilar prices in Beavaria and Lazyria. A strong Beavarian preference for cloth, and a strong Lazyrian desire for wine could lay the same foundation for trade that cost differences did. Another way prices could differ, leading to trade, is if costs in the two countries change when specialization occurs. The specialized production may lead to economies of scale so great that they cause relative price ratios in the two countries to differ. To show this on a diagram would require a decreasing-cost production possibilities curve, one that is bowed inward.

The theory of comparative advantage shows how two countries trading in two commodities can achieve higher levels of consumption with trade than without it. Trade is the only way a country can ever consume at a point lying outside its own production possibilities curve. The absolute productivity of the factors of production, how much a country can produce, how efficient it is—all of these are irrelevant for showing the gains from trade. The only question that counts is whether the residents of a country *gain* or *lose* from producing for themselves goods that they could import. Remember, however, that the wealth of a country *does* depend on the productivity (efficiency) with which it uses its resources. Gaining from trade is not necessarily the same thing as being rich.

MANY COUNTRIES, MANY COMMODITIES

What happens in the real world of many countries and many commodities? A country with many goods that potentially could be traded should be able to rank them on the basis of their relative comparative advantage. The resulting list will not give the clear predictions that the two-country, two-commodity model did, but it will provide a strong indication of the way trade will develop. Products at the top of the list, where the comparative advantage is strong, will plainly be candidates for export. Products at the bottom of the list are poor choices and cannot be exported successfully because of competition abroad. In the middle of the list is a gray area, where comparative advantage is not obvious. Whether these goods will be exported is less certain. In this gray area, small price changes may mean the difference between exporting a good and importing it. Even when complicated by the presence of over 150 countries and millions of commodities, however, the principle remains the same. International trade will lead to higher overall consumption by allowing nations to produce what they can do best, using their factors of production in activities where the return is highest.

THE DYNAMIC GAINS FROM TRADE

The gains from trade we have been considering are *static*, involving the greater output that is possible when a country's resources are allocated to the activities where they perform best. There are other **dynamic gains from trade** as well, and although these often receive less emphasis, they may in the long run be the most important. For example, trade means more competition, and competition is the spur to obtaining more output from a given quantity of inputs. Sluggish management, oligopolistic business practices, obsolete techniques, and an inadequate R&D effort may all be corrected by the stern but ultimately improving pressures of competition from abroad. For example, the opening of free trade among the nations of the European Community is believed to have provided a great stimulus toward efficiency in many formerly stagnant European industries. Even though many American business people do not appreciate the competition from Japan, Korea, and Taiwan, this competition has led to streamlining, cost cutting, and innovation in a number of important markets. Have imports of Japanese cars forced improvement in the quality of American cars? It seems obvious that they have. Trade may not be the "engine of growth," as some have said, but it certainly appears to make an economy's engine run more smoothly.

Some economists, like Richard Cobden (1804–1865), the nineteenth-century English proponent of free trade, and some politicians, such as Cordell Hull (1871–1955), Franklin Roosevelt's Secretary of State who led a world crusade to increase international trade, have gone further. Both suggested that eliminating trade barriers would encourage a mutual dependence among nations and therefore more peaceful behavior. It is a breathtaking thought, and it may be correct. The erection of barriers to trade certainly is often seen as an unfriendly act, while unencumbered trade does take some acrimony out of international relations. Compelling evidence that such a link exists can be found in Japan's entry into World War II. It is hard to avoid the conclusion that a greater welcome for Japanese goods in world markets during the 1920s and 1930s would have obstructed the rise of Japanese militarism.

► PROTECTIONISM

The theory of comparative advantage is strong. It shows that a country can obtain a combination of goods outside its own production possibilities curve if it trades. The trade enables people to enjoy a higher level of living through greater consumption and more efficient use of resources. Why then would any rational person support **protectionism**, that is, trade barriers such as tariffs and quotas against imports? Many reasons have been advanced, and some of them have become almost a tradition in politics and economics. We now consider a number of these claims.

THE INFANT-INDUSTRY ARGUMENT

The **infant-industry argument** posits that a tariff should be applied for a short period of time, allowing a newly established industry to mature. According to this view, an industry with the potential for a real comparative advantage might never grow out of its infancy. Foreign competition will make it impossible to survive the high costs of starting up, when tooling, training, and the ironing out of difficulties all have to be accomplished. A temporary tariff will allow it to survive its infancy. Then, when the industry has grown up and can survive on its own, the tariff can be removed. In this form, the infant-industry argument is technically valid.

Some further considerations should be (but seldom are) taken into account before such protection is granted. First, many economists feel that subsidies instead of tariffs should be used in an infant-industry case. In most countries a tariff, once passed into law, stays in effect permanently unless the law is changed. This may be a long time, because it is never very clear to the public how much a tariff costs. A subsidy, however, must be enacted by the legislature on an annual basis and is thus subject to regular examinations for need.

Second, as the new industries mature they may acquire influence, lobbyists, and political power. With these weapons they may succeed in retaining their tariff protection after the need for it has passed. There are many cases of tariffs for infant-industries not being removed even when they could no longer be justified—both the American and the European steel industries are well-known examples.

Finally, whether the assistance comes from a tariff or a subsidy, it comes at the expense of the consumer or taxpayer who pays higher prices or higher taxes. Even if the tariff or subsidy is then removed, the public has incurred costs. Should not these costs to the consumer/taxpayer eventually be repaid by the assisted firm? Traditionally, the assistance comes as a gift, and no repayment is ever made. This contrasts strangely to the situation *within* a country, when the argument about foreign competition cannot be made, and where industries that wish to start up in some new field are not protected. They must simply find enough capital to run at a loss temporarily until the initial problems of growing up are overcome.

Recent ideas for industrial policy, already discussed in Chapter 26, often involve infant-industry approaches to international trade. Industries that may eventually display economies of scale and positive externalities of learning and technological change can be encouraged not only by subsidies but by barriers against imports from abroad. We were rather skeptical of industrial policies when they were surveyed earlier; the skepticism is enlarged when trade protectionism is involved because of the additional economic damage that is thereby inflicted.

THE DEFENSE ARGUMENT

It is said that protection must be granted to industries manufacturing aircraft, firearms, shipping, electronics, ocular glass, oil, and the like, because if foreign competition drove these industries out of existence, the nation's capability for defense would suffer. The argument dates from as far back as Adam Smith and it has always had a certain appeal, but the objections to it are strong. As in the case of infant industries, subsidies are preferable because one can see just how much is being spent and can have an annual opportunity to reconsider the policy. As with infant industries, bargaining power counts for a great deal. Everyone wants to be considered a valuable part of the national defense. At various times and places, claims for protection on the ground of defense have been made by the watch industry, by candlemakers (emergency lighting), by textile manufacturers (uniforms), and by toothpick makers (good dental hygiene for the troops, of course). Finally, in the era of nuclear weapons it is hard to conceive of a modern war so serious and also so long-lasting that it stops international trade. Stockpiling of some essential items should suffice, and expensive support for domestic production of essential goods would be wasteful.

Recently the defense argument has been used in suggesting a response to cartels and price-fixing arrangements among suppliers of essential raw materials, such as oil. According to this approach, protection must be given to domestic producers in the countries subject to bullying by organized foreign suppliers. The trade barriers would enable the local producers to develop domestic sources of supply. Here it seems even more clear that direct government subsidies designed to encourage exploration are preferable to tariffs. This would avoid forcing consumers to pay even more than they have to for the scarce commodities that foreigners are willing to sell. Moreover, it seems better policy to allow the consumption of the foreign resource, so conserving the country's own supplies, while at the same time encouraging domestic exploration through subsidies.

MAINTAINING EMPLOYMENT: THE CHEAP-LABOR ARGUMENT

Probably the most familiar of all the arguments for protection is that a developed country's industries are at a disadvantage when competing against foreign goods manufactured by low-wage labor. Trade barriers must be put in place to maintain employment, which will otherwise be lost. In 1991, the average hourly wage in many industries was $12 to $20 in the United States, France, Germany, and Japan. At that time the same industries in countries such as South Korea, Taiwan, Mexico, and Brazil were paying $0.75 to $5.00.[2] Proponents of the argument say the low wages will have two adverse results. First, goods manufactured by this cheap labor will undersell output produced by higher-cost labor, making it impossible to compete. Second, firms in the countries with the high-cost labor may transfer their operations overseas so they, too, can employ cheap labor. Either way, so it is said, rich-country employment levels are undercut by cheap labor abroad. Many members of the public find this argument persuasive.[3]

On consideration, however, grave weaknesses appear in the theory that cheap labor abroad will be ruinous for expensive-labor countries. First, it implies that high-wage countries will have difficulty selling any exports at all because their labor is so expensive. Yet in the 1990s the three countries with the world's highest exports by value—the United States, Germany, and Japan in that order—were all very high-wage countries. How is this possible? It happens because labor is not the only factor of production and is thus not the only component of costs. High-wage developed countries possess large endowments of capital, benefit from rapid technological change, and have productive labor forces that are skilled and educated—that is why their labor earns the high wages. These countries are likely to have a substantial advantage in the export of products that utilize these factors. So costs can be relatively low and industry strongly competitive even if labor is expensive. Consider this arithmetic: U.S. labor that is paid $16 per hour may be very productive because it is better educated, more technically skilled, better housed and fed, and more adaptable to changing conditions. It may produce 100 units of output per man/hour. In that case it would not be at a disadvantage if another country's cheap labor ($4.00 per hour) produces less than 25 units per man/hour.

Indeed, it is extremely common for low-wage countries to turn the cheap-labor argument on its head, erecting barriers against imports from countries with abundant capital, or advanced technology, or a highly skilled and educated labor force. On average, the world's less-developed countries have considerably higher barriers against imports than do the industrial countries.

Lastly, even if foreign labor were always both cheaper *and* more productive, many labor-intensive activities would still survive unscathed in the rich countries. For example, a large part of the U.S. economy is "naturally protected" against imports by the high cost or the impossibility of importing the good in question. Table 27.1 illustrates the relative invulnerability of the U.S. labor force to imports. In 1992 total U.S. employment was 117.6 million. Of this

---

2.   It should be noted that in the early 1960s, Japan was a low-wage country, with average pay there only one-fifteenth the figure in the United States. Now the average Japanese worker is paid approximately the same amount as the average American worker.

3.   The theory of "factor-price equalization" in international trade analyzes the tendency of imports produced by cheap labor to exert downward pressure on the wages of those who produce goods in competition with imports. Those in cheap labor countries find the opposite is happening. Their labor is more in demand to produce exports; their wages tend to rise. The name factor-price equalization indicates that there is a pressure to drive the wages of unskilled labor toward equality around the world.

figure, those working in the services shown in the table (80% of total employment) were subject to little or no competition from imports. Importation of construction services is not very usual; transport and public utility services must be rendered in place, as is true of several other services in the list. Government services cannot be imported.

TABLE 27.1
U.S. service employment by sectors, 1992, in millions.

Construction	7.0
Transport, public utilities	8.2
Wholesale, retail trade	24.4
Finance, insurance, real estate	7.8
Other services	40.8
Government (federal, state, local)	5.6
Total	93.8

Source: Bureau of Statistics, U.S. Department of Labor, from *Statistical Abstract of the United States 1993,* Table 647.

Furthermore, the U.S. economy is becoming *more* service-oriented, so the opportunity for foreign labor to undercut American labor with lower wages is actually diminishing. Even the removal of all forms of protection could not possibly cause the massive distress that has sometimes been predicted.

DIFFICULTIES IN ADJUSTING TO FREE TRADE

A minority of U.S. industries are labor-intensive, subject to foreign competition, and without sufficient productivity advantages over foreign producers to offset their high labor costs. (Shoes and parts of the textile industry are good examples.) Dismantling all tariffs, quotas, and other forms of protection will most certainly be injurious to such industries, some of which might not be able to survive. People employed in these industries will naturally fight hard for protection. Their letters are found in the daily newspaper and on the desks of their Representatives and Senators. Their employers and their unions have lobbyists in Washington toiling for the life-giving transfusion that a tariff or quota would provide. Members of Congress courageous enough to take a stand against tariffs make permanent political enemies out of workers whose jobs are in jeopardy. Yet economic reasoning tells us that the workers, managers, and capital employed in such industries do not have a comparative advantage. If the factors of production such industries employed were switched to occupations where they would have higher productivity, everyone would benefit in the long run.

No one ever argues that kerosene lamp making should be protected by taxes on electric lights. That would be absurd, because electric lights are better for the consumer and lamp makers ought to be able to make a far better living in some other occupation. No one suggests that states or counties should have their own trade barriers. How preposterous. Monopolies would flourish because markets would be so small in scale that they could not support competition. Consumers would be exploited by the high prices and would simply have to do without the goods that could not be produced locally. Lacking the spur of competitive forces, firms would have no need for innovation. Perhaps colleges would be forbidden to hire professors from other states, or even from outside the city. What would such colleges be like? It is not hard to guess.

In one single situation, however—international trade, with its implications of "them or us"—many people still prefer to restrict trade and to keep inefficient industries operating in spite of the costs to the consumer and the nation.

Adjustment Can Be Difficult

Transferring from old to new occupations can be a painful experience. It may be difficult or impossible for some workers to acquire knowledge of new job opportunities. Job training may be needed, some workers will be past middle age and reluctant to start over again, and some families will not want to move. For these reasons, many economists support **trade adjustment assistance**, first adopted in the United States in 1962. Such assistance is intended to make labor (and other factors of production) more mobile and more employable, making the transfer out of declining industries smoother and less painful.

Unfortunately, the results in the United States have not been satisfactory. The major problem has been that the assistance has largely been in the form of increased unemployment compensation, which does nothing to make a displaced worker more employable. As already noted in Chapter 25, the education and training that would ease the transition to another job was sadly neglected in all U.S. programs until 1988. A new and much improved program of adjustment assistance was passed in that year, but at the time of writing, full funding for the program (which would have involved a tariff that would have violated several U.S. treaties with other countries) had not been made available.

In recent years, the argument has grown in volume that multinational firms now export jobs instead of products, taking their operations to countries where labor is cheap. A significant new element in the debate is the switch in position made by the trade union movement, in particular the AFL-CIO. Organized labor in the United States was long critical of trade protectionism, but from the 1970s it came to support higher trade barriers to stop the export of jobs. It is clear that among a large segment of the public, the fear of losing an existing job to import competition predominates over the predicted gain in other jobs in industries that export—even if there is a net gain in jobs, and if the new ones are better paying.

As we have seen, economists tend to *favor* the development of labor-intensive industries in cheap labor countries and running them down in the countries where labor is expensive. They see in the transfers the working of comparative advantage, which in the end will make stronger both the economies gaining the labor-intensive jobs and those losing them. When such jobs are lost in the richer country, labor is freed for higher-productivity employment in industries that *have* a comparative advantage.

THE PROBLEM FACING POORLY TRAINED BLUE-COLLAR WORKERS IN MANUFACTURING

In manufacturing industries, a major problem faces workers with few skills and little educational attainment. When these industries face competition from abroad, their workers must compete with a giant global pool of unskilled labor. The United States, with its generally high wages, has no advantage in producing goods that require mostly inputs of unskilled labor, simple and easily copied technology, and natural resource inputs that are widely available. As imports of these products rise, the United States and other rich countries find that high wages cannot be continued by the firms facing competition from imports. Rich countries are rapidly losing such jobs, which are being transferred to cheap labor countries just as the theory of comparative advantage suggests.

If, however, the unskilled workers of a rich country have been provided with limited skills and poor reading and math ability, it will be difficult to shift them into other activities. A country that neglects its education and training will face long-term difficulties of declining incomes for the workers who are "locked in" to their jobs by their limited abilities. Furthermore, a country that devotes small amounts to research and development spending will discover that high-tech jobs are going elsewhere. Finally, a country that allows its public infrastructure of transport to decline will find its productivity suffers even more.

A poorly trained blue-collar worker in manufacturing in such a country—all too closely resembling the present-day United States—may face rather bleak prospects.

Indeed, the gap between the earnings of those with a college degree and those without a high school diploma continues rapidly to widen. Trade barriers against products made by cheaper labor are not the answer. That perpetuates the unskilled jobs, and creates inefficiencies and costs to consumers, as explored next. Instead, the answer is to construct a public infrastructure of education, transport, and other services that befits a rich country and adds to the growth of its productivity.

Whatever the merits of the debate, during recent years it has resulted in Congressional support for breathtakingly severe bills to erect barriers against imports of products such as textiles, clothing, shoes, and other products. Because of presidential vetoes, no such bill has yet been passed. If new protectionist barriers are erected, there is serious danger that foreigners would retaliate in a trade war of the sort that occurred in the Great Depression of the 1930s, when countries fruitlessly attempted to protect their own industries at the expense of foreign competition. In 1993, Ross Perot went very much further, urging passage of what he called a "scientific tariff" that would bring up the costs of goods imported from cheap-labor countries to the extent needed to offset the cheap labor. Under such a plan, tariffs on goods from Mexico or China or India could conceivably face tariffs of 700% or more, high enough to halt all trade with these countries—including U.S. exports, because these countries could no longer afford to buy them.

▶ TARIFFS, QUOTAS, AND VERs: THE ECONOMICS OF TRADE BARRIERS

For as long as nations have traded, there have been special interest groups and politicians who wish to limit international trade. But as we have seen, the country that puts up barriers to trade pays a penalty in terms of reduced levels of living. This section analyzes the specific results of tariffs, quotas, and other barriers to trade used to protect a country's industries.

TARIFFS

The most well-known method of protection is the **tariff** or duty, which has a very old heritage. Long before the word (which is Arabic, meaning originally "information" or "explanation") received its current meaning, taxes on imports were being collected on many of the world's frontiers. Visitors to the remains of Hadrian's Wall, the Roman defense line that cut across the hills of England near the Scottish border, will find the ruins of little rooms beside almost every gate. These were offices of the Roman officials who taxed goods coming into the empire. A tariff nowadays is a tax on imports, or on exports where that is permitted.[4]

---

4.   U.S. taxation of American exports is prohibited by Article I of the U.S. Constitution. Article I, section 9, clause 5 says, "No tax or duty shall be laid on articles exported from any State." This clause was a reaction against the colonial economic policies followed by the ministers of King George III before 1776.

Tariffs are of two types: **specific tariffs**, meaning a certain amount per unit of the imported good (10¢ per yard, $15 per ton), or **ad valorem tariffs**, meaning a percentage of a good's value. Specific duties are obviously easier to administer because there is no problem of valuation. But they mean that a low-price good will pay more tax as a percentage of the original price than will a high-price good of the same kind. Duties of the same dollar amount on an imported Yugo and an imported Mercedes would be a form of regressive taxation hitting the poor harder than the well-to-do. Also, during periods of inflation when prices are rising, specific duties must be constantly changed if they are to provide the same amount of protection as before. To a believer in protection, this is a disadvantage because bills to change tariff rates usually face a slow passage through the legislature. Finally, specific duties cannot be used to tax art works, antiques, and other items that share the property of uniqueness. *Ad valorem* duties overcome all these problems. They collect more on higher-price than on lower-price goods, there is no need to change them in periods of inflation, and they can apply as easily to art works and the like as to anything else. The value involved is estimated and the tariff assessed accordingly. One disadvantage of an *ad valorem* tariff is that every single item must be valued by a customs official, creating expense and red tape.

QUOTAS AND VERS

Quotas are a more modern barrier to trade. They are a form of government regulation under which only a certain quantity of a good will be permitted to enter a country. Quotas can be stated in volume terms (600 tape decks) or value terms ($100,000 worth of tape decks). They were first used as an emergency measure during World War I by countries experiencing financial difficulties. These countries found quotas, unlike tariffs, allowed complete certainty in restricting imports to a desired level. The foreign exporter might cut prices in the face of tariffs, but that would do no good against a quota. Quotas disappeared in the 1920s, but were returned to use by France in 1930–1931 mainly as a means to discriminate against the Japanese. By the 1930s, France and many other countries had signed so-called **most-favored nation** treaties under which a country had to give the same tariff treatment to all countries.[5] So, when cheap Japanese goods began to enter France in large quantities, the French were treaty-bound not to raise their tariffs unilaterally against Japan. But the agreements made no mention of quotas, and the French rushed to apply the new device to imports from that country.

Ever since the 1930s, quotas have been increasing in popularity as a tool of protectionism. In the United States and Europe, this trend has come in the guise of so-called **voluntary export restraints (VERs)** in which foreign exporters undertake to limit their exports to the importing countries. Two examples are the worldwide Multifiber Arrangement (MFA) that limits imports of textiles and clothing, and the voluntary restraints that foreign steel producers have placed on shipments to the United States and Europe. These restraints are actually voluntary only in the sense that in a western movie the outlaw surrenders voluntarily to the sheriff rather than be shot. The U.S. and European governments applied heavy pressure to achieve their VERs, the pressure sometimes extending to threats of imposing outright quotas.

A DIAGRAM OF THE ECONOMIC EFFECTS OF TARIFFS, QUOTAS, AND VERS

The economic effects of tariffs, quotas, and VERs can be seen in Figure 27.3. Here are shown the domestic supply (S) and demand (D) for a product that potentially can be traded. If there were no international trade at all, a price P_e would be charged for a quantity Q_e. Now assume that international trade opens. If some more efficient producers are located abroad, then the world

---

5. Most favored nation agreements are almost universal in the 1990s, and mean that a tariff cut granted to one country must automatically be granted to all treaty partners. The single remaining exception in the developed countries is the unwillingness to extend most-favored nation treatment to some political opponents. For example, the United States still has not extended such treatment to a number of former communist countries.

price will be somewhat lower than the domestic price. This lower world price is shown as P_w on the vertical axis. Notice the effects of this price. As shown along the supply curve, domestic producers will produce a quantity equal to Q_1. At the low price P_w, home demand exceeds supply by the distance Q_1Q_4, and Q_1Q_4 is the amount that will be imported.

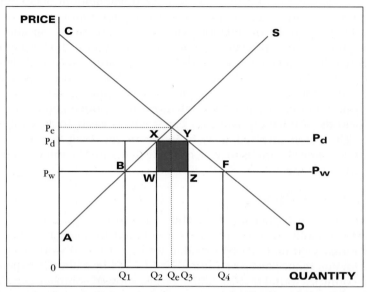

Figure 27.3. A diagrammatical analysis of tariffs, quotas, and VERs. Supply and demand curves allow us to identify the major effects, which are generally similar, of the major protectionist policies.

Now assume that the producers of this good lobby successfully for a tariff equal to P_wP_d. (P_wP_d could be a specific tariff of that amount, or, because it is 20% of the original world price P_w, it might also be an *ad valorem* tariff of 20%.) Several consequences of the new tariff can be seen on the diagram. First, the price must rise, and consumers will pay P_d instead of P_w. Consumption will be reduced at this higher price; there is a decline in the quantity demanded from Q_4 to Q_3. Domestic producers are stimulated by the effects of the tariff and raise their output from Q_1 to Q_2. Imports decline from their old level Q_1Q_4 to Q_2Q_3. One other result appears on the diagram. A tariff equal to P_wP_d is being collected by the government on every unit imported. P_wP_d is equal to WX, and Q_2Q_3 is equal to WZ. The total tariff revenue collected is equal to the tariff per unit WX times the number of units imported WZ. Multiplying two sides of a rectangle gives the area of that rectangle; thus the shaded area WXYZ shows the revenue collected by the government.[6] Consumers not only pay that bill, but also a higher amount P_wP_d to domestic producers on each unit of output from 0 to Q_2. Producers therefore garner extra revenue P_wP_dXW paid by consumers. In summary, tariffs raise prices, cut consumption, stimulate domestic producers by raising their revenues, and generate tariff revenue for the government.

There is a welfare effect as well, with an allocative inefficiency (deadweight loss) that we have come to expect when prices are altered by government intervention. (See Chapter 4 for the details of how to measure allocative inefficiency.) At the world price P_w, the producer surplus is the triangle above the supply curve but under the price, AP_wB. After the price is raised by the tariff, the producers' surplus becomes AP_dX. Consumer surplus, the area over the price but under the demand curve, is, however, cut back from the original P_wCF to the new P_dCY. The lost consumer surplus is thus the trapezoid P_wP_dYF. Part of this is gained by the country's producers because P_wP_dXB is the increase in producer surplus. Another part goes to the country's

---

6.   Until the twentieth century, most U.S. government revenue came from tariffs, which accounts for the importance of various tariff bills in the history books. In a few less-developed countries, tariffs still account for over half of all government revenue.

government as the tariff revenue WXYZ. This leaves two triangles of lost consumer surplus not counterbalanced by any gain, BXW + ZYF. These two triangles measure the allocative inefficiency or deadweight loss of a tariff.

Quotas Shown Diagrammatically

How does a quota compare to a tariff? Figure 27.3 can be used to demonstrate that a quota has exactly the same price-raising results as a tariff and that it inflicts further costs on society as well. On the diagram, assume once more that before protection the price of the good is P_w and the amount imported is Q_1Q_4. Now the legislature passes a quota limiting imports to the lower level Q_2Q_3. The result of restricting imports will be that at the old price P_w, the quantity demanded will exceed the quantity supplied (Q_4 is greater than domestic supply Q_1 plus imports Q_2Q_3), so that a shortage will develop. The market's reaction to a shortage will be to force prices up. The only price where this upward pressure disappears is P_d, where imports Q_2Q_3 (= XY) are just sufficient to fill the gap between demand and domestic supply. In short, a quota has the same upward impact on prices that a tariff has; the only difference is that the tariff collection is a tax on the good while the quota works indirectly through the mechanism of supply and demand.

Several other economic effects of tariffs also apply equally to quotas. Consumption is reduced at the high price P_d from Q_4 to Q_3, and consumers pay more to producers. Domestic producers find business more profitable and raise their output from Q_1 to Q_2. So far the effects of tariffs and quotas are identical. One major difference exists, however: tariffs generate revenue for the government, but quotas do not. Firms fortunate enough to obtain a part of the quota will be able to buy the good on the world market for P_w per unit and then resell it in the protected market for P_d. Revenues equal to the rectangle WXYZ are the result.

In some countries (Australia and New Zealand prominent among them) these revenues are captured by the government because licenses to import a share of the quota are auctioned off to the highest bidders. Alternatively, crooked customs officials may demand bribes from firms trying to import goods under a quota. Whatever the outcome, it is the consumer who pays the bill.

Quotas differ from tariffs in one further way. If economies of scale or technical change bring prices down in foreign countries, they will also come down in the country charging a tariff, which is levied on the price of the good imported. A quota will not permit this to happen, however. No matter how much the foreign price drops, only a fixed amount of the good is permitted to enter the country, and consumers cannot benefit from increasing productivity abroad. These gains go to those who have an import license, and who buy at falling prices abroad and sell at the high price at home. In short, quotas share all the major disadvantages of tariffs and have some of their own as well.

VERs Shown Diagrammatically

A voluntary export restraint (VER) differs from a quota in two major respects. First, the foreign government must establish its own licensing arrangements for its exporters, who are given targets for exports that they may not exceed. Second, these licenses permit foreign firms to sell at the high price P_d in the importing country. Thus, on Figure 27.3 foreigners lose because they sell a smaller quantity (imports are only Q_2Q_3 instead of Q_1Q_4), but they gain because they are able to sell their imports Q_2Q_3 at the higher domestic price P_d. They thus garner the revenue WXYZ. Depending on the elasticities of supply and demand, these revenues to foreign firms from higher prices may even exceed the losses due to a lower quantity of exports. In that case, foreign firms may be willing accomplices to voluntary restraints—it might increase their profits. Even at worst, any losses from a VER will be reduced because of this revenue. So a VER is often easier to negotiate and less likely to cause ill feeling and retaliation than is an outright quota—but it also ensures that some of the revenues generated by the protection will be transferred from the pockets of domestic consumers to foreign producers.

THE COSTS OF TRADE BARRIERS

Trade barriers are expensive for the consuming public. In 1993 the Institute for International Economics in Washington, D.C., estimated that the costs of protection for the United States was $70.3 billion per year, or about $1000 per family per year. The most expensive barriers by a significant margin are those for textiles and clothing. Other highly protected industries include steel, dairy products, sugar, peanuts, benzenoid chemicals, and footwear.

OTHER BARRIERS TO TRADE

There is a long list of other devices by which international trade can be hindered or reduced. The most familiar is government buying policy. Many countries have laws that require their governments to give preference to domestic producers when making purchases. In the United States, for example, the Buy American Act of 1933 requires the federal government to purchase U.S. products unless their price is over 6% higher than foreign prices for the same good. The differential must be more than 50% on defense spending. Similarly, the Ship American Act of 1934 requires 50% of all U.S. government goods shipped abroad to be carried in U.S.-flag vessels.[7]

Various local taxes and regulations can also be used to build barriers to trade. Take the auto industry as an example. Vehicle license fees and road-use taxes often apply to a car's horsepower or weight in Europe and Asia, rather than to the car's price as in the United States. As American-produced cars tend to be heavier and higher in horsepower, they often labor under a substantial tax disadvantage when exported.[8] Perhaps the most familiar of local regulations is the mark-of-origin requirement, under which goods must bear a label telling the buyer in what country they were manufactured. Such laws appear to facilitate discrimination against foreign goods, which is presumably their main purpose.

▶ TRADE POLICY

The greatest of all the dangers posed by the widespread imposition of tariffs, quotas, and VERs is that other countries will retaliate with their own barriers. The notorious exemplar of how trade wars hurt everyone was the Smoot-Hawley Tariff passed by the United States in 1930. President Hoover asked Congress in 1929 for a revision of U.S. tariffs. The House of Representatives voted a bill sponsored by Representative Willis C. Hawley of Oregon with a moderate rise in tariffs. But month after month in the Senate, new tariffs were added to the bill under the leadership of Reed Smoot of Utah. Eventually the tariff was raised on 800 items. The increases brought the U.S. average rate of tariff to 59.1%, the highest ever in the United States and nearly twice the figure of 20 years before.

The Great Depression had already begun, but Hoover did not suggest changes in the Smoot-Hawley legislation to take account of that. In March 1930, after many months of congressional horse trading, the bill went to Hoover for his signature. Over a thousand economists, a large majority of the American Economics Association, sent the White House a letter stating that the bill not only would damage American consumers, but would certainly invite retaliation on American exports by foreign governments which would see the measure as causing serious damage to their countries. In the language of the times, it was a "beggar-thy-neighbor" policy—any perceived advantage to the United States would come at the expense of its trading partners.

---

7.   Such legislation also affects private shippers to some extent. In the United States, the Jones Act bans the importation of ships to be used in trade between American ports. So the big tankers that carry Alaskan oil to the West Coast must be built in American shipyards.

8.   In the era of high energy prices, such laws are justified to encourage conservation, and one hopes they will someday find more use in the United States. However, the European and Asian laws were not passed to conserve fuel, but to protect domestic industry, and they had been in effect for many years before the energy crisis.

To the dismay of everyone who correctly understood what its effects would be, President Hoover signed the bill. The psychological effect was large and immediate, further weakening business confidence abroad. The evil consequences forecast for the bill rapidly came true. Twelve large trading countries, refusing to be beggared, retaliated with their own heavy tariffs. Spain put a tariff on U.S. autos that virtually stopped their import; the Swiss public boycotted American goods; Italy announced it would buy no more from the United States than the U.S. did from Italy; Canada hit 125 U.S. export items with higher duties.

Trade plummeted. The total imports of 75 countries had been almost $3 billion per month at the start of the year 1929. They fell below $2 billion in June 1930; below $1 billion in July 1931, and ended up at about half a billion dollars in March 1933. In volume, the total exports of the United States fell more than those of any other major country, and in 1932 they were only 53% of their 1929 volume. (The volume of trade declined by less than its value, because prices fell as well. The lower prices actually served to raise trade barriers, however, because most tariffs of the time were specific rather than *ad valorem*.) Although much of the collapse in trade can be blamed on the fall in income during the Great Depression, even the decline in income was related to trade because of the psychological impact of Smoot-Hawley on global investment as confidence collapsed. It was one of the world's greatest mistakes of economic policy.

GATT (THE GENERAL AGREEMENT ON TARIFFS AND TRADE)

Reversing the protectionism of the 1930s was a very long and involved process, in which the most important development was the formation just after World War II of an organization called **GATT (the General Agreement on Tariffs and Trade)**. GATT, based in Geneva, Switzerland, and currently with 118 member countries, is devoted to the goal of reducing protectionism and encouraging trade.

GATT sponsors conferences or "rounds" of trade negotiations to reduce protection. Seven such rounds have already taken place, and another is currently in progress. The "Kennedy Round" of the 1960s cut tariffs 35% by 1972. This was followed by the Tokyo Round 1975–1979, which cut tariffs another 33% by 1987.

These rounds lowered tariffs so successfully that the other barriers (quotas, VERs, government buying policies, and regulations on trade in services such as insurance, shipping, airlines, and the like) became the most important impediments to trade. Thus the present set of negotiations, started at Punta del Este, Uruguay, in 1987 and called the **Uruguay Round** even though the negotiations were immediately moved to Geneva, focused on these more difficult issues. The Uruguay Round proved to be the most difficult of all the GATT negotiations. Scheduled for completion in 1990, it was not finally signed until 1994, has still to be ratified by the GATT members, and will not go into effect until 1995. The major stumbling block in the negotiations was that the United States, Canada, Australia, New Zealand, Argentina, and other exporters of agricultural commodities insisted that Europe and Japan reduce their stern protection of agriculture as part of the negotiations. Europe especially was intransigent, insisting on its right to pay farmers high prices, buy their surplus production, and export the surplus at cut rates. It refused to reduce these trade-distorting subsidies as much as the agricultural exporters insisted on. (The U.S. conscience is not clear, by the way. Heavy U.S. protection applies to sugar, peanuts, and dairy products; some agricultural export subsidies are used to obtain markets.) An eventual compromise did not bring as much progress as had been hoped, but at least a first-ever breakdown of a GATT round did not occur.

For the United States, it is expected that the $70-billion bill that consumers pay because of U.S. trade barriers will be cut almost in half, to $37.5 billion. The gains will be mostly due to the reduced barriers to textiles and clothing imports ($17 billion), with the rest spread widely among hundreds of other protected items. For the world as a whole, consumers are expected to gain somewhat more than $450 billion, about 30% from a decline in tariffs and about 70% from the reduction or elimination of other types of barriers. The greatest gains are likely to accrue to the countries that export agricultural commodities

Regional Trade Agreements

Ever since GATT was established, its rules have permitted free-trade agreements. Such agreements involve the mutual elimination of trade barriers by the members. The European Community (EC, also called the Common Market) dating from 1960 was the first and is still the most well-known free-trade agreement. Its 12 members have eliminated their barriers against one another's trade. Their removal has had a major effect on the amount of trade these countries carry on with each other. Whereas in 1960 only 34.5% of the trade of the present 12 members was with each other, that figure had risen by 1990 to 60.4%—one-fifth of all world trade. The members are further diminishing rules against the movement of capital and labor and are moving toward a common currency. U.S. agreements with Israel in 1985, Canada in 1989, and a NAFTA (North American Free Trade Area) of 1993 among the United States, Canada, and Mexico, all show U.S. interest in regional agreements. These agreements do not involve free movement of labor or currency unification; they are not as ambitious as the European developments have been.

THE STRUGGLE OVER NAFTA

The U.S. debate over the ratification of NAFTA was the most heated on an international trade issue since World War II. Opponents of the agreement insisted, against the weight of the economic evidence, that Mexico's cheap labor would lure very large numbers of American firms to Mexico, involving the loss of jobs for many American workers. Supporters pointed to the jobs that would be created by the growth of American exports to Mexico. It looked for weeks as if the NAFTA treaty would be lost in the House of Representatives and would mark a turn toward trade protectionism in the United States, but enough votes were mustered at the last minute to pass the treaty by the thin margin of 234–200. The treaty will cut tariffs to zero over a period of 15 years, though about 50% of them were abolished immediately. Many restrictions on trade are being dropped, including the Mexican limits on foreign delivery of services and many U.S. barriers to the import of fresh fruits and vegetables.

NEW DEVELOPMENTS

The EC has already agreed to expand its tariff-free zone to include seven more European countries. This new European Economic Area now comprises 19 countries with 380 million people and 46% of world trade; the internal trade barriers within this zone will be abolished as soon as all the members ratify the agreement. Four countries included in the new zone, Austria, Finland, Norway, and Sweden, have applied for full EC membership.

A new U.S. free trade agreement with numerous Latin American countries is in the works. A treaty with Chile is likely to be the first. Later arrangements could include Mercosur (the free-trade association among Argentina, Brazil, Paraguay, and Uruguay) and the Andean Pact countries (Bolivia, Colombia, Ecuador, Peru, and Venezuela). Together with Mexico and Canada, a giant Pan-American free trade area would be the result.

A Japanese bloc in the Far East also seems likely. ASEAN, the Association of Southeast Asian Nations (Brunei, Indonesia, Malaysia, Philippines, Singapore, and Thailand) already is a larger market for Japanese goods than is the United States. Japan's influence in China and other Asian rim nations seems set to grow, perhaps into a "Yen block."

Economists used to look with complete approval on these agreements. The principle seemed sound that if protection was bad, then reducing it, even among just two or three countries, would be an improvement. Nowadays the confidence that free-trade agreements are always benign is eroding. The danger is that barriers will be raised against outsiders and lowered against favored partners. The more such agreements proliferate, the greater the likelihood that countries may end up importing from higher-cost suppliers that face no trade barriers, while lower-cost suppliers outside the walls lose their access. The old imperialist trade preferences of yesteryear (France but no one else having free trade with French colonies, Britain with British colonies, and so forth) may be set for an unfortunate and damaging resurrection if the advances of the GATT Uruguay Round are not adhered to.

THE GLOBALIZATION OF TRADE

There is a current in international trade contrary to that indicated by the higher trade barriers and the threat of exclusive regional trade agreements. Technological change in communications and transport have brought as never before the rise of the global firm—multinational enterprises with branches in many countries. By far the largest number of multinational enterprises have their home offices in the United States, Britain, Japan, Germany, France, and the Netherlands.

They originated in the mid-nineteenth century, though their great growth came in the period after World War II. Multinationals arose mostly because of the convenience and cost advantage of dealing with foreign branches of the same firm rather than independent firms. Transactions costs of dealing with other firms could be reduced by keeping decisions within the multinational. Commercial secrecy involving technology was much easier to maintain; transfers of new technology to foreign branches of the same firm ran far less risk that the technology would end up in unauthorized hands than if the technology was sold or licensed. A closer check could be kept on servicing of a product, important in keeping the reputation associated with a brand name. Perhaps there were economies of scale in management, inventory stocking, advertising, and other activities. A multinational firm could deliberately locate its production facilities in a manner that would minimize labor, transport, and raw materials costs. It could spread the risk of its operations among many countries; a recession or revolution that might be disastrous to a firm operating in just one country would be less serious to a multinational operating in many.

The globalization of firms has had great consequences. Modern trade is no longer a matter of a Japanese car, an American computer, a Chinese shirt. Many of the products themselves contain parts or ingredients made in other countries, either in the branches of a multinational or by a network of independent suppliers that can be tapped because the firm is global. Transactions among the branches of the world's multinational firms have now grown so large that they account for about 25% of world trade; global sales of U.S. multinational firms are actually greater than U.S. exports.

Examples are everywhere. The Ford Escort manufactured in Europe contains parts from 15 different nations and is assembled in both Britain and Germany. Nowadays a Honda, Mazda, or Toyota sold in the United States is likely to be U.S.-made in a Japanese-owned factory. When in 1992 the patriotic townspeople of Greece, New York, voted to buy an American rather than a Japanese earth mover, they accepted the bid for a higher-priced John Deere and rejected the bid for a lower-priced Komatsu. They then discovered, to their amazement, that the Komatsu was made in the U.S.A. by a branch of a Japanese multinational, while the John Deere was made in Japan by the Japanese branch of an American multinational. The globalization of firms challenges many common stereotypes.

Globalized firms are not a deviation from the standard principles of international trade; comparative advantage determines where the production will be undertaken. Production of labor-intensive components will occur in cheap-labor countries; high-tech inputs will flow from countries with an advantage in technology. If trade barriers are erected, the multinational that wants to tap supplies of inputs outside the country will lobby against the barriers. Organized labor often opposes what it sees as the loss of jobs when a multinational transfers a labor-intensive operation overseas. But it may not realize that the same firm, having lowered its costs, is now increasing the production and hiring at its home-based higher-tech divisions. (True, these jobs might not be unionized, explaining some part of the union opposition.) To the extent that globalization decreases costs, consumers get cheaper products produced under a brand name they trust.

CONCLUSION

The theory of comparative advantage in trade is a strong one. According to this theory, levels of living are advanced when countries export the items that they produce with relatively greater efficiency and import the items that they produce with relatively less efficiency.

Yet the self-interest of those who would gain from trade barriers is also strong. They are often better organized and more vocal than consumers, and so they carry weight with the governments that grant them tariffs, quotas, VERs, and other barriers to trade. Keeping these barriers low is one of the great challenges of modern economics.

The trade flows examined in this chapter are only a part of international economics, however. When items are exported and imported, there are usually financial counterparts—payments from one country to another—that involve the foreign exchange market. The organization of this market, which in total value of transactions is the largest in the world, is the subject of the next chapter.

SUMMARY

1) In international trade, country A is said to have a comparative advantage over country B in the production of a good when A can produce the good at lower cost in terms of opportunities foregone than can B. When countries follow their comparative advantage, they produce the items that they can make at lower opportunity cost, and export some of their production, while importing the items that must be produced at higher opportunity cost. By following their comparative advantage, they will increase their total output from a given stock of resources and raise their consumption.

2) Dynamic gains from trade include the greater efficiency that flows from increased competition, the spread of knowledge, and the diffusion of technology.

3) Trade barriers against imports are adopted for many reasons. The infant-industry argument holds that new industries need protection against imports to give them time to become competitive. The defense argument suggests that certain industries need to be protected against foreign competition because national output is needed to defend the country. The cheap-labor argument maintains that cheap labor abroad will lead to imports that damage domestic industries. It is clear, however, that the main impetus for protectionist policies is the self-interest of the parties that would derive economic benefits from the trade barriers.

4) The main barriers to international trade are tariffs, quotas, and voluntary export restraints (VERs). Tariffs are a tax on imports. Quotas involve controls on the quantity of imports. VERs place controls on exports, usually in response to political and economic pressure from the importing country. All reduce the quantity imported and raise the price of both imports and domestic production.

5) Trade policy in the United States has been marked by a number of intense political struggles. The Smoot-Hawley Tariff of 1930, highest in the country's history, spawned international retaliation and had a role in the collapse of world trade in the early 1930s. The General Agreement on Tariffs and Trade (GATT) was established after World War II, in part to bring about reductions in the world's high barriers to trade. The most recent agreement, the "Uruguay Round," was signed in 1994, but it proved very difficult to negotiate and has still to be ratified. Regional trade agreements, including the European Community (EC or Common Market) and the North American Free Trade Agreement or NAFTA, are permitted under GATT rules but have also stimulated considerable controversy.

6) Trade has become globalized. The role of multinational firms with branches in many countries has grown, and transactions among the branches of such firms now account for some 25% of world trade; global sales of U.S. multinational firms are actually greater than U.S. exports. This development has led to new political alliances and considerable changes in trade flows based on lower costs.

Chapter Key Words

Absolute advantage: When country A can produce a good with fewer resources than are needed to produce the same good in country B, country A is said to have an absolute advantage in the production of that good. When comparing two countries, it is possible that one of them would have the absolute advantage in all the goods that could be traded.

Ad valorem tariffs: See *tariff*.

Comparative advantage: The theory first formulated by David Ricardo in the nineteenth century. Idea that consumption can be increased by exporting the items that a country produces with relatively less cost and importing the items that a country produces with relatively greater cost. When country A can produce more of both goods 1 and 2 than can country B from the same quantity of resources, A has the absolute advantage in both goods. But if its margin of superiority is greater for good 1 than for good 2, country A is said to have a comparative advantage in good 1, and country B has a comparative advantage in good 2.

Dynamic gains from trade: Gains from international trade due to an improvement in the efficiency with which an economy operates.

GATT (General Agreement on Tariffs and Trade): International organization based in Geneva, Switzerland, that conducts negotiations to reduce trade barriers. Sponsor of the *Uruguay Round*, which see.

Infant-industry argument: An industry just beginning operation (an infant) may encounter inefficiencies due to lack of experience. Without temporary barriers against imports, it is said, the industry will not survive.

Most-favored nation: A treaty arrangement whereby a country that gives tariff concessions to one country (the most-favored nation) must apply these concessions to all countries.

NAFTA (North American Free Trade Agreement): An agreement reached in 1993 to eliminate almost all barriers to trade among the United States, Canada, and Mexico, to be phased in over 15 years. Provoked a major political battle and ratified by a very narrow margin.

Protectionism: A policy of barriers to international trade, including *tariffs, quotas*, and *voluntary export restraints*, which see.

Quotas: Fixed limits on the quantity of imports.

Specific tariffs: See *tariff*.

Tariff: A tax on imports. Tariffs can be specific, such as 20¢ per pound of product, or *ad valorem*, such as 10% of a product's value.

Terms of trade: The price ratio of imports to exports in international trade. Important in the theory of comparative advantage.

Trade adjustment assistance: Government programs to ease the transition of workers from industries harmed by foreign trade to those with better prospects. Involves retraining to increase mobility, as well as extended unemployment compensation.

Uruguay round: The latest GATT round of trade negotiations to reduce trade barriers. So named because its first meeting was at Punta del Este, Uruguay. Signed in 1994 to take effect in 1995.

Voluntary export restraints (VERs): Agreements between importing countries and exporting countries that exporters will restrain their exports. Often imposed by threat of a quota, rather than being truly voluntary.

Chapter Questions

1) U.S. companies produce sophisticated microprocessors, but they make very few memory chips. South Korean companies do the opposite. For each type of chip, which country do you think has an absolute advantage? Which country do you think has a comparative advantage?

2) The United States can produce one airliner or use the same resources to produce 2,000 cars. Japan can make one airliner or 4,000 cars. Draw production possibilities curves for both countries, showing airplanes on the vertical axis and thousands of cars on the horizontal axis. If the United States and Japan begin trading, which country will produce cars and which will produce airliners? On your diagrams, show a new world price of one airliner equals 3,000 cars. Can each country now have more airplanes and more cars?

3) In Italy, athletic shoes cost $20 and designer shoes cost $40 to produce. In the developing world taken as a whole, the athletic shoes cost only $2 while the designer shoes cost only $6. Because both types of shoes are cheaper in the developing world, the Italian shoe industry will die out without protection. Do you agree with this statement?

4) A spokesperson for an organization favoring freer trade comes before the Congressional committee you chair. She says, "We favor free trade even with countries whose relative prices are all about the same as ours. The gains from trade are not limited to just a higher quantity of goods." What other gains from trade is she refering to?

5) In usual circumstances, which of the following people should worry about competition from cheap foreign labor? Why?
     a) An engineer at a U.S. manufacturing plant.
     b) A janitor at a U.S. office.
     c) An unskilled U.S. factory worker.

6) Suppose the United States abolishes its trade barriers on a certain product. Under what circumstances would workers be most affected by the new policy, and what might be done about it?

7) Removing a tariff causes gains for some people and losses for others. Show the supply and demand for an imported good on which a tariff is charged. If the tariff is removed, what will be the change in consumer surplus, producer surplus, and government revenue? Is there a net gain or loss from lowering the tariff?

8) Suppose that the government shifts from a tariff to a quota and then to a VER. What happens to the tariff revenue as the barrier changes from tariff to quota to VER? Be specific about your assumptions.

9) Reducing trade barriers is thought to be a good thing. Is there then any cause for worry if some countries elect to trade freely with one another by forming customs unions or free trade areas?

International Finance

OVERALL OBJECTIVE: To examine how foreign exchange rates are determined, and what differences they may make for policy purposes

MORE SPECIFICALLY:

- To discuss the difference between floating (or flexible) exchange rates and fixed exchange rates.
- To show that floating rates move according to the dictates of the supply and demand for a currency, and that recessions and inflations cause the supply and demand curves to move.
- To explain that under fixed rates—whether the traditional gold standard, or the Bretton Woods Agreement after World War II, or the EC's Exchange Rate Mechanism, or proposals for target zones—some mechanism must exist to keep exchange rates from moving, or from moving very far.
- To consider the consequences of currency depreciation or devaluation, and appreciation or revaluation.
- To understand that fixed exchange rates are vulnerable to speculative "hot-money" flows.
- To examine the system used for measuring international economic transactions called the balance of payments.

The preceding chapter considered why international trade takes place and analyzed how protectionist barriers may interfere with trade. Now we turn to the mechanism through which international payments are made—the **foreign exchange rate** and its determinants.

Almost all international trade involves the market for foreign exchange. If you buy any product abroad, unless you undertake inconvenient barter with a merchant overseas, you will directly or indirectly enter the world of foreign exchange. Say you want to purchase a case of "Auld Reekie" Scotch jam direct from the Reekie Jelly Company, Ltd., in Edinburgh. Immediately you have a problem. The price of the jam is quoted in British pounds sterling, not in dollars—£100 for the 50-jar case. But you have dollars in your bank account, not pounds. You or Reekie must undertake to exchange currency, most likely in a bank. So either you buy the pounds and send them to Edinburgh yourself, or you send the Reekie Company dollars and let them handle the exchange of currencies from dollars to pounds. Either way, your jam purchase has involved buying and selling foreign currency in the foreign exchange market. This huge market worldwide was seeing average transactions of about $880 billion per day in 1993. It is the largest market in the world.

The foreign exchange market has evolved considerably over the decades, and since the early 1970s exchange rates have been set quite differently than was the case before that time. Most countries formerly established the prices of their currencies (that is, their exchange rates) by "fixing" them, that is, establishing and defending a rate fixed against some other currency. More than two-thirds of all countries still do fix their rates. The remaining countries—including the United States and Japan, which are responsible for more than half of world trade—use **floating** (or **flexible**) **exchange rates**. Floating rates move according to the dictates of supply and demand. A major purpose of the chapter is to explore the advantages and disadvantages of fixed and floating rates. As we shall see, there is a wealth of experience to draw on.

► WHEN CURRENCIES WERE MADE OF PRECIOUS METALS

For many centuries, currencies consisted of coins made out of precious metals, such as gold or silver. The value of the coins was established by the weight of precious metal they contained. A currency dealer sure of the purity of the metal only needed to know the weight of the "full-bodied" coins of different countries in order to determine the exchange rate between them. So, a trader wanting to obtain marks for pounds would get two for one, because a mark was originally equal to a half a pound of silver while a pound, as the name implies, was originally equal to a pound of silver.[1]

As time passed, coins did not contain as much precious metal as their face value, A £1 coin might be minted from only £½ worth of silver or gold mixed with another, much cheaper, alloy. This development allowed for large increases in the money supply. Governments saw advantages in putting currencies into circulation at their face value but incurring a lower cost in terms of precious metals in their coins. If carried to extremes, this practice could increase the money supply so much that inflation was the result. In fact, the first inflations known to history were due to "debasing" the currency.[2]

---

1.   Of course, appropriate checks had to be made to determine if the metal was pure and the coins still had their original weight—for someone might have clipped or shaved them, removing a little of the metal around the edges. (That is the reason for the milled edges on coins, it being easier to ascertain whether "clippers" and "shavers" had been at work.)

2.   It was very difficult for foreign merchants to determine what the proportion of precious metal actually was, and thus how much foreign money the merchant would be willing to pay for debased coins. When Archimedes of Syracuse leaped from his bath shouting "eureka, I have found it," what he had found was the principle that metals of equal weight but different density displace a different volume of water— so providing a test of how alloyed the metal in a coin was. Among the early inflations were those generated by Cleopatra and her father in Egypt, and by Nero shortly afterward in the Roman Empire. Nero's inflation allowed that debased ruler to orchestrate the rebuilding of Rome after the great fire.

Paper bank notes complicated the situation even further when they eventually became common from the latter part of the eighteenth century. These, of course, contained no precious metal at all. In order to facilitate the buying and selling of these paper notes in exchange for foreign money, the principle of supply and demand had to replace weighing among currency dealers. Prices for currency came to be established in terms of other moneys much as prices were established for any commodity. Just as the value of wheat is reckoned in terms of dollars, so can the value of the British pound also be reckoned in dollars. These currency prices were flexible up or down; in the parlance of economists they were floating rates.

► FLOATING (FLEXIBLE) EXCHANGE RATES

When the price of moneys is determined by supply and demand, exchange rates are said to be *floating* or *flexible*. Figure 28.1 illustrates the market for the exchange of U.S. dollars against French francs. Anyone who wants to buy francs with dollars comes to this market. So does anyone who wants to buy dollars and sell francs. The intersection of the supply curve and the demand curve determines the price.

On the vertical axis of the figure is the franc price of one dollar. On the horizontal axis is the quantity of dollars traded. The supply curve shows the quantity of dollars being put on the foreign exchange market at various prices. Where do the dollars that come to the market originate? Some are there because of exports of French goods. French exporters are being paid in dollars and take them to banks for exchange, or alternately American importers of these goods take dollars to their banks in America to buy francs for payment. Either way, a supply of dollars is being put on the foreign exchange market. Other sources of supply are tourists from the United States who want to travel in France, and sales of French stocks, bonds, and property to Americans who want to buy assets in France. Consider the shape of the supply curve. The less valuable dollars are (that is, if $1 will buy only two francs rather than six or eight), the less eager Americans will be to buy French goods, travel in France, or invest there. A price of two francs per dollar is a poor bargain for Americans, so the quantity of dollars supplied to the foreign exchange market in order to buy francs will be low. A high price of eight francs per dollar will increase the American desire to obtain francs and will generate a large quantity of dollars supplied.

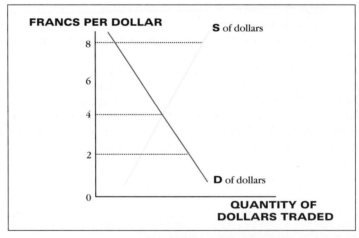

Figure 28.1. Floating (flexible) rates are determined by supply and demand. A supply of dollars emanates from Americans who want to buy French goods and services, or assets in France. The French demand dollars in order to buy U.S. goods and services, or assets in the United States. Just as the price for any commodity is determined by supply and demand, so is the price of dollars in the foreign exchange market.

The demand curve for dollars in Figure 28.1 shows the quantity of dollars demanded by those who have francs to sell at various prices for the dollar. Demand for dollars will be forthcoming from any French resident who wants to import U.S. goods, use U.S. airlines, shipping, or insurance policies, travel in the United States, or buy U.S. stocks, bonds, and property. If dollars are cheap (that is, if it takes only two francs or so to buy a dollar), then the quantity of dollars demanded will be high. If dollars are expensive, so that eight francs are needed to buy one, then the quantity of dollars demanded will be low.

Where the two curves cross in Figure 28.1, the quantity of dollars demanded and supplied is equal. At this point, an equilibrium foreign exchange rate between the dollar and the franc is established. As with any market price, only at the intersection of the demand and supply curves will there be no pressure for the price of dollars (the exchange rate) to fall or to rise. In Figure 28.1, that equilibrium exchange rate is seen to be $1 = four francs.

Floating rates are free to change with the day-to-day fluctuations in supply and demand. In Figure 28.2, a greater desire by the French for American goods raises the demand for dollars from D_1 to D_2. As the figure shows, the old price of four francs per dollar can no longer be an equilibrium price. At that price, the quantity demanded exceeds the quantity supplied, and the price will rise to a new equilibrium at a higher franc price of dollars than before (shown here as five francs to the dollar instead of four). The movement to a higher price of dollars in terms of francs is called a **depreciation** of the franc, five of which are needed to buy a dollar rather than four, and an **appreciation** of the dollar, one of which now buys five francs rather than four. Newspapers use simpler language to say the same thing. "Dollar up against franc," they will say in New York. "Franc falls against dollar," they will say in Paris.

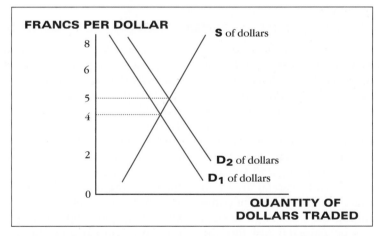

Figure 28.2. **A change in demand alters the exchange rate.** Here an increase in the demand for dollars causes the value of the dollar to rise (appreciate) and the franc to fall (depreciate). It now takes more francs than before to buy a dollar, or looking at the mirror image of the matter, a dollar buys more francs.

The same results can occur if the supply curve changes its position, as in Figure 28.3. A greater desire by Americans to buy French goods raises the supply of dollars brought to the foreign exchange market from S_1 to S_2. As shown in the figure, the old price of four francs per dollar cannot hold; it is not an equilibrium price. At four francs to the dollar, the quantity supplied exceeds the quantity demanded, and the price will fall to a new equilibrium at a lower franc price of dollars than before (shown here as three francs to the dollar instead of four). A lower price of dollars in terms of francs is called an *appreciation* of the franc, only three of which are needed to buy a dollar rather than the four needed formerly, and a *depreciation* of the dollar, one of which now buys only three francs rather than four.

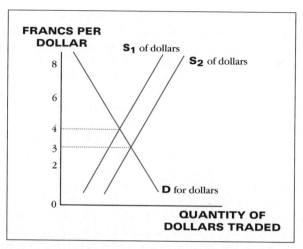

Figure 28.3. A change in supply alters the exchange rate. Here an increase in the supply of dollars causes the value of the dollar to fall (depreciate) and the franc to rise (appreciate). It now takes fewer francs than before to buy a dollar, or looking at the mirror image of the matter, a dollar buys fewer francs.

THE GREAT IMPORTANCE OF FINANCIAL FACTORS IN FOREIGN EXCHANGE TRANSACTIONS

It used to be the case that most of the demand and supply for currencies in the foreign exchange market came from exports and imports of goods and services. In recent years, that has ceased to be true. Most foreign currency movements are now connected with capital investment and financial factors including the search for higher interest rates, hedging, and speculation. For example, yearly capital flows in foreign exchange markets have become immense, swamping the currency transfers related to trade. A net capital inflow into the United States of $660 billion took place during the years 1982–1988, amounting to about 15% of U.S. gross saving. (If that capital inflow of foreign savings had not occurred, the United States with its huge federal borrowing and its low personal savings would have suffered a major rise in interest rates.) Foreigners now have a portfolio of investment in the United States of about $1.8 trillion, divided as follows: U.S. government bonds, 23%; corporate bonds, 11%;

corporate stocks, 11%; direct investment involving ownership of U.S. companies, 8%; and bank deposits plus miscellaneous, 37%.

Even this large net inflow is completely dwarfed by the churning in international financial markets. Remember that the $660 billion over a seven year period is less than *one day's* total activity in the world's foreign exchange markets. Most of that churning is related to hedging and speculation. For example, if you are an American who has to pay a bill in German marks in a few days, you can buy the marks now and hold them in a bank account to hedge against the risk that the mark might rise against the dollar before the bill is due. If you believe that real interest rates on the mark will be higher than on the dollar for the next few weeks, you can buy marks with your dollars and keep them on deposit in a German bank. If you believe the dollar might fall tomorrow, even if just temporarily by half a cent or so, you can speculate by buying marks with your dollars. If you are right and the dollar does fall, you can repurchase the dollars more cheaply than you sold them. Your expectation of what monetary policy will be in Germany and the United States during the coming weeks will therefore be a critical factor, because interest rate changes will affect the exchange rate. Nowadays, interest rate differences, hedging, and speculation provide most of the funds coming on the world's foreign exchange markets, perhaps $30 to every dollar directly connected with exporting and importing.

A specific demand for dollars has arisen for another reason. Since World War II the U.S. dollar has served as an international medium of exchange. This means foreigners want to hold dollars to facilitate carrying out international business. Say a firm in Switzerland exports a shipment of watches to a firm in Thailand. Both parties to the transaction have

dollar accounts in their banks and may find it convenient to make payment through these accounts. The Thai buyer simply writes a dollar check to the Swiss seller. Each may have an account with an American bank, or more likely each has a dollar account in a foreign bank. Dollars held in foreign bank accounts are known as **Eurodollars**. Such deposits originally sprang up in Europe, hence the name, but have become increasingly common in Asia and the Caribbean. Dollar deposits are held abroad not only for convenience in international trade and finance, but for safety by those who prefer not to hold dollars within the legal jurisdiction of the United States. Holders of Eurodollars will gain whenever interest rates on Eurodollar accounts are higher than on bank accounts in the United States.

THE ECONOMICS OF EXCHANGE RATE MOVEMENTS

Movements in exchange rates have been wide in recent years. For example, in 1987 one U.S. dollar would purchase 1.33 Canadian dollars. By early 1992, one U.S. dollar would buy only 1.17 Canadian dollars. But by November 1993, the U.S. dollar had recovered most of the lost ground, with U.S. $1 = Can. $1.29. Further examples of wide exchange rate movements can be found in Table 28.1, which shows the highs and lows for the dollar in the period ending 1991–1993.

TABLE 28.1
U.S. dollar exchange rates, 1991–1993 highs and lows.*

	1991–1993 High	1991–1993 Low
German Marks per U.S. Dollar	1.84	1.39
Japanese Yen per U.S. Dollar	142	101
U.S. Dollars per British Pound	1.43	2.00

*For the period ending December 1, 1993.
Source: Wall Street Journal, various issues.

Changes in exchange rates among the major currencies of as much as 1% a day, 5% a month, and 20% a year became common in the 1980s. The two years from 1985 to 1987 were particularly dramatic: Americans who could buy 260 yen for a dollar at the start of the period could only get 140 yen at the end, a decline in the dollar of almost half, and almost a doubling of the yen. The uncertainty (and actual economic damage, as we shall explain) caused by these wide movements in exchange rates have led to considerable criticism of exchange rates that float according to the movements in supply and demand.

What Causes the Shifts?

The swings in foreign exchange rates are the direct result of shifts in supply and demand caused for any reason whatsoever. Often, however, the causes of shifts can be identified as the result of macroeconomic conditions. Here are three such circumstances.

1) *There is more inflation in one country than in another.* Let us use the example of the United States and Germany. Higher U.S. prices make German goods attractive to U.S. buyers and make U.S. goods less attractive to German buyers. In the foreign exchange market, the supply of dollars will rise from S_1 to S_2 in Figure 28.4 as Americans buy more German marks to facilitate their purchase of German products; the demand for dollars will fall from D_1 to D_2 as Germans buy fewer U.S. goods and hence need fewer U.S. dollars. The higher U.S. inflation has caused the mark price of dollars to fall—the mark has appreciated (gained value), the dollar has depreciated (lost value). In general, when prices rise faster in one country than in its trading partners, we expect the inflating country's currency to depreciate.

2) *There is more income growth in one country than in another.* Changing incomes work in the same direction. A booming U.S. economy will cause U.S. consumers, who now have higher incomes, to want to buy more goods (including goods imported from Germany). That will raise the supply of dollars on the foreign exchange market from S_1 to S_2 in Figure 28.4. The relatively faster U.S. economic growth will cause the mark to appreciate (dollar to depreciate).

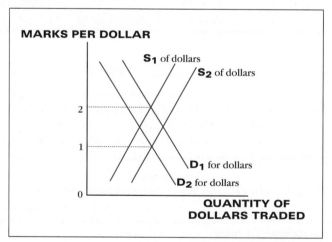

Figure 28.4. Inflation or increases in income causes a currency to depreciate. Price rises in the United States but not in Germany raise the supply of dollars as Americans purchase more German goods, but lower the demand for dollars as Germans buy fewer U.S. goods. The mark appreciates and the dollar depreciates. An increase in U.S. income would cause Americans to want to buy more German goods, so raising the supply of dollars. Again, the mark appreciates and the dollar depreciates.

Turn the example around. What if a *recession is more severe in one country than in another*. Say a recession hits the United States harder than Germany. We would expect the dollar to appreciate and the mark to depreciate. Here the income mechanism is more important (prices are more sticky in a downward direction). Falling incomes leave less available to Americans for spending on imports from Germany. The supply of dollars falls (from S_2 to S_1 in Figure 28.4), and the price of dollars rises. Possibly U.S. prices might fall relative to German ones, in which case German goods will look less attractive to Americans and U.S. goods more so. The supply of dollars brought to the foreign exchange market falls yet further. Germans also see the price changes; the cheaper U.S.

goods lead them to demand more dollars in order to buy them. In the diagram, D_2 moves to D_1. Driven by the income and price changes brought about by the recession, the dollar appreciates and the mark depreciates.

3) *Differentials in interest rates.* Perhaps U.S. interest rates are higher than elsewhere because of a Federal Reserve monetary policy of tight money; perhaps the cause of the higher interest rates is a large federal budget deficit that has increased the demand for funds on U.S. credit markets. Now consider what you might do if you live in the German city of Frankfurt and discover that the interest rate paid on dollar deposits or government bonds in the United States is now 8%, but in Germany a bank deposit in marks, or a German government bond, pays you only 3%. You will surely be tempted to buy dollars, deposit them in the United States, and earn the higher interest rates paid there.

REAL, NOT NOMINAL, RATES ARE THE IMPORTANT ONES

Warning. The interest rates discussed here are real, adjusted for inflation. Remember that a nominal rate of interest of 5% in a country where inflation is proceeding at 5% per year would mean that the real rate of interest is zero. Foreigners would *not* be expected to move their deposits to countries where real rates are low or even negative, even if nominal rates are high.

Expectational Factors

Expectations play a significant part in exchange rate movements. Drawing on actual cases, say the citizens of Argentina believe the country's undisciplined government will soon lose its financial restraint, print money, and generate an inflation. These citizens will use their Argentine money to buy dollars (or other "hard" foreign currencies expected to retain their value) and move them overseas in what is called "capital flight." Or say Peru's business community fears that that country's government intends to nationalize private firms. They, too, will join the capital flight. Say it is August 1990, and Kuwait's sheiks suspect Iraq may be planning an invasion: again, capital flight will cause Kuwaiti dinars to flood onto the foreign exchange market. Where will this capital go? To countries where the security of assets is high, taxes are low, business conditions are good, oil shocks are thought likely to do little damage, inflation is low, and the exchange rate of the currency is expected to rise rather than fall. Countries with these advantages will find foreigners buying their currencies, and the rising demand appreciates that currency's value. Countries losing the flight capital find *their* currencies are depreciating.

THE IMPACT OF CURRENCY APPRECIATION OR DEPRECIATION

When floating rates change substantially—as frequently they do—the appreciations or depreciations may have detrimental economic consequences. These are (1) an increase in uncertainty and risk, (2) an effect on exports and imports, and (3) an effect on inflation and unemployment.

Uncertainty and Risk

Even if rates never moved at all, the amount of commerce carried on between Maine and California would surely be reduced if the two had separate currencies. The two currencies would have to be exchanged by banks, for a fee, every time a transaction was made. This bothersome and expensive process is familiar to any American traveling to Europe or even to Canada. (Banks always levy a service charge on any exchange of foreign moneys. If you travel to Europe and exchange $1,000 worth of local currency every time you cross a European border, by the time you finish a 12-country trip, nearly half your money will be eaten up by the commissions alone. The bank at Toronto's airport has a minimum charge of Can$3 on any purchase of Canadian dollars, making it prohibitively expensive to obtain Can$10 or $20 for a taxi.)

If the exchange rate between two currencies floats and moves frequently in large jumps, then the situation is worse. Uncertainty and risk of loss from an unfavorable movement in the rate would increase, and all forms of commerce would become less attractive. An inability to count on stable rates is a major deterrent to both importing and exporting. Buyers and sellers would be more hesitant to sign contracts, and travelers would be less inclined to make the trip.

These objections are often accorded too much weight, however, for two reasons. First, experience with floating rates in the 1970s and 1980s demonstrated that, in spite of unprecedentedly wide and rapid swings in exchange rates, international trade grew in all years except during the early 1980s world recession. Of course, trade might have grown even faster in the absence of exchange rate fluctuations—that is hard to know. At the least, however, the severest critics, who predicted that great movements in exchange rates would create so much uncertainty and risk as to cause substantial reductions in trade, were not correct. Second, the firms engaged in international trade came to understand and use the system of "buying insurance" against changes in an exchange rate. The availability of insurance against fluctuations make the risk and uncertainty more manageable. How it works is explained in the accompanying box.

INSURING AGAINST EXCHANGE RATE CHANGES WITH FORWARD CONTRACTS

Insurance against exchange rate changes can be purchased in the form of a "forward exchange" contract. Say you will be receiving British pounds for the sale of computers next month, but you fear that the pound will decline before you receive your pounds and exchange them for dollars. Today you can sell pounds in the forward exchange market, at today's forward market price. When you deliver the pounds a month from now, the bank will pay you the price in dollars guaranteed in your agreement. The bank will charge a small premium for its services. Merchants with such contracts can be confident that they will not lose from movements in the rates, because they have already "locked in" a rate by buying forward.[3] True, buying such insurance—"forward cover" it is called—always costs money (though not much), and it is not available for every currency because some are traded only in small amounts on thin markets. Forward cover also eliminates the chance for a gain if the currency you will be receiving appreciates. Yet for the important currencies, forward markets are well developed, and prudent use of them means that the risk of changing rates is eliminated.

Recently a new form of forward contract has arisen, the so-called "currency option." (A currency option is a forward contract that does not need to be exercised.) If the exchange rate moves in your favor, you do not use the option and obtain a speculative gain. If the exchange rate moves against you, the option can be exercised, so providing you with insurance against loss. Options are much more expensive than regular forward contracts, often amounting to about 3% of the value of a given transaction.

---

3.   On the day the bank signed the forward contract with you, it went into the foreign exchange market and bought dollars for pounds at that day's rate. It then held them at interest for a month. So it has the dollars with which to pay you after a month has gone by, and it runs no risk of an adverse change in the exchange rate.

The Effects on Exports and Imports

The macroeconomic impact of currency's appreciation or depreciation on a nation's trade can be large. If Beavaria's currency is appreciating (rising in value), foreigners see Beavaria's higher-priced goods as less desirable and reduce their imports of these goods. Beavaria's exports fall. Conversely, Beavaria's own consumers come to prefer foreign goods that are now cheaper; Beavaria's imports rise. So, in countries whose currencies are appreciating, firms that produce for export and firms that face competition from imports are both damaged. Investment in these industries is likely to fall. The firms damaged by the imports and their workers, who are also voters, are likely to lobby for tariffs and other protective restraints on imports. Protectionism thrives when exchange rates are elevated. (Consumers of foreign goods, those who travel abroad, or those who want to buy foreign assets are, however, helped.)

The large appreciation of the dollar, in real terms by about half from its low point in 1980 to its high in February 1985 illustrates these principles well. The appreciation was quite damaging for U.S. trade. U.S. exports fell 9% between 1981 and 1985, while U.S. imports rose 28% in the same period. In 1981, U.S. imports exceeded exports by $28 billion; the negative margin rose to $113 billion in 1984 and to $159 billion in 1987. In these years Germany and Japan, whose currencies had depreciated against the dollar, found themselves running substantial surpluses of exports over imports. U.S. foreign trade took several years to recover from this extended episode of currency appreciation. Eventually, the dollar fell substantially, and exports were once again relatively healthy.[4] The Japanese, whose yen was much higher in value, found their export industries in distress because of the appreciation of the yen. They had to take extraordinary steps to cut their costs of production and also accepted lower profit margins in order to sustain their sales in the United States.

DUTCH DISEASE

In the era of floating rates, it became apparent that unexpected economic events could cause a currency to appreciate, in turn causing substantial harm to exports. This phenomenon received the name **Dutch disease** because it was first studied in connection with the discovery of oil and natural gas under the bed of the North Sea, some of which was in a zone allocated by agreement to the Netherlands. Dutch fuel exports grew rapidly, while fuel imports declined. Demand for the Dutch guilder rose, demand for other currencies fell, and the guilder appreciated strongly, from 3.6 guilders per dollar in 1970 to 1.9 in 1978. The effects caused serious damage for the Netherlands' other export industries, which were penalized by the high foreign exchange rate. Dutch disease has also affected a number of other oil-exporting countries. When oil prices rose sharply in 1973 and again in 1979, Nigeria benefited along with all other oil-producing states. But Nigeria's great cocoa, palm oil, and peanut industries were decimated by the appreciation of the Nigerian currency, the Naira. Dutch disease ruined a wide range of Nigeria's non-fuel exports, which have yet to recover.

4.　　Controversy surrounds the question of why the U.S. trade deficit responded so slowly to the decline in the dollar after 1985. Some said foreigners tried to maintain their market share in the United States by price cutting and that U.S. export markets once lost took time to regain. Others argued that the foreign exchange rates had lost their effectiveness in influencing trade flows. This latter argument now appears implausible because eventually the effects of the cheaper dollar were pronounced. Probably the dollar was so very high in value around 1985 that a substantial drop had to occur before exports and imports responded appreciably.

The Effect on Inflation and Unemployment

Finally, floating rates can easily influence the rate of inflation and the level of unemployment in a country. If a country's currency *appreciates*, inflation is dampened because more foreign goods can be purchased for the same amount of domestic money. Unemployment, however, may be worsened because of the damage to the country's export industries and to producers of goods subject to competition from imports. If a currency *depreciates*, inflation can accelerate because all foreign goods immediately cost more in terms of domestic currency. On the contrary, unemployment is likely to fall as export industries find the foreign demand for their products is increasing and as industries that compete with imports find that imports are falling.

► FIXED EXCHANGE RATES

Many people have argued in the past, and argue today, that exchange rates should be fixed rather than floating, with governments establishing and defending a rate fixed against some other currency. Historically, the case was based on claims that convenience required low or no variability in exchange rates and that exchange rate movements were economically disruptive, as well as on tradition from the days when full-bodied currencies were minted from precious metals. For much of the nineteenth and twentieth centuries, most governments did not allow prices for currencies to be established by free-market forces. This was the era of fixed exchange rates, with the fixing done by means of a **gold standard** for national currencies. No one can doubt that exchanging currencies in the days of the gold standard and its fixed exchange rates was much more convenient than it is now. The fixed rates and currency denominations were in part selected to make life easier. Just before World War I, a traveler would have found that, with very little variation, the rates were the same as they had been for many years. (See the accompanying box.)

**THE CONVENIENCE OF EXCHANGE RATES
JUST BEFORE THE FIRST WORLD WAR**

One U.S. dollar = 50 British pence; two U.S. cents = one British penny.
50 U.S. cents = one Japanese yen = one Russian ruble.
25 U.S. cents = one British shilling = one German mark = one Swedish krona =
    one Norwegian krone = one Danish krone.
20 U.S. cents = one French franc = one Italian lira = one Austro-Hungarian krone.

Some slight changes in values did occur from time to time, but in general these rates could be depended upon. The convenience of rates in the era of the gold standard contributes, no doubt, to the enthusiasm of those who want to return to fixed rates.

We shall first examine fixed exchange rates during the period from the late 1940s to the time of their replacement by floating rates in the years 1971–1973. Because fixed rates are so attractive to many observers, it is important to see how that system actually worked in practice. Then we shall consider the idea that floating rates should be managed by governments so that, though exchange rates would not be fully fixed, changes in rates would be slowed. Finally, we shall look at the European currency system that has reintroduced the principle of fixed exchange rates in modified form to the nations of the European Community. Assessment of the ideas for lessening the flexibility of exchange rates can borrow to a considerable degree from the analysis carried out in the next section of the fixed rates in place during the quarter-century after World War II.

The Bretton Woods System

At the Bretton Woods Conference of 1944, held in New Hampshire's White Mountains, the World War II allies agreed to a fixed-rate system for international moneys. This arrangement continued a modified form of the gold standard that had been in existence since early in the nineteenth century. In the **Bretton Woods system**, countries agreed to establish a **par value** for their currencies in terms of foreign currency, and then to defend that value with government intervention when necessary. The par value was established by the act of setting an official price of gold. Thus the United States enacted legislation stating that an ounce of gold was worth \$35.[5] The law in Great Britain declared that an ounce of gold was worth £12½. Therefore, \$35 = £12½, and £1 = \$2.80, which was the dollar/pound par value through most of the Bretton Woods period. With all countries declaring a gold value, each had a fixed par value against all others. (Canada's dollar was outside this system, floating, in the 1950s and 1960s, and so were the currencies of a few other countries including Peru and Thailand.) This system remained in general use until 1971–1973.

A diagram is helpful in demonstrating how exchange rates were kept fixed under the Bretton Woods standard. In the absence of par values and government intervention to defend them, the forces of demand and supply would have determined the price of currency, as in the floating rate system described in the last section. Figure 28.5 shows demand and supply in the dollar/franc market.

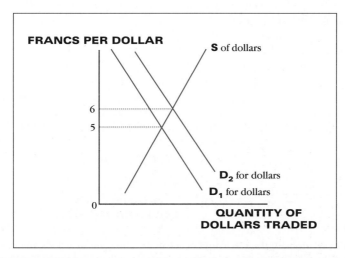

Figure 28.5. Unless something is done, a change in demand alters the exchange rate. In the figure, a rise in demand for dollars would alter the exchange rate with the French franc, appreciating the dollar and depreciating the franc. If the two countries want to fix the exchange rate, they will have to take steps to prevent the rate from changing.

If the French decide they want to consume more U.S. goods and services, then the demand for dollars would increase from its former level D_1 to its new higher position at D_2. With the old market price at the Bretton Woods par value of five francs to the dollar, the new demand would raise that price to \$1 = Ffr 6 in the absence of any intervening force. The dollar would appreciate, the franc would depreciate. Under the Bretton Woods standard, there was such an intervening force, however. In those days, governments agreed to intervene if their currencies changed in value by more than a very small amount. These "intervention points" were close together. Thus if a currency appreciated just 1% above the par value or depreciated just 1% below it, as seen in Figure 28.6, governments would act.

---

5.   This is troy weight, not the normal, avoirdupois, weight. There are 12 troy ounces to a troy pound, and a troy pound is not the same weight as an avoirdupois pound.

The upper line in the figure represents the "upper intervention point" where governments would take steps to prevent further rises in the dollar (and falls in the franc). The lower line is the "lower intervention point" where steps would be taken to keep the dollar from falling (and franc from rising). What steps? Governments would employ their **foreign exchange reserves** that over time had been accumulated against just this eventuality. These reserves consisted of hard currencies such as the dollar, pound, mark, or franc, held in bank accounts by countries other than the issuer and used to alter the demand for or supply of currencies. So the French government might use its stock of dollar reserves to buy francs on the foreign exchange market. Consider the effect of doing so. In Figure 28.6, if Q_1Q_2 of France's dollar reserves were put on the market, that would just fill the gap between the quantity supplied and the quantity demanded at a price of 5.05 francs per dollar. As long as Q_1Q_2 dollars were added to the market supply Q_1 at a price of 5.05, the price would not rise above that upper intervention point. The commitment of reserves keeps the dollar from appreciating and the franc from depreciating.[6]

In practice, even under the Bretton Woods standard's fixed exchange rates, these rates could differ from par value anywhere between the upper intervention point and the lower intervention point. A combination of supply and demand could give a rate for today of $1 = Ffr 4.97, while tomorrow a rise in demand for dollars or a fall in their supply could appreciate the dollar and depreciate the franc to a rate of $1 = 5.03, with no intervention taking place in either case.

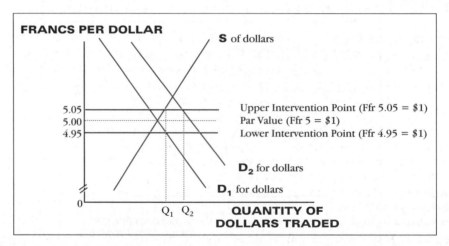

Figure 28.6. Slight variations in the rate could occur under the Bretton Woods standard.
Governments agreed to keep exchange rates from moving more than 1% beyond intervention points around a par value. They did so by committing their foreign exchange reserves when necessary. In the figure, a rise in the dollar and fall in the franc could be prevented if official sales of Q_1Q_2 dollars were made on the foreign exchange market. Between the intervention points, the exchange rate was free to move according to supply and demand.

EXPANSION AND CONTRACTION, DEVALUATION AND REVALUATION

The Bretton Woods standard faced the same problems that affect government price controls on commodities, maximum rent legislation, and minimum wages—adverse consequences when the supply and demand curves came to differ significantly from those that would yield the fixed price. Figure 28.7 shows a demand curve for dollars (D) and a supply curve for dollars (S) that yield a satisfactory exchange rate within the intervention points. No intervention is needed. Now

---

6.   Gold also played a role. France could sell some of its official stock of gold for dollars, then use the dollars to buy francs. That would also increase the supply of dollars and stop the dollar's rise (franc's fall).

assume that for a period of several years, France suffers from more serious inflation than does the United States. French consumers will see U.S. goods as an ever-better buy; an import to France costing $1 in the United States would still cost a French consumer five francs if there were no U.S. inflation. This will push outward the demand curve for dollars from D to D_H in Figure 28.7. At the same time, U.S. consumers see French goods becoming more and more expensive vis-à-vis domestic products; an import costing five francs in France might, after inflation, cost six francs in France, or $1.20 at the fixed exchange rate. As French exports become less competitive, their lower sales will mean a reduced supply of dollars from S to S_L.

France now has to use considerable amounts of its reserves to keep the exchange rate from rising past $1 = Ffr 5.05. See how Q_1Q_2 of dollar reserves has to be used in the foreign exchange market to buy francs, thus filling the gap between supply and demand at the upper intervention point of 5.05 francs per dollar. If this intervention were halted, the price of the dollar would at once rise (to 5.20 francs in the figure). For some time, the requisite flow of dollar reserves Q_1Q_2 might be maintained, depending on the quantity of reserves that the French have accumulated. No country, however, ever had enough reserves to keep expending them for a very long time in large amounts. Other steps would be needed.

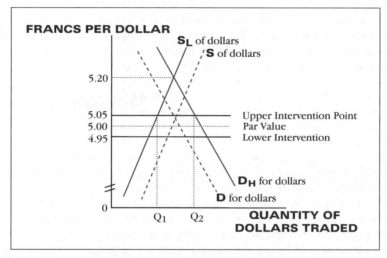

Figure 28.7. A Need for Intervention to Halt a Loss of Reserves. As long as foreign exchange reserves are adequate to fill the gap Q_1Q_2 between the supply and demand curves, the exchange rate can be held at the intervention point. But these reserves are limited, and more fundamental changes will be needed to halt their loss.

Expanding or Contracting the Economy

More commonly, it was expected that *before* the demand and supply curves reached the point where intervention would be necessary to keep the exchange rate from changing, countries would take steps to expand or contract their economies in order to stabilize the situation. Start with the demand and supply curves for dollars D_H and S_L in Figure 28.7. Intervention with Q_1Q_2 dollars must occur to keep the dollar from rising to 5.20 francs. No intervention at all would be needed, however, if the demand for dollars could be decreased, or the supply increased, or both. These shifts would follow if the United States expanded its economy with monetary and fiscal policy, or if France contracted its economy, or if both happened together. Trace first the effect of a U.S. expansion. Higher U.S. national income would increase American desires to purchase French imports and would raise the supply of dollars on the foreign exchange market, say from S_L to S. Any increase in U.S. prices because of the expansionary policies would cause French consumers to want fewer U.S. goods and would lower the demand for dollars, say from D_H to D. The higher supply and lower demand would depreciate the dollar and appreciate the franc back within the range set by the horizontal lines in the figure. France could have accomplished the same end by contractionary policy. A falling national income would lead to lower demand for dollars, while any lower prices in France would lead to a higher supply of dollars as Americans buy more French goods. The policy changes could be made by either country or both together.

The expansion and contraction could certainly work, and often did in the era of the Bretton Woods standard. Unfortunately for the stability of the exchange rate system, however, the medicine could be bitter. Expansion might mean more inflation than is desired or is politically acceptable. Contraction could mean recession with associated unemployment. Countries more and more questioned the degree to which they were willing to subordinate domestic goals to international considerations. In the final analysis they were frequently unwilling to allow their macroeconomies to be pawns to the requirements of fixed exchange rates.

Devaluation or Revaluation

There was one other possibility. The country using reserves to support its currency, as in Figure 28.7, could *devalue* its currency to end the need for intervention. Less usual but with the same effect, the country whose currency was rising could *revalue upward*.

What do these terms mean? **Devaluation** under the Bretton Woods standard meant raising the official gold price. Thus in 1971 the United States devalued the dollar by raising the fixed price for gold from $35 per ounce to $38, and once more to $42.22 in 1973. The mechanics of the devaluation are as follows: (1) Originally $35 U.S. dollars = 1 ounce of gold, while 175 French francs = 1 ounce of gold. (2) Thus $35 = Ffr 175. Because 175/35 = 5, therefore $1 = Ffr 5. (3) After the United States raises the price of gold, $42.22 = 1 ounce of gold = 175 francs. (4) Because 175/42.22 = 4.14, therefore after the dollar devaluation $1 = Ffr 4.14.

The rarer act of upward **revaluation** was never engaged in by the United States, but Britain, Germany, Switzerland, the Netherlands, and Japan all did so at one time or another. That is, they lowered the price of gold, as when Germany announced that an ounce of gold would be worth 105 Deutsche marks instead of 140 DM. If originally 35 U.S. dollars = 1 ounce of gold = 140 DM, then because 140/35 = 4, $1 = 4 DM. After Germany revalues, then 35 U.S. dollars = 1 ounce of gold = 105 DM. Because 105/35 = 3, then $1 = 3 DM.

Whether these actions are taken alone by one country as a devaluation, or in combination with other countries that revalue upward at the same time, the economic result is the same. Par value is changed, and the upper and lower intervention points are dragged along with it. In the case of Figure 28.7, which shows a weak franc and a strong dollar, the French would devalue the franc, or the United States would revalue the dollar upward, or both, so that the supply and demand situation no longer would require the government's reserves to be devoted to intervention. Figure 28.8 shows the outcome: use of reserves to defend the intervention points is no longer necessary.

Devaluation is not necessarily a permanent cure. Although the need for intervention disappears temporarily, there is no guarantee that future inflation will be controlled any better than in the past. Thus, if France continues to inflate faster than the United States, then the whole problem will repeat itself as the demand and supply for dollars keep changing. Soon the curves will once more cross outside the intervention point, and once again reserves will have to be devoted to defending the franc. Under a fixed exchange rate, it is vitally important to take corrective action as well as to devalue if intervention is to be ended.

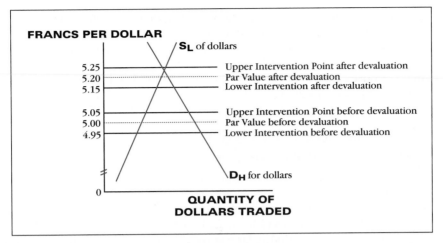

Figure 28.8. Devaluation of the franc ends the need for intervention. To halt the outflow of its foreign exchange reserves, France can devalue the franc (or the United States could revalue the dollar upward, or both). Now there are different intervention points.

ARBITRAGE

It should be noted that the country that devalues (or revalues) cannot do it against just one country. It must do so against all. If it does not, an opportunity for **arbitrage** will arise, with a class of dealers called "arbitrageurs" entering the market to exploit the profit opportunities that spring up. Say France wants to devalue only against the United States but not against Germany. To make arithmetic simple, assume the old structure of rates was $1 = 5 Ffr = 3 Deutsche marks. What if France now tries to devalue against just the dollar, so that $1 = 6 FFr but 5 FFr still = 3 DM. Perceptive dealers (arbitrageurs) with 10 dollars can buy 60 francs. With 60 francs they can buy 36 marks. With 36 marks they can buy $12.00, pocketing the extra two dollars. Then they can reenter the market with $10, buy 60 francs, with the francs buy 36 marks, with the marks buy $12, and again pocket the extra $2 before starting another round. This endless flow of profit to arbitrageurs is not sustainable. More and more arbitrage will occur; the underlying supply and demand curves shift; France begins to experience a loss of reserves as it defends the rates. Arbitrage thus makes it necessary to devalue against all countries, not just one.

The Breakdown of the Bretton Woods System

Under fixed exchange rates, adjustments were never very easy or very welcome, and eventually the difficulties involved in implementing them brought the collapse of the system. Countries losing reserves hesitated to deflate their economies because that might cause a recession; countries gaining reserves disliked expanding their economies for fear of an inflation. The United States and Great Britain, whose currencies were used to finance world trade by many other nations as well, were especially reluctant to devalue for reasons of prestige, and for fear that their currencies might no longer be used in international trade if they did so. Also, devaluations tended to become competitive as countries that lived by exporting were loath to see one of their number cheapen its exports unilaterally. Eventually, however, the United States had to face the fact that the dollar was fundamentally overvalued, that deflating the economy sufficiently to correct the situation was politically intolerable, and a big devaluation would cause a crisis of confidence in the system. The final breakdown in 1971–1973 came when the United States announced that it would allow the dollar to float and would stop using reserves to defend its value. Other countries followed suit more or less immediately, and the fixed rate system was replaced by floating rates. Exchange rates between currencies were thereafter determined by supply and demand.

THE REAPPEARANCE OF FIXED RATES: MANAGING EXCHANGE RATE MOVEMENTS

Fixed rates did not disappear entirely, even when all the major countries floated their rates. Many less-developed countries tied their currencies to the dollar, pound, or franc. They ensured that rates would vary little by intervening with their foreign exchange reserves to keep the rate fixed in value against one of those currencies (which, again, would be Q_1Q_2 in Figure 28.7). Among the major trading countries—those that do the largest part of world trade—a move developed toward what was called **managed floating**, that is, some intervention in exchange markets to keep rates from moving too far or too fast.

Fearing the results of large movements in exchange rates, governments started to intervene actively to keep the price of their currency from moving too far from what was considered to be "normal." The practice of managing exchange rate movements sometimes carries the picturesque name **dirty floating**. Unofficially, governments select and defend upper and lower limits to the movement of the exchange rate. Figure 28.9 shows the defensive strategies that can be employed. Here the dollar has depreciated to $1 = 1.00 German marks, perhaps because inflation in the United States has led to more U.S. purchases of German goods and an increase in the supply of dollars from S_1 to S_2. Both American and German officials may believe this involves an unacceptably low dollar and high mark. The Americans may worry that Germans will no longer buy American dollar bonds for fear of losing money if the dollar continues to fall; the Germans may be concerned about the damage to German exports.

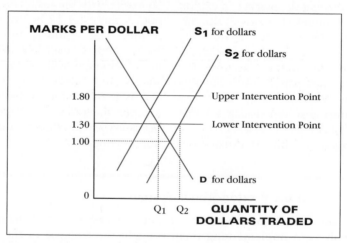

Figure 28.9. Managed floating. Here governments establish unofficial upper and lower limits and defend these limits with their foreign exchange reserves.

The depreciation may be reduced or prevented from occurring in the first place if the German government is willing to use its own marks to buy dollars on the foreign exchange markets. (The U.S. government may also be willing to use marks held in its foreign exchange reserves for the same purpose, but, of course, Germany can provide marks much more easily than the United States can. The German central bank can always create as many marks as it wants to by means of its monetary policy.)[7] As shown in the figure, at a price of 1.30 marks per dollar, the quantity of dollars supplied exceeds the quantity demanded. If governments bring enough marks to the market to buy Q_1Q_2 dollars, then this will act as a prop to the dollar, the price of which will remain at $1 = 1.30$ DMs.[8]

A little intervention could go a long way if temporary and reversible factors were the cause of the original shift in supply or demand. Perhaps the market believed incorrectly that the United States *favored* the fall in the dollar as a means to increase its exports. Conversely, in the early 1980s, Ronald Reagan was believed to favor a strong dollar, and that is said to have contributed to the boom in the dollar's exchange rate in that period. Either way, a currency's exchange rate may overshoot its equilibrium because of too much enthusiasm among speculators. Here, a little bit of government intervention may calm the markets. If, however, the curves D and S_2 reflect fundamental market forces, then government intervention is unlikely to have permanent success. The rate will be affected as long as governments can keep buying Q_1Q_2 dollars, but eventually a problem will develop. The U.S. government's willingness to intervene is strictly limited by the amount of marks it has available to sell; German willingness will be limited directly by the number of dollars it is willing to hold—if the intervention does not work, it will find itself the owner of many dollars purchased at a price above what they turn out to be worth, meaning losses for the German central bank and ultimately for the taxpayer. Less directly, if Germany creates new marks to buy dollars, the money creation might start to be inflationary.

An episode of coordinated intervention by the major industrial countries took place in September 1985, when an agreement was reached by the United States, Britain, Germany, France, and Japan to try to bring down the then-high value of the dollar. Called the Plaza Accord because it was reached at the Plaza Hotel in New York City, it resulted in the sale of dollars on the currency markets by all these countries. The accord did not of itself change basic economic conditions, but it did show a new sense of purpose and shook any remaining confidence in the market that the dollar would continue to rise. By May 1986, the dollar had depreciated in value back to about its 1975–1984 average. In 1987, the major governments believed that the dollar was now falling too low, and that the decline should be stabilized. A further agreement was then reached (at the Louvre Museum/Palace in Paris) to support the dollar.

Policy Coordination and Target Zones

This Louvre Agreement contained a policy innovation. It was seen that the level of intervention that could reasonably be expected was far too low to have much permanent effect on the market.[9] So the idea surfaced that the major countries might engage in coordination of their monetary (and fiscal) policies. A proposal to this effect had long been championed by Ronald McKinnon of Stanford University, a long-time proponent of "new fixing" with **target zones** for exchange rate movements and harmonized world monetary policies. The principles involved in this system of coordination with managed floating are shown in Figure 28.10.

---

7. During the Bretton Woods era, and thereafter until the mid-1980s, the dollar was the currency used for government intervention in the foreign exchange markets. More recently, the intervention was sometimes in currencies other than the dollar, and the United States began to build foreign exchange reserves of its own.

8. A formal system for supplying foreign currencies to governments that want to defend their exchange rate—the network of "swap agreements"—was built up from the 1960s. A swap is a loan of currency to be sold on the foreign exchange market, to be repaid several months later. The United States currently has swap agreements with most major countries, and most of these countries also have swap arrangements with each other.

9. Even so, mainly because foreign governments bought large quantities of dollars, the total holdings of international reserves reached $671 billion in 1987. The figure seems (and was) quite high, but remember that more than this is traded *every day* in the world's currency markets. From this perspective, it was a drop in the bucket.

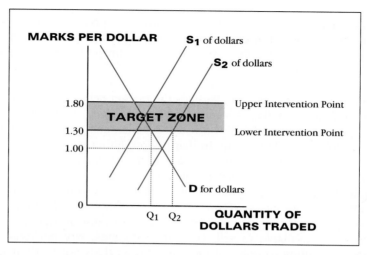

Figure 28.10. A target zone. Here governments agree on a target zone within which they will try to confine exchange rates. If the equilibrium of supply and demand falls outside the zone, the governments will first intervene with their foreign exchange reserves and later with monetary and fiscal policy coordination to pull the rates back into the zone.

Here, governments have set a target zone within which they hope to keep the exchange rates. As before when we discussed managed floating, intervention will be needed if demand and supply reach an equilibrium that is outside the zones. Recall what would happen if the supply of dollars rose from S_1 to S_2 because an inflation in the United States was causing Americans to want more German goods. Germany could keep the mark from appreciating below the lower intervention point by buying Q_1Q_2 dollars on the market and adding them to its foreign exchange reserves.

The need for such intervention could, however, be lessened or eliminated completely if the governments agreed to coordinate their economic policies. Coordination could mean tighter U.S. monetary policy and easier German monetary policy. Trace the effects in Figure 28.11: the reduced U.S. inflation and lower U.S. incomes would reduce the supply of dollars coming on to the foreign exchange markets, say from S_2 to S_3. Higher U.S. interest rates would also reduce any supply of dollars coming to the market for investment in Germany, thus contributing to the same movement. Meanwhile, Germans would want more dollars to buy U.S. goods as expansionary monetary policy raised incomes there, and perhaps raised the rate of inflation as well. Furthermore, the higher U.S. interest rates would prove attractive to German investors. The demand for dollars would rise, say from D_1 to D_2. The falling supply and rising demand would pull the mark/dollar exchange rate back within the intervention points.

With enough coordination of policies, government intervention with foreign exchange reserves would not even be needed. Rates would stay within the target zones without the intervention. Supporters of this coordination-cum-fixing note that if the United States, Japan, and the nations of the European Community did so, all others would probably follow and a situation akin to the Bretton Woods standard would be restored.

Though the Louvre Agreement did include some clauses concerning policy coordination, great barriers remain: Coordinating is difficult if the two countries have widely different views of what their economic policies should be. If the United States is unwilling to increase its unemployment, the proposed deflation will not be acceptable. If Germany fears inflation more and unemployment less, it may be unwilling to expand its economy. The more fixed exchange rates are, the less independence of policy countries can have. They must all begin to make the same choices concerning inflation and unemployment, or else the necessary coordination will not be achieved.[10]

---

10.   In fact, much increase in coordination was not achieved as a result of the Louvre Agreement. During most of 1987 the support given to the dollar and an interest rate differential that began to open once again in the dollar's favor gave it a somewhat higher value, until the stock market crash of October 1987 began another retreat. The dollar was at historic lows against some currencies in 1990.

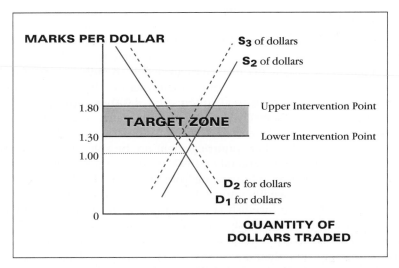

Figure 28.11. Policy coordination to pull exchange rates back within the target zone. Expansionary and contractionary monetary and fiscal policies change the position of the supply and demand curves for a currency. Thus, coordinated policy action by governments can work to keep exchange rates within some target zone.

The EC's Move Toward Monetary Union

In recent years, the European Community moved to reestablish fixed exchange rates among the member countries. In 1979 it implemented the **exchange rate mechanism (ERM)** of the European Monetary System, with limits that served as intervention points just as in Figure 28.10. (By 1992 only Greece among all the EC countries was not a member of the ERM. Meanwhile three nonmembers, Norway, Sweden, and Finland, had all tied their currencies to the ERM bands in 1990–1991.) The intervention points were 2.25% on either side of a central rate that was bargained politically. Therefore, rates among the European currencies could vary by 4.50% from the lower to the upper point before governments were required to intervene.[11] Under the ERM rules, the governments of both the strong and the weak currency countries were required to intervene when a limit was reached.

The ERM was by no means the complete equivalent of a fixed rate system, however. Realignments of the rates—mini-devaluations and revaluations—occurred rather frequently; 12 were negotiated between 1979 and 1987. The realignments were necessary because differing national monetary policies still caused different European rates of inflation and unemployment, which in turn led to shifting supply and demand curves for the various currencies. These recurring realignments made the ERM into something of a hybrid combination of fixed and floating exchange rates.

By 1992, Europe was ready to make a major advance. The members of the EC decided to establish a European central bank by 1999 at the latest. That bank would initially have more power over national monetary policies, while eventually it might acquire complete control over those policies. The member countries would then lose their power to make different decisions on how to combat inflation and unemployment. European rates of inflation and levels of unemployment would converge much more closely. With similar monetary policies everywhere in the EC, exchange rates among the member countries would automatically be stable, and it would be only a short further step to replacing individual currencies with a single European currency. But these ambitious plans hit an unexpected snag, when in 1992–1993 the EC's Exchange Rate Mechanism found itself in sudden difficulty.

---

11.   Except for the British pound, Italian lira, Spanish peseta, Portuguese escudo, and Swedish krona, which had wider limits of 6% on each side of the central rate. The governments of the countries did not want the constant intervention in exchange markets that would have been necessary otherwise. The wider limits allowed for this.

Turmoil in the ERM

Considerable turmoil enveloped the exchange rate mechanism (ERM) of the European Monetary System in 1992–1993, as a result of which European currency unification will probably be delayed. The problem arose largely because German deficit spending to pay for the expenses of unifying East and West caused an outbreak of German inflation. When the German central bank moved to stop the inflation with high (real) interest rates, other countries with lower inflation rates did not want to saddle themselves with the high rates. Germany's high rates led to considerable buying of marks by foreigners.

Speculators suspected that other countries might not be able to maintain their ERM bands. They attacked the Swedish krona in September 1992, though Sweden initially refused to yield. To discourage its commercial banks from borrowing from the central bank and then buying Deutsche marks with the loan proceeds, Sweden imposed a marginal lending rate of 25%, then 75%, then finally an astonishing 500%. The Swedish central bank also borrowed heavily in order to buy krona and so support its price. Obviously the stratospheric interest rates and heavy borrowing could not be maintained for very long. Sweden gave up and floated the krona in November. Meanwhile, speculators turned their attentions progressively to Italy's lira, Britain's pound, Spain's peseta, Portugal's escudo, and Ireland's pound. None of these countries was willing to boost interest rates to the extent needed to defend the value of its currency. The peseta had to be devalued three times, the escudo twice, and the Irish pound once, while Italy and Britain both took the drastic step of withdrawing altogether from the ERM and floating their exchange rates against the currencies that remained in the system. In 1993 speculators again challenged the peseta and the escudo and launched new attacks on the Danish krone, Belgian franc, and French franc as well.

In August 1993, Europe's finance ministers retreated. They widened the ERM's bands from 2.25% on either side of parity to 15%. In effect, that floated the challenged currencies, with intervention to maintain any given rate now far less necessary. This extended period of turmoil put the timetable for a European central bank and single currency into grave doubt.

THE DISADVANTAGES OF FIXED RATES

Fixed rates have certain disadvantages, as these European events demonstrated so clearly. The two major ones are so-called "hot money" flows carried out by speculators and the inability of a country suffering from an economic slump to benefit from the depreciation of its currency.

Hot-Money Flows

The fixed-rate Bretton Woods system was frequently a prey to currency speculators and their hot money flows, and it was eventually broken by them. Later, the ERM in Europe became another victim of currency speculation. Hot-money flows occur as follows: Say that Britain is inflating much faster than Germany, so that Britain's foreign exchange reserves are rapidly being expended in support of the pound. Put yourself in the place of a multinational company's treasurer. You know that Britain's reserves are perilously low, close to exhaustion. You know that the traditional solution to this problem is devaluation of the pound (or possibly upward revaluation of the Deutsche mark, or both)—in the ERM this would be called a realignment. You have some pounds on deposit in London, and if you keep them there you risk losing purchasing power by the amount of the devaluation. It is sheer good sense for you to exchange these pounds for German marks. The expense of doing so is minimal—just a relatively small commission paid to your bank. The risk of loss is nil, because everyone knows the pound is in danger, not the mark. Above all, there is a good chance of turning a tidy profit, because if a devaluation does occur you can buy the pounds back again much more cheaply than the price at which you sold them. When multiplied by all the corporate treasurers who act on the same facts, and by thousands of speculators who see a chance for a quick profit, the sale of pounds becomes an avalanche. The speculative hot-money flows rapidly build up pressure against the pound and may make a possible devaluation inevitable.

Hot money was the nemesis of the old fixed rate system before 1973. It was the main factor in the crises that forced the great devaluations of the pound in 1967 and the franc in 1969. Above all, it played a major role in the decisions of 1971 and 1973 to float the dollar. Had fixed rates been in use during the oil crisis of 1973–1974 and 1979–1980, it is extremely likely that hot-money flows would have reached gigantic levels.[12]

Floating the exchange rate largely avoids hot-money problems. Supply and demand adjust rates quickly to take account of changes in confidence. In the example of the pound and mark in a fixed rate system, a decline in the pound led people to speculate against it on the ground that devaluation might occur. Under a regimen of floating rates, however, the start of a movement into marks and away from pounds at once makes marks more expensive and pounds cheaper. Two results occur. First, the profits from speculation are automatically reduced. Second, the cheaper pound promotes British exports and discourages imports at the same time the more expensive German mark is accomplishing the reverse; this puts a limit on both the pound's fall and the mark's rise.

In the EC, another way to avoid hot-money flows among the member countries would be to establish a unified European currency. We have already seen that there are plans for this. Many observers inside and outside of the EC would recommend that the unification be done sooner rather than later, if it is to be done at all. The present system of semifixed rates under periodic speculative pressure appears to be a poor compromise between floating rates and a unified currency. It seems almost to invite attacks by speculators.

A Fixed Rate Can Be Disadvantageous to Countries That Suffer from a Slump

Some economists are concerned about the effects of fixed exchange rates on countries that suffer from an economic slump. Consider the situation at present if the French economy slumps while Britain's initially does not. France imports fewer British goods, so the fall in British exports initially causes the slump to spread to Britain as well. But exchange rate changes will now occur (by 15% up or down), so limiting the damage. The lower French demand for British pounds will cause the pound to lose value. The cheaper pound will prove more attractive to French consumers, who will buy more British imports than otherwise. This stimulation of British exports will keep the slump from being as serious in Britain as it would otherwise be.

Now compare the situation if the exchange rate between the pound and the franc is fixed (or if a single European currency is in use). Now no change in the British/French exchange rate can occur. The slump will spread to Britain. That might still be acceptable if unemployed Britons could move easily to find jobs in still prosperous Germany or Italy, for example, or if a fiscal system exists to transfer resources to slumping areas. Both these considerations are true of the United States, where the unemployed often move to other regions of the country to find work and where the federal tax and spending system transfers funds from prosperous states to poor ones. But neither advantage is much evident in Europe. People are reluctant to move between countries because of language and cultural differences, and the EC has only a rudimentary system of stabilizing income transfers between countries. Until there is greater mobility of populations and a more developed system of income transfers, fixed exchange rates or a single currency for the EC are likely to involve problems of unemployment. That in turn is likely to cause political difficulties, as the members with the higher unemployment lobby for expansionary monetary and fiscal policy in their own country and in the other members as well.

The Link Between Monetary and Fiscal Policy and the Exchange Rate System

In assessing their ability to use monetary and fiscal policy to stabilize their economies, governments have to consider whether their exchange rates are fixed or floating, and whether

---

12.   An old idea to reduce hot-money flows is to levy a transfer tax, akin to a sales tax, on foreign exchange transactions. The idea has never been adopted.

capital moves easily across boundaries.[13] The type of exchange rate used and the ease of capital flows can make a difference in the effectiveness of monetary and fiscal policy.

First we look at monetary policy. If the exchange rate is fixed and there are no capital flows, then with tight money, the economy cools, imports fall, and foreign currency reserves accumulate. When deposited in their banks by exporters, these reserves cause an expansion of domestic currency. As a result, the original tight monetary policy is offset by monetary expansion. If there are capital flows, then the tight monetary policy raises interest rates, which attracts foreign currency, which when converted to local currency and deposited in banks offsets the tight money. Again the tight monetary policy is offset by monetary expansion.

If the foreign exchange rate is floating and there are no capital flows, tight money lowers the demand for imports and thus for foreign currency. The domestic currency appreciates, reinforcing the cooling effect. If there are capital flows, the higher interest rates caused by the tight monetary policy attract foreign currency and appreciate the domestic currency even more, reducing exports and diverting some spending to imports, and thus cooling the economy further.

Next, consider the effectiveness of fiscal policy. If the foreign exchange rate is fixed and there are no capital flows, then a contractionary fiscal policy of raising taxes and lowering government spending lowers the nation's income and so diminishes the demand for imports. That leads to an accumulation of foreign currency reserves. These reserves when deposited by exporters lead to an increase in the domestic money supply. The contractionary fiscal policy is offset by monetary expansion. If there are capital flows, then the contractionary fiscal policy lowers interest rates, which sends domestic currency out of the country, which means a cut in the money supply, which means the contraction is tighter than it would otherwise be.

If the foreign exchange rate is floating and there are no capital flows, contractionary fiscal policy lowers the nation's income and hence the demand for imports and the demand for foreign currency. The domestic currency appreciates, reducing exports and increasing imports, which lowers domestic production of import substitutes. That reinforces the cooling effect of the fiscal policy. If there *are* capital flows, the lower level of spending caused by the contractionary fiscal policy results in lower interest rates, which repels foreign currency and depreciates the domestic currency. The depreciation works to expand exports and stimulates import-competing industries, so undoing the contractionary impact of the fiscal policy.

In fact, capital flows have become considerably more important in recent years at the same time that floating exchange rates have become the rule among the world's big trading blocs. We can conclude that these international considerations have significantly increased the potency of monetary policy and reduced the effectiveness of fiscal policy. Once again we see that governments must take into account as never before the international constraints on their economic policy.

CONCLUSION

What exchange rate regime to prefer—fixed, managed floating, or free-floating—remains a controversial area of economics. Unfortunately, each regime has distinct advantages and difficulties. Which to adopt will turn on how different a country's views of inflation and unemployment are from those of its trading partners, and how much it believes variation in rates cuts trade and investment. It seems clear that enthusiasm for a return to fixed rates now runs higher in Europe than it does in Japan and the United States. Among economists the question is by no means settled. Skepticism abounds. Would not a return to fixed rates invite destructive hot-money flows? Did not the exchange-rate turmoil of 1992–1993 in Europe show exactly that? If coordination of economic policy would stop the flows (as indeed it would), then why worry about fixing the rates? Coordinating policy is all that would be necessary. Yet why would countries be willing to coordinate if the cost of doing so might be too much inflation for some governments, and too much unemployment for others? Finally, the skeptics must also admit that floating, with its inconvenience, risk, and damage from large exchange-rate movements has

---

13.   This section is based on tables in *The Economist,* September 19, 1992.

exhibited major disadvantages. All these various negatives explain why there is no consensus position among economists about what reforms to support.

APPENDIX
MEASURING INTERNATIONAL ECONOMIC TRANSACTIONS

This appendix discusses how international economic transactions are measured. Measurement involves drawing up a record of all transactions between residents of a country and foreigners during the course of a year. This is often called the **balance of payments**. The record shows in money terms how purchasing power is spent abroad (or given away) and how purchasing power from other countries is received at home.

In accordance with bookkeeping principles, spending abroad is called a *debit* (–), while spending at home carried on by foreigners abroad is a *credit* (+). In Table 28A.1, a record of international economic transactions is constructed step by step. Although somewhat simplified, it is taken directly from the U.S. figures for 1992. Each line in the table is numbered and discussed separately.

TABLE 28A.1
U.S. international transactions, 1992
(in billions of dollars).

	Credits (+)	Debits (−)
Current Transactions		
1. Exports of merchandise	440.1	
2. Imports of merchandise		536.3
3. Balance of trade (lines 1 + 2)		**96.2**
4. Military transactions, net		2.8
5. Service and investment income, net	65.4	
6. Unilateral transfers, net		32.9
7. Balance on current account (lines 3+4+5+6)		**66.4**
Capital Transactions		
8. Private capital payments (increase in U.S. private assets abroad)		53.3
9. Private capital receipts (increase in foreign private assets in the U.S.)	88.9	
10. Gold shipments	0	
11. Changes in foreign government holdings of dollar assets	40.7	
12. Changes in U.S. government assets (foreign currency reserves)	2.3	
13. Statistical discrepancy (errors and omissions)		12.2

Source: U.S. Federal Reserve Bulletin, January 1994, Table 3.10. Figures are rounded.

1) *Exports of merchandise.* This item is *visible* exports of goods such as corn, cars, and computers.
2) *Imports of merchandise.* These are the visible imports: bananas, bauxite, and VCRs.
3) *The balance of trade.* This important figure, constantly in the news, is obtained by subtracting the dollar value of merchandise imports from merchandise exports. For many decades dating back to the nineteenth century, the figure for the United States was always positive, until in 1971 it went into deficit for the first time. Following the devaluation of the dollar in 1971 and 1973, some improvement took place, but by 1976 it was back into deficit, the negative balance growing larger as the dollar appreciated in the early 1980s.

The record high trade deficit was $159 billion in 1987—it had fallen back to $74 billion by 1991, but it is now rising again. The United States is both the world's largest exporter and its largest importer.

4) *Military transactions, net.* This is U.S. government exports of military items netted against its imports of these items. Military exports by private manufactures are not included in this line. They are classified as merchandise trade.

5) *Service and investment income.* This is a net figure that measures trade in what is called *invisibles*. It includes such items as income from transport on American ships and aircraft used by foreigners, or by Americans on foreign ships and aircraft; travel by foreigners in the United States or by Americans abroad; interest and dividends on foreign stocks and bonds owned by Americans, and U.S. stocks and bonds owned by foreigners; and profits earned by U.S. firms abroad and foreign firms in the United States. This figure remains strongly in surplus: The United States is the world's largest exporter of services.

6) *Unilateral transfers, net.* This encompasses U.S. government foreign aid (–$14.7 billion in 1992) and gifts by U.S. immigrants to relatives abroad, pensions paid to people who worked in the United States but retired overseas, and gifts and pensions paid from foreign countries to U.S. residents. (The net figure for these was –$18.2 billion in 1992).

7) *The balance on current account.* This is the sum of lines 3, 4, 5, and 6. This sum must be financed by capital flows, including all the items below line 7. If this line is negative, then spending on imports in all their forms is greater than earnings from exports in all their forms. The excess of imports over exports must somehow be financed by reductions in the stock of financial capital. Similarly, if line 7 is positive, then spending on imports in all their forms is *less* than the earnings from exports, and the stock of financial capital must increase. The capital transactions are traced in lines 8–13. An important conclusion is that these lines 8–13 must always sum to the same amount, but with reversed sign, as the current account balance of line 7. The capital transactions show how it is possible to spend more (or less) abroad than the revenue that is received from abroad.

8) *Private capital payments.* This item is a large one covering several sorts of transactions. An outflow of funds from the United States to foreign countries is generated by American purchases of foreign stocks, private or government bonds, the direct acquisition of companies or property abroad, loans from U.S. lenders to foreign borrowers, and the transfer of funds from dollar accounts in U.S. banks to other currency accounts in foreign banks. It is here that outflows of hot money will be detected when there is danger of devaluation under fixed exchange rates. These movements are also quite sensitive to differences in interest rates between countries. If holders of dollar securities or dollar deposits see that interest rates are higher in Great Britain than they are in the United States, they will be tempted to transfer their funds from New York to London.

9) *Private capital receipts.* This is the counterpart of American investment abroad and represents inflows of foreign capital for the purchase of U.S. stocks and bonds, the acquisition of U.S. bank deposits, the takeover of U.S. companies or property, and private loans from foreign banks to U.S. borrowers.[14]

10) *Gold shipments.* The old way to settle international debts was by payment in gold. When U.S. gold stocks were declining rapidly in the 1960s, however, it was clear that new methods for financing would have to be found. U.S. gold holdings, kept largely in Fort Knox, Tennessee, and in the basement of the Federal Reserve Bank of New York, had reached about 650 million ounces in 1950 and were still 509 million ounces in 1957. Several years of rapid outflow had depleted the stock to only 276 million ounces in 1972. That was when the U.S. government decided not to settle international debts with gold

---

14.   It is in these last two areas of the balance of payments, private capital payments and receipts (numbers 8 and 9), that the effect of the large Eurodollar market will be found. Eurodollars, discussed earlier, enter the balance of payments when foreigners exchange their currency to obtain dollar deposits or when they sell their dollar deposits to get foreign currency. In some years, large interest rate differentials have made these transfers very sizeable.

in the future, and so in 1992, 262 million ounces of the yellow metal still remained in storage.

11) *Changes in assets held by foreign central banks and other official agencies in the United States.* This item covers increases or decreases in dollars held by foreign central banks and other official agencies. Foreign citizens who hold more dollars than they desire will exchange these dollars for other currencies. Foreign central banks could simply allow the dollar to depreciate because of these sales, but in a world of managed floating these banks will often step in to buy dollars with their own currency. This keeps the exchange rate from moving very far, but it also means that the foreign central banks end up holding more dollars, either as bank deposits or in the form of dollar bonds issued by the U.S. government. The enlarged holding of dollar reserves is entered as a positive item in the accounts. The figure was especially high in 1987 as a result of the efforts under the Louvre Agreement to prop the value of the dollar. As the table shows, $41 billion of foreign central bank purchases of dollars took place in 1992.

12) *Changes in U.S. government assets.* These are mainly U.S. reserves of foreign exchange. If reserves of marks, yen, and other foreign currencies decrease, then the U.S. government has spent them to acquire dollars. Dollars flow in, and a positive figure is entered in the accounts.

THE IMF'S SPECIAL DRAWING RIGHTS (SDRS)

Included in the government assets discussed in items 11 and 12 are the Special Drawing Rights (SDRs) of the International Monetary Fund (IMF). SDRs are unusual in that they are internationally created reserve assets. They can be transferred between countries just as foreign exchange reserves are and as gold used to be. SDRs were born in 1967, and the plan was put into actual operation between 1968 and 1970. Paper assets were created on the books of the IMF and distributed among the member countries. IMF membership is held by almost all members of the United Nations, some (former) communist countries excepted. SDRs were allocated by a formula that gave most of them to rich nations. Although an SDR can be thought of as a piece of paper stamped "one million dollars" which can be used to pay international bills, there are in fact no such pieces of paper. All transactions are pure bookkeeping, carried out in the ledgers of the IMF. SDRs have several important advantages. They are not subject to devaluation because their value is based on the average worth of several major currencies. (In recent years, the value of one SDR has ranged from a little less than $1.30 to a little more than $1.40.) Furthermore, SDRs bear interest. It has proven difficult to create new ones, however, since an 85% vote of the IMF's members is needed to increase the total and this level of unanimity has been difficult to attain. The argument against the creation of new SDRs is that doing so would give rise to world inflationary pressures. No new creation of SDRs has occurred since a figure of 21.4 billion of them was reached in 1981.

13) *Statistical discrepancy.* This entry is "errors and omissions." Any balance sheet must make provision for errors and omissions, but this item is particularly large in the international balance of payments. Some transactions, legal as well as illegal, go undetected. Even the best sampling practices fail to account for some transfers of currency, and there are serious problems in accurate valuation of the goods and services entering international trade. For example, customs officials may have valued a Japanese television set at $300. This is the figure entered as a merchandise import in that year's international accounts. But the importing and exporting firms may have valued the TV at $350, so that 50 more dollars were converted into yen than the statistics for imports indicated. In numerous recent years "errors and omissions" have been larger than ever before as chaotic conditions in currency markets led to hot-money flows of unorthodox kinds. The figure for 1992 is small by recent precedent; for example, in 1990 it was +$48.0 billion, representing a huge unrecorded inflow of dollars that entered the country somehow. The large size of this figure in many recent years indicates that the reliability of the statistics in international trade and finance can be improved upon.

CONCLUSION

All current transactions and all capital transactions sum to zero. Any current debits must be balanced by capital inflows; current credits must be balanced by capital outflows. The counterparts to international trade and investment are the international financial flows that give rise to the enormous market in foreign exchange. International trade, investment, financial movements, and exchange rates are all thus interlinked, and flows in one sector give rise to flows in others. International trade and international finance grew increasingly more important in the last century, but that now appears to be only a beginning. Trade continues to rise as a proportion of GDP almost everywhere. The foreign exchange market is now the world's largest market for a single "product." Multinational firms operate across national boundaries to an unprecedented degree. Moves to erect barriers to trade or dismantle them, or to fix exchange rates or float them, are more crucial to economic well-being than ever before. Truly, the national economies of the world are becoming globalized.

SUMMARY

1) Floating (or flexible) foreign exchange rates are set by the forces of supply and demand. Exchange rates floated during the long era when currency consisted of coins made from precious metal, and floating rates also apply to much of international commerce today. Floating rates move according to the dictates of the supply and demand for a currency, and recessions and inflations cause the supply and demand curves to move. (Typically, an inflation causes a country's exchange rate to depreciate, or decrease in value, while a recession causes it to appreciate, or increase in value.)

2) Under fixed exchange rates, some mechanism has to exist to keep exchange rates from moving, or from moving very far. Under the traditional gold standard, the mechanism was movements in gold. Under the Bretton Woods system after World War II, or the EC's Exchange Rate Mechanism, or proposals for target zones, the mechanism involved government intervention to buy and sell currency to keep its price high or low.

3) Because governments can intervene only so long as foreign exchange reserves are available, a country may be forced to devalue its currency (that is, set new limits to its price). Fixed exchange rates are usually vulnerable to speculative "hot-money" flows triggered because speculators know that government exchange reserves are not unlimited. Hot money caused the breakdown of the Bretton Woods system and has caused great difficulty for European countries attempting to fix their exchange rates in the EC's Exchange Rate Mechanism.

4) Under proposals for target zones, governments would use their monetary and fiscal policies to expand or contract their economies to keep their exchange rates within some target area. Expanding an economy increases imports and so depreciates the currency, while contracting the economy diminishes imports and appreciates the exchange rate.

5) The system used for measuring international economic transactions in a given year is called the balance of payments. In accordance with bookkeeping principles, a country's spending abroad is called a debit (–), while spending at home carried on by foreigners abroad is a credit (+). The balance of payments is divided into two categories; the balance on current account, which is a country's balance of its exports and imports plus or minus its military transactions, service and investment income, and its unilateral transfers; and the capital transactions that arise to finance any imbalance on current account.

Chapter Key Words

Appreciation: Rise in a country's foreign exchange rate under a system of floating rates.

Arbitrage: The act of buying where rates are cheap and selling where rates are dear. Tends to keep foreign exchange rates the same in New York, London, Tokyo, and other markets.

Balance on current account: A country's balance of trade plus or minus its military transactions, service and investment income, and its unilateral transfers.

Balance of payments: A country's record of its international economic transactions during a given year.

Balance of trade: A country's net balance of merchandise exports and merchandise imports.

Bretton Woods System: The system of fixed exchange rates whereby countries agreed to establish a par value for their currencies in terms of foreign currency, and then to defend that value with government intervention when necessary. Named for a conference held in 1944 at the Mt. Washington Hotel, Bretton Woods, New Hampshire.

Depreciation: Fall in a country's foreign exchange rate under a system of floating rates.

Devaluation: Change in a country's official price of gold that makes its own currency cheaper in terms of other currencies.

Dirty floating: See *managed floating*.

Dutch disease: The tendency for some economic event such as a discovery of an oil field to lead to an appreciation of the currency, so harming the country's ability to export.

Eurodollars: Dollars held in bank accounts outside the United States, originally in Europe (hence the name) and now increasingly in Asia and the Caribbean.

Exchange rate mechanism (ERM): The system implemented by the European Community in 1979, and later greatly enlarged, under which member countries agreed to keep their exchange rates fixed against one another. Under heavy pressure in 1992–1993.

Flexible foreign exchange rates: See *floating (or flexible) foreign exchange rates*.

Floating (or flexible) foreign exchange rates: The system under which foreign exchange rates are free to vary according to supply and demand. Widely used until superseded by the gold standard of the nineteenth century, then infrequently used before 1971–1973, but in operation thereafter among the world's major trading blocs.

Foreign exchange rate: The price at which one currency exchanges for another. Varies infrequently under a system of fixed foreign exchange rates, but frequently under floating rates.

Foreign exchange reserves: Foreign currencies held by governments, used under fixed exchange rates and managed floating to defend the *par value*, which see.

Gold standard: The system under which countries agree to buy and sell gold at a fixed price in terms of their own currency (the U.S. figure was $35 per ounce between 1934 and 1971). As each country equates a certain amount of its own currency to an ounce of gold, foreign exchange rates between currencies are thereby also fixed. In wide use from the late nineteenth century until superseded by floating rates in 1971–1973.

Managed floating: Government intervention in a system of floating rates to slow the movement of exchange rates to equilibrium. Sometimes called dirty floating.

Par value: Established by the act of setting an official price of gold, used under the *Bretton Woods system*, which see, to establish foreign exchange rates among countries. Defended by means of gold transfers and spending of foreign exchange reserves.

Revaluation: A change in a country's fixed exchange rate that makes its own currency more valuable in terms of other currencies.

Target zones: The range within which countries attempt to keep their exchange rates by means of coordinating their economic policies.

Chapter Questions

1) Suppose that a strange craze for German brew sweeps Canada. The result is a shift in demand for German marks. Will the quantity of marks supplied increase? Why? Has the Canadian dollar appreciated or depreciated against the mark?

2) Italy has characteristically been a high-inflation country. If Italy's inflation rate rises relative to Germany's, what would happen in the foreign exchange market for marks and lira? Would the lira appreciate or depreciate?

3) The President appoints a new Fed chairman who is known to favor lower interest rates in order to stimulate the economy. What will happen in the foreign exchange market for dollars on the day the appointment is announced. Why?

4) You are the British finance minister under the Bretton Woods system. Your country is in the midst of a recession, and the corresponding low interest rate makes the pound unattractive. In fact, the pound is nearing the lower intervention point. What are your two choices for dealing with this situation? Do you like either choice? What other measure might you take in concert with the other Bretton Woods countries?

5) Working at the foreign exchange desk of a major bank, you keep close tabs on the fundamentals of the market for dollars. Since the dollar floats, it can fluctuate substantially in a short time. Lately you have been selling dollars because you believe it has nowhere to go but down. All the other investors you have talked with agree with you that basic fundamentals will be pushing the dollar down for some time to come. But one afternoon an unknown buyer enters the market with a considerable demand, and the dollar rises somewhat. What may have happened?

6) In 1992 the ERM faced a major crisis when speculators attacked the Swedish krona. No amount of foreign exchange intervention could have stopped the krona's fall against the mark. But the German and Swedish governments could have used coordinated monetary policy to stop the krona's decline. What would they have done, and how would it have worked? Why do you think they did not pursue this strategy?

7) Canada's economy is tightly linked to the U.S. economy. Suppose the United States is going into recession. If you were a Canadian voter, would you vote for a candidate promoting a fixed exchange rate with the U.S. dollar or one promoting a floating rate? Why?

Reforming the Command Economies

OVERALL OBJECTIVE: To compare the market system with the command system for making economic decisions, explain why crisis overtook the command economies, and explore the challenges involved in transforming them into market systems.

MORE SPECIFICALLY:

- To see how command economies relied on output targets for factories and farms, and input norms that allocated the factors of production, rather than on market prices.
- To explore the inefficiencies that arose in command economies, including the low level of technical change, the slow response to changing consumer wants, and the chronic shortages.
- To discuss the difficulties involved in reforming command economies, with a particular focus on Russia.
- To assess the privatization measures in Russia and other former communist economies, and analyze the decisions that have led to considerable inflation in Russia.
- To compare the economic reforms in China, where very high economic growth is being registered, to those in Russia where much less success has been realized.

On November 6, 1917, Communists led by Vladimir Lenin (1870–1924) seized control of the Russian government. Karl Marx had been dead for 34 years. Faced with this sudden opportunity to implement principles they had contemplated for decades, they began the transformation of Imperial Russia's rather backward market economy into a "command" system run by **central planning**. Central planning represented the first significant creation of a new economic system since the market system had replaced traditional economies over the previous several centuries.

The command system was intended to eliminate the substantial income disparities found in market economies, to promote growth of heavy industry by raising investment (thereby increasing incomes in the future), and to organize farming to support this advance. All land in what had been Imperial Russia was nationalized in 1918, as were the country's factories. Banks were taken over, and private bank accounts were confiscated. The first "five-year plan" of national goals dated from 1927, as did the establishment of collective farms and state farms (the latter run in the same manner as factories). Lenin had died shortly before, and the powerful dictator Josef Stalin (1879–1953) was at the helm. The pure form of the command economy is often called after him a "Stalinist system."

After World War II the Stalinist command system was extended to areas that had been "liberated" by Soviet forces, and where Communist governments had been installed. These included Albania, Bulgaria, Czechoslovakia, East Germany, Hungary, Poland, Romania, and Yugoslavia. In Asia, China's Communist leaders adopted similar economic methods in the late 1940s, and so did Mongolia, North Korea, and Vietnam. Laos and Cambodia later followed suit. Cuba under Fidel Castro in the late 1950s moved to central planning. Later the idea was exported to a number of other less-developed countries, including Afghanistan, Angola, Congo-Brazzaville, Ethiopia, Guinea, Guinea-Bissau, Mozambique, Nicaragua, and South Yemen.

Now, three-quarters of a century after the Russian Revolution, the world is seeing the demise of the command system. Full-scale central planning does still survive in Cuba and North Korea, but only vestiges of it remain over much of its old range, including China and the states that once made up the Soviet Union. Yet, even if its last remnants disappear, every student of economics can obtain a better understanding of the market system by studying central planning. As the only serious alternative to a market system that has had a modern trial, it tells us much about our own system. The first part of the chapter examines how the command system worked in practice, emphasizing the Soviet Union. The second part of the chapter examines the difficulties command economies face as they move to a market economy.

▶ THE LESSONS LEARNED FROM CENTRAL PLANNING

Central planning was an apt name for the command system. In the Soviet Union, government ministries were established in Moscow to supervise industries or industry groups. Originally there were two such ministries, one for heavy industry and one for light. By 1989 there were 52 industrial ministries, employing some 18 million bureaucrats. Decisions concerning what to produce, how to produce, and how to distribute the production were made by the government and put into practice by these ministries.

The typical economic ministry was in charge of a single industry. The ministry itself was located in Moscow, and directions flowed from that city through the length and breadth of the Soviet Union. Coordinating the activity of the various ministries was the State Planning Commission, called **Gosplan** (Gos means "state" in Russian), which ironed out difficulties and also had charge of drawing up the five-year plans.

How did central planning work under this ministerial system? The five-year plans were projections, not used for operational purposes. Gosplan, the ministries, and the firms all functioned under a one-year plan, usually with 12 monthly check-up periods. The annual plan instructed each firm what to produce and how this was to be accomplished. Prices had virtually no part in giving these signals. In the heyday of the command system, about 20,000 separate items were planned in this way.

The plan allocated inputs to the firms, including their raw materials, semifinished goods from other firms, fuel, and the like. It also allocated the output of the firms, either as inputs to other firms or to the general public for consumption. The plan consisted of two parts—**output targets** and **input norms** for every firm. On the basis of past performance and expectations of the future, output targets were handed down from the relevant ministry in Moscow. The firm made its own estimates of how much input would be needed to meet these targets, and communicated these to the ministry, which reviewed them and tried to "tighten up" in the sense of persuading the firm to produce a larger output from a reduced input. Then, after a period of negotiation between the firms and their ministries, all final output targets and input norms were sent to Gosplan, which had the responsibility for maintaining consistency. Consistency meant ensuring that all input and output figures meshed among sectors and at all stages of production. It would have been a problem to find that although production of a million tons of steel had been planned, the planned production of iron ore would be enough for just 800,000 tons of steel. Gosplan did its work, allocations were made, contracts were signed, and the planning year began.

Whenever a firm's input was not sufficient for production of the planned output, either because of bottlenecks in supplying firms, or because of a planning mistake, a dilemma arose. It was impossible to redo the whole plan whenever there were shortfalls. It took virtually a full year just to prepare the original plan itself. Unless steps were taken, however, missed output targets at one firm would mean lower inputs at other firms, and lower outputs there, too. The shortages would spread through the whole economy. Recognizing this, Soviet planners made every attempt to solve inconsistencies at the source so the shortages would not spread. They examined carefully the possibility of more efficient or intensive use of equipment. They looked for slack in the plan—perhaps a plant could actually get by with slightly less input, or perhaps substitutes were available and could be used. The planners then made the same investigations at the firm supplying the input. Many bottlenecks could be broken at the source by these tactics, and a general rule was to avoid changing the plan whenever possible. Sometimes, however, improvements in efficiency could not be made and the bottleneck remained. For emergencies of this sort the government maintained stocks of some critical commodities, and if the shortage looked to be serious, these were used.

PRICES IN SOVIET PLANNING

Did prices play any role for the firms in the Soviet system? Under the command system, prices of both input and output were fixed for firms by Gosplan and kept at the same level for long periods of time. For example, prices in 1989 for some basic foodstuffs had not been changed for 20 years, and the bread price had been fixed since 1917. More commonly, prices received some adjustment every 10 to 15 years. The prices were established on the basis of cost per unit—cost pricing, so to speak—but the Soviets did not measure costs as a Western economist would. Rent and interest charges, for example, were excluded from cost for doctrinal reasons.

In the command system, firms seldom or never altered their operations because of prices. Whether or not their production was in demand, whether or not the goods were sold, they were rewarded quite independently of prices in the manner described below. Prices were generally kept well under market-clearing levels; because they did not reflect the scarcity either of goods or factors, they failed to direct production toward the most profitable items and away from the loss-makers. In addition, the planners generally encouraged the output of capital goods and military production. The below-market prices and lack of emphasis on consumer goods explained the empty shelves in stores and the long queues for consumer items that were in effect rationed by shortage. The consumer goods that could be found were infamous for their poor quality and for their lack of variety—the short-changing of consumers became typical of all command economies.

In a Soviet Plant

What did central planning mean for the day-to-day operation of a Soviet plant? The most interesting question is what motivated management to carry out the dictates of the plan. The chief device was the *premium*, or monetary **bonus**, paid to management personnel for meeting or exceeding the plan's targets. Decisions were seldom made without considering their impact on the size of the bonus. The difference between 99% fulfillment of the plan and 100% could be a sizeable 30% of the plant director's income.

A visitor to a plant operating on the bonus system encountered several interesting characteristics that could be traced to the bonus. As the end of the month approached, a feeling of urgency began to permeate the plant. Would the target be reached? Would it be missed unless there was a speed-up? If there was any danger of losing the bonus, the whole factory would begin to run at an ever faster pace—Russians called it "storming"—until the planning period ended and the pace slacked off. This was a predictable response to a rewards system, and "storming" is common in market economies, too, when bonuses are used. (Storming also occurs worldwide in colleges and universities at exam time.) In Soviet enterprises, product quality suffered as a result of storming much as it does in college exams. British journalist Martin Walker quoted a worker in a factory that made TVs:

> We never use a screwdriver in the last week. We hammer the screws in. We slam solder on the connections, cannibalize parts from other televisions if we have run out of the right ones, use glue or hammers to fix switches that were never meant for that model. And all the time the management is pressing us to work faster, to make the target so we will all get our bonuses.[1]

No wonder that in Moscow, over 2,000 TVs catch fire every year.

The target itself could not be expressed in *complete* detail. A plan for a tractor factory might have said "100 tractors per month," or it might even have specified some detail such as "25 large tractors with dual rear wheels suitable for use in Siberia at –30°C., and 75 medium-size tractors with dust filters for use on dry plains." But it did *not* specify exactly how the tractors were to be built—how many rivets would hold the rear fenders in place, how thick the steel framing was to be, and so forth. The planners would have been buried under a mountain of detail if they had ever attempted such explicit instructions, so some leeway had to be given to a firm to decide these questions.

This, in turn, meant that plant managers had an opportunity to adjust their output to achieve the greatest possible success depending on how the plan targets were expressed. For example, the plan for a metal works was expressed in tons of metal roofing. Over a period of five years, that factory was able to increase its tonnage output of roofing by 20%. Measured in square meters, the area that could be covered increased by only 10%. The factory had switched toward heavier roofing, the easiest way to hit its plan target. Many similar examples were reported. Plants turning out cement blocks produced many light blocks when the plan was in numerical terms and shifted to large and heavy blocks when the plan was later altered to tonnage. Cloth was planned by the linear meter, hence bolts of cloth were narrow. When planned by quantity, nails were small. When planned by weight, there was an overabundance of spikes. In the 1970s, the *Soviet Builders' Gazette* wrote that Russia made twice as much window glass but built only half as many houses as the United States. How could this have been? The *Gazette* explained that the plan for glass was expressed in square meters, hence a very thin product was produced. Forty-six percent of it was broken in transit and during installation. Shortages of spare parts and inadequate servicing were additional results of the system's structure. The results, irrational for society as a whole, were understandable from the point of view of plant managers.

---

1.   *The Economist*, April 28, 1990.

The Safety Factor

A common, perhaps almost universal, occurrence in Soviet central planning was the **safety factor**. Plant managers realized that with no slack in the output targets or input norms, any little interruption in the supply of inputs might mean loss of the bonus at the end of the planning period. An understandable reaction was to provide some padding here and there. Perhaps the input norm could be fattened enough to give some leeway. Extra raw materials in the store room were invaluable if a bottleneck developed in a supplying firm. Some authorities quoted a figure of about 10% hoarding of scarce materials by firms that were able to manipulate their norms. Firms also attempted to have their output targets planned at a level below actual capacity. Realizing that the safety factor was present in most Soviet firms, the ministries involved often tried to compensate by advancing the expected output from a given input by a small percentage every year.[2]

One sector of the Soviet economy had another way to meet plan targets. That was the consumer-goods sector where, if necessary, product quality could be reduced. This was not possible for many industries supplying inputs to other firms. Obviously, managers of plants making machinery who discover the steel received from a supplier had weak spots in it instantly complained to the responsible ministry. Neither managers nor ministries were able to afford slippage in machine output because of supply problems. What, however, of the managers of plants that produced cigarettes or clothing or home furnishings? A little less tobacco per cigarette, fewer stitches per shirt, or using poor lumber were possibilities where products were not inputs in other industries and would not harm the productivity of other producers. Consumers as a group did not have the access to a ministry that a producing firm did. Hence plant managers found it relatively safe to cut quality if necessary to hit their targets.

Planning and New Productive Methods

The effect of Soviet central planning on a firm's willingness to introduce new productive methods was an interesting study in contrasts. In some ways the record was quite good. Statistics showed an impressive number of new ideas thought up and submitted by employees. When the ideas found favor, there were no patent laws or commercial secrecy to prevent the widespread and immediate adoption of the innovation.

There were, however, serious obstacles to innovation, due largely to the design of the planning process. For example, any halt for retooling, retraining workers, and overcoming initial defects was likely to lower total output in the short run. If plan targets were missed for a few months, managers lost their bonus and the ministry frowned. A further difficulty was the likelihood that the ministry authorizing the investment would also raise the firm's plan targets. Furthermore, innovations always involved the risk that they would fail, with damaged reputations and loss of bonus. Thus it is hardly surprising that in the 1970s the Soviet press reported that more than 600 important industrial processes and blueprints had been unaltered for as many as 30 years. The slow pace of technical change was a major cause of the unusual longevity of capital equipment. Less than 2% of it was being replaced each year toward the end of central planning, compared to 5% in the United States and about 10% in Japan.

Eventually it became clear that central planning performed poorly when many course corrections were required and when small improving innovations were desirable. Any initial mistake in a design could become an almost permanent fixture. This had not made so much difference during World War II when mass production of standardized military goods was the goal, but later it was a decided disadvantage.

---

2.   It was common enough for firms actually to fudge their production figures to hit their target and obtain the bonus. Such fudging added uncertainty to the Soviet Union's figures for GDP (which, with wide variations in the estimates, were thought to be about one-third the U.S. figure per capita).

Empire Building in the Ministries

In response to the bottlenecks and resulting shortages of necessary inputs at the plant level, numerous ministries took rather extraordinary steps to defend themselves by developing independent sources of supply within the ministry's own plants. The practice was called "empire building." Critical inputs provided within the ministry itself meant less dependence on firms not under its direct control. Widespread duplication of operations was the result, and in 1983 about a fifth of the output of Soviet ministries was outside their field of specialty.

An outstanding example was machine tools. Unavailability could cause serious difficulties for many ministries. So, machine-tool plants proliferated, and at one point the actual Ministry of Machine Tools controlled only 55 of the Soviet Union's 171 tool-making plants. The other plants were operated by 19 separate ministries. Similarly, at one time the Ministry of Tractors and Agricultural Machine Building was making only 16% of the Soviet Union's tractors, with the rest produced by 24 other ministries. Inventories in Soviet state enterprises were considerably more than twice as great as in Western firms. As empire building proliferated, the duplication and waste became legendary, and the efficiency of investment sank to very low levels.

The need for reform was patently obvious even before the end of the 1950s. But almost 40 years of attempts to do so, although they introduced many variations on traditional practices, never resulted in much improvement.

SOVIET AGRICULTURE: COLLECTIVE AND STATE FARMS

In 1930 a government decree did away with the Soviet Union's private farms. The process of doing so was difficult. Many peasants (the "kulaks") protested by slaughtering their livestock. The kulaks themselves were soon eliminated by Stalin's government.

The reasons for the collectivization of farming were three-fold. First, it was an attempt to control prices on farms, keeping them low so that the new industrial labor force in the cites would receive a cheap supply of food. The lower incomes earned by farmers would also encourage a flow of workers from farming to industry. Second, Soviet planners believed that private agriculture could not achieve the economies of scale that large-size government farms could. Third, it was hoped that surplus agricultural products could be exported to pay for imports of machinery and equipment. Most other Communist countries used similar reasoning, and eventually over one-third of the world's farmers worked under collective farming arrangements.

Two types of farming were established, the *state farms* and the *collective farms*. **State farms** eventually held almost half the tillable acres of the Soviet Union. They were very large in size, often 70,000 to 80,000 acres, sometimes even 120,000 acres with boundaries sometimes 25 miles on a side. (In the United States, 500-acre farms are a more typical size.) A state farm was run just as a firm in any other industry. The director, the junior managers, and the workers received wages, salaries, and bonuses. The usual input norms and output targets came from a ministry for agriculture. The total output of the state farms was delivered to the government except for the produce from the small *private plots*, ¾-acre patches that state farm families could cultivate for themselves.

Collective farms were run quite differently. They were smaller, averaging about 7,000 acres. The collectives were operated by their members who occupied government land without rent. In theory, the farms were worker-managed, but members elected a chairman who held the actual powers to make decisions. The most interesting feature of the collective was the way income was earned and distributed. The collective was required to sell a portion of its output to the government. After this compulsory delivery was made, the farm could sell the remainder of its produce on the "collective farm market," a place for trade maintained in towns throughout the Soviet Union. This market was ruled by supply and demand, with prices free to fluctuate. Farms near big cities usually maintained permanent stalls in these markets, although anyone was free to buy or sell in them. Sales to the government and on the free market furnished the income of the collective, divided up among the members by a system of cash payments for different tasks. If the farm did poorly, then the income of the farmers was low. In effect, the risks of farming were borne by the collective's members.

Collective farm families also had their private plots, larger than on the state farms at a little over one acre. On this land, which the farmers did not own but were entitled to use, they grew vegetables, raised chickens, and tended a few cows and pigs. The private plots were never popular with many high government officials, but they played a large role in Soviet agriculture. Surplus production from the plots were sold by individual farmers on the collective farm market to consumers in the towns. Prices on the collective market were usually from 30% to 100% higher than in state stores.

Farmers typically fed their families from their private plots and they also provided a fruitful source of cash income. The land area of the plots, which amounted to only 3–4% of all Soviet farm acreage, was intensively used. It yielded over one-fourth of the Soviet Union's food production by value, including almost two-thirds of the potatoes, one-third of the eggs, milk, vegetables, and meat, about one-fifth of the sheep, pigs, and cattle, and a quarter to a third of farmers' total income.

All in all, the structure of agriculture acted as a brake on the Soviet Union's economic performance. Farming benefits greatly from a flexible labor force, and owner-operated farms are best at that. Proper supervision of labor was difficult on the collectives. The backward nature of agriculture was apparent from the fact that the Soviet Union had more farmers than the United States, Canada, Australia, the EC, and Japan put together, but produced less than a quarter of the total combined output of these countries.

LABOR IN THE SOVIET UNION

How was labor allocated and paid in the Soviet Union? The output targets of the central plan determined the need for all types of labor so, except in a few experimental programs, the central planning authorities established the number of workers needed in particular occupations and made available a wage fund to pay these workers. Wages for specific occupations and for different levels of skill were established by the various ministries. These were printed in the official "tariff qualification handbook" for the Soviet Union and amounted to fixed wages for the entire country. There were fairly large differences in pay between industries and between geographical regions. Substantial increments could be earned by workers who agreed to locate in the far north or in Siberia. Wages were not the only incentive for attracting workers into new areas and new industries. The Soviet Union traditionally suffered from a severe housing shortage, and very often an apartment for the worker's family was a first-class drawing card for labor. Higher pensions and special bonuses for long service were also common in occupations that the government wanted to encourage.

POLLUTION PROBLEMS

Serious problems of pollution affected the Soviet Union (and Eastern Europe as well) during the era of central planning. It might have seemed reasonable to assume that, as the factories were state-owned, social costs could be considered along with private costs by the government, and that pollution would therefore be controlled. Recall, however, the importance of meeting output targets in Soviet planning. As long as rapid economic growth remained the primary planning target, there was a built-in motive to pollute.

Many sorts of pollution emerged. The Soviet Union's emphasis on heavy industry made it smog-prone, many rivers and lakes were badly fouled, and industrial waste disposal was a major problem. The turn by the Soviet Union to a particularly unsafe design for nuclear reactors from about the late 1970s, resulting in the Chernobyl disaster, was another case in point. Barring only the absence of nuclear accidents, Poland's problems were even worse. Several further cases have already been discussed in Chapter 10.

DIFFERENCES IN CHINA'S USE OF PLANNING, 1949–1980

When Chiang-Kai-Shek was expelled from the mainland to Taiwan in 1949, China moved to central planning and a command system. There were originally many similarities between Chinese and Soviet planning. In the early 1950s, Chinese plans were even run by Russian planners. But following the political break with the Soviet Union in the early 1960s, differences became substantial. Chinese emphasis on work for the good of society led to far less use of income differences as an incentive for workers and managers, and major efforts were made to prevent the emergence of a managerial class—that same class that in the Soviet Union was the recipient of the state's bonuses.

All industry was state-owned and state-run, except for the many small enterprises run by the communes on a cooperative basis. Plans and plan targets were provided to each firm. But in a major departure from the Soviet experience, bonuses were not paid to managers for successful plan fulfillment. Instead, reliance was put on the Communist Party Committee in each plant to criticize or praise managers on the basis of their performance. These *cadres* of communists, the representatives of many personnel of the plant who were party members, were expected to watch out for the interests of society as a whole. They guarded against managers too deeply imbued with self-interest and too little concerned with national goals. At times these cadres took on special importance, as during the *Great Leap Forward* of 1958–1960 and the *Cultural Revolution* of 1966–1969.

The Great Leap Forward brought the rural communes in 1958. Because no signals were given by the price mechanism, people in these new communes ate more food than before. That plus related disorganization and mismanagement of food distribution helped to cause a devastating famine of 1959–1961, during which perhaps 25 to 30 million people died. The economics of that famine were significant. The starvation was caused by mismanagement and distortions of incentives, not by a poor harvest—in fact, the crop of 1958 was relatively good. By the 1970s all of China's land was either in 50,000 communes averaging 13,000 people each, collectively farmed according to a plan, or was included in a few large state farms.

By the early 1960s, a move toward decentralization took place, with the plans for most enterprises drawn up and issued at the provincial and even the local level. Targets were issued only after extended consultation with the Communist Party Committees within the firms. The decentralization could be understood only in the context of the huge size of the units involved. China at that time had 25 provinces, and each one of them had a larger population than the majority of the world's independent countries. The attempt was made to obtain inputs and utilize outputs within a local planning area, corresponding to the move toward economic self-sufficiency often embraced by Chairman Mao-Tse-Tung and his followers. Industrial ministries continued to operate in Beijing, but their importance in the planning process was less than in the USSR.

► POOR PERFORMANCE SPURS REFORM

In the end, economics and politics combined to bring radical change to the command economies and their central planning mechanisms. The economic reasons were clear, as exemplified by the USSR. Though the early record of Soviet growth had been good, it was also misleading. It demonstrated that a limited number of goals (heavy investment, a large output of standardized military equipment and standardized civilian output) could be achieved with great success, but in time these results proved inadequate to raise levels of living for most of the population. Growth was very slow. In the USSR during the 1980s it sank to less than a third of what it had been from 1928 to 1940.[3] Several main causes of the poor performance were apparent.

1) For a long time it had been possible to transfer labor in large quantities from agriculture to industry without sacrificing farm output, but these possibilities eventually declined. Raw materials, which provided a basis for strong growth, became less accessible and harder to exploit.

2) Because prices did not reflect the scarcity of goods or the factors of production, they had no ability to direct production toward the most profitable items and away from the loss-makers. The absence of private property and the inability to shift production meant that neither the quantity of goods nor their quality changed in response to market forces. There was little or no incentive to work harder, to come up with a better product, and to take risks. Shortages caused by central-planning failures, some of them chronic, meant bottlenecks in production.

3) Inability to register improvements in efficiency, particularly from technical change, meant that productivity fell relative to that of the market economies. New investment was not giving the results it should have. Though the percentage of GDP used for investment stayed high, just over a quarter of GDP in the mid-1980s, the efficiency of that investment was very low. Factories used 70% more capital stock per unit of output than in the United States. A particular problem was the lack of innovation to improve the effectiveness of investment. This was due to the absence of incentives to innovate, poor communications among firms and ministries, and the spreading shortages of inputs. Market systems with their encouragement of a process of many trials and errors proved to be much better at stimulating technical progress.

4) The rigidity of the bureaucratic apparatus, intent on protecting its perquisites, made the situation worse.

5) Because the Soviet Union engaged in very little international trade with the West, the stimulation to be expected from the import of new technologies, new knowledge, and new incentive goods was lost.

6) The emphasis on capital goods output and military production, and willingness by the administrators of the system to ignore the interests of consumers, brought shortages in consumer goods and poor quality as well. With so little to buy, neither workers nor managers were motivated to work very hard. The lack of democratic governments to act as a safety valve for popular discontent added enormously to the alienation of the general population. Morale plummeted.

► THE REFORM MOVEMENT

As late as 1989–1990, the economies of the Communist countries still consisted largely of state enterprises that produced over 90% of industrial output. A great wave of political upheaval that swept over most of these centrally planned economies at that time moved them rapidly from the command system toward market principles. Making this transition remains one of the most difficult economic challenges of this century.

The reform of the world's command economies has been a complex and mammoth undertaking, involving conversion of tens of thousands of state companies into private firms that react to the profit motive and to the signals of prices set by supply and demand. No comparable experience exists. Yet there is broad consensus on what sorts of reform measures are needed, and in actual practice it is the details that differ rather than the concepts. This section explores the

---

3   Gur Ofer, "Soviet Economic Growth: 1928–1985," *Journal of Economic Literature*, Vol. 25, December 1987, p. 1778. My thanks to Professor Ofer for several of the ideas that figure in this chapter.

consensus and the actual results, with emphasis on what has happened in the largest of the reforming economies, Russia.

ADOPTING MARKET PRICING

Market prices have to be phased in to replace the central planning mechanism. This was done first in Poland, Hungary, and Czechoslovakia, and then on January 2, 1992, in Russia. By now, market pricing has been adopted widely (though with exceptions) in much of Eastern Europe and the old Soviet Union.

PRIVATIZING THE FIRMS

The state firms must be privatized. One way to accomplish **privatization** is to turn them into corporations and auction their shares to the highest bidder. Alternatively, the shares can be given away so that the entire population has the chance to participate in the ownership. Giving the shares away attracts great public support, but selling them raises revenues for governments that have had to develop new forms of taxation. Therefore, a combination of both sale and gift has usually been adopted. With these changes a new framework of law on private property, corporations, contracts, bankruptcy, and taxation has become necessary. Joint ventures with Western firms, or even full Western ownership in some cases, provides foreign capital, and laws have rapidly been changed to permit this. Privatizing and commercializing the state enterprises means an end to the old custom of never allowing firms to close down. That in turn means bankruptcy laws.

Some of the firms involved are huge conglomerates. Privatizing them will require a restructuring that converts most of them into smaller units that can be more easily managed. Even just assessing how much they are worth for the purpose of selling them is a monumental task. The more rapidly these firms can be privatized (thus shifting their output rapidly toward consumer goods) or closed down (so the resources they absorb can be reemployed), the better the restructuring will work.

ESTABLISHING A CAPITAL MARKET

For market prices to determine which firms get capital and which do not, a capital market is needed. Central banks must be limited to conducting monetary policy, supervising the banking system, and managing the currency. This means their commercial functions must be transferred to new private banks, and foreign banks should be permitted entry. These commercial banks will have to charge what the market will bear for loans and pay depositors an interest rate also determined by the market. Establishing access to credit for enterprises that are newly privatized or altogether new is a major challenge for the reformers. Most of Eastern Europe has already established capital markets, while Russia and many of the Soviet Union's other successor states have been slower.

FREEING EMPLOYMENT DECISIONS

Labor markets have to be freed in order to allow labor to flow from where it is not needed to where it is. This requires wages to be determined by markets rather than by government command. Furthermore, firms must be able to lay off unneeded workers, and the resulting temporary unemployment will require some kind of safety net. Many authorities believe that an incomes policy will be necessary while the transition is being made. Interestingly, Czechoslovakia before its breakup, Hungary, Poland, Romania, Yugoslavia, and several states of the old Soviet Union all adopted tax-based incomes policies akin to the TIP schemes suggested in Chapter 25. These countries have instituted a progressive income tax on wage increments to control inflation of wage costs. To make workers mobile, willing to shift from job to job as labor is more or less needed, the close tie between jobs and housing—especially strong in the old Soviet Union—will have to be broken. Other benefits, including access to food supplies in countries that decide to utilize rationing, may depend on holding a job. Attempting to find a new one might then be very risky.

TRADE LIBERALIZATION AND CURRENCY CONVERTIBILITY

To further the process of economic reform, the government monopolies over foreign trade had to be lifted. Indeed all the Eastern European countries, Russia, and most other successor states have set out to do exactly this. To facilitate trade by private firms, it was also necessary to alter currency arrangements. Traditionally, the currencies of the Communist countries were not convertible, that is, the law prohibited their exchange for foreign moneys except under strictly controlled circumstances. By 1993–1994 this had changed almost everywhere, and currencies had become more or less convertible. Trade is now being undertaken at world market prices, and the Communist countries' old trade arrangement (called COMECON) is now defunct. But the attempt to trade at world market prices, however valuable it is in concept, has not worked well. The deep recession in Russia and the other successor states has meant that these countries have had to cut their imports from Eastern Europe. The total of these imports has declined by over half.

SEQUENCING

Great debates developed over the proper timing of the reforms. Should it all be done at once, as **shock therapy** (also known as a *big bang*), or would that cause unbearable social disruption? Or if the reforms were attempted by increments, would the absence of some of the supporting measures mean that any given step accomplished little? In some countries, advocates of shock therapy initially held the upper hand. The first to implement this policy was Poland, in January 1990. The therapy was supposed to unleash private entrepreneurial effort and cut the ground from under the old bureaucrats. By 1993–1994, shock therapy was less in favor. Few observers had been fully prepared for the decline in employment that actually occurred, and the further joblessness anticipated from dismantling the large state enterprises has caused a general slowing of the pace of reform in a number of the old Communist countries.

► PROBLEMS IN REFORMING THE ECONOMY OF THE FORMER SOVIET UNION

Reform in the 16 republics that are the Soviet Union's successor states has proved particularly difficult because of the large number of antagonistic nationalities, the great size of the economy, and the hesitancy of the proffered reforms. This section discusses the failure of the *perestroika* reforms in the Soviet Union and the ongoing battle to reform the Russian economy.

THE FAILURE OF PERESTROIKA

Perestroika means reform in Russian. But President Gorbachev's *perestroika* economic reforms of the late 1980s largely failed. Beginning in 1985, the central planning structure was decentralized, removing much of the central guidance, but without providing the spur of competition or the signals of market prices. From about the middle of 1989, total output started to fall, at first slowly, then more alarmingly. Meanwhile, the efforts to increase openness and allow more political debate (**glasnost**) seemed to lead to more rather than less frustration and disenchantment.

When Boris Yeltsin was elected president of the new Russian Republic in June 1991, he committed himself to comprehensive reform. Though a 500-day plan for shock therapy failed to get through Parliament, a good deal of progress was registered rather quickly.

THE BATTLE TO REFORM THE RUSSIAN ECONOMY

Russia is the largest of the Soviet Union's successor states, with over 60% of the old area's GDP. On January 2, 1992, it dropped price controls on 90% of all goods. Prices increased by about 2½ times in a day. With some exceptions, the price reform was pervasive.

Privatizing Russia's Firms

Russia's goal of privatizing firms out of government hands is immense and unprecedented. When and if the privatization is finished, it will have involved 10,000 medium and large firms and nearly a quarter-million small ones, considerably more than the total number of firms privatized by governments in the entire rest of the world during all of the 1980s. The first move, taken pre-Yeltsin in 1990, was to lift the restrictions on street trading. Bazaar markets developed rapidly in most parts of the country. Next, small businesses were allowed to be in private hands, and about a third of these (about 82,000, including almost all retail stores and restaurants) were privatized in 1992–1993. By 1993 about 42% of the labor force was employed in the private sector, versus 15% in 1991. That sector now produces about 35-40% of Russian GDP.[4] But the stage still to come is the difficult one. Though some 700 medium and large firms were in private hands by March 1993, that was only about 7% of the total for these firms.

The main model for Russian privatization involves the idea that big state firms should become corporations owned by their shareholders. (Smaller firms can go in other ways such as auctioning to single owners and leasing.) A large percentage of the corporate shares are being sold to the highest bidders, for the simple reason that the government needs the money. It was decided that some shares had to be given away to the public as a whole instead of sold to those who could bid the most. Doing so would avoid concentrating ownership in the hands of the old elites from the Communist days, and rewarding those who acquired large resources from illegal activities. Russia in the fall of 1992 distributed **vouchers** permitting the public to purchase shares in state enterprises. A portion of firms' stock can be sold *only* for these vouchers. The vouchers can be transferred, so investment funds intent on buying them from the public sprang up almost at once, over 300 toward the end of 1992. (One result was that the vouchers increased in real value about four times during 1993). Economists welcomed the appearance of the investment funds because no improvement in efficiency could be expected unless some group acquires sufficient control over shares to force management changes to take place.

Nationally, the privatization of wholesale and retail trade, most services, food, construction, and light industry is slated to be finished in 1994. Some businesses will, however, require specific government decisions as to how the privatization is carried out. These include any monopoly, big employers of more than 10,000 workers, military and medical enterprises, and the alcohol, wine, tobacco, energy, and communications industries,

The first sale of a large group of firms occurred in January 1993. Privatizing has gone much faster in large cities where reformers are in the ascendant than in small cities and towns where the old officials retain more influence. In Moscow, St. Petersburg, Volgagrad, and especially Nizhny Novgorod, most retail stores are now privatized. But in some far-flung areas the proportion of firms privatized is still just 2% or less. Sales are hard to accomplish when capital is short, savings are scarce, capital markets do not exist, and valuations are hard to determine.

In some important cases, privatization has been difficult to implement. In practice many state firms are monopoly producers that have never faced competition from the outside world or from domestic rivals. In the old Soviet Union, about 30–40% of the value of production was produced by about 2,000 enterprises at single locations under monopoly conditions.[5] The difficulty of privatizing these monopolies has been underestimated. For the profitable ones, a jump from the frying pan of central planning to the fire of monopoly capitalism does not seem optimal. Privatizing them will have to be supervised closely to guard against exploitation of consumers, but little has been done. Antitrust laws must basically be built from the ground up, and these laws will be resisted by the new owners who will not want to lose their monopoly rents. So foreign trade will probably have to be depended on to control monopoly power. As we shall see shortly,

---

4. CIA data cited in *The Economist*, December 11, 1993.

5. *The Economist*, August 11, 1990.

the barriers to trade are presently high. The unprofitable large firms will be difficult or impossible to sell. Most of these huge losers will have to be restructured into smaller units that are more easily managed, or closed down. Executing these tasks poses a tremendous challenge for the reformers.

FARMS ARE BEING PRIVATIZED, TOO

Farms are also being privatized, and by 1992 there were 70,000 new family farms. In October 1993 a presidential decree permitted land to be bought, sold, inherited, and mortgaged, and included provisions for full property-ownership rights. The decree will also permit the collective farms to be divided up among their members. The government has not made much credit available, however, and the collectives have been obstructionist. People who want to leave get only the worst land or land that is not easy to reach. On about half of the old farms (with about two-thirds of the land), farmers have opted either for private farm associations where the members use machinery and fertilizer jointly but own and manage their own farms, or private farming. About 40% of the farms have been made over into private cooperatives. Only some 10% of the farms remain as completely state-owned. But machinery is too large and distribution is inefficient, leading to large losses during storage and transport. The latest step involves the distribution of vouchers for land, buildings, and equipment just as for industrial enterprises, all handled by a land bank. Russia has a huge potential to be an agricultural exporter, though whether Western countries will lower their trade barriers to allow this development is questionable.

An alternative method for privatization involves worker-management control, of the sort that received a long trial in Yugoslavia. This worker-management model appears to be well out of the main stream of the Russian reform movement, mainly a way to preserve the authority of the old plant managers and wreck the voucher scheme. It has been supported especially by the old-guard conservative elements who are opposed to more fundamental reform.

The Need to Control the Central Bank

The old guard still has a weapon, the Russian central bank, which has not been brought under control by the reformers. It has been a destabilizing element over the past several years.

The reason why is that the central bank has been creating credits, in effect new money, to keep the old state enterprises afloat. This is exactly what the Hungarian economist Janos Kornai meant when he coined the phrase **soft budget constraint**. The state enterprise managers demand soft open-ended and negotiable subsidies, arguing that otherwise their firms will have to close and severe unemployment will develop.

A major problem in the Russian economy today is this flow of credits from the central bank to unprofitable state enterprises. The bank is clearly more concerned about maintaining production in the heavy state industries than with the effects of the resulting inflation on the economy. The bank's conservative head, Viktor Gerashchenko—he had been chief of the old Soviet central bank—insists that the credits needed to keep the enterprises afloat will be kept coming. Without executive permission the central bank has issued huge amounts of these credits as subsidies, amounting to over a third of GDP. Very large money creation in this form dates from December 1992. The main reason for the serious inflation in Russia is that all the new credits have run up the money supply.

The 1992 inflation rate was about 2500%. Ominously, but not surprisingly, the velocity of circulation increased. Inflation on this scale harmed rational long-term investment including foreign investment, diverted activity into finding hedges such as exchanging dollars for rubles, and so promoted corruption and capital flight. Corruption is currently rampant, and the scramble for dollars includes large illegal exports across Russia's new and poorly policed land borders.

For a time in 1993, the Russian government was able to persuade the central bank to reduce its money creation, and government subsidies to industry declined to about 10% of GDP. But the reformer most responsible, finance minister Boris Fyodorov, resigned in January 1994 when he failed to gain permanent control of the bank. Almost immediately a new program of credits for agriculture and industry was announced, with the amounts involved almost as large as the whole 1993 deficit.

Whenever the inflationary money creation is halted, Russia will run up against an unfortunate trade-off. When the central-bank credits to failing industries are stopped, many bankruptcies and considerable loss of jobs will follow, because by best estimate over 40% of Russian industry is currently unprofitable, kept alive only by the new money. Already Russia has been going through a huge output decline. Experts estimate that Russian output fell 38% in the three years 1991–1993, including 23% in 1992 alone. This has not been the catastrophe it might have been for two main reasons. First, the greatest part of the decline in output has been in military goods production. Military hardware orders were down by about 60% in 1992. Many military plants have moved to the production of civilian goods such as TVs, VCRs, washing machines, refrigerators, and other consumption goods. For some firms, the shift has been complete or nearly so, while for many it has not been, with the plants simply running more slowly, but in any case few have closed. Second, much of the rest of the output decline has been in industries that are uneconomic and waste resources. Because of the pricing structure for energy, Russia was recently using 6 times as much energy and 15 times more steel per dollar of GDP than was the United States. Large segments of the Russian economy can be looked at as value-subtractors—the resources used if sold abroad at world prices would bring more income than the value of the final goods sold at home. Here again, considerable output has been lost as these value-subtractors cut production, but because of the central bank credits most of the jobs still exist. Overall, unemployment is still surprisingly low, reported to be under 2% at the end of 1993.

When the central bank credits cease and bankruptcies follow in the large state firms, then *real* restructuring of the economy will have to be undertaken. This will be the most difficult part of the economic transition. The problem is akin to closing military bases in the United States and transforming them to other uses, except that 40% of the Russian economy consists of these large enterprises.

Moving a country along its production possibilities curve is a delicate operation. Figure 29.1 divides Russia's output into "state sector" goods (items for the military, old-style low-quality consumer goods, etc.) and "modern sector" consumer goods. If the market works perfectly, then the transition from X to Y is immediate and there is no cost of transitional unemployment. If it takes time for new enterprises to hire the labor and other resources that are freed, the shift is slow and the cost is high, with a dip in production that takes the country on a lower path from X to Y. Already actual unemployment is believed to be well above the reported figure, because benefits are so small that there is little reason to register as unemployed.

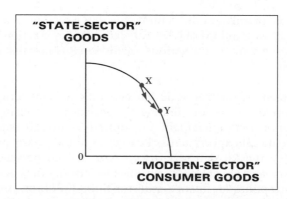

Figure 29.1. Transition may be costly. Moving along a production possibilities curve from X to Y can be costly. There may be transitional unemployment and a drop in total production, indicated by the arrow dipping below the curve. For several reasons, this situation may be especially serious in today's Russia.

Unfortunately, several negative considerations are likely to make the transition costly.

1) When the inflation is defeated, there will be a macro problem. The reduced real wages and declining orders from the state sector will lower aggregate demand until the transition can be made, incomes increase, aggregate demand rises again, and the products of privatized industry can be purchased. Government public works projects to fill the gap are severely constrained by budget problems, as we shall see.

2) Small firms cannot obtain proper loans to finance their expansion. The banking system is by no means freed as yet. The 2,000 or so new private banks that have recently been established have mostly (80%) been set up by state enterprises to handle the central bank credits being funneled to them. These banks do not attract many deposits from the public because real interest rates have been so negative, and many do not even accept deposits from individuals or make loans to them. Providing loans to small firms in a noninflationary way will be extremely difficult because of budget problems.

3) There is no mechanism in place for dealing with really large unemployment. Russia could not cope with a mass of unemployed workers, which would be a prescription for defeat of the reforms and a return to central planning. A crisis social fund must be available to buy time as the big enterprises are restructured or closed down, but it is not available except at the cost of hyperinflationary money creation. That no safety net can presently be put in place is completely understandable, however. Government revenue is inadequate to the task.

The Government's Revenue Problems

Each of these three negative factors could be dealt with if government could mobilize sufficient revenue. Serious inflations tend to erode government revenue in any case because tax collections lag. Income taxes, for example, are collected on last year's income. For Russia, the problem is much more acute. Tax revenue has fallen substantially because state enterprises stopped being a source of revenue. Russia adopted a 28% value-added tax in 1992, the highest rate in the world, but in part this only replaced the taxes applied under the Communist system, and much revenue has been lost because of the decline of production. Furthermore, local governments have been holding back tax revenues collected at the local level, understandably because they have had to take responsibility for education, local transport, and medical care. Local government budgets have rapidly run into deficit, a deficit that cannot now be financed by borrowing because domestic credit markets are undeveloped and real interest rates have been negative. Bond sales to foreign private investors are unlikely because of risk. Given all this, additional government revenue from taxation and borrowing will be difficult to acquire before recovery is considerably advanced.

Help from the West

To overcome these negative factors, help from the West could have been important, but it proved politically difficult to raise the money and disbursement was slow. Admittedly, much of what was granted went down the drain because the aid was not used to address the major problems. The major needs appear to be for a stabilization fund to give Russia a sound ruble usable in international trade, a small business loan program so new businesses can acquire the capital to grow, and a social fund that would establish a safety net against unemployment when the big state firms downsize or close. Aid could buy time for the large state firms to restructure toward producing sellable products, let the government establish some job training for the workers in these plants, and fund some temporary employment-creating public works projects.

Critics argue that all such aid is tantamount to throwing the money away. That is certainly possible. But a plausible contrary view is that aid in these forms is a public investment for the West. It may pay off in an eventual huge market for Western exports, just as Marshall Plan assistance generated prosperity in Europe. To the extent that 20% or 25% unemployment might lead to the resurrection of Communist rule, aid would also be insurance against a return of the Cold War and the associated higher defense budgets. To be sure, with the resurgence of Russian nationalism in 1994 the chances that much more aid would be donated seemed to be significantly reduced.

One major contribution the West can make could be to remove its trade barriers against Russian goods, because Western protection could stifle Eastern growth. Russia has been given favorable tariff treatment, "most-favored nation" instead of the high Smoot-Hawley tariff rates from the 1930s that applied until 1992. But the treatment is subject to annual renewal (also required of China), and is fettered by limits on exports of strategic goods that are still in effect even though the need for most of the rules is now past. Furthermore, Russian exports of steel, textiles and clothing, and almost any agricultural commodity to Europe, Japan, or the United States runs up against high trade barriers. Lowering these barriers would be a major step, with a permanent effect whereas aid by its nature is temporary.

Finally, the West's private foreign investment can play a major role in a Russian recovery, though not until the inflation is defeated and the rules and regulations relating to such investment are hammered out more adequately than they now are. There is still no law on concessions in the oil and gas fields, for example, and tax terms negotiated in several months of bargaining are often suddenly overturned. Export licenses are still required in numerous areas, and these have been administered rather capriciously. As a result, investment is low: In 1992 U.S. companies invested nearly four times as much in Hungary as the $400 million they invested in Russia. Much more has been announced—perhaps 10 times more—but the problem is that waiting to invest is not very costly, the risk from waiting is small, and the risk of investing now is high.

Favorable Factors

For all the negatives, there are a number of favorable factors. With most prices freed and privatization proceeding rapidly, incentives are now in place so that wages can be used to buy consumer goods, and queueing for scarce commodities has been much reduced. Once income starts to grow, the domestic market for services of all kinds such as restaurants will be huge. Autos, tourism, home entertainment, and supermarkets can be large growth areas. Consumer goods production by small and medium sized firms could rise greatly if credit were available for entrepreneurs to set them up and expand such enterprises. Russia possesses a greater stock of natural resources than any other country. Export of these resources should easily be able to take up the slack for Russia's old and inferior exports of manufactured goods if the trading regimen is positive. The natural resources are also assets that can be used to repay loans, making lending to Russia economically less risky than to countries lacking such rich assets.

The Russian people are well-educated, including a large pool of scientists and engineers (and the world's largest group of women trained in these fields) whose talent is now very inexpensive at world prices. They are thoroughly familiar with manufacturing. Their real wages are very low and likely to stay low for a considerable time as the state enterprises contract, not only beneath wages in the United States, Europe, and Japan, but lower than in Singapore and Hong Kong and Korea and Taiwan and Mexico. In all these, low wages have driven industrial production of goods for export, and it could also do so in Russia. It is noteworthy that strikes and riots have not broken out on any scale.

For Russia, the outlook is murky. Important political questions must be settled before the reforms have much of a chance to succeed, and these reforms will have to be in place for at least some significant period of time before sustained recovery can set in. We must fervently hope that the reforms do go forward, and do prosper, for the prospect of Russia wracked by declining levels of living, political unrest, and angry nationalist fervor would be unfavorable not just there, but for the whole world.

REFORMS ELSEWHERE IN THE OLD COMMUNIST BLOC

Economic reform is proceeding almost everywhere in the old Communist bloc, though the pace and the details differ greatly. Some of the highlights are summarized in this section.

The *old Soviet Union* is now a *Commonwealth of Independent States* (CIS) including all the republics except for Georgia and the three Baltic states (Estonia, Latvia, Lithuania). The process of reform is furthest along in Armenia, the Baltics, Kyrgyzstan, and Russia. Next to Russia, Ukraine's economy is the largest. Ukrainian reform has gone slowly, with not one state firm privatized, a budget deficit of 40% of GDP, large credits advanced by the central bank to keep the state firms afloat, and high resulting inflation running at well over 2000% per year in 1993. Many shortages are reported in shops and stores, and long queues prevail. Whatever else this proves, it shows that a country starting with the original Soviet system does not necessarily do better by going slowly with its reforms.

The *Czech Republic* and *Slovakia*, formed when Czechoslovakia split apart at the start of 1993, have moved heavily toward privatization by means of coupons distributed to the public with which people can make bids to buy shares of stock. (Managers and workers are, however, getting on average about half the shares in the enterprises for which they work.) Many private investment funds have arisen to buy the coupons in exchange for a guaranteed rate of return to participants. It is the fastest privatization yet attempted anywhere. The breakup of the old Czechoslovakia is likely to be painful for Slovakia, which is poorer, more conservatively governed, saddled with most of the old country's large military producers, and likely to get far less foreign investment than its neighbor. Privatization will probably be slowed down there. Unemployment in 1993 was four times higher in Slovakia than it was in the Czech Republic. A common currency lasted only six weeks after the split.

Hungary was the earliest of the centrally planned countries to embark on economic reform, in the late 1960s. It has attracted substantial amounts of foreign investment in recent years, its inflation is relatively limited, and its foreign trade is doing well. Yet it has not moved to mass privatization, preferring to sell to foreign investors, to the old managers, or even to old owners from before the days of Communist rule. That has led to the problem of many unsellable firms still on the government's hands. Hungary is a neighbor to the old Yugoslavia, the troubles in which have harmed its economic development. Growth has been slower than most observers anticipated.

Poland was the original practitioner of a strategy of shock therapy, in 1990 adopting orthodox/heterodox tactics including monetary and fiscal tightness, fixing the foreign exchange rate and making the currency convertible, limiting wage increases to less than inflation, freeing most prices and most trade, starting privatization, and establishing an antimonopoly office that began to break up monopolies. But the control of credit was so stringent that it interfered with the financing of production and plunged the country into recession. Serious strikes followed. The legislature was unable to pass a mass privatization program, though even so the private sector grew enormously (to nearly half of GDP and over half of employment) as new firms were started up. By 1993 it seemed that recovery was coming, with surging exports and substantial foreign investment. Even though privatization has been much more deliberate than in the Czech Republic, the GDP decline had been halted, and it looked at the time of writing as if Poland might be the first of the old Communist countries of Eastern Europe to make an economic recovery.

Romania. An advanced privatization scheme involving large-scale distribution of ownership certificates was going very slowly in 1993. GDP declined much more in 1992 (about 16%) than in Hungary or Czechoslovakia.

Bulgaria. A major decline in GDP took place during 1992, about the same as in Romania. But inflation, high after the reforms were first instituted, was slowing. Plans for privatization have been delayed.

Albania has the least east progress to report for a country not at war. Albania exhibits the greatest poverty in the region, with food queues seen frequently.

Old Yugoslavia. The rump Yugoslavia of Serbia and Montenegro, together with the newly independent states of Bosnia-Herzegovina, Croatia, Macedonia, and Slovenia have had to face wartime economic problems, including money creation to pay the bills and a UN embargo on trade with the rump Yugoslavia. State controls remain in place in that area. Inflation was over 60,000% in the first nine months of 1992, and during the month of November 1993 it was 20,190%, an annualized rate of 45 octillion percent and close to the highest monthly rate in the 1923 German hyperinflation. The privatization moves in Croatia seemed designed to centralize state controls. Slovenia, away from the fighting, has done relatively well.

General Trends

Prices. Prices for most goods and services have now been freed in these countries.

Investment. Investment is now generally open to foreigners, but the distribution of it has been uneven. Hungary has received the most.

Land: Bulgaria, the Czech Republic, Slovakia, Hungary, and Romania all have new laws recognizing the rights of the landholders who held the land just prior to collectivization and have mechanisms that can lead to a return of land to them. The old Soviet Union will find this much harder to accomplish because the land there was nationalized much earlier, in 1917, long before that happened in Eastern Europe.

Foreign trade. The collapse of trade among the old Communist countries has had major negative effects on economic growth; most of their recent income decline has been due to just this.[6] All have substantially opened their borders to foreign trade and eliminated most quotas. Poland and the Czech Republic have virtually no import restrictions. They, with Hungary and Slovakia, have set up a Central European Free Trade Area (CEFTA) with one another that will eliminate all remaining barriers over 10 years. These four have also been given associate status with the EC, though exports of their textiles, steel, and agricultural commodities are limited or excluded from the EC. That is damaging because these are the very industries where their comparative advantage probably lies. All of Eastern Europe except Romania now receive most-favored nation tariff treatment from the United States.

Currencies. Most of the Eastern European countries now have some sort of convertible currency, Poland's tied to the dollar, Yugoslavia's to the mark (but the tie now suspended because of the war), the Czech Republic and Hungary to market baskets of other currencies, and Bulgaria and Romania floating freely. Several new currencies have recently been introduced by some of the states that make up the former Soviet Union.

▶ THE CHINESE REFORMS

China's economic reforms came earlier than those of Russia and Eastern Europe, and the country has reaped considerable benefits from its early start. Chinese economic growth has recently been spectacular by any standards.

THE REFORMS IN AGRICULTURE

The Chinese leadership was forward in transforming agriculture. Enthusiasm for doing so was great because of the famine when the communes were established and because of the slow growth of output thereafter. Starting in 1977–1978, a giant land reform was undertaken that lasted until 1984. Land was distributed by lot to farmers, who received small farms of an acre or less. In spite of the sacrifice of economies of scale (these plots were too small), output rose because new and attractive incentives were provided. From 1978 the government started to pay more for its compulsory deliveries, while from 1984 farmers could enter into negotiated contracts for what these crops would be. Food prices were steadily increased. A large rise in output was the result. In the years 1978 to 1987, grain output grew at 4% a year; *total* agricultural output rose at the highest sustained rate (about 8%) in the world. Because agricultural production still made up about 35% of GDP in the mid-1980s (though down from over 60% in the 1950s), this was a major development. Contracts to use land had been given to farmers since the start of the reform; by 1984 the duration of these contracts was generally 15 years.

Farmers now have more security of tenure, and transfers to heirs can be made. They are able to sell at more remunerative prices than ever before under the Communist system. They can choose what to plant, and they can sell their crops on the open (free) market after their state contract quotas have been filled. (The state prices for grain in 1990 were less than half the free market price, with subsidies used to keep prices even lower for consumers in the cities.) The situation has become closer to that of a very small family farm in a market economy.

---

6.   Across the Atlantic, Cuba—which has generally not engaged in reform—lost about 85% of its overseas markets because of this collapse in international trade. Hundreds of goods are currently in short supply in Cuba.

INDUSTRIAL REFORMS

In industry, the original central planning dating from the early days of Chairman Mao was changed significantly in the 1980s, with the number of items that were centrally planned cut drastically. By 1993 fewer than 20 items were centrally planned, compared to 700 or so in 1978. Industrial output from nonstate enterprises rose from 14% in 1979 near the start of the reforms to over half in the early 1990s. Central planning more and more gave way to local government and provincial planning, with "local bargaining" of contracts carried out by firms and these smaller units of government. The contracts determined what share of profit will be retained by the firms, with the firms retaining any profits above what they have agreed to pay to government. The lure of higher earnings for firms had the predictable result on industrial output, which grew 12% per year in the five years centered in the mid-1980s. **Township enterprises** appeared in many rural areas. Some of these are private, some are owned cooperatively by the village, some are worker-owned, and some belong to local governments. Often financed by bank loans, competitive and unplanned, they have grown to produce half of all rural output and over a quarter of all China's output. Over 20% of the rural labor force works in these light industrial enterprises. They buy and sell their output, and depend on their profits. They can lay off workers, and they can fail. Profits fund bonuses for the workers and managers and are used for investment including village infrastructure.

Even in the state sector, compensation of managers and workers is closely tied to profitability—some observers say even more directly than in most Western corporations. The state enterprises can keep their after-tax profits, and can buy and sell input and output beyond what is planned. These reforms rapidly increased output even in that less efficient sector.

Price reform proceeded more slowly, though by 1993 price controls were much reduced; three-quarters of raw materials prices are now set by the market. As freer prices were allowed, inflation began to set in about 1988, and the central government accommodated (monetized) the price increases by means of easy money. Most of the new money came as loans from the state banking system to the large state enterprises, akin to the recent situation in Russia. For some time the money creation did not cause much inflation because people and firms were choosing to hold more financial assets rather than spend the money. But eventually serious inflation did break out, the first in China since the consolidation of Communist rule. Big "austerity" cutbacks in government spending and much tighter credit were imposed in 1989–1991. That in turn caused a recession in the free-market sector of the economy. It was clear that not only was a complete price reform badly needed, but that macroeconomic policies had to be designed to resist disruptive inflation. Inflation was defeated for a time, falling from 20% in 1988 to 2% in 1990, but it has now broken out again.

Unfortunately the political (and human) disaster of the Tiananmen Square massacre in 1989, when the leadership took a hard line with student protestors, had its economic repercussions as well. Economic policy turned back toward the past. There was a sharp cutback in reform, with price reform halted and privatization stopped. The proportion of centrally planned goods was expanded, managers and local officials quickly lost power to the national government, and a single state price became more common for many goods. The contract system lost favor with the central government though it is still in place. A move was even made toward some recollectivization of agriculture. Here the intent appeared to be a government decision to facilitate larger scale operations and more mechanization, as well as a political crackdown on the liberalization accomplished over the last decade.

Yet the pace of reform picked up once again in 1991, with new reforms that year and the next in foreign trade and trade in foreign currencies. The country's low wages are proving an advantage in labor-intensive manufacturing, and exports grew by over six times in real terms between 1978 and 1991. China's share of world trade more than doubled, and about 80% of all exports are now manufactured goods. China's textile and clothing exports have made it a major player in those markets. Companies can keep a large share of their foreign exchange earnings.

Foreign investors have noticed the low wages too, and investment by means of joint enterprise is surging. Foreign investment is now responsible for about a quarter of China's manufactured exports.

In some respects the reforms have had only a limited impact. Free movement of people is still not permitted, which helps to explain the phenomenon of China's rural factories. In effect these factories have a captive labor force. Capital markets remain rudimentary: Though there is an interest charge on capital, it is well below the cost of capital in China. Little progress has been made in improving the environment. China is badly polluted, one reason being that it is the world's leading producer of coal, and much of that is not of the best quality. The only reason why pollution has not reached massive levels is that China is still poor and its output levels remain relatively low.

Thus the pace of Chinese reform has been erratic. Even so, progress has been rapid: China has had a 9% growth rate in GDP over the last decade, and registered 13% growth in both 1992 and 1993. This performance ranks with Japan's best. The growth has undoubtedly changed Chinese life. Food consumption has risen greatly; most urban households now have a TV and a washing machine; half have a refrigerator. In 1981 only 6 in 100 households had washing machines, and fewer than 1 in 100 had TVs and refrigerators. However fitful the Chinese reforms have been, the one-fifth of the world's population that lives in China continues its progress toward a market system and much higher levels of living.

CONCLUSION

The decline of and possibly even the demise of central planning and the command system is one of the most striking developments of the twentieth century. Emerging from dissatisfaction with the market's problems with income distribution and its inability to guarantee economic growth, command economies proved to generate more problems than they did solutions. Captured as they were by party officials and bureaucrats, they did not solve even the income distribution questions raised by Marx and Lenin. Plagued by slow growth, in the end the command system brought less, not more, economic progress to most of the countries that used it. The multiple inefficiencies presented obstacles that eventually sapped morale and ruined incentives to work and to innovate. Reform leading to the adoption of a market system had to wait for political upheaval. Important as this upheaval has been, however, it has not provided a complete answer to the predicament these countries face. What to include in the reform of a command economy and what the pace and sequencing of the reform should be are among the great economic problems of the generation, just as how to avoid violent protest or a return to dictatorship are among the great political questions.

SUMMARY

1) A command system run by central planning was introduced by the Communists in the years following their seizure of the Russian government in 1917. Command principles were present in purest form during the dictatorship of Josef Stalin, who died in 1953.

2) Central planning was run by ministries that issued output targets concerning what should be produced, and input norms detailing the factor inputs that would be available. Coordination between the targets and the norms was managed by Gosplan, the state planning agency. Prices had little relevance; plant managers responded instead to the bonuses they received for meeting their output targets. Various inefficiencies were the result, including empire building by the ministries, a low level of technical change, slow response to changing consumer wants, chronic shortages, and very serious pollution of the environment.

3) A great wave of political and economic reform has swept over almost all of the former command economies. The reforms include the adoption of market pricing, the privatizing of the state firms, establishment of capital markets, freeing of employment decisions, and the adoption of currency convertibility. But debates surround the sequencing of these reforms, and they have advanced far further in some countries (the Czech Republic, Hungary, Poland) than in others (Russia, Ukraine, much of the rest of the former Soviet Union).

4) A great obstacle to Russian reform has been the continuing control of the central bank by old-guard conservative forces. The result has been substantial creation of new money to keep afloat the many remaining state enterprises, with inflationary results.

5) China's economic reforms came earlier than those of Russia and Eastern Europe, and the country has reaped considerable benefits from its early start. The reforms have been less centralized than elsewhere in the Communist world, with many variations and considerable local initiative (including the mostly rural township enterprises). Though erratic, Chinese economic growth has recently been very high by any standards.

Chapter Key Words

Bonus: Under central planning, the main method of reward for Soviet plant managers who fulfill plan targets. Important for understanding the performance of Soviet firms.

Central planning: A device for operating a command economy by means of centrally determined *output targets* and *input norms*, which see. Substitutes government direction for the market as an allocative tool.

Collective farms: A farm structure in central planning wherein farm members are organized cooperatively, sharing farm income on the basis of how much each works.

Glasnost: The successful effort to increase openness and allow more political debate in the old USSR.

Gosplan: The chief organ of Soviet central planning. Agency in charge of coordinating plans among the industrial ministries.

Input norms: The central-planning directives that establish how much input of productive factors a firm will be allowed in a given year.

Output targets: The central-planning directives that establish how much output a firm must produce in a given year. Failure to fulfill the target means forfeiture of the bonus.

Perestroika: Reforms instituted by President Gorbachev in the late 1980s. *Perestroika* means reform in Russian.

Privatization: The transfer of state firms to private ownership, either by means of sale or gift of corporate shares to the public or by transfer to workers and managers.

Safety factor: Typical behavior by Soviet firms that attempted to build up their input norms and reduce their output targets beyond what actually could be achieved to ensure that plans could actually be met.

Shock therapy: Also known as *big bang*. Terms used by economists to describe an attempt to reform a centrally planned economy all at once. Pioneered by Poland. Has led to considerable unemployment in the short run.

Soft budget constraint: The idea that firms could accumulate large losses, knowing that they would be bailed out by a compliant central bank.

State farms: Farms that under central planning were organized and operated on the same principles as factories, with output targets, input norms, and bonuses.

Township enterprises: Chinese rural factories; a major element in rapid Chinese economic success in recent years.

Vouchers: Certificates issued to members of the public entitling their holders to acquire shares in the newly privatized state firms.

Chapter Questions

1) You are the manager of a firm in a centrally planned economy. Do the prices of your inputs and output tell you how much to buy and how much to produce? If not, how do you make these decisions?

2) A Soviet worker assembles cars, and receives a large share of pay through bonuses. Just before the bonuses come out, does the worker do high quality or low quality work? Why?

3) You work in a Soviet tractor factory. For years you have bolted tractor wheels on by hand. Fed up with this work, you modify a drill to bolt wheels automatically. If you tell your manager about your innovation, will he want everyone in the factory to start using it?

4) Capital goods increase future output, while extra consumption goods do not do so. Because the USSR emphasized production of capital goods rather than consumption goods, why did it not increase output substantially over time?

5) The leaders of the East European country of Polungavia opt to sequence their market reforms rather than use shock therapy. They first privatize many firms by giving vouchers to the public, and then they work on setting up a capital market. Can you see any problem with this strategy?

6) In 1992, output fell in both the United States and Russia. Did this make the United States better or worse off? How about Russia?

7) Many Westerners feel their countries have enough problems of their own without spending money on aid to Russia. Are there any policies the West could follow that would aid Russia and benefit the West at the same time?

8) Why are Chinese enterprises, especially in rural areas, growing even when they are owned by the state, while for so many years Russian state enterprises stagnated?

Economic Development of the LDCs

OVERALL OBJECTIVE: To explore conditions in the less-developed countries (LDCs) and evaluate the steps that might be taken to hasten the development of these countries.

MORE SPECIFICALLY:

- To demonstrate that much of the world lives in poverty, with only a little over 12% of the world's total income generated by approximately 70% of the world's population.
- To call attention to the role of capital in the development of the LDCs and the need to mobilize saving to finance capital accumulation.
- To discuss the reasons for the decline of comprehensive economic planning in the LDCs, at the same time emphasizing that government policies are important for development.
- To consider specific subjects of development economics such as appropriate technology, education (especially of women, whose important role has often been neglected in the LDCs), health and nutrition, population control, and rural development.
- To emphasize the role of international trade in the development process, directing attention to developed-country trade barriers as a hindrance to economic development in the LDCs.
- To discuss the distressing problem that development of the LDCs is likely to cause further environmental problems, while realizing that deliberate attempts to slow the growth of the LDCs would be intolerable to their people.

Life in **less-developed countries (LDCs)** can be hard, as all first-time visitors soon discover.[1] Families may be farming with only a few hand tools, getting barely enough to eat; there are likely to be many children underfoot with little chance of gaining more than a few months of primary school; home is a hut or a shack; women and girls must haul water long distances because there is no inside plumbing; incomes are so low (say $300 per year) that there is nothing for saving, and nothing for a doctor or dentist even if these were available. Villages and cities are governed from the local capital by officials who are overworked, often corrupt, and appointed by a political party controlled by a wealthy elite.

Much of the world lives more or less under these conditions. Table 30.1 shows that in 1991, only a little over 12% of the world's total income was generated by approximately 70% of the world's population, while the 15% of the population that lives in the high-income developed countries generated nearly 80% of the world's income.

TABLE 30.1
World population and income, 1991.

Area	Percent of World Population	Percent of World Income
Latin America and Caribbean	8.3	5.0
Sub-Saharan Africa	9.1	0.8
East Asia and Pacific	31.2	5.0
South Asia	21.5	1.7
High-Income Economies	15.4	78.8
(USA)	(4.7)	(26.2)

Source: Calculated from World Bank, *World Development Report,* 1993, Washington, D.C., 1993, tables A.2 and 1. World income is defined as gross national product (see Chapter 15 for details). Geographical groupings do not add to 100% because of the exclusion from the table of the Middle East, North Africa, the former Communist countries of Eastern Europe, and the states that made up the old USSR.

INCOME IS NOT QUITE SO LOW IN THE LDCs AS THESE FIGURES INDICATE

For a technical reason, the actual measured statistics for output and income underestimate the levels of living in the LDCs. Take, for example, the measured national income (GNP) of India, which statisticians calculated was equal to $360 per person in 1990. Consider this for a moment. An income of $360 per person is just 99¢ per day. How could you live for less than a dollar a day? Something must be amiss.

Indeed it is. The problem is in the measurement. The figure of $360 was obtained by measuring India's total income in Indian rupees, and then converting this income into U.S. dollars at the prevailing exchange rate. But a dollar will buy much more in India than it will in the United States. The exchange rate does not pick up that the average price of goods in India that do not enter international trade is only about 13%

1. The LDCs together are often called the "Third World," the other two groups being the developed market economies and the command economies (the former Soviet Union and eastern Europe) that are now reforming themselves. Additional distinctions include the NICs (newly industrializing countries) such as Hong Kong, Singapore, South Korea, Taiwan, Malaysia, and Thailand, and the rich oil-producing states such as Saudi Arabia, Libya, and Kuwait.

of the price that would have to be paid in the United States for these goods. It is possible to give a more correct portrayal by adjusting Indian GNP to reflect the higher purchasing power of the dollar in India. When India's 1990 GNP per person was adjusted in this way, it was actually worth $1,072, which is much more realistic than the $360 when the figure is not adjusted for purchasing power.

The United Nations now calculates GNP adjusted for purchasing power for almost all countries. Whereas the unadjusted 1990 average GNP per person for all less-developed countries was $810, the GNP adjusted for purchasing power was $2,170, or nearly three times as much. Typically, the poorer the country, the greater the difference.

Economic development certainly carries costs as well as benefits. High national income does not cure all problems and brings some of its own. Pollution, congestion, and the tension of everyday life in the developed countries are among the negative results of economic growth. These negatives have led some to condemn economic progress as not necessarily bringing happiness. An excellent reply to these critics was given by Princeton's Arthur Lewis in his *Theory of Economic Growth*.[2] Lewis argued that the advantage of economic growth

> is not that wealth increases happiness, but that it increases the range of human choice....What distinguishes men from pigs is that men have greater control over their environment, not that they are more happy.

Lewis emphasized the following desirable aspects of growth in his analysis:

1) It allows people the choice of having more leisure if they want it. In an LDC where the population gets just barely enough to eat, it is much more difficult to opt for this choice.
2) Higher incomes allow people to pursue other activities beyond obtaining food, shelter, clothing, and other items of mere subsistence. Art, music, sports, literature, TV, and films are alternatives that become possible with growth.
3) Economic progress improves the position of women. Said Lewis,
   > It is open to men to debate whether economic progress is good for men or not, but for women to debate the desirability of economic growth is to debate whether women should have the chance to cease to be beasts of burden and to join the human race.
4) Economic growth allows the tender shoots of humanitarian feelings and environmental concern to germinate and multiply. A society on the verge of perpetual want may well be a callous and polluted society. The subsistence farmer who sees a beggar has little to give. Disease and short life expectancy cheapen life itself. Pollution is generally accepted because it costs money to clean it up, and the money is not there.

Another argument in favor of economic growth involves the question of who gains and who loses. In a stagnant economy, one person's gain is often another person's loss. Progress is seen as a political battle; for every person whose life improves, there is another whose life worsens as a result. In such an environment, political tensions may become so intense that authoritarian governments will arise in response. Rapid economic growth will ease this sort of tension. In a growing economy, when some people get more, other people need not necessarily get less. They may get more, too. In short, without development, politics is a game of taking from some and giving to others. With development, it is a game of benefiting some a bit more than others.

2..   W. Arthur Lewis, *The Theory of Economic Growth*, Homewood, Ill., 1955.

Development economists cannot say what the exact causes of development are or why its timing differs so greatly among countries. The process is complex, and the debates over what to do and what not to do can be intense. Even so, a considerable amount of useful knowledge about development has accumulated over the past half century, knowledge that can improve the odds for success. The following sections discuss the importance of capital and human capital, of efficient resource allocation, of the choice of appropriate technologies, of rural development, and of international trade. It then concludes by discussing the environmental consequences of rapid economic growth, fears of which are now receiving considerable attention.

▶ CAPITAL AND THE LDCs

The first factor known to enhance the prospects for economic development is to increase productivity by *saving* and *investing* a larger proportion of a nation's income in order to increase the stock of capital. Capital, whether directly productive or for social improvement, is lacking in the underdeveloped world. Additions to the capital stock are a more important contributor to economic growth in the LDCs than to growth in the developed countries, primarily because capital is so scarce in the LDCs.[3] There are less machinery per worker, less adequate housing and transport, reduced stocks of inventory and spare parts.

The inadequate supply of capital is essentially caused by the low level of income. A sort of vicious circle is involved: productivity and incomes are low because there is little capital to work with; saving is low because incomes are low; low saving means low investment; the limited investment means an inadequate capital stock; the small amount of capital per worker results in limited productivity and low income. Attaining high levels of saving is difficult when people are poor; borrowing from foreign banks is expensive, and foreign aid is in short supply. A major task is to save and invest enough to increase the size of the capital stock per person (capital deepening, so called). In addition to that, the innovation and technical change that in the long run make investment more productive must be pursued. With saving, investment, and technical change, the productivity of the labor force can be increased. We have already seen in Chapter 26 that productivity growth, even more than growth in the physical quantities of inputs, is the key to higher incomes per person.

The nature of the barriers to development posed by inadequate stocks of capital is readily apparent. Housing is often one of the most neglected areas. The typical developed country usually spends about a quarter of all its capital investment on housing. The LDC going through the difficult process of shifting a large percentage of its population from rural to urban living might have to spend even more than this to reach adequate standards. Failure to do so is a familiar phenomenon everywhere in the LDCs, and shanty-town slums are a standard feature of urban life.

Another neglected area of capital spending tends to be public works and utilities—the transport systems, power plants, telephone systems, water works, educational facilities, and hospitals that make up the so-called infrastructure of an economy. The results are highly predictable and visible. Run-down power plants gasp and die at peak load, sometimes coming on again after a few minutes, sometimes not for hours. Water supplies may be limited to just a few periods each day. Ill-kept highway surfaces, pot-holed and laced with corrugations, shorten the life of cars and trucks. Long-distance telephone calls may go through so infrequently that large firms may simply hold a line open all day, accepting the cost as less than not being able to make a connection. Single-track railway lines are often heavily congested, and ships undergo long waits

---

3.   In speaking of capital in the LDCs, there are problems of definition. Items fitting the standard definition (manmade resources that contribute to a larger output of goods and services in the future) in one country may not fit it in another. The same spending that is unambiguously consumption in North America, Western Europe, or Japan may actually form capital in Africa or Asia. An example of this definitional problem can be found in the ordinary bicycle. We might call this a consumption good. But what about the many LDCs that use bicycles to transport goods along paths where trucks cannot penetrate? A bicycle can carry an enormous load if you wheel it along—farm produce, oil drums, livestock. These definitional problems can distort the statistics, though no one would deny that capital even when defined broadly is still scarce in the LDCs.

at overcrowded ports. Inventories of spare parts are capital, too, and shortages of parts can mean equipment idled, trucks off the road, trains that do not run, and inconvenience for consumers.

Financing Capital Formation

Funds for investment are difficult to obtain in LDCs. The possible choices for financing investment include (1) domestic saving that can then be loaned to business or the government by banks; (2) taxation; (3) government creation of new money to pay its bills (inflation); (4) capital imports; and (5) foreign aid. Each of these routes to investment has its own special problems, and whatever alternative is chosen, finding sufficient funds to finance economic development is likely to be difficult.

Domestic saving. As we saw in Chapter 16, saving depends on available income. But the poorer a country is, the less likely it will be able to save very much. Socioeconomic pressures can further depress domestic saving. If society is stratified into classes (the Indian caste system, for example), saving will be of little help in advancing socially. A major incentive to save is destroyed. The "extended family" system may also cut saving. An extended family consists of parents, children, grandparents, aunts, uncles, and cousins all living together, each with an obligation to help the other. This may work well as a system of social security, but if good fortune should come to one family member, relatives will be there to claim their share. (In some cases, the extended family may actually encourage saving by pooling funds to promote a business venture or the education of a talented member. This has occurred frequently in several cultures such as the Igbo [Ibo] of Nigeria, the Lebanese, and overseas Chinese.)

Saving may also be inhibited by inflation. Serious inflation is a common problem in the LDCs, and it is normal behavior to avoid its impact by buying land, buildings, or other tangible goods to avoid the erosion of purchasing power as prices rise. Funds used in this way do not enter the banking system and are thus not available for lending to investors. Finally, religious scruples against receiving a rate of interest, especially strong among orthodox Muslims, may discourage saving.

Many schemes to increase household saving have been tried in LDCs. These include credit cooperatives, government combined plans for insurance and saving, small post office savings accounts, "bicycle bankers" who encourage rural residents to deposit small sums, and so forth. The underlying poverty and the social hindrances to saving have proven to be major obstacles in many LDCs, however, particularly in the poorest.

Taxation. Given the problems in mobilizing private saving, governments have often emphasized taxation to finance economic development. Here, too, there are some serious difficulties. Income, output, and sales are all low; hence most forms of tax revenue are bound to be low, too. So it is not surprising that total tax proceeds as a percentage of GNP range from 30% to 40% for the United States, Great Britain, Germany, and other developed countries, while running at only 10% or 20% for most LDCs. The income tax itself, central to revenue collection in the developed world, is particularly difficult to collect in poor countries. Low rates of literacy, lack of written records, cheating the tax collector, political opposition from wealthy landowners or merchants, and shortages of honest, skillful administrators all mean that the income tax brings in far less revenue in LDCs (only 20% to 30% of all tax revenue) than in developed countries (60% to 80%).

Value-added taxes collected on transactions (discussed in Chapters 15 and 23) undoubtedly have a future in the LDCs, but they have the disadvantage of requiring significant administrative competence. Collecting them in the many thousands of village markets of the poorest LDCs presents an immense challenge.

Taxes on imports and exports are popular because they are easy to collect at points of entry to a country. Taxes on imports, often high, are used in all LDCs. Many countries also tax their exports. Where a country or group of countries has some monopoly power over the production of an essential item—oil, for example, or as the LDCs once hoped, copper, tin, and uranium—

such taxes can be big revenue earners. There is, however, always a danger that taxation of exports will spur consumers to search for substitutes. Chile's high taxes on nitrate exports led eventually to the discovery of synthetic nitrates in Germany, ruining the Chilean market. Tax policies on Brazilian coffee caused the crop to spread east across the Atlantic, so that it is now an important export of Côte d'Ivoire, Kenya, and Ethiopia. The combination of reduced demand and increased supply has also been a major factor in limiting the impact of the OPEC oil cartel. Even so, large sums can be collected from export taxes when there is some market control, and the idea of heavy taxes on exports of essential raw materials remains current. Taken together, taxes on imports and exports often add up to more than 30%–40% of all tax revenue in LDCs, as compared to only 3% for the United States.

One method of taxing exports deserves further attention because it is widespread in the LDCs. This is the system of "marketing boards," the boards legally empowered to purchase at a fixed price all production for export of some agricultural commodity. The board's fixed price can be set permanently lower than the expected world price for the coming year. For example, if Ghana's Cocoa Marketing Board predicts that next year's world market price for cocoa will be $10,000 per ton, it might establish a fixed producer price of $5,000 per ton. The difference between the world price and the marketing board price is a kind of tax revenue. At one point in the 1980s, Ghana's board was paying cocoa farmers just 34% of the value of their crop; similar high levels of taxation by means of marketing boards have existed in numerous other LDCs as well. The unintended result is that farmers shift to untaxed commodities and undertake to smuggle output into neighboring countries. Ghana's high taxes on cocoa nearly ruined its industry before reforms were at last adopted.

Inflation. LDC governments often attempt to finance their spending by the inflationary means of budget deficits and money creation. These governments almost always have the power to create money by running the printing presses even if more sophisticated monetary policies for doing so have not yet emerged. Usually money creation will be attempted when the tax mechanism is performing poorly because of widespread tax avoidance, and where government feels it must spend more than it can afford. (Spending may have been run up by food subsidies to the urban population, wage increases for the unionized public officials and employees of state enterprises, better pay and higher technology for the military, and so forth.) By means of money creation to fund budget deficits, these governments can bid away resources from the private sector to the public sector. That will, of course, mean prices increase. Although inflation caused by these means can certainly result in a transfer of resources to the public sector, it is a dangerous policy device. Social unrest may be generated among the losers from the inflation. Expectations of rapid inflation may become so pervasive that entrepreneurs switch away from saving and investment toward buying speculative items that are expected to rise in price along with the inflation. Those who can use the local currency to buy dollars or other currencies will do so, causing a "capital flight" to ensue.

Since the start of the 1980s, hyperinflations in the LDCs have grown much more common. They have proved very hard to stop when governments believe that money creation is the path of least resistance. Brazil, Argentina, and Peru are all good examples of countries where governments have traditionally preferred to print money rather than deal with opposition from powerful unions, testy public servants, and militaries prone to intervene in politics.

Importing Private Capital (Including the "Debt Crisis"). Another possibility for financing development is importing the necessary capital by borrowing overseas. During the nineteenth century this was the standard method for funding the construction of railroads; British lenders were prime agents in the growth of the United States, Canada, Australia, and other countries. The idea of borrowing to fund development is sound because a country can use the borrowed money to raise productivity, generating a higher national income that provides the funds to pay back the loan with interest.

More recently, the hope of easier development by means of private borrowing was dashed by the **debt crisis**, in the course of which the ability of the LDCs to borrow on world capital markets declined sharply. In the 1970s there was a boom in LDC borrowing from private banks in the developed countries. Unfortunately, several factors emerged to cause a crisis. First, the major world recession of the early 1980s lowered the LDCs' export earnings and made it harder to "service" their debt. (Servicing debt means making timely payments of interest and repayment of principal.) Both the banks and the biggest LDC borrowers (Mexico and Brazil atop the list) had grown complacent and over-optimistic. Second, the LDCs attempted to cope with the fall in their revenues by protecting spending for public services, food subsidies, the military, and so forth. That was perhaps understandable from a political point of view, but as a result investment spending fell sharply. The fall in investment reduced the rate of growth and eventually made it harder yet to service the debt.

Worse, much of the debt was contracted at variable (floating) rates of interest. This, too, was understandable—banks had been badly burned in the 1970s when the interest rates they had to pay depositors rose, but the loans they had made carried fixed rates. They protected themselves by means of the new floating-rate contracts. But in the early 1980s, interest rates rose again to unprecedented levels, over 20% for a time.[4] This forced LDC borrowers to pay punishing charges for their loans.

In August 1982, Mexico announced that it could not make further payments on its debt. The move sparked a worldwide debt crisis of defaults by other countries, bringing on a dangerous potential for bank failures and financial collapse. Eventually banks did manage to set aside reserves against much of their lending to the LDCs, and the prospect of collapse receded. But the banks also stopped lending to the LDCs, and the resulting shortage of funds continues to haunt their development prospects a decade later. Many plans for reform have been advanced. The ones that provided for a reduction of the debt burden on the LDCs by means of payments from developed-country taxpayers to the banks, for all that they would end the crisis, would also reward LDC governments that contributed to the problem through their profligacy. Countries that struggled successfully to meet their obligations (such as South Korea) would receive no reward. The largest debtors are also usually far from being the poorest countries, and if assistance is to be given, arguably it should go to the very poor, not to middle-income countries. Finally, the banks would be rewarded, too, by a taxpayer bailout, even though they contributed to the difficulty by careless over-extension of their lending. The current Brady Plan for debt relief envisages lengthened maturities and lower interest rates on the existing debt, plus some developed-country lending by banks and governments to restore the flow of capital to the LDCs. Progress has been slow, however, and much remains to be done in ending the crisis.

Foreign aid. Government-to-government "bilateral" transfers of capital and provision of technical assistance, together with similar flows from the "multilateral" agencies such as the World Bank, can be very useful in improving the infrastructure of schools, transport, and power projects. The international agencies can often deliver the aid without the political considerations that have affected bilateral assistance. Grants can be made to the poorest recipients of aid, whereas loans will suffice for the better-off.

In spite of these advantages, aid has not grown in real terms for many years now, and the real value of U.S. aid has dropped considerably. Substantial criticism has grown up around the subject not only among donors but also among recipients. Aid is now so politicized that two countries—Israel (not poor) and Egypt—receive nearly half of all U.S. aid. Sub-Saharan Africa, with its desperate problems, receives little.

---

4.   The reasons for the rise were discussed in Chapters 20–23.

► EFFICIENT RESOURCE ALLOCATION

The second factor in development is the ability to allocate resources efficiently. Prices that reflect opportunity costs provide an inexpensive mechanism for doing so. Administrative costs are low, incentives are clear, and rapid signaling of scarcity and glut are provided. A free-market system vastly reduces the opportunities for corruption, because much dishonest practice is based on the ability to exploit the difference between a price fixed by government and a price on a black (uncontrolled) market. The LDCs have passed through a lengthy period of high barriers to trade, low fixed government prices paid to farmers, price controls on food and transportation, artificially low interest rates for favored borrowers, measures such as minimum-wage laws and regulations against layoffs, and social security legislation that boosted labor costs before the country could afford it. Often the value of the local currency has been kept artificially high by government action, one unit of local currency buying more dollars or other foreign exchange than would be true in a free market.

These interferences with a free-market outcome have their justifications. Trade barriers appeal to those who fear that exports are subject to slow growth in demand, to damaging fluctuations in price, and that they lead to economic "dependency" on foreign countries. Low fixed prices paid to farmers are justified on the grounds that supply is not very responsive to price, that richer farmers benefit from high prices more than the smaller ones, that fixed low prices help low-income consumers, and that rapid industrialization means income must be transferred from farming to manufacturing. Price controls are explained as security for the poor. Artificially low interest rates are justified as encouraging investment. Minimum-wage and anti-layoff laws are defended as a way to provide workers with a "living wage." The high value of the exchange rate is defended as making it easier to import expensive capital goods. With the local currency overvalued, the dollars or other foreign exchange needed to purchase such imports appear cheaper.

One of the most significant pieces of empirical work in modern development economics was the finding that such interferences with markets are damaging, and that countries with badly distorted prices that do not reflect the forces of supply and demand suffer from reduced growth, even if the distortions were adopted for otherwise laudable reasons. A World Bank study of 1983 showed a strong correlation between distorted price systems and slow growth in the sample of 31 countries studied.[5]

THE DECLINE OF COMPREHENSIVE ECONOMIC PLANNING

Comprehensive **economic planning** was once a central policy tool in the LDCs. After India's first five-year plan of 1952, which owed something to Soviet central planning and received its name from the Soviet original, the idea spread through the LDCs. Most countries ended up with development plans. Comprehensive plans attempted to establish government direction of the growth path an economy would take, using the government's own spending, its control over interest rates and foreign trade, and sometimes licensing of private investment to ensure that the path would be followed. Often state-owned enterprises were established to make adherence to the plan easier.

Although most LDCs have retained their planning apparatus, its importance has diminished. The 1970s and 1980s treated plans badly: oil shocks, food shocks, and world recession could be better accommodated by market responses to price changes than by a slow and ponderous planning bureaucracy. (Some contributors to the bureaucratic failures included an acute shortage of qualified personnel to run the plans, incompetency, red tape, the brain-drain to developed countries, and the visits by foreign advisors who stayed a few weeks and then departed, leaving the responsibility for mistakes to the locals.) The emphasis of plans on capital investment in physical facilities such as factories tended to become less welcome as development

---

5.   World Bank, *World Development Report, 1983*, pp. 57–63.

economists emphasized the importance of market forces, trial and error, and flexibility in determining how an economy should grow. The plans almost always involved government price-fixing, tariffs, quotas, licenses, and exchange controls; these controls led frequently to shortages, the emergence of black markets, the corruption among public officials, and widespread economic distortions as prices failed to reflect scarcity and abundance. The barriers and their consequences often reduced still further the already low efficiency of LDCs' economies.

Almost inevitably, so it now seems, the focus of planning was too often on investment in state industrial projects rather than on changing attitudes, motivations, and institutions. These state enterprises, often politicized loss-makers, proved to be models of inefficiency. (Many countries—Argentina, Bangladesh, Brazil, Ghana, Mexico, and Nigeria, among others—have moved to sell off their state enterprises into private ownership, just as the former Communist economies are doing.) Where state-operated enterprises remain in government hands, they should be made to behave like private companies, operating under the same rules. Considerable restructuring of these operations is needed, so that their managers are rewarded on the basis of performance. They should not be permitted to force private firms out of the market by price cuts made possible by government subsidies. Yet if these state operated enterprises are *sold*, little gain may ensue if they become unregulated private monopolies in the hands of the rich or foreigners. Careful regulation of monopoly power will be necessary.

By the 1990s, many official development plans had become no more than glorified forecasts or exhortations to action, with little effect on the economy. The plans still create an image of concern, of action, of doing something on a national scale. They serve to focus debate on the choices an LDC must make. Their very failures reveal the need for better data and better planners. For these reasons, plans continue to be drawn up and publicized in the world's poor countries.

Certain *aspects* of planning remain in good repute and have not lost their support. Some coordination of investment in an LDC may be a necessary component to increasing industrialization. Consider a plant whose market is too small for efficient operation. That plant could be made more efficient if users of the product were promoted at the same time in the same development plan. Say, for example, there is a small market for electricity in some upcountry region of an LDC. Even if an electricity-generating plant were built, it would be small in scale, each kilowatt it produced would be high in cost, and the development of industries that used electricity would presumably be slowed. In the language of economists, the generating station would convey external diseconomies, since its own small size will inhibit other producers from establishing themselves. But consider the effect if an aluminum smelter is planned along with a new generating facility for electricity. Aluminum smelting requires large amounts of electricity, hence large-scale demand will automatically be present. A generator of sufficient size to realize economies of scale can now be provided, and other users of electricity will benefit also from the reduction in costs. Linking the generator and the aluminum smelter in one package is a sensible investment strategy found in development plans almost everywhere in the LDCs.

Government Remains Important

Concerns about government mistakes and the inefficiencies of state operated enterprises do not amount to a general condemnation of government activity, as some conservatives would argue. Government participation in the development process is essential, and that participation is likely to be more critical the poorer a country is. Government has the responsibility to provide law and order including the establishment and protection of property rights, and to see to the establishment of an infrastructure of finance and banking, a power grid, large irrigation systems, transport, and communications. These activities will require government control or operation if they are provided in inadequate amounts by the private sector or would otherwise be private monopolies. Government will also need to provide public goods such as education, health, family planning, agricultural research, and extension services. Finally, large inequalities of income are typical of the LDCs, and government will have the further responsibility for programs that raise the productivity and employability of the poorest part of the population.

Appropriate Technology as a Problem of Economic Efficiency

It has been recognized for many years that the choice of **appropriate technology**, that is, technology that reflects a country's factor proportions, is important in making capital more efficient and raising its productivity. Technology is a broad term describing the introduction of new inventions, new products, new methods, and new ways of carrying out production. Many LDCs unfortunately face barriers to technological change that remain to be overcome.

In the agricultural sector of the economy, fragmentation of farms into ever smaller plots may be encouraged by traditional inheritance customs that divide property equally among heirs. Improved agricultural techniques may thus be discouraged. Adversarial landlord-tenant relations built into a country's social structure may have the same adverse effects. The shortage of funds for lending, and the resulting very high interest rates, may mean that improvements in agricultural technology are disregarded. All changes in farming patterns are more risky in any case when people produce only just enough for survival, as mistakes that cut into food supply can lead to famine. Markets themselves, where goods are brought for sale, may be "bazaar-style," with long and inefficient bargaining rather than announced prices that do not involve haggling. This too can delay the introduction of new techniques.

An important question of development economics is how to identify the appropriate technique for a given country to adopt. Where labor is abundant and cheap and capital is scarce and expensive—the situation in many LDCs—the principles of microeconomics suggest that output will be achieved at the lowest cost if firms adopt labor-using and capital-saving techniques. It may seem primitive to use 5,000 workers with picks, shovels, and barrows to build a dam instead of 5 bulldozers, 20 trucks, and 100 workers. But if the wages of 5,000 workers amount to less than the capital costs for the trucks and bulldozers for the time period involved in building the dam, then the so-called primitive method is the more rational one. Yet there are social barriers to using labor-intensive methods in the LDCs. Managers and government officials may prefer working with trained people rather than with a mass of unskilled laborers. There may also be a strong prejudice against the backward image of "coolie labor" and in favor of the modernity of up-to-date equipment from the rich countries. This last reason is thought to be especially important. So techniques that are expensive in terms of capital end up being adopted instead of the labor-intensive techniques that economists would often recommend. Sometimes the choice of labor-intensive techniques may actually be wrong from an economic point of view. The workers may be malnourished and in poor health, so their productivity may decline with the hard work. In that case, hiring them may prove to be a high-cost alternative.

► HUMAN RESOURCES AND ECONOMIC DEVELOPMENT

The third area critical for economic progress is development of the quality of a country's human resources. Economists stress educational improvement, better health and nutrition, and reduced population pressure. Improvements in these areas are likely to be reflected in a more productive labor force.

EDUCATION IN THE LDCs

Education is an investment in human capital that is important in the development process. A worker who cannot read, add, or subtract is almost certain to be a low-productivity worker. A basic ability to read and do simple math tends to make farmers and small business people much more productive. The same skills improve the ability of mothers to care for their children, and hence a growing share of females with primary school training tends significantly to improve children's health and nutritional status. But providing education in LDCs is fraught with difficulties. One problem is its very high relative cost in the LDCs, much higher in proportion to national incomes than in North America or Western Europe. The high cost is the result of demand

and supply. There is a need to educate relatively more people because rapid population growth means a large percentage of children in the population. Teachers are scarce, and so are the government revenues to support education.

In some countries the cost has made it impossible to enroll all children in primary school. On average, in the low-income LDCs (a group that includes about 40 nations), a quarter of all children of the relevant age are still not in school. Yet great progress has been made since 1960. In that year, 63% of all children of school age were being left out. Many problems remain. Overly large classes, acute shortages of textbooks, and prejudice against educating females continue to dog the efforts of the LDCs. High dropout rates also present a serious problem. A recent sampling in Latin America showed over one-third of the students entering the first grade of primary school dropped out before reaching the second grade, and less than a quarter of all students completed the full six years. Dropping out is usually due to economic reasons such as the need for a family to maintain its labor force for farming.

Another difficulty is that a country's elite typically favors greater government spending on secondary and university education. Especially due to the scarcity of trained instructors, education at these levels is much more expensive relative to primary schooling than in the developed countries. In the average developed country, secondary school costs per student are 9% more than for primary school, while university costs per student are a little more than double. In the average LDC, secondary education is nearly three times more expensive, while university is four times more. In sub-Saharan Africa, the figures are about 26 times and 53 times.[6] In the 1980s, primary education in the Third World received only about half the funding devoted to university education in those countries. This appears to be a serious misallocation of resources because the benefits per dollar spent on primary schools are, according to most studies, considerably greater than for higher levels of education. For example, the World Bank has stated that the rate of return on a dollar spent on primary schooling was 28% for a sample of countries studied, but only 14% for a dollar spent on university training.[7]

There would thus seem to be a strong argument for shifting funds away from university education and toward primary schooling, where the rate of return is much higher. Needless to say, this move would be politically difficult because of the opposition of the urban elites who so often hold political power. But it would also help to solve two other ongoing complications faced by many LDCs: that an overly large proportion of secondary school and university graduates may find that they are unemployable because of the underlying poverty of the economy in which they live, and the closely connected phenomenon of the **brain drain**—a flow of emigration to developed countries from the more educated part of the labor force.

HEALTH AND NUTRITION

Improving health care is a major challenge for the LDCs. Most of them will be quite unable for many years to come to afford the expensive hospital-centered care familiar in the developed countries. Paramedical personnel can, however, accomplish much and accomplish it cheaply, as China's "barefoot doctor" program has established. Improving water supplies and sanitation is usually much more cost-effective than curative medicine. On the negative side, malaria the great killer is making a comeback because mosquitoes have developed some immunity to the major prevention measures of the past. Worse yet, AIDS has reached epidemic proportions in parts of Africa.

Malnutrition is closely correlated with poverty; the poorest go the hungriest and are therefore the least productive. Attacking malnutrition is difficult because the poor often cannot afford to buy the nutritious foods that are needed. Economic growth itself is the main release from malnutrition, but growth in market systems—even developed ones—commonly leaves some people out. In the LDCs, some countries have registered significant successes with programs

---

6.   The figures are from the World Bank's *World Development Report 1988*, p. 135.

7.   World Bank, *World Development Report, 1987*, p. 64.

similar to America's food stamps for the poor. This is much better than subsidizing food supplies for everyone, a very expensive plan much used where the political support of urban elites is being bought. General food subsidies direct a country's resources partly to those that do not need them, and an LDC is by definition a country that cannot afford waste on this scale. Recent decisions to abandon general food subsidies and to substitute food stamp programs have been made by Mexico and Sri Lanka, among others.

Famines would, one might have supposed, be obsolete after several decades of economic growth in the LDCs. Unhappily, they are still with us. The reason is usually not the lack of food. For the most part famines are caused by droughts that often do not strike all areas of a country at the same time. In any case, food can be imported. But if there is a class of very poor with no savings to fall back on, any interruption to income may mean falling over the edge into famine. In such circumstances, food aid from abroad can prove vital. Experience shows, however, that it is better to pay for the food with work done rather than give it away. The work of those who are fed can build defenses against drought (terracing, forestation) and famine (better roads) that will leave people more protected in the future. Experience also reveals that it is damaging just to give away large quantities of food aid without cushioning the blow for farmers. Any fall in their incomes due to the decline in their output would be partly offset by a price rise caused by the resulting scarcity, but because of the food giveaways the price rise does not occur.

ECONOMIC DEVELOPMENT AND RAPID POPULATION GROWTH

It took roughly four million years for the earth to reach its first billion of population about the year 1800, 130 years to reach the second billion in 1930, 30 years to the third billion in 1960, 15 years to the fourth billion in 1975, and just 12 years to 1987 to reach the fifth billion. The growth *rate* of population was almost nothing, 0.03% per annum, between A.D. 1000 and 1750. It was about 0.5% per annum in 1900, 1% in 1930, and just over 2% in the 1970s. In 37 countries, population growth in the late 1980s exceeded 3% per year.

Every hour some 9,000 people are added to the world's population. Most of these births are in the LDCs; in 1950, two out of three people lived in poor countries, while in 2025 the proportion will be five out of six. Half of the world's population is under 24 years of age; in time, most of these people, too, will start to bear children. Every week world population increase is equal to another city the size of Houston, every year another country the size of Mexico. In the year 2000, 7 of the world's 10 largest cities will be in the LDCs. Mexico City's projected population in that year of 26 million will be as large as New York and London together were in 1985.

Educating the increasing number of young people may strain government budgets while feeding and caring for them strain private budgets. Raising per capita national income when the population is large and growing relative to the available land and natural resources may be difficult. The pressure on land may bring environmental degradation. Yet everywhere population grows faster because birth rates continue to stay high while death rates have been rapidly reduced because of advances in the control of fatal diseases and improvements in nutrition. (The great killer diseases such as smallpox, yellow fever, typhoid, typhus, plague, and cholera are all largely under control. Mortality from famine has been reduced by better transport and distribution of food, aided by international relief efforts.) A death rate of 25 per 1000 of population per year is now considered quite high, and death rates for the low-income LDCs averaged just 13 in 1991, almost as low as the 10–12 registered by most developed countries.[8] But birth rates have fallen far less rapidly, averaging 38 per 1000 of population in the low-income LDCs during 1991. So population continues to grow, in 1991 by 38–13 = 25 per 1000, or 2.5%. In some countries the growth is much faster. For example, Nigeria, Africa's most populous country, has an annual

---

8.   Sometimes the death rate can be much *lower* than in developed countries. The figure for Singapore and Taiwan is 5, for South Korea 6. This anomaly is caused by the preponderance of young people in the population. Development texts show how to adjust both birth and death rates to take account of the age distribution of the population. The figures we use above are not adjusted for age distribution and are thus called "crude" birth and death rates.

birth rate of 44 per 1000 and a death rate of 14; 44–14 means population growth of 3% per year, very high by historical standards for that country or the world. The high growth rates in the LDCs has given rise to the term **population explosion** to describe the situation.

Rapid population growth was undoubtedly an advantage for some of today's developed countries, such as Australia, Canada, New Zealand, and the United States, during their formative periods. These countries were blessed with good land and/or natural resources, good government, and an excellent, improving infrastructure of education, transport, and communications. For them, larger populations meant a larger labor force and hence an augmentation of productive resources. Their original inhabitants were not very numerous, and their thinly populated land was as a practical matter wide open for new settlement. They all attracted hard-working immigrants, often already educated in their mother country, and often already possessing a skill, which made their labor unusually productive. They also all attracted massive inflows of foreign capital.

Though some economists and many politicians contend that a growing population conveys the same advantages to LDCs, for most of these countries such an argument is difficult to accept. Overcrowded, short on capital, burdened with inadequate skills and managerial ability, most LDCs are unlikely to find that population growth is beneficial.

Disadvantages of Rapid Population Growth

Consider first the problem called by demographers (those who study populations) the **burden of dependency**. The faster people multiply, the higher the proportion of children in the overall population. Often in LDCs about 40% of the population is less than 15 years old, as compared to a typical figure of 30% or less in rich countries. Even though in LDCs many of these children do work, they produce little and are dependents who have to be fed, clothed, housed, and educated if possible. True, in the developed countries there is a larger percentage of people over 65 years of age than in LDCs, and this group is usually out of the active labor force. The lower numbers of elderly in the LDCs do not, however, counterbalance the very young age group, so that nonproductive population (in age groups 0–14 and 65+) average 45% of the total population for low-income LDCs and only 33% for developed countries. Some sample burdens of dependency are shown in Table 30.2. Though the LDCs have the higher burden, they also have fewer resources to meet the food, housing, and education needs of their young.

TABLE 30.2
The burden of dependency: percent of population in age groups 0–14 and 65+, 1991.

Canada	33	Egypt	43
France	34	India	40
Germany	32	Kenya	51
Italy	31	Mexico	40
Japan	30	Nigeria	52
United Kingdom	35	Pakistan	46
United States	34	Sudan	48
		Syria	51
		Tanzania	50
All Developed Countries	33	All Low-Income LDCs	45

Source: World Bank, *World Development Report, 1993*, pp. 288–289.

Rapid population growth has further detrimental effects on economic development. Population increase means a growing labor force. A given capital stock will then have to be expanded or else each worker, now working with less capital, will be less productive than before.

The fall in the productivity of labor will cause wage incomes to decrease as well. So a country must use some of its material resources simply to maintain the stock of capital per worker at its old level. If, however, population growth is limited, the same resources will allow a greater quantity of capital per worker, leading to higher labor productivity and growing wage income.

Finally, the looming possibility of environmental degradation caused by an overly large population commands attention. The added billions of people will continue to cut the rain forests, build factories, and buy products that pollute the air and water. In the end, all of mankind is likely to suffer. To the extent that larger populations generate more pollution, rapid population growth is likely to be more costly than was appreciated until very recently.

Why Birth Rates Have Stayed High

With these disadvantages to population growth, why have birth rates stayed high in many of the LDCs? Many reasons have their roots in microeconomics. Parents may view children as being necessary for farm operations. In many situations, bearing children amounts to the creation of a personal labor force. A large family is frequently the only system of social security for the parents. A high priority may thus be placed on producing children who will provide support in their parents' old age. Until economic development changes these circumstances, birth rates are likely to *stay* high. Even after people come to prefer a smaller family size, population growth may continue to be rapid because of the expense or unavailability of means for birth control.

ENDEMIC CORRUPTION IN THE LDCs

A final area of human resource improvement involves reducing the rampant corruption found in many LDCs. Corruption often permeates business transactions and daily life. Poorly paid government officials are expected to administer vast systems of credit controls, price controls, tariffs, foreign exchange controls, and licensing and permits for most every business transaction on any scale. The potential to receive bribes in the administration of these controls can lead public employees to impede progress to make bribes fatter and more forthcoming. Widespread corruption ruins the morale of the public servants who are honest, delays all forms of business, boosts costs, and means that many public officials are basically working for private gain.

The Peruvian economist Hernando de Soto conducted a revealing experiment to show how bad the situation can be.[9] De Soto's researchers established a small garment factory (two sewing machines) in Lima, Peru, and then set out to obtain the government permits necessary for them to begin production. To fulfill 11 requirements, it took 289 days and visits to seven ministries. Government officials solicited bribes on 10 occasions. When the researchers tried the same experiment in Tampa, Florida, all the necessary permits were obtained in $3\frac{1}{2}$ hours. Lessening the degree of corruption in the LDCs will be a major task, but it is a vital one.

▶ RURAL DEVELOPMENT

The fourth factor that improves the prospects for economic development is enhancing the performance of farmers and the rural sector in general. In the typical poor country, most people are small farmers working under conditions of low output per person with few tools and machinery, and using traditional techniques. The average American agricultural worker produces 20 to 40 times more per day than the average farmer of numerous African and Asian countries. It follows that rural development in the LDCs must be encouraged.

Comparative data indicate that on average the lower the overall growth of an LDC, the poorer has been its performance in the farm sector. A stagnant agricultural sector is, rather conclusively, an inhibiting factor for economic development. It is easy to see why. Agriculture often employs most of the population, can provide food that would otherwise have to be

---

9.   See Hernando de Soto, *The Other Path: The Invisible Revolution in the Third World,* New York, 1989.

imported, and can engender exports. Rural areas can provide a market for a country's new production of industrial goods. Because farming is often smaller-scale than manufacturing, it conserves on management ability.

Yet rural neglect and a bias toward urban areas were marked features of LDC economic policy during the initial decades of the development experience. Farmers were often heavily taxed, and the prices of their products were kept artificially low by government, partly because they had less political clout than did urban workers, and partly because the first generation of politicians in the LDCs believed that large-scale manufacturing was the key to economic success. Especially in Latin America, landholding was badly skewed, with tiny plots farmed by half or more of the population that owned only 10% or less of the land. Most of the land was controlled by the rich; a large portion was farmed by tenants.

Nowadays rural reform is a centerpiece in many countries' development efforts, and loans to this sector figure importantly in World Bank lending and in foreign aid. Though circumstances differ, rural improvement programs will often include a land reform that aims to guarantee title to tenant farmers, and government attempts to give farmers better access to credit. Loans are usually scarce in rural areas: Banks find keeping track of small loans to scattered farmers is burdensome; the default rate is often high; governments frequently prohibit land from being used as the collateral for loans; and in any case most farmers own little land. So interest rates are high. Innovative lending arrangements wherein a tiny sum is lent to one of a group of several farmers, another getting a loan when the first one is paid back, have attracted wide attention. The farmers in effect police themselves, keeping risks low. The bicycle bankers referred to earlier in the chapter are often active in setting up such programs, which are most popular in Asia.

An outstanding success in LDC agriculture over the last 20 years has been the **green revolution** associated with the development of high-yield varieties (HYVs) of rice and wheat. The HYVs yield much more than traditional varieties; their short and sturdy stalks can carry a considerably greater weight, so that fertilizer and irrigation water can be usefully applied in much greater quantity than before.

In spite of this success, however, the rural areas of the LDCs continue to be a cause for concern. They are a huge reservoir of population, and if governments persist in their traditional bias of favoritism toward the cities then the already huge migration of people from farms to cities will continue to swell the teeming slums of the world's poor countries. Looked at in this way, rural development appears to be a matter of urgent priority in most LDCs.

▶ PROMOTING INTERNATIONAL TRADE

A final contributor to economic development is international trade. With foreign trade a country can attain levels of consumption higher than can be achieved domestically. We have seen that a country will improve its standard of living by following the lines of comparative advantage, exporting what it produces with relative efficiency and importing what it does less well. Imports are more crucial to development than is often realized. Obviously some capital goods are unavailable locally and must be imported, and the technology embodied in the capital goods may also be procurable only through imports. Imports contribute more than that, however. They also give people the opportunity to acquire highly desirable new consumption goods that are not available otherwise. Worldwide, this provides a sizable stimulant to productive human effort. To obtain these advantages, it is necessary to export, for only by doing so will the foreign exchange be available to pay for the imports.

Unfortunately, the LDC share of the world's total exports, about one-quarter in 1955, had dropped to one-fifth by 1965, and it remains stuck at that figure. How the LDCs will achieve faster export, and hence import, growth is a major puzzle. Demand for the traditional tropical commodities has been increasing slowly (sugar, coffee, tea), while for some items demand has actually fallen (palm oil). The future for most of these commodities does not look very promising, especially because the income elasticity of demand for these commodities is low. (That is, higher incomes in the developed countries fail to boost demand much for several of the important tropical staples.) A few minerals have experienced reasonable growth in demand, but others (copper, tin) have not, and in any case many LDCs are poorly endowed with minerals, and they are depletable.

Manufactured goods, especially those that can be made with the cheap labor that the LDCs have in abundance, can be exported to the developed countries. Here appears to be the best bet, and such goods have been central to the successful development efforts of South Korea, Taiwan, Malaysia, and Indonesia, and before that, Japan. Developed-country barriers to trade have, however, made concentration on export growth more risky than it would otherwise be. Even so, exporting remains an attractive means for a low-income economy to break out of poverty.

Government policies to remove barriers to exporting are an essential part of the development effort. Reasonable practices include promoting exports by disseminating information and making credit available to small firms that otherwise could not get it because credit markets are poorly developed. A period of infant-industry protection by means of temporary tariffs, or government subsidies, may make sense if a country's capital markets are small. Evidence from the World Bank presented in Table 30.3 makes the case that economic growth has been most rapid in the countries that have adopted strongly outward-oriented policies to encourage foreign trade. The strongly inward-oriented countries that shelter their industries behind high trade barriers have done far less well.

TABLE 30.3
Growth of real GNP per capita, 1974–85, and 1986–92.

	1974–85	1986–92
Strongly Outward-Oriented Countries	8.0	7.5
Strongly Inward-Oriented Countries	2.3	2.5

Source: International Monetary Fund, *World Economic Outlook 1993*, p. 76. It should be noted that only a few Asian countries are "strongly outward-oriented." The limited size of the sample has caused some economists to criticize these data.

The main reason why outward orientation seems to work is that trade tends to increase competition, stimulate investment, lead to scale economies, and promote the flow of technology. Export-promotion programs must, however, be carefully limited to industries that have a present or predicted future comparative advantage in exporting. To do otherwise is to *decrease* efficiency and *lessen* the chances for economic development. The point must also be made that the lowest-income LDCs face the greater obstacles to development, and that export promotion works less well the poorer a country is. For international trade to expedite economic growth, it helps greatly if a country already possesses some minimal industrial base and some minimal degree of technical skills.

DEVELOPED-COUNTRY TRADE BARRIERS AGAINST LDC MANUFACTURED EXPORTS

A major difficulty for the LDCs hoping to export manufactures is the growing proclivity of the developed countries to erect trade barriers against them. Most LDC manufactured-goods exports, about 70% in the mid-1980s, go to the developed countries. The LDCs still only produce $12\frac{1}{2}$% of world manufacturing output, but that figure is a third more than it was a decade earlier, and the rapid growth has unleashed protectionist sentiments. Rich-country tariffs are high on textiles and clothing, which LDCs can often produce competitively. Tariffs on raw materials are usually low or nonexistent, while tariffs on the finished products using those raw materials are often substantial. The high developed-country tariffs on the processed items means processing industries that make chocolate from cocoa, instant coffee from coffee beans, or furniture from wood, are much more likely to locate in the developed countries than in the LDCs. Developed countries often use their laws aggressively against the import of products subsidized by foreign governments. At the start of the 1990s, of the 76 U.S. penalty tariffs levied on goods found to be subsidized 58 were directed against LDCs, even though few of these subsidies do any substantial harm to U.S. firms. The penalties affect a wide range of commodities including bricks, cement, tile, steel, chemicals, textiles, and clothing. Many voluntary export restraints (VERs) have also been forced on the LDCs, which, lacking sufficient bargaining power on trade issues, are often unable to resist. Of the 261 existing developed-country VERs in 1988, 123 were aimed at LDCs. VERs, quotas, and other nontariff barriers affect a far greater proportion of LDC exports than they do developed-country exports, as shown in Table 30.4.

TABLE 30.4
Percentage share of imports subject to non-tariff barriers.

	Percent of Imports from	
	Developed Countries	LDCs
EC	10.7	21.7
Japan	12.4	14.5
United States	9.2	16.1
All developed countries	11.3	20.6

Source: World Bank, *World Development Report,* 1986, p. 23. The data apply to the year 1984.

The Multi-Fiber Arrangement (MFA) in Textiles and Clothing

The most pervasive protection of all is directed against the LDCs' exports of textiles and clothing. These are areas of considerable potential for the LDCs because cheap labor is an advantage in their production, and because the market is huge. Textiles and clothing make up 10% of world trade, and they comprise nearly a third of all LDC exports to developed countries. But this route to development is beset with barriers. A **Multi-Fiber Arrangement** (MFA) dating from 1974 has been renewed at intervals. The present MFA IV places strict and very detailed quota limits on shipments by product type from the LDCs to the developed countries.

With the sole exception of Japan, the restrictions are *not* placed on developed-country exports of textiles and clothing, only on the exports of the LDCs. Some countries face over 100 categories of quotas, such as "men's undershirts, white," with even the imports of various sizes regulated. In the United States alone, consumers pay an estimated $27 billion more because of the MFA and the high tariffs on these imports. Scrapping the MFA would lead to an estimated rise in employment in LDC textile production of 20% to 45% depending on the country. It seems hard to believe that the governments of the developed countries would ever participate in a scheme so damaging to the world's poor—yet the U.S. Congress has several times passed quota bills even *more* restrictive than are embodied in the MFA, and only presidential vetoes have kept them from being enacted.

The LDCs' Own High Barriers

Distressingly, the LDCs also maintain their own high barriers against imports, on average higher than the developed-country barriers. Particular attention has focused on the protection against imports of services. To improve their development prospects, LDCs must improve their transport, telecommunications, computer facilities, banking, and insurance. Traditionally the barriers against importing these services from developed countries have been hard to penetrate. Often the reluctance to import is based on some concept of nationalism—politicians will intone that "foreigners cannot be allowed to control the telephone system." Yet there are two points to keep in mind: if LDCs are to persuade the developed countries to reduce the barriers against the goods they produce with their cheap labor, they, too, ought to be willing to abide by the forces of comparative advantage. Furthermore, backward service industries are a blight on the LDCs. Importing some services would arguably raise the efficiency of many economies.

PRIMARY PRODUCT EXPORTING AND ITS PROBLEMS

Exports of primary products (agricultural commodities, minerals) have not been as successful for the LDCs as manufacturing has been. Yet self-evidently for many of the poorest countries, their comparative advantage is likely to be in primary products for years to come. It therefore comes as a shock to one's sense of fair play to discover that developed countries, especially the United States, Japan, and the EC, have adopted agricultural policies that diminish the LDCs' chances of developing by means of agricultural exports. LDCs were responsible for 45% of the world's exports of food products in 1961–1963, compared to 46% from the developed countries. By 1982–1984, however, LDCs had only 34% of these exports, compared to 63% for the developed countries at the same time.[10] The major cause of this shift has been the agricultural support programs engaged in by developed countries. These programs typically boost prices for farmers and lead to surplus production. With prices kept artificially high, imports must, of course, be restricted. Recently it has also become common for the rich countries to subsidize the export of the surplus commodities they have acquired as part of their price-support programs. The LDCs find themselves losing their export markets, while at the same time their domestic markets are being eroded by the subsidized exports. (Against that, they do get cheap food imports.)

Numerous tropical commodities (bananas, cocoa, coffee) are not affected. But others that could provide good earnings for the LDCs are. Among cases in point, the United States maintains cotton quotas that limit imports to about 5% of domestic consumption; a peanut quota of 775 metric tons (unchanged since 1953) that amounts to about 0.0005% of consumption, or about 1 foreign peanut per person per year; and sugar protection that has caused U.S. prices to be about 22¢ per pound even when world prices have been as low as 4–5¢ per pound. Because of the sugar quotas, U.S. sugar imports were cut 70% between 1982 and 1987. Europe and Japan also protect their domestic producers (of beet sugar). The overall result of the barriers against sugar has been to push world prices down by as much as 50%. There are about 12,600 U.S. sugar producers, each collecting on average slightly over a quarter of a million dollars per year because of the restrictions. The quotas have been a tremendous lobbying success for them, but a disaster for countries such as the Dominican Republic, which earned $330 million from its sugar exports to the United States in 1981, but only $65 million in 1987, and where half the cane cutters have lost their jobs. (Recently the former Soviet Union was importing more sugar from the Dominican Republic than was the United States, which is only a few hundred miles away.) In St. Kitts-Nevis, a two-island country further east in the Caribbean, half the labor force has been laid off because of the repeated reductions in its sugar quota. As a side-effect of high-priced sugar, sweetener made from high-fructose corn syrup (HFCS), which can be manufactured from corn, has been made artificially competitive with sugar. That product now holds 60% of the American sweetener market, which it would not do if sugar could be freely imported. As we have seen elsewhere in the book, government interference in markets often has unexpected consequences.

Japan completely forbids rice imports as part of its support program for rice farmers that raises the price they receive to eight or nine times the world price for rice. Naturally farmers produce rice well in excess of domestic demand, which the government buys up and then dumps on world markets at whatever price it will bear. Many LDCs produce rice that could be exported to Japan, and they are the losers.

The worst situation of all is in the EC, or Common Market, where the giant mountains of surplus commodities farmers have produced in response to high EC support prices have resulted in the capture of several important world markets by an area that does not have the comparative advantage. The EC's share of all world food exports, less than 3% in 1970, is now

---

10.   Margaret Kelly, Naheed Kirmani, Miranda Xafa, Clemens Boonekamp, and Peter Winglee, "Issues and Developments in International Trade Policy," *IMF Occasional Paper No. 63,* 1988, p. 28.

over 18%. The EC is now the world's largest agricultural exporter, having passed the United States in 1986. In products of interest to the LDCs, it is the world's largest exporter of sugar, veal, poultry, tied for number 2 in beef, and number 3 in wheat, whereas 20 years ago it was a major importer of most of these. For the LDCs, it seems altogether too much like being kicked when you are down.

The world gains from dismantling the barriers against international trade in agriculture have been estimated at $64 billion annually, more than double the yearly total amount of foreign aid. Yet few lobbies are as powerful as those for the maintenance of price supports in the developed countries, and the dismal consequences for the LDCs that flow from this policy seem set to continue for some time yet.

▶ THE ENVIRONMENT AND ECONOMIC DEVELOPMENT

Environmental considerations were patently of little concern to development economics until recently. Almost everyone appreciated that consciousness of environmental problems lags well behind economic growth. Escaping from poverty is what drove poor farmers into the "dark satanic mills" of the English Midlands, and their counterparts such as Pittsburgh and the Ruhr, as industrialization took place in the eighteenth and nineteenth centuries. The smoke, grime, and fogs fed by coal fires, the polluted water, the hideous long hours in the factories, the child labor were understood to be the short-run cost of economic improvement and a better life brought by higher incomes. Industrial wastelands there certainly were, but wastelands where incomes were rising and, gradually, poverty was retreating.

Thoughts such as these explain why for many years there was only slight concern in the LDCs for environmental degradation, and why until recently, few LDCs attempted to control their pollution. Mrs. Gandhi, when she was Prime Minister of India, claimed that the *worst* pollution is poverty. From the point of view of the masses in the LDCs, that opinion is undoubtedly correct. In this view the lack of concern with the environment would be a temporary thing, disappearing as income increased. In the long run it would prove to have been relatively harmless, with problems correcting themselves as the LDCs grew out of their poverty and turned toward cleaning up.

The first concerns for environmental matters centered on the realization that population increase could harm the prospects for development by intensifying the scarcity of land and water while at the same time reducing their quality. People driven to cut forests, clear marginal hillside land for farming, and overgraze pastures could cause erosion and degradation of land, reduced agricultural production, and a silting up of waterways. A poor population might become even poorer. Though these consequences were serious, it was nonetheless still believed that they were felt only in the countries where the environmentally damaging activities were taking place. National policies could be adopted (or not adopted) in response; it was an LDC's own business.

Now the situation is changed. The ozone hole, acid rain, the possibility of global warming, even once-obscure chemical terms such as chlorofluorocarbons (CFCs) now are everyday words. Some of the environmental damage caused by local activities is now understood to have consequences for the whole world. Unfortunately, as the LDCs grow in terms of their population and their income, this damage will mount. Clearing the rain forests for farmland contributes to potential global warming (by adding carbon dioxide when the slash is burned and by reducing the vegetation that absorbs CO_2.) Increasing numbers of autos and trucks emit "greenhouse gases" with the same effect. More refrigerators and air-conditioning that use CFCs damage the ozone layer because CFC atoms destroy ozone molecules. The possibility that development of the LDCs (together with further economic growth in the developed countries) will harm the global environment is a major new factor on the economic scene. For example, China and India account for only 15% of CFC use at present, but that is expected to reach 50% by the year 2000 as their use grows and reductions occur in the developed countries. If there come to be as many refrigerators per family in China and India as in the United States, the damage to the ozone layer could become very serious.

Self-evidently, the LDCs simply cannot be told to stop developing. The *worst* pollution still is poverty. So some way will have to be found whereby rich and poor countries cooperate to avert environmental harm. Some steps can certainly be taken by the LDCs themselves, such as removal of the generous subsidies that many countries employ to keep energy prices artificially low. These subsidies lead to overly great use of energy, thereby contributing to acid rain and the potential for global warming.

But it will surely be necessary for the developed countries to fund most of the expenditures for an international effort to control environmental damage. That raises the prospect for protecting the environment while at the same time reducing the burden of LDC debt to the developed countries. The environmental and debt issues can be linked together. Potentially, developed-country taxpayers could pay off some of the LDCs' debts to banks in return for an LDC commitment to greater environmental protection. Such "debt for nature" swaps have already begun, most funded by private groups. They appear to have a bright future. One conclusion is all too likely: if something along these lines is *not* attempted, failure to cope with long-term environmental issues could be quite injurious to the LDCs' prospects for development while at the same time delivering long-term environmental damage to the rest of the world as well.

ENVIRONMENTAL CONCERNS AND INTERNATIONAL TRADE

Some environmentalists now see trade barriers as an effective weapon to enforce agreements to reduce pollution, protect endangered species, and the like. Offending countries may otherwise not cooperate, and polluting industries may be tempted to move to these countries to escape the regulation. Working out mutual agreements with such countries may seem politically more difficult than would be putting a stop to their trade.

The clear danger of trade barriers to enforce environmental agreements is that they are expensive to the public, which pays a higher price for the imports, and are profitable to the industries in the countries that erect the barriers. Economists who study the issue note that pollution control costs, at least as they exist at present, are too small to have much of an impact by comparison with labor cost and technology advantages. No large flow of polluting industries from developed countries to the LDCs appears to have sprung up.

▶ THE FUTURE FOR DEVELOPMENT

The barriers to development in the LDCs are complex. Inadequate knowledge, organizational difficulties, social and religious constraints on women, ethnic minorities and entrepreneurs, government policies that distort economic incentives, rule by an economic elite or by the military, and corruption are all difficult to incorporate into the standard models of economics. Yet these barriers are major reasons why the actual level of growth in many countries stays well below the levels that could be reached if these barriers were breached.

It would help greatly if the common perception that gains for the LDCs must be losses for the developed countries, and vice versa, could be eradicated. This false perception explains much about the suspicion and indifference that too often marks the relations of the rich and poor countries. More emphasis needs to be placed on policies involving mutual gains to both the rich and the poor, a recognition that could transform development into a more cooperative venture than it now is.

If the rich countries would adopt policies more conducive to their own growth such as lower budget deficits and interest rates in the United States, deregulation of price-boosting government policies in Europe, encouragement of consumption in Japan, and lower barriers to international trade, then not only would these countries benefit, but so would LDCs, which could increase their exports. The export increase would raise incomes in the LDCs, which would then buy more exports from the developed countries and add to their growth. Recognition that the debt crisis facing the LDCs and developed-country banks can be usefully linked to the environmental crisis by means of debt-for-environment deals could be a great help. The spread of democratic ideals and the adoption of rule by ballot, not bullet, are relevant to economic progress. A free press to expose wrongdoing and a government that is accountable at the polls are effective weapons. They can help enormously in bringing about abolition of many forms of government controls that have stifled enterprise in the LDCs.

In the final analysis, the developed countries cannot ignore the 70% of the world's population that is poor. It appears ever more likely that the challenges to peace and order in the twenty-first century will come from the planet's poor countries, not its rich ones. Even if the moral imperative and obvious justice of helping the poor to better themselves fails to move the voters and public officials of the developed countries, the stark fact that continuing widespread poverty is dangerous certainly *ought* to do so. Recognizing that the developed countries must do a better job of promoting growth in the LDCs is, after all, no more than recognizing their own self-interest.

SUMMARY

1) Most of the world's population lives in poverty. Only a little over 12% of the world's total income is generated by approximately 70% of the world's population that lives in the less-developed countries (LDCs).

2) A major cause of underdevelopment is an inadequate supply of capital, in turn due to inadequate saving and investment. Domestic saving is inhibited by low income, by tax systems that are unable to mobilize sufficient revenue, and by high levels of inflation in many LDCs. Savings can be imported from abroad, but the "debt crisis" of the 1980s has severely retarded the flow of bank lending, and foreign aid is limited in amount and heavily politicized.

3) Comprehensive economic planning was once a central policy tool in the LDCs, but it has fallen out of favor because of its focus on inefficient state enterprises. But government must still play a role in the development process wherever private enterprise cannot or will not provide an adequate infrastructure of finance and banking, a power grid, large irrigation systems, transport, and communications. Government will also need to provide public goods such as education, health, family planning, agricultural research, and extension services.

4) The choice of appropriate technology, that is, technology that reflects a country's factor proportions, is important in making capital more efficient and raising its productivity. Inadequate education (especially of women), health, and nutrition are important causes of low labor productivity, and hence low income. Rapid population growth brings a burden of dependents who must be cared for and makes it hard to raise the quantity of capital per worker.

5) In many LDCs, most of the population consists of farmers working under conditions of low output per person with few tools and machinery and using traditional techniques. It follows that rural development is a component of the development process that should not be neglected.

6) For some LDCs, foreign trade can provide large markets for labor-intensive manufactured goods, thus providing a route to higher incomes. Strongly outward-oriented economies have a much better growth record than do the strongly inward-oriented countries that shelter their industries behind high barriers to trade. But the ability to utilize foreign trade as a method of development runs up against trade barriers in the developed countries, especially to the import of textiles and clothing, and the barriers of the LDCs against their own products are even higher.

7) Exports of primary products (agricultural commodities, minerals) have not been as successful for the LDCs as manufacturing has been. Trade barriers against certain commodities are very high, while demand for a wide variety of primary products has grown slowly.

8) Until recently, environmental considerations have been of little concern to LDCs. "Poverty is the worst pollution," as Mrs. Gandhi once said. More recently, however, economists have realized that development of the LDCs is likely to cause further environmental problems of a global nature, such as ozone depletion and perhaps global warming. Self-evidently, the LDCs cannot be told to stop developing. It will probably be necessary for the developed countries to fund most of the expenditures for an international effort to control environmental damage.

9) The developed countries cannot ignore the LDCs. The acute poverty in these countries is dangerous for peace and order, so it is self-interest on the part of the developed countries to participate in the development effort.

Chapter Key Words

Appropriate technology: The idea that the technology employed in a country should reflect that country's factor proportions, emphasizing labor intensity when labor is the abundant factor of production.

Brain drain: The flow of talented people from LDCs to developed countries, understandable because they will thus receive higher income but regrettable for its impact on economic development.

Burden of dependency: An effect of rapid population growth. The number of unproductive children that must be supported by the economy is larger in most LDCs than in most developed countries.

Debt crisis: A period during the 1980s when many LDCs, which had borrowed large sums from developed-country banks, proved unable to service their debt. A large rise in interest rates was one cause, and world recession that dampened the LDCs' ability to export was another. Various plans to reduce the intensity of the crisis were in effect from the late 1980s, and helped to control it.

Economic planning: An attempt to establish government direction of the growth path an economy will take, using the government's own spending, its control over interest rates and foreign trade, and sometimes licensing of private investment to ensure that the path will be followed.

Green revolution: Refers to the introduction of several "miracle seeds" or "high-yield varieties," mainly rice and wheat, which with proper fertilizer applications and irrigation yield far more than the seeds formerly in use.

Less-developed countries (LDCs): Countries with low income, low saving, low capital formation, and usually a high level of population growth. Such countries contain about 70% of the world's population. Underdeveloped countries is a common synonym.

Multi-fiber arrangement (MFA): An international agreement to limit textile and clothing imports from the LDCs to the developed countries.

Chapter Questions

1) Most people would agree that money cannot buy happiness. Why then do economists favor growth?

2) The traditional source of capital is saving. Why can poor countries not just save more and so acquire more capital?

3) You are the minister of trade of Primaria, an LDC. Your major export is Primarium ore, an industrial input of which Primaria is the world's only supplier. Primaria would like to acquire more capital in order to diversify its economy. Should you tax exports of Primarium ore?

4) One way to pay for more capital is for the government to create more money that it could then use to purchase the new capital. Will this strategy actually lead to an increase in the capital stock?

5) For 20 years you have worked in the ministry of planning in a small LDC. With the fall of Communism, your ministry has come under attack, and the president is considering its elimination. Before doing so, he asks you if there are any beneficial roles your ministry can still perform. What do you say?

6) The many small villages of Dispersia are often connected only by narrow footpaths. To improve transportation, the government proposes to build a heliport in each village. Is this appropriate technology? Can you devise a better plan?

7) The elimination of a number of diseases has reduced your country's death rate to 10 per 1,000 people per year. Your birth rate has held steady at 40 per 1,000 people per year. What is the population growth rate? What problem does this create?

8) If you were a worker in an LDC, would your future be brighter if you made computer chips for export or harvested sugar cane? Why? Would any change in U.S. policy alter this outlook?

9) Poverty involves terrible human suffering in LDCs. Why then is there any reason to worry about the pollution that comes with growth?

INDEX